Rick Steves'®

ITALY

2013

CONTENTS

SIGHTS

1. Accademia Gallery
2. Bridge of Sighs
3. Ca' d'Oro
4. Ca' Pesaro Internat'l Gallery of Modern Art
5. Ca' Rezzonico
6. Campanile (Bell Tower)
7. Clock Tower
8. Correr Museum
9. Doge's Palace
10. Frari Church
11. Jewish Ghetto & Museum
12. La Fenice Opera House
13. La Salute Church
14. Palazzo Grassi
15. Palazzo Mocenigo Costume Museum
16. Peggy Guggenheim Collection
17. Piazzale Roma
18. Punta della Dogana Museum
19. Rialto Bridge
20. St. Mark's Basilica
21. St. Mark's Square
22. San Giorgio Maggiore Church
23. San Polo Church
24. San Zaccaria Church
25. Santa Maria Formosa Church
26. Scala Contarini del Bovolo
27. To Scuola Dalmata di San Giorgio
28. Scuola San Rocco
29. Train Station

200 Meters
200 Yards

Florence

To Fortezza da Basso

VIA FIUME
VIA FAENZA
MERCATO CENTRALE
Pi Me Cer
16

SANTA MARIA NOVELLA TRAIN STATION
34
ATAF LOCAL BUS OFFICE

VIA ALAMANNI

BUS STATION
35

Piazza della Stazione
PEDESTRIAN UNDERPASS

VIA NAZIONALE

VIA DELL'ARIENTO

Piazza dell' Unità Italiana

VIA S. ANTONINO
VIA AMARINO

MEDICI CHAPELS
14
SA LORE

VIA DEL MELARANCIO

SANTA MARIA NOVELLA
30

VIA DELLA SCALA

VIA DEI PANZANI

VIA DE' CONTI
VIA DELL'ALLORO
DEL GIGLIO

LAURENT LIBRAR

ZANNETTI

VIA DI CANACCI
VIA DELLA SCALA
VIA BENEDETTA

PERFUMERY
31

Piazza Santa Maria Novella

VIA DEGLI AVELLI

VIA DEI BANCHI

VIA DE' CERRETAN

SANTA MARIA MAGGIORE

VIA PALAZZUOLO

VIA DEI BANCHI
BELLE DONNE
TREBBIO
RONDINELLI

VIA PECORI

OGNISSANTI

VIA DELLA PORCELLANA
VIA DI PAOLINO

VIA DEL SOLE
ANTINORI
GIACOMINI

SAN GAETANO

VIA DE' TOSINGHI

Piazza Ognissanti

VIA DELLA SPADA

V. CORSI

PESCIONI
VECCHIETTI

BRUNELLESCHI

Piaz dell Repub
22

LUNGARNO VESPUCCI

VIA DE' FOSSI
VIA DEL MORO

VIA DELLA

RUCELLAI PALACE

VIGNA NUOVA

VIA DEGLI STROZZI

STROZZI PALACE

VIA D. ANSELMI

Piazza Goldoni

VIA DE FEDERIGHI

PURGATORIO
INFERNO

VIA DELLA
VIA DEL PARIONE

PARIONCINO

SANTA TRINITÀ

MONALDA
SASSETTI

POST
20

VIA PELLICCERIA

PONTE ALLA CARRAIA

LUNGARNO CORSINI

Piazza Sta. Trinità

VIA PORTA ROSSA

L. SODERINI

TORNABUONI

VIA DEL
VIA DELLE TERME

CORNINO
MANETTO

Piazza Sauro

LUNGARNO GUICCIARDINI

BORGO S. APOSTOLI
FIORDALISO
BOMBARDE
RICASOLI

LUNGARNO ACCIAIUOLI

VIA POR SAN

To Porta San Frediano

VIA SANTO SPIRITO
GEPPI

PONTE STA. TRINITÀ

S. STEF

BORGO STELLA

VIA DE' SERRAGLI
MAFFIA
V. COVERELLI

Piazza Frescobaldi

TORRE DEI BELFREDELLI

PONTE VECCHIO
26

VASA CORRID

VIA S. MONACA
6

OLTRARNO

VIA D. SPRONE

BORGO SAN JACOPO

Piazza S. Felicità

VIA

VIA SANT'AGOSTINO

SANTO SPIRITO
32

VIA DE' VELLUTINI
VIA DELVELLUTI
V. SGUAZZA

VIA DE' RAMAGLIANTI

COSTA DI SAN G

Piazza Santo Spirito

VIA DE' MAGGIO
VIA D. S. MARTINO
MICHELOZZI

VIA TOSCANELLA

SDRUCCIOLO DE' PITTI

GROTTO BACCHUS

VIA DELLE CALDAIE

BORGO TEGOLAIO
VIA MAZZETTA

VIA GUICCIARDINI

EXIT GARDENS

To Porta Romana

Piazza de' Pitti
5

PITTI PALACE
25

Boboli Gardens

To Forte di Belvedere &
3

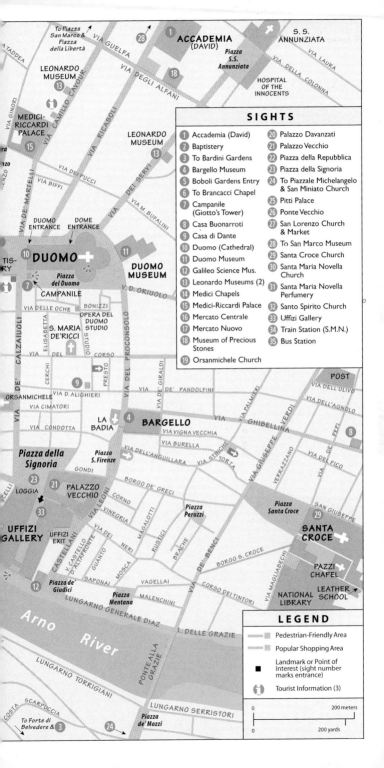

SIGHTS

1. Accademia (David)
2. Baptistery
3. To Bardini Gardens
4. Bargello Museum
5. Boboli Gardens Entry
6. To Brancacci Chapel
7. Campanile (Giotto's Tower)
8. Casa Buonarroti
9. Casa di Dante
10. Duomo (Cathedral)
11. Duomo Museum
12. Galileo Science Mus.
13. Leonardo Museums (2)
14. Medici Chapels
15. Medici-Riccardi Palace
16. Mercato Centrale
17. Mercato Nuovo
18. Museum of Precious Stones
19. Orsanmichele Church
20. Palazzo Davanzati
21. Palazzo Vecchio
22. Piazza della Repubblica
23. Piazza della Signoria
24. To Piazzale Michelangelo & San Miniato Church
25. Pitti Palace
26. Ponte Vecchio
27. San Lorenzo Church & Market
28. To San Marco Museum
29. Santa Croce Church
30. Santa Maria Novella Church
31. Santa Maria Novella Perfumery
32. Santo Spirito Church
33. Uffizi Gallery
34. Train Station (S.M.N.)
35. Bus Station

LEGEND

- Pedestrian-Friendly Area
- Popular Shopping Area
- ■ Landmark or Point of Interest (sight number marks entrance)
- Tourist Information (3)

0 — 200 meters
0 — 200 yards

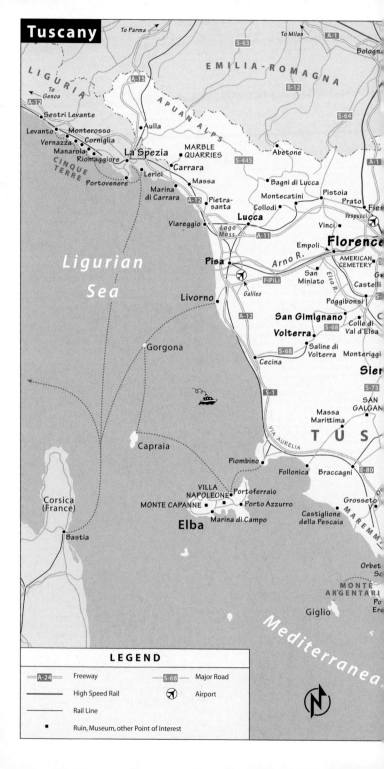

Tuscany

To Parma
To Milan
A-1
Bologna

S-63

EMILIA-ROMAGNA

LIGURIA

A-15

S-12

APUAN ALPS

S-12

To Genoa

A-12

Sestri Levante

Levanto

Monterosso

Vernazza

Corniglia

Manarola

Riomaggiore

CINQUE TERRE

Portovenere

Aulla

La Spezia

Lerici

Carrara

Marina di Carrara

Massa

Pietra-santa

A-12

Viareggio

MARBLE QUARRIES

S-445

Abetone

S-64

A-1

Bagni di Lucca

Montecatini

Pistoia

Collodi

Lucca

Prato

Fies

Vespucci

Lago Mass.

A-11

Vinci

Florence

Empoli

AMERICAN CEMETERY

Pisa

Arno R.

FIPILI

San Miniato

Elsa R.

Castelli

Galileo

Livorno

A-12

Poggibonsi

San Gimignano

Colle di Val d'Elsa

Volterra

S-68

Gorgona

Saline di Volterra

Monteriggi

Cecina

S-68

Sier

S-1

S-73

SAN GALGAN

Massa Marittima

VIA AURELIA

TUS

Capraia

Piombino

Follonica

Braccagni

E-80

Corsica (France)

Bastia

VILLA NAPOLEONE

MONTE CAPANNE

Portoferraio

Porto Azzurro

Elba

Marina di Campo

Castiglione della Pescaia

Grosseto

MAREMM

Orbet

Sc

MONTE ARGENTARI

Po

Giglio

Ere

Ligurian Sea

Mediterranea

LEGEND

A-24 Freeway		S-68 Major Road
High Speed Rail		✈ Airport
Rail Line		
■ Ruin, Museum, other Point of Interest		

N

Rome

SIGHTS

1 To Ancient Appian Way
2 Ara Pacis
3 Arch of Constantine
4 Baths of Caracalla
5 Baths of Diocletian
6 Bocca della Verità
7 To Borghese Gallery
8 Campo de' Fiori
9 Capitoline Museums
10 Capuchin Crypt
11 Castel Sant'Angelo
12 Circus Maximus
13 Colosseum
14 Galleria Doria Pamphilj
15 National Museum of Rome
16 Palatine Hill (Entrance)
17 Pantheon
18 Piazza Navona
19 Porta Portese Flea Market
20 Roman Forum (Entrance)
21 To St. Paul's Outside the Walls & Montemartini Mus.
22 St. Peter's Basilica
23 St. Peter-in-Chains
24 Santa Maria della Vittoria
25 Santa Maria in Trastevere
26 Santa Susanna
27 Sistine Chapel
28 Spanish Steps
29 Synagogue & Jewish Museum
30 Termini Train Station
31 Testaccio District
32 Trajan's Column, Market & Museum of the Imperial Forums
33 Trevi Fountain
34 Vatican Museum (Entrance)
35 Victor Emmanuel Monument
36 Villa Farnesina

Italy

Italia

Bella Italia! Italy has Europe's richest, craziest culture. If you take Italy on its own terms, you'll experience a cultural keelhauling that actually feels good.

Some people, often with considerable effort, manage to hate this country. Italy bubbles with emotion, corruption, stray hairs, inflation, traffic jams, strikes, rallies, holidays, crowded squalor, and irate ranters shaking their fists at each other one minute and walking arm-in-arm the next. Have a talk with yourself before you cross the border. Promise yourself to relax and accept it all as a package deal.

After all, Italy is the cradle of European civilization—established by the Roman Empire and carried on by the Roman Catholic Church. As you explore Italy, you'll stand face-to-face with some of the world's most iconic images from this 2,000-year history: the Colosseum of Ancient Rome, the medieval Leaning Tower of Pisa, Michelangelo's *David* and Botticelli's *Venus*, the playful Baroque exuberance of the Trevi Fountain...and the Italian city that preserves this legacy in a state of elegant decay: Venice.

Beyond these famous sights, though, Italy offers Europe's richest culture. Traditions still live within a country that is vibrant and fully modern. Go with an eye open to both the Italy of the past and of the present.

Italy is diverse, encompassing German-flavored Alps, Mediterranean beaches, sun-baked Sicily, romantic hill towns, the urban jungle of Naples, the business center of Milan, and the art-drenched cities of Venice, Florence, and Rome. The country is reasonably small and laced with freeways and train lines, so you're never more than a day's journey away from any of these places. Each of Italy's 20 regions has its own distinct character, whether it's scenic Tuscany, busy Lombardy, or the place where it all mixes together—Lazio, home of the capital, Rome.

Many travelers discover that there are two Italys: The North is industrial, aggressive, and "time is money" in its outlook. The weather is temperate, and the people are more like Northern Europeans. The South is hot and sunny, crowded, poor, relaxed, farm-oriented, and traditional. Families here are very close-knit and usually live in the same house for many generations. Loyalties are to family, city, region, soccer team, and country—in that order. (For more on the two Italys, see "Rome vs. Milan: A Classic Squabble" on page 298).

Economically, Italy has had its problems, but somehow

things have always worked out. Today, Italy is the world's tenth-largest industrial power, and the fifth-largest in Europe. Ferraris, Fiats, Maseratis, and Lamborghinis are world-renowned (though they're not really major exports). Tourism is big business—Italy is considered the world's fifth most-visited tourist destination.

Cronyism, which complicates my work, is an integral part of the economy. Much of Italy's business is hidden in a large "black market" unreported to government officials. Labor unions are strong, strikes are frequent, and the country today is faced with pressure to compete globally.

While most Italians are nominally Catholic, the true dominant religion is life—motor scooters, soccer, fashion, girl-watching, boy-watching, good coffee, good wine, and *il dolce far niente* (the sweetness of doing nothing). The Italian character shows itself on the streets, in the maniacal yet skilled drivers and the classy dressers who star in the ritual evening stroll, or *passeggiata*.

Italians are more social and communal than most other Europeans. In small towns, everyone knows everyone. People get out of their apartments to socialize on the main square. Young women walk hand in hand, and young teen-agers shove or punch each other playfully or hang all over each other.

Because they're so outgoing and their language is so fun, Italians are a pleasure to communicate with. Be melodramatic and talk with your hands. Hear the melody; get into the flow. Italians want to connect, and they try harder than any other Europeans. Play with them. Even in non-touristy towns, where English is rare and Italian

Italy Almanac

Official Name: Repubblica Italiana (Italian Republic), or Italia for short.

Population: 61 million, comprised almost entirely of indigenous Italians who speak Italian (German and French are spoken in some Alpine regions) and are nominally Roman Catholic (90 percent).

Latitude and Longitude: 43°N and 12°E (similar to Oregon and Maine).

Area: 116,000 square miles, including the islands of Sicily, Sardinia, and others.

Geography: Italy is shaped like a boot, 850 miles long and 150 miles wide, jutting into the central Mediterranean. (By comparison, Florida is 500 miles long.) The terrain is generally mountainous or hilly, with the Alps in the north and a north-south "spine" of the Apennine Mountains. The highest point is Mont Blanc (15,771 feet), on the border with France. Outside the Alps, the highest point is Monte Cimone (7,100 feet). Italy has 5,000 miles of coastline. Major rivers include the Po (the longest at 400 miles), Arno, Adige, and Tiber. Italy has three active volcanoes: Vesuvius, Etna, and Stromboli.

Regions: Italy is divided into 20 regions (including Tuscany, Umbria, Veneto, and Lazio). Locally, there are some 8,000 "communes," each with a community council and mayor.

Major Cities: Rome (the capital, 2.7 million), Milan (1.3 million), and Naples (1 million).

Economy: The Gross Domestic Product is $1.8 trillion; the GDP per capita is $30,000. About 73 percent of the economy consists of service jobs (especially tourism), 25 percent is industry (textiles, chemicals), and 2 percent is agriculture (fruit, vegetables, olives, wine, plus fishing). There are 12,000 miles of train lines (mostly government-run) and 4,300 miles of expressway (autostrada).

Government: Italy is a republic, with three branches of government. The chief executive is Prime Minister Mario Monti. The bicameral legislature is elected by (mostly) direct voting. Since World War II, the fragmented country has had 62 national governments.

Flag: Three vertical bands of green, white, and red.

Italian Inventions: Opera, cologne, thermometer, barometer, pizza, wireless telegraph, espresso machine, typewriter, batteries, nitroglycerin, yo-yos...and the ice-cream cone.

Museums: 3,000.

Average "Gio": The average Italian is 43 years old, has 1.3 kids, and will live to the ripe old age of 80 (one in five Italians is older than 65). Every day, he or she consumes two servings of pasta, a half-pound of bread, and two glasses of wine. Despite Italian cuisine, Gio isn't fat—less than 10 percent of Italians are considered obese.

is the norm, showing a little warmth lets you hop right over the language barrier.

Like most Europeans (and Americans), Italians enjoy watching TV (game shows, sitcoms, etc.), going to movies (American films are almost always dubbed, not subtitled), and listening to their homegrown pop music. Though Italy is the birthplace of opera and much classical music, it's not much more "cultured" today than America is.

Italian food, however, is a cut above. If America's specialty is fast food, Italy's is slow food: locally grown ingredients, in season, bought daily, prepared with love, and

enjoyed in social circumstances with friends and family. Even in modern cities, big supermarkets are rare. Instead, people buy their bread from the baker and their meats from the butcher, enjoying a chance to catch up on gossip with the shopkeeper. Italians buy foods in season, celebrating the arrival of fresh artichokes in the spring and porcini mushrooms in the fall.

The three-hour meal is common. For many Italians, dinner is the evening's entertainment. They eat in courses, lingering over each one. A typical meal might start with an antipasto plate of cold cuts and veggies. Next comes the pasta, then the meat dish, then a salad. No meal is complete without dessert (Italian gelato is considered the best ice cream in the world), accompanied by coffee or a digestif.

Wine complements each course. Italy is the world's number-one wine producer (just ahead of France). It'd be a shame to visit Italy without sampling the specialties from each region, whether it's the famous Chianti from central Italy, a white Soave from the Veneto, Bardolinos from the North, or a Lacryma Christi from the South.

Italian "bars" are not taverns, but cafés...and social watering holes. In the morning, they serve coffee, orange juice, and croissants to workers on the go. At lunch, it's sandwiches *(panini)* and mini-pizzas for university students. In the afternoon, housewives might drop in for an ice-cream bar. At night, men and women enjoy a glass of wine and watch TV while the kids play a video game in the corner.

Besides food, travelers enjoy sampling Italy's other wares. While no longer a cheap country, Italy is still a hit with shoppers. Find glassware in Venice; gold, silver, leather, and prints in Florence; and high fashion in Rome and Milan.

Italians are obsessed with sports—though not American sports. Italian sports idols are soccer players (Francesco Totti, Antonio Cassano), skiers (Giorgio Rocca), and cyclists (Paolo Savoldelli). Motor racing—Formula 1/Grand Prix—is huge. And since many Italians grow up zipping through narrow streets on small Vespas, it's little wonder that motorcycle racing *(moto,* led by Valentino Rossi) is a major sport here. A favorite participant sport is bocce, played casually at parks throughout Italy. The players take turns tossing small metal balls on a dirt court, aiming at a small wooden ball.

Italy's undisputed number-one sport is soccer (called *il calcio*). Soccer fans *(tifosi)* are passionate. Star players are paid millions and treated like movie stars. Little kids everywhere grow up pretending to score the winning goal just like them. On big game nights, bars are packed with men crowded around TV sets. After a loss, they drown their sorrows. After a victory, fans celebrate by driving through the city streets honking horns and waving team flags. Many Italians place their national, regional, and personal pride on the backs of their athletes. It's a cliché that remains true: In a Europe at peace, the soccer field is the battleground.

But even as Europe evolves, Italy remains a mix of old and new. Appreciate the extreme changes Italian society has gone through in just half a century: the "economic miracle" of the 1950s and 1960s, a wave of domestic terrorism (from the left and the right) in the 1970s and 1980s, stronger integration in the European Union in the 1990s, and the current economic downturn and debt crisis. Italian politics are a reckless pendulum that swings between right- and left-wing extremes. It seems that nobody holds office for very long, but it's always possible to bounce back.

Italy, home of the Vatican, is still 90 percent Catholic... but not particularly devout. Most people would never think of renouncing their faith, but they don't attend church regularly.

They baptize their kids at the local church (there's one every few blocks), but they hold modern opinions on social issues, often in conflict with strict Catholic dogma. Italy is now the land of legalized abortion, the lowest birth rate in Europe, nudity on TV, socialist politics, and a society whose common language is decidedly secular.

Some traditions thrive. Italian families and communities are still more close-knit than many others in the modern world. Many Italians, especially in rural regions, still follow the traditional siesta schedule (called *reposo* in Italy). At about 1:00 p.m., shops close and people go home for a three-hour break to have lunch, socialize with friends and family, and run errands. (While a few old-timers take a short nap in front of the TV, most Italians are quite busy during this time.) And on festival days, locals still dress up in medieval garb to paddle gondolas (Venice), race horses (Siena), battle over a bridge (Pisa), or play rugby or soccer (Florence). But these days, the traditional ways are carried on by choice. Italians are wary of the dangers of a fast-paced global lifestyle. Their history is long, and they're secure in their place in the world.

Accept Italy as Italy. Zero in on the fine points. Don't dwell on the problems. Savor your cappuccino, dangle your feet over a canal (if it smells, breathe through your mouth), and imagine what it was like centuries ago. Ramble through the rabble and rubble of Rome and mentally resurrect those ancient stones. Look into the famous sculpted eyes of Michelangelo's *David* and understand Renaissance Man's assertion of himself. Sit silently on a hilltop rooftop. Get chummy with the winds of the past. Write a poem over a glass of local wine in a sun-splashed, wave-dashed Riviera village. If you fall off your moral horse, call it a cultural experience. Italy is for romantics.

INTRODUCTION

This book will help you make the most of your trip. It breaks Italy into its top destinations—offering a balanced, comfortable mix of exciting cities and cozy towns, from brutal but *bella* Rome to *tranquillo*, traffic-free Riviera villages. It covers the predictable biggies and stirs in a healthy dose of "Back Door" intimacy. Along with marveling at Michelangelo's masterpieces, you'll enjoy a snack of *bruschetta* (fresh garlic rubbed on toast) prepared by a village boy. I've been selective, including only the most exciting sights and experiences. For example, after visiting many hill towns, I recommend just my favorites.

You'll get all the specifics and opinions necessary to wring the maximum value out of your limited time and money. If you plan a month or less in Italy, and you have a normal appetite for information, this book is all you need. If you're a travel-info fiend like me, you'll find that this book sorts through all the superlatives and provides a handy rack upon which to hang your supplemental information.

Italy is my favorite European country. Experiencing its culture, people, and natural wonders economically and hassle-free has been my goal for three decades of traveling, tour guiding, and writing. With this book, I pass to you the lessons I've learned, updated for 2013.

The best of Italy is, of course, only my opinion. But after spending half my adult life researching Europe, I've developed a sixth sense for what travelers enjoy.

Map Legend

⚞ Viewpoint	✈ Airport	)▬▬(Tunnel
↑ Entrance	Ⓣ Taxi Stand	⋯⋯⋯ Pedestrian Zone
✪ Tourist Info	Ⓣ Tram Stop	▬ ▬ ▬ Railway
WC Restroom	Ⓑ Bus Stop	⋯⋯⋯⋯ Ferry/Boat Route
✿ Synagogue	Ⓟ Parking	
⬚ Church	)(Mtn. Pass	⊢─┼─┤ Tram
Ⓥ Vaporetto Stop	⬚ Park	▦▦▦▦ Stairs
Ⓣ Traghetto Crossing	▪ Statue/Point of Interest	· · · · · Walk/Tour Route
Ⓖ Gondola Station		
Ⓐ Alilaguna Stop	⛫ Castle	─ ─ ─ ─ Trail

Use this legend to help you navigate the maps in this book.

About This Book

Rick Steves' Italy 2013 is a personal tour guide in your pocket. This book is organized by destinations. Each destination is a mini-vacation on its own, filled with exciting sights, strollable neighborhoods, affordable places to stay, and memorable places to eat. In the following chapters, you'll find these sections:

Planning Your Time suggests a schedule for how to best use your limited time.

Orientation includes specifics on public transportation, helpful hints, local tour options, easy-to-read maps, and tourist information.

Sights describes the top attractions and includes their cost and hours.

Self-Guided Walks take you through interesting neighborhoods, with a personal tour guide in hand.

Sleeping describes my favorite hotels, from good-value deals to cushy splurges.

Eating serves up a range of options, from inexpensive cafés to fancy restaurants.

Connections outlines your options for traveling to destinations by train, bus, plane, and cruise ship. In car-friendly regions, I've included route tips for drivers.

The **Italian History** chapter gives you a helpful overview of Italy's history, art, and architecture.

The **appendix** is a traveler's tool kit, with telephone tips, useful phone numbers, transportation basics (on trains, buses, boats, car rentals, driving, and flights), recommended books and films, a festival list, a climate chart, a handy packing checklist, a hotel reservation form, and Italian survival phrases.

Browse through this book, choose your favorite destinations, and link them up. Then have a *buono* trip! Traveling like a temporary local, you'll get the absolute most out of every mile, minute,

Key to This Book

Updates

This book is updated every year—but as soon as you pin down Italy, it wiggles. For the latest, visit www.ricksteves.com /update. For a valuable list of reports and experiences—good and bad—from fellow travelers, check www.ricksteves.com /feedback.

Abbreviations and Times

I use the following symbols and abbreviations in this book:

Sights are rated:

▲▲▲	**Don't miss**
▲▲	**Try hard to see**
▲	**Worthwhile if you can make it**
No rating	**Worth knowing about**

Tourist information offices are abbreviated as **TI,** and bathrooms are **WCs.** To categorize accommodations, I use a **Sleep Code** (described on page 21).

Like Europe, this book uses the **24-hour clock.** It's the same through 12:00 noon, then keep going: 13:00, 14:00, and so on. For anything over 12, subtract 12 and add p.m. (14:00 is 2:00 p.m.).

When giving **opening times,** I include both peak season and off-season hours if they differ. So, if a museum is listed as "May-Oct daily 9:00-16:00," it should be open from 9 a.m. until 4 p.m. from the first day of May until the last day of October (but expect exceptions).

For **transit** or **tour departures,** I first list the frequency, then the duration. So, a train connection listed as "2/hour, 1.5 hours" departs twice each hour and the journey lasts an hour and a half.

and dollar. As you visit places I know and love, I'm happy that you'll be meeting some of my favorite Italian people.

Planning

This section will help you get started planning your trip—with advice on trip costs, when to go, and what you should know before you take off.

Travel Smart

Many people travel through Italy thinking it's a chaotic mess. They feel that any attempt at efficient travel is futile. This is dead wrong—and expensive. Italy, which seems as orderly as spilled spaghetti, actually functions quite well. Only those who understand this and travel smart can enjoy Italy on a budget.

Top Destinations in Italy

This book can save you lots of time and money. But to have an "A" trip, you need to be an "A" student. Read it all before your trip, noting holidays, specific advice on sights, and days when sights are closed. A smart trip is a puzzle—a fun, doable, and worthwhile challenge.

Be sure to mix intense and relaxed periods in your itinerary. To maximize rootedness, minimize one-night stands. It's worth taking a long drive after dinner (or a train ride with a dinner picnic) to get settled in a town for two nights. Hotels are more likely to give a better price to someone staying more than one night. Every trip—and every traveler—needs slack time (laundry, picnics, people-watching, and so on). Pace yourself. Assume you will return.

Reread this book as you travel, and visit local TIs. Upon arrival in a new town, lay the groundwork for a smooth departure; write down (or print out from an online source) the schedule for the train, bus, or boat that you'll take when you depart. Drivers can study the best route to their next destination.

Get online at Internet cafés or your hotel, and carry a mobile phone (or use a phone card): You can find tourist information, learn the latest on sights (special events, English tour schedule, etc.), book tickets and tours, make reservations, reconfirm hotels, research transportation connections, and keep in touch with your loved ones.

Enjoy the friendliness of the Italian people. Connect with the culture. Set up your own quest for the best piazza, bell tower, or gelato. Slow down and be open to unexpected experiences. Ask questions—most locals are eager to point you in their idea of the right direction. Keep a notepad in your pocket for confirming prices, noting directions, and organizing your thoughts. Wear your money belt, learn the currency, and figure out how to estimate prices in dollars. Those who expect to travel smart, do.

Trip Costs

Six components make up your trip costs: airfare, surface transportation, room and board, sightseeing and entertainment, shopping and miscellany, and gelato.

Airfare: A basic round-trip flight from the US to Milan or Rome can cost, on average, about $1,000-1,800 total, depending on where you fly from and when (cheaper in winter). Smaller budget airlines provide bargain service from several European capitals to many cities in Italy. If your trip covers a wide area, consider saving time and money in Europe by flying into one city and out of another; for instance, into Milan and out of Rome.

Surface Transportation: For a three-week whirlwind trip of all of my recommended destinations, allow $550 per person for buses and second-class trains ($750 for first-class trains). For a three-week car rental, tolls, gas, and insurance, allow $900 per person (based on two people sharing). Leasing is worth considering for trips of three weeks or more. Car rentals and leases are cheapest if arranged from the US. Train passes are normally available only outside of Europe, though you may save money by simply buying tickets as you go. For more on public transportation and car rental, see "Transportation" in the appendix.

Room and Board: You can thrive in Italy in 2013 on $120 a day per person for room and board (more in big cities). This allows $15 for lunch, $25 for dinner, and $80 for lodging (based on two people splitting the cost of a $160 double room that includes breakfast). Students and tightwads can enjoy Italy for as little as $65 a day ($35 for a bed, $30 for meals and snacks).

Sightseeing and Entertainment: In big cities, figure about $15-22 per major sight (museums, Colosseum), $7-10 for minor

Italy's Best Three-Week Trip (by Train and Bus)

Day	Plan	Sleep in
1	Arrive in Milan	Milan
2	Milan to Lake Como	Varenna
3	Lake Como	Varenna
4	To Dolomites via Verona	Bolzano/Castelrotto
5	Dolomites	Bolzano/Castelrotto
6	To Venice	Venice
7	Venice	Venice
8	To Cinque Terre	Vernazza
9	Cinque Terre	Vernazza
10	Pisa, then to Florence	Florence
11	Florence	Florence
12	Florence, late to Siena	Siena
13	Siena	Siena
14	To Assisi (by bus)	Assisi
15	To Orvieto and Civita	Orvieto
16	To Sorrento	Sorrento
17	Naples and Pompeii	Sorrento
18	Capri or Amalfi Coast	Sorrento
19	Morning to Rome	Rome
20	Rome	Rome
21	Rome	Rome
22	Fly home	

With limited time: Skip the Dolomites.
To modify for drivers: The big sights of Italy (Rome, Florence, Venice, Sorrento/Naples/Capri/Amalfi, and Cinque

ones (climbing church towers), and $25-30 for splurge experiences (e.g., walking tours and concerts). An overall average of $35 a day works for most people. Don't skimp here. After all, this category is the driving force behind your trip—you came to sightsee, enjoy, and experience Italy.

Shopping and Miscellany: Figure $3 per postcard (including postage) and $4 per coffee, soft drink, or gelato. Shopping can vary in cost from nearly nothing to a small fortune. Good budget travelers find that this category has little to do with assembling a trip full of lifelong and wonderful memories.

Sightseeing Priorities

Depending on the length of your trip, and taking geographic proximity into account, here are my recommended priorities:

Italy's Best Three-Week Trip

(LAKES) VARENNA
CASTELROTTO (DOLOMITES)
MILAN
VERONA
VENICE
100 Kilometers
100 Miles
RAVENNA
CINQUE TERRE
PISA
FLORENCE
SIENA
ASSISI
CIVITA
ORVIETO AREA
Adriatic Sea
ROME
Mediterranean Sea
NAPLES
POMPEII
SORRENTO
PAESTUM
AMALFI COAST
● Overnights
• Other Stops

Terre) are inconvenient by car and easy by public transportation. Those wanting to drive in Italy will find a car most helpful for the hill towns of Tuscany and Umbria and the Dolomites. I'd start by touring most of the country by train, then use a car to explore a region or two (even if it means backtracking a few extra hours by train or car).

4 days:	Florence, Venice
6 days, add:	Rome
8 days, add:	Cinque Terre
10 days, add:	Civita and Siena
14 days, add:	Sorrento, Naples, Pompeii, Amalfi Coast, Paestum
18 days, add:	Milan, Lake Como, Varenna, Assisi
21 days, add:	Dolomites, Verona, Padua

This includes nearly everything on the above map.

When to Go

Italy's best travel months (also its busiest and most expensive) are May, June, September, and October. These months combine the convenience of peak season with pleasant weather.

Italy at a Glance

These attractions are listed (as in this book) roughly from north to south.

▲▲▲**Venice** Romantic island city, powerful in medieval times; famous for St. Mark's Basilica, the Grand Canal, and singing gondoliers.

▲**Near Venice** Several interesting towns: Padua (with Giotto's gloriously frescoed Scrovegni Chapel), Verona (Roman amphitheater plus Romeo and Juliet sights), and Ravenna (top Byzantine mosaics).

▲**The Dolomites** Italy's rugged rooftop with a Germanic flair, featuring Bolzano (home of Ötzi the Ice Man), Castelrotto (charming village), and Alpe di Siusi (alpine meadows laced with lifts and hiking trails).

▲**The Lakes** Two relaxing lakes, each with low-key resort towns and a mountainous backdrop: Lake Como, with quaint Varenna and upscale Bellagio; and Lake Maggiore, with straightforward Stresa, manicured islands, and elegant villas.

▲▲**Milan** Powerhouse city of commerce and fashion, with the prestigious La Scala opera house, Leonardo's *The Last Supper*, and three airports.

▲▲▲**The Cinque Terre** Five idyllic Riviera hamlets along a rugged coastline (and part of a national park), connected by scenic hiking trails and dotted with beaches.

Riviera Towns near the Cinque Terre More Italian Riviera fun, including the beach towns of Levanto, Sestri Levante, the larger Santa Margherita Ligure, and trendier Portofino nearby, and to the south, resorty Portovenere and workaday La Spezia (transportation hub).

▲▲▲**Florence** The cradle of the Renaissance, with the world-class Uffizi Gallery, Brunelleschi's dome-topped Duomo,

The most grueling thing about travel in Italy—particularly in the south—is the summer heat in July and August, when temperatures hit the high 80s and 90s. Most mid-range hotels come with air-conditioning—important in the summer—but it's usually available only from June through September.

Peak season (roughly May-Oct in the north and May-June and Sept-Oct in the south) offers the longest hours and the most

Michelangelo's *David,* and Italy's best gelato.

▲**Pisa and Lucca** Two classic towns: Pisa, with its famous Leaning Tower and surrounding Field of Miracles, and Lucca, with a charming walled old center.

▲▲▲**Siena** Florence's smaller and (some say) more appealing rival, with its grand Il Campo square and striking striped cathedral.

▲▲**Hill Towns of Central Italy** Picturesque, wine-soaked villages of Italy's heartland, including San Gimignano, Volterra, Montalcino, Pienza, Montepulciano, and Cortona.

▲▲**Assisi** St. Francis' hometown, perched on a hillside, with a divinely Giotto-decorated basilica.

▲▲**Orvieto and Civita** More hill-town adventures, featuring Orvieto's classic views and ornate cathedral plus the adorable pocket-sized village of Civita di Bagnoregio.

▲▲▲**Rome** Italy's capital, the Eternal City, studded with Roman remnants (Forum, Colosseum, Pantheon), romantic floodlit-fountain squares, and the Vatican—home to one of Italy's top museums and the Sistine Chapel.

▲▲**Naples** Gritty, in-love-with-life port city featuring vibrant street life and a top archaeological museum, with the famous Pompeii ruins a day-trip away.

▲**Sorrento and Capri** The seaside resort port of Sorrento, and a short cruise away, the jet-set island getaway of Capri, with its Blue Grotto.

▲**Amalfi Coast and Paestum** String of seafront villages—including hilly Positano and Amalfi—tied together by a scenic mountainous coastal road, plus nearby Paestum, with its well-preserved ancient Greek temples.

exciting slate of activities—but terrible crowds. During peak times, many resort-area hotels maximize business by requiring that guests take half-pension, which means buying a meal per day (usually dinner) in their restaurants. August, the month when many Italians take their summer vacations, isn't as bad as many make it out to be, but big cities tend to be quiet (with discounted hotel prices), and beach and mountain resorts are jammed (with higher

INTRODUCTION

hotel prices). Note that Italians generally wear shorts only at beach resort towns. If you want to blend in, wear lightweight long (or Capri) pants in Italy, even in summer, except at the beach.

Between November and April, you can usually expect pleasant weather, and you'll miss most of the sweat and stress of the tourist season. Off-season, expect shorter hours, more lunchtime breaks, and fewer activities. However, spring and fall can be cool, and many hotels—thanks to a national interest in conserving energy—aren't allowed to turn on their heat until winter. In the winter, it often drops to the 40s in Milan and the 50s in Rome (see the climate chart in the appendix).

Know Before You Go

Your trip is more likely to go smoothly if you plan ahead. Check this list of things to arrange while you're still at home.

You need a **passport**—but no visa or shots—to travel in Italy. You may be denied entry into certain European countries if your passport is due to expire within three to six months of your ticketed date of return. Get it renewed if you'll be cutting it close. It can take up to six weeks to get or renew a passport (for more on passports, see www.travel.state.gov). Pack a photocopy of your passport in your luggage in case the original is lost or stolen.

Book rooms well in advance if you'll be traveling during peak season (spring and fall) and any major holidays (see page 1106).

Call your **debit- and credit-card companies** to let them know the countries you'll be visiting, to ask about fees, request your PIN (it will be mailed to you), and more. See page 15 for details.

Do your homework if you want to buy **travel insurance.** Compare the cost of the insurance to the likelihood of your using it and your potential loss if something goes wrong. Also, check whether your existing insurance (health, homeowners, or renters) covers you and your possessions overseas. For more tips, see www .ricksteves.com/insurance.

If you're taking an **overnight train** and need a couchette *(cuccetta)* or sleeper—and you must leave on a certain day—consider booking it in advance through a US travel agent (such as www .raileurope.com), even though it may cost more than buying it in Italy. Other Italian trains, such as the high-speed ES trains, require a seat reservation, but for these it's usually possible to make arrangements in Italy just a few days ahead. (For more on train travel, see the appendix.)

If you're planning on **renting a car** in Italy, you'll need your driver's license and an International Driving Permit (see page 1095). Driving is prohibited in some city centers; obey the signage or risk getting a huge fine (see page 1098).

Make reservations ahead of time for major sights. Book at least a month in advance for **Florence**'s Uffizi Gallery (Renaissance paintings) and a few days ahead for the Accademia (Michelangelo's *David*); or for an easy but pricey way to avoid making reservations, you can buy a Firenze Card when you arrive in Florence (see page 471). For **Milan,** book several months ahead for da Vinci's *Last Supper* (see page 321); for **Padua,** book well in advance for Giotto's Scrovegni Chapel (see page 153); and for **Rome,** a week ahead for the Borghese Gallery (Bernini sculptures; see page 861). The Vatican Museum takes online reservations, and while not mandatory, these can save you substantial time in line (see page 851).

If you plan to hire a **local guide,** reserve ahead by email. Popular guides can get booked up.

If you're bringing a **mobile device,** download any apps you might want to use on the road, such as translators, maps, and transit schedules. Check out **Rick Steves Audio Europe,** featuring audio tours of major sights, hours of travel interviews on Italy, and more (via www.ricksteves.com/audioeurope, iTunes, Google Play, or the Rick Steves Audio Europe smartphone app; for details, see page 1101).

Check the **Rick Steves guidebook updates** page for any recent changes to this book (www.ricksteves.com/update).

Because **airline carry-on restrictions** are always changing, visit the Transportation Security Administration's website (www.tsa.gov/travelers) for an up-to-date list of what you can bring on the plane with you...and what you have to check.

Practicalities

Emergency and Medical Help: In Italy, dial 113 for English-speaking police help. To summon an ambulance, call 118. If you get sick, do as the Italians do and go to a pharmacist for advice. Or ask at your hotel for help—they'll know of the nearest medical and emergency services.

Theft or Loss: To replace a passport, you'll need to go in person to your embassy (see page 1082). If your credit and debit cards disappear, cancel and replace them (see "Damage Control for Lost Cards" on page 15). File a police report either on the spot or within a day or two; it's required to submit an insurance claim for lost or stolen railpasses or travel gear, and can help with replacing your passport or credit and debit cards. For more information, see www.ricksteves.com/help. Precautionary measures can minimize the effects of loss—back up your photos and other files frequently.

More Help: A service of the Italian government, **EasyItalia,** offers English-language tourist information, emergency assistance, and help with everything from flight cancellations to car-rental trouble (call toll-free 800-000-039 from a land line or pay phone, otherwise call 039-039-039, phone answered daily 9:00-22:00; or use their online form at www.easy-italia.com for a response within 48 hours).

Time Zones: Italy, like most of continental Europe, is generally six/nine hours ahead of the East/West Coasts of the US. The exceptions are the beginning and end of Daylight Saving Time: Europe "springs forward" the last Sunday in March (two weeks after most of North America), and "falls back" the last Sunday in October (one week before North America). For a handy online time converter, see www.timeanddate.com/worldclock.

Business Hours: Traditionally, Italy uses the siesta plan, where people usually work from about 9:00 to 13:00 and from 15:30 to 19:00, Monday through Saturday. However, many businesses have adopted the government's recommended 8:00 to 14:00 workday. In tourist areas, shops are open longer. Stores are usually closed on Sunday, and often on Monday, as well as for a couple of weeks around August 15. Banking hours are generally Monday through Friday from 8:30 to 13:30 and 15:30 to 16:30, but can vary wildly.

Saturdays are virtually weekdays, with earlier closing hours. Sundays have the same pros and cons as they do for travelers in the US: Sightseeing attractions are generally open but public transportation options are fewer (e.g., no bus service to or from the smaller hill towns), and there's no rush hour. Rowdy evenings are rare on Sundays.

Watt's Up? Europe's electrical system is 220 volts, instead of North America's 110 volts. Most newer electronics (such as laptops, battery chargers, and hair dryers) convert automatically, so you won't need a converter, but you will need an adapter plug with two round prongs, sold inexpensively at travel stores in the US. Avoid bringing older appliances that don't automatically convert voltage; instead, buy a cheap replacement in Europe.

Discounts: Discounts are not listed in this book. However, many sights offer discounts for youths (up to age 18), students (with proper identification cards, www.isic.org), families, seniors (loosely defined as retirees or those willing to call themselves a senior), and groups of 10 or more. Always ask. Some discounts are available only for EU citizens.

Tobacco Shops: Tobacco shops (known as *tabacchi*, often indicated with a big *T* sign) are ubiquitous across Italy as handy places to pay for street parking, and to buy postage or tickets for city buses and subways.

Money

This section offers advice on how to pay for purchases on your trip (including getting cash from ATMs and paying with plastic), dealing with lost or stolen cards, VAT (sales tax) refunds, and tipping.

What to Bring

Bring both a credit card and a debit card. You'll use the debit card at cash machines (ATMs) to withdraw local cash for most purchases, and the credit card to pay for larger items. Some travelers carry a third card as a backup, in case one gets demagnetized or eaten by a temperamental machine.

For an emergency reserve, bring several hundred dollars in hard cash in easy-to-exchange $20 bills. Avoid using currency exchange booths (because of their lousy rates and/or outrageous fees).

Cash

Cash is just as desirable in Europe as it is at home. Small businesses (hotels, restaurants, shops, etc.) prefer that you pay with cash. Some vendors will charge you extra for using a credit card, and some won't take credit cards at all. Cash is the best—and sometimes only—way to pay for bus fare, taxis, and local guides.

Throughout Europe, ATMs are the standard way for travelers to get cash. Stay away from "independent" ATMs such as Travelex, Euronet, and Forex, which charge huge commissions and have terrible exchange rates.

To withdraw money from an ATM (known as a *bancomat*), you'll need a debit card (ideally with a Visa or MasterCard logo for maximum usability), plus a PIN code. Know your PIN code in numbers; there are only numbers—no letters—on European keypads. For security, it's best to shield the keypad when entering your PIN at an ATM. Although you can use a credit card for ATM transactions, it's generally more expensive (and only makes sense in an emergency), because it's considered a "cash advance" rather

---

Exchange Rate

1 euro (€) = about $1.40

To convert prices in euros to dollars, add about 40 percent: €20 = about $28, €50 = about $70. (Check www.oanda.com for the latest exchange rates.) Just like the dollar, one euro is broken down into 100 cents. You'll find coins ranging from €0.01 to €2, and bills ranging from €5 to €500.

than a withdrawal. Try to withdraw large sums of money to reduce the number of per-transaction bank fees you'll pay.

Pickpockets target tourists. To safeguard your cash, wear a money belt—a pouch with a strap that you buckle around your waist like a belt—and tuck under your clothes. Keep your cash, credit cards, and passport secure in your money belt, and carry only a day's spending money in your front pocket.

Credit and Debit Cards

For purchases, Visa and MasterCard are more commonly accepted than American Express. Just like at home, credit or debit cards work easily at larger hotels, restaurants, and shops. I typically use my debit card to withdraw cash to pay for most purchases. I use my credit card only in a few specific situations: to book hotel reservations by phone, to cover major expenses (such as car rentals, plane tickets, and long hotel stays), and to pay for things near the end of my trip (to avoid another visit to the ATM). While you could use a debit card to make most large purchases, using a credit card offers a greater degree of fraud protection (because debit cards draw funds directly from your account).

Ask Your Credit- or Debit-Card Company: Before your trip, contact the company that issued your debit or credit cards.

• Confirm your card will work overseas, and alert them that you'll be using it in Europe; otherwise, they may deny transactions if they perceive unusual spending patterns.

• Ask for the specifics on transaction **fees.** When you use your credit or debit card—either for purchases or ATM withdrawals—you'll often be charged additional "international transaction" fees of up to 3 percent (1 percent is normal) plus $5 per transaction. If your card's fees are too high, consider getting a card just for your trip: Capital One (www.capitalone.com) and most credit unions have low-to-no international fees.

• If you plan to withdraw cash from ATMs, confirm your daily **withdrawal limit,** and, if necessary, ask your bank to adjust it. Some travelers prefer a high limit that allows them to take out more cash at each ATM stop (saving on bank fees), while others prefer to set a lower limit in case their card is stolen. Note that foreign banks also set maximum withdrawal amounts for their ATMs.

• Get your bank's emergency phone number in the US (but not its 800 number, which isn't accessible from overseas) to call collect if you have a problem.

• Ask for your credit card's **PIN** in case you encounter Europe's "chip-and-PIN" system; the bank won't tell you your PIN over the phone, so allow time for it to be mailed to you.

Chip and PIN: If your card is declined for a purchase in Europe, it may be because Europeans are increasingly using chip-and-PIN cards, which are embedded with an electronic chip (rather than the magnetic stripe used on our American-style cards). While chip and PIN is not yet common in Italy, much of Europe is adopting it. Some merchants rely on it exclusively. You're most likely to encounter chip-and-PIN problems at automated payment machines, such as those at train and subway stations, toll roads, parking garages, luggage lockers, and self-serve gas pumps. If a machine won't take your card, find a cashier who can make your card work (they can print a receipt for you to sign), or find a machine that takes cash.

But don't panic. Most travelers who are carrying only magnetic-stripe cards never encounter any problems. Still, it pays to carry plenty of euros (you can always use an ATM with your magnetic-stripe debit card). Memorizing the PIN lets you use it at some chip-and-PIN machines—just enter your PIN when prompted.

If you're still concerned, you can apply for a chip card in the US (though I think it's overkill). While big US banks offer these cards with high annual fees, a better option is the no-annual-fee GlobeTrek Visa, offered by Andrews Federal Credit Union in Maryland (open to all US residents; see www.andrewsfcu.org).

Dynamic Currency Conversion: If merchants offer to convert your purchase price into dollars (called dynamic currency conversion, or DCC), refuse this "service." You'll pay even more in fees for the expensive convenience of seeing your charge in dollars.

Damage Control for Lost Cards

If you lose your credit, debit, or ATM card, you can stop people from using your card by reporting the loss immediately to the respective global customer-assistance centers. Call these 24-hour US numbers collect: Visa (tel. 303/967-1096), MasterCard (tel. 636/722-7111), and American Express (tel. 623/492-8427). European toll-free numbers (listed by country) can also be found at the websites for Visa and MasterCard.

At a minimum, you'll need to know the name of the financial institution that issued you the card, along with the type of card (classic, platinum, or whatever). Providing the following information will allow for a quicker cancellation of your missing card: full card number, whether you are the primary or secondary cardholder, the cardholder's name exactly as printed on the card, billing address, home phone number, circumstances of the loss or theft, and identification verification (your birth date, your mother's maiden name, or your Social Security number—memorize this, don't carry a copy). If you are the secondary cardholder, you'll also need to provide the primary cardholder's identification-verification details. You can generally receive a temporary card within two or three business days in Europe (see www.ricksteves.com/help for more).

If you report your loss within two days, you typically won't be responsible for any unauthorized transactions on your account, although many banks charge a liability fee of $50.

Tipping

Tipping in Italy isn't as automatic and generous as it is in the US, but for special service, tips are appreciated, if not expected. As in the US, the proper amount depends on your resources, tipping philosophy, and the circumstances, but some general guidelines apply.

Restaurants: In Italy, the service charge *(servizio)* is usually built into your bill's grand total in one of two ways. If the menu states *servizio incluso* (or nothing at all), the listed prices already include service. If the menu states *servizio non incluso,* or *servizio* with a specific percentage, a fixed percentage (usually 10-15 percent of the total) will be added as a line item to the bottom of the bill. In either case, the total you pay already includes a basic tip. As a result, some Italians never tip, but adding a little extra is a nice thing to do to reward good service. To tip, round up the bill about €1 per person (or €2/person for classy places). Ideally, hand the tip to the server in cash, even if you pay with a credit card. If you order at a counter rather than from waitstaff, there's no need to tip.

Taxis: To tip the cabbie, round up. For a typical ride, round up your fare a bit (to pay a €4.50 fare, give €5). If the cabbie hauls your bags and zips you to the airport to help you catch your flight, you might want to toss in a little more. But if you feel like you're being driven in circles or otherwise ripped off, skip the tip.

Services: In general, if someone in the service industry does a super job for you, a small tip (the equivalent of a euro or two) is appropriate...but not required. If you're not sure whether (or how much) to tip for a service, ask your hotelier or the TI; they'll fill you in on how it's done on their turf.

Getting a VAT Refund

Wrapped into the purchase price of your Italian souvenirs is a Value-Added Tax (VAT) of 21 percent (rises to 23 percent in July 2013). You're entitled to get most of that tax back if you purchase more than €155 (about $220) worth of goods at a store that participates in the VAT-refund scheme. Typically, you must ring up the minimum at a single retailer—you can't add up your purchases from various shops to reach the required amount.

Getting your refund is usually straightforward and, if you buy a substantial amount of souvenirs, well worth the hassle. If you're lucky, the merchant will subtract the tax when you make your purchase. (This is more likely to occur if the store ships the goods to your home.) Otherwise, you'll need to:

Get the paperwork. Have the merchant completely fill out the necessary refund document, called a "cheque." You'll have to present your passport. Get the paperwork done before you leave the store to ensure you'll have everything you need (including your original sales receipt).

Get your stamp at the border or airport. Process your VAT document at your last stop in the EU (for instance, at the airport) with the customs agent who deals with VAT refunds. Before checking in for your flight, find the local customs office, and be prepared to stand in line. It's best to keep your purchases in your carry-on for viewing, but if they're too large or dangerous to carry on (such as knives), have your purchases easily accessible in the bag you're about to check, ready to show the customs agent. You're not supposed to use your purchased goods before you leave. If you show up at customs wearing your new leather shoes, officials might look the other way—or deny you a refund.

Collect your refund. You'll need to return your stamped document to the retailer or its representative. Many merchants work with a service, such as Global Blue (www.global-blue.com) or Premier Tax Free (www.premiertaxfree.com), which have offices at major airports, ports, or border crossings (either before or after security, probably strategically located near a duty-free shop). These services, which extract a 4 percent fee, can refund your money immediately in cash or credit your card (within two billing cycles). If the retailer handles VAT refunds directly, it's up to you to contact the merchant for your refund. You can mail the documents from home, or more quickly, from your point of departure (using a stamped, self-addressed envelope you've prepared or one that's been provided by the merchant). You'll then have to wait—it can take months.

Customs for American Shoppers

You are allowed to take home $800 worth of items per person duty-free, once every 30 days. You can also bring in a liter of alcohol duty-free. As for food, you can take home many processed and packaged foods: vacuum-packed cheeses, dried herbs, jams, baked goods, candy, chocolate, oil, vinegar, mustard, and honey. Fresh fruits and vegetables and most meats are not allowed. Any liquid-containing foods must be packed in checked luggage, a potential recipe for disaster. To check customs rules and duty rates, visit www.cbp.gov.

Sightseeing

Sightseeing can be hard work. Use these tips to make your visits to Italy's finest museums meaningful, fun, efficient, and painless.

Plan Ahead

Set up an itinerary that allows you to fit in all your must-see sights. For a one-stop look at opening hours, see the "At a Glance" side-bars for each major city (Venice, Milan, Florence, Siena, and Rome). Most sights keep stable hours, but you can easily confirm the latest by checking with the TI or visiting museum websites. Or call sights in the morning and ask: "Are you open today?" (*"Aperto oggi?"*; ah-PER-toh OH-jee) and "What time do you close?" (*"A che ora chiuso?"*; ah kay OH-rah kee-OO-zoh). I've included telephone numbers for this purpose.

Sometimes you can make reservations for an entry time (for example, at Florence's Uffizi Gallery or Rome's Vatican Museum). Some cities offer museum passes for admission to several muse-ums (e.g., Roma Pass and Firenze Card) that let you skip ticket-buying lines. At some popular places (such as Rome's Colosseum or Venice's Doge's Palace), you can get in more quickly by buying your ticket or pass at a less-crowded sight (Rome's Palatine Hill or Venice's Correr Museum). Booking a guided tour can help you avoid lines at many popular sights.

Don't put off visiting a must-see sight—you never know when a place will close unexpectedly for a holiday, strike, or restoration. On holidays (see list on page 1106), expect reduced hours or clo-sures—find out if a particular sight will be open by phoning ahead or checking its website. In summer, some sights may stay open late. Off-season, many museums have shorter hours.

Going at the right time helps avoid crowds. This book offers tips on specific sights. Try visiting popular sights very early or very late. Evening visits are usually peaceful, with fewer crowds.

Study up. To get the most out of the sight descriptions in this book, read them before you visit.

At Sights

Here's what you can typically expect:

Some important sights require you to check daypacks and coats. To avoid checking a small backpack, carry it under your arm like a purse as you enter. From a guard's point of view, a backpack is generally a problem while a purse is not.

Flash photography is often banned, but taking photos with-out a flash is usually allowed. Flashes damage oil paintings and distract others in the room. Even without a flash, a handheld camera will take a decent picture (or buy postcards or posters at the museum bookstore).

You may have to pay cash for the admission fee; some sights don't take credit cards. Some sights have found a clever way to squeeze more money out of visitors by hosting special exhibits in addition to their permanent collection. Most of these come at an extra cost (which you'll likely have to pay even if you don't want to see the special exhibit). The prices I've listed in this book generally include these obligatory temporary exhibits. Come expecting this higher price...and consider yourself lucky if you happen to visit on the rare occasion when you can get in for less.

Expect changes—artwork can be on tour, on loan, out sick, or shifted at the whim of the curator. To adapt, pick up any available free floor plans as you enter, and ask museum staff if you can't find a particular item. Say the title or artist's name, or point to the photograph in this book and ask, *"Dov'è?"* (doh-VEH; meaning "Where is?").

Many sights rent audioguides, which generally offer dry-but-useful recorded descriptions in English (about $4-7). If you bring along your earbuds, you can enjoy better sound and avoid holding the device to your ear. To save money, you can bring a Y-jack and share one audioguide with your travel partner. I've produced free downloadable audio tours of some of Italy's major sights; see page 1101.

It helps to know the terms. Art historians and Italians refer to the great Florentine centuries by dropping a thousand years. The Trecento (300s), Quattrocento (400s), and Cinquecento (500s) were the 1300s, 1400s, and 1500s. Also, in Italian museums, art is dated with *sec* (for *secolo,* or century, often indicated with Roman numerals), A.C. (for *Avanti Cristo,* or B.C.), and D.C. (for *Dopo Cristo,* or A.D.). O.K.?

Important sights may have an on-site café or cafeteria (usually a good place to rejuvenate during a long visit). The WCs at sights are free and generally clean.

Many places sell postcards that highlight their attractions. Before you leave, scan the postcards and thumb through the biggest guidebook (or skim its index) to be sure that you haven't overlooked something that you'd like to see.

Most sights stop admitting people 30-60 minutes before closing time, and some rooms may close early (often about 45 minutes before the actual closing time). Guards usher people out, so don't save the best for last.

Every sight or museum offers more than what is covered in this book. Use the information in this book as an introduction—not the final word.

Find Religion

Churches offer some amazing art (usually free), a cool respite from heat, and a welcome seat.

A modest dress code (no bare shoulders or shorts for anyone, even kids) is enforced at larger churches, such as Venice's St. Mark's and the Vatican's St. Peter's, but is often overlooked elsewhere. If you are caught by surprise, you can improvise, using maps to cover your shoulders and a jacket for your knees. (I wear a super-lightweight pair of long pants rather than shorts for my hot and muggy big-city Italian sightseeing.)

Some churches have coin-operated audioboxes that describe the art and history; just set the dial on English, put in your coins, and listen. Coin boxes near a piece of art illuminate the art (and present a better photo opportunity). I pop in a coin whenever I can. It improves my experience, is a favor to other visitors trying to appreciate a great piece of art in the dark, and is a little contribution to that church and its work. Whenever possible, let there be light.

Sleeping

I favor hotels and restaurants that are handy to your sightseeing activities. Rather than list hotels scattered throughout a city, I describe two or three favorite neighborhoods and recommend the best accommodations values in each, from dorm beds to fancy doubles with all of the comforts.

Sleeping in Italy is expensive. Cheap big-city hotels can be depressing. Tourist information services cannot give opinions on quality of hotels. A major feature of this book is its extensive listing of good-value rooms. I like places that are clean, central, relatively quiet at night, reasonably priced, friendly, small enough to have a hands-on owner and stable staff, run with a respect for Italian traditions, and not listed in other guidebooks. (In Italy, for me, satisfying six out of eight of these criteria means it's a keeper.) Some places listed are old and rickety, and I've described them as such. I'm more impressed by a convenient location and a fun-loving philosophy than flat-screen TVs and shoeshine machines.

Book your accommodations well in advance if you'll be traveling during busy times. See page 1106 for a list of major holidays and festivals in Italy; for tips on making reservations, see page 24.

Rates, Deals, and Tips

I've described my recommended accommodations using a Sleep Code (see sidebar). Prices listed are for one-night stays in peak season and assume you're booking directly (not through a TI or online hotel-booking engine). Using an online booking service

Sleep Code

(€1 = about $1.40, country code: 39)

Price Rankings

To help you easily sort through my listings, I've divided the accommodations into three categories based on the price for a double room with bath during high season:

$$$ **Higher Priced**
$$ **Moderately Priced**
$ **Lower Priced**

I always rate hostels as $, whether or not they have double rooms, because they have the cheapest beds in town. Prices can change without notice; verify the hotel's current rates online or by email.

Abbreviations

To pack maximum information into minimum space, I use the following code to describe accommodations in this book. Prices listed are per room, not per person. When a price range is given for a type of room (such as double rooms listing for €100-150), it means the price fluctuates with the season, size of room, or length of stay; expect to pay the upper end for peak-season stays.

S = Single room (or price for one person in a double).

D = Double or twin room. "Double beds" are often two twins sheeted together and are usually big enough for nonromantic couples.

T = Triple (generally a double bed with a single).

Q = Quad (usually two double beds; adding an extra child's bed to a T is usually cheaper).

b = Private bathroom with toilet and shower or tub.

s = Private shower or tub only (the toilet is down the hall).

According to this code, a couple staying at a "Db-€140" hotel would pay a total of €140 (about $195) for a double room with a private bathroom. Unless otherwise noted, breakfast is included, hotel staff speak basic English, and credit cards are accepted. Some cities charge a hotel tax of €1-4 per person per night that must be paid in cash. This tax is typically not included in the prices I've listed in this book.

There's almost always Wi-Fi and/or Internet access available, either free or for a fee.

costs the hotel about 20 percent and logically closes the door on special deals. Book direct.

Some cities—such as Venice, Florence, Padua, and Rome—levy a tax on hotel rooms to generate income for municipal projects. This tax is generally not included in the prices in this book and must be paid in cash at checkout. It varies from €1 to €4 per person, per night, depending on the city and how many stars the hotel has.

These days, many hotels change prices from day to day according to demand. Given the economic downturn, hoteliers are often willing and eager to make a deal. I'd suggest emailing several hotels to ask for their best price. Comparison-shop and make your choice.

As you look over the listings, you'll notice that some accommodations promise special prices to my readers who book direct (without using a room-finding service or hotel-booking website, which take a commission). To get these rates, you must mention this book when you reserve, and then show the book upon arrival. Rick Steves discounts apply to readers with ebooks as well as printed books.

In general, prices can soften if you do any of the following: offer to pay cash, stay at least three nights, or mention this book. You can also try asking for a cheaper room or a discount, or offer to skip breakfast.

Types of Accommodations
Hotels
Double rooms listed in this book will range from about €50 (very simple, toilet and shower down the hall) to €300 (maximum plumbing and more), with most clustered around €130 (with private bathrooms). Prices are higher in big cities and heavily touristed cities, and lower off the beaten path.

Solo travelers find that the cost of a *camera singola* is often only 25 percent less than a *camera doppia*. Three or four people can economize by requesting larger rooms. (If a double room is €110, a quad would be about €150.) Most listed hotels have a variety of rooms that can accommodate from one to five people. If there's space for an extra cot, they'll cram it in for you (charging you around €25).

The Italian word for "hotel" is *hotel*, and in smaller, non-touristy towns, *albergo*. A few places have kept the old titles *locanda* or *pensione*, indicating that they offer budget beds. English works in all but the cheapest places.

You'll save €30 if you request a room without a shower and just use the shower down the hall. Generally rooms with a bath or shower also have a toilet and a bidet (which Italians use for quick

Chill Out

Nearly all hotels, except for the rock-bottom basic ones, have air-conditioning. Because Europeans are generally careful with energy use, you'll find government-enforced limits on air-conditioning and heating. There's a one-month period each spring and fall when neither is allowed. Air-conditioning sometimes costs an extra per-day charge, is worth seeking out in summer (though it may be on only at certain times of the day), and is rarely available from fall through spring. Fancier hotel rooms usually include air-conditioning in the price. Conveniently, many business-class hotels drop their prices in July and August, just when the air-conditioned comfort they offer is most important.

Most hotel rooms with air conditioners come with a control stick (like a TV remote) that generally has the same symbols and features: fan icon (click to toggle through wind power, from light to gale); louver icon (choose steady airflow or waves); snowflake and sunshine icons (cold air or heat, depending on season); clock ("O" setting: run x hours before turning off; "I" setting: wait x hours to start); and the temperature control (21 degrees Celsius is comfortable).

sponge baths). The cord that dangles over the tub or shower is not a clothesline. You pull it when you've fallen and can't get up.

Double beds are called *matrimoniale*, even though hotels aren't interested in your marital status. Twins are *due letti singoli*. Convents offer cheap accommodation but only *letti singoli*.

When you check in, the receptionist will normally ask for your passport and keep it for a couple of hours. Hotels are legally required to register each guest with the police. Relax. Americans are notorious for making this chore more difficult than it needs to be.

Assume that breakfast is included in the prices I've listed, unless otherwise noted. If the breakfast costs money, you may want to skip it. While convenient, it's usually expensive—€5-6 per person for a simple continental buffet with (at its most generous) bread, ham, cheese, yogurt, juice, and unlimited *caffè latte*. A picnic in your room followed by a coffee at the corner café can be a lot cheaper.

More pillows and blankets are usually in the closet or available on request. In Italy, towels and linen aren't always replaced every day. Hang your towel up to dry. Some hotels use lightweight "waffle" or very thin tablecloth-type towels; these take less water and electricity to launder and are preferred by many Italians.

Most hotel rooms have a TV, phone, and Wi-Fi; sometimes there's an Internet terminal in the lobby. Simpler places rarely have

Making Hotel Reservations

Given the good value of the accommodations I've found for this book, reserve your rooms several weeks in advance—or as soon as you've pinned down your travel dates—particularly if you'll be traveling during peak season. Note that some national holidays jam things up and merit your making reservations far in advance (see "Holidays and Festivals" on page 1106).

Requesting a Reservation: It's usually easiest to book your room through the hotel's website; many have a reservation-request form built right in. (For the best rates, be sure to use the hotel's official site and not a booking agency's site.) Just type in your preferred dates and the website will automatically display a list of available rooms and prices. Simpler websites will generate an email to the hotelier with your request. If there's no reservation form, or for complicated requests, send an email from your personal address. Other options include calling (see "Phoning" below, and be mindful of time zones) or faxing. Most recommended hotels are accustomed to guests who speak only English.

The hotelier wants to know these key pieces of information about your stay (also included in the sample request form in the appendix):

- number and type of rooms
- number of nights
- date of arrival
- date of departure
- any special needs (e.g., bathroom in the room or down the hall, twin beds vs. double bed, air-conditioning, quiet, view, ground floor, etc.)

When you request a room, use the European style for writing dates: day/month/year. For example, for a two-night stay in July 2013, I would request "1 double room for 2 nights, arrive 16/07/13, depart 18/07/13." Consider carefully how long you'll stay; don't just assume you can tack on extra days once you arrive. Make sure you mention any discounts—for Rick Steves readers or otherwise—when you make the reservation.

If you don't get a response to your email, it usually means the hotel is already fully booked—but try sending the message again or call to follow up.

Confirming a Reservation: Most places will request your credit-card number to hold the room. To confirm a room using a hotel's secure online reservation form, enter your contact information and credit-card number; the hotel will email a confirmation.

If you sent an email to request a reservation, the hotel will reply with its room availability and rates. This is not a confirmation. You must email back to say that you want the room at the given rate. While you can email your credit-card information (I do), it's safer to share that confidential info via phone call, two emails (splitting your number between them), or the hotel's secure online reservation form.

Canceling a Reservation: If you must cancel your reservation, it's courteous to do so with as much notice as possible. Simply make a quick phone call or send an email. Family-run places lose money if they turn away customers while holding a room for someone who doesn't show up. Understandably, many hoteliers bill no-shows for one night.

Cancellation policies can be strict: For example, you might lose a deposit if you cancel within two weeks of your reserved stay, or you might be billed for the entire visit if you leave early. Internet deals may require prepayment, with no refunds for cancellations. Ask about cancellation policies before you book.

If canceling via email, request confirmation that your cancellation was received to avoid being accidentally billed.

Reconfirming Your Reservation: Always call to reconfirm your room reservation a few days in advance from the road. Smaller hotels and B&Bs appreciate knowing your estimated time of arrival, especially if you'll be arriving late (after 17:00). On the small chance that a hotel loses track of your reservation, bring along a hard copy of their confirmation.

Reserving Rooms as You Travel: You can make reservations as you travel, calling hotels a few days to a week before your arrival. If everything's full, don't despair. Call a day or two in advance and fill in a cancellation. If you'd rather travel without any reservations at all, you'll have greater success snaring rooms if you arrive at your destination early in the day. When you anticipate crowds (weekends are worst), call hotels at about 9:00 or 10:00 on the day you plan to arrive, when the receptionist knows who'll be checking out and just which rooms will be available. If you encounter a language barrier, ask the fluent receptionist at your current hotel to call for you.

Phoning: To call Italy from the US or Canada, dial 011-39 and then the local number. (The 011 is our international access code, and 39 is Italy's country code.) If you're calling Italy from another European country, dial 00-39-local number. (The 00 is Europe's international access code.) To make calls within Italy, simply dial the local number. Land lines start with 0; mobile lines start with 3. For more tips on calling, see page 1074.

a room phone, but often have Wi-Fi. Pricier hotels are more likely to have elevators and small stocked mini-fridges in the rooms called *frigo bars* (FREE-goh; pay for what you use).

Hotels in resort areas will often charge you for half-pension, called *mezza pensione,* during peak season (which can run from May through mid-October for resorts). Half-pension means that you pay for one meal per day per person (lunch or dinner, though usually dinner), whether you want to or not. Wine is rarely included. If half-pension is required, you can't opt out and pay less. Some places offer half-pension as an option; it can be worth considering. If they charge you less per meal than you've been paying for an average restaurant meal on your trip, half-pension is a fine value—if the chef is good. Ask other guests about the quality or check out their restaurant yourself.

If you're arriving early in the morning, your room probably won't be ready. You can drop your bag safely at the hotel and dive right into sightseeing.

Hoteliers can be a great help and source of advice. Most know their city well, and can assist you with everything from public transit and airport connections to finding a good restaurant, the nearest launderette, or an Internet café. But even at the best places, mechanical breakdowns occur: Air-conditioning malfunctions, sinks leak, hot water turns cold, and toilets gurgle and smell. Report your concerns clearly and calmly at the front desk. For more complicated problems, don't expect instant results.

If you suspect night noise will be a problem (if, for instance, your room is over a café), ask for a quiet room in the back or on an upper floor. To guard against theft in your room, keep valuables out of sight. Some rooms come with a safe, and other hotels have safes at the front desk. I've never bothered using one.

Checkout can pose problems if surprise charges pop up on your bill. If you settle up your bill the afternoon before you leave, you'll have time to discuss and address any points of contention (before 19:00, when the night shift usually arrives).

Above all, keep a positive attitude. Remember, you're on vacation. If your hotel is a disappointment, spend more time out enjoying the city you came to see.

Hostels

You'll pay about €25 per bed to stay at a hostel. Travelers of any age are welcome if they don't mind dorm-style accommodations and meeting other travelers. Most hostels offer kitchen facilities, Internet access, Wi-Fi, and a self-service laundry. Nowadays, concerned about bedbugs, hostels are likely to provide all bedding, including sheets. Family and private rooms may be available on request.

Independent hostels tend to be easygoing, colorful, and informal (no membership required); see www.hostelz.com, www.hostelseurope.com, www.hostels.com, and www.hostelbookers.com. **Official hostels** are part of Hostelling International (HI) and share an online booking site (www.hihostels.com). HI hostels typically require that you either have a membership card or pay extra per night.

Private Rooms and Apartments

In small towns, there are often few hotels to choose from, but an abundance of *affitta camere,* or rental rooms. This can be anything from a set of keys and a basic bed to a cozy B&B with your own Tuscan grandmother. Local TIs can give you a list of possibilities (or try the free Ciao Italia Bed & Breakfast, which books B&Bs and hostels in Rome, Florence, and Venice at www.ciao italia-bb.com). These rooms are usually a good budget option, but since they vary in quality, shop around to find the best value. It's always OK to ask to see the room before you commit.

Apartment rentals, a great value for families or multiple couples traveling together, are also listed at TIs and are common in small towns. Rentals are generally by the week, with prices starting around €100 per day. A bigger place for a group of four to five rents for around €200. Apartments generally offer a couple of bedrooms, a sitting area, and a teensy *cucinetta* (kitchenette), usually stocked with dishes and flatware. After you check in, you're basically on your own. While you won't have a doorman to carry your bags or a maid to clean your room each day, you will get an inside peek at an Italian home, and you can save lots of money—especially if you take advantage of the cooking facilities—with no loss of comfort.

Cross-Pollinate is an online booking agency representing B&Bs and apartments in a handful of European cities, including Rome, Venice, and Florence. They handpick their listings, presenting each one as if recommending it to a friend. Search their website for a listing you like, then submit your reservation online. If the place is available, you'll be charged a small deposit and emailed the location and check-in details. Policies vary from owner to owner, but in most cases you'll pay the balance on arrival in cash (US tel. 800-270-1190, www.cross-pollinate.com, info@cross-pollinate.com).

Agritourism

Agriturismo (agricultural tourism), or rural B&Bs, began in the 1980s as a way to encourage small farmers in the countryside to survive in a modern economy where, like in the US, so many have been run out of business by giant agricultural corporations. By renting rooms to travelers, farmers can remain on their land and continue to produce food. A peaceful home base for exploring the region, these rural Italian B&Bs are ideal for those traveling by car—especially families.

It's wise to book several months in advance for high season (May-Sept). Weeklong stays are preferred in July and August, but shorter stays are possible off-season. To sleep cheaper, avoid the peak season for *agriturismi*. A farmhouse that rents for as much as $2,000 a week at peak times can go for as little as $700 in late September or October. In the winter, you might be charged extra for heat, so confirm the price ahead of time. Payment policies vary, but generally a 25 percent deposit is required (lost if you cancel), and the balance is due one month before arrival.

As the name implies, *agriturismi* are in the countryside, although some are located within a mile of town. Most are family-run. *Agriturismi* vary wildly in quality—some properties are rustic, while others are downright luxurious, offering amenities such as swimming pools and riding stables. The rooms are usually clean and comfortable. Breakfast is often included, and *mezza pensione* (half-pension, which in this case means a home-cooked dinner) might be built into the price whether you want it or not. Most places serve tasty homegrown food; some are vegetarian or organic, others are gourmet. Kitchenettes are often available to cook up your own feast. Make sure you know how to operate the appliances. To maximize your time, ask the owner for suggestions on local restaurants, sights, and activities.

To qualify officially as an *agriturismo,* the farm must still generate more money from its farm activities, thereby insuring that the land is worked and preserved. Some farmhouse B&Bs aren't actual farms, though are fine places to stay. But if you want the real thing, make sure the owners call their place an *agriturismo.*

In this book, I've listed some *agriturismi* and farmhouses under the towns that they're nearest to, but there are many, many more. Local TIs can give you a list of farms in their area, and many *agriturismi* now have their own websites. For a sampling, visit www.agriturismoitaly.it or do a Web search for *agriturismo.* One booking agency among many is Farm Holidays in Tuscany (closed Sat-Sun, tel. 0564-417-418, www.byfarmholidays.com, info@byfarmholidays.com).

Eating

The Italians are masters of the art of fine living. That means eating...long and well. Lengthy, multicourse lunches and dinners and

endless hours sitting in outdoor cafés are the norm. Americans eat on their way to an evening event and complain if the check is slow in coming. For Italians, the meal is an end in itself, and only rude waiters rush you. When you want the bill, mime-scribble on your raised palm or ask for it: *"Il conto?"* You may have to request it more than once. To save time, ask for the check when you receive the last item you've ordered.

Even those of us who liked dorm food will find that the local cafés, cuisine, and wines become a highlight of our Italian adventure. Trust me: This is sightseeing for your palate, and even if the rest of you is sleeping in cheap hotels, your taste buds will relish an occasional first-class splurge. You can eat well without going broke. But be careful: You're just as likely to blow a small fortune on a disappointing meal as you are to dine wonderfully for €25.

Restaurants

When restaurant-hunting, choose places filled with locals, not the place with the big neon signs boasting, "We Speak English and Accept Credit Cards."

Venturing even a block or two off the main drag leads to higher-quality food for less than half the price of the tourist-oriented places. Locals eat better at lower-rent locales. Family-run places operate without hired help and can offer cheaper meals. Good restaurants don't open for dinner before 19:00.

Before you sit down, look at a menu to see what extra charges a restaurant tacks on. Many (but not all) restaurants in Italy add a cover charge *(coperto)* of €1.50-3.50 per person to your bill. Sometimes this is phrased as "bread and cover" *(pane e coperto)*. It's not negotiable, even if you don't eat the bread. Think of it as covering the cost of using the table for as long as you like. (Italians like to linger, and most restaurants don't depend on turning the table

Eating with the Seasons

Italian cooks love to serve you fresh produce and seafood at its tastiest. If you must have porcini mushrooms outside of fall, they'll be frozen. Each region in Italy has its specialties, which you'll see displayed in open-air markets. To get a plate of the freshest veggies at a fine restaurant, request *"Un piatto di verdure della stagioni, per favore."*

Here are a few examples of what's fresh when:

April-May:	Calamari, squid, green beans, asparagus, artichokes, and zucchini flowers
April-May and Sept-Oct:	Black truffles
May-June:	Mussels, asparagus, zucchini, cantaloupe, and strawberries
May-Aug:	Eggplant
Oct-Nov:	Mushrooms, white truffles, and chestnuts
Nov-Feb:	Radicchio
Fresh year-round:	Clams, meats, and cheese

over multiple times in an evening.) Restaurants with a separate service charge (*servizio*, usually around 10-15 percent) are in the minority. Places with both a cover *and* a service charge are best avoided—that's a clue that a restaurant is counting on a nonlocal clientele who can't gauge value. The same goes for the opposite: Places that advertise "no cover, no service charge" to attract tourists are likely raising their prices to compensate.

Although the tip is generally built into the bill, you may want to add a euro or two per person to reward good service; see "Tipping" on page 16.

You can save a lot by getting fixed-priced meals, which are frequently exempt from cover and service charges. However, the cheapest ones tend to be bland and heavy, pairing a very basic pasta with reheated schnitzel and roast meats (usually around €15-20, often called *menù turistico*, or sometimes, usually falsely, *menù del giorno*—menu of the day). It's worth paying more for an inventive fixed-price meal that shows off the chef's creativity. While fixed-price meals can be easy and convenient, galloping gourmets order à la carte with the help of a menu translator. (The *Rick Steves' Italian Phrase Book &*

MENU TURISTICO € 19,00

ANTIPASTO di MARE

PRIMI PIATTI
RISOTTO alla PESCATORA
SPAGHETTI alla MARINARA
SPAGHETTI allo SCOGLIO
TRENETTE al PESTO

SECONDI PIATTI
PESCE ai FERRI
FRITTO MISTO
GRIGLIATA di CARNE

CONTORNI
PATATE FRITTE o INSALATA

Dictionary has a menu decoder with enough phrases for intermediate eaters.) When going to an especially good restaurant with an approachable staff, I like to find out what they're eager to serve, or I'll simply say, "Make me happy" (in this case, it's just fine to set a price limit).

A full meal consists of an appetizer (antipasto, €5-10), a first course (*primo piatto*, pasta or soup, €7-15), and a second course (*secondo piatto*, expensive meat and fish dishes, €10-25). Vegetables *(contorni, verdure)* may come with the *secondo* or cost extra (€5-6) as a side dish.

The euros can add up in a hurry. Light and budget eaters get a *primo piatto* each and share an antipasto. (Italians admit the *secondo* is the least interesting part of their cuisine.) Another good option is sharing an array of *antipasti*—either by ordering several specific dishes or, at restaurants that offer self-serve buffets, by choosing a variety of cold and cooked appetizers from an *antipasti* buffet spread out like a salad bar. At buffets, you pay per plate, not by weight; a typical serving costs about €8 (generally Italians don't treat buffets as all-you-can-eat, but take a one-time moderate serving; watch others and imitate).

To maximize the experience and flavors, small groups can mix *antipasti* and *primi piatti* family-style (skipping *secondi*). If you do this right (e.g., under-ordering because courses are often bigger than necessary), you can eat well in better places for less than the cost of a tourist *menù* in a cheap place.

Some special dishes come in large quantities meant for two people; the shorthand way of showing this on a menu is "X2" (meaning "for two people"). The price listed generally indicates the cost per person.

Seafood and steak may be sold by weight (priced by the kilo—1,000 grams, or just over two pounds; or by the *etto*—100 grams). The letters *s.q.* mean "according to quantity." Fish is usually served whole with the head and tail; you can't just get half a fish or a fillet unless it already comes prepared as just a fillet (*filetto*, sometimes *trancio*—slice, as in tuna or swordfish). However, you can ask your waiter to select a smaller fish for you. Sometimes, especially for steak, restaurants require a minimum order of four or five *etti*. Beware, or be shell-shocked by €50 entrées. Make sure you're really clear on the price before ordering.

Wine Bars *(Enoteche)*

An *enoteca* is a popular, fast, and affordable option for lunch. Surrounded by the office crowd, you can get a fancy salad, a plate of meats and cheeses, and a glass of fine wine (see blackboards for the day's selection and price per glass—and go for the top end). A good *enoteca* aims to impress visitors with its wine, and will

Wine Labels and Lingo

The ancient Greeks who colonized Italy more than 2,000 years ago called it *"Oenotria"*—land of the grape. Little has changed over the centuries. Ideal condi- tions for grapes (warm climate, well-draining soil, and an abundance of hillsides) make the Italian peninsula a paradise for grape-growers, winemakers, and wine drinkers. Italy makes and consumes more wine per capita than any other country.

In almost every part of Italy you'll find wine varieties designed to go with the regional cuisine. Choosing a wine can be intimidating, but the Italian government tries to help you choose something decent, even if you're clueless. In general, wines are designated by one of four categories:

Vino da Tavola (table wine) is the lowest grade. It's inexpensive, but Italy's wines are so good that, for many people, a basic *vino da tavola* is just fine with a meal. Many restaurants, even modest ones, take pride in their house wine (*"vino della casa"*), bottling their own or working with wineries.

Denominazione di Origine Controllata (DOC), a cut above table wine, is usually cheap, but can be surprisingly good. Hundreds of wines have earned the DOC designation. In Tuscany, for example, many such wines come from the Chianti region, located between Florence and Siena.

Denominazione di Origine Controllata e Guarantita (DOCG) is the highest grade, and can be identified by the pink or green label on the neck and the scary price tag on the shelf. Only a limited number of wines in Italy can be called DOCG. They're generally a good bet if you want a quality wine, but you don't

generally choose excellent-quality ingredients for the simple dishes it offers with the wine (though prices can add up quickly). Some of my favorite Italian eating experiences have been at *enoteche*.

Bars/Cafés

Italian "bars" are not taverns, but inexpensive cafés. These neighborhood hangouts serve coffee, mini-pizzas, sandwiches, and drinks from the cooler. Many dish up plates of fried cheese and vegetables from under the glass counter, ready to reheat. This budget choice is the Italian equivalent of English pub grub.

For quick meals, bars usually have trays of cheap, pre-made sandwiches (*panini* or *tramezzini*)—some are delightful grilled. (Others have too much mayo between crustless slices of Wonder know anything else about the winemaker. (**Riserva** is a DOC or DOCG wine matured for a longer, more specific time.)

Indicazione Geographica Tipica (IGT) is a broad group of wines that range from basic to some of Italy's best. It includes the "Super Tuscans"—wines that don't follow the strict "recipe" required for DOC or DOCG status, but that give local vintners more opportunity to be creative. Super Tuscans are made from a mix of international grapes (such as cabernet sauvignon) grown in Tuscany and aged in small oak barrels for only two years. The result is a lively full-bodied wine that dances all over your head... and is worth the steep price for aficionados.

Visit an *enoteca* (wine bar) and sample these wines side-by-side to figure out what you like—and what suits your pocketbook.

Words to Live By, or...How to Describe Wine in Italian

As you can see from many of the words listed below, adding a vowel to the English word often gets you close to the Italian one. Have some fun, gesture like a local, and you'll have no problems speaking the language of the *enoteca. Salute!*

dry	*secco*	SAY-koh
sweet	*dolce*	DOHL-chay
earthy	*terroso*	tay-ROH-zoh
tannic	*tannico*	TAH-nee-koh
young	*giovane*	JOH-vah-nay
mature	*maturo*	mah-TOO-roh
sparkling	*spumante*	spoo-MAHN-tay
fruity	*fruttoso*	froo-TOH-zoh
full-bodied	*corposo*	kor-POH-zoh
elegant	*elegante*	ay-lay-GAHN-tay

Bread.) To save time for sightseeing and room for dinner, stop by a bar for a light lunch, such as a ham-and-cheese *panino* (called *toast);* have it grilled twice if you want it really hot. To get food "to go," say, *"Da portar via"* (for the road). Many bars are small—if you can't find a table, you'll need to stand up or find a ledge to sit on outside. Most charge extra for table service. All bars have a WC *(toilette, bagno)* in the back, and customers—and the discreet public—can use it.

Bars serve great drinks—hot, cold, sweet, caffeinated, or alcoholic. Chilled bottled water, still *(naturale)* or carbonated *(frizzante),* is sold cheap to go.

Coffee: If you ask for *"un caffè,"* you'll get espresso. Cappuccino is served to locals before noon and to tourists any time of day. (To an Italian, cappuccino is a breakfast drink and a travesty after eating anything with tomatoes.) Italians like their coffee only warm—to get it hot, request *"Molto caldo"* (MOHL-toh KAHL-doh; very hot) or *"Più caldo, per favore"* (pew KAHL-doh pehr fah-VOH-ray; hotter, please).

Experiment with a few of the options:

- Cappuccino: Espresso with foamed milk on top
- *Caffè latte:* Tall glass with espresso mixed with hot milk, no foam (ordering just a "latte" gets you only milk)
- *Caffè freddo:* Sweet and iced espresso
- Cappuccino *freddo:* Iced cappuccino
- *Caffè hag:* Instant decaf (any coffee drink is available decaffeinated—ask for it *decaffeinato:* day-kah-fay-ee-NAH-toh)
- *Caffè macchiato* (mah-kee-AH-toh): Espresso with only a little milk (*macchiato* means "marked" or "stained")
- *Latte macchiato:* Hot milk with a shot of espresso
- *Caffè americano:* Espresso diluted with water
- *Caffè corretto:* Espresso with a shot of liqueur (normally grappa, amaro, or Sambuca)

More Hot Drinks: *Cioccolato* is hot chocolate. *Tè* is hot tea. *Tè freddo* (iced tea) is usually from a can—sweetened and flavored with lemon or peach.

Juice: *Spremuta* means freshly squeezed, as far as *succo* (fruit juice) is concerned (order *una spremuta*); it's usually orange juice, and February through April it's almost always made from blood oranges. (Note: *Spumante* is sparkling wine.)

Beer: Beer on tap is *alla spina*. Get it *piccola* (33 cl, 11 oz), *media* (50 cl, about a pint), or *grande* (a liter). Italians drink mainly lager beers. You'll find local brews (Peroni or Moretti) and imports such as Heineken as well. A *lattina* is a can and a *bottiglia* (boh-TEEL-yah) is a bottle.

Wine: To order a glass (*bicchiere;* bee-kee-AY-ree) of red (*rosso*) or white (*bianco*) wine, say, *"Un bicchiere di vino rosso/bianco."* *Corposo* means full-bodied. House wine (*vino della casa*) comes in a carafe: quarter-liter pitcher (8.5 oz, *un quarto*), half-liter pitcher (17 oz, *un mezzo*), or one-liter pitcher (34 oz, *un litro*). An *ombra* is the smallest glass. Trendy wines with small production (such as Brunello di Montalcino) are good but overpriced.

Other Drinks: Some restaurants make their own after-dinner alcoholic brew (called a *digestivo*), using a secret combination of herbs to aid digestion. Popular commercial brands are Fernet Branca and Montenegro. If your tastes run sweeter, try an anise-flavored liqueur called Sambuca, served *con moscha* (with three "flies"—coffee beans).

Prices: You'll notice a two- or three-tiered pricing system. Drinking a cup of coffee while standing at the bar is cheaper than drinking it at an indoor table (you'll pay still more at an outdoor table). Many places have a *listino prezzi* (price list) with two columns—*al bar* and *al tavolo* (table)—posted somewhere by the bar or cash register. If you're on a budget, don't sit down without first checking out the financial consequences. Ask, "Same price if I sit or stand?" by saying, *"Costa uguale al tavolo o al banco?"* (KOH-stah oo-GWAH-lay ahl TAH-voh-loh oh ahl BAHN-koh). Throughout Italy, you can get cheap coffee at the bar of any establishment, no matter how fancy, and pay the same low, government-regulated price (generally only a euro if you stand).

If the bar isn't busy, you can probably just order and pay when you leave. Otherwise: 1) Decide what you want; 2) find out the price by checking the price list on the wall, the prices posted near the food, or by asking the barista; 3) pay the cashier; and 4) give the receipt to the barista (whose clean fingers handle no dirty euros) and tell him or her what you want.

Budget Eating

Italy offers many budget options for hungry travelers, but beware of cheap eateries that sport big color photos of pizza and piles of different pastas. They have no kitchens and simply microwave disgusting prepackaged food.

Stop by a *rosticcería* for great cooked deli food. Self-service cafeterias (called "free flow" in Italian) offer the basics without add-on charges. Those on a hard-core budget equip their room with a pantry stocked at the market (fruits and veggies are remarkably cheap) or pick up a kebab (or the equivalent), then dine in at picnic prices.

Pizzerias

Pizza is cheap and readily available. Stop by a pizza shop for stand-up or take-out pizza. *Pizza a taglio* ("by the slice") is usually round,

Naples-style pizza. *Pizza rustica* is thick, rustic, baked in a square pan, and sold by the weight (clearly explain how much you want—100 grams, or *un etto*, is a hot and cheap snack; 200 grams, or *due etti*, makes a light meal).

Key pizza vocabulary: *capricciosa* (generally ham, mushrooms, olives, and artichokes), *funghi* (mushrooms), *marinara* (tomato sauce, oregano, garlic, no cheese), *quattro formaggi* (four different cheeses), and *quattro stagioni* (different toppings on each of the four quarters, for those who can't choose just one menu item). If you ask for pepperoni on your pizza, you'll get *peperoni* (green or red

INTRODUCTION

Ordering Food at *Tavola Caldas*

plate of mixed veggies	*piatto misto di verdure*	pee-AH-toh MEES-toh dee vehr-DOO-ray
"Heated, please."	*"Scaldare, per favore."*	skahl-DAH-ray, pehr fah-VOH-ray
"A taste, please."	*"Un assaggio, per favore."*	oon ah-SAH-joh, pehr fah-VOH-ray
artichoke	*carciofi*	kar-CHOH-fee
asparagus	*asparagi*	ah-spah-RAH-jee
beans	*fagioli*	fah-JOH-lee
breadsticks	*grissini*	gree-SEE-nee
broccoli	*broccoli*	BROH-koh-lee
cantaloupe	*melone*	may-LOH-nay
carrots	*carote*	kah-ROT-ay
green beans	*fagiolini*	fah-joh-LEE-nee
ham	*prosciutto*	proh-SHOO-toh
mushrooms	*funghi*	FOONG-ghee
potatoes	*patate*	pah-TAH-tay
rice	*riso*	REE-zoh
spinach	*spinaci*	speen-AH-chee
tomatoes	*pomodori*	poh-moh-DOH-ree
zucchini	*zucchine*	zoo-KEE-nay

(Excerpted from *Rick Steves' Italian Phrase Book & Dictionary*)

peppers, not sausage); request *diavola* or *salsiccia piccante* instead (the closest thing in Italy to American pepperoni). Kids like the bland *margherita* (cheese with tomato sauce).

Döner Kebabs
Perhaps the best value in some cities—such as Venice and Florence—for a cheap, hot meal is a *döner kebab*. Look for little hole-in-the-wall kebab shops, where you can get a hearty take-out dinner wrapped in pita bread for €3.50. Pay an extra euro to super-size it, and it'll feed two. Ask locally for the favorite place in your neighborhood, as the quality can vary substantially.

Tavola Caldas ("Hot Tables")
For a fast, cheap, and healthy lunch, find a *tavola calda* bar with a buffet spread of meat and vegetables, and ask for a mixed plate of vegetables with a hunk of mozzarella *(piatto misto di verdure con*

How Was Your Trip?

Were your travels fun, smooth, and meaningful? If you'd like to share your tips, concerns, and discoveries, please fill out the survey at www.ricksteves.com/feedback. I value your feedback. Thanks in advance—it helps a lot.

mozzarella). Don't be limited by what's displayed. If you'd like a salad with a slice of cantaloupe and a hunk of cheese, they'll whip that up for you in a snap. Belly up to the bar and, with a pointing finger and key words in the chart in this chapter, you can get a fine mixed plate of vegetables. If something's a mystery, ask for *un assaggio* (oon ah-SAH-joh) to get a little taste.

Picnics

Picnicking saves lots of euros and is a great way to sample regional specialties. In the process of assembling your meal, you get to deal with the Italians in the market scene. For a colorful experience, gather your ingredients in the morning at the produce market; you'll probably visit several small stores or market stalls to put together a complete meal (note that many close around noon). While it's fun to visit the small specialty shops, an *alimentari* is your one-stop corner grocery store (most will slice and stuff your sandwich for you if you buy the ingredients there). The rare *supermercato* gives you more efficiency with less color for less cost. At busier supermarkets you'll need to take a number for deli service.

Juice-lovers can get a liter of O.J. for the price of a Coke or coffee. Look for "100% *succo*" (juice) on the label. Hang on to the half-liter mineral-water bottles (sold everywhere for about €1). Buy juice in cheap liter boxes, then drink some and store the extra in your water bottle. (Like locals, I refill my water bottle with tap water—*acqua del rubinetto.*)

Picnics can be an adventure in high cuisine. Be daring. Try the fresh mozzarella, *presto* pesto, shriveled olives, and any UFOs the locals are excited about. Shopkeepers are happy to sell small quantities of produce. They seem to enjoy giving you a taste *(un assaggio).* It's customary to let the merchant choose the produce for you. Say *"Per oggi"* (pehr OH-jee; "For today") and he or she will grab you something ready to eat, weigh it, and make the sale. A typical picnic for two might be fresh rolls, 100 grams (*un etto*, about a quarter pound) of cheese, 100 grams of meat, two tomatoes, three carrots, two apples, yogurt, and a liter box of juice. Total cost—about €10.

Traveling as a Temporary Local

We travel all the way to Italy to enjoy differences—to become temporary locals. You'll experience frustrations. Certain truths that we find "God-given" or "self-evident," such as cold beer, ice in drinks, bottomless cups of coffee, hot showers, and bigger being better, are suddenly not so true. One of the benefits of travel is the eye-opening realization that there are logical, civil, and even better alternatives. A willingness to go local ensures that you'll enjoy a full dose of Italian hospitality.

Europeans generally like Americans. But if there is a negative aspect to Italians' image of Americans, it's that we are loud, wasteful, ethnocentric, too informal (which can seem disrespectful), and a bit naïve. Think about the rationale behind "crazy" Italian decisions. For instance, many hoteliers turn off the heat in early April and can't turn on air-conditioning until summer. The point is to conserve energy, and it's mandated by the Italian government. You could complain about being cold or hot...or bring a sweater in winter, and in summer, be prepared to sweat a little like everyone else.

While Italians, flabbergasted by our Yankee excesses, say in disbelief, *"Mi sono cadute le braccia!"* ("I throw my arms down!"), they nearly always afford us individual travelers all the warmth that we deserve.

Judging from all the happy feedback I receive from travelers who have used this book, it's safe to assume you'll enjoy a great, affordable vacation—with the finesse of an independent, experienced traveler.

Thanks, and *buon viaggio!*

Back Door Travel Philosophy
From *Rick Steves' Europe Through the Back Door*

Travel is intensified living—maximum thrills per minute and one of the last great sources of legal adventure. Travel is freedom. It's recess, and we need it.

Experiencing the real Europe requires catching it by surprise, going casual..."through the Back Door."

Affording travel is a matter of priorities. (Make do with the old car.) You can eat and sleep—simply, safely, and enjoyably—anywhere in Europe for $120 a day plus transportation costs. In many ways, spending more money only builds a thicker wall between you and what you traveled so far to see. Europe is a cultural carnival, and time after time, you'll find that its best acts are free and the best seats are the cheap ones.

A tight budget forces you to travel close to the ground, meeting and communicating with the people. Never sacrifice sleep, nutrition, safety, or cleanliness to save money. Simply enjoy the local-style alternatives to expensive hotels and restaurants.

Connecting with people carbonates your experience. Extroverts have more fun. If your trip is low on magic moments, kick yourself and make things happen. If you don't enjoy a place, maybe you don't know enough about it. Seek the truth. Recognize tourist traps. Give a culture the benefit of your open mind. See things as different, but not better or worse. Any culture has plenty to share.

Of course, travel, like the world, is a series of hills and valleys. Be fanatically positive and militantly optimistic. If something's not to your liking, change your liking.

Travel can make you a happier American, as well as a citizen of the world. Our Earth is home to seven billion equally precious people. It's humbling to travel and find that other people don't have the "American Dream"—they have their own dreams. Europeans like us, but with all due respect, they wouldn't trade passports.

Thoughtful travel engages us with the world. In tough economic times, it reminds us what is truly important. By broadening perspectives, travel teaches new ways to measure quality of life.

Globetrotting destroys ethnocentricity, helping us understand and appreciate other cultures. Rather than fear the diversity on this planet, celebrate it. Among your most prized souvenirs will be the strands of different cultures you choose to knit into your own character. The world is a cultural yarn shop, and Back Door travelers are weaving the ultimate tapestry. Join in!

VENICE

Venezia

Soak all day in this puddle of elegant decay. Venice is Europe's best-preserved big city. This car-free urban wonderland of a hundred islands—laced together by 400 bridges and 2,000 alleys—survives on the artificial respirator of tourism.

Born in a lagoon 1,500 years ago as a refuge from barbarians, Venice is overloaded with tourists and is slowly sinking (not because of the tourists). In the Middle Ages, the Venetians became Europe's clever middlemen for East-West trade and created a great trading empire. By smuggling in the bones of St. Mark (San Marco) in A.D. 828, Venice gained religious importance as well. With the discovery of America and new trading routes to the Orient, Venetian power ebbed. But as Venice fell, her appetite for decadence grew. Through the 17th and 18th centuries, Venice partied on the wealth accumulated through earlier centuries as a trading power.

Today, Venice is home to 58,000 people in its old city, down from about twice that number just three decades ago. While there are about 270,000 people in greater Venice (counting the mainland, not counting tourists), the old town has a small-town feel. Locals seem to know everyone. To see small-town Venice away from the touristic flak, escape the Rialto-San Marco tourist zone and savor the town early and late, without the hordes of vacationers day-tripping in from cruise ships and nearby beach resorts. A 10-minute walk from the madness puts you in an idyllic Venice that few tourists see.

Planning Your Time

Venice is worth at least a day on even the speediest tour. Hyper-efficient train travelers take the night train in and/or out. Sleep in the old center to experience Venice at its best: early and late. For a one-day visit, cruise the Grand Canal, do the major sights on St. Mark's Square (the square itself, Doge's Palace, Correr Museum, and St. Mark's Basilica), see the Frari Church for art, and wander the back streets on a pub crawl. Enjoy an evening gondola ride. Venice's greatest sight is the city itself. While doable in a day, Venice is worth two. It's a medieval cookie jar, and nobody's looking. Make time to simply wander.

Orientation to Venice

The island city of Venice is shaped like a fish. Its major thorough-fares are canals. The Grand Canal winds through the middle of the fish, starting at the mouth where all the people and food enter,

passing under the Rialto Bridge, and ending at St. Mark's Square (Piazza San Marco). Park your 21st-century perspective at the mouth and let Venice swallow you whole.

Venice is a car-less kaleido-scope of people, bridges, and odorless canals. There are six districts (*sestieri*, shown on map on page 42):

San Marco (from St. Mark's Square to the Accademia Bridge), Castello (the area east of St. Mark's Square), Dorsoduro (the belly of the fish, on the far side the Accademia Bridge), Cannaregio (between the train station and the Rialto Bridge), San Polo (west of the Rialto Bridge), and Santa Croce (the "eye" of the fish, across the canal from the train station).

To find your way, navigate by landmarks, not streets. Many street corners have a sign pointing you to *(per)* the nearest major landmark, such as San Marco, Accademia, Rialto, and Ferrovia (train station). Obedient visitors stick to the main thoroughfares as directed by these signs...and miss the charm of back-street Venice.

Beyond the city's core lie several other islands, including San Giorgio (with great views of Venice), Giudecca (more views), San Michele (old cemetery), Murano (famous for glass), Burano (lace-making), Torcello (old church), and the skinny Lido beach.

Tourist Information

With this book, a free city map from your hotel, and the events schedule on the TI's website, there's little need to make an in-person visit to a TI in Venice. That's fortunate, because the city's

VENICE

Venice Overview

N

¼ Mile

500 Meters

To
Mestre & Mainland:
Treviso Airport,
Padua, Vicenza
& Verona

Lagoon

Lagoon

To Murano &
Burano &
Torcello

To Marco Polo Airport

To Lido

SAN MICHELE
(CEMETERY)

SAN PIETRO

STADIUM

SANTA ELENA

ARSENALE

NAVAL MUSEUM

PUBLIC GARDENS

S.S. GIOVANNI & PAOLO

SCUOLA DALMATA

SAN ZACCARIA

RIVA SCHIAVONI

ST. MARK'S

DOGE'S PALACE

SAN MARCO

SAN GIORGIO

FONDAMENTA NUOVE

CASTELLO

RIALTO

CA' D'ORO

MERCERIE

BOVOLO STAIRS

PUNTA DELLA DOGANA MUSEUM

SALUTE

Grand Canal

CANNAREGIO

GHETTO

JEWISH MUSEUM

GUGLIE BRIDGE

CA' PESARO

SANTA CROCE

FRARI CHURCH

SAN POLO

SCUOLA SAN ROCCO

CA' REZZONICO

ACCADEMIA

DORSODURO

ZATTERE

PEGGY GUGGENHEIM COLLECTION

MOLINO STUCKY (HILTON)

REDENTORE

LA GIUDECCA

ZITELLE

CALATRAVA BRIDGE

TRAIN STN. & i

Piazzale Roma

SAN SEBASTIANO

PARKING GARAGE

TRONCHETTO

SANTA

STAZIONE MARITTIMA

Main Cruise ships dock & Ferries to Greece

DCH

TIs are crowded and clunky. If you need to check or confirm something, try phoning the TI at 041-529-8711 or visit www .turismovenezia.it (click on "Venezia," then the English icon, and you'll have a world of help). This website is far more helpful than the actual TI office.

If you must visit a TI, you'll find offices at the **train station** (next to track 1, daily 8:00-18:30), on **St. Mark's Square** (daily 9:00-15:30, in far-left corner with your back to the basilica), nearby at the **San Marco-Vallaresso vaporetto dock** (shares office with bookshop and Alilaguna ticket sales, daily 11:00-18:00), or at the **airport** (daily 9:00-20:00).

Maps: Of all places, you need a good map in Venice. Hotels give away freebies (no better than the small color ones at the front of this book). The TI sells a decent €2.50 map and miniguide—but you can find a wider range at bookshops, newsstands, and postcard stands. The cheap maps are pretty bad, but if you spend €5, you'll get a map that shows you everything. Investing in a good map can be the best €5 you'll spend in Venice.

Helpful History Timelines: For historical orientation, local guide Michael Broderick (listed later, under "Tours in Venice") has produced three poster-size timelines that cleverly map the city's history and art (sold at local bookstores; see www.venice scapes.org).

Arrival in Venice

A two-mile-long causeway (with highway and train lines) connects Venice to the mainland. Mestre, the sprawling mainland section of Venice, has fewer crowds, cheaper hotels, and plenty of inexpensive parking lots, but zero charm. Don't stop in Mestre unless you're parking your car or transferring trains.

By Train

All trains to "Venice" stop at Venezia Mestre (on the mainland). Most continue on to Santa Lucia Station (a.k.a. Venezia S.L.) on the island of Venice itself. If your train only stops at Mestre, worry not. Your train ticket to Venice will get you to Venezia S.L. Just hop any train coming by and finish your journey (6/hour, 10 minutes). If, for some reason, you need a ticket from Mestre to Santa Lucia, you can buy one at a machine for €1.

Venice's Santa Lucia train station (Ferrovia) plops you right into the old town on the Grand Canal, an easy vaporetto ride or fascinating 40-minute walk to St. Mark's Square. If the station's TI is crowded when you arrive, skip it and visit one of the two TIs at St. Mark's Square instead. It's not worth a long wait for a minimal TI map (buy a good one from a newsstand or pick up a free

Arrival in Venice

one at your hotel). Confirm your departure plan (use the machines or just study the *partenze*/departures posters on walls).

Consider storing unnecessary heavy bags. **Baggage check** is at track 1 (€5/5 hours, €11/24 hours, daily 6:00-23:50, no lockers). **WCs** (€0.80) are at track 1 and in the back of the big bar/cafeteria area inside the station.

Minimize your time in the station—the banks of user-friendly automated ticket machines are handy but cover Italian destinations only. They take euros and credit cards, display schedules, and issue tickets. If you need international tickets or live help, the ticket windows are open from 6:00 to 20:30. Or you could take care of these tasks online or for a fee at downtown travel agencies (see page 50).

To get from the train station to downtown Venice, walk straight out of the station to the canal. You'll see vaporetto docks and ticket booths on both sides. For vaporetto #2 (fast boat down Grand Canal), go left. For vaporetto #1 (slow boat down Grand Canal), go right. See page 51 for details on vaporetto tickets and passes. A water taxi from the train station to a hotel in central Venice will cost about €60.

By Bus

Venice's "bus station" is actually an open-air parking lot called Piazzale Roma. If you arrive at the Piazzale Roma bus station, find the vaporetto docks (just left of the modern bridge) and take #1 or the faster #2 down the Grand Canal to reach the Rialto, Accademia, or San Marco (St. Mark's Square) stops. If your hotel is near the train station, you can walk there by crossing the modern Calatrava Bridge.

The square is a jumble of different operators, platforms, and crosswalks over busy lanes of traffic. But bus stops are well-signed. The ticket windows for ACTV (local public buses, including #5 to Marco Polo Airport) are by the vaporetto stop. The ATVO ticket office is in the big, white building, on the right side of the square as you face away from the canal (for express buses to Marco Polo and Treviso airports and to Padua; office open daily 6:40-19:35).

Piazzale Roma has two big parking garages and the People Mover monorail (going to the cruise port and then the parking-lot island of Tronchetto). A baggage-storage office is next to the monorail at #497m (€5/24 hours, daily 6:00-21:00).

By Car

The freeway dead-ends after crossing the causeway to Venice. At the end of the road you have two parking choices: garages at Tronchetto or Piazzale Roma. As you drive into the city, sign boards with green and red lights indicate which lots are full. (You can also park in Mestre, on the mainland, but this is less convenient.)

Parking at Tronchetto: This garage is much bigger, a bit farther out, a bit cheaper, and well-connected by vaporetto (€3-4/hour, €21/24 hours, discounts for longer stays, tel. 041-520-7555, www.veniceparking.it).

After parking in the big Tronchetto garage, cross the street. While you can head left for a long walk to the ill-conceived People Mover (which takes you to Piazzale Roma for €1), it's easiest to go right to the vaporetto dock (not well-signed, look for *ACTV*). At the dock, catch vaporetto #2 in one of two directions: via the Grand Canal (more scenic, stops at Rialto, 40 minutes to San Marco), or via Giudecca (around the city, faster, no Rialto stop, 30 minutes to San Marco).

Don't be waylaid by aggressive water taxi boatmen. They charge €100 to take you where the vaporetto will take you for €7. Also avoid the travel agencies masquerading as TIs; deal only with the ticket booth at the vaporetto dock or the HelloVenezia public transport office. If you're going to buy a local transport pass, do it now.

If you're staying near the train station and don't mind a walk, you can take the €1 People Mover monorail instead of paying €7 for the two-stop vaporetto ride. The monorail brings you from Tronchetto to the bus station at Piazzale Roma, then it's a five-minute walk across the Calatrava Bridge to the train station (buy monorail tickets with coins from machine, 3-minute trip, runs Mon-Sat 7:00-23:00, Sun 8:30-21:00).

Parking at Piazzale Roma: The two garages here are closer in and more convenient—but a bit more expensive and likelier to be full. Both garages face the busy square (Piazzale Roma) where the road ends. The big white building on your right is a 2,200-space public parking garage, the Autorimessa Communale (€25/24 hours, tel. 041-272-7211, www.asmvenezia.it). In a back corner of the square is the private Garage San Marco (€30/24 hours, tel. 041-523-2213, www.garagesanmarco.it). At either of these, you'll have to give up your keys.

Parking in Mestre: Parking in the garage across from the train station in Mestre (on the mainland) only makes sense if you have light bags and are staying within walking distance of the Santa Lucia train station (€8/day Mon-Fri, €12-16/day Sat-Sun; www.sabait.it).

By Plane or Cruise Ship

For information on Venice's airport and cruise ship terminal, see the end of this chapter.

Helpful Hints

Theft Alert: The dark, late-night streets of Venice are generally safe. Even so, pickpockets (often elegantly dressed) work the crowded main streets, docks, and *vaporetti*. Your biggest risk of pickpockets is inside St. Mark's Basilica or on a tightly packed vaporetto.

A handy *polizia* station is on the right side of St. Mark's Square (near Caffè Florian). To call the police, dial 113. The Venice TI handles complaints—which must be submitted in writing—about local crooks, including gondolier, restaurant, or hotel rip-offs (fax 041-523-0399, complaint.apt@turismovenezia.it).

It's illegal for street vendors to sell knock-off handbags and it's also illegal for you to buy them; both you and the vendor can get big fines.

Daily Reminder

Sunday: While anyone is welcome to worship, most churches are closed to sightseers on Sunday morning. They reopen in the afternoon: St. Mark's Basilica (14:00-17:00, until 16:00 Nov-March), Frari Church (13:00-18:00), and the Church of San Zaccaria (16:00-18:00). The Church of San Polo and Naval Museum are closed all day, and the Rialto open-air market consists mainly of souvenir stalls (fish and produce sections closed). It's a bad day for a pub crawl, as most pubs are closed.

Monday: All sights are open except the Rialto fish market, Ca' Pesaro, Palazzo Mocenigo Costume Museum, Lace Museum (on the island of Burano), and Torcello Museum (on the island of Torcello). The Accademia and Ca' d'Oro close at 14:00. Don't side-trip to Verona today, as most sights there are closed in the morning, if not all day.

Tuesday: All sights are open except the Peggy Guggenheim Collection, Ca' Rezzonico (Museum of 18th-Century Venice), and Punta della Dogana.

Wednesday/Thursday/Friday: All sights are open.

Saturday: All sights are open except the Jewish Museum.

Notes: The Accademia is open earlier (daily at 8:15) and closes later (19:15 Tue-Sun) than most sights in Venice. Some sights close earlier off-season (such as the Correr Museum, Campanile bell tower, St. Mark's Basilica, and the Church of San Giorgio Maggiore). Modest dress is recommended at churches and required at St. Mark's Basilica—no bare shoulders, shorts, or short skirts.

Crowd Control: The city is inundated with cruise-ship crowds and tours from mainland hotels daily from 10:00 to about 17:00. Crowds can be a serious problem at **St. Mark's Basilica.** Go early or late. You can bypass the line if you have a bag to check (see page 77). While major sights are most crowded in the late morning, exploring the back lanes is delightful during this time of day. The sights that have crowd problems get even more packed when it rains.

At the **Doge's Palace,** avoid the long line by purchasing your ticket at the never-crowded Correr Museum. You can also visit late in the day.

For the **Campanile,** ascend first thing in the morning or late (it's open until 21:00 July-Sept), or skip it entirely if you're going to the similar San Giorgio Maggiore bell tower.

For the **Accademia,** you'll enjoy fewer crowds by going early or late.

VENICE

Medical Help: Venice's Santi Giovanni e Paolo hospital (tel. 118) is a 10-minute walk from both the Rialto and San Marco neighborhoods, located on Fondamenta dei Mendicanti toward Fondamente Nove. You can take vaporetto #4.1 from San Zaccaria-Jolanda, or #5.2 from the train station or Piazzale Roma, to the Ospedale stop.

Be Prepared to Splurge: Venice is expensive for residents as well as tourists, as everything must be shipped in and hand-trucked to its destination. I find that the best way to enjoy Venice is just to succumb to its charms and blow a little money.

Take Breaks: Venice's endless pavement, crowds, and tight spaces are hard on tourists, especially in hot weather. Schedule breaks in your sightseeing. Grab a cool place to sit down, relax, and recoup—meditate on a pew in an uncrowded church, or stop in a café.

Etiquette: On St. Mark's Square, a "decorum patrol" admonishes snackers and sunbathers. Picnicking is forbidden (keep a low profile). The only place for a legal picnic is in Giardinetti Reali, the small park along the waterfront west of the Piazzetta near St. Mark's Square.

Dress Modestly: When visiting St. Mark's Basilica or other major churches, men, women, and even children must cover their shoulders and knees (or risk being turned away). Remove hats when entering a church.

Public Toilets: Handy public WCs (€1.50) are near major landmarks, including: St. Mark's Square (behind the Correr Museum and at the waterfront park, Giardinetti Reali), Rialto, and the Accademia Bridge. Use free toilets whenever you can—in a museum you're visiting or a café you're eating in. You could also get a drink at a bar (cheaper) and use their WC for free.

Best Views: On St. Mark's Square, enjoy views from the soaring Campanile or the balcony of St. Mark's Basilica (both require admission). The Rialto and Accademia bridges provide free, expansive views of the Grand Canal, along with a cooling breeze. Or get off the main island for a view of the Venetian skyline: Ascend the Church of San Giorgio Maggiore's bell tower, or venture to Giudecca Island to visit the swanky bar of the Molino Stucky Hilton Hotel (free shuttle boat leaves from near the San Zaccaria-M.V.E. vaporetto dock).

Pigeon Poop: If your head is bombed by a pigeon, resist the initial response to wipe it off immediately—it'll just smear into your hair. Wait until it dries, and it should flake off cleanly. But if the poop splatters on your clothes, wipe it off immediately to avoid a stain.

Water: I carry a water bottle to refill at public fountains. Venetians pride themselves on having pure, safe, and tasty tap water piped in from the foothills of the Alps. You can actually see the mountains from Venice's bell towers on crisp, clear winter days.

Updates to this Book: For news about changes to this book's coverage since it was published, see www.ricksteves.com/update.

Services

Internet Access: Almost all hotels have Wi-Fi, many have a computer that guests can use, and most provide these services for free. Otherwise, handy if pricey little Internet places are scattered around town (usually on back streets, marked with an @ sign, and charging €5/hour).

Post Office: The main post office is on Marzaria San Salvador, a few blocks toward St. Mark's Square from the Rialto, just beyond the Bata shoe store (Mon-Fri 8:30-19:10, Sat 8:30-12:30, closed Sun). You'll find branch offices around town. Use post offices only as a last resort, as simple transactions can take 45 minutes if you get in the wrong line. You can buy stamps from tobacco shops and mail postcards at any of the red postboxes in town.

Bookstores: In keeping with its literary heritage, Venice has classy and inviting bookstores. The small **Libreria Studium,** a block behind St. Mark's Basilica, has a carefully chosen selection of new English books, including my guidebooks (daily 9:00-19:30, on Calle de la Canonica at #337—see map on page 75, tel. 041-522-2382). Used-

bookstore lovers shouldn't miss the funky **Acqua Alta** ("high water") bookstore, whose quirky owner Luigi has prepared for the next flood by displaying his wares in a selection of vessels, including bathtubs and a gondola (daily 9:00-21:00, large and classically disorganized selection includes prints of Venice, just beyond Campo Santa Maria Formosa on Calle Lunga Santa Maria Formosa at #5176, tel. 041-296-0841). For a solid selection of used books in English, visit **Marco Polo,** on Calle del Teatro Malibran, close to the St. Mark's side of the Rialto Bridge on the way to Corte del Milion (Mon-Sat 9:30-13:00 & 15:30-19:30, closed Sun, tel. 041-522-6343).

Laundry: You'll find coin-operated launderettes near the train station and off Campo Santa Maria Formosa. I've listed details for a self-service *lavanderia* and a competitively priced

VENICE

full-service laundry near St. Mark's Square (see page 105), and for a self-serve laundry near the train station (page 117). Or ask your hotelier for the nearest launderette.

Travel Agencies: If you need to get train tickets, make seat reservations, or arrange a *cuccetta* (koo-CHET-tah—a berth on a night train), save a time-consuming trip to Venice's crowded train station by using a downtown travel agency. Most trains between Venice, Florence, and Rome require reservations, even for railpass holders. A travel agency can also give advice on cheap flights (book at least a week in advance for the best fares).

Near St. Mark's Square, **Oltrex Change and Travel** sells train tickets and books reservations for a €4 fee (tickets sold daily 9:00-18:00; on Riva degli Schiavoni, one bridge past the Bridge of Sighs—see map on page 75; tel. 041-524-2828, Luca and Beatrice).

Near Rialto, **Kele & Teo Travel** sells train tickets for a €4 per-person service charge (Mon-Fri 9:00-18:00, Sat 9:00-12:00, closed Sun; leaving the Rialto Bridge heading for St. Mark's, it's half a block away, tucked down a side street on the right; tel. 041-520-8722).

English Church Services: The **San Zulian Church** offers a Mass in English (generally May-Sept Mon-Fri at 9:30 and Sun at 11:30, Sun only Oct-April, 2 blocks toward Rialto off St. Mark's Square, tel. 041-523-5383). **St. George's Anglican Church** welcomes all to its English-language Eucharist (Sun at 10:30, located on Campo San Zio in Dorsoduro, midway between Accademia and Peggy Guggenheim Collection, www.stgeorgesvenice.com).

Getting Around Venice
On Foot

The city's "streets" are narrow pedestrian walkways connecting its docks, squares, bridges, and courtyards. To navigate, look for yellow signs on street corners pointing you to *(per)* the nearest major landmark. The first landmarks you'll get to know are San Marco (St. Mark's Square), Rialto (the bridge), Accademia (another bridge), Ferrovia (the train station), and Piazzale Roma (the bus station). Determine whether your destination is in the direction of a major signposted landmark, then follow the signs through the maze.

Dare to turn off the posted routes and make your own discoveries. While 80 percent of Venice is, in fact, not touristy, 80 percent of the tourists never notice. Escape the crowds and explore on foot. Walk and walk to the far reaches of the town. Don't worry about getting lost—in fact, get as lost as possible. Keep reminding yourself, "I'm on an island, and I can't get off." When it comes time to find your way, just follow the arrows on building corners or simply ask a local, *"Dov'è San Marco?"* ("Where is St. Mark's?") People in the tourist business (that's most Venetians) speak some English. If they don't, listen politely, watch where their hands point, say *"Grazie,"* and head off in that direction. If you're lost, refer to your map, or pop into a hotel and ask for their business card—it probably comes with a map and a prominent "You are here."

If you need to find a specific address, it helps to know its district, street, house number, and nearby landmarks. Every building in Venice has a house number. The numbers relate to the district (each with about 6,000 address numbers), not the street.

Some helpful street lingo: *Campo* means square, *campiello* is a small square, *calle* is a street, *fondamenta* is the embankment along a canal or the lagoon, *rio* is a small canal, *rio terà* is a street that was once a canal and has been filled in, *sotoportego* is a covered passageway, and *ponte* is a bridge. Don't get hung up on the exact spelling of street and square names, which may sometimes appear in the Venetian dialect and other times in standard Italian.

By Vaporetto

Venice's public transit system, run by a company called ACTV, is a fleet of motorized bus-boats called *vaporetti*. They work like city

buses except that they never get a flat, the stops are docks, and if you get off between stops, you might drown.

For most travelers, only two vaporetto lines matter: line #1 and line #2. These lines leave every 10 minutes or so and go up and down the Grand Canal, between the "mouth of the fish" at one end and San Marco at the other. Line #1 is the slow boat, taking 45 minutes and making every stop along the way. Line #2 is the fast boat that zips down the Grand Canal in 25 minutes, stopping only at Tronchetto (parking lot), Piazzale Roma (bus station), Ferrovia (train station), Rialto Bridge, San Tomà (Frari Church), San Samuele, Accademia Bridge, San Marco (west end of St. Mark's Square), and San Zaccaria (east end of St. Mark's Square).

Catching a vaporetto is very much like catching a city bus. You can buy either single-ride tickets (valid for 1 hour) or passes (valid for a variety of durations, from 12 hours to 7 days) from any ticket window or HelloVenezia office. HelloVenezia, run by ACTV, is a string of shops selling tickets and passes at the same prices as ticket windows (www.hellovenezia.com).

VENICE

Venice

To Mestre & Mainland

Canale de Cannaregio

GHETTO

Campo de Gheto Novo

CANNA

GUGLIE BRIDGE

SAN LEONARDO

SAN MARCUOLA

SAN GEREMIA

LISTA DI SPAGNA

Grand Canal

SAN ZAN DEGOLA

BEMBO

SANTA LUCIA STATION (FERROVIA)

SCALZI

To Tronchetto & Mainland

SCALZI BRIDGE

SAN SIMEONE GRANDE

SAN GIACOMO

SAN SIMEONE PICCOLO

SANTA CROCE

SAN

CALATRAVA BRIDGE

PEOPLE MOVER

GARAGE

Piazzale Roma BUS STATION

CA'AMAI

Campo San Stin

SAN ROCCO

SAN POLO

To Stazione Marittima & Tronchetto (Parking)

SAN NICOLO DA TOLENTINO

TINTORETTO

FRARI

SAONERI

SCUOLA SAN ROCCO

SAN TOMA

SAN PANTALON

C. LARGA FOSCARI

SANTA MARGARITA

CA' FOSCARI

Campo Santa Margarita

CA' REZZONICO

PALAZZO GRASSI

SANTA MARIA DEI CARMINI

Campo San Barnaba

SAN BARNABA

OGNISSANTI

DORSODURO

TOLETTA

CORFU

ACCADEMIA BRIDGE

SAN TROVASO

FOND. ZATTERE AL PONTE LONGO

ACCADEMIA GALLERY

AGNESE

RIO TERA FOSCARINI

200 Meters

200 Yards

Giudecca Canal

VENICE

VENICE

VENICE

Handy *Vaporetti* from San Zaccaria, near St. Mark's Square

Several *vaporetti* leave from the San Zaccaria docks, located 150 yards east of St. Mark's Square. There are four separate San Zaccaria docks spaced about 70 yards apart: Danieli, Jolanda, M.V.E., and Pietà. Although I list which specific dock these lines leave from, they often change from season to season—confirm before boarding.

- Line #1 goes up the Grand Canal, making all the stops, including San Marco-Vallaresso, Rialto, Ferrovia (train station), and Piazzale Roma (but it does not go as far as Tronchetto). In the other direction, it goes from San Zaccaria-Danieli to Arsenale and Giardini before ending on the Lido.
- Line #2 begins at San Zaccaria-M.V.E. and zips over to San Giorgio Maggiore, the island church across from St. Mark's Square (5 minutes, €4 ride). From there, it continues on to stops on the island of Giudecca, the parking lot at Tronchetto, and then down the Grand Canal.
- Line #4.1 goes to San Michele and Murano in 45 minutes (usually departs from the San Zaccaria-Jolanda dock).
- Line #7 is the summertime express boat to Murano (25 minutes, most likely from the San Zaccaria-Jolanda dock).
- The Molino Stucky shuttle boat takes even non-guests to the Hilton Hotel, with its popular view bar (free, 20-minute ride, leaves at 0:20 past the hour from near the San Zaccaria-M.V.E. dock).
- Lines #5.1 and #5.2 are the *circulare* (cheer-koo-LAH-ray), making a loop around the perimeter of the island, with a stop at the Lido—perfect if you just like riding boats. Line

Before you board, validate your ticket by holding it up to the small white machine on the dock until you hear a pinging sound. The machine readout shows how long your ticket is valid—and inspectors do come by now and then to check tickets. If you board without a ticket (because ticket windows at odd hours or small stops may be closed), seek out the conductor immediately to buy a single ticket on board (or risk a €50 fine). If you purchase a vaporetto pass, you're supposed to touch the pass to the machine each time you board the boat.

Large stops—such as San Marco, San Zaccaria, and Piazzale Roma—have multiple docks, and each dock has its own name, such as San Marco-Vallaresso, San Zaccaria-Jolanda, and Piazzale Roma-Parisi. Helpful electronic boards at larger stops display which boats are coming next and when, and give information for all docks at that stop. Make a point to take advantage of these.

#5.1 goes counterclockwise (usually from the San Zaccaria-Danieli dock), and #5.2 goes clockwise (usually from the San Zaccaria-Jolanda dock).
- The Alilaguna airport shuttle to and from the airport stops here as well (generally at the San Zaccaria-Jolanda dock).

At smaller stops, check the charts and signs to figure out which dock your boat will use. Signs on each dock show the vaporetto

lines that stop there and the direction they are headed: Along the Grand Canal, a #1 or #2 boat might be headed toward St. Mark's Square (signposted *San Marco*), or back toward the mainland (signposted *Ferrovia*, *Piazzale Roma*, or *Tronchetto*). Sorting out the different directions of travel can be confusing, especially as boats on some circular routes travel in one direction only (true for lines #5.1 and #5.2, plus the non-Murano sections of lines #4.1 and #4.2).

To clear up any confusion, ask a ticket-seller or conductor for help (sometimes they're stationed on the dock to help confused tourists), or look at the most current ACTV timetable (in English and Italian, free at ticket booths but often unavailable—can be downloaded from the ACTV website, www.actv.it).

These are your ticket and pass options:

Individual Vaporetto Tickets: A single ticket costs €7. Tickets are good for one hour in one direction; you can hop on and off at stops and change boats during that time. Tickets are electronic and refillable—don't toss your ticket after the first use. You can put more money on it at the automated kiosks and avoid waiting in line at the ticket window. The fare is reduced to €4 for a few one-stop runs *(corsa semplice)* that are hard to do by foot, including the route from San Marco to La Salute, from Fondamente Nove to Murano-Colonna, and from San Zaccaria-M.V.E. to San Giorgio Maggiore.

Vaporetto Passes: You can buy a pass for unlimited use of *vaporetti*: €18/12 hours, €20/24 hours, €25/36 hours, €30/48 hours, €35/72 hours, €50/7-day pass (pass is supposed to be validated each time you board by touching it to the small white machine on the dock). Because single tickets cost a hefty €7 a pop, these passes can pay for themselves in a hurry. Think through your Venice itinerary before you step up to the ticket booth to pay for your first vaporetto trip. The 48-hour pass pays for itself with five rides (for example: to your hotel, on a Grand Canal joyride, into the lagoon and back, and to the train station). Keep in mind that outlying stops, such as Santa Elena and Biennale, are unstaffed—another good reason to buy a pass. And it's fun to be able to hop on and off spontaneously, and avoid long ticket lines. On the other hand, many tourists just walk and rarely use a boat.

Anyone under 30 years old can get a 72-hour pass for €18 if they also buy a **Rolling Venice** discount card for €4 (see page 74). Those settling in for a longer stay can ride like a local by buying the **CartaVenezia** ID card (€40/5 years, which lets you ride for €1.10 per trip). See www.actv.it for details.

Passes are also valid on ACTV's mainland buses, including bus #5 to the airport (but not the airport buses run by ATVO, a separate company).

Vaporetto Tips: For fun, take my Grand Canal Cruise. Boats can be literally packed during the tourist rush hour (during mornings heading in from Piazzale Roma, and in evenings heading out to Piazzale Roma). Riding at night, with nearly empty boats and chandelier-lit palace interiors viewable from the Grand Canal, is an entirely different experience.

By *Traghetto*

Only four bridges cross the Grand Canal, but *traghetti* (shuttle gondolas) ferry locals and in-the-know tourists across the Grand Canal at seven handy locations (marked on the color map of Venice at the front of this book). Just step in, hand the gondolier €2, and enjoy the ride—standing or sitting. Note

that some *traghetti* are seasonal, some stop running as early as 12:30, and all stop by 18:00.

By Water Taxi

Venetian taxis, like speedboat limos, hang out at busy points along the Grand Canal. Prices are regulated and listed on the TI's website: €15 for pick-up, then €2 per minute; €5 per person for more than four passengers; and €10 between 22:00 and 6:00. Extra bags cost €3 apiece. (For information on taking the water taxi to/from the airport, see "Venice Connections," at the end of this chapter). Despite regulation, prices can be soft; negotiate and settle on the price or rate before stepping in. For travelers with lots of luggage or small groups who can split the cost, taxi boat rides can be a worthwhile and time-saving convenience—and skipping across the lagoon in a classic wooden motorboat is a cool indulgence. For a little more than €100 an hour, you can have a private, unguided taxi-boat tour.

By Gondola

If you're interested in hiring a gondolier for your own private cruise, see page 98.

Tours in Venice

Avventure Bellissime Venice Tours—This company offers several English-only two-hour walks, including a basic St. Mark's Square introduction called the "Original Venice Walking Tour"

(€22, includes church entry, most days at 11:00, Sun at 14:00; 45 minutes on the square, 15 minutes in the church, one hour along back streets), a 70-minute private boat tour of the Grand Canal (€43, daily at 16:30, eight people maximum), and excursions on the mainland (10 percent discount for Rick Steves readers, see descriptions at www.tours-italy.com,

Is Venice Sinking?

Venice has battled rising water levels since the fifth century. But today, the water seems to be winning. Several factors, both natural and man-made, cause Venice to flood about 100 times a year—usually from October until late winter—a phenomenon called the *acqua alta*.

On my last trip I asked a Venetian how much the city is sinking. He said, "Less than the sea is rising." Venice sits atop sediments deposited at the ancient mouth of the Po River, which are still compacting and settling. Early industrial projects, such as offshore piers and the railroad bridge to the mainland, affected the sea floor and tidal cycles in ways that made the city more vulnerable to flooding. Twentieth-century industry worsened things by pumping out massive amounts of groundwater from the aquifer beneath the lagoon for nearly 50 years before the government stopped the practice in the 1970s. In the last century, Venice has sunk by about nine inches.

Meanwhile, the waters around Venice are rising, a phenomenon that's especially apparent in winter. The highest so far was in November 1966, when a huge storm (the same one that famously flooded Florence) raised Venice's water level to more than six feet above the norm. The notorious *acqua alta* happens when an unusually high tide combines with strong sirocco winds and a storm. Although tides are miniscule in the Mediterranean, the narrow, shallow Adriatic Sea has about a three-foot tidal range. When a storm—an area of low pressure—travels over a body of water, it pulls the surface of the water up into a dome. As strong sirocco winds from Africa blow storms north up the Adriatic, they push this high water ahead of the front, causing a surging storm tide. Add to that the world-wide sea-level rise that's resulted from recent climate change (melting ice caps, thermal expansion of the water, more frequent and more powerful storms) and it

tel. 041-970-499, info@tours-italy.com, Monica or Jonathan).

Classic Venice Bars Tour—Debonair guide Alessandro Schezzini is a connoisseur of Venetian *bacari*—classic old bars serving wine and traditional *cicchetti* snacks. He organizes two-hour Venetian pub tours (€30, any night on request at 18:00, depart from top of Rialto Bridge, better to book by email—alessandro @schezzini.it—than by phone, mobile 335-530-9024, www .schezzini.it). Alessandro's tours include sampling *cicchetti* with wines at three different *bacari*. (If you think of this tour as a light makes a high sea that much higher.

If the *acqua alta* appears during your visit, you'll see the first puddles in the center of paved squares, pooling around the limestone grates at the square's lowest point. These grates cover cisterns that long held Venice's only source of drinking water. That's

right: Surrounded by the lagoon and beset by constant flooding, this city had no natural source of fresh water. For centuries, residents carried water from the mainland with much effort and risk. In the ninth century, they devised a way to collect rainwater by using paved, cleverly sloped squares as catchment systems, with limestone filters covering underground clay tubs.

Venice's population grew markedly once citizens were able to access fresh water by simply dropping buckets down into these "wells." Several thousand cisterns provided the city with drinking water up until 1886, when an aqueduct was built (paralleling the railroad bridge) to bring in water from nearby mountains. Now the wells are capped, the clay tubs are rotted out, and rain drains from squares into the lagoon—or up from it, as the case may be.

So what is Venice doing about the flooding? Since the 1966 flood, officials knew something had to be done, but it took about four decades to come up with a solution. In 2003, a consortium of engineering firms began construction on the MOSE Project, which is expected to be partially operational by 2014. Named for the acronym of its Italian name, *Modulo Sperimentale Elettromeccanico*, it's also a nod to Moses and his (albeit temporary) mastery over the sea.

Underwater "mobile" gates are being built on the floor of the sea that will lie flat at the entrances of the three inlets that lead from the open sea into Venice's lagoon. When the seawater rises above a certain level, air will be pumped into the gates, causing them to rise and shut out the Adriatic.

dinner with a local friend, it's a particularly good value.)

Artviva—This company offers a busy program of tours, including Venice in a day, four themed tours (Grand Canal, Venice Walk, Doge's Palace, Gondola Tour), and a "Learn to Be a Gondolier" tour (for details, see www.italy.artviva.com).

Venicescapes—Michael Broderick's private theme tours of Venice are intellectually demanding and beyond the attention span of most mortal tourists. But serious students of Venice find him passionate and engaging. Your time with Michael is like a rolling, graduate-level lecture (see his website for various 4-6-hour itineraries, 2 people-$250-290 or the euro equivalent, $60/person after that, admissions and transport not included, book in advance, tel. 041-520-6361, www.venicescapes.org, info@venicescapes.org).

Local Guides—Plenty of licensed, trained guides are available. If you organize a small group from your hotel at breakfast to split the cost (figure on €70/hour with a 2-hour minimum), the fee becomes more reasonable. The following guides work with individuals, families, and small groups:

Walks Inside Venice is a dynamic duo of women enthusiastic about teaching (€70/hour per group with this book, 3-hour minimum; Roberta: mobile 347-253-0560; Sara: mobile 335-522-9714; www.walksinsidevenice.com, info@walksinsidevenice.com). Roberta has been a big help in the making of this book. They also do regularly scheduled small-group, English-only walking tours (€60, departs daily at 14:30, 2.5 hours).

Elisabetta Morelli is a fine licensed guide (€70/hour, 2-hour minimum, tel. 041-526-7816, mobile 328-753-5220, www.elisabetta morelli.it, bettamorelli@inwind.it).

Venice with a Guide is a co-op of 10 good guides (www.venicewithaguide.com).

Alessandro Schezzini, mentioned earlier for his Classic Venice Bars Tour, isn't a licensed guide, so he can't take you into sights. But his relaxed, 1.5-hour back-streets tour gets you beyond the clichés and into off-beat Venice (€15/person, departs daily at 16:00, mobile 335-530-9024, www.schezzini.it, alessandro @schezzini.it). He also does lagoon tours.

Tour Leader Venice, a.k.a. **Treviso Car Service,** offers small-group tours beyond Venice to 16th-century villas, wine-and-cheese tastings, and the Dolomites. Within Venice, their guided excursions include visits to the Rialto produce market, the lagoon, artisan shops, and a one-hour gondola tour (also provides airport transfers—see page 139, mobile 348-900-0700 or 333-411-2840; in Venice: www.tourleadervenice.com, info@tourleadervenice.com; beyond Venice: www.trevisocarservice.com, tvcarservice@gmail .com; Igor, Andrea, and Marta).

Self-Guided Cruise in Venice

▲▲▲Grand Canal Cruise

Take a joyride and introduce yourself to Venice by boat. Cruise the Canal Grande all the way to San Marco, starting at the train station (Ferrovia) or the bus station (Piazzale Roma).

If it's your first trip down the Grand Canal, you might want to stow this book and just take it all in—Venice is a barrage on the senses that hardly needs narration. But these notes give the cruise a little meaning and help orient you to this great city.

This tour is designed to be done on the slow boat #1 (which takes about 45 minutes). The express boat #2 travels the same route, but it skips many stops and takes only 25 minutes, making it hard to sightsee. Also, some #2 boats terminate at Rialto; confirm that you're on a boat that goes all the way to San Marco.

To help you enjoy the visual parade of canal wonders, I've organized this tour by boat stop. I'll point out both what you can see from the current stop, and what to look forward to as you cruise to the next stop. You can download this self-guided cruise as a free Rick Steves audio tour (see page 11).

A Few Tips: You're more likely to find an empty seat if you catch the vaporetto at Piazzale Roma. You can break up the tour by hopping on and off at various sights described in greater depth elsewhere in this book (but remember, a single-fare vaporetto ticket is good for just one hour; passes let you hop on and off all day). The trip is best in a boat with seats in the bow, but many boats no longer offer these great front-row view seats. If they do, make a beeline for these seats as soon as you board. From the front, you can easily look left, right, and forward. If you find yourself stuck on the side or in the cabin, do your best. Avoid sitting in the back, only because you'll miss the wonderful forward views.

Overview

The Grand Canal is Venice's "Main Street." At more than two miles long, nearly 150 feet wide, and nearly 15 feet deep, it's the city's largest canal, lined with its most impressive palaces. It's the remnant of a river that once spilled from the mainland into the Adriatic. The sediment it carried formed barrier islands that cut Venice off from the sea, forming a lagoon.

Venice was built on the marshy islands of the former delta, sitting on wood pilings driven nearly 15 feet into the clay (alder was the preferred wood). About 25 miles of canals drain the city, dumping like streams into the Grand Canal. Technically, Venice has only three canals: Grand, Giudecca, and Cannaregio. The 45 small waterways that dump into the Grand Canal are referred to as rivers (e.g., Rio Novo).

Venice is a city of palaces, dating from the days when the city was the world's richest. The most lavish palaces formed a grand architectural cancan along the Grand Canal. Once frescoed in reds and blues, with black-and-white

Grand Canal

VENICE

- **To Jewish Ghetto**
- STRADA
- Canale de Cannaregio
- GUGLIE BRIDGE
- LISTA DI SPAGNA
- SAN GEREMIA
- PALAZZO FLANGINI
- SANTA LUCIA TRAIN STATION (FERROVIA)
- SCALZI
- PALAZZO CALBO-CROTTA
- SCALZI BRIDGE
- Grand Canal
- PALAZZO CORRER CONTARINI
- PALAZZO GIOVANELLI
- SAN MARCUOLA
- PALAZZO GRITTI
- CASINÒ PALAZZO VENDRAMIN CALERGI
- TURKISH "FONDACO" EXCHANGE
- PAL. GRITTI
- PALAZZO MARCELLO
- PALAZZO DONÀ BALBI
- SAN ZAN DEGOLÀ
- PALAZZO CA' TRÒN
- SAN SIMEONE PICCOLO
- SANTA CROCE
- CALATRAVA BRIDGE
- SAN
- PIAZZALE ROMA & PEOPLE MOVER TO STAZIONE MARITTIMA & TRONCHETTO
- FRARI
- SAN TOMÀ
- PALAZZO GIUSTINIANI
- PALAZZO CAPPELLO-LAYARD
- PALAZZO BARBARIGO
- PALAZZO BALBI
- FIRE STATION
- CA' FOSCARI
- PALAZZO GIUSTINIAN
- CA' REZZONICO
- PALAZZO MOCENIGO
- PALAZZO VECCHIA
- PALAZZO MORO LIN
- PALAZZO GRASSI
- PALAZZO MALIPIERO-CAPPELLO
- PALAZZO LOREDAN
- PALAZZO FALIER
- PALAZZO GIUSTINIAN LOLIN
- PALAZZO CONTARINI DEGLI SCRIGNI
- PALAZZO QUERINI
- ACCADEMIA BRIDGE & GALLERY
- PALAZZO BARBARO
- PALAZZO BARBARIGO
- FONDAMENTA ZATTERE AL PONTE LONGO
- Giudecca Canal
- DORSODURO
- To Zattere

Vaporetto Stops

1. Ferrovia
2. Riva de Biasio
3. San Marcuola
4. San Stae
5. Ca' d'Oro
6. Mercato Rialto
7. Rialto
8. San Silvestro
9. Sant'Angelo
10. San Tomà
11. Ca' Rezzonico
12. Accademia
13. Santa Maria del Giglio
14. Salute
15. San Marco
16. San Zaccaria

VENICE

200 Meters
200 Yards

Lagoon

FONDAMENTE NOVE

CANNAREGIO

NOVA

PALAZZO MARCELLO

PALAZZO MOLIN

PALAZZO ZULLAN

4

SAN STAE

PALAZZO BARBARIGO

PALAZZO FONTANA

PALAZZO DONÀ

PALAZZO GIUSTI

CA' PESARO

PALAZZO FAVRETTO

CA' D'ORO

STRADA NOVA

PALAZZO SAGREDO

PALAZZO MICHIEL COLONNE

PALAZZO CORNER DELLA REGINA

PALAZZO BRANDOLIN

5

PALAZZO VALMARANA

PALAZZO CA' DA MOSTO

FISH MARKET

6

FRUIT & VEGETABLE MARKET

PALAZZO CIVRAN

POLO

GERMAN EXCHANGE (FORMER POST)

RIALTO BRIDGE

A

7

PALAZZO DOLFIN-MANIN

SAL S. LIO

S. MARIA FORMOSA

PALAZZO PAPADOPOLI

PALAZZO BARZIZZA

PALAZZO BEMBO

MERCERIE

PALAZZO DONÀ

8

PALAZZO CORNER-CONTARINI

PALAZZO FARSETTI-DANDOLO

CASTELLO

PALAZZO BERNARDO

PALAZZO GRIMANI

PALAZZO BENZON

PALAZZO MARTINENGO

PALAZZO CORNER-SPINELLI

MERCERIE

ST. MARK'S BASILICA

CAMPANILE

SAN MARCO

BRIDGE OF SIGHS

DOGE'S PALACE

SAN MARCO

16

CALLE LARGA XXII MARZO

HARRY'S AMERICAN BAR

15

A

St. Mark's Basin

To Lido

GRITTI PALACE HOTEL

CA' GRANDE

PALAZZO FLANGINI

13

Grand

PALAZZO DARIO

PALAZZO GENOVESE

Canal

14

LA SALUTE CHURCH

PUNTA DELLA DOGANA (CUSTOMS HOUSE)

PEGGY GUGGENHEIM COLLECTION

To San Giorgio Maggiore & Giudecca

borders and gold-leaf trim, they made Venice a city of dazzling color. This cruise is the only way to truly appreciate the palaces, approaching them at water level, where their main entrances were located. Today, strict laws prohibit any changes in these buildings, so while landowners gnash their teeth, we can enjoy Europe's best-preserved medieval city—slowly rotting. Many of the grand buildings are now vacant. Others harbor chandeliered elegance above mossy, empty (often flooded) ground floors.

The Grand Canal Cruise Begins

This tour starts at the Ferrovia vaporetto stop (at Santa Lucia train station). It also works if you board upstream from Ferrovia at Piazzale Roma, a short walk from Ferrovia over the Calatrava Bridge. Just start the tour when your vaporetto reaches Ferrovia.

Ferrovia: The **Santa Lucia train station,** one of the few mod-

ern buildings in town, was built in 1954. It's been the gateway into Venice since 1860, when the first station was built. "F.S." stands for "Ferrovie dello Stato," the Italian state railway system.

More than 20,000 people a day commute in from the mainland, making this the busiest part of Venice during rush hour. The **Calatrava Bridge,** spanning the Grand Canal between the train station and Piazzale Roma upstream, was built in 2008 to alleviate some of the congestion and make the commute easier (see page 92).

Opposite the train station, atop the green dome of **San Simeon Piccolo** church, St. Simeon waves *ciao* to whoever enters or leaves the "old" city. The pink church with the white Carrara-marble facade, just beyond the train station, is the **Church of the Scalzi** (Church of the Barefoot, named after the shoeless Carmelite monks), where the last doge (Venetian ruler) rests. It looks relatively new because it was partially rebuilt after being bombed in 1915 by Austrians aiming (poorly) at the train station.

Riva de Biasio: Venice's main thoroughfare is busy with all kinds of boats: taxis, police boats, garbage boats, ambulances, construction cranes, and even brown-and-white UPS boats. Somehow they all manage to share the canal in relative peace.

About 25 yards past the Riva de Biasio stop, you'll look left down the broad **Cannaregio Canal** to see what was the **Jewish Ghetto** (described on page 91). The twin, pale-pink, eight-story "skyscrapers"—the tallest buildings you'll see at this end of the canal—are reminders of how densely populated the world's original ghetto was. Set aside as the local Jewish quarter in 1516, this area became extremely crowded. This urban island developed into one of the most closely knit business and cultural quarters of all the Jewish communities in Italy, and gave us our word "ghetto" (from *geto*, the copper foundry located here).

San Marcuola: At this stop, facing a tiny square just ahead, stands the unfinished church of San Marcuola, one of only five churches fronting the Grand Canal. Centuries ago, this canal was a commercial drag of expensive real estate in high demand by wealthy merchants. About 20 yards ahead on the right stands

the stately gray **Turkish "Fondaco" Exchange,** one of the oldest houses in Venice. Its horseshoe arches and roof-line of triangles and dingleballs are reminders of its Byzantine heritage. Turkish traders in turbans docked here, unloaded their goods into the warehouse on the bottom story, then went upstairs for a home-style meal

and a place to sleep. Venice in the 1500s was very cosmopolitan, welcoming every religion and ethnicity, so long as they carried cash. (Today the building contains the city's Museum of Natural History—and Venice's only dinosaur skeleton.)

Just 100 yards ahead on the left, Venice's **Casinò** is housed in the palace where German composer Richard *(The Ring)* Wagner died in 1883. See his distinct, strong-jawed profile in the white plaque on the brick wall. In the 1700s, Venice was Europe's Vegas, with casinos and prostitutes everywhere. *Casinòs* ("little houses" in Venetian dialect) have long provided Italians with a handy escape from daily life. Today they're run by the state to keep Mafia influence at bay. Notice the fancy front porch, rolling out the red carpet for high rollers arriving by taxi or hotel boat.

San Stae: The San Stae Church sports a delightful Baroque facade. Opposite the San Stae stop is a little canal opening—on the second building to the right of that opening, look for the peeling plaster that once made up **frescoes** (you can barely distinguish the scant remains of little angels on the lower floors). Imagine the facades of the Grand Canal at their finest. Most of them would have been covered in frescoes by the best artists of the day. As colorful as the city is today, it's still only a faded, sepia-toned remnant of a long-gone era, a time of lavishly decorated, brilliantly colored palaces.

Just ahead, jutting out a bit on the right, is the ornate white facade of **Ca' Pesaro** (which houses the International Gallery of Modern Art—see page 88). *"Ca'"* is short for *casa* (house). Because only the house of the doge (Venetian ruler) could be called a palace *(palazzo)*, all other Venetian palaces are technically *"Ca'."*

In this city of masks, notice how the rich marble facades along the Grand Canal mask what are generally just simple, no-nonsense brick buildings. Most merchants enjoyed showing off. However, being smart businessmen, they only decorated the side of the buildings that would be seen and appreciated. But look back as you pass Ca' Pesaro. It's the

only building you'll see with a fine side facade. Ahead, on the left, with its glorious triple-decker medieval arcade (just before the next stop) is Ca' d'Oro.

Ca' d'Oro: The lacy **Ca' d'Oro** (House of Gold) is the best example of Venetian Gothic architecture on the canal. Its three

stories offer different variations on balcony design, topped with a spiny white roofline. Venetian Gothic mixes traditional Gothic (pointed arches and round medallions stamped with a four-leaf clover) with Byzantine styles (tall, narrow arches atop thin columns), filled in with Islamic frills. Like all the palaces, this was originally painted and gilded to make it even more glorious than it is now. Today the Ca' d'Oro is an art gallery (described on page 93).

Look at the Venetian chorus line of palaces in front of the boat. On the right is the arcade of the covered **fish market,** with the open-air **produce market** just beyond. It bustles in the morning but is quiet the rest of the day. This is a great scene to wander through—even though European Union hygiene standards have made it cleaner but less colorful than it once was.

Find the ***traghetto*** gondola ferrying shoppers—standing like Washington crossing the Delaware—back and forth. There are seven *traghetto* crossings along the Grand Canal, each one marked by a classy low-key green-and-black sign. As a public service, all gondoliers are obliged to row the *traghetto* a few days a month. Make a point to use them. At €2 a ride, *traghetti*

offer the cheapest gondola ride in Venice (but at this price don't expect them to sing to you).

Mercato Rialto: This stop was opened in 2007 to serve the busy market (boats only stop here between 8:00 and 20:00). The long and officious-looking building at this stop is the Venice courthouse. Straight ahead in the distance, rising above the huge post office, is the tip of the Campanile (bell tower), crowned by its golden angel at St. Mark's Square, where this tour will end. The **German Exchange** (100 yards directly ahead, on left side) was the trading center for German metal merchants in the early 1500s (once a post office, it will soon be a shopping center).

You'll cruise by some trendy and beautifully situated wine bars on the right, but look ahead as you round the corner and see the impressive Rialto Bridge come into view.

A major landmark of Venice, the **Rialto Bridge** is lined with shops and tourists. Constructed in 1588, it's the third bridge built

on this spot. Until the 1850s, this was the only bridge crossing the Grand Canal. With a span of 160 feet and foundations stretching 650 feet on either side, the Rialto was an impressive engineering feat in its day. Earlier Rialto Bridges could open to let big ships in, but not this one. When this new bridge was completed, much of the Grand Canal was closed to shipping and became a canal of palaces.

When gondoliers pass under the fat arch of the Rialto Bridge, they take full advantage of its acoustics: *"Volare, oh, oh..."*

Rialto: Rialto, a separate town in the early days of Venice, has always been the commercial district, while San Marco was the religious and governmental center. Today, a winding street called the Mercerie connects the two, providing travelers with human traffic jams and a mesmerizing gauntlet of shopping temptations. This is the only stretch of the historic Grand Canal with landings upon which you can walk. They unloaded the city's basic necessities here: oil, wine, charcoal, iron. Today, the quay is lined with tourist-trap restaurants.

Venice's sleek, black, graceful **gondolas** are a symbol of the city (for more on gondolas, see page 98). With about 500 gondoliers joyriding amid the churning *vaporetti*, there's a lot of congestion on the Grand Canal. Pay attention—this is where most of the gondola and vaporetto accidents take place. While the Rialto is the highlight of many gondola rides, gondoliers understandably prefer the quieter small canals. Watch your vaporetto driver curse the better-paid gondoliers.

Ahead 100 yards on the left, two gray-colored **palaces** stand side by side (the City Hall and the mayor's office). Their horseshoe-shaped, arched windows are similar and their stories are the same height, lining up to create the effect of one long balcony.

San Silvestro: We now enter a long stretch of important **merchants' palaces,** each with proud and different facades. Because ships couldn't navigate beyond the Rialto Bridge, the biggest palaces—with the major shipping needs—line this last stretch of the navigable Grand Canal.

Palaces like these were multi-functional: ground floor for the warehouse, offices and showrooms upstairs, and the living quarters above the offices on the "noble floors" (with big windows designed to allow in maximum light). Servants lived and worked on the top floors (with the smallest windows). For fire-safety reasons, the kitchens were also located on the top floors. Peek into the noble floors to catch a glimpse of their still-glorious chandeliers of Murano glass.

Sant'Angelo: Notice how many buildings have a foundation of waterproof white stone *(pietra d'Istria)* upon which the bricks sit high and dry. Many canal-level floors are abandoned as the rising water level takes its toll. The **posts**—historically painted gaily with the equivalent of family coats of arms—don't rot underwater. But the wood at the waterline, where it's exposed to oxygen, does. On the smallest canals, little blue gondola signs indicate that these docks are for gondolas only (no taxis or motorboats).

San Tomà: Fifty yards ahead, on the right side (with twin obelisks on the rooftop) stands Palazzo Balbi, the palace of an early-17th-century captain general of the sea. These Venetian equivalents of five-star admirals were honored with twin obelisks decorating their palaces. This palace, like so many in the city, flies three flags: Italy (green-white-red), the European Union (blue with ring of stars), and Venice (a lion on a field of red and gold). Today it houses the administrative headquarters of the regional government.

Just past the admiral's palace, look immediately to the right, down a side canal. On the right side of that canal, before the bridge, see the traffic light and the **fire station** (the 1930s Mussolini-era building with four arches hiding fireboats parked and ready to go).

The impressive **Ca' Foscari,** with a classic Venetian facade (on the corner, across from the fire station), dominates the bend in the canal. This is the main building of the University of Venice, which has about 25,000 students. Notice the elegant lamp on the corner—needed in the old days to light this intersection.

The grand, heavy, white **Ca'**

Rezzonico, just before the stop of the same name, houses the Museum of 18th-Century Venice (see page 87). Across the canal is the cleaner and leaner **Palazzo Grassi,** the last major palace built on the canal, erected in the late 1700s. It was purchased by a French tycoon

and now displays a contemporary art collection.

Ca' Rezzonico: Up ahead, the Accademia Bridge leads over the Grand Canal to the **Accademia Gallery** (right side), filled with the best Venetian paintings (see page 85). The bridge was put up in 1934 as a temporary structure. Locals liked it, so it stayed. It was rebuilt in 1984 in the original style.

Accademia: From here, look through the graceful bridge and

way ahead to enjoy a classic view of **La Salute Church,** topped by a crown-shaped dome supported by scrolls (see page 87). This Church of Saint Mary of Good Health was built to thank God for delivering Venetians from the devastating plague of 1630 (which had killed about a third of the city's population).

The low, white building among greenery (100 yards ahead, on the right, between the Accademia Bridge and the church) is the **Peggy Guggenheim Collection.** The American heiress "retired" here, sprucing up a palace that had been abandoned in mid-construction. Peggy willed the city her fine collection of modern art (see page 87).

As you approach the next stop, notice on the right how the fine line of higgledy-piggledy palaces evokes old-time Venice. Two doors past the Guggenheim, Palazzo Dario has a great set of characteristic **funnel-shaped chimneys.** These forced embers through a loop-the-

loop channel until they were dead—required in the days when stone palaces were surrounded by humble, wooden buildings, and a live spark could make a merchant's workforce homeless. Notice this early Renaissance building's flat-feeling facade with "pasted-on" Renaissance motifs. Three doors later is the **Salviati building,** which once served as a glassworks. Its fine mosaic, done by Art Nouveau in the early 20th century, features Venice as a queen being appreciated by the big shots of society.

Santa Maria del Giglio: Back on the left stands the fancy Gritti Palace hotel. Hemingway and Woody Allen both stayed here (but not together).

Take a deep whiff of Venice. What's all this nonsense about stinky canals? All I smell is my shirt. By the way, how's your captain? Smooth dockings? To get to know him, stand up in the bow and block his view.

Salute: The huge La Salute Church towers overhead as if squirted from a can of Catholic Reddi-wip. Like Venice itself, the church rests upon pilings. To build the foundation for the city, more than a million trees were piled together, reaching beneath the mud to the solid clay. Much of the surrounding countryside was deforested by Venice. Trees were imported and consumed locally—to fuel the furnaces of Venice's booming glass industry, to build Europe's biggest merchant marine, to form light and flexible beams for nearly all of the buildings in town, and to prop up this city in the mud.

As the Grand Canal opens up into the lagoon, the last building on the right with the golden ball is the 17th-century **Customs House,** which now houses the Punta della Dogana Museum of Contemporary Art (listed on page 87). Its two bronze Atlases hold a statue of Fortune riding the ball. Arriving ships stopped here to pay their tolls.

San Marco: Up ahead on the left, the green pointed tip of the Campanile marks **St. Mark's Square,** the political and religious center of Venice...and the final destination of this tour. You could get off at the San Marco stop and go straight to St. Mark's Square. But I'm staying on the boat for one more stop, just past St. Mark's Square (it's a quick walk back).

Survey the lagoon. Opposite St. Mark's Square, across the water, the ghostly white church with the pointy bell tower is **San Giorgio Maggiore,** with great views of Venice (see page 84).

Next to it is the residential island Giudecca, stretching from close to San Giorgio Maggiore past the Venice youth hostel (with a nice view, directly across) to the Hilton Hotel (good nighttime view, far right end of island).

Still on board? If you are, as we leave the San Marco stop, prepare for a drive-by view of St. Mark's Square. First comes the bold white facade of the old mint (marked by a tiny cupola, where Venice's golden ducat, the "dollar" of the Venetian Republic, was made) and the library facade. Then come the twin columns, topped by St. Theodore and St. Mark, who've welcomed visitors since the 15th century. Between the columns, catch a glimpse of two giant figures atop the **Clock Tower**—they've been whacking their clappers every hour since 1499. The domes of **St. Mark's Basilica** are soon eclipsed by the lacy facade of the **Doge's Palace.** Next you'll see the **Bridge of Sighs** (leading from the palace to the prison—check out the maximum security bars), many gondolas with their green breakwater buoys, and then the grand harborside promenade—the **Riva.**

Follow the Riva with your eye, past elegant hotels to the green area in the distance. This is the largest of Venice's few **parks,** which hosts the annual Biennale festival (see page 99). Much farther in the distance is the **Lido,** the island with Venice's beach. Its sand and casinos are tempting, but its car traffic disrupts the medieval charm of Venice.

San Zaccaria: OK, you're at your last stop (likely San Zaccaria-Danieli or San Zaccaria-M.V.E.). Quick—muscle your way off this boat! (If you don't, you'll eventually end up at the Lido.)

At San Zaccaria, you're right in the thick of the action. A number of other *vaporetti* depart from here (see page 54). Otherwise, it's a short walk back along the Riva to St. Mark's Square. Ahoy!

Sights in Venice

For information on sightseeing passes, see below. Venice's city museums offer youth and senior discounts to Americans and other non-EU citizens.

Sightseeing Passes for Venice

Venice offers a combo-ticket and an array of passes. For most people, the best choice is the Museum Pass, which covers entry into the Doge's Palace, Correr Museum, and more. Note that some major sights (Accademia, Peggy Guggenheim Collection, Scuola San Rocco, Campanile, and the three sights within St. Mark's Basilica that charge admission) are not covered on any pass.

Combo-Ticket: To visit either the Doge's Palace or the Correr

VENICE

Venice at a Glance

▲▲▲**St. Mark's Square** Venice's grand main square. **Hours:** Always open. See page 74.

▲▲▲**St. Mark's Basilica** Cathedral with mosaics, saint's bones, treasury, museum, and viewpoint of square. **Hours:** Mon-Sat 9:45-17:00, Sun 14:00-17:00 (until 16:00 Nov-March). See page 76.

▲▲▲**Doge's Palace** Art-splashed palace of former rulers, with prison accessible through Bridge of Sighs. **Hours:** Daily April-Oct 8:30-18:30, Nov-March 8:00-17:30. See page 79.

▲▲▲**Rialto Bridge** Distinctive bridge spanning the Grand Canal, with a market nearby. **Hours:** Bridge—always open; market—souvenir stalls open daily, produce market closed Sun, fish market closed Sun-Mon. See page 88.

▲▲**Correr Museum** Venetian history and art. **Hours:** Daily April-Oct 10:00-19:00, Nov-March 10:00-17:00. See page 82.

▲▲**Accademia** Venice's top art museum. **Hours:** Mon 8:15-14:00, Tue-Sun 8:15-19:15. See page 85.

▲▲**Peggy Guggenheim Collection** Popular display of 20th-century art. **Hours:** Wed-Mon 10:00-18:00, closed Tue. See page 87.

▲▲**Frari Church** Franciscan church featuring Renaissance masters. **Hours:** Mon-Sat 9:00-18:00, Sun 13:00-18:00. See page 89.

▲▲**Scuola San Rocco** "Tintoretto's Sistine Chapel." **Hours:** Daily 9:30-17:30. See page 90.

▲**Campanile** Dramatic bell tower on St. Mark's Square with elevator to the top. **Hours:** Daily Easter-June and Oct 9:00-19:00, July-Sept 9:00-21:00; Nov-Easter 9:30-16:45. See page 83.

▲**Bridge of Sighs** Famous enclosed bridge, part of Doge's Palace, near St. Mark's Square. **Hours:** Always viewable. See page 84.

▲**La Salute Church** Striking church dedicated to the Virgin Mary. **Hours:** Daily 9:00-12:00 & 15:00-17:30. See page 87.

▲**Ca' Rezzonico** Posh Grand Canal palazzo with 18th-century Venetian art. **Hours:** April-Oct Wed-Mon 10:00-18:00, Nov-March

Wed-Mon 10:00-17:00, closed Tue year-round. See page 87.

▲**Punta della Dogana** Museum of contemporary art. **Hours:** Wed-Mon 10:00-19:00, closed Tue. See page 87.

▲**Ca' Pesaro International Gallery of Modern Art** in a canalside palazzo. **Hours:** Tue-Sun 10:00-18:00, closed Mon. See page 88.

▲**Scuola Dalmata di San Giorgio** Exquisite Renaissance meeting house. **Hours:** Mon 14:45-18:00, Tue-Sat 9:15-13:00 & 14:45-18:00, Sun 9:15-13:00. See page 93.

Church of San Zaccaria Final resting place of St. Zechariah, plus a Bellini altarpiece and an eerie crypt. **Hours:** Mon-Sat 10:00-12:00 & 16:00-18:00, Sun 16:00-18:00. See page 84.

Church of San Polo Ninth-century church with works by Tintoretto, Veronese, and Tiepolo. **Hours:** Mon-Sat 10:00-17:00, closed Sun. See page 90.

Nearby Islands
▲**San Giorgio Maggiore** Island across the lagoon featuring church with Palladio architecture, Tintoretto paintings, and fine views back on Venice. **Hours:** May-Sept Mon-Sat 9:30-12:30 & 14:30-18:00, Sun 8:30-11:00 & 14:30-18:00; Oct-April until 17:00. See page 84.

San Michele Cemetery island on the lagoon. **Hours:** Daily April-Sept 7:30-18:00, Oct-March 7:30-16:30. See page 94.

Murano Island famous for glass factories and glassmaking museum. **Hours:** Glass Museum open daily April-Oct 10:00-18:00, Nov-March 10:00-17:00. See page 94.

Burano Sleepy island known for lacemaking and a lace museum. **Hours:** Lace Museum open April-Oct Tue-Sun 10:00-18:00, Nov-March Tue-Sun 10:00-17:00, closed Mon year-round. See page 95.

Torcello Near-deserted island with old church, bell tower, and museum. **Hours:** Most sights open daily March-Oct 10:30-18:00, Nov-Feb 10:00-17:00, museum closed Mon. See page 95.

Museum, you must buy a €16 combo-ticket that includes both. To bypass the long line at the Doge's Palace, buy your combo-ticket at the never-crowded Correr Museum.

Museum Pass: Busy sightseers may prefer this more expensive pass, which covers these museums: the Doge's Palace; Correr Museum; Ca' Rezzonico (Museum of 18th-Century Venice); Palazzo Mocenigo Costume Museum; Casa Goldoni (home of the Italian playwright); Ca' Pesaro (modern art); Museum of Natural History in the Santa Croce district; the Glass Museum on the island of Murano; and the Lace Museum on the island of Burano. At €20, this pass is the best value if you plan to see the Doge's Palace and even just one of the other covered museums. You can buy it at any of the participating museums.

Chorus Pass: This pass gives church lovers admission to 16 of Venice's churches and their art (generally €3 each)—including the Frari Church—for €10, although the typical tourist is unlikely to see more than two of them.

Venice Card: This pass combines the 11 city-run museums and the 16 churches covered by the Chorus Pass, plus a few minor discounts, for €40, but it's hard to make it pay off.

Rolling Venice: This youth pass offers discounts at dozens of sights and shops, but its best deal is for transit. If you're under 30 and want to buy a three-day transit pass, it'll cost you just €18—rather than €35—with the Rolling Venice pass (€4 for ages 14-29, sold at TIs and HelloVenezia shops).

Transportation Passes: Venice sells transit-only passes that cover *vaporetti* and mainland buses. For a rundown on these, see "Getting Around Venice," earlier.

San Marco District

▲▲▲**St. Mark's Square (Piazza San Marco)**—This grand square is surrounded by splashy, historic buildings and sights: St. Mark's Basilica, the Doge's Palace, the Campanile bell tower, and the Correr Museum. The square is filled with music, lovers, pigeons, and tourists by day, and is your private rendezvous with the Venetian past late at night, when Europe's most magnificent dance floor is *the* romantic place to be.

With your back to the church, survey one of Europe's great urban spaces, and the only square in Venice to merit the title "Piazza." Nearly two football fields long, it's surrounded by the offices of the republic. On the right are the "old offices" (16th-century Renaissance). At left are the "new offices" (17th-century High Renaissance). Napoleon called the piazza "the most beautiful drawing room in Europe," and added to the intimacy by building the final wing, opposite the basilica, that encloses the square.

For a slow and pricey evening thrill, invest €12-20 (includ-

St. Mark's Square

To Rialto
To Rialto
CALLE D'FABBRI
SAN GALLO
SAN GALLO
FOND. ORSEOLO
CALLE FIUBERA
RAMO SALIZ
Bacino Orseolo
MARZARIA OROLOGIO
SPADARIA
ATENEO SAN BASSO
C. ANGELO
C. CANONICA
Rio G. APOLLONIA
Rio de Palazzo
C. FIGHER
C. DE CHIESA
To S.M. Formosa
Campo Santi Filippo & Giacomo

9 Piazzetta dei Leoni
7

C. ALBANESI
C. DE LE RASSE
Rio del Vin

Rio de le Procuratie
OLD OFFICES
CLOCK TOWER

ST. MARK'S BASILICA

DIOCESAN MUSEUM

BRIDGE OF SIGHS

8

CORRER MUSEUM
5 Piazza San Marco
2 **3**
TETRARCHS
CAMPANILE
7TH COLUMN
6
DOGE'S PALACE
PRISON

POST
FREZZERIA
NAPOLEON'S WING
NEW OFFICES
4
Piazzetta
PONTE DE PAGLIA
RIVA DEGLI SCHIAVONI

To Accademia
SAL. SAN MOISE
CALLE LARGA DE L'ASCENSION
i
SAN MARCO COLUMN
SAN THEODORE COLUMN

To Accademia
To S.M.

VENICE

San Zaccaria-Danieli
V

To Lido →

CALLE VALLARESSO
DEL RIDOTTO
Giardinetti Reali
WC
i

HARRY'S AMERICAN BAR

V San Marco-Giardinetti
A

V San Marco-Vallaresso

Grand Canal

T

St. Mark's Basin

To Accademia

PUNTA DOGANA (CUSTOMS HOUSE)

N

100 Meters
100 Yards

Eateries & Entertainment
1 Caffè Florian
2 Gran Caffè Quadri
3 Gran Caffè Lavena; Galleria San Marco Glassblowing
4 Gran Caffè Chioggia
5 Eden Bar
6 Caffè Aurora

Other
7 Libreria Studium Bookstore
8 Oltrex Change & Travel
9 St. Mark's Basilica Bag Check

ing the cover charge for the music) for a drink at one of the ele-
gant cafés with the dueling orchestras (see "Cafés on St. Mark's Square," page 80). For an unmatched experience that offers the best people-watching, it's worth the small splurge.

The **Clock Tower** (Torre dell'Orologio), built during the Renaissance in 1496, marks the entry to the main shopping drag, called the Mercerie (or "Marzarie," in Venetian dialect), which connects St. Mark's Square with the Rialto Bridge. From the piazza, you can see the bronze men (Moors) swing their huge clappers at the top of each hour.

In the 17th century, one of them knocked an unsuspecting worker off the top and to his death—probably the first-ever killing by a robot. Notice one of the world's first "digital" clocks on the tower facing the square (with dramatic flips every five minutes). You can go inside the Clock Tower with a pre-booked guided tour that takes you close to the clock's innards and out to a terrace with good views over the square and city rooftops (€12.50 combo-ticket includes Correr Museum— where tour starts—but not Doge's Palace; tours in English Mon-Wed at 10:00 and 11:00, Thu-Sun at 14:00 and 15:00; no kids under age 6; reserve by calling 848-082-000, booking online at http://torreorologio.visitmuve.it, going in person at the Correr Museum a day in advance, or even just showing up at the Correr prior to a scheduled tour to see if space is available).

You can download a free Rick Steves audio tour of St. Mark's Square (see page 1101).

▲▲▲St. Mark's Basilica (Basilica di San Marco)—Built in the 11th century to replace an earlier church, this basilica's dis-

tinctly Eastern-style architecture underlines Venice's connection with Byzantium (which protected it from the ambition of Charlemagne and his Holy Roman Empire). It's decorated with booty from returning sea captains—a kind of architectural Venetian trophy chest. The interior glows mysteriously with gold mosaics and colored marble. Since about A.D. 830, the saint's bones have been housed on this site.

Cost and Hours: Basilica entry is free, three interior sights charge admission (see below), open Mon-Sat 9:45-17:00, Sun 14:00-17:00 (Sun until 16:00 Nov-March), interior brilliantly lit daily 11:30-12:30, St. Mark's Square, vaporetto: San Marco or San Zaccaria. No photos are allowed inside. Tel. 041-270-8311, www .basilicasanmarco.it.

Three separate exhibits within the church charge admission: the **Treasury** (€3, includes free audioguide), **Golden Altarpiece** (€2), and **San Marco Museum** (€5). The San Marco Museum has the original bronze horses (copies of these overlook the square), a balcony offering a remarkable view over St. Mark's Square, and various works related to the church.

Dress Code: Modest dress (no bare knees or bare shoulders) is strictly enforced, even for kids. Shorts are OK if they cover the knees.

Bag Check (and Skipping the Line): Small purses and shoulder-slung bags are allowed inside, but larger bags and backpacks are not. Check them for free for up to one hour at the nearby church called Ateneo San Basso, 30 yards to the left of the basilica, down narrow Calle San Basso (see map page 77; daily 9:30-17:00). Note that Ateneo San Basso will not let you check small bags that would be allowed inside.

Those with a bag to check actually get to skip the line, as do their companions (up to three or so). Leave your bag at Ateneo San Basso and pick up your claim tag. Take your tag to the basilica's tourist entrance. Keep to the left of the railing where the line forms and show your tag to the gatekeeper. He'll let you in, ahead of the line. After touring the church, come back and pick up your bag.

Theft Alert: St. Mark's Basilica is the most dangerous place in Venice for pickpocketing—inside, it's always a crowded jostle.

Tours: Free, hour-long English **tours** (heavy on the mosaics' religious symbolism) are offered many days at 11:00 (meet in atrium, schedule varies, see schedule board). You can download a free Rick Steves audio tour of St. Mark's Basilica (see page 1101).

Visiting the Basilica: St. Mark's Basilica has 4,750 square yards of Byzantine mosaics, though many were designed by artists from the Italian Renaissance and later. Start outside in the square, far enough back to take in the whole facade. Then zero in on the details. The mosaic over the far left door shows the theft of ❶ **St. Mark's relics** that put Venice on the pilgrimage map.

The best and oldest mosaics are in the atrium (turn right as you enter and stop under the last dome). Facing the piazza, look domeward for the story of ❷ **Noah, the ark, and the flood** (two by two, the wicked being drowned, Noah sending out the dove, a happy rainbow, and a sacrifice of thanks).

Step inside the church and follow the one-way tourist route. Notice how the marble floor is richly decorated in mosaics. As in many Venetian buildings, because the best foundation pilings were made around the perimeter, the floor rolls. The church is laid out with four equal arms, topped with domes, radiating out from the center to form a ❸ **Greek cross** (+). Those familiar with Eastern Orthodox churches will find common elements in St. Mark's: a central floor plan, domes, mosaics, and iconic images of Mary and Christ as Pantocrator—ruler of all things.

Find the chandelier near the entrance doorway, and run your eyes up to the ❹ **Pentecost** mosaic in the dome above. In a golden heaven, the dove of the Holy Spirit shoots out a pinwheel of spiritual lasers, igniting tongues of fire on the heads of the 12 apostles below.

VENICE

St. Mark's Basilica

To San Zaccaria

CALLE DE LA CANONICA

Not to Scale

11 → MAIN ALTAR (MARK'S BONES BENEATH)

8

6

7

NORTH TRANSEPT

CENTRAL

5

DOME

SOUTH TRANSEPT

9

TREASURY

10

C. RIZZA

ENTRY (WORSHIP ONLY) →

BAG CHECK

SAN BASSO

Piazzetta dei Leoni

NARTHEX

4

3 NAVE

BAPTISTERY

12

2

ATRIUM

To Rialto

MARZARIA OROLOGIO

LIONS

1

↓ TOUR BEGINS

↑ ENTRANCE

To Doge's Palace

CLOCK TOWER

Piazza San Marco

To Campanile

1 Exterior – Mosaic of Mark's Relics

2 Atrium – Mosaic of Noah's Ark & the Great Flood

3 Nave – Mosaics & Greek-Cross Floor Plan

4 Pentecost Mosaic

5 Central Dome – Ascension Mosaic

6 Rood Screen

7 Doge's Pulpit

8 Nicopeia Icon

9 Discovery of Mark Mosaic

10 Treasury

11 Golden Altarpiece

12 Stairs up to Loggia: San Marco Museum & Bronze Horses

Shuffle under the central dome, and look up for the ❺ **Ascension** mosaic. Christ—having lived his miraculous life and having been crucified for man's sins—ascends into the starry sky on a rainbow.

Look around at the church's furniture: the ❻ **rood screen,** topped with 14 saints, separates the congregation from the high altar. The ❼ **pulpit** on the right was reserved for the doge, who led prayers and made important announcements.

In the north transept, today's Venetians pray to a painted wooden icon of Mary and baby Jesus known as ❽ **Nicopeia,** or "Our Lady of Victory." This Madonna has helped Venice persevere through plagues, wars, and crucial soccer games.

In the south transept (to right of main altar), find the dim ❾ **Discovery of Mark** mosaic high up on the west wall. This mosaic re-creates the happy scene in 1094 when Mark's misplaced relics were found within a hollow column.

Additional Sights: The ❿ **Treasury** (ask for the included and informative audioguide when you buy your ticket) and ⓫ **Golden Altarpiece** give you the easiest way outside of Istanbul or Ravenna to see the glories of the Byzantine Empire. Venetian crusaders looted the Christian city of Constantinople and brought home piles of lavish loot (perhaps the lowest point in Christian history until the advent of TV evangelism). Much of this plunder is stored in the Treasury (Tesoro) of San Marco. As you view these treasures, remember that most were made in about A.D. 500, while Western Europe was stuck in the Dark Ages. Beneath the high altar lies the body of St. Mark ("Marce") and the Golden Altarpiece (Pala d'Oro), made of 250 blue-backed enamels with religious scenes, all set in a gold frame and studded with 15 hefty rubies, 300 emeralds, 1,500 pearls, and assorted sapphires, amethysts, and topaz (c. 1100).

In the ⓬ **San Marco Museum** (Museo di San Marco) upstairs you can see an up-close mosaic exhibition, a fine view of the church interior, a view of the square from the balcony with bronze horses, and (inside, in their own room) the original horses. Art historians don't know how old the horses are—they could be from ancient Greece (fourth century B.C.) or from ancient Rome, during its Fall (fourth century A.D.). Legend says these well-traveled horses were taken to Rome by Nero. We know they were taken to Constantinople/Istanbul by Constantine, to Venice by crusaders, to Paris by Napoleon, back "home" to Venice when Napoleon fell, and finally indoors and out of the acidic air. The staircase up to the museum is in the atrium, near the basilica's main entrance, marked by a sign that says *Loggia dei Cavalli, Museo.*

▲▲▲**Doge's Palace (Palazzo Ducale)**—The seat of the Venetian government and home of its ruling duke, or doge, this

Cafés on St. Mark's Square

In the Venetian culture, coffee was huge. It was said that the freedoms a gentleman could experience in Venice went far beyond what any one person could actually indulge in. But one extravagance all could enjoy was the ritual of coffee's public consumption: showing off with an affordable luxury, participating in something new and trendy, sharing the ideas of the Enlightenment.

Exotic coffee was made to order for the fancy café scene. Traders introduced coffee, called the "wine of Islam," from the East. The first coffeehouses opened in the 17th century, and by 1750 there were dozens of cafés lining Piazza San Marco and 200 operating in Venice.

Today, several fine old cafés survive and still line the square. Those with live music feature similar food, prices, and a three- to five-piece combo playing a selection of classical and pop hits, from Brahms to "Bésame Mucho." If you sit outside and get just a drink, expect to pay €12-20, including a €6 cover charge when the orchestra is playing (no cover charge otherwise). A coffee—your cheapest option—costs about €6 if you sit at an outside table, plus the €6 cover charge when the music plays, bringing it to €12 total (even at the venerable Caffè Florian). It's perfectly acceptable to nurse a cappuccino for an hour—you're paying for the music with the cover charge. Do remember that a law limits what a café can charge for coffee at the bar—no matter how fancy the place or how high the demand. So, you can sip your coffee at the bar at a nearly normal price—even with the orches-

was the most powerful half-acre in Europe for 400 years. The Doge's Palace was built to show off the power and wealth of the Republic. The doge lived with his family on the first floor, near the halls of power. From his once-lavish (now sparse) quarters, you'll follow the one-way tour through the public rooms of the top floor, finishing with the Bridge of Sighs and the prison. The place is wall-papered with masterpieces by Veronese and Tintoretto. Don't

worry much about the great art. Enjoy the building.

Cost and Hours: €16 combo-ticket also includes Correr Museum, daily April-Oct 8:30-18:30, Nov-March 8:00-17:30, last entry one hour before closing, café, next to St. Mark's Basilica, just off St. Mark's Square, vaporetto stops: San Marco or San Zaccaria, tel. 041-271-5911, http://palazzoducale.visitmuve.it.

Avoiding Lines: If the line is long at the Doge's Palace, buy tra playing. For locations of the following cafés, see the map on page 75.

Caffè Florian (on the right as you face the church) is the most famous Venetian café and one of the first places in Europe to serve coffee (daily 10:00-24:00, shorter hours in winter). It's been a popular spot for a discreet rendezvous in Venice since 1720. The orchestra here plays a more classical repertoire than at the other cafés. The outside tables are the main action, but do walk inside through the richly decorated, old-time rooms where Casanova, Lord Byron, Charles Dickens, and Woody Allen have all paid too much for a drink.

Gran Caffè Quadri, opposite the Florian, has an equally illustrious roster of famous clientele, including the writers Stendhal and Dumas, and composer Richard Wagner. **Gran Caffè Lavena,** near the Clock Tower, is newer and less storied. Drop in to check out its dazzling but politically incorrect chandelier.

Gran Caffè Chioggia, on the Piazzetta facing the Doge's Palace, charges slightly less, with one or two musicians, usually a pianist, playing cocktail jazz.

Eden Bar and **Caffè Aurora** are less expensive and don't have live music.

VENICE

your combo-ticket at the Correr Museum across the square; then you can go straight to the Doge's Palace turnstile, skirting along to the right of the long ticket-buying line and entering at the "prepaid tickets" entrance. It's also possible to buy your ticket online—at least 48 hours in advance—on the museum website.

Tours: The audioguide tour is dry but informative (€5, 1.5 hours, need ID or credit card for deposit). For a 1.25-hour live guided tour, consider the Secret Itineraries Tour, which takes you into palace rooms otherwise not open to the public (€20, includes Doge's Palace admission but not Correr Museum admission; €14 with combo-ticket; three English-language tours each morning). Though the tour skips the palace's main hall, you're welcome to visit the hall afterward on your own. Reserve ahead for this tour in peak season—it can fill up as much as a month in advance. Book online at http://palazzoducale.visitmuve.it or reserve by phone (tel. 848-082-000, from the US dial 011-39-041-4273-0892), or you can try just showing up at the info desk.

Visiting the Doge's Palace: You'll see the restored facades from the **courtyard.** Notice a grand staircase (with nearly naked

Moses and Paul Newman at the top). Even the most powerful visitors climbed this to meet the doge. This was the beginning of an architectural power trip.

In the **Senate Hall,** the 120 senators met, debated, and passed laws. Tintoretto's large *Triumph of Venice* on the ceiling (central painting, best viewed from the top) shows the city in all its glory. Lady Venice is up in heaven with the Greek gods, while barbaric lesser nations swirl up to give her gifts and tribute.

The **Armory**—a dazzling display originally assembled to intimidate potential adversaries—shows remnants of the military might that the empire employed to keep the East-West trade lines open (and the local economy booming).

The giant **Hall of the Grand Council** (175 feet by 80 feet, capacity 2,600) is where the entire nobility met to elect the senate and doge. It took a room this size to contain the grandeur of the Most Serene Republic. Ringing the room are portraits of the first 76 doges (in chronological order). The one at the far end that's blacked out is the notorious Doge Marin Falier, who opposed the will of the Grand Council in 1355. He was tried for treason, beheaded, and airbrushed from history.

On the wall over the doge's throne is Tintoretto's monsterpiece, *Paradise,* the largest oil painting in the world. Christ and Mary are surrounded by a heavenly host of 500 saints. The painting leaves you feeling that you get to heaven not by being a good Christian, but by being a good Venetian.

Cross the covered **Bridge of Sighs** over the canal to the **prisons.** Circle the cells. Notice the carvings made by prisoners—from olden days up until 1930—on some of the stone windowsills of the cells, especially in the far corner of the building.

Cross back over the Bridge of Sighs, pausing to look through the marble-trellised windows at all of the tourists.

▲▲**Correr Museum (Museo Correr)**—This uncrowded museum gives you a good, easy-to-manage overview of Venetian history and art. The doge memorabilia, armor, banners, statues (by Canova), and paintings (by the Bellini family and others) re-create the festive days of the Venetian Republic. There are English descriptions and breathtaking views of St. Mark's Square throughout the museum. But the Correr Museum has one more thing to offer, and that's a quiet refuge—a place to rise above St. Mark's Square when the piazza is too hot, too rainy, or too overrun with tourists.

Cost and Hours: €16 combo-ticket also includes the Doge's Palace and two lesser museums inside the Correr (National Archaeological Museum and the Monumental Rooms of the Marciana National Library); daily April-Oct 10:00-19:00, Nov-March 10:00-17:00, last entry one hour before closing; free and mandatory for bags bigger than a large purse, no photos, elegant café, enter at far end of square directly opposite basilica, tel. 041-240-5211, http://correr.visitmuve.it.

Avoid long lines at the crowded Doge's Palace by buying your combo-ticket at the Correr Museum. For €12.50 you can see the Correr Museum and tour the Clock Tower on St. Mark's Square, but this ticket doesn't include the Doge's Palace (and the €16 combo-ticket mentioned above doesn't include the Clock Tower). For more on reserving a Clock Tower tour, see page 75.

▲**Campanile (Campanile di San Marco)**—This dramatic bell tower replaced a shorter tower, part of the original fortress that guarded the entry of the Grand Canal. That

tower crumbled into a pile of bricks in 1902, a thousand years after it was built. Today you'll see construction work being done to strengthen the base of the rebuilt tower. Ride the elevator 325 feet to the top of the bell tower for the best view in Venice (especially at sunset). For an ear-shattering experience, be on top when the bells ring. The golden archangel Gabriel at the top always faces into the wind. Beat the crowds and enjoy the crisp morning air at 9:00 or the cool evening breeze at 18:00.

Cost and Hours: €8, daily Easter-June and Oct 9:00-19:00, July-Sept 9:00-21:00, Nov-Easter 9:30-16:45, tel. 041-522-4064, www.basilicasanmarco.it.

La Fenice Opera House (Gran Teatro alla Fenice)—During

Venice's glorious decline in the 18th century, this was one of seven opera houses in the city, and one of the most famous in Europe. For 200 years, great operas and famous divas debuted here, applauded by ladies and gentlemen in their finery. Then in 1996, an arson fire completely gutted the theater. But La Fenice ("The Phoenix") has risen from the ashes, thanks to an eight-year effort to rebuild the historic landmark according to photographic archives of the interior. To see the results at their most glorious, attend an evening **performance** (theater box office open daily 9:30-18:00, tel. 041-2424, www.teatrolafenice.it).

You can also **tour the opera house** during the day. All you really see is the theater itself; there's no "backstage" tour of dressing rooms, or an opera museum. The auditorium, ringed with box seats, is impressive: pastel blue with sparkling gold filigree, muses depicted on the ceiling, and a starburst chandelier. It's also a bit saccharine and brings sadness to Venetians who remember the place before the fire. Other than a minor exhibit of opera scores and Maria Callas memorabilia, there's little to see from the world of opera. A dry 45-minute audioguide recounts two centuries of construction.

Cost and Hours: €8 tours, generally open daily 9:30-13:30, but can vary wildly, depending on the performance schedule—to confirm, call box office number (listed above) or check www .festfenice.com. La Fenice is on Campo San Fantin, between St. Mark's Square and the Accademia Bridge.

Behind St. Mark's Basilica

▲**Bridge of Sighs**—This much-photographed bridge connects the Doge's Palace with the prison. Travelers popularized this

bridge in the Romantic 19th century. Supposedly, a condemned man would be led over this bridge on his way to the prison, take one last look at the glory of Venice, and sigh. Though overhyped, the Bridge of Sighs is undeniably tingle-worthy—especially after dark, when the crowds have dispersed and it's just you and floodlit Venice.

Getting There: The Bridge of Sighs is around the corner from the Doge's Palace. Walk toward the waterfront, turn left along the water, and look up the first canal on your left. You can walk across the bridge (from the inside) by visiting the Doge's Palace.

Church of San Zaccaria—This historic church is home to a sometimes-waterlogged crypt, a Bellini altarpiece, a Tintoretto painting, and the final resting place of St. Zechariah, the father of John the Baptist.

Cost and Hours: Free, €1 to enter crypt, €0.50 coin to light up Bellini's altarpiece, Mon-Sat 10:00-12:00 & 16:00-18:00, Sun 16:00-18:00 only, 2 canals behind St. Mark's Basilica.

Across the Lagoon from St. Mark's Square

▲**San Giorgio Maggiore**—This is the dreamy church-topped island you can see from the waterfront by St. Mark's Square. The striking church, designed by Palladio, features art by Tintoretto, a bell tower, and good views of Venice.

Cost and Hours: Free entry to church; May-Sept Mon-Sat 9:30-12:30 & 14:30-18:00, Sun 8:30-11:00 & 14:30-18:00; Oct-April until 17:00. The bell tower costs €3 and is accessible by elevator (runs from 30 minutes after the church opens until 30 minutes before the church closes).

Getting There: To reach the island from St. Mark's Square, take the five-minute ride on vaporetto #2 (€4, 6/hour, ticket valid for one hour; leaves from San Zaccaria-M.V.E. dock located east of Bridge of Sighs by equestrian statue, direction: Tronchetto).

Dorsoduro District

▲▲**Accademia (Galleria dell'Accademia)**—Venice's top art museum, packed with highlights of the Venetian Renaissance, features paintings by the Bellini family, Titian, Tintoretto, Veronese, Tiepolo, Giorgione, Canaletto, and Testosterone. It's just over the wooden Accademia Bridge from the San Marco action.

The Accademia is the greatest museum anywhere for Venetian Renaissance art and a good overview of painters whose works you'll see all over town. Venetian art is underrated and, I think, misunderstood. It's nowhere near as famous today as the work of the florescent Florentines, but—with historical slices of Venice, ravishing nudes, and very human Madonnas—it's livelier, more colorful, and simply more fun. The Venetian love of luxury shines through in this collection, which starts in the Middle Ages and runs to the 1700s. Look for grand canvases of colorful, spacious settings, peopled with happy locals in extravagant clothes having a great time.

Medieval highlights include elaborate altarpieces and golden-haloed Madonnas, all painted at a time when realism, depth of field, and emotion were considered beside the point. Medieval Venetians, with their close ties to the East, borrowed techniques such as gold-leafing, frontal poses, and "iconic" faces from the religious icons of Byzantium (modern-day Istanbul).

Among early masterpieces of the Renaissance are Mantegna's studly *St. George* and Giorgione's mysterious *The Tempest*. As the Renaissance reaches its heights, so do the paintings, such as Titian's magnificent *Presentation of the Virgin*. It's a religious scene, yes, but it's really just an excuse to display secular splendor (Titian was the most famous painter of his day—perhaps even more famous than Michelangelo). Veronese's sumptuous *Feast in the House of Levi* also has an ostensibly religious theme (in the middle, find Jesus eating his final meal)—but it's outdone by the luxury and optimism of Renaissance Venice. Life was a good thing and beauty was to be enjoyed. (Veronese was hauled before the Inquisition for painting such a bawdy Last Supper...so he fine-tuned the title). End your tour with Guardi's and Canaletto's painted "postcards" of the city—landscapes for visitors who lost their hearts to the romance of Venice.

Cost and Hours: €11, dull audioguide-€5, Mon 8:15-14:00, Tue-Sun 8:15-19:15, last entry 45 minutes before closing, no photos allowed. At Accademia Bridge, vaporetto: Accademia, tel. 041-522-2247, www.gallerieaccademia.org.

Avoiding Lines: In peak season, visit early or late to miss the crowds (300 people are allowed in at any one time).

Renovation: This museum seems to be in a constant state of disarray. A major expansion and renovation has been dragging on for years, and the halls feel like a gallery from the 1960s. Paintings come and go, but still, the museum contains sumptuous art—the best in Venice. Be flexible: You'll probably just end up wandering around and matching descriptions to blockbuster paintings when you find them.

▲▲Peggy Guggenheim Collection—The popular museum of far-out art, housed in the American heiress' former retirement palazzo, offers one of Europe's best reviews of the art of the first half of the 20th century. Stroll through styles represented by artists whom Peggy knew personally—Cubism (Picasso, Braque), Surrealism (Dalí, Ernst), Futurism (Boccioni), American Abstract Expressionism (Pollock), and a sprinkling of Klee, Calder, and Chagall.

Cost and Hours: €12, usually includes temporary exhibits, audioguide-€7, Wed-Mon 10:00-18:00, closed Tue, no photos inside, pricey café, 5-minute walk from the Accademia Bridge, vaporetto: Accademia or Salute, tel. 041-240-5411, www.guggenheim-venice.it.

▲La Salute Church (Santa Maria della Salute)—This impressive church with a crown-shaped dome was built and dedicated to the Virgin Mary by grateful survivors of the 1630 plague.

Cost and Hours: Free entry to church, €3 to enter the Sacristy; daily 9:00-12:00 & 15:00-17:30. It's a 10-minute walk from the Accademia Bridge; the Salute vaporetto stop is at its doorstep, tel. 041-241-1018, www.seminariovenezia.it.

▲Ca' Rezzonico (Museum of 18th-Century Venice)—This grand Grand Canal palazzo offers the best look in town at the life of Venice's rich and famous in the 1700s. Wander under ceilings by Tiepolo, among furnishings from that most decadent century, enjoying views of the canal and paintings by Guardi, Canaletto, and Longhi.

Cost and Hours: €8, audioguide-€4; April-Oct Wed-Mon 10:00-18:00, Nov-March Wed-Mon 10:00-17:00, closed Tue year-round; ticket office closes one hour before museum does, café, at Ca' Rezzonico vaporetto stop, tel. 041-241-0100, http://carezzonico.visitmuve.it.

▲Punta della Dogana—This museum of contemporary art, opened in 2009, makes the Dorsoduro a major destination for

art lovers. Housed in the former Customs House at the end of the Grand Canal, it features cutting-edge 21st-century art in spacious rooms. This isn't Picasso and Matisse, or even Pollock and Warhol—those guys are ancient history. But if you're into the likes of Jeff Koons, Cy Twombly, Rachel Whiteread, and a host of newer artists, the museum is world-class. The displays change completely about every year, drawn from the museum's large collection. In fact, the art spreads over two locations—the triangular Customs House and Palazzo Grassi.

Cost and Hours: €15 for one locale, €20 for both; Wed-Mon 10:00-19:00, closed Tue, last entry one hour before closing; audio-guide-€5 or €8 for both museums, small café, tel. 199-139-139, www.palazzograssi.it.

Getting There: Punta della Dogana is near La Salute Church (Dogana *traghetto* or vaporetto: Salute). Palazzo Grassi is a bit upstream, on the east side of the Grand Canal (vaporetto: San Samuele).

Santa Croce District

▲Ca' Pesaro International Gallery of Modern Art—This museum features 19th- and early 20th-century art in a 17th-century canalside palazzo. The collection is strongest on Italian (especially Venetian) artists, but also presents a broad array of other well-known artists. The highlights are in one large room: Klimt's beautiful/creepy *Judith II,* with eagle-talon fingers; Kandinsky's *White Zig Zags* (plus other recognizable shapes); the colorful *Nude in the Mirror* by Bonnard that flattens the 3-D scene into a 2-D pattern of rectangles; and Chagall's surprisingly realistic portrait of his hometown rabbi, *The Rabbi of Vitebsk.* The adjoining room VII features small-scale works by Matisse, Max Ernst, Mark Tobey, and a Calder mobile.

Cost and Hours: €8, Tue-Sun 10:00-18:00, closed Mon, last entry one hour before closing, 2-minute walk from San Stae vaporetto stop, tel. 041-524-0662, http://capesaro.visitmuve.it.

Palazzo Mocenigo Costume Museum—The Museo di Palazzo Mocenigo offers a walk through six rooms of a fine 17th-century mansion with period furnishings, family portraits, ceilings painted (c. 1790) with family triumphs (the Mocenigos produced seven doges), Murano glass chandeliers in situ, and a paltry collection of costumes with sparse descriptions.

Cost and Hours: €5, Tue-Sun 10:00-17:00, closed Mon, last entry one hour before closing, a block in from San Stae vaporetto stop, tel. 041-721-798, http://mocenigo.visitmuve.it.

San Polo District

▲▲▲Rialto Bridge—One of the world's most famous bridges, this distinctive and dramatic stone structure crosses the Grand Canal with a single confident span. The arcades along the top of the bridge help reinforce the structure...and offer some enjoyable shopping diversions, as does the **market** surrounding the bridge (produce

Frari Church

To Scuola
San Rocco

Not to scale

Campo
San Rocco

To
Accademia

3 ALTAR

1

2 S A C R I S T Y

TRANSEPT

CHAPTER HOUSE

CHOIR

TICKETS

ENTRY

N A V E

Campo
dei
Frari

4

5

To
Rialto

1 DONATELLO –
Statue of
John the Baptist

2 GIO. BELLINI –
Madonna and
Child with Saints
and Angels

3 TITIAN – The
Assumption
of the Virgin

4 Canova Monument

5 Tomb of Titian

market closed Sun, fish market closed Sun-Mon).

▲▲Frari Church (Basilica di Santa Maria Gloriosa dei Frari)—My favorite art experience in Venice is seeing art in the setting for which it was designed—as it is at the Frari Church. The Franciscan "Church of the Brothers" and the art that decorates it are warmed by the spirit of St. Francis. It features the work of three great Renaissance masters: Donatello, Giovanni Bellini, and Titian—each showing worshippers the glory of God in human terms.

Cost and Hours: €3, Mon-Sat 9:00-18:00, Sun 13:00-18:00, last entry 30 minutes before closing, modest dress recommended, on Campo dei Frari, near San Tomà vaporetto and *traghetto* stops, tel. 041-272-8618, www.basilicadeifrari.it.

Audioguides: You can rent an audioguide for €2, or you can download a free Rick Steves audio tour of the Frari (see page 1101).

Concerts: The church occasionally hosts evening concerts and small theatrical performances (€8-20, buy tickets at church, for details see the church website on previous page).

Visiting the Frari Church: In **Donatello's wood statue of St. John the Baptist** (just to the right of the high altar), the prophet of the desert—dressed in animal skins and nearly starving from his diet of bugs 'n' honey—announces the coming of the Messiah. Donatello was a Florentine working at the dawn of the Renaissance.

Bellini's *Madonna and Child with Saints and Angels* painting (in the sacristy farther to the right) came later, done by a Venetian in a more Venetian style—soft focus without Donatello's harsh realism. While Renaissance humanism demanded Madonnas and saints that were accessible and human, Bellini places them in a physical setting so beautiful that it creates its own mood of serene holiness. The genius of Bellini, perhaps the greatest Venetian painter, is obvious in the pristine clarity, rich colors (notice Mary's clothing), believable depth, and reassuring calm of this three-paneled altarpiece.

Finally, glowing red and gold like a stained-glass window over the high altar, **Titian's** *The Assumption of the Virgin* sets the tone of exuberant beauty found in the otherwise sparse church. Titian the Venetian—a student of Bellini—painted steadily for 60 years... you'll see a lot of his art. As stunned apostles look up past the swirl of arms and legs, the complex composition of this painting draws you right to the radiant face of the once-dying, now-triumphant Mary as she joins God in heaven.

Feel comfortable to discreetly freeload off passing tours. For many, these three pieces of art make a visit to the Accademia Gallery unnecessary (or they may whet your appetite for more). Before leaving, check out the Neoclassical pyramid-shaped Canova monument and (opposite that) the grandiose tomb of Titian. Compare the carved marble *Assumption* behind Titian's tombstone portrait with the painted original above the high altar.

▲▲Scuola San Rocco—Sometimes called "Tintoretto's Sistine Chapel," this lavish meeting hall (next to the Frari Church) has some 50 large, colorful Tintoretto paintings plastered to the walls and ceilings. The best paintings are upstairs, especially the *Crucifixion* in the smaller room. View the neck-breaking splendor with the mirrors available in the Grand Hall.

Cost and Hours: €8, audioguide-€1, daily 9:30-17:30, last entry 30 minutes before closing, tel. 041-523-4864, www.scuola grandesanrocco.it.

Church of San Polo—This nearby church, which pales in comparison to the two sights just listed, is only worth a visit for art lovers. One of Venice's oldest churches (from the ninth century), San

VENICE

A Dying City?

Venice's population (58,000 in the historic city) is half what it was just 30 years ago, and people are leaving at a rate of

a thousand a year. Of those who stay, 25 percent are 65 or older.

Sad, yes, but imagine raising a family here: Apartments are small, high up, and expensive. Humidity and occasional flooding make basic maintenance a pain. Home-improvement projects require navigating miles of red tape, and you must follow regulations intended to preserve the

historical ambience. Everything is expensive because it has to be shipped in from the mainland. You can easily get glass and tourist trinkets, but it's hard to find groceries or get your shoes fixed. Running basic errands involves lots of walking and stairs—imagine crossing over arched bridges while pushing a child in a stroller and carrying a day's worth of groceries.

With millions of visitors a year (150,000 a day at peak times), on any given day Venetians are likely outnumbered by tourists. Despite government efforts to subsidize rents and build cheap housing, the city is losing its residents. The economy itself is thriving, thanks to tourist dollars and rich foreigners buying second homes. But the culture is dying. Even the most hopeful city planners worry that in a few decades Venice will not be a city at all, but a museum, a cultural theme park, a decaying Disneyland for adults.

Polo features works by Tintoretto, Veronese, and Tiepolo and son.
Cost and Hours: €3, Mon-Sat 10:00-17:00, closed Sun.

Cannaregio District

Jewish Ghetto—Tucked away in the Cannaregio District is the ghetto where Venice's Jewish population once lived, segregated from their non-Jewish neighbors. While today's Jewish population is dwindling, the neighborhood still has centuries of history, not to mention Jewish-themed sights and eateries.

In medieval times, Jews were grudgingly allowed to do business in Venice, but they weren't permitted to live here until 1385 (subject to strict laws and special taxes). Anti-Semitic forces tried to oust them from the city, but in 1516, the doge compromised by restricting Jews to a special (undesirable) neighborhood. It was located on an easy-to-isolate island near the former foundry *(geto)*—in time the word "ghetto" caught on across Europe as a term for any segregated neighborhood.

The population swelled with immigrants from elsewhere in Europe, reaching 5,000 in the 1600s, the Golden Age of Venice's Jews. Restricted within their tiny neighborhood (the Gheto Novo, or "New Ghetto"), they expanded upward, building six-story "skyscrapers" that still stand today. The community's five synagogues were built atop the high-rise tenements. (As space was very tight and you couldn't live above a house of worship, this was the most practical use of precious land.) Only two synagogues are still active. You can spot them (with their five windows) from the square, but to visit them you have to book a tour through the Jewish Museum.

This original ghetto becomes most interesting after touring the **Jewish Museum** (Museo Ebraico) at #2902b, a worthwhile stop with just three rooms. Exhibits include silver menorahs, cloth covers for Torah scrolls, and a concise bilingual exhibit on the Venetian Jewish community up through 1797 (€3, June-Sept Sun-Fri 10:00-19:00, Oct-May Sun-Fri 10:00-17:30, closed Jewish holidays and Sat year-round, bookstore, small café, Campo de Gheto Novo, tel. 041-715-359, www.museoebraico. it). You can see three of the ghetto's five **synagogues** with the 45-minute English tour (€8.50, tours run hourly on the half-hour June-Sept Sun-Fri 10:30-17:30, Oct-May Sun-Fri 10:30-16:30, no tours Sat and Jewish holidays). Group sizes are limited (the 11:30 and 12:30 tours are the most popular), so show up 20 minutes early to be sure you get in.

Getting There: From either the San Marcuola vaporetto stop or the train station, walk five minutes to the Ponte de Guglie bridge that crosses the Cannaregio Canal. Cross the bridge and turn left. About 50 yards north of the bridge, a small covered alleyway (Calle del Gheto Vechio) leads between the *farmacia* and the Gam-Gam Kosher Restaurant, through a newer Jewish section, across a bridge, and into the historic core of the ghetto at Campo de Gheto Novo.

Calatrava Bridge (a.k.a. Ponte della Costituzione)—This controversial bridge, designed by Spanish architect Santiago Calatrava, is just upstream from the train station. Only the fourth bridge to cross the Grand Canal, it carries foot traffic between the train station and bus terminal at Piazzale Roma. After delays, cost overruns, and questions about its stability, the bridge finally opened in 2008.

The bridge draws snorts from Venetians. Its modern design is a sore point for a city with such rich medieval and Renaissance architecture. With an original price tag of €4 million, the cost rose to around €11 million. Then someone noticed that people in wheelchairs couldn't cross, so the bridge was retrofitted with a special carriage on a track. And, to add practical insult to aesthetic injury, critics say the heavy bridge is crushing the centuries-old foundations at either end, threatening nearby buildings.

Ca' d'Oro—This "House of Gold" palace, fronting the Grand Canal, is quintessential Venetian Gothic (Gothic seasoned with Byzantine and Islamic accents—see "Ca' d'Oro" on page 66). Inside, the permanent collection includes a few big names in Renaissance painting (Ghirlandaio, Signorelli, and Mantegna), a glimpse at a lush courtyard, and a grand view of the Grand Canal.

Cost and Hours: €6, dry audioguide-€4, Mon 8:15-14:00, Tue-Sun 8:15-19:15, free peek through hole in door of courtyard, at vaporetto: Ca' d'Oro, www.cadoro.org.

Castello District

▲**Scuola Dalmata di San Giorgio**—This little-visited "school" (which means "meeting place") features an exquisite wood-paneled chapel decorated with the world's best collection of paintings by Vittorio Carpaccio (1465-1526).

The Scuola, a reminder that cosmopolitan Venice was once Europe's trade hub, was one of a hundred such community centers for various ethnic, religious, and economic groups, supported by the government partly to keep an eye on foreigners. It was here that the Dalmatians (from present-day Croatia) worshipped in their own way, held neighborhood meetings, and preserved their culture.

Cost and Hours: €4, Mon 14:45-18:00, Tue-Sat 9:15-13:00 & 14:45-18:00, Sun 9:15-13:00, midway between St. Mark's Square and the Arsenale, on Calle dei Furlani at #3259a, tel. 041-522-8828.

Naval Museum and Arsenale—The mighty Republic of Venice was home to the first great military industrial complex: a state-of-the-art shipyard that could build a powerful warship of standardized parts in an assembly line (and did so to intimidate visiting heads of state). While the Arsenale is still a military base and is therefore closed to the public, its massive and evocative gate, the Porta Magna, is worth a look (to see the gate, turn left at the Naval Museum—described next—and follow the canal). At the waterfront end of the canal, in front of the Arsenale, stands the Naval Museum (Museo Storico Navale). It's very old-school and military-run, but anyone into maritime history or sailing will find its several floors of exhibits interesting. You'll see the evolution of warships, displays on old fishing boats, and gondolas (all described in English).

Cost and Hours: Museum-€2, Mon-Sat 8:45-13:30, closed Sun, tel. 041-244-1399.

Santa Elena—For a pleasant peek into a completely non-touristy, residential side of Venice, walk or catch vaporetto #1 from St. Mark's Square to the neighborhood of Santa Elena (at the fish's tail). This 100-year-old suburb lives as if there were no tourism. You'll find a kid-friendly park, a few lazy restaurants, and beautiful sunsets over San Marco.

La Biennale—From roughly June through November, Venice hosts an annual world's fair—contemporary art in odd years, modern architecture in even years—in buildings and pavilions scattered throughout Giardini park and the Arsenale. The festival is an excuse for temporary art exhibitions, concerts, and other cultural events around the city (for more information, see "Experiences in Venice," later in this chapter, and www.labiennale.org).

Venice's Lagoon

The island of Venice sits in a lagoon—a calm section of the Adriatic protected from wind and waves by the natural breakwater of the Lido. Beyond the church-topped island of San Giorgio Maggiore (directly in front of St. Mark's Square—see page 85), four interesting islands hide out in the lagoon: Cimitero, Murano, Burano, and Torcello.

San Michele (a.k.a. Cimitero) is the cemetery island—the final resting place of Venetians and a few foreign VIPs, from poet Ezra Pound to composer Igor Stravinsky. The stopover is easy, since boats come every 10 minutes. If you even half-enjoy wandering through old cemeteries, you'll dig this one—it's full of flowers, trees, and birdsong, and has an intriguing chapel (cemetery open daily April-Sept 7:30-18:00, Oct-March 7:30-16:30; reception to the left as you enter, free WC to the right, no picnicking).

Murano is famous for its glassmaking. From the Colonna vaporetto stop, skip the glass shops in front of you, walk to the right, and wander up the street along the canal, **Fondamenta dei Vetrai** (Glassmakers' Embankment). The Faro district of Murano, on the other side of the canal, is packed with glass factories *(fabriche)* and their furnaces *(fornaci)*. You'll pass dozens of glass shops along the canal. A cut above is the venerable **Venini** shop, at #47, which shows off the ultimate in modern Venetian glass design (Mon-Sat 9:30-17:30, closed Sun).

Murano's **Glass Museum** (Museo Vetrario) traces the history of this delicate art (€8, daily April-Oct 10:00-18:00, Nov-March

10:00-17:00, last entry 30 minutes before closing, tel. 041-739-586, http://museovetro.visitmuve.it).

Burano, known for its lacemaking and countless lace shops, offers a delightful pastel village alternative to big, bustling Venice. The main drag from the vaporetto stop into town is packed with tourists and lined with shops, some of which sell Burano's locally produced white wine. Wander to the far side of the island, and the mood shifts. Explore to the right of the leaning tower for a peaceful yet intensely pastel, small-town lagoon world. Benches lining a little promenade at the water's edge make another pretty picnic spot.

Burano's **Lace Museum** (Museo del Merletto di Burano) showcases the island's lace heritage (€5.50, April-Oct Tue-Sun 10:00-18:00, Nov-March Tue-Sun 10:00-17:00, closed Mon year-round, tel. 041-730-034, http://museomerletto.visitmuve.it).

Torcello is the birthplace of Venice, where some of the first mainland refugees settled, escaping the barbarian hordes. Yet today, it's the least-developed island (pop. 20) and in its mostly natural state, marshy and shrub-covered. There's little for tourists to see except the church (a 10-minute walk from the dock), which is the oldest in Venice and has impressive mosaics, a climbable bell tower, and a modest museum of Roman sculpture and medieval sculpture and manuscripts (tickets for each sight cost €3-5 or €8 for all sights plus an audioguide; most sights open daily March-Oct 10:30-18:00, Nov-Feb 10:00-17:00, museum closed Mon; museum tel. 041-730-761, church/bell tower tel. 041-730-119).

Getting There: You can travel to any of the four islands by vaporetto. Since single vaporetto tickets (€7) expire after one hour, getting a vaporetto pass for this lagoon excursion makes more sense (such as a 12-hour pass for €18; see page 51 for more on vaporetto tickets).

The Route from Fondamente Nove: The following route takes you to all four islands. Start at the Fondamente Nove vaporetto stop on the north shore of Venice (the "back" of the fish); it's a 15-minute walk from the Rialto or Campo Santa Maria Formosa. At this stop, lines #4.1 and #4.2 converge before heading out to Murano. Catch either one (every 10 minutes).

From Fondamente Nove the boats cross to San Michele (whose stop is called Cimitero) in six minutes, then continue another three minutes to Murano-Colonna.

On the way to Murano, you can make a quick visit to the cemetery (Cimitero stop). You'll arrive at Murano-Colonna, but leave Murano from a different stop (Murano-Faro). At Murano-Faro, board vaporetto #12 for the 30-minute trip to Burano. From Burano, you can side-trip to Torcello on vaporetto #9 (5-minute trip each way). From Burano, you can make a quick return to Venice on

VENICE

Lagoon Tour

1 Kilometer

1 Mile

Lagoon

CHURCH COMPLEX

10-MIN. WALK

Torcello

LINE 9 5 MIN.

Laghi

Mazzorbo

Burano

See Burano detail map below

LINE 12

Crevan

To Sant'Erasmo

San Francesco del Deserto

Sant' Erasmo

Burano detail map

Mazzorbo

To Torcello

LINE 9

LINE 12

To Sant'Erasmo

To Murano

LINE 12

SAN MAURO

MARCELLO

COMARE

F. S. MAURO

Burano

C. PITTONA

VIA B. GALUPPI

FONDAMENTA DELLA GIUDECCA

FISH MARKET

WC

Piazza Galuppi

VIGNA

F. TERANOVA

POST

Sant' Erasmo

Lagoon

100 Meters

100 Yards

R. T. PIZZO

Park

FONDAMENTA DEL PIZZO

San Martino Church & Leaning Bell Tower

vaporetto #12, arriving at Fondamente Nove (45 minutes).

If you'd prefer a longer boat ride from Burano, you can take the #12 in the other direction. It runs once an hour from Burano to Punta Sabbioni on the island of Sant'Erasmo, where you connect to the #14, which takes you to the San Zaccaria-Pietà dock and St. Mark's Square. This route is more complicated, but will give you a fine lagoon cruise experience.

Experiences in Venice

Gondola Rides

Riding a gondola is simple, expensive, and one of the great experiences in Europe. Gondoliers hanging out all over town are eager

to have you hop in for a ride. A rip-off for some, this is a traditional must for romantics.

The price for a gondola starts at €80 for a 40-minute ride during the day. Prices jump about 30 percent after 19:00—when it's most romantic and relaxing. Prices are standard and listed on the gondoliers' association website (go to www.gondolavenezia .it, click on "Using the Gondola," and look under "*charterage*"). You can divide the cost—and the romance—among up to six people per boat, but only two get the love seat. Adding a singer and an accordionist will cost an additional €120.

Because you might get a narration plus conversation with your gondolier, talk with several and choose one you like. You're welcome to review the map and discuss the route. Doing so is also a good way to see if you enjoy the gondolier's personality and language skills. Establish the price, route, and duration of the trip before boarding, enjoy your ride, and pay only when you're finished. While prices are pretty firm, you might find them softer during the day. Most gondoliers honor the official prices, but a few might try to scam you out of some extra euros, particularly by insisting on a tip.

If you've hired musicians and want to hear a Venetian song (*un canto Veneziano*), try requesting "*Venezia La Luna e Tu.*" Asking to hear "*O Sole Mio*" (which comes from Naples) is like asking a lounge singer in Cleveland to sing "The Eyes of Texas."

Glide through nighttime Venice with your head on someone's shoulder. Follow the moon as it sails past otherwise unseen buildings. Silhouettes gaze down from bridges while window glitter spills onto the black water. You're anonymous in the city of masks, as the rhythmic thrust of your striped-shirted gondolier turns old crows into songbirds. This is extremely relaxing (and, I think, worth the extra cost to experience at night). Suggestion: Put the camera down and make a point for you and your partner to enjoy a threesome with Venice. Warning: Women, beware...while gondoliers can be extremely charming, local women say that anyone who falls for one of these Venetian Romeos "has slices of ham over her eyes."

For cheap gondola thrills during the day, stick to the €2 one-minute ferry ride on a Grand Canal *traghetto*. At night, *vaporetti* are nearly empty, and it's a great time to cruise the Grand Canal on the slow boat #1. Or hang out on a bridge along the gondola route and wave at romantics.

Festivals

Venice's most famous festival is **Carnevale,** the celebration Americans call Mardi Gras (Jan 6-Feb 12 in 2013, www.carnevale .venezia.it). Carnevale, which means "fare-well to meat," originated centuries ago as a wild two-month-long party leading up to the austerity of Lent. In Carnevale's heyday—the 1600s and 1700s—you could do pretty much anything with anybody from any social class if you were wearing a mask. These days it's a tamer 18-day celebration, culminating in a huge dance lit with fireworks on St. Mark's Square. Sporting masks and costumes, Venetians from kids to businessmen join in the fun. Drawing the biggest crowds of the year, Carnevale has nearly been a victim of

its own success, driving away many Venetians (who skip out on the craziness to go skiing in the Dolomites).

Every year, the city hosts the **Venice Biennale International Art Exhibition,** a world-class contemporary fair, alternating between art in odd years and architecture in even years. The exhibition spreads over the Arsenale and Giardini park. When the Biennale focuses on visual art (in 2013), representatives from 70 nations offer the latest in contemporary art forms: video, computer art, performance art, and digital photography, along with painting and sculpture (take vaporetto #1 or #2 to Giardini-Biennale; for details and an events calendar, see www.labiennale.org). The actual exhibition usually runs from June through November, but other events—film, dance, theater—loosely connected with the Biennale are held throughout the year (starting as early as Feb) in various venues on the island.

Other typically Venetian festival days filling the city's hotels with visitors and its canals with decked-out boats are **Feast of the Ascension Day** (May 9 in 2013), **Feast and Regatta of the Redeemer** (third Sun in July and the preceding evening), and the **Historical Regatta** (old-time boats and pageantry, first Sat and Sun in Sept). **Vogalonga** is a colorful regatta that attracts more than 1,500 human-powered watercraft; teams of often-costumed participants follow a 20-mile course through the canals and lagoon (late May-early June, www.vogalonga.it). Smaller regattas include the **Murano Regatta** (early July) and the **Burano Regatta** (mid-Sept).

Venice's patron saint, **St. Mark,** is commemorated every April 25. Venetian men celebrate the day by presenting roses to the women in their lives (mothers, wives, and lovers).

Every November 21 is the **Feast of Our Lady of Good Health.** On this local "Thanksgiving," a bridge is built over the Grand Canal so that the city can pile into La Salute Church and remember how Venice survived the gruesome plague of 1630. On this day, Venetians eat smoked lamb from Dalmatia (which was the cargo of the first ship admitted when the plague lifted).

Shopping in Venice

Shoppers like Murano glass (described earlier), Burano lace (fun lace umbrellas for little girls), Carnevale masks (fine shops and artisans all over town), art reproductions (posters, postcards, and books), prints of Venetian scenes, traditional stationery (pens and marbled paper products of all kinds), calendars with Venetian scenes, silk ties, scarves, and plenty of goofy knickknacks (Titian mousepads, gondolier T-shirts, and little plastic gondola condom holders).

Shops are typically open from 9:00 to 19:30, and more stores are open on Sunday here than in the rest of the country. If you're buying a substantial amount from nearly any shop, bargain—it's accepted and almost expected. Offer less and offer to pay cash; merchants are very conscious of the bite taken by credit-card companies.

Popular **Venetian glass** is available in many forms: vases, tea sets, decanters, glasses, jewelry, lamps, mod sculptures (such as solid-glass aquariums), and on and on. Shops will ship it home for you, but you're likely to pay as much or more for the shipping as you are for the item(s), and you may have to pay duty on larger purchases. Make sure the shop insures their merchandise (*assicurazi-*

one), or you're out of luck if it breaks. If your item arrives broken and it has been insured, take a photo of the pieces, send it to the shop, and they'll replace it for free. For a cheap, packable souvenir, consider the glass-bead necklaces sold at vendors' stalls throughout Venice.

Some visitors feel that because they're in Venice, they ought to grab the opportunity to buy glass. Remember that you can buy fine glass back home, too (Venice stopped forbidding its glassblowers from leaving the republic a few centuries ago), under less time pressure.

If you'd like to watch a quick glassblowing demonstration, try **Galleria San Marco,** a tour-group staple on St. Mark's Square at #139, which offers great demos every few minutes. They let individual travelers flashing this book sneak in with tour groups to see the show (and sales pitch). If you buy anything, show this book and they'll take 20 percent off the listed price. The gallery faces the square behind the orchestra nearest to the church; come to the door at #139, go through the shop, and climb the stairs (daily 9:00-18:00, tel. 041-271-8671, info@galleriasanmarco.it, manager Marino Busetto, see map on page 75).

If you're serious about glass, visit the island of **Murano,** its glass museum, and many shops. You'll find greater variety on Murano, but prices are usually the same as in Venice.

Along Venice's many shopping streets, you'll notice fly-by-night street vendors selling knockoffs of famous-maker handbags (Louis Vuitton, Gucci, etc.). These vendors are willing to bargain.

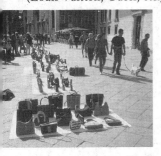

But buyer beware: If you're caught purchasing fakes, you could get hit with a fine. Legitimate manufacturers are raising a stink about these street merchants, and the government is trying to rid the city of them. Their hope: The threat of a huge fine will scare potential customers away—so unlicensed merchants will be driven out of business and off the streets.

Nightlife in Venice

You must experience Venice after dark. The city is quiet at night, as tour groups stay in the cheaper hotels of Mestre on the mainland, and the masses of day-trippers return to their beach resorts and cruise ships. Gondolas cost more, but are worth the extra expense (see page 98). At night, *vaporetti* are nearly empty, and it's a great time to cruise the Grand Canal on the slow boat #1.

Venice has a busy schedule of events, church concerts,

festivals, and entertainment. Check at the TI or the TI's website
(www.turismovenezia.it) for listings. The free monthly *Un Ospite
di Venezia* lists all the latest happenings in English (free at fancy
hotels, or check www.aguestinvenice.com).

Baroque Concerts—Venice is a city of the powdered-wig
Baroque era. For about €25, you can take your pick of traditional
Vivaldi concerts in churches throughout town. Homegrown
Vivaldi is as ubiquitous here as Strauss is in Vienna and Mozart
is in Salzburg. In fact, you'll find frilly young Vivaldis hawking concert tickets on many corners. Most shows start at 20:30
and generally last 1.5 hours. You'll see posters in hotels all over
town (hotels sell tickets at face-value). A one-stop shop for concerts is the Vivaldi Store (east end of Rialto Bridge, at Fontego dei
Tedeschi #5537, tel. 041-522-1343). Tickets for Baroque concerts in
Venice can usually be bought the same day as the concert, so don't
bother with websites that sell tickets with a surcharge. The general
rule of thumb: Musicians in wigs and tights offer better spectacle;
musicians in black-and-white suits are better performers.

The **Interpreti Veneziani orchestra**, considered the best
group in town, generally performs 1.5-hour concerts nightly at
21:00 at the San Vidal Church (€25, church ticket booth open
daily 9:30-21:00, north end of Accademia Bridge, tel. 041-277-
0561, www.interpretiveneziani.com). If you're attending a concert
at **Scuola San Rocco** (tickets €15-30), arrive 30 minutes early to
enjoy the art (which you'd have to pay €8 to see during the day).

Other Performances—Venice's most famous theaters are **La
Fenice** (grand old opera house, box office tel. 041-2424, see page
83), **Teatro Goldoni** (mostly Italian live theater), and **Teatro della
Fondamenta Nuove** (theater, music, and dance).

Musica a Palazzo is a unique evening of opera at a Venetian
palace on the Grand Canal. You'll spend about 45 delightful minutes in each of three sumptuous rooms as eight musicians (generally four instruments and four singers) perform. They generally
present three different operas on successive nights—enthusiasts
can experience more than one. With these kinds of surroundings,
under Tiepolo frescoes, you'll be glad you dressed up. As there are
only 70 seats, you must book by phone or online in advance (€60,
nightly shows at 20:30, Palazzo Barbarigo-Minotto, Fondamenta
Duodo o Barbarigo, vaporetto: Giglio, mobile 340-971-7272, www
.musicapalazzo.com).

Venezia is advertised as "the show that tells the great story
of Venice" and "simply the best show in town." I found the performance to be slow-moving and a bit cheesy, and the venue was
disappointing (€39, nightly May-Oct at 20:00, Nov-April at 19:00;
80 minutes, just off St. Mark's Square on Campo San Gallo, tel.
041-241-2002, www.teatrosangallo.net).

St. Mark's Square—For tourists, St. Mark's Square is the high-light, with lantern light and live music echoing from the cafés. Just being here after dark is a thrill, as **dueling café orchestras** entertain (see sidebar on page 80). Every night, enthusiastic musicians play the same songs, creating the same irresistible magic. Hang out for free behind the tables (allowing you to move easily on to the next orchestra when the musicians take a break), or spring for a seat and enjoy a fun and gorgeously set concert. If you sit a while, it can be €12-20 well spent (for a drink and the cover charge for music). Dancing on the square is free—and encouraged.

Several venerable cafés and bars on the square serve expensive drinks outside but cheap drinks inside at the bar. The scene in a bar like **Gran Caffè Lavena** (in spite of its politically incorrect chandelier) can be great. The touristy **Bar Americano** is lively until late (under the Clock Tower). You'll hear people talking about the famous **Harry's American Bar,** which sells overpriced food and American cocktails to dressy tourists near the San Marco-Vallaresso vaporetto stop. But it's a rip-off...and the last place Hemingway would drink today. It's far cheaper to get a drink at any of the bars just off St. Mark's Square; you can even get prosecco to go in a plastic cup.

Wherever you end up, streetlamp halos, live music, floodlit history, and a ceiling of stars make St. Mark's magic at midnight. You're not a tourist, you're a living part of a soft Venetian night... an alley cat with money. In the misty light, the moon has a golden hue. Shine with the old lanterns on the gondola piers, where the sloppy lagoon splashes at the Doge's Palace...reminiscing.

Sleeping in Venice

For hassle-free efficiency and the sheer magic of being close to the action, I favor hotels that are handy to sightseeing activities. I've listed rooms in four neighborhoods: St. Mark's bustle, the Rialto action, the quiet Dorsoduro area behind the Accademia art museum, and near the train station (handy for train travelers, but far from the action). I also mention several apartment rentals, big fancy hotels, cheap dorms, and places on the mainland. For additional listings of B&Bs and apartments, try **Cross-Pollinate,** a reputable online booking agency (www.cross-pollinate.com; see page 27).

Book your accommodations well in advance if you'll be traveling during busy times. Contact the hotel directly, not through any room-finding service (they can't give opinions on quality).

Note that hotel websites are particularly valuable for Venice, because they often include detailed directions that can help you get

VENICE

Sleep Code

(€1 = about $1.40, country code: 39)
S = Single, **D** = Double/Twin, **T** = Triple, **Q** = Quad, **b** = bathroom, **s** = shower only. Unless otherwise noted, credit cards are accepted, breakfast is included, and English is generally spoken. There's almost always Wi-Fi and/or Internet access available, either free or for a fee. Venice charges a hotel tax of €1-4 per person, per night. This tax is typically not included in the prices I've listed here.

To help you easily sort through these listings, I've divided the accommodations into three categories based on the price for a standard double room with bath:

$$$ Higher Priced—Most rooms €180 or more.
 $$ Moderately Priced—Most rooms between €130-180.
  $ Lower Priced—Most rooms €130 or less.

Prices can change without notice; verify the hotel's current rates online or by email.

to your rooms with a minimum of wrong turns in this navigationally challenging city.

Over the past decade, Venice has seen the opening of several big new hotels, countless little boutique hotels, and the conversion of many private homes to short-term rental apartments, nearly doubling Venice's hotel capacity. Now the city is overbuilt for hotels. Demand is soft and, therefore, so are prices. Most hotels change prices from day to day, according to demand.

The prices I've listed are for one-night stays in peak season (April, May, June, Sept, and Oct) and assume you're booking directly (not through a TI or online hotel-booking engine). Prices can spike up during festivals. Almost all places drop prices from November through March (except during Carnevale—Jan 26-Feb 12 in 2013—and Christmas) and in July and August. A €180 double can cost €80-90 in winter. Off-season, don't pay the rates I list.

To save money during a relatively slow time, consider arriving without a reservation and dropping in at the last minute. Big, fancy hotels put empty rooms on an aggressive push list, offering great prices. Many hotels in Venice list rooms on www.venere.com, especially for last-minute vacancies (two to three weeks before the date). Before you bite, check to see if rates are lower than the prices in this book.

For tips on making reservations, see page 24.

Near St. Mark's Square

To get here from the train station or Piazzale Roma bus station, ride the vaporetto to San Zaccaria—either the slow #1 or the fast #2 (from the Tronchetto parking lot, it's #2 only). Consider using your ride to follow my tour of the Grand Canal (see page 60); to make sure you arrive via the Grand Canal, confirm that your boat goes "*via Rialto*."

To locate the following hotels, see the map on page 106.

Nearby Laundries: Lavanderia Gabriella offers full service a few streets north of St. Mark's Square (€15/load includes wash, dry, and fold; drop off Mon-Fri 8:00-12:30, closed Sat-Sun; pick up 2 hours later or next working day; with your back to the door of San Zulian Church, go over Ponte dei Ferali, take first right down Calle dei Armeni, then first left on Rio Terà de le Colonne to #985; tel. 041-522-1758, Elisabetta).

Effe Erre, a modern self-service *lavanderia,* is near the recommended Hotel al Piave on Ruga Giuffa at #4826 (€12/load, daily 6:30-24:00, mobile 349-058-3881, Massimo).

East of St. Mark's Square

Located near the Bridge of Sighs, just off the Riva degli Schiavoni waterfront promenade, these places rub drainpipes with Venice's most palatial five-star hotels.

$$$ Hotel Campiello, lacy and bright, was once part of a 19th-century convent. Ideally located 50 yards off the waterfront, on a tiny square, its 16 rooms offer a tranquil, friendly refuge for travelers who appreciate comfort and professional service (Sb-€130, Db-€180, 10 percent cash discount with this book if you reserve direct, air-con, elevator; just steps from the San Zaccaria vaporetto stop, Castello 4647; tel. 041-520-5764, fax 041-520-5798, www.hcampiello.it, campiello@hcampiello.it; family-run for four generations, currently by Thomas, Nicoletta, and Marco). They also rent three modern family apartments, under rustic timbers just steps away (up to €380/night).

$$$ Hotel Fontana is a nice, old-time, family-run place with 15 rooms near a school, two bridges behind St. Mark's Square (Sb-€120, Db-€180, family rooms, 10 percent cash discount, quieter rooms on garden side, 2 rooms have terraces for €20 extra, air-con, elevator, free Internet access, on Campo San Provolo at Castello 4701, tel. 041-522-0579, fax 041-523-1040, www.hotelfontana.it, info@hotelfontana.it, cousins Diego and Gabriele).

$$$ Hotel la Residenza is a grand old palace facing a peaceful square. It has 15 small rooms on three levels and a huge, luxurious lounge that comes with a piano and a stingy breakfast. This is a good value for romantics—you'll feel like you're in the Doge's Palace after hours (Sb-€105, Db-€175-220, air-con, on Campo

VENICE

Hotels & Restaurants near St. Mark's Square

Hotels

1. Hotel Campiello
2. Hotel Fontana
3. Locanda al Leon
4. To Hotel la Residenza
5. Albergo Doni
6. Casa per Ferie Santa Maria della Pietà
7. Hotel al Piave
8. Locanda Silva
9. Locanda Casa Querini
10. Hotel Riva
11. Corte Campana B&B
12. Hotel Flora
13. Hotel Bel Sito
14. Hotel Mercurio
15. Hotel Casa Verardo
16. Hotel Donà Palace
17. Hotel all'Angelo
18. Hotel al Ponte dei Sosperi
19. Hotel Ca' Dei Conti

VENICE

<u>Eateries & Other</u>
- 20 Ristorante Antica Sacrestia
- 21 Birreria Forst Café
- 22 Bar Verde
- 23 Ristorante alla Basilica
- 24 Rizzo Café
- 25 Ristorante alla Conchiglia
- 26 Trattoria da Giorgio ai Greci
- 27 Gran Caffè Lavena (Gelato)
- 28 Todaro Gelateria
- 29 Co-op Supermarket
- 30 Lavanderia Gabriella
- 31 Lavanderia Effe Erre
- 32 Paolo Brandolisio's Wood-Carving Shop

Bandiera e Moro at Castello 3608, tel. 041-528-5315, fax 041-523-8859, www.venicelaresidenza.com, info@venicelaresidenza.com, Giovanni).

$$ Locanda al Leon, which feels a little like a medieval tower house, rents 13 reasonably priced rooms just off Campo Santi Filippo e Giacomo (Db-€150-160, Tb-€190, Qb-€230, these prices with cash and this book, air-con, Campo Santi Filippo e Giacomo, Castello 4270, tel. 041-277-0393, fax 041-521-0348, www.hotelalleon.com, leon@hotelalleon.com, Giuliano and Marcella).

$ Albergo Doni is dark and quiet—a bit of a time-warp—with 13 well-worn, once-classy rooms up a creaky stairway. It's run by friendly Tessa and her brother, an Italian stallion named Nikos (S-€75, D-€105, Db-€130, T-€135, Tb-€170, €5 discount in 2013 with this book, ceiling fans, 3 Db rooms have air-con, 3 nice overflow apartments are same price but no breakfast, on Fondamenta del Vin at Castello 4656, tel. & fax 041-522-4267, www.albergodoni.it, albergodoni@hotmail.it).

$ Casa per Ferie Santa Maria della Pietà is a wonderful church-run facility renting 55 beds in 16 rooms just a block off the Riva, with a fabulous lagoon-view roof terrace that could rival the most luxurious hotels in town. Institutional with generous public spaces and dorm-style comfort, there are no sinks, toilets, or showers in any of its rooms, but there's plenty of plumbing down the hall (€40 beds in 4-8-bed dorms, S-€55, D-€100, straight price all year, only twin beds, reserve with credit card but pay cash, partial air-con, profits go to church care for poor, 100 yards from San Zaccaria-Pietà vaporetto dock, down Calle de la Pietà from La Pietà Church, tel. 041-522-2171, www.pietavenezia.org, info .admin@pietavenezia.org).

North of St. Mark's Square

$$ Hotel al Piave, with 28 fine, air-con rooms above a bright and classy lobby, is fresh, modern, and comfortable. You'll enjoy the neighborhood and always get a cheery welcome (Db-€150, Tb-€200; family suites-€280 for 4, €300 for 5, or €310 for 6; €10 Rick Steves discount when booked directly and paid in cash, on Ruga Giuffa at Castello 4838, tel. 041-528-5174, fax 041-523-8512, www.hotelalpiave.com, info@hotelalpiave.com, Mirella, Paolo, Ilaria, and Federico speak English).

$$ Locanda Silva is a big, basic, beautifully located hotel with a functional 1960s feel, renting 23 decent old-school rooms (S-€70, Sb-€85, D-€90, Db-€140, Tb-€160, Qb-€180, book direct and request 10 percent Rick Steves discount, another 10 percent off if you stay at least 2 nights, discounts valid only with cash, closed Dec-Jan, air-con, on Fondamenta del Remedio at Castello 4423, tel. 041-522-7643, fax 041-528-6817, www.locandasilva.it, info

@locandasilva.it, Sandra, Katia and Massimo).

$$ Locanda Casa Querini rents six bright, high-ceilinged rooms on a quiet square tucked away behind St. Mark's. You can enjoy your breakfast or a sunny happy-hour picnic sitting at their tables right on the sleepy little square (Db-€150, third person-€20-25, one cheaper small double, these prices promised in 2013 with this book and cash, air-con, halfway between San Zaccaria vaporetto stop and Campo Santa Maria Formosa at Castello 4388 on Campo San Zaninovo/Giovanni Novo, tel. 041-241-1294, fax 041-523-6188, www.locandaquerini.com, info @locandaquerini.com; Silvia, Patrizia, and Caterina).

$ Hotel Riva, with gleaming marble hallways, big exposed beams, fine antique furnishings, and lots of stairs, is romantically situated on a canal along the gondola serenade route. This has long been a standby in this book, but how it'll stack up when it reopens after a major renovation remains to be seen (see website for latest prices, on Ponte de l'Anzolo at Castello 5310, tel. 041-522-7034, www.hotelriva.it, info@hotelriva.it, Daniella).

$ Corte Campana B&B, run by enthusiastic and helpful Riccardo, rents three quiet and characteristic rooms just behind St. Mark's Square. One room has a private bath down the hall (Db-€125, Tb-€165, Qb-€190, prices are soft, cash only, 2-night minimum, at least €10/night less for stays of 4 nights, air-con, free Internet access, on Calle del Remedio at Castello 4410, tel. & fax 041-523-3603, mobile 389-272-6500, www.cortecampana.com, info@cortecampana.com).

West of St. Mark's Square

$$$ Hotel Flora sits buried in a sea of fancy designer boutiques and elegant hotels almost on the Grand Canal. It's formal, with uniformed staff and grand public spaces, yet the 40 rooms have a homey warmth and the garden oasis is a sanctuary for well-heeled, foot-weary guests (generally Db-€260, check website for special discounts or email Sr. Romanelli for 10 percent Rick Steves discount off standard prices, air-con, elevator, family apartment, San Marco 2283a, tel. 041-520-5844, fax 041-522-8217, www.hotelflora .it, info@hotelflora.it).

$$$ Hotel Bel Sito offers pleasing yet well-worn Old World character, 34 rooms, generous public spaces, a peaceful courtyard, and a picturesque location—facing a church on a small square between St. Mark's Square and the Accademia (Sb-€110, Db-€185, air-con, elevator; near Santa Maria del Giglio vaporetto stop—line #1, San Marco 2517; tel. 041-522-3365, fax 041-520-4083, www .hotelbelsitovenezia.it, info@hotelbelsito.info, manager Rossella).

$$ Hotel Mercurio, a block in front of La Fenice Opera House, offers a warm welcome and 29 peaceful, comfortable

VENICE

VENICE

Hotels & Restaurants near the Rialto Bridge

Hotels
1. Pensione Guerrato
2. Hotel al Ponte Antico
3. Locanda la Corte
4. To Alloggi Barbaria
5. Hotel Giorgione
6. Foresteria della Chiesa Valdese

16. "Bancogiro Stretch"
17. "Cicchetti Strip"
18. Pronto Pesce
19. Al Mercà
20. Ristorante Vini da Pinto
21. Trattoria alla Madonna

22. Trattoria Pizzeria al Nono Risorto
23. Osteria da Alberto
24. Grom Gelateria
25. Co-op Supermarket
26. Billa Supermarket
27. Small Deli

rooms, some with canal views (Sb-€130, Db-€170, Tb-€200, Qb-€230-250, €10 less when booked direct and paid in cash, air-con, on Calle del Fruttariol at San Marco 1848, tel. 041-522-0947, fax 041-241-1079, www.hotelmercurio.com, info@hotelmercurio.com, Monica, Vittorio, and Natale).

Near the Rialto Bridge

Vaporetto #2 brings you to the Rialto quickly from the train station, the Piazzale Roma bus station, and the parking-lot island of Tronchetto. You can also take the slower vaporetto #1 (but not from Tronchetto).

To locate the following hotels, see the map on page 110.

West of the Rialto Bridge

$$ Pensione Guerrato, above the colorful Rialto produce market and just two minutes from the Rialto Bridge, is run by friendly, creative, and hardworking Roberto and Piero. Their 800-year-old building—with 24 spacious, air-conditioned, and charming rooms—is simple, airy, and wonderfully characteristic (D-€90, Db-€140, Tb-€160, Qb-€175, Quint/b-€185, these prices with this book and cash, check website for special discounts, Rick Steves readers can ask for €5/night discount below Web specials, on Calle drio la Scimia at San Polo 240a, tel. & fax 041-528-5927, www.pensioneguerrato.it, info@pensioneguerrato.it, Monica and Rosanna). My tour groups book this place for 60 nights each year. Sorry. The Guerrato also rents family apartments in the old center (great for groups of 4-8) for around €55 per person.

East of the Rialto Bridge

$$$ Hotel al Ponte Antico is exquisite, professional, and small. With nine plush rooms, a velvety royal living/breakfast room, and its own dock for water taxi arrivals, it's perfect for a romantic anniversary. Because its wonderful terrace overlooks the Grand Canal, Rialto Bridge, and market action, its non-canal-view rooms may be a better value (Db-€320, superior Db-€400, deluxe canal-front Db-€490, air-con, 100 yards from Rialto Bridge at Cannaregio 5768, tel. 041-241-1944, fax 041-241-1828, www.alponteantico.com, info@alponteantico.com, Matteo makes you feel like royalty).

$$ Locanda la Corte is perfumed with elegance without being snooty. Its 17 attractive, high-ceilinged, wood-beamed rooms—Venetian-style, done in earthy pastels—circle a small, quiet courtyard (standard Db-€150, deluxe Db-€170, 10 percent discount with cash and this book, suites and family rooms available, air-con, on Calle Bressana at Castello 6317, tel. 041-241-1300, fax 041-241-5982, www.locandalacorte.it, info@locandalacorte.it, Marco, Abel, and Tommy the cat).

$ Alloggi Barbaria rents eight backpacker-type rooms on one floor around a bright but institutional-feeling common area. Beyond Campo Santi Giovanni e Paolo, it's a long walk from the action, in a residential neighborhood, and only a step above a youth hostel (Db-€90-100, third or fourth person-€25 each, pay cash for best price, family deals, limited breakfast, air-con, on Calle de le Capucine at Castello 6573, tel. 041-522-2750, fax 041-277-5540, www.alloggibarbaria.it, info@alloggibarbaria.it, Giorgio and Fausto).

Near the Accademia Bridge

As you step over the Accademia Bridge, the commotion of touristy Venice is replaced by a sleepy village laced with canals. This quiet area, next to the best painting gallery in town, is a 15-minute walk from the Rialto or St. Mark's Square.

The fast vaporetto #2 connects the Accademia Bridge with the train station (15 minutes), Piazzale Roma bus station (20 minutes), Tronchetto parking lot (25 minutes), and St. Mark's Square (5 minutes). For hotels south of the Accademia Bridge, vaporetto #5.1 to Zattere (or the Alilaguna speedboat from the airport to Zattere) is a good option.

To locate the following hotels, see the map on page 114.

South of the Accademia Bridge

$$$ Pensione Accademia fills the 17th-century Villa Maravege like a Bellini painting. Its 27 rooms are comfortable, elegant, and air-conditioned. You'll feel aristocratic gliding through its grand public spaces and lounging in its wistful, breezy gardens (Sb-€145, standard Db-€250, bigger "superior" Db-€300, Qb-€360, 10 percent Rick Steves discount when booked direct; on Fondamenta Bollani at Dorsoduro 1058; facing Accademia art museum, go right to where the small canal hits the big one; tel. 041-521-0188, fax 041-523-9152, www.pensioneaccademia.it, info@pensione accademia.it).

$$$ Hotel Belle Arti has a grand entry and a formal, stern staff. With the ambience of a modern American hotel, its 64 rooms feel out of place in musty Old World Venice (Sb-€150, Db-€240, Tb-€270, air-con, elevator; 100 yards behind Accademia art museum at Dorsoduro 912a; tel. 041-522-6230, fax 041-528-0043, www.hotelbellearti.com, info@hotelbellearti.com).

$$ Pensione la Calcina, the home of English writer John Ruskin in 1876, maintains a 19th-century formality. It comes with three-star comforts in a professional yet intimate package. Its 27 nautical-feeling rooms are squeaky clean, with nice wood furniture, hardwood floors, and a peaceful canalside setting facing Giudecca Island (Sb-€140, Sb with view-€170, Db-€150-250,

VENICE

VENICE

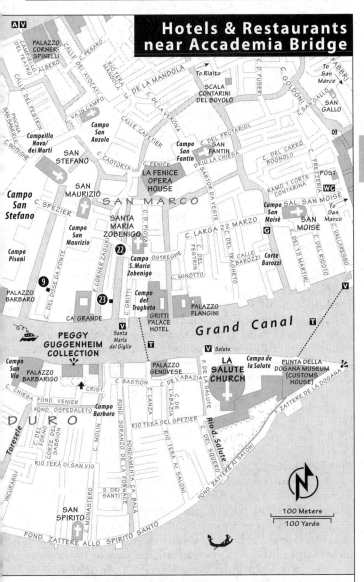

Hotels & Restaurants near Accademia Bridge

Eateries & Nightlife

13 Ristorante/Pizzeria Accademia Foscarini
14 Enoteca Cantine del Vino Già Schiavi
15 Terrazza del Casin dei Nobili
16 To Ae Oche Pizzeria & Billa Supermarket
17 Ristoteca Oniga
18 Osteria Enoteca Ai Artisti
19 Pizzeria al Profeta
20 Enoteca e Trattoria la Bitta
21 Grom Gelateria
22 Small Deli
23 Musica a Palazzo
24 Interpreti Veneziani Orchestra

Db with view–€290-350, Qb-€320, air-con, rooftop terrace, buffet breakfast outdoors on platform over lagoon, near Zattere vaporetto stop at south end of Rio de San Vio at Dorsoduro 780, tel. 041-520-6466, fax 041-522-7045, www.lacalcina.com, info@lacalcina.com).

$$ Casa Rezzonico, a tranquil getaway far from the crowds, rents seven quiet rooms with a grassy private garden terrace (Sb-€130, Db-€170, Tb-€200, Qb-€230, ask for Rick Steves discount when you book, air-con, near Ca' Rezzonico vaporetto stop—line #1, on Fondamenta Gherardini at Dorsoduro 2813, tel. 041-277-0653, fax 041-277-5435, www.casarezzonico.it, info@casarezzonico.it, Matteo).

$$ Hotel Galleria has nine tight, velvety rooms, most with views of the Grand Canal. Some rooms are quite narrow. It's run with a family feel by Luciano and Stefano (S-€85, D-€130, skinny Grand Canal view Db-€160, palatial Grand Canal view Db-€185, breakfast in room, ceiling fans, free mini-bar, 30 yards from Accademia art museum, next to recommended Foscarini pizzeria at Dorsoduro 878a, tel. 041-523-2489, fax 041-520-4172, www.hotelgalleria.it, info@hotelgalleria.it).

$$ Don Orione Religious Guest House is a big cultural center dedicated to the work of a local man who became a saint in modern times. Filling an old monastery, it feels institutional, like a modern retreat center—clean, peaceful, and strictly run, with 74 rooms. It's beautifully located, comfortable, and a fine value (Sb-€88, Db-€146, Tb-€188, Qb-€226, profits go to mission work in the developing world, groups welcome, air-con, elevator, on Rio Terà A. Foscarini, Dorsoduro 909a, tel. 041-522-4077, fax 041-528-6214, www.donorione-venezia.it, info@donorione-venezia.it). From the Zattere vaporetto stop, turn right, then turn left. It's just after the church at #909a.

$ Ca' San Trovaso rents seven simple rooms split between the main building and a nearby annex. The location is peaceful, on a small desolate-feeling canal (Sb-€90, Db-€115, Db with bigger canal view and air-con-€130, Tb-€145, these prices with cash, breakfast in your room, air-con in most rooms, no common space except small roof terrace, near Zattere vaporetto stop, off Fondamenta de le Romite at Dorsoduro 1350/51, tel. 041-277-1146, mobile 339-445-8821, fax 041-277-7190, www.casantrovaso.com, info@casantrovaso.com, Mark and his son Alessandro).

$ Casa di Sara, a colorfully decorated B&B, is hidden in a leafy courtyard in a humble back-street area. Their four quiet rooms and tiny roof terrace offer the maximum in privacy (Sb-€85, Db-€110, Tb-€130, mobile 342-596-3563, fax 041-241-2296, www.casadisara.com, info@casadisara.com, Aniello).

North of the Accademia Bridge

$$$ Novecento Hotel rents nine plush rooms on three floors. This boutique hotel is decorated circa-1920s throughout, with a big, welcoming lounge and an elegant living room (Db-€240-260, air-con, lots of stairs; on Calle del Dose, off Campo San Maurizio at San Marco 2683; tel. 041-241-3765, fax 041-521-2145, www .novecento.biz, info@novecento.biz).

$$ Istituto Ciliota is a big, efficient, and sparkling-clean place—well-run, well-located, and church-owned—with an Ikea-style charm, 30 dorm-like rooms, and a peaceful garden. If you want industrial-strength comfort at a good price with no stress and little character, this is a fine value. Rooms come with twin beds and a fridge. During the school year, half the rooms are used by students (Sb-€80, twin Db-€80-160 but generally €140, air-con, cheaper with longer stays, on Calle delle Muneghe just off Campo San Stefano near the Accademia Bridge and vaporetto stop, tel. 041-520-4888, www.ciliota.it, info@ciliota.it).

$$ Foresteria Levi, run by a foundation that promotes research on Venetian music, offers 20 quiet, institutional yet comfortable and spacious rooms (some are lofts). Prices vary wildly—ask for the Rick Steves deal (Db-€100-190, fans, elevator, on Calle Giustinian at San Marco 2893, tel. 041-786-711, fax 041-786-766, www.foresterialevi.it, info@foresterialevi.it). It's 80 yards from the Accademia Bridge on the St. Mark's side.

$ Albergo San Samuele is a backpacker place: dumpy but in a great locale. It rents 12 basic rooms in a crumbling old palace near Campo San Stefano. Sleep here only if their price is far less than other listings (S-€70, D-€90, Db-€110, extra bed-€15, no breakfast, on Salizada San Samuele at San Marco 3358, tel. 041-520-5165, fax 041-522-8045, www.hotelsansamuele.com, info @hotelsansamuele.com).

Near the Train Station

I don't recommend the train station area. It's crawling with noisy, disoriented tourists with too much baggage and people whose life's calling is to scam visitors out of their money. It's so easy just to hop a vaporetto upon arrival and sleep in the Venice of your dreams. Still, some like to park their bags near the station, and if so, these places stand out (for locations, see the map on page 118).

Nearby Laundry: Orange, the nearest self-service laundry, is across the Grand Canal from the station (€14/load, daily 7:30-22:30, follow directions to recommended Albergo Marin, on Ramo de le Chioverete at Santa Croce 665b).

$$$ Hotel Abbazia, in the dreary hotel zone near the train station, fills a former abbey with both history and class. The

VENICE

Hotels near the Train Station

1. Hotel Abbazia
2. Locanda Ca' San Marcuola
3. Locanda Herion
4. Albergo Marin & Launderette
5. Hotel S. Lucia
6. Hotel Henry
7. Hotel Rossi
8. Pizzeria Vesuvio
9. Enoteca Cicchetteria Do Colonne
10. Antica Birraria la Corte
11. To Osteria L'Orto dei Mori
12. To Osteria Ai 40 Ladroni
13. Timon Enoteca Osteria
14. To Osteria al Bacco
15. Brek Cafeteria

Road to Mestre & Mainland

To Road to Mestre & Mainland

To Tronchetto

FOND. PE

CALLE DELLA MISERICORDIA

RAMO DEI SCALZI

C. PRIULI DEL CAVALETTI

C. DE LA 2 CORTI

SCALZI

SANTA LUCIA TRAIN STATION (FERROVIA)

WC

Ferrovia W V

Ferrovia V Scalzi

SCALZI BRIDGE

Ferrovia V

FOND. DE SAN SIMEONE PICCOLO

NOVA DE S.

SAN SIMEONE PICCOLO

CAMP DE LE CHIOVERETE

C. DE BERGAMASCHI

To Stazione Marittima & Tronchetto

RAMPA SAN BASILIO

PONTE DELA Santa Chiara

Canale de Santa Chiara

Canale de la Liberta

PEOPLE MOVER

PARKING GARAGE

P

Rio Tera San Andrea

CO-OP SUPER-MARKET

Piazzale Roma V

CALATRAVA BRIDGE

FOND. DE LA CROCE

F. DEI TOLENTINI

CASE NOVE

CAMPO D. LA

C. DE CA'AMAI

Piazzale Roma

Giardino Papadopoli

Rio Novo

F. PAPADOPOLI

BUS STATION

Campiello de Lana

F. CONDULMER

SAN NICOLO DA TOLENTINO

SANTA CROCE

Canale de Santa Maria Maggiore

FONDAMENTA DEL 3 PONTE

F. DEL PASSAMONTE

F. MINOTTO

F. D. GAFFARO

C. S. BIAGIO

GALLO

C. BASEGO

F. DEL RIO NUOVO

Rio de la Cazziola

100 Meters
100 Yards

VENICE

refectory makes a grand living room for guests, a garden fills the old courtyard, and the halls leading to 50 rooms are monkishly wide (Db-€200, larger Db-€230—choose Venetian or modern style, ask for 10 percent Rick Steves discount when you book direct, air-con, no elevator but plenty of stairs, fun-loving staff, 2 blocks from the station on the very quiet Calle Priuli dei Cavaletti, Cannaregio 68, tel. 041-717-333, fax 041-717-949, www.abbazia hotel.com, info@abbaziahotel.com).

$$ Locanda Ca' San Marcuola is a peaceful and characteristic, if well-worn, oldie-but-goodie renting 14 fine rooms a few steps from the Grand Canal (Db-€140, €10 more for slightly bigger room overlooking small canal, air-con, near San Marcuola vaporetto stop, tel. 041-716-048, www.casanmarcuola.com, info @casanmarcuola).

$ Locanda Herion rents 16 beige-tiled, homey rooms for a decent price (Db-€120, 10 percent discount with cash, air-con, on Campiello Augusto Picutti at Cannaregio 1697a, tel. 041-275-9426, fax 041-275-6647, www.locandaherion.com, info@locandaherion .com). Exiting the train station, turn left to follow Rio Terà Lista de Spagna. It's near the San Marcuola vaporetto stop.

$ Albergo Marin has a depressing lobby, but its 19 good-value, quiet rooms are handy to the train station (Sb-€110, D-€100, Db-€120, Tb-€150, 5 percent cash discount, fans on request, on Ramo de le Chioverete at Santa Croce 670b, tel. 041-718-022, fax 041-721-485, www.albergomarin.it, info@albergomarin.it, Giacomo). From the station, cross the stone bridge over the Grand Canal and go right along the embankment. Take the first left, then the first right, then right again to #670b.

$ Hotel S. Lucia, 150 yards from the train station, is oddly modern and sterile, with bright and spacious rooms and tight showers. Its 15 rooms are simple and clean. Guests enjoy their sunny garden area out front (S-€60, D-€90, Db-€110, Tb-€130, 5 percent cash discount, breakfast-€5, air-con, closed Nov-Feb, on Calle de la Misericordia at Cannaregio 358, tel. 041-715-180, fax 041-710-610, www.hotelslucia.com, info@hotelslucia.com, Gianni and Alessandra). Exit the station, head left, then take the second left onto Calle de la Misericordia.

$ Hotel Henry, a tiny family-owned hotel, rents 15 simple and flowery rooms without any public spaces. It's in a quiet residential neighborhood near the Jewish Ghetto, a 10-minute walk from the train station (D-€80, Db-€100, Tb-€130, Qb-€160, these prices good with cash and this book through 2013, 10 percent discount with 3-night stay, no breakfast, air-con, on Calle Ormesini at Campiello Briani, Cannaregio 1506e, tel. 041-523-6675, fax 041-715-680, www.alloggihenry.com, info@alloggihenry.com, Manola and Henry).

$ Hotel Rossi sits quietly at the end of a dead-end street. It's tired and quiet, renting 17 inexpensive, well-worn rooms (S-€56, D-€80, Db-€95, Tb-€115, air-con, a short walk from the station and a block away from the main street at Lista di Spagna 262, tel. 041-715-164, www.hotelrossi.ve.it, into@hotelrossi.ve.it).

Big, Fancy Hotels that Discount Shamelessly

Here are several big, plush, four-star places with greedy, sky-high rack rates (around Db-€300) that often have great discounts (as low as Db-€120) for online booking through their websites. All are on the map on page 106, except for Hotel Giorgione. If you want sliding-glass-door, uniformed-receptionist kind of comfort and formality in the old center, these are worth considering: **$$$ Hotel Giorgione** (big, garish, shiny, near Rialto Bridge, www .hotelgiorgione.com, see map on page 110); **$$$ Hotel Casa Verardo** (elegant and quietly parked on a canal behind St. Mark's, more stately, www.casaverardo.it); **$$$ Hotel Donà Palace** (sitting like Las Vegas in the touristy zone a few blocks behind St. Mark's Basilica, works with neighbors **$$$ Hotel all'Angelo** and **$$$ Hotel al Ponte dei Sosperi** to rent 100 overpriced but often discounted rooms, all on Calle Larga San Marco, www.dona palace.it); and **$$$ Hotel Ca' Dei Conti** (5 minutes northeast of St. Mark's Square, palatial and perfectly located but €500 rooms are worth it only when deeply discounted, www.cadeiconti.com).

Cheap Dormitory Accommodations

$ Foresteria della Chiesa Valdese is ramshackle, chilly, and run-down yet charming. It rents 70 beds—mostly in tight (6-10-bed) dorms, but with nine fine doubles and some larger private rooms sleeping up to six. It comes with generous public spaces and classic paintings on the walls and ceilings. Its profits support the charity work of the Methodist Church. They take reservations for the rooms, but only accept walk-ins for the dorms (dorm bed-€34, Db-€100-135, Tb-€115-130, Qb-€175, 5b-€190, €5/person less for multi-night stays; includes breakfast, sheets, towels, and lockers; must check in and out when office is open—8:30-20:00, no air-con, elevator, near Campo Santa Maria Formosa on Fondamenta Cavagnis at Castello 5170, see map on page 110, tel. 041-528-6797, fax 041-241-6238, www.foresteriavenezia.it, info@foresteria venezia.it).

$ Venice's youth hostel, on Giudecca Island with 260 beds and grand views across the Bay of San Marco, is a godsend for backpackers shell-shocked by Venetian prices. It's an old-school hostel—big rooms stacked with bunk beds (€26 beds with sheets and breakfast in 8-20-bed dorms, cheaper for hostel members, lockers, towels-€5, room lock-out 10:00-13:30, office open 24 hours, Fondamenta Zitelle 86, tel. 041-523-8211, fax 041-523-5689, www.ostellovenezia.it, info@ostellovenezia.it). Take vaporetto #4.1 from the bus or train stations (from the Tronchetto parking lot, take vaporetto #2) to the Zitelle stop, then walk right along the embankment to #86.

On the Mainland

While I prefer to stay in the heart of the action, these two places combine fine prices with easy bus links into Venice and are particularly good options for those who need to park a car.

$ Villa Dolcetti is a 1635 building with six comfortable rooms in a suburb of Venice. Art lovers Diego and Tatiana provide a buffet breakfast, free parking, and lots of sightseeing advice (Db-€75, superior Db-€85, Tb-€90-110, these prices for Rick Steves readers booking direct, air-con, tel. 041-563-1077, www.villadolcetti.com, info@villadolcetti.com). It's in the town of Oriago di Mira, at Via Venezia 85. Steps away is a bus stop on the Venice-Padua line that connects you to Venice's Piazzale Roma (2/hour, 25 minutes).

$ Villa Mocenigo Agriturismo, about 10 miles from Marco Polo Airport, is a working, family-run farm in a peaceful rural location between Venice and Padua. Its 10 rooms are furnished with antiques, and regional specialties are served for dinner (Sb-€40-55, Db-€60-74, extra bed-€20-25, dinner about €20/person, air-con, free parking, Via Viasana 59 in Mirano-Venezia, tel. 041-433-246, mobile 335-547-4728, www.villamocenigo.com, info @villamocenigo.com). Email for directions. Buses to Venice leave directly from the villa (3/hour, 45 minutes).

Eating in Venice

While touristy restaurants are the scourge of Venice, the following places are popular with actual Venetians and respect the tourists who happen in. First trick: Walk away from triple-language menus. Second trick: For freshness, eat fish. Most seafood dishes are the catch-of-the-day. (But remember that seafood can be sold by weight—per 100 grams or *etto*—rather than a set price.) Third trick: Eat later. A place may feel really touristy at 19:00, but if you come back at 21:00 it can be filled with locals. Tourists eat barbarically early, which is fine with the restaurants because they fill tables that would otherwise be used only once in an evening.

Near the Rialto Bridge
North of the Bridge

These restaurants are located beyond Campo Santi Apostoli, along the Strada Nova, the main drag going from Rialto toward the train station. Unless otherwise noted, for locations see the map on page 110.

Trattoria da Bepi, bright and alpine-paneled, feels like a classic, where Loris carries on his mother's passion for good, traditional Venetian cuisine. Ask for the seasonal specialties: The seafood appetizer plate and crab dishes are excellent. There's good seating inside and out. If you trust Loris, you'll walk away with a wonderful dining memory (€8-10 pastas, €14-18 *secondi*, €2 cover, Fri-Wed 12:00-14:30 & 19:00-22:00, closed Thu, half a block off Campo Santi Apostoli on Salizada Pistor at #4550, tel. 041-528-5031).

La Cantina is an elegant *enoteca*—both rustic and sophisticated. There's no menu. Rather than cook (there's no kitchen here), Francesco and Andrea prepare wonderful gourmet plates of meat, cheese, and fish. Though it's not cheap (meat-and-cheese plates-€15/person, seafood plates-€30/person), you'll enjoy the very best ingredients paired with fine wines. You can sit inside and watch the preparation scene, or enjoy the parade of passersby from great seats right on the Strada Nova. For a budget alternative, have a *cicchetti* (€1.50) at the bar with a glass of fine wine (closed Sun, facing Campo San Felice on Strada Nova near Ca' d'Oro, tel. 041-522-8258).

Vini da Gigio has an enthusiasm for good food and a traditional Venetian menu (€12-16 pastas, €18-22 *secondi*, no cover, Wed-Sun 12:00-14:30 & 19:00-22:30, closed Mon-Tue, 4 blocks from Ca' d'Oro vaporetto stop on Fondamenta San Felice at #3628a—behind the church on Campo San Felice, tel. 041-528-5140).

Pizzeria Vesuvio serves some of the best and most popular pizza in town. A neighborhood favorite, it has classy indoor seating and pleasant tables outside (long hours, closed Tue, on Rio Terà Farsetti up from San Marcuola vaporetto stop, tel. 041-795-688).

Enoteca Cicchetteria Do Colonne is a local dive with a loyal following and a good spread of *cicchetti* and sandwiches. It's handy for a drink and a snack. While the food is mediocre, the scene (both at the bar and at the tables outside) feels real and is fun (daily, up from San Marcuola vaporetto stop just before Strada Nova on Rio Terà del Cristo, a block from Pizzeria Vesuvio—listed above, see map on page 118, tel. 041-524-0453).

East of the Bridge

Osteria di Santa Marina, serving pricey, near-gourmet cuisine in a dressy dining room, is highly regarded by Venetians. The presentation is impressive, but you feel there's more pretense than love of food. Cheap-eating tricks are frowned on in this elegant, borderline stuffy restaurant (€15 pastas, €25 *secondi*, €3 cover, €75-80 fixed-price meals, Mon-Sat 12:30-14:30 & 19:30-22:00, closed

Sun, reserve for dinner, eat indoors or outdoors on pleasant Campo Marina at #5911, between Rialto Bridge and Campo Santa Maria Formosa, tel. 041-528-5239).

Rosticceria San Bartolomeo is a cheap—if confusing—self-service diner. This throwback budget eatery has a surly staff: Don't take it personally. Take out, grab one of the few tiny tables, or munch at the bar—I'd skip their upper-floor restaurant option (€6-7 pastas, great fried *mozzarella al prosciutto* for €1.50, fruit salad, €1 glasses of wine, prices listed on wall behind counter, no cover and no service charge, daily 9:00-21:30, tel. 041-522-3569). To find it, imagine the statue on Campo San Bartolomeo walking backward 20 yards, turning left, and going under a passageway—now, follow him.

Osteria al Portego is a friendly neighborhood eatery. Carlo serves good meals and excellent *cicchetti*—best enjoyed early, around 18:00 (from 19:00 to 21:00, their six tables are reserved for those ordering from the menu; the *cicchetti* are picked over by 21:00). The *cicchetti* here can make a great meal, but consider sitting down for a dinner from their fine menu. Reserve ahead if you want a table (€13 pastas, €1 glasses of house wine, daily 10:30-15:00 & 18:00-22:00, near Campo Marina at #6015 on Calle Malvasia, tel. 041-522-9038). From Rosticceria San Bartolomeo (listed above), continue over a bridge to Campo San Lio, turn left, and follow Calle Carminati straight 50 yards over another bridge.

Near Campo Santa Maria Formosa: **Osteria alle Testiere** is my top dining splurge in Venice. Hugely respected, Luca and his staff are dedicated to quality, serving up creative, artfully presented market-fresh seafood (there's no meat on the menu), homemade pastas, and fine wine in what the chef calls a "Venetian Nouvelle" style. With only 22 seats, it's tight and homey, with the focus on food and service. They have daily specials, 10 wines by the glass, and one agenda: a great dining experience. This is a good spot to let loose and trust your host. Reservations are a must for their three seatings: 12:30, 19:00, and 21:30 (€20 pastas, €26 *secondi*, plan on spending €50 for dinner, closed Sun-Mon; on Calle del Mondo Novo, just off Campo Santa Maria Formosa, at #5801; tel. 041-522-7220).

Osteria al Mascaron is where I've gone for years to watch Gigi, Momi, and their food-loving band of ruffians dish up rustic-yet-sumptuous pastas with steamy seafood to salivating foodies. The seafood pastas seem pricey at €24-32, but they're meant for two (it's OK to ask for single portions). The €16 *antipasto misto* plate—have fun pointing—and two glasses of wine make a terrific light meal (€2.50 cover, Mon-Sat 12:00-15:00 & 19:00-23:00, closed Sun, reservations smart Fri-Sat; on Calle Lunga Santa Maria Formosa, a block past Campo Santa Maria Formosa, at

#5225; tel. 041-522-5995).

Fast and Cheap Eats: The veggie stand on Campo Santa Maria Formosa is a fixture. For *döner kebabs* (€3.50) and pizza to go (€2/slice), head down Calle Lunga Santa Maria Formosa to **Peter Pan** at #6249 (daily 11:00-24:00).

Rialto Market Area

As with market neighborhoods anywhere, you'll find lots of hardworking hole-in-the walls with a line on the freshest of ingredients and catering to local shoppers needing a quick, affordable, and tasty bite. This area is very crowded by day, nearly empty early in the evening, and packed with young Venetian clubbers later.

Most of these places are informal, serving *cicchetti* and/or light meals. At each place, look for the list of snacks and wine by the glass at the bar or on the wall. When you're ready for dessert, try dipping a Burano biscuit in a glass of strawberry-flavored *fragolino* or another sweet dessert wine. Most bars are closed 15:00-18:00, and offer glasses of house wine for under €1, better wine for around €2.50, and *cicchetti* for €1-2.

My listings below include a strip of trendy places fronting the Grand Canal, a stretch of dark and rustic pubs serving regional tapas, three little places on the market (one for sandwiches, one for seafood, and a cheap and cheery low-end restaurant), a venerable old Venetian diner, and a couple of solid places for pasta and pizza (see map on page 110). Most of these eateries are within 200 yards of the market and each other.

The Bancogiro Stretch:
Five Places Overlooking the Grand Canal

Just past the Rialto Bridge, between Campo San Giacomo and the Grand Canal, this strip of five popular places has some of the best canalside seating in Venice. I call this the "Bancogiro Stretch" (Bancogiro is the strip of old banking buildings they front). Each place has a unique character and formula. During meals, they charge more and limit table seating to those ordering full lunches or dinners; but between meal times you can enjoy a drink or a snack at fine prices. After dinner hours, the Bancogiro Stretch becomes a youthful and trendy night spot. Before or after dinner, this strip is one of the best places in town for a *spritz*.

Here's the rundown (in the order you'd reach them from the Rialto Bridge): **Bar Naranzaria** serves Japanese and Italian dishes (€15-20 plates); **Caffè Vergnano**, your cheapest option—especially during meal times—is just a café with no cover (€9-12 salads, pizzas, and pastas, and a busy microwave oven); **Osteria al Pescador** is a more serious restaurant; **Bar Ristorante Bancogiro** is really good, with the only full kitchen on the strip, romantic dining

The Stand-Up Progressive Venetian Pub-Crawl Dinner

My favorite Venetian dinner is a pub crawl *(giro d'ombra)*—a tradition unique to Venice, where no cars means easy crawling. *(Giro* means stroll, and *ombra*—slang for a glass of wine—means shade, from the old days when a portable wine bar scooted with the shadow of the Campanile bell tower across St. Mark's Square.)

Venice's residential back streets hide plenty of characteristic bars *(bacari)* with countless trays of interesting toothpick munchies *(cicchetti)* and blackboards listing the wines that are uncorked and served by the glass. This is a great way to mingle and have fun with the Venetians. Bars don't stay open very late, and the *cicchetti* selection is best early, so start your evening by 18:00. Most bars are closed on Sunday. For a stress-free pub crawl, consider taking a tour with the charming Alessandro Schezzini (see page 60).

***Cicchetti* bars** have a social stand-up zone and a cozy gaggle of tables where you can generally sit down with your *cicchetti* or order from a simple menu. In some of the more popular places, the crowds happily spill out into the street. Food generally costs the same price whether you stand or sit.

I've listed plenty of pubs in walking order for a quick or extended crawl. If you've crawled enough,

---

upstairs (no canal views), a passion for the best cheese, and good *cicchetti* options at the bar (€16 pastas, €22 *secondi*, nice €15 cheese plate, €3.50 cover, closed Mon, tel. 041-523-2061); and the more modern **Bar Ancora**, which seems to be most popular with the local bar crowd (€13 pastas, €17 *secondi*, *cicchetti* at the bar).

The *Cicchetti* Strip: Four Venetian Tapas Bars

The 100-yard-long stretch starting two blocks inland from the Rialto Market (along Sotoportego dei Do Mori and Calle de le Do Spade) is beloved among Venetian *cicchetti* enthusiasts for its delightful bar munchies, good wine by the glass, and fun stand-up conviviality. These four places serve food all day, but the spread is best at around noon (generally open daily 12:00-15:00 & 18:00-20:00 or 21:00; two of the places I list are closed Sun). While each place offers a fine bar-and-stools scene, you might instead choose to treat one like a restaurant, order from their rustic menu, and grab a table. Scout these four places in advance to help decide which ambience is right for the experience you have in mind. Then most of these bars make a fine one-stop, sit-down dinner.

While you can order a plate, Venetians prefer going one-by-one...sipping their wine and trying this...then give me one of those...and so on. Try deep-fried mozzarella cheese, gorgonzola, calamari, artichoke hearts, and anything ugly on a toothpick. *Crostini* (small toasted bread with a topping) are popular, as are marinated seafood, olives, and prosciutto with melon. Meat and fish (*pesce;* PESH-ay) munchies can be expensive; veggies (*verdure*) are cheap, at about €3 for a meal-sized plate. In many places, there's a set price per food item (e.g., €1.50). To get a plate of assorted appetizers for €8 (or more, depending on how hungry you are), ask for *"Un piatto classico di cicchetti misti da €8"* (oon pee-AH-toh KLAH-see-koh dee cheh-KET-tee MEE-stee dah OH-toh ay-OO-roh). Bread sticks (*grissini*) are free for the asking.

Bar-hopping Venetians enjoy an *aperitivo,* a before-dinner drink. Boldly order a Bellini, a *spritz con Aperol,* or a prosecco, and draw approving looks from the natives.

Drink the house wines. A small glass of house red or white wine (*ombra rosso* or *ombra bianco*) or a small beer (*birrino*) costs about €1. The house keg wine is cheap—€1 per glass, about €4 per liter. *Vin bon,* Venetian for fine wine, may run you from €2 to €6 per little glass. There are usually several fine wines uncorked and available by the glass. A good last drink is *fragolino,* the local sweet wine—*bianco* or *rosso.* It often comes with a little cookie (*biscotti*) for dipping.

pick one, dig in, and drink up.

Bar all'Arco, a bustling one-room joint, is particularly enjoyable for its tiny open-face sandwiches (closed Sun; Francisco, Anne, Matteo).

Osteria ai Storti, with a cool photo of the market in 1909, is run by Alessandro, who speaks English and enjoys helping educate travelers (€8 pastas, €12 *secondi,* 20 yards from Cantina Do Mori—listed below, around the corner on Calle San Matio).

Cantina Do Mori has been famous with locals (since 1462) and savvy travelers (since 1982) as a convivial place for fine wine. They serve a forest of little edibles on toothpicks and *francobolli* (a spicy selection of 20 tiny, mayo-soaked sandwiches nicknamed "stamps"). Go here to be abused in a fine atmosphere—the frowns are part of the shtick (closed Sun).

Cantina Do Spade is expertly run by Francesco, who clearly lists the *cicchetti* and wines of the day (also good for sit-down meals, 30 yards down Calle de le Do Spade from Osteria ai Storti at #860).

Other Good Eateries near the Rialto Market

Pronto Pesce is the perfect place to sample fish while watching the market action. Bruno and Umberto speak English and like to explain what's good. They serve a €10 mixed fish plate with bread (daily from 13:00 until it's sold out) that locals plan their day around. Consider their "express plates" of pasta (€10-12, served daily 12:45-14:15), fish risotto specials, artful fish hors d'oeuvres, and many other fresh fish tidbits. This fancy hole-in-the-wall is fun for a quick bite—eat standing up or take it to go (Tue-Sat 10:00-15:00 & 17:30-19:30, closed Sun-Mon, facing the fish market on Calle de le Becarie o Panataria at #319, tel. 041-822-0298).

Al Mercà ("At the Market"), a few steps away and off the canal, is a lively little nook with a happy crowd, where law-office workers have lunch and young locals gather in the evening for drinks and little snacks. The price list is clear, and I've found the crowd to be welcoming to tourists interested in connecting (stand at the bar or in the square—there are no tables and no interior, Mon-Sat 9:30-14:30 & 18:00-21:00, closed Sun, on Campo Cesare Battisti at #213).

Ristorante Vini da Pinto is a cheap, tourist-friendly eatery with a basic menu and forgettable food at decent prices. It has good service and relaxing outdoor seating (daily, long hours, facing the fish market, tel. 041-522-4599).

Trattoria alla Madonna is a big, bustling, classic Italian eatery with old-school formal waiters, a huge menu, and about a hundred tables. Tour groups find it efficient, and local families have come here for lunch after church for generations. There's no romance—just solid, reliable, traditional food from a menu that hasn't changed since World War II (€10 pastas, €13 *secondi*, €2 cover, closed Tue, tel. 041-522-3824, tucked away on Calle della Madonna, 2 minutes west of Rialto Bridge).

Antica Birraria la Corte is an everyday eatery on the delightful Campo San Polo, between the Rialto Bridge and the Frari Church. Popular for its €8-11 pizza, calzones, and wonderful selection of hearty €10 salads, it fills the far side of this cozy, family-filled square. While the interior is a sprawling beer hall, it's a joy to eat on the square, where metal tables teeter on the cobbles, the wind plays with the paper mats, and children run free (€11-12 pastas, €14-19 *secondi*, €2 cover, daily 12:00-15:30 & 18:00-22:30, Campo San Polo 2168, tel. 041-275-0570, see the map on page 118).

Trattoria Pizzeria al Nono Risorto is unpretentious, inexpensive, youthful, and famous for serving good pizza in a nice setting. You'll sit in a gravelly garden under a leafy canopy, surrounded by Italians enjoying huge €8 salads, pastas, and pizzas, and €12-17 grilled meat or fish dishes (Thu 19:00-22:30, Fri-Tue 12:00-14:30 & 19:00-22:30, closed Wed, reservations smart on weekends; from Rialto fish market, get out your map and walk 3 minutes away from the Rialto to Campo San Cassiano—it's just over the bridge on Sotoportego de Siora Bettina at #2338; tel. 041-524-1169).

Near St. Mark's Square: Dining Fine and Cheap 'n' Cheery

For locations, see the map on page 106.

Ristorante Antica Sacrestia is a classic restaurant where the owner, Pino, takes a hands-on approach to greeting guests. His staff serve creative €33-50 fixed-price meals and a humdrum €20 *turistico* one. You can also order à la carte; try the delightful €21 antipasto spread. This is a good place if you're looking for quality pizza in a lovely setting near St. Mark's for lunch, or a romantic splurge for dinner. Seating is tight in the front room, while the back room is more spacious. There's no cover or service charge, and my readers are welcome to a free *sgroppino* (lemon vodka after-dinner drink) upon request (€12-16 pastas and pizzas, €17-30 *secondi*, Tue-Sun 11:30-15:00 & 18:00-23:00, closed Mon, immediately behind San Zaninovo/Giovanni Novo Church on Calle de la Sacrestia at #4442, tel. 041-523-0749).

"Sandwich Row": On Calle de le Rasse, just steps away from the tourist intensity at St. Mark's Square, is a handy strip I call "Sandwich Row." Lined with sandwich bars, it's the closest place to St. Mark's to get a decent sandwich at an affordable price with a place to sit down (most places open daily 7:00-24:00, €1 extra to sit; from the Bridge of Sighs, head down the Riva and take the second lane on the left). I particularly like **Birreria Forst,** a café that serves a selection of meaty €3 sandwiches with tasty sauce on wheat bread, or made-to-order sandwiches for €4 (daily 10:00-21:00, air-con, rustic wood tables, Calle de le Rasse at #4540, tel. 041-523-0557), and **Bar Verde,** a more modern sandwich bar with fun people-watching views from its corner tables (big €5 sandwiches, splittable €9 salads, fresh pastries, at the end of Calle de le Rasse at #4526, facing Campo Santi Filippo e Giacomo).

Ristorante alla Basilica, just one street behind St. Mark's Basilica, is a church-run, indoor, institutional-feeling place that serves a solid €14 fixed-price lunch (including water) daily from 11:45 to 15:00. It's not self-serve—you'll be seated and can choose a pasta, a *secondi,* and a vegetable side dish off the menu (air-con, on Calle dei Albanesi at #4255, tel. 041-522-0524).

Rizzo, like most Venetian "bars," is an eat-at-the-counter café with sandwiches, pizza, pastries, and other reasonably priced snacks. It stands out for its handy location, north of St. Mark's Square on the main drag of Calle dei Fabbri, and its tiny grocery shelf with yogurt and other quick bites (Mon-Sat 8:00-20:00,

VENICE

Romantic Canalside Settings

Of course, if you want a meal with a canal view, it generally comes with lower quality or a higher price. But if you're determined to take home a canalside memory, these places can be great.

Near the Rialto Bridge: The five places I call the "Bancogiro Stretch" offer wonderful canalside dining and a great place to enjoy a drink and/or a snack between meals or after dinner (see page 125).

Rialto Bridge Tourist Traps: Venetians are embarrassed by the lousy food and aggressive "service" at the string of joints dominating the best romantic, Grand Canal-fringing real estate in town. Still, if you want to linger over dinner with a view of the most famous bridge and the songs of gondoliers oaring by (and don't mind eating with other tourists), this can be enjoyable. Don't trust the waiter's recommendations for special meals. The budget ideal would be to get a simple pizza or pasta and a drink for €15, and savor the ambience without getting ripped off. But few restaurants will allow you to get off that easy. To avoid a dispute over the bill, ask if there's a minimum charge before you sit down (most places have one).

Near the Accademia: **Ristorante/Pizzeria Accademia Foscarini,** next to the Accademia Bridge, offers decent pizzas overlooking the canal with no cover or service charge (see below).

East of St. Mark's Square: **Ristorante alla Conchiglia** and **Trattoria da Giorgio ai Greci,**

closed Sun, on Calle dei Fabbri at #933a, tel. 041-522-3388).

Picnicking: Though you can't picnic on St. Mark's Square, you can legally take your snacks to the nearby Giardinetti Reali, the small park along the waterfront west of the Piazzetta.

In Dorsoduro

All of these recommendations are within a 10-minute walk of the Accademia Bridge (for locations, see the map on page 114). Dorsoduro is great for restaurants and well-worth the walk from the more touristy Rialto and San Marco areas. The first two listings are near the Accademia (and best for lunch). The next two are in Zattere, overlooking the Giudecca Canal. And the last four (best for dinner) are near Campo San Barnaba.

Near the Accademia Bridge

Ristorante/Pizzeria Accademia Foscarini, next to the Accademia several blocks behind St. Mark's, both have a few tables next to one of the smaller canals frequented by gondoliers. While tourist traps, they are lit up like Venetian Christmas trees after dark, and you can't argue with their setting (on Fondamenta San Lorenzo near the Ponte dei Greci bridge).

Overlooking the Giudecca Canal (From Venice Looking Out and from Giudecca Looking In): **Terrazza del Casin dei Nobili** is located in Zattere—on the Venice side of the wide Giudecca Canal—and gets the warm, romantic evening sun (vaporetto: Zattere, see page 132). For a cheaper perch on the same canal, consider **Ae Oche Pizzeria,** described on page 132. **I Figli delle Stelle Ristorante,** on the island of Giudecca, is a classy restaurant offering romantic canalside seating and a wonderful experience (vaporetto: Zitelle, see page 133).

On Fondamente Nove with a View of the Open Lagoon: **Ristorante Algiubagio** offers a good opportunity to eat well while overlooking the lagoon (see page 134).

On Burano: **Trattoria al Gatto Nero** sits on a tranquil canal under a tilting bell tower in the pastel townscape of Burano. If you're touring the lagoon and want to enjoy Burano without the crowds, go late and consider a dinner here (see page 95).

Bridge and Galleria, offers decent €10-11 pizzas in a great canal-side setting. Their toasted *farciti* stuffed sandwich is a local favorite (€6.50 at the table). Though the pizzas may be forgettable, this place is both scenic and practical—on each visit to Venice, I grab a pizza lunch here while I ponder the Grand Canal bustle. They also serve a €10 breakfast (no cover or service charge, May-Oct Wed-Mon 7:00-22:30, Nov-April Wed-Mon 7:00-21:00, closed Tue year-round, on Rio Terà A. Foscarini at #878c, tel. 041-522-7281, Paolo).

Enoteca Cantine del Vino Già Schiavi is much-loved for its €1 *cicchetti* and €3.50 sandwiches (order from list on board). It's also a good place for a €1-2 glass of wine and appetizers. You're welcome to enjoy your wine and finger food at the bar or out on the sidewalk. This is primarily a wine shop with great prices for bottles to go—and plastic glasses for picnickers (Mon-Sat 8:00-20:30, closed Sun, 100 yards from Accademia art museum on San Trovaso canal; facing Accademia, take a right and then a forced left at the canal to the second bridge—it's at #992, tel. 041-523-0034).

In Zattere

Terrazza del Casin dei Nobili takes full advantage of the warm, romantic evening sun. They serve finely crafted, regional special-ties with creativity at tolerable prices. The canalside seating is breezy and beautiful, but comes with the rumble of *vaporetti* from the nearby stop. The interior is bright and hip (good €9-10 piz-zas, €10-13 pastas, €15-25 *secondi*, €2 cover, Fri-Wed 12:00-23:00, closed Thu; from Zattere vaporetto stop, turn left to #924; tel. 041-520-6895, Ruggiero and Eleonora). On Wednesday and Sunday evenings in summer, there's live music nearby on the Zattere promenade.

Ae Oche Pizzeria is playful, with casual tables on the canal and a sprawling pizza parlor interior. It's a hit with young Venetians for its fun atmosphere and good prices (daily 12:00-15:00 & 19:00-23:00, a couple of hundred yards from the Zattere vaporetto stop, tel. 041-520-6601).

On or near Campo San Barnaba

This small square is a delight—especially in the evening. As these places are within a few steps of each other—and the energy and atmosphere can vary—I like to survey the options before choos-ing (although reservations may be necessary to dine later in the evening).

Ristoteca Oniga is all about fresh fish, with a chic-and-shipshape interior, great tables on the square, and the enthusiastic direction of Raffaele. The menu is accessible and always includes a good vegetarian dish (€12 pastas, €20 *secondi*, €2 cover, closed Tue, reservations smart, Campo San Barnaba, tel. 041-522-4410).

Osteria Enoteca Ai Artisti serves well-presented quality dishes either in its tight little wine-snob interior or at six petite, romantic canalside tables. They serve good wines by the glass from their prize-winning list (€15 pastas, €20 *secondi*, closed Sun, Fondamenta della Toletta, tel. 041-523-8944).

Pizzeria al Profeta is a casual place popular for great pizza and steak. It's big, woody interior seems to stoke conviviality, as does its leafy garden out back (€8-10 pizzas, closed Tue; from Campo San Barnaba, walk to the end of Calle Lunga San Barnaba; tel. 041-523-7466).

Enoteca e Trattoria la Bitta is dark and woody, with a soft-jazz bistro feel, tight seating, and a small, forgettable back patio. They serve beautifully presented, traditional Venetian food with—proudly—no fish. Their helpful waitstaff and small, handwritten daily menu are clearly focused on quality, with local ingredients and a "slow food" ethic. As it has an avid following, there are two seatings (19:00 and 21:00), reservations are required, and service can be intense (€10 pastas, €16-25 *secondi*, €2 cover, dinner only, Mon-Sat 18:30-23:00, closed Sun, cash only, just off Campo San Barnaba on Calle Lunga San Barnaba, tel. 041-523-0531, Debora and Marcellino).

In Cannaregio

Cannaregio offers the classic chance in Venice to "get off the beaten path." Beyond the Jewish Ghetto, this neighborhood—more residential than touristic—features a grid layout with straight and spacious canalside walks (part of an expansion from the 1400s). Although it lacks the higgledy-piggledy feel of the older part of town, it's worth the long walk for a look. Rather than come here just for a meal, I'd make time to explore and then grab a bite while in the neighborhood. Cannaregio is most peaceful at sunset. For locations, see the map on page 118.

Osteria L'Orto dei Mori is a chic place serving nicely presented, creative Venetian cuisine. You can eat in the elegant, modern interior or on a great neighborhood square with 10 tables surrounded by a classic scene of wellhead, bridges, and canal (€13 pastas, €25 *secondi*, €3 cover, closed Tue, on Rio della Sensa at Calle Larga, on Campo dei Mori, tel. 041-524-3677).

Osteria Ai 40 Ladroni ("The Forty Thieves") is a characteristic old standby with a few tables on the canal, a rustic interior, and a convivial garden out back. The action is near the bar (€10 pastas, €15 *secondi*, they're proud of their mixed seafood *antipasti*, closed Mon, Fondamenta della Sensa at Calle del Capitello, reserve for dinner, tel. 041-715-736).

Timon Enoteca Osteria, while nothing earthshaking, has a relaxing canalside setting with nice wines and *cicchetti* (a block past the Jewish Ghetto on Fondamenta Ormesini at Calle Malvasia, tel. 041-524-6066).

Osteria al Bacco is simple and rustic, with a typical Venetian menu and a couple of canalside tables (€10 pastas, €16 *secondi*, €2 cover, closed Mon, on Fondamenta Capuzine at Calle Girolamo, tel. 041-721-415).

Elsewhere in Venice

On Giudecca Island: **I Figli delle Stelle Ristorante** offers a delightful dining experience with an excuse to ride the boat from St. Mark's Square across to the island of Giudecca. Simone and his staff artfully serve Venetian classics with a dash of Rome and Puglia and a passion for fish and lamb. While they have inside seating, the reason to venture here is to sit canalside with fine views of Venice across the broad Giudecca Canal and all the water traffic. Reserve ahead to specify "first line" seating along the water, "second line" seating a few steps away, or a table inside (€15 pastas, €22 *secondi*, €3.50 cover, daily 12:30-14:30 & 19:00-22:30, 50 yards from Zitelle vaporetto dock—from San Marco ride line #4.2 or #2, tel. 041-523-0004).

On Fondamente Nove: **Ristorante Algiubagio,** though not cheap, is a good place to eat well overlooking the northern lagoon. The name is a combination of the owners' four names—Alberto, Giulio, Barbara, and Giovanna—who strive to impress visitors with quality, creative Venetian cuisine made using the best ingredients. Reserve a table on the lagoon facing the island of San Michele or in their classy cantina dining room (€16-18 pastas, €24-25 *secondi,* €3.50 cover, €30-42 fixed-price meals, Wed-Mon 12:00-15:00 & 19:00-22:30, closed Tue; on Fondamente Nove, to the left of the vaporetto dock as you face the water, at #5039; tel. 041-523-6084). This is a convenient place to eat if you're taking the vaporetto out to the islands in the lagoon.

Near Campo Santa Maria Nova: **Osteria da Alberto,** with excellent daily specials, €13 seafood dishes, €11 pastas, a good house wine, and a woody and characteristic interior, is one of my standbys. It's smart to reserve at night—I'd request a table in the front (€2 cover, Mon-Sat 12:00-15:00 & 18:30-22:30, closed Sun; on Calle Larga Giacinto Gallina, midway between Campo Santi Apostoli and Campo Santi Giovanni e Paolo, next to Ponte de la Panada bridge at #5401—see map on page 110; tel. 041-523-8153, run by Graziano and Giovanni).

Near the Train Station: There are piles of eateries near the station. The buffet in the station itself is quite good, with peaceful garden seating out back in summer, big €3-4 sandwiches, and slices of pizza for €3. A block away is a small branch of the efficient and economic **Brek,** a popular self-service cafeteria chain (€5 pastas, €7-9 *secondi,* daily 11:30-22:00, head left as you leave the station and walk about 50 yards past the bridge along Rio Terà Lista di Spagna to #124—see map on page 118).

Cheap Meals

The keys to eating affordably in Venice are pizza, *döner kebabs,* bars/cafés, cafeterias, and picnics. *Panini* and *tramezzini* (sandwiches, described on page 32) are sold fast and cheap at bars everywhere and can stave off midmorning hunger. There's a great "sandwich row" of cheap cafés near St. Mark's Square (see page 129). For speed, value, and ambience, you can get a filling plate of typically

Venetian appetizers at nearly any bar. For quick, fun eating, I like small, stand-up mini-meals at *cicchetti* **bars** best (several are recommended in this chapter). Those on a hard-core budget equip their room with a pantry stocked at the market (fruits and veggies are remarkably cheap) or pick up a kebab (or the equivalent), then dine in at picnic prices.

Pizza

While not the home of pizza, Venice is enthusiastic about it. For tourists, a great way to enjoy a delightful Venetian setting at a painless price is to have a pizza with a beer or carafe of house wine at a canalside restaurant. Pizza ranges from €4 for takeout to €6 in a cheap restaurant to €12 in a finest restaurant. Personally, I like to go top-end on pizza: Invest the extra euros, and enjoy a great setting, classy service, and the best quality.

If you're in the mood for pizza, here are my recommendations (all of these places are described in more detail earlier):

For fun-loving, youthful places featuring inexpensive and good pizzas, big pizza parlor-type interiors, and relaxing outdoor seating, try **Pizzeria al Profeta** (with a leafy garden, near Campo San Barnaba), **Ae Oche Pizzeria** (with casual tables overlooking the Giudecca Canal), **Antica Birraria la Corte** (on a big, breezy neighborhood square), or **Trattoria Pizzeria al Nono Risorto** (near the Rialto Bridge with a garden full of tables).

For simple pizza from little more than a bar—with great tables on the Grand Canal under the Accademia Bridge—check out **Ristorante/Pizzeria Accademia Foscarini.**

For top-shelf pizza served in a more formal restaurant setting, consider **Terrazza del Casin dei Nobili** (with elegant seating overlooking the Giudecca Canal), **Ristorante Antica Sacrestia** (in a classy restaurant near St. Mark's Square), and **Pizzeria Vesuvio** (with fine outdoor seating too, near the Jewish Ghetto).

Picnics

The **fruit and vegetable market** that sprawls for a few blocks just past the Rialto Bridge is a fun place to assemble a picnic (best Mon-Sat 8:00-13:00, closed Sun). The adjacent **fish market** is wonderfully slimy (closed Sun-Mon). Side lanes in this area are speckled with fine little hole-in-the-wall munchie bars, bakeries, and cheese shops.

A handy (but often mobbed) **Co-op** supermarket is between St. Mark's and Campo Santa Maria Formosa, on the corner of Salizada San Lio and Calle del Mondo Novo at #5817. It has a great selection of picnic supplies, including packaged salads for €2 (daily 8:30-20:00). The largest supermarket in town is the **Co-op** at Piazzale Roma, next to the vaporetto stop at #504-507 (daily

8:30-20:00). It's an easy walk from the train station, as is the **Billa** supermarket on Campo San Felice (at #3660, along the Strada Nova between the train station and Rialto area, Mon-Sat 8:30-20:00, Sun 9:00-20:00). Another **Billa** supermarket is convenient for those staying in Dorsoduro: It's at #1492, as far west as possible on the Zattere embankment, by the San Basilio vaporetto stop and the cruise-ship docks (Mon-Sat 8:00-20:00, Sun 9:00-19:00).

The only legal place to picnic in public in Venice is Giardinetti Reali, the waterfront park near St. Mark's Square. Eating anywhere outdoors, you may be besieged by pigeons. A picnic in your room can be a better bet.

Gelato

You'll find good *gelaterie* in every Venetian neighborhood, offering one-scoop cones for about €1.50. Look for the words *artigianale* or *produzione propria*, which indicates that a shop makes its own gelato.

The popular, inventive, upscale **Grom** ice-cream chain has two branches in Venice, one on Campo San Barnaba at #2761 (beyond the Accademia Bridge), and another one on the Strada Nova at #3844, not far from the Rialto (cheapest cone-€2.50, both open long hours daily). A competing gourmet gelato shop, **Gelatoteca Suso,** serves up delectable flavors such as fig and nut (daily 12:00-23:00, next to recommended Rosticceria San Bartolomeo on Calle de la Bissa).

On St. Mark's Square, two venerable cafés have gelato counters: **Gran Caffè Lavena** (April-Oct daily until 24:00, no gelato Nov-March, first café to left of the Clock Tower, behind the first orchestra, at #134) and **Todaro** (on the corner of the Piazzetta at #5, near the water and just under the column topped by St. Theodore slaying a crocodile).

Venice Connections

By Train

From Venice by Train to: Padua (2/hour, 30-50 minutes), **Vicenza** (2/hour, 45-75 minutes), **Verona** (2/hour, 1.25-2.25 hours), **Ravenna** (roughly hourly, 3-3.5 hours, transfer in Ferrara or Bologna), **Florence** (hourly, 2-3 hours, often crowded so make reservations), **Bolzano/Dolomites** (to Bolzano about hourly, 3-3.5 hours, transfer in Verona; catch bus from Bolzano into mountains), **Milan** (hourly, 2.5-3.5 hours), **Cinque Terre/Monterosso** (5/day, 6 hours, change in Milan), **Rome** (roughly hourly, 3.75 hours, also 1 direct night train, 7 hours), **Naples** (almost hourly, 5.5-7 hours with changes in Bologna or Rome), **Brindisi** (5/day, 9 hours, change in Rome or Bologna).

International Destinations: Interlaken (5/day, 6-8.5 hours, 2-5 changes, no pleasant overnight option), **Luzern** (7/day, 6.5-7 hours, 1 direct, others change in Milan and Arth-Goldau), **Bern** (3/day, 6 hours, change in Milan or Brig), **Munich** (4-6/day, 7 hours, change in Verona; 1 direct night train, 9 hours; most trains reservable only via www.bahn.de), **Salzburg** (4/day, 6-7 hours, 1-2 changes, 1 direct night train, 7 hours), **Paris** (2/day, 10-12 hours with change in Milan; 1 direct night train, 13.5 hours, important to reserve ahead, no railpasses accepted, www.thello.com), **Ljubljana** (3/day, 7.5 hours—buy ticket at train station, take bus from Piazzale Roma to Villach in Austria, then transfer to train; 1 direct night train, 4 hours, but arrives at 2:00 in the morning), and **Vienna** (3/day, 8 hours—same system as Ljubljana; 1 direct night train, 11 hours).

By Plane

Marco Polo is Venice's main airport. Some budget flights, including Ryanair, use the smaller airport in the nearby city of Treviso. (For more on budget carriers, see page 1100.)

Marco Polo Airport

Venice's small, modern airport is on the mainland shore of the lagoon, six miles north of the city (airport code: VCE). There's one sleek terminal, with a TI (daily 9:00-20:00), car-rental agencies, ATMs, a bank, and a few shops and eateries. For flight information, call 041-260-9260, visit www.veniceairport.com, or ask your hotel.

Getting Between the Airport and Venice

Here are four ways to transfer between the airport and downtown Venice:

- Alilaguna boats—Slowest trip, medium cost
- Water taxis—Fastest trip, most expensive
- Airport shuttle buses to Piazzale Roma (Venice's bus station)—Faster than Alilaguna, slower than water taxi, least expensive
- Private shuttle bus to Piazzale Roma—Medium speed, medium cost

Each of these options is explained in detail (next). An advantage of the Alilaguna boats is that you can reach most of this chapter's recommended hotels very simply, with no changes—except hotels near the train station, which are better served by the bus to

Piazzale Roma.

Both Alilaguna boats and water taxis leave from the airport's boat dock, an eight-minute walk from the terminal. Exit the arrivals hall and turn left, following signs along a paved, level, covered sidewalk (easy for wheeled bags).

When flying out of Venice, allow yourself plenty of time to get to the airport. Water transport can be slow. Plan to arrive at the airport two hours before your flight, and remember that getting there can easily take another two hours. Alilaguna boats are small and can fill up. In an emergency, you can always hop in a water taxi and get to the airport in 30 minutes.

Alilaguna Airport Boats

These boats make the scenic (if slow) journey across the lagoon, each shuttling passengers between the airport and a number of different stops on the island of Venice (€15, €25 round-trip, €1 surcharge if bought on boat, roughly 2/hour, 1-1.5-hour trip depending on destination). Alilaguna boats are not part of the ACTV vaporetto system, so they aren't covered by city transit passes. But they do use the same docks and ticket windows as the regular *vaporetti*.

There are three Alilaguna lines—blue, red, and orange. Stops near recommended hotels include: San Marco, San Zaccaria, Zattere, Guglie, Rialto, and Fondamente Nove. For a full schedule, visit the TI, see the website (www.alilaguna.it), call 041-240-1701, ask your hotelier, or scan the schedules posted at the docks.

From the Airport to Venice: You can buy Alilaguna tickets at the airport's TI, the ticket desk in the terminal, and at the ticket booth at the dock. Any ticket-seller can tell you which line to catch to get to your destination. Boats from the airport run roughly twice an hour from 7:00 to midnight.

From Venice to the Airport: Ask your hotelier what dock and what line is best. Boats start leaving Venice as early as 3:40 in the morning so that passengers can catch early flights. Scope out the dock and buy your ticket in advance to avoid last-minute stress.

Water Taxis

Luxury taxi speedboats zip directly between the airport and the closest dock to your hotel, getting you within steps of your final destination in about 30 minutes. The official price is €110 for up to four people; add €10 for every extra person (10-passenger limit). You may get a higher quote—politely talk it down. A taxi can be a smart investment for small groups and those with an early departure.

From the airport, arrange your ride at the water-taxi desk or with the boat captains lounging at the dock. From Venice, book your taxi trip the day before you leave. Your hotel will help (since they get a commission), or you can book directly with the Consorzio Motoscafi water taxi association (tel. 041-522-2303, www.motoscafivenezia.it).

Airport Shuttle Buses

Buses between the airport and Venice are fast, frequent, and cheap. They take you across the bridge from the mainland to the island, dropping you at Venice's bus station, at the "mouth of the fish" on a square called Piazzale Roma. From there, you can catch a vaporetto down the Grand Canal—convenient for hotels near the Rialto Bridge and St. Mark's Square. If you're staying near the train station, you can walk from Piazzale Roma to your hotel.

Two bus companies run between Piazzale Roma and the airport: ACTV and ATVO. ATVO buses take 20 minutes and go nonstop. ACTV buses make a few stops en route and take slightly longer (30 minutes). They are equally good; just jump on whichever one's leaving next (either bus: €5, runs about 5:00-24:00, 2/hour, just 1/hour early and late, check schedules at www.atvo.it or www.actv.it).

From the Airport to Venice: Both buses leave from just outside the arrivals terminal. Buy tickets from the TI, the ticket desk in the terminal, ticket machines, or the driver. ATVO tickets are not valid on ACTV buses and vice versa. Double-check the destination; you want Piazzale Roma. If taking ACTV, you want bus #5.

From Venice to the Airport: At Piazzale Roma, buy your ticket from the ACTV windows or ATVO office before heading out to the platforms. The newsstand in the center of the lot also sells tickets. ACTV buses leave from platform A1; ATVO buses leave from platforms near the center of the lot and are well-signed.

Private Shuttle Bus

Treviso Car Service offers a private minivan service between Marco Polo Airport and Piazzale Roma or the cruise port (minivan-€55, seats up to 8; car-€50, seats up to 3; mobile 348-900-0700 or 333-411-2840, www.tourleadervenice.com, info@tourleadervenice.com; they also offer tours—see page 60).

Treviso Airport

Several budget airlines, such as Ryanair, Wizz Air, and Germanwings, use Treviso Airport, 12 miles northwest of Venice (airport code: TSF, tel. 042-231-5111, www.trevisoairport.it). Regular ATVO buses take you from the airport to Piazzale Roma (€7, about 2/hour, 1.25 hours, www.atvo.it). Buy your tickets at the ATVO desk in the airport and stamp them on the bus. Treviso

Car Service offers minivan service to Piazzale Roma (minivan–€75, seats up to 8; car–€65, seats up to 3; for contact info, see private shuttle bus listing above).

By Cruise Ship

Most cruise ships visiting Venice dock at Stazione Marittima, which is roughly between the Tronchetto parking garage and Santa Lucia train station. The terminal forms "the fish's mouth" of Venice. Some smaller ships also tie up at the Santa Marta and San Basilio docks, which are south of the main port. The Venice port website has a map of the different docks (www.port.venice.it/en /terminals.html).

Getting into Town

The handy Alilaguna blue line conveniently connects Stazione Marittima directly to St. Mark's Square (San Marco-Giardinetti dock) in just 20 minutes (€8 one-way, €15 round-trip, €3 per big bag, 2/hour in each direction, from cruise port 8:10-16:10, from St. Mark's Square 9:10-16:10; before boarding at the cruise terminal, buy ticket at kiosk in front of building #103 at the top of the harbor; www.alilaguna.it). Because this service is understandably popular, the boats can fill up; if you're arriving on a cruise ship, get to this dock as quickly as possible.

To reach the Grand Canal (and the start of my self-guided Grand Canal Cruise) from Stazione Marittima, hop on the People Mover monorail (€1) to Piazzale Roma. The People Mover station is a five-minute walk inland from the port (you'll see its elevated platform).

If money is no object, you can spring for a water taxi to anywhere in town (€80).

If all of these options are jammed up (as can happen when multiple cruise ships arrive all at once), you can walk to the Grand Canal in about 15 minutes, or all the way to St. Mark's Square in about 45 minutes.

If your ship is docked outside the main port, take vaporetto #2 from San Basilio to get into Venice.

Getting to Marco Polo Airport

The shuttle buses between Piazzale Roma and the airport are quick and inexpensive (described earlier). From the cruise port, take the People Mover monorail to Piazzale Roma to catch the bus. To go from Stazione Marittima to the airport, you can also take a land taxi (€40) or the Alilaguna blue line, though that can take two hours (€15). From the Santa Marta or San Basilio docks, you can take a land taxi to the airport (€40).

NEAR VENICE

Padua • Verona • Ravenna

Venice is just one of many towns in this corner of Italy, but few visitors venture off the lagoon. Several important towns and possible side-trips make zipping directly from Venice to Milan (or Florence) a route strewn with temptation.

Planning Your Time

The towns of Padua, Verona, and Ravenna are great stops. Each gives the visitor a low-key slice of Italy that complements the intensity and earthshaking (yet exhausting) sightseeing thrills of Venice, Florence, and Rome. If you can't make it to all three, pick the one that most inter-

ests you. Art lovers will want to head to Padua to see Giotto's celebrated Scrovegni Chapel, or to Ravenna for its sumptuous Byzantine mosaics. History buffs should see Verona's impressive Roman ruins. Verona is also the pick for star-crossed lovers retracing Romeo and Juliet's steps. Architecture fans could consider a quick trip to Palladio-designed Vicenza, located about halfway between Padua and Verona.

Spending a day as a side-trip from Venice or town-hopping between Venice and Milan is exciting and efficient. Padua and Verona are on the same train line and only 40-60 minutes apart. Connected by two trains per hour, they're easy to visit. Of the towns included in this chapter, only Ravenna (2.5 hours from Padua and 3-3.5 hours from Venice) is not on the main Venice-Milan train line.

If you're Padua-bound, remember that you need to reserve ahead to see the Scrovegni Chapel. Mondays are not ideal for a trip to Verona or Vicenza, when many of the top sights are closed.

Padua

Living under Venetian rule for four centuries seemed only to sharpen Padua's independent spirit. Nicknamed "the brain of Veneto," Padua (Padova in Italian) has a prestigious university (founded in 1222) that hosted Galileo, Copernicus, Dante, and Petrarch. Padua's old town center is elegantly arcaded, filled with students, and sprinkled with surprises. Padua's museums and churches hold their own in Italy's artistic big league—yet its hotels are reasonably priced and the city doesn't feel touristy.

Planning Your Time: Padua in Six Hours

Day-trippers can do a quick but enjoyable blitz of Padua—including a visit to the Scrovegni Chapel—in six hours. Trains from Venice are cheap, take 30-50 minutes, and run frequently. Once in Padua, everything is a 10-minute walk or a quick tram ride apart.

Your Scrovegni Chapel reservation will dictate the order of your sightseeing (see "Reservations" on page 153). When planning your day, also consider these factors: The station has a reliable baggage check desk; the open-air markets are vibrant in the morning, dead in the evening; student life is best at the university late in the day; and the Basilica of St. Anthony is open all day, but the reliquary chapel closes from 12:45 to 14:30.

Ideally, I'd do it this way: 9:00—Market action and sightseeing in town center, 11:00—Basilica of St. Anthony, 13:00—Lunch, 15:00—Scrovegni Chapel tour.

Orientation to Padua

Padua's main tourist sights lie on a north-south axis through the heart of the city, from the train station to Scrovegni Chapel to the market squares (the center of town) to the Basilica of St. Anthony. It's roughly a 10-minute walk between each of these sights, or about 30 minutes from end to end. Padua's wonderful single tram line makes lacing things together quick and easy (see "Getting Around Padua," later).

Tourist Information

Padua has three TIs, though budget woes may cause any or all of these to close in 2012: in the **center** (in the alley behind Caffè Pedrocchi at Vicolo Cappellatto Pedrocchi 9, Mon-Sat 9:00-13:30 & 15:00-19:00, closed Sun, tel. 049-876-7927), at the **train station** (Mon-Sat 9:15-19:00, Sun 9:00-12:30, tel. 049-875-2077), and near the **Basilica of St. Anthony,** across the street on Piazza del Santo (April-Oct daily 9:00-13:30 & 15:00-18:00, closed Nov-March, tel. 049-875-3087).

At any TI, pick up a map, a list of sights, and the seasonal Padova Today entertainment listing. The TI's free I-PADova audio tour is creative and works really well. You can download it for free from their website (www.turismopadova.it) and follow any of the five routes in town. It's smart to print out the audio tour map ahead of time.

The Padova Card gives you entry to all the recommended sights—except the university's Anatomy Theater and the Oratory of St. George—and unlimited tram rides (€16/48 hours, €21/72 hours). The card covers the Scrovegni Chapel, but you still need to make a reservation in advance to enter. While the card is sold at TIs and at included sights, it makes more sense to get it online at the Scrovegni Chapel website (www.cappelladegliscrovegni.it) when you are reserving and paying for your chapel entrance. Then, simply take your confirmation number to the chapel ticket desk before your appointed time, and pick up both your Padova Card and your chapel ticket.

Arrival in Padua

By Train: The efficient station is a user-friendly shopping mall with whatever you might need (Despar supermarket open daily 7:00-21:00). WCs and baggage deposit (€4, daily 6:30-18:00, bring photo ID) are along track 1.

For a travel agency, go to Leonardi Viaggi-Turismo, which is only a block from the station and offers ticketing services for trains, planes, and boats for a small fee (Mon-Fri 9:00-13:00 &

Padua

NEAR VENICE

Padua Key

❶ Hotel Majestic Toscanelli
❷ Albergo Verdi
❸ Hotel Al Fagiano
❹ Hotel Belludi 37
❺ Hotel/Rist. Casa
  del Pellegrino
❻ Hotel Al Santo & Antica
  Trattoria dei Paccagnella
❼ Ostello Città di Padova
❽ Osteria dei Fabbri
❾ Osteria L'Anfora
❿ Enoteca dei Tadi
⓫ Rist. Dante alle Piazze
⓬ La Lanterna Ristorante
⓭ Bar dei Osei
⓮ Brek Cafeteria
⓯ PAM Supermarket & Brek
⓰ Pizzeria Pago Pago
⓱ Zairo Rist./Pizzeria
⓲ Pollodoro la Gastronomica
⓳ Gelato Pretto
⓴ Gelateria Grom (2)
㉑ Caffè Pedrocchi
㉒ Internet Café
㉓ Feltrinelli's Int'l Bookstore
㉔ Launderette & Internet Café
㉕ Buses to Venice &
  Marco Polo Airport

14:30-19:00, Sat 9:00-13:00, closed Sun, up the main drag, Corso del Popolo 14, tel. 049-650-455).

To get downtown, simply hop on Padua's handy **tram** (see "Getting Around Padua," next page). Purchase your ticket (€1.20) at the tobacco shop in the station. Leaving the station, the tram stop is 100 yards to the right at the foot of the bridge. A **taxi** into town (a good option after dark) costs about €8.

By Bus: The bus station is 100 yards east of the train station. Buses arrive here from Venice's Piazzale Roma and Marco Polo Airport.

Helpful Hints

Pronunciation: You say Padua (PAD-joo-wah), they say Padova (PAH-doh-vah).

Internet Access: Befitting a college town where every student has a laptop, Padua has few Internet cafés. The central TI offers free access for 15 minutes (if you fill out a form and show your passport). There's an Internet terminal at Ki-Point (across Via Marsala from recommended launderette listed below, Mon-Fri 9:00-19:00, closed Sat-Sun). You can also walk to **Internet Point** (€2/hour, Mon-Sat 10:00-24:00, Sun 16:00-24:00, 10-minute walk east of the Ponte Romani tram stop at Via Altinate 145, tel. 049-659-292).

Bookstore: Feltrinelli's International Bookstore, with books in English, is a block from the main university building (Mon-Sat 9:00-19:30, Sun 10:00-13:00 & 15:30-19:30, Via San Francesco 7, tel. 049-875-4630).

Launderette: Lavami is modern and entirely automated (daily 7:00-22:00, Via Marsala 22 near intersection with Via dell'Arco, tel. 049-876-4532).

Local Guide: Charming and helpful **Cristina Pernechele** is a great teacher (€110/half-day, mobile 338-495-5453, cristina @pernechele.eu).

Best Gelato: In Padua, my favorite is **Gelato Pretto**. It's the creation of Michelin three-star chefs who are bringing gourmet to gelato. Servers are almost evangelical about their exclusive taste creations (which cost a bit more than the already expensive standard flavors). Ask for several tastes before choosing your favorite (daily 11:00-24:00, Via Umberto 1, tel. 049-875-0776). If eating dinner out, consider letting this be your dessert and enjoy it while strolling the wonderful streets and piazzas of Padua. **Grom** is also popular for its unusual flavors and exotic ingredients. While it's tasty, organic, and green, it's also expensive and part of a big chain—the Starbucks of Italian gelato joints (two locations: Via Roma 101, tel. 049-876-4262; and Piazza dei Signori 33, tel. 049-875-4373).

Getting Around Padua

Ignore the city buses. Visitors should pretend there is only the **tram** and rely on it. There's just one line, which efficiently and without stress connects everything you care about (€1.20 ticket good for 75 minutes; buy tickets from machines at stops, tobacco shops, or newsstands; departs every 8 minutes during the day Mon-Sat, every 20 minutes evenings and Sun). The rubber-wheeled trams run on a single rail.

Before boarding, note the tram direction on posted schedules and above the front window (Pontevigodarzere is northbound, Capolinia Sud is southbound). Stops that matter to tourists include: Stazione FS (train and bus stations), Eremitani (Scrovegni Chapel), Ponti Romani (old town center, market squares, university), Tito Livio (ghetto, old town center, Hotel Majestic Toscanelli), Santo (Basilica of St. Anthony and neighborhood hotels), and Prato della Valle (hostel).

Padua's **hop-on, hop-off tour buses** are not worth the time or money.

Sights in Padua

▲▲▲Basilica of St. Anthony

Friar Anthony of Padua, "Christ's perfect follower and a tireless preacher of the Gospel," is buried here. Construction of this impressive Romanesque/Gothic church (with its Byzantine-style domes) started immediately after St. Anthony's death in 1231. As a mark of his universal appeal and importance in the medieval Church, he was sainted within a year of his death. Speedy. And for nearly 800 years, his remains and this glorious church have

St. Anthony of Padua
(1195-1231)

One of Christendom's most popular saints, Anthony is known as a powerful speaker, a miracle worker, and the finder of lost articles.

Born in Lisbon to a rich, well-educated family, his life changed at age 25, when he saw the mutilated bodies of some Franciscan martyrs. Their sacrifice inspired him to join the poor Franciscans and dedicate his life to Christ. He moved to Italy and lived in a cave, studying, meditating, and barely speaking to anyone.

One day, he joined his fellow monks for a service. The appointed speaker failed to show up, so Anthony was asked to say a few off-the-cuff words to the crowd. He started slowly, but, filled with the Spirit, he became more confident and amazed the audience with his eloquence. Up in Assisi, St. Francis heard about Anthony and sent him on a whirlwind speaking tour.

Anthony had a strong voice, knew several languages, had an encyclopedic knowledge of theology, and could speak spontaneously as the Spirit moved him. It's said he even stood on the shores of the Adriatic Sea in Rimini and enticed a school of fish to listen. Anthony also was known as a prolific miracle worker.

In 1230, Anthony retired to Padua, where he founded a monastery and initiated reforms for the poor. An illness cut his life short at age 36. Anthony said, "Happy is the man whose words issue from the Spirit and not from himself!"

NEAR VENICE

attracted pilgrims to Padua.

Cost and Hours: The basilica is free and open April-Oct daily 6:20-19:45; Nov-March Mon-Fri 6:20-19:00, Sat-Sun 6:20-19:45. The following sights within the basilica close for lunch (12:45-14:30): Chapel of the Reliquaries (free), museum (€3), and Oratory of St. George (€3).

Information: A modest dress code is enforced. An information desk with Anthony-related pamphlets is in the cloisters

(public WC and picnic area nearby, Santo tram stop, tel. 049-822-5652, www.basilicadel santo.org). The information desk has free English pamphlets on the saint's life and the basilica; make a donation in the Chapel of the Reliquaries to get a more-detailed booklet. A TI is on the square facing the church.

Basilica Exterior

St. Anthony looks down from the red-brick facade and blesses all. He holds a book, a symbol of all the knowledge he accumulated as a quiet monk before starting his preaching career.

A golden angel—the weathervane atop the spire—points her trumpet into the wind. (While you can never really be sure with angels, locals say they know it's a woman because she always tells the truth.)

Guarding the church is Donatello's life-size equestrian statue of the Venetian mercenary general, Gattamelata. Though it looks like a thousand other man-on-a-horse statues, it was a landmark in Italy's budding Renaissance—the first life-size, secular, equestrian statue cast from bronze in a thousand years.

The church is technically outside of Italy. When you pass the banisters that mark its property line, you're passing into Vatican territory.

Interior

Entering the basilica, grab a pew in the center of the nave. Sit and appreciate the space. Gaze past the crowds and through the incense haze to Donatello's glorious crucifix rising from the altar, and realize that this is one of the most important pilgrimage sites in Christendom.

Along with the crucifix, Donatello's bronze statues—Mary with Padua's six favorite saints—grace the high altar. Late in his career, the great Florentine sculptor spent more than a decade in Padua (1444-1455), creating the altar and Gattamelata.

St. Anthony's Tomb

Head to the left side of the nave to find the gleaming marble masterpiece that is the focus of the visiting pilgrims—the tomb of St. Anthony. Pilgrims file slowly through this side chapel around the tomb, so focused on the saint that they hardly notice the nine fine marble reliefs. These Renaissance masterpieces were carved during the 16th century, and show scenes and miracles from the life of the saint. As you enjoy each scene, notice the Renaissance mastery of realism and 3-D perspective and the intricate frames, which celebrate life with a burst of exuberance. Note also the vivid faces with their powerful emotions.

First Relief: This depicts St. Anthony receiving the Franciscan tunic. The architectural setting (such as the perspective of the arches on the left and the open door) illustrates the new ability to show depth by using mathematics. The cityscape above is Padua in about 1500.

Second Relief: A jealous husband has angrily stabbed his wife. Notice the musculature, the emotion, and the determination

Basilica of St. Anthony

- CHAPEL OF THE RELIQUARIES
- ❸
- APSE
- NOVITIATE CLOISTER
- 50 Feet
- CHAPEL OF BENEDICTION
- MAIN ALTAR
- CLOISTERS ENTRANCE
- ST. ANTHONY'S TOMB ■ ❷
- CHAPEL OF ST. JAMES
- MAGNOLIA TREE
- **BASILICA**
- N A V E
- MAGNOLIA CLOISTER
- GENERAL CLOISTER
- **CLOISTERS** ❹
- MULTIMEDIA EXHIBIT
- LOW BANISTER
- CLOISTERS ENTRANCE
- WC
- STATUE OF GATTAMELATA
- BASILICA ENTRANCE
- ❶ ☛
- ❺
- MUSEUM CLOISTER (PICNIC AREA)
- MUSEUM
- TOUR BEGINS
- ORATORY OF ST. GEORGE
- *Piazza del Santo*
- To University & Town Center
- LOW BANISTER
- VIA ORTO BOTANICO
- VIA CAPPELLI
- VIA BELLUDI
- To Santo Tram Stop & Prato della Valle
- To Botanic Garden

NEAR VENICE

❶ View of Basilica
❷ St. Anthony's Tomb
❸ Chapel of the Reliquaries
❹ Cloisters
❺ Oratory of St. George

in the faces of loved ones. Above, Anthony intercedes with God to bring the woman back to life.

Third Relief: This panel shows Anthony bringing a young man back to life. Above is the Palazzo della Ragione looking as it still does today.

Fourth Relief: This scene, by the famous Florentine sculptor Jacopo Sansovino, shows three generations: a dead girl, her distraught mom, and a grandmother who's seen it all. A boy on the right realistically leans on his stick. Of course, Anthony will eventually change the mood, but right now it's pretty dire. Above is a relief of this basilica.

Fifth Relief: A fisherman holds a net, having sadly retrieved a drowned boy. The mother looks at Anthony, who blesses and revives the boy. Across from here is the saint's actual tomb. Under thoughtful lighting, it reads *Corpus S. Antonii*. Prayer letters are dropped behind the iron grill.

Sixth Relief: This shows "the miracle of the miser's heart." Anthony's helper dips his hand into a moneylender's side to demonstrate the absence of his heart. At his foot, the square tray with coins and a heart illustrates the scriptural verse "for where your treasure is, there your heart will be also."

Seventh Relief: Anthony holds the foot of a young man who confessed to kicking his mother. Taking a lesson from the saint about respecting your mother a little too literally, the man had cut off his own foot. The hysterical mother implores Anthony's help, and the saint's prayers to God enabled him to re-attach the foot.

Stand in the corner for a moment, observing the passionate devotion that pilgrims and Paduans alike have for Anthony. Touching his tomb or kneeling in prayer, the faithful believe Anthony is their protector—a confidant and intercessor for the poor. And they believe he works miracles. Believers leave offerings, votives, and written prayers to ask for help or to give thanks for miracles they believe Anthony has performed. By putting their hands on his tomb while saying silent prayers, pilgrims show devotion to Anthony and feel the saint's presence.

Popular Anthony is the patron saint of dozens of things: travelers, amputees, donkeys, pregnant women, infertile women, and flight attendants. Most pilgrims ask for his help in his role as the "finder of things"—from lost car keys to a life companion. You'll see dozens of photos posted on his tomb in prayer or as thanks, including many of fervently wished-for newborns.

Eighth Relief: This scene makes the point that—unlike St. Francis, who was a rowdy youth—Anthony was holy even as a toddler. He tosses the glass (representing his faith), which, rather than shattering, breaks the marble floor.

Ninth Relief: A jealous husband (the bearded man behind Anthony) accuses his wife of cheating. The wife asks Anthony to identify her baby's father. Anthony asks the child, who speaks and says that the husband is his real dad and his mother was not messing around. Everyone is relieved—whew!

Stand in the corner and take a moment to appreciate how the entire chapel is an integrated artistic wonder. Now leave the chapel (between scenes eight and nine) and step into the oldest part of the church—the original chapel, where Anthony was first buried in 1231. To the left of the altar, note the fine (and impressively realistic for the 14th century) view of medieval Padua, with this church outside the wall (finished by 1300 and looking like it does today).

Below the cityscape, in a circa-1380 fresco, Anthony on his cloud promises he'll watch over Padua.

As you exit this chapel, you'll notice many tombs nearby. People wanted to be buried near a saint. If you could afford it, this was about the best piece of real estate a dead person could want. (The practice was ended with Napoleonic reforms in 1806.)

Chapel of the Reliquaries

Continue your circuit of the church by going behind the altar into the apse, to the Chapel of the Reliquaries. The most prized relic is in the glass case at center stage—Anthony's tongue. When Anthony's remains were exhumed 32 years after his death (in 1263), his body had decayed to dust, but his tongue was found miraculously unspoiled and red in color. How appropriate for the great preacher who, full of the Spirit, couldn't stop talking about God.

Start under the dome in front of the staircase at St. Anthony's holy, and holey, tunic *(tonaca)*. Then work clockwise around the chapel: His rough-hewn wood coffin is on the left wall. His pillow—a comfy rock—is up the stairs (chest level in first glass case). The center display case contains (top to bottom) the saint's lower jaw with all his teeth impressively intact *(il mento,* located about 8 feet high), his uncorrupted tongue *(lingua,* at about eye level), and, finally, his vocal chords *(apparato vocale,* at about waist level) discovered intact when his remains were examined in 1981. In the last display case, a fragment of the True Cross *(la croce)* is held in a precious crucifix reliquary.

Above the relics, decorating the cornice, is the *Glorification of St. Anthony.* In this Baroque fantasy—made in 1691 of carved marble and stucco, a cloud of angels and giddy *putti* tumble to the left and right in jubilation as they play their Baroque-era musical instruments to celebrate Anthony's arrival in heaven.

Leaving this relic chapel, continue circling the apse. You'll come to the Chapel of Benediction. Here, under a powerful modern fresco of the Crucifixion (by Pietro Annigoni, who died in 1982), a priest is waiting to bless anyone who cares to be blessed.

Next is a door leading to the cloisters. Before heading out, walk just beyond this passage to the Chapel of St. James (exactly opposite the tomb of St. Anthony). This chapel features an exquisite 14th-century fresco by Altichiero da Zevio. Study the vivid commotion around the Crucifixion, clearly inspired by Giotto (this was done 70 years after the Scrovegni Chapel). The faces are real—right off the streets of 14th-century Padua. Next, head out into the cloisters.

Cloisters

From the right side of the nave as you face the altar, follow signs to *chiostro;* from outside, find signs on the right side of the church. The main cloister is dominated by an exceptionally bushy magnolia tree, planted in 1810 (the magnolia tree was exotic for Europe when it was imported from America in 1760). Also in the cloister are the graves of the most illustrious Padovans, such as Gabriel Fallopius, the

scientist who gave his name to his discovery, the Fallopian tube. When Napoleon decreed that graves should be moved out of cities, this once grave-covered courtyard was cleared of tombstones. But the bodies were left in the ground, perhaps contributing to the magnolia tree's fecundity. Today the tree remains an explosion of life.

Wander around the series of three cloisters. Picnic tables invite pilgrims and tourists to enjoy meals within the solitude of one of the cloisters (it's covered and suitable even when rainy, also has WCs). The **multimedia exhibit** on the life of St. Anthony is kitschy, as pilgrimage multimedia exhibits tend to be (30 minutes, free, you move three times as you use headphones to listen to the story of each tableau).

At the far end, a fascinating little **museum** is filled with votives and folk art recounting miracles attributed to Anthony. The abbreviation *PGR* that you'll see on many votives stands for *per grazia ricevuta*—for answered prayers.

Oratory of St. George

The small but sumptuous Oratory of St. George faces the little square in front of the basilica. The oratory ("ora" means prayer) is not actually a church, though it's certainly a fine place to pray— it's filled with vivid, circa-1370 frescoes showing scenes not of Anthony, but from the life of St. Catherine. Because many lovers credit St. Anthony with finding them their partners—and this is the closest place to St. Anthony where you can be married—it's popular for weddings. While you can see it all from the door, paying the entry fee lets you sit and enjoy this peaceful spot.

Near the Basilica

Prato della Valle—The square is 150 yards southwest of the basilica (down Via Luca Belludi). Once a Roman theater and later Anthony's preaching grounds, this square claims to be the largest in Italy. It's a pleasant, 400-yard-long, oval-shaped piazza with fountains, walkways, dozens of statues of Padua's eminent citizens, and grass. It's also a lively **market** scene: fruit and vegetables

(Mon-Fri 8:00-13:00), clothing, shoes, and household goods (Sat 8:00-19:00), and antiques (third Sun 8:00-19:00). This place is often busy with special events and festivals. Ask at the TI or your hotel if anything's going on at Prato della Valle.

Botanic Garden (Orto Botanico)—Green thumbs appreciate this nearly five-acre botanical garden, which contains the university's vast collection of rare plants. Founded in 1545 to cultivate medicinal plants, it's the world's oldest academic botanical garden still in its original location. A visitors center—in a little cottage to the right of the garden's entrance—houses models of the garden's layout and computer terminals that describe the history and composition of the garden in English.

Cost and Hours: Garden—€4; April-Oct daily 9:00-13:00 & 15:00-19:00; Nov-March Mon-Sat 9:00-13:00, closed Sun; entrance 150 yards south of Basilica of St. Anthony—with your back to the facade, take a hard left, Santo tram stop, tel. 049-827-2119, www.ortobotanico.unipd.it.

▲▲▲Scrovegni Chapel (Cappella degli Scrovegni)

Wallpapered with Giotto's beautifully preserved cycle of nearly 40 frescoes, this glorious, renovated chapel holds scenes depicting the

lives of Jesus and Mary. You must make reservations in advance to see the chapel (see "Reservations," below).

Cost and Hours: €13 combo-ticket with the Civic Museums (includes the worthwhile Pinacoteca and Multimedia Room). The chapel is open March-Oct Mon 9:00-19:00, Tue-Sun 9:00-22:00; Nov-Feb daily 9:00-19:00. When the Civic Museums are closed—after 19:00 and on Monday—tickets are €8.

Entry Times: Every 15 minutes (on the quarter-hour), groups of 25 visitors are admitted for a 15-minute video presentation in an anteroom, followed by 15 minutes in the chapel itself. After 19:00, visitors can enter every 20 minutes and get 20 minutes inside (last entry at 21:40).

Reservations: To protect the paintings from excess humidity,

Giotto di Bondone
(c. 1267-1337)

Though details of his life are extremely sketchy, we know that as a 12-year-old shepherd boy, Giotto was discovered painting pictures of his father's sheep on rock slabs. He became the wealthiest and most famous painter of his day. His achievement is especially remarkable because painters at that time weren't considered anything more than craftsmen and weren't expected to be innovators.

After making a name for himself by painting the life of St. Francis frescoes in Assisi, the Florentine tackled the Scrovegni Chapel (c. 1303-1305). At age 35, he was at the height of his powers. His scenes were more realistic and human than anything done for a thousand years. Giotto didn't learn technique by dissecting corpses or studying the mathematics of 3-D perspective; he had innate talent. And his personality shines through in the humanity of his art.

The Scrovegni frescoes break ground by introducing nature—rocks, trees, animals—as a backdrop for religious scenes. Giotto's people, with their voluminous, deeply creased robes, are as sturdy and massive as Greek statues, throwbacks to the Byzantine icon art of the Middle Ages. But these figures exude stage presence. Their gestures are simple but expressive: A head tilted down says dejection, an arm flung out indicates grief, clasped hands indicate hope. Giotto created his figures not just by drawing outlines and filling them in with single colors; he filled the outlines in with subtle patchworks of lighter and darker shades, and in doing so pioneered modern modeling techniques. Giotto's storytelling style is straightforward, and anyone with knowledge of the episodes of Jesus' life can read the chapel like a comic book.

The Scrovegni represents a turning point in European art and culture—away from scenes of heaven and toward a more down-to-earth, human-centered view.

only 25 people are allowed in the chapel at a time. Prepaid reservations are required. It's easiest to reserve online at www.cappella degliscrovegni.it (website also sells Padova Cards—described on page 143, tel. 049-201-0020).

Without a reservation, it's sometimes possible to buy a ticket for the same day at the ticket office (especially for single visitors), but don't count on it. If you neglected to make a reservation and really want to see the chapel, drop by and see if anything is available (a Post-it note stuck to the desk indicates the next available entry time). Local tour guides, who have to book blocks of tickets, are generally happy to unload unneeded tickets to those who ask.

Helpful Hint: If you packed binoculars, bring them along for a better—and more comfortable—view of the uppermost frescoes.

Getting There: From the train station, it's a 10- to 15-minute walk, or a quick, two-stop tram ride to the Eremitani stop. You'll enter through the Civic Museums building, where you'll find the ticket counter and mandatory bag check.

Getting In: You'll be instructed to pick up your tickets at the ticket office at least an hour before your visit. In practice, I've found that you can arrive later, but give yourself a minimum of 30 minutes to weather any commotion at the desk. Present your confirmation number at the ticket desk, verify your time, pick up your ticket, and check any bags or purses.

While waiting for your reserved time, blitz the Pinacoteca and Multimedia Room (described later). Read the chapel description (below) before you enter, since you'll only have a short time in the chapel itself.

The chapel is well-signed: From the ticket counter, go outside and walk 100 yards down the path. Be at the chapel doors at least five minutes before your scheduled visit. The doors are automatic, and if you're even a minute late, you'll forfeit your visit and have to rebook and repay to enter.

At your appointed time, you first enter an anteroom to watch a very instructive 15-minute video (with English subtitles) and to establish humidity levels before continuing into the chapel. No photos are allowed. Although you have only a short visit inside the chapel, it is divine. You're inside a Giotto time capsule, looking back at an artist ahead of his time.

Background

Painted by Giotto and his assistants from 1303 to 1305 and considered by many to be the first piece of modern art, this work makes it clear: Europe was breaking out of the Middle Ages. A sign of the Renaissance to come, Giotto placed real people in real scenes, expressing real human emotions. These frescoes were radical for their 3-D nature, lively colors, light sources, emotion, and humanism.

The chapel was built out of guilt for white-collar crimes. Reginaldo degli Scrovegni (skroh-VEHN-yee) charged sky-high interest rates at a time when the Church forbade the practice. He even caught the attention of Dante, who placed him in one of the levels of hell in his *Inferno*. When Reginaldo died, the Church denied him a Christian burial. His son Enrico tried to buy forgiveness for his father's sins by building this superb chapel. After

NEAR VENICE

Scrovegni Chapel

❶ Joachim Driven from the Temple
❷ Joachim Returns to the Sheepfold
❸ Mary's Birth Announced to St. Anne
❹ Birth of Jesus
❺ Slaughter of the Innocents
❻ Jesus Astounding the Scholars
❼ Jesus Drives Out the Money Changers
❽ Last Supper
❾ Betrayal of Christ
❿ Jesus Beaten and Humiliated
⓫ Jesus Carrying the Cross
⓬ Lamentation (Deposition)
⓭ Last Judgment

seeing Giotto's frescoes for the Franciscan monks of St. Anthony, Enrico knew he'd found the right artist to decorate the interior (and, he hoped, to save his father's soul). The Scrovegni residence once stood next to the chapel, but was torn down in 1824.

Giotto's Frescoes in the Scrovegni Chapel

Giotto painted the entire chapel in 200 working days over two years, but you'll get only 15 minutes to see it.

As you enter the long, narrow chapel, look straight to the far end—the rear wall is covered with Giotto's big *Last Judgment*. Christ in a bubble is flanked by crowds of saints and by scenes of heaven and hell. This is the final, climactic scene of the story told in the chapel's 38 panels—the three-generation history of Jesus, his mother Mary, and Mary's parents.

The story begins with Jesus' grandparents, on the long south wall (with the windows) in the upper-left corner. ❶ In the first frame, a priest scolds the man who will be Mary's father (Joachim, with the halo) and kicks him out of the temple for the sin of being childless. ❷ In the next panel to the right, Joachim returns dejectedly to his sheep farm. ❸ Meanwhile (next panel), his wife is in the bedroom, hearing the miraculous news that their prayers have been answered—she'll give birth to Mary, the mother of Jesus.

From this humble start, the story of Mary and Jesus spirals clockwise around the chapel, from top to bottom. The top row (both south and north walls) covers Mary's birth and life.

Jesus enters the picture in the middle row of the south (windowed) wall.

❹ The first frame shows his birth in a shed-like manger. In the next frame, the Magi arrive and kneel to kiss his little toes. Then the child is presented in the tiny temple. Fearing danger, the family gets on a horse and flees to Egypt. ❺ Meanwhile, back home, all the baby boys are slaughtered in an attempt to prevent the coming of the Messiah *(Slaughter of the Innocents).*

Spinning clockwise to the opposite (north) wall, you see (in a badly damaged fresco) ❻ the child Jesus astounding scholars with his wisdom. Next, Jesus is baptized by John the Baptist. His first miracle, at a wedding, is turning jars of water into wine. Next, he raises a mummy-like Lazarus from the dead. Riding a donkey, he enters Jerusalem triumphantly. ❼ In the temple, he drives out the wicked money changers.

Turning again to the south wall (bottom row), we see scenes from Jesus' final days. ❽ In the first frame, he and his followers gather at a table for a Last Supper. Next, Jesus kneels humbly to wash their feet. ❾ He is betrayed with a kiss and arrested. Jesus is tried. ❿ Then he is beaten and humiliated.

⓫ Finally (north wall, bottom row), he is forced to carry his own cross, is crucified, and prepared for burial, while his followers mourn (⓬ *Lamentation*). Then he is resurrected and ascends to heaven, leaving his disciples to carry on.

❸ The whole story concludes on the rear wall, where Jesus reigns at the Last Judgment. The long south wall (ground level) features the Virtues that lead to heaven, while the north wall has the (always more interesting) Vices. And all this unfolds beneath the blue, starry sky overhead on the ceiling.

Some panels deserve a closer look:

Joachim Returns to the Sheepfold (south wall, upper left, second panel): Though difficult to appreciate from ground level, this oft-reproduced scene is groundbreaking. Giotto—a former shepherd himself—uses nature as a stage, setting the scene in front of a backdrop of real-life mountains, and adding down-home details like Joachim's jumping dog, frozen in midair.

Betrayal of Christ, a.k.a. *Il Bacio*, "The Kiss" (south wall, bottom row, center panel): Amid the crowded chaos of Jesus' arrest, Giotto focuses our eyes on the central action, where Judas ensnares Jesus in his yellow robe (the color symbolizing envy), establishes meaningful eye contact, and kisses him.

Lamentation, a.k.a. *Deposition* (north wall, bottom row, middle): Jesus has been crucified, and his followers weep and wail over the lifeless body. John the Evangelist spreads his arms wide and shrieks, his cries echoed by anguished angels above. Each face is a study in grief. Giotto emphasizes these saints' human vulnerability.

Last Judgment (big west wall): Christ in the center is a glorious vision, but the real action is in hell (lower right). Satan is a Minotaur-headed ogre munching on sinners. Around him, demons give sinners their just desserts in a scene right out of Dante...who was Giotto's friend and fellow Florentine. Front and center is Enrico Scrovegni, in a violet robe (the color symbolizing penitence), donating the chapel to the Church in exchange for forgiveness of his father's sins.

Before the guard scoots you out, take a look at the actual altar. Though Enrico's father's tomb is lost, Enrico Scrovegni himself is in the tomb at the altar. The three statues are by Giovanni Pisano—Mary (in the center) supports baby Jesus on her hip with a perfectly natural, maternal, S-shape. She's flanked by anonymous deacons.

Civic Museums (Musei Civici Agli Eremitani)

The Eremitani, the building next to the Scrovegni Chapel, was once an Augustinian hermit's monastery and now houses three museums. While you can skip the ground-floor Archaeological Museum (with Roman and Etruscan artifacts and no English descriptions), the Pinacoteca and the Multimedia Room are worth visiting. Another part of the museum, Palazzo Zuckermann, is across the street.

Cost and Hours: €13 combo-ticket with Scrovegni Chapel,

€10 without the chapel. The Pinacoteca, Archaeological Museum, and Palazzo Zuckermann are open Tue-Sun 9:00-19:00, closed Mon. The Multimedia Room is open daily 9:00-19:00. Palazzo Zuckerman is open Tue-Sun 10:00-19:00, closed Mon. No photos are allowed, and there's a mandatory and free bag check. The museums are on Piazza Eremitani (Eremitani tram stop, Eremitani tel. 049-820-4551, Palazzo Zuckerman tel. 049-820-5664).

Pinacoteca

The museum's highlight is upstairs, in the Pinacoteca (picture gallery). The collection has 13th- to 18th-century paintings by Titian, Tintoretto, Giorgione, Tiepolo, Veronese, Bellini, Canova, Guariento, and other Veneto artists. But I'd make a beeline for the room with the Giotto crucifix. Ask for it: *"La Croce di Giotto?"*

Originally hung in the Scrovegni Chapel between the Scrovegni family's private zone and the public's worshiping zone, this crucifix is painted on wood by Giotto. If you actually sit on the floor and look up, the body really pops. The adjacent "God as Jesus" piece was the only painting in the otherwise frescoed chapel. (This is hung here because of preservation concerns. Its copy is the only non-original art in the chapel.) Studying these two masterpieces affirms Giotto's greatness.

Behind the crucifix room is a collection of 14th- and 15th-century art. While the works here are exquisite—and came well after Giotto—they're clearly not as modern.

Multimedia Room

The Multimedia Room, dedicated to taking a closer look at the Scrovegni Chapel, is adjacent to the Civic Museum (in the same building). To head straight from the museum entrance to the Multimedia Room, use the entrance to the right of the main entry, step into the courtyard, make a sharp right, and head down the stairs.

Rows of computer screens offer a virtual Scrovegni Chapel visit and provide cultural insights into daily life in the Middle Ages. There are explanations of the individual panels, Giotto's fresco technique, close-ups of the art, and a description of the restoration. They show a 12-minute video (English headphones available) that is similar—but not identical—to the one that precedes your chapel visit. For me, it's worth just taking some time to enjoy a second video that features a mesmerizing, slow montage of close-ups of the Giotto frescoes.

Between the museum and the chapel are the scant remains of Roman Padua. The remnants are from the wall of an arena with nicely fitting pipes that once channeled water so that the arena could be flooded for special spectacles.

NEAR VENICE

Palazzo Zuckermann

This little-visited wing of the Civic Museum, just across a busy street, is included in the same ticket. Its first two floors offer a commotion of applied and decorative arts—such as clothes, furniture, and ceramics—from the Venetian Republic (1600s-1700s). On the top floor, the Bottacin collection takes you to the 19th century with coins and delightful (but no-name) pre-Impressionist paintings.

More Sights in the Center

Palazzo della Ragione—This grand 13th-century palazzo, commonly called *il Salone* (great hall), once held the medieval law courts. The first floor consists of a huge hall—265 feet by 90 feet— that was at one time adorned with frescoes by Giotto. A fire in 1412 destroyed those paintings, and the palazzo was redecorated with the 15th-century art you see today: a series of 333 frescoes depicting the signs of the zodiac, labors of the month, symbols representing characteristics of people born under each sign, and, finally, figures of saints to legitimize the power of the courts in the eyes of the Church.

The hall is topped with a hull-shaped roof, which helps to support the structure without the use of columns—quite an architectural feat in its day, considering the building's dimensions. The curious black stone in the corner opposite the big wooden horse is the "Stone of Shame," which was the seat of debtors being punished during the Middle Ages. It was introduced as a compassionate alternative to prison by St. Anthony in 1230. Instead of being executed or doing prison time, debtors sat upon this stone, surrendered their possessions, and denounced themselves publicly before being exiled from the city. The computer kiosks (choose "English") provide excellent information with entertaining videos.

Cost and Hours: €4, Feb-Oct Tue-Sun 9:00-19:00; Nov-Jan Tue-Sun 9:00-18:00; closed Mon year-round, enter through the east end of Piazza delle Erbe and go up the long staircase, Ponti Romani tram stop, tel. 049-820-5006. The WCs are through the glass doors at the opposite end of the hall from the wooden horse.

▲▲**Market Squares: Piazza delle Erbe, Piazza della Frutta, and Piazza dei Signori**—The stately Palazzo della Ragione (described above) provides a dramatic backdrop for Padua's almost exotic-feeling produce market that fills the surrounding squares, **Piazza delle Erbe** and **Piazza della Frutta**, each morning and all day Saturday (Mon-Fri roughly 8:00-13:00, Sat 8:00-19:00, closed Sun). Second only to the produce market in Italy's gastronomic capital of Bologna, this market has been renowned for centuries as having the freshest and greatest selection of herbs, fruits, and vegetables. The presentation is an art in itself. As you wander, appreciate the local passion for good food: Residents can tell the month by the seasonal selections, and merchants share recipe tips with shoppers. You'll notice some Sri Lankans working here (Italy took in many refugees from Sri Lanka's civil war).

Don't miss the ground floor of the Palazzo della Ragione. Wandering through this H-shaped arcade—where you'll find various butchers, *salumerie* (delicatessens), cheese shops, bakeries, and fishmongers at work—is a sensuous experience. For centuries, this was a market for luxury items (furs, fine cloths, silver, and gold—notice the imposing iron gates used to lock it up each evening). Then, the devastating loss to the French in 1797 marked the end of good times and, with no market for luxury items, the arcade was used to sell perishables—meat and cheese—out of the sun.

Students gather in the squares after the markets have closed, spilling out of colorful bars and cafés—drinks in hand. Pizza by the slice is dirt cheap. A typical snack stand selling all kinds of fresh, hot, and ready-to-eat seafood appetizers sets up in Piazza della Frutta between 17:00 and 20:30 (daily except Sun). Belly up to the bar with your drink and try whatever Massimiliano's serving.

Just a few steps away is a classic old pharmacy that dates to 1841. **Ai Due Cantini d'Oro,** stocking retail items like it did before World War II, sells odd foods and specialty items for every dietary need (Piazza della Frutta 46, tel. 049-875-0623).

Piazza dei Signori, just a block away, is a busy clothing market in the morning and the most popular gathering place in the evening for students out for a drink. The circa-1400 clock decorates the former palace of the ruling family. The aggressive lion with unfurled wings on the column was a reminder of the Venetian determination to assert its control. Today

that lion can be seen as representing the Veneto region's independence from Rome: Italy's north (Veneto and Lombardy) is tired of subsidizing the south. Grumbling about this issue continues to stir talk of splitting the country.

Drinking a *Spritz* with the Student Crowd—Each early evening, before dinner, students enliven Padua by enjoying a convivial drink in their favorite places. Piazza dei Signori (described earlier) is more trendy, with people of all ages, while the scene on Piazza della Erbe is more bohemian and alternative. Or you could sit in front of the university, nurse your drink, and watch the graduates get roasted with their crazy gangs of friends (see "Graduation Antics in Padua" sidebar, later).

The drink of choice is a *spritz,* an aperitif generally made with Campari (a red liqueur infused with bitter herbs), white wine, and sparkling water, and garnished with a blood-orange wedge. While men opt for the heavier and more bitter Campari *spritz*, most Paduan women seem to prefer a sweeter and lighter *spritz* made with Aperol (an orange-flavored liqueur with less alcohol content).

Grab a table and be part of the scene. This is a classic opportunity to enjoy a real discussion with smart, English-speaking students who see tourists not as pests, but as interesting people from far away. For an instant conversation starter, ask about the current political situation in Italy, the right-wing party's policy on immigrants, or the cultural differences between Italy's north and south.

Caffè Pedrocchi—The white-columned, Neoclassical Pedrocchi building is much more than just a café on the ground floor. A complex of meeting rooms and entertainment venues, it stirs the Italian soul (at least, patriotic Italian souls). Built in 1831 during the period of Austrian rule, Caffè Pedrocchi was inaugurated for the fourth Italian Congress of Scientists, which convened during the mid-19th century to stir up nationalistic fervor as Italy struggled to become a united nation. As a symbol of patriotic hope, it was the target (no surprise) of a student uprising plot in 1848. You can still see a bullet hole (framed in silver) in the wall of the Sala Bianca, where one of the insurgents was killed.

Each of the café's three dining rooms is decorated and furnished in a different color: red, white, or green—representing the colors of the Italian flag. In the outer, unheated Sala Verde (Green Room), people are welcome to sit and relax without ordering anything or having to pay. This is where Italian gentlemen read their newspapers and gather with friends to chat about the old days. In the red room, the clock over the bar is flanked by marble reliefs of morning and night, signaling that it was once open 24 hours a day (in the 19th century). The maps of the hemispheres with south up top reflect the anti-conventional spirit of the place. The menu offers teahouse fare, including salads, sandwiches, and the writer Stendhal's beloved *zabaglione,* a creamy custard made with *marsala* wine. Remember that in Italy, you can order a coffee at the bar of any place, no matter how fancy, and pay the same low, government-regulated price (Sun-Tue 9:00-21:00, Wed-Sat 9:00-23:00, two entrances across from Via VIII Febbraio 14 and 20 near Ponti Romani tram stop, tel. 049-878-1231).

Piano Nobile: This upper, "noble floor" of the Pedrocchi building is more elaborate. The rooms are all in different styles, such as Greek, Etruscan, or Egyptian, with good English descriptions throughout. These rooms were intended to evoke memories of the glory of past epochs, which a united Italy had hopes of reliving.

Museum of the Risorgimento: The Piano Nobile hosts a small museum that traces Padua's role in Italian history, from the downfall of the Venetian Republic (1797) to the founding of the Republic of Italy (1948). Exhibits, a few with English descriptions, include uniforms, medals, weaponry, old artillery, Fascist propaganda posters, and a 30-minute propagandistic video (in Italian, but mostly fascinating footage without narration). The video, played on demand, is a "Luce" production (meaning a Mussolini production) and features great scenes of the town in the 1930s, including clips of Il Duce's visit and later WWII bombardments. The war and propaganda posters in the last room are haunting. An old woman pleads to those who might question the Fascist-driven war effort: "Don't betray my son." Another declares, "The Germans are truly our friends." And another asks, "And you...what are you doing?" (€4, Tue-Sun 9:30-12:30 & 15:30-18:00, closed Mon, tel. 049-878-1231). To reach the Piano Nobile, find the stairway in the far wing of the café building.

▲**Baptistery**—This richly frescoed little building was originally the private chapel of Padua's ruling family. Then, in 1405, Venice took over, killing the family, and making the building a baptistery. Located next to Padua's skippable Duomo, the Baptistery was frescoed (c. 1370) by Giusto de' Menabuoi.

While created 70 years after Giotto, the Baptistery feels older. Because the artist was working for a private family, he needed to be politically correct and not threaten or offend the family's allies, especially the Church. While still mind-blowing, the Baptistery's art seems relatively conservative compared to Giotto's Scrovegni Chapel. Giotto, supported by the powerful Scrovegni family and the Franciscans, could get away with being more progressive and bold.

The Baptistery's complex design must have made perfect and

cohesive sense to the faithful in centuries past. Almighty Christ is in majesty on top, while approachable Mary and the multitude of saints provide the devout with access to God. Find the world as it was known in the 14th century (the disk below Mary's feet). It kicks off a cycle of scenes illustrating creation (clockwise from the creation of Adam). The four evangelists (Matthew, Mark, Luke, and John) with their books and symbols fill the corners. A vivid crucifixion scene faces a gorgeous annunciation. And the altar niche features a dim, blue-toned, literal Apocalypse from the book of Revelation.

Cost and Hours: €2.80, daily 10:00-18:00.

University of Padua—The main building of this prestigious university, known as Palazzo Bò, is adjacent to Caffè Pedrocchi. Founded in 1222, it's one of the first, greatest, and most progressive universities in Europe. Back when the Church controlled university curricula, a group of professors and students broke free from the University of Bologna to create this liberal school, which would be independent of Catholic constraints and accessible to people of alternative faiths.

A haven for free thought, the university attracted intellectuals from all over Europe, including the great astronomer Copernicus, who realized here that the universe didn't revolve around him. And Galileo—notorious for disagreeing with the Church's views on science—called his 18 years on the faculty here the best of his life.

Cost and Hours: While it's free to visit the university (weekdays and Sat mornings only), you must sign up for a 30-minute tour (€5) to see the Anatomy Theater. Only 30 people may enter at a time. Tours run three times a day (March-Oct Mon, Wed, and Fri at 15:15, 16:15, and 17:15; Tue, Thu, and Sat at 9:15, 10:15, and 11:15; no tours on Sun, reduced schedule Nov-Feb—call number below, Ponti Romani tram stop, www.unipd.it). School groups often book the entire visit, and many of the guides speak no English.

Confirm tour times and availability by calling 049-827-3047 or stopping by the ticket window (opens 15 minutes before each tour, located just inside the palace, in the hall reached from the Fascist-era courtyard described above). The bar there is fun for a cheap drink and to see photos of university life.

Visiting the University: The gawking public is not really welcomed in the university, but on weekdays and Saturday mornings, you can poke into two **courtyards** (when closed, just peer through the gate). Find the entrance at Via VIII Febbraio 7, under the "Gymnasium"

Graduation Antics in Padua

With 60,000 students, Padua's university always seems to be hosting graduation ceremonies. There's a constant trickle of happy grads and their friends and families celebrating the big event.

During the school year, every 20 minutes or so, a student steps into a formal room (upstairs, above the university courtyard) to officially meet with the leading professors of his or her faculty. When they're finished, the students are given a green laurel wreath. They pose for ceremonial group photos and family snapshots. It's a sweet scene. Then, craziness takes over.

The new graduates replace their somber clothing with raunchy outfits, as gangs of friends gather around them on Via VIII Febbraio, the street in front of the university. The roast begins. The gang rolls out a giant butcher-paper poster with a generally obscene caricature of the student and a litany of *This Is Your Life* photos and stories. The new grad, subject to various embarrassing pranks, reads the funny statements out loud. The poster is then taped to the university wall for all to see. (Find the plastic panels to the right of the main entry, facing Via VIII Febbraio. Graduation posters are allowed to stay there for 24 hours. The panels are emptied each morning, but by nighttime a new set of posters is affixed to the plastic shields.)

During the roast, the friends sing the catchy but obscene local university anthem, reminding their newly esteemed friend not to get too huffy: *Dottore, dottore, dottore del buso del cul. Vaffancul, vaffancul* (loosely translated: "Doctor, doctor. You're just a doctor of the a-hole...go f-off, go f-off"). After you've heard this song (with its fanfare and oom-pah-pah catchiness) and have seen all the good-natured fun, you can't stop singing it.

The crazy show is usually staged late in the afternoon. Outdoor café tables afford great seats to enjoy the spectacle.

inscription (30 yards from Caffè Pedrocchi, facing City Hall). You'll pop into a 16th-century courtyard, the school's historic core. It's littered with the coats of arms of important faculty and leaders of the university over the ages. Classrooms, which open onto the square, are still used. Today, students gather here, surrounded by memories of illustrious alumni, including the first woman ever to receive a university degree (in 1678).

A passageway leads from here to an adjacent second courtyard from the Fascist era (c. 1938). The relief celebrates heroic students in World War I. Off of this courtyard, notice the richly decorated stairway, frescoed Fascist-style in the 1930s with themes celebrating art, science, and the pursuit of knowledge.

The big attraction among tourists is Europe's first great **Anatomy Theater** (from 1594), which you can visit only on a guided tour. Try to get a ticket, but keep in mind that it's not worth any heroics to see. The first two rooms of the tour are underwhelming: One features the supposed "pulpit of Galileo" (c. 1550) and portraits of 40 famous alums. The second is the Aula Magna, a ceremonial room for festivities. The historic Anatomy Theater itself is more impressive. Despite the Church's strict ban on autopsies, more than 300 students would pack this theater to watch professors dissect human cadavers (the bodies of criminals from another town). This had to be done in a "don't ask, don't tell" kind of way, because the Roman Catholic Church only started allowing the teaching of anatomy through dissection in the late 1800s.

Sleeping in Padua

Rooms in Padua's hotels are more spacious and a better value than those in Venice. Keep in mind that when large conventions take over the town—several times a year—all hotels raise prices. Generally, prices are very flexible and might even be lower than what I've written here; check hotel websites for *offerti* (specials). I've listed two hotels in the center and a group of accommodations near the basilica. All are reachable from the station by the tram; only Albergo Verdi is more than a five-minute walk from the nearest tram stop.

In the Center

$$$ **Hotel Majestic Toscanelli** is a central, fancy hotel with 34 pleasant, air-conditioned rooms and a touch of charm, buried in a characteristic ghetto with wonderful cobbled ambience. This area is popular with students at night, and it can be noisy; request a quiet room on the back side (Sb-€95-110, Db-€150-160, ask for 10 percent Rick Steves discount, check their website for routine special discounts, free Wi-Fi, parking-€19/day, Via dell'Arco 2, Tito Livio tram stop, tel. 049-663-244, fax 049-876-0025, www.toscanelli.com, majestic@toscanelli.com, Mario Morosi and family). From the tram stop, follow the passageway next to #26, then

Sleep Code

(€1 = about $1.40, country code: 39)

S = Single, **D** = Double/Twin, **T** = Triple, **Q** = Quad, **b** = bathroom, **s** = shower only. Unless otherwise noted, credit cards are accepted, breakfast is included, and English is spoken. Padua levies a hotel tax of about €2 per person, per night, which must be paid in cash (not included in the rates I've quoted).

To help you easily sort through these listings, I've divided the accommodations into three categories based on the price for a standard double room with bath:

$$$ **Higher Priced**—Most rooms €125 or more.

$$ **Moderately Priced**—Most rooms between €90-125.

$ **Lower Priced**—Most rooms €90 or less.

Prices can change without notice; verify the hotel's current rates online or by email.

jog left down Via Marsala and turn right on Via dell'Arco.

$$ Albergo Verdi, a modern little place, is crammed into an old building on a small back street beyond Piazza dei Signori. While public spaces are tight, the 14 rooms are comfortable (Sb-€70, Db-€90-100, extra person-€30, air-con, free Internet access, pay Wi-Fi, Via Dondi dall'Orologio 7, Ponti Romani tram stop, tel. 049-836-4163, fax 049-878-0175, www.albergoverdipadova .it, info@albergoverdipadova.it). From Piazza dei Signori, walk through the arch under the clock tower and go to the far end of Piazza del Capitaniato; the hotel is on the side street to your right.

Near Basilica of St. Anthony

Santo is the nearest tram stop for the following hotels. Use the Prato della Valle tram stop for the hostel.

$$ Hotel Al Fagiano feels like an art gallery with crazy, sexy, modern art everywhere. The hotel is all about the union of a man and a woman (quite romantic). They rent 40 bright and cheery air-conditioned rooms, each uniquely decorated with Rossella Fagiano's canvases (Sb-€64, Db-€100, Tb-€115, 10 percent Rick Steves discount when booked direct, €7 per person less without breakfast, free Wi-Fi, parking-€10/day, 50 yards from the Santo tram stop at Via Locatelli 45, tel. 049-875-3396, fax 049-878-9460, www.alfagiano.com, info@alfagiano.com, Anita and artist Rossella).

$$ Hotel Belludi 37 is a slick, borderline-pretentious place renting 15 modern rooms shoehorned into an old building. The decor is dark, woody, fresh, and stylish (S-€57, Sb-€80, Db-€125, bigger Db-€140, ask for 10 percent Rick Steves discount, save €7/person without breakfast, air-con, Wi-Fi, a block from the Santo tram stop at Via Luca Belludi 37, tel. 049-665-633, fax 049-658-685, www.belludi37.it, info@belludi37.it).

$ Hotel Casa del Pellegrino, with 160 spotless, cheap, institutional rooms and straight pricing, is owned by the friars of St. Anthony. It's home to the pilgrims who come to pay homage to the saint in the basilica next door. Any visitor to Padua is welcome, making it popular with professors and students (S-€44, Sb-€62, D-€58, Db-€75, Tb-€85, Qb-€100, family rooms-€110, ask for a room off the street, breakfast-€5, air-con, elevator, free Wi-Fi, parking-€5/day, Via Cesarotti 21, tel. 049-823-9711, fax 049-823-9780, www.casadelpellegrino.com, info@casadelpellegrino.com). For better accommodations, request one of the 24 "superior" rooms in the *dipendenza*, the hotel's modern wing (€5 extra/night).

$ Hotel Al Santo, run with charm by Valentina and Antonio, offers 15 spacious rooms with all the comforts on two floors above their restaurant, a few steps from the basilica (Sb-€60, Db-€85, Tb-€110, Qb-€130, double-paned windows, quieter rooms off street, some rooms have views of basilica, air-con, elevator, free Wi-Fi, parking-€14/day, Via del Santo 147, tel. 049-875-2131, fax 049-878-8076, www.alsanto.it, alsanto@alsanto.it).

Hostel: **$ Ostello Città di Padova,** near Prato della Valle, is well-run and has 90 beds in 4- and 6-bed rooms (beds with sheets and breakfast-€19; family rooms-€88; free Wi-Fi, laundry-€5.50/load, lockers, reception open 7:15-9:30 & 15:30-23:30, rooms locked during afternoon but reception staffed if you need to leave bags, 23:30 curfew; Via Aleardi 30, Prato de Valle tram stop, tel. 049-875-2219, fax 049-654-210, www.ostellopadova.it, ostello padova@ctg.it). From the tram stop, exit the square ahead of you to the right and make an immediate left down Via Memmo; after the church, continue straight one block on Via Torresini and turn right on Via Aleardi.

Eating in Padua

The university population means cheap, good food abounds. My recommended restaurants are all centrally located in the historic core. You'd think there would be fine dining on the charming market squares, but on the piazzas it's a take-out-pizza-and-casual-bar scene (dominated by students after dark). La Lanterna, at the neighboring Piazza dei Signori, is the best on-square option—but it's still basically pizza. The dreamily atmospheric ghetto neighborhood (just two blocks off the market squares) thrives after dark with trendy bars and a lively student *spritz* scene.

Fine Dining near the Center

Osteria dei Fabbri, with shared rustic tables, offers a good mix of class and accessibility, quality, and price. The dining room is spacious, and the dishes are traditional Venetian (€9 pastas, €14 *secondi*, €2.50 cover, Mon-Sat 12:30-14:30 & 19:30-22:30, closed Sun, Via dei Fabbri 13, on a side street on south side of Piazza Erbe, tel. 049-650-336).

Osteria L'Anfora is a classic place serving classic dishes in an informal, fun-loving space. Don't be put off by the woody, ruffian decor and the fact that it's a popular hangout for a pre-meal drink. They take food seriously and serve it at good prices, and the energy and commotion add to a great dining experience (€9 pastas, €14-16 *secondi*, €2 cover, meals served Mon-Sat 12:30-15:00 & 19:30-22:30, closed Sun, no reservations taken, Via dei Soncin 13, tel. 049-656-629).

Antica Trattoria dei Paccagnella, near the basilica, serves up nicely presented local dishes. There's friendly service, modern art on the walls, and no pretense. It's thoughtfully run by two brothers, Raffaele and Cesare—who happily explain why they are so excited about "hen" (€9 pastas, €13 *secondi*, daily 12:00-14:30 & 19:00-22:00, Via del Santo 113, tel. 049-875-0549).

Enoteca dei Tadi is a small place with seven tables filling a cozy back room behind a convivial little bar (avoid their basement). Roberta and Anna serve traditional Paduan dishes and have earned a local following for their small but tasty menu. The selection is driven by what's fresh and in season, and they offer good wines by the glass (Tue-Sun 18:00-24:00, closed Mon, Via dei Tadi 16, mobile 338-408-3434).

Ristorante Dante alle Piazze is a respected fixture in town for its dressy white-tablecloth dining. They are passionate about their meat and fish dishes. Reservations are smart at night (€9-11 pastas, €13-24 *secondi*, €2.50 cover, Tue-Sat 12:00-15:00 & 19:00-24:00, Sun 12:00-15:00, closed Mon, Via Daniele Manin 8, tel. 049-836-0973).

Cheap Eats near the Center

La Lanterna has a forgettable interior, but a pizza here on Piazza dei Signori includes a rare-in-Padua chance to sit in a grand square under the stars, surrounded by great architecture. Its pizzas are a local favorite—takeaway available—and reservations are recommended (€7-9 pizzas, €8 pastas, €14 *secondi*, €2 cover, Fri-Wed 12:00-14:30 & 18:00-24:00, closed Thu, Piazza dei Signori 39, tel. 049-660-770).

Bar dei Osei, on Piazza della Frutta, is a very simple sandwich bar with some of the best outdoor seats in town. While

Paduans love their delicate *tremazzini*—white bread sandwiches with crusts cut off (€1.50/€1.80 with table service), I'd choose their *porchetta*—savory roasted pork sandwiches (€3.50/€3.80). You'll find a two-foot-long mother lode waiting on the counter for you; tell friendly Marco how big a slice you'd like. Wines are listed on the board (Mon-Sat 7:00-21:00, closed Sun).

Brek, with one entrance next to the Ponti Romani tram stop and another tucked into a corner of Piazza Cavour at #20, is an easy self-service chain *ristorante* with healthy and affordable choices. It's big, bright, practical, and family-friendly (€4-5 pastas, no cover, daily 11:30-15:00 & 18:30-22:00, tel. 049-875-3788).

Brek Foccacceria (part of the same chain), across from Caffè Pedrocchi and next door to the PAM supermarket, is a café selling big sandwiches and slices of pizza that you can eat at outdoor tables (daily 8:00-22:00, Piazzetta della Garzeria 6, tel. 049-876-1651).

Stock up on picnic items at the outdoor markets, or visit the **PAM supermarket,** in the tiny *piazzetta* east of Caffè Pedrocchi (Mon-Sat 8:00-21:00, closed Wed after 14:00 and all day Sun, Piazzetta Garzeria 3).

Near the Basilica of St. Anthony

Pizzeria Pago Pago dishes up wood-fired Neapolitan pizzas (a local favorite) and daily specials depending on what's in season. Get there early for dinner or wait (€5.50-7.50 pizzas, €2.50 cover, Wed-Mon 12:00-14:00 & 19:00-24:00, closed Tue; 2 blocks from Basilica of St. Anthony, up Via del Santo and right onto Via Galileo Galilei to #59; tel. 049-665-558, Gaetano and Modesto).

Casa del Pellegrino Ristorante caters to St. Anthony pilgrims with simple, basic, and hearty meals, served in a cheery dining room just north of the basilica. *Baccalà* (cod) is a favorite here (€4-6 pastas, €7.50-9.50 *secondi*, €14 fixed-price meal, €2 cover, daily 12:00-14:00 & 19:30-21:30, Via Cesarotti 21, tel. 049-876-0715).

Zairo is a huge indoor/outdoor *ristorante*/pizzeria with reasonable prices, delicious homemade pastas, Veneto specialties, snappy service, and a local clientele (€6-8 pastas, Tue-Sun 12:00-14:30 & 19:00-24:00, closed Mon, east side of the vast Prato della Valle square at #51, tel. 049-663-803).

Pollodoro la Gastronomica, my pick of the take-out delis near the basilica, sells roast chicken, pastas, pizza, and veggies, and will make sandwiches (Wed-Sat and Mon 9:00-14:00 & 17:00-20:00, Sun 9:00-14:00 only, closed Tue, 100 yards from basilica at Via Belludi 34, tel. 049-663-718). You can picnic at the nearby cloisters of the basilica.

Padua Connections

From Padua by Train to: Venice (2/hour, 30-50 minutes), **Vicenza** (2/hour, fewer on weekends, 15-25 minutes), **Milan** (1-2/hour, 2-3 hours), **Verona** (2/hour, 40-60 minutes), **Ravenna** (roughly hourly, 2.5 hours, change in Bologna or Ferrara).

By Bus to: Venice (45 minutes, €4.10, hourly at :25 past the hour from 5:25 to 22:25), and Venice's **Marco Polo Airport** (65 minutes, €8, €10 if bought on board; buses depart at :25 past each hour from platform 11 at Padua's bus station, next to the train station; recheck times at www.fsbusitalia.it). If flying into the airport, take this bus to get directly to Padua (buy tickets at windows in arrivals hall or at airport TI).

By Minibus to Airports: A minibus service runs from Padua to **Marco Polo Airport** (€31/person) or **Treviso Airport** (€40/person, reservations required, tel. 049-870-4425, www.airservice padova.it).

NEAR VENICE

Near Padua: Vicenza

To many architects, Vicenza (vih-CHEHN-zah) is a pilgrimage site. Entire streets look like the back of a nickel. This is the city of Andrea Palladio (1508-1580), the 16th-century Renaissance architect who gave us the Palladian style that is so influential in countless British country homes. But as grandiose as Vicenza's Palladian facades may feel, there is little marble here. The city lacked the wealth to build with much more than painted wood and plaster.

If you're an architecture buff, Vicenza merits a quick day trip on any day but Monday, when major sights are closed. If you're packing light, it's an easy stop, located on the same train line as Padua, Verona, and Venice. But because you can't store bags at the train station, it's not worth stopping if you have lots of luggage.

Tourist Information: The TI is next to the Olympic Theater at Piazza Matteotti 12 (daily 9:00-13:00 & 14:00-18:00, tel. 0444-320-854, www.visitvicenza.org). Ask for the free brochure on Palladio's buildings. Architecture fans appreciate the €2.50 *Vicenza and the Villas of Andrea Palladio*.

Arrival in Vicenza: From the **train station**, I'd head straight for the most distant sight, the Olympic Theater (with a TI next door), and then see other sights on the way back. Go straight out the train station's front door, and use the crosswalk on the right side of the roundabout. From here, it's a five-minute walk straight ahead up wide Viale Roma to the PAM supermarket at the bottom

Vicenza

of Corso Palladio; turn right through the gate and then it's a good 10 minutes more down the Corso to the Olympic Theater (a taxi costs €8). **Drivers** can park in one of the cheap parking lots (Parcheggio Bassano and Parcheggio Cricoli), and catch a free shuttle bus to the center.

Helpful Hints: All of the sights mentioned (except the villas outside of town) are covered by the **Card Musei** combo-ticket (€8.50, €12 family pass, good for 3 days, sold at Olympic Theater and Palazzo Leoni Montanari). In a pinch, the TIs may be willing to store bags for you while you walk around town.

Sights in Vicenza

Helpful bilingual signs in front of Palladio's buildings explain their history. Arrows around town point you to his major works, and you can also pick up a map from the TI.

▲▲**Olympic Theater (Teatro Olimpico)**—Palladio's last work, one of his greatest, shouldn't be missed. This indoor theater is a wood-and-stucco festival of classical columns, statues, and an oh-wow stage bursting with perspective tricks

Cost and Hours: Entry only with €8.50 Card Musei, which covers other Vicenza sights; audioguide available, Tue-Sun 9:00-17:00, closed Mon, last entry 30 minutes before closing, very occasionally closed when theater is in use, entrance to left of TI at Piazza Matteotti 11, tel. 0444-222-800, www.comune.vicenza.it. When you step back outside, look up the town's main drag—named after Palladio. It's the same main street you saw on the stage of his theater.

▲**Church of Santa Corona and Diocesan Museum**—A block away from the Olympic Theater and currently closed for restoration, this "Church of the Holy Crown" was built in the 13th century to house a thorn from the Crown of Thorns, given to the Bishop of Vicenza by the French King Louis IX. The church has two artistic highlights: the art embellishing its high altar and Giovanni Bellini's fine painting, *Baptism of Christ*. While the church is closed, its paintings are on display at the nearby Diocesan Museum.

Cost and Hours: €5, Tue-Sun 10:00-13:00 & 14:00-18:00, closed Mon, Piazza Duomo 12, tel. 0444-226-400, www.museodiocesanovicenza.it.

Archaeological and Natural History Museum—Located next door to the Church of Santa Corona, this museum's ground floor features Roman antiquities (mosaics, statues, and artifacts excavated from Rome's Baths of Caracalla, plus swords) and a barbarian warrior skeleton complete with sword and helmet. Prehistoric scraps are upstairs. Look for English description sheets near exhibit entryways throughout.

Cost and Hours: Covered by Card Musei, Tue-Sun 9:00-17:00, closed Mon, Contrà Santa Corona 4, tel. 0444-222-815, www.museicivicivicenza.it.

Palazzo Leoni Montanari—Across the street from the Church of Santa Corona, this small museum is a palatial riot of Baroque, with cherub-cluttered ceilings jumbled like a preschool in heaven. A quick stroll shows off Venetian paintings and a floor of Russian icons.

Cost and Hours: €5, Tue-Sun 10:00-18:00, closed Mon, last entry 30 minutes before closing, Contrà Santa Corona 25, tel. 800-578-875, www.palazzomontanari.com.

Piazza dei Signori—Vicenza's main square has been the center of town ever since it was the site of the ancient Roman forum. The commanding **Basilica Palladiana,** with its 270-foot-tall, 13th-century tower, dominates the square (may be under renovation during your visit). It was a meeting place for local big shots. It was young Palladio's proposal—to redo Vicenza's dilapidated Gothic palace of justice in the Neo-Greek style—that established him as the city's favorite architect. The rest of Palladio's career was a one-man construction boom. The basilica hosts special exhibitions that sometimes involve a fee, but you can often pop in for a free look.

Villas on the Outskirts of Vicenza— Vicenza is surrounded by dreamy Venetian villas. Venice's commercial empire receded in the 1500s when trade began to pick up along the Atlantic seaboard and dwindle in the Mediterranean. Venice redirected its economic agenda to agribusiness, which led to the construction of lavish country villas, such as **Villa la Rotonda**, the inspiration for Thomas Jefferson's Monticello (www.villalarotonda.it), and **Villa Valmarana ai Nani** (www.villavalmarana.com). Located southeast of the town center, both houses are furnished with period pieces and come with good English descriptions (closed Mon). Pick up the free English brochure on Palladio's villas from the TI if you plan to visit.

Vicenza Connections

From Vicenza by Train to: Venice (2/hour, 45-75 minutes), **Padua** (2/hour, fewer on weekends, 15-25 minutes), **Verona** (2/hour, 30-60 minutes), **Milan** (1-2/hour, 1.75-2.5 hours). Unless you crave speed or need to burn a railpass day, you'll save a lot of money by taking the slow *R* trains to Vicenza instead of the fast *ES* trains.

Verona

Romeo and Juliet made Verona a household word. Alas, a visit here has nothing to do with those two star-crossed lovers. You can pay to visit the house that falsely claims to be Juliet's (with an almost believable balcony and a courtyard swarming with tour groups), join in the tradition of rubbing the breast of Juliet's statue to help find a lover (or to pick up the sweat of someone who can't), and even make a pilgrimage to what isn't "La Tomba di Giulietta."

Fiction aside, Verona has been an important crossroads for 2,000 years and is therefore packed with genuine history. R&J fans will take some solace in the fact that two real feuding families, the Montecchi and the Cappellos, were the models for Shakespeare's Montagues and Capulets. And, if R&J had existed and were alive today, they would still recognize much of their "hometown."

Verona's main attractions are its wealth of Roman ruins; the remnants of its 13th- and 14th-century political and cultural boom; its 21st-century, quiet, pedestrian-only ambience; and its world-class opera festival, held each summer. After Venice's festival of tourism, the Veneto region's second city is a cool and welcome sip of pure Italy, where dumpsters are painted by schoolchildren as class projects and public spaces are the domain of locals, not tourists. If you like Italy but don't need blockbuster sights, this town is a joy.

Orientation to Verona

Verona's old town fills an easy-to-defend bend in the River Adige. The vibrant and enjoyable core of Verona lies along Via Mazzini between Piazza Brà (pronounced "bra") and Piazza Erbe, Verona's market square since Roman times. Each evening the two main streets from Piazza Brà to Piazza Erbe, Via Mazzini and Corso Porta Borsari, are enlivened by a wonderful *passeggiata*...bustling with a slow and elegant parade of strollers. For a good day trip to Verona, visit the Roman Arena and then take my self-guided walk.

Tourist Information

Verona's TI is just off **Piazza Brà**—from the square, head to the big yellow building with columns and cross the street to Via degli Alpini 9 (Feb-Nov Mon-Sat 9:00-19:00, Dec-Jan Mon-Sat 9:00-18:00; Sun 10:00-16:00 year-round; tel. 045-806-8680, www.tourism.verona.it). Pick up the free city map for a list of sights and opening hours, and confirm the walking-tour schedule. If you're staying the night, ask about concerts or pick up the monthly entertainment guide, *Carnet Verona* (free at TI, €2 at newsstands).

Verona Card: This tourist card covers entrance to all the recommended Verona sights (€15/2 days, €20/5 days, sold at TIs and at participating sights). If you visit the Roman Arena (€6), climb Torre dei Lamberti (€6), explore Castelvecchio (€6), and tour two churches (€5), you'll pay €23. At €15, the card saves a day-tripper intent on blitzing the city almost a third off their sightseeing costs.

The €6 **Church Card,** sold at four churches (San Zeno, Duomo, Sant'Anastasia, and San Fermo) that require admission (€2.50 each), pays off if you visit three (www.chieseverona.it). There's no need to get both tourist cards.

Arrival in Verona

By Train: Verona's main train station is called Verona Porta Nuova. In the main hall, you'll find WCs (€0.80) and a baggage check office (€5/5 hours, €12.50/24 hours, daily 7:00-23:00). Buses and taxis are immediately outside.

Avoid the boring 15-minute walk from the station to Piazza Brà. Buses are cheap, easy, and leave every couple of minutes. Buy a ticket from the tobacco shop inside the station (€1.10/1 hour, €3.50 day pass valid until midnight), or get it from the driver (€2/1 hour). Find platform A in front of the station and hop on bus #11, #12, or #13. After 20:00, and all day Sunday, though, you'll want bus #90, #92, or #98. If in doubt, confirm that your bus is headed to the city center by asking, *"Per il centro?"* (pehr eel CHEN-troh). Validate your ticket by stamping it in the machine on the bus.

Drivers don't announce stops, but you'll know Piazza Brà because of the mass exodus and the can't-miss-it Roman Arena. The TI is just a few steps beyond the bus stop (against the medieval wall). You can catch return buses to the station (same numbers) from the stop on the piazza side of the street, or from another bus stop just outside the city wall on Corso Porta Nuova (on the right).

Taxis pick up only at taxi stands (at Piazza Brà and train station) and cost about €8 for the quick ride between the train station and the center of town.

By Car: The old town center (where nearly all my recommended hotels are located) is closed to traffic. Your hotel can get you permission to drive in—ask when you book. Otherwise your license plate could be photographed, and a €100 ticket might be waiting in the mail when you get home.

Drivers will find reasonably priced parking in well-marked lots and garages just outside the center. The underground **Cittadella garage,** at Piazza Cittadella (a block off Piazza Brà, behind the TI), is huge, convenient, and easy to find (€2/hour, €15/24 hours). The lot in front of the train station costs less (€10/24 hours), but you'll spend your savings on the bus to the center. Street parking costs €1.50 per hour (spaces marked with blue lines, buy ticket at a tobacco shop or an automated machine, place ticket on dashboard, maximum two hours). The Città di Nimes parking lot (a 5-minute walk from the train station, near the wall) costs €5/day.

By Plane: Efficient buses connect Verona's airport (known as Catullo or Verona-Villafranca, 12 miles southwest of the city, airport code: VRN) with its train station (€6, buy tickets on board or at tobacco shop, daily about 5:40-23:00, 3/hour, 15 minutes, bus stop is by front door of train station, www.aeroportoverona.it).

Helpful Hints

Sightseeing Schedules: Many sights (except churches) are closed on Mondays, at least in the morning.

Opera: From mid-June through early September, Verona's opera festival brings the city to life, with 15,000 music fans filling the Roman Arena for almost nightly performances. The city is packed and festive—restaurants have prescheduled seatings for dinner and hotels jack up their prices (cheap upper-level seats-€25; book tickets online at www.arena.it, at the TI, or by calling 045-800-5151; day-of-show tickets often available; box office open Mon-Fri 9:00-12:00 & 15:15-17:45, Sat-Sun 9:00-12:00; during opera season, open daily 10:00-17:45, or until 21:00 on performance days; Via Dietro Anfiteatro 6B).

Internet Access: There are two good Internet cafés just outside the wall from Piazza Brà: **Casino Internet Point** (daily 10:00-24:00, €2/hour, 100 yards behind the TI at 49 Via Adigetto); and **Khan Servizi Internet Point** (daily 9:30-21:00, €2/hour, just off Piazza Cittadella and 200 yards from Porta Nuova on Vicolo Ghiaia).

Tours in Verona

Walking Tours—The TI organizes 1.5-hour tours in English (March-Oct Fri-Sun 11:30, no tours off-season, €10/person). Tours meet inside the Piazza Brà TI and stroll all the way through the old town (call to confirm schedule, no reservation necessary, tel. 045-806-8680).

Private Guides—Two excellent and enthusiastic Verona guides enjoy giving private tours of the town and region to readers of this book (€110/2 hours, €220/5 hours, prices are per group, tours tailored to your interests—villas, wine tasting, and so on). They are **Marina Menegoi** (mobile 328-958-1108, mmenegoi@gmail.com) and **Valeria Biasi** (ask for Rick Steves discount, mobile 348-903-4238, www.aguideinverona.com, valeria@aguideinverona.com). For families with children, Valeria offers an interactive game in the city called Safari (€130/2.5 hours).

Self-Guided Walk

Welcome to Verona Town Walk

This walk covers the essential sights in the town core, starting at Piazza Brà and ending at the cathedral. Allow two hours (including the tower climb and dawdling).

❶ Piazza Brà

If you're wondering about the name, it comes from the local dialect

and means "big open space." A
generation ago this piazza was
noisy with cars. Now it's open
and people friendly—it's become
the community family room and
natural festival grounds.

Grab a bench near the central fountain called "The Alps."
This was a gift from Verona's
sister city Munich, which is
just over the mountains to the north. You'll see in the middle of
the fountain the symbols of the two cities separated by the Alps,
carved out of pink marble from this region.

The ancient arena looming over the piazza is a reminder that
the city's history goes back to Roman times. On this walk, we'll
meander across what was the ancient city, from the arena on this
side to the theater across the river.

With the fall of Rome in the fifth century, Verona became
a favored capital of barbarian kings. In the Middle Ages, noble
families had to choose sides in the civil struggles between emperors (Ghibellines) and popes (Guelphs). During this time (1200s),
the town bristled with several hundred San Gimignano-type towers, built by different families to symbolize their power. When
the Scaligeri family rose to power here in the 14th century, they
established stability on their terms and made the other noble families lop off their proud towers—only the Scaligeri were allowed to
keep theirs. To add insult to injury, the Scaligeri paved the city's
roads with bricks from the other families' toppled towers. But
inter-family feuds made it impossible for the Scaligeri to maintain a stable government, and in 1405 the town essentially gave
itself to Venice, which ruled Verona until Napoleon stopped by
in 1796. During the 19th century, a tug-of-war between France
and Austria actually divided the city for a time, with the river
marking the border of each country's domain. Eventually Verona,
like Venice, fell into Austrian hands. Reminders of Austrian rule
remain: The huge yellow Neoclassical city hall facing Piazza Brà
(look for the flags) was built by the Austrians to serve as their
19th-century military headquarters. Their former arsenal stands
just across the river, and an Austrian fortress caps the hill looking over the city. But the big statue is of Italy's first king, Victor
Emmanuel II, celebrating Italian independence and unity, won in
the 1860s.

Apart from all its history, Piazza Brà is about strolling—the
evening *passeggiata* is a national sport in Italy. The broad, shiny
sidewalk (named "Liston" after a Venetian promenade; note the
fine Venetian-style marble pavement slabs) was built by 17th-

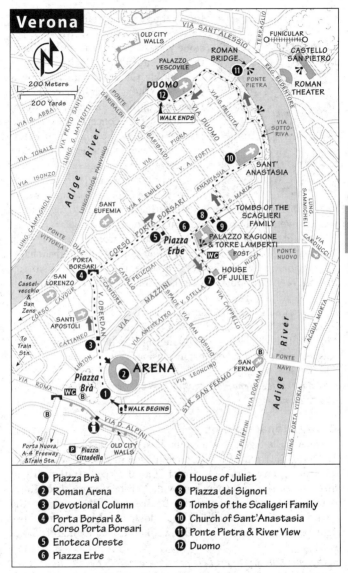

Verona

200 Meters

200 Yards

WALK ENDS

WALK BEGINS

① Piazza Brà
② Roman Arena
③ Devotional Column
④ Porta Borsari & Corso Porta Borsari
⑤ Enoteca Oreste
⑥ Piazza Erbe

⑦ House of Juliet
⑧ Piazza dei Signori
⑨ Tombs of the Scaligeri Family
⑩ Church of Sant'Anastasia
⑪ Ponte Pietra & River View
⑫ Duomo

NEAR VENICE

century Venetians, who made it big and wide so that promenading socialites could see and be seen in all their finery.

❷ Roman Arena

The Romans built this stadium outside their town walls, just as modern stadiums are usually located outside downtown districts. With 72 aisles, this elliptical 466-by-400-foot amphitheater is the third largest in Italy (and it was originally 50 percent taller). Most of the stone you see is original. Dating from the first century A.D., it looks great in its pink marble. Over the centuries, crowds of up to 25,000 spectators have cheered Roman gladiator battles, medieval executions, rock concerts, and modern plays—including the popular opera festival (held every summer), which take advantage of the arena's famous acoustics. While there's little to see inside except for the impressive stonework, it's memorable to visit a Roman arena that is still a thriving concert venue. If you climb to the top, you'll enjoy great city views.

The gladiators posing with tourists out front are mostly from Albania, and part of a local gang; they're notorious for overcharging for photos. While they're a nuisance, the police say it's better that they're scamming a living here than finding even more disreputable ways to get by.

Cost and Hours: €6, don't bother with the combo-ticket that includes the unimpressive Maffei Museum, Tue-Sun 8:30-19:30, Mon 13:30-19:30, closes at 14:00 during mid-June-early Sept opera season, last entry one hour before closing, WC near entry, tel. 045-800-3204.

• *As you exit the arena, look to your right. Where the street splits you'll see a column.*

❸ Devotional Column

In the Middle Ages, this column blessed a marketplace held here. Ten yards in front of it, a bronze plaque in the sidewalk shows the Roman city plan—a town of 20,000 placed strategically in the bend of the river, which provided protection on three sides. A wall enclosed the peninsula. The center of the grid was the forum, today's Piazza Erbe. (Look down Via Mazzini, the busy main pedestrian drag—the bell tower in the distance marks Piazza Erbe.)

• *After viewing the bronze plaque, turn around so your back is to the arena. Head straight down Via Oberdan and continue a couple of blocks (passing a derelict Fascist-era theater, the Astra) until you see an ancient gate to your right, the Porta Borsari. Walk up to it.*

❹ Porta Borsari and Corso Porta Borsari

You're standing before the main entrance to Roman Verona; back then, this gate functioned as a tollbooth (*borsari* means purse, referring to the collection of tolls here). Below the spiral, fluted columns (which parents nickname "*tortiglioni*"—a pasta kids can relate to), carved into the rock, is a tribute to the emperor who restored this gate. Outside the adjacent Caffè Rialto, the stone on the curb is from a tomb—in Roman times, the roads outside the walls were lined with tombstones, because burials were not allowed within the town itself. Turn around, look down Corso Cavour, and imagine it in Roman times, leading away from the city gate and lined with tombs. Step into the café. A glass panel in the floor shows the original Roman foundations and pavement stones.

Back outside, cross under the Roman gate and head into the ancient city. Walk down Corso Porta Borsari, the Roman main drag, toward what was the forum. Make it a scavenger hunt. As you walk, discover bits of the town's illustrious past—chips of Roman columns, medieval reliefs, fine old facades, fossils in marble—as well as its elegant present of fancy shops, in a setting that prioritizes pedestrians over cars. On the right, you'll pass the recommended Osteria del Bugiardo, at #17, a popular wine bar and a good place to take a break and hang out with Verona's young and trendy.

• *Between Corso Porta Borsari 13 and 15, detour right down Vicolo San Marco in Foro, following the* Pozzo dell'Amore *sign. Twenty yards ahead on your right, you'll find...*

❺ Enoteca Oreste

This funky wine-and-grappa bar is still run by Oreste (with his Chicagoan wife, Beverly) like a 1970s, old-style *enoteca*. Browse and sample and clown around with Oreste. This historic *enoteca* was once the private chapel of the archbishop of Verona. Traces of the past hide between the bottles—ask Beverly to tell you the story (Tue-Sun 8:00-20:00, closed Mon, Vicolo San Marco in Foro 7, tel. 045-803-4369).

• *Return to Corso Porta Borsari and continue one block until you hit a big square.*

❻ Piazza Erbe

This bustling market square is a photographer's delight. Its pastel buildings corral the fountains, pigeons, and people who have

NEAR VENICE

congregated here since Roman times, when this was a forum. Notice the Venetian lion hovering above the square atop a column, reminding locals of the conquest of 1405. During medieval times, the stone canopy in the center of the square held the scales where merchants measured the weight of goods they bought and sold, such as silk and wool. A fountain has bubbled here for 2,000 years. The original Roman statue lost its head and arms. After a sculptor added a new head and arms, the statue became Verona's Madonna. She holds a small banner that reads, roughly, "The city of Verona deserves respect and justice."

If you were standing here in the Middle Ages, you would have been surrounded by proud noble family towers. Medieval nobles showed off with towers. Renaissance nobles showed off with finely painted facades on their palaces. Find remnants of the 16th-century days when Verona was nicknamed "the painted city."

Locals like to start their evening with an *aperitivo* here. Each bar caters to a different market segment. Survey the scene and, if or when the time is right, chose the terrace that suits you and join in the ritual. It's simple: Grab a spot, adjust your seat for the best view, and order a *spritz* to drink (€4 with a plate of olives and chips).

• *At the far end of Piazza Erbe is a market column featuring St. Zeno, the patron of Verona, who looks at the crazy crowds flushing into the city's silly claim to touristic fame: the House of Juliet (100 yards down Via Cappello to #23—just follow the crowds). Side-trip there now (but watch your wallet—it's a pickpocket's haven).*

❼ House of Juliet

The tiny, admittedly romantic courtyard is a spectacle in itself:

Tourists from all over the world pose on the balcony, while those hoping for love wait their turn to polish Juliet's bronze breast. Residents marvel that each year, about 1,600 Japanese tour groups break their Venice-Milan ride for an hour-long stop in Verona just to see this courtyard (free, gates open roughly 9:00-19:00 or longer). It's fun to stand in the corner and observe the scene, knowing that all of this commotion was started by a clever tour guide in the early 1970s as a way to attract visitors to Verona.

The courtyard walls have long been filled with amorous graffiti—the latest trend is to affix a paper note to the gates or walls with chewing gum. The wall of padlocks is another new gimmick, enabling lovers to blow money in an attempt to prove that their hearts are thoroughly locked up. (The shop that sells the locks also sells pens to write on them.) The red mailbox is for love letters to Juliet. There's actually a Juliet Club that reviews these—and all the letters mailed from around the world to "Juliet, Verona, Italy." Each year, the club awards the author of the sweetest letter a free vacation to Verona.

Information boxes offer a good story (for €1): "While no documentation has been discovered to prove the truth of the legend, no documentation has disproved it either." The "museum," which displays art inspired by the love story, plus costumes and the bed from Franco Zeffirelli's film *Romeo and Juliet*, is certainly not worth the €6 entry fee.

Was there ever a real Juliet Capulet? You just walked down Via Cappello, the street of the cap makers. Above the courtyard entry (looking out) is a coat of arms featuring a hat—representing a family that made hats and which would be named, logically, Capulet.

The public's interest in a fictional Romeo and Juliet—or at least Juliet—is a sign that there's a hunger for a Juliet in our world. Observing the mobs clamoring to polish her breast or blow kisses from her bogus balcony, I try to appreciate what she means to people, and to psychoanalyze what she provides to those who come to Verona specifically for this: the message that love will prevail. In love, you can lose, and still be a winner. Juliet is brave, tragic, honest, outspoken, timeless, and passionate. She's a mover and a shaker, a dreamer, and a fighter. In a way, this is a pagan temple where the spirit of Juliet gives people something to believe in...or maybe it's just a bunch of baloney appreciated by a simple-minded crowd.

• *Return to Piazza Erbe. From the middle of the piazza, head right on Via della Costa—look for the whale's rib suspended under an arch. It was likely a souvenir brought home by a traveling merchant, reminding the townspeople that there was a big world out there. Walk down Via della Costa, into the big square.*

❽ Piazza dei Signori

Literally the "Lords' Square," this is Verona's sitting room, quieter and more harmonious than Piazza Erbe. The buildings—which

span five centuries—define the square and are all linked by arches. The long portico on the left is inspired by a building in Florence: Brunelleschi's Hospital of the Innocents, considered the first Renaissance building.

Locals call the square Piazza Dante for the statue of the Italian poet Dante Alighieri that dominates it. Dante—always pensive, never smiling—seems to wonder why the tourists choose Juliet over him. Dante was expelled from Florence when that city sided with the pope (who didn't appreciate Dante's writing) and banished its greatest poet. Verona and its ruling Scaligeri family, however, were at odds with the pope (siding instead with the Holy Roman Emperor), and granted Dante asylum.

With the whale's rib behind you, you're facing the brick, crenellated, 14th-century Scaligeri residence. Behind Dante is the yellowish, 15th-century Venetian Renaissance-style Portico of the Counsel. In front of Dante to his right is the 12th-century Romanesque **Palazzo della Ragione** (closed to the public, except for its tower).

Follow the white *WC* signs into the courtyard of the Palazzo della Ragione. The impressive stairway is the only surviving Renaissance staircase in Verona. For a grand city view, you can climb to the top of the palazzo's 13th-century **Torre dei Lamberti** (€6 for stairs or elevator, daily June-Sept 8:30-20:30, Oct-May 8:30-19:30, ticket office next to staircase). The elevator saves you 245 steps—but you'll still need to climb about 45 more to get to the first viewing platform. It's not worth continuing up the endless spiral stairs to the second viewing platform.

• *Exit the courtyard the way you entered and turn right, continuing downhill. Within a block, you'll find the...*

❾ Tombs of the Scaligeri Family

These exotic and very Gothic 14th-century tombs, with their fine, original, wrought-iron protective cages, evoke the age when one family ruled Verona. The Scaligeri were to Verona what the Medici family was to

Florence. These were powerful people. They changed the law so that they could be buried within the town. They forbade the presence of any noble family's towers but their own. And, by building tombs atop pillars, they arranged to be looked up to, even in death.

• *Continue 15 yards to the next corner and take a left on Vicolo Cavalletto. At the first corner, turn right along Corso Sant'Anastasia toward the big, unfinished brick facade of Verona's largest church. For a fragrant and potentially tasty diversion, pop into the two classic grocery stores:* **Gastronomia** *and* **Albertini**, *both located on your left in the next block. Gastronomia can rustle up tasty sandwiches (about €3-4).*

⑩ Church of Sant'Anastasia

This church was built from the late 13th century through the 15th

century. Although the facade was never finished (the builders ran out of steam), the interior was—and still is—brilliant. Step inside to see the delightful way this region's medieval churches were painted. Note the grimacing hunchbacks holding basins of holy water on their backs (near main entrance at base of columns). And don't miss Pisanello's fresco of *St. George and the Princess of Trebizond* (1438; at the tip of the arch, high above chapel to right of altar). Once colorful, it has oxidized over time to its current monochrome state. For a closer look at its wonderful detail, check out the images on the computer terminal below. Ask for the English brochure, which describes the story of the church.

Cost and Hours: €2.50, March-Oct Mon-Sat 9:00-18:00, Sun 13:00-18:00; Nov-Feb closes daily at 17:00, www.chieseverona .it.

• *Leaving the church, make two lefts, and walk along the right side of the church to Via Sottoriva. To the right, the Sottoriva arcade was once busy with colorful wine bars and* osterie, *some of which still exist (see "Eating in Verona," later). But for now, head to the left on Via Sottoriva. In a block, you'll reach a small riverfront area with stone benches that usually have a few modern-day Romeos and Juliets gazing at each other rather than at the view. Belly up to the river view.*

NEAR VENICE

⓫ Ponte Pietra and River View

The white stones of the Ponte Pietra footbridge are from the original Roman bridge that stood here. After the bridge was bombed in World War II, the Veronese

fished the marble chunks out of the river to rebuild it. From here, you can see across the river to the Roman Theater, built into the hillside behind the green hedge (see page 188). Way above the theater (behind the cypress trees) is the fortress, Castello San Pietro.

The wide spot in the river here was called the "Millers' Widening," where boats stopped and unloaded grain to be milled. Water wheels once lined the river and powered medieval Verona, employing technology imported from the Holy Land by 10th-century Crusaders.

Continue up the river toward the bridge. You'll pass the recommended **Gelateria Ponte Pietra,** where Mirko, Mariam, and Stefano dish out fine gelato. Walk to the high point on the bridge and enjoy the view.

• *From the bridge, look back 200 yards at the tall white spire...that's where you're heading.*

⓬ Duomo

Started in the 12th century, this church was built over a period of several hundred years. Before entering, note the fine Romanesque

carvings on its facade. Also notice the elevated tomb (high above on the left)—a donor was buried this way at his request. Step inside, and pick up the leaflet that explains the church's highlights.

Directly ahead is Titian's 16th-century *Assumption of the Virgin* (Mary calmly rides a cloud—direction up—to the shock and bewilderment of the crowd below). To the right of the Titian (through the last wooden door, left of high altar) are the ruins of an older church. These are the 10th-century foundations of the Church of St. Elena, turned intriguingly into a modern-day chapel featuring exposed fourth-century mosaic floors from the Roman church that originally stood here. Don't miss the adjacent baptistery, with its clean Romanesque lines, hanging 14th-century crucifix, and fine marble font. Try to identify the eight biblical scenes carved on its panels before referring to my answers. (Answers: Annunciation; first Christmas, with animals licking baby Jesus and giving him a barnyard welcome; announcement to shepherds of Jesus' birth; Epiphany, with the Three Kings giving their gifts to Baby Jesus; Herod commanding that all male infants be killed; Slaughter of the Innocents; flight to Egypt; and finally, facing the entry door, John the Baptist baptizing Christ.) The peaceful Romanesque cloister is to the right as you leave the church, with mosaics from a fifth-century Christian church exposed below the walk.

Cost and Hours: €2.50; March-Oct Mon-Fri 10:00-17:30, Sat 10:00-16:00, Sun 13:30-17:30; shorter hours and closed Mon off-season.

Sights in Verona

▲▲**Evening _Passeggiata_**—For me, the highlight of Verona is the _passeggiata_ (stroll)—especially in the evening. Make a big circle from Piazza Brà through the old town on Via Mazzini (one of Europe's many "first" pedestrian-only streets) to the colorful Piazza Erbe, and then back down Corso Porta Borsari to Piazza Brà. This is a small town, where people know each other, and they're all out on parade. Like peacocks, the young and nubile spread their wings. The classy shop windows are integral to the _passeggiata_ as, for the ladies, shopping is a sport. Their never-finished wardrobes are considered a work in progress, and this is when they gather ideas. If you're going to complement your stroll with a sit in a café or bar, the best plan is to enjoy a _spritz_ drink—not on Piazza Brà, but on Piazza Erbe (the oldest and most elegant bars are on the end farthest from Juliet's balcony).

▲**Castelvecchio**—Verona's powerful Scaligeri family built this castle (1343-1356) as both a residence and a fortress. The castle has

two parts: the family palace, and the quarters for their private army (separated, for the nervous family's security, by a fortified wall and an internal moat). Today, it's the city's art gallery, with an extensive collection of mostly paintings. The religious statues, once brightly painted, were the city's medieval forte. The paintings were the city's Renaissance forte. Through the enjoyable collection—which includes minor works by many major masters (such as Bellini, Mantegna, and Veronese) you can trace the evolution of painting from the 13th through the 17th centuries.

You'll also find armor and have a chance to roam the ramparts with fine views of the city and river. Verona was an independent city-state from 1176 to 1387. Then came a long period of subjugation under other powers which, in more modern times, included the Austrians. From the ramparts you can see remnants of Austrian rule: the arsenal across the river and the castle atop the distant hill.

Cost and Hours: €6, Tue-Sun 9:00-19:00, closed Mon, Corso Castelvecchio 2, tel. 045-806-2611, see map on page 190 for location. Info sheets with good English descriptions are available throughout, but the €4 audioguide is still worthwhile.

Nearby: Next to Castelvecchio, the **Ponte Scaligero** bridge is free, open to the public, and fun to stroll across. Destroyed by the Germans in World War II, it was rebuilt in the 1950s using many of its original bricks, which were dredged out of the river. Today it's understandably a favorite for wedding-day photos.

▲**Basilica of San Zeno Maggiore**—This church, outside the old center, is dedicated to the patron saint of Verona, whose remains are buried in the crypt under the main altar. In addition to being a fine example of Italian Romanesque, the basilica features Mantegna's *San Zeno Triptych* (1456-1459) with its marvelous perspective, peaceful double-columned cloisters, and a set of 48 paneled 11th-century bronze doors nicknamed "the poor man's Bible." Pretend you're an illiterate medieval peasant and do some reading. Facing the altar, on the walls of the right-side aisle, you can see frescoes painted on top of other frescoes and graffiti dating from the 1300s. These were done by people who fled into the church in times of war or flooding and scratched prayers into the walls. Druidic-looking runes are actually decorated letters typical of the Gothic period, like those in illuminated manuscripts.

Cost and Hours: €2.50, March-Oct Mon-Sat 8:30-18:00, Sun 12:30-18:00; Nov-Feb Tue-Sat 10:00-13:00 & 13:30-17:00, Sun 12:30-17:00, closed Mon; located on Piazza San Zeno, a good 15-minute walk upriver beyond Castelvecchio; www.chiese verona.it.

Roman Theater (Teatro Romano)—Dating from about the time of Christ, this ancient theater was discovered in the 19th century and restored. Admission includes the Roman Museum, located high in the building above the theater (reach it via elevator—start at the stage and walk up the middle set of stairs, then continue straight on the path through the bushes).

The museum displays a model of the theater, a small chapel, and Roman artifacts, including mosaic floors, busts and other statuary, clay and bronze votive figures, and architectural fragments. There's not much to see. Unless you've never seen a Roman ruin, I'd skip it.

Cost and Hours: €4.50, Tue-Sun 8:30-19:30, Mon 13:30-19:30, last entry 45 minutes before closing, theater located across the river near Ponte Pietra footbridge, tel. 045-800-0360. From mid-June through August, the theater stages Shakespeare plays—only a little more difficult to understand in Italian than in Elizabethan English.

Giusti Garden (Giardino Giusti)—This Renaissance garden is a little oasis with manicured box hedges and towering cypress trees, and a city view from the top of its hill. For most people, however, it's not worth the hike, time, or money.

Cost and Hours: €6, daily April-Sept 9:00-20:00, Oct-March 9:00-17:00, across the river, beyond Ponte Nuovo.

Sleeping in Verona

I've listed rates you'll pay in the regular season—most of April through May, and September through October. Prices soar (at least €20-30 more per night) from mid-June through early September (opera season), in early April (during the Vinitaly wine festival—see "The Wines of Verona" sidebar, later), and during big trade

---

Sleep Code

(€1 = about $1.40, country code: 39)
S = Single, **D** = Double/Twin, **T** = Triple, **Q** = Quad, **b** = bathroom, **s** = shower only. Hotels accept credit cards and provide breakfast unless otherwise noted. Everyone speaks English. Many towns in Italy levy a hotel tax of about €2 per person, per night, which must be paid in cash (not included in the rates I've quoted).

To help you easily sort through these listings, I've divided the accommodations into three categories, based on the price for a standard double room with bath:

$$$ **Higher Priced**—Most rooms €125 or more.
$$ **Moderately Priced**—Most rooms between €90-125.
$ **Lower Priced**—Most rooms €90 or less.

Prices can change without notice; verify the hotel's current rates online or by email.

NEAR VENICE

Verona Hotels & Restaurants

1. Hotel Aurora
2. Casa della Giovane
3. Hotel Milano & Hotel Giulietta e Romeo
4. Hotel Europa
5. Hotel Colomba d'Oro & Hotel/Ristorante Torcolo
6. Albergo Arena
7. To L'Ospite Apartments
8. To Villa Francescatti Hostel
9. Enoteca Can Grande
10. Trattoria al Pompiere
11. Antico Café Dante
12. Bottega del Vin
13. Osteria al Duca
14. Osteria Sottoriva
15. Osteria del Bugiardo
16. Osteria Vini Zampieri
17. Pizzeria da Salvatore
18. Pizzeria Du de Cope
19. Doner Kebab Shop
20. Brek Cafeteria
21. PAM Supermarket
22. Gelateria Savoia
23. Gelateria Ponte Pietra
24. Gastronomia & Albertini Groceries
25. Internet Cafés (2)

fairs or major holidays. Unless your goal is opera, consider coming before mid-June or after early September. Prices are lower from November to March. Hotel websites clearly explain their rates.

Near Piazza Erbe

$$$ Hotel Aurora, at the corner of Piazza Erbe and Via Pelliciai, has friendly family management, a terrace overlooking the piazza, and 18 fresh, air-conditioned rooms (Sb-€125, Db-€140, Tb-€160, Qb-€200, elevator, free Wi-Fi, Piazzetta XIV Novembre 2, tel. 045-594-717, fax 045-801-0860, www.hotelaurora.biz, info@hotel aurora.biz, Rita). Coming from the train station, stay on the bus until the San Fermo stop (two stops past Piazza Brà) to get within an easy walk of the hotel.

$ Casa della Giovane, run by an association that houses poor women, also rents rooms and dorm beds to female tourists (and their children up to age 10). Buried deep in the old town and up several flights of stairs, the place offers 55 cheap beds in a clean, institutional, and peaceful setting (women only, €22/bed in 11-bed dorm, Sb-€35, Db-€60, Tb-€90, no breakfast, 23:00 curfew, free Wi-Fi, reception open 9:00-23:00, Via Pigna 7, tel. 045-596-880, fax 045-800-5449).

Near Piazza Brà

You'll find several options in the quiet streets just off Piazza Brà, within 200 yards of the bus stop. From the square, yellow signs point you to the hotels. The first three are big, business-class places with the service and formality you'd expect. The Torcolo is more homey and friendly.

$$$ Hotel Milano, a few doors from Hotel Giulietta e Romeo, is an arty hotel with 52 rooms. The lobby and fancier rooms are tricked out in black and chrome (rates vary wildly—see website—generally about Sb-€75-100, Db-€120-150, air-con, elevator, free Wi-Fi, garage parking-€15/day, Vicolo Tre Marchetti 11, tel. 045-591-692, fax 045-801-1299, www.hotelmilano-vr.it, info@hotelmilano-vr.it).

$$$ Hotel Colomba d'Oro is a sprawling, stately, elegant (if impersonal) place renting 51 fine rooms. It has generous public spaces and overlooks a quiet and central street (Sb-€100-150, Db-€120-180, prices peak July-Aug, extra bed-€30, pay Wi-Fi, Via C. Cattaneo 10, tel. 045-595-300, info@colombahotel.com, www.colombahotel.com).

$$ Hotel Europa offers sleek, modern comfort in springtime colors. Most of its 46 rooms are non-smoking, and a few rooms have little balconies overlooking the *piazzetta* below (Db-€100-120 most of year but up to €200 July-Aug, 10 percent discount if you mention this book when reserving direct, air-con, elevator, free Wi-Fi, a couple of blocks off Piazza Brà at Via Roma 8, tel. 045-594-744, fax 045-800-1852, www.veronahoteleuropa.com, info@veronahoteleuropa.com).

$$ Hotel Giulietta e Romeo is on a quiet side street just 50 yards behind the Roman Arena. Nine of its 40 sexy, ultra-modern rooms have balconies (Sb-€110, Db-€120, bigger Db-€150, prices shoot up to €200/€260 during opera season, non-smoking, air-con, elevator, free Wi-Fi, free loaner bikes, fitness room, garage €20/day, Vicolo Tre Marchetti 3, tel. 045-800-3554, fax 045-801-0862, www.hotelgr.it, info@hotelgr.it).

$$ Hotel Torcolo offers 19 comfortable, lovingly maintained, non-smoking rooms with Grandma's furnishings (Sb-€60-95, Db-€75-120 most of the year but up to €140 July-Aug, breakfast is extra, air-con, fridge in room, elevator, Wi-Fi, garage-€15/day; from Piazza Brà promenade, head down the alley to the right of #16 and walk to Vicolo Listone 3; tel. 045-800-7512, fax 045-800-4058, www.hoteltorcolo.it, hoteltorcolo@virgilio.it, well-run by Silvia, Diana, and helpful Caterina).

Near Castelvecchio

$ Albergo Arena, while dreary, is a good value for those on a budget. Located in a peaceful courtyard off a busy street a few blocks from Piazza Brà, it offers 17 very basic, quiet rooms (S-€45, Sb-€60, D-€75, Db-€85, air-con, free Wi-Fi, just west of Castelvecchio at Stradone Porta Palio 2, tel. & fax 045-803-2440, www.albergoarena.it, info@albergoarena.it, Francesco).

Across the River

$$ L'Ospite, a 10-minute walk across the river from Piazza Erbe, has six cozy, immaculate, fully equipped apartments and lots of stairs. The rooms, warmly managed by English-speaking Federica De Rossi, sleep from two to four, with air-conditioning and free Wi-Fi (Db-€95, Tb/Qb-about €40-55/person, discounts for cash and longer stays, no reception or daily cleaning; Via XX Settembre 3; tel. 045-803-6994, mobile 329-426-2524, www.lospite.com, info@lospite.com). Coming from the station by bus, get off three stops past Piazza Brà at the XX Settembre stop (across the street from the apartments).

$ Villa Francescatti is a good, church-affiliated hostel in a pretty hillside setting (€18/bed in 6- or 8-bed sex-segregated rooms with hall bath, €20/bed in family rooms with private bathrooms, cash only, includes breakfast, €8 dinners, laundry €5/load, free Wi-Fi in common areas, rooms closed from 9:00 to 17:00 but reception open all day, 24:00 curfew; Salita Fontana del Ferro 15, bus #73 or #91 from station to Piazza Isolo plus short steep walk, tel. 045-590-360, fax 045-800-9127, www.ostelloverona.it, info @villafrancescatti.it).

Eating in Verona

Every restaurant listed here is within a 10-minute walk of the others. They're mostly small and intimate, and found along side streets. It's tempting to grab a table next to the *passeggiata* action along Piazza Brà, but you'll be sacrificing service, value, and quality for your view of the floodlit Roman Arena and Verona on parade. Except for Brek Cafeteria, restaurants on the piazza tend to charge a cover and service fee, making even pizza a pricey choice.

Fine Dining

Enoteca Can Grande is enthusiastically run by Giuliano and Corrina, who enjoy turning people on to great, well-matched food and wine. You can sit on a quiet street or in a plush little dining area inside. Their star offering is a €40 set menu, a festival of *antipasti* treats, an imaginative pasta, your choice of a meat or fish course, and dessert. They also offer a junior version at lunch for €20: a pasta and your choice of salad or dessert (Wed-Mon 12:00-15:30 & 18:00-22:30, closed Tue, closed Mon instead of Tue during opera season; a block off Piazza Brà at Via Dietro Liston 19D—if the equestrian statue jogged slightly right, he'd head straight here; tel. 045-595-022).

Trattoria al Pompiere, which has a commitment to regional traditions, is bigger, with formal waiters weaving among its tight tables. All the bustle is surrounded by walls plastered with photos of local big shots. A favorite of local foodies, Marco and his gang serve gourmet meats and cheeses as *antipasti,* ideal for a mixed plate to complement the huge selection of fine wines. Reservations are wise (€12-13 pastas, €16-17 *secondi*, lunch from 12:30, dinner from 19:30, closed Sun, chivalry lives—ladies' menus come without prices; find Via Cappello 8, across from Juliet statue, and head down side street to Vicolo Regina d'Ungheria 5; tel. 045-803-0537).

Antico Café Dante is a dressy, high-end place with a 19th-century pedigree and elegant service on the classiest square in town. You can enjoy reliably high-quality, classic Veneto cuisine either at dressy tables on the square, or inside. While not cheap, if you want to dress up and enjoy a slow, romantic, and memorable meal, this is a good value (open daily, lunch from 12:30, dinner from 19:30, Piazza dei Signori 2, tel. 045-800-0083).

Bottega del Vin is pricey, venerable, and a bit pretentious. Under a high ceiling and walls of wine bottles, brisk black-vested waiters match traditional dishes (polenta, duck, game) with glasses

The Wines of Verona

Wine connoisseurs love the high-quality wines of the Verona area. The hills to the east are covered with grapes to make Soave; to the north is Valpolicella country; and Bardolino comes from vineyards to the west.

Valpolicella grapes, which are used to make the fruity, red Valpolicella table wine (found everywhere), are also the basis for full-bodied red Amarone and the sweet dessert wine Recioto. To produce Amarone, grapes are partially dried *(passito)* before fermentation, then aged for a minimum of four years in oak casks, resulting in a rich, velvety, full-bodied red. Recioto, which in local dialect means "ears," uses only the grapes from the top of the cluster (so they sort of look like the "ears" of the cluster's "head"). Because these grapes get the most sun, they mature the fastest and have the highest concentration of sugar. Before pressing, the grapes are dried for months until all moisture has gone out; the wine is then aged for one to three years.

Bardolino, from the vineyards near Lake Garda, is a light, fruity wine, like a French Beaujolais. It's a perfect picnic wine.

Soave, which might be Italy's best-known white wine, goes well with seafood and risotto dishes. While Soave can vary widely in quality, the best are called "Soave Classico" and come from the heart of the region, near the Soave Castle. Soave is sometimes aged in oak casks, giving it a mellow, rounded flavor.

Sample these and many others at the numerous *enoteche* (wine-tasting bars) or at any restaurant around town. In early April, Verona hosts Vinitaly, the most important international convention of domestic and international wines. Vintners vie for prestigious awards for the past year's vintage. Tourists are welcome to attend at the end of the week, and are shuttled to the convention hall from Piazza Brà. Hotels book up months in advance. Check with the TI and www.vinitaly.com for details.

If you're visiting the area in the fall, consider a day trip to nearby Monteforte d'Alpone, east of Verona. The town hosts a fun, raucous wine festival in September—ask at the TI for more information on this and other regional wine festivals.

of fine wine. Choose from 20 open bottles. The waitstaff, ambience, and food have deep roots in local culture. I like their front room best. Reservations are smart for dinner (€15 pastas, €18-24 *secondi*, good daily specials, daily 12:00-24:00 but closed Sun evening; off Via Mazzini at Via Scudo di Francia 3; tel. 045-800-4535).

Budget Restaurants

Osteria al Duca is a fun, family-run place with a lively atmosphere and good traditional dishes. Locals line up for its affordable, two-course, €16 fixed-price meal with lots of choices. I much prefer their ground floor (*piano terra*—worth requesting). Reservations are advised (Mon-Sat 12:00-15:00 & 18:30-22:30, closed Sun, half-block east of Scaligeri family tombs at Via Arche Scaligere 2, tel. 045-594-474, Alessandro or Daniela).

Ristorante Torcolo is a warm family restaurant, with mom (Paola) running the kitchen, and father and son (Roberto and Luca) serving. It's dressy but without pretense, and the service is professional, yet fun-loving. There's a happy energy, stoked by carts of tempting boiled meat and desserts rolling through the dining room. They serve all the classic dishes, with an accessible menu and an extensive wine list. Eat in their dressy dining hall, or on the tiny courtyard outside (€9 pastas, €15 *secondi*, €35 fixed-price meal featuring traditional Verona dishes, €3 cover, closed Mon, just behind the Piazza Brà scene on a quiet street, Via Carlo Cattaneo 11, tel. 045-803-3730).

Eating in *Osteria* (Old Bars)

Wandering around the old town, you'll see plenty of Verona's thriving little watering holes. While these characteristic old bars focus more on wine than on food, most serve memorable, characteristic and affordable plates. Menus are simple and rustic—sometimes just bar munchies and the daily pasta. Service is relaxed and the clientele is young and local. For drinks it's mostly wine or water—fine wines are served by the glass, with bottles open and prices listed on blackboards. (I saw one sign suggesting that patrons "don't drive too much to drink.")

I've listed three places below: a classic antique *osteria* with more of a menu; a trendy, more modern place in the old center; and a small one-man show just off Piazza Brà, where you're most likely to make a new friend.

Osteria Sottoriva survives from an era when Verona's river served as the town thoroughfare, and business deals could be made over a glass of wine at rustic riverside eateries. Located in a fine old covered arcade (the portico of Via Sottoriva), Sottoriva offers simple soups and pastas, with both indoor and outdoor seating (daily from 18:30, behind the Church of Sant'Anastasia at Via Sottoriva 9, tel. 045-801-4323).

Osteria del Bugiardo is jammed with a hip young crowd that spills out into the pedestrian-filled Corso Porta Borsari. They have a buffet of little sandwiches, can whip up a plate of top quality cheeses and wine, and serve a good pasta-of-the-day. While they showcase Buglioni wines, they're also proud of their extensive list of wines by the glass (€7 pastas, €11 *secondi*, daily 10:00-23:00, Corso Porta Borsari 17).

Osteria Vini Zampieri, with a tiny bar and five tables, keeps

A Mobile Feast Through Verona

Verona is a great town to sample the *aperitivo* ritual. All over town, locals enjoy a refreshing *spritz,* ideally on Piazza Erbe between 18:00 and 20:00. Chose a nice perch here, for about €4, you'll get the drink of your choice and a few nibbles (olives and/or potato chips) and a chance to feel very local as you enjoy the *passeggiata* scene.

Consider this for a fun sampling of many dimensions of the Verona eating and socializing scene: Start with an *aperitivo* on **Piazza Erbe** (the most refined bars are the farthest from Juliet's balcony), then walk across Ponte Nuovo to **Pizzeria da Salvatore** and enjoy the town's best pizza. If you have to wait for a table, have another *spritz* at the neighboring bar. Then stroll along the river to **Osteria Sottoriva,** and enjoy a little sampling of bar food with a glass of Amarone (wine to meditate with) under the old arcade. Finish by meandering through the old center back to Piazza Brà for a gelato at **Gelateria Savoia.** *Buon appetito!*

a tradition of stoking conviviality with good wine since 1937. Energetically run, its young manager, Leo, is passionate about organic wines, slow food, and Italian microbrews. Even though they barely serve food, Leo can put together a nice ham-and-cheese plate or whip up a simple pasta to complement your drink (daily 11:00-late, a few steps off Piazza Brà and next to Via Mazzini at Via Alberto Maria 23, tel. 045-597-053). You're welcome to play foosball downstairs on what Italians call the *calcio balilla* ("the little boy soldiers of Mussolini").

Pizza

Pizzeria da Salvatore, Verona's first pizzeria, opened in 1961, when pizza was considered a foreign food...from Naples. They serve the best pizza in town, and a visit here gives a nice excuse to stroll across the river into a part of town with no tourists. It's family-friendly, not fancy or romantic, and you'll share a table with others. Come early, or plan to leave your name on the list and wait a while—they don't take reservations (€6-€9 pizzas, Tue-Sun 19:00-23:00, closed Mon, across Ponte Nuovo to Piazza San Tomaso 6, tel. 045-803-0366).

Pizzeria Du de Cope is a high-energy, informal place (with paper placemats) that buzzes with smartly attired young waiters and locals who consider the pizza here to be the best in the old town center (big €11 salads, €9-13 pizzas, daily 12:00-14:00 & 19:00-23:00, flamboyant desserts, families welcome, no reservations, at Galleria Pelliciai 10, tel. 045-595-562).

Cheap Eats

Döner kebab shops serve hearty, cheap kebabs to munch on stools or take out all over town (most open daily roughly noon-midnight). "Piadina" kebabs are worth the €4, and the super-sized kebabs can fill a couple on a very tight budget for a total of €5. The best kebabs, according to local assessments, are behind the Roman Arena at Via Leoncino 44. There's another good place on the other side of Piazza Brà, near Hotel Europa, at Via Teatro Filarmonico 6. The benches in the center of Piazza Brà are handy for a scenic place to munch your cheap meal.

Brek Cafeteria, a well-run and modern chain, offers a cheap and easy self-serve option with tables right on Piazza Brà—an inexpensive way to eat while enjoying this view (€5 pastas, €6 *secondi*, cheap salad plates, daily 11:30-15:00 & 18:30-22:00, indoor/outdoor seating, facing equestrian statue at Piazza Brà 20).

Supermarket near Piazza Brà: **PAM supermarket** is just outside the historic gate on Piazza Brà (Mon-Sat 8:00-21:00, Sun 9:00-20:00, exit Piazza Brà through the gate and take the first right to Via dei Mutilati 3).

Gelato: The venerable **Gelateria Savoia** has been a local favorite since 1939. It's in an arcade just off Piazza Brà, marked by a happy crowd licking their distinctive *semi-freddo*—a specialty of bitter-almond amaretto, cream and cookie (open long hours daily, just off Piazza Brà at Via Roma 1). On the other side of town, near Ponte Pietra and the Duomo, is **Gelateria Ponte Pietra** (Tue-Sun 14:30-19:30, until 23:00 in summer, closed Mon, at #23; see the end of my self-guided walk, earlier).

Verona Connections

You have three options for getting train tickets in the Verona station: the standard station ticket office (with slow-moving lines), a bank of modern machines (good English descriptions, cash and credit cards accepted), and the Deutsche Bahn ticket office (20 yards from baggage check office in the tunnel, offering tickets at the same cost as the station office but with German efficiency and no lines).

Every hour, at least two trains connect Verona with Venice, Padua, and Vicenza: one's a slow, cheap, regional train; the other is 20 minutes faster, twice as expensive, and requires reservations—meaning you need to choose a particular departure when you buy your ticket (with a slow-train ticket, however, you can just hop on any departure you like).

From Verona by Train to: Venice (2/hour, 1.25-2.25 hours), **Padua** (2/hour, 40-60 minutes), **Vicenza** (2/hour, 30-60 minutes), **Florence** (listed as *Firenze* on train schedules, about hourly,

1.5 hours direct or 2.5 hours with transfer in Bologna), **Bologna** (hourly, 1.5 hours, a few faster trains), **Milan** (2/hour, 1.5-2 hours, a few faster trains), **Rome** (at least hourly, 4-5 hours, often with transfer in Bologna), **Bolzano** (about hourly, 1.75-2.25 hours, avoid "fast" trains that take the same amount of time but cost much more). For more information, visit www.trenitalia.com.

Ravenna

Ravenna is on the tourist map for one reason: its 1,500-year-old churches, decorated with best-in-the-West Byzantine mosaics.

The city's churches and mosaics date from the time (c. A.D. 400-600) when it was the center of Western civilization—a civilization in transition, from Roman to barbarian to Byzantine to medieval. You'll see all these layers in Ravenna.

In 402, barbarian tribes were zeroing in on the city of Rome. The Roman emperor moved his capital to Ravenna, a city well-known as a home port for the imperial navy (today's Classe). Because of its location, Ravenna kept close ties with the other Roman capital at Constantinople (called Byzantium).

Ravenna was conquered by the Goths from Hungary in 476, and the 1,000 years of the Roman Empire came to an end. But Ravenna continued on as the Goths' capital. They kept much of the Roman infrastructure and legitimized their rule by building sophisticated palaces and churches in the Roman style.

In 540, the Byzantine emperor Justinian conquered the Goths. This reunited Italy with the still-thriving Empire to the east. Justinian turned Ravenna into a pinnacle of civilization. It remained a flickering light in Europe's Dark Ages for another 200 years, until the Lombard tribe of Germany booted out the Byzantines (in 751). Ravenna melted into the backwaters of medieval Italy, staying out of historical sight for a thousand years.

In your sightseeing, you'll see art from each of these periods: Roman (Mausoleum of Galla Placidia, Neonian Baptistery), Gothic (Arian Baptistery, Basilica di Sant'Apollinare in Nuovo, Archiepiscopal Museum), Byzantine (Basilica di San Vitale, House of Stone Carpets, Church of Sant'Apollinare in Classe), and medieval (Tomb of Dante, Basilica di San Francesco).

Today, Ravenna's economy booms with a big chemical industry, the discovery of offshore gas deposits, and the construction of a new ship canal. The bustling town center is Italy's best for bicyclists. Residents go about their business, while busloads of tourists slip quietly in and out of town for the best look at the glories of Byzantium this side of Istanbul—specifically, the richest collection anywhere of mosaics from the fifth and sixth centuries. Many are pleasantly surprised by the peaceful charm of this untouristy town.

Planning Your Time

Ravenna is a worthwhile four-hour stop, or even an overnight, particularly for mosaic lovers. Its inexpensive lodgings offer good value for your money. The town is also a doable, though long, day trip from Florence, Venice, or Padua. You could stop here on your way between Venice (or Padua) and Florence.

Orientation to Ravenna

Central Ravenna is quiet, with a pedestrian-friendly core and more bikes than cars. Keep to the sides of the streets; bikes take the center lane (subtly indicated by white brick paving) down the brick "pedestrian" streets. Listen for the outta-my-way bells.

On a quick visit to Ravenna, follow my self-guided walk and visit the Basilica di San Vitale, its adjacent Mausoleum of Galla Placidia, and the Basilica di Sant'Apollinare Nuovo. While the main sights are easily walkable from the station, it's also fun to do the city by bike. A handy bike-rental place is at the train station. If arriving by car, park near the station and pretend you arrived by train.

Tourist Information

The TI is a 15-minute walk (or a 5-minute pedal) from the train station (Mon-Sat 8:30-19:00, until 18:00 Oct-March, Sun 10:00-16:00 year-round, Via Salara 8, tel. 0544-35404, www.turismo.ra.it).

Combo-Ticket: Five of Ravenna's best mosaic sights are covered by a single combo-ticket; just pay €11.50 at the first sight you visit (€9.50 July-Feb). Included are the Basilica di San Vitale, Mausoleum of Galla Placidia, Basilica di Sant'Apollinare Nuovo, Archiepiscopal Museum (with its Chapel of Sant'Andrea), and Neonian Baptistery. All five sights are church-run and have virtually the same hours (daily April-Sept 9:00-19:00, Oct-March 9:00 or 9:30-17:00).

Helpful Hints

Baggage Storage: The **Co-op San Vitale** bike-rental shop, listed below, has lockers (€3-5 depending on size for up to 24 hours).

Laundry: A self-service launderette is a five-minute walk from the train station (€3.50 wash, €3.50 dry, daily 7:00-22:00, go left as you exit the station, then take your first left over the grade crossing to Via Candiano 16, mobile 331-130-2072).

Bike Rental: Co-op San Vitale, in front of the train station, rents

1. Hotel Bisanzio
2. M Club B&B
3. Casa Masoli B&B
4. A Casa di Paola
5. Hotel Italia
6. Albergo I Cherubini
7. To Ostello Dante
8. Ca' de Ven Ristorante
9. Ristorante la Gardèla
10. Ristorante Marchesini
11. Free Flow Bizantino & Covered Market
12. Pizzeria Cupido
13. Pretty Market
14. Bike Rental
15. Launderette

NEAR VENICE

bikes (€1.10/hour, €8.50/day, Mon-Fri 7:00-19:00, closed Sat-Sun, photo ID required, tel. 054-437-031). Many hotels have loaner bikes. The **TI** loans 20 yellow one-speed bikes for free on a first-come, first-served basis (bring your passport). Ask the TI for the free "Cycler" bike-trail map, which includes rides to the sea, parks, and historical sights.

Parking: Don't drive into the center, or you'll be fined. Two inexpensive lots are near the historic core: one accessible from the west side of Via Roma, at Via Mura di Porta Serrata (€1.50/day), and another at Largo Giustiniano just north of the Basilica di San Vitale (€2.80/day). Or find a free lot near the station. Many lots are free overnight (20:00-8:00) and most are free on Sunday.

Local Guide: Private guide Claudia Frassineti is excellent (€95/half-day, mobile 335-613-2996, www.abacoguide.it, claudia.frassinetti@gmail.com).

Self-Guided Walk

Welcome to Ravenna (A Four-Hour Tour)

A visit to Ravenna can be as short as a four-hour loop from the train station. This walk brings you from the train station to Ravenna's top draw (Basilica di San Vitale), quickly taking in a few other sights on the way. When done, you'll be well-oriented and can use any remaining time to visit more of Ravenna's sights.

Start at the train station. The station and surrounding neighborhood were bombed in World War II. Walk (or pedal) the main drag, Viale Farini, from the station directly into town. You'll pass the St. John the Evangelist church on the left, with a rebuilt facade. This was the palace church of the fifth-century Empress Galla Placidia. She and her children were caught at sea in a storm, prayed to St. John (the protector of sailors), and survived. In thanks, she had this church built at the site of their first safe step ashore. At least that's the story. It is true that in ancient times, the town harbor came right up to here. Historic churches are so common in Ravenna that we'll skip this one.

The next big building is the high school, with students' motorbikes parked in front. After that, the boulevard becomes Via Diaz, an arcaded pedestrian shopping street. Remember that the lighter cobbles are for the bikes.

• *At Via degli Ariani, side-trip to the right 50 yards to find the...*

Arian Baptistery

Built during the reign of the Goths (c. 526), this small octagonal building marks the center of their Arian-style Christian faith (see sidebar).

Cost and Hours: Free, daily 8:30-19:30, off-season until 16:00, tel. 0544-543-711, www.turismo.ravenna.it.

Visiting the Baptistery: Theodoric the Great, the Gothic king of Italy (r. 493-526), built the church next door, with this as his baptistery. Imagine the small baptismal pool that once stood beneath this gloriously decorated dome.

The mosaic-covered dome shows Christ standing waist-deep in the River Jordan, being baptized by John the Baptist (in leopardskin robe), as the dove of the Holy Spirit descends. The body builder on the left is the personified River Jordan, next to a vase from which the river springs. Notice the realism in John's stance. The 12 apostles, dynamic, with feet in motion, proceed around the dome. The empty throne between Paul (with scroll) and Peter (with keys) is a reminder that Judgment Day will come.

The mosaic is Arian, stressing Jesus' human rather than divine nature. Jesus is naked, with his genitals only partly obscured by the water. This emphasizes his mortal body, not his divine spirit. He's a beardless youth, suggesting his recent creation by God. The descending dove spews water to purify Jesus, marking the exact moment when Arians believed Jesus' divine nature emerged. Besides heretical Arian elements, there's also the pagan river god, shown in (pagan) Roman fashion as a bearded old man with a vase and river plant.

To modern eyes, these subtle details mean little. But to Emperor Justinian and the Nicenes, these were red flags announcing heresy. While most Arian art was destroyed when Justinian took control, this ceiling is one of the rare survivors.

The adjacent church is closed to the public. It was the cathedral of the Goths, with a simple main structure surviving from the sixth century and a Renaissance portico.

• *Now, return to the pedestrian boulevard, turn right, and continue to...*

Piazza del Popolo

Marking the town center, this square was created by Ravenna's Venetian rulers in the 15th century. The river once flowed to about where the two columns stand. But it got mucky and full of mosquitoes. (Dante died here...of malaria.) One column was topped by a Venetian lion until 1509 when, with the support of Rome, Ravenna won its independence from Venice. Ravenna's citizens pulled down that symbol of Venetian rule and did the local equivalent of tarring and feathering it. The lion was replaced by St. Vitale

(a first-century Christian martyr). The column on the left is topped by Ravenna's first bishop, St. Apollinare. This square is a fine place to join the old guys on benches, watching the community parade by.

• *At the end of Piazza del Popolo, turn left down Via Cairoli two blocks and find the...*

Basilica di San Francesco

Pop into this basilica to see its flooded mosaic-covered crypt below the main

The Arian Heresy

Ravenna's art reflects a centuries-long battle of ideas among Europe's Christians that came to a violent head right here. As you wonder at the beauty of Ravenna's mosaics, you're also witnessing an epic clash between two different interpretations of Christianity.

Around 320 A.D. in Alexandria, a devout Christian priest named Arius (c. 256-336) began preaching a seemingly simple idea: Jesus, being the Son of God, was therefore created by God the Father. This idea touched off a firestorm of debate and division unmatched in Christianity until the Protestant Reformation. Arius had raised questions about the very nature of the Christian God: Is God a single entity (as the head of a monotheistic religion should be); three different persons (God the Father, Jesus Christ, and the Holy Spirit); or something in between?

To keep the peace, Roman Emperor Constantine convened a Council at Nicea (in 325 A.D., near modern Istanbul). Arius was accused of doubting the divinity of Christ, by making him separate from and inferior to God the Father. The Council branded Arius a heretic and burned his books. After splitting many theological hairs, they issued the Nicene Creed, which defined God as a Trinity: There was one God, existing in three persons "of the same substance." (Don't make me try to explain it further, or this book may end up getting burned by some sect somewhere.) The three-in-one Trinity became the standard throughout the Empire, and Arian sects were brutally suppressed.

altar. Today's water table is one yard above the Roman crypt's floor level—so there's a pond with goldfish over the fifth-century mosaics (spend a coin to turn on the light). The interior is simple and Franciscan; the altar features a fourth-century Christian sarcophagus with Jesus in the center and the 12 apostles.

Cost and Hours: Free, daily 7:00-12:00 & 15:00-18:00, Piazza San Francesco, tel. 054-433-256.

• *With your back to the church, cut right through the small wooded park. On your right, next to the double archway, is the...*

Tomb of Dante

After he was exiled from Florence for his political beliefs, Dante lived out the rest of his life in Ravenna. The Florentines forgave Dante posthumously and wanted to bring their famous poet's bones home to rest. To protect Dante's relics from theft by the Florentines, in 1519 Ravenna hid his

But that did not settle the matter. Constantine's own son, a fervent Arian, sent missionaries north across the Danube to convert the barbarian Goths to Arian-style Christianity. A century later, as Rome was falling, those same Goths came knocking on Italy's doorstep. They overran Ravenna (476) and made Arian Christianity the official religion of state, though they tolerated the Nicene Christianity of their Italian subjects.

The churches the Goths built—the Arian Baptistery, Basilica di Sant'Apollinare Nuovo, and Chapel of Sant'Andrea (at the Archiepiscopal Museum)—reflected their Arian faith. Arian mosaics of Jesus emphasized his humanness rather than his divinity. (Don't confuse the Arian sect with Nazi Germany's idea of an Aryan race.)

In 540, the Byzantine Emperor Justinian drove out the Goths. To unite his empire, he demanded both political and theological conformity. Anything with the slightest whiff of Arianism was wiped out. Mosaics were stripped from the walls, statues defaced, and churches were renamed for saints famous for fighting heretics. In their place came art that reflected Byzantine tastes and Trinitarian theology. You'll see evidence of this shift at many of Ravenna's top sights.

Ravenna was Arianism's Waterloo. Sects were snuffed out, Trinitarians triumphed, and the Nicene Creed (in some form) is still said in many Christian churches today.

NEAR VENICE

bones in the Monastery of San Francesco. There they lay forgotten for three centuries, until they were rediscovered and eventually placed here in 1865. In the garden next door, find the mound *(tumulo)* where Dante's bones were hidden during World War II. The Dante memorial—often mistaken for a tomb—in Florence's Santa Croce Church is empty.

Cost and Hours: Free, daily April-Sept 9:30-18:30, Oct-March 9:00-12:00 & 14:00-17:00, Via D. Alighieri 9, tel. 0544-33662.

• *Turn your back to Dante's tomb and walk straight until you reach Piazza del Popolo again. Cross to the far right side of the piazza, where Via IV Novembre leads a block to the colorful...*

Covered Market

The Mercato Coperto, built in 1921, is good for picnic fixings (Mon-Sat 7:00-14:00, closed Sun) and has a busy self-serve cafeteria (closed Sat-Sun, more seating and WC upstairs).

• *With your back to the market's front door, jog right around the building onto Via Cavour, Ravenna's favored street for evening strolling and shopping. The Porta Adriana city gate will come into view ahead of you. Three blocks down, at #117, turn right on Via M. Fanti. As the street ends, continue straight through the squared-off archway. Now follow* Basilica di San Vitale *signs around the left of the building and inside to the ticket office for the...*

▲▲▲Basilica di San Vitale

Imagine: It's A.D. 540. The city of Rome has been looted, the land is crawling with barbarians, and the infrastructure of Rome's thousand-year empire is crumbling fast. Into this chaotic world comes the emperor of the East (Justinian), bringing order and stability, briefly reassembling the empire, and making Ravenna a beacon of civilization.

After buying your ticket, you'll descend to the basilica's floor level, which is lower than today's ground level. First you'll see the basilica itself with its dazzling mosaics and then, across the yard, the small Mausoleum of Galla Placidia.

Cost and Hours: €11.50 combo-ticket (€9.50 July-Feb) also covers Mausoleum of Galla Placidia, Basilica di Sant'Apollinare Nuovo, Archiepiscopal Museum, and Neonian Baptistery; open daily April-Sept 9:00-19:00, Oct-March 9:00-17:30, last entry at 18:45, tel. 0544-541-688, www.ravennamosaici.it.

Information: There's no audioguide, but the gift shop, behind the basilica altar, sells a DVD which also plays continually on a screen at the entrance.

❍ Self-Guided Tour: Step inside the church. The basilica—standing as a sanctuary of order in the midst of the madness after the fall of Rome—is covered with lavish mosaics: gold and glass chips the size of your fingernail. It's impressive enough to see a 1,400-year-old church. But it's rare to see one decorated in brilliant mosaics, still managing to convey the intended feeling that "This peace and stability was brought to you by your emperor and God." The art is an intricate ensemble of images that, with the help of a medieval priest, would teach volumes.

Stand before the altar. The centerpiece, high above, is God in heaven, portrayed as Christ sitting on a celestial orb. He oversees his glorious creation, symbolized by the four rivers.

Running the show on earth is Justinian (left side), sporting both a halo and a crown to indicate that he's both leader of the Church and the state. Here, Justinian brings together the military leaders and the church leaders, all united by the straight line of eyes. The bald bishop of Ravenna—the only person who was actually here—is portrayed most realistically (with a name tag above reading *Maximanus*).

Facing the emperor (from the right side) are his wife, Theodora, and her entourage. Decked out in jewels and pearls, the former dancer who became Justinian's mistress (and then empress) carries a chalice with which to consecrate the new church.

The border inside the apse is decorated with horns of plenty (cornucopia), promising prosperity in return for the people's obedience to the Church and State (Justinian and Theodora).

Sit in a wooden pew, front and center. Get in a medieval frame of mind and study the scene: On the floor a 16th-century inlaid marble labyrinth leads to the center, evocative of the belief that the pilgrimage of life on earth leads to salvation through Christ. The inlaid shell is the scallop shell of St. James—symbol of pilgrims.

While the decor behind you is Baroque and of no particular artistic importance, the walls and ceilings above and in front sparkle with colorful biblical scenes told with a sixth-century exuberance. (The Viennese artist Gustav Klimt sat right here around 1900 and was inspired by the glint of the light on the gold leaf.)

Okay. Now take a longitudinal, ground-up tour from your seat: The inlaid floor maze leads to the sixth-century marble altar (busy with iconography). Above that is Christ on the globe. Appreciate the symmetry. Two angels hold rays of sun (Christ is the origin of light). The scene is flanked by two cities: Bethlehem and Jerusalem (where Jesus was born and died). Above each city are potted grape vines producing wine, symbols of the blood of Christ. The circle with the monogram of Christ (I for Jesus and X for Christ) symbolizes perfection and eternity.

The ceiling above is a festive celebration of God's creation, with 80 different birds from the sixth century—most still flying around Ravenna today. (Bird-watchers—who visit with binoculars—can easily identify these by their exquisitely detailed and accurate feathers.) All creation swirls around Christ as the sacrificial lamb, supported by four angels.

Leading to the apse, arcing high above, is a triumphal arch.

Its 15 medallions depict 12 apostles, two sons of St. Vitale, and a
medieval bearded Christ.

The mid-sixth century was a
time of transition, and many consider Ravenna's mosaics to be both
the last ancient Roman and the
first medieval European works of
art. The beardless Christ (as he was depicted by ancient Romans)
above the altar and the standard medieval portrayal atop the arch
(with a beard) were created within the same generation.

The church's octagonal design—clearly Eastern in origin—inspired at least two churches, including Hagia Sofia, the
church-turned-mosque-turned-museum built 10 years later in
Constantinople (today's Istanbul). Emperor Charlemagne, the
greatest ruler in Europe in A.D. 800, traveled to Ravenna, and was
so impressed that when he returned to his capital, Aix-la-Chapelle
(present-day Aachen in Germany), he built a church that many
consider to be the first great stone building in northern Europe,
modeled after this one.

The pilasters surrounding you are brick, covered by sliced
marble veneers. Similar marble sheets once covered all the walls.
Many were scavenged by Charlemagne to provide flooring for his
great church.

• *From the basilica, head across the grounds to the Mausoleum of Galla
Placidia. Look to the right to see a bit of contemporary mosaic art—a
glassy round of hay (described on the adjacent plaque). Left over from a
recent international festival of mosaics, it reminds visitors that the art
form survives today.*

▲▲Mausoleum of Galla Placidia

Just across the courtyard from the Basilica di San Vitale is a tiny,
humble-looking mausoleum, with the oldest—and, to many, the
most precious—mosaics in Ravenna. Ninety-five percent of the
mosaics here are originals, dating from the late Roman period,
when Ravenna was capital of a declining West.

Cost and Hours: Covered by Basilica di San Vitale combo-
ticket, same hours and contact info as listed earlier for basilica.

Visiting the Mausoleum: The Mausoleum of Galla Placidia
(plah-CHEE-dee-ah) was likely designed to be the burial place
of this daughter, sister, and mother of emperors, who died around
A.D. 450. But Galla Placidia died in Rome, and wasn't buried here.
The three sarcophagi, built for the imperial family but likely only
used by later Christian leaders, stand empty today. The original
floor was about four feet lower, explaining the stunted feel of the
interior. The art's realistic portrayal of tunics and sandals gives us a

peek at the fashions of fifth-century Romans.

The little light that sneaks through the thin alabaster panels brings a glow and a twinkle to the early Christian symbolism that fills the small room. Opposite the door is St. Lawrence being martyred on a fiery grill. He's legendary for mocking his executors, reportedly saying something like "I'm done on this side. You can turn me over now." He was famous as an example of the strength of the feisty early Christians. Note the four Gospels clearly labeled on the bookshelf, another inspiration for these first believers as they were persecuted by the Romans.

The dome is filled with stars. Along with Mark's lion, Luke's ox, Matthew's Archangel, and John's eagle, the golden cross rises from the east, bringing life to all. Doves drink from fountains, symbolic of souls finding nourishment in the Word of God. In both transepts are deer, reminding worshippers of Psalms 42: "Like the thirsty deer longs for spring water, so my soul longs for you, my God."

Look toward the back of the mausoleum. Cover the light from the door with your hand (or close the curtain) to see the standard Roman portrayal of Christ—beardless and as the Good Shepherd.

Jesus, dressed in gold and purple like a Roman emperor, is the King of Paradise—receiving the faithful (represented by lambs). The Eastern influence (perhaps inspired by the designs on fine Persian carpets or silks) is apparent in the vault's decorative patterns.

• *Our walk is done. Got a train to catch? Head straight back to the station. If you have more time, visit the other sights included on your basilica ticket on your way: the Neonian Baptistery, the Archiepiscopal Museum, and the Basilica di Sant'Apollinare Nuovo.*

More Sights in Ravenna

▲▲**Basilica di Sant'Apollinare Nuovo**—This austere sixth-century church has a typical early-Christian-basilica floor plan and two huge and wonderfully preserved side panels.

Cost and Hours: Covered by Basilica di San Vitale combo-ticket, daily April-Sept 9:00-19:00, Oct-March 9:30-17:00, on Via di Roma, tel. 0544-541-688, www.ravennamosaici.it.

Visiting the Basilica: Start by seeking out the two side panels. One is a procession of haloed virgins, each bringing gifts to the Madonna and the Christ Child. Opposite, Christ is on his throne with four angels, awaiting a solemn procession of 26 martyrs. Ignoring the Baroque altar from a thousand years later, you can clearly see the rectangular Roman hall of justice (basilica) floor plan—which was adopted by Christian churches and used throughout the Middle Ages.

This basilica started (c. 500) as an Arian church—the palace church of King Theodoric of the Goths. Theodoric decorated it with scenes of himself and his royal palace amid Christ and the saints. Look for original, surviving Arian art in the front (on the left, Mary and baby Jesus; on the right, Jesus and four angels) and in the rear (two cityscapes: Classe and Ravenna).

When Justinian arrived, he transformed the church in the Byzantine (and Nicene) style. If you study the arcades in the cityscapes you can see where Arian figures were erased, leaving only bits of hands and fingers on the columns, and blotted-out haloes behind the curtains. The brilliant white-robed figures parading on both sides were remade in the mid-500s with a Byzantine rather than Arian message. But the uppermost panels (hard to see without binoculars) are original Theodoric Arian: prophets (between windows), miracles of Christ (on the left), and scenes from the last week of Jesus' life and his Resurrection (on the right).

Nearby: You can have a quick lunch at the air-conditioned, efficient Sant'Apollinare Self-Serve cafeteria on the church grounds (Mon-Fri 11:30-14:30, closed Sat-Sun).

▲**Archiepiscopal Museum**—This museum, in Ravenna's Duomo, contains the sixth-century Chapel of Sant'Andrea. Built as the private prayer chapel for Theodoric's bishop (c. 500), today it anchors a fine collection of Roman, Byzantine-Christian, and pagan statues, reliefs, and mosaics.

Cost and Hours: Covered by Basilica di San Vitale combo-ticket, daily April-Sept 9:00-19:00, Oct-March 9:30-17:00, on Piazza Arcivescovado, tel. 0544-541-688, www.ravennamosaici.it.

Visiting the Museum: You'll enter the chapel under a sixth-century mosaic showing Christ as a religious warrior, stepping triumphantly on a lion and snake (ancient symbols of evil) and carrying the cross as if it were a weapon. The book he holds reads in Latin, "I am the way, the truth, and the life." This is a strong pro-Trinity statement (Jesus, God, and the Holy Spirit are one) against the Arian heresy. The main chamber of the charming chapel is covered in rich mosaics, with lots of sixth-century symbolism and realistic portrait medallions.

In the next room is the museum's other highlight, an exquisite sixth-century Byzantine ivory throne, decorated with scenes from the life of Christ. It was carved for Bishop Maximian, Justinian's Trinitarian appointee, the man who oversaw construction of the Basilica di San Vitale, and whose bald head appears in its mosaics. In another room is an interesting circular calendar designed to keep track of the dates for Easter in the 500s and 600s.

▲**Neonian Baptistery**—Also known as the Baptistery of the Orthodox, this octagonal space dates from about the year 400.

Imagine pagan adults immersed in the pool under glorious ceiling mosaics as they convert to Christianity. The mosaic portrays the common baptistery theme: John the Baptist baptizing Christ, with the personification of the River Jordan looking on. The scene is ringed by empty chairs waiting to welcome you into the eternal heavenly banquet. Twelve apostles with dancing feet—their tunics and cloaks alternating between gold and white—give the room a joyful visual sense of rhythm. The acanthus flowers dividing the apostles were the botanic inspiration for the Corinthian capital, the Roman capital of choice. Decoration on the lower walls features dark purple disks made of precious porphyry stone and a gold leafy arcade creating almond frames for the prophets.

Cost and Hours: Covered by Basilica di San Vitale combo-ticket, daily April-Sept 9:00-19:00, Oct-March 9:30-17:00, next to Ravenna's Duomo, tel. 0544-541-688, www.ravennamosaici.it.

House of Stone Carpets (Domus dei Tappeti di Pietra)—Discovered in 1993, the stone mosaic floors of this sixth-century Byzantine house show both pictorial images and abstract designs. Excavations revealed many layers, dating back to the second century B.C. All were peeled away and preserved elsewhere. Only the sixth-century floor (12 rooms on one level) was put back and exhibited here, very close to its original location. Because this was a private home, its art could break from the conservative norms for public art of the age. The highlight is the wonderfully realistic

Dance of the Four Seasons. Don't miss the fourth-century Christ as a Shepherd, which some consider the earliest portrayal of Jesus (it's hung on a wall; part of the face was lost to modern excavations). A visit here is almost meaningless without the €1 audioguide.

Cost and Hours: €4; March-Oct daily 10:00-18:30, July-Aug Tue and Fri until 22:30; Nov-Feb Tue-Fri 10:00-17:00, Sat-Sun 10:00-18:00, closed Mon; ask for the 10-minute English-language video—the computer-generated images help visitors envision the place in action; entrance through Church of Sant'Eufemia, on Via Barbiani just off Via Cavour near Piazza Baracca, tel. 0544-32512, www.ravennantica.it.

More Mosaics: The same association that runs the House of Stone Carpets also runs two other mosaic sights: **TAMO** has little in the way of historical artifacts, but tells the story of mosaic-making (€4, daily 10:00-18:30, Via Rondinelli 2); **Rasponi Crypt** displays a floor of mosaics pieced together from different sites, crazy-quilt style (€2, daily 10:00-13:00 & 15:00-18:30, Piazza San Francesco).

Near Ravenna

▲▲**Church of Sant'Apollinare in Classe**—The final major sight for Byzantine mosaic fans is a sixth-century church standing a couple of miles outside of Ravenna in the suburb of Classe. It's impressive, but comes in fourth place after the Basilica di San Vitale, Mausoleum of Galla Placidia, and Basilica di Sant'Apollinare Nuovo. On a quick day trip, it's skippable.

Cost and Hours: €3, Mon-Sat 8:30-19:30, Sun 13:00-19:30, last entry at 19:00, Via Romea Sud, tel. 0544-473-569, www.turismo.ravenna.it.

Getting There: The church is two miles out of town—an easy bike ride. To go by bus, buy two local bus tickets (€1 each) at any tobacco shop, then catch bus #4A or #4B across the street from the train station (on the corner by the park; 3/hour Mon-Sat, 2/hour on Sun, 15 minutes; save second ticket for return trip). The bus also leaves from Piazza Caduti (stop is on the corner). To return to Ravenna from the church, walk back toward town along the main road about 100 yards to find the bus shelter on the right.

Visiting the Church: The statue of Emperor Augustus, standing in front of the church, is a reminder that Classe was a strategic navy base in Roman times. In early Christian days, Classe was a big pilgrimage destination and home to a large Christian community. Today, little remains other than its church, and even that was nearly bombed-out in World War II when the Germans used its medieval tower as a lookout.

The artistic treasure here is the mosaic work in the apse, 90 percent of which is original from the sixth century. The scene is an abstract portrayal of the Transfiguration of Jesus. The cross with a tiny portrait of Christ in its center beams light. God's hand above affirms that "This is the Truth." The three lambs represent James, John, and Peter. The landscape is of pine trees, which once forested the region. And St. Apollinare, the first local bishop, is celebrated because it was he who brought Christianity to the area.

The rest of the church—its mosaics lost to time—is pretty plain. While many churches this old have settled and the bases of their columns are no longer visible, here the floor level remains unchanged and you can admire the columns' original bases. Near the entrance, a bilingual display panel gives detailed information on the church.

Overrated Sight—The nearby beach town of Rimini is a crowded mess.

Sleeping in Ravenna

In the Pedestrian Zone, near Piazza del Popolo

$$$ Hotel Bisanzio is a business-class splurge renting 38 rooms in the city center (Sb-€86, small Db-€108, mid-size Db-€124, large Db-€136, air-con, free Wi-Fi, usually free on-street parking with hotel permits; Via Salara 30, tel. 054-421-7111, fax 054-432-539, www.bisanziohotel.com, info@bizanziohotel.com). From Piazza del Popolo, take Via IV Novembre to the market, turn left

Sleep Code

(€1 = about $1.40, country code: 39)
S = Single, **D** = Double/Twin, **T** = Triple, **Q** = Quad, **b** = bathroom, **s** = shower only. Unless otherwise noted, credit cards are accepted, English is spoken, and prices include breakfast. Many cities in Italy levy a hotel tax of €2 per person, per night, which must be paid in cash (not included in the rates I've quoted).

To help you easily sort through these listings, I've divided the accommodations into three categories, based on the price for a standard double room with bath:

  $$$ Higher Priced—Most rooms €100 or more.
   $$ Moderately Priced—Most rooms between €60-100.
    $ Lower Priced—Most rooms €60 or less.

Prices can change without notice; verify the hotel's current rates online or by email.

onto Via Cavour, then take the first right.

$$ M Club B&B is a creative, comfortable, and stylish five-room place with an elegant breakfast room, spacious bedrooms, and thoughtful touches. Each unique room is described on their website (straight pricing: Db-€70-120 depending on size, big Qb suite-€130, free Wi-Fi, loaner bikes, Piazza Baracca 26, tel. 333-955-6466, fax 054-421-5250, www.m-club.it, info@m-club.it, Michael). The M Club faces the Porta Adriana gate at the far end of the old town from the train station (a 15-minute walk).

$$ Casa Masoli B&B's six elegantly outfitted rooms include giant bathrooms in a wood-paneled Art Deco style. You're in a family home here; grandmotherly Signora Masoli works quietly alongside daughter Anna and grandchildren Chiara and Alessandro (Sb-€50, Db-€70, Tb-€90, 4th and 5th person-€20 each, peaceful garden, air-con, free Wi-Fi, library, Via G. Rossi 22, mobile tel. 335-609-9471 or 339-544-8405, www.casa masoli.it, anna@casamasoli.it). From Piazza del Popolo, walk up Via S. Ferruzzi, jogging left onto Via G. Rossi after a couple of blocks.

$$ A Casa di Paola is a converted private home (Paola's mother has an apartment on the ground floor) with eight nicely decorated rooms and comfy common spaces (Sb-€50, Db-€70, Tb-€90, Qb-€120, Quint/b-€140, air-con, free Internet access and Wi-Fi, Via P. Costa 26, tel. 054-439-425, mobile tel. 347-730-6386, www.acasadipaola.it, info@acasadipaola.it).

Near the Train Station

These places are convenient, but have less atmosphere.

$$ Hotel Italia, just 100 yards from the train station, feels like a chain hotel but is actually family-owned. Its 45 rooms lack character but provide comfort and lots of space (Sb-€60, Db-€90, Tb-€110, Qb-€130, air-con, free Wi-Fi, free loaner bikes, free parking on first-come, first-served basis, turn left out of station, Viale Pallavicini 4, tel. 0544-212-363, fax 0544-217-004, www .hotelitaliaravenna.com, info@hotelitaliaravenna.com, Mauro).

$ Albergo I Cherubini, near the train station, has 18 basic, no-frills rooms and dark hallways. Ask for a room off the street (S-€30, D-€50, Db-€65, Tb-€75, Qb-€90, fans, free Wi-fi, Via R. Brancaleone 42, tel. & fax 054-439-403, www.albergoristorante icherubini.it, info@albergoristoranteicherubini.it, Donatella).

Hostel: **$ Ostello Dante,** a 15-minute walk from the station, has Wi-Fi, loaner bikes, and a game room (140 beds, €18/bed in 4-bed rooms, Db-€48, family rooms with bath-€22/person, €3/night extra for non-hostel members, includes breakfast and sheets, towels-€1, laundry-€5/load, 11:00-14:30 lockout, 23:30 curfew or pay €1 for magnetic entrance key, closed Nov-Feb, Via Nicolodi 12,

bus #70 from train station, tel. & fax 054-442-1164, www.hostel
ravenna.com, hostelravenna@hotmail.com).

Eating in Ravenna

Ca' de Ven ("House of Wine"), the most famous restaurant in
town, is affordable. It fills a 16th-century warehouse with communal seating and residents enjoying quality wine and traditional
regional cuisine, including *piadina* (peeah-DEE-nah; unleav-
ened bread served plain or with pizza-type stuffing). Their dessert specialty, *torta di marzapane*—a decadent almond-and-cocoa
brownie—is good with sweet red wine. Reserve ahead for dinner
(€4-6 *piadina*, €8-9 pastas, €12-13 *secondi,* no cover, Tue-Sun 11:00-
14:15 & 18:00-22:00, closed Mon, 2-minute walk from Piazza del
Popolo on Via Cairoli, which turns into Via C. Ricci, Via C. Ricci
24, tel. 054-430-163).

Ristorante la Gardèla is a favorite. Their *cappelletti,* a cheese-
stuffed pasta, is served *in brodo* (soup) or *in ragu* (meat sauce). If
Ravenna had a town dining room, this would be it. The fun-loving
waitstaff has been here for years and the restaurant has all the nice
touches without the pretense. While there are a few tables outside and upstairs, I like the jolly main floor (€5-6 pastas, €7-10 *secondi,* €15 and €25 set menus, €1.50 cover, Fri-Wed 12:00-14:30 &
19:00-22:00, closed Thu, from Piazza del Popolo follow Via IV
Novembre past Piazza della Costa to corner of Via Ponte Marino
3, tel. 054-421-7147).

Ristorante Marchesini is an upscale self-serve restaurant
(over a delicatessen) offering delicious salads and homemade pastas
(€7 pastas, €10 *secondi,* €1.50 cover, Mon-Sat 12:00-14:30, closed
Sun, 5-minute walk from Piazza del Popolo, on corner of Piazza
Caduti at Via Mazzini 6—ride elevator to first floor, tel. 054-421-
2309).

Free Flow Bizantino, inside the covered market, is a self-serve
cafeteria serving lunch only (€4 pastas, €5 *secondi,* €8 three-course
lunch, Mon-Fri 11:45-14:45, closed Sat-Sun, tel. 0544-32073).

Pizzeria Cupido is good for a cheap and traditional lunch or
snack. Try their *piadina* or *crescione* (calzone-like) sandwich. These
tasty sandwiches (€3.50-5) come stuffed with a variety of meats,
cheeses, and vegetables. Consider one filled with *squacquerone,* a
soft regional cream cheese (no cover, Sun-Wed 11:00-16:00, Thu-
Sat 11:00-20:00, just up Via Cavour from the market at Via Cavour
43, mobile tel. 393-670-8225).

Supermarkets: For lunch, assemble a picnic at the **covered
market** (Mon-Sat 7:00-14:00, closed Sun) and enjoy your feast in
the shady gardens of the Rocca Brancaleone fortress (daily until
18:00; 5-minute walk from station, follow Via Maroncelli until you

NEAR VENICE

see the walls). If the covered market is closed, visit **Pretty Market,** on Via di Roma at the corner of Via A. Moriani (Mon-Sat 7:30-20:30, Sun 9:00-13:30 & 16:30-20:30).

Ravenna Connections

Ravenna's train-station ticket office is open daily 6:00-20:30. The station has no automated ticket machines.

From Ravenna by Train to: Venice (roughly hourly, 3-3.5 hours), **Padua** (roughly hourly, 2.5 hours), **Florence** (about hourly, 2.5 hours by fast train, no slow train option). All of these trips require a change in either Ferrara or Bologna.

THE DOLOMITES

Dolomiti

Italy's dramatic rocky rooftop, the Dolomites, offers some of the best mountain thrills in Europe. Bolzano is the gateway to the Dolomites, and Castelrotto is a good home base for your exploration of Alpe di Siusi, Europe's largest alpine meadow.

The sunny Dolomites are well-developed, and the region's famous valleys and towns suffer from après-ski fever. The cost for the comfort of reliably good weather is a drained-reservoir feeling. Lovers of other parts of the Alps may miss the lushness that comes with the unpredictable weather farther north. But the bold, light-gray cliffs and spires flecked with snow, above green meadows and beneath a blue sky, offer a powerful, unique, and memorable mountain experience. Dolomite, a sedimentary rock similar to limestone, gives these mountains their distinctive shape and color.

A hard-fought history has left the region bicultural, with an emphasis on the German. Most locals speak German first, and some wish they were still part of Austria. In the Middle Ages, as part of the Holy Roman Empire, the region faced north. Later, it was firmly in the Austrian Habsburg realm. By losing World War I, Austria's South Tirol became Italy's Alto Adige. Mussolini did what he could to Italianize the region, including giving each town an Italian name. But even as recently as the 1990s, secessionist groups agitated violently for more autonomy—with some success (see sidebar).

The government has wooed locals with economic breaks, which have made this one of Italy's richest areas (as local prices attest), and today all signs and literature in the province of Alto Adige/Südtirol are in both languages. Many include a third language, Ladin—an ancient Romance language still spoken in a few traditional areas. (I have listed both the Italian and German, so the confusion caused by this guidebook will match that experienced in your travels.)

In spite of all the glamorous ski resorts and busy construction cranes, the regional color survives in a warm blue-aproned, ruddy-faced, felt-hat-with-feathers way. There's yogurt and yodeling for breakfast. Culturally as much as geographically, the area is reminiscent of Austria. In fact, the Austrian region of Tirol is named for a village that is now part of Italy.

Planning Your Time

Train travelers can side-trip into the mountains from Bolzano (1.5 hours north of Verona). To get a feel for the alpine culture, spend at least one night in Castelrotto. But with two nights there, you can actually get out and hike. Tenderfeet ride the bus, catch a cable car, and stroll. For serious mountain thrills, do a six-hour hike. And for a memory that won't soon fade away, spend a night in a mountain hut. Always remember to check the latest transportation

Ich bin ein Italiener

With the exception of Bolzano, where Italian has become the primary language, you'll hear mostly German in Dolomite villages. Overall, seven in ten Italians living in the South Tirol speak German as their mother tongue. Many are fair-skinned and blue-eyed, prefer dumplings and strudel to pasta and gelato, and feel a closer bond with their ancestors in Austria than with their swarthy countrymen to the south. Most have a working knowledge of Italian, but they watch German-language TV, read newspapers *auf Deutsch,* and live in Tirolean-looking villages.

At the end of World War I, the region was ceded by Austria (loser) to Italy (winner). Mussolini suppressed the Germanic cultural elements as part of his propaganda campaign to praise all things Italian. Many German-speakers hoped that Hitler would "liberate" them from Italy, but Hitler's close alliance with Mussolini prevented that from happening. Instead, in June 1939, residents were given six months to make a hard choice—move north to the Fatherland and become German citizens, or stay in their homeland *(Heimat)* under Italian rule. The vast majority (212,000, or 85 percent) made the decision to leave, but because of the outbreak of World War II, only 75,000 actually moved.

At the war's end, German-speakers were again disappointed when the Allied powers refused to grant them autonomy or the chance to become Austrian citizens. Instead, the victors decided to stick with the prewar arrangement.

The region rebuilt and the two linguistic groups patched things up, but for the remainder of the 20th century, there was always an underlying problem: German-speakers were continually outvoted by the Italian-speaking majority in the regional government (comprising two provinces, Italian-speaking Trentino and German-speaking Alto Adige/Südtirol). German-speakers lobbied the national government for more control on the provincial (not regional) level, even turning to demonstrations and violence. Over the years, Rome has slowly and grudgingly granted increased local control.

Today, Alto Adige/Südtirol has a large measure of autonomy written into the country's 2001 constitution, though it's still officially tied to Trentino. Roads, water, electricity, communications, and schools are all under local control, including the Free University of Bozen-Bolzano, founded in 1998.

timetables before you embark on an outing.

If you have a car, you can drive the three-hour loop from Bolzano or Castelrotto (Val Gardena-Sella Pass-Val di Fassa) and ride one of the lifts to the top for a ridge walk. Connecting Bolzano and Venice by the Great Dolomite Road takes two hours longer than by the autostrada, but is far more scenic (see "More Sights in the Dolomites" at the end of this chapter).

Hiking season is mid-June through mid-October. The region is particularly crowded, booming, and blooming from mid-July through mid-September (but once you're out on the trails, you'll leave the crowds behind). It's packed with Italian vacationers in August. Spring is usually dead, with lifts shut down, huts closed, and the most exciting trails still under snow. Many hotels and restaurants close in April and November. Ski season (Dec-Easter) is busiest of all. For more information, visit www.visitdolomites .com.

Bolzano

Willkommen to the Italian Tirol! If Bolzano (Bozen in German) weren't so sunny, you could be in Innsbruck. This enjoyable old town of 100,000 is the most convenient gateway to the Dolomites, especially if you're relying on public transportation. It's just the place to take a Tirolean stroll.

Orientation to Bolzano

Tourist Information

Bolzano's TI is helpful (Mon-Fri 9:00-19:00, Sat 9:30-18:00, closed Sun, Piazza Walther/Waltherplatz 8, tel. 0471-307-000, www.bolzano-bozen.it). Pick up the city map and the *Historic and Cultural Route* brochure (also downloadable from website).

Consider buying the **museummobil Card**, which covers most museums in the South Tirol (including the archaeology museum, with its famous Ice Man), plus trains, buses, the Funivia del Renon/Rittner Seilbahn cable car, and more (€28/3 days, available at local TIs and some hotels, www.mobilcard.info). This card saves you several euros if you visit the Ice Man, ride the cable car, take the train round-trip from Bolzano to Klobenstein, and take the bus round-trip from Bolzano to Castelrotto. The **Mobilcard** is a transit-only pass that covers trains, buses, and lifts (€15/1 day, €23/3 days, sold at TIs and transit offices, www.mobilcard.info).

Serious hikers visit the **Alpine Information Center** (Alpine Auskunft) run by the Alpenverein Südtirol, a local hiking club. It offers a map library (also available at http://trekking.suedtirol.info) and advice on trails and mountain huts. It's deep in the old town in an arcade that you enter at Via Dr. Streiter/Dr.-Streiter-Gasse 16; ring the bell and go upstairs (Mon-Thu 9:00-12:00 & 13:00-17:00, Fri 9:00-12:00, closed Sat-Sun, tel. 0471-999-955, www.alpine -auskunft.it).

Arrival in Bolzano

There are two train stations for Bolzano—you want just *Bolzano*, not *Bolzano Süd*. To get to the TI and downtown from the train station, veer left up the tree-lined Viale della Stazione/Bahnhofsallee, and walk past the bus station (on your left) two blocks to **Piazza Walther/Waltherplatz.** You'll see the TI on the right side of the square. The medieval heart of town is on the far side of the square: The arcaded Via dei Portici/Laubengasse is Bolzano's old main street. It leads to Piazza Erbe/Obstplatz, which has an open-air produce market (see "Markets," below); the Ice Man is a couple of blocks farther beyond.

Helpful Hints

Sleepy Sundays: The city is really dead on Sunday (young locals add "and during the rest of the week, too").

Markets: Piazza Erbe/Obstplatz hosts an ancient and still-thriving open-air produce market (Mon-Fri all day, Sat morning only, closed Sun). Wash your produce in the handy drinking fountain in the middle of the market. Another market (offering more variety, not just food) is held Saturday mornings on Piazza della Vittoria.

Internet Access: Multi Kulti Internet Point is a short walk from Piazza Walther/Waltherplatz at Via Dr. Streiter/Dr.-Streiter-Gasse 9 (€3/hour, Mon-Sat 9:00-23:00, closed Sun, tel. 0471-056-056).

Baggage Storage: While there's no baggage-storage service at the train station, there is a tiny *deposito bagagli* at the bus station just a block away (€3/24 hours, €10 refundable deposit, out back from where the buses leave, at the entrance to the bathrooms, daily 7:00-13:00 & 14:00-19:30).

Laundry: Lava e Asciuga launderette is at Via Rosmini/Rosmini Strasse 81, about two blocks west of the South Tirol Museum of Archaeology (€3 wash, €3 dry, English instructions, daily 7:30-22:30, last wash 21:00, mobile 340-220-2323).

Bike Rental: The city has a well-developed bike-trail system. Rental bikes are curiously cheap here. Plenty of bikes are available for rent just off Piazza Walther/Waltherplatz on Viale della Stazione/Bahnhofsallee on the right side (€1/6 hours, €2/6-24 hours, €5/24 hours, €10 refundable deposit,

Bolzano

CORSO DELLA LIBERTÀ

VIA BATTISTI

Piazza della Vittoria

VICTORY MONUMENT

Petrarcha Park

PONTE TALVERA

SOUTH TIROL MUSEUM OF ARCHAEOLOGY (ÖTZI THE ICE MAN)

VIA MUSEO

MUSEO CIVICO

EUROPA GALLERY

VIA LEONARDO

Piazza Sernesi

MUSEUM OF MODERN ART

VIA OSPEDALE

VIA CASSA DI RISPARMIO

VIALE VENEZIA

VIA SAN QUIRINO

Talvera River

VIA ROSMINI

VIA CARDUCCI

VIA CARDUCCI

VIA DANTE

VIA FLUME

VIA ZARA

VIA MARCONI

VIALE DRUSO

VIALE TRISTE

VIA VERONA

Isarco/

Bike

THE DOLOMITES

① Hotel Figl
② Hotel Greif
③ Stadt Hotel Città
④ Parkhotel Laurin
⑤ Hotel Feichter
⑥ Kolpinghaus Bozen
⑦ Youth Hostel Bolzano
⑧ Weisses Rössl Restaurant
⑨ Ca' de Bezzi/Gasthaus Batzenhäusl
⑩ Hopfen & Co. Restaurant
⑪ Paulaner Stuben
⑫ Enoteca Il Baccaro
⑬ Gasthaus Fink
⑭ DeSpar Supermarkets (3)
⑮ Internet Café
⑯ Alpine Info Center
⑰ Launderette
⑱ Bike Rental

ID required, April-Sept Mon-Sat 7:30-19:50, Oct until 18:50, closed Sun and Nov-March, tel. 0471-997-578). The TI also has 10 bikes to rent for €5 per day (€10 refundable deposit, ID required, ask for a map).

Self-Guided Walk

Welcome to Bolzano

Everything mentioned in Bolzano is a 10-minute walk from the train station and the main square, Piazza Walther/Waltherplatz.
• Start in...

Piazza Walther/Waltherplatz: The square's namesake, Walther von der Vogelweide, honored by the statue in the center, was a 12th-century politically incorrect German poet who courageously stood up to the Holy Roman Emperor. Walther's spunk against a far bigger power represents the Germanic pride of this region. The statue is made of marble quarried in the village of Laas, north of Bolzano. The US chose this same marble for the 86,000 crosses and Stars of David needed to mark the WWII dead buried at Normandy and other battlefields across Europe.

When not hosting Bolzano's Christmas market, flower market (May Day), or Speck Fest (a spring ham festival), Piazza Walther/Waltherplatz is simply the town's living room. And locals care about it. It was the site of Italy's first McDonald's, which—in the early 1990s—became the first McDonald's to be shut down by locals protesting American fast food. Today, the square is home to trendy cafés such as Café Walther, where (outside of meal times). you're welcome to nurse a "Venetian" *spritz* or a pricier cocktail as long as you like.

• *Cross the street to the big church.*

The Cathedral: The cathedral's glazed-tile roof is typical of the Germanic world, a reminder that from the sixth century until 1919, German was the region's official language. Then, suddenly: *Buon giorno!* Walk around to the right to the Romanesque Lion's Gate. The church was flattened in World War II (a distinct downside of being located near a train station in 20th-century Europe). Stepping inside, you get a Teutonic—not Italian—feel. The mostly Gothic interior is broken by an impressive Baroque tabernacle. Most of the art here is by Bavarian artists. There's a stiff, pre-Michelangelo, 15th-century *pietà* to the left of the altar. The sandstone pulpit (c. 1500), with its reliefs of the four Church fathers (whose presence gave credibility to sermons preached here) is reminiscent of Vienna's St. Stephen's Cathedral.

• *Leaving the church, walk diagonally across Piazza Walther/ Waltherplatz and find the street to the right of the big Sparkasse bank building. Go down it for one block, to...*

Piazza del Grano/Kornplatz: Nine hundred years ago, this was Bolzano's main square. The building to your right was the bishop's castle. The traditional food stand selling *Vollkornbrot* (dense, whole-grain bread) and pretzels is another reminder of German heritage. Find the flower beds at the top of the square; a bronze relief on a large stone shows Bolzano's street plan in the 12th century—a one-street arcaded town huddled within a forti- fied wall.

• *Continue uphill into the original medieval town, passing the "Wurstel Boutique" on your left (yet another reminder of this region's Germanic orientation).*

Via dei Portici/Laubengasse: This was the only street in 12th-century Bolzano. Step into the center (dodging bikes).

Looking east and west, you see the width of the original town. Thirty yards to the left is the old city hall—the street's only Gothic building (with frescoed pointed arches). The other buildings are all basically the same: Each had a storm cellar, cows out back, a ground-level shop, and living quarters upstairs. Bay windows were designed for maximum light—just right for clerks keeping track of accounts and for women doing their weaving. The arcades *(Lauben)*, typical of Tirol, sheltered merchants and their goods from both snow and sun. Narrow side passages lead to neighboring streets. The only balcony marks the one Baroque building—once the mercantile center (with a fine worth-a-look courtyard), now a skippable museum.

• *Turn left on Via dei Portici/Laubengasse and continue to the end, where you'll find a bustling market.*

Piazza Erbe/Obstplatz: This square hosts an open-air pro- duce market, liveliest in the morning (Mon-Fri all day, Sat morn- ings, closed Sun). The historic market fountain gives Bolzano its only hint of the sea—a 17th-century statue of Neptune. Stroll around and see what's in season. All of the breads, strudel, and hams *schmecken sehr gut*.

• *From the market, Via Museo/Museumstrasse (called Butcher Street until the 19th century, when a museum opened) leads straight to Frozen Fritz.*

Sights in Bolzano

▲▲South Tirol Museum of Archaeology (Museo Archeologico dell'Alto Adige/Südtiroler Archäologiemuseum)—

This excellent museum features the actual corpse of Ötzi the Ice Man. His frozen body was discovered high in the mountains on the Italian/Austrian border by a German couple in 1991. Police initially believed the corpse was a lost hiker, and Ötzi was chopped roughly out of the glacier, damaging his left side. But upon discovering his pre-Bronze Age hatchet, officials realized what they had found: a 5,300-year-old, nearly perfectly preserved man with clothing and gear in excellent condition for his age. Later, researchers pinned down the cause of death—an arrowhead buried in Ötzi's left shoulder.

As the body was found right on the border, Austria and Italy squabbled briefly over who would get him. Tooth enamel studies have now shown that he did grow up on the Italian side. An Austrian journalist dubbed him Ötzi, after the Ötztal valley, where he was discovered.

With Ötzi as the centerpiece, the museum takes you on an intriguing journey through time, recounting the evolution of humanity—from the Paleolithic era to the Roman period and finally to the Middle Ages—in vivid detail. The exhibit offers informative displays and models, video demonstrations of Ötzi's extraction and his personal effects, and interactive computers.

You'll see Ötzi himself—still frozen—as well as an artist's reconstruction of what he looked like when alive. In his mid-40s at the time of his death, Ötzi was 5 feet, 3 inches tall, with brown hair and brown eyes. He weighed about 110 pounds and likely had trouble with his knees.

Glass cases display his incredibly well-preserved and fascinating clothing and gear, including a finely stitched two-color coat, his goathide loincloth, a fancy hat, shoes, a well-crafted hatchet, 14 arrows, a bow, and fire-making gadgets.

Cost and Hours: €9, tours-€2.50; Tue-Sun 10:00-18:00, closed Mon except July-Aug and Dec; last entry 30 minutes before closing, no photos, no café, near the river at Via Museo/Museumstrasse 43, tel. 0471-320-100, www.iceman.it.

Dominican Church (Chiesa dei Domenicani/Dominikanerkirche)—Drop by this 13th-century church to see its Chapel of St. John (San Giovanni/St. Johannes; chapel is through the archway and on the right), frescoed in the 14th century by the Giotto School.

Cost and Hours: Free, €0.50 coin lights dim interior, Mon-Sat 9:30-17:00, Sun 12:00-18:00, on Piazza Domenicani, two blocks west of Piazza Walther.

Lift to Oberbozen and the Ritten—The **Funivia del Renon/Rittner Seilbahn** cable car whisks you over the hills from Bolzano to the touristy resort village of Oberbozen, where Sigmund Freud and wife once celebrated their wedding anniversary. The reasonably priced, 12-minute ride is the main attraction, offering views of the town, surrounding mountains, made-for-yodeling-farmsteads and 18-wheelers downshifting along the expressway from Austria. The cable car's valley station is a five-block walk east from the Bolzano train station along Via Renon/Rittner Strasse or from Piazza Municipio/Rathausplatz in the old center (€10 round-trip, departures year-round Mon-Sat 6:30-22:38, Sun 7:10-22:38; leaves every 4 minutes, every 12 minutes after 21:00; closes for maintenance for a week in March and Nov; for info call regional transport hotline at tel. 840-000-471 or visit www.sii.bz.it). While the cable car is fun, it is no replacement for a trip to Castelrotto and Alpe di Siusi.

At the end of the ride, **Oberbozen** (elevation 4,000 feet) is mostly a collection of resort hotels. From Oberbozen, a narrow-gauge train makes the 16-minute trip to **Klobenstein,** a larger and slightly less touristy village at 3,800 feet (€3.50 one-way, €6 round-trip, €15 round-trip for both cable car and train, leaves daily at least hourly). The local TI has branches in both villages (www.ritten.com). In Oberbozen, the TI is in the train station building, just steps from the lift station (Mon-Fri 9:00-12:30 & 15:00-18:00, Sat 9:00-12:30, closed Sun in summer, tel. 0471-345-245). The Klobenstein TI is a five-minute walk from the train station (Mon-Fri 8:30-18:00, Sat 8:30-12:00, closed Sun, tel. 0471-356-100).

The lift station and TIs have brochures suggesting short walks. More interesting than Oberbozen itself (though not a must-see) are the nearby **"earth pyramids,"** which are a 30-minute walk downhill from the cable-car station and can be glimpsed from the cable car itself. The pyramids, created by eroding glacial debris dumped at the end of the last ice age, are Bryce Canyon-like pinnacles that rise out of the ridge. Klobenstein has its own earth pyramids a 45-minute walk from town. Another walk is the Freudpromenade, a fairly level, 1.5-hour stroll between Oberbozen and Kloben-stein (you can take the train back).

Sleeping in Bolzano

THE DOLOMITES

All of the listed hotels are in the city center, within walking distance of the train and bus stations.

$$$ Hotel Figl, warmly run by Anton and Helga Mayr, has 23 comfy, bright, modern rooms and an attached café on a pedestrian square located a block from Piazza Walther/Waltherplatz. With rooms better than its humble public spaces and exterior, it's a fine value (Sb-€90-95, Db-€125-135, junior suite-€135-145, discount with this book for longer stays—ask when you reserve, breakfast-€4-14, air-con, elevator, non-smoking, free Internet access and Wi-Fi, parking- €15/day, Piazza del Grano/Kornplatz 9, tel. 0471-978-412, fax 0471-978-413, www.figl.net, info@figl .net, include a backup fax number if you email).

$$$ Hotel Greif, a luxury boutique hotel, is right on Piazza Walther/Waltherplatz. Each of the 33 individually designed rooms makes you feel like you're in a modern-art installation (its fine website gives a room-by-room tour). It's not cozy, but it is striking, and a stay here comes with one of the best breakfasts in Italy (comfort Sb-€157, Db-€176, comfort Db-€204, superior Db-€248, discounted Sat-Sun by request, ask for the 10 percent Rick Steves discount when you book online—availability limited, includes buffet breakfast, most rooms non-smoking, air-con, Internet access and Wi-Fi, Piazza Walther/Waltherplatz, entrance on Via della Rena/Raingasse, tel. 0471-318-000, fax 0471-318-148, www.greif.it, info@greif.it). Drivers follow signs to *P3-Parking Walther* (€17/day) and enter the hotel from level 1 of the garage.

$$$ Stadt Hotel Città, a venerable old hotel with 99 modern if basic rooms, is ideally situated on Piazza Walther/Waltherplatz. The hotel's café spills out onto the piazza, offering a prime spot for people-watching (Sb-€102, Db-€148, bigger Db with view-€190, Tb-€190, air-con, elevator, free Internet access and Wi-Fi, parking-€16/day, Piazza Walther/Waltherplatz 21, tel. 0471-975-221, fax 0471-976-688, www.hotelcitta.info, info@hotelcitta.info, Francesco and Alessandra). This place is an especially good value if you plan to spend an afternoon in their free-for-guests Wellness Center (mid-Sept-May Mon-Sat 16:30-22:00, likely closed Sun; closed May-mid-Sept; Turkish bath, whirlpool, Finnish sauna, biosauna, massage by appointment)—a fine way to unwind after a day of hiking in the Dolomites.

$$$ Parkhotel Laurin is an Old World luxury hotel located very close to the train station, with 100 tastefully decorated rooms, marble bathrooms, a chic dining room and terrace, a swimming pool, an extensive garden, attentive staff, and frescoes throughout the grand lobby depicting the legend of King Laurin (small Sb-€104, standard Sb-€118, standard Db-€151, comfort Db-€187, discounted Sat-Sun by request, Internet access and Wi-Fi, parking-€14/day, Via Laurin/Laurinstrasse 4, tel. 0471-311-000, fax 0471-311-148, www.laurin.it, info@laurin.it).

$$ Hotel Feichter is an inexpensive, well-kept, family-run place with simple but sufficient amenities in a great location. Some of the 30 rooms share a communal terrace overlooking the rooftops of Bolzano. Papà Walter, Mamma Hedwig, Hannes, Irene, and Wolfi Feichter have run this homey hotel since 1969 (Sb-€60, Db-€95, Tb-€115, parking-€5/day, ground-floor café serves lunches; from station, walk up Via Laurin/Laurinstrasse, which becomes Via Grappoli/Weintraubengasse—hotel is on the right at #15; tel. 0471-978-768, fax 0471-974-803, www.hotelfeichter.it, info@hotelfeichter.it).

$$ Kolpinghaus Bozen, modern, clean, and church-run, has 34 rooms with two twin beds (placed head to toe) and 71 air-conditioned single rooms with all the comforts. Though institutional, it's a great deal...and makes me feel thankful (Sb-€63, Db-€95, Tb-€140, elevator, free Internet access or Wi-Fi—varies by floor, laundry-€6/big load, parking-€12/day, 4 blocks from Piazza Walther/Waltherplatz near Piazza Domenicani at Largo A. Kolping/Adolph-Kolping-Strasse 3, tel. 0471-308-400, fax 0471-973-917, www.kolpingbozen.it, info@kolpingbozen.it). The line of people in front of the building at lunchtime consists mainly of office workers waiting for the cafeteria to open (€10.50 three-course lunch, Mon-Fri 11:45-14:00, Sat 12:00-13:30, closed Sun).

$ Youth Hostel Bolzano is the most comfortable and inviting hostel that I've seen in Italy. It has 18 four-bed rooms (each with two bunk beds and a full bathroom) and 10 delightful singles with bath. The bright, clean, modern rooms make it feel like a dorm in a fancy university. With no age limit, easy reservations online, great lockers, and cheap Internet access, it is the utopian hostel (bed in quad-€21, Sb-€25, €2 extra for 1-night stays, includes linens and buffet breakfast, towels-€2, laundry-€4/load, kitchen, free luggage storage, 9:00 checkout; 100 yards to the right as you leave the train station at Via Renon/Rittner Strasse 23; tel. 0471-300-865, fax 0471-300-858, www.ostello.bz, bolzano@ostello.bz).

Eating in Bolzano

All of these recommendations are in the center of the old town. Prices are consistent (you can generally get a good plate of meat and veggies for €10). While nearly every local-style place serves a mix of Germanic/Tirolean and Italian fare, I favor eating Tirolean here in Bozen.

Weisses Rössl offers affordable, mostly Tirolean food with meat, fish, and fine vegetarian options. Located in a traditional woody setting, it's good for dining indoors among savvy locals (€11-14 main courses, €7-12 lunch specials, Mon-Fri 11:00-15:00 & 17:30-23:30—light meals only available between 15:00-17:30, Sat 11:00-15:00 only, closed Sun, 2 blocks north of Piazza Municipio at Via Bottai/Bindergasse 6, tel. 0471-973-267).

Ca' de Bezzi/Gasthaus Batzenhäusl is historic. It's Bolzano's oldest inn, with two Teutonic-feeling upper floors; by contrast, the patio and back room are refreshingly modern and untouristy. They make their own breads and pastas, and serve traditional Tirolean fare (€12-14 main courses, daily 10:00-1:00, limited menu outside mealtimes, one of the rare places open on Sun, Via Andreas Hofer/Andreas-Hofer-Strasse 30, tel. 0471-050-950).

Tirolean Cuisine

During your visit to the Dolomites, take a break from Italian-style pizzas and pastas to sample some of the region's traditional cuisine...with a distinctly Austrian flavor. For simplicity, I've generally listed Italian names here, though local menus are in both Italian and German (and usually also English).

Wurst and sauerkraut are the Tirolean clichés. More adventurous eaters seek out *speck,* a raw (prosciutto-style) ham smoked for five months then thinly sliced and served as an antipasto or in sandwiches. *Canederli*—large dumplings with bits of *speck,* liver, spinach, or cheese—are often served in broth, or with butter and cheese. (Never cut a dumpling with a knife—it'll destroy the chef.)

The stars of Tirolean cuisine are the hearty meat dishes—which, unlike traditional Italian main courses, are nearly always served with side dishes of doughy dumplings or vegetables and potatoes. Try *stinco di maiale* (roasted pork shank, usually garnished with potatoes) and *crauti rossi* (a sweetish sauerkraut made from red cabbage). *Carrè affumicato* is pork shank that is first smoked, then boiled. *Selvaggine,* or wild game, comes in the form of *capriolo* (fawn), *cervo* (venison), or *camoscio* (chamois/antelope). Game is eaten smoked and thinly sliced in *antipasti;* in meat sauce *(ragù)* with fresh pasta or as ravioli stuffing; or in entrées, as tender chunks grilled or roasted in a rich sauce *(spezzatino).*

For dessert, strudel is everywhere, filled with the harvest from this region's renowned apple orchards. Cakes and pies are loaded with other locally grown fruits, raisins, and nuts. *Kaiserschmarrn* is an interesting alternative: a tall, eggy crêpe prepared with raisins and topped with powdered sugar and red currant jam.

Bier (birra) is king in the Alto Adige (the best-known brand, Forst, is brewed in nearby Merano), but the wines of the area are well-matched to the local fare. *Magdalaner* is a light, dry red made from Schiava grapes. *Lagrein scuro* is a full-bodied red, dry and fruity, similar to a cabernet sauvignon or merlot. *Gewürztraminer* is a dry white wine with a spicy fruit flavor. For something stronger, try grappa made from Williams pears (and served with a wedge of fresh pear), or *grappa Nocino*—a darker, sweeter brew similar to Jägermeister. *Guten Appetit und Prost!*

Hopfen and Company fills an 800-year-old house with happy eaters, drinkers, and the beer lover's favorite aroma: hops...or *Hopfen*. A tavern since the 1600s, it's a stylish, fresh microbrewery today. This high-energy, boisterous place is packed with locals who come for its homemade beer, delicious Tirolean food, and reasonable prices. You'll enjoy the friendly English-speaking waitstaff (€10-15 main courses, €7-11 heavy traditional beer dumplings with salad, great €8 salads, daily 9:30-24:00, Piazza Erbe/Obstplatz 17, tel. 0471-300-788).

Paulaner Stuben is a restaurant-pizzeria-*Bierstube* serving good food and a favorite Bavarian beer. It has good outside seating and a take-me-to-Germany *Stube* (€6-7 pizzas and pastas, €7-8 salads, €10-14 main courses, Mon-Sat 11:30-24:00, limited menu from 15:00-18:00, closed Sun, Via Argentieri/Silbergasse 16—or use back entrance at Via dei Portici/Laubengasse 51, tel. 0471-980-407).

Enoteca Il Baccaro, a nondescript hole-in-the-wall wine bar, is an intriguing spot for a glass of wine (€1-4) and bar snacks amid locals. Wines available by the glass are listed on the blackboard (Mon-Fri 9:00-14:00 & 15:30-20:30, Sat 9:00-15:30, closed Sun, located a half-block east of Hopfen and Company on a hidden alley off Via Argentieri/Silbergasse 17, look for *vino* or *wein* sign next to fountain on south side of street and enter courtyard, tel. 0471-971-421).

Gasthaus Fink, a busy diner, serves typical Tirolean and Italian dishes. It has both indoor and outdoor seating on a quiet pedestrian street a few doors off Piazza Walther/Waltherplatz (€8 pastas, €10 antipasto plates, €14 *secondi,* Fri-Tue 9:00-22:00, Wed 9:00-15:00 only, closed Thu, Via della Mostra/Mustergasse 9, tel. 0471-975-047).

Picnic: Assemble the ingredients at the **Piazza Erbe/Obstplatz** market and dine in the park along the Talvera River (the green area with benches past the museum). Or visit one of the three **DeSpar supermarkets:** The largest, with longest hours, is at the end of the Galleria Greif arcade (enter arcade from Piazza Walther/Waltherplatz by Hotel Greif and walk to far end—the supermarket is downstairs; Mon-Fri 8:30-19:30, Sat 8:30-19:00, closed Sun). Smaller branches are on Piazza Erbe/Obstplatz and at Via Bottai/Bindergasse 29 (both open Mon-Fri 8:30-19:15, Sat 8:30-18:00, closed Sun).

Bolzano Connections

From Bolzano by Train to: Milan (about hourly, 3.5-4 hours, change in Verona), **Verona** (about hourly, 1.75-2.25 hours, take €8.70 "R" trains, avoid "fast" trains that take same time for €15-25),

Venice (about hourly, 3-3.5 hours, change in Verona), **Florence** (every 1-2 hours, 3.5-5 hours, change in Verona and/or Bologna), **Innsbruck** (1-2/hour, 2-2.5 hours, some change in Brennero), **Munich** (called "Monaco" in Italy, 5/day direct, 3.75 hours).

By Bus to: Castelrotto (2/hour Mon-Fri, 1-2/hour Sat, hourly Sun, 50 minutes, last departure Mon-Fri at 20:10, Sat-Sun at 19:10, pick up free schedule at bus station, €3.50 each way, buy tickets from driver, toll-free tel. 800-846-047 or toll tel. 840-000-471, www.sii.bz.it). The bus leaves from Bolzano's bus station (one block west of train station), stops at the train station, and then winds high into the mountains, dropping you in the center of Castelrotto.

If you're heading directly to **Alpe di Siusi,** take the same bus, get off just past the Seiseralm Bergbahn cable-car station, and ascend on the cable car. For more on Alpe di Siusi, see page 242.

Castelrotto

The ideal home base for exploring Alpe di Siusi, Castelrotto (Kastelruth in German; town population: 2,000; district population: 6,000; altitude: 3,475 feet) has more village character than any other town I know in the region. With a traffic-free center, a thousand years of history, an oversized and hyperactive bell tower, and traditionally clad locals, it seems lost in another world. Against a backdrop of mountains, Castelrotto conveys the powerful message that simple pleasures are enough. Stay two nights!

Orientation to Castelrotto

Tourist Information

The helpful TI is on the main square at Piazza Kraus 2 (Mon-Sat 8:30-12:00 & 14:30-18:00, closed Sun except July-Aug 9:00-12:00, shorter hours off-season, tel. 0471-706-333, www.seiseralm.it). If you plan to do any hiking, pick up the TI's list of suggested hikes, including estimated walking times and trail numbers.

For a longer stay, consider the **Combi-Card** (€38/any 3 days out of a 7-day validity period, €48/unlimited usage for 7 days, expires 1 week after time stamp, sold at TI). This card cov-

THE DOLOMITES

① Alla Torre (Gasthof zum Turm) Hotel, Rest. & Internet Café

② Hotel Cavallino d'Oro (Goldenes Rössl) & Rest.

③ Hotel Wolf (Hotel al Lupo)

④ Residence Garni Trocker & Internet Cafe

⑤ Haus Trocker

⑥ To Tirler Hof B&B

⑦ To Villa Pircher, Residence Burghof & Sasso's Wine Bar

⑧ Saalstuben Restaurant

⑨ Zur Alten Schmiede Pizzeria

⑩ Stern Café

⑪ Rubin's Wine Bar

⑫ Supermarkets (3)

⑬ Library (Internet)

⑭ RC Sports & Rent

⑮ ATM, WC & Phones

⑯ Mendel Haus

⑰ Kastelruther Spatzen-Laden Shop

ers the Alpe di Siusi Express bus, Seiseralm Bergbahn cable car, Compatsch-Saltria shuttle bus (Almbus #11), other shuttle buses, regional orange SAD buses—such as the one to Bolzano from Castelrotto, and all trains in the Südtirol/Alto Adige region.

Helpful Hints

Annual Events: The Oswald-von-Wolkenstein Riding Tournament, held on the first weekend of June, features equestrian medieval-style tournament games, followed by a feast. The town also holds religious processions with locals dressed in traditional costumes, usually on Corpus Christi (May 30 in 2013); the feast day of the village protectors, Sts. Peter and Paul (June 29); and on the local Thanksgiving (first weekend in Oct). Mid-October is packed for Kastleruther Spatzenfest, a concert weekend for local musical heartthrobs, Kastleruther Spatzen.

Closures: The periods between ski season and hiking season (April and Nov) are quiet, with lifts closed for maintenance and most hotels and restaurants shut down so locals can take their own vacations.

Internet Access: You can get online at the recommended **Alla Torre** hotel, which has an Internet café (Thu-Tue 8:00-23:00, closed Wed, closed April and Nov, behind TI at Kofelgasse 8, tel. 0471-706-349), or the recommended **Residence Garni Trocker** (daily 8:00-20:00, on Fostlweg 3). Or visit the public **library** (Mon 14:00-18:00, Tue 9:00-12:00, Thu 15:00-19:00, Fri 9:00-12:00, tel. 0471-708-023).

Recreation: A heated outdoor swimming pool with alpine views and nearby tennis courts is near town (€6, mid-May-mid-Sept 9:00-20:00, tel. 0471-705-090, ask at your hotel for details). You can rent a horse at **Ober-Lanzinerhof Tezfen** (tel. 339-868-6868, Karin speaks some English).

For more excitement, tandem paragliding flights—you and the pilot—depart from Alpe di Siusi and land either where you started or in Castelrotto (tel. 335-603-6400, www.tandem-pilot.com, Ruben and Kurt). You can rent skis and snowboards at **RC Sports and Rent** (Via Panider/Paniderstrasse 10, tel. 0471-711-079, Robert—mobile 339-293-9725, Christian—mobile 328-303-8045).

Arrival in Castelrotto

The **bus station** *(Bushof)* is a few steps below the town's main square. The bus parking lot has a shelter with timetables. An ATM, WC, and phones are located in a building to the right. Take the stairs or elevator to get to the main square and TI.

Drivers can park in one of the two underground parking lots—one is near the bus station; the other is on Wolkensteinstrasse just past the recommended Saalstuben Restaurant (first hour free). Each of the recommended hotels also has free parking: For Alla Torre and Hotel al Lupo, email for directions. For Hotel Cavallino d'Oro, drive through the traffic-free town center, drop off your luggage in front of the hotel, and then park in their garage. The recommended private homes will advise you of your options (see "Sleeping in Castelrotto," later).

The Dramatic Dolomites

Located in northeastern Italy, the Dolomites have been called the most beautiful mountains on earth, and certainly they are among the most dramatic.

They differ from the rest of the Alps because of their dominant rock type, dolomite, which forms sheer vertical walls of white, gray, and pink that rise abruptly from green valleys and meadows. There is one national park (Dolomiti Bellunesi National Park) in this region, and many regional parks, such as Alpe di Siusi. Rail lines, roads, and a huge system of lifts make this group of mountains very accessible.

Once dubbed the "Pale Mountains" or the "Venetian Alps," this mountain range was named after French mineralogist Dolomieu, who in the late 1700s first described the rock type responsible for the region's light-colored bluffs and peaks. These sedimentary rocks (similar to limestone) were formed in warm tropical seas during the Triassic Period (about 250 million years ago). The marine sediments, along with the fossilized remains of coral reefs and other animals, were buried, hardened, and later scooped upward along with the rest of the Alps by the tectonic-plate action of Africa slowly smashing into Europe. Today, marine fossils are found atop the region's highest peaks, including the skyscraping, nearly 11,000-feet-high Marmolada (east of Bolzano).

During World War I, the front line between the Italian and Austro-Hungarian forces ran through these mountains, and many paths were cut into the range for military use. Today mountaineers follow a network of metal rungs, cables, and ladders called the *Via Ferrata*. One famous wartime trail is the "Road of Tunnels," which passes through 52 tunnels. Along with being a paradise for hikers and climbers, the Dolomites are a popular skiing destination. The 1956 Olympics in Cortina di Ampezzo put the region on the map. A popular winter activity for intrepid skiers is the "Sella Ronda"—circling the Sella massif using a system of lifts and 28 miles of ski runs.

Whether you experience the Dolomites with your hand on a walking stick, a ski pole, or an *aperitivo* while mountain-gazing from a café, it's easy to enjoy this spectacular region.

THE DOLOMITES

Self-Guided Walk

Welcome to Castelrotto

Castelrotto has little to distract you other than the surrounding mountains and hikes. This quick walk will trace the town's history, from the ruling Krauses to yodelers who rule. Note that shops in Castelrotto close for siesta 12:00-15:00—a good time for a long lunch, a hike in the hills...or a siesta of your own.

• *Start in the...*

Main Square: Piazza Kraus is named for the family who ruled the town 1550-1800. Their palace, now the City Hall and TI, overlooks the square and sports the Kraus family coat of arms.

Castelrotto uses its square well. The farmers' market takes place here Friday mornings in the summer (June-Oct), and a clothing market fills the square most Thursday mornings. Before and after Sunday Mass, the square is crowded with villagers and farmers (who fill the church) dressed in traditional clothing. The main Mass (Sat at 20:00—at 19:30 in winter—and Sun at 10:00) is in German. Another Mass takes place in Italian throughout the tourist season (at 11:00) for visitors.

• *A landmark in the square is the...*

Bell Tower: At 250 feet, the freestanding bell tower dominates the town. It was once attached to a church, which burned in

1753. While the bell tower was quickly rebuilt, the present-day church was constructed a century later next to the gutted church (which was then torn down to make space for the square). The wire between the church and tower connects the noisy bells. The sacristan can easily ring them using an electric switch.

When you feel the pride that the locals have in their tower—which symbolizes their town—you'll better understand why Italy is called "the land of a thousand bell towers." The bells of Castelrotto—a big part of the town experience—ring on the hour from 6:00 until 22:00. While sleepy tourists wonder why they clang so very early in the morning, locals—who grew up with the chimes—find them comforting. The bells mark the hours, summon people to work and to Mass, announce festivals, and warn when storms threaten. In the days when people used to believe that thunder was the devil approaching, the bells called everyone to pray. (Townspeople thought the bells' sound cleared the clouds.) Bells ring big at 7:00, noon, and 19:00. The biggest of the eight bells (7,500 pounds) peals only on special days. On Fridays, the bells ring at 15:00, commemorating Christ's sacrifice at the supposed hour of his death. The colorful poles in front of the church (yellow-and-white for the Vatican, red-and-white for Tirol) fly flags on festival days.

• *Also on the square is the...*

Church: Before entering, notice the plaque on the exterior. This commemorative inscription honors the tiny community's WWI dead—*Dorf* means from the village itself, and *Fraktion* is from an outlying district. Stepping into the church, you're surrounded by harmonious art from about 1850. The church is dedicated to Sts. Peter and Paul, and the paintings that flank the high altar show how each was martyred (crucifixion and beheading). The pews (and smart matching confessionals) are carved of walnut wood.

• *Back outside, belly up to the...*

Fountain: Opposite the bell tower, Castelrotto's fountain dates from 1884. St. Florian, the protector against fires, keeps an eye on it today as he did when villagers (and their horses) first came here for a drink of water.

• *With your back to the bell tower, look a half-block down the lane to see the finely frescoed...*

Mendel Haus: This house has a traditional facade and a wood-carvers' shop. Its frescoes (from 1886) include many sym-

bolic figures, as well as an emblem of a carpenter above the door—a relic from the days when images, rather than address numbers, identified the house. Notice St. Florian again; this time, he's pouring water on a small painting of this very house engulfed in flames. Inside Mendel Haus are fine carvings, a reminder that this region—especially nearby Val Gardena—is famous for its woodwork. You'll also see many witches, folk figures that date back to when this area was the Salem of this corner of Europe. Women who didn't fit society's mold—including midwives, healers, redheads, and so on—were burned as witches.

• *Walk downhill to the left of Mendel Haus, then turn right and climb the stairs. At the top of the stairs, turn left on Dolomitenstrasse. In 20 yards, on the left at the end of the street, is a shop dedicated to Castelrotto's hometown heroes...*

Kastelruther Spatzen-Laden: The ABBA of the Alps, the folk-singing group Kastelruther Spatzen is a gang of local boys who put Castelrotto on the map. They have a huge following here and throughout the German-speaking world. The lead singer, Norbert, is a Germanic heartthrob on par with Tom Jones. At the big Castelrotto festival on the second weekend in October, they put on hometown concerts—filling this place with fans from as far away as the Alsace, Switzerland, and the Netherlands. They also have an open-air concert in June and a Christmas concert.

Inside this shop—where you'll undoubtedly hear their inimitable music—is a folk musician's Carnaby Street. Downstairs is a folksy little museum slathered with gifts, awards, and gold records. The group has won 13 Echo Awards..."more than Robbie Williams." Watch the continuously playing video (€2 museum downstairs, refunded if you spend €5 in the shop, Mon-Fri 9:00-12:00 & 14:00-18:00, Sat 9:00-12:00, closed Sun, Via Dolomitenstrasse 21, tel. 0471-707-439, www.spatzenladen.it).

Sights in Castelrotto

Calvario Stroll—For a scenic stroll, take a short walk around the town's hill, originally the site of the ancient Roman fortress and later the fortified home of the medieval lord. One lane circles the hill while another spirals to the top past seven little chapels, each depicting a scene from Christ's Passion and culminating in the Crucifixion. Facing the TI, take the road under the arch to the right, and then follow signs to *Kofel* (to go around the hill) or *Kalvarienberg* (to get directly to the top). This 15-minute stroll is great after dark—romantically lit and under the stars. (The lead singer of Kastelruther Spatzen enjoyed his first kiss right here.) On a warm day, take the Friedensweg (Peace Trail) from the top of the hill to go back to the town square or below the village. This 30-minute forest walk is decorated with peace-themed artwork by local elementary students.

Marinzen Lift—The little Marinzen chairlift zips you up the mountain to the Marinzenhütte café, which has an animal park for kids (open when the cable car runs). You can come back on the lift, or it's a one-hour hike down (€7 one-way, €9 round-trip, runs daily late May-mid-Oct 9:00-17:00, July-Aug Wed until 22:00, closed off-season and rainy mornings, tel. 0471-707-160, www.seiseralm.it). From the town square, head downhill toward Wolkensteinstrasse, turn left and go another 50 yards down the road toward San Michele, and find the chairlift a few steps off the road on the right, behind the Co-op supermarket.

Nightlife in and near Castelrotto

If you're here on the weekend, the "Nightliner" shuttle bus connects you with local hot spots (Fri-Sat hourly 20:40-4:00 in the morning, schedules at TI and hotels; €2.50/ride, €4/all-night pass). **Rubin's,** next door to the Hotel Schgaguler in Castelrotto (tel. 0471-712-100), and **Sasso's,** on Schlernstrasse in the nearby town of Siusi/Seis (tel. 0471-708-068), are trendy wine bars. A popular hangout for the younger crowd in Siusi/Seis is **Santners,** at the Seiseralm Bergbahn cable-car station (tel. 0471-727-913).

Sleeping in Castelrotto

(€1 = about $1.40, country code: 39)
$$$ Alla Torre (in German, **Gasthof zum Turm**) is comfortable, clean, and alpine-traditional, with great beds and modern bathrooms (small Db-€80-120, big Db-€100-140, Tb-€150-210, one-night stay-€4 extra, price depends on season—highest in Aug, elevator, free Wi-Fi, free parking, closed April and Nov, behind TI at Kofelgasse 8, tel. 0471-706-349, fax 0471-707-268, www .zumturm.com, info@zumturm.com, Gabi and Günther).

$$$ Hotel Cavallino d'Oro (in German, **Goldenes Rössl**), on the main square, has plenty of Tirolean character and plush, welcoming public rooms. Run by friendly and helpful Stefan and Susanne, the entire place is dappled with artistic, woodsy touches and historic photos. If you love antiques by candlelight, this 650-year-old hotel is the best in town (Sb-€55-77, Db-€106-154, Db suite-€130-190 depending on season, 2 percent discount with cash, discount for 4-night stay, elevator, free Internet access and Wi-Fi, laundry, free parking, Piazza Kraus 1, tel. 0471-706-337, fax 0471-707-172, www.cavallino.it, cavallino@cavallino.it). Stefan converted his wine cellar into a Roman steam bath and Finnish sauna (free for guests, great after a hike, can book an hour for exclusive use)—complete with heated tile seats, massage rooms, a solarium for tanning, and tropical plants.

$$$ Hotel Wolf (in Italian, **al Lupo**) is pure Tirolean, with all the comforts in 23 neat-as-a-pin rooms, most with balconies (Sb-€55-70, Db-€95-120, prices vary with season and view, elevator, pay Wi-Fi, coin-op laundry, free parking, closed April-mid-May and Nov-mid-Dec, a block below main square at Wolkensteinstrasse 5, tel. 0471-706-332, fax 0471-707-030, www.hotelwolf.it, info@hotel wolf.it, Arno).

$$ Residence Garni Trocker is run by the Moser family, who rent 13 great rooms in a place that's bomb-shelter solid yet warm-wood cozy. Their compound is beautifully laid out with a café-bar, garden, and top-notch plumbing (Sb-€34-48, Db-€65-97 depending on season, apartments available, pay Internet access in lobby, Fostlweg 3, tel. 0471-705-200, fax 0471-707-427, www.residencetrocker.com, garni@residencetrocker.com, Stefan). Non-smokers should request a room far from the smoking rooms. Sunday is the family's day of rest; if you're coming on a Sunday, be sure to let them know in advance what time you'll arrive.

$ Haus Trocker, on the edge of town, is a modern home where the delightful Frau Trocker rents two lovely rooms that share one WC. Frau Trocker doesn't speak English, but after you meet her you won't care. Her son Roland can translate for you if he's around (D-€50; from the bus station, walk away from the church spire, past Hotel Kastel Seiseralm to Fostlweg 6, then look for yellow *Zimmer* sign at top of steps; mobile 348-921-0335).

$ Tirler Hof, the storybook Jaider family farm, has 40 cows, four Old World-comfy guest rooms, and a great mountain view. The ground-floor double has a private bath. The top-floor rooms share a bathroom and a great balcony. Take a stroll before breakfast (D/Db-€60, discount for stays longer than one night, cash only, open year-round, definitely most practical for drivers; it's the first farm outside of town on the right on road to San Michele, Via Panider/Paniderstrasse 44; tel. 0471-706-017, info@tirler hof.it).

Near Castelrotto, in Siusi/Seis

These two accommodations are in the hamlet of Siusi/Seis, just five minutes from Castelrotto by bus (see "By Bus from Castelrotto" on page 243). Siusi/Seis has shops, restaurants, a TI, and other services—and the cable car to Alpe di Siusi. Both places listed below will pick you up from the Siusi/Seis bus station.

$$ At Villa Pircher, the friendly Pircher family rents out two view apartments just a short walk or bus ride from the cable-car station. Numerous trails begin nearby (Db-€49-75, price varies by season and number of people, no minimum stay, laundry service, parking, one stop past the Siusi/Seis bus station at Laranzweg 13, tel. 0471-707-440, mobile 339-191-3063, www.villapircher.com, info@villapircher.com, Thomas speaks some English).

$$ Residence Burghof offers fully equipped apartments in a rural setting with beautiful views only 10 minutes from the village. When he's not teaching skiing, English-speaking Patrick Fill and his family run this Tirolean retreat (Sb-€48-64, Db-€51-91, Tb-€70-131, price depends on season, discounts for 3-night stay, family rates, sauna, Wi-Fi, free parking, rental bikes available, Burgfriedenstrasse 20, tel. 0471-706-243, fax 0471-706-056, www.residence-burghof.com, info@residence-burghof.com).

Eating in Castelrotto

Note that the first two options are also listed earlier under "Sleeping in Castelrotto."

Cavallino d'Oro Restaurant offers a variety of beautifully presented, homemade Tirolean cuisine—including wild game, *canederli* dumplings, and strudel—in a dressy but relaxed and woodsy ambience. The waiters, Marco and Monica, are very helpful; quiz them before you order. Reservations are smart (€30 meals, daily 18:00-21:00, tel. 0471-706-337).

Alla Torre Restaurant, homier and with the best terrace in town, is another fine option for traditional and international dishes (Thu-Tue 12:00-14:00 & 18:00-20:45, closed Wed, closed April and Nov, tel. 0471-706-349).

Saalstuben Restaurant dishes up a selection of reasonably priced Austrian-Italian dishes indoors or on their terrace. If you believe in dessert first, try the Kaiserschmarrn (€9.75), a favorite of Austrian Emperor Franz Josef. You won't need anything else (summer daily 11:30-14:00 & 17:30-21:00, closed Thu in winter, Wolkensteinstrasse 12, tel. 0471-707-394).

Zur Alten Schmiede Pizzeria is a great place to enjoy an evening drinking Forst, the local beer, and playing darts (€6-9 pizzas and pastas, Tue-Sun 11:30-14:00 & 17:30-24:00 but kitchen closes at 23:00, closed Mon, outdoor seating, near bus station entrance at Paniderstrasse 7, tel. 0471-707-390).

Dessert: For strudel, locals like the no-nonsense **Stern** café, with its terrace seating (Tue-Sun 7:30-19:00, closed Mon; on Plattenstrasse—facing TI, go left through arch; tel. 0471-706-382).

Picnics: You can put together a picnic at **Euro Spar** (Mon-Sat 8:00-19:00, closed Sun, on Wolkensteinstrasse, tel. 0471-706-222), **M-Preis** (Mon-Sat 8:00-19:00, closed Sun, Paniderstrasse 21, tel. 0471-710-014), or **Co-op/Konsum-Market** (sells locally produced food, Mon-Sat 7:30-12:30 & 15:00-19:00, closed Sun and off-season Sat afternoons, Paniderstrasse 24, tel. 0471-706-330).

Castelrotto Connections

From Castelrotto by Bus to: Bolzano (2/hour Mon-Fri, 1-2/hour Sat, hourly Sun, 50 minutes, runs Mon-Sat 6:15-19:00, Sun 7:00-19:00; €3.50 one-way; in Bolzano, the bus stops at the more central Bahnhofplatz, or train station—get off here to avoid the 200-yard walk from the bus station, where the bus terminates), **Canazei** (late June-mid-Sept only, 3-4/day, 2-2.25 hours), and **Ortisei/St. Ulrich** and **St. Cristina** (8/day, 30 minutes to Ortisei, then another 10 minutes to St. Cristina). Get bus schedules at the

THE DOLOMITES

TI, call toll-free tel. 800-846-047, toll tel. 840-000-471, or check www.sii.bz.it or www.silbernagl.it. For **Alpe di Siusi** connections, see "Orientation to Alpe di Siusi," later.

To Munich: On Saturdays only late May-September, a bus departs Alpe di Siusi at 6:00 and Castelrotto at 6:25, and heads for Munich's main train station (arrives 11:00, €38) and airport (arrives 12:00, €46). You can be picked up at your hotel for an extra €5. For information and booking, contact the Castelrotto TI.

Alpe di Siusi

Europe's largest high-alpine meadow, Alpe di Siusi (Seiser Alm in German) separates two of the most famous Dolomite ski-resort valleys. Eight miles wide, 20 miles long, and soaring up to 6,500 feet high, Alpe di Siusi is dotted by farm huts and wildflowers (mid-June-July), surrounded by dramatic—if distant—Dolomite peaks and cliffs, and much appreciated by hordes of walkers.

Compatsch, the modern little tourist town at the entrance of the meadow, has a TI, food, two small shopping strips, and services (described later). Don't confuse the village of Siusi/Seis at the bottom of the cable car with Alpe di Siusi—the alpine meadow at the top.

The Sasso Lungo Mountains (Langkofel in German, Long Stone in English) at the head of the meadow provide a storybook Dolomite backdrop, while the spooky Schlern peak stands boldly staring into the haze of the peninsula. The Schlern, looking like a devilish *Winged Victory,* gave ancient peoples enough willies to spawn legends of supernatural forces. The Schlern witch, today's tourist-brochure mascot, was the cause of many a broom-riding medieval townswoman's fiery death.

Alpe di Siusi is my recommended one-stop look at the Dolomites because of Castelrotto's charm as a home base, its quintessential Dolomite mountain views, its easy accessibility for those with and without cars, and its variety of walks, hikes, and mountain-bike routes. While most hikers will enjoy the easy meadow strolls, the nearby Schlern tempts and rewards those with more energy and an adventurous spirit.

The meadow is famous for its wildflowers—a fragrant festival (best in June) blooming with flowers that grow only 5,900-7,800 feet above sea level. The cows munching away in this vast meadow produce 2.5 million gallons of milk annually, much of which is sent to Bolzano to make cheese. After tourism, dairy is the leading industry here. While cows winter in Castelrotto, they summer in Alpe di Siusi. The meadow is also dotted with small, idyllic hotels and chalet restaurants. It's extremely family-friendly, with playgrounds at each stop and plenty of animals to pet. Being here on a sunny summer day comes with the ambience of a day at the beach.

Orientation to Alpe di Siusi

Getting to Alpe di Siusi

By Car: A nature preserve, Alpe di Siusi is closed to cars during the day (9:00-17:00), unless you're staying in one of the area hotels. (Show your reservation confirmation as proof.) Parking at Compatsch (€14.50/day) requires that you arrive before the road closes at 9:00 in the morning, though you can drive back down at any time. Park officials encourage visitors to use the free parking lot located at the Seiseralm Bergbahn cable-car station in Siusi/Seis (see below); park your car and take the cable car *(cabinovia)* up to Compatsch.

By Cable Car from Siusi up to Alpe di Siusi: A cable car (Seiseralm Bergbahn) runs hikers and skiers from the village of Siusi/Seis to Compatsch, the gateway to the meadow (late May-mid-Sept daily 8:00-19:00, off-season 8:00-18:00, closed Nov and April-late May, 15-minute ride to the top, €10 one-way, €14.50 round-trip, www.seiseralmbahn.it). From Compatsch, you can take a shuttle bus farther into Alpe di Siusi to Saltria (€1.50/ride, €3/day).

By Bus from Castelrotto: Bus #3 links Castelrotto with Siusi/Seis and stops at the front door of the Seiseralm Bergbahn cable-car station (4/hour mid-June-mid-Oct during morning and afternoon peak times, otherwise 2/hour, 5 minutes). Less-frequent bus #4 connects the cable-car station with Siusi/Seis, Castelrotto, and Ortisei/St. Ulrich (2/hour, June-Oct only). Buses cost €1-4 per ride.

Regional buses (such as the orange SAD bus to and from Bolzano) stop at Siusi/Seis and just below the cable-car station (frequent in summer, 4/day in each direction off-season, €2 one-way).

The Alpe di Siusi Express is a shuttle bus that runs from Castelrotto all the way to Compatsch—denying you the fun experience of approaching the high meadow by cable car (6/day, 20 minutes, €10 one-way, €14.50 round-trip, see www.silbernagl.it for schedules).

Alpe di Siusi

THE DOLOMITES

Sasso Lungo
3181

Sella
3152

Sella
Pass

To Cortina di
Ampezzo

5

Selva Gardena/
Wolkenstein

FLORIAN

SALTRIA
1675

Monte
Pana

A l p e   d i

Sta.
Cristina

MEZDI

SS-242

PUFLATSCH
2176

Compatsch
1835

ARNIKA
2061

4

Ortisei/
St. Ulrich

A.V.S.
1950

HOTEL
SEELAUS

Val Gardena
Grödnertal

MARINZEN
1486

TIRLER
HOF B&B

To Ponte Gardena / Waidbruck,
Chiusa / Klausen
& A-22 Autostrada

Castelrotto/
Kastelruth
1060

SP-24

To Ponte Gardena / Waidbruck
& S-12 to Bolzano

● Town	•••• Lift
▭ Road	▲ Mtn. Hut
---- Trail	(Mütte/Rifugio)

Note: This 3-D view looks southeast & is not to scale. Elevations in meters

Marmolada 3342

PLATTKOFEL

2

ZALLINGER 2054

WILLIAMS 2100

1

MAHLKNECHT/ MOLIGNON 2060

Tierser Alpl 2441

S i u s i

PANORAMA 2014

SALTNER DAIRY FARM "TSCHAPIT" 1830

SCHLERNHAUS 2450

SPITZBÜHL 1979

3

Mt. Pez 2563

Schlern 2450

SEISERALM O BERGBAHN

Siusi /Seis 1002

To Bolzano via Tiers & A-22 Autostrada

1 Panorama to Zallingerhütte Hike
2 Panorama to Plattkofelhütte Hike
3 Summit Hike of Schlern
4 "Trail of the Witches"
5 Loop Around Sasso Lungo

THE DOLOMITES

Getting Around Alpe di Siusi

Shuttle Buses: As the meadow is essentially car-free, the park's buses shuttle visitors to and from key points along the tiny road all the way from Compatsch—at the entry to the meadow—to the end of the line at Saltria, at the foot of the postcard-dramatic Sasso peaks (every 20 minutes 9:00-18:30, 15 minutes from Compatsch to Saltria, €1.50, buy from driver). At the end of the day, buses can be jam-packed.

Cable Cars and Chair Lifts: The entire meadow is served by various lifts (marked on maps). These are worth the roughly €5-8 per ride to get you into the higher and more scenic hiking areas (or back to the shuttle buses quickly). Keep in mind that lifts stop running fairly early (typically at about 17:00)—which can be a major disappointment if you're running out of steam and time, and are still high up after a long day's hike.

Compatsch

This tourist village (6,048 feet) at the entrance to the meadow is served by the Seiseralm Bergbahn cable car from the town of Siusi/ Seis. You can drive to Compatsch if you are staying at a hotel in Alpe di Siusi (or if you arrive very early or leave very late, outside of park opening hours). Parking costs €14.50 per day.

Compatsch has a **TI** (Mon-Fri 8:15-12:30, Sat 8:15-12:00, closed Sun, tel. 0471-727-904, www.seiseralm.it/en). The cable-car station has WCs, sporting-goods stores, and restaurants. In the center of Compatsch, you'll also find a tiny grocery store (open early-June-mid-Oct), ATMs, hotels, restaurants, and shops.

Sleeping near the Park Entrance: There are many chalets and huts with rooms for rent in Alpe di Siusi (which generally cost as much as a normal hotel; ask TI for details).

$$$ Hotel Seelaus, a 10-minute walk downhill from Compatsch, is a cozy, friendly, family-run place with an Austrian feel and down comforters (Sb-€65-130, Db-€120-240, Tb-€165-330, suite-€140-265; prices vary with season and type of room; family rates and week-stay discounts; includes buffet breakfast and hearty dinner, free and easy parking, and use of Wellness Center with sauna, hydro-massage, and mini-pool; free Wi-Fi, Via Compatsch 8, tel. 0471-727-954, fax 0471-727-835, www.hotel seelaus.it, info@hotelseelaus.it, Roberto). If you arrive in Siusi/ Seis by bus, Roberto can pick you up—arrange in advance.

Helpful Hints

Bike Rental: You can rent mountain bikes at **Sporthaus Trocker** (€8/1 hour, €25/day, mid-May-mid-Oct, between Plaza Hotel and the local bank, tel. 0471-727-824, www.sporthaustrocker.it). There's a world of tiny paved and gravel lanes to pedal on. Pick up their suggested routes and consider those I've described later. Rentable baby buggies are popular for those hiking with toddlers.

Horse Rides: Trocker rents horses and provides guides (about €28/1 hour, €38/2 hours, €54/3 hours, mid-June-Sept, near cable-car station, follow gravel road between Pensione Animone and station to end, tel. 0471-727-807, no English spoken).

> **Horse-drawn carriage rides** are available to the left of the TI (May-Oct 9:00-16:00). Prices vary widely; check the sign near the road for details.

Local Guide: American transplant **Kat Reno** loves sharing her knowledge of South Tirol history and folklore. She offers private walks, hikes, and other alpine adventures (half-day walking tour-€140, mobile 346-663-8340, dolomitefun@live.com).

Hiking in Alpe di Siusi

Easy meadow walks abound in Alpe di Siusi, giving novice hikers classic Dolomite views from baby-stroller trails. Experienced hikers should consider the tougher and more exciting treks. Before attempting a hike, call or stop by the TI to confirm your understanding of the time and skills required. As always, when hiking in the mountains, assume weather can change quickly, and pack accordingly. Many lifts operate only mid-June through mid-October—check with the TI for specifics on open lifts. Meadow walks, for flower lovers and strollers, are pretty—for advanced hikers, they're pretty boring. Chairlifts are springboards for more dramatic and demanding hikes. Trails are very well-marked, and the brightly painted numbers are keyed into local maps. Signs also display the next mountain hut along the trail. When asking for directions, most locals will know the trail by the huts it connects rather than its number. For simple hikes, you can basically string together three or four hut names. For anything more serious, invest in a good map, about €6 at the TI. The Kompass Bolzano map #54 covers everything in this chapter (scale 1:50,000). The Wanderkarte map of Alpe di Siusi (produced by Tabacco) offers more detail and focuses on just Alpe di Siusi (scale 1:25,000).

Walks and Hikes from Compatsch
Panorama to Zallingerhütte: The "Easy" Route—This is a basic four-hour walk that is moderately strenuous. It promises fine vistas from both ends of the meadow, fun stops along the way, and lifts up and down on each end. Start by riding the €5 lift to

THE DOLOMITES

Panorama (6,600 feet), then hike 1.25 hours to Mahlknechthütte/ Molignonhütte (6,725 feet)—from the chairlift, follow trail #2 across the meadow to the paved road and then join trail #7. Continue hiking two hours to Zallingerhütte (6,725 feet). From here it's a 10-minute walk to Williamshütte (6,888 feet), where you catch the €8 Florian lift back to Saltria and the shuttle-bus stop (for Compatsch). Both Mahlknechthütte and Zallingerhütte have great restaurants for a drink or meal. For shorter or cheaper versions, you can ride the lift up and stroll back down.

Panorama to Plattkofelhütte: The High Route—For a more thrilling two-hour extension of the previous hike, climb from Mahlknechthütte (6,725 feet) up to Plattkofelhütte (7,544 feet), follow the high trail #4 along the ridge for an hour, with commanding views both left and right, and then hike steeply back down to Williamshütte (6,888 feet).

Summit Hike of Schlern (Sciliar)—For a challenging 12-mile (six-hour) hike—with a possible overnight in a traditional mountain refuge (generally open mid-June-Sept)—consider hiking to the summit of Schlern and spending a night in Rifugio Bolzano/ Schlernhaus. This route is popular with serious hikers as the best hike in the region.

Start at the Spitzbühl chairlift (€5 one-way, €7 round-trip, 5,659 feet, free parking lot, first bus stop in park, www.seiseralm.it), which drops you at Spitzbühl (6,348 feet). Trail #5 takes you through a high meadow, down to the Saltner dairy farm (6,004 feet—you want the Saltner dairy farm at Tschapit, not the one near Zallingerhütte), across a stream, and steeply up the Schlern mountain. About three hours into your hike, you'll meet trail #1 and walk across the rocky tabletop plateau of Schlern to the mountain hotel **Rifugio Bolzano/Schlernhaus** (7,544 feet, €24-30 bunks, some double rooms available, breakfast-€8, open early June-Sept, cold water only, summer-only tel. 0471-612-024, off-season tel. 0471-724-094, can reserve by email before hut opens in June, www.schlernhaus.it, info@schlernhaus .it). From this dramatic setting, you can enjoy a meal and get a great view of the Rosengarten range. Hike 20 more minutes up the nearby peak (Monte Pez, 8,400 feet) where you'll find a lofty meadow, cows in the summer, and the region's ultimate 360-degree alpine panorama. From Rifugio Bolzano/Schlernhaus, you can hike back the way you came or walk farther along the Schlern (7 miles, 2 hours; past **Rifugio Alpe di Tires/Tierser Alpl**, 8,006 feet, €21-31 bunks, half-board available for €39-€49, open June-mid-Oct, showers-€3, tel. 0471-727-958 or 0471-707-460, mobile

333-654-6865, www.tierseralpl.com, info@tierseralpl.com) and descend back into Alpe di Siusi, to the road where the bus or cable car will return you to your starting point or hotel.

The "Trail of the Witches"—Take the cable car from Compatsch to Puflatsch (€5 one-way, €7 round-trip) for the two-hour loop north to Arnikahütte (with a café) and back (elevation gain about 660 feet). An engraved map at the Engelrast (Angel's Rest) observation point near the top of the lift gives the names of the surrounding mountains. Walking among the legendary stone seats of witches, you'll enjoy fine views of the valley all the way down to Castelrotto.

Loop Around Sasso Lungo—Another dramatic but medium-difficulty hike is the eight-hour walk around the Sasso Lungo (Langkofel) mountains, called the Federico Augusto/Friederich August trail. The trail has sections of loose rocks; good shoes are essential. Ride the bus to Saltria (end of the line), take the chairlift to Williamshütte, walk past the **Zallingerhütte** (overnight possible, €47/person in dorm room, Db-€63, includes breakfast and dinner, open late-May-mid-Oct, tel. 0471-727-947), and circle the Sasso Lungo group (get details and advice from the TI). On the opposite side, at Sella Pass, you ride a lift up Sasso Lungo to the Leo Demetz hut (8,790 feet), cross the saddle between Sasso Lungo and Sasso Piatto, and zigzag back into Alpe di Siusi with breathtaking views of rock climbers.

Trail Running—The Running Park Seiser Alm includes 46 miles of signed running trails in the meadow. Year after year, the clean air and high mountain altitude attract many international runners, including the Kenyan marathon team (during a one-day event usually held in July, they invite the public to run with them...or at least try). Contact the Compatsch TI for trail info and maps.

Biking in Alpe di Siusi

Mountain bikes are easy to rent, welcome on many lifts, and permitted on Alpe di Siusi lanes. The Compatsch TI has a good information flier that lists the best routes (I've listed three here). Get local advice to confirm difficulty levels and your plan before starting any ride.

Mountain-Bike Rides from Compatsch
Easy High Alp Ride (2.5 Hours, Medium)—This ride stays in Alpe di Siusi and gives you the best basic look at this high meadow, with little altitude gain and easy lanes throughout.

Start from Compatsch (6,048 feet), bike or ride the lift to Panorama (6,600 feet), and take road #7, which runs generally uphill to Punta d'Oro/Goldknopf, and then follows a series of hills

THE DOLOMITES

and dips to Mahlknechthütte/Molignonhütte (6,725 feet). Then take road #8 downhill to Saltria (5,575 feet) and back to Compatsch (6,048 feet).

Alpe di Siusi Meadow and Val Gardena (4 Hours, Medium to Difficult)—This route covers the great views of the Alpe di Siusi meadow, gets you into Val Gardena (a classic Südtirol valley) to see two resort towns, and then a lift gets you easily back to your starting point.

Start at Compatsch (6,048 feet), and take the road to Saltria (5,575 feet); from the bus stop, ride the unpaved road down to Monte Pana (5,366 feet). From here, an asphalt road zigzags steeply to St. Cristina (4,592 feet on valley floor far below), then heads down the valley to Ortisei/St. Ulrich (4,264 feet), where you take the cable car to Mezdi (6,560 feet, runs late May-Oct, €10.50 one-way, €15.20 round-trip). Complete your loop by rolling back down on a good road to Compatsch (6,048 feet).

Dramatic High Ridge Ride (4 Hours, Difficult)—This ride takes you into the dramatic rocks so characteristic of the Dolomites, with grand views and only the sound of your hardworking body and the rocks under your tires. If you get an early start, you can leave the bike at the Alpe di Tires/ Tierser Alpl hut (8,006 feet) while you hike to Rifugio Bolzano/Schlernhausern near the summit of the mighty Schlern—Monte Pez (2 hours, 8,400 feet).

Start at Compatsch (6,048 feet), ride the paved road downhill for 3.5 miles to Saltria (5,575 feet), then take road #8 for a huge uphill slog to the Tierser Alpl hut (8,006 feet; or you can ride the lift to Williamshütte to avoid half the altitude gain). From the Tierser Alpl hut, return the way you came until just below Hotel Floralpina/Seiser Alm Haus, where you'll take the left fork and follow road #7 to Mahlknechthütte/Molignonhütte (6,725 feet) and on through Punta d'Oro/Goldknopt (6,560 feet), and back down to Compatsch (6,048 feet).

More Sights in the Dolomites

▲▲Great Dolomite Road (Grande Strada delle Dolomiti)—This is the definitive Dolomite drive: Belluno-Cortina-Pordoi Pass-Val di Fassa-Bolzano (about 125 miles). Connecting Venice with Bolzano this way (the Venice-Belluno autostrada is slick) takes two hours longer than the direct Venice-Verona-Bolzano autostrada. No public transit does this trip. In spring and early summer, passes labeled "closed" are often bare, dry, and, as far as local drivers are concerned, wide-open. Call 0471-200-198 for road conditions (in Italian or German only).

▲▲**Abbreviated Dolomite Loop Drive**—See the biggies in half the miles (allow four hours, Bolzano-Castelrotto-Val Gardena-Sella Pass-Val di Fassa-Bolzano). Val Gardena (Grödner Tal) is famous for its skiing and hiking resorts, traditional Ladin culture, and wood-carvers (the wood-carving company ANRI is from the Val Gardena town of St. Cristina). It's a bit overrated, but even if its culture has been suffocated by the big bucks of hedonistic European fun-seekers, it remains a good jumping-off point for trips into the mountains. Within an hour, you'll reach Sella Pass (7,349 feet). After a series of tight hairpin turns a half-mile or so over the pass, you'll see some benches and cars. Pull over and watch the rock climbers.

The town of Canazei, at the head of the valley and the end of the bus line, has the most ambience and altitude (4,642 feet). From there, a lift (€5 one-way, €8.50 round-trip) and a gondola (€6.50 one-way, €11 round-trip; or both lifts for €10 one-way, €17 round-trip; late April-late Oct daily 8:30-12:30 & 14:00-17:30, both closed late Oct-late April) take you to Col dei Rossi Belvedere, where you can hike the Bindelweg trail past Rifugio Belvedere along an easy but breathtaking ridge to Rifugio Viel del Pan (Canazei TI for lift info: Tel. 0462-609-600, www.fassa.com, infocanazei@fassa.com). This three-hour round-trip hike has views of the highest mountain in the Dolomites—the Marmolada—and the Dolo-mighty Sella range.

▲▲**Reifenstein Castle**—For one of Europe's most intimate looks at medieval castle life, let the friendly lady of Reifenstein (Frau Steiner) show you around her wonderfully preserved castle. She leads a one-hour tour in German and Italian, squeezing in whatever English she can (€7, open May-Oct; tours Sun-Fri at 10:30, 14:00, and 15:00; mid-July-mid-Sept also at 16:00, always closed Sat, best to call ahead to reserve tour, minimum of 4 people needed for tour to run, picnic spot at drawbridge, tel. 339-264-3752, or TI tel. 0472-765-325, www.sterzing.com).

To drive to the castle, follow the A-22 autostrada toward Brenner Pass, exit at Vipiteno (Sterzing), and follow signs toward *Bolzano,* taking three rights. The castle is just west of the freeway; park at the base of the castle's rock. Of the two castles here, Reifenstein is the one to the west. While this is easy by car, it's probably not worth the trouble by train (6/day from Bolzano, one-hour train ride followed by a one-hour hike).

▲**Glurns**—Drivers connecting the Dolomites and Lake Como by the high road via Meran and Bormio can spend the night in the amazing little town of Glurns (45 minutes west of touristy Meran, between Schluderns and Taufers). Glurns still lives within its square wall on the Adige River, with a church bell tower that has a thing about ringing, and real farms rather than boutiques.

THE DOLOMITES

The town's short archways seem to cause the locals, whose families go back eons, to take on a Quasimodo-like posture. There are several small hotels in the town, but I'd stay in a private home (such as **Family Hofer,** 4 rooms, €27/person with breakfast, less for 3 nights, cash only, 100 yards from town square, near church, just outside wall on river, Via Adige 1, tel. 0473-831-597, fax 0473-835-864, www.hofer.bz.it, privatzimmer.hofer@rolmail.net).

THE LAKES

Commune with nature where Italy is joined to the Alps, in the lovely Italian lakes district. In this land of lakes, the million-euro question is: Which one? For the best mix of accessibility, scenery, and offbeatness, Varenna on Lake Como is my top choice, followed by Stresa on Lake Maggiore. You'll get a complete dose of Italian-lakes wonder and aristocratic-old-days romance. Bustling Milan, just an hour away from either lake, doesn't even exist. Now it's your turn to be *chiuso per restauro* (closed for restoration). If relaxation's not on your agenda, the lakes shouldn't be either. If you must choose between Lake Como and Lake Maggiore, the former is a better place to linger, while the latter makes a good day trip from Milan.

Lake Como

Lake Como (Lago di Como)—lined with elegant 19th-century villas, crowned by snowcapped mountains, and busy with ferries, hydrofoils, and slow, passenger-only boats—is a good place to take a break from the intensity and obligatory-turnstile culture of central Italy. It seems like half the travelers you'll meet have tossed their itineraries into the lake and are actually relaxing.

Lake Como is Milan's quick getaway, and the sleepy mid-lake village of Varenna is the gateway to the lake and the handiest base of operations. With good connections to Milan, Malpensa Airport, and mid-lake destinations, Varenna is my favorite home base for the lakes. Today, the hazy, lazy lake's only serious industry

The Lakes

SWITZERLAND
TICINO
LOMBARDY
PIEDMONT
ITALY

To Luzern
To Pontre-sina
To Bern
Tirano
Locarno
Bellinzona
Sondrio
Domo-dossola
Colico
Lake Como
Lake Maggiore
Lugano
Menaggio
Varenna
Bellagio
See Central Lake Como detail map
Mt. Motta-rone
Stresa
See Stresa Area detail map
Lake Lugano
Orta
Como
Lecco
Arona
To Brescia & Venice
Lake Orta
Bergamo
Gallarate
Saronno
Orio al Serio
Monza
Malpensa
To Turin
Novara
Milan
Linate
To Venice
To Genoa & Cinque Terre
To Florence

Rail
High Speed Rail
Bus
Boat

15 Kilometers
15 Miles

is tourism. Thousands of lakeside residents travel daily to nearby Lugano, in Switzerland, to find work. The lake's isolation and flat economy have left it pretty much the way the 19th-century Romantic poets described it: heaven on earth.

Planning Your Time

Even though there are no essential activities, plan for at least two nights so you'll have an uninterrupted day to see how slow you can get your pulse.

Getting Around Lake Como

By Boat: Lake Como is well-served by boats and hydrofoils. The lake service is divided into three parts: south-north from Como to Colico; mid-lake between Varenna, Bellagio, Menaggio, and Cadenabbia (Villa Carlotta); and the southeastern arm to Lecco (Villa Balbianello). Unless you're going through Como, you'll probably limit your cruising to the mid-lake service (boat info: toll-free tel. 800-551-801 or tel. 031-579-211, www.navigazionelaghi.it). Boats go about every 30 minutes between Varenna, Menaggio, and

Boat Schedule Literacy Tips

Feriali	Monday-Saturday
Festivi	Sundays and holidays
Partenze da...	Departing from
Traghetto or *autotraghetto*	Car ferry (walk-on passengers, too)
Aliscafo or *servizio rapido*	Hydrofoil
Battello ship	Slow passenger-only boat going to Como
Battello navetta	Shuttle serving mid-lake only

Bellagio (€3.70 per hop, 15-20 minutes, daily approximately 7:00-22:30, confirm return trip when you disembark). Overnight stopovers aren't allowed, so buy individual tickets for each ride if you aren't planning to return the same day. The one-day €15 mid-lake pass saves you a little over the cost of three rides. It can be used to make unlimited trips between seven different villages bordering the lake, either on the *autotraghetto* (car ferry) or the passenger-only *battello* (but note that many travelers take only two rides in a day—a round-trip between Varenna and Bellagio).

The free schedule (available at TIs, hotels, and boat docks) lists boat times. Rates are displayed on posters at ticket windows. Confusingly, the schedule requires you to scan four different time-tables to know all the departures:

- car and passenger ferry (mid-lake ferryboat, or *autotraghetto*)
- hydrofoil (*servizio rapido,* costs a third more, enclosed, stuffy, speedy, less scenic)
- all-lake slow boat *(battello ship)*
- mid-lake shuttle ferry *(battello navetta)*

If you find the schedule impossible to decipher, simply ask at each dock when the next boat is leaving and which slip it's leaving from (Bellagio has several docks). Be sure to note whether you are traveling on a weekday (*feriali,* Mon-Sat) or a Sunday or holiday *(festivi).* Review your possible connections (ask your hotelier for help) before you set out so you can pace your day smartly. It's a shame to miss a boat and lose out on a hike or an eagerly antici-pated meal because of confusing timetables.

By Car: With scarce parking, traffic jams, and expensive

THE LAKES

car ferries, this is no place to drive if you don't have to. While you can drive around the lake, the road is narrow, congested, and lined with privacy-seeking walls, hedges, and tall fences. Parking in Bellagio is more difficult than in Varenna. If you have a car in Varenna, leave it there and use the boat.

While you can rent cars in Bellagio, for most travelers, it's best to take the train to Milan and pick up a car there, either at the central train station or at one of Milan's three airports.

Varenna

This town of 800 people offers the best of all lake worlds. Easily accessible by train, on the less-driven side of the lake, Varenna has a romantic promenade, a tiny har-

bor, narrow lanes, and its own villa. It's just the right place to savor a lake-side cappuccino or *aperitivo*. There's wonderfully little to do here, and it's very quiet at night, unless you're here during one of the hundred or so annual American wedding parties. The *passerella* (lakeside promenade, lit at foot level and safe after dark) is adorned with caryatid lovers pressing silently against each other in the shadows. Varenna is a popular destination with my readers and European vacationers—book well in advance for visits in summer (May-Oct). Between November and mid-March, Varenna practically shuts down; hotels close for the winter, and restaurants and shops reduce their hours.

Orientation to Varenna

Tourist Information

Don't count on any tourist information. You may find a small office with sporadic hours at the train station, on the main square, or at the boat dock. Proloco Varenna, on the main square, is generally open only during high season (April-Sept Tue-Sat 10:00-12:00 & 15:00-17:00, Sun 10:00-12:00, closed Mon; Oct-March may be open Sat 10:00-17:00; just past the tobacco shop, tel. 0341-830-367, www.varennaitaly.com, prolocovarenna@tin.it). Your hotel may have the latest edition of the *Varenna Tourist Info* booklet, with updated info on sights around Varenna and a list of restaurants, bars, and services in town.

Arrival in Varenna

By Train: From any destination covered in this book, you'll get to Lake Como via Milan. The quickest, easiest, and cheapest

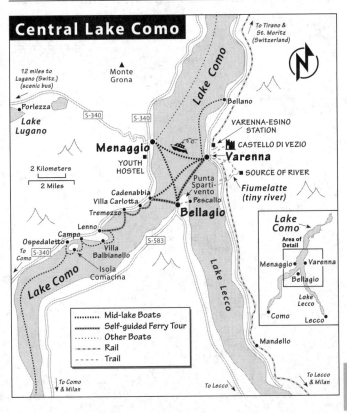

Milan connection to any point mid-lake (Varenna, Bellagio, or Menaggio) is via the train to Varenna. On arrival, set up and limit your activities to the scenic mid-lake area (Varenna and Bellagio).

Here are the specifics: Leaving from Milan's central train station, catch a train heading for Sondrio or Tirano—sometimes the departure board also says "Lecco/Tirano." (Tirano is often confused with Torino...wrong city.) And, if you're heading for Varenna, be sure you don't accidentally catch a train to Verona. All Sondrio trains stop in Varenna, as noted in the fine print on the *Partenze* (departures) schedule posted at Milan's train station. Trains leave Milan about every two hours (€6.40, 1 hour, likely schedule—but confirm these times: 6:20, 8:20, 10:20, 12:20, 14:20, 16:20, 17:20, 19:20, 20:20, and 21:25; no railpasses accepted). Get a second-class ticket, since first-class train cars are rare on the Sondrio-Tirano route. If you plan to head back to Milan on the train, also buy a return ticket—Varenna's station has no ticket office or ticket machine (though it does have a travel agency that sells train tickets; see "Helpful Hints," later). Stamp the ticket in the yellow box at the front of the tracks or risk a €50 fine. Sit on

Varenna

100 Meters
100 Yards

VARENNA-ESINO
TRAIN
STATION

Torento Esino

To Tirano

Wooded

TRAVEL
AGENCY

To Tirano
& 14

VIA PER ESINO

8

Steep
Trail!

WALK
BEGINS

VIA EMBARCADERO

VIA CORRADO VENINI

7

VIA PER VEZIO

BANK

(MAIN ROAD)

VIA RIVA DEI MARMISTI

2

15

18

CAR /
PASSENGER
FERRY DOCK

P A S S

Lido
(Beach)

WC

TICKETS

Harbor

HYDROFOIL &
SLOW BOAT DOCK

Lake

Passerella
(Lakeside Promenade)

To Menaggio

To Bellagio,
Cadenabbia & Como

THE LAKES

the left for maximum lake-view beauty. Get off at Varenna-Esino. Even though train schedules simply list Varenna, Varenna-Esino is what you'll see at the train station—same place.

Long trains serve Varenna's tiny station and stop for only about a minute. Know what time you're supposed to arrive in Varenna, so you can be ready to disembark with luggage in hand. Otherwise you'll be carried on to the next town and have to backtrack. You may have to open the train door yourself, and because trains can be longer than the station, your car may actually stop before or after the platform (causing you to mistakenly think that you're not there yet). Look out the window. If part of the train is at the station, you'll need to get out and walk to the platform. Tips: Board mid-train to land next to a platform. Leave from the door by which you entered, since you know it's working. If necessary, pull hard on the red handle to open the door.

By Train from Malpensa Airport (Milan): You can take the

1. Hotel du Lac
2. Albergo Milano & Ristorante la Vista
3. Villa Cipressi & Ristorante la Contrada
4. To Eremo Gaudio
5. Albergo/Ristorante del Sole
6. Villa Elena
7. Hotel/Rist. Montecodeno
8. Albergo Beretta
9. Ristorante il Cavatappi
10. Varennamonamour
11. Osteria Quatro Pass
12. Nilus Bar & Bar il Molo
13. Gelateria Riva
14. To Ristorante il Caminetto & Cooking Course
15. Pub l'Orso
16. Ristorante Isola Nuova
17. Vecchia Varenna
18. Hotel/Ristorante Olivedo
19. Grocery Stores (2)
20. Ornithology & Natural Science Museum; Internet Café
21. Laundry
22. Villa Monastero Entrance
23. Barilott Bar

Malpensa Express train from Malpensa Airport to Milan's central train station (see page 338), then transfer to a Varenna-bound train (described above).

By Boat via Como: For a less convenient but more scenic trip, you can also get to Varenna from Milan via the town of Como (or vice versa). Trains take you from Milan to Como (hourly, 30-90 minutes). It's a 10-minute walk to the dock, where you catch either the speedy hydrofoil or the leisurely *battello* (slow boat—great for enjoying the scenery) for the ride up the lake to Varenna (slow boat: 3/day, €9.30, 2 hours, last departure about 15:00; hydrofoil: 5/day Mon-Sat, 2/day Sun, €13, 1 hour, last departure about 19:00).

By Taxi: A taxi costs roughly €130-165 between Varenna and downtown Milan or Milan's airports. For a reputable taxi service, see "Taxi," page 260.

By Car: In Varenna, the easiest, although most expensive option for parking is the new multilevel lot at the end of town, across from Villa Monastero (€2/hour, €20/24 hours). Because the town is promoting use of the garage, the other parking options described here may change or disappear altogether. Bottom line: Save yourself time and headache and park in the garage.

In town, you can look for the color-coded lines to decipher the parking options: white is free anytime; yellow is for residents only; and blue means you pay (look for signs, €1.50/hour, payment times vary—often 8:00-19:00, otherwise free). Buy tickets from the newsstand on the main square, the tobacco shop just south of the square, or Bar Cambusa near the ferry dock, or put coins in the parking meter. Leave the ticket on your dashboard; overnight until 8:00 is OK.

Parking is free Monday-Friday at the train station, but you'll have to pay on Saturdays and Sundays during high season (8:00-19:00, feed coins into meter in center of lot and put printed ticket on dashboard). Parking on the main square is for residents only. If you park elsewhere in town and aren't sure if your spot is legal, check with your hotelier.

Getting Around Varenna

Varenna is small, and everything is within a 15-minute walk (except for the Eremo Gaudio hotel). From the dock, walk up to the main road to avoid carting your luggage across the cobblestones.

If you'd prefer a taxi, you'll find them waiting at the train station and dock. From either arrival point, a taxi should charge about €9 for a ride to your hotel (see "Taxi," below).

Helpful Hints

Money: One bank is near Varenna's main square; another is located inland from the boat dock. Both have cash machines (see town map).

Internet Access: Try **Barilott,** which also sells some train and local bus tickets, fresh *panini,* and wines by the glass (Internet access-€5/hour, free Wi-Fi for customers, Mon-Sat 7:00-20:00, closed Sun, Via IV Novembre 6, tel. 0341-815-045, Claudia and Fabrizio).

Post Office: It's just off the main square (Mon-Fri 8:30-14:00, Sat 8:30-12:30, closed Sun).

Laundry: Lavanderia Pensa Barbara can wash and dry your laundry within 24 hours (€3.50/kilo—about 2 pounds, no self-service, no underwear but socks are OK, Mon-Fri 9:00-12:30 & 15:00-19:30, Sat 9:00-12:30, closed Sun, Via Venini 31, tel. 0341-830-478, mobile 340-466-2977).

Taxi: Reliable **Marco Barili** (or his wife Nelly) will meet you at the train station if you know your exact arrival time in Varenna. He can also get you to Milan and its airports and, unlike other drivers, he doesn't add surcharges for baggage or early/late departures (€135 to central Milan or Linate Airport, €150 to Malpensa Airport for up to 4 people—or €210 for 5-8 passengers in a minibus, €130 to Bergamo's Orio al Serio Airport, tel. 0341-815-061, taxi.varenna@tiscali.it).

Travel Agency: For bus and boat tours, consider Varenna's travel agency, **I Viaggi del Tivano,** next to Albergo Beretta, a block below the train station. They book planes, trains, and automobiles, and can offer half-day and daylong tours of the region and into Switzerland from April through October; book tours by noon the day before. This agency, along with the Barilott tobacco shop off the main square, are the only places in town that sell train tickets to Milan; no tickets are sold at the small train station (office open Mon-Fri 9:00-18:00, Sat 9:00-12:00, closed Sun, can book rental cars here but pick up in Lecco, no service charge for Milan train tickets, €5 service charge for long-distance train tickets, Via Esino 3, tel. 0341-814-009, www.tivanotours.com, info@tivanotours.com, helpful Cristina and Eleonora).

Self-Guided Walk

Welcome to Varenna

Since you came here to relax, this short walk gives you just the town basics.

Bridge Just Below Train Station: This main bridge spans the tiny Esino River. The river divides two communities: Perledo (which sprawls up the hill—notice the church spire high above) and the old fishing town of Varenna (huddled around its harbor). The train station, called Varenna-Esino, is named for a third community situated eight miles higher in the hills. Cross the bridge and follow the river down to the lakeside promenade by the ferry dock. The town's public beach (or *lido*) is just over the cute pedestrian bridge (€2 entry). The inn facing the ferry dock, Hotel Olivedo, has greeted ferry travelers since the 19th century and is named for the olive groves you can see growing halfway up the hill. Natives claim this is the farthest north that olives grow in Europe. Near the dock is a playground and a small square that hosts a market on Wednesdays.

• *Across from Hotel Olivedo is Varenna's...*

Ferry Landing: Since the coming of the train in 1892, Varenna has been *the* convenient access point from "mid-lake" (the communities of Bellagio, Menaggio, and Varenna) to Milan. From this viewpoint, you can almost see how Lake Como is shaped like a man. The head is the north end (to the right, up by the Swiss Alps). Varenna is the man's left hip (to the east). Menaggio, across the lake, is the right hip (to the west). And Bellagio (hiding behind the smaller wooded hill to your left) is where the legs come together, at the point called Punta Spartivento—literally, "point that divides the wind." In a more colorful description, a traditional poem says, "Lake Como is a man, with Colico the head, Lecco and Como the feet, and Bellagio the testicles." (In the regional dialect, this rhymes—ask a native to say it for you.)

The farthest ridges high above the right hip mark the border of Switzerland. The region's longtime poverty shaped the local character (much like the Great Depression shaped the outlook of a generation of Americans). Many still remember that this side of the lake was the poorest, because those on the Menaggio side controlled the lucrative cigarette-smuggling business over the Swiss border. Today, the entire region is thriving—thanks to tourism.

• *Walk past the ferry dock to Varenna's elevated shoreline walk, called the...*

Passerella: A generation ago, Varenna built this elegant lakeside promenade, which connects the ferry dock with the old town center. Strolling this lane, you'll come to the tiny, two-dinghy, concrete breakwater of a villa. Lake Como is lined with swanky 19th-century villas; their front doors face the lake to welcome visitors arriving by boat. At this point, the modern *passerella* cuts between this villa's water gate and its private harbor. From here, enjoy a good Varenna town view. These buildings are stringently protected by preservation laws; you can't even change the color of your villa's paint.

Just over the hump (which allows boats into a covered moorage), look up at another typical old villa—with a private *passerella*, a lovely veil of wisteria, and a prime lakeview terrace. Many of these villas are owned by the region's "impoverished nobility." They were bred and raised not to work and, therefore, are now unable to pay for the upkeep of their sprawling houses. Lately, these villas are being bought by the region's nouveau riche.

• *At the community harbor, walk to the end of the pier for a town overview, then continue under the old-time arcades toward the multihued homes facing the harbor.*

Varenna Harborfront: There are no streets in the old town— just the characteristic stepped lanes called *contrade*. Varenna was originally a fishing community. Even today, old-timers enjoy Lake Como's counterpart to the Norwegian lutefisk: *missoltino*, air-dried and salted lake "sardines." They're served with the region's polenta (different from Venice's because buckwheat is mixed in with the corn).

Imagine the harbor 200 years ago—busy with coopers expertly fitting chestnut and oak staves into barrels, stoneworkers carving the black marble that was quarried just above town, and fishing boats dragged onto the sloping beach. The little stone harbor dates from about 1600. Today, the fishing boats are just for recreation, and residents gather here with their kids to relax by the lake.

At the south end of the harbor (across from La Frulleria), belly up to the banister of the terrace for another colorful town view. Another traditional ditty goes, "If you love Lake Como, you know Bellagio is the pearl...but Varenna is the diamond."

• *Continue straight, leaving the harbor. A lane leads around Hotel du Lac (its fine lakeside terrace welcomes even non-guests for a drink) to the tiny pebbly town beach. From here, climb uphill to the town square, called...*

Piazza San Giorgio: Several churches face Varenna's town square. The main church (Chiesa di San Giorgio) dates from the 13th century. Romantic Varenna is an understandably popular spot for weddings—rice often litters the church's front yard. Stepping inside, you'll find a few humble but centuries-old bits of carving and frescoes. The black floor and chapels are made from the local marble.

On the square, to the right of the WWI monument, is the Proloco Varenna office and the Ornithology and Natural Science Museum, with its small collection of stuffed birds and other wildlife (typically open Sat-Sun only).

The Hotel Royal Victoria, also on the main square, recalls the 1839 visit of Queen Victoria, who registered herself as the Countess of Clare in an attempt to remain anonymous.

The trees in the square are planted to make a V for Varenna. The street plan survives from Roman times, when gutters flowed down to the lake. The little church on the lake side of the square is the baptistery. Dating from the ninth century, it's one of the oldest churches on the lake, but is rarely open for visits.

Your walk is over. From this square, you can head south to visit the gardens (described later, under "Sights in Varenna"), north to go to the train station or ferry dock, east to hike up to the castle, or west to go to the beach (take either of the lanes flanking the Hotel Royal Victoria down to the water).

Sights in Varenna

Castle—A steep and stony trail leads to Varenna's ruined hilltop castle, Castello di Vezio, located in a peaceful, traffic-free, one-chapel town. Take the small road, Via per Vezio (about 100 feet south of—and to the right of—Hotel Montecodeno), and figure on a 20-minute walk one-way. The castle is barren, but livened up by occasional art exhibits and a falconry-training center.

Cost and Hours: €4, April-Sept Mon-Fri 10:00-18:00, Sat-Sun 10:00-19:00; March and Oct closes one hour earlier; closed Nov-Feb and in bad weather, low-key falconry shows usually around 15:30 but check website or call in morning for times, bar and restaurant at entrance, dinner by reservation only, mobile 333-448-5975, www.castellodivezio.it, info@castellodivezio.it, Nicola.

Gardens—Two separate manicured lakeside gardens—the terraces of Villa Cipressi and the adjacent, more open grounds of

Villa Monastero—are open to the public. Formerly a noble residence, Villa Monastero, filled with overly ornate furnishings from the late 1800s, is also open to the public as a museum.

Cost and Hours: Villa Cipressi—€5; May-Nov; Villa Monastero—gardens-€5, gardens and museum-€8, April-Oct daily 9:00-19:00, closed Nov-March, villa closed for lunch 13:00-14:00, bar in garden serves snacks 9:00-18:00, tel. 0341-295-450, www.villa monastero.eu.

Swimming—There are three spots to swim in Varenna: the free little beach behind the Hotel Royal Victoria off Piazza San Giorgio, the central lakefront area by Nilus Bar, and the *lido*. The *lido* is by far the best-equipped for swimmers. Just north of the boat dock, it's essentially a wide concrete slab with sand and a swimming area off an old boat ramp. It has showers, bathrooms, a restaurant, a bar, and lounge chairs for rent (entry-€2, lounge chair-€3/half-day, sunshades-€4, tel. 0341-815-3700). Swimming by the boat dock is strictly forbidden for safety reasons.

Speedboat Tours—**Taxiboat** organizes "villa-viewing trips" around the lake, gives personalized tours on the water, and provides a water-taxi service. Their 30-minute "Varenna seen from the water" tour (€50, up to 12 people) is fun, and chartering the boat for 1.25 hours (€150, up to 5 people) gets you a mid-lake tour (April-Sept, mobile 349-229-0953, www.taxiboatlecco.com, info@taxi boatlecco.com, Luca). A similar company works out of Bellagio.

THE LAKES

Near Varenna

▲▲Self-Guided Ferry Tour: Lake Como—The best simple day out is to take the *battello navetta* (mid-lake ferry) on its

entire 50-minute Varenna-Bellagio-Cadenabbia-Villa Carlotta-Tremezzo-Lenno route. On the return trip, stop at any sights that interest you (Lenno to see Villa del Balbianello, Cadenabbia for Villa Carlotta, and/or Bellagio). This commentary describes what you'll see along the way.

Leaving Varenna: Looking back at Varenna from the lake, you'll see the castle rising above the town, with new Varenna on the left (bigger buildings and

modern ferry dock), and old Varenna on the right (tighter buildings). The big development high on the hillside is an ugly example of cronyism (without the mayor involved, this would never have happened). Under the castle is a grove of olives (reputedly the

most northern ones grown in Italy). Because the lake is protected from the north wind, exotic flowers grow well in the lake's many fine gardens. To the right of Varenna's castle are the town cemetery, a lift up to the recommended Eremo Gaudio hotel (a former hermitage), and a spurt of water gushing out of the mountain just above lake level. This is the tiny Fiumelatte, Italy's shortest river.

Mid-Lake: The Swiss Alps rise to the north. Across the lake is Menaggio, and just over the ridge from that is Lugano and the "Swiss Riviera." The winds alternate between north and south. In pre-industrial times, traders harnessed the wind to sail up and down the lake. Notice the V-shaped, fjord-like terrain. Lake Como is glacier-cut. And at more than 1,200 feet deep, it's Europe's deepest lake. You'll cruise past the Punta Spartivento, the point that literally splits the wind, and where the two "legs" of the lake join (Lake Lecco is on the left, to the east, and Lake Como on the right).

Approaching Bellagio: Survey the park to the left of Punta Spartivento—it's a pleasant walk from town. Bellagio has 10 times the number of hotel rooms as Varenna, as you can see upon approach. The town, with its strip of three-star hotels, is book-ended by Villa Serbelloni (5 stars) on the left, dominating the lake-front, and the sprawling Grand Hotel Bretagne (4 stars) on the

right. In the 19th century, aristocratic Russians hung out in
the Serbelloni, and well-heeled
English chose the Bretagne.
These days, the Serbelloni is the
second-most luxurious hotel on
the lake after Villa Este, while
Bretagne is mired in a long renovation project.

Approaching Cadenabbia: From Bellagio, you cross the
lake to Cadenabbia. Above Cadenabbia, the Church of St. Martin
seems stranded halfway up the mountain. This side of the lake has
nearly all the area's traffic, thanks to a big road that ended up sepa-
rating many fine lakefront gardens from their villas. Farther north
is the village of Dongo, where Mussolini and his girlfriend were
captured in the last months of World War II as they tried to escape
into Switzerland. They were shot here on the lake, and their bodies
were hung ingloriously in Milan for public viewing.

Villa Carlotta: Because of lake taxes and high maintenance
costs, owners of once-elite villas have been forced to turn them

into hotels or to open their
doors to the paying pub-
lic. This is an example of
the latter. One of the finest properties on the lake,
Villa Carlotta is most visited for its Canova statue
and lush garden (see listing
on page 280).

Tremezzo: Notice the Grand Hotel Tremezzo, with its striking Liberty-style (Art Nouveau) facade and swimming pool float-
ing on the lake. Above the town is a villa built in the 19th-century
Romantic Age to resemble a medieval castle. After the Tremezzo
stop (just before the Tremezzo church), you'll see a fine public park
with a fountain. When the road separated this land from its villa,
its owners gave it to the community. Here the lake is dotted by a
string of fine old villas with elegant landings and gated boathouses.
Built in the days before motors,
they are now too small for most
modern lake boats. Tullio Abbate
is famous in this area for building
speedy, high-end lake boats.

Lenno: This is your last
stop. About 400 yards farther
along the shore is a tiny dock for
shuttle boats headed for Villa del

THE LAKES

Balbianello (of *Star Wars: Episode II* and *Casino Royale* fame—see page 281).

Sailing Home: Get off the boat at Lenno; from here you can return to Bellagio or Varenna, stopping along the way as you like.

Hiking—The town of Fiumelatte, about a half-mile south of Varenna, was named for its milky river. It's the shortest river in Italy (at 800 feet) and runs—like most of the area tourist industry—only from April through September (though even then it may be dry, depending on the weather). The *La Sorgente del Fiumelatte* brochure, available at Varenna's TI or at the travel agency, lays out a walk from Varenna to the Fiumelatte, then to the castle, and back. It's a 30-minute hike to the source *(sorgente)* of the river (at Varenna's monastery, take the high road, drop into the tranquil and evocative cemetery, and climb steps to the wooded trail leading to the peaceful and refreshing cave from which the river spouts).

For a longer hike in the opposite direction with lake views, ask the TI about the Wayfarers' Path (hike one-way up the lake, about 1.5 hours, not quite as steep as Fiumelatte hike). You can return by train from Bellano (€1.20, Bellano not included on mid-lake pass, check schedule before you go), or take the ferry to Menaggio and catch a connecting boat back to Varenna.

▲**Cooking Course**—Chef Moreno of the recommended Ristorante il Caminetto picks you up in Varenna, zips you up the mountain to his restaurant (experience Italian driving!), and then teaches you some basics of Italian cooking. Learn how to handcraft fresh pasta or prep regional specialties. Classes last about three hours, plus time to *mangiare* (€48 includes trip, lesson, and lunch complete with wine, cookies, and coffee; Mon, Tue, Thu, and Fri; 10:00 pick-up from Varenna landing, return by 16:00, reservations mandatory, tel. 0341-815-225, www.ilcaminettoonline .com, info@ilcaminettoonline.com). People love the experience and find Moreno a charming teacher and host.

Sleeping in Varenna

Reservations are tight in August, snug May through October, and wide open most of the rest of the year. Many places close in winter. High-season prices are listed here; prices get soft off-season (Nov-April).

$$$ Hotel du Lac, filling a refined and modernized 19th-century villa, is the finest hotel in town. From its exclusive private perch on the point, it offers a quiet lakefront breakfast terrace, generous public spaces, a friendly, professional staff, and 16 delightful rooms—all but three with lake views (standard Db-€190, bigger Db-€245, these high-season prices are for May-mid-Oct, €20 less in shoulder season, closed off-season, air-con, Wi-Fi, parking-€15,

THE LAKES

Sleep Code

(€1 = about $1.40, country code: 39)
S = Single, **D** = Double/Twin, **T** = Triple, **Q** = Quad, **b** = bathroom, **s** = shower only. Unless otherwise noted, you can assume the price includes breakfast, credit cards are accepted, and English is spoken. Varenna, like many cities in Italy, has started charging a tourist tax. The tax, which is €1 per person per night, must be paid in cash at check-out.

To help you sort easily through these listings, I've divided the accommodations into three categories based on the price for a standard double room with bath:

$$$ Higher Priced—Most rooms €150 or more.
$$ Moderately Priced—Most rooms between €100-150.
$ Lower Priced—Most rooms €100 or less.

Prices can change without notice; verify the hotel's current rates online or by email.

Via del Prestino 11, tel. 0341-830-238, fax 0341-831-081, www .albergodulac.com, albergodulac@tin.it).

$$$ Albergo Milano, located right in the old town, is graciously run by Egidio and his Swiss wife, Bettina. Fusing the best of Italy with the best of Switzerland, this well-run, romantic hotel has eight comfortable rooms with extravagant views, balconies, or big terraces (Sb-€125, Db-€150-170, €10 extra for view terrace, €5/ day cash discount, no elevator, pay Wi-Fi, closed mid-Nov-Feb; from the station, take main road to town and turn right at steep alley where sidewalk and guardrail break; Via XX Settembre 35, tel. 0341-830-298, fax 0341-830-061, www.varenna.net, hotelmilano @varenna.net). This place whispers *luna di miele*—honeymoon (see website for 3-night honeymoon deal). Nearby is **$$ Casa Rossa,** an annex with six comfortable rooms and two apartments that work well for families (Db-€135-165, proportionately more for third or fourth person, breakfast served at main hotel). Their recommended Ristorante la Vista is worth considering for dinner.

$$ Villa Cipressi is a sprawling, centuries-old lakeside mansion with 33 warmly outfitted, modern rooms. Its public spaces are often busy with wedding parties. Rooms without views face the street and can be noisy. The villa sits in a huge, quiet terraced garden that non-guests pay to see (Sb-€135, non-view Db-€165, view Db-€185-195, extra cot-€40, extra bed-€60, ask for Rick Steves discount, elevator, Internet access, Wi-Fi, garden access, free mountain bike use for guests, Via IV Novembre 22, tel. 0341-830-113, fax 0341-830-401, www.hotelvillacipressi.it, info@hotel villacipressi.it, Davide).

$$ Eremo Gaudio stands out with a commanding lake view high above Varenna. Once an orphanage, it became a hermitage run by the Catholic Church, and then—since 2000—a modern hotel accessed by a private funicular. Perfect for monks with champagne tastes, it's peaceful, with awe-inspiring view balconies and a breakfast terrace. Thirteen bright, plain-but-comfy rooms climb up the main building, and 15 less dramatic but equally comfortable rooms huddle below at the foot of the funicular (upper rooms: Sb-€110, Db-€120, Db with balcony-€148; lower rooms: Db-€120-148; 5 percent discount with cash and 2-night stay, closed Nov-Feb, all rooms have lake views, air-con May-Oct, requires walking up steep hills and steps—taking a taxi from station is recommended, quarter-mile south of Varenna's main square at Via Roma 25, tel. 0341-815-301, fax 0341-815-314, www.eremo gaudio.it, eremogaudio@yahoo.it). Suppers are served on the terrace, weather permitting.

$$ Albergo del Sole is a no-frills hotel over a basic restaurant right on the town square. Run by fun-loving Enzo, the hotel has seven comfy rooms and no hint of a lake view (Sb-€70-85; Db-€120, €105 off-season; fans, hardwood floors, shiny bathrooms, Wi-Fi, no elevator, Piazza San Giorgio 17, tel. & fax 0341-815-218, albergo.sole@virgilio.it).

$ Villa Elena, a grandmotherly, low-energy place on the main square, offers a tranquil rest and the best budget beds in town. English-speaking Signora Seta ("Silk") Vitali, who lives downstairs, rents her three characteristic, antique-filled rooms at the same price—room #1 has a shabby bathroom and view terrace (first come, first served); room #3 also has a private bathroom, but room #2 does not. With only twin beds, it's not for romantics, but it is a great value (D-€50 with or without bath, cash only, no breakfast, it's the house with the vine-covered pergola at Piazza San Giorgio 7 near Via San Giovanni, tel. 0341-830-575, www.villa elenavarenna.it, info@villaelenavarenna.it).

$ Hotel Montecodeno, with 11 decent rooms and no views, is a functional concrete box just off the main road between the train station and lake (Sb-€75-80, Db-€100, extra bed-€10, air-con, Internet access, pay Wi-Fi, attached restaurant serves fresh fish and a €23 "Rick Steves" fixed-price meal if you show this book; if you stay 3 nights and pay cash, you get one meal included per guest or a 15 percent cash discount—take your pick; Via della Croce 2, tel. 0341-830-123, fax 0341-815-227, www.hotelmontecodeno.com, info@hotelmontecodeno.com, kind Marina Castelli and Lucia). Their nearby apartment sleeps up to five (€35-40/person).

$ Albergo Beretta, on the main road a block below the station, has 10 pleasant rooms, several with balconies (and street noise). Second-floor rooms are quietest. This place, above a coffee shop that doubles as the reception, feels homey but lacks any lakeside glamour (D-€60, Db-€70, larger room-€80, extra bed-€12, breakfast-€6 but free with 2-night stay and this book, no elevator, Via per Esino 1, tel. & fax 0341-830-132, www.hotelberetta.it, hotelberetta@iol.it, Signora Tosca doesn't speak English, but Giulia does).

Eating in Varenna

Dining with a Lake View

Ristorante la Vista, at Albergo Milano, feels like a private hotel restaurant but also welcomes non-guests. On a balmy evening, their terrace overlooking the town and the lake is hard to beat. Egidio (or Egi—pronounced "edgy") and his staff give traditional cuisine a creative twist, and his selection is great for foodies with discerning tastes. I'd go with his €38 three-course fixed-price dinner (Mon and Wed-Sat 19:00-22:00, closed Sun and Tue, reservations required, Via XX Settembre 35, tel. 0341-830-298).

Ristorante la Contrada, with its terrace-side location, is run by the Villa Cipressi and takes advantage of the villa's elegant garden, trickling fountain, and lake view. Indoor seating glows with a warm and romantic air, and the garden is a delight on warm summer evenings. Fresh daily specialties and professional service make this a worthwhile splurge. However, weddings and conference groups can crowd the place and distract from the service (€35 meals plus wine, daily 12:30-14:00 & 19:15-21:30, may close for weddings, Via IV Novembre 22, tel. 0341-830-113).

Dining Without a Lake View

Ristorante il Cavatappi, a tiny place on a quiet lane just off the town square, serves old-time specialties, such as the antipasto *missoltino*, the air-dried lake fish that natives like more than tourists do. Helpful owner-chef Mario is happy to be considered a lunatic gourmet. With just five tables, he can connect personally with diners. Talk with him, make a plan, then let him loose. Plan on spending €28-38 plus wine (daily 12:30-14:30 & 19:30-21:45, reservations recommended for dinner, tel. 0341-815-349).

Varennamonamour, a new upscale eatery hiding just up from the water, is sure to become popular with fashionable Italians. Its original menu (mainly fish) has a nouvelle cuisine flair, with some unlikely pairings such as guinea fowl and pumpkin dumplings. The cream-and-brown modern decor harmonizes well with the original exposed stone walls to create a classy, welcoming space (€13 pastas, €16 *secondi*, Wed-Sat 12:00-15:00 & 19:00-22:00, Sun 12:00-15:00, closed Tue, Contrada Scoscesa 7, tel. 033-181-4016).

Osteria Quatro Pass is a welcoming bistro known for its homemade pasta and fish. It offers 10 candlelit tables under picturesque vaults, plus sidewalk seating (Thu-Tue 12:00-14:00 & 19:00-22:00, closed Wed, Via XX Settembre 20, tel. 0341-815-091, Lollo).

Eating Simply on the Harbor

The harborfront is lined with several simple eateries, all with great lakefront seating.

Nilus Bar, with a young waitstaff, serves dinner crêpes, pizzas, big mixed salads, hot sandwiches, soup of the day, and cocktails with a smile. Pricing includes cover and service (March-Nov Wed-Mon 12:00-22:30, hours can vary and bar open longer, closed Tue and Dec-Feb, cash only, tel. 0341-815-228, Fulvia and Giovanni).

Bar il Molo, next door, is good for a casual meal on the harbor or a gelato with a view (€9 pizzas and pastas, salads, toasted sandwiches, daily 11:00-24:00, tel. 0341-830-070). They also have a room full of gifty edibles for sale.

At **Gelateria Riva,** you can get a cup or cone to go, then grab a pillowy seat on the bulkhead. Duillo is the only guy in town who prepares his gelato fresh every day. Try his *nocciola* (hazelnut) before making your choice. Ask the day before if you want to watch the gelato being made (daily 13:00-21:00, open later June-Aug, closed off-season).

Eating Simply Without a Lake View

Ristorante del Sole, facing the town square, serves respectable, well-priced meals and Neapolitan-style pizzas (€5-9). Making few concessions to the tourist crowds, this family-friendly restaurant caters to residents, providing a fun atmosphere, a cozy, walled-in garden in back, and tables on the square (daily 12:00-15:00 & 19:00-22:00, pizza until 24:00, Piazza San Giorgio 21, tel. 0341-815-218).

Ristorante il Caminetto is a homey, backwoods mountain trattoria in Gittana, a tiny town high above Varenna. Getting there entails a curvy 10-minute drive—they'll pick you up for free in Piazza San Giorgio at 19:30, deliver you to the restaurant, and then dish up classic fare at small-town prices. Specialties such as grilled meats and risotto with porcini mushrooms and berries are made with pride by husband and wife Moreno and Rossella. This is a good place to set a price and trust your host to bring whatever's best (€16-20 *dégustation* menu, wine extra, Thu-Tue 12:30-14:30 & 19:30-21:30, closed Wed, reservations mandatory to confirm pickup from Varenna at 19:30, Viale Progresso 6, tel. 0341-815-225 or 0341-815-127, mobile 347-331-2238).

Other Eateries

Pub l'Orso is the new hot-spot in town for wine or beer and a light meal (closed Mon). Oozing character, it's behind Hotel Olivedo in a renovated shed that used to be a marble-polishing shop. **Ristorante Montecodeno,** a cozy little place on the big road in the new part of town, serves a plate of eight different tasty lake fish specialities (including *missoltino*) prepared by chef Ferruccio. **Ristorante Isola Nuova** is a newish restaurant with a fresh atmosphere, buried in the old town with no sea view (closed Tue). The venerable **Vecchia Varenna** is the only classy restaurant actually on the harbor (old place with new management). And at **Hotel Olivedo,** a grand old hotel facing the ferry dock, you can eat in a classic dining hall.

Picnics: Varenna's two little grocery stores have all you need for a tasty balcony or breakwater picnic-dinner. The *salumeria* on the square is best for meats, cheese, and bread; try their homemade salami (Tue-Sat 7:30-12:30 & 16:00-19:30, Sun-Mon 7:30-12:30 only). The store just north of the main square by the pharmacy stocks fresh fruits and veggies (daily 7:30-12:30, Tue-Sat also 16:00-19:30).

Varenna Connections

If leaving Varenna by train, you can't purchase tickets at the station. Instead, you can buy them from the travel agency, I Viaggi del Tivano (next door to the recommended Albergo Beretta hotel; see "Helpful Hints," earlier) or the Barilott tobacco shop just off the main square. Stamp your ticket in the yellow machine at the station before boarding. If both places are closed, win the sympathy of the conductor and buy your ticket as soon as you're on board for an additional fee. (Seek him out. If he finds you, you'll likely be charged a stiff penalty.)

Varenna to Milan by Train: Trains leave Varenna for Milano Centrale (1 hour, €6.25, likely schedule for daily and direct trains: 5:36, 6:23, 6:39, 7:37, 8:37, 10:37, 12:37, 14:37, 16:37, 18:37, 20:37, 21:37, and 22:21; if you board a train at a time not listed here, it's likely a local milk-run train that will take twice as long; railpasses not valid on TRENORD trains).

Varenna to Stresa by Train: Trains run about every two hours (2.75-4 hours, transfer in Milan).

Varenna to St. Moritz in Switzerland by Train: From Varenna, you have easy access to the Bernina Express scenic train to St. Moritz. Note that this is only realistic from April through October. First, take the train to Tirano, and then transfer to the Bernina Express train to St. Moritz (4/day, allow 4-5 hours with transfer; for details see www.rhb.ch—click "E" for English). For information and a timetable for this route, stop by the I Viaggi del Tivano travel agency (see "Helpful Hints," earlier), or ask your hotelier for the handy tourist information book produced by local travel agencies. Don't forget your passport for trips into Switzerland.

Bellagio

The self-proclaimed "Pearl of the Lake" is a classy combination of tidiness and Old World elegance. If you don't mind that "tramp in

a palace" feeling, it's a fine place to shop for ties and umbrellas while surrounding yourself with the more adventurous posh travelers. Heavy curtains between the harborfront arcades create welcome shade and keep visitors and their poodles from sweating. Thriving yet still cute, Bellagio is

a much more substantial town than Varenna (which has one-tenth the number of hotel beds and almost no shops).

Orientation to Bellagio

Tourist Information
The TI is right downtown, at the passenger boat dock (April-Oct Mon-Sat 9:00-12:30 & 13:00-18:00, Sun 10:00-14:00; Nov-March shorter hours and closed Sun and Tue; tel. 031-950-204, www.bellagiolakecomo.com).

Arrival in Bellagio
Bellagio is best reached via ferry from Varenna (€3.60); or by ferry, hydrofoil, or slow boat from Como. (For ferries, see pages 254; for hydrofoils and slow boats, see page 259.)

By Boat: Bellagio has two docks a few minutes' walk apart. The northern docks are for the passenger-only slow boat (*battello* or *battello navetta*) and the hydrofoil *(servizio rapido)*. The southern dock is for all "ferry boats" *(traghetti):* both the car ferry (cars and foot passengers) and the passenger-only ferry. Ask around to make sure you're waiting at the correct dock. Remember that if you want to know all your departure options beyond Varenna, Cadenabbia, and Menaggio, you need to study four different timetables (see "Getting Around Lake Como," page 254). Confirm your intentions at the kiosk near either dock.

By Car: Parking is difficult, but you can try for a spot near the lakeside or in the parking lot at the ferry dock (white lines are

Bellagio

❶ Hotel Florence	❿ Rist. Terrazza Barchetta
❷ Hotel/Rist./Snack Bar Metropole	⓫ Enoteca Cava Turacciolo
❸ Hotel Centrale	⓬ Aperitivo Et Al
❹ Albergo Europa	⓭ Gelateria del Borgo
❺ Bellagio B&B Apartments	⓮ Caligari Alimentari
❻ Il Borgo Apartments	⓯ To La Punta Ristorante
❼ To Giardini di Villa Melzi Apartments	⓰ Internet Café
❽ The Florence Ristorante	⓱ Launderette
❾ Trattoria San Giacomo	⓲ Villa Serbelloni Park Tickets
	⓳ Bellaggio Water-Taxi Lake Tours

always free, yellow lines are for residents only, blue lines cost €1.50/hour—pay with coins in gray or blue machines and stick ticket in car window).

Helpful Hints

Internet Access: Bellagio Point has a slick Internet café, complete with great sandwiches, wine-tasting options, and free Wi-Fi if you buy a drink (€2/15 minutes, daily 10:00-22:00, Salita Plinio 8, tel. 031-950-437, www.bellagiopoint.com). Julio also rents apartments (listed later, under "Sleeping in Bellagio").

Post Office: It's on the south end of Lungo Lago Mazzini (Mon-Fri 8:30-14:00, Sat 8:30-12:30, closed Sun).

Laundry: La Lavandera is bright and new. Don't be discouraged if it looks closed; the lights come on automatically when you enter (€8.50 wash/dry, open daily 24 hours, Salita Carlo Grandi 21—this street is also marked as Via Specula, tel. 339-410-6852).

Sights in Bellagio

Villa Serbelloni Park—If you need a destination, you can take a guided tour of this park, which overlooks the town. The villa itself, owned by the Rockefeller Foundation, is not open to the public.

Cost and Hours: €9, April-Oct, tours Tue-Sun at 11:00 and 15:30, no tours Mon and when rainy, 1.5 hours, first two-thirds of walk is uphill, show up at the little tour office in the medieval tower on Piazza della Chiesa 15 minutes before tour time to buy tickets, confirm time at office, tel. 031-951-555.

Strolling—Explore the steep-stepped lanes rising from the harborfront. While Johnnie Walker and jewelry sell best at lake level,

the natives shop up the hill. Piazza della Chiesa, near the top of town, has a worth-a-look church (with its art described in an English-language handout).

The administrative capital of the mid-lake region, Bellagio is located where the two southern legs of the lake split off. For an easy break in a park with a great view, wander right on out to the crotch. Meander past the rich and famous Hotel Villa Serbelloni, and walk five minutes to Punta Spartivento ("point that divides the wind"). You'll find a Renoir atmosphere complete with an inviting bar-restaurant, a tiny harbor, and a chance to sit on a park bench and gaze north past Menaggio, Varenna, and the end of the lake to the Swiss Alps.

For another stroll, head south from the car-ferry dock down the tree-shaded promenade. Ten minutes later, you'll pass the town's concrete swimming area. The grassy, pebbly public San Giovanni beach (no showers) is another 20 minutes farther south from there.

Villa Melzi Gardens—A 10-minute walk south from the ferry dock, this picture-perfect lakeside expanse of exotic plants, flowers, trees, and Neoclassical sculpture was assembled by the vice president of Napoleon's Italian Republic in the early 19th century.

Cost and Hours: €6, March-Oct daily 9:30-18:30, last entry at 17:30, mobile 339-457-3838, www.giardinidivillamelzi.it.

Hikes and Walks—The TI has free brochures for three well-crafted walking tours, varying from one to three hours, which explore the city and environs. Sites include villas, gardens, churches, an old-fashioned dairy shop, medieval towers, and a nautical instruments museum. The TI also sells a hiking map for €3 that shows four different hikes ranging in difficulty and duration.

Bellagio Water-Taxi Lake Tours—With a small stand at the boat docks, Jennine and Luca offer tours and private service in their luxurious and powerful boat. Their basic 2.5-hour tour, guided by Luca, includes a fun hour on mid-lake, with a float-by of Richard Branson's villa, as well as a stop at Villa del Balbianello (see listing on page 281), where you'll take an English tour.

Cost and Hours: €50 with a 10 percent discount for readers of this book, price includes entry and tour of villa—worth €12, generally at 14:00 but check blackboard for day's offerings or call, mobile 338-524-4914, www.bellagiowatertaxis.com, bellagio watertaxis@tin.it.

Sleeping in Bellagio

(€1 = about $1.40, country code: 39)
This is a "boom or bust" lake resort, with high-season prices (those listed here) straight through from May to September, plus a brief shoulder season (with discounted prices) in April and from October to November. Off-season (Dec-March), nearly everything is closed down.

$$$ Hotel Florence has a prime lakefront setting in the center of town. The 150-year-old, family-run place features 30 rooms, hardwood floors, bold earth tones, and a rich touch of Old World elegance (Sb-€125, Db-€145-210, Db suite-€240-270, prices depend on view and balcony, closed Nov-March, handheld showers, fans on request, Wi-Fi, tel. 031-950-342, fax 031-951-722, www.hotelflorencebellagio.it, info@hotelflorencebellagio.it, run by Austrian Ketzlar family).

$$$ Hotel Metropole, dominating Bellagio's waterfront between the ferry docks, is a grand old place with plush public spaces. Its modern rooms have all the comforts, but also an institutional feel with ugly bathrooms. Many of its 42 rooms have lake views (Db-€160, €190 with balcony, €220 with terrace, air-con, elevator, Wi-Fi, stunning roof terrace, tel. 031-950-409, fax 031-951-534, www.albergometropole.it, info@albergometropole.it).

$$ Hotel Centrale, managed with pride and care by Giacomo Borelli, warmly welcomes its guests into a true-blue family operation: Signore Borelli's wife and two sons help out, his mama painted the art, and grandpa crafted much of the Art Deco-era furniture. This place has generous public spaces and many thoughtful touches—and its 17 comfortable rooms are a great value, even without lake views (Sb-€90-110, Db-€110-130, €5/night discount with this book, air-con, elevator, free Wi-Fi, Salita Plinio 7, tel. 031-951-940, fax 031-952-682, www.hc-bellagio.com, info@hc-bellagio.com).

$ Albergo Europa, run with low energy, is in a concrete annex behind a restaurant, away from the waterfront. Its 10 rooms have no charm but are comfortable (Db-€60-90, breakfast-€8, no elevator, free parking, Via Roma 21, tel. & fax 031-950-471, www.hoteleuropabellagio.it, info@hoteleuropabellagio.it, Marchesi family).

$ Bellagio B&B Apartments, with three units for rent, are located behind the *gelateria* at the top of town. Julio also runs the Bellagio Point Internet café, which serves as the reception (Db-€60, more for 3 or 4 people, 3-night minimum, no breakfast, Wi-Fi, reception at Salita Plinio 8, apartments at Salita Cavour 37, tel. 031-951-680, fax 031-953-0025, www.bellagiobedand breakfast.com, info@bellagiobedandbreakfast.com). Julio also has three large apartments a 15-minute walk from Bellagio (toward Como); email him for rates.

$ Il Borgo Apartments rents six modern *Better Homes and Gardens*-quality apartments with kitchenettes in the old center at great prices. Easygoing Flavio is available for check-in daily 9:00-12:00, or by appointment (Db-€90, 2 bigger apartments for up to 6 people-€110, cash discount, no breakfast, 2-night minimum required, air-con, Wi-Fi, Salita Plinio 4, tel. 031-952-497, mobile 338-193-5559, fax 031-951-585, www.borgoresidence.it, info@borgo residence.it).

$ Giardini di Villa Melzi Apartments provides modern accommodations in three double bedrooms and three studios with kitchenettes in the little harbor of Loppia, about a 15-minute walk south of Bellagio. A free pass allows guests to take a shortcut to Bellagio through the Villa Melzi Gardens (Db-€630/week, 30 percent advance deposit required, one-week minimum but shorter stays sometimes possible, cash only, free parking, Via Melzi d'Eril

23, tel. 339-221-4394, www.bellagiowelcome.com, info@bellagio
welcome.com, Ornella).

Eating in Bellagio

On the Lakefront

These places offer wonderful lakeside tables and, considering the
setting, reasonable prices.

Hotel Metropole Ristorante, while a mediocre food value,
has a full menu and is a relaxing delight for a meal with good service (€14 pastas, €16 *secondi,* April-Oct daily 12:00-14:30 & 19:00-
21:30, closed Nov-March, tel. 031-950-409).

Hotel Metropole Snack Bar, next to the hotel's restaurant,
is quite good, with simple pastas (€9), fine salads, and sandwiches
(no cover charge, daily 12:00-21:30, good service, great locale).

The Florence is nicely situated under a trellis of flowers across
from the Florence Hotel and away from the ferry fumes. This is a
lovely perch for a drink or meal (€16 pastas, €20 *secondi*, no cover
charge, simpler lunch menu of salads and such, bar open all day).

In the Old Town Without Lake Views

Trattoria San Giacomo is a high-energy place that's respected for
its traditional cuisine, such as *riso e filetto di pesce* (rice and perch
fillet in butter and sage). It has daily seasonal specials and an inviting €25 fixed-price meal based on regional specialties. Choose
between fun seating on a steep, cobbled lane or tight seating inside
(Mon and Wed-Thu 12:00-14:30 & 19:00-21:30, Fri-Sun open later
midday and evenings, closed Tue, Salita Serbelloni 45, tel. 031-
950-329, Aurelio).

Ristorante Terrazza Barchetta, set on a terrace with no lake
view and bedecked with summery colors, puts a creative twist
on regional favorites such as lake fish. Don't confuse it with the
street-level bar-trattoria—head up the stairs to the second floor.
Reservations are recommended (€15 pastas, €20 *secondi,* Wed-Mon
12:00-14:30 & 19:00-22:30, closed Tue, Salita Mella 13, tel. 031-
951-389).

Other Options

Wine-Tasting: Step into the vaulted stone cellar rooms of the funky
Enoteca Cava Turacciolo to taste three regional wines with a
sampling of cheeses, meats, and breads (€18/person with this book,
Thu-Tue 10:30-1:00, closed Wed, Salita Genazzini 3, tel. 031-950-
975, Norberto and Rosy). **Aperitivo Et Al,** slick and jazzy, is a
trendier wine bar, offering mixed *salumi* and *formaggi* plates (€12),
big fresh salads (€10), and light lunches, along with a great selection of wines by the glass (€14 three-glass tasting—totaling a half-

bottle of wine per person, add antipasto plate for €24, also Super Tuscan wine-tastings, Wed-Mon 11:30-24:00, closed Tue, free Wi-Fi, Salita Serbelloni 34, tel. 031-951-523).

Gelato: Residents agree that you won't find the best *gelateria* in town among the sundaes served on the waterfront. Instead, climb to the top of town to **Gelateria del Borgo** (daily April-Oct 10:00-22:30, closed Nov-March, Via Garibaldi 46, tel. 031-950-755, Stefania and Gianfranco).

Picnics: You'll find benches at the park, along the waterfront in town, and lining the promenade south of town. Pick up your picnic supplies at **Caligari Alimentari.** They have roast chicken, ribs, and focaccia, and are happy to make fresh sandwiches to your order (Tue-Sat 7:30-13:00 & 16:00-19:30, Sun 7:30-13:00, closed Mon, shorter hours off-season, on corner of Via Garibaldi and Via Carlo Bellosio, tel. 031-951-815).

Punta Spartivento: This dramatic natural park, a 10-minute walk north of town (see "Strolling," page 275), is a great place for either a picnic or a meal at **La Punta Ristorante** (€9 pastas, €13 fish, €22 meat courses, March-Oct daily 12:00-14:30 & 19:00-22:00, bar open 14:30-19:00 for snacks only, closed Nov-Feb, tel. 031-951-888).

Menaggio

Menaggio has more urban bulk than its neighbors. Since many visitors find Lake Como too dirty for swimming, consider spend-

ing time in Menaggio's fine public pool (look for the "Lido"). This is the starting point for a few hikes. Only a few decades ago, cigarette smugglers used these trails at night to sneak back into Italy from Switzerland with their tax-free booty. The TI has information about mountain biking and catching the bus to trailheads on nearby Mount Grona (TI in Piazza Garibaldi open daily 9:00-12:30 & 14:30-18:00, closed Wed Nov-March, closed Sun year-round, tel. 0344-32-924, www .menaggio.com).

Getting to Menaggio: Buses may make the trip (€13, 1 hour) between Milan's Malpensa Airport and Como—ask at the Airport 2000 ticket desk in the arrivals hall; at Como, change to public bus #C10 to get to Menaggio (€3.30, 1-2/hour, 1 hour). Alternatively, take the Malpensa Express from the airport as far as Saronno, where you change for a train to Como (station: Como Lago), then catch the local bus #C10 for Menaggio as above.

Sleeping in Menaggio

(€1 = about $1.40, country code: 39)

$ La Marianna B&B has eight rooms and a fine restaurant in Cadenabbia, about a mile south of Menaggio on a busy road (Db with view-€95, optional €30 dinner, lakeside terrace at restaurant, air-con, free Wi-Fi, tel. 0344-43095, www.la-marianna.com, inn @la-marianna.com, Ty and Paola). Guests receive a 25 percent discount in the restaurant. The hourly Como-Menaggio bus #C10 stops here, and the ferry dock for mid-lake towns via Bellagio is 300 yards away.

$ La Primula Youth Hostel has a great location on the lake, a two-minute walk from the ferry dock (€18/person in dorm room, Db-€54, family room with bathroom and 4 beds-€78, €3 extra/ night for nonmembers, pizzas from €5, Internet access and Wi-Fi, sailing school, kayak and mountain bike rentals, rock-climbing nearby, tel. & fax 0344-32356, www.lakecomohostel.com, info @lakecomohostel.com). The bus from Como (55 minutes) stops right by the hostel.

Menaggio Connections

From Menaggio to Milan: It's a 20-minute ferry to Varenna (boats hourly), where trains connect to Milan (every 1-2 hours, 1 hour, see "Varenna Connections," page 272). More fast trains depart from Como than Varenna. From Menaggio, take hourly local bus #C10 (€3.30, 1-2/hour, 1 hour) to Como, where you can catch the train (hourly, 30-90 minutes).

From Menaggio to Switzerland: Public bus #C12 departs about every hour or two from Piazza Roma for Lugano (€10 round-trip, 1 hour, buy tickets at newspaper shop in Piazza Garibaldi). In summer, the yellow Palm Express bus runs once daily to **Lugano** (1 hour) and **St. Moritz** (3 hours). Off-season (mid-Oct-mid-June), the bus runs only on weekends. Advance reservations are required (www.postbus.ch)—and remember to bring your passport.

More Sights on Lake Como

Villa Carlotta

If you plan to tour one of Lake Como's famed villas, this is the best for gardens and flowers (its forte). I see the lakes as a break from Italy's art, but if you're in need of a place that charges admission, Villa Carlotta offers an elegant Neoclassical interior, Antonio Canova's famous *Maddalena Penitente* statue, and a garden (the highlight—at its best in spring).

Cost and Hours: €8.50, daily April-mid-Oct 9:00-18:00, last

2 weeks of March and mid-Oct-mid-Nov 10:00-17:00, closed mid-Nov-mid-March, no photos inside the villa, tel. 034-440-405, www.villacarlotta.it.

Nearby: Tremezzo and **Cadenabbia** are pleasant lakeside resorts, each one an easy walk away. Boats serve both places (5-minute walk from either dock to the villa) and are reached by *traghetto* (ferry, dock in Cadenabbia) or the *battello* (slow boat, dock in Tremezzo).

To visit **Villa del Balbianello** (see below) after you see Villa Carlotta, catch the blue #C10 bus (turn right when exiting the villa and walk to the trash cans; bus departs at 11:10, 11:58, 13:05, 13:57, 14:36, 15:06, and 15:36; €1.20, pay on bus). Get off at the second stop in Lenno, walk 30 yards, turn left, and follow the signs.

Villa del Balbianello

On a romantic promontory overlooking Lake Como and facing Bellagio is the dreamiest villa on the lake. Built for a cardinal at the end of the 18th century on the remains of an old Franciscan church, the villa was the cardinal's palace of delights, where he could study and brainstorm with his friends. Today it reflects the exotic vision of its last owner, explorer Guido Monzino, who died in 1988—leaving his villa, his rich art collection, and mementos of his expeditions to the state. The upper floor serves as a museum of his expeditions, with memorabilia from his North Pole and Mount Everest adventures. The real masterpiece here is the terraced garden and elegant loggia, where the land fits the architecture and landscaping in a lovely way. This is a favorite choice for movie directors when they need a far-out villa to feature; scenes from *Casino Royale* and *Star Wars: Episode II* were filmed here.

Cost and Hours: Garden only-€6, garden with villa tour-€12, tours depart hourly Thu-Sun and Tue 10:00-18:00, closed Mon and Wed, tel. 024-676-151, www.fondoambiente.it.

Getting There: You can reach it on **foot** (on Tue and Sat-Sun only) by walking six-tenths of a mile from Lenno through the park. Otherwise, catch the more glamorous **speedboat shuttle** from Lido di Lenno (€5 one-way, €6 round-trip, Igor can also be hired for private tours, mobile 333-410-3854).

Isola Comacina

This remote little island, just south of Bellagio, offers peace, ancient church foundations, a small archaeological museum, goats, sheep, nice swimming, and a lovely view of Lake Como. It takes 30-45 minutes to walk around the island, but longer to savor it. Bring a picnic or try the snack bar at the dock. The island is accessible every day in summer (€6, daily July-Aug 10:00-18:30, March-June and Sept-Oct 10:00-17:00; information at TI in mainland town

THE LAKES

of Ossuccio, tel. 034-456-369, www.isola-comacina.it, info@isola
-comacina.it).

Getting There: The *isola* can be reached from Varenna (1 hour), Menaggio (50 minutes), or Bellagio (35 minutes). Look for trips to Isola Comacina (€5) on the Colico-Como *battello* schedule (listed in Lago di Como boat timetable, free at ticket booths at ferry docks, see page 254). Check return times carefully (Como-Colico direction) and don't miss your boat. Usually only one trip a day each way works out for a visit. Allow about six hours, including travel time. Or ask about organized excursions on Sundays (€18.50 including transport, tel. 034-456-369).

Como

On the southwest tip of the lake, Como has a good, traffic-free old town, an interesting Gothic/Renaissance cathedral, and a pleasant lakefront with a promenade (TI open June-Sept Mon-Sat 9:00-13:00 & 14:30-18:00, closed Sun, shorter hours off-season, tel. 031-330-0128, www.lakecomo.it). It's an easy 10-minute walk from the boat dock to the train station (trains to Milan depart hourly, 30-90 minutes). Boats leave Como about hourly for mid-lake (ferries-€8-10, 2 hours, departures 7:35-16:45; hydrofoils-€11-13, 1 hour, departures 8:45-19:10, fewer on Sun; tel. 02-467-6101, www.navigazionelaghi.it).

Sleeping in Como: For a cheap overnight, try the **$ Villa Olmo Hostel** (€18, includes breakfast and sheets, €3/night extra for non-members, family room-€19.50/person, dinners-€6.50-10.50, free Wi-Fi and pay Internet access, laundry service available, baggage storage, free parking, bike rental, reception open 7:00-10:00 & 16:00-24:00, lockout 10:00-16:00, 24:00 curfew, closed mid-Nov-Feb, 20-minute walk from train station or dock, Via Bellinzona 2, tel. & fax 031-573-800, www.aighostels.com, ostellocomo@tin.it).

All-Day Lugano Side-Trip

From Varenna or Bellagio, you can make a loop that lets you nip into Switzerland to see the elegant lake resort of Lugano, pass through the town of Como, and cruise a good part of Lake Como. Here's a good day plan: 9:00—ferry to Menaggio; 10:00—bus to Lugano (45 minutes, bring your passport); 11:30—explore Lugano, train to Como (2/hour); 16:00—fast boat from Como to Varenna (departures also at about 17:00, 18:00, and 19:00). For information on Lugano, see www.ricksteves.com/lugano.

Lake Maggiore

Lake Maggiore is ringed by mountains, snowcapped in spring and fall, and lined with resort towns such as Stresa. While crassly

touristic, Stresa is a handy base from which to explore the exotic garden islands of Lake Maggiore. And many consider it a pleasant last stop before flying home from nearby Malpensa Airport.

A visit to this region is worth the trouble for two islands, both with exotic gardens and lovely villas built by the Borromeo family. The Borromeos—through many generations since 1630—lovingly turned their islands into magical retreats, with elaborate villas and fragrant gardens. Isola Bella has a palace and terraced garden; Isola Madre has a villa and sprawling English-style (more casual) garden. A third island, Isola Superiore (a.k.a. Isola Pescatori), is simply small, serene, and residential. The Borromeos, who made their money from trade and banking, enjoyed the arts—from paintings (hung in lavish abundance throughout the palace and villa) to plays (performed in an open-air theater on Isola Bella) and marionette shows (you'll see the puppets that once performed here).

Tourists flock to the lakes in May and June, when flowers are in bloom, and in September. Concerts held in scenic settings draw music lovers, particularly during the Musical Weeks in August (get details from Stresa TI). For fewer crowds, visit in April, July, August (when Italians prefer the Mediterranean beaches), or October. In winter, the snow-covered mountains (with resorts a 1.5-hour drive away) attract skiers.

Planning Your Time

This region is best visited on a sunny day, when the mountains are clear, the lake is calm, and the heat of the sun brings out the scent of the blossoms. The two top islands for sightseeing are Isola Bella and Isola Madre. Isola Superiore has no sights, but is a peaceful place for lunch. You can stay the night in Stresa (accommodations listed later), but a day trip is sufficient for most.

Day Trip from Milan: Catch the one-hour, early train from Milan to Stresa (usually at 8:28, may require reservations; the next departure isn't until 11:25). Upon arrival in Stresa, walk 10 minutes downhill to the boat dock, and catch a boat to Isola Madre. Then work your way back to Isola Superiore for a lazy lunch, and on to Isola Bella for the afternoon, before returning to the town of Stresa and back to Milan.

THE LAKES

Getting Around Lake Maggiore

Boats link the islands and Stresa, running about twice hourly. Allow roughly 10 minutes between stops. Since short round-trip hops add up fast (€7 each for Isola Bella and Isola Superiore, €9 for Isola Madre), it's best to simply buy the **all-day pass:** €10 for two islands (Bella and Superiore), or €15 for all the islands plus Pallanza (a town on the opposite shore) and Villa Taranto. A **combo-ticket** combining the villas on Isola Bella and Isola Madre with the all-day boat pass is available for €30 (credit cards accepted).

Boats run daily April through September. The map on page 286 shows the route: Stresa, Carciano/Lido, Isola Bella, Isola Superiore, Baveno (lakeside town), Isola Madre, Pallanza, and Villa Taranto. This route is part of a longer one. To follow the boat schedule (free, available at boat docks, TI, and maybe your hotel), look at the Arona-Locarno timetable for trips from Stresa to the islands, and the Locarno-Arona timetable for the return trip to Stresa. Off-season, the boats cover a shorter route; check the time-table (public boat info: tel. 800-551-801 or 0322-233-200, www.navigazionelaghi.it, infomaggiore@navigazionelaghi.it).

Buy boat tickets directly from the dock ticket booth under the gallery to the left of the TI. Don't be fooled by the private taxi-boat drivers, most dressed in navy-blue uniforms and white hats (they look like Italian traffic cops); with their little sales booth on the sidewalk in front of the public boat launch, they'll try to talk you into paying way too much for private tours on their smaller boats.

Stresa

Stresa—which means "thin stretch"—was named for the original strip of fishermen's huts that lined the shore. Today, grand old hotels run along that same shore. The old town—basically a traffic-free touristy shopping mall—is just a few blocks deep, stretching inland from the main boat dock. A fine waterfront promenade leads past the venerable old hotels to the Lido (with the Carciano boat dock and a mountain cable car). Stresa's stately 19th-century lakeside hotels date back to the days when this town was on the "Grand Tour" circuit. In any Romantic-age resort like Stresa, hotels had names designed to appeal to Victorian aristocrats...like Palace (rather than Palazzo), Astoria, Bristol, and Victoria.

Nineteen-year-old Ernest Hemingway first came to Stresa in 1918. Wounded in Slovenia as an ambulance driver for the Italian Red Cross, he was taken to the Grand Hotel des Iles Borromees. This was the first hotel on the shore (from 1862), and it served—like its regal neighbors—as an infirmary during World War I. Hemingway returned to the same hotel in 1948, stayed in the same room (#205, now called the "Hemingway suite"—you can stay there for a couple of thousand dollars a night), and signed the guest book as "an old client." Another "old client" was Winston Churchill, who honeymooned here.

Orientation to Stresa

Tourist Information
The helpful TI, located to the right of the ticket window at the boat dock, has free maps and boat schedules (March-Oct daily 10:00-12:30 & 15:00-18:30; Nov-Feb Mon-Fri 10:00-12:30 & 15:00-18:30, Sat 10:00-12:30, closed Sun; Piazza Marconi 16, tel. 0323-30150, www.stresaturismo.it).

Internet Access: The **Newdata Internet Point** is a block off Piazza Cadorna in the old center (daily 9:30-12:30 & 15:00-22:00, until 19:30 in winter, Via de Vit 15A, tel. 0323-30323, www.new data.too.it).

Arrival in Stresa
At the train station, ask for a free city map at the newsstand (to the far right of the tracks as you exit the train). To get downtown, exit right from the station and take your first left (on Viale Duchessa di Genova). This takes you straight down to the lake (the boat dock is about four blocks to your right; ask for boat schedule at ticket window). The TI is next door on the same dock. Taxis charge a fixed rate of €8 for even the shortest ride in town.

Sights in Stresa

Islands and Gardens
▲▲**Isola Bella**—This island, nearest Stresa, has a formal garden and a fancy Baroque palace. Looking like a stepped pyramid from

the water, the island was named by Charles Borromeo (sponsor of Milan's Duomo) for his wife, Isabella. The island itself is touristy, with a gauntlet of souvenir stands and a corral of restaurants. A few back streets provide evidence that people actually live here. While the Borromeo family now lives in Milan, they spend a few weeks on Isola Bella each summer (when their blue-and-red family flag flies from the top of the garden).

Cost and Hours: Palace and garden-€13, picture gallery-€3 extra, €18 combo-ticket includes the villa at Isola Madre (but not Isola Bella's picture gallery), daily late-March-late-Oct 9:00-18:00,

Stresa & the Borromeo Islands

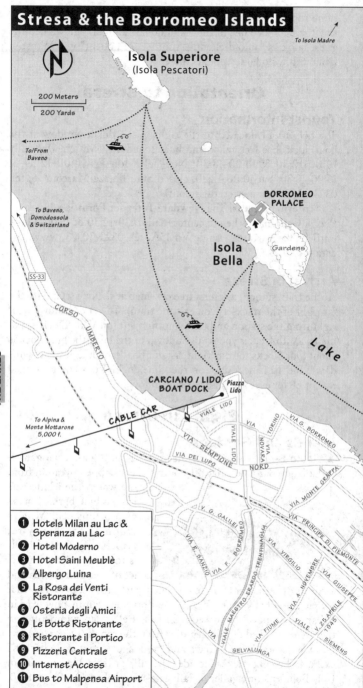

1 Hotels Milan au Lac & Speranza au Lac
2 Hotel Moderno
3 Hotel Saini Meublè
4 Albergo Luina
5 La Rosa dei Venti Ristorante
6 Osteria degli Amici
7 Le Botte Ristorante
8 Ristorante il Portico
9 Pizzeria Centrale
10 Internet Access
11 Bus to Malpensa Airport

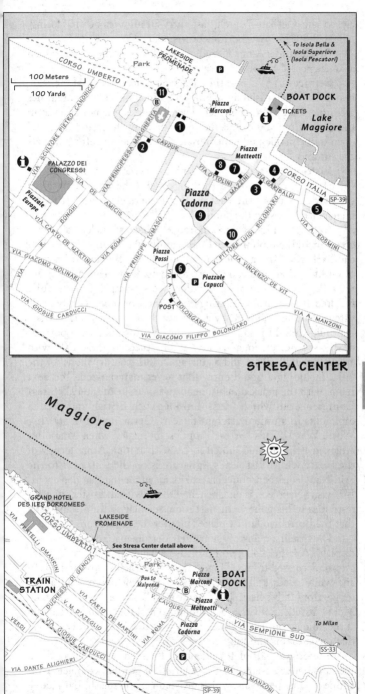

STRESA CENTER

closed late-Oct-late-March, last entry 30 minutes before closing, tel. 0323-30556, www.borromeoturismo.it.

Audioguide: A fine €3 audioguide describes the palace, which also has posted English descriptions.

Services: A WC is at the garden entrance. Note that there are two docks on this island (one for each direction). Departure times are indicated by clocks at each dock. Picnicking is not allowed in the garden, but you can picnic at the point of the island (free and open to the public); take the mosaic sidewalk to the left of the palace entrance.

Visiting the Island: Your visit is a one-way tour, starting with the palace and finishing with the garden. (There's no way to see the garden without the palace.) From the dock, head left to the huge palace, passing the public WCs.

In the lavishly decorated Baroque **palace**, stairs lead to stucco crests of Italy's top families (balls signify the Medici, bees mean the Barberini, and a unicorn symbolizes the Borromeos' motto: Humility). Here, you can choose to pay for a supplementary ticket to walk through the picture gallery (containing 130 beautifully restored 16th-century paintings from the Borromeo family's private collection, followed by an ornate throne room). Otherwise, continue straight into the next room, where you'll see a portrait of the first Borromeo, and into a richly stuccoed grand hall, with an 80-foot-high dome and featuring an 18th-century model of the villa, including a grand entry that never materialized. The next room, with the musical instruments, was the site of the 1935 Stresa Conference, in which Mussolini met with British and French diplomats in a united attempt to scare Germany out of starting World War II. This "Stresa Front" soon fizzled when Mussolini attacked Ethiopia and joined forces with Hitler. A photocopy of the treaty with Mussolini's signature is on the wall next to the exit. Napoleon's bedroom comes with an engraving that depicts his 1797 visit (Napoleon is on a bench with his wife and sister enjoying festivities in his honor). The last rooms display souvenirs and gifts that the Borromeo family picked up over the generations.

Downstairs, many of the famous Borromeo marionettes are on display. (A larger collection is on Isola Madre.) The 18th-century grotto, decorated from ceiling to floor with shell motifs and black-and-white stones, still serves its original function of providing a cool refuge from Italy's heat. The dreamy marble statues are by Gaetano Monti, a student of Canova. Climbing out of the basement, look up at the unique cantilevered stairs; they're from a 16th-century fortress that predates this building.

The ornate hall of 16th-century Flemish tapestries leads to the finale of this island visit: the beautiful **garden**, complete with Chinese white peacocks, which give it an exotic splash. Baroque—

which is exactly what you see here—is all about controlling nature. The terraced gardens are crowned by the Borromeo family unicorn. Circle around the garden to the left to visit the bookshop and café, or head to the right to go straight to the exit. Gardeners continue on to the second exit to pass through Elisa's Greenhouse, named for Napoleon's sister and home to tropical plants.

▲**Isola Superiore (Pescatori)**—This sleepy island—home to

35 families—is the smallest and most residential of the three. It has a couple of good seafood restaurants, picnic benches, views, and, blissfully, nothing much to do—all under arbors of wisteria. A delight for photographers and painters, the island is never really crowded, except at lunchtime.

▲▲**Isola Madre**—Don't come here unless you intend to tour the sight, because that's all there is: an interesting furnished villa and a lovely garden filled with exotic birds and plants.

Cost and Hours: Villa and garden-€11, €18 combo-ticket includes Isola Bella, late-March-late-Oct daily 9:00-18:00, closed late-Oct-late-March, last entry 30 minutes before closing, no photos in villa, WC next to chapel, tel. 0323-233200, www.borromeoturismo.it.

Visiting the Island: Visiting is a one-way affair, starting with a long stroll through the garden and finishing with the villa. The sightseeing route is clearly signed, taking you through the gardens and villa, and ending at the chapel. The €2.50 audioguide is devoted almost entirely to the garden—a good investment to properly appreciate the plantings.

Eight gardeners (with the help of water continually pumped from the lake) keep this English-style **garden** paradise lush. It's a joy, even for those bored by flowers and foliage. You'll see trees from around the world, and an exotic bird menagerie with golden and silver pheasants and Chinese peacocks. In front of the villa, a once-magnificent Himalayan cypress tree paints your world a streaky green. The 150-year-old tree, knocked down by a tornado in 2006 but successfully saved, is an attraction in its own right, with steel guy-wires now anchoring it firmly in place.

The 16th-century **villa** is the first of the Borromeo palaces. A century older than the Isola Bella villa, it's dark, somber, and dates

THE LAKES

from the Renaissance. The clever angled hinges keep the doors from flapping in the lake breeze. The family's huge collection of dolls, marionettes, and exquisite 17th-century marionette theater sets—painted by a famous La Scala opera set designer—fills several rooms. A corner room is painted to take you into an 18th-century Venetian Rococo sitting room under a floral greenhouse. Some of the garden's best flowers are in view immediately after leaving the villa.

Eating: While eating is best on Isola Superiore, Isola Madre has one eatery, **La Piratera Ristorante Bar** (€25 fixed-price tourist meal, daily 8:00-18:00, sit-down meals 12:00-15:00 and simple sandwiches to go anytime, picnic at rocky beach a minute's walk from restaurant, just to your right as you exit the gardens, tel. 0323-31171).

▲Villa Taranto Botanical Gardens—Garden lovers will enjoy this large landscaped park, located on the mainland a 10-minute boat ride beyond Isola Madre (across the lake from Stresa). The gardens are a Scotsman's labor of love. Starting in the 1930s, Neil McEacharn created this garden of delights—bringing in thousands of plants from all over the world—and here he stays, in the small mausoleum. The park's highlight is a terraced garden with a series of cascading pools. Villa Taranto is directly across the street from the boat dock.

Cost and Hours: €9.50, daily April-Sept 8:30-18:30, Oct 8:30-17:00, closed Nov-March, boat from Stresa-€11, tel. 0323-404-555, www.villataranto.it.

Mountain Cable Car—From Stresa's Lido, a cable car takes you up—in two stages and a 20-minute ride—to the top of Mount Mottarone (about 5,000 feet). From here, you get great views of neighboring peaks and, by taking a short hike, a bird's-eye view of the small, neighboring Lake Orta.

Cost and Hours: €17.50 round-trip, €10.50 one-way, daily 9:30-17:40 in summer, 8:30-17:00 in winter, closed Nov, 2-3/hour, bar midway up, tel. 0323-30295, www.stresa-mottarone.it.

Activities: To visit the **Alpine Gardens,** get off at the midway Alpina stop, where a 10-minute walk leads to the gardens (turn left as you leave; €3, April-Oct daily 9:30-18:00, closed Nov-March). The gardens come with great lake views and picnic spots, but can't compare to what you'll see on the islands.

If you plan to **hike** down, pick up the Trekking Map from the TI and allow 3.5 hours from the top of Mount Mottarone, or

THE LAKES

1.5 hours from the Alpine Gardens.

You can rent a **bike** at the base of the cable-car lift (full-suspension mountain bike or road bike-€5/hour, €22/half-day, €27/day, €45/weekend, includes helmet, tel. 338-839-5692, Giorgio) and bring it on the cable car with you (€11 extra). It's a treacherous ride, enjoyable only for serious bikers. While the ride is nice on top, you'll fight traffic on congested, rough, and windy roads for the rest of the descent.

Day Trips from Stresa

▲Scenic Boat and Rail Trip to Locarno and Centovalli—This enjoyable all-day excursion from Stresa involves three segments. Before you embark on the trip, confirm all times, particularly the departure of the last boat from Locarno. Take the train from Stresa to Domodossola, then catch the "Centovalli" train for a 1.5-hour ride that links together remote mountain villages on your way to Locarno, in the Italian-speaking Swiss canton of Ticino (bring your passport). Spend an hour or so exploring this town, on the far end of Lake Maggiore. Then take the boat past loads of small lakeside hamlets back to Italy. As a relaxing finale, you'll cruise into your home port of Stresa. The trip can also be done in reverse (with the boat trip first). A special €32 "Lago Maggiore Express" ticket covers both the train and boat (you must reserve in advance; fax 0322-249-530 or email infomaggiore@navigazionelaghi.it—indicate the date you'll travel, number of passengers, and a return email address or fax number; call 800-551-801 or 0322-233-200, www.lagomaggioreexpress.com).

▲Lake Orta—Just on the other side of Mount Mottarone is the small lake of Orta. The lake's main town, Orta San Giulio,

has a beautiful lakeside piazza ringed by picturesque buildings. The piazza faces the lake with a view of Isola San Giulio. Taxi boats (€4 round-trip) make the five-minute trip throughout the day. The island is worth a look for the Church of San Giulio and the circular "path of silence," which takes about 10 minutes. In peak season, Orta is anything but silent, but off-season or early or late in the day, this place is full of peace and magic (TI open Sat-Sun 9:30-17:30, closed Mon-Fri, on Via Panoramica next to the parking lot downhill from the train station, tel. 0322-905-163).

The train ride from Stresa to Orta-Miasino (a short walk from the lakeside piazza) takes 1.5-2 hours and requires a change or two (9/day). Public buses from Stresa's Piazza Marconi to Orta depart

THE LAKES

from near the TI (around €9 round-trip, 3/day mid-June-mid-Sept, confirm schedule at TI or at www.safduemila.com).

Sleeping in Stresa

(€1 = about $1.40, country code: 39)
Because Stresa town is just a resort, I'd day-trip from Milan. But here are good options if you'd like to stay.

$$ Hotel Milan au Lac and its sister hotel next door, the yellow-brick **Speranza au Lac,** are impersonal four-star corporate-style hotels that cater mostly to tour groups, with 175 predictably comfortable rooms across from the boat dock (to the right as you leave the boat). Reception for both hotels is in Hotel Milan au Lac (Db-€100-198 depending on season and view, generally open April-Oct, air-con, elevator, tel. 0323-31178, fax 0323-32729, www.milansperanza.it, info@milansperanza.it).

$$ Hotel Moderno offers 54 peaceful and well-maintained pastel rooms on a pedestrian street a block from the main square (Sb-€98, Db-€145, discount for Rick Steves readers depending on availability, closed Nov-mid-March, air-con, elevator, Internet access, Wi-Fi, Via Cavour 33; from the main square, with your back to the lake, find the church—hotel is behind the church on pedestrian street parallel to main road; tel. 0323-933-773, fax 0323-933-775, www.hms.it, moderno@hms.it).

$$ Hotel Saini Meublè is a cozy, 14-room place with rustic stonework and hardwood floors, located in a pedestrian zone a couple of blocks from the boat dock in the old center (Sb-€82, Db-€102, lower prices off-season, these rates promised to my readers through 2013, elevator, Internet access and Wi-Fi; from Piazza Matteotti head up Via Mazzini and turn left on Via Garibaldi, Via Garibaldi 10, tel. 0323-934-519, fax 0323-31169, www.hotelsaini.it, info@hotelsaini.it). Gianni (Johnny) greets you at reception.

$ Albergo Luina, with new owners, offers seven basic rooms above a restaurant (Sb-€62, Db-€95, breakfast-€4; 2 blocks off Piazza Matteotti—with back to lake, go left up small street; Via Garibaldi 21, tel. & fax 0323-30285, luinastresa@yahoo.it).

Eating in Stresa

La Rosa dei Venti, on the main drag, has great €7 pizzas and lakefront dining. They proudly offer homemade pastas and creative risottos for €7 (big €9 salads, €15 *secondi*, Wed-Mon 12:00-14:30 & 18:15-22:30, closed Tue, everything made to order, 2 blocks south of the boat dock at Corso Italia 50, tel. 0323-31431).

Osteria degli Amici serves up tasty €10 risottos and pastas, with fast and friendly service under a canopy of grape and kiwi leaves (€7 wood-fired pizzas, daily 12:00-14:15 & 18:30-22:30, closed Wed Sept-June, deep in the old town past Piazza Cadorna at Via Bolongaro 33, tel. 0323-30453).

Le Botte offers a variety of Piedmont's regional specialties in a pub-grub casual atmosphere (€9 pastas, €13 *secondi,* daily 12:00-15:00 & 19:00-22:30 in summer, closed Thu Oct-March and all of Dec-Feb, Via Mazzini 6/8, tel. 0323-30462).

Ristorante il Portico is a cheerful, energetic place featuring several €16-26 multicourse tasting samplers and daily market specials on sidewalk tables or in their airy, fresh dining room. It's smart to reserve (piping-hot €6 pizzas, €7 pastas, €9 *secondi,* daily 12:00-16:00 & 19:00-24:00, closed off-season, Via Ottolini 9, tel. 0323-934-510).

The main square, **Piazza Cadorna,** is a carnival of residents selling things to tourists. Still, at night it has a certain charm. It seems anyone who claims to be a musician can get a gig singing for diners. The **Pizzeria Centrale** (on a platform in the center) is a good place to enjoy the ambience. Their pizzas are decent, but don't order any serious food here.

Stresa Connections

From Stresa by Train to: Milan (about hourly, 1-hour fast train—but there can be gaps in service so check timetable carefully, 1.5-hour slow train), **Varenna** (roughly every two hours, 2.75-4 hours, transfer in Milan), **Venice** (7/day, 4-4.5 hours, transfer in Milan), **Domodossola** (near the Swiss border, almost hourly, 30 minutes).

To Malpensa Airport: For a **train-bus combination,** take the train toward Milan (departs hourly) and get off at Gallarate (after about 40 minutes), where cheap shuttle buses run to Malpensa's Terminal 1 (€1.50, pay driver, about 1-2/hour, 25 minutes). From Gallarate, the bus departs from the train station and runs 5:55-20:15; from Malpensa's Terminal 1, the bus runs 5:34-19:50; tel. 0331-258-411, www.sea-aeroportimilano.it/en). For an early-morning flight, the first Stresa-Milan train departs at 5:25, connecting with Gallarate's first bus departure for Malpensa (confirm schedules locally).

Alibus Airport buses run between Stresa and Malpensa (€12, mid-April-Sept, 50 minutes; leaves Stresa from in front of the church next to Hotel Milan au Lac—near the ferry dock and TI—at 6:30, 9:30, 11:30, 13:30, 16:30, and 19:30; leaves airport from bus stop 22 outside Terminal 1 at 8:30, 11:30, 13:30, 15:30, 18:30, and 21:00; confirm schedule, must reserve by 11:00 the previous day or by 11:00 Sat if booking for Sun or Mon bus—call 0323-552-172, book online at www.safduemila.com, or email alibus @safduemila.com).

Taxis to the airport cost €100 (1-5 people, €110 if traveling between 22:00-7:00) and take about an hour; your hotel can arrange the taxi for you, but will charge extra for booking it. It's easy to arrange a taxi on your own at the train station's taxi stand. Salvo Taxi is reliable (mobile 335-707-8894).

MILAN

Milano

For every church in Rome, there's a bank in Milan. Italy's second city and the capital of Lombardy, Milan is a hardworking, fashion-conscious, time-is-money city of 1.3 million. It's a melting pot of people and history. Milan's industriousness may come from the Teutonic blood of its original inhabitants, the Lombards, or from the region's Austrian heritage. Milan is Italy's fashion, industrial, banking, TV, publishing, and convention capital. The economic success of post-war Italy can be blamed on this city of publicists and pasta power lunches.

As if to make up for its rough, noisy big-city-ness, its people are works of art. Milan is an international fashion capital with a refined taste. Window displays are gorgeous, cigarettes are chic, and even the cheese comes gift-wrapped. Yet thankfully, Milan is no more expensive for tourists than other Italian cities.

Three hundred years before Christ, the Romans called this place Mediolanum, or "the central place." By the fourth century A.D., it was the capital of the western half of the Roman Empire. Emperor Constantine issued the Edict of Milan from here, legalizing Christianity. After some barbarian darkness, medieval Milan rose to regional prominence under the Visconti and Sforza families. By the time of the Renaissance, it was nicknamed "the New Athens," and was enough of a cultural center for Leonardo da Vinci to call home. Then came 400 years of foreign domination (Spain, Austria, France, more Austria). Milan was a center of the 1848 revolution against Austria, and helped lead Italy to unification in 1870.

Mussolini left a heavy fascist touch on the architecture here (such as the central train station). His excesses also led to the

Greater Milan

To Malpensa Airport,
Varenna, Stresa, Venice, etc.

CENTRAL
STATION

Airport
Buses

V.A. DORIA

Monumental
Cemetery

PORTA
GARIBALDI
STATION

PIRELLI
TOWER

VIA VITRUVIO

VIA LIB.

VIA PASANI

To Como &
Malpensa
Airport

CORSO SEMPIONE

VIA LEGNANO

Repubblica

VIA TURATI

CORSO BUENOS AIRES

Lima

To Fiera
di Milano
Trade Fair

Parco
Sempione

Turati

BRANCA
TOWER

Porta
Venezia

LAST
SUPPER
S. MARIA
D. GRAZIE

SFORZA
CASTLE

BRERA ART
GALLERY

Monte-
napoleone

VIA MONTE NAPOLEONE

Conc.

NORD
STN.

Cadorna

RING
ROAD

To
Leonardo's
Horse &
Meazza
Stadium

Tram #16
Stop

C. MAGENTA

LA SCALA

VIA MERAVIGLI

GALLERIA

Duomo

DUOMO

S.
Amb.

DA VINCI
NATIONAL SCIENCE
MUSEUM

See Milan Hotels & Restaurants map

CORSO
PORTA VITTORIA

VIA TORINO

Missori

VELASCO
TOWER

See Central Milan map

PORTA
GENOVA
STATION

CORSO TICINESE

CORSO ITALIA

CORSO PORTA ROMANA

VIALE CALDARA

NAVIGLI
DISTRICT

VIALE
B. D'ESTE

Porta
Romana

.5 Kilometer

.5 Mile

WWII bombing of Milan. But the city rose again. The 1959 Pirelli Tower (the skinny skyscraper in front of the station) was a trendsetter in its day. Today, Milan is people-friendly, with a great transit system and inviting pedestrian zones. And the city is busy with construction projects in an effort to beef up both its infrastructure and cultural offerings as it prepares to host the 2015 World's Fair.

Many tourists come to Italy for the past. But Milan is today's Italy, and no trip to this country is complete without visiting it. While it's not big on the tourist circuit, the city has plenty to see. And fortunately, seeing Milan—so manageable and well-organized—is not difficult.

For pleasant excursions from the city, consider visiting Lake Como or Lake Maggiore—both are about an hour from Milan by train (see The Lakes chapter).

Planning Your Time

OK, it's a big city, so you probably won't linger. Compared to Rome and Florence, Milan's art is mediocre, but the city does have unique and noteworthy sights: the Duomo and Galleria Vittorio Emanuele, Pinacoteca Ambrosiana, La Scala Opera House, Brera Art Gallery, Michelangelo's last *Pietà* in the Sforza Castle, and Leonardo's *Last Supper*. It's best to reserve several months in advance to see *The Last Supper* (see page 321); if you haven't booked ahead, your best option is to take a bus-and-walking tour (see "Tours in Milan," later).

With two nights and a full day, you can gain an appreciation for the town and see the major sights. On a short visit, I'd focus on

the center. Tour the Duomo, hit what art you like, browse through the elegant shopping area and the Galleria Vittorio Emanuele, and try to see an opera. Technology buffs like the Leonardo da Vinci National Science and Technology Museum, while history and art buffs dig the city's early Christian churches, Brera Gallery, Pinacoteca Ambrosiana, and the Museum of Art and Science. People-watchers and pigeon-feeders could spend their entire visit never losing sight of the Duomo. And if you dig burial grounds, rattle through Milan's evocative Monumental Cemetery. To maximize your time in Milan, use the Metro and note which places stay open through the siesta.

Since Milan is a cold Italian plunge, and most flights to the US leave Milan early in the morning, you could save it for the end of your trip and start your journey softly by going directly by train from Milan to Lake Como (one-hour ride to Varenna), Lake Maggiore (1-1.5 hours to Stresa), or the Cinque Terre (3-4 hours to Monterosso). Then spend the last night or two of your trip in Milan before flying home.

Monday is a terrible sightseeing day, since many museums are closed (including the church that houses Leonardo's *Last Supper*). August is oppressively hot and muggy, and locals who can vacate at this time, do, leaving the city pretty quiet. Those visiting in August find that the nightlife is sleepy and many shops and restaurants are closed. Some hotels are closed; other hotel rooms are on the discounted push list.

A Three-Hour Tour: If you're just changing trains in Milan's Centrale Station (as, sooner or later, you probably will), consider this blitz tour: Check your bag at the station, pick up a city map at the station TI, ride the subway to the Duomo (for specifics, see "Arrival in Milan," later), peruse the square, explore the cathedral's

Rome vs. Milan: A Classic Squabble

In Italy, the North and South bicker about each other, hurling barbs, quips, and generalizations. All the classic North/South traits can be applied to Milan (the business capital) and Rome (the government capital). Although the differences have become less pronounced lately, the sniping continues.

The Milanesi say the Romans are lazy. Roman government jobs come with short hours—cut even shorter by too many coffee breaks, three-hour lunches, chats with colleagues, and phone calls to friends and relatives. Milanesi contend that "Roma *ladrona*" (Rome, the big thief) is a parasite that lives off the taxes of people up North. There's still a strong Milan-based movement seriously promoting secession from the South.

Romans, meanwhile, dismiss the Milanesi as uptight workaholics with nothing else to live for—gray like their foggy city. Romans do admit that in Milan, job opportunities are better and based on merit. And the Milanesi grudgingly concede the Romans have a gift for enjoying life.

While Rome is more of a family city, Milan is the place for high-powered singles on the career fast track. Milanese yuppies

rooftop and interior, have a scenic coffee in the Galleria Vittorio Emanuele, spin on the floor mosaic of the bull for good luck, see a museum or two (most are within a 10-minute walk of the main square), and return by subway to the station. Art fans could make time for *The Last Supper* (if they've made reservations), the Michelangelo *Pietà* in the Sforza Castle (no reservations necessary), the Brera Art Gallery, or the Pinacoteca Ambrosiana (with its Leonardo exhibit).

Orientation to Milan

My coverage focuses on the old center. Most sights and hotels are within a 10-minute walk of the cathedral (Duomo), which is a straight eight-minute Metro ride from the central train station.

Tourist Information

Milan has two TIs: The main TI is at Piazza Castello 1 (near Sforza Castle) and the other is at the Milano Centrale train station, in front of track 13 (both share same hours: Mon-Fri 9:00-18:00, Sat 9:00-13:30 & 14:00-18:00, Sun 9:00-13:30 & 14:00-17:00, main TI mix with each other...not the city's longtime residents. Milan is seen as wary of foreigners and inward-looking, and Rome as fun-loving, tolerant, and friendly. In Milan, bureaucracy (like social services) works logically and efficiently, while in Rome, accomplishing even small chores can be exasperating. Everything in Rome—from finding a babysitter to buying a car—is done through friends. Meanwhile, people in Milan are more private.

Milanesi find Romans vulgar. The Roman dialect is considered one of the coarsest in the country. Much as they try, Milanesi just can't say "Damn your dead relatives" quite as effectively as the Romans. Still, Milanesi enjoy Roman comedians and love to imitate the accent.

The Milanesi feel that Rome is dirty and Roman traffic nerve-wracking. But despite the craziness, Rome maintains a genuine village feel. People share family news with their neighborhood grocer. Milan lacks people-friendly piazzas, and entertainment comes at a high price. But in Rome, *la dolce vita* is as close as the nearest square, and a full moon is enjoyed by all.

tel. 02-7740-4343, train TI tel. 02-7740-4318, www.visitamilano .it, iat.info@provincia.milano.it). You can book Autostradale and Zani Viaggi city tours (see "Tours in Milan," later) at the companies' offices on Piazza Castello, near the main TI.

At either TI, confirm your sightseeing plans and pick up a free map. Also ask for the two free booklets listing Milan's sights (including hours, prices, and directions), events, concerts, films in English, expatriate groups, and cultural insights. *Hello Milano* is a monthly newspaper in English (www.hellomilano.it); *Milano Mese* is less helpful (scant event descriptions in English, events listed by category rather than date).

I've listed enough sights to keep you very busy for two days, but there's much more to see in Milan. Its many thousand-year-old churches make it clear that Milan was an important beacon in the Dark Ages. The TI, local guidebooks, and newspapers can point you in the right direction if you have more time.

Arrival in Milan

By Train at Milano Centrale: The huge, sternly decorated, fascist-built (in 1931) central train station is a sight in itself.

MILAN

Recently cleaned, the halls feel more monumental than ever. Notice how the art makes you feel that a powerful state is a good thing. In the front lobby, heroic people celebrate "modern" transportation (circa-1930 ships, trains, and cars) opposite reliefs depicting old-fashioned sailboats and horse carts.

The station has three levels of **shops and services.** On the ground level to the left (with your back to the tracks), you'll find taxis, travel agencies, shuttle buses to the airports, and a baggage check (marked *deposito bagagli*, €5/5 hours, €12.50/24 hours, 5-day maximum, daily 6:00-23:50, passport required, 45-pound bag limit). A supermarket is outside on the right (daily 8:00-22:00). ATMs are in front of the station, outside and to the right. Also in front of the station are the Metro and car-rental offices (clearly marked). The 24-hour pharmacy has a big green neon cross. The WCs are by track 22 (€1, daily 6:00-24:00).

From the track level, down the moving walkways, you'll find the **Trenitalia ticket office** (daily 5:50-22:20) and user-friendly ticket sales machines (gray-and-blue for local train services only, red-white-and-green for all Italian trains, credit cards and cash accepted, you can't buy international tickets from machines).

The **365 Travel Agency**—which sells train tickets, supplements, and night-train berth reservations—has three offices at the station. One is across from the baggage-check *deposito* desk (has longest hours, daily 6:40-21:00, agency tel. 02-6738-2603, www.agenzie365.it); another is outside facing the airport shuttle buses on Piazza Luigi di Savoia; and a third is on the opposite side of the station near the Sisley fashion store (with your back to the tracks, exit to the right). Their seven percent commission can be a reasonable price to pay to skip the Trenitalia ticket lines.

Taking the Metro to the Duomo and Back: For a quick visit, it's a straight shot on the underground from the station to the Duomo (buy €1.50 ticket at kiosk or from machines, validate in orange machine). Follow signs for yellow line 3 (direction: San Donato); after an eight-minute ride (four stops), you'll be facing the cathedral. To return, ride the same yellow line 3 back the other way (direction: Comasina).

By Train at Milano Porta Garibaldi: Italo trains—Italy's new, privately run high-speed service to Florence, Rome, and Naples (see page 1084)—use Porta Garibaldi Station, north of the city center and not far from Milano Centrale (see map on page 296). The high-speed TGV trains from Paris also use this station. As Milan's busiest commuter station, Porta Garibaldi is also served by many bus lines and Metro line 2 (green).

By Car: Driving is bad enough in Milan to make the €20/day fee for a downtown garage a blessing. If you're driving, do Milan (and Lake Como) before or after you rent your car, not while you've got it. If you have a car, use the well-marked suburban *parcheggi* (parking lots), which offer affordable (€6/day) and safe parking at city-edge subway stations, with extremely easy access to the center by Metro.

By Plane: Frequent shuttle trains and buses connect the airports and Milano Centrale train station. See "Milan Connections" at the end of this chapter.

Helpful Hints

Theft Alert: Be on guard. Milan's thieves target tourists, especially at the central train station, getting in and out of the subway, and around the Duomo. They can be dressed as tourists, businessmen, or beggars, or they can be gangs of too-young-to-arrest children. Watch out for ragged people carrying newspaper and cardboard—they'll thrust this item at you as a distraction while they pick your pocket. If you're ripped off and plan to file an insurance claim, fill out a report with the police (Police Station, "Questura," Via Fatebenefratelli 11, Metro: Turati, open daily 24 hours, tel. 02-62261). For police emergencies, call 113. For lost or stolen credit cards, see page 15.

US Consulate: It's at Via Principe Amedeo 2/10 (Metro: Turati, tel. 02-290-351 for recorded info and phone tree, http://milan.usconsulate.gov).

Medical Help: Dial 118 for medical emergencies. There are two medical clinics with emergency care facilities: the International Health Center in Galleria Strasburgo 3 (Mon-Thu 9:00-19:00, Fri 9:00-18:00, closed Sat-Sun, between Via Durini and Corso Europa, third floor, Metro: San Babila, tel. 02-7634-0720) and the American International Medical Center at Via Mercalli 11 (Mon-Fri 9:00-17:30, closed Sat-Sun, Metro: Missori or Crocetta, call for appointment, tel. 02-5831-9808, mobile 335-570-1055). A 24-hour pharmacy is in the central train station; look for the neon-green cross.

Street Markets: Milan has two very popular flea markets. **Fiera di Sinigallia** spills into a lot at Porta Genova every Saturday (8:30-17:00, later in summer, Metro: Porta Genova). If you continue along Viale d'Annunzio to Viale Papiniano, you'll run into the **Papiniano** market (Tue morning and Sat all day). Small street markets are held every morning except Sunday in various neighborhoods; *Hello Milano* has a complete listing (free at TI).

Internet Access: A **Mondadori Mediacenter** shop is near the Duomo on Piazza del Duomo at the corner of Via Marconi (daily 9:00-23:00, see map on page 304). Purchase an Internet card (*tessera*, €3/hour) on the ground floor, then go up two flights of stairs to the second floor to register. The shop also

MILAN

sells a wide selection of international newspapers.

Bookstores: The handiest major bookstore is **Libreria Feltrinelli,** under the Galleria Vittorio Emanuele. Books in English—fiction and guidebooks—are at opposite ends of the store (Mon-Sat 10:00-23:00, Sun 10:00-20:00; enter at Ricordi Mediastore next to McDonald's in center of Galleria and go downstairs, or through Autogrill restaurant on Piazza del Duomo, store is in basement level; also sells maps, tel. 02-8699-6903). The **American Bookstore** is at Via Camperio 16, near the Sforza Castle (Mon 13:30-19:00, Tue-Sat 10:30-19:00, closed Sun, tel. 02-878-920).

Travel Agencies: You can buy train tickets and reserve an overnight berth *(cuccetta)* at the **365 Travel Agency**'s train station locations (listed earlier, under "Arrival in Milan") or at a downtown travel agency such as **American Express,** near the Duomo (Mon-Fri 9:00-17:30, closed Sat-Sun, Italian train tickets only, Via Larga 4, two blocks southeast of the Duomo, tel. 02-721-041).

Getting Around Milan

By Public Transit: Use Milan's great subway system. The clean, spacious, fast, and easy three-line Metro zips you nearly anywhere you may want to go, and trams and city buses fill in the gaps. The handiest Metro line for a quick visit is the yellow line 3, which connects the central train station to the Duomo. The other lines are red (1) and green (2). "ATM" is the acronym for the Milan public transit system.

A **ticket,** valid for 1.25 hours, can be used for one subway, tram, or bus ride, including a transfer either within the same or another system, but not a round-trip on the same system (€1.50; sold at newsstands, tobacco shops, shops with *ATM* sticker in window, and at machines in subway stations).

Validate tickets in the yellow or orange machines at the turnstiles, and keep them until you exit the Metro system. If you're caught riding on an unvalidated ticket, the fine is €33.

Other ticket options include: a *carnet* (€13.80 for 10 rides—one magnetic ticket that can be validated 10 times); a **24-hour pass** (€4.50, worthwhile if you take at least four rides); and a **48-hour pass** (€8.25). Passes use the same validation machines as standard tickets.

For transit information, visit the ATM Point (at Duomo stop, near Arengario exit, to right of Duomo as you face it, opposite La Scala ticket office, Mon-Sat 7:45-19:15, closed Sun, tel. 800-808-181, www.atm-mi.it).

I've keyed sightseeing to the subway system. Though most sights are within a few blocks of each other, Milan is an exhaust-

Milan Metro

To
Malpensa Airport,
Varenna, Stresa,
Venice,
etc.

YELLOW
3 Comasina

RED
1 Sesto F.S.

To Linate
& Bergamo
Airports

To
Malpensa
Airport

**CENTRAL TRAIN
STATION**
Centrale F.S.

Lambrate
F.S.

**PORTA GARIBALDI
TRAIN STATION**
Garibaldi F.S.

Gioia

Loreto

To Cologno
Nord &
Gessate

Moscova

Repubblica

Lima

Turati

Pta.
Venezia

To RHO,
QT8, Lotto,
Molino Dorino
& Bisceglie

Lanza

Montenapoleone

Palestro

Cadorna

DUOMO

San Babila

Conciliazione

Cairoli

Cordusio

Duomo

**LAST
SUPPER**

Missori

Sant'Ambrogio

Crocetta

Sant'Agostino

3 S. Donato
YELLOW

Porta Genova F.S.

2 Assago &
Abbiategrasso
GREEN

Not to Scale

| METRO LINES |
MILAN'S OLD CENTER	**1** RED
BUS	**2** GREEN
RAIL	**3** YELLOW

MILAN

ing city for walking. With the Metro, you'll rarely wait more than five minutes for a train. The well-marked trams can also be useful, especially to get to *The Last Supper* (tram #16) and the Monumental Cemetery (#12 or #14).

By Taxi: Small groups go cheap and fast by taxi (drop charge-€3.20, €0.70/kilometer; €5.20 drop charge on Sun and holidays, €6.20 from 21:00 to 6:00 in the morning). It can be easier to walk to a taxi stand than to flag down a cab. Handy stands are at Piazza del Duomo and in front of the Sforza Castle.

Tours in Milan

Bus Tours—The three-hour **Autostradale** bus-and-walking tour is a good value, has a live guide describing the city's monuments in English, and guarantees you'll see Leonardo's *Last Supper*—

Milan

Piazza Sempione

ARENA

VIA LEGNANO

To Five Diamonds Lounge Bar, Malpensa Airport & Como

BRANCA TOWER

Parco Sempione

VIALE MOLIERE

See Milan Hotels & Restaurants detail map

PALAZZO DELL'ARTE

VIA GADIO

FORO

Lanza M

BUONAPARTE

SFORZA CASTLE

MUSEUM OF ARTS & SCIENCE

4

Piazza Castello

To Fiera di Milano Trade Fair

V. 20 SETTEMBRE

VIA VICENZO MONTI

FORO

CADORNA STATION

M Cadorna

BUONAPARTE

1

i

2

Largo Cairoli

M Cairoli

VIA GIOVANNI BOCCACCIO

TEATRO DAL VERME

8

VIA G. PUCCINI

LAST SUPPER

S. MARIA D. GRAZIE

V. CARDOSSO

CORSO MAGENTA

PALAZZO LITTA

V. S. GIOVANNI SUL MURO

VIA MERAVIGLI

To Leonardo's Horse & Meazza Stadium

PALAZZO DELLE STELLINE

CORSO MAGENTA

V. SANT' AGNESE

VIA NIRONE

VIA LUINI

VIA BRISA

BORSA

VIA SAN VITTORE

OSPEDALE S. GIUSEPPE

VIA GIOSUE CARDUCCI

VIA TERRAGGIO

VIA BORROMEI

S. VITTORE AL CORPO

BASILICA DI S. AMBROGIO

V. L. NECCHI

V. SANT'ORSOLA

VIA CAPPUCCIO

DA VINCI NATIONAL SCIENCE MUSEUM

M Sant' Ambrogio

UNIVERSITA CATTOLICA

VIA SANTA MARTA

PUSTERLA DI S. AMBROGIO

VIA LANZONE

VIA STAMP.

VIA OLONA

VIA CAM.

VIA AUSONIO

VIA EDMONDO DE AMICIS

VIA CORENTI

VIA SAN VITO

M Sant'Agostino

VIA ARIBERTO

S. VINCENZO

VIA MORA

VIA C. DA SESTO

VIA CALOGERO

200 Meters

200 Yards

S. LORENZO

VIALE PAPINIANO

V. CON ZUGNA

CORSO GENOVA

V. SIMONETTA

V. MOLINO D. ARMI

To Navigli District

MILAN

1 Autostradale Tour Office
2 Zani Viaggi Tours
3 Via Montenapoleone (High-Fashion Shops)
4 Museum of Ancient Art Entrance
5 Stairs to Duomo Roof
6 Elevators to Duomo Roof (2)
7 Internet Café
8 American Bookstore

MILAN

useful if you haven't booked ahead for this important sight. The jam-packed itinerary also includes visits to the Duomo, Galleria Vittorio Emanuele, Sforza Castle, and La Scala Opera House (€55, departs Tue-Sun at 9:30 and Fri-Sat at 14:00, no Mon tours). They also offer an express version of the same tour, which skips the walking portion and lasts 1.5 hours (€35, Tue-Sun at 11:00). Tours leave from Piazza del Duomo, next to the taxi stand at the far end of the square from the church. There are four ways to reserve this tour: Book online at least two days in advance at www.autostradale .it; ask your hotelier to book it for you; call the main TI at 02-7740-4343; or drop into the Autostradale office next to the TI at Piazza Castello 1 (Mon-Fri 8:30-18:00, Sat-Sun 9:00-16:00). Tickets may be available for the same-morning departure. To confirm details, call 02-7200-1304 or 02-3391-0794.

Zani Viaggi does a similar tour that includes *The Last Supper*. Guides lead two-language tours (one of which is always English), departing Tuesday through Sunday at 9:30 and 14:30 from their office at Foro Bonaparte 76, near the Sforza Castle (€60, 3.5 hours, no Mon tours; ticket office open Mon-Fri 9:00-19:00, Sat-Sun 9:00-15:00; online reservations must be made at least two days in advance, tel. 02-867-131, www.zaniviaggi.it, excursions@zaniviaggi.it).

CitySightseeing Milano has hop-on, hop-off buses that do a circuit of the major sights accompanied by a recorded commentary; you can get off at a stop, tour the sight, and hop back on the bus to resume your tour (€20/48 hours, buy ticket on board; April-Oct daily 9:30-19:00, 2/hour; Nov-March daily 9:30-17:30, almost hourly; tel. 02-867-131. www.city-sightseeing.it). While you can hop on at any of their stops, it's easy at the Duomo (next to the taxi stand) and La Scala.

Local Guide—**Lorenza Scorti** is a hardworking young woman who knows her city's history and how to teach it. She can be booked well in advance (necessary in May and Sept) or on short notice (€125/3-hour tour, €250/day, same price for individuals or groups, evenings OK, tel. 02-4801-7042, mobile 347-735-1346, lorenza.scorti@libero.it).

Sights in Milan

▲▲Duomo (Cathedral)

The city's centerpiece is the fourth-largest church in Europe, after the Vatican's, London's, and Seville's. Back when Europe was fragmented into countless tiny kingdoms and dukedoms, the dukes of Milan wanted to impress their counterparts in Germany and France. Their goal was to earn Milan recognition and respect from both the Vatican and the kings and princes of northern Europe by building a massive, richly ornamented cathedral. Even after

Renaissance-style domes were in vogue elsewhere in Italy, conservative Milan's cathedral stayed on Gothic target. The dukes—thinking northerners would relate better to Gothic—loaded it with pointed arches and spires. For good measure, the cathedral was built not from ordinary stone, but from marble, top to bottom. Pink Candoglia marble was rafted in from a quarry about 60 miles away, across Lake Maggiore and down a canal to a port at the cathedral.

Cost and Hours: Free entry; separate charges for treasury (€2), baptistery (€4), and roof climb (by **elevator**-€12, daily 9:00-18:00, may close later in high season, enter outside at north or south transept; or take **stairs**-€7, daily 9:00-20:15, until 19:30 in winter, last stair entry at 18:15, enter outside on north side, across from La Rinascente department store). Church open daily 7:00-19:30, Metro: Duomo, tel. 02-7202-2656, www.duomomilano.it. The Duomo Point info center behind the cathedral on the right-hand side sells tickets for the Duomo's south elevator (daily 9:00-20:30, may stay open later in high season, tel. 02-7202-3375, staff are helpful and most speak English).

Audioguide: €5 for 1.5-hour audioguide, €2.50 if rented in last hour before closing (available from kiosk located inside to right of entrance, open Mon-Fri 9:30-17:30, Sat 9:30-16:00, closed Sun, ID required).

Dress Code: Modest dress is required. Don't wear shorts or anything sleeveless. Even kids with bare shoulders or knees are likely to be turned away at the door.

MILAN

Self-Guided Tour

At 525 by 300 feet, the place is immense, with more than 2,000 statues inside and 52 one-hundred-foot-tall, sequoia-size pillars representing the weeks of the year and the liturgical calendar. If you do two laps, you've done your daily walk. It was built to hold 40,000 worshippers, the entire population of Milan when construction began.

Built from 1386 to 1810, with the final touches added in 1965, this construction project originated the Italian phrase for "never-ending": "like building a cathedral." It started out Gothic (best seen in the apse behind the altar) and was finished in the early 1800s under Napoleon (particularly the noteworthy west facade, which is wonderful late in the day, with the sun low in the sky). While the church is a good example of the Flamboyant, or "flamelike," over-ripe final stage of Gothic, architectural harmony is not its forte.

Milan at a Glance

▲▲Duomo Milan's showpiece cathedral, with an amazing roof you can walk on, amid a forest of spires. **Hours:** Church—daily 7:00-19:30, rooftop elevator—daily 9:00-18:00, may close later in high season; rooftop stairs—daily 9:00-20:15, until 19:30 in winter, last entry at 18:15. See page 306.

▲▲Galleria Vittorio Emanuele Glass-domed arcade on the main square, perfect for window-shopping and people-watching. **Hours:** Always open. See page 313.

▲▲La Scala Opera House and Museum The world's most prestigious opera house. **Hours:** Museum daily 9:00-12:30 & 13:30-17:30. See page 314.

▲▲Pinacoteca Ambrosiana Oldest museum in Milan, with works by Raphael, Leonardo, Botticelli, Titian, and Caravaggio, and a special exhibit of Leonardo sketches (until 2015). **Hours:** Tue-Sun 10:00-18:00, closed Mon. See page 316.

▲Piazza del Duomo Milan's main square, full of energy, history, and pickpockets. **Hours:** Always open. See page 312.

▲Brera Art Gallery World-class collection of Italian paintings (13th-20th centuries), including Raphael, Caravaggio, Gentile da Fabriano, Piero della Francesca, Mantegna, and the Bellini brothers. **Hours:** Tue-Sun 8:30-19:00, closed Mon. See page 317.

▲Risorgimento Museum History of Italian unification. **Hours:** Tue-Sun 9:00-13:00 & 14:00-17:30, closed Mon. See page 318.

▲Sforza Castle Milan's castle containing a museum whose highlight is an unfinished Michelangelo *Pietà*. **Hours:** Tue-Sun 9:00-17:30, closed Mon. See page 319.

▲Via Dante Human traffic frolics to lilting accordions on one of Europe's longest pedestrian-only boulevards. **Hours:** Always open. See page 320.

MILAN

Exterior

Walk around the entire church exterior and notice the statues, made between the 14th and 20th centuries by sculptors from all over Europe. There are hundreds of these statues—each different and quite creative. Look at the statues on the tips of the many spires...they seem so relaxed, like they're just hanging out, waiting for their big day. Functioning as drain spouts, the 96 fanciful

▲**The Last Supper** Leonardo da Vinci's masterpiece, viewable only with a reservation—book several months in advance. **Hours:** Tue-Sun 8:15-18:45 (last entry), closed Mon. See page 321.

▲**Leonardo da Vinci National Science and Technology Museum** Leonardo's designs illustrated in wooden models, plus a vast collection of historical, scientific, and technological bric-a-brac and machines. **Hours:** Tue-Fri 9:30-17:00, Sat-Sun 9:30-18:30, closed Mon. See page 323.

▲**Monumental Cemetery** Evocative outdoor art gallery with tombs showcasing expressive art styles from 1870-1930. **Hours:** Tue-Sun 8:00-18:00, closed Mon. See page 325.

Church of Santa Maria presso San Satiro Pilgrim church with impressive 3-D paintings. **Hours:** Mon-Fri 7:30-11:30 & 15:30-18:30, Sat 15:30-19:00, Sun 10:00-12:00 & 15:30-19:00. See page 315.

Poldi Pezzoli Museum Italian paintings (15th-18th centuries), weaponry, and decorative arts. **Hours:** Wed-Mon 10:00-18:00, closed Tue. See page 318.

Bagatti Valsecchi Museum 19th-century Italian Renaissance furnishings. **Hours:** Tue-Sun 13:00-17:45, closed Mon. See page 318.

Branca Tower Great 360-degree views over the city. **Hours:** Erratic—call or confirm at TI before heading there, closed Mon and in bad weather. See page 320.

Museum of Art and Science Leonardo da Vinci's art and inventions, with hands-on exhibits on authenticating and dating various forms of art. **Hours:** Mon-Fri 10:00-18:00, closed Sat-Sun. See page 320.

Leonardo's Horse Gargantuan equestrian monument built according to Leonardo's designs. **Hours:** Tue-Sun 9:00-17:30, closed Mon. See page 324.

MILAN

gargoyle monsters are especially imaginative.

As you stand outside at the back, behind the altar, imagine the glory of this first wall. These were the earliest stones, laid in 1390. The sun-in-rose window was the proud symbol of the city's leading Visconti family; it's flanked by the angel telling Mary she's going to bear the Messiah. And behind you is a shrine to the leading religion of the 21st century: soccer. The Football Team store is filled with colorful vestments and relics of local soccer saints (go upstairs, daily 10:00-19:00).

Return to the front and enjoy the statues enlivening the facade. The lower ones—full of energy and movement—are early Baroque, from about 1600. Of the five doors, the center one is biggest. Made in 1907 in the Liberty style, it features the Joy and Sorrow of the Virgin Mary. Sad scenes are on the left, joyful ones on the right, and on top is the coronation of Mary in heaven by Jesus with all the saints and angels looking on.

Interior

Enter the church. Stand at the back of the fourth-longest nave in Christendom. The apse at the far end was started in 1386. The wall behind you wasn't finished until 1520. Even though the Renaissance had begun, builders stuck with the Gothic style. The two single stone-marble pillars behind you are the most precious ones in the church.

Notice two tiny lights: The little red one above the altar marks where a nail from the cross of Jesus is kept. This relic was brought to Milan by St. Helen (Emperor Constantine's mother) in the fourth century, when Milan was the capital of the Western Roman Empire. It's on display for three days a year (in mid-Sept). Now look high to the right and find a tiny pinhole of white light. This is designed to shine a 10-inch sunbeam at noon onto the bronze line that runs across the floor, indicating where we are on the zodiac (but local guides claim they've never seen it work).

Stained-Glass Windows: Wander deeper into the church up the right aisle. Check out the windows—15th-century mosaics of brilliant and expensive colored glass (stained, not painted). Bought by wealthy families seeking the Church's favor, they face the south and get the most light. The altars below generally honor the patron who made that window possible. Pick out familiar scenes in the windows. The purpose was to teach the illiterate masses the way to salvation through stories of the Old Testament and the life of Jesus. On the opposite wall (left side), many of the windows date from the time of Napoleon and are either made of dimmer, cheaper painted glass or are replacements for ones bombed out in World War II.

One window is clearly more modern, dating from the 1980s and celebrating the three top local cardinals, two of whom became saints (St. Ambrose, St. Charles Borromeo, and Cardinal Ferrari).

Altar: Belly up to the bar facing the high altar. While the church is Gothic, the area around the altar was made Baroque—the style of the Vatican in the 1570s (a Roman Catholic statement to counter the Protestant churches of the north, which were mostly Gothic). Napoleon crowned himself King of Italy under this dome in 1805. Now look to the rear up at the ceiling and see the fancy "carving" (between the ribs)—nope, that's painted. It looks expensive, but paint is more affordable than carved stone.

St. Bartolomeo Statue: Find the bald statue lit by the open door, by the wall in the south transept. This is a grotesque 16th-century statue of St. Bartolomeo, an apostle and first-century martyr skinned alive by the Romans. Walk behind the poor guy wearing his skin like a robe to see his face, hands, and feet. Carved by a student of Leonardo da Vinci, this is a study in human anatomy learned by dissection, forbidden by the Church at the time.

Floor: Walk toward the altar and around the corner 30 steps, to a gate blocking entry to the apse. Look down at the fine 16th-century inlaid-marble floor. The pieces around the altar are original. You can tell that the black marble (quarried from Lake Como) is harder because it looks and feels less worn than the other colors (the white is from Lake Maggiore, the pink from Verona).

Windows: The apse is lit by three huge windows, all 19th-century painted copies. The originals, destroyed in Napoleonic times, were made of precious stained glass.

Other Sights in the Duomo

Treasury: Steps lead under the altar to the treasury and to the tombs of St. Charles Borromeo (1538-1584) and his family. Charles was bishop of Milan, and the second most important hometown saint after St. Ambrose. Silver reliefs around the ceiling show scenes from Charles' life. The treasury, or *tesoro*, features empty reliquaries and carved ivories.

Paleo-Christian Baptistery: In the rear of the church (buy ticket at bookshop kiosk, same hours as the Duomo), you can climb down into the church that stood here long before the present one. Milan was an important center of early Christianity. In Roman times, Mediolanum's street level was 10 feet below today's level. You'll see the scant remains of an eight-sided baptistery (where

saints Augustine and Ambrose were baptized) and a little church. Back then, since you couldn't enter the church until you were baptized (which didn't happen until age 18), churches had a little "holy zone" just outside for the unbaptized. This included a baptistery like this one.

Cathedral Rooftop: This is the most memorable part of a Duomo visit. You'll wander through a fancy forest of spires with great views of the city, the square, and—on clear days—the crisp and jagged Italian Alps. And, 330 feet above everything, La

Madonnina overlooks it all. This 15-foot-tall gilded Virgin Mary is a symbol of the city.

Climb the stairs or take the elevator; the entrances to both are outside the church (for specifics, see "Cost and Hours," earlier).

Near the Duomo

▲▲**Duomo Museum (Museo del Duomo)**—This fine museum, currently closed for extensive renovation, offers an excellent opportunity to understand Milan's cathedral and see its original art close up. It's likely to reopen in 2015.

▲**Piazza del Duomo**—Milan's main square is a classic European scene and a popular local gathering point. Professionals scurry, fashion-conscious kids loiter, young thieves peruse. Teens hang out near the Galleria entrance in the afternoons, waving at the balcony above in hopes of being filmed by MTV cameras located in an upper-floor studio.

Standing in the square (midway between the statue and the Galleria), you're surrounded by history. The statue is Victor Emmanuel II, first king of Italy. He's looking at the grand Galleria named for him. The words above the triumphal arch entrance read: "To Victor Emmanuel II, from the people of Milan."

Behind the statue (opposite the cathedral) is the center of medieval Milan: Piazza Mercanti. Dating from 1220, the medieval City Hall (look for its red-brick arches) marked the center of town back when the entire city stood within its immense fortified walls. The merchant's square is a strangely peaceful place today, with a fine smattering of old-time Milano architecture that escaped the bombs of World War II.

Opposite the Galleria are twin fascist buildings. Mussolini made grandiose speeches from their balconies. Study the buildings' relief panels, which tell—with fascist melodrama—the history of Milan. Between these buildings and the cathedral (set back a bit) is the historic ducal palace, Palazzo Reale. This building, now a venue for temporary art exhibits, was redone in the Neoclassical style by Maria Theresa in the late 1700s, when Milan was ruled by the Austrian Habsburgs. For a fine view of the Duomo and the piazza, climb the steps to the balcony of the skinny fascist-style building closest to the cathedral (can be closed for frequent *manifestazioni*—demonstrations—or any other perceived security threat). Behind the Duomo is a vibrant pedestrian shopping zone along Corso Vittorio Emanuele.

▲▲**Galleria Vittorio Emanuele**—A symbol of Milan is its great four-story glass-domed arcade on the cathedral square. Built dur-

ing the heady days of Italian unification (c. 1870), it was the first building in town to have electric lighting. Here you can turn an expensive cup of coffee into a good value by enjoying Europe's best people-watching (or get the same view for peanuts from the strategically placed McDonald's).

The venerable **Bar Camparino** (at the entry), with a friendly staff and an Art Deco interior typical of the 1920s, is the former haunt of famous opera composer Giuseppe Verdi and conductor Arturo Toscanini, who used to stop by after their performances at La Scala. It's a fine place to enjoy a drink and people-watch (€3 for an espresso is a great deal if you relax and enjoy the view, or €1 at the bar just to enjoy the sumptuous interior). Once called the Campari café, this is considered the birthplace of the famous Campari bitter (€3.90 standing or €9.20 seated, Tue-Sun 7:30-20:00, closed Mon and Aug, tel. 02-8646-4435).

Wander around the gallery. Its art celebrates the establishment of Italy as an independent country. Around the central dome,

patriotic mosaics symbolize the four major continents. The mosaic floor is also patriotic. The white cross in the center represents the king. The she-wolf with Romulus and Remus (on the south side—facing Rome) honors the city that, since 1870, has been the national capital. On the west side (facing Torino, the provisional capital of Italy from 1861-1865), you'll find that city's symbol: a *torino* (little bull). For good luck, locals step on his irresistible little testicles. Two local girls explained to me that it works better if you spin. Find the poor little bull and observe for a few minutes...

it's a cute scene. With so much spinning, the mosaic is replaced every few years.

Piazza della Scala—This smart little traffic-free square, out the back between the Galleria and the opera house, is dominated by a statue of Leonardo da Vinci. The statue (from 1870) is a reminder that Leonardo spent many years in Milan working for the Sforza family (who dominated Milan as the Medici family dominated Florence). Under the great Renaissance genius stand four of his

MILAN

greatest "Leonardeschi." (He apprenticed a sizable group of followers.) The reliefs show his various contributions as painter, architect, and engineer. Leonardo, wearing his hydro-engineer hat, re-engineered Milan's canal system, complete with locks. (Until the 1920s, Milan was one of Italy's major ports, with canals connecting the city to the Po River and Lake Maggiore.)

▲▲La Scala Opera House and Museum—The statue of Leonardo behind the Galleria is looking at a plain but famous Neoclassical building, arguably the world's most prestigious opera house: Milan's Teatrale alla Scala. La Scala opened in 1778 with an opera by Antonio Salieri (of *Amadeus* fame). At Milan's famous opera house and its adjacent museum, opera buffs can see the museum's extensive collection and get a glimpse of the theater.

Cost and Hours: Museum—€6, daily 9:00-12:30 & 13:30-17:30, last entry 30 minutes before closing, Piazza della Scala, tel. 02-8879-7473, www.teatroallascala.org.

Museum: Well-described in English, the collection features things that mean absolutely nothing to the hip-hop crowd: Verdi's top hat, Rossini's eyeglasses, Toscanini's baton, Fettuccini's pesto, original scores, diorama stage sets, costumes, busts, portraits, and death masks of great composers and musicians. The museum allows you to peek into the actual theater. The stage is as big as the seating area on the ground floor. (You can see the towering stage box from Piazza della Scala across the street.) A recent five-year renovation corrected acoustical problems caused by WWII bombing and subsequent reconstruction. The royal box is just below your vantage point, in the center rear. Notice the massive chandelier made of Bohemian crystal.

Events in the Opera House: The show goes on at the world-famous La Scala Opera House. Schedules vary, but the opera season is nearly year-round (show time 20:00), and ballet and classical concerts are held from October through June. No performances are held in August (for information, call Scala Infotel Service, daily 9:00-18:00, tel. 02-7200-3744; for automated booking, call 02-860-775 and press 2 for English; or book online at www.teatroallascala.org). On the opening night of an opera, a dress code is enforced for men (suit and tie).

Tickets generally go on sale one month before a performance. Seats sell out quickly. On performance days, 140 sky-high gallery tickets are sold at a discount only at the box office (located down the left side of the theater toward the back on Via Filodrammatici, and marked with *Biglietteria Serale* sign). If you want a same-day discounted (but still not cheap) ticket, show up at 13:00 to get your name on the list. Return at 17:00 for the roll call. You must be present when your name is called in order to receive a voucher, which you'll then show at the ticket window to purchase a discounted ticket. One hour before show time, the box office sells any remaining tickets at a 25 percent discount. You can also buy tickets—but not the discounted ones—at a handy ticket office in the Duomo Metro station (daily 12:00-18:00, entrance is to right of the Duomo as you face it, underground, follow signs to *ATM Point*), as well as on the Internet (Web sales end one hour before show time).

Via Speronari—A block off Piazza del Duomo, this is one of Milan's oldest streets, and the most charming drag in the old center. Via Speronari—named for the spurs once made and sold here—is worth a wander. Street names around here recall their medieval crafts: *speronari*—spurs, *spadari*—swords, *armorari*—armor. The weaponry made on these streets was high fashion among Europe's warrior class...like having an Armani dagger. While right in the city center, the neighborhood feels vital because it's also a residential street. Banks of doorbells indicate that families live above the shops. Start at the corner of Via Mazzini and Via Speronari, one block southwest of the Duomo. A shop on your right—*L'Ortolan Pusae Vecc de Milan*—brags in the old Milanese language that this is the oldest fruit-and-veggie store in the city. The neighboring Princi bakery is understandably popular. Its brioches are rarely more than a few minutes old. The *tavola calda*—hot table—across the street sells fresh, hearty takeout to hungry businesspeople.

Nearby: Where Via Speronari hits Via Torino, go 20 yards to the left to find the...

Church of Santa Maria presso San Satiro (Church of St. Mary at St. Satiro)—Hiding behind its Baroque facade, this church was the scene of a temper tantrum in 1242, when a losing gambler vented his anger by hitting the baby Jesus in the Madonna-and-Child altarpiece. Blood "miraculously" spurted out, and the beautiful little church has been on the pilgrimage trail ever since. While I've never seen any blood, I'd swear I've seen a 3-D background behind the basically flat altar (a *trompe l'oeil* illusion—only about a foot deep). This church—squeezed between the earlier church of San Satiro and a street—had no room for a real apse, so the Renaissance architect Donato Bramante created the illusion of an apse.

In the north transept, you'll find that original ninth-century church of San Satiro (brother of St. Ambrose, patron saint of Milan). This tiny church—with surviving bits of Byzantine fresco—predated the rest. From this chapel, look back at the main altar to see Bramante's 3-D work collapsed. On the opposite side (near entry)—with dimensions mirroring this old chapel—an eight-sided baptistery by Bramante from the 1480s shows the mathematically based values of the Renaissance. If you have a prayer in need of an extra boost, pop a coin into the box and

MILAN

"light" an electric candle.

Cost and Hours: Free entry, Mon-Fri 7:30-11:30 & 15:30-18:30, Sat 15:30-19:00, Sun 10:00-12:00 & 15:30-19:00, Via Torino at Via Speronari, tel. 02-874-683.

▲▲**Pinacoteca Ambrosiana (with Leonardo exhibit)**—This oldest museum in Milan was inaugurated in 1618 to house Cardinal Federico Borromeo's painting collection. And until 2015, the museum is both more expensive and more important, thanks to a long-running special exhibit displaying 22 pages from Leonardo's notebook. Think of your visit in two parts: the permanent collection of paintings (including the Leonardo Hall), and the last room, which has the notebook pages. While it's exciting to see the pages, the permanent material is still the highlight. Pick up the English-language map locating major works, and rent the €1 audioguide (80 minutes), which explains highlights of both the permanent and special exhibits.

Cost and Hours: €15, Tue-Sun 10:00-18:00, closed Mon, last entry at 17:00, near Piazza del Duomo at Piazza Pio XI 2, tel. 02-8069-2221, www.ambrosiana.eu.

Visiting the Museum: Pinacoteca Ambrosiana began as a teaching academy, which explains its many replicas of famous works of art. Highlights include original paintings by Botticelli, Caravaggio, and Titian. As Cardinal Borromeo was a friend of Jan Brueghel, you'll find an entire room (#7) filled with delightful works by Brueghel and other Flemish masters. Study the wonderful detail in Brueghel's *Allegory of Fire* and *Allegory of Water*. The Flemish paintings are extremely detailed—many painted on copper to heighten the effect—and offer an insight into the psyche of the age. If the cardinal were asked why he enjoyed paintings that celebrated the secular life, he'd likely say, "Secular themes are God's book of nature."

Filling an entire wall, Raphael's charcoal-on-canvas cartoon served as an outline for the famous *School of Athens* fresco at the Vatican Museum. (A cartoon—*cartone* in Italian—is a large sketch that functions as a model for the making of a fresco.) While the Vatican's much-adored fresco is attributed entirely to Raphael, it was painted mostly by his students. But this *cartone* was wholly sketched by the hand of Raphael. To make the fresco, his assistants riddled this cartoon with pinpricks along the outlines of the characters, stuck it to the wall of the pope's study, and then applied a colored powder. When they removed the *cartone*, the characters' shapes were marked on the wall, and completing the fresco was a lot like filling in a coloring book. If you've seen the original fresco at the Vatican, you'll notice that the figure of Michelangelo (as a brooding stonecutter lounging on the steps in the foreground) is missing from the cartoon. Raphael added him to the fresco as a tribute after seeing his awe-inspiring work on the ceiling of the Sistine Chapel.

As Leonardo da Vinci spent many of his most productive years working in Milan, the city has an affinity for the Renaissance genius. The **Leonardo Hall,** with more of the gallery's permanent collection, features da Vinci's *Portrait of a Musician*, a copy of *The Last Supper*, and several fine Leonardo-type paintings by Luini and other disciples. During his Milan years, Leonardo created *The Last Supper* and painted several other famous canvases. Of these other paintings, only the *Portrait of a Musician*—as delicate, mysterious, and thought-provoking as the *Mona Lisa*—remains in Milan. The large fresco filling the far wall—with Christ receiving the crown of thorns—is by Luini. I find the painting of *The Last Supper* most interesting. When the cardinal realized that Leonardo's marvelous frescoed original was fading, he commissioned a careful copy to be created here for posterity. Today, this copy gives a rare chance to appreciate the original colorful richness of the now-faded masterpiece.

The Leonardo Hall leads into the somber library called Federiciana Hall, where you'll find the special Leonardo exhibit. The gallery, which owns da Vinci's *Codex Atlanticus,* is showing 22 of its 1,100 pages in themed exhibits changing quarterly until 2015. Soft period music accompanies your time with the 22 glass cases, each displaying a well-lit page from the notebook (the audioguide, which explains each page of the current exhibit, is essential to fully enjoy your visit). Don't enter the special exhibit until you are done with the permanent collection, as it's a one-way system and re-entry isn't allowed.

In the Brera Neighborhood

▲**Brera Art Gallery**—Milan's top collection of Italian paintings (13th-20th centuries) is world-class, but it can't top Rome's or Florence's. Established in 1809 to house Napoleon's looted art, it fills the first floor above a prestigious art college.

Cost and Hours: €6, more during special exhibits, Tue-Sun 8:30-19:00, closed Mon, last entry 45 minutes before closing, free lockers just before the ticket counter, no photos, Via Brera 28, Metro: Lanza or Montenapoleone, tel. 02-722-631, www.brera .beniculturali.it. Since there are no English descriptions, consider renting the audioguide (€5, ID required).

Visiting the Museum: Enter the grand courtyard of a former monastery, where you'll be greeted by the nude *Napoleon with Tinkerbell* (by Antonio Canova). Climb the stairway (following signs to *Pinacoteca,* past all the art students), buy your ticket, and pick up an English map of the museum's masterpieces.

The gallery's highlights include works by Gentile da Fabriano, hinting at the realism of the coming Renaissance (check out the lifelike flowers and realistic, bright gold paint—he used real gold powder, Room IV). Andrea Mantegna's *The Dead Christ* is a textbook example of feet-first foreshortening (Room VI). Room XVIII hosts a permanent glass-enclosed restoration lab, allowing you to see various restoration works in progress.

In Room XXI, notice how Crivelli employs Renaissance technique (he was a contemporary of Leonardo), yet clings to the mystique of the Gothic Age (that's why I like him so much). Find eight Crivellis. Also, don't miss Raphael's *Wedding of the Madonna,* Piero della Francesca's *Madonna and Child with Four Angels* (Room XXIV), and the gritty-yet-intimate realism of Caravaggio's *Supper at Emmaus* (Room XXIX). Room XXXV features several of Canaletto's picture-postcards of Venetian cityscapes. This is Impressionism—not a single line in these works, just strategically placed daubs of paint that render palazzos and canals bathed in Venetian light with photographic precision. To spice things up, look for Francesco Hayez's hot and heavy *The Kiss (Il Bacio)* in Room XXXVII.

Java junkies will seek out the great, cheap cappuccino machine: Go through Napoleon's courtyard and straight through the art school to the end of the long hall; the machine's on your left. It's fun to explore the art school on the ground floor, mill about among the many young students, and wonder if there's a 21st-century Leonardo in your midst.

▲**Risorgimento Museum**—With a quick 30-minute swing through this quiet one-floor museum, you'll get an idea of the interesting story of Italy's rocky road to unity: from Napoleon (1796) to the victory in Rome (1870). However, there isn't much information in English. It's just around the block from the Brera Art Gallery at Via Borgonuovo 23.

Cost and Hours: €2, Tue-Sun 9:00-13:00 & 14:00-17:30, closed Mon, Metro: Montenapoleone, tel. 02-8846-4176, www .museodelrisorgimento.mi.it.

Near Montenapoleone

Poldi Pezzoli Museum—This classy house of art features top Italian paintings of the 15th through 18th centuries, old weaponry, and lots of interesting decorative arts, such as a roomful of old sundials and compasses.

Cost and Hours: €9, Wed-Mon 10:00-18:00, closed Tue, last entry one hour before closing, free English audioguides, Via Manzoni 12, Metro: Montenapoleone, tel. 02-794-889, www .museopoldipezzoli.it.

Bagatti Valsecchi Museum—This unique 19th-century collection of Italian Renaissance furnishings was assembled by two

MILAN

aristocratic brothers who spent a wad turning their home into a Renaissance mansion. Museum guards pack flashlights for closer examination of fine wood carvings. The museum's beautiful but outrageously expensive café in its Renaissance courtyard might be worth the €5 cover charge just to be seen noshing with Milan's stylish elite.

Cost and Hours: €8, half-price on Wed, open Tue-Sun 13:00-17:45, closed Mon, free English audioguides and good English descriptions throughout, Via Gesù 5, Metro: Montenapoleone, tel. 02-7600-6132, www.museobagattivalsecchi.org.

Sforza Castle and Nearby

▲**Sforza Castle (Castello Sforzesco)**—The castle of Milan tells the story of the city in brick. Built in the late 1300s as a military fortress, it guarded the gate to the city wall and defended Milan from enemies "within and without." It was beefed up by the Sforza duke in 1450 in anticipation of a Venetian attack. Later, it was the Renaissance palace of the Sforza family and was even home to their in-house genius, Leonardo. During the many years of foreign rule (16th-19th centuries), it was a barracks for occupying Spanish, French, and Austrian soldiers. Today, it houses several museums.

Cost and Hours: €3, free entry 16:30-17:00 and Fri 14:00-17:00; open Tue-Sun 9:00-17:30, closed Mon, WCs and limited free lockers are downstairs from the ticket counter—get key and give ID at ticket desk, English info fliers throughout and at information office beside the Porta Umberto entrance, Metro: Cairoli, tel. 02-8846-3700, www.milanocastello.it.

Visiting the Castle: The **gate** stands above a ditch that was once filled with water. A relief celebrates Umberto I, the second king of Italy. Above that, a statue of St. Ambrose, the patron of Milan (and a local bishop in the fourth century), oversees the action. Notice the chart, just outside the gate, showing how the city was encircled first by a crude medieval wall, and then by a state-of-the-art 16th-century wall—of which this castle was a key element. It's apparent from the enormity of these walls that Milan was a strategic prize. Today, the walls are gone, giving the city two circular boulevards.

This immense, often-bombed-and-rebuilt brick fortress—exhausting at first sight—can only be described as heavy. But its courtyard has a great lawn for picnics and siestas. Its main museum, the **Museum of Ancient Art,** is fascinating, unlike the other museums in the castle. Enter the museum just past the ticket counter. It fills the old Sforza family palace with interesting medieval armor, furniture, early Lombard art, an Egyptian collection, and—for your finale—Michelangelo's unfinished *Pietà Rondanini* in Room XV.

This is a rare opportunity to enjoy a Michelangelo with no crowds. Michelangelo died while still working on this piece—his fourth *Pietà*. A *pietà*, by definition, is a representation of a dead Christ with a sorrowful Virgin Mary. This unfinished statue is surrounded by a fortress-like concrete wall to limit its viewing to a few tourists at a time, and is unique in that it shows the genius of Michelangelo midway through a major rework—Christ's head is cut out of Mary's right shoulder, and an earlier arm is still just hanging there. But there's a certain power to this rawness. Walk around the back to see the strain in Mary's back (and Michelangelo's rough chisel work) as she struggles to support her son. The sculpture's elongated form hints at the Mannerist style that would follow. Notice the ancient Roman altar underneath the *Pietà*. This sculpture was owned by the Rondanini family until just after World War II.

At the far end of the castle's grounds is the monumental **Arco della Pace**, a triumphal arch. They built the arch facing Paris to welcome Napoleon's rule, because locals believed he would bring with him the ideals of the French Revolution. When they learned he was just another megalomaniac, they turned the horses around, their tails facing France. The neighborhood near the arch is becoming a trendy nighttime district; see "Nightlife in Milan," later.

Branca Tower—This tower, a five-minute walk from the Sforza Castle through Milan's equivalent of Central Park, offers a commanding city view. You'll ride an elevator that takes you as high as the Mary that crowns the cathedral.

Cost and Hours: €4, hours are erratic, call or confirm at TI before heading out, closed Mon and in bad weather, tel. 02-331-4120.

Museum of Art and Science (Museo d'Arte e Scienza)—This oddly eclectic hands-on museum offers a look at Leonardo's works during the 20 years he spent in Milan. It includes reproductions of his paintings and sketches, and inventions such as a clever drum machine and war machines in miniature. Another part of the museum describes how to tell the difference between genuine art and copies or fakes. Oddly, a third collection features African and Buddhist art.

Cost and Hours: €8, Mon-Fri 10:00-18:00, closed Sat-Sun, English descriptions throughout, Via Q. Sella 4; tel. 02-7202-2488, www.museoartescienza.com.

▲**Via Dante**—This grand pedestrian boulevard and popular shopping street leads from the Sforza Castle toward the town center and the Duomo. Since Via Dante was carved out of a medieval tangle of streets to celebrate Italian unification (c. 1870), all the facades lining it are relatively new. Over the vigorous complaints of merchants, the street became traffic-free in 1995. Today, they'd have it no other way. Enjoy strolling this beautiful people zone, where you'll hear the whir of bikes and the lilting melodies of accordion players instead of traffic noise. Photo exhibits are frequently displayed up and down the street. In front of the Sforza Castle, a commanding statue of Giuseppe Garibaldi, one of the heroes of the unification movement, looks down one of Europe's longest pedestrian zones. From here you can walk to the Duomo and beyond (about 1.5 miles) down streets that are all nearly traffic-free. Stroll and appreciate Italian design both in people and in windows (ignore the Foot Locker).

The Last Supper and Nearby
▲Leonardo da Vinci's *The Last Supper (Cenacolo)*

MILAN

Housed in the Church of Santa Maria delle Grazie, this is one of the ultimate masterpieces of the Renaissance. Milan's leading family, the Sforza, hired da Vinci to decorate the dining hall of the Dominican monastery that adjoins the church. This gift was essentially a bribe to the monks so that the Sforzas could locate their family tomb in the church. Ultimately, the French drove the Sforzas out of Milan, they were never buried here, and the Dominicans got a great fresco for nothing. Note that this is a rare sight, and entry must be booked several months in advance (see "Reservations," on next page).

Cost and Hours: €8, includes €1.50 reservation fee (9:30 and 15:30 visits require €3.25 extra for provided guided English tour). Open Tue-Sun 8:15-18:45 (last entry), closed Mon. Show up 20 minutes before your scheduled entry time. When an attendant calls your time, get up and move into the next room.

Reservations: Reservations are mandatory. Even though the hype surrounding *The Da Vinci Code* novel and movie has died down, spots are still booked several months in advance—so plan ahead. To minimize the humidity problem—even though the damage has already been done—only 900 visitors a day are allowed in. That's 25 tourists popping in every 15 minutes for exactly 15 minutes. Prior to your appointment time, you wait in several rooms to dehumidify, while doors close behind you and open up slowly in front of you. The posted information about Leonardo is mainly in Italian.

If you book by **phone,** you'll have a greater selection of days and time slots to choose from, since the website doesn't reflect cancellations, but you won't be able to reserve same-day tickets (tel. 02-9280-0360, or from the US dial 011-39-02-9280-0360, office open Mon-Sat 8:00-18:30, closed Sun; the number is often busy— once you get through, dial 2 for an English-speaking operator; the process takes about two minutes and you'll hang up with an appointed entry time and a number; pay with credit card upon booking).

If you book **online** using the official website, www.cenacolo vinciano.net, choose "Cenacolo Vinciano." You'll see a calendar that shows available time slots for the current month. If the days are blank, it means that all the slots for those days have been filled. Be careful when you select the date—on this calendar the first day of the week is Monday. If you can't find a spot when you need it, try calling instead, because cancellations show up on the website as booked slots.

Last-Minute Tickets: While "reservations are required," if spots are available (more likely on weekdays and first thing in the morning) you can sometimes book one at the desk (even if *Sold Out* sign is posted). If fewer than 25 people show up for a particular time slot, you can get lucky. But those who show up without a reservation generally kill lots of time waiting around. Note that the Autostradale and Zani Viaggi bus tours (see "Tours in Milan," earlier) include entry to *The Last Supper.*

Audioguide: Consider the fine €3 audioguide. Its spiel fills every second of the time you're in the room—so try to start listening to it just before you enter (ideally in the waiting room while studying the reproduction of *The Last Supper*).

Photography: No photos are allowed.

Getting There: Take the Metro to Cadorna or Conciliazione (plus a 5-minute walk), or hop on tram #16 (catch it just off Piazza del Duomo on corner of Via Mazzini and Via Dogana), which drops you off in front of the Church of Santa Maria delle Grazie. The Science and Technology Museum (next listing) is two blocks away.

Visiting *The Last Supper:* Because of Leonardo's experimental fresco technique, deterioration began within six years of *The Last Supper's* completion. The church was bombed in World War II, but—miraculously, it seems—the wall holding *The Last Supper* remained standing. A 21-year restoration project (completed in 1999) peeled away 500 years of touch-ups, leaving Leonardo's masterpiece faint but vibrant.

In a big, vacant whitewashed room, you'll see faded pastels and not a crisp edge. The feet under the table look like negatives. But the composition is dreamy—Leonardo captures the psychological drama as the Lord says, "One of you will betray me," and the apostles huddle in stressed-out groups of three, wondering, "Lord, is it I?" Some are scandalized. Others want more information. Simon (on the far right) gestures as if to ask a question that has no answer. In this agitated atmosphere, only Judas (fourth from left and the only one with his face in shadow)—clutching his 30 pieces of silver and looking pretty guilty—is not shocked.

The circle meant life and harmony to Leonardo. Deep into a study of how life emanates in circles—like ripples on a pool hit by a pebble—Leonardo positioned the 13 characters in a semicircle. Jesus is in the center, from whence the spiritual force of God emanates, or ripples out.

The room depicted in the painting seems like an architectural extension of the church. The disciples form an apse, with Jesus as the altar—in keeping with the Eucharist. Jesus anticipates his sacrifice, his face sad, all-knowing, and accepting. His feet even foreshadowed his death by crucifixion. Had the door, which was cut out in 1652, not been added, you'd see how Leonardo placed Jesus' feet atop each other, ready for the nail.

The room was a refectory or dining room for the Dominican friars. Traditionally, they'd gather here to eat, with a Last Supper scene on one wall facing a Crucifixion scene on the opposite wall.

The perspective is mathematically correct. In fact, restorers found a tiny nail hole in Jesus' left eye, which anchored the strings Leonardo used to establish these lines. The table is cheated out to show the meal. Notice the exquisite lighting. The walls are lined with tapestries (as they would have been), and the one on the right is brighter in order to fit the actual lighting in the refectory (which has windows on the left). With the extremely natural effect of the light and the drama of the faces, Leonardo created an effective masterpiece.

▲Leonardo da Vinci National Science and Technology Museum (Museo Nazionale della Scienza e Tecnica "Leonardo da Vinci")—The spirit of Leonardo lives here. Most tourists visit for the hall of Leonardo designs illustrated in wooden models, but Leonardo's mind is just as easy to appreciate by paging

MILAN

through a coffee-table edition of his notebooks in any bookstore. The rest of this immense collection of industrial cleverness is fascinating, with planes, trains, automobiles, ships, radios, old musical instruments, computers, batteries, telephones, chunks of the first transatlantic cable, interactive science workshops, and a 1960s "pocket-sized" submarine. Many exhibits include English descriptions. Some of the best exhibits (such as the Marconi radios) branch off the Leonardo hall. Ask for an English museum map from the ticket desk—you'll need it. Allow at least 1.5 hours here. On weekends, this museum is very popular with families, so come early or be prepared to wait in line.

Cost and Hours: €10, guided tour of submarine-€8; Tue-Fri 9:30-17:00, Sat-Sun 9:30-18:30, closed Mon; Via San Vittore 21, bus #50 or #58 from the Sforza Castle, or tram #16—catch it just off Piazza del Duomo in direction: San Siro, or Metro: Sant'Ambrogio; tel. 02-485-551, www.museoscienza.org.

Away from the Center

Leonardo's Horse—The largest equestrian monument in the world is a modern reconstruction of a model created in 1482 by Leonardo da Vinci for the Sforza family. The clay prototype was destroyed in 1499 by invading French forces, who used it for target practice. In 1982, American Renaissance-art collector Charles Dent decided to build the 15-ton, 24-foot-long statue from Leonardo's design, planning to present it to the Italians in appreciation for their role in the Renaissance and in homage to Leonardo's genius.

Unfortunately, Dent died before the project could be completed. In 1997, American sculptor Nina Akamu created a new clay model that became the template for the final statue; it was unveiled in 1999. The exhibit, described in English, includes statue casts and photos of the construction.

Cost and Hours: Free, Tue-Sun 9:00-17:30, closed Mon, located on outskirts near Meazza soccer stadium and San Siro racetrack; from corner of Via Mazzini and Via Dogana, take tram #16, direction: San Siro, to Stratico Palatino stop—ask conductor when to get off, then head right on Via Palatino, and left on Piazzale dello Sport to #9; or you can walk a half-mile from Metro: Lotto.

Soccer—The Milanesi claim that their soccer (football, or *calcio*, in Italian) teams are the best in Europe. For a dose of Europe's soccer mania (which many believe provides a necessary testosterone vent to keep Europe out of a third big war), catch a match while you're here. A.C. Milan and Inter Milan are the ferociously competitive home teams (tickets-€10-350).

A.C. Milan tickets are sold at Intesa Sanpaolo banks (one's at Via Verdi 8, Mon-Fri 8:45-13:45 & 14:45-15:45, closed Sat-Sun), online at www.acmilan.com, or at the Milan Point Shop (Tue-Sat 10:00-19:00, closed Sun-Mon, Piazza XXVI Maggio next to Via San Gottardo). Inter Milan tickets are sold at Banca Popolare di Milano banks (one's at Piazza Meda 4, Metro: San Babila; Mon-Fri 8:45-13:45 & 14:45-15:45, closed Sat-Sun) or online at www.inter.it.

Games are held in the 85,000-seat Meazza stadium most Sunday afternoons from September to June (Metro: Lotto, or tram #16—catch it just off Piazza del Duomo, on corner of Via Mazzini and Via Dogana, direction: San Siro; take it to last stop, where you'll find the stadium). You'll need to have your passport when you buy your ticket and bring it with you to the stadium for security reasons. For more on the Italian passion for soccer, see page 876.

▲**Monumental Cemetery (Il Cimitero Monumentale)**— Europe's most artistic and dreamy cemetery experience, this grand

place was built just after unification to provide a suitable final resting spot for the city's "famous and well-deserving men." Any cemetery is evocative, but this one—with its super-emotional portrayals of the deceased and their heavenly escorts (in art styles c. 1870-1930)—is in a class by itself. It's a vast garden art gallery of proud busts and grim reapers, heartbroken angels and weeping widows, too-young soldiers and countless old smiles, frozen on yellowed black-and-white photos.

Cost and Hours: Free, Tue-Sun 8:00-18:00, closed Mon, last entry at 17:30, pick up map at the entrance gate, a long walk from Metro: Garibaldi FS, or catch tram #12 or #14 from the corner of Via Orefici and Via Cantu' near the Duomo, tel. 02-8846-5600, www.monumentale.net.

Shopping in Milan

For world-class window-shopping, visit the "**Quadrilateral**," an elegant high-fashion shopping area around Via Montenapoleone. This was the original Beverly Hills of Milan. In the 1920s, the top fashion shops moved in, and today it remains *the* place for designer labels. Most places close Sunday and for much of August. On

MILAN

Mondays, stores open only after 16:00. In this land where fur is still prized, the people-watching is as entertaining as the window-shopping. Notice also the exclusive penthouse apartments with roof gardens high above the scene. Via Montenapoleone and the pedestrianized Via della Spiga are the best streets.

Whether you're gawking or shopping, here's the best route: From La Scala, walk up Via Manzoni to the Metro stop at Montenapoleone, browse down Via Montenapoleone, cut left on Via Santo Spirito (lined with grand aristocratic palazzos—peek into the courtyard at #7), turn right to window-shop down Via della Spiga, turn right on Via Sant'Andrea and then left, back onto Montenapoleone, which leads you through a final gauntlet of temptations to Piazza San Babila. Then (for less-expensive shopping thrills), walk back to the Duomo down the pedestrian-only Corso Vittorio Emanuele. From the Duomo, go down Via Dante to the Sforza Castle.

La Rinascente, next to the Duomo, is a Nordstrom-type department store with something for everyone and an especially good toy selection. Each floor has a fine collection of designer names sold out of independent shops, all functioning within the walls of this vast and venerable store. Simply riding the escalator up and up gives a fun overview of Italian design and marketing. The seventh floor is a top-end food circus, with terrace views of the Duomo and a public WC. Its name, meaning "the place reborn," fits its history. In an earlier life, it was a fine Liberty-style building until it burned down in 1918. It was rebuilt, only to be bombed in World War II and rebuilt once again (Mon-Thu 9:30-21:00, Fri-Sat 9:30-22:00, Sun 10:00-21:00, has a VAT refund office and recommended restaurants, faces north side of the Duomo on Piazza del Duomo).

Excelsior is a bold high-end concept store, owned by the Coin department-store chain. Giving you the sensation of a design museum rather than a store, a conveyor belt takes you from level to colorful level with pulsing music and electronic art installations. If you're looking for the perfect €1,000 shirt, you've come to the right place. Otherwise, hit the delectable food hall in the basement and pick up a high-design salad—a bargain at €6 (daily 10:00-20:30, Galleria del Corso 4, two long blocks behind the Duomo, tel. 027-630-7301).

Nightlife in Milan

For evening action, check out the artsy Brera area in the old center, with several swanky sidewalk cafés to choose from and lots of bars that stay open late. Home to Brera's Art University, this district has a sophisticated, lively people-watching scene. Another great neighborhood for nightlife, especially for a younger scene, is Navigli, Milan's formerly bohemian, now gentrified "Little Venice" (Metro: Porta Genova).

An up-and-coming area—which is expected to become the "in" place for evenings out during the 2015 World's Fair—is the neighborhood near Arco della Pace along Corso Sempione. Locals believe this street will become the Champs-Elysées of Milan. It's at the far end of the Sforza Castle grounds; just head for the triumphal arch. Find out what the fuss is about as you enjoy an *aperitivo* during happy hour (18:00-21:00) at **Five Diamonds Lounge Bar,** an upmarket venue run by the owners of the recommended Ristorante Bruno (closed Mon; from Piazza Cordusio or La Scala, take tram #1, direction: Piazza Castelli; Corso Sempione 11, tel. 02-3459-3668).

There are always concerts and live music playing in the city at various clubs and concert halls. Specifics change quickly, so it's best to rely on the entertainment information in periodicals from the TI.

Sleeping in Milan

All recommended hotels are within a few minutes' walk of Milan's subway system. With Milan's fine Metro, you can get anywhere in town in a flash. Anytime in March, April, September, and October, the city can be completely jammed by conventions, and hotel prices jump way up. I've listed high-season prices, but not convention-gouging prices. (For the convention schedule, see www.fieramilano.it.) Summer is usually wide-open and prices are discounted, though many hotels close in August for vacation. Hotels cater more to business travelers than to tourists, so Fridays and Saturdays are generally cheaper and available.

Lately I've noticed a trend in which small family-style hotels in the center are being neglected, and the big, modern business-class hotels around the train station are proliferating. I've tried to collect central places, where travelers feel appreciated and the staff feels like part of the family. If the following places are booked up, go online—there are lots of hotels near the train station.

Near the Duomo

The Duomo area is thick with people-watching, reasonably priced eateries, and the major sightseeing attractions. From the central train station to the Duomo, it's just four stops on a direct Metro line (yellow line 3, direction: San Donato) to Metro: Duomo.

$$$ Hotel Grand Duca di York is stuck oddly in the middle of banks and big-city starkness three blocks southwest of Piazza del Duomo. It's got lavish public spaces and 33 modern, bright

Sleep Code

(€1 = about $1.40, country code: 39)
S = Single, **D** = Double/Twin, **T** = Triple, **Q** = Quad, **b** = bathroom, **s** = shower only. Unless otherwise noted, credit cards are accepted, English is spoken, and breakfast is included. Many cities in Italy levy a hotel tax of about €2 per person, per night, which must be paid in cash (not included in the rates I've quoted).

To help you sort easily through these listings, I've divided the accommodations into three categories based on the price for a standard double room with bath:

$$$ Higher Priced—Most rooms €150 or more.
$$ Moderately Priced—Most rooms between €110-150.
$ Lower Priced—Most rooms €110 or less.

Prices can change without notice; verify the hotel's current rates online or by email.

rooms that are thoughtfully designed and decorated (Sb-€98-128, Db-€170-190, air-con, elevator, free Wi-Fi, free minibar, near Metro stops: Cordusio or Duomo, Via Moneta 1, tel. 02-874-863, fax 02-869-0344, www.ducadiyork.com, info@ducadiyork.com).

$$$ Hotel Spadari boasts an Art Deco interior designed by the Milanese artist Giò Pomodoro ("Joe Tomato" in English). The 40 rooms have billowing drapes, big paintings, and designer doors. It's next door to the recommended Peck deli, and two blocks from the Duomo (standard Db-€220-248, deluxe Db-€280-350, no need for the pricier suites, 5 percent Rick Steves discount when you booked direct, air-con, elevator, Wi-Fi, Via Spadari 11, tel. 02-7200-2371, fax 02-861-184, www.spadarihotel.com, reservation @spadarihotel.com).

$ Hotel Vecchia Milano is a humble, clean place buried deep in the old town on a narrow lane. Although the management is indifferent, it rents 27 comfortable rooms at a great price for the location (Sb-€65-80, Db-€90-100, air-con, pay Wi-Fi, next to recommended Hostaria Borromei at Via Borromei 4, tel. 02-875-042, fax 02-8645-4292, www.hotelvecchiamilan.com, hotelvecchia milano@tiscalinet.it).

Between La Scala and the Sforza Castle

$$$ Hotel Star, comfortable and modern, rents 30 sparkling, fresh, and spacious rooms with unexpected artistic touches (Sb-€165, Db-€215, prices drop about €40 outside convention times, check website for deals, interior rooms are quieter, air-con, Wi-Fi,

MILAN

usually closed Aug, Via dei Bossi 5, tel. 02-801-501, fax 02-861-787, www.hotelstar.it, info@hotelstar.it, cheeky Vittoria).

$$$ Antica Locanda dei Mercanti offers 15 white, minimalist rooms in an 18th-century palazzo. While the rooms are all different—some with kitchens, others with spacious terraces—all have a clean, fresh-flower vibe, uncommonly romantic for Milan (Db-€195-265, €30 more for terrace rooms, breakfast extra, aircon, free Internet access and Wi-Fi, Via San Tomaso 6, Metro: Cairoli or Cordusio; tel. 02-805-4080, fax 02-805-4090, www.locanda.it, locanda@locanda.it, Alex and Eri).

$$ London Hotel, a simple 30-room hotel with overstuffed little living rooms, an inviting breakfast room, and all the amenities, is tucked away on a quiet side street just off vibrant Via Dante. It's warmly run by the friendly Gambino family: mom and pop Elda and Franco don't speak English, but daughters Tanya and Licia do (S-€70, Sb-€90, D-€120, Db-€150, Tb-€180, prices much higher during conventions, skip their €8 breakfast and grab something on Via Dante, cheaper in July and Aug, book direct for these rates and get an additional 10 percent off with cash, aircon, elevator, pay Wi-Fi, near Metro: Cairoli at Via Rovello 3, tel. 02-7202-0166, fax 02-805-7037, www.hotellondonmilano.com, info@hotellondonmilano.com).

Near the Central Train Station

The train station neighborhood is more practical than characteristic. Its hotels are utilitarian business-class hotels with prices that bounce all over depending upon the convention schedule. You'll find more shady characters than shady trees in the parks, and lots of massage parlors. But you can't beat the convenience (near station, Metro to the center, shuttles to airports), and if you hit it outside of convention times, the prices are hard to beat. Here are two decent options:

$$ Hotel Florida is a comfortable, well-maintained businessclass hotel with 55 rooms on a quiet street one block from the station. Prices plummet if you book direct and are not visiting during a convention (rack rate Db-€290 but often more like Sb-€70-100 and Db-€90-130, free Wi-Fi, Via Lepetit 33, tel. 02-670-5921, fax 02-669-2867, www.hotelfloridamilan.com, info@hotelflorida milan.com). With the tracks to your back, leave the station's upper hall to the left, cross the taxi stand, and then cross the road. The hotel is on Via Lepetit, around the corner from Ristorante Giglio Rosso.

$$ Hotel Garda has 55 tidy, spotless rooms two and a half blocks from the station (Sb-€40-140, Db-€60-170; email first to get a promo code for a 10 percent discount when booking on their website; air-con, elevator, Via N. Torriani 21, tel. 02-6698-2626,

MILAN

Hotels & Restaurants in Milan

- ❶ Hotel Grand Duca di York
- ❷ Hotel Spadari & Peck Gourmet Deli
- ❸ Hotel Vecchia Milano & Hostaria Borromei
- ❹ Hotel Star
- ❺ Antica Locanda dei Mercanti
- ❻ London Hotel
- ❼ To Train Station Area Hotels
- ❽ Trattoria Milanese
- ❾ Ristorante Bruno
- ❿ Peck Italian Bar
- ⓫ Elevator to La Rinascente Dep't Store Eateries
- ⓬ Latteria Cucina Vegetariana

MILAN

⑬ Ciao Cafeteria
⑭ Ristorante Rita
⑮ McDonald's & Bar Camparino
⑯ Odeon Gelateria
⑰ Gelateria Grom
⑱ Princi Bakeries (2)
⑲ Luini Panzerotti

⑳ Supermarket
㉑ Da Rita e Antonio
㉒ Le Briciole Ristorante
㉓ Antica Osteria Milanese
㉔ Via Dante Eateries
㉕ Obikà Mozzarella Bar
㉖ Bar Brera

MILAN

fax 02-6698-2576, www.hotelgardamilan.com, info@hotelgarda milan.com). Exit the train station and head straight across the square, veering left onto Via N. Torriani. It's ahead on your right.

Hostels

For beds costing about €21-30, consider Milan's hostels. Most are away from the center, but the first one I've listed is closer to town.

$ **Ostello la Cordata,** a good choice, has 83 beds in both private rooms and in shared dorm rooms (€21-26 for beds in 6-, 8-, and 16-bed dorms; hotel-type rooms on the third floor—Sb-€50-60, Db-€70-90, Tb-€90-123; reserve ahead, 14:30-24:00 check-in but can leave bags earlier, no curfew, elevator, free Internet access and Wi-Fi, self-serve laundry, Via Burigozzo 11, Metro: Missori—on yellow line 3, tel. 02-5831-4675, fax 02-5830-3598, www.ostellola cordata.com, info@ostellolacordata.com).

$ **AIG Piero Rotta** is larger and offers cheap, basic accommodation with a simple breakfast (€21-30 beds in 2-6-bed dorms, non-members pay €3/night more, near Metro: QT8—on red line 1, at Via Martino Bassi 2, tel. 02-3926-7095, fax 02-3300-0191, www.ostellomilano.it, milano@aighostels.com).

Eating in Milan

This is a fast-food city, but fast food in a fashion capital isn't a burger and fries. Milan's bars, delis, *rosticcerie,* and self-service cafeterias cater to people with plenty of taste and more money than time. You'll find delightful eateries all over town (note that they take Aug off).

I find the price difference between basic and classy restaurants to be negligible (for example, pastas-€7-12, *secondi*-€12-20, cover-€1-3), so it's worth springing for the places that give the best experience. To eat mediocre food on a famous street with great people-watching, choose an eatery on the pedestrian-only Via Mercanti or Via Dante. To eat with students in trendy little trattorias, explore the Brera neighborhood. To eat well near the Duomo, consider the recommended places below.

Locals like to precede a lunch or dinner with an *aperitivo* (while Campari made its debut in Milan, a simple glass of *vino bianco* or prosecco, the Italian champagne, is just as popular). Bars fill their counters with inviting baskets of munchies, which are served free with these drinks, at about 17:00. A cheap drink (if you're either likable or discreet) can become a light meal. For example, check out the wonderful buffet spread at the recommended Bar Brera.

Breakfast is a bad value in hotels and fun on Via Dante or in bars. It's OK to quasi-picnic. Bring in a banana (or whatever) and

> ## Milanese Specialties
>
> Milan's signature dishes (often served together as a *piatto unico,* or "single dish") are *risotto alla milanese* and *ossobuco.* The risotto is flavored with saffron, which gives it its intense yellow color. It's said that a 16th-century Belgian glassworker first stumbled on the use of saffron as a spice. Initially, he used saffron to tint the glass mixture for completing the stained-glass windows of the Duomo in 1574. His master joked that he'd end up adding the precious spice to his food as well. On the day of his master's daughter's wedding, the glassworker persuaded the chef to add saffron to the rice cooked for the reception. After the guests got over their initial surprise, the dish was a great success, and has been a staple on Milan's menus ever since. The subtle flavor of the saffron pairs nicely with the *ossobuco* (meaning "marrow," or literally "hole in the bone," of the veal shank). The prized marrow is extracted with special little forks and is considered the best part of the meal.

order a toasted ham-and-cheese sandwich (called *toast*) or brioche with your cappuccino.

Near the Duomo

Dining with Class

Trattoria Milanese, sophisticated and family-run, is a splurge. It has an enthusiastic and local clientele—the restaurant didn't even bother to get a phone until 1988. Expect a Milanese ambience and quality traditional cuisine (Mon-Fri 12:00-14:45 & 19:00-22:45, closed Sat-Sun and mid-July-Aug, air-con, Via Santa Marta 11, 5-minute walk from the Duomo, near Pinacoteca Ambrosiana, tel. 02-8645-1991).

Ristorante Bruno serves Tuscan cuisine with a passion for fresh fish. This place impresses with its dressy waiters, hearty food, inexpensive desserts, and a fine self-serve antipasto buffet (a plate full of Tuscan specialties for €9). You can eat inside or on the sidewalk under fascist columns (Sun-Fri 12:00-15:00 & 19:00-23:00, closed Sat and Aug, moderate prices, air-con, Via M. Gonzaga 6, reservations wise, tel. 02-804-364). Giuseppe (from Volterra) and Graziella take good care of their clientele.

Hostaria Borromei is where Milanese yuppies go for power lunches to impress clients with market-fresh traditional Italian dishes. Dine under an awning of vines in an elegant mellow-yellow interior courtyard or in their cantina-chic dining rooms. Reservations are recommended (€15 pastas, €20 *secondi,* €3 cover and service charge, Mon-Fri 12:30-14:45 & 19:30-22:45, Sat-Sun 19:30-22:45, Via Borromei 4, tel. 02-8645-3760).

MILAN

Peck Italian Bar is a hit with the sophisticated office crowd, which mobs the place at lunch for its fast, excellent meals. It's owned by the same people who run the recommended high-end Peck deli (listed later), so be prepared to spend—this place's classiness alone makes it worth the money. Any time you find yourself among such a quality-conscious group of Milanesi, you know you're getting good food (€12 pastas, €18 *secondi*, Mon-Fri 7:30-20:30, Sat 9:00-20:30, closed Sun, Via Cantù 3, tel. 02-869-3017).

Dining at the Top of a Top-End Department Store with a Duomo View

The seventh floor of the La Rinascente department store, alongside the Duomo, has a Milanese-style food court, including a sunny outdoor terrace. You'll dine accompanied by views of the cathedral's rooftop (though anyone can pop up for a look at the cathedral). All three of the terrace-seating establishments recommended below are open 10:00-24:00, include cover charge with service, and can be accessed after store hours from elevators on Via S. Radegonda. (During open hours, you can go through the department store to take escalators to the top, but it's faster to take the elevators.)

Obikà is a swanky mozzarella bar offering this heavenly cheese in all its various forms—cow's milk, buffalo, and smoked—in salads or on splittable €10-19 antipasto sampler plates, accompanied by *salumi*, tapenades, and vegetables (another Obikà is north of the Duomo, see "In the Brera Neighborhood," later).

At the opposite end of the terrace, **Ristorante Maio** has pricey full-meal service (€13 pastas and pizzas, €22 *secondi*). In between is **Il Bar,** living-room cozy with cushy divans and low coffee tables, and serving light meals (salads, pasta), coffee, desserts, and cocktails.

Eating Simply

Latteria Cucina Vegetariana, with a 50-year history, is a bright hole-in-the-wall that serves a good vegetarian Italian lunch. This busy joint is overrun with tables where neighborhood workers enjoy soup, salads, pastas, and imaginative veggie entrées at affordable prices. Try the €13 *piatto misto al forno* for a delicious assortment of soufflés, quiches, and roasted and sautéed veggies (€10-15 meals, Mon-Sat 12:00-16:00, closed Sun, just off Via Torino at Via dell'Unione 6, 2 blocks southwest of the Duomo, tel. 02-874-401). Giorgio is a hit with camera-toting eaters.

Ciao, a self-service cafeteria, offers a low-stress, affordable meal above a fast-food arcade on Piazza del Duomo (daily 11:30-23:00, sometimes closes 22:30, inexpensive pasta and good salad bar, easy public WC). It's to the right of the Galleria entrance—

enter through the ground floor Autogrill and go up to the second floor.

Ristorante Rita is a smart budget option (€4-5 pastas and *secondi*) without the Italian fast-food feel. While the downstairs has a take-out place, there's a sleek, modern restaurant upstairs with good food and cafeteria prices (Mon-Sat 12:00-15:00, closed Sun, on Via Marconi between Piazza del Duomo and Piazza Diaz, tel. 02-8699-7387).

Fast-food cheapskates enjoy the best people-watching in Milan inside the Galleria at **McDonald's** (long hours daily, salad/pasta plate and tall orange juice for around €5).

Gelato: Floodlit Mary gazes down on the **Odeon Gelateria** from the top of the Duomo for good reason (next to a McDonald's on Piazza del Duomo, on far side of square opposite Duomo facade, open nightly until 24:00, off-season until 19:30 if it's raining). While Odeon is convenient, **Gelateria Grom** (two blocks toward La Scala on Via Santa Margherita) is the connoisseurs' choice.

Picnics Milan-style

For a fun adventure, assemble an elegant dinner picnic by hitting the colorful deli, cheese, and produce shops on Via Speronari.

The **Princi bakery** is mobbed with locals vying for focaccia, olive breadsticks, and luscious pastries. Notice the stacked-wood-oven action in the back. For most pastry items (like the brioche), pay the cashier first; for items sold by weight (such as pizza and cake), get it weighed before you pay. Consider a piping-hot pasta lunch (12:00-15:00 only) for €6 per plate (Mon-Sat 7:00-20:00, Sun 10:00-19:30, on Via Speronari, off Via Torino, a block southwest of Piazza del Duomo; a larger Princi bakery, more like a café, is near the Sforza Castle and is listed later).

Peck Gourmet Deli is an aristocratic deli with a fancy café/lunchroom/pastry and gelato shop upstairs, a gourmet grocery and *rosticceria* on the main level, and an expensive *enoteca* wine cellar in the basement. Even if all you can afford is the aroma, peek in. Check out the classic circa-1930 salami slicers and the gourmet assembly line in the kitchen in the back (Mon 15:30-19:30, Tue-Sat 9:15-19:30, closed Sun, Via Spadari 9, tel. 02-802-3161). The *rosticceria* serves fancy food to go for a superb picnic dinner in your hotel. It's delectable, beautiful, sold by weight (order by the *etto*—100-gram unit, 250 grams equals about a half-pound), and pricey. Try the risotto.

Luini Panzerotti serves up piping-hot mini-calzones *(panzerotti)* stuffed with mozzarella, tomatoes, ham, or whatever you like for €3-5 (Mon 10:00-15:00, Tue-Sat 10:00-20:00, closed Sun and Aug, Via S. Radegonda 16, tel. 02-8646-1917). From the back of the Duomo, head north and look for the lines of hungry locals out front. Order from the small menus posted behind the cash registers. Traditionally, Milanesi munch their hot little meals on nearby Piazza San Fedele. Don't overlook the *dolce* half of their menu—Panzerotti is popular for its sweets all day long.

Billa Superfresco Supermarket is within a few blocks of the Duomo (Mon-Sat 8:00-21:00, Sun 9:00-20:00, small deli on ground level, big supermarket in basement, on Via Torino at intersection with San Maurilio).

Near the Sforza Castle

Da Rita e Antonio is a favorite neighborhood restaurant, serving up well-prepared, reasonably priced Milanese specialties such as *costoletta* (breaded veal chop) and *ossobuco* (veal shank and risotto), as well as delicious €9 Neapolitan-style pizzas. It's a high-energy, brightly lit, dressy place, complete with waiters in bow ties and vests (€10 pastas, €20 *secondi*, great tiramisu, Tue-Fri and Sun 12:00-14:30 & 19:00-23:00, Sat 19:00-23:00, closed Mon, Via G. Puccini 2a, tel. 02-875-579). Facing the Sforza Castle from the end of Via Dante, it's about 100 yards to your left, built into the far side of the pink-and-white theater.

Le Briciole, run by the Campenella family, is small and folksy, drawing a local crowd for its quality Ligurian cuisine (pesto, seafood) and friendly family feel (€13 homemade pastas, Mon-Sat 12:15-14:30 & 19:15-22:30, closed Sun; Via Camperio 17, a block in front of castle, on small street at end of Via Dante, tel. 02-804-114; Anamaria and Sara).

Antica Osteria Milanese is a hardworking family place with a smart local following and spacious, stylish seating. They serve good-quality typical Milanese favorites (€8 pastas, €13 *secondi*, €2 cover, Mon-Sat 12:15-14:30 & 19:30-22:15, closed Sun, Via Camperio 12, tel. 02-861-367, Alessandro).

Fancy Via Dante Bars and Cafés: Thriving and central, Via Dante is lined with hardworking eateries where you can join locals for a lively lunch. Or, for about the price of your forgettable hotel breakfast, you can start your day watching the parade of Milanesi heading to work.

Princi bakery, near the castle, works the same as the one on Via Speronari (listed earlier), only it's more of a restaurant, with seating both inside and on the street. While the bakery and café are open all day, they serve hot cafeteria-style lunches only 12:00-15:30 (Mon-Sat 7:00-20:00, Sun 9:00-19:30, Via Ponte Vetero 10, tel. 02-7201-6067).

In the Brera Neighborhood

The Brera neighborhood surrounding the Church of St. Carmine is laced with narrow, inviting pedestrian streets. Make an evening of your visit by having an *aperitivo* (pre-dinner drink) with snacks at recommended Bar Brera or any bar—most serve munchies with pre-dinner drinks 17:00-21:00. Afterwards, stroll along restaurant row (Via Fiori Chiari) to survey the sidewalk cafés. To locate these eateries, see the map on page 330.

Obikà is a trendy mozzarella eatery with a sleek, minimalist sushi-bar feel. It features fresh cow, buffalo, and smoked mozzarella; big organic gourmet salads; and top-quality *salumi*. Show up at happy hour (daily 18:30-21:00) to enjoy a generous buffet and select from a long list of €10 drinks (€10 pastas, Mon-Fri 12:00-15:30 & 18:30-24:00, Sat-Sun 12:00-24:00, on corner of Via Mercato and Via Fiori Chiari, at Via Mercato 28, tel. 02-8645-0568).

Bar Brera, across the street from the Brera Art Gallery, serves salads, sandwiches, and pastas to throngs of art students. Come during the first hour of happy hour (daily 18:00-21:00), have a seat, order a drink, and then help yourself to the buffet (17:00-19:00), which has a generous variety of *antipasti*, from marinated veggies to prosciutto (buffet is free if you buy drinks; bar open daily 7:00-2:00 in the morning, great streetside seating, Via Brera 23, tel. 02-877-091).

Milan Connections

By Train
From Milano Centrale by Train to: Venice (at least hourly, most departures at :05 or :35 past the hour, most are direct on high-speed ES trains, 2.5-3.5 hours), **Florence** (hourly, 1.75 hours), **Genoa** (about hourly, 1.5-2 hours, also look for trains to La Spezia or Livorno that stop at Genoa), **Rome** (hourly, 3-8 hours, overnight possible), **Brindisi** (4 direct/day, 2 are night trains, 9-15 hours, more with changes), **Cinque Terre/La Spezia** (about hourly, 3 hours direct or with change in Genoa; trains from La Spezia to the villages go nearly hourly), **Cinque Terre/Monterosso al Mare** (8/day direct, otherwise hourly, 3-4 hours, more with change in Genoa), **Varenna** on Lake Como (1 hour; €6.25; small line direct to Lecco/Sondrio/Tirano leaves at 8:20, 10:20, 14:20, 16:20, 17:20, 19:20, 20:20, and 21:20; confirm these times—if you take a train at a time not listed here, it will require a change in Lecco and an extra 30 minutes; railpasses may not be valid on TRENORD trains), **Stresa** on Lake Maggiore (about hourly; 1-hour fast train may require reservations; also 1.5-hour slow train; also look for trains to Domodossola and some international destinations that stop at Stresa), **Como** (at least hourly, 30-90 minutes, boats go from Como to Varenna until about 19:00), **Naples** (direct trains hourly, 5 hours, more with change in Rome, overnight possible);

MILAN

see www.trenitalia.com for details.

From Milano Porta Garibaldi by Train to: Florence (8/day, 2 hours), **Rome** (8/day, 3.5 hours), **Naples** (5/day, 4.75 hours); see www.italotreno.it for details.

International Destinations: Amsterdam (hourly with several changes, fastest via Basel or Zurich, 15 hours), **Barcelona** (14-20 hours, several with 1-5 changes), **Bern** (change required in Brig, at least 3.5 hours), **Frankfurt** (change in Basel or Zurich, at least 9-10 hours), **London** (3/day, 12-18 hours with changes), **Munich** (7/day, 8-12 hours with changes), **Nice** (5/day with change in Ventimiglia, night train possible, 5-6.5 hours), **Paris** (2-3/day direct from Milano Porta Garibaldi, 7 hours; night train possible from Milano Centrale), **Lyon** (8/day, 6-8.5 hours with changes), **Vienna** (1/day direct, more with 1-3 changes, 11-14 hours). With dozens of budget airlines serving Europe's hub cities, flying to your international destination is often the most efficient and economical option (see "Cheap Flights," on page 1100).

By Plane

To get flight information for Malpensa or Linate airports or the current phone number of your airline, call 02-74851 or 02-232-323 and wait for English options, or check www.sea-aeroporti milano.it.

Malpensa Airport

Most international flights land at the manageable Malpensa Airport (airport code: MXP), 28 miles northwest of Milan. Customs guards fan you through, and even the security dog seems friendly. You'll most likely land at Terminal 1 (international flights), rather than Terminal 2 (charter flights); buses connect the two. Both have ATMs (at Terminal 1, between exit 4 and 5 at Banca Nazionale del Lavoro), banks, and exchange offices. Terminal 1 has a pharmacy, eateries, and a hotel reservation service disguised as a TI (daily 7:00-20:00; when you exit the baggage-carousel area, go right to reach services and exit; tel. 02-5858-0080). The tobacco shop sells phone cards—handy for confirming your hotel reservation.

You have three easy ways to get to downtown Milan: by train, shuttle bus, or taxi.

By Train: The Malpensa Express has two different lines serving downtown Milan. One line serves Milan's central train station—Milano Centrale—with rail links across Italy and beyond (€11, may have limited €7 special, 1-2/hour, 40-50 minutes). The other line zips between the airport and Milan's Cadorna station, which is both a Metro stop and a small train station; it's relatively close to the Duomo and Sforza Castle (€11, credit cards accepted, not covered by railpasses, 2/hour, 40 minutes; usually departs air-

Train Connections from Milan

port at :26 and :56 past the hour, generally departs Cadorna at :28 and :58 past the hour, tel. 800-500-005, www.malpensaexpress.it).

At the airport, as you pop out through customs, you'll see a *Treno per Malpensa* kiosk selling tickets and a big electric board on the wall indicating how many minutes until the next departure. Follow signs (*Treni* and *Malpensa Express*) down the stairs to the tracks. Check to make sure your train is going to the right destination—*Milano Centrale* or *Milano Cadorna*.

If you're leaving Milan to go to the airport, either go to Milan's central station or take the Metro to the Cadorna stop, surface, and buy a ticket at the Malpensa Express office in the station. Purchase your ticket before you board, or you'll pay €2.50 extra to buy it on the train. At Milano Centrale, check the departure board for the track number. Trains depart Cadorna from track 1; note that there are a few late-night departures to and from Cadorna by bus after midnight—ask when you buy your ticket. If your departure is by bus, the stop is outside the station; after you exit, find the stop 50 yards to the left on Via Paleocapa.

Malpensa Airport also has direct, high-speed rail links to **Florence** (2/day, 2.75 hours), **Rome** (1/day, 4.5 hours), and **Naples** (1/day, 6 hours). Check www.trenitalia.com for details.

By Shuttle Bus: Two bus companies offer virtually identical, competing services between Malpensa Airport and Milan's central train station. They each charge about €10 for the one-hour trip (buy ticket from driver) and depart from the same places: in front of the airport (outside exit 5, at stops 2 and 3) and from Piazza Luigi di Savoia (on the east side of Milan's central train station—with your back to the tracks, exit to the left). You'll generally find a bus leaving about every 20 minutes, every day, nearly all day (from downtown roughly 3:45-0:30 in the morning and from the airport roughly 5:30-00:15 in the morning; Malpensa Shuttle tel. 02-5858-3185, www.malpensashuttle.it; Autostradale tel. 02-3391-0794, www.autostradale.it). They're almost comically competitive, with one offering three rides for the price of two. Play around a bit and you may save some money.

By Taxi: Taxis into Milan cost a fixed rate of €90; avoid hustlers in airport halls (catch taxis outside exit 6). Considering how far the city is from the airport and how good the train and bus services are, Milan is the last place I'd take an airport taxi. To get from Milan to the airport, I'd take the Metro to the central train station (or a taxi to the Cadorna station) and then catch the Malpensa Express train.

Getting Between Malpensa and Linate: The Malpensa Shuttle company runs a bus between the airports about hourly (€13, from Malpensa to Linate runs 7:50-00:25 in the morning, 1.25 hours, catch bus outside Malpensa's exit 3, stop 20, buy tickets from Airport 2000 offices; from Linate to Malpensa buses depart 4:30-21:30, bus stops at Malpensa's Terminal 1—you must request stop if you need Terminal 2; tel. 02-5858-3185, www.malpensa shuttle.it).

Linate Airport

Most European flights land at Linate (airport code: LIN), five miles east of Milan. The airport has a bank (just past customs; ATM, decent rates) and a hotel-finding service disguised as a TI (daily 7:30-23:30, tel. 02-7020-0443).

You can get to downtown Milan by bus or taxi (or to Malpensa Airport by bus; see above).

By Bus: Two different buses—Starfly and ATM—take you from Linate Airport to downtown. The Starfly bus zips you to the central train station (€4, buy ticket from driver, 3/hour, 30 minutes, bus runs from airport 6:00-22:00, from station 6:00-21:30, leaves from east side of train station at Piazza Luigi di Savoia, tel. 02-587-237, www.autostradale.it). The cheaper ATM city bus gets you to the San Babila Metro stop (specifically to Corso Europa, just around the corner from Piazza San Babila and its Metro station; from here it's one stop to the Duomo on red line 1, direction: Molino Dorino or Bisceglie, or a 7-minute walk). The bus costs €1, departs every 10 minutes, and takes 20 minutes (departures leave city center 5:35-00:35, from airport 6:00-01:05, www.atm-mi.it). Either bus company works fine: Wait for the one that's handier to your hotel, or hop on the first one that shows up. From where it drops you off, take the Metro or a taxi to your hotel. Both buses leave the airport from outside the arrivals hall.

By Taxi: Taxis from Linate to the Duomo cost about €25.

Bergamo (Orio Al Serio) Airport

Some budget airlines, such as Ryanair and Wizzair, use Bergamo Airport as their Milan hub (about 30 miles from Milan, airport code: BGY, tel. 035-326-323, www.sacbo.it).

An express bus, Orioshuttle, connects the airport to Milan's central train station (€10, daily 4:00-23:15, 2/hour, 1 hour, buy tickets from driver or online at http://ticketonline.orioshuttle.com, tel. 035-330-706). A different company, Oriobus Express, covers the same route (€9.90, €15 round-trip, daily 4:30-1:00 in the morning, 2/hour, 1 hour, tel. 02-3391-0794, www.autostradale.it).

MILAN

THE CINQUE TERRE

The Cinque Terre (CHINK-weh TAY-reh), a remote chunk of the Italian Riviera, is the traffic-free, lowbrow, underappreciated alternative to the French Riviera. There's not a museum in sight—just sun, sea, sand (well, pebbles), wine, and pure, unadulterated Italy. Enjoy the villages, swimming, hiking, and evening romance of one of God's great gifts to tourism. For a home base, choose among five *(cinque)* villages, each of which fills a ravine with a lazy hive of human activity—calloused locals, sunburned travelers, and no Vespas. While the Cinque Terre is now discovered (and can be quite crowded midday, when tourist boats and cruise-ship excursions drop by), I've never seen happier, more relaxed tourists.

The chunk of coast was first described in medieval times as "the five lands." In the feudal era, this land was watched over by castles. Tiny communities grew up in their protective shadows, ready to run inside at the first hint of a Turkish Saracen pirate raid. Marauding pirates from North Africa were a persistent problem until about 1400. Many locals were kidnapped and ransomed or sold into slavery, and those who remained built fires on flat-roofed watchtowers to relay warnings—alerting the entire coast to imminent attacks. The last major raid was in 1545.

As the threat of pirates faded, the villages prospered, catching fish and cultivating grapes. Churches were enlarged with a growing population. But until the advent of tourism in this generation, the towns remained isolated. Even today, traditions survive, and each of the five villages comes with a distinct dialect and its own proud heritage.

Sadly, a few ugly, noisy Americans give tourism a bad name

The Cinque Terre

To A-12 Autostrada (Carrodano Exit)
To A-12 Autostrada (Brugnato Exit)
To Genova
SP-1
A-12
To La Spezia & Pisa
SP-566
Beverino
SP-1
To Sestri Levante, Santa Margherita & Genoa
2 Kilometers
2 Miles
Pignone
SP-1
Pian di Barca
Levanto
SP-370
To New Town (Fegina)
To Monterosso's Old Town
SP-38
SP-1
SP-63
This portion of road between Monterosso & Vernazza closed in 2013
Monterosso al Mare
SANDY BEACH
Vernazza
Corniglia
SP-51
Walking trail between Manarola & Corniglia closed in 2013
CORNIGLIA STATION
To La Spezia & A-12
Manarola
VIA DELL'AMORE
VIA LITORANEA
To La Spezia & A-12
Riomaggiore
Ligurian Sea
SP-370
To Portovenere

here. Even hip, young residents are put off by loud, drunken tourists. They say—and I agree—that the Cinque Terre is an exceptional place. It deserves a special dignity. Party in Viareggio or Portofino, but be mellow in the Cinque Terre. Talk softly. Help keep it clean. In spite of the tourist crowds, it's still a real community, and we are its guests.

In this chapter, I cover the five towns in order from south to north—from Riomaggiore to Monterosso. Since I still get the names of the towns mixed up, I think of them by number: #1 Riomaggiore (a workaday town), #2 Manarola (picturesque), #3 Corniglia (on a hilltop), #4 Vernazza (the region's cover girl, the most touristy and dramatic), and #5 Monterosso al Mare (the closest thing to a beach resort of the five towns).

Flooding Damage and Closures: On October 25, 2011, the Cinque Terre region was hit hard by a devastating flood (see sidebar on page 376). Two towns in particular—Monterosso and Vernazza—were seriously damaged. After a winter of hard work, both Monterosso and Vernazza reopened for tourism in 2012; nearly all of the trails, beaches, hotels, and restaurants of the entire Cinque Terre are wide-open for visitors, though a few businesses may lag behind. After this exhausting period of rebuilding, locals are offering visitors, who provide their livelihood, a warm and hearty welcome. For all the latest on the recovery in **Vernazza,** see www.savevernazza.com; for **Monterosso,** see www.rebuildmonte rosso.com.

Arrival in the Cinque Terre

By Train: Big, fast trains from elsewhere in Italy speed right past the Cinque Terre (though some stop in Monterosso and Riomaggiore). Unless you're com-

ing from a nearby town, you'll have to change trains at least once to reach Manarola, Corniglia, or Vernazza.

Generally, if you're coming from the north, you'll change trains in Sestri Levante or Genoa (specifically, Genoa's Piazza Principe station). If you're coming from the south or east, you'll most likely have to switch trains in La Spezia (change at La Spezia Centrale station—don't make the mistake of getting off at La Spezia Migliarina). No matter where you're coming from, it's best to check in the station before you leave to see your full schedule and route options (use the computerized kiosks or ask at a ticket window). Don't forget to validate your ticket by stamping it—ka-CHUNK!—in the machines located on train platforms and elsewhere in the station. Conductors here are notorious for levying stiff fines on forgetful tourists. For more information on riding the train between Cinque Terre towns, see "Getting Around the Cinque Terre," later.

By Car: If you're driving in the Cinque Terre (but, given the narrow roads and lack of parking, I wouldn't), see "Cinque Terre Connections" at the end of this chapter for directions.

Planning Your Time

The ideal stay is two or three full days; my recommended minimum stay is two nights and a completely uninterrupted day. The Cinque Terre is served by the local train from Genoa and La Spezia. Speed demons arrive in the morning, check their bags in La Spezia, take the five-hour hike through all five towns, laze away the afternoon on the beach or rock of their choice, and zoom away on the overnight train to somewhere back in the real world. But be warned: The Cinque Terre has a strange way of messing up your momentum. (The evidence is the number of Americans who have fallen in love with the region and/or one of its residents...and are still here.) Frankly, staying fewer than two nights is a mistake that you'll likely regret.

The towns are just a few minutes apart by hourly train or boat. There's no checklist of sights or experiences—just a hike, the towns themselves, and your fondest vacation desires. Study this chapter in advance and piece together your best day, mixing hiking, swimming, trains, and a boat ride. For the best light and coolest temperatures, start your hike early.

Market days perk up the towns from 8:00 to 13:00 on Tuesday in Vernazza, Wednesday in Levanto, Thursday in Monterosso and Sestri Levante, and Friday in La Spezia. (Levanto, Sestri Levante, and La Spezia are covered in the next chapter.)

The winter is really dead—most hotels and some restaurants close in December and January. The long Easter weekend (March 29-April 1 in 2013) and June and July are the peak of peak periods, the toughest times to find rooms. In spring, the towns can feel inundated with Italian school groups day-tripping on spring excursions (they can't afford to sleep in this expensive region).

For more information on the region, see www.cinqueterre.it.

Cinque Terre Park Cards

Visitors hiking between the towns on coastal trails need to pay a park entrance fee. This fee keeps the trails safe and open, and pays for viewpoints, picnic spots, WCs, and more. The popular coastal trail generates enough revenue to subsidize the development of trails and outdoor activities higher in the hills.

You have two options for covering the park fee: the Cinque Terre Park Card or the Cinque Terre Treno Park Card. Both are valid until midnight on the expiration date. Write your name on your card or risk a big fine. The configuration and pricing of these cards seem to always be in flux—be aware that the following details may change before your visit. Cuts to park funding may cause the park to stop offering these cards in 2013.

The **Cinque Terre Park Card** costs €5 for one day of hiking or €9 for two (covers trails and shuttle buses but not trains, buy at trailheads and at most train stations, no validation required).

The **Cinque Terre Treno Park Card** covers what the Cinque Terre Park Card does, plus the use of the local trains (from Levanto to La Spezia, including all Cinque Terre towns). It's sold at TIs inside train stations, but not at trailheads (€10/1 day, €19/2 days, validate card at train station by punching it in the yellow machine). With this card, you have to hike and take three train trips every day just to break even.

Cards cost a bit more on weekends and in August. Those under 18 or over 70 get a discount, as do families of four or more (see www.parconazionale5terre.it).

Getting Around the Cinque Terre

Within the Cinque Terre, you can connect towns in three ways: by train, boat, or foot. Trains are cheaper, boats are more scenic, and hiking lets you enjoy more pasta. From a practical point of view, you should consider supplementing the often frustrating train with the sometimes more convenient boat. The trail between Riomaggiore and Manarola is a delight and takes just a few minutes, making the train not worth waiting for. The trail from Manarola to Corniglia is likely closed through much of 2013 (after a huge 2011 landslide).

By Train

Along the coast here, trains go in only two directions: "*per* [to] *Genova*" (the Italian spelling of Genoa), northbound; or "*per La Spezia*," southbound. Assuming you're on vacation, accept the unpredictability of Cinque Terre trains (they're often late...unless you are, too—in which case they're on time). Relax while you wait—buy a cup of coffee at a station bar. When the train comes (know which direction to look for: La Spezia or Genova), casu-

ally walk over and hop on. This is especially easy in Monterosso, with its fine café-with-a-view on track #1 (direction: Milano/Genova), and in Vernazza, where you can hang out at the Blue Marlin Bar with a prepaid drink and dash when the train pulls in.

Use the handy TV monitors in the station, which display upcoming departures for the next hour or so (as well as notes about which track they're on and whether they're late—*in ritardo*). Most of the northbound trains that stop at all Cinque Terre towns and are headed toward Genova will list Sestri Levante as the *destinazione*.

By train, the five towns are just a few minutes apart. Know your stop. Once the train leaves the town just before your destination, go to the door and get ready to slip out before the mobs flood in, making it impossible to get off. Words to the wise for novice tourists, who often miss their stop: The stations are small and the trains are long, so (especially in Vernazza) you might have to get off deep in a tunnel. Also, the doors don't open automatically—you may have to open the handle of the door yourself (twist the black handle, or lift up the red one). If a door isn't working, go quickly to the next car to leave. (When leaving a town by train, if you find the platform jammed with people, walk down the platform into the tunnel, where things quiet down.)

It costs about €1.80 per ride within the region. Tickets are good for 75 minutes in one direction, so you could conceivably use one for a brief stopover. To make the ticket good for six hours (in one direction only), you need to buy a ticket good for 40 kilometers

Events in the Cinque Terre in 2013

For more festival information, check www.cinqueterre.it and www.turismoinliguria.it. The food festivals in particular are subject to change.

March 31-April 1	All towns: Easter Sunday and Monday
April 25	All towns: Liberation Day (stay away from the Cinque Terre this day, as locals literally shut down the trails)
May 1	All towns: Labor Day (another local holiday that packs the place)
Mid-May	Monterosso: Lemon Festival (usually the third Sunday)
May 9	All towns: Ascension Day
May 30	Monterosso: Feast of Corpus Domini (procession on carpet of flowers at 18:00)
Mid-June	Monterosso: Anchovy Festival
June 24	Riomaggiore and Monterosso: Feast day of St. John the Baptist (procession and fireworks; big fire on Monterosso's old town beach the day before)
June 29	Corniglia: Feast day of Sts. Peter and Paul
July 20	Vernazza: Feast day of patron saint, St. Margaret, with fireworks
Aug 10	Manarola: Feast day of patron saint, St. Lawrence
Aug 14	Monterosso: Fireworks on eve of feast of the Assumption
Aug 15	All towns: Feast of the Assumption (*Ferragosto*)
Mid-Sept	Monterosso: Anchovies and Olive Oil Festival (usually the second weekend)

(€3.50). Stamp the ticket at the station machine before you board. Machines are often broken or out of ink (good luck explaining that to conductors), but riding without a validated ticket can be expensive (usually €50). You can buy several tickets at once and use them as you like, validating as you go. If you have a Eurail Pass, don't spend one of your valuable travel days on the cheap Cinque Terre.

Cinque Terre Train Schedule: Since the train is the Cinque Terre's lifeline, many shops and restaurants post the current schedule, and most hotels offer copies of it (one also comes with the Cinque Terre Park Card). But beware: The printed schedules can be misleading (half the listed departures don't go every day); the monitors in the stations are your best source of actual, current departure information. Note that fast trains leaving La Spezia zip right through the Cinque Terre; some stop only in Monterosso (town #5) and Riomaggiore (town #1). But any train that stops in Manarola, Corniglia, and Vernazza (towns #2, #3, and #4)—including the trains on the schedule below—will stop in all five towns.

The times below are accurate as of this printing, but confirm schedules locally. These are the daily train times (a few do not run on Sunday; more trains are added in the busiest season, June-Sept):

Trains leave La Spezia Centrale for all or most of the Cinque Terre villages at 7:12, 10:06, 11:10, 12:00, 13:15, 14:09, 15:10, 15:58, 17:10, 17:20, 18:06, 19:10, 20:18, 21:25, 23:10, and 00:50.

Going back to La Spezia, trains leave Monterosso at 6:20, 8:15, 9:29, 11:00, 11:55, 12:19, 13:28, 14:20, 15:22, 16:17, 17:30, 18:18, 19:22, 20:07 or 20:20, 21:32, 22:22, and 23:45 (these same trains depart Vernazza about four minutes later).

Again, convenient TV monitors posted at several places in each station clearly show exactly what times the next trains are leaving in each direction (and, if they're late, how late they are expected to be). I trust these monitors much more than my ability to read any printed schedule.

By Boat

From Easter through October, a daily boat service connects Monterosso, Vernazza, Manarola, Riomaggiore, and Portovenere.

Boats provide a scenic way to get from town to town and survey what you just hiked. And boats offer the only efficient way to visit the nearby resort of Portovenere (see next chapter; the alternative is a tedious train-bus connection via La Spezia). In peaceful weather, the boats can be more reliable than the trains, but if seas are rough, they don't run at all. Because the boats nose in and tourists have to gingerly disembark onto little more than a plank, even a small chop can cancel some or all of the stops.

I see the tour boats as a syringe, injecting each town with a boost of euros. The towns are addicted, and they shoot up hourly through the summer. (Between 10:00 and 15:00—especially on weekends—masses of gawkers unload from boats, tour buses, and cruise ships, inundating the villages and changing the feel of the region.)

Boats depart Monterosso about hourly (10:30-17:00), stopping at the Cinque Terre towns (except at Corniglia) and ending up an hour later in Portovenere. (Portovenere-Monterosso boats run 8:50-17:00.) The ticket price depends on the length of the boat ride (short hops-€4, longer hops-€8, one-way with stops-€10, five-town all-day pass-€15). Round-trip tickets are slightly cheaper than two one-way trips. You can buy tickets at little stands at each town's harbor (tel. 0187-732-987 and 0187-818-440). Another all-day boat pass for €25 extends to Portovenere and includes a 40-minute scenic ride around three small islands (2/day). Boats are not covered by the Cinque Terre Park Card. Boat schedules are posted at docks, harbor bars, Cinque Terre park offices, and hotels (www .navigazionegolfodeipoeti.it).

By Shuttle Bus
Green shuttle buses connect each Cinque Terre town with its distant parking lot and various points in the hills (for example, a shuttle runs from Corniglia's train station to its hilltop town center). Note that these shuttle buses do not connect the towns with each other. Most rides cost €1.50 (and are covered by the Cinque Terre Park Card)—pick up bus schedules from TIs or note the times posted on bus doors and at bus stops. Departures often coordinate with train arrival times. Some (but not all) departures from Vernazza, Manarola, and Riomaggiore go beyond the parking lots and high into the hills. To soak in the scenery, you can pay for a round-trip ride and just cruise both ways (30-45 minutes round-trip). Be aware that cuts to park funding may eliminate or reduce the frequency of these buses in 2013.

Hiking the Cinque Terre
All five towns are connected by good trails, marked with red-and-white paint, white arrows, and some signs. You'll experience the area's best by hiking all the way from one end to the other (although, unfortunately, the Manarola-Corniglia stretch is likely

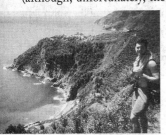

closed in 2013). While you can detour to dramatic hilltop sanctuaries, I'd keep it simple by following trail #2—the low route between the villages. The entire seven-mile hike can be done in about four hours, but allow five for dawdling. Germans (with their task-oriented *Alpenstock* walking sticks) are notorious for marching too fast through the region. Take it slow...smell the cactus flowers and herbs, notice the lizards, listen to birds singing in the olive groves, and enjoy vistas on all sides.

Trails can be closed in bad weather or because of landslides.

The Cinque Terre National Park: Peaks and Valleys

Since its creation in 1999, the Cinque Terre National Marine Park has brought plenty of good things to the area: money (visitors pay about €5 a day to hike the trails), new regulations to protect wildlife, and improved walkways, trails, beaches, breakwaters, and docks. Travelers have been able to take advantage of park-sponsored information centers and tiny folk museums.

The vision for the park was exciting—to have everyone thinking creatively about how to improve the area for the good of nature, the local communities, and their many visitors. Park administrators were well on their way to creating something unique in Europe. But, as so often happens in Italy, power and money corrupted the men entrusted to lead. Those working under them could see what was happening—but rather than try to stop the sleaze, many of them scrambled to get in on the easy money. The result is a vision gone completely out of focus and a park that's in disarray.

The park president, Franco Bonanini, was a powerful man—nicknamed "The Pharaoh" for his grandiose ideas. He initially impressed people as a visionary committed to the region and its precious park. But with a group of local bureaucrats—including Riomaggiore's mayor—he created a medieval-style system of favorites and enemies. This cabal was focused more on preserving their power than improving the park. As they started and stopped construction projects, funneling money here and there,

Remember that hikers need to pay a fee to enter the trails (see "Cinque Terre Park Cards," earlier). If you're hiking the entire five-town route, consider that the trail between Riomaggiore (#1) and Manarola (#2) is easiest. The hike between Manarola and Corniglia (#3) has minor hills (likely closed in 2013). The trail from Corniglia to Vernazza (#4) is demanding, and the path from Vernazza to Monterosso (#5) is the most challenging. For that hike, you might want to start in Monterosso in order to tackle the toughest section while you're fresh—and to enjoy the region's most dramatic scenery as you approach Vernazza. If you plan to hike all five towns, it's best to start early in the day, beginning at Monterosso (#5) and ending with Riomaggiore (#1).

Other than the wide, easy Riomaggiore-Manarola segment, the trail is generally narrow, steep, rocky, and comes with lots of steps. Be warned that I get many emails from readers who say the trail was tougher than they expected. The rocks and metal grates can be slippery in the rain. While the trail is a bit of a challenge, it's perfectly doable for any fit hiker...and worth the sweat.

Maps aren't necessary for the basic coastal hikes described

they derailed the park vision. In 2011, they were at last removed from power, but the damage had been done. Plans for future projects were scuttled, and improvements already in place or underway—information offices, baggage deposits, mountain-biking opportunities, little museums, elevators for people with limited mobility, and even maintenance of the trails—were abandoned. The persistent woes were only made more complicated by the floods in October of 2011.

Today, the park is run by a man from the central government whose plan, it seems, is to run the park as a business. But a park is a park, not a business. Ironically—and sadly, for the residents—using the park to wring money out of visitors while giving little back is not good for the livelihoods of the region's hardworking townspeople. For 2013, no one knows exactly how the park will be functioning (for the latest, see www.parconazionale5terre.it).

Despite the hassles, the Cinque Terre is still my favorite chunk of Mediterranean coastline. Thankfully, the villages and dramatic stretches of land between them transcend any corrupt modern-day pharaohs. The people are endearing. The food, culture, and natural setting are uniquely enjoyable. But what's happened is disheartening. I thrill at the thought of people working together for a grand and noble vision that helps a community's economy by wisely treating a park as a park, rather than a moneymaker. And so far, the Cinque Terre has failed in that regard.

here. But for the expanded version of this hike (12 hours, from Portovenere to Levanto) and more serious hikes in the high country, pick up a good hiking map (about €5, sold everywhere). The *Cinque Terre Walking Guide* (by a German publisher, but sold locally in an English-language edition) is worth seeking out for anyone planning a serious hike.

To leave the park cleaner than you found it, bring a plastic bag *(sacchetto di plastica)* and pick up a little trail trash along the way. It would be great if American visitors—who get so much joy out of this region—were known for this good deed.

Riomaggiore-Manarola (20 minutes): Facing the front of the train station in Riomaggiore (#1), go up the stairs to the right, following signs for *Via dell'Amore*. The photo-worthy promenade—wide enough for baby strollers—winds along the coast to

Via dell'Amore

The Cinque Terre towns were extremely isolated until the last century. Villagers rarely married anyone from outside their town. After the blasting of a second train line in the 1920s, a trail was made between the first two towns: Riomaggiore and Manarola. The gunpowder warehouses built on each end, safely away from the townspeople, house cute little bars today.

Happy with the trail, the villagers asked that it be improved as a permanent connection between neighbors. But persistent landslides kept the trail closed more often than it was open. After World War II, the trail was reopened, and became established as a lovers' meeting point for boys and girls from the two towns. (After one extended closure in 1949, the trail was reopened for a Christmas marriage.) A journalist who noticed all the amorous graffiti along the path coined the trail's now-established name, Via dell'Amore: "Pathway of Love."

This new lane changed the social dynamics between the two villages, and made life much more fun and interesting for courting couples. Today, many tourists are put off by the cluttered graffiti that lines the trail. But it's all part of the history of the Cinque Terre's little lovers' lane.

You'll see padlocks locked to wires, cables, and fences. Closing a padlock with your lover at a lovey-dovey spot—often a bridge—is a common ritual in Italy (it was re-popularized by a teen novel a few years ago). In case you're so inclined, the hardware store next to Bar Centrale in Riomaggiore sells these locks. (You'll notice many of the locks come with the park logo.)

Major construction work—including the addition in 1994 of tunnels—has made the trail safer and keeps it open permanently. Notice how the brick-lined arcades match the train tunnel below. Rock-climbers from the north ("Dolomite spiders") were imported to help with the treacherous construction work. As you hike, look up and notice the massive steel netting bolted to the cliffside. Look down at the boulders that fell before the nets were added, and up at the boulders that have been caught...and be thankful for those Dolomite spiders.

Continuing the romance theme, benches along the way are named for lovers from Greek mythology. The many agave plants sport carved love notes—etched by amorous couples who likely don't know that the plant, which flowers once and then dies, is named for a tragic Greek story.

Manarola (#2). While there's no beach along the trail, stairs lead down to sunbathing rocks. A long tunnel and mega-nets protect hikers from mean-spirited falling rocks. A wine bar—Bar & Vini A Piè de Mà—is located at the Riomaggiore trailhead and offers light meals, awesome town views, and clever boat storage under the train tracks (for more info, see page 364). There's a picnic zone with a water fountain, shade, and a seagull that must have been human in a previous life hanging out just above the Manarola station (WC at Manarola station).

Manarola-Corniglia (45 minutes, likely closed in 2013): The walk from Manarola (#2) to Corniglia (#3) is a little longer, more rugged, and steeper than the Via dell'Amore. It's also less romantic. To avoid the last stretch (switchback stairs leading up to the hill-capping town of Corniglia), end your hike at Corniglia's train station and catch the shuttle bus to the town center (2/hour, €1.50, free with Cinque Terre Park Card, usually timed to meet the trains).

Corniglia-Vernazza (1.5 hours): The hike from Corniglia (#3) to Vernazza (#4)—the wildest and greenest section of the coast—is very rewarding but very hilly (going the other direction, from Vernazza to Corniglia, is steeper). From the Corniglia station and beach, zigzag up to the town (via the steep stairs, the longer road, or the shuttle bus). Ten minutes past Corniglia, toward Vernazza, you'll see Guvano beach far beneath you (once the region's nude beach). The scenic trail leads past a bar and picnic tables, through lots of fragrant and flowery vegetation, into Vernazza. If you need a break before reaching Vernazza, stop by Franco's Ristorante and Bar la Torre; it has a small menu but big views.

Vernazza-Monterosso (1.5 hours): The trail from Vernazza (#4) to Monterosso (#5) is a scenic up-and-down-a-lot trek and the most challenging of the bunch. Trails are narrow, steep, and crumbly, with a lot of steps (some readers report "very dangerous"), but easy to follow. Locals frown on camping at the picnic tables located midway. The views just out of Vernazza, looking back at the town, are spectacular.

Longer Hikes: Above the trails that run between the towns, higher-elevation hikes crisscross the region. Shuttle buses make the going easier, connecting coastal villages and trailheads in the hills. Ask locally about the more difficult six-mile inland hike to Volastra. This tiny village, perched between Manarola and Corniglia, hosts lots of Germans and Italians in the summertime. Just below its town center, in the hamlet of Groppo, is the Cinque Terre Cooperative Winery (open daily). For the whole trip on the high road between Manarola and Corniglia, allow two hours one-way. In return, you'll get sweeping views and a closer look at the vineyards. Shuttle buses run from Manarola to Volastra (€2.50 or free with Cinque Terre Park Card, pick up schedule from park office, 8/day, more departures in summer, 15 minutes); consider taking the bus up and hiking down.

Swimming, Kayaking, and Biking

Every town in the Cinque Terre has a beach or a rocky place to swim. Monterosso has the biggest and sandiest beach, with umbrellas and beach-use fees (but it's free where there are no umbrellas). Vernazza's is tiny—better for sunning than swimming. Manarola and Riomaggiore have the worst beaches (no sand), but Manarola offers the best deep-water swimming.

Wear your walking shoes and pack your swim gear. Several of the beaches have showers (no shampoo, please). Underwater sight-seeing is full of fish—goggles are sold in local shops. Sea urchins can be a problem if you walk on the rocks, and sometimes jellyfish wash up on the pebbles.

You can rent kayaks or boats in Riomaggiore, Vernazza, and Monterosso. (For details, see individual town listings in this chapter.) Some readers say kayaking can be dangerous—the kayaks tip easily, training is not provided, and lifejackets are not required.

Sleeping in the Cinque Terre

If you think too many people have my book, avoid Vernazza. You get fewer crowds and better value for your money in other towns. Monterosso is a good choice for sun-worshipping softies, those who prefer the ease of a real hotel, and the younger crowd (more nightlife). Hermits, anarchists, wine lovers, and mountain goats like Corniglia. Sophisticated Italians and Germans choose Manarola. Riomaggiore—bigger than Vernazza and less resorty than Monterosso—has the cheapest beds.

While the Cinque Terre is too rugged for the mobs that ravage the Spanish and French coasts, it's popular with Italians, Germans, and in-the-know Americans. Hotels charge more and are packed on holidays (including Easter); in June, July, and September; and on Fridays and Saturdays all summer. (With global warming, swel-tering August is no longer considered peak season on this stretch of the Riviera.) While you can find doubles for €65 or €70 most of the season, you'll pay extra (around €80) in June and July. The prices I've listed are the maximum for April through October. For a terrace or view, you might pay an extra €20 or more. Apartments for four can be economical for families—figure around €120.

It's smart to reserve your room in advance in May, June, July, and September, and on weekends and holidays. At other times, you can land a double room on any day by just arriving in town (ideally by noon) and asking around at bars and restaurants, or simply by approaching locals on the street. Many travelers enjoy the opportunity to shop around a bit and get the best price by bargaining. Private rooms—called *affitta camere*—are no longer an intimate stay with a family. They are generally comfortable apartments (often with small kitchens) where you get the key and come and go as you like, rarely seeing your landlord. Many landowners rent the buildings by the year to local managers, who then attempt to make a profit by filling them night after night with tourists. While air-conditioning is essential in the summer elsewhere in Italy, in the breezy Cinque Terre you can generally manage fine without it.

For the best value, visit several private rooms and snare the best. Going direct cuts out the middleman and softens prices. Staying more than one night gives you bargaining leverage. Plan on paying cash. Private rooms are generally bigger and more comfortable than those offered by pensions and have the same privacy as a hotel room.

If you want the security of a reservation, make it at a hotel long in advance (smaller places generally don't take reservations very far ahead). Query by email, not fax. If you do reserve, honor your reservation (or, if you must cancel, do it as early as possible). Since people renting rooms usually don't take deposits, they lose money if you don't show up.

Eating in the Cinque Terre

Hanging out at a sea-view restaurant while sampling local specialties could become one of your favorite memories.

Tegame alla Vernazza is the most typical main course in Vernazza: anchovies, potatoes, tomatoes, white wine, oil, and herbs. Anchovies (*acciughe*; ah-CHOO-gay) are ideally served the day they're caught. There's nothing cool about being an anchovy virgin. If you've always hated anchovies (the harsh, cured-in-salt American kind), try them fresh here. *Pansotti* are ravioli with ricotta and a mixture of greens, often served with a walnut sauce... delightful and filling.

While antipasto means cheese and salami in Tuscany, here you'll get *antipasti frutti di mare* (or *antipasti misti*), a plate of mixed "fruits of the sea" and a fine way to start a meal. Many restaurants are particularly proud of their *antipasti frutti di mare*—it's how they show off. For two diners, splitting one of these and a pasta dish can be plenty.

This region is the birthplace of pesto. Basil, which loves the temperate Ligurian climate, is ground with cheese (half parmigiano cow cheese and half pecorino sheep cheese), garlic, olive oil, and pine nuts, and then poured over pasta. Try it on spaghetti, *trenette* (the long, flat Ligurian noodle), or *trofie* (made of flour with a bit of potato, designed specifically for pesto to cling to). Many also like pesto lasagna, always made with white sauce, never red. If you become addicted, small jars of pesto are sold in the local grocery stores and gift shops. If it's refrigerated, it's fresh; this is what you want if you're eating it today. For taking home, get the jar-on-a-shelf pesto.

Focaccia, the tasty pillowy bread, also originates here in Liguria. Locals say the best focaccia is made between the Cinque Terre and Genoa. It's simply flatbread with olive oil and salt. The baker roughs up the dough with finger holes, then bakes it. Focaccia comes plain or with onions, sage, or olive bits, and is a local favorite for a snack on the beach. Bakeries sell it in rounds or slices by the weight (a portion is about 100 grams, or *un etto*).

Farinata, a humble fried-bread snack, is made from chickpea meal, water, oil, and pepper, and baked on a copper tray in a wood-burning stove. *Farinata* is sold at pizza and focaccia places.

The *vino delle Cinque Terre*, while not one of Italy's top wines, flows cheap and easy throughout the region. It's white—great with seafood. For a sweet dessert wine, the *sciacchetrà* wine is worth the splurge (€4 per small glass, often served with a cookie). You could order the fun dessert *torta della nonna* ("grandmother's cake") and dunk chunks of it into your glass. Aged *sciacchetrà* is dry and costly (up to €12/glass). While 10 kilos of grapes yield seven liters of local wine, *sciacchetrà* is made from near-raisins, and 10 kilos of grapes make only 1.5 liters of *sciacchetrà*. The word means "push and pull"—push in lots of grapes, pull out the best wine. If your room is up a lot of steps, be warned: *Sciacchetrà* is 18 percent alcohol, while regular wine is only 11 percent.

In the cool, calm evening, sit on Vernazza's breakwater with a glass of wine and watch the phosphorescence in the waves.

Nightlife in the Cinque Terre

While the Cinque Terre is certainly not noted for bumping beach-town nightlife like nearby Viareggio, you'll find some sort of travel-tale-telling hub in Monterosso, Vernazza, and Riomaggiore (Manarola and Corniglia are sleepy). Monterosso (where bars can stay open until 2:00 in the morning) has a lively scene, especially in the summertime—but no *discoteca* yet. In Vernazza, the nightlife centers in the bars on the waterfront piazza, which is the small-town-style place to "see and be seen." A town law requires all bars to shut by midnight. Bar Centrale in Riomaggiore is, well, the central place for cocktails and meeting fellow travelers.

(For details, see the "Nightlife" sections for these three villages.) Wherever your night adventures take you, have fun, but please remember that residents live upstairs.

Helpful Hints for the Cinque Terre

Tourist and Park Information: Each town (except Corniglia) has a well-staffed TI and park office (listed throughout this chapter). Be aware that budget cuts may cause TIs and park offices to reduce their hours or close in 2013.

Money: Banks and ATMs are plentiful throughout the region.

Baggage Storage: You can store bags at La Spezia's train station (€3/12 hours, 8:00-22:00, see page 446) and at Lucia's Lavarapido in Monterosso (€5/day).

Services: Every train station has a handy public WC. Otherwise, pop into a bar or restaurant.

Taxi: Cinqueterre Taxi covers all five towns (mobile 328-583-4969, www.cinqueterretaxi.com, info@cinqueterretaxi.com).

Local Guides: Andrea Bordigoni is both knowledgeable and a delight (€110/half-day, €175/day, mobile 347-972-3317, bordigo @inwind.it). Other local guides are **Marco Brizzi** (mobile 328-694-2847, marco_brizzi@yahoo.it) and **Paola Tommarchi** (paolatomma@alice.it).

Booking Agency: Miriana and Filippo at **Cinque Terre Riviera** book rooms in the Cinque Terre towns, Portovenere, and La Spezia for a 10 percent markup over the list price (can also arrange transportation, cooking classes, and weddings; Via Picedi 18 in La Spezia; tel. 0187-520-702, Miriana—mobile 340-794-7358, Filippo—mobile 393-939-1901, www .cinqueterreriviera.com, info@cinqueterreriviera.com, English spoken).

Riomaggiore (Town #1)

THE CINQUE TERRE

The most substantial non-resort town of the group, Riomaggiore is a disappointment from the train station. But once you leave that neighborhood, you'll stumble upon a fascinating tangle of pastel homes leaning on each other like drunken sailors. Just walk through the tunnel next to the train tracks, and you'll discover a more real, laid-back, and workaday town than its touristy neighbors.

Orientation to Riomaggiore

Tourist Information

The TI is in the train station at the ticket desk (daily 8:00-18:00, tel. 0187-920-633). If the TI in the station is crowded, buy your hiking pass at the Cinque Terre park shop/information office next door by the mural (daily 8:00-19:30, tel. 0187-760-515, netpoint riomaggiore@parconazionale5terre.it). For an informal information source, try Ivo and Alberto, who run Bar Centrale (see "Nightlife in Riomaggiore," later).

Arrival in Riomaggiore

The bus shuttles locals and tourists up and down Riomaggiore's steep main street and continues to the parking lot outside town (€1.50 one-way, €2.50 round-trip, free with Cinque Terre Park Card, 2/hour but almost comically erratic, main stop at the fork of Via Colombo and Via Malborghetto, or flag it down as it passes).

Helpful Hints

Internet Access: The **park shop/information office** has four Internet terminals upstairs, plus Wi-Fi (€1.50/20 minutes, daily May-Sept 8:00-22:00, Oct-April 8:00-19:30). **La Zorza Café** and **Bar Centrale** both offer free Wi-Fi with the purchase of a drink (see "Nightlife in Riomaggiore," later).

Laundry: A self-service launderette is on the main street (€3.50/wash, €3.50/dry, daily 9:00-19:30, run by Edi's Rooms next door, Via Colombo 111).

Self-Guided Walk

Welcome to Riomaggiore

Here's an easy loop trip that maximizes views and minimizes uphill walking.

• *Start at the train station. (If you arrive by boat, cross beneath the tracks and take a left, then hike through the tunnel along the tracks to reach the station.) You'll come to some...*

Colorful Murals: These murals, with subjects modeled after real-life Riomaggiorians, glorify the nameless workers who constructed the nearly 300 million cubic feet of dry-stone walls (without cement) that run throughout the Cinque Terre. These walls give the region its characteristic *muri a secco* terracing for vineyards and olive groves. The murals, done by Argentinean artist Silvio Benedetto, are well-explained in English.

• *Head to the railway tunnel entrance, and ride the elevator to the top of town (€0.50 or €1 family ticket, free with Cinque Terre Park Card, daily 8:00-19:45). If the elevator is closed (likely), hike around to the left, following the road up and then right to the...*

Top o' the Town: Here you're treated to spectacular sea views. To continue the viewfest, go right and follow the walkway (ignore the steps marked *Marina Seacoast* that lead to the harbor). It's a five-minute level stroll to the church. You'll pass under the offices of the disgraced national park president and the city hall (flying two flags), with murals celebrating the heroic grape-pickers and fishermen of the region (also by Silvio Benedetto).

• *Before reaching the church, pause to enjoy the...*

Town View: The major river of this region once ran through this valley, as implied by the name Riomaggiore (local dialect for "river" and "major"). As in the other Cinque Terre towns, the river ravine is now paved over, and the romantic arched bridges that once connected the two sides have been replaced by a practical modern road.

Notice the lack of ugly aerial antennae. In the 1980s, every residence got cable. Now, the TV tower on the hilltop behind the church steeple brings the modern world into each home. The church was rebuilt in 1870, but was first established in 1340. It's dedicated to St. John the Baptist, the patron saint of Genoa, the maritime republic that once dominated the region.

• *Continue past the church down to Riomaggiore's main street, named...*

Via Colombo: Walk about 30 feet beyond the WC, go down the stairs, and—if it's open—pop into the tiny Cinque Terre Antiche museum (€0.50, free with Cinque Terre Park Card, generally closed). Inside, sit down for a few minutes to watch a circa-1950 video of the Cinque Terre.

Continuing down Via Colombo, you'll pass a bakery, a couple of grocery shops, and the self-service laundry. There's homemade gelato next to the Bar Centrale. Above where Via Colombo dead-ends, a park-like square built over the train tracks gives the children of the town a level bit of land upon which to kick their soccer balls. The murals above celebrate the great-grandparents of these very children—the salt-of-the-earth locals who earned a humble living before the age of tourism. To the left, stairs lead down to the Marina neighborhood, with the harbor, the boat dock, a 200-yard trail to the beach *(spiaggia)*, and an inviting little art gallery. To the right of the stairs is the pedestrian tunnel, running alongside the tracks, which takes you directly back to the station and the trail to the other towns. From here, you can take a train, hop a boat, or hike to your next destination.

THE CINQUE TERRE

To Manarola

VIA DELL'AMORE

TRAIN STATION

Cliffs

MURALS

CINQUE TERRE INFO

ELEVATOR TO HIGH ROAD

PECUNIA

VIA

VIA SIGNORINI

VIA

PEDESTRIAN TUNNEL

VIA SANT'ANTONIO

PUNTA

Cliffs

Harbor

BOAT DOCK

VIA SAN GIACOMO

BREAKWATER

BOAT TICKETS

Ligurian Sea

1 Locanda del Sole
2 Locanda Ca' dei Duxi
3 Hotel & Café la Zorza
4 Locanda dalla Compagnia
5 Riomaggiore Reservations
6 La Dolce Vita Rooms
7 Edi's Rooms & Launderette
8 Camere Patrizia
9 Trattoria la Grotta
10 La Lanterna Ristorante
11 Te la Do Io la Merenda Snack Bar
12 Enoteca & Ristorante Dau Cila
13 Bar & Vini A Piè de Mà
14 Bar Centrale & Gelateria
15 Madonna di Montenero Trail
16 Park Office Kiosk

THE CINQUE TERRE

Sights in Riomaggiore

Beach—Riomaggiore's rugged and tiny "beach" is rocky, but it's clean and peaceful. Take a two-minute walk from the harbor: Face the harbor, then follow the path to your left. Passing the rugged boat landing, stay on the path to the pebbly beach. There's a shower there in the summer, and another closer to town by the boat landing—where many enjoying sunning on and jumping from the rocks.

Kayaks and Water Sports—The town has a diving center (scuba, snorkeling, kayaks; office down the stairs and under the tracks on Via San Giacomo, daily May-Sept 9:00-18:00, tel. 0187-920-011, www.5terrediving.it).

Hikes—The cliff-hanging Torre Guardiola trail, a steep 20-minute climb from the beach up to old WWII bunkers and a hilltop botanical pathway, has been closed because of a rock slide. Another trail rises from Riomaggiore scenically to the 14th-century Madonna di Montenero sanctuary, high above the town (45 minutes, take the main road inland until you see signs, or ride the green shuttle bus

Riomaggiore

12 minutes from the town center to the sanctuary trail, then walk uphill 10 minutes).

Nightlife in Riomaggiore

Bar Centrale, run by sociable Ivo, Alberto, and the gang, offers "nightlife" any time of day—making it a good stop for Italian breakfast and music. Ivo, who lived in San Francisco, fills his bar with San Franciscan rock and a fun-loving vibe. During the day, this is a shaded place to relax with other travelers; it feels a little like the village's living room. At night, it offers the younger set the liveliest action (and best mojitos) in town. They also serve €5 fast-food pastas and microwaved pizzas, and a menu featuring comfort food for homesick Americans (daily 7:30-24:00 or later, closed Mon in winter, free Wi-Fi with drink, in the town center at Via Colombo 144, tel. 0187-920-208). There's a good *gelateria* next door.

Enoteca & Ristorante Dau Cila, a cool little hideaway with a mellow jazz-and-Brazilian-lounge ambience down at the miniscule harbor, is a counterpoint to wild Bar Centrale. It's cool for

THE CINQUE TERRE

cocktails and open nightly until 24:00 (snacks and meals, fine wine by the glass; see "Eating in Riomaggiore," later).

Bar & Vini A Piè de Mà, at the beginning of Via dell'Amore, has piles of charm, €6 cocktails, often music, and stays open until midnight June through September (see "Eating in Riomaggiore," later).

La Zorza Café is a hip, youthful alternative to the other bars in town. The music is thumping and the cocktails come with a spread of little snacks (same space as the Hotel la Zorza reception, €6 drinks, daily until 1:00 in the morning, free Wi-Fi with drink, tel. 0187-920-036, fun-loving Elenia).

The marvelous **Via dell'Amore** trail (described earlier), lit only with subtle ground lighting so that you can see the stars, welcomes romantics after dark. The trail is free after 19:30.

Sleeping in Riomaggiore

Riomaggiore has arranged its private-room rental system better than its neighbors. Several agencies—with regular office hours, English-speaking staff, and email addresses—line up within a few yards of each other on the main drag. Each manages a corral of local rooms for rent. These offices keep erratic hours, so it's smart to settle up the day before you leave in case they're closed when you need to depart. Expect lots of stairs. If you don't mind the hike, the street above town has safe overnight parking (free 20:00-8:00).

Hotels

$$$ Locanda del Sole has seven modern, basic, and overpriced rooms with a shared and peaceful terrace. Located at the utilitarian top end of town, it's a five-minute walk downhill to the center. Easy (and free with this book) parking makes it especially appealing to drivers (Db-€110-120, air-con, Wi-Fi, Via Santuario 114, tel. 0187-920-773, mobile 340-983-0090, www.locandadelsole.net, info@locandadelsole.net, Enrico).

$$$ Locanda Ca' dei Duxi rents 10 good rooms from an efficient little office on the main drag (Db-€100-130 depending on view and season, extra person-€20, air-con, Wi-Fi, open year-round, Via Colombo 36, mobile 329-825-7836, www.duxi.it, info @duxi.it, Samuele and Anna). They also manage **Ca' dei Lisci**, with simpler and cheaper rooms (D-€60, Db-€70-80, www.cadeilisci .com).

$$$ Hotel la Zorza rents 11 decent, cave-like, and overpriced rooms in the tangled lanes in the center of town (Db-€110-140, Qb apartment-€150, air-con, Wi-Fi, Via Colombo 231, tel. 0187-920-036, mobile 329-825-7836, www.hotelzorza.com, info@duxi.it).

Sleep Code

(€1 = about $1.40, country code: 39)
S = Single, **D** = Double/Twin, **T** = Triple, **Q** = Quad, **b** = bathroom, **s** = shower only. Unless otherwise noted, credit cards are accepted, English is spoken, and breakfast is included (except in Vernazza). Many towns in Italy levy a hotel tax of €2 per person, per night, which must be paid in cash (not included in the rates I've quoted).

To help you sort easily through these listings, I've divided the accommodations into three categories based on the price for a standard double room with bath:

$$$ Higher Priced—Most rooms €100 or more.
$$ Moderately Priced—Most rooms between €50-100.
$ Lower Priced—Most rooms €50 or less.

Prices can change without notice; verify the hotel's current rates online or by email.

$$ Locanda dalla Compagnia rents five modern rooms at the top of town, just 300 yards below the parking lot and the little church. All rooms—nice but rather dim—are on the same tranquil ground floor, and share an inviting lounge. Franca runs it with the help of son Allessandro (Db-€80, air-con, mini-fridge, no view, Via del Santuario 232, tel. 0187-760-050, www.dallacompagnia.it, lacomp@libero.it).

Room-Booking Services

$$ Riomaggiore Reservations offers 12 rooms and 15 apartments, with American expats Amy and Maddy smoothing communications (Db-€60-90 depending on view, Db suite with top view-€120, cash only, reception open 9:00-17:00 in season, Via Colombo 181, tel. 0187-760-575, www.riomaggiorereservations.com, info @riomaggiorereservations.com).

$$ La Dolce Vita offers three fine, good-value rooms on the main drag and two apartments around town (Db-€60-80, open daily 9:30-19:30; if they're closed, they're full; Via Colombo 167, tel. 0187-762-283, mobile 329-099-2741, agonatal@libero.it, helpful Giacomo and Simone).

$$ Edi's Rooms rents 20 rooms and apartments. You pay extra for views (Db-€70-90 depending on room, apartment Qb-€100-180, reserve with credit card, office open daily in summer 8:30-20:00, in winter 10:30-12:30 & 14:30-19:00, some rooms involve climbing a lot of steps—ask before viewing or reserving, reception at Via Colombo 111, tel. 0187-760-842, tel. 0187-920-325, www.appartamenticinqueterre.net, edi-vesigna@iol.it).

Backpacker Dorms

$ Riomaggiore Reservations (also listed above) runs a mini-hostel in a fine communal apartment with nine beds in three rooms, a cool living room, terrace, and kitchen in a good, quiet location. Take care of this little treasure so it survives (€25/bed, reception open 9:00-17:00 in season, Via Colombo 181, tel. 0187-760-575, www.riomaggiorereservations.com, info@riomaggiorereservations.com).

$ Camere Patrizia rents cheap doubles and dorm bunk beds at €25 per person from its reception at Via Colombo 25, but books only through www.hostelworld.com or to drop-ins (mobile 333-165-6362).

Eating in Riomaggiore

Trattoria la Grotta, right in the town center (with no view), serves reliably good food with a passion for anchovies and mussels. You'll enjoy friendly service surrounded by historic photos and wonderful stonework in a dramatic, dressy, cave-like setting. Venessa is warm and helpful, while her mother, Isa, is busy cooking (€12 pastas, €15 *secondi*, 5 percent cash discount, Thu-Tue 12:00-14:30 & 17:30-22:30, closed Wed, Via Colombo 247, tel. 0187-920-187).

La Lanterna, with a gray-and-white interior and a few appealing harborside tables outside, is wedged into a niche in the Marina, overlooking the harbor under the tracks. Chef Massimo serves traditional plates, loves anchovies, and bakes fresh bread daily (€10 pastas, €18 *secondi*, no cover, daily 12:00-22:00, Via San Giacomo 10, tel. 0187-920-589).

Te La Do Io La Merenda ("I'll Give You a Snack") is good for a snack, pizza, or takeout. Their counter is piled with an assortment of munchies, and they have pastas, roasted chicken, and focaccia sandwiches to go (daily 9:00-21:00, Via Colombo 161, mobile 340-400-3256).

Enoteca & Ristorante Dau Cila is decked out like a black-and-white movie set in a centuries-old boat shed with extra tables outside on a rustic deck over dinghies. Try their antipasto specialty of several seafood appetizers, and listen to jazz with the waves lapping at the harbor below (€12 pastas, €18 *secondi*, March-Jan daily until 24:00, Via San Giacomo 65, tel. 0187-760-032, Luca).

Bar & Vini A Piè de Mà, at the trailhead on the Manarola end of town, is good for a scenic light bite or quiet drink at night. Enjoying a meal at a table on its dramatically situated terrace provides an indelible Cinque Terre memory (daily 10:00-20:00, June-

Sept until 24:00, tel. 0187-921-037).

Picnics: Groceries and delis lining Via Colombo sell food to go, including pizza slices, for a picnic at the harbor or beach. Look for *Co-Op* grocery store signs for the best prices.

Manarola (Town #2)

Like Riomaggiore, Manarola is attached to its station by a 200-yard-long tunnel (lined with interesting photos). During WWII air raids, these tunnels provided refuge and a safe place for rattled villagers to sleep. The town itself fills a ravine, bookended by its wild little harbor to the west and a diminutive church square inland to the east. A delightful and gentle stroll from the church down to the harbor-side park provides the region's easiest vineyard walk (described in my "Self-Guided Walk," next page).

Orientation to Manarola

The **TI** at the train station is open daily 7:00-20:00.

A **shuttle bus** runs between the low end of Manarola's main street (at the tobacco shop and newsstand) and the parking lot (€1.50 one-way, €2.50 round-trip, free with Cinque Terre Park Card, 2/hour, just flag it down). Shuttle buses also run about hourly from Manarola to Volastra, near the Cinque Terre Cooperative Winery.

To get to the **dock** and the boats that connect Manarola with the other Cinque Terre towns, find the steps to the left of the harbor view—they lead down to the ticket kiosk. Continue around the left side of the cliff (as you're facing the water) to catch the boats.

Self-Guided Walk

Welcome to Manarola

From the harbor, this 30-minute circular walk shows you the town and surrounding vineyards, and ends at a fantastic viewpoint, perfect for a picnic.

• *Start down at the waterfront.*

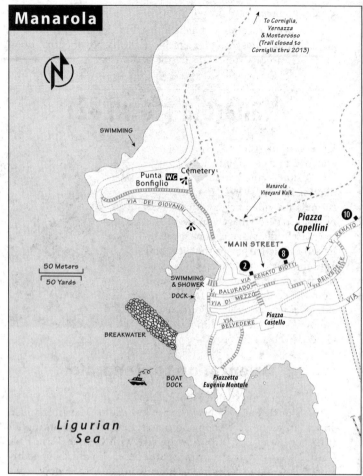

Manarola

SWIMMING

Punta Bonfiglio

WC Cemetery

VIA DEI GIOVANNI

Manarola Vineyard Walk

To Corniglia, Vernazza & Monterosso
(Trail closed to Corniglia thru 2013)

Piazza Capellini

❿

V. RENATO

V. PELVEDERE

V. PELVEDERE

"MAIN STREET"

VIA RENATO BIOTTI

V. BALURADO

VIA DI MEZZO

VIA BELVEDERE

Piazza Castello

❷

❽

50 Meters
50 Yards

SWIMMING & SHOWER

DOCK

BREAKWATER

BOAT DOCK

Piazzetta Eugenio Montale

Ligurian Sea

The Harbor: Manarola is tiny and picturesque, a tumble of buildings bunny-hopping down its ravine to the fun-loving waterfront. Notice how the I-beam crane launches the boats. Facing the water, look to the right, at the hillside Punta Bonfiglio cemetery and park (where this walk ends).

The town's swimming hole is just below. Manarola has no sand, but offers the best deep-water swimming in the area. The first "beach" has a shower, ladder, and wonderful rocks. The second has tougher access and no shower, but feels more remote and pristine

1 La Torretta Rooms
2 Marina Piccola Rooms & Restaurant
3 Albergo Ca' d'Andrean
4 Affitta Camere da Paulin
5 Aria di Mare Rooms
6 Ostello 5-Terre
7 To Hotel il Saraceno
8 Trattoria il Porticciolo
9 Trattoria dal Billy
10 Shuttle Bus to Parking Lot & Volastra

(follow the paved path toward Corniglia, just around the point). For many, the tricky access makes this beach dangerous.

• *Hiking inland up the town's main drag, you'll come to the train tracks covered by Manarola's new square, called...*

Piazza Capellini: Built in 2004, this square is an all-around great idea, giving the town a safe, fun zone for kids. Locals living near the tracks also enjoy a little less noise. Check out the mosaic that displays the varieties of local fish in colorful enamel.

• *Fifty yards uphill, you'll find the...*

Sciacchetrà Museum: Run by the national park, it's hardly a museum. But if it's open, pop in to its inviting room to see a tiny exhibit on the local wine industry (€0.50, free with Cinque Terre Park Card, generally closed, 15-minute video in English by request, 100 yards uphill from train tracks, across from the post office).

• *Hiking farther uphill, you can still hear...*

Manarola's Stream: Like the streams in Riomaggiore, Monterosso, and Vernazza, Manarola's rivulet was covered over by a modern sewage system after World War II. Before that time, romantic bridges arched over its ravine. A modern waterwheel recalls the origin of the town's name—local dialect for "big wheel" (one of many possible derivations). Mills like this once powered the local olive oil industry.

• *Keep climbing until you come to the square at the...*

Top of Manarola: The square is faced by a church, an oratory—now a religious and community meeting place—and a bell tower, which served as a watchtower when pirates raided the town (the cupola was added once the attacks ceased). Behind the church is Manarola's well-run youth hostel, originally the church's schoolhouse. To the right of the oratory, a stepped lane leads to Manarola's sizable tourist-free zone.

While you're here, check out the **church**. According to the white marble plaque in its facade, the Parish Church of St. Lawrence (San Lorenzo) dates from "MCCCXXXVIII" (1338). Step inside to see two paintings from the unnamed Master of the Cinque Terre, the only painter of any note from this region (left wall and above main altar). While the style is Gothic, the work dates from the late 15th century, long after Florence had entered the Renaissance. Note the humble painted stone ceiling, which replaced the wooden original in the 1800s. It features Lawrence, patron saint of the Cinque Terre, with his grill, the symbol of his martyrdom (he was roasted on it).

• *With the bell tower on your left, head about 20 yards down the main street below the church and find a wooden railing. It marks the start of a delightful stroll around the high side of town, and back to the seafront. This is the beginning of the...*

Manarola Vineyard Walk: Don't miss this experience. Simply follow the wooden railing, enjoying lemon groves and wild red valerian (used for insomnia since the days of the Romans). Along the path, which is primarily flat, you'll get a close-up look at the region's famous dry-stone walls and finely crafted vineyards (with dried-heather thatches to protect the grapes from the southwest winds). Smell the rosemary. Study the structure of the town, and pick out the scant remains of an old fort. Notice the S-shape of the main road—once a riverbed—that flows through town. The town's roofs are traditionally made of locally quarried slate, rather than tile, and are held down by rocks during windstorms. As the harbor comes into view, you'll see the breakwater, added just a decade ago.

Above you on the right are simple wooden religious scenes, the work of local resident Mario Andreoli. Before his father died, Mario promised him he'd replace the old cross on the family's vineyard. Mario has been adding figures ever since. After recovering from a rare illness, he redoubled his efforts. On religious holidays, everything's lit up: the Nativity, the Last Supper, the Crucifixion, the Resurrection, and more. Some of the scenes are left up year-round.

High above, a recent fire burned off the tree cover, revealing ancient terraces that line the terrain like a topographic map.

• *Follow this trail all the way to a T-intersection, where it hits the main coastal trail. Turn left. (A right takes you to the trail to Corniglia, likely closed in 2013.) Before descending back into town, take a right, detouring into...*

The Cemetery: Ever since Napoleon—who was king of Italy in the early 1800s—decreed that cemeteries were health risks, Cinque Terre's burial spots have been located outside the towns. The result: The dearly departed generally get first-class sea views. Each cemetery—with its evocative yellowed photos and finely carved Carrara marble memorial reliefs—is worth a visit. (The basic structure for all of them is the same, but Manarola's is the most easily accessible.)

In cemeteries like these, there's a hierarchy of four places to park your mortal remains: a graveyard, a spacious death condo *(loculo),* a mini bone-niche *(ossario),* or the communal ossuary. Because of the tight space, a time limit is assigned to the first three options (although many older tombs are grandfathered in). Bones go into the ossuary in the middle of the chapel floor after about a generation. Traditionally, locals make weekly visits to loved ones here, often bringing flowers. The rolling stepladder makes access to top-floor *loculi* easy.

• *The Manarola cemetery is on Punta Bonfiglio. Take the stairs just below it, then walk farther out through a park (playground, drinking water, WC, and picnic benches). Your Manarola finale: the bench at the tip of the point, offering one of the most commanding views of the entire region. The easiest way back to town is to take the stairs at the end of the point, which join the main walking path.*

Sleeping in Manarola

(€1 = about $1.40, country code: 39)

Manarola has plenty of private rooms. Ask in bars and restaurants. There's a modern three-star place halfway up the main drag, a sea-view hotel on the harbor, a big modern hostel, and a cluster of options around the church at the peaceful top of the town (a 5-minute hike from the train tracks).

$$$ La Torretta is a trendy, upscale 13-room place that caters to a demanding clientele. Probably the most elegant retreat in the region, it's a peaceful refuge with all the comforts for those happy to pay, including a communal hot tub with a view. Enjoy a complimentary snack and glass of prosecco on arrival, free wine-tastings during your stay, breakfast in your room, and a free mini-bar. Each chic room is distinct and described on their website (smaller Db-€145, regular Db-€190, Db suite-€250-400, 10 percent discount with cash, book several months in advance as it's justifiably popular, closed mid-Nov-mid-March, free Wi-Fi, on Piazza della Chiesa beside the bell tower at Vico Volto 20, tel. 0187-920-327, www.torrettas.com, torretta@cdh.it).

$$$ Marina Piccola offers 13 bright, slick rooms on the water—so they figure a warm welcome is unnecessary (Db-€120, air-con, free Wi-Fi, Via Birolli 120, tel. 0187-762-065, www.hotel marinapiccola.com, info@hotelmarinapiccola.com).

$$$ Albergo Ca' d'Andrean, run by Simone, is quiet, comfortable, and modern—except for its antiquated reservation system. While the welcome is formal at best, it has 10 big, sunny, air-conditioned rooms and a cool garden oasis complete with lemon trees (Sb-€75, Db-€105, breakfast-€6, free Wi-Fi, cash only, send personal check to reserve from US—or call if you're reserving from the road, closed Nov-Christmas, up the hill at Via A. Discovolo 101, tel. 0187-920-040, www.cadandrean.it, cadandrean @libero.it).

$$ At Affitta Camere da Paulin, charming Donatella and Eraldo (the town's retired policeman) rent very nice, well-equipped rooms with a large and inviting common living room. It's in a modern setting a few minutes' walk uphill from the train tracks (Db-€70-80, view apartment Db-€105-130, 3-night minimum stay, free Wi-Fi, Via Discovolo 126, tel. 0187-920-706, mobile 334-389-4764, www.dapaulin.it, prenotazioni@dapaulin.it).

$$ Aria di Mare Rooms rents four sunny rooms and an apartment 20 yards beyond Trattoria dal Billy at the very top of town. Three rooms have spacious terraces with knockout views and lounge chairs. Maurizio speaks a little English, while Mamma Franca communicates with lots of Italian and toothy smiles (Db-€65, 2 adults and 1 child-€80, Db apartment-€90, these prices promised through 2013, basic breakfast, free Wi-Fi, up stairs on the left at Via Aldo Rollandi 137, tel. 0187-920-367, mobile 349-058-4155, www.ariadimare.info, info@ariadimare.info, ask at Billy's if no one's home).

$ Ostello 5-Terre, Manarola's modern and pleasant hostel, occupies the former parochial school above the church square and offers 48 beds in four- to six-bed rooms. Nicola and Riccardo run a calm and peaceful place—it's not a party hostel—and quiet is greatly appreciated. They rent dorm rooms as doubles. Reserve well in advance. Full means full—they don't accommodate the desperate on the floor (Easter-mid-Oct: dorm beds-€23, Db-€65, Qb-€100; 20 percent less off-season, normally closed Dec-Feb but can open on demand, not co-ed except for couples and families, no membership necessary, open to all ages, optional €5 breakfast and bargain dinners, office closed 13:00-16:00, rooms closed 10:00-13:00, check-in until 22:00, elevator, free Internet access and Wi-Fi, safe, laundry, book exchange, Via B. Riccobaldi 21, tel. 0187-920-039, www.hostel5terre.com, info@hostel5terre.com).

For Drivers: **$$$ Hotel il Saraceno,** with seven spacious, modern rooms, is a deal for drivers. Located above Manarola in the tiny town of Volastra (chock-full of vacationing Germans and Italians in summer), it's serene, clean, and right by the shuttle bus to Manarola (Db-€100, buffet breakfast, Wi-Fi, free parking, Via Volastra 8, tel. 0187-760-081, www.thesaraceno.com, hotel@the saraceno.com, friendly Antonella).

Eating in Manarola

Many hardworking places line the main drag. The Scorza family works hard at **Trattoria il Porticciolo** (free glass of *sciacchetrà* dessert wine with this book, closed Wed, below train tracks at Via R. Birolli 92, tel. 0187-920-083). The harborside **Marina Piccola** is famous for great views, lousy service, and gouging naive tourists.

Trattoria dal Billy, hiding out high on the hill, is a hit, with good food and impressive views over the valley. With Edoardo and Enrico's black pasta with seafood and squid ink, green pasta with artichokes, mixed seafood starters, and homemade desserts, many find it worth the climb. Dinner reservations are a must (€11 pastas, €14 *secondi*, generally daily 8:00-15:00 & 19:00-23:30, closed Thu, Via Aldo Rollandi 122, tel. 0187-920-628).

Corniglia (Town #3)

This is the quiet town—the only one of the five not on the water—with a mellow main square. According to a (likely fanciful) local legend, the town was originally settled by a Roman farmer who named it for his mother, Cornelia (how Corniglia is pronounced). The town and its

THE CINQUE TERRE

ancient residents produced a wine so famous that—some say—
vases found at Pompeii touted its virtues. Regardless of the verac-
ity of the legends, wine remains Corniglia's lifeblood today. Follow
the pungent smell of ripe grapes into an alley cellar and get a local
to let you dip a straw into a keg.

Remote and less visited than the other Cinque Terre towns,
Corniglia has fewer tourists, cooler temperatures, a few restaurants, a windy overlook on its promontory, and plenty of private
rooms for rent (ask at any bar or shop, no cheaper than other
towns). If you think of the Cinque Terre as the Beatles, Corniglia
is Ringo.

Orientation to Corniglia

Arrival in Corniglia

From the station, a footpath zigzags up about 380 steps to the
town. Or take the green shuttle bus, generally timed to meet arriving trains (€1.50 one-way, €2.50 round-trip; free with Cinque Terre
Park Card—to catch the waiting bus, ideally buy the card before
you arrive in Corniglia; 2/hour). If you're driving, be aware that
only residents can park on the main road between the recommended Villa Cecio and the point where the steep switchback staircase meets the road. Beyond that area, parking is €1.50 per hour.

Self-Guided Walk

Welcome to Corniglia

We'll explore this tiny town—population 240—and end at a scenic viewpoint.

• *Begin near the bus stop, located at a...*

Town Square: The gateway to this community is "Ciappà"
square, with an ATM, phone booth, old wine press, and bus stop.
The Cinque Terre's designation as a national park sparked a revi-
talization of the town. Corniglia's young generation is more likely
now to stay put, rather than migrate into big cities the way locals
did in the past.

• *Look for the arrow pointing to the center (centro). Stroll the spine of
Corniglia, Via Fieschi. In the fall, the smell of grapes (on their way to
becoming wine) wafts from busy cellars. Along this main street, you'll
see...*

Corniglia's Enticing Shops: Alberto's Gelateria dishes up
the best homemade gelato in town. Before ordering, get a free taste
of Alberto's *miele di Corniglia,* made from local honey. His local
lemon slush takes pucker to new heights. **Enoteca il Pirun**—named
for a type of oddly shaped old-fashioned wine pitcher designed to
aerate the wine and give the alcohol more kick—is located in a cool

Corniglia

To Vernazza
200 Meters
200 Yards

LOC. CANALE
VIA SIERA
LOC. CHIOSO
VIA FIESCHI
VIA DELLA STAZIONE
VIA ALLA MARINA

HUNDREDS
OF STEPS

VIA LARDARINA

To
Manarola

❶ ❷ ❾ ❹ ❽
❸
❶ ❼
❻

Harbor

"CIAPPÀ"
SQUARE &
BUS STOP

SANTA MARIA
BELVEDERE

LARGO
TARAGIO,
ORATORY & ❺

Ligurian Sea

TRAIN
STATION

SWIMMING

❶ Pan e Vin Bar
   (Ricci Rooms Check-In)
❷ Il Carugio Rooms & Butiega Shop
❸ Villa Cecio Rooms
❹ Corniglia Hostel

❺ La Lanterna Restaurant
❻ Osteria Mananan
❼ Enoteca il Pirun
❽ La Posada Ristorante
❾ Gelateria

cantina at Via Fieschi 115. Sample some local wines (generally free for small tastes). If you buy a bottle, they may gift you with a souvenir bib. In the **Butiega** shop at Via Fieschi 142, Vincenzo sells organic local specialties (daily 8:00-19:30). For picnickers, they offer €4 made-to-order ham-and-cheese sandwiches and a fun €5 *antipasti misti* to go. (There are good places to picnic farther along on this walk.)

• *Following Via Fieschi, you'll end up at the...*

Main Square: On Largo Taragio, tables from two bars and a trattoria spill around a WWI memorial and the town's old well. It once piped in natural spring water from the hillside to locals living without plumbing. What looks like a church is the Oratory of Santa Caterina. (An oratory is a kind of a spiritual clubhouse for a service group doing social work in the name of the Catholic Church. For more information, see "Oratory of the Dead" on page 405.) Behind the oratory, you'll find a clearing that local children have made into a soccer field. The stone benches and viewpoint make this a peaceful place for a picnic (less crowded than the end-of-town viewpoint, described below).

• *Opposite the oratory, notice how steps lead steeply down on Via alla Marina to Corniglia's non-beach. It's a five-minute paved climb to sunning rocks, a shower, and a small deck (with a treacherous entry into the water). From the square, continue up Via Fieschi to the...*

End-of-Town Viewpoint: The Santa Maria Belvedere, named for a church that once stood here, marks the scenic end of

THE CINQUE TERRE

Corniglia. This is a super picnic spot. From here, look high to the west, where the village and sanctuary of San Bernardino straddle a ridge (a good starting point for a hike; accessible by shuttle bus from Monterosso or a long uphill hike from Vernazza). Below is the tortuous harbor, where locals hoist their boats onto the cruel rocks.

Sights in Corniglia

Beaches—This hilltop town has rocky sea access below its train station (toward Manarola). Once a beach, it's all been washed away and offers no services. Look for signs that say *al mare* or *Marina*. A trail leads from the town center steeply down to sunning rocks on the closest thing Corniglia has to a beach (with a shower).

The infamous **Guvano beach** (a bit along the coast toward Vernazza) is now essentially closed down. Guvano was created by an 1893 landslide that cost the village a third of its farmland. Notorious throughout Italy as a nude beach, Guvano was accessed via an unused train tunnel and attracted visitors with an appetite for drug use. Now the tunnel is closed, and the national park wants people to keep their clothes on and forget about Guvano.

Sleeping in Corniglia

(€1 = about $1.40, country code: 39)
Perched high above the sea on a hilltop, Corniglia has plenty of private rooms. To get to the town from the station, catch the shuttle bus or make the 15-minute uphill hike. The town is riddled with humble places that charge too much (generally Db-€65) and have meager business skills and a limited ability to converse with tourists—so it's almost never full.

$$ Cristiana Ricci is an exception to the rule. She communicates well and is reliable, renting four small, clean, and peaceful rooms—two with kitchens and one with a terrace and sweeping view—just inland from the bus stop (Db-€60-70, Qb-€90, €10/day less when you stay 2 or more nights, free Internet access, check in at the Pan e Vin bar at Via Fieschi 123, mobile 338-937-6547, cri_affittacamere@virgilio.it). Her mom rents a big, modern apartment (€90 for 2-4 people).

$$ Il Carugio has nine modern, sunny rooms right in the center of the village, most with sea views. The communal rooftop terrace offers a commanding view of the coast (Db-€70-80, no breakfast, tel. 0187-812-293, mobile 335-175-7946, www.il carugiodicorniglia.com, info@ilcarugiodicorniglia.com, Lidia).

$$ Villa Cecio (pronounced "chay-choe") feels like an abandoned hotel. They offer eight well-worn rooms on the outskirts of town, with saggy beds and little character or warmth (Db-€65 promised in 2013, breakfast-€5, cash preferred, great views, on main road 200 yards toward Vernazza at Via Serra 58, tel. 0187-812-043, mobile 334-350-6637, www.cecio5terre.com, info@cecio 5terre.com, Giacinto). They also rent eight similar rooms (Db-€60) in an annex on the square where the bus stops.

$ **Corniglia Hostel** was formerly the town's schoolhouse. It rents 24 beds in a pastel-yellow building up some steps from the main square, where the bus stops. The playground in front is often busy with happy kids. Despite its strict and institutional atmosphere, the hostel's prices, central location, and bright and clean rooms ensure its popularity. Its hotelesque double rooms are open to anyone (€24/bed in two 8-bed dorms, €27 with minimal breakfast; four Db-€55, €60 with breakfast; office open 7:00-13:00 & 15:00-24:00, rooms closed 13:00-15:00, 1:30 curfew, air-con, lockers, Internet access and Wi-Fi, self-serve laundry, no public spaces except lobby, Via alla Stazione 3, tel. 0187-812-559, www .ostellocorniglia.com but reserve at www.hostelworld.com, ostello corniglia@gmail.com).

Eating in Corniglia

Corniglia has few restaurants.

The trattoria **La Lanterna,** on the main square, is the most atmospheric (but without particularly charming service).

Osteria Mananan—between the Ciappà bus stop and the main square at Via Fieschi 117—serves what many consider the best food in town in its small, stony, elegant interior (Wed-Mon 12:15-14:30 & 19:45-22:00, closed Tue, no outdoor seating, tel. 0187-821-166).

Enoteca il Pirun, also on Via Fieschi, has a small restaurant above the wine bar, where Mario serves typical local dishes (€28 fixed-price meal includes homemade wine, daily 12:00-16:00 & 19:30-23:30, tel. 0187-812-315).

La Posada Ristorante offers dinner in a garden under trees, overlooking the Ligurian Sea. To get here, stroll out of town to the top of the stairs from the station (€10 pastas, €10 *secondi*, €15 tourist *menu*, nightly from 19:00, tel. 0187-821-174).

THE CINQUE TERRE

The Cinque Terre Flood...and Recovery

When you visit, the Cinque Terre will look as beautiful as always—because the locals worked hard to fix the damage caused by the flood. Here is the story:

On October 25, 2011, after a very dry summer, a freak rainstorm hit the Cinque Terre. Within four hours, the region got 22 inches of rain—a third of an average year's total. Because of the topography, which allowed the flash flooding to drain, three of the towns (Riomaggiore, Manarola, and Corniglia) were undamaged. However, two were devastated: Much of Monterosso and Vernazza were buried under 10 feet of mud and left without water, electricity, or phone connections. It was a day residents will talk about for the rest of their lives.

The destruction occurred mostly along former ravines, where, historically, streams ran through the towns. In the last century, the ravines were covered with roads, and the streams channeled into underground canals that, over time, were not properly maintained. Like congested arteries, the drainage canals couldn't handle the raging flow, so the deluge was forced aboveground. Trees, furniture, cars, buses, and tons of mud and rocks plowed through both towns. Water pressure from drain pipes below caused streets to explode upward. Medieval wells in basements became geysers. Rivers of raging mud rampaged down the streets, stranding locals and visitors, and burying the shops and restaurants on the main streets of old Monterosso and Vernazza. Four locals lost their lives.

The tourist business in 2011 had been very strong. The day of the flood, October 25, was at the end of the season, when residents of Vernazza and Monterosso were ready for a much-needed winter break. While the flood hit at the perfect time from a business point of view, locals—already exhausted after a very busy season—had to immediately plunge into a non-stop rebuilding period, pushing to be ready for the 2012 season. And they made remarkable progress.

Socially, it was a time of reshuffling for both communities. Being small towns, they were already rife with cliques and ancient grudges. Faced with the challenges presented by the flood and recovery, everyone came together—or nearly everyone. Today, many locals enjoy better relations with old enemies, but there is a new divide: between people who joined in the community-wide effort, and those who only took care of their own business needs (or even left town during the chaos). While a large portion of the businesses in both Vernazza and Monterosso were essentially destroyed, lots of homes and hotels that were on higher (or luckier) ground came through unscathed. Some of these ignored their own business needs and became heroically involved in helping the greater community—including the competition—get back on its feet.

Ecologically, the people of the Cinque Terre were taught a tough lesson. It's their beautiful land that brings the tourists. But with the affluence brought by tourism, locals abandoned their land—leaving the vineyards unplanted and the centuries-old dry-stone terracing to crumble—for less physically demanding, more profitable work in town. (Grapevines have far-reaching root systems to combat erosion, and traditional vintners keep their stone terraces in good order.) After a generation of neglect, the land was left unprotected from the violent weather, and washed down into the towns.

Psychologically, the trauma and aftermath of the flood were toughest on local seniors. Many have barely ventured beyond the

Cinque Terre during their lives. Every day, for many decades, they've warmed the same bench with the same friends. Trying to hang onto a little normalcy, one old man still came to his buried bench each afternoon in the days after the flood.

I visited Vernazza six months to the day after the flood. For 30 years, I've strolled the main drag of Vernazza as if walking through a poem. But on this visit, walking down that street—gutted of nearly all its businesses, the dreams and labors of love of its residents swept away so violently—was an emotional roller coaster for me. Feeling nostalgic, I had lunch in Piva's restaurant, where I first ate when visiting as a student in the 1970s. Piva, who cooked an amazing seafood risotto then as now, is also the town troubadour. Many nights, when the cooking's done, he pulls out his guitar and leads his happy diners in song. After showing me the new post-flood ovens and stoves in his kitchen, he showed me his well-worn guitar—a trace of mud still caked on its neck—and said, "In this restaurant, only my guitar survived the flood."

Talking with locals in the months after the flood, a phrase I heard over and over was *"piano, piano"* (little by little). Little by little, they were rebuilding. Everything is new: Restaurants and businesses at street level in affected areas were gutted and had to replace everything: stoves, tables, chairs, plates, walls lined with bottles of wine, and so on. I was told, "The reality of a tragedy like this is eventually the government aid dries up, the sympathy fades, and it's just you and a shovel." Strolling through these towns today, keep in mind everything these people have been through—and appreciate the resilience of the human spirit.

Vernazza

Trail to
Monterosso

Rocks

Cemetery

SUNNING &
SWIMMING

Harbor

SANTA
MARGHERITA
CHURCH

SUNNING →

Breakwater

Beach

9 **13**

*Piazza
Marconi*

14

18

3

VIA S.

VIA

BOAT
DOCKS
HERE

11

10

12 **19**

2

VIA VISCONTI

21

VIA

V. SAN GIOVANNI BATTISTA

22

17 **24**

VIA MARCANTONIO

CASTLE

Rocks and Cliffs

50 Meters

50 Yards

L i g u r i a n   S e a

THE CINQUE TERRE

Vernazza (Town #4)

With the closest thing to a natural harbor—overseen by a ruined
castle and a stout stone church—
Vernazza is the jewel of the Cinque
Terre. Only the occasional noisy
slurping up of the train by the
mountain reminds you of the modern world.

The action is at the harbor,
where you'll find outdoor restaurants, a bar hanging on the edge of
the castle, and a breakwater with a

1. Pensione Sorriso
2. Trattoria Gianni Rooms/Ristorante
3. Albergo Barbara
4. La Marina Rooms, Tonino Basso Rooms & Il Pirata della Cinque Terre
5. Camere Fontana Vecchia
6. Giuliano Basso Rooms
7. Vernazza Rooms
8. Blue Marlin Bar & Café
9. Ananasso Bar
10. Ristorante al Castello
11. Ristorante Belforte
12. Gambero Rosso Ristorante
13. Trattoria del Capitano
14. Ristorante Pizzeria Vulnetia
15. Trattoria da Sandro
16. Antica Osteria il Baretto
17. Ristorante Incadase da Piva
18. Bar Baia Saracena
19. Burgus Wine Bar
20. Franco's Ristorante & Bar la Torre
21. Forno (Bakery)
22. Gelateria
23. Launderette
24. Internet Point

promenade, corralled by a natural amphitheater of terraced hills. In the summer, the beach becomes a soccer field, where teams fielded by local bars and restaurants provide late-night entertainment. In the dark, locals fish off the promontory, using glowing bobbers that shine in the waves.

Proud of their Vernazzan heritage, the town's 500 residents like to brag: "Vernazza is locally owned. Portofino has sold out." Fearing the change it would bring, keep-Vernazza-small proponents stopped the construction of a major road into the town and region. Families are tight and go back centuries; several generations stay together. In the winter, the population shrinks, as many people return to their more comfortable big-city apartments to spend the money they reaped during the tourist season.

Sadly, Vernazza was hit harder than any other Cinque Terre

town by the flood on October 25, 2011. Essentially every business in town was destroyed as the flood raged through the town, burying it in mud. Every shop, restaurant, and hotel on the main drag had to be re-wired, re-plumbed, and re-equipped. Around town, you'll see photos and hear stories of what was, perhaps, the most tumultuous day ever in the town's thousand-year history (see sidebar).

The flood's impact for visitors in 2013? Almost nothing. Just enjoy. Now that things are mostly back to normal, leisure time is devoted to taking part in the *passeggiata*—strolling lazily together up and down the main street. Sit on a bench and study the passersby doing their *vasche* (laps). Explore the characteristic alleys, called *carugi*. Learn—and live—the phrase *"la vita pigra di Vernazza"* (the lazy life of Vernazza).

Orientation to Vernazza

Tourist Information

The TI/park information/train ticket office is one desk buried in a gift shop between the two tracks at the train station (daily 8:00-19:30, tel. 0187-812-524). Public WCs are nearby in the station.

Save Vernazza: Led by a group of American women who married into the community, Save Vernazza brought relief to the town in the immediate aftermath of the 2011 flood, and has since morphed into an organization to help preserve and foster healthy tourism. For the latest on the town, its recovery, and their activities—including leads on locals with rooms and apartments for rent—visit www.savevernazza.com.

Arrival in Vernazza

By Train: Vernazza's train station is only about three cars long, but the trains are much longer—so most of the cars come to a stop in a long, dark tunnel. Get out anyway, and walk through the tunnel to the station.

By Car: Because many roads and parking lots were washed out in the 2011 flood, road access and parking above Vernazza is in flux. There are plans to create a nonresident pay parking lot 500 yards above the town (but don't count on it). In the past, visitors could connect between the parking lot and downtown on a hard-working shuttle service. This may or may not be back up and running for your visit. Yellow lines mark parking spots for residents only.

Helpful Hints

Internet Access: The slick, expensive, six-terminal **Internet Point,** run by Alberto and Isabella, is in the village center (daily June-Oct 9:30-23:00, until 20:00 Nov-May, Wi-Fi, will burn your digital photos to a CD or DVD for €5). The **Il Pirata delle Cinque Terre** bar (at the top of the town) and **Burgus Wine Bar** (on the harbor) both offer free Wi-Fi with a purchase.

Laundry: Domenico's Lavanderia, at the top of town next to the post office, is completely self-serve (coin-op, €6/wash, €5/dry, daily 8:00-22:00, operated by Domenico and Barbara at the fish shop).

Massage: Kate Allen offers a super-relaxing fusion of aromatic/Swedish/holistic massage for €50 per hour in her little studio adjacent to the clinic at the top of Vernazza (mobile 333-568-4653, www.vernazzamassage5terre.com).

Best Views: A steep 10-minute hike in either direction from Vernazza gives you a classic village photo op (for the best light, head toward Corniglia in the morning, and toward Monterosso in the evening).

Self-Guided Walks

Welcome to Vernazza

This tour includes Vernazza's characteristic town squares and ends on its scenic breakwater.

• *From the train station, walk uphill until you hit what was the pre-flood parking lot, with a post office and a barrier that keeps out all but service vehicles. As you survey the post-flood reconstruction work, it is easy to imagine how this ravine could be susceptible to flash flooding. The stream in this ravine once powered Vernazza's water mill. Vernazza's shuttle buses run from here to hamlets and sanctuaries in the hills above.*

Walk to the tidy, modern square called...

Fontana Vecchia: Named after a long-gone fountain, this is where older locals remember the river filled with townswomen doing their washing. A lane leads from here up to the cemetery. Imagine the entire village sadly trudging up here during funerals. (The cemetery is peaceful and evocative at sunset, when the fading light touches each crypt.)

• *Glad to be here in happier times, begin your saunter downhill to the harbor. Just before the* Pensione Sorriso *sign, on your right (big brown wood doors), you'll see the...*

Ambulance Barn: A group of volunteers is always on call for a dash to the hospital, 40 minutes away in La Spezia. Opposite the barn is a big empty lot. Like many landowners, the owner of Pensione Sorriso had plans to expand, but since the 1980s, the government has said "No." While some landowners are frustrated, the old character of these towns survives. A few steps farther down is the town clinic. The *guarda medica* (emergency doctor—see buzzer) sleeps upstairs.

• *At the corner across from the playground, on a marble plaque in the wall on the left, you'll see a...*

World Wars Monument: This is dedicated to those killed in the World Wars. Not a family in Vernazza was spared. Listed on the left are soldiers *morti in combattimento*, who died in World War I; on the right is the World War II section. Some were deported to *Germania;* others—labeled *Part* (stands for *partigiani*, or partisans, generally communists)—were killed while fighting against Mussolini. Cynics considered partisans less than heroes. After 1943, Hitler called up Italian boys over 15. Rather than die on the front for Hitler, they escaped to the hills. They became "resistance fighters" in order to remain free.

The path to Corniglia leaves from here (behind and above the plaque). Behind you is a small square and playground, decorated with three millstones, once used to grind local olives into oil. There's a good chance you'll see an expat mom here at the village playground with her kids. I've met many American women who fell in love with a local guy, stayed, and are now happily raising families here. (But I've rarely met an American guy who moved in with a local girl.)

From here, Vernazza's tiny river goes underground. Until the 1950s, the river ran openly through the center of town. Old-timers recall the days before the breakwater, when the river cascaded down and the surf sent waves rolling up Vernazza's main drag. Back then, this place was nicknamed "Little Venice" for the series of romantic bridges that arched over the stream, connecting the two sides of the town before the main road was built.

Corralling this stream under the modern street, and forcing it to take a hard right turn here, contributed to the damage caused by the 2011 flood. Following the flood, alpine engineers were imported from Switzerland to redesign this drainage system, so any future floods will be less destructive. They also put nets above the town to protect it from more landslides.

Before the flood, the walls under the tracks served as a community information center, with historic photos of the old town, maps showing trails in the hills, a list of local volunteers and when they are on call to drive the ambulance, and an events board. Look around here for photos of the flood and the shops that it devastated. "The 25th of October" is a day that will live forever in this town's lore. The second set of tracks (nearer the harbor) was recently renovated to lessen the disruptive noise, but locals say it made no difference.

• *Follow the road downhill to...*

Vernazza's "Business Center": Here, you'll pass many locals doing their *vasche* (laps). Next, you'll pass souvenir shops, wine shops, the Blue Marlin Bar (Vernazza's top nightspot), and the tiny Chapel of Santa Marta (the small stone chapel with iron grill-work over the window), where Mass is celebrated only on special Sundays. Farther down, you'll walk by a *gelateria*, bakery, pharmacy, a grocery, and another *gelateria*. There are plenty of fun and cheap food-to-go options here.

• *On the left, in front of the second* gelateria, *a stone arch was blasted away by the flood. The hole in the rock leads to a beach created by the flood. This is where the town's stream used to hit the sea back in the 1970s.*

Continue downhill. Just before the harbor, the main street becomes very narrow. This was the bottleneck that caused water to back up into the town during the flood. And these buildings are about the only ones in town to suffer structural damage from the force of the water.

A few steps farther take you to the...

Harbor Square and Breakwater: Vernazza, with the only natural harbor of the Cinque Terre, was established as the sole place boats could pick up the fine local wine. The two-foot-high square stone at the foot of the stairs by the Burgus Wine Bar is marked *Sasso del Sego* (stone of tallow). Workers crushed animal flesh and fat in its basin to make tallow, which drained out of the tiny hole below. The tallow was then used to waterproof boats or wine barrels. For more town history, step into the Burgus to see fascinating old photos of Vernazza on the wall. Stonework is the soul of the region. Take some time to appreciate the impressive stonework of the restaurant interiors facing the harbor.

On the far side (behind Ristorante Pizzeria Vulnetia), peek into the tiny street with its commotion of arches. Vernazza's most characteristic side streets, called *carugi*, lead up from here. The trail (above the church, toward Monterosso) leads to the quintessential view of Vernazza.

Located in front of the harborside church, the tiny piazza—decorated with a river-rock mosaic—is a popular hangout spot. It's where Vernazza's old ladies soak up the last bit of sun, and kids enjoy a patch of level ball field.

Vernazza's harborfront **church** is unusual for its strange entry-way, which faces east (altar side). With relative peace and prosperity in the 16th century, the townspeople doubled the church in size, causing it to overtake a little piazza that once faced the west facade. From the square, use the "new" entry and climb the steps, keeping an eye out for the level necessary to keep the church high and dry. Inside, the lighter pillars in the back mark the 16th-century extension. Three historic portable crosses hanging on the walls are carried through town during Easter processions. They are replicas of crosses that (locals like to believe) Vernazza ships once carried on crusades to the Holy Land. In 1998, Vernazza's priest was gruesomely and mysteriously murdered. While circumstantial evidence points to fascinating conspiracy theories, no one knows whodunit (or, at least, no one's telling). Today's priest, Don Giovanni, is popular—he stopped the church bells from ringing through the night (light sleepers rejoiced). In the wake of the 2011 flood, he opened up the church as a staging ground for recovery services.

• *Finish your town tour seated out on the breakwater (perhaps with a glass of local white wine or something more interesting from a nearby bar—borrow the glass, they don't mind). Face the town, and see...*

The Harbor: In a moderate storm, you'd be soaked, as waves routinely crash over the *molo* (breakwater, built in 1972). Waves can rearrange the huge rocks—depositing them from the breakwater onto the piazza and its benches. Freak waves have even washed away tourists squinting excitedly into their cameras. (I've seen it happen.) In 2007, an American woman was swept away and killed by a rogue wave. Enjoy the waterfront piazza—carefully.

The train line (to your left) was constructed in 1874 to tie together a newly united Italy, and linked Turin and Genoa with Rome. A second line (hidden in a tunnel at this point) was built in the 1920s. The yellow building alongside the tracks was Vernazza's first train station. You can see the four bricked-up alcoves where people once waited for trains. Notice the wonderful concrete sunbathing strip (and place for late-night privacy) laid below the tracks along the rocks.

Vernazza's fishing fleet is down to just a couple of boats (with the net spools). While the 2011 flood washed away many of the town's boats and cars (one boat was actually recovered in Spain), Vernazzans are still more likely to own a boat than a car, and it's said that you stand a better chance of surviving if you mess with a local man's wife than with his boat. On a recent visit just after the flood, I ran into Tonino, who showed me photo of his boat, *Gustina*, with this caption: "Tonino loved me and the flood kidnapped me." Tonino said he was lucky to have been stranded across the street when *Gustina* was swept away, or he likely would have been swept out to sea with her.

Boats are on buoys, except in winter or when the red storm flag (see the pole at the start of the breakwater) indicates bad seas. At these times, the boats are pulled up onto the square—which is usually reserved for restaurant tables. In the 1970s, tiny Vernazza

THE CINQUE TERRE

had one of Italy's top water polo teams, and the harbor was their "pool." Later, when the league required a real pool, Vernazza dropped out.

The Castle: On the far right, the castle, which is now a grassy park with great views (and nothing but stones), still guards the

town (€1.50 donation, daily 10:00-19:00; from harbor, take stairs by Trattoria Gianni and follow *Ristorante al Castello* signs, tower is a few steps beyond). This was the town's watchtower back in pirate days, and a Nazi lookout in World War II. The castle tower looks new because it was rebuilt after the British bombed it, chasing out the Germans. The highest umbrellas mark the recommended Ristorante Al Castello. The squat tower on the water is great for a glass of wine or a meal. From the breakwater, you could follow the rope to the Ristorante Belforte and pop inside, past the actual submarine door. A photo of a major storm showing the entire tower under a wave (not uncommon in the winter) hangs near the bar.

The Town: Before the 12th century, pirates made the coast uninhabitable, so the first Vernazzans lived in the hills above (near the Reggio Sanctuary). The town itself—and its towers, fortified walls, and hillside terracing—are mostly from the 12th through the 15th centuries, when Vernazza was allied with the Republic of Genoa.

Vernazza has two halves. *Sciuiu* (Vernazzan dialect for "flowery") is the sunny side on the left, and *luvegu* (dank) is the shady side on the right. Houses below the castle were connected by an interior arcade—ideal for fleeing attacks. The "Ligurian pastel" colors are regulated by a commissioner of good taste in the regional government. The square before you is locally famous for some of the area's finest restaurants. The big red central house—on the site where Genoan warships were built in the 12th century—used to be a guardhouse.

In the Middle Ages, there was no beach or square. The water went right up to the buildings, where boats would tie up, Venetian-style. Imagine what Vernazza looked like in those days, when it was the biggest and richest of the Cinque Terre towns. Buildings had a water gate (facing today's square) and a front door on the higher inland side. There was no pastel plaster—just fine stonework (traces of which survive above the Trattoria del Capitano). Apart from the added plaster, the general shape and size of the town has changed little in five centuries. Survey the windows and notice inhabitants quietly gazing back.

The Flood in Vernazza

Vernazza is built around one street—basically a lid over the stream in its ravine. On October 25, 2011, the surrounding hills acted like a funnel, directing flash-flood waters right through the middle of town. (For more on the flood and recovery, see page 376.)

On the afternoon of the disaster, 40 locals and tourists were trapped in the Blue Marlin Bar with the water rising and no way out. The owner, Massimo, knew which bit of wall was thin, and, fortunately, a hammer had been left out nearby. With his bartender, Jeff (the only American man living in Vernazza), they broke through the wall and heroically helped all 40 trapped inside to escape through the hole and onto a staircase leading to safety. In the chaos, one Vernazza woman recalls kissing her little girl and passing her through the hole, thinking she might never see her again. Everyone in the Blue Marlin survived, but the only piano in town was swept away, along with all the bar's shipwreck decor (and a dozen years of family Christmas cards I'd sent, which Massimo had collected on his bulletin board). On my last visit, even though the space was newly plastered and quiet, that hole still yawned in the corner—a reminder of a horrific story.

On the day of the flood, members of one of our Italy tours were enjoying a free day in Vernazza. At the height of the flood, some of them were stranded in Gianni Franzi's restaurant, literally standing on tables as the water rose. Throughout town,

These images show Vernazza's harborfront: on the day before the flood; during the flood; and the cleanup six months later.

While the town has 1,500 residents in summer, only 500 stay here through the winter. Vernazza has accommodations for about 500 tourists.

Above the Town: The small, round tower above the red guardhouse—another part of the city fortifications—reminds us of the town's importance in the Middle Ages. Back then, its key ally Genoa's enemies (i.e., the other maritime republics, especially Pisa) were Vernazza's enemies. Franco's Ristorante and Bar la Torre, just behind the tower, welcomes hikers who are finishing, starting, or simply contemplating the Corniglia-Vernazza hike, with great town views. That tower recalls a time when the entire town was fortified by a stone wall.

people had taken refuge—as people do in a sudden downpour—in shops and restaurants, waiting for it to pass. But this storm wasn't passing. The downpour persisted and the water just kept rising. I heard many personal stories of the moment when, amazingly, the water receded before rising again to its ultimate height. This brief respite gave people (my tour group included) a window of time to scamper out and up nearby staircases to safety. While many thank the town's patron saint, the Madonna of Reggio, others figure a bus became lodged in the narrowest part of the main street, causing a backup that let the flooding below it recede—just temporarily.

Not everyone was so fortunate. Little Vernazza lost three residents: Pino, the gelato man; Sauro, a shopkeeper; and 80-year-old Pina, who refused to leave her apartment. Sauro also refused to leave. He was last seen hanging on to the awning of his building in a muddy torrent. Their bodies washed up together—three weeks later—on the beaches of St-Tropez, France.

After a long winter of hard work, Vernazza's harborfront had blossomed back to life. But the upper half of town still felt like a war zone, with few businesses open and many apartments and homes still unoccupied. Thankfully, the structural integrity of Vernazza's buildings was generally fine, and by the time you visit most businesses will be open. But for the Vernazzan people, the memories of the flood will linger forever.

Vineyards fill the mountainside beyond the town. Notice the many terraces. Someone—probably after too much of that local wine—calculated that the roughly 3,000 miles of dry-stone walls built to terrace the region's vineyards have the same amount of stonework as the Great Wall of China.

For six centuries, the economy was based on wine and olive oil. Then came the 1980s—and the tourists. Locals turned to tourism to make a living, and stopped tending the land. Many vineyards were abandoned, and the terraces fell into disrepair. But it's the stonework of the terracing in the surrounding hills that helps prevent flooding—a lesson learned in the worst possible way on October 25, 2011.

Although many locals still maintain their tiny plots and proudly serve their family wines, the patchwork of local vineyards is atomized and complex because of inheritance traditions. Historically, families divided their land between their children. Parents wanted each child to get some good land. Because some lots were "kissed by the sun" while others were shady, the lots were split into increasingly tiny and eventually unviable pieces—another reason why many have been abandoned.

A single steel train line winds up the gully behind the tower. It is for the vintner's *trenino*, the tiny service train. Play "Where's *trenino?*" and see if you can find two trains. The vineyards once stretched as high as you can see, but since fewer people sweat in the fields these days, the most distant terraces have gone wild again.

The Church, School, and City Hall: Vernazza's Ligurian Gothic church, built with black stones quarried from Punta Mesco (the distant point behind you), dates from 1318. Note the gray stone that marks the church's 16th-century expansion. The gray-and-red house above the spire is the local elementary school (about 25 children attend; education through age 14 is obligatory). High-schoolers go to the "big city," La Spezia. The red building to the right of the schoolhouse, a former monastery, is the City Hall. Vernazza and Corniglia function as one community. Through most of the 1990s, the local government was Communist. In 1999, residents elected a coalition of many parties working to rise above ideologies and simply make Vernazza a better place. That practical notion of government continues here today. The city was led through the trauma and challenges of the flood by Mayor Vincenzo Resasco. He worked so tirelessly and heroically that, suffering from complete exhaustion after the initial recovery period, he had to be helicoptered to the hospital.

Finally, on the top of the hill, with the best view of all, is the town cemetery.

Activities in Vernazza

Tuesday-Morning Market—Vernazza's skimpy business community is augmented Tuesday mornings (8:00-13:00) when a meager gang of cars and trucks pulls into town for a tailgate market.

Beach—The harbor's sandy cove has sunning rocks and showers by the breakwater. There's also a ladder on the breakwater for deep-water access. The sunbathing lane directly under the church also has a shower.

Boat Rental—Before the flood, Vincenzo of Nord Est rented canoes and small motorboats from his stand on the harbor, and also took people out for mini-cruises. He lost his little fleet; how he'll put it back together remains to be seen (contact him for the latest: mobile 338-700-0436, info@manuela-vernazza.com). With a rental boat, you can reach a tiny *acqua pendente* (waterfall) cove between Vernazza and Monterosso; locals call it their *laguna blu*.

Shuttle Bus Joyride—For a cheap and scenic joyride, with a chance to chat about the region with friendly, English-speaking Beppe, Simone, or Pietro, ride the shuttle bus from the top of town to the sanctuaries and hamlets San Bernadino and Reggio—the ancient birthplace of Vernazza—and back again (entire route for the cost of a round-trip ticket, 5/day—usually at 7:00, 9:45, 12:00, 15:00, and 17:30; schedule posted at park office, train station, and bus stop in front of post office; €2.50 one-way, free with Cinque Terre Park Card, churches at sanctuaries are usually closed).

Nightlife in Vernazza

Vernazza's younger generation of restaurant workers lets loose after-hours. They work hard through the tourist season, travel in the winter, speak English, and enjoy connecting with international visitors. After the restaurants close down, the town is quiet except for a couple of nightspots. For more information on the Blue Marlin, Ananasso, Il Pirata, and Ristorante Incadase, see their listings under "Eating in Vernazza," later. All Vernazza bars must close by 24:00.

Blue Marlin Bar dominates the late-night scene with a mix of locals and tourists, home-cooked food until 22:00, good drinks, and piano jam sessions. If you're young and hip, this is *the* place to hang out. There's a new piano, and if you play, you're welcome to contribute to the scene. They also host a free book-swap shelf.

Ananasso Bar offers early-evening happy-hour fun and cocktails *(aperitivi)* that both locals and visitors enjoy. Its harborfront tables get the last sunshine of the day.

Burgus Wine Bar, chic and cool with a jazzy ambience, is a popular early-evening and after-dinner harborside hangout. Sip local wine or a cocktail. Valerio and Lorenza specialize in Ligurian wines and can explain the historic town photos and museum cases of artifacts (closed Tue, free Wi-Fi with a drink, Piazza Marconi 4).

Il Pirata delle Cinque Terre, at the top of the town, was completely destroyed by the flood—but is back in business. This place features the entertaining Cannoli brothers, who fill a happy crowd of tourists with wonderful Sicilian pastries and drinks each evening. Many come for dinner and end up staying because of these two wild and crazy guys and the camaraderie they create among their diners (erratic hours driven by demand, free Wi-Fi).

Ristorante Incadase da Piva (tucked up the lane behind the pharmacy) is the haunt of Piva, Vernazza's troubadour. Piva often gets out his guitar and sings traditional local songs as well as his own compositions. If you're looking for a local Hemingway, check here.

Really Late: There's a little cave on the beach just under the church that lends itself to fun in the wee hours, when everything else is closed.

Sleeping in Vernazza

(€1 = about $1.40, country code: 39)

Vernazza, the spindly and salty essence of the Cinque Terre, is my top choice for a home base. Off-season (Oct-March), you can generally arrive without a reservation and find a place, but at other times, it's smart to book ahead (especially June-July and weekends).

People recommended here are listed for their communication skills (they speak English, have email, and are reliable with bookings) and because they rent several rooms. Consequently, my recommendations cost more than comparable rooms you'll find if you shop around. Comparison-shopping will likely save you €10-20 per double per night—and often get you a better place and view to boot. The real Vernazza gems are stray single rooms with owners who have no interest in booking in advance or messing with email. Arrive by early afternoon and drop by any shop or bar and ask; most locals know someone who rents rooms.

Anywhere you stay here requires some climbing, but keep in mind that more climbing means better views. Most do not include breakfast (for suggestions, see "Eating in Vernazza," later). Cash is preferred or required almost everywhere. Night noise can be a problem if you're near the station. Rooms on the harbor come with church bells (but only between 7:00 and 22:00).

Expect Changes: Following the 2011 flooding, most accommodations in town had to rebuild from scratch. While many are likely open for your visit, specifics have likely changed. When inquiring about rooms, carefully confirm the prices, amenities, and other information noted below.

Pensions

These pensions are located on the Vernazza map, earlier in this chapter.

$$$ Pensione Sorriso, the oldest pension in town (where I stayed on my first visit in 1975), rents 19 overpriced rooms above the train station. While the main building has the charm, it comes with train noise and saggy beds; the annex, up the street, is in a quieter apartment that feels forgotten (S-€65, Sb-€80, D-€100, Db-€140-150, Tb-€130, includes breakfast, some with air-con,

Wi-Fi, Via Gavino 4, tel. 0187-812-224, www.pensionesorriso .com, info@pensionesorriso.com, Francesca and Aldo).

$$$ Trattoria Gianni rents 27 small rooms and three apartments just under the castle. The rooms are in three buildings—one funky, two modern—up a hundred tight, winding spiral stairs. The funky ones, which may or may not have private baths, are artfully decorated à la shipwreck, with tiny balconies and grand sea views *(con vista sul mare)*. The comfy new *(nuovo)* rooms lack views. Both have modern bathrooms and access to a super-scenic cliff-hanging guests' garden. Steely Marisa requires check-in before 16:00 or a phone call to explain when you're coming. Emanuele (Gianni's

son, who now runs the restaurant), Simona, and the staff speak a little English (S-€45, D-€80, Db-€100-120, Tb-€120-140, 10 percent discount with cash and this book—request when you reserve, cancellations less than a week in advance are charged one night's deposit, closed Jan-Feb, Piazza Marconi 5, tel. 0187-812-228, tel. 0187-821-003, on Wed call mobile 393-9008-155 instead, www.giannifranzi.it, info@giannifranzi.it). Pick up your keys at Trattoria Gianni's restaurant on the harbor square.

$$ Albergo Barbara rents nine simple, clean, and modern rooms overlooking the harbor square—most with small windows and small views. It's run by English-speaking Giuseppe and his no-nonsense Swiss wife, Patricia (D-€55, Db-€65-70, big Db with nice harbor view-€110, extra bed-€10, 2-night stay preferred, closed Dec-Feb, reserve online with credit card but pay cash, free Wi-Fi, Piazza Marconi 30, tel. 0187-812-398, mobile 338-793-3261, www .albergobarbara.it, info@albergobarbara.it).

Private Rooms *(Affitta Camere)*

Vernazza is honeycombed with private rooms year-round, offering the best values in town. Owners may be reluctant to reserve rooms far in advance. Doubles cost €55-100, depending on the view, season, and plumbing—you get what you pay for. Most places accept only cash. Some have killer views, come with lots of stairs, and cost the same as a small, dark place on a back lane over the train tracks. Little English is spoken at many of these places. If you call ahead to let them know your arrival time (or call when you arrive, using your mobile phone), they'll meet you at the train station.

Note: Many of the places listed next were not yet open during my last visit to Vernazza—but they hope to be ready by 2013.

Contact those that interest you to see if they're taking guests yet. A helpful source of information is **Save Vernazza,** which began as a post-flood relief organization but has now evolved into an all-purpose Vernazza advocacy group, with info on local rooms and apartments for rent (check their website for details: www.save vernazza.com).

Well-Run Rooms in the Inland Part of Town

Some of my favorite places in town, located in the ravine above the train station, were hardest hit by the flood. Exactly how and when they will reopen is hard to say, but if they're open, they're well worth considering. For the latest, visit their websites or inquire via Save Vernazza. These rooms are located on the Vernazza map, earlier in this chapter.

$$$ **Tonino Basso**'s four rooms, which come with tranquility but no views, will likely be run by Alessandra (www.toninobasso .com).

$$ **La Marina Rooms**—which had already reopened as of summer 2012—is run by hardworking Christian, who speaks English and happily meets his guests at the station to carry their bags. There are five beautiful, top-end, pricey units: Three €90 doubles share a fine ocean-view terrace, and two €120 apartments are more spacious, with fine terraces and views (mobile 338-476-7472, www.lamarinarooms.com, mapcri@yahoo.it).

$$ **Camere Fontana Vecchia** has four spacious, quiet, non-view rooms near the post office, run by Anne (Via Gavino 15, tel. 0187-821-130, mobile 333-454-9371, www.cinqueterrecamere.com, m.annamaria@libero.it).

$$ **Giuliano Basso**'s four carefully crafted rooms are just above town, straddling a ravine among orange trees. It's proudly built out of stone by Giuliano himself—the town's last stone-layer (more train noise than others, above train station, take the ramp just before Pensione Sorriso, mobile 333-341-4792, www.cdh.it /giuliano, giuliano@cdh.it).

Other Reliable Places Scattered Through Town and the Harborside

These places are not located on this book's map; ask for directions when you reserve.

$$$ **La Malà** is Vernazza's jetsetter pad. Four pristine white rooms boast four-star-hotel-type extras and a common terrace looking out over the rocky shore. It's a climb—way, way up to the top of town—but they'll gladly carry your bags to and from the station (Db-€155, Db suite-€220, includes breakfast at a bar, air-con, Wi-Fi, mobile 334-287-5718, www.lamala.it, info@lamala .it, Giamba and Armanda). They also rent the simpler "Armanda's

Room" nearby (no view, Db-€75, ring bell at Piazza Marconi 15).

$$$ Martina Callo's four air-conditioned rooms overlook the square; they're up plenty of steps near the silent-at-night church tower (room #1: Tb-€110 or Qb-€120 with harbor view; room #2: huge Qb family room with no view-€110; room #3: Db with grand view terrace-€100; room #4: roomy Db with no view-€60; free Wi-Fi, ring bell at Piazza Marconi 26, tel. 0187-812-365, mobile 329-435-5344, www.roommartina.com, roomartina @roommartina.com).

$$ Monica Lercari rents several classy rooms with modern comforts, perched at the top of town. Guests are welcome to borrow the family rowboat or mountain bike (Db-€80, sea-view D-€100, grand sea-view terrace D-€120, "honeymoon suite" Db-€180, includes breakfast, air-con, Wi-Fi, next to recommended Ristorante al Castello, tel. 0187-812-296, alcastello vernazza@yahoo.it).

$$ Memo Rooms has three clean and spacious rooms that offer good value. They overlook the main street, in what feels like a miniature hotel. Enrica will meet you if you call upon arrival (Db-€70, Via Roma 15, tel. 0187-812-360, mobile 338-285-2385, www .memorooms.com, info@memorooms.com).

$$ Nicolina rents five recently renovated units with double-paned windows. Two rooms are in the center over the pharmacy, up a few steep steps—one has only sleeper sofas (Db-€80); two others are in a different building beyond the church with great views (Db-€100, Tb-€120, Qb-€150); and the last unit is a two-bedroom quadruple with even better views (€200). Inquire at Pizzeria Vulnetia on the harbor square (Piazza Marconi 29, tel. 0187-821-193, www.camerenicolina.it, camerenicolina.info @cdh.it).

$$ Rosa Vitali rents two four-person apartments across from the pharmacy overlooking the main street (and beyond the train noise). One has a terrace and fridge (top floor); the other has windows and a full kitchen (Db-€95, Tb-€115, Qb-€125, reception at Via Visconti 10 between the grotto and Piazza Marconi, tel. 0187-821-181, mobile 340-267-5009, www.rosacamere.it, rosa.vitali @libero.it).

$$ Francamaria and her kind husband Andrea rent eight sharp, comfortable, and creatively renovated but expensive rooms—all described in detail on her website. While their reception desk is on the harbor square (on the ground floor facing the harbor at Piazza Marconi 30—don't confuse it with Albergo Barbara at same address), the rooms they manage are all over town (Db-€80-120 depending on size and view, Qb-€125-160, extra person-€20, tel. 0187-812-002, mobile 328-711-9728, www.francamaria.com, info@francamaria.com).

More Private Rooms in Vernazza

$$ Maria Capellini rents a couple of simple, clean rooms, including one on the ground floor right on the harbor (Db with kitchen-€85, Tb-€110, cash only, fans, mobile 338-436-3411, www.maria capellini.com, mariacapellini@hotmail.it, Maria and Giacomo).

$$ Ivo's Camere rents two simple no-terrace rooms high above the main street, as well as a studio apartment (Db-€75, studio-€100, free Wi-Fi, Via Roma 6, reception at Pizzeria Fratelli Basso—Via Roma 1, tel. 0187-812-103, mobile 333-477-5521, www .ivocamere.com, post@ivocamere.com).

$$ Vernazza Rooms, run by Daria Bianchi, Chiara, and Davide, rents 12 decent rooms from their office near the station. Four rooms are above the Blue Marlin Bar looking down on the main street, and eight are below the City Hall (Db-€60-95, Qb-€100-120, fans, reception next to Blue Marlin Bar at Via del Santo 9, tel. 0187-812-151, mobile 338-581-4688 or 338-418-8696, www.vernazzarooms.com, info@vernazzarooms.com).

$$ Emanuela Colombo has two rooms—one spacious and basic on the harbor square, the other *molto* chic and located on a quiet side street (Db-€90, Tb-€110, tel. 339-834-2486, www .vacanzemanuela.it, manucap64@libero.it).

More Options: **$$ Affitta Camere Alberto Basso** (a clean, modern room with a noisy harbor/piazza view, Db-€75, check in at Internet Point, albertobasso@hotmail.com); **$$ Capitano Rooms** (3 recently remodeled rooms above the main drag, Db-€90, ask for Paolo or Barbara at the Trattoria del Capitano restaurant, tel. 0187-812-201); **$$ Eva's Rooms** (3 rooms overlooking main street with train noise, Db-€60-80, ring at Via Roma 56, tel. 0187-821-134, www.evasrooms.it, evasrooms@yahoo.it); **$$ Manuela Moggia** (3 rooms, Db-€80, Tb-€95, Qb with kitchen-€125, top of the town at Via Gavino 22, tel. 0187-812-397, mobile 333-413-6374, www.manuela-vernazza.com, info@manuela-vernazza.com); and **$$ Elisabetta Rooms** (3 tired rooms at the tip-top of town with Vernazza's ultimate 360-degree roof terrace, Db-€65, Tb-€90, Qb-€100, fans, Via Carattino 62, mobile 347-451-1834, www.elisa bettacarro.it, carroelisabetta@hotmail.com, Elisabetta and Pino).

Eating in Vernazza

As many Vernazza restaurants were wiped out by the 2011 flood, it's possible that a few of the places listed here may still be under construction or have different hours for your visit.

Breakfast

Locals take breakfast about as seriously as flossing. A cappuccino and a pastry or a piece of focaccia from a bar or bakery does it. Most of my recommended accommodations don't come with breakfast (when they do, I've noted so in my listings). Assuming you're on your own, you have four basic options: Blue Marlin Bar for its extensive menu, including bacon and eggs; Il Pirata delle Cinque Terre for sugary stuff and a lively welcome; Ananasso Bar for coffee and a sweet roll on the harborfront; or any bakery for picnic goodies.

Blue Marlin Bar (mid-town, just below the train station) serves a good array of clearly priced à la carte items including eggs and bacon (only after 8:45), adding up to the priciest breakfast in town (likely to total €10). It's run by Massimo and Carmen with the capable assistance of Jeff, an American who now lives in Vernazza. If you're awaiting a train any time of day, the Blue Marlin's outdoor seating beats the platform (Thu-Tue 7:00-24:00, closed Wed, tel. 0187-821-149).

Il Pirata delle Cinque Terre is located at the top of the town, where the dynamic Sicilian duo Gianluca and Massimo (hard-working twins, a.k.a. the Cannoli brothers) enthusiastically offer a great assortment of handcrafted authentic Sicilian pastries. Their fun and playful service makes up for the lack of a view. Gianluca is a pastry artist, hand-painting fanciful sculptured marzipan. Their sweet pastry breakfasts are a hit, with a stunning array of hot-out-of-the-oven treats like *panzerotto* (made of ricotta, cinnamon, and vanilla, €2.50) and hot cheese and pesto bruschetta (€3). They proudly serve no bacon and eggs (since "this is Italy"). While the atmosphere of the place seems like suburban Milan, it has a curious charisma among its customers—bringing Vernazza a welcome bit of Sicily (daily 6:30-24:00, Via Gavino 36, tel. 0187-812-047).

Ananasso Bar feels Old World, with youthful energy and a great location with little tables right on the harbor. They offer toasted *panini*, pastries, and designer cappuccino. You can eat a bit cheaper at the bar (you're welcome to picnic on the nearby bench or seawall rocks with a Mediterranean view) or enjoy the best-situated tables in town (Fri-Wed 8:00-late, closed Thu).

Picnic Breakfast: Drop by one of Vernazza's several little bakeries, focaccia shops, or grocery stores to assemble a breakfast to eat on the breakwater. Top it off with a coffee in a nearby bar.

Lunch and Dinner

If you enjoy Italian cuisine and seafood, Vernazza's restaurants are worth the splurge. All take pride in their cooking. Wander around at about 20:00 and compare the ambience, but don't wait too late to eat—many kitchens close at 22:00. (Immigrants, who are doing more and more of the hard work of cooking and cleaning, need to wrap things up in time to catch the last train back to La Spezia, where many of them live.) To get an outdoor table on summer

THE CINQUE TERRE

weekends, reserve ahead. Expect to spend €10 for pastas, €12-16 for *secondi*, and €2-3 for a cover charge. Harborside restaurants and bars are easygoing. You're welcome to grab a cup of coffee or glass of wine and disappear somewhere on the breakwater, returning your glass when you're done. If you dine in Vernazza but are staying in another town, be sure to check train schedules before sitting down to eat, as trains run less frequently in the evening. Anchovies are the specialty, and any restaurant loves to show off with dazzling *antipasti misti* plates of seafood and anchovies.

Above the Harbor, by the Castle

Ristorante al Castello is run by gracious and English-speaking Monica, her husband Massimo, kind Mario, and the rest of her family. Hike high above town to just below the castle for commanding views. Their *lasagne al pesto*, "spaghetti on the rocks" (noodles with shellfish), and scampi crêpes are time-honored family specialties. For simple fare and a special evening, reserve one of the dozen romantic cliff-side sea-view tables for two. Some of these tables snake around the castle, where you'll feel like you're eating all alone with the Mediterranean. Monica offers a free *sciacchetrà* or *limoncello* with biscotti if you have this book (€10 pastas, €12 *secondi*, Thu-Tue 12:00-15:00 for lunch, 19:00-22:00 for dinner, closed Wed and Nov-April, tel. 0187-812-296).

Ristorante Belforte's experimental, beautifully presented, creative cuisine includes a hearty *zuppa Michela* (€23 for a boatload of seafood), fishy *spaghetti Bruno* (€13), and *trofie al pesto* (hand-rolled noodles with pesto). Their classic *antipasto del nostro chef* (€36 for six plates) is plenty for two people. From the breakwater, follow either the stairs or the rope that leads up and around to the restaurant. You'll find a tangle of tables embedded in four levels of the lower part of the old castle. For the ultimate seaside perch, call and reserve one of four tables on the *terrazza con vista* (view terrace). Most of Belforte's seating is outdoors—if the weather's bad, the interior can get crowded (€15 pastas, €23 *secondi*, €3 cover, Wed-Mon 12:00-15:00 & 19:00-22:00, closed Tue and Nov-March, tel. 0187-812-222, Michela).

Harborside

Gambero Rosso ("Red Prawn," the same name as Italy's top restaurant guide) is considered Vernazza's most venerable restaurant. It feels dressy and costs more than the others. Try Chef Claudio's namesake risotto (€15 pastas, €20 *secondi*, €3 cover, Tue-Sun 12:00-15:00 & 19:00-22:00, closed Mon and Dec-Feb, Piazza Marconi 7, tel. 0187-812-265).

Trattoria del Capitano serves *spaghetti con frutti di mare* (pasta entangled with various types of seafood) and *grigliata mista* (a mix of seasonal Mediterranean fish) among their offerings (€10 pastas, €16 *secondi*, €2 cover, Wed-Mon 12:00-15:00 & 19:00-22:00, closed Tue except in Aug, closed Nov-Dec, tel. 0187-812-201, while Paolo and Eduardo speak English, grandpa Giacomo doesn't need to).

Trattoria Gianni is an old standby for locals and tourists who appreciate the best prices on the harbor. You'll enjoy well-prepared seafood and receive steady, reliable, and friendly service from Emanuele and Alessandro. Ask about "off-menu specials." While the outdoor seating is basic, the indoor setting is classy (€15 pastas, €15 *secondi*, €3 cover, check their *menù cucina tipica Vernazza*, Thu-Tue 12:00-15:00 & 19:00-22:00, closed Wed except July-Aug, tel. 0187-812-228).

Ristorante Pizzeria Vulnetia is simpler, serving regional specialties such as prizewinning *tegame alla Vernazza*—anchovies, tomatoes, and potatoes baked in the oven (€8 pizzas, €12 pastas, €16 *secondi*, €2 cover, Tue-Sun 12:00-15:30 & 18:30-22:00, closed Thu, Piazza Marconi 29, tel. 0187-821-193, Giuliano).

Inland, on or near the Main Street
Several of Vernazza's inland eateries manage to compete without the harbor ambience, but with slightly cheaper prices.

Trattoria da Sandro, on the main drag, mixes Genovese and Ligurian cuisine with friendly service. It can be a peaceful alternative to the harborside scene, plus they dish up award-winning stuffed mussels (€13 pastas, €15 *secondi*, Wed-Mon 12:00-15:00 & 18:30-22:00, closed Tue, Via Roma 62, tel. 0187-812-223, Gabriella and Alessandro).

Antica Osteria il Baretto is another solid bet for homey, reasonably priced traditional cuisine, run by Simone and Jenny. As it's off the harbor and a little less glitzy than the others, it's favored by locals who prefer less noisy English while they eat great homemade fish ravioli. Sitting deep in their interior can be a peaceful escape (€12 pasta, €14 *secondi*, Tue-Sat 12:00-15:00 & 19:00-22:00, closed Mon, indoor and outdoor seating, Via Roma 31).

Ristorante Incadase da Piva is a rare bit of old Vernazza. For 25 years, charismatic Piva has been known for his *tegame alla Vernazza*, his *riso Piva* (seafood risotto), and his love of music. The town troubadour, he often serenades his guests when the cooking's done. Piva is now joined by his son, Raphael, who speaks English (€10 pastas, €14 *secondi*, Fri-Wed 12:00-15:00 & 19:00-22:30, closed Thu, tucked away 20 yards off the main drag, up a lane behind the pharmacy).

Other Eating Options
Il Pirata delle Cinque Terre, popular for breakfast, is also a favorite for lunch and dinner (€9 pastas, great salads, Sicilian

THE CINQUE TERRE

specialties), and its homemade desserts and drinks. The Cannoli twins entertain while they serve, as diners enjoy delicious meals while laughing out loud in this simple café/pastry shop. The menu offers a break from the predictable Ligurian fare, and the bread is literally hot out of the oven (at the top of town; for complete description, see listing under "Breakfast," earlier).

Bar Baia Saracena ("Saracen Bay") serves decent pizza and pastas out on the breakwater. Eat here for the economy and the view (€5-7 salads, €9 pizza, tel. 0187-812-113, Luca).

Pizzerias, Sandwiches, and Groceries: Vernazza's main-street eateries were among the last businesses to reopen after the flood. Two **pizzerias** stay busy, and while they mostly do takeout, each will let you sit and eat for the same cheap price. One has tables on the street, and the other, called Ercole, hides a tiny terrace and a few tables out back. **Forno Bakery** has good focaccia and veggie tarts, and several bars sell sandwiches and pizza by the slice. **Pino's grocery store** also makes inexpensive sandwiches to order (generally Mon-Sat 8:00-13:00 & 17:00-19:30, closed Sun). Tiny jars of pesto spread give elegance to picnics.

Gelato: The town's three *gelaterias* are good. What looks like **Gelateria Amore Mio** (near the grotto, mid-town) is actually Gelateria Stalin—founded in 1968 by a pastry chef with that unfortunate name. His niece Sonia, who "speaks ice cream," and nephew Francesco now run the place, and are generous with free tastes. They also have good coffee (daily 8:00-24:00, closes at 19:00 off-season, 24 flavors, sit there or take it to go).

Monterosso al Mare (Town #5)

This is a resort with a few cars and lots of hotels, rentable beach umbrellas, crowds, and a little more late-night action than the neighboring towns. Monterosso al Mare—the only Cinque Terre town built on flat land—has two parts: A new town (called Fegina) with a parking lot, train station, and TI; and an old town (Centro Storico), which cradles Old World charm in its small, crooked lanes. In the old town, you'll find hole-

in-the-wall shops, pastel townscapes, and a new generation of creative small-businesspeople eager to keep their visitors happy.

A pedestrian tunnel connects the old with the new—but take a small detour around the point for a nicer walk. It offers a close-up view of two sights: a 16th-century lookout tower, built after the last serious pirate raid in 1545; and a Nazi "pillbox," a small, low concrete bunker where gunners hid. (During World War II, nearby La Spezia was an important Axis naval base, and Monterosso was bombed while the Germans were here.)

Strolling the waterfront promenade, you can pick out each of the Cinque Terre towns decorating the coast. After dark, they sparkle. Monterosso is the most enjoyable of the five for young travelers wanting to connect with others looking for a little evening action. Even so, Monterosso is not a full-blown Portofino-style resort—and locals appreciate quiet, sensitive guests.

Monterosso sustained serious damage in the 2011 flood, but within just a few months, it was back up and running at nearly 100 percent. Walking through the town today, you'll have to know where to look to find evidence of the devastation. Big grates on the six roads cover the historic canals (which drain runoff from the surrounding hills into the sea), and the sound of rushing water reassures townsfolk that the streams are flowing unimpeded below. The old town is filled with newly furnished and equipped shops and restaurants, and photos on walls commemorate the historic deluge. But for the most part, the town is moving on—and eager to welcome visitors.

Orientation to Monterosso

Tourist Information

The TI Proloco is next to the train station (April-Oct daily 9:00-19:00, closed Nov-March, exit station and go left a few doors, tel. 0187-817-506, www.prolocomonterosso.it). If you arrive late on a summer day, the old town's Internet café is helpful with tourist information (see later).

Rebuild Monterosso: Led by a group of American women who married into the community, Rebuild Monterosso brought relief to the town in the immediate aftermath of the flood, and has since morphed into an organization to help preserve and foster healthy tourism. For the latest on the town, its recovery, and their activities, visit www.rebuildmonterosso.com.

Arrival in Monterosso

By Train: Train travelers arrive in the new town, from which it's a scenic, flat 10-minute stroll to all the old-town action (leave station to the left; to reach hotels in the new town, turn right out of station). The bar at track 1, which overlooks both the tracks and the beach, is a handy place to hang out while waiting for your train to pull in (salads, sandwiches, drinks). As many trains run late, this can turn a frustration into a blessing.

Monterosso al Mare

To Levanto &
Autostrada
Exit: Carrodano
or Brugnato

Not to Scale

Walk from Train Station
to Piazza Garibaldi
is approx. 7 mins.

VIA PADRE SEM.

VIA MESCO

VIA PADRE SEM.

VIA MOLINELLI

NEW TOWN
(FEGINA)

TRAIN
STATION

❶

🅖 16

🅖 33

🅖 18

🅖 23

🅖 15   🅖 24

VIA FEGINA

Beach

❸ 🅖 32

🅖 14

🅖 13

VIA 4 NOV.

VIA E. MONTALE

P

Beach
(Free)

Ligurian

Trail to
Levanto

IL GIGANTE
STATUE

Beach
(Free)

BREAKWATER

❶ Hotel Villa Steno	❼ L'Antica Terrazza	❽ A Cà du Gigante
❷ Albergo Pasquale	❽ Manuel's Guesthouse	⓮ Hotel Villa Adriana
❸ Locanda il Maestrale	❾ Buranco Agriturismo	⓯ Hotel la Spiaggia
❹ Albergo Marina	❿ Hotel Souvenir	⓰ Hotel Punta Mesco
❺ Hotel la Colonnina	⓫ Albergo al Carugio	⓱ Pensione Agavi &
❻ Il Giardino Incantato	⓬ The Net (Rooms)	Affittacamere Rist. Il
& Rist. L'Alta Marea	& Pizzeria la Smorfia	Gabbiano

Shuttle buses run roughly hourly along the waterfront between the old town (Piazza Garibaldi, just beyond the tunnel), the train station, and the parking lot at the end of Via Fegina (*Campo Sportivo* stop). While the buses can be convenient—saving you a 10-minute schlep with your bags—they only go once an hour, and are likely not worth the trouble (€1.50, free with Cinque Terre Park Card).

The other alternative is to take a **taxi** (certain vehicles have permission to drive in the old city center). They usually wait outside the train station, but you may have to call (€7 from station to the old town, mobile 335-616-5842 or 335-628-0933).

Le Sirene/Raggi di Sole

Ristorante Belvedere

Ciak Restaurant

Ristorante al Pozzo

Via Venti Restaurant

Miky Restaurant

La Cantina di Miky

Ristorante Tortuga

Il Casello

Il Frantoio Focacceria

Focacceria da Ely

A Ca' du Sciensa Pub

Enoteca Eliseo

Fast Bar

Nuovo Eden Bar

Lucia's Laundry & Bag Check

Wash & Dry Laundry

By Car: Monterosso is 30 minutes off the freeway (exit: Levanto-Carrodano). Note that about three miles above Monterosso, a fork directs you to either *Centro Storico* (old part of town—Via Roma parking lot with a few spots, and possibly the new Loreto garage) or *Fegina* (the new town and beachfront parking, most likely where you want to go). At this point you must choose which area, because you can't drive directly from the new town to the old center (which is closed to cars without special permits).

Parking is easy (except July-Aug and summer weekends) in the huge beachfront guarded lot in the new town (€14/24 hours).

If you're heading to the old town, you'll find the big Loreto parking garage on Via Roma, a 10-minute downhill walk to the main square (€1.70/hour, €18/24 hours). For the cheapest Monterosso rates, park along the blue lines (a few minutes farther uphill from the Loreto garage) for €8 per day. See "Cinque Terre Connections" at the end of this chapter for directions from Milan and tips on driving in the Cinque Terre.

Helpful Hints

Thursday Morning Market: Each Thursday morning, trucks pull into the old town and fill the public area by the beach with temporary stalls where locals get the items not otherwise available in this small town.

Medical Help: The town's bike-riding, leather bag-toting, English-speaking physician is **Dr. Vitone,** who charges €50-80 for a simple visit (less for poor students, mobile 338-853-0949).

Internet Access: The Net, a few steps off the old town's main drag (Via Roma), has eight high-speed computers (€1/10 minutes) and Wi-Fi. Enzo happily provides information on the Cinque Terre, rents rooms (see "Sleeping in Monterosso," later), and can burn your photos onto a DVD for €6 (daily 9:30-23:00, off-season closes for lunch and dinner breaks, Via Vittorio Emanuele 55, tel. 0187-817-288, mobile 335-778-5085, www.monterossonet.com, enzo@monterossonet.com).

Baggage Storage: Lucia's Lavarapido, two blocks from the station, provides a wonderful bag-check service (courageously bucking concerns about terrorist bombs—which can cause entire cities to leave their visitors wondering where they'll park their bags during their visit). Just drop off your bag for €5 (see details in next listing).

Laundry: For full-service laundry in the new town, **Lucia's Lavarapido** will return your laundry to your hotel (€12/13 pounds, daily 8:30-22:00, Via Molinelli 17, mobile 339-484-0940, Lucia and Ivano). For self-service in the old town, **Wash and Dry Lavanderia** is new and modern (€6/wash and dry, daily 7:30-23:30, Via Roma 43).

Massage: Giorgio Moggia, the local physiotherapist, gives good massages at your hotel or in his studio (€60/hour, tel. 339-314-6127, giomogg@tin.it).

Self-Guided Walk

Welcome to Monterosso

• *Hike out from the dock in the old town and climb five rough steps to the very top of the concrete...*

   Breakwater: If you're visiting by boat, you'll start here anyway. From this point, you can survey Monterosso's old town and new town (stretching to the left, with train station and parking lot), and actually see all *cinque* of the *terre* from one spot: Vernazza, Corniglia (above the shore), Manarola, and a few buildings of Riomaggiore beyond that. The little fort above, which dates from 1550, is now a private home.

These days, the harbor hosts more paddleboats than fishing boats. Sand erosion is a major problem. The partial breakwater is designed to save the beach from washing away. While old-timers remember a vast beach, their grandchildren truck in sand each spring to give tourists something to lie on. (The Nazis liked the Cinque Terre, too—find two of their bomb-hardened bunkers, near left and far right.)

The fancy €300-a-night, four-star Hotel Porto Roca (on the far right) marks the trail to Vernazza. High above, you see an example of the costly roads built in the 1980s to connect the Cinque Terre towns with the freeway over the hills. The two capes (Punta di Montenero and Punta Mesco) define the Cinque Terre region. The closer cape, Punta Mesco, marks an important sea-life sanctuary, home to a rare sea grass that provides an ideal home for fish eggs. Buoys keep fishing boats away. The cape was once a quarry, providing employment to locals who chipped out the stones used to build the local towns (the green stones making up part of the breakwater below you are from there).

On the far end of the new town, marking the best free beach around, you can just see the statue named *Il Gigante*. It's 45 feet tall and once held a trident. While it looks as if it were hewn from the rocky cliff, it's actually made of reinforced concrete and dates from the beginning of the 20th century, when it supported a dancing terrace for a *fin de siècle* villa. A violent storm left the giant holding nothing but memories of Monterosso's glamorous age.

• *From the breakwater, walk into the old town. At the top of the beach, notice the openings of two big drains, ready to let flash floods rip through town without destroying things. Walking under the train tracks, venture right into the square and find the statue of a dandy holding what looks like a box cutter.*

Piazza Garibaldi: The statue honors Giuseppe Garibaldi, the dashing firebrand revolutionary who, in the 1860s, helped unite the people of Italy into a modern nation. Facing Garibaldi, with your back to the sea, you'll see (from right to left) the City Hall (with the now-required European Union flag beside the Italian one) and a big home and recreation center for poor and homeless elderly. You'll also see A Ca' du Sciensa pub (with historic town photos inside and upstairs; you're welcome to pop in for a look—see "Nightlife in Monterosso," later).

After the 2011 flood, it was on this square that the National

Guard set up an emergency tent, used for staging emergency deliveries, community meals, Christmas Eve Mass, and the New Year's Eve disco. In the aftermath of the flood, many moving stories emerged. Old ladies who couldn't help dig, helped cook. People worried that Laura, whose bakery—loved for her secret recipes—was destroyed, wouldn't be able to reopen. But she rebuilt, and that beautiful aroma of her sweet cakes again helps locals greet each new day. The motorbike of Diego's dreams, which he had bought just 10 days before the flood, was buried by the mud. He excavated it, cleaned it up, and—to the cheers of his friends—it started. The local civil protection unit is now named for 40-year-old volunteer Sandro Usai, Monterosso's one death from the flood. Sandro was last seen heroically trying to open up a grate to increase canal drainage when he was swept out to sea. When his body washed ashore a week later, his funeral was the first time the community stopped working and was silent together. Sandro posthumously received the highest civilian award the Italian government gives.

Just under the bell tower (with your back to the sea, it's on your left), a set of covered arcades facing the sea is where the old-timers hang out (they see all and know all). The crenellated bell tower marks the church.

• Go to church (the entrance is on the inland side).

Church of St. John the Baptist (Chiesa di San Giovanni Battista): This black-and-white church, with white marble from Carrara and green marble from Punte Mesco, is typical of this region's Romanesque style. Note the lacy, stone rose window above the entrance. It's as delicate as crochet work, with 18 slender mullions (the petals of the rose). The marble stripes get narrower the higher they go, creating the illusion of a church that's taller than it really is.

Step inside for more Ligurian Gothic: original marble columns and capitals with pointed arches to match. The octagonal baptismal font (in the back of the church) was carved from Carrara marble in 1359. Imagine the job getting that from the quarries to here. Nearby is a wooden statue of St. Anthony, carved about 1400, which once graced a church that stood atop Punta Mesco. The church itself dates from 1307—see the proud inscription on the middle column inside: "MilleCCCVII." Outside the church, on the side facing the main street, find the high-water mark from a November 1966 flood (the same month as the flood that devastated Florence). Nearly half a century later, the crippling October 2011 flood hit Monterosso. But the church's statues survived, thanks to townspeople who came to their rescue, carrying them through raging waters to safety. Later, when there was enough help in the streets, excess volunteers came into the church and lovingly polished the candlesticks, just to keep caring for their town.

• *Leaving the church, immediately turn left and go to church again.*

Oratory of the Dead (Oratorio dei Neri): During the Counter-Reformation, the Catholic Church offset the rising influence of the Lutherans by creating brotherhoods of good works. These religious Rotary clubs were called "confraternities." Monterosso had two, nicknamed White and Black. This building is the oratory of the Black group, whose mission—as the macabre decor filling the interior indicates—was to arrange for funerals and take care of widows, orphans, the shipwrecked, and the souls of those who ignore the request for a €1 donation. It dates from the 16th century, and membership has passed from father to son for generations. Notice the fine carved choir stalls (c. 1700) just inside the door, and the haunted-house chandeliers. Look up at the ceiling to find the symbol of the confraternity: a skull-and-crossbones and an hourglass...death awaits us all.

• *Return to the beach and find the brick steps that lead up to the hill-capping convent (starting between the train tracks and the pedestrian tunnel). Stop above the castle at a statue of St. Francis and a wolf taking in a grand view. Enjoy another opportunity to see all five of the Cinque Terre towns. From here, backtrack 20 yards and continue uphill.*

The Switchbacks of the Friars: Follow the yellow brick road (OK, it's orange...but I couldn't help singing as I skipped skyward). Climb uphill until you reach a convent church, then a cemetery, in a ruined castle at the summit. The lane *(Salita dei Cappuccini)* is nicknamed *Zii di Frati* ("switchbacks of the friars").

• *When you reach a gate marked* Convento e Chiesa Cappuccini, *you have arrived.*

Church of the Capuchin Friars: The former convent is now manned by a single caretaker friar. Before stepping inside, notice the church's striped Romanesque facade. It's all fake. Tap it—no marble, just cheap 18th-century stucco. Sit in the rear pew. The high altarpiece painting of St. Francis can be rolled up on special days to reveal a statue of Mary standing behind it. Look at the statue of St. Anthony to the right and smile (you're on convent camera). Wave at the security camera—they're nervous about the precious painting to your left.

This fine painting of the Crucifixion is attributed to Anthony van Dyck, the 17th-century Flemish master who lived and worked for years in nearby Genoa (though art historians suspect that, at best, it was painted by someone in the artist's workshop). When Jesus died, the earth went dark. Notice the eclipsed sun in the painting, just to the right of the cross. Do the electric candles work? Pick one up, pray for peace, and plug it in. (Leave €0.50, or unplug it and put it back.)

• *Leave and turn left to hike 100 yards uphill to the cemetery that fills the remains of the castle, capping the hill. Look out from the gate and enjoy the view.*

Cemetery in the Ruined Castle: In the Dark Ages, the village huddled within this castle. Slowly it expanded. Notice the town view from here—no sea. You're looking at the oldest part of Monterosso, huddled behind the hill, out of view of 13th-century pirates. Explore the cemetery, but remember that cemeteries are sacred and treasured places (as is clear by the abundance of fresh flowers). Ponder the black-and-white photos of grandparents past. *Q.R.P.* is *Qui Riposa in Pace* (a.k.a. R.I.P.). Rich families had their own little tomb buildings. Climb to the very summit—the castle's keep, or place of last refuge. Priests are buried in a line of graves closest to the sea, but facing inland, toward the town's holy sanctuary high on the hillside (above the road, with its triangular steeple peeking above the trees). Each Cinque Terre town has a lofty sanctuary, dedicated to Mary and dear to the village hearts.

• *From here, your tour is over—any trail leads you back into town.*

Sights in Monterosso

Beaches—Monterosso's beaches, immediately in front of the train station, are easily the Cinque Terre's best and most crowded. This town is a sandy resort with rentable beach extras: Figure €20 to rent two chairs and an umbrella for the day. Light lunches are served by beach cafés to sunbathers at their lounge chairs. It's often worth the euros to enjoy a private beach. If you see umbrellas on a beach, it means you'll have to pay a rental fee; otherwise the sand is free (all the beaches are marked on this book's Monterosso al Mare map). Prices get very soft in the afternoon. Don't use your white hotel towels; most hotels will give you beach towels—sometimes for a fee. The local hidden beach, which is free, gravelly, and generally less crowded, is tucked away under Il Casello restaurant at the east end of town, near the trailhead to Vernazza. There's another free beach at the far-west end, near the Gigante statue. The bocce ball court (next to Il Casello) is busy with the old boys enjoying their favorite pastime.

Kayaks—**Samba** rents kayaks on the beach (€7/hour for 1-person kayak, €12/hour for 2-person kayak, to the right of train station as you exit, mobile 339-681-2265, Domenico). The paddle to Vernazza is a favorite.

Shuttle Buses for High-Country Hikes—Monterosso's bus service (described earlier, under "Arrival in Monterosso") continues beyond the town limits, but check the schedules—only one or two departures a day head into the high country. Some buses go to the Sanctuary of Our Lady of Soviore, from where you can hike back down to Monterosso (1.5 hours, moderately steep). Rides cost €1.50 (free with Cinque Terre Park Card, pick up schedule from park office). Or you can hike to Levanto (no Cinque Terre Park card necessary, not as stunning as the rest of the coastal trail, 2.5 hours, straight uphill and then easy decline, follow signs at west end of the new town). For hiking details, ask at the train station TI.

Wine-Tasting—Buranco Agriturismo offers visits to their vine-yard and cantina daily (just about anytime). You'll taste two of their wines plus a grappa and a *limoncino*, along with home-cooked food (up to €25/person with snacks, English may be limited, fol-low Via Buranco uphill to path, 10 minutes above town, tel. 0187-817-677, www.burancocinqueterre.it). They also rent apartments; see "Sleeping in Monterosso," later.

Boat Rides—From the old-town harbor, boats run nearly hourly (10:30-17:00) to Vernazza, Manarola, Riomaggiore, and Portovenere. Schedules are posted in Cinque Terre park offices (for details, see "Getting Around the Cinque Terre—By Boat" on page 348).

Nightlife in Monterosso

A Ca' du Sciensa has nothing to do with science—it's the nick-name of the town moneybags, who had a couple of years of higher education and owned this old mansion. The antique dumbwaiter is still in use—a remnant from the days when servants toiled downstairs while the big shots wined and dined up top. This classy yet laid-back pub offers breezy square seating, bar action on the ground level, an intimate lounge upstairs, and discreet balconies overlooking the square to share with your best travel buddy. It's a good place for light meals from a fun and accessible menu: €5-6 sandwiches, salads, and microwaved pastas. They offer €6 cocktails and mojitos with free *aperitivo* snacks from 17:30 to 20:30. Luca welcomes you to wander around the place and view the old Cinque Terre photo collection (daily 10:00-24:00, Piazza Garibaldi 17, tel. 0187-818-233).

Enoteca Eliseo, the first (and I'd say best) wine bar in town, comes with operatic ambience. Eliseo and his wife, Mary, love music and wine. You can select a fine bottle from their shop shelf, and for €7 extra, enjoy it and the village action from their cozy tables. If you've ever wanted an education in grappa, talk to Eliseo—he stocks 96 varieties. Wines sold by the glass *(bicchiere)* are posted (Wed-Mon 9:00-24:00, closed Tue, Piazza Matteotti 3, a block inland behind church, tel. 0187-817-308).

Fast Bar, the best bar in town for young travelers and night owls, is located on Via Roma in the old town. Customers mix travel tales with big, cold beers, and the crowd (and the rock 'n' roll) gets noisier as the night rolls on. Come here to watch Italian or American sporting events on TV any time of day (sandwiches and snacks usually served until midnight, open nightly until 2:00, closed Nov-March, Alex, Francisco, and Stefano).

La Cantina di Miky, in the new town just beyond the train station, is a trendy bar-restaurant with an extensive cocktail and grappa menu. The seating is in three zones: overlooking the beach, in the garden, or in the cellar. Run by Manuel, son of well-known local restaurateur Miky, it sometimes hosts live music. Manuel offers a fun "five villages" wine-tasting with local meats and cheeses. Microbrews are becoming popular in Italy, and this is the best place in town for top-end Italian beers (daily until well after 24:00, Via Fegina 90, tel. 0187-802-525).

Nuovo Eden Bar, overlooking the beach by the big rock just east of the train station, is a fine place to enjoy a cocktail or fancy ice cream with a sea view. Their happy hour (daily 16:30-21:00) means €6 cocktails come with a snack. Locals consider their ice cream (either to go from the streetside stand, or fancy and sit-down) the best in town. Consider this place for a pre-dinner drink or dessert with a view.

Sleeping in Monterosso

(€1 = about $1.40, country code: 39)
Monterosso, the most beach-resorty of the five Cinque Terre towns, offers maximum comfort and ease. The TI Proloco just outside the train station can give you a list of €70-80 double rooms. Rooms in Monterosso are a better value for your money than similar rooms in crowded Vernazza, and the proprietors seem more genuine and welcoming. To locate the hotels, see the Monterosso al Mare map.

In the Old Town

$$$ Hotel Villa Steno is lovingly managed and features great view balconies, panoramic gardens and a roof terrace with sun beds, air-conditioning, and the friendly help of English-speaking Matteo and his wife, Carla. Of their 16 rooms, 12 have view balconies (Sb-€110, Db-€170, Tb-€195, Qb-€225, includes hearty buffet breakfast, €10 per night discount with cash and this book in 2013, Internet access and Wi-Fi, laundry, parking-€8—reserve in advance, Via Roma 109, tel. 0187-817-028 or 0187-818-336, www .villasteno.com, steno@pasini.com). It's a 15-minute hike (or €8 taxi ride) from the train station to the top of the old town. Readers get a free Cinque Terre info packet and a glass of the local sweet wine, *sciacchetrà*, when they check in—ask for it.

$$$ Albergo Pasquale is a modern, comfortable place with 15 rooms, run by the same family as the Hotel Villa Steno (above). It's conveniently located just a few steps from the beach, boat dock, tunnel entrance to the new town, and train tracks. While there is some train noise, it's mostly a lullaby of waves. Located right on the harbor, it has an elevator and offers easier access than most (same prices and welcome drink as Villa Steno; air-con, all rooms with sea view, Via Fegina 8, tel. 0187-817-550 or 0187-817-477, www.hotelpasquale.com, pasquale@pasini.com, Felicita and Marco).

$$$ Locanda il Maestrale rents six small, stylish rooms in a sophisticated and peaceful little inn. Although renovated with all the modern comforts, it retains centuries-old character under frescoed ceilings. Its peaceful sun terrace overlooking the old town and Via Roma action is a delight (small Db-€115, Db-€145, suite-€170, less off-season, 10 percent discount with cash and this book, air-con, Wi-Fi, Via Roma 37, tel. 0187-817-013, mobile 338-4530-531, www.locandamaestrale.net, maestrale@monterossonet.com, Stefania).

$$$ Albergo Marina, creatively run by enthusiastic husband-and-wife team Marina and Eraldo, has 23 decent rooms and a garden with lemon trees. With a free and filling buffet featuring local specialties from 14:00 to 17:00 daily, they offer a fine value (standard Db-€135, 10 percent discount with cash and this book in 2013, elevator, air-con, Wi-Fi, free use of kayak and snorkel equipment, Via Buranco 40, tel. 0187-817-613, www.hotelmarina5terre.com, marina@hotelmarina5terre.com).

$$$ Hotel la Colonnina, a comfy, modern place with 21 big and pretty rooms, generous public spaces, and several leafy, peaceful sun terraces, is buried in the town's fragrant and sleepy back streets (Db-€140-150, Tb-€200, Qb-€230, €15 more for rooms with viewless terrace, cash only, air-con, Internet access and Wi-Fi, fridges, elevator, inviting rooftop terrace with sun beds, garden, in the old town a block inland from the main square at Via Zuecca 6, tel. 0187-817-439, www.lacolonninacinqueterre.it, info@lacolonninacinqueterre.it, Christina).

$$$ Il Giardino Incantato ("The Enchanted Garden") is a charming four-room B&B in a tastefully renovated 16th-century Ligurian home in the heart of the old town. Breakfast is served in a hidden garden, which is illuminated with candles in the evening (Db-€150-170, Db suite-€200, ask for Rick Steves discount, air-con, Wi-Fi, free minibar and tea and coffee service, Via Mazzini 18, tel. 0187-818-315, mobile 333-264-9252, www.ilgiardino incantato.net, giardino_incantato@libero.it, kind and eager-to-please Fausto and Mariapia).

$$$ L'Antica Terrazza rents four classy rooms right in town. With a pretty terrace overlooking the pedestrian street and minimal stairs, Raffaella and John offer a good deal (Db-€115, 5 percent discount with cash, air-con, Internet access and Wi-Fi, Vicolo San Martino 1, tel. 380-138-0082, mobile 347-132-6213, www.antica terrazza.com, post@anticaterrazza.com).

$$$ Manuel's Guesthouse, perched high above the town among terraces, is a garden getaway ruled by disheveled artist Manuel and run by his nephew Lorenzo (who is happy to carry your bags up the hill). They have six big, bright rooms and a grand view. After climbing the killer stairs from the town center, their killer terrace is hard to leave—especially after a few drinks (Db-€100, big Db with grand-view balcony-€120, cash only, air-con, Internet access and Wi-Fi, in old town, up about 100 steps behind church, Via San Martino 39, mobile 333-439-0809 or 329-547-3775, www.manuelsguesthouse.com, manuelsguesthouse @libero.it).

$$$ Buranco Agriturismo, a 10-minute hike above the old town, has wonderful gardens and views over the vine-covered valley. Its primary business is wine and olive-oil production, but they offer three apartments at a good price. It's a rare opportunity to stay in a farmhouse but still be able to get to town on foot (2-6 people-€60/person including breakfast, €30/child under 12, dinner on request, air-con, free shuttle from station, tel. 0187-817-677, mobile 349-434-8046, www.burancocinqueterre.it, info@buranco .it, informally run by Loredana, Mary, and Giulietta).

$$ Hotel Souvenir is Monterosso's cash-only backpacker hotel. It has 30 rooms in two buildings, each utilitarian but comfortable. Both share a lounge and pleasant leafy courtyard. The basic one is popular with students (S-€30, Sb-€35, D-€55, Db-€70, T-€105, breakfast-€5); the other is less stark and pricier (Sb-€45, Db-€80, Tb-€120, includes breakfast; walk three blocks inland to Via Gioberti 24, tel. 0187-817-822, tel. 0187-817-595, hotel _souvenir@yahoo.com, Beppe).

$$ Albergo al Carugio is a simple, practical nine-room place in a big apartment-style building at the top of the old town. It's quiet, comfy, and functional (Db-€80 when you book direct and mention this book, no breakfast, air-con, Wi-Fi, Via Roma 100, tel. 0187-817-453, www.alcarugio.it, info@alcarugio.it, Andrea and Simona).

$ The Net Room Service is run by Enzo, who owns the Internet point in town (and speaks perfect English). He manages several apartments, offering Monterosso's least expensive accommodations. Enzo's office functions as your reception (Db-€60-70 any time of year, 2- or 3-night minimum stay, Via Vittorio Emanuele 55, tel. 0187-817-288, www.monterossonet.com, info @monterossonet.com).

In the New Town

$$$ A Cà du Gigante, despite its name, is a tiny yet stylish refuge with nine rooms. About 100 yards from the beach (and surrounded by blocky apartments on a modern street), the interior is tastefully done with modern comfort in mind (Db-€160, Db sea-view suite-€180, 10 percent discount with 3-night stay and this book in 2013, occasional last-minute deals, air-con, free parking, Via IV Novembre 11, tel. 0187-817-401, www.ilgigantecinqueterre.it, gigante@ilgigantecinqueterre.it, Claudia).

$$$ Hotel Villa Adriana is a big, modern, bright hotel on a church-owned estate set in a peaceful garden with a pool, free parking, and a no-stress style. They rent 54 rooms at the same price as much simpler places on the water (Sb-€110, Db-€140-160, all with showers, includes big breakfast, air-con, Wi-Fi, Via IV Novembre 23, tel. 0187-818-109, www.villaadriana.info, info @villaadriana.info).

$$$ Hotel la Spiaggia is a venerable old 19-room place facing the beach and run with attitude by Andrea Poggi and his gentle daughter Maria. Half of the rooms come with air-con and half with sea views, but all are the same price—request what you like when you reserve (Db-€160, extra bed-€30, €10 discount for 2-night stays, includes breakfast and parking, elevator, Via Lungomare 98, tel. 0187-817-567, www.laspiaggiahotel.com, hotellaspiaggia @libero.it, friendly Ele at the desk).

$$$ Hotel Punta Mesco is a tidy, well-run little haven renting 17 quiet, modern rooms. While none have views, 10 rooms have small terraces. For the price, it may offer the best comfort in town (Db-€132, Tb-€178, 5 percent discount with cash, air-con, Wi-Fi, free loaner bikes, free parking, Via Molinelli 35, tel. 0187-817-495, www.hotelpuntamesco.it, info@hotelpuntamesco.it, Diego and Anna).

$$$ Pensione Agavi has 10 spartan, bright, hostel-like, over-priced rooms, about half overlooking the beach near the big rock. This is not a place to party—it feels like an old hospital with narrow hallways (D-€80, Db-€110, Tb-€145, same price with or without view, 10 percent discount for 2 nights or more, no breakfast, cash only, refrigerators, turn left out of station to Fegina 30, tel. 0187-817-171, mobile 333-697-4071, hotel.agavi@libero.it, Hillary).

$$ Affittacamere Ristorante il Gabbiano is a charming, family-run restaurant right on the beach, renting five quiet, air-conditioned rooms upstairs. Three rooms face the sea, with small balconies (Db-€100, the largest can be Tb-€130, Qb-€160), while two are at the back (Db-€90). The Gabbiano family restaurant serves as your reception (cash only, refrigerators in rooms, Via Fegina 84, tel. 0187-817-578, lella-v71@hotmail.it).

$ Le Sirene/Raggi di Sole, with nine simple rooms in two humble buildings, is about the cheapest place in town. It's run from a hole-in-the-wall reception desk a block from the station, just off the water. I'd request the Le Sirene building, which doesn't have train noise and is a bit more spacious and airy than Raggi di

Sole (Db-€90, third person-€45, fans, Via Molinelli 10, mobile 393-935-7683, www.sirenerooms.com, sirenerooms@gmail.com, Ermanna).

Eating in Monterosso

Restaurants

Ristorante Belvedere, big and sprawling, is *the* place for a good-value meal indoors or outdoors on the harborfront. Their *amfora belvedere*—mixed seafood stew—is huge, and can easily be split among up to four diners (€48). Share with your group and add pasta for a fine meal. Mussel fans will enjoy the *tagliolini della casa* (€8). Their *antipasti misti* (2-person minimum, €15/person), a fishy treat, can nearly make an entire meal. It's energetically run by Federico and Roberto (€9 pastas, €12 *secondi*, Wed-Mon 12:00-14:30 & 19:00-22:00, usually closed Tue, on the harbor in the old town, tel. 0187-817-033).

L'Alta Marea offers special fish ravioli, the catch of the day, and huge crocks of fresh, steamed mussels. Young chef Marco cooks with charisma, while his wife, Anna, takes good care of the guests. This place is quieter, buried in the old town two blocks off the beach, and has covered tables out front for people-watching (€9 pastas and pizza, €12-15 *secondi*, 10 percent discount with cash and this book, Thu-Tue 12:00-15:00 & 18:00-22:00, closed Wed, Via Roma 54, tel. 0187-817-170).

Ciak, high-energy and tightly packed, is a local institution with reliably good food and higher prices. It's known for its huge, sizzling terra-cotta crock for two crammed with the day's catch and accompanied by risotto or spaghetti, or served swimming in a soup *(zuppa)*. Other popular choices are fish ravioli with shrimp sauce and the seafood *antipasto Lampara*. Stroll a couple of paces past the outdoor tables up Via Roma to see what Signore Ciak (who wears his Popeye cap in the kitchen) has on the stove. His son, Lorenzo, made the new tables himself after the 2011 flood (Thu-Tue 12:00-15:00 & 19:00-22:30, closed Wed, tel. 0187-817-014).

Ristorante al Pozzo is a favorite among locals. It's family-run, with good old-fashioned quality, as Gino (with his long white beard) cooks, and his engaging English-speaking son, Manuel, serves. They have one of the best wine lists in town, serve only homemade pasta, and are known for their raw fish and wonderful seafood *antipasti misti* (€10-15 pastas, €15-20 *secondi*, closed Thu, Via Roma 24, tel. 0187-817-575).

Via Venti is a quiet little trattoria, hidden in an alley deep in the heart of the old town, where Papa Ettore creates imaginative seafood dishes using the day's catch and freshly made pasta. Ilaria and her partner Michele serve up delicate and savory gnocchi (tiny potato dumplings) with crab sauce, tender ravioli stuffed with fresh fish, and pear-and-cheese pasta. There's nothing pretentious here... just good cooking, service, and prices (€11 pastas, €16 *secondi*, Fri-Wed 12:00-15:00 & 18:30-22:30, closed Thu, tel. 0187-818-347). From the bottom of Via Roma, with your back to the sea and the church to your left, head to the right down Via XX Settembre and follow it to the end, to #32.

Miky is packed with well-dressed locals who know their seafood and want to eat it in a classy environment. For elegantly presented, top-quality food, this is my Cinque Terre favorite. It's clearly a proud family operation: Miky (dad), Simonetta (mom), and charming Sara (daughter, who greets guests) all work hard. All their pasta is "pizza pasta"—cooked normally but finished in a bowl that's encased in a thin pizza crust. They cook the concoction in a wood-fired oven to keep in the aroma. Miky's has a fine wine list with many available by the glass if you ask. If I were ever to require a dessert, it would be their mixed sampler plate, *dolce mista*—€10 and plenty for two (€15 pastas, €22 *secondi*, €8 sweets, Wed-Mon 12:00-15:00 & 19:00-23:00, closed Tue, reservations wise in summer, diners tend to dress up a bit, in the new town 100 yards north of train station at Via Fegina 104, tel. 0187-817-608).

La Cantina di Miky, a few doors down (toward the station), serves Ligurian specialties that follow in Miky's family tradition of quality. Run by son Manuel—and Christine from New Jersey—it's more trendy, youthful, and informal than Miky's. You can sit downstairs, in the garden, or overlooking the sea (€16 anchovy tasting plate, €13 pastas, €15 *secondi*, creative desserts, large selection of Italian microbrews, daily 12:00-24:00 or later, Via Fegina 90, tel. 0187-802-525). This place doubles as a cocktail bar in the evenings—see "Nightlife in Monterosso," earlier.

Ristorante Tortuga is the top option in Monterosso for sea-view elegance, with gorgeous outdoor seating on a bluff and an elegant white-tablecloth-and-candles interior. If you're looking for a place to propose, this offers the prettiest and most romantic dining in town. When you're out and about, drop by to consider which table you'd like to reserve for later. House specialties include *cannelloni tortuga* and *filetto sciacchetrà* (€15 pastas, €20 *secondi*, Tue-Sun 12:00-14:30 & 18:00-22:00, closed Mon, just outside the tunnel that connects the old and new town, tel. 0187-800-065, mobile 333-240-7956, Silvia and Giamba).

Il Casello is the only place for a fun meal on a terrace overlooking the old-town beach. With outdoor tables on a rocky outcrop, it's a pleasant spot for a salad, pasta, or *secondi* (€10 pastas, €15 *secondi*, daily April-Oct, closed Nov-March, mobile 333-492-7629, Bacco).

Light Meals, Take-Out Food, and Breakfast

Lots of shops and bakeries sell pizza and focaccia for an easy picnic at the beach or on the trail. **Pizzeria la Smorfia**—the local favorite for pizza—cooks up good pizza to eat in or take out. Pizzas come in two sizes; the large can feed three (closed Thu, Via Vittorio Emanuele 73).

At **Il Frantoio,** Simone makes tasty pizza to go or to munch perched on a stool (closed Thu, just off Via Roma at Via Gioberti 1).

Focacceria da Ely makes airy focaccia and thick-crust pizzas for casual seating or takeout (daily 10:30-20:00, until 24:00 in summer, Emigliano).

For a quick bite right at the train station (or on the beach), consider **Il Massimo della Focaccia**. Massimo and Daniella serve local quiche-like tortes, sandwiches, focaccia pizzas, and desserts. With benches just in front, this is a good bet for a €4 light meal with a sea view (daily, Via Fegina 50 at the entry to the station).

Breakfast: Most hotels include breakfast in the room rate. But if you're out looking for breakfast, consider **Bar Gio,** near the train station on the waterfront (continental breakfasts), or **Bar Davi,** under the arch on Via Roma in the old town (with an American-style option, daily from 7:00).

Cinque Terre Connections

By Train

The five towns of the Cinque Terre are on a pokey milk-run train line (described in "Getting Around the Cinque Terre—By Train" on page 346). Erratically timed but roughly hourly trains connect each town with the others, plus La Spezia, Genoa, and Riviera towns to the north. While a few of these local trains go to more distant points (Milan or Pisa), it's much faster to change in La Spezia, Monterosso, or Sestri Levante to a bigger train (local train info tel. 0187-817-458, www.trenitalia.com).

From La Spezia Centrale by Train to: Rome (7/day, 3-4.5 hours, more with changes, €45; an evening train—departing around 20:00—gives you a complete day in the region while still getting you to Rome that night), **Pisa** (about hourly, 1-1.5 hours, €5), **Florence** (5/day direct, otherwise nearly hourly, 2.5 hours, €11.30), **Milan** (about hourly, 3 hours direct or with change in Genoa, €22), **Venice** (about hourly, 5-6 hours, 1-3 changes, €50).

From Monterosso by Train to: Venice (about hourly, 6-7 hours, 1-3 changes, €52), **Milan** (8/day direct, otherwise hourly with change in Genoa, 3-4 hours, €22), **Genoa** (hourly, 1.2-2 hours, €8), **Turin** (8/day, 3-4 hours, €20), **Pisa** (hourly, 1-2 hours, €6-10), **Sestri Levante** (hourly, 20-40 minutes, most trains to Genoa stop here, €3), **La Spezia** (2-3/hour, 15-30 minutes), **Levanto** (2-3/hour,

4 minutes), **Santa Margherita Ligure** (at least hourly, 45 minutes, €4.50), **Rome** (hourly, 4.5 hours, change in La Spezia, €50). For destinations in **France,** change trains in Genoa.

By Car
Because these towns are close together and have frequent transportation connections, bringing a car to the Cinque Terre is not the best idea. If your plans require it, however, here are some basic tips: Stay in a hotel that includes parking, use public transportation or hike between towns, and for day-trip parking, go to Monterosso (€14-18/day), Riomaggiore (€22/day), or Manarola (€15/day). Don't drive to Vernazza, as the flood blew out its parking lot. Even if it's rebuilt, finding a spot will likely be tough. Parking anywhere on the Cinque Terre is truly a mess in July and August.

Milan to the Cinque Terre (130 miles): Drivers speed south on autostrada A-7 from Milan, skirt Genoa, and drive a little bit of Italy's curviest and narrowest freeways, passing the Cinque Terre toward the port of La Spezia (A-12). Another option is to take the slightly straighter A-1 via the city of Parma, followed by A-15 to La Spezia. This route takes the same amount of time (about 2.5 hours), even though it covers more miles.

The route from autostrada A-12 depends partly on the status of repairs to the 2011 flood damage. As of this writing (mid-2012), this is the best approach, but confirm details locally:

To reach **Monterosso** (about 30 minutes from the autostrada), exit A-12 at *uscita Carrodano*, northwest of La Spezia. Remember that the highway divides as you approach Monterosso—you must choose between the road to Centro Storico (the old town) or the one to Fegina (the new town and beachfront parking).

For **Vernazza**, **Riomaggiore, Corniglia,** or **Manarola,** leave the freeway at La Spezia. The drive down to Vernazza is scenic, narrow, and scary; it's better to park at the new lot next to the La Spezia train station and ride the train in. While there is a secondary road connecting Vernazza and Monterosso, it's not recommended (the main road, SP-63, was washed out by the flood and will likely remain closed in 2013—ask locally). For a map of the region, see page 343.

Within the Cinque Terre: On busy weekends, holidays, and in July and August, both Vernazza and Monterosso fill up, and police at the top of town will deny entry to anyone without a hotel reservation. It's smart to have a confirmation in hand. If you don't, insist (politely) that they allow you to enter—but only if you actually have a room reserved (the police might call your hotel to check your story).

Parking Tips: Riomaggiore, Manarola, and Monterosso each have a parking lot and a once-an-hour shuttle bus to get you into town, though all parking areas are no more than a 10-minute walk uphill from the center.

White signs post valid hours for pay parking, which usually don't charge 24:00-8:00. Anyone can park where there are blue lines. Parking is cash only in all towns (except Riomaggiore, where some readers have been overcharged on their credit cards—best to pay in cash).

If you plan to find parking in any of the Cinque Terre towns, try to arrive between 10:00 and 11:00, when overnight visitors are usually departing. Or you can park your car in Levanto or La Spezia (both covered in next chapter), then take the train into the town of your choice. In these bigger towns, confirm that your parking spot is OK, and leave nothing inside to steal.

A few hotels offer parking for free or a daily charge. In **Monterosso,** consider Hotel Villa Steno, A Cà du Gigante, or Hotel Punta Mesco. For **Riomaggiore,** try Locanda del Sole, Locanda Ca' dei Duxi, or Villa Argentina. In Volastra (a shuttle ride above **Manarola**), try Hotel il Saraceno. Rooms listed in this book for Corniglia and Vernazza do not offer parking.

RIVIERA TOWNS NEAR THE CINQUE TERRE

*Levanto • Sestri Levante • Santa Margherita Ligure •
Portofino • La Spezia • Carrara • Portovenere*

The Cinque Terre is tops, but several towns to the north have a breezy beauty and more beaches. Towns to the south offer a mix of marble, trains, and yachts.

Levanto, the northern gateway to the Cinque Terre, has a long beach and a scenic, strenuous trail to Monterosso al Mare. Sestri Levante, on a narrow peninsula flanked by two beaches, is for sun-seekers. Santa Margherita Ligure is more of a real town, with actual sights, beaches, and easy connections with Portofino by trail, bus, or boat. All three towns are a straight shot to the Cinque Terre by train.

South of the Cinque Terre, you'll likely pass through the workaday town of La Spezia (don't stay here unless you're desperate), the southern gateway to the Cinque Terre. Carrara is a quickie for marble lovers who are driving between Pisa and La Spezia. The picturesque village of Portovenere, near La Spezia, has scenic boat connections with Cinque Terre towns.

Public transportation is the best way to get around this region. All the places in this chapter are well connected by train and/or boat.

North of the Cinque Terre

Levanto

Graced with a long, sandy beach, Levanto is packed in summer and popular with surfers. The rest of the year, it's just a small, sleepy town, with less charm and fewer tourists than the Cinque Terre. With quick connections to Monterosso (4 minutes by train), Levanto makes a decent home base if you can't snare a room in the Cinque Terre.

Levanto has a new section (with a regular grid street plan) and a twisty old town (bisected by a modern street), plus a few pedestrian streets and a castle (not tourable). From Levanto, you can take a no-wimps-allowed hike to Monterosso (2.5 hours) or hop a boat to the Cinque Terre towns and beyond.

Orientation to Levanto

Tourist Information

The helpful TI is on Piazza Mazzini (daily 9:00-13:00 & 15:00-18:00, tel. 0187-808-125, www.comune.levanto.sp.it).

Arrival in Levanto

By Train: It's a 10-minute walk from the Levanto train station to the TI in town (head down stairs in front of station, turn right, cross bridge, then follow Corso Roma to Piazza Mazzini).

By Car: Drivers can use the cheap short-term parking in the lots in front of and on either side of the train station (€6/8 hours, €9/24 hours, note that you have to pay at the machines each day—so long-term parking is difficult). Another option is the lot across the river from the hospital on the way into town (first left after the hospital, cross bridge and immediately turn left), or north of the church on Via del Mercato (free during high season, except Wed before 14:00). For long-term parking, try the lots at Piazza Mazzini or behind the TI (€18/day).

Helpful Hints

Markets: Levanto's modern covered *mercato*, which sells produce and fish, is on Via del Mercato, between the TI and train station (Mon-Sat 8:00-13:00, closed Sun). On Wednesday morning, an **open-air market** with clothes, shoes, and housewares fills the street in front of the *mercato*.

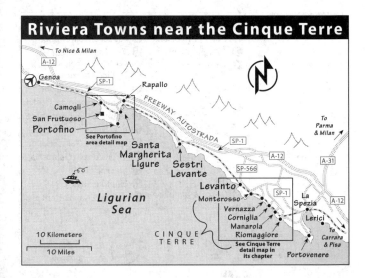

Riviera Towns near the Cinque Terre

Internet Access: Try **Viaggi Beraldi** at Via Garibaldi 102 (€2/30 minutes, Mon-Sat 9:00-12:30 & 15:30-19:30, closed Sun, tel. 0187-800-818).

Baggage Storage: None is available at the station. Baggage storage is available in La Spezia (see page 446), Monterosso (page 402), and possibly Santa Margherita Ligure (page 431).

Laundry: A self-service launderette stuffed with snack and drink vending machines is at Piazza Staglieno 38 (wash-€5 including soap, dry-€5, open 24 hours daily, mobile 338-701-6341).

Bike Rental: Cicli Raso North Shore rents bikes (€8-20/day depending on type of bike, daily 9:30-12:30 & 15:30-19:30, closed Sun Nov-April, Via Garibaldi 63, tel. 0187-802-511, www.cicliraso.com).

Sports Rentals: Rosa dei Venti rents kayaks, canoes, surfboards, and windsurfing equipment right on the beach (Marco mobile 349-520-7538, Nicola mobile 349-520-7538, www.levantorosa deiventi.it).

Sights in Levanto

Beach—The beach is just two blocks away from the TI. As you face the harbor, the boat dock is to your far left, and the diving center is to your far right (rental boats available at either place in summer). You can also rent a kayak or canoe on the beach, just below the east end of the Piazza Mazzini parking lot.

During the summer, three parts of the beach are free: both sides of the boat dock, and behind the TI. The rest of the beach is broken up into private sections that charge admission. You can

Levanto

1. Albergo Primavera
2. Villa Margherita
3. Garden Hotel
4. A Durmi Guesthouse
5. Ristorante la Loggia Rooms
6. Villa Clelia B&B
7. La Rosa dei Venti Rooms
8. To Erba Persa Agriturismo
9. Ostello Ospitalia del Mare
10. Osteria Tumelin
11. Da Rino Trattoria
12. Ristorante Moresco
13. Taverna Garibaldi & Bike Rental
14. La Picea Pizzeria
15. Focacceria il Falcone
16. Il Laboratorio del Pesto
17. Dimarket Supermarket
18. Crai Supermarkets (2)
19. Il Pinguino Gelateria
20. Il Porticciolo Gelateria
21. Internet Café
22. Launderette
23. Canoe & Kayak Rental

always stroll along the beach, even through the private sections—just don't sit down. Off-season, roughly October through May, the entire beach is free, and you can lay your towel anywhere you like.

Old Town and Trailhead—The old town, several blocks from the TI and beach, clusters around Piazza del Popolo. Until a few decades ago, the town's open-air market was held at the 13th-century loggia (covered set of archways) in the square. Explore the back streets.

To reach the trailhead to Monterosso: From Piazza del Popolo, head uphill to the striped church, Chiesa di Sant'Andrea (with your back to the loggia, go straight ahead—across the square and up Via Don Emanuele Toso to the church). From the church courtyard, follow the sign to the *castello* (a private residence), go under the stone arch, and continue uphill. Or, if you're coming from the seaside promenade (Via Gaetano Semenza), head under the arches and up the stairs, and follow the signs to the *castello*. Either route leads you to a sign that points you toward Punta Mesco, the rugged tip of the peninsula. From here, you can hike up to Monterosso (2.5 hours). This lovely, rugged-and-wild hike is no joke—bring lots of water and wear good shoes. Most of the trail is a gradual up-and-down, but the last stretch into Monterosso is almost entirely big steps, so those with knee problems might consider starting in Monterosso instead. The elevation gain overall is more than double that of the toughest Cinque Terre hikes. The Cinque Terre hiking pass is not necessary here.

Hike or Bike to Bonassola—Cross the river bridge located by the TI to wander along this waterfront path, good for walking or cycling. You'll encounter shaded tunnels and two sunny beaches on the way to the small but modern town of Bonassola with its sandy beach (25 minutes by foot, 10 minutes by bike, public beaches located a minute's walk down from trail).

Sleeping in Levanto

In this popular beach town, many hotels want you to take half-pension (lunch or dinner) in summer, especially in July and August. Prices listed here are the maximum for high season (July-Aug); smaller rooms or those without views may be less. Expect to pay €10-30 less per night for April-June and September-October, and even less for the rest of the year. The longer your stay, the greater your bargaining power. The high number of four-person rooms in Levanto makes it particularly welcoming to families who want to explore the Cinque Terre. Many hotels rent out large apartments with kitchenettes (without a half-pension requirement), and parking is free or very reasonable.

$$$ Albergo Primavera is family-run, with 17 recently redecorated, tasteful rooms—10 with balconies but no views—just a half-block from the beach (Db-€130, request a quiet room off the street, includes hearty breakfast buffet with local hams and cheeses, air-con, Internet access and Wi-Fi, free loaner bikes, Via Cairoli 5, tel. 0187-808-023, fax 0187-801-588, www.primavera hotel.com, info@primaverahotel.com). Friendly Carlo, cheerful Daniela, and older daughter Giuditta speak some English, and younger daughter Gloria does her homework in the dining room.

Sleep Code

(€1 = about $1.40, country code: 39)
S = Single, **D** = Double/Twin, **T** = Triple, **Q** = Quad, **b** = bathroom,
s = shower only. Unless otherwise noted, credit cards are
accepted, English is spoken, and breakfast is included.

To help you sort easily through these listings, I've divided
the accommodations into three categories based on the price
for a standard double room with bath:

$$$ Higher Priced—Most rooms €110 or more.
$$ Moderately Priced—Most rooms between €50-110.
$ Lower Priced—Most rooms €50 or less.

Prices can change without notice; verify the hotel's
current rates online or by email.

Carlo also does airport transfers for a reasonable rate.

$$$ Villa Margherita is 300 yards out of town, but the shady
gardens, 11 characteristic colorfully tiled rooms (some with lit-
tle view terraces), and tranquility are worth the walk (Db-€160,
Tb-€185, 5 percent discount with cash and this book, elevator one
flight up from street level, Internet access, free Wi-Fi, free parking,
10-minute walk to town with stairs, 5-minute walk to train station,
free shuttle service from station if you tell them when you'll arrive,
Via Trento e Trieste 31, tel. 0187-807-212, fax 0187-803-717, mobile
328-842-6934, www.villamargherita.net, info@villamargherita
.net). They also rent apartments around town and a fancy villa (for
up to 14 people) set on a peninsula by the sea (www.levanto.net).

$$$ Garden Hotel offers 17 simple, bright, and modern
rooms, all with balconies (but most lack views due to the elevated
street), a block from the beach on busy Corso Italia (Db-€120, new
fifth-floor rooms with views and terraces go for Db-€148, 5 percent
discount with cash and this book, lower floors closed mid-Nov-
mid-March, air-con, elevator for some floors, free Internet access
and Wi-Fi, free parking but not on-site—can unload bags and
then park near the station, Corso Italia 6, tel. 0187-808-173, fax
0187-803-652, www.nuovogarden.com, info@nuovogarden.com,
Davide and Damiano).

$$ A Durmì is a happy little *affitta camere* (guesthouse) owned
by Graziella, Gianni, and their two daughters, Elisa and Chiara.
Their sunny patios, green leafy gardens, six immaculate modern
new rooms, and five sunlit apartments make a welcoming place to
stay (Db-€100, extra bed-€20; apartments-€150—no minimum
stay required; rooms cleaned daily, breakfast-€7, air-con, power
showers, Internet access and Wi-Fi, bar, parking-€5/day, Via D.

Viviani 12, tel. 0187-800-823, mobile 349-105-6016, www.adurmi
.it, info@adurmi.it).

$$ Ristorante la Loggia has four pleasant, cozy, summery rooms perched above the old loggia on Piazza del Popolo (Db-€70, cash only, request balcony, quieter rooms in back, two basic side-by-side apartments great for families of 4-8, lots of stairs, air-con, free parking, Piazza del Popolo 7, tel. & fax 0187-808-107, mobile 335-641-7701, Nerina does not speak English).

$$ Villa Clelia B&B has six peaceful, dark, air-conditioned rooms (named for the winds—*scirocco, maestrale,* and so on) with mini-fridges and terraces in a garden courtyard just 50 yards from the sea (Db-€70-90, minimal in-room breakfast, free parking, with loggia on your left it's straight ahead at Piazza da Passano 1, tel. 0187-808-195, mobile 328-797-6403, www.villaclelia.it, info@villaclelia.it). They also have seven central apartments that economically sleep up to five (€700/week, 3-night minimum stay). B&B rooms are cleaned daily; you're on your own at the apartments.

$$ La Rosa dei Venti is an *affitta camere* just a couple of blocks from the beach. Enthusiastic Rosanna and her son Marco rent five super-clean rooms with dark hardwood floors, comfy rugs, and a hodgepodge of glittery seashore decor (Db-€100, Tb-€135, includes homemade breakfast and free parking, free Wi-Fi, behind Enoteca Tumelin across from Piazza del Popolo, Via della Compera, tel. 0187-808-165, Marco's mobile 328-742-8268, www .larosadeiventilevanto.com, info@larosadeiventilevanto.com).

$$ Erba Persa Agriturismo, a rustic farmhouse run by sunny Grazia Lizza and her gardener husband Claudio, hosts cats, dogs, pet rabbits, and donkeys among their plots of organic fruits and vegetables. It's a 10-minute walk from the train station and about a 20-minute walk from town (D-€50, Db with balcony and view-€70, Tb-€80, free Internet access, free parking, free mosquitoes, Via N. S. della Guardia 21, mobile 339-400-8587 or 348-344-7695, fax 0187-801-376, www.erbapersa.it, erbapersa@alice.it).

***Hostel:* $ Ostello Ospitalia del Mare**, a budget gem, is run by the city tourist association. It has 70 beds, airy rooms, an elevator, and a terrace in a well-renovated medieval palazzo a few steps from the old town (beds-€19-27 in 4-, 6-, and 8-bed rooms with private bath, Db-€65; includes breakfast, towels, and sheets; Internet access and free Wi-Fi, self-service laundry-€7.50, microwave, fridge, non-members welcome, co-ed unless you strenuously object, no curfew, no lockout; office open daily April-Oct 8:00-13:00 & 16:00-20:00, until 23:00 weekend nights, slightly shorter hours off-season; may close Nov-March, Via San Nicolò 1, tel. 0187-802-562, fax 0187-803-696, www.ospitaliadelmare.it, info @ospitaliadelmare.it).

Eating in Levanto

Osteria Tumelin, a local favorite, is more expensive than other options, but has a dressy, sophisticated ambience and a wide selection of fresh seafood. Reservations are smart on weekends or if you want to dine outside (daily 12:00-14:30 & 19:00-22:30, closed Thu Oct-May, aquarium containing giant lobster and moray eels in first dining room on the right, Via D. Grillo 32, across street from loggia, tel. 0187-808-379).

Da Rino, a small trattoria on a quiet pedestrian lane, dishes up reasonably priced fresh seafood and homemade Ligurian specialties prepared with care. Consider the grilled *totani* (squid), *pansotti con salsa di noci* (cheese ravioli with walnut sauce), and *trofie al pesto* (local pasta with pesto sauce). Dine indoors, or at one of the few outdoor tables. On busy nights, they open up a second dining room across the street (€8 pastas, €13 *secondi,* cash only, daily 19:00-22:00, closed Tue Nov-mid-March, Via Garibaldi 10, tel. 0187-813-475).

Ristorante la Loggia, next to the old loggia, makes fine gnocchi with scampi and saffron sauce. Their daily fish specials are served in a homey wood-paneled dining room or on a little terrace overlooking the square (€10 pastas, €15 *secondi,* Thu-Tue 12:30-14:00 & 19:00-22:00, closed Wed, closed Nov-Feb, Piazza del Popolo 7, tel. 0187-808-107).

Ristorante Moresco serves large portions of pasta and seafood at reasonable prices in a vaulted, candlelit room decorated with Moorish-style frescoes. The best value is their €25 four-course tasting *menu* (doesn't include drinks, 2-person minimum). Skip the house white wine and order something more drinkable from their wine list (daily 12:00-14:00 & 19:00-21:00, until 23:00 in summer, may close Sun evenings in winter, reservations appreciated, Via Jacopo 24, tel. 0187-807-253, busy Roberto and Francesca).

Taverna Garibaldi is a good-value, cozy place on the most characteristic street in Levanto, serving focaccia with various toppings, made-to-order *farinata* (savory chickpea crêpe), 34 types of pizza, and salads (€8 light meals, daily in summer 19:00-22:00, closed Tue Sept-June, Via Garibaldi 57, tel. 0187-808-098).

La Picea serves up wood-fired pizzas to go, or dine at one of their few small tables (Tue-Sun 16:30-21:45, closed Mon, just off the corner near Via Varego at Via della Concia 18, tel. 0187-802-063).

A Picnic or Bite on the Go: Focaccerie, rosticcerie, and delis with take-out pasta abound on Via Dante Alighieri. **Focacceria il Falcone** has a great selection of focaccia with different toppings (daily 9:30-22:00, Oct-May closes at 20:00 and on Mon, Via Cairoli 19, tel. 0187-807-370). For more picnic options, try the *mercato* (mornings except Sun; see "Helpful Hints," page 418). It's fun to grab a crusty loaf of bread, then pair it with a pot of freshly made Genovese *pesto* from **Il Laboratorio del Pesto** (sometimes closed Wed afternoons, Via Dante 14, tel. 0187-807-441). The **Dimarket supermarket** just below the train station has a good deli counter and opens at 7:00—handy for those taking an early train. There are two **Crai supermarkets:** One is just off Via Jacopo da Levanto at Via del Municipio 5 (Mon-Sat 8:00-13:00 & 17:00-20:00, Sun 8:00-13:00 & 16:30-19:30); the other is nearby on Piazza Staglieno (for a shaded setting, lay out your spread on a bench in the grassy park at this piazza). Another excellent picnic spot is Piazza Cristoforo Colombo, located east of the swimming pool, with benches and sea views.

And for Dessert: Compare **Il Pinguino Gelateria** at Piazza Staglieno 2 (daily until late) with **Il Porticciolo Gelateria,** at the end of Via Cairoli at Piazzetta Marina (daily in summer, closed Mon Sept-June, mobile 393-228-1570).

Levanto Connections

From Levanto: To get to the Cinque Terre, you can take the **train** (2-3/hour, 4 minutes to Monterosso). A slower, more scenic option is the **boat,** which stops at every Cinque Terre town—except Corniglia—before heading to Portovenere (2/day Easter-Oct, none Nov-Easter; €7 one-way to Monterosso, 10:00 departure includes Cinque Terre, Portovenere, and Lerici Island tour for €28; 14:30 departure includes Cinque Terre and 1-hour stop in Portovenere for €18; 1 return boat each day from Portovenere departs at about 17:00; pick up boat schedule and price sheet from TI or boat dock, tel. 0187-732-987 or on weekends 0187-777-727, www.navigazione golfodeipoeti.it).

Sestri Levante

This peninsular town is squeezed as skinny as a hot dog between its two beaches. The pedestrian-friendly Corso Colombo, which runs down the middle of the peninsula, is lined with shops that sell take-away pizza, pastries, and beach paraphernalia. Don't be discouraged by the ugly modern town in front of the train station; the peninsula, about a seven-minute walk away, has charm to spare.

Hans Christian Andersen enjoyed his visit here in the mid-1800s, writing, "What a fabulous evening I spent in Sestri

Levante!" One of the bays—Baia delle Favole—is named in his honor (*favole* means "fairy tale"). The small mermaid curled on the edge of the fountain behind the TI is another nod to the beloved Danish storyteller.

During the last week of May, the town holds a street festival, culminating in a ceremony for locals who write the best fairy tales (four prizes for four age groups, from pre-kindergarten to adult). The "Oscar" awards are little mermaids.

Orientation to Sestri Levante

Tourist Information: From the train station, it's a five-minute walk to the TI, where you can pick up a map (Tue-Sat 9:30-13:00 & 14:00-17:30, closed Sun-Mon; go straight out of station on Via Roma, turn left at fountain in park, TI in next square—Piazza Sant'Antonio 10; tel. 0185-457-011).

Market Day: It's on Saturday at Piazza Aldo Moro (8:00-13:00).

Baggage Storage: None is available at the station.

Sights in Sestri Levante

Stroll the Town—From the TI, take Corso Colombo (to the left of Bermuda Bar, eventually turns into Via XXV Aprile, then Via alla Penisola), which runs up the peninsula. Follow this street— lively with shops, eateries, and delightful pastel facades—for about five minutes. Just before you get to Piazza Matteotti with the large white church at the end, turn off for either beach (free Silenzio beach is on your left). Or continue on the street to the left of the church and head uphill. You'll pass the evocative arches of a ruined chapel (bombed during World War II, and left as a memorial). A few minutes farther on, past a stony Romanesque church, the road winds to the right to the Grand Hotel dei Castelli. Consider a drink at their view café (so-so view, reasonably priced drinks, daily 10:00-24:00, café entrance is at end of parking lot). The rocky, forested bluff at the end of the town's peninsula is actually the huge private backyard of this fancy hotel.

Beaches—These are named after the bays *(baie)* that they border. The bigger beach, Baia delle Favole, is divided up much of the year (May-Sept) into sections that you must pay to enter. The fees, which can soar up to €30 per day in August (no hourly rate), generally include chairs, umbrellas, and fewer crowds. There are several small free sections: at the ends and in the middle (look for *libere* signs, and ask *"Gratis?"* to make sure that it's free). For less-expensive sections of beach (where you can rent a chair for about €8-10), ask for *spiaggia libera attrezzata* (spee-AH-jah LEE-

Sestri Levante

To Rapallo & Santa Margherita Ligure

To Santa Margherita Ligure

To Santa Margherita Ligure & Portofino

TRAIN STATION

Piazza Caduti

LUNGO G. DESCALZO

VIA OLIVE

VIALE MAZZINI

VIA V. ROMA

VIA ERALDO

To Cinque Terre

VIA NAZIONALE

To A-12 Freeway

Ligurian Sea

To Cinque Terre

Piazza Italia

VIALE V. VENETO

Giardini Ventre

V. XX SETT

VIA C. COLOMBO

Piazza Sant' Antonio

VIA DANTE

VIA C. APRILE

Piazza Repubblica

PACE

Baia delle Favole

BOAT DOCK

VIA PILADE QUEIROLO

PROMENADE & BIKE PATH

Beaches

VIA RIMEMBRANZA

Piazza Aldo Moro

VIA DELLA CHIUSA

VIA XXV

VICO CORO

Piazza Matteotti

VIA POZZETTO

VIA PENISOLA

VIA PORTO

VIA CAPPUCCINI

GRAND HOTEL DEI CASTELLI

FREE BEACH

Baia del Silenzio

ROMANESQUE CHURCH

RUINED CHAPEL

N

200 Meters
200 Yards

❶ Hotel Due Mari
❷ Hotel Helvetia
❸ Hotel Celeste
❹ Hotel Genova
❺ Albergo Marina
❻ Villa Jolanda

❼ L'Osteria Mattana
❽ Polpo Mario
❾ Ristorante Mainolla & Bacciolo Gelato
❿ Ice Cream's Angels
⓫ Supermarkets (2)
⓬ Rosticceria Bertolone

behr-ah ah-treh-ZAHT-tah). The usual beach-town activities are clustered along this *baia:* boat rentals, sailing lessons, and bocce courts—ask if you can get in on a game.

The town's other beach, Baia del Silenzio, is narrow, virtually all free, and packed, providing a good chance to see Italian families at play. There isn't much more to do here than unroll a beach towel and join in. At the far end of Baia del Silenzio (under Hotel Helvetia) is Citto Beach bar, which offers front-row seats with bay views (drinks daily June-Aug 10:00-24:00, May and Sept-Oct until 20:00, sandwiches and salads at lunchtime only, closed Nov-April, Gilberto).

RIVIERA TOWNS

Sleeping in Sestri Levante

(€1 = about $1.40, country code: 39)
Prices listed here are the maximum for the high season (July-Aug). Prices are €10-20 less per night April-June and September-October, and soft the rest of the year. Some hotels are closed off-season, so call ahead.

$$$ Hotel Due Mari, located in an old Genoese palazzo with sprawling public spaces, has three stars, 65 fine rooms, and a rooftop terrace with a super view of both beaches. Ideally, reserve well in advance. The extra services and grand communal spaces are the draw (small Db-€110, bigger Db-€140-200 depending on view and type of room, half-pension in aristocratic restaurant required July-Aug-€35/person, closed mid-Oct-Dec, air-con, Internet access and Wi-Fi, elevator, garden, outdoor and heated indoor sea-water swimming pools, wet sauna, small gym, parking-€15/day, take Corso Colombo to the end, hotel is behind church in Piazza Matteotti—take the left-hand alleyway flanking church, Vico del Coro 18, tel. 0185-42695, fax 0185-42698, www.duemarihotel.it, info@duemarihotel.it).

$$$ Hotel Helvetia, overlooking Baia del Silenzio, feels posh and romantic, with 21 bright rooms, a large sun terrace with a heated, cliff-hanging swimming pool, and a peaceful garden atmosphere (viewless Db-€190, Db with view/balcony-€270, closed Nov-March, air-con, elevator, free Wi-Fi, off-site parking-€15/day with free shuttle, from Corso Colombo turn left on Via Palestro and angle left at the small square to Via Cappuccini 43, tel. 0185-41175, fax 0185-457-216, www.hotelhelvetia.it, helvetia@hotelhelvetia.it, Alex).

$$$ Hotel Celeste, a dream for beach lovers, rests along the waterfront. Its 41 rooms are modern and plainly outfitted—you pay for the sea breeze (Db-€165 with view and balcony, €25 optional half-pension, air-con, elevator, Internet access, free Wi-Fi, deals on beach chairs, attached beachside bar, Lungomare Descalzo 14, tel. 0185-485-005, fax 0185-41-166, www.hotelceleste.com, info@hotelceleste.com, Franco).

$$$ Hotel Genova, run by the Bertoni family, is a ship-shape hotel with 27 shiny-clean, modern, and cheery rooms, sunny lounge, rooftop sundeck, free loaner bikes, and a good location just two blocks from Baia delle Favole (Sb-€75, Db-€130, superior Db-€150, Tb-€189, ask for quieter room in back, air-con, elevator, Internet access and Wi-Fi, parking-€4/day; from the train station, walk straight ahead, turn right at the T-intersection, and find the cream building ahead on the right, Viale Mazzini 126; tel. 0185-41057, fax 0185-455-739, www.hotelgenovasestrilevante.com, info@hotelgenovasestrilevante.com, Stefano).

$$ Albergo Marina's friendly Magda and her brother Santo rent 23 bright, peaceful, and clean rooms done in sea-foam green. Though the hotel is located on a busy boulevard, all rooms are at the back, facing a quiet courtyard and parking lots, and priced right (Db-€65-80, half-pension optional, air-con, elevator, self-service laundry, pool table; exit the train station and angle left down Via Eraldo, at Piazza Repubblica take an easy left onto Via Fasce and find the hotel ahead on the right, Via Fasce 100; tel. & fax 0185-487-332, www.marinahotel.it, marinahotel@marina hotel.it).

$$ Villa Jolanda is a homey, kid-friendly, basic *pensione* with 17 simple rooms, five with little balconies but no views, new bathrooms, and a garden courtyard/sun terrace—perfect for families on a budget...and the owner's cats (Sb-€30-45, Db-€75-95, Qb-€100-120, 3-night minimum stay required with advance reservation, €6.50 breakfast isn't worth it but owner Mario's €23 home-cooked dinners are, free parking, located near Baia del Silenzio—take alley just to the right of the church on Piazza Matteotti, Via Pozzetto 15, tel. & fax 0185-41354, www.villaiolanda.com, info @villaiolanda.com).

Eating in Sestri Levante

Everything I've listed is on classic Via XXV Aprile, which also abounds with *focaccerie,* take-out pizza by the slice, and little grocery shops. Assemble a picnic or try one of the places below.

At **L'Osteria Mattana,** where everyone shares long tables in two dining rooms (the second one is in the back, past the wood oven and brazier), you can mix with locals while enjoying traditional cuisine, listed on the chalkboard menus (Tue-Fri 19:30-22:00, Sat-Sun 12:30-14:30 & 19:30-22:30, closed Mon except in Aug, cash only; follow Corso Colombo from TI as it turns into Via XXV Aprile, restaurant on right at #36; tel. 0185-457-633, Marco).

Polpo Mario is classier but affordable, with a fun people-watching location on the main drag (€40 fixed-price tasting menu, Tue-Sun 12:15-15:00 & 19:00-23:00, closed Mon, Via XXV Aprile 163, tel. 0185-480-203).

Ristorante Mainolla offers pizzas, big salads, focaccia sandwiches, and reasonably priced pastas near Baia del Silenzio (daily in summer 12:00-16:00 & 19:00-22:00, closed Tue off-season, Via XXV Aprile 187, mobile 338-157-0877).

Gelato: Locals flock to **Ice Cream's Angels** at the intersection of Via XXV Aprile and Via della Chiusa. Riccardo and Elena artfully load up your cone with intermingling flavors, and top it with a dollop of Nutella chocolate-hazelnut cream (open daily until late in summer, closed Tue off-season, mobile 348-402-1604). **Bacciolo**

RIVIERA TOWNS

enjoys a similar popularity among residents (closed Thu, Via XXV Aprile 51, on the right just before the church).

Supermarket: You can stock up on picnic supplies at two locations of **Carrefour Express** on Piazza della Repubblica, at #1 and #28 (daily 8:00-13:30 & 15:30-20:00).

Deli: For a take-out meal, head to **Rosticceria Bertolone** for roasted anything—beef, pork, chicken, or vegetables. Assemble an entire meal from their deli and ask them to heat it for you (Mon-Sat 7:30-13:00 & 16:00-19:30, closed Wed afternoon and all day Sun, Via Fasce 12, tel. 0185-487-098).

Sestri Levante Connections

By **train,** Sestri Levante is just 20 to 40 minutes away from Monterosso (hourly connections with Monterosso, nearly hourly with other Cinque Terre towns) and 30 minutes from Santa Margherita Ligure (2/hour).

Boats depart to the Cinque Terre, Santa Margherita Ligure, Portofino, and San Fruttuoso from the dock *(molo)* on the peninsula (boats run Easter-Oct, see "Santa Margherita Ligure Connections," page 440, for details; to get to the dock: facing the church in Piazza Matteotti, take the road on the right with the sea on your right, about halfway down Via Pilade Queirolo; tel. 0185-284-670, mobile 336-253-336, www.traghettiportofino.it).

Santa Margherita Ligure

If you need the Riviera of movie stars, park your yacht at Portofino. Or you can settle down in the nearby and more personable Santa Margherita Ligure (15 minutes by bus from Portofino and one hour by train from the Cinque Terre). While Portofino's velour allure is tarnished by snobby residents and a nonstop traffic jam in peak season, Santa Margherita tumbles easily downhill from its train station. The town has a fun Old World resort character and a breezy harborfront.

On a quick day trip from Milan or the Cinque Terre, walk the beach promenade and see the small old town of Santa Margherita Ligure before catching the bus (or boat) to Portofino to see what all the fuss is about. With more time, Santa Margherita makes a fine overnight stop.

Orientation to
Santa Margherita Ligure

Tourist Information

Pick up a map at the harborside TI on Piazza Veneto (daily April-Sept 9:30-12:30 & 14:30-19:30, Oct-March closes at 17:30 and all day Sun, tel. 0185-287-485, www.turismoinliguria.it).

Arrival by Train

To get from the station to the city center, take the stairs marked *Mare* (sea) down to the harbor. The harborfront promenade is as wide as the skimpy beach. (The real beaches, which are pebbly, are a 10-minute walk farther on, past the port.)

The TI is right on the waterfront at Piazza Veneto (with the roundabout, flags, and park). The pedestrian-friendly old town is a block away: From the piazza, head inland on Largo Antonio Giusti and take a near-immediate left onto Via Torino, which opens onto Piazza Caprera, a square with a church and morning fruit vendors in the midst of pedestrian streets.

Helpful Hints

Internet Access: Papiluc Bar has two terminals (€3/30 minutes, daily 6:30 until late, Via del Arco 20, tel. 0185-282-580).

Post Office: It's just down the road from the train station on Via Roma (Mon-Fri 8:25-19:10, Sat 8:25-12:35, closed Sun, Via Roma 36).

Baggage Storage: There's no official left-luggage office, but day-trippers arriving by train may be able to stash their bags at the station's café-bar (outside the station on the left).

Bike Rental: GM Rent is at Via XXV Aprile 11 (€10/5 hours, €20/24 hours, also rents scooters and Smart Cars, daily 10:00-13:00 & 16:30-20:00, mobile 329-406-6274, www.gmrent.it, Francesco).

Taxi: Taxis wait outside the train station, and charge a minimum of €13 for a ride from the train station to anywhere in town (they justify the high price by the short tourist season).

Driver: Helpful taxi driver **Alessandro** is also available for airport transfers and local excursions (mobile 338-860-2349, www.alessandrotaxi.com, alessandrotaxi@yahoo.it).

Parking: The recommended **Hotel Mediterraneo** and **Villa Anita** offer free parking to their guests, and a few hotels have limited spots for a fee. When you reserve your room, mention that you'll have a car. Otherwise, try a private lot (about €10-15/half-day, €15-20/24 hours) such as **Autorimessa Europa**, next to the post office (Via Roma 38, tel. 0185-287-818). An hourly parking lot is by the harbor, in front of the fish market (pay at blue machine in front of Laurin Hotel, Mon-Sat 8:00-20:00, Sun 8:00-23:00, first hour-€2, successive hours-€2.50). The TI has a list of parking spots (generally free where there are white lines) and paid parking lots.

Local Guide: Roberta De Beni knows the Ligurian Coast, its history, and its art very well (€100/half-day, €165/day, mobile 349-530-4778, diodebe@inwind.it).

Self-Guided Walk

Welcome to Santa Margherita Ligure

Explore Santa Margherita Ligure on the following stroll.

• *Begin on the water at Piazza della Libertà (just beyond Piazza Veneto). Walk out to the tip of the boat dock and turn around to survey the...*

Town View: From here you can take in all of Santa Margherita Ligure, from the villas dotting the hills and the castle built in the 16th century (closed except for special exhibitions) to the exclusive hotels. Sharing the dock with you is a statue of "Santa Margherita Virgin Martyr."

• *Wander along the harborfront (down Corso Marconi) past the castle and to the...*

Marina: What's left of the town's fishing fleet ties up here. The fishing industry survives, drag-netting octopus, shrimp, and miscellaneous "blue fish"—plus mountains of anchovies attracted to midnight lamps. The fish market (inside the rust-colored building with arches and columns) wiggles weekdays at about, oh, maybe 16:00-20:00 or so. Residents complain that it's easier to buy their locally caught fresh fish in Milan than here.

• *Behind the fish market, up a flight of stairs by the war memorial, stands the...*

Oratory of Sant'Erasmo: This small church is named for St. Erasmus (a.k.a. "St. Elmo"), the protector of sailors. Notice the fine and typically local black-and-white pebble mosaic *(riseu)* in front of the church (with maritime themes). The church is actually an "oratory," where a brotherhood of faithful men who did anonymous good deeds congregated and worshipped. It's decorated with ships and paintings of storms that—thanks to St. Erasmus—the local seafarers survived. The huge crosses are carried through town on special religious holidays (the church is supposedly open only during Mass, but often open at other times, too).

• *Next, double back to climb the looooong stairway (Via Tre Novembre) overlooking the bay to reach the...*

Church of San Giacomo: Even though this is a secondary church in a secondary town, it's impressively lavish (daily 7:30-19:00, may close earlier in winter, avoid visiting during Mass—usually

Santa Margherita Ligure

100 Meters
100 Yards

TRAIN STATION

1. Hotel Jolanda
2. Hotel Tigullio et de Milan
3. Hotel Mediterraneo
4. Hotel Laurin
5. To Villa Anita, Rist. A' Lampara & Via Tomaso Bottaro Eateries
6. Hotel Nuova Riviera
7. La Locanda di Colombo
8. Hotel Fasce
9. La Cambusa Ristorante
10. Dal Baffo Ristorante
11. Da Pezzi Ristorante
12. Da Gennaro Pizzeria
13. Simonetti Gelateria
14. Gelateria Centrale
15. Seghezzo Grocery
16. D'Oro Centry Supermarket
17. Bike Rental
18. Internet Café

7:45-9:00). The region's aristocrats amassed wealth from trade in the 11th to the 15th centuries. When Constantinople fell to the Turks, free trade in the Mediterranean stopped and Genovese traders became bankers—making even more money. A popular saying of the day was, "Silver is born in America, lives in Spain, and dies in Genoa." Bankers here served Spain's 17th-century royalty and aristocracy, and the accrued wealth paid for a Golden Age of art. Wander the church, noticing the inlaid-marble floors and chapels.
• Step out of the church and enjoy the sea view. Then turn left and step into...

RIVIERA TOWNS

Rise of a Resort: The History of Santa Margherita Ligure

This town, like the entire region (from the border of France to La Spezia), was once ruled by the Republic of Genoa. In the 16th century, when Arab pirates from North Africa plagued the entire coastal area, Genoa built castles in the towns and lookout towers in the neighboring hills.

At the time, Santa Margherita was actually two bickering towns—each with its own bay. In 1800, Napoleon came along, took over the Republic of Genoa, and turned the rival towns into one city—naming it Porto Napoleone. When Napoleon fell in 1815, the town stayed united and took the name of the patron saint of its leading church, Santa Margherita.

In 1850, residents set to work creating a Riviera resort. They imported palm trees from North Africa and paved a fine beach promenade. Santa Margherita (and the surrounding area) was studded with fancy villas built by the aristocracy of Genoa (which was controlled by just 35 families). English, Russian, and German aristocrats also discovered the town in the 19th century. Mass tourism only hit in the last generation. Even with the increased crowds, the town decided to stay chic and kept huge developments out. Its neighbor, Rapallo, chose the extreme opposite—giving the Italian language a new word for uncontrolled growth ruining a once-cute town: *rapallizzazione.*

Durazzo Park (Parco di Villa Durazzo): This park was an abandoned shambles until 1973, when the city took it over (free, daily 9:00-19:00, off-season until 17:00). Today it's a delight, with a breezy café enjoyed mostly by locals (generally daily from 10:30 except closed Tue May-Aug) and free Wi-Fi (ask at the cafe for the password). The garden has two distinct parts: the carefully coiffed Italian garden (designed to complement the villa's architecture) and the calculatedly wild "English garden" below. The Italian garden is famous for its varied collection of palm trees and an extensive collection of camellias. It's OK to feed the large turtles in the central pond (they like bits of fish or meat).

• *In the building next to the café, you'll see...*

Villa Durazzo: This was the home of a local journalist and writer, Vittorio G. Rossi (1898-1978), whose office has been preserved as he left it. Typical of the region, this palazzo has some period furniture, several grand pianos, chandeliers, and paintings strewn with cupids on the walls and ceilings. Look for King Umberto's letter offering condolences on Rossi's death. For most people, it's probably not worth the entry fee (€5.50, more for special exhibits; daily 9:00-13:00 & 14:30-18:30, Oct-March until 17:00, last entry 30 minutes before closing, WC opposite entry on left, tel. 0185-293-135, www.villadurazzo.it, villa.durazzo@comune sml.it). Classical music concerts are held here in July and August (ask at TI or villa ticket desk, or call for the schedule).

• *Your self-guided walk is over. Enjoy the park.*

Sights in Santa Margherita Ligure

Basilica of Santa Margherita (Basilica di Nostra Signora della Rosa)—The town's main church is textbook Italian Baroque. Its 18th-century facade hides a 17th-century interior. The chapels to the right of the high altar contain religious "floats" used in local festival parades. The wooden groups in the niches higher up used to be part of the processions, too. The altar is typical of 17th-century Ligurian altars—shaped like a boat, with lots of shelf space for candles, flowers, and relics. Remember, Baroque is like theater. After the Vatican II decrees of the 1960s, priests began to face their flocks instead of the old altars. For this reason, all over the Catholic world, modern tables serving as post-Vatican II altars stand in front of earlier altars that are no longer the center of attention during the Mass.

Cost and Hours: Free, daily 7:30-12:00 & 15:00-18:30, tel. 0185-286-555.

Via Palestro—This promenade (a.k.a. *caruggio*—"the big street" in local dialect) is *the* strolling street for window-shopping, people-watching, and studying the characteristic Art Nouveau house painting from about 1900. Before 1900, people distinguished their buildings with pastel paint and distinctive door and window frames. Then they decided to get fancy and paint entire exteriors with false balconies, weapons, saints, beautiful women, and 3-D Gothic concentrate.

As you wander from the Basilica of Santa Margherita inland, pop into the fanciest grocer-deli in town—the recommended **Seghezzo** (immediately to the right of the church on Via Cavour). Locals know that this venerable institution has whatever odd ingredient the most obscure recipe calls for.

Farther up Via Palestro, you might drop into the traditional old **Panificio** bakery for a slice of fresh focaccia. Saying *"Vorrei un etto di focaccia"* will get you a Ligurian olive-oily, 100-gram, €1.50 hunk of every kid's favorite beach munchie. Locals claim the best focaccia in Italy is made along this coast.

RIVIERA TOWNS

Markets—On weekday afternoons, fishing boats unload their catch, which is then sold to waiting customers at **Mercato del Pesce** (roughly Mon-Fri 17:00-20:00, opens an hour earlier for wholesalers, Oct-April might open at 15:30). Find it in the rust-colored building with arches and columns on Corso Marconi, on the harbor, just past the castle. The open-air market, a commotion of clothes and produce, is held every Friday morning along Corso Matteotti, inland from Piazza Mazzini (8:00-13:00). Piazza Caprera (facing the main church) daily hosts a few farmers selling their produce from stalls.

Beaches—The handiest free Santa Margherita beaches are just below the train station toward the boat dock. But the best beaches are on the south side of town. Among these, I like "Gio and Rino beach" (just before Covo di Nord Est)—not too expensive, with fun, creative management and a young crowd. Also nice is the beach on the south side of Hotel Miramare, which offers a more relaxing sun-worshipping experience. Both beaches have free entry and rentable chairs and umbrellas. They're a 20-minute walk from downtown, or take the bus from either the train station or Piazza Veneto (€1.50 each way if bought in advance from kiosk, newsstands, tobacco shops, or the green ATP ticket office next to the TI; €3 if bought on board).

Paraggi beach, which is halfway to Portofino (with an easy bus connection—see "Portofino," later in this chapter, and the map on page 441), is better than any Santa Margherita beach, but it's *very* expensive. One Paraggi beach operator, Bosetti, offers a reasonable rate (€25/day, no hourly rates, includes umbrella, lounge chair, and towel), while rates at other beaches may soar up to €50 per day in July and August. In high season, the Paraggi beach may be all booked up by big shots from Portofino, which has no beach—only rocks. Off-season, the entire Paraggi beach is all yours and free of charge. A skinny patch of sand smack-dab in the middle of Paraggi beach is free year-round.

Sleeping in Santa Margherita Ligure

(€1 = about $1.40, country code: 39)

All of these accommodations are in the center; for specific locations, see the map on page 433. La Locanda di Colombo, Hotel Jolanda, and Hotel Tigullio et de Milan are closest to the station. Prices listed here are the maximum price for the high season of July-August. Expect April-June and September-October to be €10-15 cheaper, and the rest of the year to be cheaper still.

$$$ Hotel Jolanda, just around the corner from La Locanda di Colombo, is a solid, professionally run hotel with 50 rooms, a revolving door, a good breakfast buffet, and a friendly staff. With lavish public spaces and regal colors, this place makes you feel like nobility (Db-€150, superior Db-€170, 10 percent discount with this book if you mention it when you reserve, Internet access and Wi-Fi, air-con, elevator, free one-hour use of small weight room, wet and dry saunas, Jacuzzi, 10 free loaner bikes on request, Via Luisito Costa 6, tel. 0185-287-512, fax 0185-284-763, www.hotel jolanda.it, info@hoteljolanda.it).

$$$ Hotel Tigullio et de Milan, run by Giuseppe of Hotel Jolanda, has equally fine rooms with creamy hues and lower prices. You don't get all the luxurious extras, but the breezy sun terrace on top—with a bar in summertime—makes for a relaxing retreat (Db-€140, bigger Db with terrace-€150, 10 percent discount with this book if you mention it when you reserve, air-con, elevator but lots of stairs down to reception, a few free parking spots, Via Rainusso 3, tel. 0185-287-455, fax 0185-281-860, www.hotel tigullio.eu, info@hoteltigullio.eu).

$$$ Hotel Mediterraneo, run by the Melegatti family, offers 30 spacious rooms (a few with balconies or sun terraces) in a family-friendly, creaky, and comfy 18th-century palazzo a five-minute walk from Piazza Veneto. They have a park-like sun garden with lounge chairs and lots of semi-private space. Kindly Pia Pauli presides over the dining room and makes great homemade Ligurian specialties for dinner (Sb-€100, Db-€150, Tb-€180, great breakfast, five-course dinner-€30/person, free laundry service with 3-day stay or longer, free parking, free loaner bikes, closed Jan-March, take street immediately to the right of Basilica of Santa Margherita and find hotel straight ahead at Via della Vittoria 18A, tel. 0185-286-881, fax 0185-286-882, www.sml-mediterraneo.it, info@sml-mediterraneo.it).

$$$ Hotel Laurin offers slick, modern, air-conditioned, American-style lodgings fixated on harborfront views. All of its 43 rooms face the sea, most have terraces, and there's a small pool on the sundeck, as well as a gym and wet sauna. As it's a Best Western, it feels corporate (Sb-€159, Db-€230, 10 percent discount if you book direct—mention this book when you reserve and show book on arrival, double-paned windows, elevator, 15-yard walk past the castle or €15 taxi ride from station, Corso Marconi 3, tel. 0185-289-971, fax 0185-285-709, www.laurinhotel.it, info@laurin hotel.it).

$$$ Villa Anita is an elegant-yet-homey family hotel run by hospitable Daniela and her friendly son, Sandro. They rent 12 tidy rooms—nearly all with terraces, and several with new, high-tech bathrooms—overlooking a peaceful residential neighborhood just a five-minute walk from the seaside boulevard. Daniela makes great cakes, and the in-house chef offers a varying menu of Ligurian specialties (Db-€150, dinner-€18/person, family rooms, hot tub and playground, air-con, free Wi-Fi, free parking, €15 cab ride from station, Via Tigullio 10, tel. 0185-286-543, fax 0185-283-005, www.hotelvillaanita.com, info@hotelvillaanita.com).

$$$ Hotel Nuova Riviera is an old villa surrounded by a garden, with nine institutional-feeling rooms, warmly run by the Sabini family (Db-€130, Tb-€140, Qb-€165, these prices good in 2013 if you book direct and mention this book when you reserve, additional 5 percent discount with cash, fans, some balconies, no elevator, 15-minute walk from station or easy cab ride; if you're driving, follow signs to hospital, then watch for hotel signs on Piazza Mazzini; if you're walking, enter Piazza Mazzini and see signs from there; Via Belvedere 10, tel. & fax 0185-287-403, www.sabinirentals.com, info@sabinirentals.com, chatty Cristina). They also run a nearby annex with six renovated rooms and one apartment with a tiny corner kitchen (Db-€85, Tb-€110, Qb-€125, cash only, breakfast at Hotel Nuova Riviera is optional and extra, tel. 0185-290-083).

$$$ La Locanda di Colombo has six stylish and contemporary rooms and two small, relaxing patios (Db-€150, tell them "Rick sent me" to get a 5 percent discount on stays of 1-3 days, 10 percent discount on longer stays; air-con, disabled access, Via XXV Aprile 12, tel. 0185-293-129, fax 0185-291-937, www.lalocandadicolombo.it, sml@lalocandadicolumbo.it, welcoming hosts Massimiliano and Raffaella).

$$$ Hotel Fasce, a 16-room hotel surrounded by flowers and greenery, is run enthusiastically by intense Englishwoman Jane Fasce, her husband Aristide, and son Alessandro. Jane gets mixed reviews from my readers—some find her helpful, while others find her rules too strict...my advice is to toe the line (Sb-€100, Db-€128, Tb-€170, Qb-€200, see website for deals, no-nonsense 21-day cancellation policy, two rooms have private bathroom located across the hall, no elevator, free Wi-Fi, free loaner bikes, rooftop garden, laundry service-€18, parking-€20, free round-trip train tickets to Cinque Terre with 3-night stay if you book room direct or through their website, 10-minute walk or €15 cab ride from station at Via Bozzo 3, tel. 0185-286-435, fax 0185-283-580, www.hotelfasce.it, hotelfasce@hotelfasce.it).

Eating in Santa Margherita Ligure

For information on some of the regional specialties, see page 355.

Ristorante "A' Lampara" is the locals' favorite for *casalinga* (home-style) Genovese cuisine, prepared by the endearing Barbieri family: Mamma Maria Luisa oversees the dining room, son Mario cooks, and daughter Natalina serves. Try their specialties, such as *ravioli di pesce* (homemade fish ravioli with red mullet sauce) or *pansotti con salsa di noci*—cheese ravioli with walnut sauce (Fri-Wed 12:30-14:00 & 19:30-22:00, closed Thu, veggie options, reservations smart for dinner in summer; follow Corso Marconi 4 blocks past the fish market, turn right onto Via Maragliano, and find #33 a block and a half ahead on left; tel. 0185-288-926).

La Cambusa is perched above the culinary heart of Santa Margherita Ligure—the fish market. Popular with tourists and resident romantics, its terrace has an unbeatable view over the harbor. In cooler weather, the terrace is covered and heated. Pick your favorite yacht while tucking into their seafood dishes with a Ligurian twist (€13 pasta, €20 main dishes, July-Sept daily 9:00-15:00 & 19:00-24:00 except closed Thu morning, Oct-June closed all day Thu, Via T. Bottaro, tel. 0185-287-410; Luciano, wife Antonella, and serious but efficient Vittorio).

Dal Baffo is a bustling mom-and-pop eatery popular for its traditional Ligurian specialties, including homemade pasta, wood-fired pizzas (folks queue up to watch the *pizzaioli* make their €7 pies to go), fresh fish, and grilled steaks at reasonable prices (Wed-Mon 12:00-15:00 & 19:00-23:30, closed Tue; from Piazza Caprera, head inland—both pedestrian streets eventually turn into busy Corso Matteotti; Corso Matteotti 56, tel. 0185-288-987).

Da Pezzi, with a cheap cafeteria-style atmosphere, is packed with locals at midday and at night. They're munching *farinata* (crêpes made from chickpeas, available Oct-May) standing at the bar, or enjoying pesto and fresh fish in the dining room. Consider the deli counter with its Genovese picnic ingredients (Sun-Fri 12:00-14:00 & 18:15-21:00, closed Sat, Via Cavour 21, tel. 0185-285-303, Giancarlo and Giobatta).

Waterfront Dining: All along Via Tomaso Bottaro, you'll find restaurants, pizzerias, and bars serving food with a harbor view. **Da Gennaro Pizzeria,** at Piazza della Libertà 30 by the boat dock, makes popular Neapolitan-style pizzas. **Bar Giuli,** the only place actually on the harbor, serves forgettable salads and sandwiches for a reasonable price (about 150 yards south of the fish market).

Gelato: The best *gelateria* I found in town—with chocolate-truffle *tartufato*—is **Simonetti** (daily 8:30 until late, closed Mon off-season, under the castle, closest to the water at Piazza della Libertà 48). **Gelateria Centrale,** just off Piazza Veneto near the cinema, serves up their specialty—*pinguino* (penguin), a cone with your choice of gelato dipped in chocolate (daily 7:00-late, closed Wed Sept-May).

Groceries: **Seghezzo** is classiest and great for a meal to go—ask them to *riscaldare* (heat up) their white *lasagne al pesto* or grilled veggies (daily June-Aug 7:30-13:00 & 15:30-20:00, closed Wed Sept-May, right of the church on Via Cavour, tel. 0185-287-172). The **D'Oro Centry** supermarket, just off Piazza Mazzini at #35, has better prices (Mon-Sat 8:00-13:30 & 15:30-19:30, Sun 8:00-13:00, tel. 0185-286-470).

Santa Margherita Ligure Connections

From Santa Margherita Ligure by Train to: Sestri Levante (2/hour, 30 minutes, €2.40), **Monterosso** (at least hourly, 45 minutes, €4.50), **La Spezia** (hourly, 1-1.5 hours, €5.50), **Pisa** (1-2/hour, 2-2.5 hours, InterCity/IC goes direct, other connections may require transfer in La Spezia, €14.50), **Milan** (8/day, 2-2.5 hours, more with transfer in Genoa, €19), **Ventimiglia**/French border (4/day, 4 hours; or hourly with change in Genoa, €13), **Venice** (8/day, 6-7 hours with 1-3 changes, €41-50). For **Florence,** transfer in Pisa (8/day, 3.5-4 hours, €20-26). See "Getting Around the Cinque Terre—By Train" on page 346 for details.

By Boat to the Cinque Terre: For the latest, pick up a schedule of departures and excursion options from the TI, visit the ticket shack on the dock, call 0185-284-670 or 335-709-0870, or check online at www.traghettiportofino.it. The routes mentioned below run at least once weekly from May through September or October, increasing in frequency in July and August.

The "Gita 3" boat does an all-day trip that includes two stopovers: one hour in Vernazza and three hours in Portovenere, plus a scenic trip around an island (April-mid-Oct depart Sun at 8:45, plus Tue and Thu late July-mid-Sept, €21 one-way, €32 round-trip).

The half-day "Gita 4" boat sails to the Cinque Terre with a one-hour stopover in Vernazza (July-Sept depart Tue and Fri at 13:30, €17 one-way, €24.50 round-trip).

The "Super Cinque Terre, Gita 5" boat offers day-trip cruises from Santa Margherita Ligure to the Cinque Terre, departing at 8:45 and stopping in three Cinque Terre towns: three hours in Monterosso, and an hour each in Vernazza and Riomaggiore (May-Sept Wed, plus Sat July-Sept, €21 one-way, €32 round-trip).

Portofino

Santa Margherita Ligure, with its aristocratic architecture, hints at old money, whereas nearby Portofino, with its sleek shops, reeks of new money. Fortunately, a few pizzerias, *focaccerie*, bars, and grocery shops are mixed in with Portofino's jewelry shops, art galleries, and haute couture boutiques, making the town affordable. The *piccolo* harbor, classic Italian architecture, and wooded peninsula can even turn glitzy Portofino into an appealing package. It makes a fun day trip from Santa Margherita Ligure.

Ever since the Romans founded Portofino for its safe harbor, it has had a strategic value

(appreciated by everyone from Napoleon to the Nazis). In the 1950s, *National Geographic* did a beautiful exposé on the idyllic port, and locals claim that's when the Hollywood elite took note. Liz Taylor and Richard Burton came here annually (as did Liz Taylor and Eddie Fisher). During one famous party, Rex Harrison dropped his Oscar into the bay (it was recovered). Ava Gardner came down from her villa each evening for a drink—sporting her famous fur coat. Greta Garbo loved to swim naked in the harbor, not knowing that half the town was watching. Truman Capote also called Portofino home. But VIPs were also here a century earlier. In one of his books, Friedrich Nietzsche wrote about philosophizing with the mythical prophet Zarathustra on the path between Portofino and Santa Margherita.

My favorite Portofino plan: Visit for the evening. Leave Santa Margherita on the bus at about 16:30 and hike the last 20 minutes from Paraggi beach. Explore Portofino. Splurge for a drink on the harborfront, or get a take-out fruity sundae (*paciugo*; pah-CHOO-goh) and sit by the water. Then return by bus to Santa Margherita for dinner (confirm late departures). Portofino does offer fancy harborside dining, but the quality doesn't match the high prices.

Getting to Portofino

Portofino makes an easy day trip from Santa Margherita by bus, boat, bike, or foot.

By Bus: Catch bus #82 from Santa Margherita's train station or at bus stops along the harbor (main stop in front of TI, €1.50, 2-3/hour, 15 minutes, goes to Paraggi or Portofino). Buy tickets at the bar next to the station, at Piazza Veneto's green bus kiosk (next to the TI; daily 7:15-19:45), from the green machine on the side of the kiosk, or at any newsstand, tobacco shop, or shop that displays a *Biglietti Bus* sign. You can usually buy tickets on the bus—for double the cost. If you're at the Piazza Veneto kiosk, grab a bus schedule, which will come in handy if you travel in the evening (last bus around 23:00, #82).

In Portofino, get tickets at the newsstand or from the machine next to the bus stop (go uphill and you'll come to Piazza Martiri della Libertà, machine and bus stop on right side, directions in English).

By Boat: The boat makes the 15-minute trip with more class and without the traffic jams (€5.50 one-way, €8.50 round-trip, €0.50 more on Sun and holidays; daily May-Sept nearly hourly departures 10:15-16:15, Oct-April at 10:15 and 14:15 only; dock is a 2-minute walk from Piazza Veneto off Piazza Martiri della Libertà, call to confirm or pick up schedule from TI or your hotel, tel. 0185-284-670, mobile 336-253-336, check at www.traghetti portofino.it). This company also runs boats from Santa Margherita to the Cinque Terre (see page 440). The boat from Portofino back to Santa Margherita departs nearly hourly in summer (May-Sept daily 12:00-18:00; Oct-April at 12:00 and 16:00 only).

The boats run between Rapallo and the San Fruttuoso Abbey, stopping en route at Santa Margherita Ligure and Portofino. (Another boat line runs from Recco, Camogli, and Punta Chiappa to the abbey.)

By Bike: The 25-minute bike ride from Santa Margherita to Portofino is doable for cautious cyclists. While there are no steep hills to struggle up, the road is narrow, with many blind corners. Many of my recommended hotels provide free loaner bikes (though they may not be in the best condition); you can also rent your own wheels (see page 431).

On Foot: To hike the entire distance from Santa Margherita Ligure to Portofino, you have two options: You can follow the sidewalk along (and sometimes hanging over) the sea (1 hour, 2.5 miles)—although traffic can be noisy. Or, if you're hardy and ambitious, you can take a quieter two-hour hike by leaving Santa Margherita at Via Maragliano, then follow the Ligurian-symbol trail markers (look for red-and-white stripes—they're not always obvious, sometimes numbered according to the path you're on, usually painted on rocks or walls, especially at junctions). This hike takes you high into the hills. Keep left after Cappelletta delle Gave. Several blocks past a castle, you'll drop down into the Paraggi beach, where you'll take the Portofino trail the rest of the way.

Bus and Hike Option: For a shorter hike (20 minutes) into Portofino, ride bus #82 from Santa Margherita only as far as the small but ritzy Paraggi beach. (Ask on board where to get off, as the Paraggi stop is not labeled—watch for an inland bay with green water and a sandy beach.) At the far end of the beach, cross the street, climb the steps, and follow the hilly, paved trail marked *Pedonali per Portofino* high above the road. Twenty minutes later, you'll enter Portofino at a yellow-and-gray-striped church labeled *Divo Martino*—which I figure means "the divine Martin" and has something to do with Dean Martin giving us all "Volare" (which I couldn't get out of my head for the rest of the day).

Orientation to Portofino

Tourist Information: Portofino's TI is downhill from the bus stop, on your right under the portico. Pick up a free town map and a rudimentary hiking map (June-Sept Tue-Sun 10:00-13:00 & 14:00-18:00, closed Mon; Oct-May Tue-Sat 9:30-13:30 & 14:00-17:00, closed Sun-Mon; Via Roma 35, tel. 0185-269-024).

Sights in Portofino

Museo del Parco—For an artsy break, walk around the harbor to the right, where you can stroll around a park littered with 148 contemporary sculptures by top artists (€5, June-Oct Wed-Mon 10:00-13:00 & 15:00-19:00, closed Tue, closed Nov-May and in bad weather, mobile 337-333-737).

Hikes—One option is the paved stone path that winds up and down to the **lighthouse** *(faro)* at a scenic point with a bar (bar open May-Sept, hedges block views until the end, 25-minute walk). Consider popping into **Castello Brown,** a medieval castle, on the way. It features lush gardens and a black-and-white portrait gallery of stars and famous personages who once frequented Portofino, including Clark Gable, Sophia Loren, Kim Novak, Grace Kelly, John Wayne, Ernest Hemingway, Humphrey Bogart, and Lauren Bacall. Original decorations and photos are explained in English

(€5, March-Oct daily 10:00-19:00, Nov-Feb Sat-Sun until 17:00 in winter, tel. 0185-267-101, www.castellobrown.it).

Or you could stroll the hilly pedestrian promenade through the trees from Portofino to **Paraggi beach**, and, if you're lucky, see a wild boar en route (20 minutes, path starts to the right of yellow-and-gray-striped Divo Martino church—look for clock tower, parallels main road, ends at ritzy Paraggi beach, where it's easy to catch bus back to Santa Margherita Ligure).

Another option is to hike out to **San Fruttuoso Abbey** and the nearby underwater Christ statue (described next; the hike there is steep at beginning and end, takes about 2.5 hours from Portofino—pick up the trailhead at the inland-most point of town, past Piazza della Libertà and the *carabinieri* station; you can also hike all the way there from Santa Margherita in about 4.5 hours via Portofino).

Near Portofino

San Fruttuoso Abbey (Abbazia di San Fruttuoso)—This 11th-century abbey is accessible only by foot (a 2.5-hour hike from Portofino, 4.5 hours from Santa Margherita) or boat (from either Portofino or Santa Margherita; abbey entry-€5, more for special exhibits; June-Sept daily 10:00-17:45; Oct-May daily 10:00-15:45 except closed Mon in winter; last entry 45 minutes before closing, tel. 0185-772-703). But the abbey itself isn't the main attraction. The more intriguing draw is 60 feet underwater, offshore from the abbey: the statue *Christ of the Abyss (Cristo degli Abissi)*. A rowboat will take you from the dock below the Portofino boat dock to the statue, where you can look down through a lens to just barely see the arms of Jesus—outstretched, reaching upward. Some people bring goggles and dive in for a better view. The statue was placed there in 1954 for the divine protection of the region's divers. As the rowboats don't run in rough seas, call the abbey to confirm before making the trip (about €4, 20-minute round-trip, rowboats run only during boat arrival hours from Portofino—generally daily May-Sept 9:00-17:00).

From Easter through September, boats continue north from San Fruttuoso Abbey to Punta Chiappa and Camogli (€5 one-way, can return to Santa Margherita by train or buy round-trip boat tickets, call 0185-772-091 or inquire at Portofino or Santa Margherita TI for information).

South of the Cinque Terre

La Spezia

While just a quick train ride away from the fanciful Cinque Terre (20-30 minutes), the working town of La Spezia feels like "reality Italy." Primarily a jumping-off point for travelers, the town is slim on sights, and has no beaches.

The pedestrian zone on Via del Prione to the gardens along the harbor makes a pleasant stroll. The nearly deserted **Museo Amedeo Lia** displays Italian paintings from the 13th to 18th centuries, including minor works by Venetian masters Titian, Tintoretto, and Canaletto (€6.50, Tue-Sun 10:00-18:00, closed Mon, last entry 30 minutes before closing, English descriptions on laminated sheets in most rooms, audioguide-€3, WCs down the hall from ticket desk, no photos allowed, 10-minute walk from station at Via del Prione 234, tel. 0187-731-100, http://mal.spezianet.it).

Stay in the Cinque Terre if you can. But if you're in a bind, I've listed several La Spezia accommodations. I've also listed (under "Eating in La Spezia") some places to grab a meal while you wait for a train.

Orientation to La Spezia

Tourist Information

The TI is in a separate building in front of the north end of the train station, by the pine trees (daily May-Sept 9:00-19:00, Oct-April 9:00-16:00, tel. 0187-742-218, www.turismoprovincia.la spezia.it). The Cinque Terre National Park office is on the platform of track 1 (daily 7:30-19:30, until 17:00 off-season, Internet access €1.50/20 minutes, tel. 0187-762-600, www.parconazionale5terre .it). A second TI is near the waterfront (with same phone and hours as the train station TI, Viale Italia 5).

Arrival in La Spezia

By Train: Get off at the La Spezia Centrale stop. You can check your bags at the train station (see "Helpful Hints," next). Exit the station down the road to the left, where several recommended hotels and eateries are located. From beside the TI, a less-convenient set of stairs descends to Via Fiume. Another exit takes you out onto Via Fiume by way of the parking garage.

By Car: A handy but pricey parking option is under the

RIVIERA TOWNS

train station. The upper level, accessed near the station entrance, is more expensive (€35/day) than the lower levels, accessed from Via Fiume and Via Milano (€18/12 hours, €24/day, www.mobpark .it, tel. 0187-187-5305). You can park for free at Piazza d'Armi (a 20-minute walk to station, or take €1 shuttle bus to Piazza Brin, a five-minute walk to station; 3/hour).

Helpful Hints

Market Days: A colorful covered market sets up in Piazza Cavour (Mon-Sat 8:00-13:00). On Fridays, a huge all-day open-air market sprawls along Viale Garibaldi, about six blocks from the station.

Baggage Storage: A left-luggage service is at the train station along track 1 (facing the tracks on platform 1, go left; it's next to the WC). It's secure, though it isn't always staffed—ring the bell to the left of the doorway to call the attendant. Since you may have to wait, allow plenty of time to pick up your baggage before departing (€3/12 hours, daily 8:00-22:00, they'll photocopy your passport).

1. Hotel Firenze e Continentale
2. Hotel Astoria
3. Hotel Venezia
4. Albergo Parma
5. Casa da Nè/ Tre Frè Rooms
6. L'Arca di Noè B&B
7. Ristorante Roma da Marcellin
8. Il Pomodoro Pizzeria
9. Covered Market
10. Supermarket & Launderette
11. Piazza d'Armi (Free Parking)
12. Piazza d'Armi Shuttle Drop-Off
13. Portovenere Bus Stop

Laundry: A handy self-service launderette is just below the train station. Head down toward town, and immediately at the first piazza take a sharp right on Via Fiume—it's on your left at #95 (€7 one-hour wash and dry, Mon-Sat 8:00-22:00, Sun 9:00-22:00, mobile 348-543-7924, Edoardo).

Supermarket: Le Dune DiMeglio is at Via Fiume 125, near the recommended launderette (daily 8:00-20:00, tel. 0187-704-059).

Booking Agency: Cinque Terre Riviera books rooms and apartments in La Spezia, the Cinque Terre, and Portovenere for a 10 percent markup (Mon-Fri 9:30-13:00 & 15:00-19:30, closed Sat-Sun, check website for day trips and cooking lessons, Via Picedi 18, tel. 0187-520-702, www.cinqueterreriviera.com, info@cinqueterreriviera.com).

Getting to the Cinque Terre: Trains leave at least twice hourly for the Cinque Terre, though not all trains stop at all towns. The Cinque Terre Treno Park Card (covers train ride to Cinque Terre as well as hiking fee—see page 345) is sold at the train-station ticket window and at the national park office in the station (see "Tourist Information," at the beginning of this section). For more details, see "Getting Around the Cinque Terre" on page 345. It's also possible to take boat excursions to the Cinque Terre, Portovenere, and outer islands from the La Spezia dock; for current schedules, check at the TI, dock, or www.navigazionegolfodeipoeti.it.

Sleeping in La Spezia

(€1 = about $1.40, country code: 39)
Remember, sleep in La Spezia only as a last resort. These hotels and rooms are within a five-minute walk of La Spezia's station—except the last two listings, which are for drivers only. Prices listed are the high-season rates.

Hotels

$$$ Hotel Firenze e Continentale is grand and Old World, but newly restored with a mountain-view breakfast room to boot. Just to the left of the station, its 68 rooms have all the usual comforts (Sb-€130, Db-€200, email for best rate, 10 percent discount in 2013 if you book directly and mention this book, cheaper during slow times, non-smoking rooms, double-paned windows, air-con, elevator, indoor parking-€22/day, Via Paleocapa 7, tel. 0187-713-200, fax 0187-714-930, www.hotelfirenzecontinentale.it, info@hotel firenzecontinentale.it).

$$ Hotel Astoria, with 47 decent rooms, has a combination lobby and breakfast room as large as a school cafeteria. It's a fine backup if the hotels nearer the train station are full (older Db without air-con-€90; Db-€130 for the 10 summery, modern rooms with air-con and double-paned windows; elevator, free parking garage; take Via Milano left of Albergo Parma, go 3 blocks, and turn left to reach Via Roma 139; tel. 0187-714-655, fax 0187-714-425, www.albergoastoria.com, info@albergo astoria.com).

$$ Hotel Venezia, across the street from Hotel Firenze e Continentale, is run with indifference but its 19 rooms are pleasantly modern (Sb-€55, Db-€90, air-con, elevator, free parking out front but must request when you reserve, Via Paleocapa 10, tel. & fax 0187-733-465, www.hotelvenezialaspezia.it, hotelvenezia @telematicaitalia.it).

$$ Albergo Parma, with 36 rooms, is a dingy slumbermill, but the price is right (D-€50, Db-€60, breakfast-€4, no fans, double-paned windows, just below train station and down the stairs at Via Fiume 143, tel. 0187-743-010, fax 0187-743-240, www.albergo parma.com, albergoparma@libero.it, Aurelio speaks a bit of English, Silvana doesn't).

Private Rooms

Affitta camere, meaning rented rooms with no official reception, abound near the station. Expect good deals, modest English skills, and no breakfast (buy yourself a coffee and pastry at a nearby bar).

$$ Casa da Nè/Tre Frè, next door to the recommended Hotel Venezia, has 11 chic rooms with comfy linens and orange trees outside the door. It's located so close to the station that some rooms look out at the tracks; luckily, the windows are double-paned (Db-€80, air-con, Wi-Fi, Via Paleocapa 4, mobile 347-351-3239, www.trefre.it, info@trefre.it, Paolo).

$$ L'Arca di Noè B&B is homey, with three bright and artsy rooms that share two bathrooms for one of the best deals on the Cinque Terre. A group could take the entire massive apartment (D-€55, Q-€85, includes breakfast, air-con, communal kitchen, 5-minute walk from station at Via Fiume 39, mobile 320-485-2434 or 348-916-9378, g.brunella@email.it, Brunella and Alessandra).

Near La Spezia

$$ Il Gelsomino, for drivers only, is a homey B&B in the hills above La Spezia overlooking the Gulf of Poets. It has three tranquil rooms: one with a bay-view terrace, one with hillside views, and a third that lacks views or a terrace. Don't confuse it with another B&B called Il Gelsomino d'Oro (Db-€70, Tb-€90/Qb-€110, reconfirm a day in advance with your arrival time, large breakfast, Via dei Viseggi 9, tel. & fax 0187-704-201, www.ilgelsomino.biz, ilgelsomino@inwind.it, gracious Carla and Walter Massi).

$ Santa Maria del Mare Monastery, a last resort for drivers, rents 15 comfortable rooms to spiritual travelers high above La Spezia in a scenic but institutional setting (donation only, recommended offerings: dorm bed-€35, Db-€60, includes breakfast, additional €15/person for a meal, Via Montalbano 135B, tel. 0187-711-382, fax 0187-708-490, mobile 347-848-3993, www.santamaria delmare.it, madre@santamariadelmare.191.it).

Eating in La Spezia

Ristorante Roma da Marcellin, a one-minute walk from the station, has a cool, leafy terrace that's ideal for relaxing while you await your train. Grandpa Ottorino cooks up the freshest catch, as well as homemade ravioli and spaghetti *frutti di mare* (daily 12:15-15:00 & 19:30-23:00; as you exit the station, turn left—it's across from Hotel Firenze e Continentale at Via Paleocapa 18; tel. 0187-715-921).

Il Pomodoro Pizzeria, just a few doors farther down on the corner of Via Zampino, offers more reasonable prices and an extensive selection of pizzas from €5. Practice your Italian with the chalkboard display of pastas of the day (Mon-Fri 12:00-14:00 & 19:00-23:00, Sat 19:00-23:00, closed Sun, Piazza S. Bon 5, tel. 0187-739-911).

La Spezia Connections

From La Spezia by Train to: Monterosso (2-3/hour, 15-30 minutes, €2.60), **Carrara** (2/hour, 25 minutes, €2.40), **Viareggio** (2/hour, 30-60 minutes, €4), **Pisa** (hourly, 1-1.5 hours, €5-9), **Florence** (4/day direct, otherwise nearly hourly, 2.5 hours, change in Pisa, €9), **Rome** (every 2 hours, 3.5-5 hours, €35-45), **Milan** (about hourly, 3 hours direct or with change in Genoa, €22-29), **Venice** (nearly hourly, 5 hours, 1-3 changes, €50-55).

By Bus to Portovenere: City buses generally depart from Viale Garibaldi (2/hour, 30 minutes, €2 each way, buy tickets at tobacco shops or newsstands, bus stop 11P—just past Corso Cavour; but note that Friday buses depart from Corso Cavour). From the La Spezia train station, exit left and head downhill, following the street to the first square (Piazza S. Bon). Continue down the pedestrian stretch of Via Fiume to Piazza Garibaldi, then turn right at the fountain in the square onto Viale Garibaldi; the bus stop for Portovenere-bound buses is after the first stoplight on the right side of the street. A timetable is posted by the bus stop.

Carrara

Perhaps the world's most famous marble quarries are just east of La Spezia in Carrara. Michelangelo himself traveled to these valleys to pick out the marble that he would work into his masterpieces. The towns of the region are dominated by marble. The quarries higher up are vast digs that dwarf the hardworking trucks and machinery coming and going. The **Marble Museum** traces the story of marble-cutting here from pre-Roman times until today (€4.50, May-Sept Mon-Sat 9:30-13:00 & 15:30-18:00, Oct-April Mon-Sat 9:00-12:30 & 14:30-17:00, closed Sun year-round, Viale XX Settembre 85, tel. 0585-845-746, http://urano.isti.cnr.it:8880/museo/home.php).

For a guided visit, **Sara Paolini** is excellent (€80/half-day tour, mobile 373-711-6695, sarapaolini@hotmail.com). She is accustomed to meeting drivers at the Carrara freeway exit, or she can pick you up at the train station.

Portovenere

While the gritty port of La Spezia offers little in the way of redeeming touristic value, the nearby resort of Portovenere is

enchanting. This Cinque Terre-esque village clings to a rocky promontory that juts into the sea and protects the harbor from the crashing waves. On the harbor, next to colorful bobbing boats, a row of restaurants—perfect for al fresco dining—feature local specialties such as *trenette* pasta with pesto and *spaghetti con frutti di mare*.

Local boats take you on a 40-minute excursion around three nearby islands or over to Lerici, the town across the bay. Lord Byron swam to Lerici (not recommended). Hardy hikers enjoy the five-hour (or more) hike to Riomaggiore, the nearest Cinque Terre town.

Getting There: Portovenere—not to be confused with Portofino—is an easy day trip from the Cinque Terre by **boat** (Easter-Oct, 4-6/day 9:20-15:40, 1 hour, €12 one-way, €25 day pass includes hopping on and off and either Lerici or a jaunt around three small islands near Portovenere, www.navigazionegolfo deipoeti.it). You can also cruise between Portovenere and Santa Margherita Ligure, with stops in Vernazza and Sestri Levante, using another boat line (www.traghettiportofino.it)—see "Santa Margherita Ligure Connections" on page 440. Pick up a schedule of departures and excursion options from the TI, or ask at your hotel. Or you can take the **bus** from La Spezia (2/hour, 30 minutes, €2, in La Spezia buy tickets at tobacco shops or newsstands; in Portovenere get tickets at TI; for directions to the bus stop in La Spezia, see page 450). **Parking** is a nightmare here from May through September, but Albergo Il Genio offers free parking. In peak season, buses shuttle drivers from the parking lot just outside Portovenere to the harborside square. Otherwise, test your luck with the spots on the seaside (€1.50/hour).

Tourist Information: The TI is easy to find in the main square (June-Sept Thu-Tue 10:00-12:00 & 16:00-19:00, closed Wed; Oct-May Thu-Tue 10:00-12:00 & 15:00-18:00, closed Wed; Piazza Bastreri 7, tel. 0187-790-691).

Sleeping in Portovenere: If you've forgotten your yacht, try **$$$ Albergo Il Genio,** in the building where the main street hits the piazza (Db-€130, some rooms with views, no elevator, Internet access, free parking but request when you reserve, Piazza Bastreri 8, tel. & fax 0187-790-611, www.hotelgenioportovenere.com, info@hotelgenioportovenere.com). If your *vita* is feeling *dolce,* consider **$$$ Grand Hotel Portovenere,** which has striking sea views (from €125 for a viewless Db off-season to €300 for a view suite in summer, optional half-pension-€30-39/person, Internet access, tel. 0187-792-610, fax 0187-790-661, Via Garibaldi 5, www .portovenerehotel.it, ghp@village.it).

FLORENCE

Firenze

Florence, the home of the Renaissance and birthplace of our modern world, has the best Renaissance art in Europe. In a single day, you could look Michelangelo's *David* in the eyes, fall under the seductive sway of Botticelli's *Birth of Venus,* and climb the modern world's first dome, which still dominates the skyline.

Get your bearings with a Renaissance walk. Florentine art goes beyond paintings and statues—enjoy the food, fashion, and street markets. You can lick Italy's best gelato while enjoying some of Europe's best people-watching.

Planning Your Time

If you're in Italy for three weeks, Florence deserves at least one well-organized day: see the Accademia *(David),* tour the Uffizi Gallery (Renaissance art), visit the underrated Bargello (best statues), and do the Renaissance Walk (explained on page 476; to avoid heat and crowds, do this walk in the morning or late afternoon). Art lovers will want to chisel out another day of their itinerary for the many other Florentine cultural treasures. Shoppers and ice-cream lovers may need to do the same.

Plan your sightseeing carefully; follow the tips and tricks in this chapter to save time and avoid lines. This is particularly important if you'll be in town for only a day or two during the crowded summer months.

The Uffizi Gallery and Accademia nearly always have long ticket-buying lines, especially in peak season (April-Oct) and on holiday weekends. Crowds thin out weekdays in the off-season. You can easily avoid the wait by making reservations (see page 473) or buying a Firenze Card (see page 471).

FLORENCE

Florence Overview

SAN LORENZO

RICASOLI

S.M.N. TRAIN STN.

DAVID (ACCADEMIA)

CERRETANI

DUOMO

SANTA MARIA NOVELLA

VIA DE' CALZAIUOLI ←

PALAZZO VECCHIO

Piazza della Signoria

SANTA CROCE

PONTE VECCHIO

UFFIZI

LUNGARNO

BRANCACCI CHAPEL

OLTRARNO

Arno River

SANTO SPIRITO

GUICCIARDINI

PITTI PALACE

Not to Scale

Note that both the Uffizi and Accademia are closed on Monday. Some sights close early; see the early-closing warning in the "Daily Reminder" on page 462. Other museums close early only on certain days (e.g., the first Sunday of the month, second and fourth Monday, etc.). In general, Sundays and Mondays are bad, with many museums either closed or with shorter hours.

Connoisseurs of smaller towns should consider taking the bus to Siena for a day or evening trip (1.25 hours one-way, confirm when last bus returns). Siena is magic after dark. For more information, see the Siena chapter.

Orientation to Florence

The best of Florence lies on the north bank of the Arno River. The main historical sights cluster around the red-brick dome of the cathedral (Duomo). Everything is within a 20-minute walk of the train station, cathedral, or Ponte Vecchio (Old Bridge). The less famous but more characteristic Oltrarno area (south bank) is just over the bridge. Though small, Florence is intense. Prepare for scorching summer heat, slick pickpockets, few WCs, steep prices, and long lines. Easy tourist money has corrupted some locals, making them greedy and dishonest (check your bill carefully). The big news for visitors to Florence is the energetic young mayor's passion for traffic-free zones. Once brutal for pedestrians, the city is now a delight on foot.

Tourist Information

Florence has two separate TI organizations, which are equally helpful.

One TI has two different branches, both with a focus on the city. The main branch is across the square from the **train station** and very crowded (Mon-Sat 8:30-19:00, Sun 8:30-14:00; with your back to tracks, exit the station—it's 100 yards away, across the square in wall near corner of church at Piazza Stazione 4; if you see a "tourist information" desk inside the train station, it's a hotel-booking service in disguise; tel. 055-212-245, www.firenze turismo.it). The other branch is very centrally located at **Piazza del Duomo**, at the west corner of Via Calzaiuoli (it's inside the Bigallo Museum/Loggia; Mon-Sat 9:00-19:00, Sun 9:00-14:00).

The other TI organization covers both the city and the greater province of Florence. Its main branch is a couple of blocks **north of the Duomo** (Mon-Sat 8:30-18:30, closed Sun, just past Medici-Riccardi Palace at Via Cavour 1 red, tel. 055-290-832, international bookstore across street); a second branch is at the **airport** (daily 8:30-20:30).

At any TI, peruse these free, handy resources in English (though, since they overlap quite a bit, you probably don't need them all):

- city map (also ask for the transit map, which has bus routes of interest to tourists on the back; your hotel likely has freebie maps, too)
- current museum-hours listing (very important, since no guidebook—including this one—has ever been able to accurately predict the hours of Florence's sights for the coming year; you can also download this list at www.firenze turismo.it)
- a list of current exhibitions
- a printout of what's happening that day
- the compact *Firenze Info* booklet, loaded with useful practical details
- the *Firenze: The Places of Interest* fold-out, with brief descriptions of sightseeing options
- information on entertainment, including the TI's monthly *Florence & Tuscany News* (good for events and entertainment listings)
- the glossy monthly *Florence Concierge Information* magazine (stuffed with ads for shopping and restaurants, but also includes some practical information)

FLORENCE

FLORENCE

- *The Florentine* newspaper (published every other Thu in English, for expats and tourists, with great articles giving cultural insights; download latest issue at www.theflorentine .net)

The Florence magazine and newspaper just mentioned are often available at hotels throughout town.

The TIs across from the train station and on Via Cavour sell the €50 **Firenze Card,** an expensive but handy sightseeing pass that allows you to skip the lines at top museums (see page 471).

Arrival in Florence

By Train

Florence's main train station is called **Santa Maria Novella** (*Firenze S.M.N.* on schedules and signs). Built in Mussolini's "Rationalism" style back between the wars, in some ways the station seems to have changed little—notice the 1930s-era lettering and architecture.

Florence also has two suburban train stations: **Firenze Rifredi** and **Firenze Campo di Marte.** Note that some trains don't stop at the main station—before boarding, confirm that you're heading for S.M.N., or you may overshoot the city. (If this happens, don't panic; the other stations are a short taxi ride from the center.)

Take advantage of the user-friendly, automated "Fast Ticket" machines that display schedules, issue tickets, and even make reservations for railpass-holders. Some take only credit cards; others take cards and cash. Using them is easy—it actually can be fun; just tap "English." Be aware there are two train companies: TrenItalia, with most connections, has green-and-white machines (toll tel. 892-021, www.trenitalia.it); the red machines are for the new Italo service, run by a private operator (tel. 06-0708, www .italotreno.it).

To get international tickets, you'll need to either go to a ticket window (in the main hall) or a travel agency.

To orient yourself to Santa Maria Novella Station and nearby services, stand with your back to the tracks. Look left to see a 24-hour pharmacy (*Farmacia,* near McDonald's) and baggage storage halfway down track 16 (€5/5 hours, then €0.70/hour for 6-12 hours and €0.30/hour for over 12 hours, daily 6:00-23:50, passport required, maximum 40 pounds, no explosives—sorry).

Directly ahead of you is the main hall (*salone biglietti,* with ticket windows). Avoid the station's fake "Tourist Information" office, funded by hotels, if it's still around. To reach the real TI, walk away from the tracks and exit the station; it's straight across the square, 100 yards away, by the stone church. (If there's construction, circle around the torn-up square to the left to reach it.) For cheap eats, the large cafeteria near McDonald's has various food stands. Better yet, the handy Margherita/Conad supermarket—with sandwiches and salads to go—is just around the corner (with your back to the tracks, leave the station to the right, go down the steps, and it's immediately on your right on Via Luigi Alamanni; Mon-Sat 8:00-20:00, closed Sun).

Getting to the Duomo and City Center: The Duomo and town center are to your left (with your back to the tracks). Out the doorway to the left, you'll find city buses and the taxi stand. Taxis cost about €8 to the Duomo, and the line moves fast, except on holidays. To walk into town (10-15 minutes), exit the station to the left and find the stairs/escalators down to the underground passageway/mall called Galleria S.M. Novella. Head toward the Church of Santa Maria Novella. (Warning: Pickpockets—often dressed as tourists—frequent this tunnel, especially the surface point near the church.) You come out on the other side of the square; head down Via dei Panzani, which leads directly to the Duomo.

By Bus

The bus station is next to the train station, with the TI across the square. Exit the station through the main door, and turn left along the busy street toward the brick dome. The train station is on your left, while downtown Florence is straight ahead and a bit to the right. For more information on buses, see page 465.

By Car

The autostrada has several exits for Florence. Get off at the *Nord*, *Sud*, or *Certosa* exits and follow signs toward—but not into—the *Centro*.

Don't even attempt driving into the city center. Florence has a traffic-reduction system that's complicated and confusing even to locals. Every car passing into the *Zona Traffico Limitato (ZTL)* is photographed; those who haven't jumped through bureaucratic hoops to get a permit can expect to receive a €100 ticket in the mail. If you get lost and cross the line several times...you get several fines. The no-go zone (defined basically by the old medieval wall, now a boulevard circling the historic center of town—watch for *Zona Traffico Limitato* signs) is roughly the area between the river, main train station, Piazza della Libertà, Piazza Donatello, and Piazza Beccaria.

Parking: The city center is ringed with big, efficient parking lots (signposted with the standard big *P*), each with taxi and bus service into the center. Check www.firenzeparcheggi.it for details on parking lots, availability, and prices. From the freeway, follow the signs to *Centro*, then *Stadio*, then *P*. I usually head for "Parcheggio del Parterre," just beyond Piazza della Libertà (€2/hour, €20/day, €65/week, open 24 hours daily, tel. 055-500-1994,

600 spots, automated, pay with cash or credit card, never fills up completely). To get into town, find the taxi stand at the elevator exit, or ride one of the minibuses that connect all of the major parking lots with the city center (see www.ataf.net for routes).

You can park for free along any suburban curb near a bus stop that feels safe and take the bus into the city center from there. Check for signs that indicate parking restrictions—for example, a circle with a slash through it and "*dispari giovedi*, 0,00-06,00" means "don't park on Thursdays between midnight and six in the morning."

Free parking is easy up at Piazzale Michelangelo (see page 501), but don't park where the buses drop off passengers; park on the side of the piazza farthest from the view. To get from Piazzale Michelangelo to the center of town, take bus #12 or #13.

Car Rental: If you're picking up a rental car upon departure, don't struggle with driving into the center. Taxi with your luggage to the car-rental office, and head out from there.

By Plane

Amerigo Vespucci Airport, also called Peretola Airport, is about five miles northwest of the city (open 5:10-24:00, no overnighting allowed, TI, cash machines, car-rental agencies, airport code: FLR, airport info tel. 055-306-1630, flight info tel. 055-306-1700—domestic only, www.aeroporto.firenze.it). Shuttle buses (far right of airport as you exit arrivals hall) connect the airport with Florence's SITA bus station, 100 yards west of the train station on Via Santa Caterina da Siena (2/hour, 30 minutes, €5, buy ticket on board and validate immediately, daily 6:00-23:30, first bus leaves for airport from Florence at 5:30). If you're changing to a different intercity bus in Florence (for instance, one bound for Siena), stay on the bus through the first stop (at the train station); it will continue on to the bus station nearby. Allow about €25 and 30 minutes for a taxi.

By Cruise Ship

For detailed instructions for arriving at Florence's port, Livorno, see page 535.

Helpful Hints

Theft Alert: Florence has particularly hardworking thief gangs who hang out where you do: near the train station, the station's underpass (especially where the tunnel surfaces), and at major sights. American tourists—especially older ones—are considered easy targets. Some thieves even dress like tourists to fool you. Be on guard at two squares frequented by drug pushers (Santa Maria Novella and Santo Spirito). Bus #7 (to the nearby town of Fiesole, with great Florence views) is a favorite with tourists and, therefore, with thieves.

Medical Help: There's no shortage of English-speaking medical help in Florence. To reach a doctor who speaks English, call **Medical Service Firenze** at 055-475-411; the phone is answered 24/7. Rates are reasonable. For a doctor to come to your hotel within an hour of your call, you'd pay €100-200 (higher rates apply on Sun, holidays, or for late visits). You pay only €50 if you go to the clinic when the doctor's in (Mon-Fri 11:00-12:00 & 17:00-18:00, Sat 11:00-12:00, closed Sun, no appointment necessary, Via L. Magnifico 59, near Piazza della Libertà). A second clinic is available at Via Porta Rossa 1 (Mon-Sat 13:00-15:00, closed Sun).

Dr. Stephen Kerr is an English doctor specializing in helping sick tourists (drop-in clinic open Mon-Fri 15:00-17:00, other times by appointment, €50/visit, Piazza Mercato Nuovo 1, between Piazza della Repubblica and Ponte Vecchio, tel. 055-288-055, mobile 335-836-1682, www.dr-kerr.com). The TI has a list of other English-speaking doctors.

There are 24-hour **pharmacies** at the train station and on Borgo San Lorenzo (near the Baptistery).

Museum Strategies: If you want to see a lot of museums, the pricey Firenze Card—which saves you from having to wait in line or make reservations for the Uffizi and Accademia—can be a good value (see page 471).

Churches: Some churches operate like museums, charging an admission fee to see their art treasures. Modest dress for men, women, and even children is required in some churches (including the Duomo, Santa Maria Novella, Santa Croce, Santa Maria del Carmine—with the Brancacci Chapel, and the Medici Chapels), and recommended for all of them—no bare shoulders, short shorts, or short skirts. At many churches, you can borrow or buy a cheap, disposable poncho for instant respectability. Be respectful of worshippers and the paintings; don't use a flash. Churches usually close from 12:00 or 12:30 to 15:00 or 16:00.

Addresses: For reasons beyond human understanding, Florence has a ridiculously confusing system for street addresses, with separate numbering for businesses (red) and residences (black). In print, this designation is sometimes indicated by a letter following the number: "r" = red; no indication or "n" = black, for *nero*. While usually black, B&Bs can be either. The red and black numbers each appear in roughly consecutive order on streets but bear no apparent connection with each other. While the numbers are sometimes color-coded on street signs, in many cases they appear in neither red nor black, but

Daily Reminder

Sunday: The Duomo's dome, Museum of Precious Stones, and the Mercato Centrale are closed.

These sights close early: Duomo Museum (at 13:40) and the Baptistery's interior (at 14:00).

A few sights are open only in the afternoon: Duomo (13:30-16:45), Santa Croce Church (14:00-17:30), Church of San Lorenzo (13:30-17:30 except closed Nov-Jan), Brancacci Chapel and Church of Santa Maria Novella (both 13:00-17:00), and Santo Spirito Church (16:00-17:30).

The Museum of San Marco and the Bargello are closed on the first, third, and fifth Sundays of the month. Palazzo Davanzati and the Medici Chapels close on the second and fourth Sundays. Need a calendar? Look in the appendix.

Monday: The biggies are closed, including the Accademia (David) and the Uffizi Gallery, as well as the Pitti Palace's Palatine Gallery, Royal Apartments, and Gallery of Modern Art.

The Museum of San Marco and the Bargello close on the second and fourth Mondays. At the Pitti Palace, the Argenti/Silverworks Museum and the Boboli and Bardini gardens close on the first and last Mondays. Palazzo Davanzati is closed on the first, third, and fifth Mondays. The San Lorenzo Market is closed Mondays in winter.

Target these sights on Mondays: the Duomo and its dome, Duomo Museum, Campanile, Baptistery, Medici-Riccardi Palace, Brancacci Chapel, Mercato Nuovo, the Mercato Centrale, Casa Buonarroti, Galileo Science Museum, the Palazzo Vecchio, and churches (including Santa Croce and Santa Maria Novella). Or take a walking tour.

Tuesday: Casa Buonarroti, Brancacci Chapel, and the Museum of Santa Maria Novella are closed. The Galileo Science Museum closes early (13:00).

in blue! I'm lazy and don't concern myself with the distinction (if one number's wrong, I look nearby for the other) and can easily find my way around.

Chill Out: Schedule several cool breaks into your sightseeing where you can sit, pause, and refresh yourself with a sandwich, gelato, or coffee. Carry a water bottle to refill at Florence's twist-the-handle public fountains. Try the *fontanello* (dispenser of free cold water) on Piazza della Signoria, behind the statue of Neptune (to the left of the Palazzo Vecchio).

Internet Access: Bustling, tourist-filled Florence has many small Internet cafés. **VIP Internet** has cheap rates, numerous terminals, and long hours (€1.50/hour, daily 9:00-24:00, near recommended hotel Katti House at Via Faenza 49 red, tel.

Wednesday: All sights are open, except for the Medici-Riccardi Palace, Santo Spirito Church, and the Museum of Santa Maria Novella.

Thursday: All sights are open, except for the Museum of Santa Maria Novella. These sights close early: the Palazzo Vecchio (14:00) and off-season, the Duomo (16:00 Oct-May).

Friday: All sights are open.

Saturday: All sights are open, but the Duomo's dome closes earlier than usual, at 17:40.

Early-Closing Warning: Some of Florence's sights close surprisingly early most days. Palazzo Davanzati closes at 13:50 and the Museum of San Marco closes at 13:50 on weekdays (open later on Sat and when open on Sun). Off-season, the Medici Chapels and Bargello close at 13:50. The Museum of Precious Stones closes at 14:00, as does the Mercato Centrale (except in winter, when it stays open until 17:00 on Sat).

Late-Hours Relief: The Accademia and the Pitti Palace's Palatine Gallery and Royal Apartments are open until 18:50 (and the Uffizi until 18:35) daily except Monday.

Many sights are open until 19:00 on a particular day or days: San Lorenzo Market (daily, but closed Mon in winter), the Duomo's dome (Mon-Fri), and the Baptistery (Mon-Sat, except first Sat of month until 14:00).

These sights are open until 19:30: Campanile (daily), Duomo Museum (Mon-Sat), and the Boboli and Bardini gardens at the Pitti Palace (daily except some Mon, June-Aug only). The Mercato Nuovo is open daily until 20:00, as is the San Miniato Church (but closes at 19:00 in winter),

In summer (April-Sept), the best late-hours sightseeing is at the Palazzo Vecchio, which stays open until 24:00 (except on Thu, when it closes at 14:00); off-season, it's still open relatively late (Wed-Mon until 19:00).

055-264-5552). **Internet Train,** the dominant chain, is pricier, with bright and cheery rooms, speedy computers, and decent hours (€4.30/hour, cheaper for students, reusable card good for any other Internet Train location, open daily roughly 9:00-20:00, www.internettrain.it). Find branches near Piazza della Repubblica (Via Porta Rossa 38 red), behind the Duomo (Via dell'Oriolo 40), and on Piazza Santa Croce (Via de'Benci 36 red). Internet Train also offers Wi-Fi, phone cards, and other services.

Most hotels have Wi-Fi. If you have a smartphone with an Italian mobile number, you can access free Wi-Fi for an hour at various hotspots around town (the TI can give you a list of hotspots and instructions).

Bookstores: Local guidebooks (sold at kiosks) are cheap, and give you a map and a decent commentary on the sights. For brand-name guidebooks in English (including mine), try **Feltrinelli International** (Mon-Sat 9:00-19:30, closed Sun, a few blocks north of the Duomo and across the street from TI and Medici-Riccardi Palace at Via Cavour 12 red, tel. 055-219-524); **Edison Bookstore** (also has CDs, plus novels on the Renaissance and much more on its four floors; Mon-Sat 9:00-24:00, Sun 10:00-24:00, facing Piazza della Repubblica, tel. 055-213-110); **Paperback Exchange** (cheaper, all books in English, bring in your used book for a discount on a new one, Mon-Fri 9:00-19:30, Sat 10:30-19:30, closed Sun, just south of the Duomo on Via delle Oche 4 red, tel. 055-293-460); or **BM Bookshop** (with perhaps the city's largest collection of English books and guidebooks—including mine; Mon-Sat 9:30-19:30, closed Sun, near Ponte alla Carraia at Borgognissanti 4 red, tel. 055-294-575).

Services: WCs are scarce. Use them when you can, in any café or museum you patronize.

Laundry: The **Wash & Dry Lavarapido** chain offers long hours and efficient, self-service launderettes at several locations (about €7 for wash and dry, bring plenty of coins, daily 8:00-22:00, tel. 055-580-480). These are close to recommended hotels: Via dei Servi 102 red (near *David*), Via del Sole 29 red and Via della Scala 52 red (between train station and river), Via Ghibellina 143 red (Palazzo Vecchio), and Via dei Serragli 87 red (across the river in Oltrarno neighborhood). For more options, the TI has a complete list of launderettes.

Bike Rental: The **city of Florence** rents bikes cheaply at several locations: the train station, Piazza Santa Croce, and Piazza Ghiberti (€2/1 hour, €5/5 hours, €10/day, tel. 055-650-5295; information at any TI). **Florence by Bike** rents two-wheelers of all sizes (€3.50/hour, €9/5 hours, includes bike lock and helmet, child seat-€3 extra; April-Oct daily 9:00-19:30; Nov-March Mon-Sat 9:00-13:00 & 15:30-19:30, closed Sun; Via San Zanobi 120 red, tel. 055-488-992, www.florencebybike.it, info@florencebybike.it).

Travel Agency: While it's easy to buy train tickets to destinations within Italy at handy machines at the station, travel agencies can be more convenient and helpful for getting international tickets, reservations, and supplements. The cost may be the same, or there may be a minimal charge. Ask your hotelier for the nearest travel agency.

Updates to this Book: For updates to this book, check www.ricksteves.com/update.

Getting Around Florence

I organize my sightseeing geographically and do it all on foot. I think of Florence as a Renaissance treadmill—it requires a lot of walking. You likely won't need public transit, except maybe to head up to Piazzale Michelangelo and San Miniato Church for the view, or to Fiesole.

Buses: The city's full-size buses don't cover the old center well (the whole area around the Duomo is off-limits to motorized traffic). The TI hands out a map of transit routes. Of the many bus lines, I find these to be of most value for seeing outlying sights:

Buses **#12** and **#13** go from the train station to Porta Romana, up to San Miniato Church and Piazzale Michelangelo, and on to Santa Croce.

Bus **#7** goes from Piazza San Marco (near the Accademia and Museum of San Marco) to Fiesole, a small town with big views of Florence.

The train station and Piazza San Marco are two major hubs near the city center; to get between these two, either walk (about 15 minutes) or take bus #1, #6, #14, or #23.

Fun little **minibuses** (many of them electric, *elettrico*) wind through the tangled old center of town and up and down the river—just €1.20 gets you a 90-minute joyride. These buses, which run every 10 minutes, are popular with sore-footed sightseers and eccentric local seniors.

Bus **#C1** stops behind the Palazzo Vecchio and Piazza Santa Croce, then heads north up to Piazza Libertà.

Bus **#C2** twists through the congested old center from the train station to Piazza Beccaria.

Bus **#C3** goes up and down the Arno River, with stops near Ponte Vecchio, the Carraia bridge to Oltrarno, and beyond.

Bus **#D** goes from the train station to Ponte Vecchio, cruises through Oltrarno, and finishes at Ponte San Niccolò.

The minibuses connect many major parking lots with the historical center (tickets sold at machines at lots).

Buy bus tickets at tobacco shops *(tabacchi)*, newsstands, or the ATAF bus office just east of the train station, on Piazza della Stazione (€1.20/90 minutes, €4.70/4 tickets, €5/24 hours, €12/3 days, 1-day and 3-day passes aren't always available in tobacco shops, validate in machine on the bus, tel. 800-424-500, www .ataf.net). You can buy tickets on board, but you'll pay more (€2) and you'll need exact change. City buses are free with the Firenze Card (see page 471). Follow general bus etiquette: Board at front or rear doors, exit out the center.

Taxi: The minimum cost for a taxi ride is €5, or €6 after 22:00 and on Sundays (rides in the center of town should be charged as

FLORENCE

Florence at a Glance

▲▲▲**Accademia** Michelangelo's *David* and powerful (unfinished) *Prisoners*. Reserve ahead or get a Firenze Card. **Hours:** Tue-Sun 8:15-18:50, closed Mon. See page 474.

▲▲▲**Duomo Museum** Underrated cathedral museum with sculptures. **Hours:** Mon-Sat 9:00-19:30, Sun 9:00-13:40. See page 486.

▲▲▲**Bargello** Underappreciated sculpture museum (Michelangelo, Donatello, Medici treasures). **Hours:** Tue-Sat 8:15-13:50, until 16:50 during special exhibits (typically April-Oct); also open first, third, and fifth Mon and second and fourth Sun of each month. See page 487.

▲▲▲**Uffizi Gallery** Greatest collection of Italian paintings anywhere. Reserve well in advance or get a Firenze Card. **Hours:** Tue-Sun 8:15-18:35, closed Mon. See page 490.

▲▲**Museum of San Marco** Best collection anywhere of artwork by the early Renaissance master Fra Angelico. **Hours:** Tue-Fri 8:15-13:50, Sat 8:15-16:50; also open 8:15-13:50 on first, third, and fifth Mon and 8:15-16:50 on second and fourth Sun of each month. See page 477.

▲▲**Medici Chapels** Tombs of Florence's great ruling family, designed and carved by Michelangelo. **Hours:** Tue-Sat April-Oct 8:15-16:50, Nov-March 8:15-13:50; also open second and fourth Mon and first, third, and fifth Sun of each month. See page 479.

▲▲**Duomo** Gothic cathedral with colorful facade and the first dome built since ancient Roman times. **Hours:** Mon-Fri 10:00-17:00, Thu until 16:00 Oct-May, Sat 10:00-16:45, Sun 13:30-16:45. See page 484.

▲▲**Palazzo Vecchio** Fortified palace, once home to the Medici, wallpapered with history. **Hours:** Fri-Wed 9:00-19:00, until 24:00 April-Sept; Thu 9:00-14:00 year-round. See page 493.

▲▲**Galileo Science Museum** Fascinating old clocks, telescopes, maps, and Galileo's finger in a bottle. **Hours:** Wed-Mon 9:30-18:00, Tue 9:30-13:00. See page 494.

▲▲**Santa Croce Church** Precious art, tombs of famous Florentines, and Brunelleschi's Pazzi Chapel in 14th-century church. **Hours:** Mon-Sat 9:30-17:30, Sun 14:00-17:30. See page 495.

▲▲**Church of Santa Maria Novella** Thirteenth-century Dominican church with Masaccio's famous 3-D painting. **Hours:**

Church—Mon-Thu 9:00-17:30, Fri 11:00-17:30, Sat 9:00-17:00, Sun 13:00-17:00; museum—Fri-Mon 9:00-16:00, closed Tue-Thu. See page 496.

▲▲Pitti Palace Several museums in lavish palace plus sprawling Boboli and Bardini gardens. **Hours:** Palatine Gallery, Royal Apartments, and Gallery of Modern Art: Tue-Sun 8:15-18:50, closed Mon; Boboli and Bardini gardens, Costume Gallery, Argenti/Silverworks Museum, and Porcelain Museum: Daily 8:15-18:30, until 19:30 June-Aug, gardens close as early as 16:30 in winter, closed first and last Mon of each month. See page 497.

▲▲Brancacci Chapel Works of Masaccio, early Renaissance master who reinvented perspective. **Hours:** Mon and Wed-Sat 10:00-17:00, Sun 13:00-17:00, closed Tue. Reservations required, though often available on the spot. See page 500.

▲▲San Miniato Church Sumptuous Renaissance chapel and sacristy showing scenes of St. Benedict. **Hours:** Daily Easter-mid-Oct 8:00-20:00 or possibly later, in winter 8:30-13:00 & 15:30-19:00. See page 502.

▲Medici-Riccardi Palace Lorenzo the Magnificent's home, with fine art, frescoed ceilings, and Gozzoli's lovely Chapel of the Magi. **Hours:** Thu-Tue 9:00-18:00, closed Wed. See page 480.

▲Climbing the Duomo's Dome Grand view into the cathedral, close-up of dome architecture, and, after 463 steps, a glorious Florence vista. **Hours:** Mon-Fri 8:30-19:00, Sat 8:30-17:40, closed Sun. Long and slow lines, go early, no reservations accepted. See page 485.

▲Campanile Bell tower with views similar to Duomo's, 50 fewer steps, and fewer lines. **Hours:** Daily 8:30-19:30. See page 485.

▲Baptistery Bronze doors fit to be the gates of paradise. **Hours:** Doors always viewable; interior open Mon-Sat 12:15-19:00 except first Sat of each month 8:30-14:00, Sun 8:30-14:00. See page 486.

▲Ponte Vecchio Famous bridge lined with gold and silver shops. **Hours:** Bridge always open (shops closed at night). See page 494.

▲Casa Buonarroti Early, lesser-known works by Michelangelo. **Hours:** Wed-Mon 10:00-17:00, closed Tue. See page 496.

▲Piazzale Michelangelo Hilltop square with stunning view of Duomo and Florence, with San Miniato Church just uphill. **Hours:** Always open. See page 501.

tariff #1). A taxi ride from the train station to the Duomo costs about €8. Taxi fares and supplements (e.g., €2 extra if you call a cab rather than hail one) are clearly explained on signs in each taxi. It can be hard to find a cab on the street; to call one, dial 055-4390 or 055-4242.

Tours in Florence

Tour companies big and small offer plenty of tours that go out to smaller towns in the Tuscan countryside (the most popular day trips: Siena, San Gimignano, Pisa, and into Chianti country for wine-tasting). They also do Florence city tours, but for most people, the city is really best on foot (and the book you're holding provides as much information as you'll get with a generic bus tour). To sightsee on your own, download my series of free audio tours that illuminate some of Florence's top sights and neighborhoods: my Renaissance Walk, the Accademia, and the Uffizi Gallery (see page 1101 for details).

For insight with a personal touch, consider the tour companies and individual Florentine guides listed here. Hardworking and creative, they offer a worthwhile array of organized sightseeing activities. Study their websites for details. If you're taking a city tour, remember that individuals save money with a scheduled public tour (such as those offered daily by Florencetown or ArtViva). If you're traveling as a family or small group, however, you're likely to save money by booking a private guide (since rates are based on roughly €55/hour for any size of group).

Walking (and Biking) Tours

ArtViva Walking Tours—This company offers a variety of tours (up to 12/day year-round) featuring downtown Florence, museum highlights, and Tuscany and Cinque Terre day trips. Their guides are native English-speakers. The three-hour "Original Florence" walk hits the main sights but gets offbeat to weave a picture of Florentine life in medieval and Renaissance times. Tours go rain or shine with as few as four participants (€25, daily at 9:15). Museum tours include the Uffizi Gallery (€39, includes admission, 2 hours), Accademia (called "Original *David*" tour, €35, includes admission, 1 hour), and "Original Florence in One Day" (€94, includes admission to Uffizi and Accademia plus 3-hour town walk, 6 hours). Their brochure and website list more activities, including biking and hiking tours, wine tours, and cooking classes (Mon-Sat 8:00-18:00, Sun 8:30-13:30, near Piazza della Repubblica at Via de' Sassetti 1, second floor, above Odeon Cinema, tel. 055-264-5033 during day or mobile 329-613-2730 from 18:00-20:00, www .artviva.com).

Florencetown Tours on Foot or by Bike—This well-organized company runs a variety of English-language tours. The boss, Luca Perfetto, offers student rates (10 percent discount) to anyone with this book, with an additional 10 percent off for second tours (if booking on their website, enter the code "RICK2013" when prompted). Three tours—their basic town walk, bike tour, and cooking class— are worth considering: The "Walk and Talk Florence" tour, which takes 2.5 hours, hits all the basic spots, including the Oltrarno neighborhood (€19, daily at 10:00). The "I Bike Florence" tour gives you 2.5 hours on a vintage one-speed bike following a fast-talking guide on a blitz of the town's top sights (€25, daily at 10:00 and 15:00, helmets optional, 15 stops on both sides of the river; in bad weather, the bike tours go as a €19 walking tour). The cooking class costs €79 and includes a market tour; see the listing later. Their office is two blocks from the Palazzo Vecchio at Via de Lamberti 1 (find steps off Via de' Calzaiuoli on the river side of Orsanmichele Church); they also have an "info point" kiosk on Piazza della Repubblica, at the corner with Via Pellicceria (tel. 055-012-3994, www.florence town.com).

Walks Inside Florence—Three art historians—Paola Barubiani and her partners Emma Molignoni and Marzia Valbonesi—provide quality guiding. Their company offers a daily 2.5-hour introductory tour (€50/person, 6 people maximum; outside except for a visit inside to see *David*, Accademia entry fee not included) and three-hour private tours (€180, €60/hour for more time, price is for groups of up to 4 people). They also offer an artisans-and-shopping tour, a guided evening walk, cooking classes with a market visit, private cruise excursions from the port of Livorno, and more— see their website for details (ask about Rick Steves discount for any tour, Paola's mobile 335-526-6496, www.walksinside florence.com, paola@walksinsideflorence.it).

Florentia—Top-notch private walking tours—geared for thoughtful, well-heeled travelers with longer-than-average attention spans—are led by Florentine scholars. The tours range from introductory city walks and museum visits to in-depth thematic walks, such as the Oltrarno neighborhood, Jewish Florence, and family-oriented tours (tours start at €250, includes personal assistance by email as you plan your trip, reserve in advance, www .florentia.org, info@florentia.org).

Context Florence—This scholarly group of graduate students and professors leads "walking seminars," such as a 3.5-hour study of Michelangelo's work and influence (€75/person, plus museum admission) and a two-hour evening orientation stroll (€40/person). I enjoyed the fascinating three-hour fresco workshop (€75/person plus materials, you take home a fresco you make yourself). See

FLORENCE

their website for other innovative offerings: Medici walk, lecture series, food walks, kids' tours, and programs in Venice, Rome, Naples, London, and Paris (tel. 06-967-27371, US tel. 215/609-4888 or 800-691-6036, www.contexttravel.com, info@context travel.com).

Cooking Classes and Market Tour

For something special, consider this five-hour experience offered by **Florencetown.** You'll start with a trip to the Mercato Centrale for shopping and tasting, then settle into their kitchen for a cooking lesson that finishes with a big feast of everything you've cooked. You'll meet butchers and bakers, and make bruschetta, pasta, a main course, and dessert (likely tiramisu). Groups are intimate and small (from 1-25 people, €79/person, 10 percent Rick Steves discount, Mon-Sat 10:00-15:00, runs rain or shine, chef Giovanni, Via de Lamberti 1, tel. 055-012-3994, www.florencetown.com).

Local Guides for Private Tours

Alessandra Marchetti, a Florentine who has lived in the US, gives private walking tours of Florence and driving tours of Tuscany (€60-75/hour, mobile 347-386-9839, aleoberm@tin.it).

Paola Migliorini and her partners offer museum tours, city walking tours, private cooking classes, wine tours, and Tuscan excursions by van—you can tailor tours as you like (€60/hour without car, €70/hour in an 8-seat van, tel. 055-472-448, mobile 347-657-2611, www.florencetour.com, info@florencetour.com); they also do private tours from the cruise-ship port of Livorno.

Karin Kibby, an Oregonian living in Livorno who leads Rick Steves tours, also offers day trips throughout Tuscany, including private excursions for cruise-ship passengers docking at Livorno. She'll work with you to find the best solution for your budget and interests (2-10 people, mobile 333-108-6348, karinkintuscany @yahoo.it).

Roberto Bechi, a great guide based in Siena, can come pick you up in Florence for off-the-beaten-path tours of the Tuscan countryside (see contact information on page 586).

Hop-on, Hop-off Bus Tours

Around town, you'll see big double-decker sightseeing buses double-parking near major sights. Tourists on the top deck can listen to brief recorded descriptions of the sights, snap photos, and enjoy a drive-by look at major landmarks (€16/1 calendar day, €22/48 hours, pay as you board, www.firenze.city-sightseeing.it). As the name implies, you can hop off when you want and catch the next bus (usually every 30 minutes). But since the most important sights are buried in the old center where big buses can't go,

Florence doesn't really lend itself to this kind of tour bus. Look at the route map before committing.

Driving Tours

500 Touring Club offers a unique look at Florence: from behind the wheel of one of the most iconic Italian cars, a vintage, restored Fiat 500. After a lesson *in la doppietta* (double-clutching), you'll head off in a guided convoy, following a lead car with live commentary via the radio and photo stops at the best viewpoints. Tours depart from a 15th-century villa on the edge of town; the Fiats are restored models from the 1960s and 1970s. Itineraries vary from basic sightseeing to countryside excursions with wine-making and lunch; see their website for options (2-hour tour-€60/person, US tel. 347/535-0030, Italian mobile 346-826-2324, Via Gherardo Silvani 149a, www.500touringclub.com, info@500touringclub .com, Andrea).

Sights in Florence

Avoid long ticket-buying lines at many sights and museums (especially the Uffizi and Accademia) by buying a Firenze Card, making advance reservations, or buying a combo-ticket. Unfortunately, no single option works for every sight, so it's well worth your time to study the following options and plan ahead.

Firenze Card

The Firenze Card (€50) is pricey but convenient. This three-day sightseeing pass gives you admission to many of Florence's sights, including the Uffizi Gallery and Accademia. Just as important, it lets you skip the ticket-buying lines without making reservations. For busy sightseers, the card can save some money. And for anyone, it can certainly save time. For people seeing five or six major sights in a short time, the card is well worth it. (But if you only want to see the Uffizi and Accademia, you'll save at least €20 by making individual reservations instead; see "Advance Reservations," later.)

With the card, you simply go to the entrance at a covered sight (if there's a "with reservations" door, use it), show the card, and they let you in (though there may be delays on especially crowded days).

The Firenze Card is valid for 72 hours from when you validate it at your first museum (e.g., Tue at 15:00 until Fri at 15:00). It

Summary of Sightseeing Strategies

To spend more time sightseeing and less time waiting in ticket-buying lines, consider these options, all of which are explained in more detail in these pages.

If you plan to see the...

Uffizi and Accademia only: Make reservations in advance for these two sights—it's cheaper than getting the Firenze Card.

Uffizi and Accademia, plus many other sights: Get the Firenze Card. Besides the Uffizi and Accademia, the card covers the Bargello, Museum of San Marco, Medici Chapels, Medici-Riccardi Palace, Palazzo Vecchio, Pitti Palace, and others you can pop into on a whim.

Duomo and its related sights (Baptistery, Campanile, and Duomo Museum): Get the combo-ticket.

Duomo plus dome-climb: The only way to skip the dome-climb ticket line is with the "Terraces of the Cathedral and Dome" tour.

includes regular admission price as well as any temporary exhibits (which are commonly tacked on at major sights such as the Uffizi). The card is good for one visit per sight. It also gives you free use of Florence city buses. The card is not shareable, and there are no family or senior discounts for Americans or Canadians.

To figure out if the Firenze Card is a good deal for you, tally up the entry fees of what you want to see. For example, here's a list of popular sights and their admission fees:

• Uffizi Gallery (€6.50 base price, usually €11 with temporary exhibits, as much as €15 with €4 reservation fee)
• Accademia (same fees as Uffizi)
• Palazzo Vecchio (€6.50)
• Bargello (€4 base, €7 with exhibits)
• Medici Chapels (€6 base, €9 with exhibits)
• Museum of San Marco (€4)
• Medici-Riccardi Palace (€7)

If you saw these sights in three days—which a busy sightseer might reasonably expect to do —you'd pay about €60 without the card, including the exhibit and reservation fees.

Other covered sights featured in this book include the Pitti Palace (both Palatine Gallery and Boboli Gardens), Brancacci Chapel, Museum of Precious Stones, Palazzo Davanzati, Galileo Science Museum, and Museum of Santa Maria Novella. The card is great for popping into lesser sights you otherwise wouldn't pay for. For a complete list of included sights, see www.firenze card.it.

Notable sights *not* covered by the Firenze Card include the various Duomo-related sights (dome climb, Campanile, Duomo Museum, and Baptistery—covered by their own, separate, time-saving combo-ticket described later), Church of Santa Maria Novella, Santa Croce Church, Casa Buonarroti, Casa di Dante, and the two Leonardo museums.

Getting the card makes the most sense from April through October, when crowds are worst. Off-season travelers could do without it.

You can buy the card at TIs and many participating sights. The handiest places are the TI at Via Cavour 1 red (a couple of blocks north of the Duomo), the Museum of Santa Maria Novella (next to the church of that name), and the Uffizi's door #2. See the full list of outlets at www.firenzecard.it.

Validate your card only when you're ready to tackle the covered sights on three consecutive days. Make sure the sights you want to visit will be open (many sights are closed Sun or Mon). For details, see the "Daily Reminder" on page 462.

Advance Reservations

Florence has an optional reservation system (€4 booking fee) for its state-run sights—including the Accademia, Uffizi Gallery, Bargello, Medici Chapels, and the Pitti Palace. (The Brancacci Chapel technically *requires* an advance reservation, but you can work around that—see page 500.) I'd recommend reservations only for the Uffizi and Accademia. For the Uffizi, book a month in advance for April-Oct travel (less off-season). For the Accademia, book a few days ahead for April-Oct (less off-season. From November to March, you can probably get in without a reservation after 16:00, but why risk it? After seeing hundreds of bored tourists waiting in lines, it's hard not to be amazed at their cluelessness.

Here are your reservation options:

• **Through Your Hotel:** When you make your hotel reservation, ask if they can book your museum reservations for you. Some hoteliers may charge a €3-5 fee above the €4 booking fee. They'll reserve by phone and give you a confirmation number that you'll take to the museum, where you'll pay cash for your ticket. This is your easiest reservation option.

• **By Phone:** From the US, dial 011-39-055-294-883, or within Italy call 055-294-883. The lines are open (Italian time) Mon-Fri 8:30-18:30, Sat 8:30-12:30, closed Sun. The reservation line is often busy. Be persistent. When you get through, an English-speaking operator walks you through the process—a few minutes later you say *grazie,* having secured an entry time and a confirmation number. You'll need to present your confirmation number at the museum and pay cash for your ticket plus the €4 reservation fee.

• **Online:** Sites such as www.uffizi.com and www.tickitaly .com are easy and reliable, but they require paying in advance with a credit card and charge a hefty €10-per-ticket reservation fee. The city's official site (www.firenzemusei.it) is only €4, but it's troublesome and not user-friendly.

• **Reserve in Florence:** Try to score a same-day reservation (€4) at the booking window at Orsanmichele Church (daily 10:00-17:00, along Via de' Calzaiuoli—see location on map on page 477); the My Accademia Libreria bookstore across from the Accademia (Tue-Sun 8:15-17:30, closed Mon, Via Ricasoli 105 red—see map on page 482); or the Uffizi's door #2—skirt to the left of the long ticket-buying line (Tue-Sun 8:15-18:35).

• **Private Tour:** Take a tour that includes your museum admission (see listings of tour companies on page 470).

Combo-Tickets:
The Duomo and Related Sights

The Duomo interior (free to enter), as well as the Campanile, Baptistery, and dome climb, suffer from long lines in peak season. They don't take reservations and aren't covered by the Firenze Card. To beat the lines, you have two options:

A **combo-ticket** (€15, valid four days) gives you slightly-reduced admission to the Campanile, Baptistery, Duomo Museum, and Duomo crypt (which also gets you into the Duomo interior via the church's uncrowded exit door). Buy your combo-ticket at the least-crowded sight—the Duomo Museum—and waltz right in to the other included sights without waiting in lines. Note that it does *not* include the dome-climb.

To skip lines at the dome-climb and Duomo, take the **"Terraces of the Cathedral and Dome" tour** (€15). You get a quick tour of the Duomo and then can continue directly up the dome. Book the tour at the Duomo Museum. For more details, see page 485.

Sights North of the Arno River
North of the Duomo (Cathedral)

▲▲▲**Accademia (Galleria dell'Accademia)**—When you look into the eyes of Michelangelo's magnificent sculpture of *David*, you're looking into the eyes of Renaissance Man.

In 1501, Michelangelo Buonarroti, a 26-year-old Florentine, was commissioned to carve a large-scale work. The figure comes from a Bible story. The Israelites are surrounded by barbarian warriors, who are led by a brutish giant named Goliath. When the

FLORENCE

giant challenges the Israelites to send out someone to fight him, a young shepherd boy steps forward. Armed only with a sling, David defeats the giant. This 17-foot-tall symbol of divine victory over evil represents a new century and a whole new Renaissance outlook.

Originally, *David* was meant to stand on the roofline of the Duomo, but was placed more prominently at the entrance of the Palazzo Vecchio (where a copy stands today). In the 19th century, *David* was moved indoors for his own protection, and stands under a wonderful Renaissance-style dome designed just for him.

Nearby are some of the master's other works, including his powerful (unfinished) *Prisoners, St. Matthew,* and a *Pietà* (possibly by one of his disciples). Florentine Michelangelo Buonarroti, who would work tirelessly through the night, believed that the sculptor was a tool of God, responsible only for chipping away at the stone until the intended sculpture emerged. Beyond the magic marble are some mildly interesting pre-Renaissance and Renaissance paintings, including a couple of lighter-than-air Botticellis, the plaster model of Giambologna's *Rape of the Sabine Women,* and a musical instrument collection with an early piano.

Cost and Hours: €6.50, up to €11 with mandatory exhibits, plus €4 reservation fee; Tue-Sun 8:15-18:50, closed Mon, last entry 30 minutes before closing; no photos, Via Ricasoli 60, reservation tel. 055-294-883, www.polomuseale.firenze.it. To avoid long lines in peak season, get the Firenze Card (described earlier) or make reservations (see page 473).

Avoiding Lines: In peak season (April-Oct), the museum is most crowded on Sunday, Tuesday, and between about 11:00 and 13:00. It's smart to buy a Firenze Card or reserve ahead (see pages 471 and 473 for info on both options). Those with reservations or the Firenze Card line up at the entrance labeled *With Reservations.* If you show up without a reservation or Firenze Card, and there's a long line, try dropping by the My Accademia Libreria reservation office, just across the street from the exit, to see if they have any reservations available later that day (€4 reservation charge). On off-season weekdays (Nov-March) before 8:30 or after 16:00, you can sometimes get in with no reservation and no lines.

Audioguides: The museum rents a €6 audioguide (€10/2 people; rent from souvenir counter in ticket lobby). You can download a free Rick Steves audio tour of the Accademia; see page 1101.

Nearby: Piazza S.S. Annunziata, behind the Accademia,

A Renaissance Walk Through Florence

During the Dark Ages, it was especially obvious to the people of Italy—sitting on the rubble of Rome—that there had to be a brighter age on the horizon. The long-awaited rebirth, or Renaissance, began in Florence for good reason. Wealthy because of its cloth industry, trade, and banking; powered by a fierce city-state pride (locals would pee into the Arno with gusto, knowing rival city-state Pisa was downstream); and fertile with more than its share of artistic genius (imagine guys like Michelangelo and Leonardo attending the same high school)—Florence was a natural home for this cultural explosion.

Take a two-hour walk through the core of Renaissance Florence from the Duomo (cathedral) to Ponte Vecchio on the Arno River. You can download a free Rick Steves audio tour of this walk (see page 1101).

Begin at the Duomo to marvel at the dome that kicked off the architectural Renaissance. Step inside the Baptistery to view a ceiling covered with preachy, flat, 2-D, medieval mosaic art. Then, to learn what happened when art met math, check out the realistic 3-D reliefs on the doors; the man who painted them, Giotto, also designed the bell tower—an early example of a Renaissance genius who excelled in many areas.

Continue toward the river on Florence's great pedestrian mall, Via de' Calzaiuoli—part of the original grid plan given to the city by the ancient Romans. Stop by any gelato shop for some cool refreshment. Down a few blocks, compare medieval and Renaissance statues on the exterior of the Orsanmichele Church. Via de' Calzaiuoli connects the cathedral with the central square (Piazza della Signoria), the city palace (Palazzo Vecchio), and the Uffizi Gallery, which contains the greatest collection of Italian Renaissance paintings in captivity. Finally, walk through the Uffizi courtyard—a statuary thinktank of Renaissance greats—to the Arno River and Ponte Vecchio.

displays lovely Renaissance harmony. Facing the square are two fine buildings: the 15th-century Santissima Annunziata church (worth a peek) and Filippo Brunelleschi's Hospital of the Innocents (Spedale degli Innocenti, not worth going inside), with terra-cotta medallions by Luca della Robbia. Built in the 1420s, the hospital is considered the first Renaissance building. I love sleeping on this square (at the recommended Hotel Loggiato dei Servti) and picnicking here during the day (with the riffraff, who remind me of the persistent gap—today as in Medici times—between those who appreciate fine art and those just looking for some cheap wine).

▲▲Museum of San Marco (Museo di San Marco)—Located one block north of the Accademia, this 15th-century monastery houses the greatest collection anywhere of frescoes and paintings by the early Renaissance master Fra Angelico. The ground floor features the monk's paintings, along with some works by Fra Bartolomeo. Upstairs are 43 cells decorated by Fra Angelico and his assistants. While the monk/painter was trained in the medieval religious style, he also learned and adopted Renaissance techniques and sensibilities, producing works that blended Christian symbols and Renaissance realism. Don't miss the cell of Savonarola, the charismatic monk who rode in from the Christian right, threw out the Medici, turned Florence into a theocracy, sponsored "bonfires of the vanities" (burning books, paintings, and so on), and was finally burned himself when Florence decided to change channels.

Cost and Hours: €4, covered by Firenze Card, Tue-Fri 8:15-13:50, Sat 8:15-16:50; also open 8:15-13:50 on first, third, and fifth Mon and 8:15-16:50 on second and fourth Sun of each month; last entry 30 minutes before closing, reservations possible but unnecessary, no photos, on Piazza San Marco, tel. 055-238-8608, www.polomuseale.firenze.it.

Museum of Precious Stones (Museo dell'Opificio delle Pietre Dure)—This unusual gem of a museum features room after room of exquisite mosaics of inlaid marble and other stones. The Medici loved colorful stone tabletops and floors; you'll even find landscapes and portraits (find Cosimo I in Room I). Upstairs, you'll see wooden work benches from the Medici workshop (1588), complete with foot-powered power tools. Rockhounds can browse 500 different stones (lapis lazuli, quartz, agate, marble, and so on) and the tools used to cut and inlay them. Borrow the English descriptions in each room.

Cost and Hours: €4, covered by Firenze Card, Mon-Sat 8:15-14:00, closed Sun, last entry 30 minutes before closing, around corner from Accademia at Via degli Alfani 78, tel. 055-265-1357.

Church of San Lorenzo—This red-brick dome—which looks like the Duomo's little sister—is the Medici church and the burial place of the family's founder, Giovanni di Bicci de' Medici (1360-1429).

Cost and Hours: €3.50, buy ticket just inside cloister next door, €6 combo-ticket covers Laurentian Library; March-Oct

Mon-Sat 10:00-17:30, Sun 13:30-17:30; Nov-Jan Mon-Sat 10:00-17:30, closed Sun; last entry 30 minutes before closing.

Visiting the Church: The facade is big, ugly, and unfinished, because Pope Leo X (also a Medici) pulled the plug on the project due to dwindling funds—after Michelangelo had labored on it for four years (1516-1520). Inside, though, is the spirit of Florence in the 1420s, with gray-and-white columns and arches in perfect Renaissance symmetry and simplicity. The Brunelleschi-designed church is lit by an even, diffused light. The Medici coat of arms (with the round pills of these "medics") decorates the ceiling, and everywhere are images of St. Lawrence, the Medici patron saint who was martyred on a grill.

Highlights of the church include two finely sculpted Donatello pulpits (in the nave). In the Martelli Chapel (left wall of the left transept), Filippo Lippi's *Annunciation* features a smiling angel greeting Mary in a sharply 3-D courtyard. Light shines through the vase in the foreground, like the Holy Spirit entering Mary's womb. The Old Sacristy (far left corner), designed by Brunelleschi, was the burial chapel for the Medici. Bronze doors by Donatello flank the sacristy's small altar. Overhead, the dome above the altar shows the exact arrangement of the heavens on July 4, 1442, leaving scholars to hypothesize about why that particular date was used. Back in the nave, the round inlaid marble in the floor before the main altar marks where Cosimo the Elder—Lorenzo the Magnificent's grandfather—is buried. Assistants in the church provide information on request, and the information brochure is free and in English.

Nearby: Outside the church, just to the left of the main door, is a **cloister** with peek-a-boo Duomo views and the **San Lorenzo Museum.** This collection of fancy reliquaries is included in your church admission, but is hardly worth the walk, except to see Donatello's grave. Also in the cloister is the **Laurentian Library** (€3, €6 combo-ticket with church, includes special exhibits, generally Mon and Fri-Sat 9:30-13:30, Tue-Thu 9:30-17:15, closed Sun). The library, largely designed by Michelangelo, stars his impressive staircase, which widens imperceptibly as it descends. Michelangelo also did the walls in the vestibule (entrance) that feature empty niches, scrolls, and oddly tapering pilasters. Climb the stairs and enter the Reading Room—a long, rectangular hall with a coffered-wood ceiling—designed by Michelangelo to host scholars enjoying the Medici's collection of manuscripts.

A **street market** bustles outside the church (listed after the Medici Chapels, next). Around the back end of the church is the entrance to the Medici Chapels and the New Sacristy, designed by Michelangelo for a later generation of dead Medici.

▲▲**Medici Chapels (Cappelle Medicee)**—The burial site of

the ruling Medici family in the Church of San Lorenzo includes the dusky Crypt; the big, domed Chapel of Princes; and the magnificent New Sacristy, featuring architecture, tombs, and statues almost entirely by Michelangelo. The Medici made their money in textiles and banking, and patronized a dream team of

Renaissance artists that put Florence on the cultural map. Michelangelo, who spent his teen years living with the Medici, was commissioned for the family's final tribute.

Cost and Hours: €6, €9 with mandatory exhibits, covered by Firenze Card; Tue-Sat April-Oct 8:15-16:50, Nov-March 8:15-13:50; also open second and fourth Mon and first, third, and fifth Sun of each month; last entry 30 minutes before closing; reservations possible but unnecessary, audioguide-€6 (€10/2 people), modest dress required, no photos, tel. 055-238-8602, www.polo museale.firenze.it.

▲**San Lorenzo Market**— Florence's vast open-air market sprawls around the Church of San Lorenzo. Most of the leather stalls are run by Iranians selling South American leather that was tailored in Italy. Prices are soft (daily 9:00-19:00, closed Mon in winter, between the Duomo and train station).

▲**Mercato Centrale (Central Market)**—Florence's giant iron-and-glass-covered central market, a wonderland of picturesque produce, is fun to explore. While the nearby San Lorenzo Market—with its garment stalls in the streets—feels like a step up from a haphazard flea market, the Mercato Centrale retains a Florentine elegance. Wander around. You'll see parts of the cow you'd never dream of eating (no, that's not a turkey neck), enjoy generous free samples, watch pasta-making, and have your pick of plenty of fun eateries sloshing out cheap and tasty pasta to locals (Mon-Sat 7:00-14:00, in winter open Sat until 17:00, closed Sun year-round). For eating ideas in and around the market, see "Eating in Florence," later.

▲**Medici-Riccardi Palace (Palazzo Medici-Riccardi)**—Lorenzo the Magnificent's home is worth a look for its art. The tiny Chapel of the Magi contains colorful Renaissance gems such as the *Procession of the Magi* frescoes by Benozzo Gozzoli. The former library has a Baroque ceiling fresco by Luca Giordano, a prolific artist from Naples known as "Fast Luke" *(Luca fa presto)* for his speedy workmanship. While the Medici originally occupied this 1444 house, in the 1700s it became home to the Riccardi family, who added the Baroque flourishes. While the

palace is rarely mobbed, you may encounter a slight bottleneck at the Chapel of the Magi (Cappella di Gozzoli). Only 10 people are allowed in at a time, but the line moves quickly.

Cost and Hours: €7, covered by Firenze Card, Thu-Tue 9:00-18:00, closed Wed, last entry 30 minutes before closing, ticket entrance is north of the main gated entrance, audio/videoguide-€4, no photos in Chapel of the Magi, Via Cavour 3, tel. 055-276-0340, www.palazzo-medici.it.

Leonardo Museums—Two different-but-similar entrepreneurial establishments several blocks apart show off reproductions of Leonardo's ingenious inventions. Either one is fun for anyone who wants to crank the shaft and spin the ball bearings of Leonardo's fertile imagination. While there are no actual historic artifacts, each museum shows several

dozen of Leonardo's inventions and experiments made into working models. You might see a full-size armored tank, walk into a chamber of mirrors, operate a rotating crane, or watch experiments in flying. The exhibits are described in English, and what makes these places special is that you're encouraged to touch and play with the models—it's great for kids. The museum on Via dei Servi is a bit larger.

Cost and Hours: Admission to each museum is €7. Museo Leonardo da Vinci—daily 10:00-19:00, Nov-March until 18:00, Via dei Servi 66 red, tel. 055-282-966, www.mostredileonardo.com. Le Macchine di Leonardo da Vinci—April-Oct daily 9:30-19:30; Nov-March Mon-Fri 11:00-17:00, Sat-Sun 9:30-19:30; for €1 extra they'll throw in a slice of pizza and a Coke, in Galleria Michelangelo at Via Cavour 21, tel. 055-295-264, www.macchinedileonardo.com.

FLORENCE

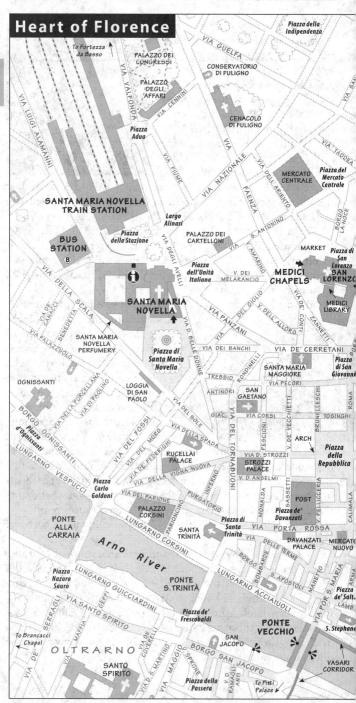

Heart of Florence

To Fortezza da Basso

PALAZZO DEI CONGRESSI

Piazza della Indipendenza

VIA GUELFA

VIA VALFONDA

PALAZZO DEGLI AFFARI

CONSERVATORIO DI FULIGNO

VIA CENNINI

CENACOLO DI FULIGNO

Piazza Adua

VIA FIUME

VIA NAZIONALE

VIA DELL'ARIENTO

VIA FAENZA

MERCATO CENTRALE

Piazza del Mercato Centrale

BORGO LA NOCE

VIA TADDEA

VIA LUIGI ALAMANNI

SANTA MARIA NOVELLA TRAIN STATION

Largo Alinari

S. ANTONINO

MARKET

Piazza di San Lorenzo

MEDICI CHAPELS

SAN LORENZO

BUS STATION B

Piazza della Stazione

VIA DEGLI AVELLI

PALAZZO DEI CARTELLONI

V. AMARINO

V. DEI MELARANCIO

VIA DE' CONTI

VIA DE' ZANNETTI

MEDICI LIBRARY

Piazza dell'Unità Italiana

VIA DELLA SCALA

VIA DE' CANACCI

SANTA MARIA NOVELLA

VIA D. BELLE DONNE

VIA PANZANI

DEL GIGLIO

V. DELL'ALLORO

VIA DE' CERRETANI

SANTA MARIA MAGGIORE

Piazza di San Giovanni

VIA BENEDETTA

VIA PALAZZUOLO

SANTA MARIA NOVELLA PERFUMERY

Piazza di Santa Maria Novella

TREBBIO

RONDINELLI

ANTINORI

VIA PECORI

BRUNELLESCHI

ROMA

OGNISSANTI

VIA DELLA PORCELLANA

VIA DI PAOLINO

LOGGIA DI SAN PAOLO

VIA DEL SOLE

SAN GAETANO

GIAC.

VIA CORSI

V. DE' VECCHIETTI

ARCH

TOSINGHI

Piazza della Repubblica

BORGO OGNISSANTI

Piazza d'Ognissanti

VIA DEL FOSSI

VIA DEL MORO

VIA DELLA SPADA

PESCIONI

VIA D. STROZZI

STROZZI PALACE

V. D. ANSELMI

MONALDA

SASSETTI

POST

V. PELLICCERIA

CALIMALA

LUNGARNO VESPUCCI

VIA DE FEDERIGHI

RUCELLAI PALACE

VIA DELLA VIGNA NUOVA

INFERNO

Piazza Carlo Goldoni

VIA DEL PARIONE

PALAZZO CORSINI

PURGATORIO

Piazza de' Davanzati

PONTE ALLA CARRAIA

LUNGARNO CORSINI

SANTA TRINITÀ

Piazza di Santa Trinità

VIA PORTA ROSSA

DAVANZATI PALACE

MERCATO NUOVO

Arno River

PONTE S. TRINITÀ

BORGO

DELLE TERME

S. APOSTOLI

MANETTO

VIA POR S. MARIA

ARMA

Piazza Nazaro Sauro

LUNGARNO GUICCIARDINI

LUNGARNO ACCIAIUOLI

Piazza de' Salt.

LAMB.

VIA SERRAGLI

VIA SANTO SPIRITO

Piazza de' Frescobaldi

PONTE VECCHIO

S. Stephane

To Brancacci Chapel

VIA DE' COVERELLI

VIA D. S. MARTINO

SAN JACOPO

BORGO SAN JACOPO

VASARI CORRIDOR

OLTRARNO

VIA MAGGIO

SPRONE

V. D. RAMAGLI

SANTO SPIRITO

Piazza della Passera

To Pitti Palace

Duomo and Nearby

FLORENCE

▲▲Duomo (Cattedrale di Santa Maria del Fiore)—Florence's Gothic cathedral has the third-longest nave in Christendom. The church's noisy neo-Gothic facade from the 1870s is covered with pink, green, and white Tuscan marble. In the interior, you'll see a huge *Last Judgment* by Giorgio Vasari and Federico Zuccari (inside the dome). Much of the church's great art is stored in the Duomo Museum behind the church.

The cathedral's claim to artistic fame is Brunelleschi's magnificent dome—the first Renaissance dome and the model for domes to follow. Think of the confidence of the age: The Duomo was built with a big hole in its roof, awaiting a dome...but it was built before the technology to span the hole with a dome even existed. No *problema*. They knew that someone soon could rise to the challenge...and the local architect Filippo Brunelleschi did. First, he built the grand white skeletal ribs, which you can see, then filled them in with interlocking bricks in a herringbone pattern. The dome grew upward like an igloo, supporting itself as it proceeded from the base. When the ribs reached the top, Brunelleschi arched them in and fixed them in place with the cupola at the top. His dome, built in only 14 years, was the largest since Rome's Pantheon.

Massive crowds line up to see the huge church: Although it's a major sight, it's not worth a long wait. To avoid the lines, either go late (crowds subside by late afternoon), buy a combo-ticket, or take the "Terraces" tour (ticket and tour options explained below).

Cost and Hours: Free entry, Mon-Fri 10:00-17:00, Thu until 16:00 Oct-May, Sat 10:00-16:45, Sun 13:30-16:45, modest dress code enforced, tel. 055-230-2885, www.operaduomo.firenze.it.

Crowd-Beating Tips: There are two ways to avoid lines at the Duomo, both of which involve paying for related sights (and let you skip the lines there, too). Each one costs €15; the combo-ticket covers more (including the highly recommended Duomo Museum), while the "Terraces" tour features the church interior, outdoor view terrace, and dome climb.

The **combo-ticket** covers most of the sights associated with the Duomo: the crypt, Duomo Museum, Baptistery, and Campanile (sold at all of these sights, but generally no lines to buy at the museum). A €23 version of the combo-ticket includes all the same sights and adds the dome; however, it must be purchased at the dome entrance, which can have lines, negating your time savings. Any combo-ticket is valid for one entrance to each sight, for four days. Once you've purchased the ticket, just show up at the exit door of the Duomo—it's around the right side as you face the main entrance, near the Campanile—show your ticket to the guard and he'll let you inside (allowing you to avoid the line at the entrance).

Alternatively, taking the **"Terraces of the Cathedral and Dome" tour** allows you to skip the long lines to enter the cathedral and to climb the dome. After a short guided tour of the interior, you'll climb up onto the exterior terrace, where great views reward the hike up the stairs (see "Climbing the Duomo's Dome," next). When the tour is finished, you can continue on your own up to the top of the dome (€15, 45 minutes; offered Mon-Fri at 10:30, 12:00, and 15:00 except no 15:00 tour Nov-March; Sat at 10:30 and 12:00, no tours on Sun; buy tickets at nearby Duomo Museum and they'll tell you where to meet your guide, tickets sold same-day only but there's generally no problem getting a spot). If you're planning to climb the dome anyway (€8), the tour is a fine value—and it's the only way to skip the line.

▲Climbing the Duomo's Dome—For a grand view into the cathedral from the base of the dome, a peek at some of the tools used in the dome's construction, a chance to see Brunelleschi's "dome-within-a-dome" construction, a glorious Florence view from the top, and the equivalent of 463 plunges on a Renaissance StairMaster, climb the dome. Michelangelo, setting out to construct the dome of St. Peter's in Rome, drew inspiration from the dome of Florence. He said, "I'll make its sister...bigger, but not more beautiful."

Cost and Hours: €8, cash only, Mon-Fri 8:30-19:00, Sat 8:30-17:40, closed Sun, last entry 40 minutes before closing, enter from outside church on north side, tel. 055-230-2885.

Crowd-Beating Tips: To avoid the long, dreadfully slow-moving line, arrive by 8:30, drop by very late, or take the "Terraces" tour of the Duomo (described earlier).

▲Campanile (Giotto's Tower)—The 270-foot bell tower has 50 fewer steps than the Duomo's dome (but that's still 413 steps—no elevator); offers a faster, relatively less-crowded climb; and has a view of that magnificent dome to boot. On the way up, there are several intermediate levels where you can catch your breath and enjoy ever-higher views. The stairs narrow as you go up, creating a mosh-pit bottleneck near the very top—

but the views are worth the hassle. While the various viewpoints are enclosed by cage-like bars, the gaps are big enough to let you snap great photos.

Cost and Hours: €6, daily 8:30-19:30, last entry 40 minutes before closing; to skip the line, consider the Duomo combo-ticket (see page 474).

▲**Baptistery**—Michelangelo said its bronze doors were fit to be the gates of paradise. Check out the gleaming copies of Lorenzo Ghiberti's bronze doors facing the Duomo (the original panels are in the Duomo Museum). Making a breakthrough in perspective, Ghiberti used mathematical laws to create the illusion of receding

distance on a basically flat surface.

The doors on the north side of the building were designed by Ghiberti when he was young; he'd won the honor and opportunity by beating Brunelleschi in a competition (the rivals' original entries are in the Bargello).

Inside, sit and savor the medieval mosaic ceiling, where it's always Judgment Day and Jesus is giving the ultimate thumbs-up and thumbs-down.

Cost and Hours: €5, €7 with mandatory exhibits, interior open Mon-Sat 12:15-19:00 except first Sat of month 8:30-14:00, Sun 8:30-14:00, last entry 30 minutes before closing, audio-guide-€2, tel. 055-230-2885. First buy your tickets at the office just across the piazza, then enter on the north side. The bronze doors are on the outside, so they are always "open" and viewable. To beat the line, consider the Duomo combo-ticket (see page 474).

▲▲▲**Duomo Museum (Museo dell'Opera del Duomo)**— The underrated cathedral museum, behind the church (at Via del Proconsolo 9), is great if you like sculpture, with many of the original creations that defined the 1400s (the Quattrocento) in Florence, when the city blossomed and classical arts were reborn. On the ground floor, look for a late Michelangelo *Pietà* that was intended as his sculptural epitaph, and statues from the original Baptistery facade. The museum also features Ghiberti's original bronze "Gates of Paradise" panels (the ones on the Baptistery's doors today are replicas). While copies now decorate the exteriors of the Duomo (cathedral) and Campanile (bell tower, called Giotto's Tower), the original sculptured masterpieces from both are now restored and displayed safely indoors at the Duomo Museum. Upstairs, you'll find Brunelleschi's models for his dome, as well as Donatello's anorexic *Mary Magdalene* and playful choir loft. Though overlooked by most visitors to Florence, this refurbished museum is a delight.

Cost and Hours: €6; Mon-Sat 9:00-19:30, Sun 9:00-13:40, last entry 40 minutes before closing, one of the few museums in Florence always open on Mon, audioguide-€5, Via del Proconsolo 9, tel. 055-282-226, www.operaduomo.firenze.it.

Tours: The audioguide costs €5. Guided English tours are generally offered daily in summer for €3 (as they use volunteer guides, schedules vary—stop by or call to ask).

Crowd-Beating Tips: While there's never a line here, the Duomo Museum is a good place to buy the Duomo combo-ticket (which allows you to bypass lines at the Duomo and related sights) and also sells tickets for the "Terraces of the Cathedral and Dome" tour (which allows you to skip the long cathedral-entry and dome-climbing lines). For more on these two options, see "Crowd-Beating Tips" on page 484.

Nearby: If you find this church art intriguing, head to the left around the back of the Duomo to find Via dello Studio (near the south transept), then walk a block toward the river to #23a (freestanding yellow house on the right). You can look through the open doorway of the **Opera del Duomo art studio** and see workers sculpting new statues, restoring old ones, or making exact copies. They're carrying on an artistic tradition that dates back to the days of Brunelleschi. The "opera" continues.

Between the Duomo and Piazza della Signoria

▲▲▲**Bargello (Museo Nazionale)**—This underappreciated

sculpture museum is in a former police station-turned-prison that looks like a mini-Palazzo Vecchio. The Renaissance began with sculpture—the great Florentine painters were "sculptors with brushes." You can see the birth of this revolution of 3-D in the Bargello (bar-JEL-oh), which boasts the best collection of Florentine sculpture. It's a small, uncrowded museum and a pleasant break from the intensity of the rest of Florence.

The Bargello has Donatello's very influential, painfully beautiful *David* (the first male nude to be sculpted in a thousand years), works by Michelangelo, and rooms of Medici treasures. Moody Donatello, who embraced realism with his lifelike statues, set the personal and artistic style for many Renaissance artists to follow. The best pieces are in the ground-floor room at the foot of

FLORENCE

the outdoor staircase (with fine works by Michelangelo, Cellini, and Giambologna) and in the "Donatello room" directly above (with plenty by Donatello, including two different *David*s, plus Ghiberti and Brunelleschi's revolutionary dueling door panels and yet another *David* by Verrocchio).

Cost and Hours: €4, €7 with mandatory exhibits, covered by Firenze Card, Tue-Sat 8:15-13:50, until 16:50 during special exhibits (generally April-Oct); also open first, third, and fifth Mon and the second and fourth Sun of each month; last entry 30 minutes before closing, reservations possible but unnecessary, audioguide-€6 (€10/2 people), photos in courtyard only, Via del Proconsolo 4, reservation tel. 055-238-8606, www.polomuseale.firenze.it.

Casa di Dante (Dante's House)—Dante Alighieri (1265-1321),

the poet who gave us *The Divine Comedy,* is the Shakespeare of Italy, the father of the modern Italian language, and the face on the country's €2 coin. However, most Americans know little of him, and this museum is not the ideal place to start. Even though it has English information, this small museum (in a building near where he likely lived) assumes visitors have prior knowledge of the poet. It's not a medieval-flavored house with period furniture—it's just a small, low-tech museum about Dante. Still, Dante lovers can trace his interesting life and works through pictures, models, and artifacts. And because the exhibits are as much about medieval Florence as they are about the man, novices can learn a little about Dante and the city he lived in.

Cost and Hours: €4; April-Sept daily 10:00-18:00; Oct-March Tue-Sun 10:00-17:00, closed Mon; last entry 30 minutes before closing, near the Bargello at Via Santa Margherita 1, tel. 055-219-416, www.museocasadidante.it.

▲Orsanmichele Church—In the ninth century, this loggia (covered courtyard) was a market used for selling grain (stored upstairs). Later, it was enclosed to make a church.

Outside are dynamic, statue-filled niches, some with accompanying symbols from the guilds that sponsored the art. Donatello's *St. Mark* and *St. George* (on the northeast and northwest corners) step out boldly in the new Renaissance style.

The interior has a glorious Gothic tabernacle (1359) housing the painted wooden panel that depicts *Madonna delle Grazie* (1346). The iron bars spanning the vaults were the Italian Gothic answer to the French Gothic external buttresses. Look for the rectangular holes in the piers—these were once wheat chutes that connected to the upper floors. The museum upstairs (limited hours) displays most of the originals from the niches outside the building, by Ghiberti, Donatello, Brunelleschi, and others.

Cost and Hours: Free, daily 10:00-17:00, museum also free but open only Mon, niche sculptures always viewable from the outside. You can give the *Madonna della Grazie* a special thanks if you're in town when an evening concert is held inside the Orsanmichele (tickets sold on day of concert from door facing Via de' Calzaiuoli; also books Uffizi and Accademia tickets, ticket window open daily 10:00-17:00).

▲**Mercato Nuovo (a.k.a. the Straw Market)**—This market loggia is how Orsanmichele looked before it became a church. Originally a silk and straw market, Mercato Nuovo still functions as a rustic yet touristy market (at the intersection of Via Calimala and Via Porta Rossa). Prices are soft, but the San Lorenzo Market (listed earlier) is much better for haggling. Notice the circled X in the center, marking the spot where people hit after being hoisted up to the top and dropped as punishment for bankruptcy. You'll also find *Porcellino* (a statue of a wild boar nicknamed "little pig"), which people rub and give coins to in order to ensure their return to Florence. This new copy, while only a few years old, already has a polished snout. At the back corner, a wagon sells tripe (cow innards) sandwiches—a local favorite (daily 9:00-20:00).

▲**Piazza della Repubblica and Nearby**—This large square sits

on the site of the original Roman Forum. Florence was a riverside garrison town set below the older town of Fiesole—essentially a rectangular fort with the square marking the intersection of the two main roads (Via Corso and Via Roma). The square's lone column—nicknamed "the belly button of Florence"—once marked the intersection (the Roman streets were about nine feet below the present street level). All that survives of Roman Florence is this column and the city's street plan. Look at any map of Florence today, and you'll see the ghost of Rome in its streets: a grid-plan city center surrounded by what was the Roman wall. The Braille model of the city makes the design clear.

Venerable cafés and stores line the square. During the 19th century, intellectuals met in cafés here. The La Rinascente department store, facing Piazza della Repubblica, is one of the city's mainstays (WC on fourth floor, continue up the stairs from there to the bar with a rooftop terrace with great Duomo and city

FLORENCE

views).

▲**Palazzo Davanzati**—This five-story, late-medieval tower house offers a rare look at a noble dwelling built in the 14th century. Currently only the ground, first, and second floors are open to visitors, though the remaining floors can be visited with an escort (usually at 10:00, 11:00, and 12:00; ask when you arrive or call ahead to be sure there's space). Like other

buildings of the age, the exterior is festooned with 14th-century horse-tethering rings made out of iron, torch holders, and poles upon which to hang laundry and fly flags. Inside, though the furnishings are pretty sparse, you'll see richly painted walls, a long chute that functioned as a well, plenty of fireplaces, a lace display, and even an indoor "outhouse." While there's little posted information, you can borrow English descriptions in each room.

Cost and Hours: €2, covered by Firenze Card, Tue-Sat 8:15-13:50; also open first, third, and fifth Sun and second and fourth Mon of each month; Via Porta Rossa 13, tel. 055-238-8610.

On and near Piazza della Signoria

The main civic center of Florence is dominated by the Palazzo Vecchio, Uffizi Gallery, and marble greatness of old Florence littering the cobbles. Piazza della Signoria still vibrates with the echoes of Florence's past—executions, riots, and great celebrations. Today, it's a tourist's world with pigeons, postcards, horse buggies, and tired hubbies. If it would make your weary companion happy, stop in at the recommended but expensive **Rivoire** café to enjoy its fine desserts, pudding-thick hot chocolate, and the best view seats in town. It's expensive—but if you linger, it can be a great value.

▲▲▲**Uffizi Gallery**—This greatest collection of Italian paintings

anywhere features works by Giotto, Leonardo, Raphael, Caravaggio, Titian, and Michelangelo, and a roomful of Botticellis, including the *Birth of Venus.* Northern Renaissance masters (Dürer, Rembrandt, and Rubens) are also well represented. The museum is not nearly as big as it is great. Few tourists spend more than two hours inside. Most of the paintings are displayed on one comfortable, U-shaped floor in chronological order from the 13th through 17th centuries. The left wing, starring the

Uffizi Gallery Overview

Not to Scale

To Duomo

DAVID COPY

PALAZZO VECCHIO

Piazza della Signoria

TERRACE (LOGGIA BELOW)

FAMOUS FLORENTINES LINE THE COURTYARD

VIA DI NINNA

To Santa Croce →

CAFÉ

STAIRS DOWN TO WC & FOREIGN PAINTERS SECTION

CORRIDOR

COURTYARD

ELEVATOR

STAIRS UP FROM ENTRY & WC

EARLY ITALIAN

EXIT

GIFT SHOP, WC & POST BELOW

STAIRS DOWN TO WC & EXIT

BOTTICELLI

LEONARDO

CORRIDOR

❶

❷

MANNERISM

VENUS DE' MEDICI

VIA DI CASTELLANI

❸

HIGH RENAISSANCE

NORTHERN RENAISSANCE

VIEW OF PONTE VECCHIO →

STATUES

GALILEO SCIENCE MUSEUM

← To Ponte Vecchio

LUNGARNO A. M. L. DE'MEDICI

Arno River

❶ Reservation Entrance
❷ Unreserved Ticket (Main) Entrance
❸ Reservation Ticket Office

Florentine Middle Ages to the Renaissance, is the best. The connecting corridor contains sculpture, and the right wing focuses on the High Renaissance and Baroque.

Essential stops are (in this order): Gothic altarpieces (narrative, pre-Realism, no real concern for believable depth) including Giotto's altarpiece, which progressed beyond "totem-pole angels"; Paolo Uccello's *Battle of San Romano,* an early study in perspective with a few obvious flubs (under restoration but hopefully back on display in 2012); and Fra Filippo Lippi's cuddly Madonnas. The Botticelli room is filled with masterpieces and classical fleshiness (the famous *Birth of Venus* and the *Allegory of Spring*), plus two minor works by Leonardo da Vinci. The octagonal classical sculpture room has a copy of Praxiteles' *Venus de' Medici*, considered the epitome of beauty in Elizabethan Europe. Next comes the view of Ponte Vecchio through the window, dreamy at sunset. Rounding it off are Michelangelo's only surviving easel painting, the round *Holy Family;* Raphael's noble *Madonna of the Goldfinch;* and Titian's voluptuous *Venus of Urbino.* Enjoy Duomo views from the café terrace. The lower floor contains temporary exhibitions and works by Caravaggio and foreign painters.

Cost and Hours: €6.50, €11 with mandatory exhibits, extra €4 for recommended reservation, cash required to pick up tickets reserved by phone; Tue-Sun 8:15-18:35, closed Mon, last entry 30 minutes before closing, no photos, museum info tel. 055-238-8651, reservation tel. 055-294-883, www.uffizi.firenze.it.

Avoiding Lines: To avoid the notoriously long ticket-buying lines, either get a Firenze Card or book ahead (for details on both, see page 471). During summer and on weekends, the Uffizi can be booked up a month or more in advance. Sometimes, by the end of the day (an hour before closing), you can just walk right in, but generally you'll encounter lines even off-season (and waits up to three hours in peak season, April-Oct). The busiest days are Tuesday, Saturday, and Sunday.

Getting In: There are several entrances (see map). Which one you use depends on whether you have a Firenze Card, a reservation, or neither. Firenze Card-holders enter at door #1 (labeled *Reservation Entrance*), close to the Palazzo Vecchio. Read the signs carefully, as there are two lines at this entrance; get in the line for individuals, not groups. People buying a ticket on the spot line up with everyone else at door #2. (The wait can be up to two hours.)

To buy a Firenze Card, or to see if there are any same-day reservations available (€4 extra, but could save you time in the ticket line), enter door #2 to the left of the ticket-buying line (marked *Booking Service and Today*).

If you've already made a reservation and need to pick up your ticket, go to door #3 (labeled *Reservation Ticket Office,* across the courtyard from doors #1 and #2). Tickets are available for pick-up 10 minutes before your appointed time. If you booked online, you've already prepaid with your credit card and just need to exchange your voucher for a ticket. If you (or your hotelier) booked by phone, you need to give them your confirmation number and pay for the ticket (cash only). Once you have your ticket, walk briskly past the 200-yard-long ticket-buying line—pondering the IQ of this gang—to door #1. Show your ticket and walk in.

Audioguides: A 1.5-hour audioguide costs €6 (€10/2 people; must leave ID). You can also download a free Rick Steves audio tour of the Uffizi (see page 1101).

In the Uffizi's Courtyard: Enjoy the courtyard (free), full of artists and souvenir stalls. (Swing by after dinner when it's completely empty.) The surrounding statues honor earthshaking Florentines: artists (Michelangelo), philosophers (Niccolò Machiavelli), scientists (Galileo), writers (Dante), cartographers (Amerigo Vespucci), and the great patron of so much Renaissance thinking, Lorenzo "the Magnificent" de' Medici.

Nearby: The Loggia dei Lanzi, across from the Palazzo Vecchio and facing the square, is where Renaissance Florentines once debated the issues of the day; a collection of Medici-approved sculptures now stand (or writhe) under its canopy, including Cellini's bronze *Perseus*. The plaque on the pavement in front of the fountain marks the spot where the monk Savonarola was burned in MCDXCVIII, or 1498.

▲▲Palazzo Vecchio—This castle-like fortress with the 300-foot spire dominates Florence's main square.

In Renaissance times, it was the Town Hall, where citizens pioneered the once-radical notion of self-rule. Its official name—the Palazzo della Signoria—refers to the elected members of the city council. In 1540, the tyrant Cosimo I de' Medici made the building his personal palace, redecorating the interior in lavish style. Today the building functions once again as the Town Hall, home to the mayor's office and the city council.

Entry to the ground-floor courtyard is free, so even if you don't go upstairs to the museum, you can step inside and feel the essence of the Medici. Paying customers can see Cosimo's (fairly) lavish royal apartments, decorated with (fairly) top-notch paintings and statues by Michelangelo and Donatello. The highlight is the Grand Hall (Salone dei Cinquecento), a 13,000-square-foot hall lined with huge frescoes and interesting statues. People who pay to climb the tower are rewarded with a magnificent city view.

Cost and Hours: Courtyard—free to enter; museum—€6.50, €8 combo-ticket with Brancacci Chapel, covered by Firenze Card; tower only-€6.50 (418 steps), museum plus tower-€10; Fri-Wed 9:00-19:00, until 24:00 April-Sept; Thu 9:00-14:00 year-round; ticket office closes one hour earlier, Piazza della Signoria, tel. 055-276-8224, www.museicivicifiorentini.it.

Nighttime Terrace Visits: In summer, you can join an escort for an unnarrated walk along the "patrol path"—the balcony that runs just below the crenellated top of the building (€2 plus regular admission ticket, every 30 minutes between 20:00 and 23:00, no tours Oct-March). Note that this tour doesn't go to the top of the

FLORENCE

tower, but just to the top of the main building.

▲Ponte Vecchio—Florence's most famous bridge has long been lined with shops. Originally these were butcher shops that used the river as a handy disposal system. Then, when the powerful and princely Medici built the Vasari Corridor (described next) over the bridge, the stinky meat market was replaced by the more elegant

gold and silver shops that remain there to this day. A statue of Benvenuto Cellini, the master goldsmith of the Renaissance, stands in the center, ignored by the flood of tacky tourism. This is a very romantic spot late at night (when lovers gather, and a top-notch street musician performs).

Vasari Corridor—This elevated and enclosed passageway, constructed in 1565, gave the Medici a safe, private commute over Ponte Vecchio from their Pitti Palace home to their Palazzo Vecchio offices. It's open only by special appointment, and while enticing to lovers of Florence, the actual tour experience isn't much. Entering from inside the Uffizi Gallery, you walk along a modern-feeling hall (wide enough to carry a Medici on a sedan chair) across Ponte Vecchio, and end in the Pitti Palace. Half the corridor is lined with Europe's best collection of self-portraits, along with other paintings (mostly 17th- and 18th-century) that seem like they didn't make the cut to be hung on the walls of the Uffizi. The best way to get inside the corridor is to go with a tour company such as Florencetown (€89, daily at 15:30, tel. 055-012-3994, www.florencetown.com) or ArtViva (€84, Tue and Sat at 13:30, tel. 055-264-5033, www.artviva.com). The three-hour tours, which include a tour of the Uffizi, are expensive because of steep city entrance fees and the requirement that groups be accompanied by attendants and a guide.

▲▲Galileo Science Museum (Museo Galilei e Istituto di Storia della Scienza)—When we think of the Florentine Renaissance, we think of visual arts: painting, mosaics, architec-

ture, and sculpture. But when the visual arts declined in the 1600s (abused and co-opted by political powers), music and science flourished in Florence. The first opera was written here. And Florence hosted many scientific breakthroughs, as you'll see in this fascinating collection of Renaissance and later clocks, telescopes, maps, and ingenious gadgets. Trace the technical innovations as modern science emerges from 1000 to 1900. One of the most talked-about bottles in Florence is the one here that contains Galileo's finger. Exhibits include various tools for gauging the world, from a compass and thermometer to Galileo's telescopes. Other displays delve into clocks, pumps, medicine, and chemistry. It's friendly, comfortably cool, never crowded, and just a block east of the Uffizi on the Arno River.

Cost and Hours: €9, €22 family ticket, cash only, covered by Firenze Card, Wed-Mon 9:30-18:00, Tue 9:30-13:00, last entry 30 minutes before closing, Piazza dei Giudici 1, tel. 055-265-311, www.museogalileo.it.

Tours: The €5 audioguide is well-produced, and offers both a highlights tour as well as dial-up info (with video) on each exhibit. The 1.5-hour English-language guided tour covers the collection plus behind-the-scenes areas, and includes hands-on demonstrations of some of the devices (€50 flat fee for 2-14 people, cash only, doesn't include museum entry, book at least a week in advance, great for kids, tel. 055-234-3723, groups@museogalileo.it).

East of Piazza della Signoria

▲▲Santa Croce Church—This 14th-century Franciscan church, decorated with centuries of precious art, holds the tombs of great Florentines. The loud 19th-century Victorian Gothic facade faces a huge square ringed with tempting shops and littered with tired tourists. Escape into the church and admire its sheer height and spaciousness.

On the left wall (as you face the altar) is the **tomb of Galileo Galilei** (1564-1642), the Pisan who lived his last years under house arrest near Florence. Having defied the Church by saying that the earth revolved around the sun, his heretical remains were only allowed in the church long after his death. Directly opposite (on the right wall) is the **tomb of Michelangelo Buonarroti** (1475-1564).

The first chapel to the right of the main altar features the famous fresco by Giotto of the *Death of St. Francis*. With simple but eloquent gestures, Francis' brothers bid him a sad farewell.

In the hallway near the bookstore, notice the photos of the devastating flood of 1966. Beyond that is the leather school (free entry).

Exit between the Rossini and Machiavelli tombs into the delightful cloister (open-air courtyard). On the left, enter Brunelleschi's Pazzi Chapel, which captures the Renaissance in miniature.

Cost and Hours: €6, €8.50 combo-ticket with nearby Casa Buonarroti, Mon-Sat 9:30-17:30, Sun 14:00-17:30, last entry 30 minutes before closing, audioguide-€5 (€8/2 people), modest dress required, 10-minute walk east of the Palazzo Vecchio along Borgo de' Greci, tel. 055-246-6105, www.santacroceopera.it. The **leather school** is free and sells tickets to the church. If the church has a long line, come here to avoid it (daily 10:00-18:00, has own entry behind church plus an entry within the church, www.leather school.com).

▲**Casa Buonarroti (Michelangelo's House)**—Fans enjoy a house standing on property once owned by Michelangelo. The house was built after Michelangelo's death by the artist's grand-nephew, who turned it into a little museum honoring his famous relative. You'll see some of Michelangelo's early, less-than-monumental statues and a few sketches. Be warned: Michelangelo's descendants attributed everything they could to their famous relative, but very little here (beyond two marble relief panels and a couple of sketches) is actually by Michelangelo.

Cost and Hours: €6.50, €8.50 combo-ticket with Santa Croce Church, Wed-Mon 10:00-17:00, closed Tue, English descriptions, Via Ghibellina 70, tel. 055-241-752.

Santa Maria Novella Sights near the Train Station

▲▲**Church of Santa Maria Novella**—This 13th-century Dominican church is rich in art. Along with crucifixes by Giotto and Brunelleschi, it contains every textbook's example of the early Renaissance mastery of perspective: *The Holy Trinity* by Masaccio. The exquisite chapels trace art in Florence from medieval times to early Baroque. The outside of the

church features a dash of Romanesque (horizontal stripes), Gothic (pointed arches), Renaissance (geometric shapes), and Baroque (scrolls). Step in and look down the 330-foot nave for a 14th-century optical illusion. Next to the church are the cloisters and the museum, located in the old Dominican convent of Santa Maria Novella. The museum's highlight is the breathtaking Spanish Chapel, with walls covered by a series of frescos by Andrea di Bonaiuto.

Cost and Hours: Church—€3.50, Mon-Thu 9:00-17:30, Fri 11:00-17:30, Sat 9:00-17:00, Sun 13:00-17:00, last entry 30 minutes before closing, audioguide-€5 (€8/2 people), modest dress required, no photos, tel. 055-219-257, www.museicivicifiorentini.it; museum—€2.70, covered by Firenze Card, Fri-Mon 9:00-16:00, closed Tue-Thu, tel. 055-282-187.

Farmacia di Santa Maria Novella—This palatial perfumery has long been run by the Dominicans of Santa Maria Novella. Thick with the lingering aroma of centuries of spritzes, it started as the herb garden of the Santa Maria Novella monks. Well-known even today for its top-quality products, it is extremely Florentine. Pick up the history sheet at the desk, and wander deep into the shop. The first room features perfumes, the middle (green) room offers items for the home, and the third room, which sells herbal products and dates from 1612, is the most historic. From here, you can peek at one of Santa Maria Novella's cloisters with its dreamy frescoes and imagine a time before Vespas and tourists.

Cost and Hours: Free but shopping encouraged, inconsistent hours but likely daily 9:30-19:30, a block from Piazza Santa Maria Novella, 100 yards down Via della Scala at #16—located on map on page 456, tel. 055-216-276, www.smnovella.com.

Sights South of the Arno River

To locate these sights, see the map on page 498.

▲▲**Pitti Palace**—The imposing Pitti Palace, several blocks southwest of Ponte Vecchio, is not only home to the second-best collection of paintings in town, the **Palatine Gallery,** but also happens to be the most sumptuous palace you can tour in Florence. The building itself is mammoth, holding several different museums and anchoring two gardens. Stick primarily to the gallery, forget about everything else, and the palace becomes a little less exhausting.

You'll walk through one palatial room after another, walls sagging with masterpieces by 16th- and 17th-century masters, including Rubens, Titian, and Rembrandt. Its Raphael collection is the second-biggest anywhere—the Vatican beats it by one. Each room has some descriptions in English, though the paintings themselves have limited English labels.

The collection is all on one floor. To see the highlights, walk straight down the spine through a dozen or so rooms. Before you exit, consider a visit to the Royal Apartments. These 14 rooms (of which only a few are open at any one time) are where the Pitti's rulers lived in the 18th and 19th centuries. Each room features a different color and time period. Here, you get a real feel for the splendor of the dukes' world.

The rest of the Pitti Palace is skippable, unless the various

Oltrarno, South of the Arno River

sights match your interests: the **Gallery of Modern Art** (second floor, features Romantic, Neoclassical, and Impressionist works by 19th- and 20th-century Tuscan painters), **Argenti/Silverworks Museum** (on the ground and mezzanine floors; displays Medici treasures from jeweled crucifixes to gilded ostrich eggs), **Costume Gallery**, **Porcelain Museum**, and **Boboli and Bardini gardens** (behind the palace; enter from Pitti Palace courtyard).

The main reason to visit the Pitti Palace is to see the Palatine Gallery, but you can't buy a ticket for the gallery alone; to see it you'll need to buy ticket #1, which includes the Palatine Gallery, Royal Apartments, and Gallery of Modern Art. Ticket #2 covers the Boboli and Bardini gardens, Costume Gallery, Argenti/Silverworks Museum, and Porcelain Museum. Behind door #3 is a combo-ticket covering the whole shebang.

Cost and Hours: Ticket #1—€8.50, Tue-Sun 8:15-18:50, closed Mon. Ticket #2—€7, daily 8:15-18:30, except closed first and last Mon of each month, until 19:30 June-Aug, gardens close as early as 16:30 in winter, last entry 30-60 minutes before closing. An €11.50 combo-ticket (valid 3 days) covers the entire palace complex. All tickets are cash only and increase in price with mandatory special exhibits. Reservations are possible but unnecessary, and everything is covered by the Firenze Card. The €6 audioguide (€10/2 people) explains the sprawling palace. No photos are allowed in the Palatine Gallery. Tel. 055-238-8614, www.polo museale.firenze.it.

Getting In: If there's a long line, you can bypass it by making a €3 "reservation" on the spot for immediate entry. The ticket office is at the far right of the massive facade; just march up to the head of the line and go to the window on the right, marked *reservation desk*. You can also skip lines if you have a Firenze Card. Once you have your ticket, enter through the main doorway in the center of the facade. Firenze Card-holders should go directly to the main

FLORENCE

entrance (where you may be ushered to the head of the security checkpoint); then go to the bookstore on the left side of the courtyard to have your card swiped and get your tickets.

▲▲**Brancacci Chapel**—For the best look at works by Masaccio (one of the early Renaissance pioneers of perspective in painting), see his restored frescoes here. Instead of medieval religious symbols, Masaccio's paintings feature simple, strong human figures with facial expressions that reflect their emotions. The accompanying works of Masolino and Filippino Lippi provide illuminating contrasts.

Your ticket includes a 40-minute film in English on the church, the frescoes, and Renaissance Florence (reserve a viewing time when you book your entry). The film starts promptly at the top of the hour (first shown at 10:00, last shown at 15:00). Computer animation brings the paintings to life—making them appear to move and giving them 3-D depth—while narration describes the events depicted in the panels. Yes, it's a long time commitment, and the film takes liberties with the art. But it's visually interesting and your best way to see the frescoes close up. The film works great either before or after you visit the frescoes.

Cost and Hours: €4, covered by Firenze Card, free and easy reservations required but it's usually possible to just show up and get an entry time if you arrive before 15:30, €8 combo-ticket with Palazzo Vecchio, includes worthwhile 40-minute film in English—reserve viewing time when you book entry, Mon and Wed-Sat 10:00-17:00, Sun 13:00-17:00, closed Tue, last entry 30 minutes before closing, in Church of Santa Maria del Carmine, reservations tel. 055-276-8224 or 055-276-8558, ticket desk tel. 055-284-361, www.museicivicifiorentini.it.

Reservations: Reserving an entry time is required (and free), but if you come before 15:30, you can usually just show up and be assigned a time more or less right away. Officially, reservation times begin every 15 minutes, with a maximum of 30 visitors per time slot (you have 15 minutes inside the chapel). But when it's not too busy, they generally let people come and go at will, and stay as long as they like.

The most crowded time is around 16:00, just before closing time; the least crowded time tends to be 12:00-14:00. If, before you head out for the sight, you want to find out if there's a long line, you can call ahead to the ticket desk just to ask how busy it is (tel. 055-284-361).

Firenze Card users don't need a reservation at all, and can

walk in whenever they like.

If it's worth the peace of mind for you to reserve in advance, you must call the chapel at least a day ahead (tel. 055-276-8224 or 055-276-8558, English spoken, call center open Mon-Sat 9:30-17:00, Sun 9:30-12:30). If the line is busy, keep trying—it's best to call around 13:00-15:00.

Dress Code: Shorts and bare shoulders are OK in the chapel, but modest dress is requested when visiting the rest of the church.

Santo Spirito Church—This church has a classic Brunelleschi interior—enjoy its pure Renaissance lines (and ignore the later Baroque altar that replaced the original). Notice Brunelleschi's "dice"—the stone cubes added above the column capitals that contribute to the nave's playful lightness. The church's art treasure is a painted, carved wooden crucifix attributed to 17-year-old Michelangelo. The sculptor donated this early work to the monastery in appreciation for allowing him to dissect and learn about bodies. The Michelangelo *Crocifisso* is displayed in the sacristy, through

a door midway down the left side of the nave (if it's closed, ask someone to let you in). Copies of Michelangelo's *Pietà* and *Risen Christ* flank the nave (near the main door). Beer-drinking, guitar-playing rowdies decorate the church steps.

Cost and Hours: Free, Mon-Tue and Thu-Sat 9:30-12:30 & 16:00-17:30, Sun 16:00-17:30 only, closed Wed, Piazza di Santo Spirito, tel. 055-210-030.

▲**Piazzale Michelangelo**—Overlooking the city from across the river (look for the huge statue of *David*), this square has a

superb view of Florence and the stunning dome of the Duomo (see photo on page 453).

It's worth the 30-minute hike, drive (free parking), or bus ride (either #12 or #13 from the train station—takes 20-30 minutes, or even more in bad traffic). It makes sense to take a taxi or ride the bus up, and then enjoy the easy downhill walk back into town. An inviting café with great views is just below the overlook. The best photos are taken from the street immediately below the overlook (go around to the right and down a few steps). Off the west side of the piazza is a somewhat hidden terrace, an excellent place to retreat from the mobs. After dark, the square is packed with schoolkids licking ice cream and each other. About 200 yards beyond all the tour groups and teenagers is the stark, beautiful, crowd-free, Romanesque San Miniato Church (next listing).

The hike down is quick and enjoyable. Take the steps between the two bars on the San Miniato Church side of the parking lot (Via San Salvatore al Monte), and in a couple of minutes you walk through the old wall (Porta San Miniato) and emerge in the delightful little Oltrarno neighborhood of San Niccolò.

▲▲**San Miniato Church**—According to legend, the martyred St. Minias—this church's namesake—was beheaded on the banks of the Arno in A.D. 250. He picked up his head and walked here (this was before the #12 bus), where he died and was buried in what became the first Christian cemetery in Florence. In the 11th century, this church was built to house Minias' remains. The church's green-and-white marble facade (12th century) is classic Florentine Romanesque,

one of the oldest in town. The church has wonderful 3-D paintings, a plush ceiling of glazed terra-cotta panels by Luca della Robbia, and an exquisite Renaissance chapel (on the left side of the nave). The highlight for me is the brilliantly preserved art in the sacristy (upstairs to right of altar, in the room on right) showing scenes from the life of St. Benedict (circa 1350, by a follower of Giotto). Drop €2 into the electronic panel in the corner to light the room for five minutes. The evening Mass with the monks chanting in Latin offers a meditative worship experience—a peaceful way to end your visit.

Cost and Hours: Free, daily Easter-mid-Oct 8:00-20:00 or possibly later, in winter 8:30-13:00 & 15:30-19:00, tel. 055-234-2731, www.sanminiatoalmonte.it.

Getting There: It's about 200 yards above Piazzale Michelangelo. From the station, bus #12 takes you right to the San Miniato al Monte stop (hop off and hike up the grand staircase); bus #13 from the station takes you to Piazzale Michelangelo, from which you'll hike up the rest of the way up.

Gregorian Chants: To experience this mystical medieval space at its full potential, time your visit to coincide with a Mass of Gregorian chants. In general, these are held each evening in summer (Easter-mid-Oct) at 18:30, and in winter at 17:00 or 17:30—but as the schedule is subject to change, double-check with any TI, check the church's website, or call ahead.

Shopping in Florence

Florence is a great shopping town—known for its sense of style since the Medici days. Many people spend entire days shopping. Smaller stores are generally open 9:00-13:00 and 15:30-19:30, usually closed on Sunday, often closed on Monday, and sometimes closed for a couple of weeks around August 15. Many stores have promotional stalls in the market squares.

Busy street scenes and markets abound, especially near San Lorenzo, near Santa Croce, on Ponte Vecchio, and at Mercato Nuovo (the covered market square three blocks north of Ponte Vecchio, described on page 489). Prices are soft in the markets—go ahead and bargain. Leather, gold, silver, art prints, and tacky plaster mini-*David*s are most popular.

For shopping ideas, ads, and a list of markets, see *The Florentine* newspaper or *Florence Concierge Information* magazine (free from TI and many hotels). For a list of bookstores, see page 464.

For ritzy Italian fashions, browse along Via della Vigna Nuova (runs west from Via de' Tornabuoni), Via del Parione, and Via Strozzi (runs east from Via de' Tornabuoni to Piazza della Repubblica). The main **Ferragamo** store fills a classy 800-year-old building with a fine selection of shoes and bags (daily 10:00-19:30, Via de' Tornabuoni 2).

Typical chain department stores are **Coin,** the Italian equivalent of Macy's (Mon-Sat 10:00-19:30, Sun 10:30-19:30, on Via de' Calzaiuoli, near Orsanmichele Church); the similar, upscale **La Rinascente** (Mon-Sat 9:00-21:00, Sun 10:30-20:00, on Piazza della Repubblica); and **Oviesse,** a discount clothing chain, the local JCPenney (Mon-Sat 9:00-19:30, Sun 10:00-19:30, near train station at intersection of Via Panzani and Via del Giglio).

Sleeping in Florence

Competition among hotels is stiff. When things slow down, fancy hotels drop their prices and become a much better value for travelers than the cheap, low-end places.

Nearly all of my recommended accommodations are located in the center of Florence, within minutes of the great sights. If arriving by train, you can either walk (usually around 10 minutes) or take a taxi (roughly €8-10) to reach most of my recommended accommodations, as buses don't cover the center very well. For additional listings of B&Bs and apartments, try **Cross-Pollinate,** a trustworthy online booking agency (www.cross-pollinate.com; see page 27).

Florence is notorious for its mosquitoes. If your hotel lacks air-conditioning, request a fan and don't open your windows,

FLORENCE

Sleep Code

(€1 = about $1.40, country code: 39)

S = Single, **D** = Double/Twin, **T** = Triple, **Q** = Quad, **b** = bathroom, **s** = shower only. You can assume a hotel takes credit cards unless you see "cash only" in the listing. Unless otherwise noted, hotel staff speak basic English and breakfast is included.

Florence charges a hotel tax of €1 per star (according to the hotel's official star rating), per person, per night. So a couple staying at a three-star hotel would pay €3 each, or €6 total, per night. This tax is generally not included in the prices I've listed here.

To help you easily sort through these listings, I've divided the accommodations into three categories based on the price for a standard double room with bath during high season:

$$$ Higher Priced—Most rooms €160 or more.
$$ Moderately Priced—Most rooms between €100-160.
$ Lower Priced—Most rooms €100 or less.

Prices can change without notice; verify the hotel's current rates online or by email.

especially at night. Many hotels furnish a small plug-in bulb *(zanzariere)*—usually set in the ashtray—that helps keep the blood-suckers at bay. If not, you can purchase one cheaply at any pharmacy *(farmacia)*.

Museumgoers take note: If you don't plan to get a Firenze Card (see page 471), ask if your hotelier will reserve entry times for you to visit the popular Uffizi Gallery and the Accademia (Michelangelo's *David*). Request this service when you book your room; it's fast, easy, and offered free or for a small fee by most hotels—the only requirement is advance notice. Ask them to reserve your visits for any time the day after your arrival. If you'd rather make the reservations yourself, see page 473 for details.

North of the Arno River
Between the Duomo and the Train Station

$$$ Hotel Centrale is indeed central, just a short walk from the Duomo. The 31 spacious but slightly overpriced rooms—with a tasteful mix of old and new decor—are over a businesslike conference center (Db-€170, bigger superior Db-€212, Tb-€210, suites available, 10 percent discount with this book, ask for Rick Steves rate when you reserve, 20 percent discount if booked 3 months in advance, air-con, elevator, free Internet access and Wi-Fi, Via dei Conti 3, check in at big front desk on ground floor, tel. 055-215-761, fax 055-215-216, www.hotelcentralefirenze.it, info@hotel

FLORENCE

centralefirenze.it, Margherita and Roberto).

$$ Hotel Accademia, which comes with marble stairs, parquet floors, and attractive public areas, has 21 pleasant rooms and a floor plan that defies logic (Db-€145, Tb-€170, 10 percent discount with this book if you book direct and pay cash, air-con, free Internet access and Wi-Fi, Via Faenza 7, tel. 055-293-451, fax 055-219-771, www.hotelaccademiafirenze.com, info@hotelaccademia firenze.com, Tea and Paolo).

$ Hotel Lorena, just across from the Medici Chapels, has 19 rooms (six of which have shared bathrooms) and a tiny lobby. Though it's a bit like a youth hostel, it's cheap and conveniently located. Chatty Roberto speaks little English, but is eager to please (S-€35, Sb-€50, D-€60, Db-€75, Tb-€95, very flexible rates, breakfast-€5, air-con, free Wi-Fi, Via Faenza 1, tel. 055-282-785, fax 055-288-300, www.hotellorena.com, info@hotellorena.com).

$ Katti House and the nearby **Soggiorno Annamaria** are run by house-proud mama-and-daughter team Maria and Katti, who rent a total of 15 rooms on a bustling pedestrian street. While both offer comparable comfort, Soggiorno Annamaria has a more historic setting, with frescoed ceilings, unique tiles, timbered beams, and quieter rooms. Katti House serves as reception for both places, but mostly you interact with Maria; while she's a fine hostess, she speaks virtually no English so communication can be challenging (Sb-€85, D-€85, Db-€100, skimpy breakfast served in your room, air-con, free Internet access and Wi-Fi—only in Katti, Via Faenza 21, if no answer check in at Trattoria Katti next door, tel. & fax 055-213-410, www.kattihouse.com, info@kattihouse.com).

North of the Duomo
North of the Mercato Centrale
After dark, this neighborhood can feel a little deserted, but I've never heard of anyone running into harm here. It's a short walk from the train station and an easy stroll to all the sightseeing action. While workaday, it's practical, with plenty of good budget restaurants and markets nearby.

$$ Grand Tour Firenze has six charming rooms on a nondescript street between the train station and the Accademia. This cozy B&B will make you feel right at home; it's thoughtfully appointed and the owners, Cristina and Giuseppe, live there. The delightful and spacious suites come with a garden ambience on the ground floor (Db-€110, suite-€130, 10 percent discount when you book direct and pay cash, includes breakfast voucher for the corner bar—or skip it to save €10/person, air-con, free Wi-Fi, Via Santa Reparata 21, tel. 055-283-955, www.florencegrandtour.com, info @florencegrandtour.com). They run another more romantic, pricier place a couple of blocks away.

Florence Hotels

1 Hotel Centrale
2 Hotel Accademia
3 Hotel Lorena
4 Katti House & Soggiorno Annamaria
5 Grand Tour Firenze
6 Galileo Hotel
7 Hotel Il Bargellino
8 Casa Rabatti
9 Soggiorno Magliani
10 Hotel Enza
11 Hotel Loggiato dei Serviti
12 Hotel dei Macchiaioli
13 Hotel Morandi alla Crocetta
14 Hotel Europa
15 Arti e Hotel
16 Palazzo Niccolini al Duomo
17 Hotel Duomo
18 Residenza dei Pucci
19 Soggiorno Battistero
20 Residenza Giotto B&B

21 La Residenza del Proconsolo B&B
22 Residenza il Villino
23 Panella's Residence
24 B&B Il Bargello
25 Hotel Cardinal of Florence
26 Hotel Dalí
27 Oblate Sisters of the Assumption
28 Locanda de' Ciompi
29 Hotel Il Duca
30 In Piazza della Signoria B&B
31 Hotel Pendini
32 Hotel Olimpia
33 B&B Dei Mori
34 Hotel Davanzati
35 Hotel Torre Guelfa
36 Relais Ufizzi
37 Hotel Alessandra
38 Bellevue House & Albergo Margaret
39 To Villa Camerata & Hostel 7 Santi

$$ Galileo Hotel, a classy business hotel with 31 rooms on a chaotic and congested street, is run with familial warmth (Sb-€100, Db-€130, Tb-€150, ask for 10 percent Rick Steves discount when you book direct and pay cash, quadruple-pane windows effectively shut out street noise, air-con, elevator, free Internet access and Wi-Fi, Via Nazionale 22a, tel. 055-496-645, fax 055-496-447, www.galileohotel.it, info@galileohotel.it).

$ Hotel Il Bargellino, run by Bostonian Carmel and her Italian husband Pino, feels like it's in a residential neighborhood. They rent 10 summery rooms decorated with funky antique furniture and Pino's modern paintings. Guests enjoy relaxing with Carmel and Leopoldo the parrot on the big, breezy, momentum-slowing terrace adorned with lemon shrubs (S-€45, D-€80, Db-€90, ask for Rick Steves discount if you book direct and pay cash, extra bed-€25, no breakfast, free Wi-Fi, north of the train station at Via Guelfa 87, tel. 055-238-2658, www.ilbargellino.com, carmel@ilbargellino.com).

$ Casa Rabatti is the ultimate if you always wanted to have a Florentine mama. Its four simple, clean rooms are run with warmth by Marcella. This is a great place to practice your Italian, since Marcella loves to chat and speaks minimal English. Seeing nearly two decades of my family Christmas cards on their walls, I'm reminded of how long she has been keeping budget travelers happy (D-€50, Db-€60, €25 extra per bed in shared quad or quint, prices good with this book, cash only but secure reservation with credit card, no breakfast, fans available, free Wi-Fi, 5 blocks from station at Via San Zanobi 48 black, tel. 055-212-393, casarabatti @inwind.it). If Marcella's booked, she'll put you up in her daughter's place nearby, at Via Nazionale 20 (five big, airy, family-friendly rooms; €25/person, fans, no breakfast, closer to the station). While daughter Patrizia works, her mom runs the place. Getting bumped to Patrizia's gives you slightly more comfort and slightly less personality...certainly not a net negative.

$ Soggiorno Magliani is central and humble, with six bright, no-frills rooms (sharing two baths) that feel and smell like a great-grandmother's home. It's run by the friendly duo Vincenza and her English-speaking daughter Cristina, and the price is right (S-€36, D-€46, T-€65, cash only but secure reservation with credit card, no breakfast, near Via Guelfa at Via Santa Reparata 1, tel. 055-287-378, hotel-magliani@libero.it).

$ Hotel Enza rents 19 dark, musty, straightforward rooms. The prices are reasonable for predictable hotel comfort (S-€45, Sb-€55, Db-€80, these prices promised through 2013 with this book, extra bed-€20, optional breakfast-€8, air-con, free Internet access and Wi-Fi, Via San Zanobi 45 black, tel. 055-490-990, fax 055-473-672, www.hotelenza.it, info@hotelenza.it, Diana).

Near the Accademia

$$$ Hotel Loggiato dei Serviti, at the most prestigious address in Florence on the most Renaissance square in town, gives you Old World romance with hair dryers. Stone stairways lead you under open-beam ceilings through this 16th-century monastery's monumental public rooms—it's so artful, you'll be snapping photos everywhere. The 38 cells—with air-conditioning, TVs, minibars, free Wi-Fi, and telephones—would be unrecognizable to their original inhabitants. The hotel staff is both professional and warm (Sb-€140, Db-€160, superior Db-€180, family suites from €263, ask for Rick Steves rate when you book, elevator, valet parking-€21/day, Piazza S.S. Annunziata 3, tel. 055-289-592, fax 055-289-595, www.loggiatodeiservitihotel.it, info@loggiatodei servitihotel.it; Simonetta, Gianni, and two Chiaras). When full, they rent five spacious and sophisticated rooms in a 17th-century annex a block away. While it lacks the monastic mystique, the annex rooms are bigger, gorgeous, and cost the same.

$$$ Hotel dei Macchiaioli offers 15 fresh and spacious rooms on one high-ceilinged, noble floor in a restored *palazzo* owned for generations by a well-to-do Florentine family. You'll eat breakfast under original frescoed ceilings while enjoying modern comforts (Sb-€100, Db-€180, Tb-€220, 10 percent Rick Steves discount if you book direct and pay cash, air-con, free Wi-Fi, Via Cavour 21, tel. 055-213-154, www.hoteldeimacchiaioli.com, info@hoteldei macchiaioli.com, helpful Francesca and Paolo).

$$ Hotel Morandi alla Crocetta, a former convent, envelops you in a 16th-century cocoon. Located on a quiet street with 12 rooms, period furnishings, parquet floors, and wood-beamed or painted ceilings, it takes you back a few centuries and up a few social classes (Sb-€105, Db-€155, Tb-€185, low-season discounts online, air-con, free Wi-Fi, a block off Piazza S.S. Annunziata at Via Laura 50, tel. 055-234-4747, fax 055-248-0954, www.hotel morandi.it, welcome@hotelmorandi.it, well-run by Maurizio, Rolando, and Ertol).

$$ Hotel Europa, run by cheery Miriam, Roberto, and daughters Priscilla and Isabel since 1970, has a welcoming atmosphere. The breakfast room is spacious, and some of the 20 rooms have views of the Duomo (Sb-€89, Db-€150, Tb-€180, Qb-€250, a little extra for a private balcony, €10-15 more for bigger "deluxe" room, 10 percent discount if you pay cash, mention Rick Steves to get their best available room, air-con, old-timey elevator, free Wi-Fi, Via Cavour 14, tel. 055-239-6715, fax 055-268-984, www .webhoteleuropa.com, firenze@webhoteleuropa.com).

$$ Arti e Hotel rents 11 large, tastefully furnished rooms well-located on a quiet street just far enough away from the tourist scene. As there's no real public space, the emphasis is on the classy rooms (Db-€135, 10 percent discount if you book direct and pay cash—ask for their Rick Steves price, third bed-€30, air-con, elevator, free Wi-Fi, Via dei Servi 38, tel. 055-267-8553, fax 055-290-140, www.artiehotel.it, info@artiehotel.it, Carlo).

Near the Duomo

All of these places are within a block of Florence's biggest church and main landmark.

$$$ Palazzo Niccolini al Duomo, one of five elite Historic Residence Hotels in Florence, is run by Niccolini da Camugliano. The lounge (where free chamomile tea is served in the evenings) is palatial, but the 12 rooms, while splendid, vary wildly in size. If you have the money and want a Florentine palace to call home, this can be a good bet (Db-€180-€450 depending on type of room, ask for 10 percent Rick Steves discount when you book, check online to choose a room and consider last-minute deals, elevator, free Internet access and Wi-Fi, Via dei Servi 2, tel. 055-282-412, fax 055-290-979, www.niccolinidomepalace.com, info@niccolini domepalace.com).

$$$ Hotel Duomo, big and venerable, rents 24 rooms four floors up. The Duomo looms like a monster outside the hotel's windows; most (but not all) rooms come with views. The rooms are modern and comfortable enough, and the location can't be beat (Sb-€90, Db-€160, Tb-€180, 10 percent discount with this book if you pay cash, air-con, elevator, free Wi-Fi, Piazza del Duomo 1, tel. 055-219-922, www.hotelduomofirenze.it, info@hotelduomo firenze.it; Alberto, Sonia, and Karen).

$$ Residenza dei Pucci rents 12 pleasant rooms (each one different) spread over three floors. The decor, a mix of soothing earth tones and aristocratic furniture, makes this place feel upscale for this price range (Sb-€135, Db-€150, Tb-€170, Qb-€238, rates can vary, 10 percent discount with cash and this book, air-con, no elevator, free slow Wi-Fi or pay for fast Wi-Fi, reception open 9:00-20:00—let them know if you'll arrive late, Via dei Pucci 9, tel. 055-281-886, fax 055-264-314, www.residenzadeipucci.com, residenzadeipucci@residenzadeipucci.com, Mirella and Marina).

$$ Soggiorno Battistero rents seven simple, airy rooms, most with great views, overlooking the Baptistery and the Duomo square. Choose a view or a quieter room in the back when you book by email. It's a pristine, fresh, and minimalist place run by Italian Luca and his American wife Kelly, who makes the hotel particularly welcoming (Sb-€83, Db-€110, Tb-€145, Qb-€155, prices good with this book, 5 percent discount if you book direct and pay cash, breakfast served in room, air-con available June-Aug, free Wi-Fi, Piazza San Giovanni 1, third floor—new elevator planned for 2013, tel. 055-295-143, fax 055-268-189, www.soggiorno

battistero.it, info@soggiornobattistero.it).

$$ Residenza Giotto B&B offers you the chance to stay on Florence's upscale shopping drag, Via Roma. Occupying the top floor of a 19th-century building, this place has six bright, smallish rooms and a terrace with knockout views of the Duomo's tower. Reception is generally open 9:00-17:00; let them know your arrival time in advance (Sb-€90, Db-€130, view rooms-€10 extra, extra bed-€25, 10 percent discount if you book direct and pay cash, air-con, elevator, free Wi-Fi, Via Roma 6, tel. 055-214-593, fax 055-264-8568, www.residenzagiotto.it, info@residenzagiotto.it, Giorgio).

$$ La Residenza del Proconsolo B&B, run by helpful Mariano, has five older-feeling rooms a minute from the Duomo (three rooms have Duomo views). The place lacks public spaces, but the rooms are quite large and nice—perfect for eating breakfast, which is served in your room (Sb-€90, Db-€120, Tb-€140, air-con, free Wi-Fi, Via del Proconsolo 18 black, tel. 055-264-5657, mobile 335-657-4840, www.proconsolo.com, info@proconsolo.com).

East of the Duomo

$$ Residenza il Villino, popular and friendly, aspires to offer a Florentine home away from home. It has 10 charmingly rustic rooms and a picturesque, peaceful little courtyard. As it's in a "little villa" (as the name implies) set back from the street, this is a quiet refuge from the bustle of Florence (small Db-€110, Db-€130, family suite that sleeps up to six—price upon request, 5 percent discount with cash and this book, air-con, free Internet access and Wi-Fi, just north of Via degli Alfani at Via della Pergola 53, tel. 055-200-1116, fax 055-200-1101, www.ilvillino.it, info@ilvillino.it; Sergio—who looks a bit like Henry Winkler, Elisabetta, and son Lorenzo).

$$ Panella's Residence, once a convent and today part of owner Graziella's extensive home, is a classy B&B, with six chic, romantic, and ample rooms, antique furnishings, and historic architectural touches (Db-€140, bigger superior Db-€165, even bigger deluxe Db-€180, these prices are with cash, discounts for 3 or more nights, air-con, free Wi-Fi, Via della Pergola 42, tel. & fax 055-234-7202, mobile 345-972-1541, www.panellaresidence.com, panella_residence@yahoo.it).

$ B&B Il Bargello is a home away from home, run by friendly and helpful Canadian expat Gabriella. Hike up three long flights (no elevator) to reach six smart, relaxing rooms. Gabriella offers a cozy communal living room, kitchen access, and an inviting rooftop terrace with close-up views of Florence's towers (Db-€100, ask for Rick Steves rate when you book direct and pay cash, air-con, free Internet access and Wi-Fi, 20 yards off Via Proconsolo at Via de' Pandolfini 33 black, tel. 055-215-330, mobile 339-175-3110, www.firenze-bedandbreakfast.it, info@firenze-bedandbreakfast.it).

$ Hotel Cardinal of Florence is a third-floor walk-up with 17 spartan, tidy, and sun-splashed rooms overlooking either a silent courtyard (many with views of Brunelleschi's dome) or quiet street. Relax and enjoy Florence's rooftops from the sun terrace (Sb-€60, Db-€95, these prices for Rick Steves readers, additional €5 discount if you pay cash, air-con, free Wi-Fi, Borgo Pinti 5, tel. 055-234-0780, fax 055-234-3389, www.hotelcardinalofflorence .com, info@hotelcardinalofflorence.com, Mauro and Ida).

$ Hotel Dalí has 10 cheap and cheery rooms with new baths and floors in a nice location for a great price. Samanta and Marco, who run this guesthouse with a charming passion and idealism, are a delight to know (S-€40, D-€70, Db-€85, extra bed-€25, no breakfast, fans but no air-con, request quiet room when you book, no elevator, free Wi-Fi, free parking, 2 blocks behind the Duomo at Via dell'Oriuolo 17 on the second floor, tel. & fax 055-234-0706, www.hoteldali.com, hoteldali@tin.it).

$ Oblate Sisters of the Assumption run an institutional 30-room hotel in a Renaissance building with a dreamy garden, great public spaces, appropriately simple rooms, and a quiet, prayerful ambience (€45/person in single, double, triple, or quad rooms with bathrooms, €38/person with shared bathrooms, cash only, single beds only, air-con, elevator, Wi-Fi with suggested donation, €10/day limited parking—request when you book, Borgo Pinti 15, tel. 055-248-0582, fax 055-234-6291, sroblateborgopinti@virgilio .it, sisters are likely to speak French but not English, Sister Theresa is very helpful).

$ Locanda de' Ciompi, overlooking the inviting Piazza dei Ciompi antiques market in a young and lively neighborhood, is just right for travelers who want to feel like a part of the town. Riccardo runs a minimalist place—just five quiet, clean, tasteful rooms along a thin hallway (Db-€100, Tb-€115, 10 percent discount with this book if you book direct and pay cash, includes breakfast at nearby bar, air-con, free Wi-Fi, 8 blocks behind the Duomo at Via Pietrapiana 28, tel. 055-263-8034, www.locanda deciompi.it, locandadeciompi@yahoo.it).

$ Hotel Il Duca—a big, bright place on a quiet street a few blocks behind the Duomo—seems like a basic building wearing a fancy coat. Its 13 pleasant rooms are a great value, but don't expect a warm welcome or personal service (Sb-€85, Db-€90, third bed-€25, air-con, free Wi-Fi, Via della Pergola 34, tel. 055-906-2167, www.hotelilduca.it, info@hotelilduca.it, Angela).

South of the Duomo
Between the Duomo and Piazza della Signoria
These are the most central of my accommodations recommenda-

tions (and therefore a little overpriced). While worth the extra cost for many, given Florence's walkable, essentially traffic-free core, nearly every hotel I recommend can be considered central.

$$$ **In Piazza della Signoria B&B,** overlooking Piazza della Signoria, is peaceful, refined, and homey at the same time. Fit for a honeymoon, the 10 rooms come with all the special touches and little extras you'd expect in a top-end American B&B. However, the rates are high, and the "partial view" rooms require craning your neck to see anything—not worth the extra euros (viewless Db-€250, partial-view Db-€280, full-view "deluxe" Db-€300, Tb-€280, partial-view Tb-€300, ask for 10 percent discount when you book direct with this book, family apartments, lavish bathrooms, air-con, tiny elevator, free Internet access and Wi-Fi, Via dei Magazzini 2, tel. 055-239-9546, mobile 348-321-0565, fax 055-267-6616, www.inpiazzadellasignoria.com, info@inpiazzadella signoria.com, Sonia and Alessandro).

$$$ **Hotel Pendini,** with 42 rooms and three slightly tarnished stars, fills the top floor of a grand building constructed to celebrate Italian unification in the late 19th century. It overlooks Piazza della Repubblica, and as you walk into the lobby, you feel as if you are walking back in time (Sb-€139, Db-€189, deluxe Db with square view and noise-€239, air-con, elevator, free Internet access and Wi-Fi, Via degli Strozzi 2, tel. 055-211-170, www.hotel pendini.it, info@hotelpendini.it).

$$$ **Hotel Olimpia** is a friendly, well-worn, established place renting 24 quite dated rooms on the fourth floor overlooking Piazza della Repubblica (some rooms have views and noise). You pay for the location (Db-€160, air-con, elevator, pay Wi-Fi, Piazza della Repubblica 2, tel. 055-219-781, fax 055-267-0383, www.hotel -olimpia.it, hotelolimpia@tin.it, Marziano).

$$ **B&B Dei Mori,** a peaceful haven with a convivial and welcoming living room, rents five tastefully appointed rooms ideally located on a quiet pedestrian street near Casa di Dante—within a five-minute walk of the Duomo, the Bargello, or Piazza della Signoria. Accommodating Suzanne, Daniele, and Peter pride themselves on offering personal service, including lots of tips on dining and sightseeing in Florence. But if they're full, I'd skip their offer of an apartment nearby (D-€100, Db-€120, 10 percent discount for my readers—ask when you book, air-con-€5, free Wi-Fi, reception open 8:00-19:00, Via Dante Alighieri 12, tel. 055-211-438, www.deimori.com, deimori@bnb.it).

Near Ponte Vecchio

$$$ **Hotel Davanzati,** bright and shiny with artistic touches, has 22 cheerful rooms with all the comforts. The place is a family affair, thoughtfully run by friendly Tommaso and father Fabrizio,

who offer drinks and snacks each evening at their candlelit happy hour, plus lots of other extras (Sb-€132, Db-€199, Tb-€259, these rates good with this book though prices soft off-season, 10 percent discount if you pay cash, free loaner laptop in every room, free on-demand movies—including my Italy TV shows—on your room TV, air-con, free Wi-Fi, next to Piazza Davanzati at Via Porta Rossa 5—easy to miss so watch for low-profile sign above the door, tel. 055-286-666, fax 055-265-8252, www.hoteldavanzati.it, info @hoteldavanzati.it).

$$$ **Hotel Torre Guelfa** has grand (almost royal) public spaces and is topped by a fun medieval tower with a panoramic rooftop terrace. Its 31 pricey rooms vary wildly in size and layout. Room 315, with a private terrace (€245), is worth reserving several months in advance (Db-€170-190, Db junior suite-€230, ask for Rick Steves discount, family deals, check their website for promotions, air-con, elevator, free Internet access and Wi-Fi in lobby, a couple blocks northwest of Ponte Vecchio, Borgo S.S. Apostoli 8, tel. 055-239-6338, fax 055-239-8577, www.hoteltorreguelfa.com, info@hoteltorreguelfa.com, Sandro and Barbara).

$$$ **Relais Uffizi** is a peaceful little gem, with 15 classy rooms tucked away down a tiny alleyway off Piazza della Signoria. The lounge has a huge window overlooking the action in the square below (Sb-€120, Db-€180, Tb-€220, more for deluxe rooms, buffet breakfast, air-con, elevator, free Wi-Fi, Chiasso de Baroncelli/Chiasso del Buco 16, tel. 055-267-6239, fax 055-265-7909, www.relaisuffizi.it, info@relaisuffizi.it, charming Alessandro and Elizabetta).

$$ **Hotel Alessandra** is 16th-century, tranquil, and sprawling, with 27 big, tasteful rooms and an old-school, peeling-wallpaper vibe (S-€67-€88, Sb-€110, D-€110, Db-€150, Tb-€195, Qb-€215, 5 percent cash discount, air-con, free Internet access and Wi-Fi, Borgo S.S. Apostoli 17, tel. 055-283-438, fax 055-210-619, www.hotelalessandra.com, info@hotelalessandra.com, Anna and son Andrea).

Near the Train Station

$ **Bellevue House** is a third-floor (no elevator) oasis of tranquility, with six spacious, old-fashioned rooms flanking a long, mellow-yellow lobby. It's a peaceful time warp thoughtfully run by Rosanna and Antonio di Grazia (Db-€70-95, family deals; 10 percent discount if you stay two nights, pay cash, and book direct; optional €3 breakfast in street-level bar, air-con, free Wi-Fi, Via della Scala 21, tel. 055-260-8932, mobile 333-612-5973, fax 055-265-5315, www.bellevuehouse.it, info@bellevuehouse.it).

$ **Albergo Margaret,** homey yet minimalist, doesn't have a public lounge or offer breakfast. Run by the Cristantielli family, it has seven peaceful and simple rooms (D-€40, Ds-€60, Db-€75, 10 percent discount if you book direct and pay cash, extra bed-€10, air-con, free Wi-Fi, near Santa Maria Novella at Via della Scala 25, tel. & fax 055-210-138, www.hotel-margaret.it, info@hotel -margaret.it; Francesco, Anna, and Graziano).

Hostels away from the Center

These two hostels, northeast of downtown, are a bus ride from the action. A far more central hostel is in the Oltrarno (listed at the end of the next section).

$ Villa Camerata, classy for an IYHF hostel, is in a pretty villa three miles northeast of the train station, on the outskirts of Florence (€18/bed with breakfast, 4- to 6-bed rooms, non-members pay €3/night more, free Wi-Fi, self-serve laundry, Via Righi 2—take bus #11 from the train station to Salviatino or bus #17 to Via Cento Stelle, tel. 055-601-451, fax 055-610-300, www .aighostels.com, firenze@aighostels.com).

$ Hostel 7 Santi calls itself a "travelers' haven." It fills a for-mer convent, but you'll feel like you're in an old school. Still, it offers some of the best cheap beds in town, is friendly to older travelers, and comes with the services you'd expect in a big, mod-ern hostel, including free Wi-Fi and self-serve laundry. It's in a more residential neighborhood near the Campo di Marte stadium, about a 10-minute bus ride from the center (200 beds in 60 rooms, mostly 4- or 6-bed dorms with a floor of doubles and triples, €16-18/dorm bed, Sb-€45, Db-€60, Tb-€75, Qb-€85, includes sheets and towels, breakfast and dinner available but cost extra, no cur-few, free Internet access and Wi-Fi; Viale dei Mille 11—from train station, take bus #10, #17, or #20, direction: Campo di Marte, to bus stop Chiesa dei Sette Santi; tel. 055-504-8452, www.7santi .com, info@7santi.com).

South of the Arno River, in the Oltrarno

Across the river in the Oltrarno area, between the Pitti Palace and Ponte Vecchio, you'll find small, traditional crafts shops, neigh-borly piazzas, and family eateries. The following places are an easy walk from Ponte Vecchio. Only the first two are real hotels—the rest are a ragtag gang of budget alternatives.

$$$ Hotel Silla is a classic three-star hotel with 36 cheery, spacious, pastel, and modern rooms. It faces the river and overlooks a park opposite Santa Croce Church (Db-€180, bigger "superior" Db-€210, ask for Rick Steves rate when you book, extra bed-€35, air-con, elevator, free Internet access and Wi-Fi, parking-€19/ day, Via dei Renai 5, tel. 055-234-2888, fax 055-234-1437, www .hotelsilla.it, hotelsilla@hotelsilla.it; Laura, Chiara, Massimo, and Stefano).

FLORENCE

Oltrarno Hotels & Restaurants

1. To Hotel Silla & Il Gelato di Filo
2. Hotel la Scaletta
3. Istituto Gould
4. Soggiorno Alessandra
5. Casa Santo Nome di Gesù
6. Ostello Santa Monaca
7. Golden View Open Bar
8. Il Santo Bevitore Ristorante & Enoteca Il Santino Gastronomia
9. Trattoria 4 Leoni
10. To Antico Ristoro Di' Cambi, Trattoria da Sergio & Trattoria Sabatino
11. Olio & Convivium Gastronomia
12. To Trattoria Al Tranvai
13. Trattoria Casalinga
14. Borgo Antico, Volume Bar & Ricchi Caffè
15. Pop Café
16. Meta Supermarket

FLORENCE

$$ Hotel la Scaletta has 17 functional but colorful rooms hiding in a tortured floor plan, plus a fabulous rooftop terrace overlooking Boboli Gardens (Db-€130, third bed-€20, breakfast-€7, air-con, elevator, free Internet access and Wi-Fi, Via de' Guicciardini 13, tel. 055-283-028, fax 055-283-013, www.hotellascaletta .it, info@hotellascaletta.it).

$ Istituto Gould is a Protestant Church-run place with 39 clean and spartan rooms that have twin beds and modern facilities. It's located in a 17th-century palace with a beautiful garden courtyard. The complex also houses kids from troubled homes, and proceeds raised from renting rooms help fund that important work (Sb-€55, Db-€60, €20 more for garden rooms that are quieter and have air-con, Tb-€81, Qb-€100, breakfast-€6, non-air-con rooms have fans, free Wi-Fi in lobby, Via dei Serragli 49, tel. 055-212-576, fax 055-280-274, www.istitutogould.it, foresteriafirenze@dia coniavaldese.org). You must arrive when the office is open (Mon-Fri 8:45-13:00 & 15:00-19:30, Sat 9:00-13:30 & 14:30-18:00, no live check-in on Sundays but they'll email you a code).

$ Soggiorno Alessandra has five bright, comfy, and smallish rooms. Because of its double-paned windows, you'll hardly notice the traffic noise (D-€73, Db-€78, Tb-€98, Qb-€128, cheaper off-season, includes basic breakfast in room, air-con-€8, free Wi-Fi, just past the Carraia Bridge at Via Borgo San Frediano 6, tel. 055-290-424, fax 055-218-464, www.soggiornoalessandra.it, info @soggiornoalessandra.it, Alessandra).

$ Casa Santo Nome di Gesù is a grand, 29-room convent whose sisters—Franciscan Missionaries of Mary—are thankful to rent rooms to tourists. Staying in this 15th-century palace, you'll be immersed in the tranquil atmosphere created by a huge, peaceful garden, generous and prayerful public spaces, and smiling nuns. The monastic rooms have only twin beds (D-€70, Db-€85, T-€100, Tb-€120, book direct to avoid fees, no air-con but rooms have fans, memorable convent-like breakfast room, elevator, strict 23:29 curfew, Piazza del Carmine 21, tel. 055-213-856, fax 055-281-835, www.fmmfirenze.it, info@fmmfirenze.it).

Hostel: **$ Ostello Santa Monaca,** a well-run, institutional-feeling hostel a long block south of the Brancacci Chapel. As clean as its guests, its 112 beds in 15 rooms (2- to 20-bed dorms) attract a young backpacking crowd (€18-26/bed with sheets and towel, 10:00-14:00 lock-out, 2:00 in the morning curfew, free Internet access and Wi-Fi, self-serve laundry, kitchen, bike rental, Via Santa Monaca 6, tel. 055-268-338, fax 055-280-185, www.ostello santamonaca.com, info@ostellosantamonaca.com).

Rural Agriturismo South of Florence

The countryside south of Florence is loaded with enticing rural farms offering accommodations, called *agriturismi* (for details, see page 28). I've listed several good choices in the Siena, Hill Towns of Central Italy, Assisi, and Orvieto and Civita chapters. This option is a bit closer to Florence (about 45 minutes south), in the Chianti region.

$$$ I Greppi di Silli is a lovely, family-run *agriturismo* set among rolling hills south of Florence. Owners Anna and Giuliano Alfani cultivate Chianti grapes and olive trees, and offer six carefully remodeled apartments with beds for 2-6 people, some with panoramic views and/or terraces; a seventh apartment (sleeps 8) is a mile away in an old country house (Db-€115-250 or €735-1,900/week, price depends on apartment, less off-season; one-week minimum—Sat-to-Sat—in July-Aug, fewer nights possible in shoulder and low season—but generally still a 3-night minimum; breakfast-€9, pool, kids' play area, table tennis, bocce ball court, loaner bikes, weekly farm dinners-€28/person—less for kids, Via Vallacchio 19, near San Casciano and just outside the village of Mercatale Val di Pesa, about 45 minutes' drive to Florence or San Gimignano and one hour from Siena, tel. 055-821-7959, www.igreppidisilli.it, info@igreppidisilli.it).

Eating in Florence

Remember, restaurants like to serve what's fresh. If you're into flavor, go for the seasonal best bets—featured in the *piatti del giorno* ("special of the day") section on menus. For dessert, it's gelato (see sidebar later in this section).

To save money and time for sights, keep lunches fast and simple, eating in one of the countless pizzerias and self-service cafeterias. Picnicking is easy—there's no shortage of corner *supermercatos*, or you can picnic your way through the Mercato Centrale.

North of the Arno River
Near the Church of Santa Maria Novella

Trattoria al Trebbio serves traditional food, especially rabbit and steak, with simple Florentine elegance in its candlelit interior. Inside, it feels like a throwback; the room is decorated with old movie posters. Outside, tables spill out onto a romantic little square—an oasis of Roman Trastevere-like charm (€7-10 pastas, €10-14 *secondi*, daily 12:00-15:00 & 19:15-23:00, closed for lunch Tue off-season, reserve for outdoor seating, half a block off of Piazza Santa Maria Novella at Via delle Belle Donne 47, tel. 055-287-089, Antonio).

FLORENCE

Florence Restaurants

Piazza della Indipendenza

300 Meters

300 Yards

To Fortezza da Basso

PALAZZO DEI CONGRESSI

CONSERVATORIO DI FULIGNO

VIA GUELFA

PALAZZO DEGLI AFFARI

CENACOLO DI FULIGNO

Piazza Adua

9

10 **37**

7

VIA NAZIONALE

FAENZA

MERCATO CENTRALE

Piazza del Mercato Centrale

11

6

SANTA MARIA NOVELLA TRAIN STATION

Largo Alinari

PALAZZO DEI CARTELLONI

12

BUS STATION

Piazza della Stazione

Piazza dell'Unità Italiana

MARKET

MEDICI CHAPELS

Piazza di San Lorenzo

MAIN TOURIST INFO

V. DEI MELARANCIO

8

SAN LORENZO

SANTA MARIA NOVELLA

MEDICI LIBRARY

VIA PANZANI

VIA DEI BANCHI

VIA DE' CERRETANI

WC

SANTA MARIA NOVELLA PERFUMERY

2

Piazza di Santa Maria Novella

1

SANTA MARIA MAGGIORE

Piazza di San Giovanni

LOGGIA DI SAN PAOLO

SAN GAETANO

19

LOGGIA DI BIGALLO & **i**

OGNISSANTI

4

VIA DEL SOLE

VIA CORSI

5

Piazza d'Ognissanti

RUCELLAI PALACE

3

ARCH

Piazza della Repubblica

PONTE ALLA CARRAIA

Piazza Carlo Goldoni

STROZZI PALACE

ORSAN-MICHELE

PALAZZO CORSINI

SANTA TRINITA

Piazza di Santa Trinita

POST

Piazza de' Davanzati

Arno River

DAVANZATI PALACE

MERCATO NUOVO

21

PONTE S. TRINITA

LUNGARNO ACCIAIUOLI

Piazza Nazaro Sauro

PONTE VECCHIO

Piazza de' Salt.

S. Stephano

33 **27**

To Brancacci Chapel

OLTRARNO

Piazza de' Frescobaldi

SAN JACOPO

SANTO SPIRITO

BORGO SAN JACOPO

Piazza della Passera

To Pitti Palace

FLORENCE

1 Trattoria al Trebbio
2 Trattoria "da Giorgio"
3 Trattoria Marione
4 Trattoria Sostanza-Troia
5 Trattoria 13 Gobbi
6 Trattoria Zà-Zà & Trattoria Mario's
7 Trattoria la Burrasca
8 Trattoria Lo Stracotto
9 Osteria Vineria i'Brincello
10 Trattoria Nerone Pizzeria
11 Mercato Centrale & Nerbone in the Market
12 Casa del Vino
13 Pugi Pizza
14 Barbecue Döner Kebab
15 Pasticceria Robiglio
16 La Mescita Fiaschetteria
17 Il Centro Supermercati
18 To Antica Trattoria da Tito
19 Self-Service Rist. Leonardo
20 Turkuaz Döner Kebab
21 Rivoire Café
22 Frescobaldi Rist. & Wine Bar
23 Ristorante Paoli, Cantinetta dei Verrazzano & Perchè No! Gelateria
24 Osteria Vini e Vecchi Sapori
25 I Fratellini
26 L'Antico Trippaio, Pizzeria Totò & Supermarket
27 'Ino Bottega di Alimentari e Vini
28 Ristorante del Fagioli
29 Boccadama Enoteca Rist.
30 Trattoria Anita
31 Trattoria I'cche C'è C'è
32 Gelateria Grom
33 Gelateria Carrozze
34 Gelateria Carabè
35 Vivoli's Gelateria
36 Gelateria de' Neri
37 The Bermuda Triangle

Trattoria "da Giorgio" is a family-style diner on a sketchy street serving up piping-hot, delicious home cooking to happy locals and tourists alike. Their three-course, fixed-price meal, including water and a drink, is a great value (€12 at lunch, €13 at dinner). Choose from among the daily specials or the regular menu (Mon-Sat 12:00-14:30 & 18:30-22:00, closed Sun, Via Palazzuolo 100 red, tel. 055-284-302, Silvano).

Trattoria Marione serves sincerely home cooked-style meals to a mixed group of tourists and Florentines beneath hanging ham hocks. The ambience is happy, crowded, food-loving, and steamy (€8-11 pastas, €10-12 *secondi*, daily 12:00-17:30 & 19:00-23:00, Via della Spada 27 red, tel. 055-214-756, Fabio).

Trattoria Sostanza-Troia, characteristic and well established, is famous for its beef. Hearty steaks and pastas are splittable. Whirling ceiling fans and walls strewn with old photos evoke earlier times, while the artichoke pies remind locals of Grandma's cooking. Crowded, shared tables with paper tablecloths give this place a bistro feel. They offer two dinner seatings, at 19:30 and 21:00, which require reservations (dinners for about €30 plus wine, cash only, lunch Mon-Sat 12:30-14:00, closed Sun, closed Sat off-season, Via del Porcellana 25 red, tel. 055-212-691).

Trattoria 13 Gobbi ("13 Hunchbacks") is a trendy and slightly self-important eatery, atmospherically cluttered and glowing with candles around a tiny garden. Romantic in front and more kid-friendly in back, it serves beautifully presented Tuscan food (they're enthusiastic about their steak) on big, fancy plates to a mostly tourist crowd (€10-12 pastas, €14-19 *secondi*, daily 12:30-15:00 & 19:30-23:00, Via del Porcellana 9 red, tel. 055-284-015, Enrico).

Near the Mercato Centrale

The following market-neighborhood eateries all have a distinct vibe. They're within a few blocks of each other: Scout around and choose your favorite.

Trattoria Zà-Zà is a fun, characteristic, high-energy place facing the Mercato Centrale. It offers a family-friendly festival of standard Tuscan dishes such as *ribollita* and *bistecca alla fiorentina*, plus a variety of big, splittable €8 salads. Though it's more touristy than ever, the food is still great, and everyone's happy. Arrive early or make a reservation. Choose between the folkloric interior or the fine outdoor piazza. Understand your itemized bill, and don't mistake their outside seating with the neighboring restaurant's (€8-10 pastas, €10-16 *secondi*, daily 11:00-23:00, Piazza del Mercato Centrale 26 red, tel. 055-215-411). Their **bar/osteria,** nearby, has a similar menu (with a few differences, including more of an emphasis on seafood and *taglieri*—cheese-and-meat plates), a trendier-feeling interior, and a smaller, more open outdoor-dining zone.

Trattoria la Burrasca is Flintstone-chic. Friendly duo Elio and Simone offer a limited menu with good-value seasonal specials of Tuscan home cooking. It's small—10 tables—and often filled with my readers. If Archie Bunker were Italian, he'd eat at this trattoria for special nights out (€6 pastas, €7-15 *secondi*, no cover or service charge, Tue-Sun 12:00-15:00 & 19:00-22:30, closed Mon, Via Panicale 6, north corner of Mercato Centrale, tel. 055-215-827).

Trattoria Lo Stracotto is a truffle-colored eatery with sophisticated ambience just steps away from the Medici Chapels. It's run by cousins Francesco and Tommaso, who serve up tasty, traditional dishes such as *bistecca alla fiorentina* and *ribollita* (based on grandfather's recipe), and good chocolate soufflé. Enjoy the candlelit ambience and soft music as you sit either in the dining room or out on the terrace (€8-10 pastas, €9-15 *secondi*, daily 12:00-15:00 & 18:00-22:30, Piazza Madonna degli Aldobrandi 16/17, tel. 055-230-2062).

Osteria Vineria i'Brincello is a bright, happy, no-frills diner with tasty food, lots of spirit, friendly service, and no hint of snobbishness. It features a list of Tuscan daily specials hanging from the ceiling and great prices on good bottled wine (€7-8 pastas, €8-15 *secondi*, €5 takeout homemade pasta, daily 12:00-15:00 & 19:00-23:00, near corner of Via Nazionale and Via Chiara at Via Nazionale 110 red, tel. 055-282-645, Fredi cooks while Claudia serves).

Trattoria Nerone Pizzeria, serving up cheap, hearty Tuscan dishes and decent pizzas, is a tourist-friendly, practical standby in the hotel district. The lively, flamboyantly outfitted space (once the garden courtyard of a convent) feels like a good but kitschy Italian-American chain restaurant (€5-8 pizzas, €6-8 pastas, €8-12 *secondi*, daily 12:00-15:00 & 18:30-23:00, just north of Via Nazionale at Via Faenza 95 red, tel. 055-291-217, Tulio).

Eating Cheaply in or near the Mercato Centrale

Note that none of these eateries is open for dinner.

The **Mercato Centrale (Central Market)** is great for an ad-lib lunch. It offers colorful piles of picnic produce, people-watching, and rustic sandwiches (Mon-Sat 7:00-14:00, Sat in winter until 17:00, closed Sun, a block north of San Lorenzo street market). Meat, fish, and cheese are sold on the ground level, with fruit and veggies mostly upstairs. The thriving ground-level eateries within the market (such as Nerbone, described next) serve some of the cheapest hot meals in town. The fancy deli, Perini, is famous for its quality products and generous free samples. Buy a picnic of fresh mozzarella cheese, olives, fruit, and crunchy bread to munch on the steps of the nearby Church of San Lorenzo, overlooking the bustling street market.

Nerbone in the Market is a venerable café and the best place for a sit-down meal within the Mercato Centrale. Join the shoppers and workers who crowd up to the bar to grab their €4-6 plates. Of the several cheap market diners, this feels the most authentic. As intestines are close to Florentines' hearts, tripe is very big here (lunch menu served Mon-Sat 12:00-14:00, sandwiches available 8:00-12:00, closed Sun, cash only, inside the Mercato Centrale on the side closest to the Church of San Lorenzo, mobile 339-648-0251).

Trattoria Mario's, around the corner from Trattoria Zà-Zà (listed earlier), has been serving hearty lunches to market-goers since 1953 (Fabio and Romeo are the latest generation). Their simple formula: bustling service, old-fashioned good value, a lunch-only fixed-price meal, and shared tables. It's *cucina casalinga*—home cooking *con brio*. This place is high-energy and jam-packed. Their best dishes often sell out first, so go early. If there's a line, put your name on the list (€5-6 pastas, €8 *secondi*, cash only, Mon-Sat 12:00-15:30, closed Sun and Aug, no reservations, Via Rosina 2, tel. 055-218-550).

Casa del Vino, Florence's oldest operating wine shop, offers glasses of wine from among 25 open bottles (see the list tacked to the bar). Owner Gianni, whose family has owned the Casa for more than 70 years, is a class act. Gianni's *carta dei panini* lists delightful €3.50 sandwiches and €1 crostini; the *I Nostri Panini* (classic sandwiches) richly reward adventurous eaters. During busy times, it's a mob scene. You'll eat standing outside alongside workers on a quick lunch break (Mon-Fri 9:30-20:00 year-round, Sat 9:30-17:00 June-Sept only, closed Sun year-round and Sat off-season, hidden behind stalls of San Lorenzo Market at Via dell'Ariento 16 red, tel. 055-215-609).

Near the Accademia
Budget-Lunch Places Surrounding the Accademia
For pizza by the slice, try **Pugi,** at Piazza San Marco 10. For a break from pasta and pizza, grab a quick kebab lunch from **Barbecue: The Taste of Istanbul** (Via Cavour 41).

Pasticceria Robiglio, a smart little café, opens up its stately dining area and sets out a few tables on the sidewalk for lunch. They have a small menu of daily pasta and *secondi* specials, and seem determined to do things like they did in the elegant, pre-tourism days (generous €9-10 plates, a great €8 *niçoise*-like "fantasy salad," pretty pastries, smiling service, daily 12:00-15:00, longer hours as a café, a block toward the Duomo off Piazza S.S. Annunziata at Via dei Servi 112 red, tel. 055-212-784). Before you leave, be tempted by their pastries—famous among Florentines.

La Mescita Fiaschetteria is a characteristic hole-in-the-wall just around the corner from *David*—but a world away from all the tourism. It's where locals and students enjoy daily pasta specials and hearty sandwiches with good €1.50 house wine. You can trust Mirco and Alessio (as far as you can throw them)—just point to what looks good (such as their €5-6 pasta plate or €6-7 *secondi*), and you'll soon be eating well and inexpensively. The place can either be mobbed by students or in a peaceful time warp, depending on when you stop by (Mon-Sat 10:45-16:00, closed Sun, Via degli Alfani 70 red, mobile 347-795-1604 or 338-992-2640).

Picnic on the Ultimate Renaissance Square: **Il Centro Supermercati,** a handy supermarket a half-block north of the Accademia, has a curbside sandwich bar (Panineria) with an easy English menu that includes salads to go (Mon-Sat 9:00-19:30, Sun 10:00-19:00, sandwich bar may close earlier, Via Ricasoli 109). With your picnic in hand, hike around the block and join the bums on Piazza S.S. Annunziata, the first Renaissance square in Florence (don't confuse this with the less-interesting Piazza San Marco, closer to the supermarket). There's a fountain for washing fruit on the square. Grab a stony seat anywhere you like, and savor one of my favorite cheap Florence eating experiences. Or, drop by any of the places listed earlier for an easy lunch (pizza, kebab, or sandwich plus juice) to go.

Dining with Bobo away from the Center

Antica Trattoria da Tito, a 10-minute hike from the Accademia along Via San Gallo, is a long, drawn-out event of a meal. The boss, Bobo, is a fire hose of restaurateur energy who has clearly found his niche—making people happy with quality traditional food and lots of wine. His staff is as loyal as his clientele. While the food is great, there's no pretense. It's just a playground of Tuscan cuisine with "no romance allowed." As for the music he plays, Bobo says, "We are slaves of '80s." I'd come late and plan to party. To gorge on a feast of *antipasti* (meats, cheeses, fava beans, and bruschetta), consider ordering *fermami* (literally "stop me")—for €14, Bobo brings you food until you say, *"Fermami!"* A couple can get *fermami,* desserts, and a nice bottle of wine for €60 total. Ask for *vino* recommendations to experience that perfect pairing of food and wine. If you go with the flow here, you'll walk back to your hotel fat and filled with memories (€10 pastas, €12 *secondi,* €14 *gran tagliere*—big plate of cheese and meat, travelers with this book get a free after-dinner drink, Mon-Sat 12:30-15:00 & 19:00-23:00, closed Sun, reservations generally necessary, Via San Gallo 112 red, tel. 055-472-475).

Fast and Cheap near the Duomo

Self-Service Ristorante Leonardo is inexpensive, air-conditioned, quick, and handy. Eating here, you'll get the sense that they're passionate about the quality of their food. Stefano and Luciano (like Pavarotti) run the place with enthusiasm and put out free pitchers of tap water. It's just a block from the Duomo, southwest of the Baptistery (tasty €5 pastas, €6 main courses, Sun-Fri 11:45-14:45 & 18:45-21:45, closed Sat, upstairs at Via Pecori 11, tel. 055-284-446).

Döner Kebab: A good place to try this cheap Middle Eastern specialty is **Turkuaz,** a couple of blocks northeast of the Duomo (Via dei Servi 65).

Near Piazza della Signoria

Piazza della Signoria, the scenic square facing the Palazzo Vecchio, is ringed by beautifully situated yet touristy eateries serving overpriced, bad-value, and probably microwaved food. If you're determined to eat on the square, have pizza at Ristorante il Cavallino or bar food from the Irish pub next door. Piazza della Signoria's saving grace is **Rivoire** café, famous for its fancy desserts and thick hot chocolate. While obscenely expensive, it has the best view tables on the square (Tue-Sun 7:30-24:00, closed Mon, tel. 055-214-412).

Fine Dining

Frescobaldi Ristorante and Wine Bar, the showcase of Italy's aristocratic wine family, is a good choice for a formal dinner in Florence. Candlelight reflects off glasses of wine, and high-vaulted ceilings complement the sophisticated dishes. They offer the same menu in three different dining areas: cozy interior, woody wine bar, and breezy terrace. If coming for dinner, make a reservation, dress up, and hit an ATM (€11-14 appetizers and pastas, €18-24 *secondi,* lighter wine-bar menu at lunch, Tue-Sat 12:00-14:30 & 19:00-22:30, Mon 19:00-22:30, closed Sun and much of Aug, air-con, half a block north of the Palazzo Vecchio at Via dei Magazzini 2-4 red, tel. 055-284-724, Francesco is the lead waiter).

Ristorante Paoli dishes up wonderful, traditional cuisine to loads of cheerful eaters being served by jolly little old men under a richly frescoed Gothic vault. It feels old-school and Old World... it's all about the setting. Because of its fame and central location, it's filled mostly with tourists, but for a sophisticated, traditional Tuscan splurge meal, this is a fine choice. Salads are dramatically cut and mixed from a trolley right at your table. The walls are sweaty with memories that go back to 1824, and the service is flamboyant and fun-loving (but don't get taken—confirm prices). Woodrow Wilson slurped spaghetti here—his bust looks down on you as you eat (€10-15 pastas, €12-20 *secondi,* daily 12:00-15:00 &

19:00-23:00, reserve for dinner, between Piazza della Signoria and the Duomo at Via dei Tavolini 12 red, tel. 055-216-215).

Eating Cheaply and Simply near Piazza della Signoria

Cantinetta dei Verrazzano, a long-established bakery/café/wine bar, serves delightful sandwich plates in an old-time setting. Their *selection Verrazzano* is a fine plate of four little crostini (like mini-bruschetta) proudly featuring different breads, cheeses, and meats from the Chianti region (€7.50). The *tagliere di focacce,* a sampler plate of mini-focaccia sandwiches, is also fun (€14 for big plate for two). Add a €5 glass of Chianti to either of these dishes to make a fine, light meal. Office workers pop in for a quick lunch, and it's traditional to share tables. Be warned: Prices can add up here in a hurry (Mon-Sat 8:00-21:00, Sun 10:00-17:00, no reservations taken, just off Via de' Calzaiuoli, across from Orsanmichele Church at Via dei Tavolini 18, tel. 055-268-590). They also have benches and tiny tables for eating at takeout prices. Simply step to the back and point to a hot *focacce* sandwich (€3), order a drink at the bar, and take away your food or sit with Florentines and watch the action while you munch.

Osteria Vini e Vecchi Sapori, half a block north of the Palazzo Vecchio, is a colorful 16-seat hole-in-the-wall restaurant serving Tuscan food with a fun, accessible menu of delicious €7-9 pastas and €9-10 *secondi* (Tue-Sat 12:30-15:00 & 19:30-22:00, Sun 12:30-15:00, closed Mon, reserve for dinner; facing the bronze equestrian statue in Piazza della Signoria, go behind its tail into the corner and to your left; Via dei Magazzini 3 red, tel. 055-293-045, run by Mario while wife Rosanna cooks and son Thomas serves).

I Fratellini is an informal eatery where the "little brothers" have served peasants 29 different kinds of sandwiches and cheap glasses of Chianti wine (see list on wall) since 1875. Join the local crowd to order, then sit on a nearby curb or windowsill to eat, placing your glass on the wall rack before you leave (€2.50 sandwiches, daily 9:00-20:00 or until the bread runs out, closed Sun in winter, 20 yards in front of Orsanmichele Church on Via dei Cimatori, tel. 055-239-6096). Be adventurous with the menu (easy-order by number). Consider *finocchiona* (#15, a special Tuscan salami), *lardo di Colonnata* (#22, lard aged in Carrara marble), and *cinghiale* (#19, spicy wild boar) sandwiches. Order the most expensive wine they're selling by the glass (Brunello for €5; bottles are labeled).

Cheap Takeout on Via Dante Alighieri: Three handy places line up on this street, just a couple of blocks from the Duomo. **L'Antico Trippaio,** an antique tripe stand, is a fixture in the town center. Cheap and authentic as can be, this is where locals come daily for €4-6 sandwiches *(panini),* featuring specialties like *trippa alla fiorentina* (tripe), *lampredotto* (cow's stomach), and a list of

Gelato

Gelato is an edible art form. Italy's best ice cream is in Florence—one souvenir that can't break and won't clutter your luggage.

But beware of scams at touristy joints on busy streets that turn a simple request for a cone into a €10 "tourist special" rip-off. To avoid this, survey the size options and be very clear in your order (for example, "a €3 cone").

A key to gelato appreciation is sampling liberally and choosing flavors that go well together. Ask, as Italians do, for *"Un assaggio, per favore?"* (A taste, please?; oon ah-SAH-joh pehr fah-VOH-ray) and *"Che si sposano bene?"* (What marries well?; kay see spoh-ZAH-noh BEN-ay).

Artiginale, nostra produzione, and *produzione propia* mean gelato is made on the premises; also, gelato displayed in covered metal tins (rather than white plastic) is more likely to be homemade. Gelato aficionados avoid colors that don't appear in nature—for fewer chemicals and real flavor, go for mellow hues (bright colors attract children). If you see giant mounds of bright colors, skip it.

All of these places, which are a cut above, are open daily for long hours.

Near the Duomo: The recent favorite in town, **Grom** uses organic ingredients and seasonal fresh fruit, along with biodegradable spoons and tubs. This clever Italy-wide chain markets its traditional approach with a staff quick to tell customers, "This gelato reminds me of my childhood." A few purists grumble that a chain *gelateria* can't possibly compare with a local one-off,

more appetizing options. Roberto and Maurizio offer a free plastic glass of rotgut Chianti with each sandwich for travelers with this book (daily 9:00-20:00, on Via Dante Alighieri, mobile 339-742-5692). If tripe isn't your cup of offal, **Pizzeria Totò,** just next to the tripe stand, has very good €2.50-3 slices (Via Dante Alighieri 28 red, tel. 055-290-406). And a few steps in the opposite direction is a **Metà supermarket,** with cheap drinks and snacks and a fine *antipasti* case inside (daily 8:30-21:30, Sun from 9:00, Via Dante Alighieri 20-24). If you pick up lunch at any of these, the best people-watching place to enjoy your sandwich is three blocks away, on Piazza della Signoria.

Wine Bar near Ponte Vecchio

'Ino Bottega di Alimentari e Vini is a mod little shop filled but so far Grom has maintained an impressively high quality—likely because the menu follows what's in season, changing every month (Via delle Oche 24 red).

Near Ponte Vecchio: **Gelateria Carrozze** is a longtime favorite (on riverfront 30 yards from Ponte Vecchio toward the Uffizi at Piazza del Pesce 3).

Near the Accademia: A Sicilian choice on a tourist thoroughfare, **Gelateria Carabè** is particularly famous for its luscious *granite*—Italian ices made with fresh fruit. A cremolata is a granita with a dollop of gelato—a delicious combination (from the Accademia, it's a block toward the Duomo at Via Ricasoli 60 red).

Near Orsanmichele Church: **Perchè No!** is located just off the busy main pedestrian drag, Via de' Calzaiuoli, and serves a wide array of flavors (Via dei Tavolini 19).

Near the Church of Santa Croce: The venerable favorite, **Vivoli's** still has great gelato—but it's more expensive and stingy in its servings. Before ordering, try a free sample of their rice flavor—*riso* (closed Mon, Aug, and Jan; opposite the Church of Santa Croce, go down Via Torta a block and turn right on Via Stinche). Locals flock to **Gelateria de' Neri** (Via de' Neri 26 red), also owned by Vivoli's.

Near the Mercato Centrale: The **Bermuda Triangle** (a.k.a., I Gelati Del Bondi) is a hit both for its fresh ingredients and for the big-hearted energy of its owner, Vetulio (Via Nazionale 61 red, where it crosses Via Faenza, tel. 055-287-490).

Across the River: If you want an excuse to check out the little village-like neighborhood across the river from Santa Croce, enjoy a gelato at the tiny **Il Gelato di Filo** (named for Filippo and Lorenzo) at Via San Miniato 5 red, a few steps toward the river from Porta San Miniato. Gelato chef Edmir is proud of his fruity sorbet as well.

with gifty edibles. Alessandro and his staff serve sandwiches and wine—you'll get your €5-8 sandwich on a napkin with an included glass of their wine of the day as you perch on a tiny stool. They can also make a fine €12 *piatto misto* of cheeses and meats with bread (daily 11:00-16:30, immediately behind Uffizi Gallery on Ponte Vecchio side, Via dei Georgofili 3 red, tel. 055-219-208).

Between the Palazzo Vecchio and Santa Croce Church

Ristorante del Fagioli is an enthusiastically run eatery where you feel the heritage. The dad, Gigi, commands the kitchen while family members Antonio, Maurizio, and Simone keep the throngs of loyal customers returning. The cuisine: home-style bread-soups, hearty steaks, and Florentine classics. Don't worry—while *fagioli* means "beans," that's the family name, not the extent of the menu (€9 pastas, €9 *secondi,* cash only, Mon-Fri 12:30-14:30 & 19:30-24:00, closed Sat-Sun, reserve for dinner, between Santa Croce Church and the Alle Grazie bridge at Corso dei Tintori 47, tel. 055-244-285).

Boccadama Enoteca Ristorante is a stylish, shabby-chic wine bistro serving an easy-to-navigate menu of capably executed traditional Tuscan fare based on seasonal produce. Eat in the intimate dining room with candles reflecting off bottle-lined walls or at one of the few tables on the dramatic Piazza Santa Croce. As this place is popular with groups, reservations are smart (€8-9 *primi,* €12-16 *secondi,* daily 11:00-16:00 & 18:30-24:00, on south side of Piazza Santa Croce at 25-26 red, tel. 055-243-640, Marco).

Trattoria Anita, midway between the Uffizi and Santa Croce, feels old-school, with wood paneling and rows of wine bottles. Brothers Nicola, Gianni, and Maurizio offer a good lunch special: three hearty Tuscan courses for €9 on weekdays (€7-8 pastas, €7-12 *secondi,* Mon-Sat 12:00-14:30 & 19:00-22:15, closed Sun, on the corner of Via Vinegia and Via del Parlagio at #2 red, tel. 055-218-698).

Trattoria I'cche C'è C'è (EE-kay chay chay; dialect for "whatever there is, there is") is a small, family-style restaurant where fun-loving Gino and his wife Mara serve functional local food, including a €13 three-course, fixed-price meal. While filled with tourists, the place has a charming mom-and-pop warmth (€7-12 pastas, €12-18 *secondi,* Tue-Sun 12:30-14:30 & 19:30-22:30, closed Mon and two weeks in Aug, midway between Bargello and river at Via Magalotti 11 red, tel. 055-216-589).

South of the River, in the Oltrarno

In general, dining in the Oltrarno offers a more authentic experience; although it's quite close to the old center, tourists imagine that it's another world and tend to stay away. At many of these places, Florentines may even outnumber my readers. For locations, see the map on pages 516-517.

Dining with a Ponte Vecchio View

Golden View Open Bar is a lively, trendy bistro, good for a romantic meal or just a salad, pizza, or pasta with fine wine and a fine view of Ponte Vecchio and the Arno River. Its white, minimalist interior is a stark contrast to atmospheric old Florence. Reservations for window tables are essential unless you drop in early for dinner (€10 pizzas, €11-15 pastas, big €11-14 salads, €20-30 *secondi,* daily 11:30-24:00, impressive wine bar, 50 yards east of Ponte Vecchio at Via dei Bardi 58, tel. 055-214-502, run by Antonio, Marco, and Tomaso). They have four seating areas (with the same menu and prices) for whatever mood you're in: a riverside pizza place, a classier restaurant, a jazzy lounge, and a wine bar (they also serve a buffet of appetizers free with your drink from 19:00 to 21:00). Mixing their fine wine, river views, and live jazz makes for a wonderful evening (jazz nightly at 21:00 except Tue and Thu off-season).

Dining Well in the Oltrarno

Of the many good and colorful restaurants in the Oltrarno, these are my favorites. Reservations are a good idea in the evening.

Il Santo Bevitore Ristorante, lit like a Rembrandt painting and filled with dressy tables, serves creative Tuscan cuisine. They're enthusiastic about matching quality produce from the area with the right wine. This is a good break from the big, sloppy plates of pasta you'll get at many Florence eateries (€9-12 pastas, €8-12 meat-and-cheese *taglieri*, €10-17 *secondi*, good wine list by the glass or bottle, daily 12:30-14:30 & 19:30-22:30, closed Sun for lunch, come early or make reservations, no outside seating, Via di Santo Spirito 64, tel. 055-211-264). Their smaller wine bar next door, **Enoteca Il Santino Gastronomia,** feels like the perfect after-work hangout for foodies who'd like a glass of wine and some light food. Tight, cozy, and atmospheric, one wall is occupied by the bar, where you can assemble an €8-12 *tagliere* of local cheeses and *salumi* (also available to take away). They also have a few €6-8 hot dishes. Both the food and the wine is locally sourced from small producers (daily 12:30-23:00, Via di Santo Spirito 60 red, tel. 055-230-2820).

Trattoria 4 Leoni creates the quintessential Oltrarno dinner scene. The Tuscan-style food is made with an innovative twist and an appreciation for vegetables. You'll enjoy the fun energy and characteristic seating, both outside on the colorful square, Canto ai Quattro Pagoni, and inside, where you'll dine in exposed-stone sophistication. While the wines by the glass are pricey, the house wine is very good (€10 pastas, €10-15 *secondi*, daily 12:00-24:00, dinner reservations smart; from Ponte Vecchio walk four blocks up Via de' Guicciardini, turn right on Via dello Sprone, then slightly left to Via de' Vellutini 1; tel. 055-218-562).

Antico Ristoro Di' Cambi is a meat-lover's dream—thick with Tuscan traditions, rustic touches, and T-bone steaks. The bustling scene has a memorable, beer-hall energy. As you walk in, you'll pass a glass case filled with red chunks of Chianina beef that's priced by weight (for the famous *bistecca alla fiorentina*, €40/kilo, standard serving is half a kilo per person). Before you OK your investment, they'll show you the cut and tell you the weight. While the steak comes nearly uncooked, it's air dried for 21 days so it's not really raw, just very tasty and tender—making you so happy you're sitting at the top of the food chain. Sit inside the convivial woody interior or outside on a square (€8-10 pastas, €10-18 *secondi*,

Mon-Sat 12:00-14:30 & 18:30-22:30, closed Sun, reserve on week-ends and to sit outside, Via Sant'Onofrio 1 red, one block south of Ponte Amerigo Vespucci, tel. 055-217-134, run by Stefano and Fabio, the Cambi cousins).

Olio & Convivium Gastronomia is primarily a catering company for top-end events, and this is where they showcase their cooking. It started as an elegant deli whose refined olive-oil-tasting room morphed into a romantic, aristocratic restaurant. Their three intimate rooms are surrounded by fine *prosciutti*, cheeses, and wine shelves. It can seem intimidating and a little pretentious, but well-dressed foodies will appreciate this place for its quiet atmosphere. Their list of €14-25 *gastronomia* plates offers an array of taste treats and fine wines by the glass (€14-16 pastas, €20-22 *secondi*, stylish €18 lunches with wine, Tue-Sat 12:00-14:30 & 19:00-22:30, Mon 12:00-14:30 only, closed Sun, strong air-con, Via di Santo Spirito 4, tel. 055-265-8198, Monica).

Trattoria da Sergio is a tiny eatery about a block before Porta San Frediano, one of Florence's medieval gates. It has charm and a strong following, so reservations are a must. The food is on the gourmet side of home cooking—mama's favorites with a modern twist—and therefore a bit more expensive (€9-10 pastas, €12-20 *secondi*, Tue-Sun 12:00-14:00 & 19:30-22:45, closed Mon, Borgo San Frediano 145 red, tel. 055-223-449, Sergio and Marco).

Trattoria Al Tranvai, with tight seating and small dark-wood tables, looks like an old-time tram filled with the neighborhood gang. A 10-minute walk from the river at the edge of the Oltrarno, it feels like a small town's favorite eatery (€9 pastas, €10-13 *secondi*, Mon 19:00-24:00, Tue-Sat 11:00-15:00 & 19:00-24:00, closed Sun, Piazza T. Tasso 14 red, tel. 055-225-197).

Eating Cheaply in the Oltrarno

Trattoria Sabatino, farthest away and least touristy of my Oltrarno listings, is a spacious, brightly lit mess hall—disturbingly cheap—with family character and a simple menu. It's a super place to watch locals munch. You'll find it just outside Porta San Frediano, a 15-minute walk from Ponte Vecchio (€4 pastas, €5 *secondi*, Mon-Fri 12:00-15:00 & 19:15-22:00, closed Sat-Sun, Via Pisana 2 red, tel. 055-225-955, little English spoken).

Trattoria Casalinga, an inexpensive standby, comes with aproned women bustling around the kitchen. Florentines and tourists alike pack the place and leave full and happy, with euros to spare for gelato (€7 pastas, €8-10 *secondi*, Mon-Sat 12:00-14:30 & 19:00-21:45, after 20:00 reserve or wait, closed Sun and Aug, just off Piazza di Santo Spirito, near the church at Via de' Michelozzi 9 red, tel. 055-218-624, Andrea and Paolo).

Borgo Antico is the hit of Piazza di Santo Spirito, with enticing pizzas, big deluxe plates of pasta, a delightful setting, and a trendy and boisterous young crowd (€8-10 pizza and pasta, €14-18 *secondi*, daily 12:00-23:00, best to reserve for a seat on the square, Piazza di Santo Spirito 6 red, tel. 055-210-437, Andrea and Michele—feel his forearm). **Volume,** the bar next door, is run by the same gang.

Ricchi Caffè, next to Borgo Antico, has fine gelato, home-made desserts, shaded outdoor tables, and €9 pasta dishes at lunch (daily 7:00-24:00, tel. 055-215-864). After noting the plain facade of the Brunelleschi church facing the square, step inside the café and pick your favorite picture of the many ways it might be finished.

Supermarket: Facing the Pitti Palace, **Metà Supermarket** seems designed to rescue poor, hungry, and thirsty travelers (daily 9:00-20:30, Piazza de' Pitti 33 red). For other good options near Pitti Palace, see page 530.

Florence Connections

Florence is Tuscany's transportation hub, with fine train, bus, and plane connections to virtually anywhere in Italy. The city has several train stations, a bus station (next to the main train station), and an airport (plus Pisa's airport is nearby). Livorno, on the coast west of Florence, is a major cruise-ship port for passengers visiting Florence, Pisa, and other nearby destinations.

By Train
From Florence by Train to: Pisa (2-3/hour, 45-75 minutes, €7.10), **Lucca** (2/hour, 1.5 hours, €6.40), **Siena** (direct trains hourly, 1.5-2 hours, €7.70; bus is better because Siena's train station is far from the center), **Camucia-Cortona** (hourly, 1.5 hours, €8.90), **Livorno**—cruise ship port described later (hourly, 1.5 hours, some change in Pisa, €8.20), **La Spezia** (for the Cinque Terre, 5/day direct, 2.5 hours, otherwise nearly hourly with change in Pisa, €11.30), **Milan** (hourly, 1.75 hours, €53), **Milan's Malpensa Airport** (2/day direct, 2.75 hours, €58), **Venice** (hourly, 2-3 hours, may transfer in Bologna; often crowded—reserve ahead, €43), **Assisi** (8/day direct, 2-3 hours, €12), **Orvieto** (hourly, 2 hours, some with change in Campo di Marte or Rifredi station, €19), **Rome** (at least hourly, 1.5 hours, most connections require seat reservations, €45), **Naples** (3/day direct, 3 hours, €72; otherwise about hourly with change in Rome, 4.25 hours, €56-59), **Brindisi** (8/day, 8 hours with change in Bologna or Rome, €75), **Interlaken** (5/day, 5.5-6 hours, 2-3 changes), **Frankfurt** (1/day, 12 hours, 1-3 changes), **Paris** (3/day, 10-15 hours, 1-2 changes, important to reserve overnight train ahead), **Vienna** (1 direct overnight train, or 5/day with 1-3 changes,

10-16 hours). Note that these are all TrenItalia connections; the new Italo company may offer additional options (check www.italo treno.it).

By Bus

The SITA bus station (100 yards west of the Florence train station on Via Santa Caterina da Siena) is traveler-friendly—a big, old-school lot with numbered stalls and all the services you'd expect. Schedules for regional trips are posted everywhere, and TV monitors show imminent departures. Bus service drops dramatically on Sunday.

From Florence by Bus to: San Gimignano (hourly, less on Sun, 1.5-2 hours, change in Poggibonsi, €6.80), Siena (about 2/hour, 1.25-hour *rapida/via superstrada* buses are faster than the train, avoid the 2-hour *ordinaria* buses, €7.20), Volterra (4/day Mon-Sat, 1/day Sun, 2 hours, change in Colle Val d'Elsa where you catch a convenient CPT bus, €8.35), Montepulciano (2/day with a change in Bettole, 2 hours, €8.70), Florence's Amerigo Vespucci Airport (2/hour, 30 minutes, €5, pay driver and immediately validate ticket, always from platform 1). Generally, buy bus tickets in the station, as you'll pay 30 percent more if you buy tickets on the bus. Bus info: www.sitabus.it or tel. 800-373-760 (Mon-Fri 8:30-12:30 & 15:00-18:00, closed Sat-Sun).

By Taxi

For small groups with more money than time, zipping to nearby towns by taxi can be a good value (e.g., €120 from your Florence hotel to your Siena hotel).

A more comfortable alternative is to hire a private car service. Florence-based Transfer Chauffeur Service has a fleet of modern vehicles with drivers who can whisk you between cities, to and from the cruise ship port at Livorno, and through the Tuscan countryside for around the same price as a cab (tel. 055-614-2182, mobile 338-862-3129, www.transfercs.com, marco.masala@transfer cs.com, Marco).

By Plane

For information on Florence's Amerigo Vespucci Airport, see page 460. For information on Pisa's Galileo Galilei Airport, see page 561.

By Cruise Ship

Florence's port is Livorno (sometimes called "Leghorn" in English), a coastal town located about 60 miles west of Florence. Of the excursion options, Florence is the most time-consuming to reach (roughly two hours each way by public transit); it will take you the

FLORENCE

Greater Florence

To Bologna, Venice & Milan

To Lucca, Pisa & Cinque Terre

AUTOSTRADA CHURCH

FIRENZE NORD EXIT

A-11

VESPUCCI AIRPORT

RIFREDI STATION

PIAZZA LIBERTÀ & P

Fiesole

VIA SAN DOMENICO (BUS #7)

VIA PISTOIESE

VIA BARACCA

Arno River

FIRENZE SIGNA EXIT

SUPERSTRADA

VIA PISANA

VIA BACCIO MONTELUPO

S.M. NOVELLA MAIN TRAIN STN.

SITA BUS STN.

CAMPO DI MARTE STATION

FLORENCE CENTER
SEE DETAIL MAPS

To Pisa & Livorno

A-1

CERTOSA

PIAZZALE MICHELANGELO & P

PORTA ROMANA & P

VIA SENESE

VIA MARCO POLO

VIA G. AGNELLI

FIRENZE SUD EXIT

A-1

To Roma

FIRENZE CERTOSA EXIT

S-222

2 Kilometers

2 Miles

S-2

FLORENCE AMERICAN CEMETERY

SUPERSTRADA

SCENIC WINDING ROAD THROUGH CHIANTI

To San Gimignano & Siena

To Siena

whole day. **Pisa** is closer (about an hour each way), and—since Pisa is well-connected with **Lucca**—it's possible to combine those two cities into one long day. (If doing this, save Pisa until after lunch to avoid the cruise crowds in the morning, and be aware that most shops and restaurants in Lucca are closed Sun-Mon.)

No matter where you go, if you're taking the train, keep in mind that it takes 30 minutes just to get from Livorno's cruise port to the train station across town. Plan your day conservatively, as trains can be delayed.

Livorno Arrival and Connections

Livorno's port (at the western edge of town) is vast and sprawling, but most cruise ships dock in one of two places: Molo 75, at the Porto Mediceo; or the adjacent Molo Capitaneria. Livorno's city center clusters around two nearby squares: Piazza Grande (stop for bus #1 to train station) and Piazza del Municipio (TI, public WCs, stop for shuttle bus to the port). The squares are connected by a long, covered pedestrian mall (with the main TI inside).

Most cruise lines offer a **shuttle bus** to the center of Livorno, dropping you off at a bus stop near the TI kiosk in Piazza del Municipio (sometimes free, otherwise about €5-8 round-trip).

Taxis to Florence, Pisa, or Lucca are very expensive (explained later), though if splitting the cost with a group, this can be a decent way to go. With a little patience, budget-minded travelers can use public transportation to go from Livorno to any of these places, and back again before the ship departs.

The basic plan is this: Walk or ride the cruise line's shuttle bus from the port to downtown Livorno; then ride a public bus to Livorno's train station; then take the train to wherever you're going.

Public Transportation Between Livorno and Florence, Pisa, and Lucca

From Livorno Centrale Station, trains zip to Florence, Pisa, Lucca, and other points in Italy. Note that all train lines go first to Pisa, then split: north to Lucca or east to Florence.

To Florence: Hourly, usually departs at :10 after the hour, arrive in Florence at :32 past the following hour—1 hour and 22 minutes total, €8.20 on a regional train. (There are also a few departures that are a few minutes shorter, but require you to change trains at Pisa Centrale.)

To Pisa: 2-3/hour, 20 minutes, €1.90 on a regional train.

To Lucca: About hourly, 1-1.25 hours, transfer at Pisa Centrale, €3.70 on a regional train.

To Lucca and Pisa: If you want to visit Lucca and Pisa in one day, take the train to Lucca first. A handy bus connects Lucca's Piazzale Giuseppe Verdi to Pisa's Field of Miracles (hourly Mon-Sat, fewer on Sun, 30 minutes, €3).

Taxi and Shared Minibus Excursions

Taxis meet arriving cruises and offer various day trips around the area (the cabbie drops you off for a designated amount of time in one or two cities). Private taxis are costly, but you'll also find enterprising drivers with eight-seat minibuses gathering groups to split their €400 fee. At €50/person, this is actually a great deal—you'll be driven one hour into Florence, dropped off near the center for four or five hours of free time, and then taken back to the port. Here are some ballpark round-trip fares for a four-seat car: **Pisa**—€120, **Pisa and Lucca**—€220, **Florence**—€320. In general, drivers at the port prefer to take passengers who will pay them for the whole day, so it can be difficult to get someone to take you just one-way (especially the long haul into Florence).

Taxis both at the port and in the city offer the same rates. Clarify the fare beforehand, even though by law the driver must have the meter on (the quoted price will usually be less than the meter).

Near Florence: Fiesole

Perched on a hill overlooking the Arno valley, Fiesole gives weary travelers a break in the action and—during the heat of

summer—a breezy location from which to admire the city below. It's a small town with a main square, a few restaurants and shops, a few minor sights, and a great view. The ancient Etruscans knew a good spot when they saw one, and chose to settle here, establishing Fiesole about 400 years before the Romans founded Florence. Wealthy Renaissance families in pre-air-conditioning days also chose Fiesole (fee-AY-zoh-lay) as a preferred vacation spot, building villas in the surrounding hillsides. Later, 19th-century Romantics spent part of the Grand Tour admiring the vistas, much like the hordes of tourists do today. Most come here for the view—the actual sights pale in comparison to those in Florence. Shutterbugs visit in the morning for the best light.

Getting to Fiesole: From Florence's Piazza San Marco, take bus #7—enjoying a peek at gardens, vineyards, orchards, and villas—to the last stop, Piazza Mino (4/hour, fewer after 20:00, 30 minutes, €1.20, €2 if bought on bus; departs Florence from Piazza San Marco; wear your money belt—thieves frequent this bus). Taxis from Florence cost about €25-35 (ride to highest point you want to visit—La Reggia Ristorante for view terrace or Church of San Francesco—then explore downhill).

Tourist Information: The TI, immediately to the right of the Roman Archaeological Park, is a two-minute walk from the bus stop—head behind the church (daily 10:30-17:00, Via Portigiani 3, tel. 055-596-1311, www.fiesoleforyou.it).

Market Day: A modest selection of food and household items fills Via Portigiani, just off Piazza Mino, on Saturday mornings until 13:00.

FLORENCE

Sights in Fiesole

Fiesole's main sights are either free or covered by one €10 combo-ticket, available at the Roman Theater.

▲▲**Terrace and Garden with a View**—Catch the sunset (and your breath) from the view terrace just below La Reggia Ristorante. It's a steep seven-minute hike from the Fiesole bus stop: Face the bell tower and take Via San Francesco, on the left. (For similar views and a peek at residential Fiesole, climb up the opposite side of the square, along the road hugging the ridgeline.)

Church of San Francesco—For even more hill-climbing, continue up from the view terrace to this charming little church. The small scale and several colorful altar paintings make this church more enjoyable than Fiesole's Duomo (free, Mon-Sat 8:00-12:00 & 15:00-19:00, Sun 7:00-11:00 & 15:00-19:00, Via San Francesco 13, tel. 055-59175).

Franciscan Ethnographic Missionary Museum (Museo Missionario Etnografico Francescano)—This eclectic little collection, hidden beneath the church of San Francesco, includes an Egyptian mummy, ancient coins, Chinese Buddhas, and the in situ ruins of a third-century Etruscan wall (free but donation suggested, Tue-Fri 10:00-12:00 & 15:00-19:00, Sat-Sun 15:00-19:00, closed Mon, unmarked door inside church leads to cloisters and museum, tel. 055-59175).

Duomo—While this church has a drab, 19th-century exterior, the interior is worth a look, if only for the blue-and-white glazed Giovanni della Robbia statue of St. Romulus over the entry door (free, daily 10:00-17:00, across Piazza Mino from the bus stop).

Roman Theater and Archaeological Park—Occasionally used today for plays, this well-preserved theater held up to 2,000 people. The site's other ruins are, well, ruined, and lacking in explanation. But the valley view and peaceful setting are lovely (€8, ticket also covers Civic Archaeological Museum—described next, €10 combo-ticket adds Bandini Museum; April-Sept daily 10:00-19:00; March and Oct daily 10:00-18:00; Nov-Feb Wed-Mon 10:00-14:00, closed Tue; from the bus stop cross Piazza Mino, heading toward the back of the Duomo; www.museidifiesole.it).

Civic Archaeological Museum—Located within the Archaeological Park, the museum imparts insight into Fiesole's Etruscan and Roman roots with well-displayed artifacts and with a few English description sheets in the corners (€8 ticket also includes Roman theater and park, also covered by €10 combo-ticket with Bandini Museum, same hours as Roman Theater, listed above).

Bandini Museum—This petite museum displays the wooden panels of lesser-known Gothic and Renaissance painters as well as the glazed terra-cotta figures of Andrea della Robbia (€5, also covered by €10 combo-ticket with archaeological museum, Roman theater, and park, daily 10:00-18:00, shorter hours off-season, behind Duomo at Via Dupre 1).

Eating in Fiesole

These two restaurants are on Piazza Mino, where the bus from Florence stops.

Ristorante Perseus, a local favorite, lacks views but serves authentic Tuscan dishes at a fair price in a rambling interior, at a few sidewalk tables, or on a shady garden terrace in fair weather (daily 12:30-14:30 & 19:30-23:30, tel. 055-59-143, Leonardo).

Ristorante Aurora is an upscale alternative with a view terrace overlooking the city of Florence (daily 12:00-14:30 & 19:00-22:30, tel. 055-59-363).

Picnics: Fiesole is made-to-order for a scenic and breezy picnic. Grab a pastry at Fiesole's best *pasticceria,* **Alcedo** (head up the main drag from the bus stop to Via Gramsci 27). Round out your goodies at the **Co-op** supermarket on Via Gramsci before walking up to the panoramic terrace. Or, for more convenience and less view, picnic at the shaded park on the way to the view terrace (walk up Via San Francesco about halfway to the terrace, and climb the stairs to the right).

PISA and LUCCA

Florence is within easy striking distance of a number of great cities—as their fortifications attest. Along with Siena (see the Siena chapter), Pisa and Lucca show that Florence wasn't the only power and cultural star of the late Middle Ages and Renaissance.

Pisa's Leaning Tower is touristy but worth a visit. Many tourists are surprised to see that the iconic tower is only a small part of a gleaming white architectural complex—featuring a massive cathedral and baptistery—that dominates the grand green square, the Field of Miracles. The rest of the city is virtually tourist-free and merits a wander for its rich history, architecture, and student vibe.

Lucca, contained within its fine Renaissance wall, lacks any blockbuster sights, but has a charm that causes many connoisseurs of Italy to claim it as a favorite stop. The town's garden-topped city wall is perfect for a laid-back bike ride—the single must-do activity in this pleasant getaway.

The two towns are 30 minutes from each other by hourly bus. Each is about 1.5 hours (or less) by train from Florence and well-served by excellent highways.

Using public transportation, you could day-trip from Florence to both cities. But with more time, stay overnight in Lucca. Take the train to Pisa in the morning, do your sightseeing, catch the bus to Lucca late in the afternoon, enjoy the evening scene, and stay the night. Sightsee Lucca the next day, then move on to your next destination by train.

Pisa

In A.D. 1200, Pisa's power peaked. For nearly three centuries (1000-1300), Pisa rivaled Venice and Genoa as a sea-trading power, exchanging European goods for luxury items in Muslim lands. As a port near the mouth of the Arno River (six miles from the coast), the city enjoyed easy access to the Mediterranean, plus the protection of sitting a bit upstream. The Romans had made it a naval base, and by medieval times the city was a major player.

Pisa's 150-foot galleys cruised the Mediterranean, gaining control of the sea, establishing outposts on the islands of Corsica, Sardinia, and Sicily, and trading with other Europeans, Muslims, and Byzantine Christians as far south as North Africa and as far east as Syria. European Crusaders hired Pisan boats to carry them and their supplies as they headed off to conquer the Muslim-held Holy Land. The Pisan "Republic" prided itself on its independence from both popes and emperors. The city used its sea-trading wealth to build the grand monuments of the Field of Miracles, including the now-famous Leaning Tower.

But the Pisan fleet was routed in battle by Genoa (1284, at Meloria, off Livorno), and their overseas outposts were taken away. Then the port silted up, and Pisa was left high and dry, with only its Field of Miracles and its university keeping it on the map.

Pisa's three important sights—the Duomo, Baptistery, and the Tower—float regally on the best lawn in Italy. The style throughout is Pisa's very own "Pisan Romanesque." Even as the church was being built, Piazza del Duomo was nicknamed the "Campo dei Miracoli," or Field of Miracles, for the grandness of the undertaking.

The Tower recently underwent a decade of restoration and

Pisa

To Autostrada & P "Pietrasantina"

See Field of Miracles detail map

Parking-Lot Shuttle

VIALE CASCINE

LEANING TOWER

CAMPOSANTO

VIA CONTESSA MATILDE

Bus to Lucca

BAPT.

DUOMO

FIELD OF MIRACLES

Piazza Manin

Bus to Train Station

TACKY SOUVENIR STANDS

VIA CARDINALE PIETRO MAFFI

DUOMO MUSEUM

V. C. CAPPONI

3

6

OLD CITY WALLS

10

Piazza San Caterina

Piazza Martiri della Libertà

VIA SAN LORENZO

VIA G. CARDUCCI

VIA BONANNO PISANO

ROMA

VIA SANTA MARIA

11

5

12

VIA DEI MILLE

VIA FAGGIOLA

VIA MARTIRI

VIA SAN GIUSEPPE

VIA PAOLO SAVI

VIA

Piazza Cavalotti

Piazza Cavalieri

SANTO STEFANO

BORGO STRETTO

V. DINI

B. FRANCESCO

To Nazionale di San Matteo

V. NICOLA PISANO

VIA DERNA

SAN SISTO

S. FREDIANO

VIA PAOLI

V. RISORGIMENTO

8

Piazza Dante

7

14

VIA PALESTRO

VIA TRIESTE

VIA TRENTO

Piazza Carrara

2

15

Piazza Garibaldi

VIA ENRICO FERMI

LUNGARNO PACINOTTI

L. MEDICEO

VIA VOLTURNO

PONTE SOLFERINO

LUNGARNO GAMBACORTI

PONTE DI MEZZO

LUNGARNO G. GALILEI

LUNGARNO SIMONELLI

LUNGARNO SONNINO

SANTA MARIA DELLA SPINA

V. A. MARIO

9

VIA SAN MARTINO

NUNZIATINA

VIA CECI

Arno River

LUNGARNO SAO PAOLO

V. FRANCESCO CRISPI

VIA GIUSEPPE MAZZINI

CORSO ITALIA

VIA CARMINE

V. NICOLA PISANO

VIA FRANCESCO NIOSI

VIA MANZONI

VIA LAVAGNA

V. ROMITI

VIA NINO BIXIO

HARING MURAL

Piazza San Antonio

V. IE. TURATI

Piazza Vittorio Emanuele II

VIA BENEDETTO CROCE

VIA CESARE BATTISTI

BUS STATION

200 Meters

200 Yards

Bus #101

4

VIALE BONAINI

13

1

V. A. GRISCI

Piazza d. Stazione

Bus to Field of Miracles

VIA ALESSANDRA DELLA SPINA

TRAIN STATION

GARIBALDI ARENA

VIA LUIGI BIANCHI

To Lucca & Market

Pisa Key

① Hotel Alessandro della Spina
② Hotel Royal Victoria & Caffè dell'Ussero
③ Hotel Villa Kinzica
④ Hotel Milano
⑤ Pensione Helvetia
⑥ Two Steps from the Tower B&B
⑦ Antica Trattoria il Campano
⑧ Ristorante Masala

⑨ Ristorante Bagus
⑩ Pizzeria al Bagno di Nerone
⑪ Paninoteca il Canguro
⑫ Panetteria Antiche Tradizioni
⑬ La Lupa Ghiotta Tavola Calda
⑭ Via delle Colonne Produce Market & Restaurants
⑮ La Bottega del Gelato

PISA AND LUCCA

topple-prevention. To ascend, you'll have to get your ticket and book a time at least a few hours in advance (for details, see page 549).

Planning Your Time

For most visitors, Pisa is a touristy quickie—seeing the Tower, visiting the square, and wandering through the church are 90 percent of their Pisan thrills. But it's a shame to skip the rest of the city. Considering the city's historic importance and the wonderful ambience created by its rich architectural heritage and vibrant student population, the city deserves a half-day visit. For many, the lack of tourists outside the Field of Miracles is both a surprise and a relief.

If you want to climb the Tower, go straight to the ticket office upon arrival in the city to snag an appointment—usually for a couple of hours later (for directions to the Field of Miracles, see "Arrival in Pisa," later). For an extra €2, you can book a time in advance online (at least 15 days beforehand) at www.opapisa.it. If you'll be seeing both the town and the Field of Miracles, plan on a six-hour stop. If just blitzing the Field of Miracles, three hours is the minimum. Spending the night lets you savor a great Italian city scene.

If you're day-tripping to Pisa from Lucca, or doing a Lucca/Pisa day trip from Florence, note that a handy bus runs hourly (less frequent on Sun) between the Field of Miracles and Lucca, saving time and hassle (see page 560).

Orientation to Pisa

The city of Pisa is framed on the north by the Field of Miracles (Leaning Tower) and on the south by the Pisa Centrale train station. The Arno River flows east to west, bisecting the city. Walking from Pisa Centrale directly to the Tower takes about 30 minutes (but allow up to an hour if you take my self-guided walk). The two main streets for tourists and shoppers are Via Santa Maria (running south from the Tower) and Corso Italia/Borgo Stretto (running north from the station).

Tourist Information

The TI is about 200 yards from Pisa Centrale train station—exit and walk straight up the left side of the street to the big, circular Piazza Vittorio Emanuele II. The TI is on the left, around the corner from #16 (daily 9:00-19:00, closes Sun at 16:00 off-season, tel. 050-42291). There's also a TI at the airport (daily 8:30-23:30).

Arrival in Pisa

By Train

Most trains (and visitors) arrive at Pisa Centrale Station, about a mile south of the Tower and Field of Miracles. A few trains, particularly those from Lucca, also stop at the smaller Pisa San Rossore Station, which is just four blocks from the Tower (not all trains stop here, but if yours does, hop off).

Pisa Centrale: This station has a baggage-check desk—look for *deposito bagagli* (€3/bag for 12 hours, daily 6:00-21:00, they photocopy your passport to check ID). As you get off the train, it's to the right at the far end of platform 1, just after the police station.

To get from this station to the Field of Miracles, you can **walk** (get free map from TI, 30 minutes direct, one hour if you follow my self-guided walk), take a **taxi** (€7-10, tel. 050-541-600, taxi stand at station), or go by **bus.** Take bus LAM Rossa (4-6/hour, after 20:00 3/hour, 15 minutes), which stops across the street from the train station, in front of the NH Cavalieri Hotel. Buy a €1.10 bus ticket from the tobacco/magazine kiosk in the train station's main hall or at any tobacco shop (€1.50 if you buy it on board, smart to have exact change, good for 70 minutes, round-trip permitted). Before getting on the bus, confirm that it is indeed going to "Campo dei Miracoli" (ask driver, a local, or TI) or risk taking a long tour of Pisa's suburbs. The correct buses let you off at Piazza Manin, in front of the gate to the Field of Miracles; drivers make sure tourists don't miss the stop.

To return to the train station from the Tower, catch the bus in front of the BNL bank, across the street from where you got off (again, confirm the destination—"Stazione Centrale," staht-see-OHN-ay chen-TRAHL-ay). You'll also find a taxi stand 30 yards from the Tower (at Bar Duomo).

Pisa San Rossore: From this station to the Field of Miracles, it's just a four-block walk. Follow Viale delle Cascine east, continuing as it turns into Via Contessa Matilde, and follow signs to *La Torre*—or just head toward the dome of the Baptistery.

By Car

It's best to leave your car at the big Pietrasantina parking lot, designed for tour buses (which pay €110 to park) and tourists with cars (who park for free). From there, a regular city bus shuttles you to the Field of Miracles (driving in the city center will likely net you a steep fine—cameras catch you and the city sends you a ticket by mail).

To reach the parking lot, exit the autostrada at *Pisa Nord* and follow signs to *Pisa* (on the left). Pass the second traffic light and turn left toward the city center. Go straight, following the *Bus Parking* signs, until you see the gas station. The parking lot is on the left. Here you'll find a cafeteria, WC, lots of big buses, and a bus stop for the Line C shuttle that goes back and forth between the lot and the Largo Cocco Griffi bus stop, just behind the walls of the Field of Miracles (6/hour, daily 8:30-19:20, €1.50, buy round-trip ticket on board). Or, if you have more time and want to follow my self-guided walk through Pisa to the Field of Miracles, take bus LAM Rossa to Pisa Centrale train station (4-6/hour, after 20:00 3/hour, €1.10 if you buy ticket at parking-lot cafeteria, €1.50 if purchased on board, also stops near the Tower en route).

By Plane

For details on Pisa's Galileo Galilei Airport, see page 561.

Helpful Hints

Markets: An open-air produce market attracts picnickers to Piazza della Vettovaglie, one block north of the Arno River near Ponte di Mezzo, and nearby Piazza Sant'Uomobuono (Mon-Sat 7:00-18:00, main section closes at 13:00, closed Sun). A street market—with more practical goods than food—bustles on Wednesday and Saturday mornings between Via del Brennero and Via Paparrelli (8:00-13:00, just outside of wall, about 6 blocks east of the Tower).

Festivals: The first half of June has many events, culminating in a celebration for Pisa's patron saint (June 16-17).

Local Guide: Dottore Vincenzo Riolo is a great guide for Pisa and the surrounding area (€130/3 hours, mobile 338-211-2939, www.pisatour.it, info@pisatour.it).

Tours: The TI coordinates with local guides to offer walking tours most days. The theme and schedule change every day; check with the TI for the latest information.

Self-Guided Walk

Welcome to Pisa: From Pisa Centrale Train Station to the Tower

A leisurely one-hour stroll from the station to the Tower is a great way to get acquainted with the more subtle virtues of this Renaissance city. Because the hordes who descend daily on the Tower rarely bother with the rest of the town, you'll find most of Pisa to be delightfully untouristy—a student-filled, classy, Old World town with an Arno-scape much like its upstream rival, Florence. Pisa is pretty small, with just 100,000 people. But its 45,000 students keep it lively, especially at night.

• *From Pisa Centrale train station, walk north up Viale Antonio Gramsci to the circular square called...*

Piazza Vittorio Emanuele II

The Allies considered Pisa to be strategically important in World War II, and both the train station and its main bridge were targeted for bombing. Forty percent of this district was destroyed. The piazza has been recently rebuilt, and now this generous public space with grass and benches is actually a lid for an underground parking lot. The TI is on this piazza, in the arcade. The entire wall of a building just to the left of the piazza was painted by American artist Keith Haring in 1989 to create *Tuttomondo (Whole Wide World).* Haring (who died of AIDS in 1990) brought New York City graffiti into the mainstream. This painting is a celebration of diversity, chaos, and the liveliness of our world, vibrating with energy.

• *Walk up Corso Italia to the river.*

Corso Italia

Cutting through the center of town, this is Pisa's main drag. As you leave Piazza Vittorio Emanuele II, look to the right to see the circa-1960 wall map of Pisa with a steam train (on the wall of the bar on the corner). You'll also see plenty of youthful fashions, as kids are out making the scene here. Be on guard for pickpockets—too young to arrest, they can only be kicked out of town. Pushed out of their former happy hunting grounds, the Field of Miracles, they now work the crowds here, often dressed as tourists.

• *Follow the pedestrianized Corso Italia straight north to the Arno River and Ponte di Mezzo. Stop in the center of the bridge.*

Ponte di Mezzo

This modern bridge, constructed on the same site where the Romans built one, marks the center of Pisa. In the Middle Ages, this bridge (like Florence's Ponte Vecchio) was lined with shops. It's been destroyed several times by floods and in 1943 by British and American bombers. Enjoy the view from the center of the bridge of the elegant mansions that line the riverbank, recalling Pisa's days of trading glory—the cityscape feels a bit like Venice's Grand Canal. Pisa sits on shifting delta sand, making construction tricky. The entire town leans. With innovative arches above ground and below, architects didn't stop the leaning—but they have made buildings that wobble without being threatened.

• *Cross the bridge to...*

Piazza Garibaldi

This square is named for the charismatic leader of the Risorgimento, the unification movement that led to Italian independence in 1870. Knowing Pisa was strongly nationalist, Garibaldi came here when wounded to be nursed back to health. Many Pisans died in the national struggle. **La Bottega del Gelato,** Pisa's favorite gelato place, is on Piazza Garibaldi (daily 11:30-24:00). You can side-trip about 100 yards downstream to **Caffè dell'Ussero** (famous for its fine 14th-century red terra-cotta original facade, at #28, Sun-Fri 7:00-21:00, closed Sat) and browse its time-warp interior, lined with portraits and documents from the struggle for Italian independence.

• *Continue north up the elegantly arcaded...*

Borgo Stretto

Welcome to Pisa's main shopping street. On the right, the Church of St. Michael, with its fine Pisan Romanesque facade, still sports some 16th-century graffiti. I'll bet you can see some modern graffiti across the street. Students have been pushing their causes here— or simply defacing things—for five centuries.

From here, look farther up the street and notice how it undulates like a flowing river. In the sixth century B.C., Pisa was born when two parallel rivers were connected by canals. This street echoes the flow of one of those canals. An 11th-century landslide rerouted the second river, destroying ancient Pisa, and the entire city had to regenerate.

• *After a few steps, detour left onto Via delle Colonne, and walk one block down to...*

Piazza delle Vettovaglie

Pisa's historic market square, Piazza delle Vettovaglie, is lively day and night. Its Renaissance loggia has hosted the fish and vegetable market for generations. The stalls are set up in this piazza during the morning (Mon-Sat 7:00-13:00, closed Sun) and stay open later in the neighboring piazza to the west (Piazza Sant'Uomobuono, Mon-Sat 7:00-18:00, closed Sun). You could cobble together a picnic from the sandwich shops and fruit-and-veggie stalls ringing these squares.

• *Continue north on Borgo Stretto another 100 yards, passing an ugly bomb site on the right, with its horrible 1960s reconstruction. Take the second left on nondescript Via Ulisse Dini (it's not obvious—turn left immediately at the arcade's end, just before the pharmacy). This leads to Pisa's historic core, Piazza dei Cavalieri.*

Piazza dei Cavalieri

With its old clock and colorfully decorated palace, this piazza was once the seat of the independent Republic of Pisa's government.

In around 1500, Florence conquered Pisa and made this square the training place for the knights of its navy. The statue of Cosimo I de' Medici shows the Florentine who ruled Pisa in the 16th century. With a foot on a dolphin, he reminded all who passed that the Florentine navy controlled the sea—at least a little of it. The frescoes on the exterior of the square's buildings, though damaged by salty sea air and years of neglect, reflect Pisa's fading glory under the Medici.

With Napoleon, this complex of grand buildings became part of the University of Pisa. The university is one of Europe's oldest, with roots in a law school that dates back as far as the 11th century. In the mid-16th century, the city was a hotbed of controversy, as spacey professors like Galileo Galilei studied the solar system—with results that challenged the church's powerful doctrine. More recently, the blind tenor Andrea Bocelli attended law school in Pisa before embarking on his well-known musical career.

• *From here, take Via Corsica (to the left of the clock).*

The humble **Church of San Sisto,** ahead on the left (side entrance on Via Corsica), is worth a quick look. With simple bricks, assorted reused columns, heavy walls, and few windows, this was the typical Romanesque style that predated the more lavish Pisan Romanesque style of the Field of Miracles structures.

• *Follow Via Corsica as it turns into Via dei Mille, then turn right on Via Santa Maria, which leads north (and grab a quick bite at the recommended **Panetteria Antiche Tradizioni**). You'll pass through increasingly touristy claptrap, directly to the Field of Miracles and the Tower.*

Field of Miracles Tickets

Pisa has a combo-ticket scheme designed to get you into its neglected secondary sights: the Baptistery, Camposanto Cemetery, Duomo Museum, and Museum of the Sinopias (fresco pattern museum). For €5, you get your choice of one of these sights; for two of these sights or one plus the Duomo, the cost is €6; and for the works, you'll pay €10 (credit cards accepted). By comparison, the Duomo alone is a bargain (€2).

You can buy any of these tickets either behind the Leaning Tower or at the Museum of the Sinopias (near Baptistery, almost suffocated by souvenir stands). Both ticket offices have big, yellow, triangle-shaped signs.

No matter which ticket you get, you'll have to pay an additional €15 if you want to climb the Tower. Tickets for the Tower are sold at the ticket offices or online at least 15 days in advance at www.opapisa.it (€2 fee).

Sights in Pisa

▲▲▲Leaning Tower

A 15-foot lean from the vertical makes the Tower one of Europe's most recognizable images. You can see it for free—it's always viewable—or you can pay to climb its 294 stairs to the top.

Cost and Hours: €15 to go inside and climb to the top (see age restrictions in "Reservations to Climb the Tower," below); always viewable from the outside; open to climb daily April-Sept 8:00-20:00, Oct 9:00-19:00, Nov-

Feb 10:00-17:00, March 9:00-18:00; ticket office opens 30 minutes early, last entry 30 minutes before closing. For details on how to get to the Tower from the train station, see page 544.

Reservations to Climb the Tower: Entry to the Tower is by a timed ticket good for a 30-minute visit. Every 20 minutes, 45 people can clamber up the 294 tilting stairs to the top. Children under age eight are not allowed to go up. Children ages 8-12 must be accompanied by—and hold hands at all times with—an adult. Teenagers (up to and including 18-year-olds) must also be accompanied by an adult.

Reserve your timed entry in person at the ticket office (see below), or for an extra €2, book a time online at www.opapisa.it.

Online bookings are accepted no more than 45 days—and no fewer than 15 days—in advance. You must pick up your ticket(s) at least 30 minutes before your entry time. Show up 10 minutes before your appointment at the meeting point outside the ticket office.

To reserve in person, go to the **ticket office** behind the Tower, on the left in the yellow building, or to the Museum of the Sinopias ticket office hidden behind the souvenir stalls. In summer, for same-day entry, it will likely be a couple of hours before you're able to go up (see the rest of the monuments and grab lunch while waiting). The wait is usually much shorter at the beginning or end of the day.

Baggage Check: You can't take any bags up the Tower, but day-bag-size lockers are available at the ticket office—show your Tower ticket to check your bag. You may check your bag 10 minutes before your reservation time and must pick it up immediately after your Tower visit.

⊙ Self-Guided Tour: Rising up alongside the cathedral, the Tower is nearly 200 feet tall and 55 feet wide, weighing 14,000 tons and currently leaning at a five-degree angle (15 feet off the vertical axis). It started to lean almost immediately after construction began. Count the eight stories—a simple base, six stories of columns (forming arcades), and a belfry on top. The inner structural core is a hollow cylinder built of limestone bricks, faced with white marble barged here from San Giuliano, northeast of the city. The thin columns of the open-air arcades make the heavy Tower seem light and graceful.

The Tower was built over two centuries by at least three different architects. You can see how each successive architect tried to correct the leaning problem—once halfway up (after the fourth story), once at the belfry on the top.

The first stones were laid in 1173, probably under the direction of the architect Bonanno Pisano (who also designed the Duomo's bronze back door). Five years later, just as they'd finished the base and the first arcade, someone said, "Is it just me, or does that look crooked?" The heavy Tower—resting on a very shallow 13-foot foundation—was obviously sinking on the south side into the marshy, multilayered, unstable soil. (Actually, all the Campo's buildings tilt somewhat.) The builders carried on anyway, until they'd finished four stories (the base, plus three arcade floors). Then, construction suddenly halted—no one knows why—and for a century the Tower sat half-finished and visibly leaning.

Around 1272, the next architect continued, trying to correct

Pisa's Field of Miracles

To Autostrada & P "Pietrasantina"

VIALE CASCINE

VIA CONTESSA MATILDE

100 Meters
100 Yards

VIA CARLO CAMMEO

PARKING-LOT SHUTTLE

Largo Griffi

Jewish Cemetery

VIA NICOLINI

BAPTISTERY

CAMPOSANTO CEMETERY — WC — ❷ ❶

OLD CITY WALLS

LEANING TOWER

❹

PORTA S. MARIA

DUOMO

Grassy Lawn

VIA C. P. MAFFI

DUOMO MUSEUM

Piazza Archivescovado

Piazza Manin

❸ Ⓑ Ⓣ

Piazza del Duomo ❶

TACKY SOUVENIR STANDS

VIA BONANNO PISANO

MUSEUM OF THE SINOPIAS

VIA ROMA

Ⓣ BAR DUOMO

VIA SANTA MARIA

VIA TASSI

To rest of town & train station

PISA AND LUCCA

❶ Ticket Offices (2 Locations)   ❸ Bus to Train Station
❷ Tower Bag Check   ❹ Bus to Lucca

the problem by angling the next three stories backward, in the opposite direction of the lean. The project then again sat mysteriously idle for nearly another century. Finally, Tommaso Pisano put the belfry on the top (c. 1350-1372), also kinking it backward.

After the Tower's completion, several attempts were made to stop its slow-motion fall. The architect/artist/writer Giorgio Vasari reinforced the base (1550), and it actually worked. But in 1838, well-intentioned engineers pumped out groundwater, destabilizing the Tower and causing it to increase its lean at a rate of a millimeter per year.

It got so bad that in 1990 the Tower was closed for repairs, and $30 million was spent trying to stabilize it. Engineers dried the soil with steam pipes, anchored the Tower to the ground with steel cables, and buried 600 tons of lead on the north side as a counterweight (not visible)—all with little success. The breakthrough came when they drilled 15-foot-long holes in the ground on the north side and sucked out 60 tons of soil, allowing the Tower to sink on the north side and straighten out its lean by about six inches.

In addition to gravity, erosion threatens the Tower. Since its construction, 135 of the Tower's 180 marble columns have had to be replaced. Stone decay, deposits of lime and calcium phosphate, accumulations of dirt and moss, cracking from the stress of the lean—all of these are factors in its decline.

Thanks to the Tower's lean, there are special trouble spots. The lower south side (which is protected from cleansing rain and wind) is a magnet for dirty airborne particles, while the stone on the upper areas has more decay (from eroding rain and wind).

The Tower, now stabilized, has been cleaned as well. Cracks were filled, and accumulations of dirt removed with carefully formulated atomized water sprays and poultices of various solvents.

All the work to shore up, straighten, and clean the Tower has probably turned the clock back a few centuries. In fact, art historians figure it leans today as much as it did when Galileo reputedly conducted his gravity experiments here some 400 years ago.

Climbing the Tower: You wind your way up the outside of the Tower along a spiraling ramp. For your 30-minute time slot, figure about 10 minutes to climb and 10 to descend, leaving about 10 minutes for vertigo at the top. Even though it's technically a "guided" visit, that only means you're accompanied by a museum guard who makes sure you don't stay up past your scheduled appointment time.

Caution: The railings are skinny, the steps are slanted, and rain makes the marble slippery. Anyone with balance issues of any sort should think twice before ascending.

▲▲Duomo (Cathedral)

The huge Pisan Romanesque cathedral, with its carved pulpit by Giovanni Pisano, is artistically more important than its more famous bell tower.

Cost and Hours: €2, covered by various combo-tickets (see sidebar on page 549); daily April-Sept 10:00-20:00, Oct 10:00-19:00, Nov-Feb 10:00-13:00 & 14:00-17:00, March 10:00-18:00, last entry 30 minutes before closing.

Information: Shorts are OK as long as they're not too short, and shoulders should be covered (although it's not really enforced). Big backpacks are not allowed, nor is storage provided. If you have a day bag, carry it. Don't let the sparkle of the new coin-operated "phone guides" tempt you. These €2 machines still use narration from a bygone era.

❍ Self-Guided Tour: Begun in 1063, the Duomo is the centerpiece of the Field of Miracles' complex of religious buildings. Start by admiring its facade.

Exterior: The architect Buschetto created the style of Pisan Romanesque that set the tone for the Baptistery and Tower. Five decades later (1118), the architect Rainaldo added the impressive main-entrance facade (which also leans out about a foot).

The **bronze back doors** (Porta San Ranieri, at the Tower end) were designed by Bonanno Pisano (c. 1186). The doors have 24 different panels that show Christ's story using the same simple, skinny figures found in Byzantine icons. (The doors are actually copies; the originals are housed—but not always on display—in the Duomo Museum.) Cast using the lost-wax tech-

nique, these doors were an inspiration for Lorenzo Ghiberti's bronze doors in Florence.

Nave: Inside, the 320-foot nave was the longest in Christendom when it was built. The striped marble and arches-on-

columns give it an exotic, almost mosque-like feel. Dim light filters in from the small upper windows of the galleries, where the women worshipped.

At the center of the gilded coffered ceiling is the shield of Florence's Medici family. This powerful merchant and banking family took over Pisa after its glory days.

In the apse (behind the altar) is a **mosaic** (c. 1300, partly done by the great artist Cimabue) showing Christ as the Ruler of All (Pantocrator), between Mary and St. John the Evangelist. The Pantocrator image of Christ is standard fare among Eastern Orthodox Christians—that is, the "Byzantine" people who were Pisa's partners in trade.

Giovanni's Pulpit: The 15-foot-tall, octagonal pulpit is by Giovanni Pisano (c. 1250-1319), who left no stone uncarved in his pursuit of beauty. Four hundred intricately sculpted figures smother the pulpit, blurring the architectural outlines. In addition, the relief panels are actu-

ally curved, making it look less like an octagon than a circle. The creamy-white Carrara marble has the look and feel of carved French ivories, which the Pisanos loved. At the base, lions roar and crouch over their prey, symboliz-ing how Christ (the lion) triumphs over

Satan (the horse, as in the Four Horsemen of the Apocalypse). Four of the pulpit's support "columns" are statues. The central "column" features three graceful ladies representing Faith, Hope, and Charity, the three pillars of Christianity. Around the top of the pulpit, Christ's life unfolds in a series of panels saturated with carvings.

Galileo's Lamp: The bronze incense burner that hangs from the ceiling of the north transept (to the left of the altar) is a replica of the one that supposedly caught teenage Galileo's attention when a gust of wind set the lamp swinging. He timed the swings and realized that the burner swung back and forth in the same amount of time regardless of how wide the arc. (This pendulum motion was a constant that allowed Galileo to measure our ever-changing universe.)

St. Ranieri's Body: In a glass-lined casket on the altar, Pisa's patron saint lies mummified, encased in silver at his head and feet, with his hair shirt covering his body. The silver, mask-like face dates from 2000 and is as realistic as possible—derived from an FBI-style computer scan of Ranieri's skull. The son of a rich sea-trader, Ranieri (1117-1161) was a hard-partying, touring musician who one night was inspired to set fire to his musical instrument, open his arms to the heavens (à la Jimi Hendrix), and return to his father's shipping business, where he amassed a fortune. He later gave away his money, joined a monastery, and delivered spirited sermons from the Duomo pulpit.

Tomb of Holy Roman Emperor Henry VII: Pause at the tomb of this German king (c. 1275-1313), who invaded Italy and was welcomed by the Pisans as a leader of unity and peace. Unfortunately, Henry took ill and died young, leaving Ghibelline Pisa at the mercy of its Guelph rivals, such as rising Florence. Pisa never recovered.

▲▲▲Field of Miracles (Campo dei Miracoli)

Scattered across a golf-course-green lawn are five grand buildings: the cathedral (or Duomo), its bell tower (the Leaning Tower), the Baptistery, the hospital (today's Museum of the Sinopias), and the Camposanto Cemetery. The buildings are constructed from similar

materials—bright white marble—and have comparable decoration. Each has a simple ground floor and rows of delicate columns and arches that form open-air arcades, giving the Campo a pleasant visual unity.

The style is called Pisan Romanesque. Unlike traditional

Romanesque, with its heavy fortress-like feel—thick walls, barrel arches, few windows—Pisan Romanesque is light and elegant. At ground level, most of the structures have simple half-columns and arches. On the upper levels, you'll see a little of everything—tight rows of thin columns; pointed Gothic gables and prickly spires; Byzantine mosaics and horseshoe arches; and geometric designs (such as diamonds) and striped, colored marbles inspired by mosques in Muslim lands.

Architecturally, the Campo is unique and exotic. Theologically, the Campo's buildings mark the main events of every Pisan's life: christened in the Baptistery, married in the Duomo, honored in ceremonies at the Tower, healed in the hospital, and buried in the Camposanto Cemetery.

Lining this field of artistic pearls is a gauntlet of Europe's tackiest souvenir stands, as well as dozens of amateur mimes "propping up" the Leaning Tower while tourists take photos.

Secondary Sights on the Field of Miracles

The next four sights—the Baptistery, Camposanto Cemetery, Museum of the Sinopias, and Duomo Museum—share the same pricing and schedule.

Cost and Hours: It's €5 for one sight, but most visitors buy one of the various combo-tickets to save money (see sidebar on page 549). Open daily April-Sept 8:00-20:00, Oct 9:00-19:00, Nov-Feb 10:00-17:00, March 9:00-18:00, last entry 30 minutes before closing.

Locations: The Baptistery is located in front of the Duomo's facade. The Camposanto Cemetery is behind the church on the north side of the Field of Miracles. The Museum of the Sinopias is hidden behind souvenir stands, across the street from the Baptistery entrance. The Duomo Museum is housed behind the Tower.

▲**Baptistery**—The round Baptistery is the biggest in Italy. It's interesting for its superb acoustics and fine Pisano pulpit.

Visiting the Baptistery: The building is 180 feet tall—John the Baptist, on top, looks eye-to-eye with the tourists atop the nearly 200-foot-tall Leaning Tower. Notice that the Baptistery leans nearly six feet to the north (the Tower leans 15 feet to the south). The building (begun in 1153) is modeled on the circular domed Church of the Holy Sepulchre in Jerusalem, seen by Pisan Crusaders who occupied Jerusalem in 1099.

Inside, it's simple, spacious, and baptized with light. Tall arches encircle just a few pieces of religious furniture. In the center sits the beautiful, marble **octagonal font** (1246). A statue of the first Baptist, John the Baptist, stretches out his hand and says, "Welcome to my Baptistery." The font contains plenty of space for baptizing adults by immersion (the medieval custom), plus four wells for dunking babies.

The **pulpit** by Nicola Pisano, Giovanni's father, is arguably the world's first Renaissance sculpture. It's the first authenticated (signed) work by the "Giotto of sculpture," working in what came to be called the Renaissance style. The freestanding sculpture has classical columns, realistic people and animals, and 3-D effects in the carved panels. The speaker's platform stands on columns that rest on the backs of animals, representing Christianity's triumph over paganism. The relief panels, with scenes from the life of Christ, are more readable than the Duomo pulpit. Read left to right, starting from the back: Nativity, Adoration of the Magi, Presentation in the Temple, Crucifixion, Last Judgment.

The **acoustics** are impressive. Make a sound in here and it echoes for a good 10 seconds. A priest standing at the baptismal font (or a security guard today) can sing three tones within the 10 seconds—"Ave Maria"—and make a chord, singing haunting harmonies with himself. This medieval form of digital delay is due to the 250-foot-wide dome. Recent computer analysis suggests that the 15th-century architects who built the dome intended this building to function not just as a Baptistery, but also as a musical instrument. A security guard sings every half-hour, starting when the doors open in the morning. Climb 75 steps to the interior gallery (midway up) for an impressive view back down on the baptismal font.

Camposanto Cemetery—This site has been a cemetery since at least the 12th century. The building's cloistered open-air courtyard, lined with traces of fresco on the bare-brick walls, is surrounded by an arcade with intricately carved tracery in the arches and dozens of ancient Roman sarcophagi. The courtyard's grass grows on special dirt (said to turn a body into bones in a single day), shipped here by returning Crusaders from Jerusalem's Mount Calvary, where Christ was crucified. The 1,000-square-foot fresco, *The Triumph of Death* (c. 1340), captures late-medieval Europe's concern with death—predating but still accurately depicting Pisa's mood in reaction to the bubonic plague (1348), which killed one in three Pisans. Grim stuff, but appropriate for the Camposanto's permanent residents.

In 1944, the Camposanto took a direct hit from an Allied incendiary grenade (the rest of the Field of Miracles was miraculously unscathed). It melted the lead-covered arcade roof and peeled historic frescoes from the walls—one of the many tragic artistic losses of World War II (look for photos of the bombed-out Camposanto at the back). The Americans liberated the city on September 2 and later rebuilt the Camposanto.

Museum of the Sinopias (Museo delle Sinopie)—Housed in a 13th-century hospital, this museum features the preparatory sketches (sinopias) for the Camposanto's WWII-damaged frescoes (including *The Triumph of Death,* described earlier). Sinopias are sketches made in red paint directly on the wall, designed to guide the making of the final colored fresco. The master always did the sinopia himself; if he liked the results, his assistants made a "cartoon" by tracing the sinopia onto large sheets of paper *(cartone)*. Then the sinopia was plastered over, and the assistants redrew the outlines, using the cartoon as a guide. While the plaster was still wet, the master and his team quickly filled in the color and details, producing the final frescoes (now on display at the Camposanto). These sinopias—never meant to be seen—were uncovered by the bombing and restoration of the Camposanto and brought here.

Whether or not you pay to go in, you can watch two free videos in the entry lobby that serve to orient you to the square: a 10-minute, 3-D computer tour of the complex, and a 15-minute story of the Tower, its tilt, and its fix.

Duomo Museum (Museo dell'Opera del Duomo)—This museum behind the Leaning Tower is big on Pisan art, displaying treasures of the cathedral, paintings, silverware, and sculptures (from the 12th to 14th centuries, particularly by the Pisano dynasty), as well as ancient Egyptian, Etruscan, and Roman artifacts. It houses many of the original statues and much of the artwork that once adorned the Campo's buildings (where copies stand today), notably the statues by Nicola and Giovanni Pisano. You can stand face-to-face with the Pisanos' very human busts, which once ringed the outside of the Baptistery.

Also on display are the Duomo's original 12th-century bronze doors of St. Ranieri, done by Bonanno Pisano, which feature scenes from the life of Jesus. You'll also see a mythical sculpted hippogriff (a medieval jackalope) and other oddities brought back from the Holy Land by Pisan Crusaders, along with several large-scale wooden models of the Duomo, Baptistery, and Tower. The museum's grassy interior courtyard has a two-story, tourist-free view of the Tower, Duomo, and Baptistery.

Beyond the Field of Miracles

Museo Nazionale di San Matteo—On the river and in a former convent, this art museum displays 12th- to 15th-century sculptures, illuminated manuscripts, and paintings on wood by pre- and early Renaissance masters Martini, Masaccio, and others. It's a fine collection—especially its painted wood crucifixes—and gives you a chance to see Pisan innovation in 11th- to 13th-century art, before Florence took the lead.

Cost and Hours: €5, Tue-Sat 9:00-19:00, Sun 9:00-13:00, closed Mon, near Piazza San Paolo at Lungarno Mediceo, a 5-minute walk upriver from the main bridge, tel. 050-541-865.

Sleeping in Pisa

To locate these hotels, see the map on page 542.

$$$ Hotel Alessandro della Spina, in a nondescript neighborhood near Pisa Centrale train station, has 16 elegant and colorful rooms, each named after a flower (Sb-€120, Db-€140, discounts off-season and online, air-con, Internet access, free Wi-Fi, parking-€10/day; head straight out of train station, turn right on Viale F. Bonaini, and take the third right on Via Alessandro della Spina to find the hotel on your left at #5; tel. 050-502-777, fax 050-20583, www.hoteldellaspina.it, info@hoteldellaspina.it).

$$ Hotel Royal Victoria, a classy place on the Arno River, has been run by the Piegaja family since 1837. With 48 creaky, historic rooms filled with antiques, it's ideal for romantics who missed out on the Grand Tour. The location, dead-center between the Tower and Pisa Centrale train station, is the most atmospheric of my listings (D-€80, standard Db-€110, better Db-€130, suite-€190, family room-€228, 10 percent discount with this book if you pay cash and book direct, check website for special deals, air-con on request, Wi-Fi, parking garage-€20/day, lush communal terrace, Lungarno Pacinotti 12, tel. 050-940-111, fax 050-940-180, www.royalvictoria.it, mail@royalvictoria.it).

$$ Hotel Villa Kinzica has 30 tired, worn rooms with high ceilings, indifferent management, and a prime location just steps away from the Field of Miracles—ask for a room with a view of the Tower (Sb-€70, Db-€95, Tb-€109, Qb-€119, air-con, elevator, Piazza Arcivescovado 2, tel. 050-560-419, fax 050-551-204, www.hotelvillakinzica.it, info@hotelvillakinzica.it).

$ Hotel Milano, near Pisa Centrale train station, offers 10 simple, clean rooms (D-€55, Db-€78, 10 percent discount for Rick Steves readers if you pay cash and book direct, breakfast extra, air-con, Via Mascagni 14, tel. 050-23-162, fax 050-44-237, www.hotelmilano.pisa.it, info@hotelmilano.pisa.it).

$ Pensione Helvetia is a no-frills, homey, clean, and quiet inn just 100 yards from the Tower. Its 29 economical rooms are spread over four floors (no elevator); the lower your room number, the lower your altitude (S-€54, Sb-€60, D-€70, Db-€79, lower prices off-season, no breakfast but small lounge with vending machines, ceiling fans, free Wi-Fi, Via Don G. Boschi 31, reception around the corner at Hotel Francesco on Via Santa Maria, tel.

Sleep Code

(€1 = about $1.40, country code: 39)
S = Single, **D** = Double/Twin, **T** = Triple, **Q** = Quad, **b** = bathroom, **s** = shower only. Unless otherwise noted, credit cards are accepted, breakfast is included (but sometimes optional), and English is generally spoken. Many towns in Italy levy a hotel tax of about €2 per person, per night, which is generally not included in the rates I've quoted.

To help you sort easily through these listings, I've divided the accommodations into three categories based on the price for a standard double room with bath:

$$$ Higher Priced—Most rooms €120 or more.
$$ Moderately Priced—Most rooms between €80-120.
$ Lower Priced—Most rooms €80 or less.

Prices can change without notice; verify the hotel's current rates online or by email.

050-553-084, www.pensionehelvetiapisa.com, helvetiapisatravel @gmail.com).

$ Two Steps from the Tower B&B, in the historic center just a few blocks east of the Field of Miracles, offers three Ikea-style rooms (Sb-€35-40, Db-€60-65, extra bed-€15, weekly rates available, free Wi-Fi, kitchen use-€10/day, Via Cardinale Pietro Maffi 6, tel. 347-394-6559, www.2stepsfromtower.com, info@2stepsfromtower.com).

Eating in Pisa

Antica Trattoria il Campano, just off the market square, has a typically Tuscan menu and a candlelit, stay-awhile atmosphere. Their €30-€35 tasting menus include wine and generous portions of local specialties (Thu-Tue 12:30-15:00 & 19:30-22:45, closed Wed, reservations smart, Via Cavalca 19, tel. 050-580-585).

Ristorante Masala serves tasty, authentic Indian cuisine just a few blocks from the Tower. As there is a large Indian community in Pisa, this is a great place to take a break from pizza and pasta (€4-9 curries, vegetarian options, Tue-Sun 19:00-23:00, lunch Fri-Sun 12:00-14:30, closed Mon, Via Roma 52, tel. 050-48513).

At **Ristorante Bagus** the specialties are an extra-rare burger made with the famous Chianina beef and trendy twists on typical Tuscan fare (€25 fixed-price meal, Mon-Fri 12:30-14:30 & 19:30-22:00, Sat 19:30-22:00 only, closed Sun; heading south on Corso Italia, turn right on Via Nunziata and take your first right after

Piazza Griletti to Piazza dei Facchini 13; tel. 050-26196).

Pizzeria al Bagno di Nerone is a local favorite and is particularly popular with students. Belly up to the bar and grab a slice to go, or sit in their small dining room for a whole pie. Try the *cecina*, a crepe-like garbanzo-bean cake (Wed-Mon 11:30-14:30 & 18:45-22:30, closed Tue, a 5-minute walk from the Tower at Largo Carlo Fedeli 26, tel. 050-551-085).

At **Paninoteca il Canguro,** Mario makes warm, hearty sandwiches to order. Check the chalkboard for seasonal specials, such as *porchetta* (daily 10:00-24:00, Via Santa Maria 151, tel. 050-561-942).

Panetteria Antiche Tradizioni—not to be confused with another Panetteria across the street—is a sandwich/bread shop with complete fixings for a picnic on the lawn at the Field of Miracles. Build your own sandwich with homemade bread or focaccia, then choose fruit from the counter, fresh pastries from the window, and cold drinks or wine to round out your meal (daily 8:00-20:00, Via Santa Maria 66, mobile 327-570-5210).

Drop by cheery **La Lupa Ghiotta Tavola Calda** for a cheap, fast, and tasty meal a few steps from Pisa Centrale train station. It's got everything you'd want from a *ristorante* at half the price and with faster service (build your own salad—five ingredients for €4.50; Mon and Wed-Sat 12:15-15:00 & 19:15-23:30, Tue 12:15-15:00 only, closed Sun, Viale F. Bonaini 113, tel. 050-21018).

The street that houses the daily market, **Via delle Colonne** (a block north of the Arno, west of Borgo Stretto), has a few atmospheric, mid-priced restaurants and several fun, greasy takeout options.

Pisa Connections

Pisa is well-connected by trains, buses (particularly with Lucca), and highways, with a busy airport nearby.

From Pisa Centrale Station by Train to: Florence (2-3/hour, 45-75 minutes, €7.10), **Livorno** (2-3/hour, 20 minutes, €1.90), **Rome** (2/hour, many change in Florence, 3-4 hours), **La Spezia,** gateway to Cinque Terre (about hourly, 1-1.5 hours), **Siena** (2/hour, 1.75 hours, change at Empoli, €8.90), **Lucca** (1-2/hour, 30 minutes, bus is better except on Sun—see below, €3). Even the fastest trains stop in Pisa, so you might change trains here whether you plan to stop or not.

By Bus to Lucca: A handy bus connects the Field of Miracles with Lucca's Piazzale Giuseppe Verdi in 30 minutes (Mon-Sat hourly, fewer on Sun; in Pisa, wait at the Vai Bus signpost, immediately outside the wall behind the Baptistery on the right; buy €3 ticket on bus, toll-free tel. 800-602-947). This makes a half-day side-trip to Pisa from Lucca particularly easy.

By Car: The drive between Pisa and Florence is that rare case where the non-autostrada highway (free, more direct, and at least as fast) is a better deal than the autostrada.

By Plane: Pisa's **Galileo Galilei Airport** handles more and more international and domestic flights (TI open daily 8:30-23:30, cash machine, car-rental agencies, baggage storage from 8:00-20:00 only, €7/bag; self-service cafeteria, airport code: PSA, tel. 050-849-300, www.pisa-airport.com).

To get into **Pisa,** you can take bus LAM Rossa (4-6/hour, after 20:00 3/hour, 15 minutes, €1.10, departs from in front of the arrivals hall); a train (departs from the far left of the arrivals hall as you face the exits); or a taxi (€10-12).

You can connect to **Florence** easily by train (2-3/hour, 1.25 hours, €5.80, most transfer at Pisa Centrale) or by Terravision bus (about hourly, 1.25 hours, €10 one-way, ticket kiosk is at the right end of the arrivals hall as you're facing the exits, catch bus outside and to the far right of the bus parking lot, www.terravision.eu).

Lucca

Surrounded by well-preserved ramparts, layered with history, alternately quaint and urbane, Lucca charms its visitors. The city is a paradox. Though it hasn't been involved in a war since 1430, it is Italy's most impressive fortress city, encircled by a perfectly intact wall. Most cities tear down their wall to make way for modern traffic. But Lucca's wall effectively keeps out both traffic and, it seems, the stress of the modern world. Locals are very protective of their wall, which they enjoy like a community roof garden.

Lucca, known for being Europe's leading producer of toilet paper and tissue (with a monopoly on the special machinery that makes it), is nothing to sneeze at. However, the town has no single monumental sight to attract tourists—it's simply a uniquely human and undamaged, never-bombed city. Romanesque churches seem to be around every corner, as do fun-loving and shady piazzas filled with soccer-playing children.

Locals say Lucca is like a cake with a cherry filling in the middle...every slice is equally good. Despite Lucca's charm, few tourists seem to put it on their maps, and it remains a city for the Lucchesi (loo-KAY-zee).

Planning Your Time

Low-impact Lucca has no must-see sights, but its pleasant ambience, ample churches, and pristine piazzas reward any time you've got. With the better part of a day, stroll through the town center, dipping into the sights that interest you. Once you've had your fill, rent a bike and do a few spins around the ramparts (or do the loop in slow motion, by foot) before dinner.

Orientation to Lucca

Tourist Information

Lucca has two TIs. The bigger TI, on **Piazzale Giuseppe Verdi**, offers city information and a no-fee room-booking service (daily 9:00-19:00, futuristic WC-€0.60, tel. 0583-583-150, www.luccaitinera.it). It also has Internet access, baggage storage, and bike rentals (all described under "Helpful Hints," later) and guided city walks (see "Tours in Lucca," later).

The other TI is in a kiosk near the train station. As you exit the piazza in front of the station, look for it to the right on **Piazza Curtatone** (daily May-Sept 9:00-19:00, Oct-April 9:00-13:00 & 14:00-18:00, no-fee room booking, baggage storage—see "Helpful Hints," later, tel. 0583-496-639).

Arrival in Lucca

By Train: There is no baggage check at the train station, but you can leave your luggage at either TI described above, or in a pinch, at the recommended Hotel Rex, near the train station (see "Helpful Hints," later).

To reach the city center from the train station, walk toward the walls and head left, to the entry at Porta San Pietro. Taxis are sparse, but try calling 025-353 (ignore any recorded message— just wait for a live operator); a ride from the station to Piazza dell'Anfiteatro costs about €6.

By Bus: Buses from Pisa, Viareggio, and from nearby villages arrive inside the walls at Piazzale Giuseppe Verdi, where the main TI is located.

By Car: The key for drivers—don't try to drive within the walls. The old town is ringed by parking lots (with two just inside the walls, both usually full).

An easy option is to park near the tour bus lot, not far from the southwest wall. As you leave the autostrada, follow signs for *Bus Turistico Checkpoint*, which will lead you to parking lots on Via Luporini—one is for buses but the other has free and paid parking for cars. White lines denote free parking, and blue lines are paid parking (daily 8:00-20:00, €1-1.50/hour, pay at automated kiosks).

Avoid the yellow lines—these spots are for locals only. From here it's about a five-minute walk to Porta Sant'Anna.

Parking is always free in Piazzale Don Franco, a five-minute walk north of the city walls. If you must park inside the city walls, try just inside Porta Santa Maria (€1/hour). Or consider parking outside the gates near the train station or on the boulevard surrounding the city (meter rates vary; also about €1/hour). Overnight parking (20:00-8:00) on city streets and in city lots is usually free. Check with your hotel to be sure.

Helpful Hints

Combo-Tickets: A €7 combo-ticket includes visits to the Ilaria del Carretto tomb in San Martino Cathedral (€3), Cathedral Museum (€4), and San Giovanni Church (€4). A €6 combo-ticket combines the Guinigi Tower (€4) and the Clock Tower (€4). Yet another combo-ticket covers Palazzo Mansi and Villa Guinigi for €6.50 and is valid for three days (€4 each if purchased separately).

Shops and Museums Alert: Shops close most of Sunday and Monday mornings. Many museums are closed on Monday as well.

Markets: Lucca's atmospheric markets are worth visiting. Every third weekend of the month (wherever the third Sun falls), one of the largest **antiques markets** in Italy unfurls in the blocks between Piazza Antelminelli and Piazza San Giovanni (8:00-19:00). The last weekend of the month, local artisans sell **arts and crafts** around town, mainly near the cathedral (also 8:00-19:00). At the **general market,** held Wednesdays and Saturdays, you'll find produce and household goods (8:30-13:00, from Porta Elisa to Porta San Jacopo on Via dei Bacchettoni).

Concerts: San Giovanni Church hosts one-hour concerts featuring a pianist and singers performing highlights from hometown composer Giacomo Puccini (€17 at the door, some hotels offer tickets for the same price or cheaper, daily April-Oct at 19:00, Nov-March check schedule and location at www .puccinielasualucca.com).

Festival: On September 13 and 14, the city celebrates Volto Santo ("Holy Face"), with a procession of the treasured local crucifix and a fair in Piazza Antelminelli.

Internet Access: You can get online at the main TI on Piazzale Giuseppe Verdi (€2/hour, two terminals, Wi-Fi same price) or at **Betty Blue,** a wine bar handy to the recommended launderette (€4.50/hour, two terminals and cables to plug in your laptop, Thu-Tue 11:00-24:00, closed Wed, Via del Gonfalone 18, tel. 0583-492-166).

Lucca

200 Meters
200 Yards

PISA AND LUCCA

V. MAT-
To P

VIA DELLE TAGLIATE TERZA

VIALE CARLO DEL PRETE

TUNNEL
UNDER
RAMPARTS

N

RAMPARTS

SAN
FREDIANO

PASSAGIATA DELLE MURA

Piazza
S. Agostino

PALAZZO
PFANNER

P

PORTA
SAN DONATO

PANIFICIO
VIA DELLO STUFA
VIA C. BATTISTI

VIA PELLERIA

VIA ASILI

SAN
LORETO

VIA GIORGIO

VIA
VIA DEL MORO

DA
SIMO
CAFFÈ

VIA SANTA GIUSTINA

PUCCINI'S
HOUSE

VIA FILLUNGO

VIA TOMMASO

TEGNINI

CALDERIA

VIA FILLUNGO

Piazzale
San Donato

PALAZZO
MANSI

VIA TORO

VIA POGGIO

SAN
MICHELE

VIA SAN
PAOLINO

VIA GALLIASSI

Piazza
San Michele

VIA LAZZARO PAPI

PORTA VITTORIO
EMANUELE/
PORTA SANT'ANNA

Piazzale
Giuseppe
Verdi
Bus to Pisa
Bus Tickets

SAN
PAULINO

VIA VITTORIO

EMANUELE II

VIA BURLAMACCHI

BECCHERIA

V. BATTISTERO

V. CENAMI

VIA LUPORINI

VIALE

VIA DEL PILLONE

CITTADELLA

VIA DEI TABACCHI

Piazza
Napoleone

SAN
ROMANO

VIA DELLA CASERMA

Piazza
d. Giglio

SAN
GIOVANNI

V. IDELFONGSO NIERI

PASSAGIATA DELLE MURA

VIA VITTORIO VENETO

CORSO GARIBALDI

GIOSUÈ

VIALE
EUROPA

CARDUCCI

VIA FRANCESCO CARRARA

P

V. REPUBBLICA

VIA

PORTA
SAN PIETRO

To Autostrada

P

V. CAMILLO CAVOUR

To

---

① La Romea B&B
② La Locanda Sant'Agostino
③ La Bohème B&B
④ Hotel la Luna
⑤ Alla Dimora Lucense
⑥ Hotel Universo
⑦ La Magnolia B&B

⑧ Hotel Diana
⑨ Le Violette B&B
⑩ Ostello San Frediano
⑪ To Hotel San Marco
⑫ Hotel Rex
⑬ To Hotel Moderno
⑭ Sogni d'Oro Guest House

15 Ristorante Canuleia
16 Vineria I Santi
17 Osteria Via San Giorgio
18 Vecchia Trattoria Buralli
19 Trattoria da Leo
20 Bella 'Mbriana Pizzeria

21 Il Cuore Ristorante
22 Pizzeria da Felice
23 Betty Blue (Internet Access)
24 Launderette
25 Bike Rentals (3)

Baggage Storage: For train travelers, the most convenient storage spot is the TI on **Piazza Curtatone** (2 bags for €4.50/5 hours, €7/day, daily 9:00-17:30, they need to photocopy your passport). The TI on **Piazzale Giuseppe Verdi** is more convenient to the buses and has longer hours (same prices and passport procedure as other TI, daily 9:00-18:30). In a pinch, you also may be able to store bags at the recommended Hotel Rex (near the train station).

Laundry: Lavanderia Self-Service Niagara is just off Piazza Santa Maria at Via Rosi 26 (€9 wash and dry, daily 7:00-23:00).

Bike Rental: A one-hour rental gives you time for two leisurely loops around the ramparts. Several places with identical prices cluster around Piazza Santa Maria (€3/hour, €15/day, tandem bikes available, helmets available on request, daily about 9:00-19:00 or sunset). Try these easygoing shops: **Antonio Poli** (Piazza Santa Maria 42, tel. 0583-493-787, enthusiastic Cristiana) and, right next to it, **Cicli Bizzarri** (Piazza Santa Maria 32, tel. 0583-496-682, Australian Dely). At the west end of town, the **TI** on Piazzale Giuseppe Verdi rents bikes (€3/hour). At the south end, at Porta San Pietro, you'll find **Chrono** (same rates and hours as the competition, Corso Garibaldi 93, tel. 0583-490-591, www.chronobikes.com).

Local Magazine: For insights into American and British expat life and listings of concerts, markets, festivals, and other special events, pick up a copy of the *Grapevine* (€2), available at newsstands.

Cooking Class: Gianluca Pardini invites you to the hills above Lucca to learn to make Tuscan fare. You prepare and then eat a three-course meal. Depending on how many others attend, the price ranges from €50 (a steal) to a whopping €125 per person. This is great for groups of four or more (€14 cab ride from town, 3-hour lesson plus time to dine, includes wine, reserve at least 2 days in advance, Via di San Viticchio 414, tel. 0583-378-071, mobile 347-678-7447, www.italiancuisine.it, info@italiancuisine.it).

Tours in Lucca

Walking Tours—The TI offers two-hour city walks with a local guide, departing from the office on Piazzale Giuseppe Verdi (€10, Mon-Sat at 14:30, Sun at 9:30, tel. 0583-583-150).

Local Guide—Gabriele Calabrese knows and shares his hometown well (€120/3 hours, by foot or bike, mobile 347-788-0667, www.turislucca.com, turislucca@turislucca.com).

Sights in Lucca

▲▲**Bike the Ramparts**—Lucca's most remarkable feature, its Renaissance wall, is also its most enjoyable attraction—especially when circled on a rental bike. Stretching for 2.5 miles, this is an ideal place to come for an overview of the city by foot or bike.

Lucca has had a protective wall for 2,000 years. You can read three walls into today's map: the first rectangular Roman wall, the later medieval wall (nearly the size of today's), and the 16th-century Renaissance wall that still survives.

With the advent of cannons, thin medieval walls were suddenly vulnerable. A new design—the same one that stands today—was state-of-the-art when it was built (1550-1650). Much of the old medieval wall (look for the old stones) was incorporated into the Renaissance wall (with uniform bricks). The new wall was squat: a 100-foot-wide mound of dirt faced with bricks, engineered to absorb a cannonball pummeling. The townspeople cleared a wide no man's land around the town, exposing any attackers from a distance. Eleven heart-shaped bastions (now inviting picnic areas) were designed to minimize exposure to cannonballs and to maximize defense capabilities. The ramparts were armed with 130 cannons.

The town invested a third of its income for more than a century to construct the wall, and—since it kept away the Florentines and nasty Pisans—it was considered a fine investment. In fact, nobody ever bothered to try to attack the wall. Locals say that the only time it actually defended the city was during an 1812 flood of the Serchio River, when the gates were sandbagged and its ramparts kept out the high water.

Today, the ramparts seem made-to-order for a leisurely bike ride (20-minute pedal, wonderfully smooth). You can rent bikes cheaply and easily from one of several bike-rental places in town (listed earlier, under "Helpful Hints").

Piazza dell'Anfiteatro—Just off the main shopping street, the architectural ghost of a Roman amphitheater can be felt in the delightful Piazza dell'Anfiteatro. With the fall of Rome, the theater (which seated 10,000) was gradually cannibalized for its stones and inhabited by people living in a mishmash of huts. The huts were cleared away at the end of the 19th century to better appreciate the

The History of Lucca

Lucca began as a Roman settlement. In fact, the grid layout of the streets (and the shadow of an amphitheater) survives from Roman times. Trace the rectangular Roman wall—indicated by today's streets—on the map. As in typical Roman towns, two main roads quartered the fortified town, crossing at what was the forum (main market and religious/political center)—today's Piazza San Michele.

Christianity came here early; it's said that the first bishop of Lucca was a disciple of St. Peter. While churches were built here as early as the fourth century, the majority of Lucca's elegant Romanesque churches date from about the 12th century.

Feisty Lucca, though never a real power, enjoyed a long period of independence (maintained by clever diplomacy). Aside from 30 years of being ruled from Pisa in the 14th century, Lucca was basically an independent city-state until Napoleon came to town.

In the Middle Ages, wealthy Lucca's economy was built on the silk industry, dominated by the Guinigi (gwee-NEE-gee) family. Without silk, Lucca would have been just another sleepy Italian town. In 1500, the town had 3,000 silk looms employing 25,000 workers. Banking was also big. Many pilgrims stopped here on their way to the Holy Land, deposited their money for safety...and never returned to pick it up.

In its heyday, Lucca packed 160 towers—one on nearly every corner—and 70 churches within its walls. Each tower was the home of a wealthy merchant family. Towers were many stories tall, with single rooms stacked atop each other: ground-floor shop, upstairs living room, and top-floor firesafe kitchen, all connected by exterior wooden staircases. The rooftop was generally a vegetable garden, with trees providing shade. Later, the wealthy city folk moved into the countryside, trading away life in their city palazzos to establish farm estates complete with fancy villas. (You can visit some of these villas today—the TI has a brochure—but they're convenient only for drivers and are generally not worth the cost of admission.)

In 1799, Napoleon stormed into Italy and took a liking to Lucca. He liked it so much that he gave it to his sister as a gift (who ruled 1805-14). After Napoleon was toppled, Europe's ruling powers gave Lucca to Maria Luisa, the daughter of the king of Spain. Duchess Maria Luisa (who ruled 1817-24) was partially responsible for turning the city's imposing (but no longer particularly useful) fortified wall into a fine city park that is much enjoyed today. Her statue stands on Piazza Napoleone, near Palazzo Ducale.

town's illustrious past. Today, the square is a circle of touristy shops and mediocre restaurants that becomes a lively bar-and-café scene after dark. The modern street level is nine feet above the original arena floor. The only bits of surviving Roman stonework are a few arches on the northern exterior (at Via Fillungo 42 and on Via dell'Anfiteatro).

Via Fillungo—This main pedestrian drag stretches southwest from Piazza dell'Anfiteatro. *The* street to stroll, Via Fillungo takes you from the amphitheater almost all the way to the cathedral. Along the way, you'll get a taste of Lucca's rich past, including several elegant, century-old storefronts. Many of the original storefront paintings, reliefs, and mosaics survive—even if today's shopkeeper sells something entirely different.

At #97 is a classic old **jewelry store** with a rare storefront that has kept its T-shaped arrangement (when closed, you see a wooden T, and during open hours it unfolds with a fine old-time display). This design dates from a time when the merchant sold his goods in front, did his work in the back, and lived upstairs.

Di Simo Caffè, at #58, has long been the hangout of Lucca's artistic and intellectual elite. Composer and hometown boy Giacomo Puccini tapped his foot while sipping coffee here. Pop in to check out the 1880s ambience (daily 9:00-24:00).

A surviving five-story **tower house** is at #67. There was a time when nearly every corner sported its own tower (see the sidebar). The stubby stones that still stick out once supported wooden staircases (there were no interior connections between floors). So many towers cast shadows over this part of town that the street just before it is called Via Buia (Dark Street). Look away from this tower and down Via San Andrea for a peek at the town's tallest tower, Guinigi, in the distance—with its characteristic oak trees sprouting from the top.

At #45 and #43, you'll see two more good examples of tower houses. Across the street, the **Clock Tower** (Torre delle Ore) has a hand-wound Swiss clock that has clanged four times an hour since 1754 (€4 to climb up and see the mechanism flip into action on the quarter-hour—if it's actually working, €6 combo-ticket includes Guinigi Tower, daily April-Oct 9:30-18:30, Nov-March 9:30-16:30, last entry 20 minutes before closing, corner of Via Fillungo and Via del'Arancio).

The intersection of Via Fillungo and Via Roma/Via Santa

Croce marks the center of town (where the two original Roman roads crossed). As you go right down Via Roma, you'll pass the fine Edison Bookstore on your left before reaching Piazza San Michele.

Piazza San Michele—This square has been the center of town since Roman times, when it was the forum. It's dominated by the Church of San Michele. Towering above the church's fancy Pisan Romanesque facade, the archangel Michael stands ready to flap his wings—which he was known to do on special occasions.

The square is surrounded by an architectural hodgepodge. The loggia, which dates from 1495, is the first Renaissance building in town. There's a late 19th-century interior in Buccellato Taddeucci, a 130-year old pastry shop (#34). The left section of the BNL bank (#5; in front of the church) sports an Art Nouveau facade that celebrates both Amerigo Vespucci and Cristoforo Colombo.

Perhaps you've noticed that the statues of big shots that decorate many an Italian piazza are mostly absent from Lucca's squares. That's because unlike Venice, Florence, and Milan—which were dominated by a few powerful dynasties—Lucca was traditionally run by an oligarchy of a hundred leading families, with no one central figure to commemorate in stone. But after Italian unification, when leaders were fond of saying, "We have created Italy... now we need to create Italians," stirring statues of national heroes popped up everywhere—even in Lucca. The statue on Piazza San Michele is a two-bit local guy, dredged up centuries after his death because he favored strong central government.

Look back at the church facade, which also has an element of patriotism—designed to give roots and legitimacy to Italian statehood. Perched above many of the columns are the faces of heroes in the Italian independence and unification movement: Victor Emmanuel II (above the short red column on the right), the Count of Cavour (next to Victor, above the column with black zigzags), and Giuseppe Mazzini.

▲San Martino Cathedral—This cathedral, begun in the 11th century, is an entertaining mix of architectural and artistic styles. It's also home to the exquisite 15th-century tomb of Ilaria del Carretto, who married into the wealthy Guinigi family.

Cost and Hours: Cathedral—free, Ilaria tomb—€3, €7 combo-ticket includes Cathedral Museum and San Giovanni Church; Mon-Fri 9:30-17:45, Sat 9:30-18:45; Sun open sporadically between Masses: 9:00-10:15 & 11:30-18:00; Piazza San Martino.

Visiting the Cathedral: The cathedral's elaborate Pisan Romanesque **facade** features Christian teaching scenes, animals, and candy-cane-striped columns.

The central figure is St. Martin, a Roman military officer from Hungary who, by offering his cloak to a beggar, more fully understood the beauty of Christian compassion. (The impressive original, a fine example of Romanesque sculpture, hides from pollution just inside, to the right of the main entrance.) Each of the columns on the facade is unique. Notice how the facade is asymmetrical: The 11th-century bell tower was already in place when the rest of the cathedral was built, so the builders cheated on the right side to make it fit the space. Over the right portal (as if leaning against the older tower), the architect Guideo from Como holds a document declaring that he finished the facade in 1204. On the

right (at eye level on the pilaster), a labyrinth is set into the wall. The maze relates the struggle and challenge our souls face in finding salvation. (French pilgrims on their way to Rome could relate to this, as it's the same pattern they knew from the floor of the church at Chartres.) The Latin plaque just left of the main door is where moneychangers and spice traders met to seal deals (on the doorstep of the church—to underscore the reliability of their promises). Notice the date: *An Dni MCXI* (A.D. 1111).

The interior features Gothic arches, Renaissance paintings, and stained glass from the 19th century. On the left side of the nave, a small, elaborate, birdcage-like temple contains the wooden crucifix—beloved by locals—called **Volto Santo**. It's said to have been sculpted by Nicodemus in Jerusalem and set afloat in an unmanned boat that landed on the coast of Tuscany, from where wild oxen miraculously carried it to Lucca in 782. The sculpture (which is actually 12th-century Byzantine-style) has quite a jewelry collection, which you can see in the Cathedral Museum (described next).

On the right side of the nave, the sacristy houses the enchantingly beautiful **memorial tomb of Ilaria del Carretto** by Jacopo della Quercia (1407). Pick up a handy English description to the right of the door as you enter the sacristy. This young bride of silk baron Paolo Guinigi is decked out in the latest, most expensive fashions, with the requisite little dog (symbolizing her loyalty) curled up at her feet in eternal sleep. She's so realistic that the statue was nicknamed "Sleeping Beauty." Her nose is partially worn off because of a long-standing tradition of lonely young ladies rubbing it for luck in finding a boyfriend.

Cathedral Museum (Museo della Cattedrale)—This beautifully presented museum houses original paintings, sculptures, and vestments from the cathedral and other Lucca churches. The first room displays jewelry made to dress up the Volto Santo crucifix (described above), including gigantic gilded silver shoes. Upstairs, notice the fine red brocaded silk—a reminder that this precious fabric is what brought riches and power to the city. The exhibits in this museum have very brief descriptions and are meaningful only with the slow-talking €1 audioguide—if you're not in the mood to listen, skip the place altogether.

Cost and Hours: €4, €7 combo-ticket includes Ilaria tomb and San Giovanni Church; April-Oct daily 10:00-18:00; Nov-March Mon-Fri 10:00-14:00, Sat-Sun 10:00-17:00; to the left of the cathedral as you're facing it, Piazza Antelminelli, tel. 0583-490-530, www.museocattedralelucca.it.

San Giovanni Church—This first cathedral of Lucca is interesting only for its archaeological finds. The entire floor of the 12th-century church has been excavated in recent decades, revealing layers of Roman houses, ancient hot tubs that date back to the time of Christ, early churches, and theological graffiti. Sporadic English translations help you understand what you're looking at. As you climb under the church's present-day floor and wander the lanes of Roman Lucca, remember that the entire city sits on similar ruins. If it's open, climb the *campanile* (bell tower) of the church for a panoramic view of the city.

Cost and Hours: €4, €7 combo-ticket includes Ilaria tomb and Cathedral Museum, audioguide-€1; mid-March-Oct daily 10:00-18:00; Nov-mid-March Sat-Sun 10:00-17:00, closed Mon-Fri; see concert info on page 563; kitty-corner from cathedral at Piazza San Giovanni.

Church of San Frediano—This impressive church was built in 1112 by the pope to counter Lucca's bishop and his spiffy cathedral. Lucca was the first Mediterranean stop on the pilgrim route from northern Europe, and the pope wanted to remind pilgrims that the action, the glory, and the papacy awaited them in Rome. Therefore, he had the church made "Roman-esque." The pure marble facade frames an early Christian Roman-style mosaic of Christ with his 12 apostles. Step inside and you're struck by the sight of 40 powerful (if recycled) ancient Roman columns. The message: Lucca may be impressive, but the finale of your pilgrimage—in Rome—is worth the hike.

Inside, there's a notable piece of art in each corner: At rear left is the 12th-century baptistery, with some interesting Church propaganda showing the story of Moses (the evil Egyptians are played by Holy Roman Empire troops). At rear right is St. Zita's actual body, put there in 1278. At front left is a particularly elegant Virgin

Mary, depicted at the moment she gets the news that she'll bring the Messiah into the world (carved and painted by Lucchesi artist Matteo Civitali, c. 1460). And at front right is a painting on wood of the *Assumption of the Virgin* (c. 1510), with Doubting Thomas receiving Mary's red belt as she ascends so he'll doubt no more. The pinball-machine composition serves as a virtual catalog of the fine silk material produced in Lucca—a major industry in the 16th century.

Cost and Hours: Free, Mon-Sat 8:30-12:00 & 15:00-17:30, Sun 9:00-11:30 & 15:00-17:30, Piazza San Frediano, tel. 0583-493-627.

Palazzo Mansi—Minor paintings by Tintoretto, Pontormo, Veronese, and others vie for attention, but the palace itself—a sumptuously furnished and decorated 17th-century confection—steals the show. This is your chance to appreciate the wealth of Lucca's silk merchants. Since all visitors must be accompanied by a museum employee, during high season you may have to wait a bit for your chance to enter.

Cost and Hours: €4, €6.50 combo-ticket includes Villa Guinigi, hours prone to change but generally Tue-Sat 8:30-19:30, Sun 8:30-13:30, closed Mon, no photos, request English booklet at ticket desk, Via Galli Tassi 43, tel. 0583-55-570.

Guinigi Tower (Torre Guinigi)—Many Tuscan towns have towers, but none is quite like the Guinigi family's. Up 227 steps is a small garden with fragrant trees, surrounded by fantastic views.

Cost and Hours: €4, €6 combo-ticket includes Clock Tower, daily April-May 9:30-18:30, June-Sept 9:30-19:30, March and Oct 9:30-17:30, Nov-Feb 9:30-16:30, Via Sant'Andrea 41.

Puccini's House—Opera enthusiasts (but nobody else) will want to visit the home where Giacomo Puccini (1858-1924) grew up. The museum has the great composer's piano and a small collection of his personal belongings, as well as opera costumes and memorabilia.

Cost and Hours: €7; April-Oct Wed-Mon 10:00-18:00, Nov-March Wed-Mon 11:00-17:00, closed Tue year-round; Corte San Lorenzo 9, ring to be let in, tel. 0583-584-028, www.puccinimuseum.it.

Palazzo Pfanner—Garden enthusiasts (and anyone needing a break from churches) will enjoy this 18th-century palace built for a rich Swiss expat who came to Lucca to open a brewery. His sudsy legacy includes Baroque furniture, elaborate frescoes, a centuries-old kitchen, and a lavish garden.

Cost and Hours: Garden or residence-€4.50 apiece, €6 for both, April-Oct daily 10:00-18:00, closed Nov-March, Via degli Asili 33, tel. 0583-954-029, www.palazzopfanner.it.

Villa Guinigi—Built by Paolo Guinigi in 1418, the family villa is now a stark, abandoned-feeling museum displaying a hodgepodge of Etruscan artifacts, religious sculptures, paintings, inlaid wood-work, and ceramics. Monumental paintings by the multitalented Giorgio Vasari are the best reason to visit.

Cost and Hours: €4, €6.50 combo-ticket includes Palazzo Mansi, Tue-Sat 8:30-19:30, Sun 8:30-13:30, closed Mon, may have to wait in high season for a museum employee to accompany you, Via della Quarquonia, tel. 0583-496-033.

Sleeping in Lucca

Fancy Little Boutique B&Bs Within the Walls

$$$ La Romea B&B, in an air-conditioned, restored, 14th-century palazzo near Guinigi Tower, feels like a royal splurge. Its four posh rooms and one suite are lavishly decorated in handsome colors and surround a big, plush lounge with stately Venetian-style floors (Db-€100-135 depending on season, big suite-€160, extra bed-€20-25; 10 percent discount when you book direct, show this book, and pay cash; Wi-Fi; from the train station, take Via Fillungo, turn right on Via Sant'Andrea, then take the second right to Vicolo delle Ventaglie 2; tel. 0583-464-175, www.laromea.com, info@laromea.com, Giulio and wife Gaia).

$$$ La Locanda Sant'Agostino has three romantic, bright, and palatial rooms. The vine-draped terrace, beautiful break-fast spread, and quaint views invite you to relax (Db-€160, extra bed-€25, air-con, Internet access and Wi-Fi, from Via Fillungo take Via San Giorgio to Piazza Sant'Agostino 3, best to reserve by email, tel. 0583-443-100, mobile 347-989-9069, www.locanda santagostino.it, info@locandasantagostino.it).

$$$ La Bohème B&B has a cozy yet elegant ambience, offer-ing six large, charming, chandeliered rooms, each painted with a different rich color scheme (Db-€125, less off-season, 10 per-cent discount with this book if you pay cash and book direct, air-con, free Wi-Fi, Via del Moro 2, tel. & fax 0583-462-404, www.boheme.it, info@boheme.it, Sara).

Sleeping More Forgettably Within the Walls

$$$ Hotel la Luna, run by the Barbieri family, has 29 rooms in a great location, right in the heart of the city. Updated rooms are split between two adjacent buildings just off of the main shopping street. The annex may have an elevator, but I prefer the rooms in the main building, which are larger and classier (Sb-€90, Db-€125, suite-€190, these prices for Rick Steves readers who book direct, air-con, pay Internet access and Wi-Fi, parking-€15/day, Via Fillungo at Corte Compagni 12, tel. 0583-493-634, fax 0583-490-021, www.hotellaluna.com, info@hotellaluna.com, Sara).

$$$ **Alla Dimora Lucense**'s seven newer rooms are bright, modern, clean, and peaceful, with all the comforts. Enjoy their relaxing, sunny interior courtyard (Db-€125, suite for 2-4 people-€150-200; 10 percent discount if you pay cash, book direct, and show this book; air-con, Wi-Fi, half a block from Via Fillungo at Via Fontana 19, tel. 0583-495-722, fax 0583-441-210, www.dimoralucense.it, info@dimoralucense.it).

$$ **Hotel Universo,** renting 55 rooms right on Piazza Napoleone and facing the theater and Palazzo Ducale, is a 19th-century town fixture. While it clearly was once elegant, now it's old and tired, with a big Old World lounge and soft prices ("comfort" Db-€100, "superior" Db with updated bath-€130, Wi-Fi, Piazza del Giglio 1, tel. 0583-493-678, www.universolucca.com, info@universolucca.com).

$$ **La Magnolia B&B** offers five basic rooms and one apartment with an intimate atmosphere and relaxing garden. It's buried in a ramshackle old palace in a central location (Sb-€65, Db-€85, Qb-€90, includes breakfast at nearby bar, 5 percent discount with this book if you pay cash and book direct, a block behind amphitheater at Via Mordini 63, tel. 0583-467-111, www.lamagnolia.com, info@lamagnolia.com, Andrea and Laura).

$ **Hotel Diana** is a dreary little family-run hotel, with nine rooms in the main building and another six slightly nicer, soundproofed, and air-conditioned rooms in the annex just around the corner (D-€50, Db-€65, annex Db-€85, Wi-Fi, parking-€6/day, south of the cathedral at Via del Molinetto 11, tel. 0583-492-202, fax 0583-467-795, www.albergodiana.com, info@albergodiana.com).

$ At **Le Violette B&B,** friendly Anna (who's still learning English) will settle you into one of her six homey rooms near the train station inside Porta San Pietro (D-€60, Db-€75, extra bed-€15, Wi-Fi, communal kitchen, €5 to use washer and dryer, Via della Polveriera 6, tel. 0583-493-594, mobile 349-823-4645, fax 0583-429-305, www.leviolette.it, leviolette@virgilio.it).

$ **Ostello San Frediano,** in a central, sprawling ex-convent with a peaceful garden, is a cut above the average hostel, though it's still filled mainly with a young crowd. Its 29 rooms are bright and modern, and some have fun lofts (€20 beds in 6- to 8-person dorms, 140 beds, Db-€65, Tb-€80, Qb-€105, includes sheets, €3 extra/night for non-members, cash only, breakfast extra, no curfew, lockers, Internet access and Wi-Fi, cheap restaurant, free parking, Via della Cavallerizza 12, tel. 0583-469-957, fax 0583-461-007, www.ostellolucca.it, info@ostellolucca.it).

Outside the Walls

$$$ Hotel San Marco, a seven-minute walk outside the Porta Santa Maria, is a postmodern place decorated à la Stanley Kubrick. Its 42 rooms are sleek, with all the comforts (Sb-€87, Db-€136, extra bed-€10, includes nice breakfast spread, air-con, Wi-Fi, elevator, pool, bikes-€6/half-day, free parking, taxi from station-€6, Via San Marco 368, tel. 0583-495-010, fax 0583-490-513, www.hotelsanmarcolucca.com, info@hotelsanmarcolucca.com).

$$ Hotel Rex rents 25 rooms in a practical contemporary building on the train station square. While in the modern world, you're just 200 yards away from the old town and get more space for a better price (Db-€80-100; 10 percent discount with this book if you pay cash and book direct, does not apply to prepaid/non-refundable rooms booked online; air-con, Wi-Fi, free bike rental, a few steps from the train station at Piazza Ricasoli 19, tel. 0583-955-443, www.hotelrexlucca.com, info@hotelrexlucca.com).

$$ Hotel Moderno is indeed modern, with 11 good-value rooms tastefully decorated in shades of white. Although it backs up to the train tracks, the rooms are quiet (Sb-€70, Db-€90, air-con, Wi-Fi, Via Vincenzo Civitali 38—turn left out of train station and go over bridge across tracks, tel. 0583-55-840, fax 0583-53-830, www.albergomodernolucca.com, info@albergomodernolucca.com).

$ Sogni d'Oro Guest House ("Dreams of Gold"), run by Davide, is a handy budget option for drivers, with five basic rooms and a cheery communal kitchen (grocery store next door). It's a 10-minute walk from the train station and a five-minute walk from the city walls (D-€50, Db-€65, Q-€70, 10 percent discount with cash; free ride to and from station with advance notice—then call when your train arrives in Lucca; from the station, head straight out to Viale Regina Margherita and turn right, follow the main boulevard as it turns into Viale Giuseppe Giusti, at the curve turn right onto Via Antonio Cantore to #169; tel. 0583-467-768, mobile 329-582-5062, fax 0583-957-612, www.bbsognidoro.com, info@bbsognidoro.com).

Eating in Lucca

Ristorante Canuleia makes everything fresh in their small kitchen. While the portions aren't huge, the food is tasty. You can eat in their dressy little dining room or outside on the garden courtyard (€10 pastas, €17 *secondi*, Mon-Sat 12:30-14:00 & 19:30-

Specialties in Lucca

Lucca has some tasty specialties worth seeking out. *Ceci* (CHEH-chee), also called *cecina* (cheh-CHEE-nah), makes an ideal cheap snack any time of day. This garbanzo-bean crepe is sold in pizza shops and is best accompanied by a nip of red wine.

Farro, a grain (spelt) dating back to ancient Roman cuisine, shows up in restaurants in soups or as a creamy rice-like dish *(risotto di farro).*

Tordelli, the Lucchesi version of *tortelli,* is homemade ravioli. It's traditionally stuffed with meat and served with more meat sauce, but chefs creatively pair cheeses and vegetables, too.

Meat, not fish, is the star at most restaurants, especially steak, which is listed on menus as *filetto di manzo* (filet), *tagliata di manzo* (thin slices of grilled tenderloin), or the king of steaks, *bistecca alla fiorentina.* Order *al sangue* (rare), *medio* (medium rare), *cotto* (medium), or *ben cotto* (well). Anything more than *al sangue* is considered a travesty for steak connoisseurs.

Note that steaks (as well as fish) are often sold by weight, noted on menus as *s.q.* (according to quantity ordered) or *l'etto* (cost per 100 grams—250 grams is about an 8-ounce steak).

For something sweet, bakeries sell *buccellato,* bread dotted with raisins, lightly flavored with anise, and often shaped like a wreath. It's only sold in large sizes, but luckily it stays good for a few days (and it also pairs well with *vin santo*—fortified Tuscan dessert wine). An old proverb says, "Coming to Lucca without eating the *buccellato* is like not having come at all." *Buon appetito!*

21:30, closed Sun, Via Canuleia 14, tel. 0583-467-470, reserve for dinner).

Vineria I Santi is pricey but good if you appreciate quality food and fine wine, and just want to lie back and be pampered. The sexy jazz ambience would work well in a bordello. Relax in the peaceful indoors among wine bottles, or on a quiet square outside (€11 pastas, €18 *secondi,* Thu-Tue 12:30-14:30 & 19:30-22:00, closed Wed, Via dell'Anfiteatro 29, tel. 0583-496-124).

Osteria Via San Giorgio, owned by Daniela and her brother Piero, is a cheery family eatery that satisfies both fish lovers and meat lovers. Sample the splittable *antipasto fantasia*—five small courses such as *ceviche* (seafood salad), scallops au gratin, squid sautéed with potatoes, or whatever else was caught that day in Viareggio; they also offer a meatier version. Dinner-size salads are bright and fresh, pasta is homemade, and Daniela's desserts tempt (daily 12:00-16:00 & 19:00-23:00, Via San Giorgio 26, tel. 0583-953-233).

Vecchia Trattoria Buralli, on quiet Piazza Sant'Agostino, is a good bet for traditional cooking and juicy steaks, with fine indoor and piazza seating (€7 pastas, €10 *secondi,* €12-30 fixed-price meals, Thu-Tue 12:00-14:45 & 19:00-22:30, closed Wed, Piazza Sant'Agostino 10, tel. 0583-950-611).

Trattoria da Leo packs in chatty locals for typical, cheap home cooking in a hash-slingin' Mel's-diner atmosphere. This place is a high-energy winner...you know it's going to be good as soon as you step in. Arrive early or reserve in advance (€6 pastas, €10 *secondi,* Mon-Sat 12:00-14:30 & 19:30-22:30, sometimes open Sun, cash only, leave Piazza San Salvatore on Via Asili and take the first left to Via Tegrimi 1, tel. 0583-492-236).

Bella 'Mbriana Pizzeria focuses on doing one thing very well: turning out piping-hot, wood-fired pizzas to happy locals in a welcoming wood-paneled dining room. Order and pay at the counter, take a number, and they'll call you when your pizza's ready. Consider takeout to munch on the nearby walls (Wed-Mon 12:30-14:30 & 18:30-23:00, closed Tue, to the right as you face the Church of San Frediano, Via della Cavallerizza 29, tel. 0583-495-565).

Il Cuore Enogastronomia includes a delicatessen and restaurant. For a fancy picnic, drop in the deli for ready-to-eat lasagna, saucy meatballs, grilled and roasted vegetables, vegetable soufflés, Tuscan bean soup, fruit salads, and more, sold by weight and dished up in disposable trays to go. Ask them to heat your order *(riscaldare),* then picnic on nearby Piazza Napoleone. For curious traveling foodies on a budget who want to eat right there, they can assemble a €10 "degustation plate"—just point to what you want from among the array of tasty treats under the glass (Tue-Sun 9:30-19:30, closed Mon, Via del Battistero 2, tel. 0583-493-196, Cristina).

Il Cuore Ristorante, located across the way, is a trendy find for wine-tasting or a meal on a piazza. Try the €8 *aperitivo* (available 18:00-20:00), which includes a glass of wine and a plate of cheese, *salumi,* and snacks, or feast on fresh pastas and other high-quality dishes from their lunch and dinner menus (Wed-Sun 12:00-22:00 with limited menu 15:00-19:30, Tue 12:00-15:00, closed Mon, Via del Battistero, tel. 0583-493-196).

Pizzeria da Felice is a little mom-and-pop hole-in-the-wall serving *cecina* (garbanzo-bean crepes) and slices of freshly baked pizza to throngs of snackers. Grab an *etto* of *cecina* and a short glass of wine for €2.50 (Mon-Sat 10:00-20:30, closed Sun and 3 weeks in Aug, Via Buia 12, tel. 0583-494-986).

Lucca Connections

From Lucca by Train to: Florence (2/hour, 1.5 hours), **Pisa** (roughly 1-2/hour, 30 minutes, bus is better except on Sun), **Livorno** (about hourly, 1-1.25 hours, transfer at Pisa Centrale, €3.70), **Milan** (2/hour except Sun, 4-5 hours, transfer in Florence), **Rome** (1/hour except Sun, 3-4 hours, change in Florence).

From Lucca by Bus to Pisa: Direct buses from Lucca's Piazzale Giuseppe Verdi drop you right at the Leaning Tower, making Pisa an easy day trip (Mon-Sat hourly, fewer on Sun, 30 minutes, also stops at Pisa's airport, €3). Even with a car, I'd opt for this much faster and cheaper option.

SIENA

Siena was medieval Florence's archrival. And while Florence ultimately won the battle for political and economic superiority, Siena still competes for the tourists. Sure, Florence has the heavyweight sights. But Siena seems to be every Italy connoisseur's favorite town. In my office, whenever Siena is mentioned, someone moans, "Siena? I looove Siena!"

Once upon a time (about 1260-1348), Siena was a major banking and trade center, and a military power in a class with Florence, Venice, and Genoa. With a population of 60,000, it was even bigger than Paris. Situated on the north-south road to Rome (Via Francigena), Siena traded with all of Europe. Then, in 1348, the Black Death (bubonic plague) swept through Europe, hitting Siena and cutting the population by more than a third. Siena never recovered. In the 1550s, Florence, with the help of Philip II's Spanish army, conquered the flailing city-state, forever rendering Siena a non-threatening backwater. Siena's loss became our sight-seeing gain, as its political and economic irrelevance pickled the city in a purely medieval brine. Today, Siena's population is still 60,000, compared with Florence's 370,000.

Siena, situated atop three hills, qualifies as Italy's ultimate "hill town" (though it's much larger than its cousins covered in the Hill Towns of Central Italy chapter). Its thriving historic center, with red-brick lanes cascading every which way, offers Italy's best medieval city experience. Most people do Siena, just 35 miles south of Florence, as a day trip, but it's best experienced at twilight. While Florence has the blockbuster museums, Siena has an easy-to-enjoy soul: Courtyards sport flower-decked wells, alleys dead-end at rooftop views, and the sky is a rich blue dome.

For those who dream of a Fiat-free Italy, Siena is a haven. Pedestrians rule in the old center of Siena. Sit at a café on the main square. Wander narrow streets lined with colorful flags and studded with iron rings for tethering horses. Take time to savor the first European city to eliminate automobile traffic from its main square (1966) and then, just to be silly, wonder what would happen if they did it in your hometown.

Planning Your Time

On a quick trip, consider spending two nights in Siena (or three nights with a whole-day side-trip into Florence). Whatever you do, enjoy a sleepy medieval evening in Siena. The next morning, you can see the city's major sights in half a day.

Orientation to Siena

Siena lounges atop a hill, stretching its three legs out from Il Campo. This main square, the historic meeting point of Siena's

neighborhoods, is pedestrian-only—and most of those pedestrians are students from the university.

Just about everything mentioned in this chapter is within a 15-minute walk of the square. Navigate by three major landmarks (Il Campo, Duomo, and Church of San Domenico), following the excellent system of street-corner signs. The typical visitor sticks to the Il Campo-San Domenico axis. Make a point to stray from this main artery. Sienese streets go in anything but a straight line, so it's easy to get lost—but equally easy to get found. Don't be afraid to explore.

Siena itself is one big sight. Its individual sights come in two little clusters: the square (Civic Museum and City Tower) and the cathedral (Baptistery and Duomo Museum, with its surprise viewpoint). Check these sights off, and then you're free to wander.

Tourist Information

The TI on Il Campo can be an exasperating place. Think about the importance of tourism in this town—and yet this office charges €0.50 for a map and lets tour commissions color its advice (Mon-Sat 10:00-18:30, Sun 10:00-17:00, on Il Campo at #56, tel. 0577-280-551, www.terresiena.it). They hand out a few pretty booklets (including *Siena* and the regional *Terre di Siena* guide), sell maps and books, and may be able to answer a few questions. The TI

SIENA

organizes walking tours of the old town (€20, daily April-Oct at 11:00, 2 hours, no interiors, guide usually explains in both English and Italian). Ignore the second "TI" across from the Church of San Domenico, which is a useless private agency run by the local hotel association.

Arrival in Siena

By Train

The small train station, located at the base of the hill on the edge of town, has a bar, a bus office (Mon-Fri 7:15-19:30, Sat 7:15-17:45, Sun 8:30-12:30 & 14:30-18:30), and a newsstand (which sells local bus tickets—buy one now if you're taking the city bus into town), but no baggage check or lockers (stow bags at Piazza Gramsci—see "By Intercity Bus," later). A shopping mall with a supermarket (handy for picnic supplies) is across the plaza right in front of the station.

Getting from the Train Station to the City Center: To reach central Siena, you can hop aboard the city bus, ride a long series of escalators (which involves a bit of walking), or take a taxi. To reach either the bus or the escalators, head for the shopping mall across the plaza. From the tracks, go down the stairs into the tunnel that connects the platforms; this leads (with escalators) right up into the mall. Alternatively, you can exit the station out the front door, cross over to the plaza, turn left and walk to the far end of the plaza, then turn right to enter the mall's glass doors.

To ride the **city bus**, go through the shopping mall's right-hand door and use the elevator to go down to the subterranean bus stop. If you didn't buy bus tickets in the train station, you can get them from the blue machine (press "F" to toggle to English, then select "A" for type of ticket). Buses leave frequently (6/hour, fewer on Sun and after 22:00, €1.10, about a 10-minute ride into town depending on route). Smaller shuttle buses go up to Piazza del Sale, while bigger city buses head to nearby Piazza Gramsci (both are at the north end of town, walkable to most of my recommended hotels). Before boarding, double-check the destination with the driver by asking *"Centro?"* Punch your ticket in the machine onboard to validate it.

Riding the **escalator** into town takes a few minutes longer and requires more walking than the bus. From the station, follow the instructions above and enter the mall at the far-left end. Once inside, go straight ahead and ride the escalators up two floors to the food court. Continue directly through the glass doors to another escalator (marked *Porta Camollia/Centro*) that takes you gradually, up, up, up into town (free). Exiting the escalator, turn left down the big street, bear left at the fork, then continue straight through the town gate. From here, landmarks are well-signed (go

Greater Siena

To Florence (Direct Route)
SIENA NORD EXIT
To Florence via Castellina
To Florence via Gaiole, Radda & **5**
To Monte-riggione & Florence
S-222
VIA CASSIA
S-2
S-408
VIA BANDELLI
VIA FIORENTINA
AQUACALDA EXIT
SUPERSTRADA FREEWAY
TRAIN STATION
SOME BUSES STOP HERE, TOO
SCIAVO
VIA CAVOUR
CAMPING
VIA MAZZINI
VIALE PIETRO TOSELLI
To **4**
BOZZONE
STRADA DI PESCAIA
PORTA CAMOLLIA
3
B
PORTA OVILE
PIAZZA GRAMSCI (MAIN BUS STOP)
PORTA PISPINI
VIA ARETINA
FORTEZZA & **P**
STADIO & **P**
IL★CAMPO
See detail maps
PORTA SAN MARCO
CITY WALLS
P
PORTA ROMANA
PORTA TUFI
VIA PICCOLOMINI
1
SIENA OVEST EXIT
STRADA MASSETANA ROMANA
2
S-73
To A-1 Autostrada, Assisi, Rome & #438
S-2
SIENA SUD EXIT
S-223
VIA CASSIA
To A-1 Autostrada, Pienza, Montepulciano & **6**
To San Galgano
To Grosseto

1/2 Kilometer
1/2 Mile

1 Hotel Santa Caterina	**4** To Frances' Lodge Relais
2 Hotel Porta Romana	**5** To Borgo Argenina
3 Hotel Minerva	**6** To Il Canto del Sole

SIENA

up Via Camollia).

The **taxi stand** is to your right as you exit the train station, but as the city is chronically short on cabs, getting one here can take a while (about €9 to Il Campo, taxi tel. 0577-49222).

Getting to the Train Station from the City Center: If you're leaving Siena by train, you can ride a smaller shuttle bus from Piazza del Sale (which goes straight to the station), or catch an orange or red-and-silver city bus from Piazza Gramsci (which may take a more roundabout route). Multiple bus routes make this trip—look for *Ferrovia* or *Stazione* on schedules and marked on the bus. City buses drop off right in front of the station. Confirm with the driver that the bus is going to the *stazione* (stat-zee-OH-nay); remember to purchase your ticket in advance from a tobacco shop or the blue machine, then validate it on board.

By Intercity Bus

Most buses arrive in Siena at Piazza Gramsci, a few blocks north of the city center. (Some buses only go to the train station; others go first to the train station, then continue to Piazza Gramsci—to find out, ask your driver, "pee-aht-sah GRAM-chee?") The main bus companies are Sena and Tiemme/Siena Mobilità (formerly called Tra-In). Day-trippers can store baggage in the passageway underneath Piazza Gramsci called Sottopassaggio la Lizza (€5.50/day, open daily 7:00-19:00, carry-on-sized luggage no more than 33 pounds, no overnight storage). From Piazza Gramsci, it's an easy walk into the town center—just head in the opposite direction of the tree-filled park. For more on buses, see page 619.

By Car

Siena is not a good place to drive. Plan on parking in a big lot or garage and walking into town.

Drivers coming from the autostrada take the *Siena Ovest* exit and follow signs for *Centro*, then *Stadio* (stadium). The soccer-ball signs take you to the stadium lot (Parcheggio Stadio, €1.70/hour, pay when you leave) near Piazza Gramsci and the huge, bare-brick Church of San Domenico. The nearby Fortezza lot charges the same amount. Another good option is the underground Santa Caterina garage (you'll see signs on the way to the stadium lot, same price). From the garage, hike 150 yards uphill through a gate to an escalator on the right, which carries you up into the city. If you're staying in the south end of town, try the Il Campo lot, near Porta Tufi.

On parking spots, blue stripes mean pay and display; white stripes mean free parking. You can park for free in the lot west of the Fortezza; in white-striped spots behind the Hotel Villa Liberty (south of the Fortezza); and overnight in most city lots from 20:00 to 8:00. Watch for signs showing a street cleaner and a day of the week—that's when the street is closed to cars for cleaning.

Driving within Siena's city center is restricted to local cars and policed by automatic cameras. If you drive or park anywhere marked *Zona Traffico Limitato (ZTL)*, you'll likely have a hefty ticket waiting for you in the mail back home. Technically, hotel customers are allowed to drop off bags at their hotel before finding a place to park overnight, but getting permission to do so isn't worth the trouble.

Helpful Hints

Combo-Tickets: Siena always seems to be experimenting with different combo-tickets, but in general, only two are worth considering: the €10 Opa Si combo-ticket that includes the Duomo, Duomo Museum, Crypt, and Baptistery (a savings of €8 if you plan on seeing all those sights; sold only at the ticket office just right of the Duomo, near the Duomo Museum entrance); and the €13 combo-ticket covering the Civic Museum and City Tower (a €3 savings; must purchase at City Tower).

Wednesday Morning Market: The weekly market (clothes, knick-knacks, and food) sprawls between the Fortezza and Piazza Gramsci along Viale Cesare Maccari and the adjacent Viale XXV Aprile. The fact that this is more local than touristy makes it, for some, even more interesting.

Internet Access: In this university town, there are lots of places to get plugged in. **Cheap Phone Center** is hidden in a small shopping mall near Il Campo (€2/hour to use terminals, €1/hour for Wi-Fi, daily 10:00-22:00, Sun from 12:00; coming from Il Campo, go uphill past recommended Albergo Tre Donzelle, turn left at Via Cecco Angiolieri, after 20 yards look for #16). **Internet Point** is located upstairs at Via di Città 80, with the entrance around the corner on Via delle Campane (€3/hour, daily 9:00-21:00).

Post Office: It's on Piazza Matteotti (Mon-Fri 8:15-19:00, Sat 8:15-13:30, closed Sun).

Books: Libreria Senese sells books (including my guidebooks), newspapers, and magazines in English, with an emphasis on Italian-related topics (daily 9:00-20:00, Via di Città 62, tel. 0577-280-845). The **Feltrinelli** bookstore at Banchi di Sopra 52 also sells books and magazines in English (Mon-Sat 9:00-19:30, closed Sun, tel. 0577-271-104; the bigger Feltrinelli branch farther down the street at #64 has no English books).

Laundry: Onda Blu is a modern, self-service launderette just 50 yards from Il Campo (about €6 wash and dry, daily 8:00-22:00, last load at 21:00, Via del Casato di Sotto 17).

Travel Agency: Palio Viaggi, on Piazza Gramsci, sells plane tickets upstairs. Their downstairs office (go down the ramp to the door below the arch) sells train tickets, railpass reservations, and some bus tickets (only for the longer-distance Sena buses, not the regional Tiemme/Siena Mobilità buses). They charge a €1 fee per bus or train ticket, but this saves you a trip to the train station (Mon-Fri 9:00-12:45 & 15:00-18:30, Sat 9:00-12:30, closed Sun, opposite the columns of NH Excelsior Hotel at La Lizza 12, tel. 0577-280-828, info@palioviaggi.it).

Wine Classes: The **Tuscan Wine School** gives two-hour classes in English on Italian wine and food. Morning classes (11:00) cover rotating topics: wines from all over Italy, olive-oil tasting, or a "Savor Siena" food tour that visits several vendors around town (check website for specific schedule). Afternoon classes (16:00) focus on Tuscan wines, including samples of five vintages. They also offer a one-hour "crash course" at 14:00. Rebecca and her fellow sommeliers keep things entertaining and offer classes for as few as two people (€40/person, 20 percent student discount to anyone with this book, €25 for one-hour course, classes offered Mon-Sat, closed Sun, reservations recommended—especially in peak season, Via di Stalloreggi 26, 30 yards from recommended Hotel Duomo, tel. 0577-221-704, mobile 333-722-9716, www.tuscanwine school.com, info@tuscanwineschool.com). Their outlet store sells wine from local producers at cost (Mon-Sat 11:00-18:00, closed Sun).

Tours in Siena

Roberto's Tuscany Tours—Roberto Bechi, a hardworking Sienese guide, specializes in off-the-beaten-path minibus tours of the surrounding countryside (up to eight passengers, convenient pickup at hotel). Married to an American (Patti) and having run restaurants in Siena and the US, Roberto communicates well with Americans. His passions are Sienese culture, Tuscan history, and local cuisine. It's ideal to book well in advance, but you might be able to schedule a tour if you call the day before (seven different tours—explained on his website, €90/person for full-day tours, €60/person for off-season four-hour tours, entry fees extra, assistant Anna can schedule city tours as well as other guides if Roberto is booked, Anna's mobile 320-147-6590, Roberto's mobile 328-425-5648, www.toursbyroberto.com, toursbyroberto@gmail .com). Roberto also does multiday tours. If you book any tour with Roberto, he can advise you on other aspects of your trip.

Other Local Guides—Federica Olla, who leads walking tours of Siena, is a smart, youthful guide with a knack for creative teaching (€55/hour, mobile 338-133-9525, info@ollaeventi.com).

GSO Guides Co-op is a group of 10 young professional guides who offer good tours covering all of Tuscany and Umbria (€130/half-day, €260/full day, 10 percent discount for Rick Steves readers, mobile 338-611-0127, www.guidesienaeoltre.com). Among them, charming Stefania Fabrizi specializes in Siena (mobile 338-640-7796).

Bus Tours—Somehow a company called My Tour has a lock on all hotel tour-promotion space. Every hotel has a rack of their brochures, which advertise a variety of five-hour big-bus tours into the countryside (€38, depart from Piazza Gramsci).

Sights in Siena

On Il Campo, the Main Square

▲▲▲**Il Campo**—This square is the heart, both geographically and metaphorically, of Siena. It fans out from City Hall (Palazzo Pubblico) to create an amphitheater.

It's the only town square I've ever seen where people stretch out as if at the beach. Il Campo's shining moment is the famous Palio horse races, which take place in summer (see sidebar on page 592).

Originally, this area was just a field *(campo)* located outside the former city walls. Bits of those original walls, which circled the Duomo (and curved against today's square), can be seen above the pharmacy (the black-and-white stones, to the right as you face City Hall). In the 1200s, with the advent of the Sienese Republic, the city expanded—once a small medieval town circling its cathedral, it became a larger, humanistic city gathered around its towering City Hall. In this newer and relatively secular age, the focus of power shifted from the bishop to the city council.

As the city expanded, Il Campo eventually became the historic junction of Siena's various competing *contrade* (neighborhood districts) and the old marketplace. The brick surface is divided into nine sections, representing the council of nine merchants and city bigwigs who ruled medieval Siena. The square and its buildings are the color of the soil upon which they stand—a color known to artists and Crayola users as "Burnt Sienna."

City Hall: This secular building, with its 330-foot tower, dominates the square. In medieval Siena, this was the center of

the city, and the whole focus of Il Campo still flows down to it.

The **City Tower** (Torre del Mangia) is Italy's tallest secular tower. It was named after a hedonistic watchman who consumed his earnings like a glutton consumes food. His chewed-up statue is in the courtyard, to the left as you enter. (For details on climbing

Siena at a Glance

▲▲▲**Il Campo** Best square in Italy. **Hours:** Always open. See page 587.

▲▲▲**Duomo** Art-packed cathedral with mosaic floors and statues by Michelangelo and Bernini. **Hours:** March-Oct Mon-Sat 10:30-19:00, Sun 13:30-18:00; Nov-Feb Mon-Sat 10:30-17:30, Sun 13:30-17:30. See page 595.

▲▲**Civic Museum** City museum in City Hall with Sienese frescoes, the *Effects of Good and Bad Government*. **Hours:** Daily mid-March-Oct 10:00-19:00, Nov-mid-March 10:00-18:00. See page 589.

▲▲**Duomo Museum** Siena's best museum, displaying cathedral art (including Duccio's *Maestà*) and offering sweeping Tuscan view. **Hours:** Daily March-Oct 10:30-19:00, Nov-Feb 10:30-17:30. See page 600.

▲**City Tower** 330-foot tower climb. **Hours:** Daily March-mid-Oct 10:00-19:00, mid-Oct-Feb 10:00-16:00. See page 594.

▲**Pinacoteca** Fine Sienese paintings. **Hours:** Tue-Sat 8:15-19:15, Sun-Mon 9:00-13:00. See page 594.

▲**Baptistery** Cave-like building with baptismal font decorated by Ghiberti and Donatello. **Hours:** Daily March-Oct 10:30-19:00, Nov-Feb 10:30-17:30. See page 601.

▲**Santa Maria della Scala** Museum with vibrant ceiling and wall frescoes depicting day-to-day life in a medieval hospital, much of the original Fountain of Joy, and an Etruscan artifact exhibit. **Hours:** Daily March-Oct 10:30-18:00, Nov-Feb 10:30-16:00. See page 602.

Crypt Site of 12th-century church, housing some of Siena's oldest frescoes. **Hours:** Daily March-Oct 10:30-19:00, Nov-Feb 10:30-17:30. See page 602.

Church of San Domenico Huge brick church with St. Catherine's head and thumb. **Hours:** Daily 7:00-18:30. See page 603.

Sanctuary of St. Catherine Home of St. Catherine. **Hours:** Daily 9:00-18:00, church closed 12:30-15:00. See page 603.

the tower, see "City Tower" listing, later.)

The open **chapel** located at the base of the tower was built in 1348 as thanks to God for ending the Black Death (after it killed more than a third of the population). It should also be used to thank God that the top-heavy tower—just plunked onto the building with no extra foundation and no iron reinforcement—still stands. These days, the chapel is used solely to bless the Palio contestants, and the tower's bell only rings for the race.

Fountain of Joy (Fonte Gaia): This 15th-century work by Jacopo della Quercia marks the square's high point. The joy is all about how the Sienese Republic blessed its people with water. Notice Lady Justice with her scales (also holding a sword, right of center), overseeing the free distribution of water to all. Imagine residents gathering here in the 1400s to fill their jugs. The Fountain of Joy still reminds locals that life in Siena is good. Notice the pigeons politely waiting their turn to tightrope gin-

gerly down slippery spouts to slurp a drink from wolves' snouts. The relief panel on the left shows God creating Adam by help-ing him to his feet. It's said that this reclining Adam influenced Michelangelo when he painted his Sistine Chapel ceiling. This fountain is a copy—you can see most of the original fountain in an interesting exhibit at Siena's Santa Maria della Scala (described later).

▲▲**Civic Museum (Museo Civico)**—At the base of the tower is Siena's City Hall, the spot where secular government got its start in early Renaissance Europe. There you'll find city government still at work, along with a sampling of local art, including Siena's first fresco (with a groundbreaking down-to-earth depiction of the Madonna). While pricey, it's worth strolling through the dramatic halls to see fascinating frescoes and portraits extolling Siena's greats, saints, and the city-as-utopia.

Cost and Hours: €8, €13 combo-ticket with tower (must be purchased at tower), daily mid-March-Oct 10:00-19:00, Nov-mid March 10:00-18:00, last entry 45 minutes before closing, tel. 0577-292-615, www.comune.siena.it.

Visiting the Museum: Start in the Sala del Risorgimento, with dramatic scenes of Victor Emmanuel II's unification of Italy (surrounded by statues that don't seem to care).

Passing through the chapel, where the city's governors and bureaucrats prayed, enter the Sala del Mappamondo. On oppo-site walls are two large frescoes. The beautiful *Maestà* (*Enthroned*

Siena

SIENA

SIENA'S "CONTRADE" (NEIGHBORHOODS)

AQUILA (Eagle)
BRUCO (Caterpillar)
CIVETTA (Owl)
DRAGO (Dragon)
GIRAFFA (Giraffe)
LEOCORNO (Unicorn)
OCA (Goose)
PANTERA (Panther)
SELVA (Forest)
TORRE (Tower)

NOTE: MORE *CONTRADE* LIE BEYOND THE MAP BOUNDARIES.

1 Sottopassaggio la Lizza (Underground Bus Depot, Bag Storage & Bus Tickets)
2 Libreria Senese Bookstore
3 Feltrinelli Bookstore
4 Palio Viaggi Travel Agency
5 Tuscan Wine School
6 Internet Cafés (2)
7 Launderette
8 Train Station Shuttle Bus

SIENA

Siena's Palio

In the Palio, the feisty spirit of Siena's 17 neighborhoods lives on. Each *contrada* has a parish church, well or fountain, and sometimes even a historical museum. Each is represented by a mascot (porcupine, unicorn, wolf, etc.) and unique colors worn proudly by residents.

Contrada pride is evident year-round in Siena's parades and colorful banners, lamps, and wall plaques. (If you hear the thunder of distant drumming, run to it for some medieval action—there's a good chance it'll feature flag-throwers.) You are welcome to participate in these lively neighborhood festivals. Buy a scarf in *contrada* colors, grab a glass of Chianti, munch on some *panforte*, and join in the merriment.

Contrada passion is most visible twice a year—on July 2 and August 16—when the city erupts during its world-famous horse race, the Palio di Siena. Ten of the 17 neighborhoods compete (chosen by rotation and lot), hurling themselves with medieval abandon into several days of trial races and traditional revelry. Jockeys—usually from out of town—are considered hired guns, no better than paid mercenaries. Bets are placed on which *contrada* will win...and lose. Despite the shady

behind-the-scenes dealing, on the big day the horses are taken into their *contrada*'s church to be blessed. ("Go and return victorious," says the priest.) It's considered a sign of luck if a horse leaves droppings in the church.

On the evening of the race, Il Campo is stuffed to the brim with locals and tourists. Dirt is brought in and packed down over the gray pavement of the perimeter to create the track's surface, while mattresses pad the walls of surrounding buildings. The most treacherous spots are the sharp corners, where many a rider has bitten the dust.

Virgin, 1315), by Siena's great Simone Martini (c. 1280-1344), is groundbreaking as Siena's first fresco showing a Madonna not in a faraway, gold-leaf heaven, but under the blue sky of the real world that we inhabit. Facing the *Maestà* is the famous *Equestrian Portrait of Guidoriccio da Fogliano* (1330), which depicts a mercenary general surveying the imposing castle that his armies have just conquered.

Next is the Sala della Pace—where the city's fat cats met. Looking down on the oligarchy during their meetings was a fascinating fresco series showing the *Effects of Good and Bad Government*, by Sienese painter Ambrogio Lorenzetti. Compare the whistle-while-you-work happiness of the utopian community

Picture the scene: Ten snorting horses and their nervous riders line up near the pharmacy (on the west side of the square) to await the starting signal. Then they race like crazy while spectators wave the scarves of their neighborhoods. Every possible vantage point and perch is packed with people straining to see the action. One lap around the course is about a third of a mile (350 meters); three laps make a full circuit. In this literally no-holds-barred race—which lasts just over a minute—a horse can win even without its rider (jockeys perch precariously without saddles on the sweaty horses' backs, and often fall off).

When the winner crosses the line, 1/17th of Siena—the prevailing neighborhood—goes berserk. Winners receive a *palio* (banner), typically painted by a local artist and always featuring the Virgin Mary. But the true prize is proving that your *contrada* is *numero uno,* and mocking your losing rival.

All over town, sketches and posters depict the Palio. This is not some folkloric event—it's a real medieval moment. If you're packed onto the square with 60,000 people, all hungry for victory, you won't see much, but you'll feel it. Bleacher and balcony seats are expensive, but it's free to join the masses in the square. Be sure to go with an empty bladder as there are no WCs, and be prepared to surrender any sense of personal space.

While the actual Palio packs the city, you could side-trip in from Florence to see the horse-race trials—called *prove* (proh-vay)—on any of the three days before the main event (usually at 9:00 and after 19:00, free seats in bleachers). For more information, visit www.ilpalio.org.

ruled by the utopian government (in the better-preserved fresco) against the crime, devastation, and societal mayhem of a community ruled by politicians with more typical values. The message: Without justice, there can be no prosperity.

On your way out, climb up to the loggia (using the stairs just before the Sala del Risorgimento) for a sweeping view of the city and its surroundings. (For a less impressive version of this view, you could skip the stairs and simply peek behind the curtains in the Sala della Pace.)

▲**City Tower (Torre del Mangia)**—Siena gathers around its City Hall more than its church. Medieval Siena was a proud republic, and this tall tower is the exclamation point of its "declaration of independence." Its 300 steps get pretty skinny at the top, but the reward is one of Italy's best views.

Cost and Hours: €8, €13 combo-ticket with Civic Museum, daily March-mid-Oct 10:00-19:00, mid-Oct-Feb 10:00-16:00, last entry 45 minutes before closing, closed in rain, free and mandatory bag check. Wait at the bottom of the stairs for the green *Avanti* light. Admission is limited to 50 people at a time, so be prepared for long lines or for tickets to be sold out. Try to avoid midday crowds (up to an hour wait at peak times).

Near Il Campo

▲**Pinacoteca**—If you're into medieval art, you'll likely find this quiet, uncrowded, colorful museum delightful. The museum walks you through Siena's art chronologically, from the 12th through the 16th centuries, when a revolution in realism was percolating in Tuscany.

Cost and Hours: €4, Tue-Sat 8:15-19:15, Sun-Mon 9:00-13:00, last entry 30 minutes before closing, free and mandatory bag check; from Il Campo, walk out Via di Città and go left on Via San Pietro to #29; tel. 0577-281-161 or 0577-286-143, www.pinacotecanazionale.siena.it.

Visiting the Museum: In general, the collection lets you follow the evolution of painting styles from Byzantine to Gothic, then to International Gothic, and finally to Renaissance. Long after Florentine art went realistic, the Sienese embraced a timeless, otherworldly style glittering with lots of gold.

As you walk through the museum, note that Sienese art features more than just paintings. In this city of proud craftsmen, the gilding and carpentry of the frames almost competes with the actual paintings. The exquisite attention to detail gives a glimpse into the wealth of the 14th and 15th centuries, Siena's Golden Age. Take time to trace the delicate features with your eyes. The woven silk and gold clothing you'll see was worn by the very people who once walked these halls, when this was a private mansion (appreciate the colonnaded courtyard).

The core of the collection is on the second floor, in Rooms 1-19. Works by Duccio (artist of the *Maestà* in the Duomo Museum) feature groundbreaking innovations that are subtle to the layman's eyes: less gold-leaf background, fewer gold creases in robes, transparent garments, inlaid-marble thrones, and a more human Mary and Jesus.

St. Augustine of Siena, by Duccio's assistant, Simone Martini (who did the *Maestà* in the Civic Museum), sets the saint's life in pretty realistic Sienese streets, buildings, and landscapes. In each panel, the saint pops out at the oddest (difficult to draw) angles to save the day.

Also look for religious works by the hometown Lorenzetti brothers (Ambrogio is best known for the secular masterpiece, the *Effects of Good and Bad Government,* in the Civic Museum). *Città sul Mare (City by the Sea)* and *Castello in Riva al Lago (Castle on the Lakeshore)* feature the strange, medieval Cubism seen in the work of the contemporaneous *Guidoriccio da Fogliano* (in the Civic Museum). Notice the weird, melancholy light that captures the sense of the Dark Ages. These images are replicated on postcards found throughout the city.

Several colorful rooms on the first floor are dedicated to Domenico Beccafumi (1486-1551), who designed many of the Duomo's inlaid pavement panels (including *Slaughter of the Innocents*). With strong bodies, twisting poses, and dramatic gestures, Beccafumi's works epitomize the Mannerist style.

Cathedral Area

Each of the first four sights (Duomo, Duomo Museum, Crypt, and Baptistery) is covered by a separate ticket, or by the €10 Opa Si combo-ticket. If you're planning to visit only the Duomo and Duomo Museum, the combo-ticket is a bad deal; but if you're curious about the Crypt and Baptistery, the combo-ticket lets you peek into those sights for just €1 more. Individual tickets for any of these sights and the Opa Si combo-ticket are sold only at the ticket office near the entrance to the Duomo Museum—to the right as you face the cathedral facade (no tickets sold at sight entrances).

▲▲▲Duomo

If the Campo is the heart of Siena, the Duomo (or cathedral) is its soul. The white and dark-green striped church, sitting on an artificial platform atop Siena's highest point, is visible for miles around. This ornate but surprisingly secular shrine to the Virgin Mary is stacked with colorful art inside and out, from the inlaid-marble floors to the stained-glass windows. The interior is a Renaissance riot of striped columns, intricate marble inlays, Michelangelo statues, and Bernini sculptures. In the Piccolomini Library, a series of captivating frescoes by the Umbrian painter Pinturicchio tells the story of Aeneas Piccolomini, Siena's consummate Renaissance Man, who became Pope Pius II.

Cost: €3 includes cathedral and Piccolomini Library, buy ticket at Duomo Museum entrance (facing the cathedral entry, the museum is 100 yards to the right, near the south transept). To add the Duomo Museum, Crypt, and Baptistery, consider the €10 Opa Si combo-ticket. Check the line to get into the Duomo before buying tickets—if there's a long wait, you can pay an extra €1 for a (misnamed) "reservation" that lets you skip the line (not possible to book in advance).

Hours: March-Oct Mon-Sat 10:30-19:00, Sun 13:30-18:00; Nov-Feb Mon-Sat 10:30-17:30, Sun 13:30-17:30; last entry 30 minutes before closing, tel. 0577-286-300, www.operaduomo.siena.it.

Dress Code: Modest dress is required, but stylish paper ponchos are provided for the inappropriately clothed.

Audioguides: Inside the Duomo are €2 **video terminals** that give a history of the cathedral floor. In the nave, you can rent a small **tablet** computer (like a mini-iPad) with audio commentary, colorful photographs, and an extremely dry but informative tour of the cathedral and related sights (for Duomo only: €6, €10/2 people; for Duomo plus Duomo Museum, Crypt, and Baptistery: €8, €14/2 people). Considering the expense and hassle (you have to return the audioguide to the nave), it's probably not worth it for most visitors, who should find the commentary given here to be plenty.

❍ Self-Guided Tour: Grab a spot on a stone bench opposite the entry to take in this architectural festival of green, white, pink, and gold.

Exterior: Like a medieval altarpiece, the facade is divided into sections, each frame filled with patriarchs and prophets, studded with roaring gargoyles, and topped with prickly pinnacles. Imagine pilgrims arriving at this church, its facade trumpeting the coming of Christ and the correct path to salvation.

The current structure dates back to 1215, with the major decoration done during Siena's heyday (1250-1350). The lower story, by Giovanni Pisano (who worked from 1284 to 1297), features remnants of the fading Romanesque style (round arches over the doors), topped with the pointed arches of the new Gothic style that was seeping in from France. The upper half, in full-blown Gothic, was designed and built a century later.

• *Step inside, putting yourself in the mindset of a pilgrim as you take in this trove of religious art. (With a maximum capacity of 700 visitors, you may have to wait—the current number is indicated on a computer screen at the turnstile. Remember, if the line is dreadfully long, you can pay €1 for a "reservation" at the ticket office and go right in.)*

Nave: The heads of 172 popes—who reigned from Peter's time to the 12th century—peer down from above, looking over the fine inlaid art on the floor. With a forest of striped columns, a coffered dome, a large stained-glass window at the far end (described later), and an art gallery's worth of early Renaissance art, this is one busy interior. If you look closely at the popes, you'll see the same four faces repeated over and over.

For almost two centuries (1373-1547), 40 artists paved the marble floor with scenes from the Old Testament, allegories, and intricate patterns. The series starts near the entrance with historical allegories; the larger, more elaborate scenes surrounding the altar are mostly stories from the Old Testament. Many of the floor panels are roped off—and occasionally even covered—to prevent further wear and tear.

• *Look for the marble altarpiece decorated with statues.*

Piccolomini Altar: This was designed for the tomb of the Sienese-born Pope Pius III. It was commissioned when he was the cardinal of Siena, but because he later became a pope (see the fresco of his coronation with Pius wearing the golden robe—above and to the right of the Michelangelo statue), he was buried in the Vatican and this fancy tomb was never used. It's most interesting for its statues: one by Michelangelo, and three by his students. Michelangelo was originally contracted to do 15 statues, but another sculptor had started the marble blocks, and Michelangelo's heart was never in the project. He personally finished only one—the figure of St. Paul (lower right, clearly more interesting than the bland, bored popes above him).

• *Now grab a seat under the...*

Dome: The dome sits on a 12-sided base, but its "coffered" ceiling is actually a painted illusion. Get oriented to the array of sights by thinking of the church floor as a big 12-hour clock. You're the middle, and the altar is high noon: You'll find the *Slaughter of the Innocents* roped off on the floor at 10 o'clock, Pisano's pulpit between two pillars at 11 o'clock, a copy of Duccio's round stained-glass window at high noon, Bernini's chapel at 3 o'clock, the Piccolomini Altar with the Michelangelo statue (next to doorway leading to a shop, snacks, and WC) at 7 o'clock, the Piccolomini Library at 8 o'clock, and a Donatello statue at 9 o'clock.

Pisano's Pulpit: The octagonal Carrara marble pulpit (1268) rests on the backs of lions, symbols of Christianity triumphant. Like the lions, the Church eats its catch (devouring paganism) and nurses its cubs. The seven relief panels tell the life of Christ in rich detail. The pulpit is the work of Nicola Pisano (c. 1220-1278), the

"Giotto of sculpture," whose revival of classical forms (columns, sarcophagus-like relief panels) signaled the coming Renaissance. His son Giovanni (c. 1240-1319) carved many of the panels, mixing his dad's classicism and realism with the decorative detail and curvy lines of French Gothic—a style that would influence Donatello and the other Florentines.

Duccio's Stained-Glass Rose Window: This is a copy of the original window, which was moved to the Duomo Museum a couple of years ago. The famous rose window was created in 1288 and dedicated to the Virgin Mary (for more details, see page 601).

Slaughter of the Innocents: This pavement panel shows Herod (left), sitting enthroned amid Renaissance arches, as he orders the massacre of all babies to prevent the coming of the promised Messiah. It's a chaotic scene of angry soldiers, grieving mothers, and dead babies, reminding locals that a republic ruled by a tyrant will experience misery.

• *Step into the chapel just beyond the pavement panel (next to the Piccolomini Library) to see...*

St. John the Baptist **Statue:** The statue of the rugged saint in his famous rags was created by Donatello. The aging Florentine sculptor, whose style was now considered passé in Florence, came here to build bronze doors for the church (similar to Ghiberti's in Florence). He didn't complete the door project, but he did finish this bronze statue (1457). Notice the cherubs high above it, playfully dangling their feet.

• *Cross beneath the dome to find the Chigi Chapel, also known as the...*

Chapel of the Madonna del Voto: To understand why Gian Lorenzo Bernini (1598-1680) is considered the greatest Baroque sculptor, step into this sumptuous chapel (designed in the early 1660s for Fabio Chigi, a.k.a. Pope Alexander VII). Move up to the altar and look back at the two Bernini statues: Mary Magdalene in a state of spiritual ecstasy, and St. Jerome playing the crucifix like a violinist lost in beautiful music. It's enough to make even a Lutheran light a candle.

The painting over the altar is the *Madonna del Voto,* a Madonna and Child adorned with a real crown of gold and jewels (painted by an unknown Italian master in the mid-13th century). In typical medieval fashion, the scene is set in the golden light of heaven. Mary has the almond eyes, long fingers, and golden folds in her robe that are found in orthodox icons of the time. Still, this Mary tilts her head and looks out sympathetically, ready to listen to the prayers of the faithful. This is the Mary to whom the Palio is dedicated, dear to the hearts of the Sienese. In thanks, they give **offerings** of silver hearts and medallions, many of which hang now on the wall just to the left as you exit the chapel.

• *Cross back to the other side of the church to find the...*

Piccolomini Library: Brilliantly frescoed, the library captures the exuberant, optimistic spirit of the 1400s, when human-

ism and the Renaissance were born. The never-restored frescoes look nearly as vivid now as the day they were finished 550 years ago. (With the bright window light, candles were unnecessary in this room—and didn't sully the art with soot.) The painter Pinturicchio (c. 1454-1513) was hired to celebrate the life of one of Siena's hometown boys—a man many call "the first humanist," Aeneas Piccolomini (1405-1464), who became Pope Pius II. Each of the 10 scenes is framed with an arch, as if Pinturicchio were opening a window onto the spacious 3-D world we inhabit.

The library also contains intricately decorated, illuminated music scores, and a statue (a Roman copy of a Greek original) of the Three Graces, who almost seem to dance to the beat. The oddly huge sheep-skin sheets of music are from the days before individual hymnals—they had to be big so that many singers could read the music at the same time from a distance. Appreciate the fine painted decorations on the music—the gold-leaf highlights, the newly discovered (and quite expensive) cobalt for blue tones, and the miniature figures. All of this exquisite detail was lovingly crafted by Benedictine monks for the glory of God. Find your favorite—I like the blue, totally wild god of wind with the big hair (in the fourth case).

• *Exit the Duomo and make a U-turn to the left, walking alongside the church to Piazza Jacopo della Quercia.*

Unfinished Church: After rival republic Florence began its grand cathedral (1296), proud Siena planned to build one even bigger, the biggest church in all Christendom.

Construction began in the 1330s on an extension off the right side of the existing Duomo (today's cathedral would have been used as a transept). The nave of the Duomo was supposed to be where the piazza is today. Worshippers would have entered the church from the far end of the piazza through the unfinished wall. (Look way up at the highest part of the wall. That's the viewpoint accessible from inside the Duomo Museum.) Some of the nave's green-and-white striped columns were built, and are now filled in with a brick wall. White stones in the pavement mark where a row of pillars would have been.

The vision was grand, but it underestimated the complexity of constructing such a building without enough land for it to sit upon. That, coupled with the devastating effects of a plague, killed the city's ability and will to finish the project. Look through the unfinished entrance facade, note blue sky where the stained-glass windows would have been, and ponder the struggles, triumphs, and failures of the human spirit.

▲▲Duomo Museum (Museo dell'Opera e Panorama)

Located in a corner of the Duomo's grand but unfinished extension (to the right as you face the main facade), Siena's most enjoyable

museum was built to house the cathedral's art. Here you can stand eye-to-eye with the saints and angels who once languished unknown in the church's upper reaches (where copies are found today).

Cost and Hours: €6, also covered by Opa Si combo-ticket, buy tickets near Duomo Museum entry; daily March-Oct 10:30-19:00, Nov-Feb 10:30-17:30, last entry 30 minutes before closing; next to the Duomo, in the skeleton of the unfinished part of the church on the Il Campo side—look for the white banner; tel. 0577-286-300, www.operaduomo.siena.it.

Audioguides: You can rent an audio/videoguide on a tablet computer for €4 (€6/2 people). You can pay more for one that also covers the Duomo and other sights, but you have to pick it up and drop it off inside the cathedral (for details, see page 596).

◑ Self-Guided Tour: Start your tour at the bottom and work your way up.

Ground Floor: This floor is filled with the cathedral's original Gothic sculptures by Giovanni Pisano, who spent 10 years in the late 1200s carving and orchestrating the decoration of the cathedral with saints, prophets, sibyls, animals, and the original she-wolf with Romulus and Remus.

On the ground floor you'll also find Donatello's fine, round *Madonna and Child* carved relief. A slender, tender Mary gazes down at her chubby-cheeked baby, as her sad eyes say that she knows the eventual fate of her son.

On the opposite side of the room is Duccio's original stained-glass window, which until recently was located above and behind the Duomo's altar. Now the church has a copy, and art lovers can enjoy a close-up look at this masterpiece. The rose window—20 feet across, made in 1288—is dedicated (like the church and the city itself) to the Virgin Mary. The work was designed by Siena's most famous artist, Duccio di Buoninsegna (c. 1255-1319), and combines elements from rigid Byzantine icons (Mary's almond-shaped bubble, called a *mandorla,* and the full-frontal saints that flank her) with a budding sense of 3-D realism (the throne turned at a three-quarter angle to simulate depth, with angels behind).

Duccio's *Maestà*: Upstairs awaits a private audience with the *Maestà* (*Enthroned Virgin,* 1311), whose panels were once part of the Duomo's main altarpiece. Although the former altarpiece was disassembled (and the frame was lost), most of the pieces are displayed here, with the front side (*Maestà,* with Mary and saints) at one end of the room, and the back side (26 Passion panels) at the other.

The *Maestà* was revolutionary for the time in its sheer size and opulence, and in Duccio's budding realism, which broke standard conventions. Duccio, at the height of his powers, used every innovative arrow in his quiver. He replaced the standard gold-leaf background (symbolizing heaven) with a gold, intricately patterned curtain draped over the throne. Mary's blue robe opens to reveal her body, and the curve of her knee suggests real anatomy beneath the robe. Baby Jesus wears a delicately transparent garment. Their faces are modeled with light—a patchwork of bright flesh and shadowy valleys, as if lit from the left (a technique he likely learned from his contemporary Giotto during a visit to Florence).

The flip side of the *Maestà* featured 26 smaller panels—the medieval equivalent of pages—showing colorful scenes from the Passion of Christ.

Panorama dal Facciatone: About 60 claustrophobic spiral stairs take you to the first viewpoint. You can continue up another similar spiral staircase to reach the very top. Standing on the wall from this high point in the city, you're rewarded with a stunning view of Siena...and an interesting perspective. Look toward the Duomo and consider this: If Siena's grandiose plans to expand the cathedral had come to fruition, you'd be looking straight down the nave toward the altar.

▲**Baptistery**—Siena is so hilly that there wasn't enough flat ground on which to build a big church. What to do? Build a big church anyway and prop up the overhanging edge with the Baptistery. This dark and quietly tucked-away cave of art is worth a look for its cool, tranquil bronze panels and angels by Ghiberti, Donatello, and others that adorn the pedestal of the baptismal font.

SIENA

Cost and Hours: €3, also covered by Opa Si combo-ticket, buy tickets near Duomo Museum entry, daily March-Oct 10:30-19:00, Nov-Feb 10:30-17:30, last entry 30 minutes before closing.

Crypt—The cathedral "crypt" is archaeologically important. The site of a small 12th-century Romanesque church, it was filled in with dirt a century after its creation to provide a foundation for the huge church that sits atop it today. Recently excavated, the several rediscovered frescoed rooms show off what are likely the oldest frescoes in town.

Cost and Hours: €6, also covered by Opa Si combo-ticket, buy tickets near Duomo Museum entry, daily March-Oct 10:30-19:00, Nov-Feb 10:30-17:30, last entry 30 minutes before closing, entrance is halfway up the stairs between the Baptistery and Duomo Museum.

▲**Santa Maria della Scala**—This museum (opposite the Duomo entrance) was used as a hospital until the 1980s. Its labyrinthine 12th-century cellars—carved out of volcanic tuff and finished with brick—go down several floors and during medieval times were used to store supplies for the hospital upstairs. Today, the hospital and its cellars are filled with exhibits (well-described in English) and can be a welcome refuge from the hot streets. Stop in for a cool and quiet break in the air-conditioned lobby, which offers a fine bookshop and big, comfy couches, all under great 15th-century timbers.

Cost and Hours: €6, daily March-Oct 10:30-18:00, Nov-Feb 10:30-16:00, last entry 30 minutes before closing, bookstore, tel. 0577-534-511, www.santamariadellascala.com.

Visiting the Museum: It's easy to get lost in this gigantic complex, so stay focused on the main attractions—the fancily frescoed Pellegrinaio Hall (ground floor), most of the original Fountain of Joy (first basement), and the Etruscan collection in the Archaeological Museum (second basement). Just inside the complex (enter from the square) is the Church of the Santissima Annunziata.

• *From the entrance, walk down the lengthy hall to the long room with the colorful frescoes.*

The sumptuously frescoed walls of **Pellegrinaio Hall** show medieval Siena's innovative health care and social welfare system in action (c. 1442, wonderfully described in English). Starting in the 11th century, the hospital nursed the sick and cared for abandoned children, as is vividly portrayed in these frescoes. The good works paid off, as bequests and donations poured in, creating the wealth that's evident throughout this building.

• *Head down the stairs, then continue straight into the darkened rooms with pieces of Siena's landmark fountain—follow signs to* Fonte Gaia.

An engaging exhibit explains Jacopo della Quercia's early 15th-century **Fountain of Joy** (Fonte Gaia)—and displays the disassembled pieces of the original fountain itself. In the 19th century, after serious deterioration, the ornate fountain was dismantled and plaster casts were made. (From these casts, they formed the replica that graces Il Campo today.) Here you'll see the eroded original panels paired with their restored casts, along with the actual statues that once stood on the edges of the fountain.

• *Descend into the cavernous second basement.*

Under the groin vaults of the **Archaeological Museum**, you're alone with piles of ancient Etruscan stuff excavated from tombs dating centuries before Christ (displayed in a labyrinthine exhibit). Remember, the Etruscans dominated this part of Italy before the Roman Empire swept through—some historians think even Rome originated as an Etruscan town.

San Domenico Area

Church of San Domenico—This huge brick church is worth a quick look. The spacious, plain interior (except for the colorful

flags of the city's 17 *contrade,* or neighborhoods) fits the austere philosophy of the Dominicans and invites meditation on the thoughts and deeds of St. Catherine. Walk up the steps in the rear to see paintings from the life of St. Catherine. Halfway up the church on the right, find a metal bust of St. Catherine, a small case housing her thumb (on the left), and a glass box on the lowest shelf containing the chain she used to scourge herself. In the chapel (15 feet to the left) surrounded with candles, you'll see Catherine's actual head atop the altar. Through the door just beyond are the sacristy and the bookstore.

Cost and Hours: Free, daily 7:00-18:30, gift shop tel. 0577-286-848, www.basilicacateriniana.com. A WC (€0.50) is at the far end of the parking lot, to the right as you face the church entrance.

Sanctuary of St. Catherine (Santuario di Santa Caterina)— Step into the cool and peaceful site of Catherine's home. Siena remembers its favorite hometown gal, a simple, unschooled, but mystically devout soul who, in the mid-1300s, helped convince the pope to return from France to Rome. Pilgrims have visited this place since 1464, and architects and artists have greatly embellished what was probably once a humble home (her family worked as wool dyers). You'll see paintings throughout showing

St. Catherine of Siena
(1347-1380)

The youngest of 25 children born to a Sienese cloth dyer, Catherine began experiencing heavenly visions as a child. At 16 she became a Dominican nun, locking herself away for three years in a room in her family's house. She lived the life of an ascetic, which culminated in a vision wherein she married Christ. Catherine emerged from solitude to join her Dominican sisters, sharing her experiences, caring for the sick, and gathering both disciples and enemies. At age 23, she lapsed into a spiritual coma, waking with the heavenly command to spread her message to the world. She wrote essays and letters to kings, dukes, bishops, and popes, imploring them to find peace for a war-ravaged Italy. While visiting Pisa during Lent of 1375, she had a vision in which she received the stigmata, the wounds of Christ.

Still in her twenties, Catherine was invited to Avignon, France, where the pope had taken up residence. With her charm, sincerity, and reputation for holiness, she helped convince Pope Gregory XI to return the papacy to the city of Rome. Catherine also went to Rome, where she died young. She was canonized in the next generation (by a Sienese pope), and her relics were distributed to churches around Italy.

Because of her intervention in the papal schism, today Catherine is revered (along with St. Benedict) as the patron saint of Europe, and remembered as a rare outspoken medieval woman still appreciated for her universal message: that this world is not a gift from our fathers, but a loan from our children.

scenes from her life.

Enter through the courtyard, and walk down the stairs at the far end. The church on your right contains the wooden crucifix upon which Catherine was meditating when she received the stigmata. Take a pew, gaze at it, and try to imagine the scene. Back outside, the oratory across the courtyard stands where the kitchen once was. Go down the stairs (left of the gift shop) to reach the saint's room. Catherine's bare cell is behind wrought-iron doors.

Cost and Hours: Free, daily 9:00-18:00, church closed 12:30-15:00, a few downhill blocks toward the center from San Domenico—follow signs to *Santuario di Santa Caterina*—at Costa di Sant'Antonio 6, tel. 0577-288-175.

Shopping in Siena

The main drag, Via Banchi di Sopra, is a cancan of fancy shops. Here are some things to look for:

Flags: For easy-to-pack souvenirs, get some of the large, colorful scarves/flags that depict the symbols of Siena's 17 different neighborhoods (such as the wolf, the turtle, or the snail). They're good for gifts or to decorate your home (sold in varying sizes at souvenir stands).

Sweets: All over town, Prodotti Tipici shops sell Sienese specialties. Siena's claim to caloric fame is its *panforte,* a rich, chewy concoction of nuts, honey, and candied fruits that impresses even fruitcake-haters. There are a few varieties: *Margherita,* dusted in powdered sugar, is more fruity, while *panpepato* has a spicy, peppery crust. Locals prefer a chewy, white macaroon-and-almond cookie called *ricciarelli.*

Sleeping in Siena

Finding a room in Siena is tough during Easter (March 31 in 2013) or the Palio (July 2 and Aug 16). Many hotels won't take reservations until the end of May for the Palio, and even then they might require a four-night stay. While day-tripping tour groups turn the town into a Gothic amusement park in midsummer, Siena is basically yours in the evenings and off-season.

Part of Siena's charm is its lively, festive character—this means that all hotels can be plagued with noise, even (and sometimes especially) the hotels in the pedestrian-only zone. If tranquility is important for your sanity, ask for a room that's off the street, or consider staying at one of the recommended places outside the center.

Fancy Sleeps, Southwest of Il Campo

These well-run places are a 10-minute walk from Il Campo.

$$$ Pensione Palazzo Ravizza is elegant and friendly, with 38 rooms and an aristocratic feel—fitting, as it was once the luxurious residence of a noble. Guests enjoy a peaceful garden set on a dramatic bluff, along with a Steinway in the upper lounge (Sb-€170, small loft Db-€130, standard Db-€170, superior Db-€200, Tb-€230, family suites-€300, rates can vary, see website for room differences, rooms in back overlook countryside, air-con, elevator, free Wi-Fi, Via Piano dei Mantellini 34, tel. 0577-280-462, fax

Sleep Code

(€1 = about $1.40, country code: 39)

S = Single, **D** = Double/Twin, **T** = Triple, **Q** = Quad, **b** = bathroom, **s** = shower only. Breakfast is included unless otherwise noted. If your hotel doesn't provide breakfast, eat at a bar on Il Campo or near your hotel. Credit cards are generally accepted, but I note in the listings if they aren't. (If not, there are ATMs all over town.) Hotel staff generally speak English unless noted otherwise. Siena levies a hotel tax of €2 per person, per night, which must be paid in cash (not included in the rates I've quoted).

To help you easily sort through these listings, I've divided the accommodations into three categories based on the price for a standard double room with bath during high season:

$$$ Higher Priced—Most rooms €130 or more.
$$ Moderately Priced—Most rooms between €90-130.
$ Lower Priced—Most rooms €90 or less.

Prices can change without notice; verify the hotel's current rates online or by email.

0577-221-597, www.palazzoravizza.com, bureau@palazzoravizza .it, Ariol). As parking is free and the hotel is easily walkable from the center, this is a particularly good value for drivers.

$$$ Hotel Duomo has 20 spacious but slightly dated rooms, a picnic-friendly roof terrace, and a bizarre floor plan (Sb-€105, Db-€130, Db suite-€180, Tb-€180, Qb-€230, elevator with some stairs, air-con, free Wi-Fi, discounted parking-€20/day; follow Via di Città, which becomes Via di Stalloreggi, to #38; tel. 0577-289-088, fax 0577-43-043, www.hotelduomo.it, booking@hotelduomo .it, Alessandro). If you're arriving by train, take a taxi (€10) or ride bus #3 to the Porta Tufi stop, just a few minutes' walk from the hotel; you can also arrange to have Alessandro take you to/ from the train station or airport (with this book: train station-€10, Florence's Vespucci Airport-€105, Pisa's Galilei Airport-€165; he'll also take you to nearby hill towns, e.g., Florence-€105 and Pisa-€165). If you're driving, go to Porta San Marco, turn right, and follow signs to the hotel—drop your bags, then park in the nearby Il Campo lot near Porta Tufi.

Simple Places near Il Campo

Most of these listings are forgettable but inexpensive, and just a horse wreck away from one of Italy's most wonderful civic spaces.

$$ Piccolo Hotel Etruria, with 20 straightforward rooms, is overpriced for what it is—though well-located and restful (S-€50,

Sb-€60, Db-€90-110, Tb-€120-138, Qb-€145-166, higher rates are for peak-of-peak times, optional breakfast-€6, air-con June-Oct only, next to recommended Albergo Tre Donzelle at Via delle Donzelle 1-3, tel. 0577-288-088, fax 0577-288-461, www.hotel etruria.com, info@hoteletruria.com, Fattorini family).

$ Albergo Tre Donzelle is a fine budget value with 20 plain, well-worn rooms. Although the showers have seen better days, these may be the cheapest rooms in the center. Don't hang out here...think of Il Campo, a block away, as your terrace (S-€38, D-€49, Db-€60, T-€70, Tb-€85, no rooms available for Palio, breakfast-€5, free Wi-Fi; with your back to the tower, head away from Il Campo toward 2 o'clock to Via delle Donzelle 5; tel. 0577-280-358, www.tredonzelle.com, info@tredonzelle.com, Maurizio).

$ Hotel Cannon d'Oro, a few blocks up Via Banchi di Sopra, is a labyrinthine slumbermill renting 30 institutional, overpriced rooms (Sb-€71, Db-€90, Tb-€115, Qb-€136, these discounted prices good with this book through 2013, fans, free Wi-Fi in lobby and some rooms, a couple of blocks from the bus hub at Via dei Montanini 28, tel. 0577-44-321, fax 0577-280-868, www.cannon doro.com, info@cannondoro.com; Maurizio, Tommaso, and Rodrigo).

B&Bs in the Old Center

$$ Antica Residenza Cicogna is a seven-room guesthouse with a homey elegance and an ideal location. It's warmly run by the young and charming Elisa and her dad Fabio, who set out biscotti, *vin santo,* and tea all day for their guests. With artfully frescoed walls and ceilings, this is remarkably genteel for the price (Db-€95, suite Db-€120, third bed-€15, air-con, free Internet access and Wi-Fi, Via dei Termini 76, tel. 0577-285-613, mobile 347-007-2888, www .anticaresidenzacicogna.it, info@anticaresidenzacicogna.it).

$$ Palazzo Masi B&B, run by Alizzardo and Daniela, is just below Il Campo. They rent six pleasant, spacious, antique-furnished rooms with shared common areas on the second and third floors of an old building. While a bit pricey, the fine location and warm welcome are appreciated (D-€80, Db-€120 if you book direct, discounts for 4 or more nights, cash only, breakfast-€8, free Wi-Fi, discounted parking at nearby Il Campo lot-€25/24 hours; from City Hall, walk 50 yards down Via del Casato di Sotto to #29; mobile 349-600-9155, www.palazzomasi.com, info@palazzo masi.it). The place is sometimes unstaffed, so it's important to phone upon arrival.

$ B&B Alle Due Porte is a charming little establishment renting four big rooms with sweet furniture under big medieval beams. The shared breakfast room is delightful. The manager, Egisto, is a phone call and five-minute scooter ride away (Db-€85,

SIENA

Siena Hotels & Restaurants

Eateries

15 Antica Osteria Da Divo
16 Taverna San Giuseppe
17 Compagnia dei Vinattieri
18 Hostaria Il Carroccio
19 Trattoria La Torre, Ciao Cafeteria & Spizzico Pizza
20 Ristorante Guidoriccio
21 Trattoria Papei
22 Osteria Trombicche
23 La Taverna Di Cecco
24 Ristorante Alla Speranza & Bar Paninoteca San Paolo

25 Il Bandierino
26 Bar Il Palio
27 Osteria Liberamente
28 Costarella Gelateria
29 Key Largo Bar
30 Antica Pizzicheria al Palazzo della Chigiana
31 Pizzeria San Martino
32 Rosticceria Vitti
33 Consorzio Agrario Siena Grocery
34 Nannini Pastry Shop
35 Gelateria Grom
36 Enoteca Italiana

Piazza del Sale
To Train Station
BRUCO
ANCIENT CITY WALLS
SANT' ANDREA
SAN ROCCO
Fonte Nuova
Piazza d'Ovile
Piazza Fabio Bargagli Petrucci
SAN DONATO
POST
Piazza Matteotti
SANTA MARIA DELLE NEVI
McD
ORATORIO DELLE SUORE
SAPIENZA
SAN PELLEGRINO
OCA
SANTA MARIA DI PROVENZANO
GIRAFFA
Piazza Provenzano Salvani
CIVETTA
SANTA MESSE
Piazza Tolomei
SANCTUARY OF ST. CATHERINE
Piazza Indipendenza
LOGGIA
FONTE GAIA
Il Campo
UNIVERSITY
PALAZZO PICCOLOMINI
LEOCORNO
SAN GIOVANNINO DELLA STAFFA
BAPTISTERY (BELOW DUOMO)
CITY TOWER
CIVIC MUSEUM CITY HALL
Piazza del Mercato
SAN MARTINO
To Porta Romana
TORRE
DUOMO
DUOMO MUSEUM
Piazza del Duomo
ACCADEMIA MUSICALE CHIGIANA
MARKET BUILDING
SAN GIACOMO
PREFETTURA
PALAZZO DEL CAPITANO
AQUILA
To P & Porta Tufi
PINACOTECA (PAINTING GALLERY)

NOTE: MUCH OF CENTRAL SIENA IS A PEDESTRIAN ZONE

100 Meters
100 Yards

SIENA

Accommodations
1. To Pensione Palazzo Ravizza & Osteria del Gatto
2. Hotel Duomo
3. Piccolo Hotel Etruria
4. Albergo Tre Donzelle
5. Hotel Cannon d'Oro
6. Antica Residenza Cicogna
7. Palazzo Masi B&B
8. To B&B Alle Due Porte
9. B&B Siena in Centro
10. Hotel Chiusarelli
11. Alma Domus
12. Albergo Bernini
13. Hotel Villa Elda
14. Hotel Villa Liberty

windowless Db with small bed-€65, Tb-€110, free Wi-Fi, Via di Stalloreggi 51, tel. 0577-287-670, mobile 368-352-3530, www.siena tur.it, soldatini@interfree.it).

$ B&B Siena in Centro is a clearinghouse managing five good and centrally-located private apartments. Their handy office functions as a reception renting out a total of about 20 rooms; stop by here to pick up your key and be escorted to your apartment. The rooms are generally spacious, quiet, and comfortable, but with no air-conditioning or Wi-Fi. Their website lets you visualize your options (Sb-€45-60, Db-€70-90, Tb-€90-120, reception open 9:00-13:30 & 15:00-19:00, later in high season, other times by phone request, OK to leave bags at reception, Via di Stalloreggi 14, tel. 0577-43041, mobile 331-281-4137 or 347-465-9753, www .bbsienaincentro.com, info@bbsienaincentro.com; Patrizia, Paolo, Gioia, and Michela).

Near San Domenico Church

These hotels are within a 10-minute walk northwest of Il Campo. Note that Albergo Bernini and Alma Domus offer fine panoramas of the old town for reasonable prices.

$$$ Hotel Chiusarelli, with 48 classy rooms in a beautiful Neoclassical villa, has a handy location but is on a very busy street. Expect traffic noise at night—ask for a quieter room in the back (can be guaranteed with reservation). The bells of San Domenico are your 7:00 wake-up call (Sb-€108, Db-€155, Tb-€190, ask for Rick Steves discount when you book, air-con, free Wi-Fi with this book, across from San Domenico at Viale Curtatone 15, tel. 0577-280-562, fax 0577-271-177, www.chiusarelli.com, info@chiusarelli .com).

$ Alma Domus is a church-run hotel renting 43 spartan rooms with quaint balconies, some fantastic views (ask for a room *con vista*), stately public rooms, and a pleasant atmosphere. While the setting is tranquil, thin doors, echoey halls, and nearby church bells will make you glad you brought earplugs. The 10:00 checkout time is strict, but they will store your luggage in their secure courtyard (Sb-€48, Db-€80, Tb-€105, €5 extra for best views on fourth floor, central air-con, elevator, pay Internet access and Wi-Fi; from San Domenico, walk downhill toward the view with the church on your right, turn left down Via Camporegio, make a U-turn down the brick steps to Via Camporegio 37; tel. 0577-44-177, fax 0577-47-601, www.hotelalmadomus.it, info@hotelalmadomus.it, Louis).

$ Albergo Bernini makes you part of a Sienese family in a modest, clean home with 10 traditional rooms. Giovanni, charming wife Daniela, and their three daughters welcome you to their spectacular view terrace for breakfast and picnic lunches and dinners (S-€55, D-€65, Sb or small Db with view-€78, Db-€85, less in winter, optional breakfast-€3.50/small or €7.50/big, cash only, free Wi-Fi, on the main Il Campo-San Domenico drag at Via della Sapienza 15, tel. & fax 0577-289-047, www.albergobernini.com, hbernin@tin.it).

Farther from the Center

These options, a 10- to 20-minute walk from the center, are great for drivers.

Near Porta Romana City Gate

These two fine spots are about 200 yards outside the Porta Romana (see locations on the map on page 583). To get to downtown Siena from here, catch minibus line A uphill to Piazza al Mercato, just behind Il Campo (€1.10). To reach the bus and train stations, take bus #2 (which becomes #17 at Piazza del Sale; when arriving, catch #17 from the station). If driving, from the freeway, take the Siena Sud exit, continue in direction Romana, then at the first light turn left, following *Pta Romana/Centro* signs for about half a mile until you see the big city gate.

$$$ **Hotel Santa Caterina** is a three-star, 18th-century place renting 22 comfy rooms. It's professionally run with real attention to quality. While it's on a big city street, it has a delightful garden terrace with views over the countryside (Sb-€125, four small Db-€125, Db-€165, split-level Tb or Qb-€215, prices promised with this book through 2013, can be cheaper in low season, garden side is quieter, air-con, fridge in room, elevator, free Wi-Fi, parking-€15/day—request when you reserve, Via E.S. Piccolomini 7, tel. 0577-221-105, fax 0577-271-087, www.hscsiena.it, info@hscsiena.it, Lorenza and her crew).

$$ **Hotel Porta Romana** is at the edge of town, off a busy road. Some of its 15 rooms face the open countryside (request one of these), and breakfast is served in the garden (Sb-€90, Db-€110, extra person-€20, 10 percent Rick Steves discount if you book direct and pay cash, air-con in some rooms, free Internet access, free Wi-Fi with this book, free parking, inviting sun terrace, Via E.S. Piccolomini 35, tel. 0577-42299, fax 0577-232-905, www.hotelportaromana.com, info@hotelportaromana.com; Marco and Evelia).

In the Posh Neighborhood South of the Fortress

These two places are in a villa-studded residential neighborhood across a gully from San Domenico Church. They're about 5-10 minutes farther than the listings under "Near San Domenico Church," earlier, but the extra walking gets you to a swankier address.

$$$ **Hotel Villa Elda** rents 11 bright and light rooms in a recently renovated villa. It's classy, stately, pricey, and run with

a feminine charm (Db-€140-170, about €20 more for view, extra person-€30, air-con, free Wi-Fi, garden and view terrace, Viale Ventiquattro Maggio 10, tel. 0577-247-927, www.villaeldasiena.it, info@villaeldasiena.it).

$$$ Hotel Villa Liberty, across a busy street from the fortress, is a former private mansion. It has 17 big, bright, comfortable rooms and some road noise (Sb-€80, Db-€150, Tb-€180, €10 more for superior room, air-con, elevator, free Wi-Fi, bar, courtyard, free and easy street parking, facing fortress at Viale Vittorio Veneto 11, tel. 0577-44-966, fax 0577-44-770, www.villaliberty.it, info@villaliberty.it).

Just Inside Porta Ovile, at the North End of Town

$$ Hotel Minerva is your big, professional, plain, efficient option. It's the most impersonal of my listings, with zero personality but predictable comfort. While its 56 rooms are boring, they don't hide any unpleasant surprises. It works best for those with cars—parking is reasonable (€12/day), and it's only a 10-minute walk from the action (Sb-€76, Db-€122, Tb-€168, bigger suites available for more, air-con, elevator, free Internet access, pay Wi-Fi, Via Garibaldi 72, see map on page 583 for location, tel. 0577-284-474, fax 0577-43343, www.albergominerva.it, info@albergominerva.it).

Outside Siena

The following accommodations are set in the lush, peaceful countryside surrounding Siena, and are best for those traveling by car (see locations on the map on page 583).

$$$ Frances' Lodge Relais is a tranquil and delightfully managed farmhouse B&B a mile out of Siena. Each of its six rooms is bursting with character (all well-described on their website). Franca and Franco run this rustic-yet-elegant old place, which features a 19th-century orangery that's been made into a "better homes and palaces" living room, as well as a peaceful garden, eight acres of olive trees and vineyards, and great views of Siena and its countryside—even from the swimming pool (small Db-€170, Db-€190, Db suite-€220, Tb-€210-220, Tb suite-€280, Qb suite-€340, these prices promised to Rick Steves readers through 2013, possibly cheaper for longer stays, air-con-€10, free Internet access and Wi-Fi, free parking, Strada di Valdipugna 2, tel. & fax 0577-42379, mobile 337-671-608, www.franceslodge.it). To the center, it's a five-minute bus ride (€1.10, they'll call to arrange) plus a five-minute walk, or €10 by taxi. Consider having an al fresco dinner in the gazebo, complete with view (make your own picnic, or have your hosts assemble a very fancy one for €20/person).

$$$ Borgo Argenina has seven rooms in a well-maintained, pricey splurge of a B&B. Run by helpful Elena Nappa, it's 20 minutes north of Siena by car in the Chianti region (Db-€170, beautiful gardens, free Wi-Fi, tel. 0577-747-117, www.borgoargenina.it, info@borgoargenina.it).

$$ Il Canto del Sole is a restored 18th-century farmhouse turned family-friendly B&B located about six miles outside the Porta Romana city gate. Run by Laura, Luciano, and their son Marco, it features 10 bright and airy rooms and two apartments with original antique furnishings, a saltwater swimming pool, a game room, and bike rentals (Db-€120, Tb-€140, extra bed-€30, apartment-€180-220, air-con, free Wi-Fi, free parking, dinner cooked on request, Val di Villa Canina 1292, 53014 Loc. Cuna, tel. 0577-375-127, fax 0577-373-378, www.ilcantodelsole.com, info @ilcantodelsole.com).

Eating in Siena

Sienese restaurants are reasonable by Florentine and Venetian standards. You can enjoy ordering high on the menu here without going broke. For me, the best €5 you can spend in Siena is on a cocktail at Bar Il Palio, overlooking Il Campo. For pasta, a good option is *pici* (PEE-chee), a thick Sienese spaghetti that seems to be at the top of every menu.

Fine Dining in the Old Town

For only a few euros more, these four places deliver a more upscale ambience and generally better food than my later recommendations.

Antica Osteria Da Divo is *the* place for a dressy and atmospheric €45 meal. The kitchen is creative, the ambience is flowery and candlelit, some of the seating fills old Etruscan tombs, and the food is fresh, delicate, and top-notch. While the cuisine is flamboyant and almost over-the-top, Chef Pino and his wife Susanna serve up my favorite splurge dinner in town. Pino is a fanatic for fresh ingredients, enjoys giving traditional dishes his creative spin, and is understandably proud of his desserts. The wine is good, too—you can order it by the glass (€4-7) if you ask (€10-12 pastas, €20-26 *secondi*, €3 cover, Wed-Mon 12:00-14:30 & 19:00-22:30, closed Tue, reservations smart; facing Baptistery door, take the far right street and walk one long curving block to Via Franciosa 29; tel. 0577-284-381). Those dining here with this book can finish with a complimentary biscotti and *vin santo* or coffee (upon request).

Taverna San Giuseppe, a local favorite, offers modern Tuscan cuisine in a chic grotto atmosphere. While the vibe is high energy and casual, the food compares favorably with the slightly more upscale places listed here. The wine-and-cheese cellar in back is cut from an Etruscan tomb. Check the posters tacked around the entry for daily specials. Reserve or arrive early to get a table (€8-10 pastas, €15-20 *secondi*, Mon-Sat 12:00-14:30 & 19:00-22:00, closed Sun, air-con, 7-minute climb up street to the right of City Hall at Via Giovanni Dupre 132, tel. 0577-42-286, Matteo).

Compagnia dei Vinattieri serves modern Tuscan dishes with a creative twist. In this elegantly unpretentious space, you can enjoy a quiet and romantic meal under graceful brick arches. The menu is small and accessible, and the young staff will help you match your meal with the right wine. Marco, the owner, is happy to take you down to their marvelous wine cellar (€9-12 pastas, €16-18 *secondi*, leave this book on the table for a complimentary *aperitivo* or dessert drink, daily 12:30-15:00 & 19:30-23:00, near Via dei Pittori at Via delle Terme 79, tel. 0577-236-568).

Hostaria Il Carroccio, artsy and convivial, seats guests in a tight, sea-foam green dining room and serves elegantly presented, traditional "slow food" recipes with innovative flair at affordable prices (€8 pastas, €14-18 *secondi*, €30 tasting *menu*—minimum two people, cash only, reservations wise, Thu-Tue 12:30-15:00 & 19:30-22:00, closed Wed, Via del Casato di Sotto 32, tel. 0577-41-165, sweet Renata and Mauro).

Traditional and Rustic Places in the Old Town

Trattoria La Torre is a thriving, unfussy *casalinga* (home-cooking) eatery, popular for its homemade pasta, plates of which entice customers as they enter. The sound of its busy open kitchen adds to the conviviality. Ten tables are packed under one medieval brick arch. Service is brisk and casual, and despite its priceless position below the namesake tower, it feels more like a local hangout than a tourist trap. Study the menu in the window before entering; otherwise, the owner likes to just recite his long list of dishes (€7-8 pastas, €8-10 *secondi*, €2 cover, Fri-Wed 12:00-15:00 & 19:00-22:00, closed Thu, just steps below Il Campo at Via Salicotto 7, tel. 0577-287-548, Alberto Boccini).

Osteria del Gatto is a classic little hole-in-the-wall, thriving with townspeople and powered by a passion for serving good Sienese cuisine. Marco Coradeschi and his engaged staff cook and serve daily specials with attitude. As it's so small and popular, it can get loud (€8-9 pastas, €8-10 *secondi*, Mon-Fri 12:30-15:00 & 19:30-22:00, Sat 19:30-22:00 only, closed Sun, 5-minute walk away from the center at Via di San Marco 8, tel. 0577-287-133).

Ristorante Guidoriccio, just a few steps below Il Campo, feels warm and welcoming. You'll get smiling service from Ercole and Elisabetta. While mostly filled with tourists, the place has charm—especially if you let gentle Ercole explore the menu with you and follow his suggestions (€9 pastas, €13-14 *secondi*, Mon-

Sat 12:30-14:30 & 19:00-22:30, closed Sun, air-con, Via Giovanni Dupre 2, tel. 0577-44-350).

Trattoria Papei is a Sienese favorite, featuring a casual, rollicking family atmosphere and friendly servers dishing out generous portions of rib-stickin' Tuscan specialties and grilled meats. This big, sprawling place under tents in a parking lot is in all the guidebooks and often jammed—so call to reserve (€7 pastas, €8-12 *secondi*, daily 12:00-15:00 & 19:00-22:30, closed Mon June-Sept, on the market square directly behind City Hall at Piazza del Mercato 6, tel. 0577-280-894; for 50 years Signora Giuliana has ruled her kitchen, Amadeo and Eduardo speak English).

Osteria Trombicche takes you back to another age—cheap and small, with tight indoor seating and two tiny outdoor tables from which to watch the street scene. Bobby (who speaks English) and monolingual Davide serve fast, hearty food to a local crowd (€6.50 *ribollita*—bean-and-vegetable soup—in winter, €5 *panzanella*—bread salad with tomato and basil—in summer, €8-10 mixed-vegetable antipasto plates, hand-cut prosciutto, Mon-Sat 11:00-15:00 & 17:30-22:00, closed Sun, Via delle Terme 66, tel. 0577-288-089).

La Taverna Di Cecco is a simple, comfortable little eatery on an uncrowded back lane where earnest Luca and Gianni serve tasty salads and Sienese specialties made from fresh ingredients for a fair price (€8-12 pastas, €10-15 *secondi*, daily 12:00-16:00 & 19:00-24:00, Via Cecco Angiolieri 19, tel. 0577-288-518).

Places on Il Campo

If you choose to eat on perhaps the finest town square in Italy, you'll pay a premium, meet waiters who don't need to hustle, and get mediocre food. And yet I recommend it. The clamshell-shaped square is lined with venerable cafés, bars, restaurants, and pizzerias.

To experience Il Campo without paying for a full meal, consider having drinks or breakfast on the square. Some bars serve food. And if your hotel doesn't include breakfast or if you'd like something more memorable, Il Campo has plenty of options. A cappuccino and a *cornetto* (croissant) run about €5-6.

Dining and Drinks on the Square

Ristorante Alla Speranza has perhaps the best view in all of Italy. If you're looking to eat reasonably on Il Campo, this is your place (€8-10 pastas and pizzas, €13-15 *secondi*, €2 cover charge, daily 9:00-late, tel. 0577-280-190). It's smart to reserve the view table of your choice by phone—or simply stop by earlier in the day while you're sightseeing in the square.

Il Bandierino is another decent option with an angled view of

City Hall (€8-12 salads, €11-12 pizzas, €13-15 pastas; no cover but a 20 percent service fee, daily 11:00-23:00, tel. 0577-282-217).

Bar Il Palio is the best bar on Il Campo for a pre- or post-dinner drink: It has straightforward prices, no cover, decent waiters, and a fantastic perspective out over the square.

Dynamic little **Osteria Liberamente** (on the square, not above it) has a trendy vibe and is popular with young people (fine wine by the glass, €7 cocktails with good tapas, Wed-Mon 8:00 until late, closed Tue, Pino).

Drinks or Snacks from Balconies Overlooking Il Campo

Three places have skinny balconies with benches overlooking the main square for their customers. Sipping a coffee or nibbling a pastry here while marveling at the Il Campo scene is one of my favorite things to do in Europe. And it's very cheap. Survey these three places from Il Campo (with your back to the tower, they are at 10 o'clock, high noon, and 3 o'clock, respectively).

The little **Costarella Gelateria,** on the corner of Via di Città and Costa dei Barbieri, has good drinks and light snacks, such as cute little €3.50 sandwiches, though the gelato tastes artificial (daily 8:00-late, Via di Città 33). While the restaurant is for regular service, you're welcome to take anything from the bar out to the simple benches (just walk through the "table service only" section upstairs) and eat with a grand view overlooking Il Campo.

Bar Paninoteca San Paolo has a youthful pub ambience and a row of stools lining a skinny balcony overlooking the square. It serves big €7 salads and 50 kinds of €4 sandwiches, hot and cold—not authentic Italian, but quick and filling (order and pay at the counter, food served daily 12:00-2:00 in the morning, on Vicolo di San Paolo, tel. 0577-226-622).

Key Largo Bar has two long, second-story benches in the corner offering a wonderful secret perch. Buy your drink or snack at the bar (no cover and no extra charge to sit on balcony), climb upstairs, and slide the ancient bar to open the door. Enjoy stretching out, and try to imagine how, during the Palio, three layers of spectators cram into this space—note the iron railing used to plaster the top row of sardines up against the wall. Suddenly you're picturing Palio ponies zipping wildly around the corner (€4 cocktails, daily 7:00-24:00, on the corner of Via Rinaldini). If you can't get a seat on the outdoor benches, skip the otherwise nondescript, youthful interior.

Eating Cheaply in the Center

Antica Pizzicheria al Palazzo della Chigiana (look for the sign reading *Pizzicheria de Miccoli*) may be the official name, but I bet

Nightlife in Siena

Evenings are a wonderful time to be out and about in Siena, after the tour groups have left for the day.

Join the evening *passeggiata* (peak strolling time is 19:00) along Via Banchi di Sopra with gelato in hand. I like **Gelateria Grom,** which serves "Gelato like it used to be." Its seasonal flavors and all-natural ingredients make it a popular stop for any Sienese in need of something cool and sweet to lick while strolling (a little pricier than the competition, daily 11:00-24:00, Banchi di Sopra 13).

A fun trend in Siena is the *aperitivo.* All over town, you'll find bars attracting an early evening crowd by serving a free buffet of food with the purchase of a drink. For many, this can be a light dinner for the cost of a drink. Or consider starting or ending a meal with a drink or dessert on Il Campo. For suggestions, see "Places on Il Campo."

Enoteca Italiana is a good wine bar in a cellar in the Fortezza, funded in part by the government to promote Italian wine production. They have 30 different bottles open on any given day, and they offer tastings at three different prices: €3, €4, and €6.50. To get there, enter the Fortezza via the bridge, cross the running track, and—after passing a tree—go left down a ramp (Mon-Sat 12:00-24:00, closed Sun, snacks served when the bar's pricey restaurant is between mealtimes, outside terrace, tel. 0577-228-832).

locals just call it Antonio's. For most of his life, frenzied Antonio has carved salami and cheese for the neighborhood. Most of the day, a hungry line spills onto the street as people wait for their sandwiches—meat and cheese sold by weight—with a good €10 bottle of Chianti (Italian law dictates that he must sell you a bottle of wine—cheap and good—and lend you the glasses). Antonio and his boys offer a big cheese-and-meat plate (about €18 gets you 30 minutes of eating) and pull out a tiny tabletop in the corner so you can munch or sip while standing and watching the ham-hock-y scene. Or just grab a €4-5 sandwich. Even if you don't eat here, pop in to inhale the commotion or peruse Antonio's gifty traditional edibles (daily 8:00-20:00, Via di Città 95, tel. 0577-289-164).

Ciao Cafeteria, at the bottom of Il Campo, offers good-value, self-service lunches, but no ambience or views (hearty €5-7 meals, daily 12:00-15:00). The crowded **Spizzico,** a pizza counter in the front half of Ciao, serves huge €4-5 quarter-pizzas. For both places, the food and ambience recall a cut-rate truck stop—but on sunny days, people take the pizza out on Il Campo for a memorable picnic (daily 11:00-21:00, to left of City Tower as you face it).

Pizza: Spizzico (listed above) is worth considering only if you're standing on Il Campo, desperate for pizza, and unashamedly lazy. Budget eaters look for *pizza al taglio* shops, scattered throughout Siena, selling better pizza by the slice. One good bet, **San Martino,** a couple of blocks behind Il Campo, is a local-feeling spot with €2-3 slices and sandwiches (Mon-Sat 8:00-14:30 & 16:30-21:00, closed Sun, Via del Porrione 64).

Rosticcerie: For cheap take-out food, look for a *rosticceria* (explained on page 35). One affordable, central option that feels at least partly untouristed is **Rosticceria Vitti,** near Piazza Gramsci's bus terminus (point to what you want in the glass case, figure €5 for a light meal, Sun-Fri 9:00-21:30, closed Sat, Via Montanini 14/16, tel. 0577-289-291).

Supermarket: You won't find many cheap grocery shops in the touristy center of Siena. But one handy (if fancy) option is **Consorzio Agrario Siena**. Ask them to make you up a *panino.* As this place specializes in artisan Tuscan foods, both the quality and prices are high (Mon-Sat 8:00-19:30, sometimes open Sun, a block off Piazza Matteotti, toward Il Campo at Via Pianigiani 5).

Desserts and Treats

For a special dessert or a sweet treat any time of day, stop by **Nannini**—considered the top-end pastry shop and *the* place to go for quality local specialties (Mon-Sat 7:30-21:00, Sun 8:00-21:00, Banchi di Sopra 24). Across the street is the wonderful **Gelateria Grom** (see "Nightlife in Siena" sidebar)—but you have my permission to sample every *gelateria* in town to pick your own favorite.

Siena Connections

Siena has sparse train connections but is a great hub for buses to the hill towns, though frequency drops on Sundays and holidays. For most, Florence is the gateway to Siena. Even if you are a railpass-user, connect these two cities by bus—it's faster than the train, and Siena's bus station is more convenient and central than its train station. (Note: Many travelers mistake old signs for a former bus company, Tra-In, as signs for trains or the train station. Those buses have nothing to do with the railway.)

By Train

Siena's train station is at the edge of town. For details on getting between the town center and the station, see page 582.

From Siena by Train to: Florence (direct trains hourly, 1.5-2 hours, €7.70; bus is better), **Pisa** (2/hour, 1.75 hours, change at Empoli, €8.90), **Assisi** (hourly, 4-5 hours, most involve 2 changes, €11.05, bus is faster), **Rome** (1-2/hour, 3-3.5 hours, change in Florence or Chiusi, €24-53), **Orvieto** (12/day, 2-2.5 hours, change in Chiusi, €14.10). For more information, visit www.trenitalia .com.

By Bus

The main bus companies are **Tiemme** (part of a larger company called Siena Mobilità and formerly called Tra-In; mostly handles buses to regional destinations, tel. 0577-204-246, www.siena mobilita.it) and **Sena** (for long-distance connections, tel. 0577-208-282, www.sena.it). On schedules, the fastest buses are marked *rapida*. I'd stick with these. Most buses depart Siena from Piazza Gramsci; others leave from the train station (confirm when you buy your ticket).

Tiemme/Siena Mobilità Buses go to: Florence (about 2/hour, 1.25-hour *rapida/via superstrada* buses are faster than the train, avoid the 2-hour *ordinaria* buses unless you have time to enjoy the beautiful scenery en route, €7.20; to avoid line at bus-ticket office, tickets also available at tobacco shops/*tabacchi*; generally leaves from Piazza Gramsci as well as train station), **San Gimignano** (Mon-Fri 10/day direct, Sat 7/day, none direct on Sun, 1.25 hours, €6, leaves from Piazza Gramsci), **Volterra** (4/day Mon-Sat, no buses on Sun, 2 hours, change in Colle Val d'Elsa, €5.75, leaves from Piazza Gramsci), **Montepulciano** (8/day, none on Sun, 1.25 hours, €5.45, leaves from train station), **Pienza** (6/day, none on Sun, 1.5 hours, €4.40, leaves from train station), **Montalcino** (6/day Mon-Sat, 4/day Sun, 1.25 hours, €3.85, leaves from train station or Piazza del Sale), and **Pisa's Galileo Galilei Airport** (3/day, 1.75 hours, €14, one direct, two via Poggibonsi).

Sena Buses go to: Rome (9-10/day, 3 hours, €22, from Piazza Gramsci, arrives at Rome's Tiburtina station on Metro line B with easy connections to the central Termini train station), **Naples** (1/day overnight bus, 6.5 hours, bus departs at 23:59, €30), and **Milan** (4/day, 4 hours, €36, departs from Piazza Gramsci, arrives at Milan's Cadorna Station with Metro access and direct trains to Malpensa Airport). To reach the town center of **Pisa,** the train is better (described earlier).

Tickets and Information: You can buy tickets in the underground passageway (called Sottopassaggio la Lizza) beneath Piazza Gramsci—look for stairwells in front of NH Excelsior Hotel. Once down there, be sure to find the correct office: The larger one (marked *Siena Mobilità*) handles Tiemme/Siena Mobilità buses (Mon-Fri 6:30-19:30, Sat-Sun 7:00-19:30). The smaller one is for Sena buses (Mon-Sat 8:30-19:45 only; on Sun, when the Sena bus ticket office is closed, buy tickets next door at Tiemme/Siena Mobilità office). Both offices accept credit cards. You can also get tickets for both Tiemme/Siena Mobilità buses and Sena buses at the train station (look for bus-ticket kiosk just inside main door—

see page 582 for hours). If necessary, you can buy tickets from the driver, but it costs €3 extra.

Services: Sottopassaggio la Lizza also has luggage storage (at the Tiemme/Siena Mobilità office, see page 584 for details), posted bus schedules, TV monitors listing imminent departures for several bus companies, and WCs (€0.50).

HILL TOWNS OF CENTRAL ITALY

San Gimignano • Volterra • Montepulciano • Pienza •
Montalcino • Cortona • More Hill Towns and Sights

The sun-soaked hill towns of central Italy offer what to many is the quintessential Italian experience: sun-dried tomatoes, homemade pasta, wispy cypress-lined driveways following desolate ridges to fortified 16th-century farmhouses, atmospheric *enoteche* serving famously tasty wines, and dusty old-timers warming the same bench day after day while soccer balls buzz around them like innocuous flies.

Hill towns are best enjoyed by adapting to the pace of the countryside. So, slow...down...and savor the delights that this region offers. Spend the night if you can, as many hill towns are mobbed by day-trippers.

Planning Your Time

How in Dante's name does a traveler choose from Italy's hundreds of hill towns? I've listed some of my favorites in this chapter. The one(s) you visit will depend on your interests, time, and mode of transportation.

Multi-towered San Gimignano is a classic, but because it's such an easy hill town to visit (about 1.5 hours by bus from Florence), peak-season crowds can overwhelm its charms. For rustic vitality not completely trampled by tourist crowds, out-of-the-way Volterra is the clear winner. Wine aficionados head for Montalcino and Montepulciano—each a happy gauntlet of wine shops and art galleries (Montepulciano being my favorite). Fans of architecture and urban design appreciate Pienza's well-planned streets and squares. Those enamored by Frances Mayes' memoir *(Under the Tuscan Sun)* make the pilgrimage to Cortona. Urbino,

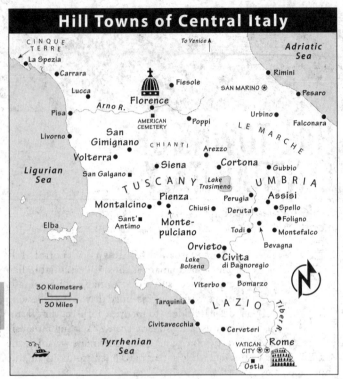

Hill Towns of Central Italy

HILL TOWNS

well off the tourist track and quite remote, is known for its huge Ducal Palace. And Assisi, Siena, and Orvieto—while technically hill towns—are in a category by themselves: Bigger and with more major artistic and historic sights, they each get their own chapter. (The Orvieto chapter also includes my all-around favorite hill town, the stranded-on-a-hilltop Civita di Bagnoregio.)

For a relaxing break from big-city Italy, settle down in an *agriturismo*—a farmhouse that rents out rooms to travelers (usually for a minimum of a week in high season). These rural B&Bs—almost by definition in the middle of nowhere—provide a good home base from which to find the magic of Italy's hill towns. I've listed several good options throughout this chapter (for more information, see "Agritourism" on page 28).

Hill Towns: Public Transportation

(Map legend: Rail, High Speed Rail, Bus)

Getting Around the Hill Towns

While you can reach just about anyplace with public buses, taxis, and loads of patience, most hill towns are easier and more efficient to visit by car.

By Bus or Train

Traveling by public transportation is cheap and connects you with the locals. While trains link some of the towns, hill towns—being on hills—don't quite fit the railroad plan. Stations are likely to be in the valley a couple of miles from the town center, usually connected efficiently by a local bus. Buses are often the only public-transportation choice to get between small hill towns. But, as with trains, they don't always drive up into the town itself. Fortunately, bus stations are sometimes connected to the town by escalator or elevator. (For more on traveling by train and bus in Italy, see the appendix.) If you're pinched for time, it makes sense to narrow your focus to one or two hill towns, or rent a car to see more.

HILL TOWNS

Driving in Tuscany: Distance & Time

To Milan
EMILIA - ROMAGNA
To Venice

20 Kilometers
20 Miles

To Cinque Terre
(La Spezia)

190m · 3.5h
160m · 3.5h

LE MARCHE

50m · 1h
50m · 1h
20m · .5h
Lucca
50m · 1h
Florence

Pisa
70m · 1.25h
(via FiPiLi)

70m · 1.5h

15m · .5h
60m · 1.25h
55m · 1.5h

40m · .75h
(via S-2)

45m · .75h
(superstrada)

45m · 2h
(via S-222)

75m · 1.5h
(via A-1)

Livorno

San Gimignano

TUSCANY

20m · .5h
30m · .75h

Volterra

Siena
45m · 1h
Cortona
40m · 1h

To Assisi

40m · 1h
25m · .75h
30m · .75h

50m · 1h
40m · 1.5h
(via S-438)

10m · .25h

20m · .75h
30m · .75h

San Galgano Monastery
55m · 1.5h
15m · .5h
Pienza
75m · .5h
Chiusi

Montalcino
Monte-pulciano
UMBRIA
To Assisi

Mediterranean Sea

60m · 1.5h
35m · 1h
60m · 1.5h

210m · 4h

Orvieto

m = miles   h = hours
Note: Your times may vary based on traffic, construction, and road conditions.

Bagnoregio (Civita)
15m · .5h
75m · 1.5h

To Rome
LAZIO
To Rome

By Car

Exploring the hill towns by car can be a great experience. But since a car is an expensive, worthless headache in cities like Florence and Rome, wait to pick up your car until the last sizeable town you visit (or pick it up at the nearest airport to avoid big-city traffic). Then use the car for lacing together the hill towns and exploring the countryside. For more on car rentals and driving in Italy, see the appendix.

A big, detailed regional road map (buy one at a newsstand or gas station) and a semi-skilled navigator are essential. Freeways (such as the toll autostrada and the non-toll *super-strada*) provide the fastest way to connect two points, but the smaller roads, including the super-scenic S-222, which runs through the heart of the Chianti region (connecting

Florence and Siena), are more rewarding. For more joyrides—from Siena to Montalcino, and from Montalcino to Montepulciano—see "The Crete Senese" on page 685.

Parking throughout this region can be challenging. Some towns don't allow visitors to park in the city center, so you'll need to leave your car outside the walls and walk into town. Signs reading *Zona Traffico Limitato (ZTL)*—often above a red circle—mark areas where no driving or parking is allowed. Parking lots, indicated by big blue *P* signs, are usually free and plentiful outside city walls (and in some cases, are linked to the town center by elevators or escalators). In some towns, you can park on the street; nearby kiosks sell "pay and display" tickets. In general, white lines indicate free parking, blue lines mean you have to pay, and yellow lines are spaces reserved for local residents. To reduce the threat of theft (no guarantees, though), choose a parking lot over street parking when possible. Your hotelier can also recommend safe parking options.

Between Florence and Siena

Two fine hill towns—one famous, the other underrated—sit in the middle of the triangle formed by three major destinations: Florence, Siena, and Pisa. If driving between those cities, it makes sense to detour either to picturesque but touristy San Gimignano, or charming and authentic-feeling Volterra. (Or you could use one of them as a home base for reaching the bigger towns.) While they're only about a 30-minute drive apart, they're poorly connected to each other by public transit (requiring an infrequent two-hour connection); if relying on buses, San Gimignano is easier to reach, but Volterra rewards the additional effort.

San Gimignano

The epitome of a Tuscan hill town, with 14 medieval towers still standing (out of an original 72), San Gimignano (sahn jee-meen-YAH-noh) is a perfectly preserved tourist trap. There are no important interiors to sightsee, and the town is packed with crass commercialism. The locals seem spoiled by the easy money of tourism, and most of the rustic is faux. The fact that this small town supports two torture museums is a comment on the caliber of the masses who choose to visit. But San Gimignano is so easy to reach and visually so beautiful that it remains a good stop. It's enchanting at night, when it's yours alone. For this reason, San Gimignano is an ideal place to go against the touristic flow—arrive late in the day, enjoy it at twilight, then take off in the morning before the deluge begins.

In the 13th century—back in the days of Romeo and Juliet—feuding noble families ran the hill towns. They'd periodically battle things out from the protection of their respective family towers. Pointy skylines, like San Gimignano's, were the norm in medieval Tuscany.

San Gimignano's cuisine is mostly what you might find in Siena—typical Tuscan home cooking. *Cinghiale* (cheeng-GAH-lay, boar) is served in almost every way: stews, soups, cutlets, and, my favorite, salami. Most shops will give you a sample before you commit to buying. The area is well known for producing some of the best saffron in Italy (collected from the purple flowers of *Crocus sativus*); you'll find the spice for sale in shops (it's fairly expensive) and as a flavoring in meals at finer restaurants. Although Tuscany is normally a red-wine region, the most famous Tuscan white wine comes from here: the inexpensive, light, and fruity Vernaccia di San Gimignano. Look for the green "DOCG" label around the neck for the best quality (see "Wines Labels and Lingo" on page 32).

Orientation to San Gimignano

While the basic ▲▲▲ sight here is the town of San Gimignano itself, there are a few worthwhile stops. From the town gate, head straight up the traffic-free town's cobbled main drag to Piazza della Cisterna (with its 13th-century well). The town sights cluster around the adjoining Piazza del Duomo.

Tourist Information

The helpful TI is in the old center on Piazza del Duomo (daily March-Oct 10:00-13:00 & 15:00-19:00, Nov-Feb 10:00-13:00 & 14:00-18:00, free maps, sells bus tickets, books rooms, handles VAT refunds, tel. 0577-940-008, www.sangimignano.com).

The town offers a two-hour **guided walk** in English and Italian several days a week (April-Oct Sat-Sun at 11:00, €20; includes admission either to the Duomo or to the Civic Museum and Tower; pay and meet at TI). They also offer a two-hour minibus tour to a countryside winery for the same price (April-Oct Tue and Thu at 17:00).

HILL TOWNS

HILL TOWNS

San Gimignano

1 Hotel l'Antico Pozzo
2 Hotel la Cisterna
3 Palazzo al Torrione
4 To Ponte a Nappo Rooms
5 Le Vecchie Mura Camere & Ristorante
6 Locanda il Pino
7 Dulcis in Fundo Ristorante
8 Trattoria Chiribiri
9 Locanda di Sant'Agostino
10 diVinorum Wine Bar
11 Gelateria Pluripremiata "di Piazza"
12 Co-op Supermarket

Arrival in San Gimignano

The **bus** stops at the main town gate, Porta San Giovanni. There's no baggage storage anywhere in town, so you're better off leaving your bags in Siena or Florence.

You can't **drive** within the walled town. There are three pay lots a short walk outside the walls: The handiest is Parcheggio Montemaggio, just outside the main gate, Porta San Giovanni (€2/hour, €20/day). The one below the roundabout and Co-op supermarket, called Parcheggio Giubileo, is least expensive (€1.50/hour, €6/day). And at the north end of town, by Porta San Jacopo, is Parcheggio Bagnaia (€2/hour, €15/day). Note that some lots—including the one directly in front of the Co-op and the one just outside Porta San Matteo—are designated for locals and have a one-hour limit for tourists.

Helpful Hints

Market Day: Thursday is market day on Piazza del Duomo (8:00-13:00), but for local merchants, every day is a sales frenzy.

Services: A public **WC** is just off Piazza della Cisterna (€0.50); others are at the Rocca fortress, just outside Porta San Matteo, and at the Parcheggio Bagnaia parking lot.

Shuttle Bus: A little electric shuttle bus does its laps all day from Porta San Giovanni to Piazza della Cisterna to Porta San Matteo. Route #1 runs back and forth through town; route #2—which runs only in summer—conveniently connects the three parking lots to the town center. Each route runs about hourly (€0.75 one-way, €1.50 for all-day pass, buy ticket in advance from TI or tobacco shop, possible to buy on bus for extra charge).

Self-Guided Walk

Welcome to San Gimignano

This quick walking tour will take you across town, from the bus stop at Porta San Giovanni through the town's main squares to the Duomo, and on to the Sant'Agostino Church.

• *Start, as most tourists do, at the Porta San Giovanni gate at the bottom end of town.*

Porta San Giovanni: San Gimignano lies about 25 miles from both Siena and Florence, a good stop for pilgrims en route to those cities, and on a naturally fortified hilltop that encouraged settlement. The town's walls were built in the 13th century, and gates like this helped regulate who came and went. Today, modern posts keep out all but service and emergency vehicles. The small square just outside the gate features a memorial to the town's WWII dead. Follow the pilgrims' route (and flood of modern tourists) through the gate and up the main drag.

About 100 yards up, on the right, is a pilgrims' shelter (12th-century, Pisan Romanesque). The eight-pointed Maltese cross indicates that this was built by the Knights of Malta, whose early mission (before they became a military unit) was to provide hospitality for pilgrims. It was one of 11 such shelters in town. Today, only the wall of this shelter remains.

• *Carry on past all manner of touristy rip-off shops, up to the town's central Piazza della Cisterna. Sit on the steps of the well.*

Piazza della Cisterna: The piazza is named for the cistern that is served by the old well standing in the center of this square.

A clever system of pipes drained rainwater from the nearby rooftops into the underground cistern. This square has been the center of the town since the ninth century. Turn in a slow circle and observe the commotion of rustic-yet-proud facades crowding in a tight huddle around the well. Imagine this square in pilgrimage times, lined by inns and taverns for the town's guests. Now finger the grooves in the lip of the well and imagine generations of maids and children fetching water. Each Thursday, the square fills with a market—as it has for more than a thousand years.

• *Notice San Gimignano's famous towers.*

The Towers: Of the original 72 towers, only 14 survive. Before effective city walls were developed, rich people fortified their own homes with these towers: They provided a handy refuge when ruffians and rival city-states were sacking the town. If under attack, tower owners would set fire to the external wooden staircase, leaving the sole entrance unreachable a story up; inside, fleeing nobles pulled up behind them the ladders that connected each level, leaving invaders no way to reach the stronghold at the tower's top. These towers became a standard part of medieval skylines. Even after town walls were built, the towers continued to rise—now to fortify noble families feuding within a town (Montague and Capulet-style).

In the 14th century, San Gimignano's good times turned very bad. In the year 1300, about 13,000 people lived within the walls. Then in 1348, a six-month plague decimated the population, leaving

HILL TOWNS

the once-mighty town with barely 4,000 survivors. Once fiercely independent, now crushed and demoralized, San Gimignano came under Florence's control and was forced to tear down its towers. (The Banca CR Firenze building occupies the remains of one such toppled tower.) And, to add insult to injury, Florence redirected the vital trade route away from San Gimignano. The town never recovered, and poverty left it in a 14th-century architectural time warp. That well-preserved cityscape, ironically, is responsible for the town's prosperity today.

• *From the well, walk 30 yards uphill to the adjoining square with the cathedral.*

Piazza del Duomo: The square faces the former cathedral. The twin towers to the right are 10th century, among the first in

town. The stubby tower opposite the church is typical of a merchant's tower: main door on ground floor, warehouse upstairs, holes to hold beams that once supported wooden balconies and exterior staircases, heavy stone on the first floor, cheaper and lighter brick for upper stories.

• *On the piazza are the Civic Museum and Tower, worth checking out (see "Sights in San Gimignano," later). You'll also see the...*

Duomo (or Collegiata): Inside San Gimignano's Romanesque cathedral, Sienese Gothic art (14th century) lines the nave with parallel themes—Old Testament on the left and New Testament on the right. (For example, from back to front: Creation facing the Annunciation, the birth of Adam facing the Nativity, and the suffering of Job opposite the suffering of Jesus.) This is a classic use of art to teach. Study the fine Creation series (top left). Many scenes are portrayed with a local 14th-century "slice of life" setting, to help lay townspeople relate to Jesus—in the same way that many white Christians are more comfortable thinking of Jesus as Caucasian (€3.50, €5.50 combo-ticket includes mediocre Religious Art Museum—skip it; April-Oct Mon-Fri 10:00-19:30, Sat 10:00-17:30, Sun 12:30-19:30; Nov-March Mon-Sat 10:00-17:00, Sun 12:30-17:00; last entry 20 minutes before closing, buy ticket and enter from the courtyard around the left side).

• *From the church, hike uphill (passing the church on your left) following signs to* Rocca e Parco di Montestaffoli. *Keep walking until you enter a peaceful hilltop park and olive grove within the shell of a 14th-century fortress.*

Hilltop Views at the Rocca: On the far side, 33 steps take you to the top of a little tower (free) for the best views of San Gimignano's skyline; the far end of town and the Sant'Agostino

Church (where this walk ends); and a commanding 360-degree view of the Tuscan countryside. San Gimignano is surrounded by olives, grapes, cypress trees, and—in the Middle Ages—lots of wild dangers. Back then, farmers lived inside the walls and were thankful for the protection.

• *Return to the bottom of Piazza del Duomo, turn left, and continue your walk across town, cutting under the double arch (from the town's first wall). In around 1200, this defined the end of town. The **Church of San Bartolo** stood just outside the wall (on the right). The Maltese cross over the door indicates that it likely served as a hostel for pilgrims. As you continue down Via San Matteo, notice that the crowds have dropped by at least half. Enjoy the breathing room as you pass a fascinating array of stone facades from the 13th and 14th centuries—now a happy cancan of wine shops and galleries. Reaching the gateway at the end of town, follow signs to the right to reach...*

Sant'Agostino Church: This tranquil church, at the far end of town (built by the Augustinians who arrived in 1260), has fewer crowds and more soul. Behind the altar, a lovely fresco cycle by Benozzo Gozzoli (who painted the exquisite Chapel of the Magi in the Medici-Riccardi Palace in Florence) tells of the life of St. Augustine, a North African monk who preached simplicity. The kind, English-speaking friars (from Britain and the US) are happy to tell you about their church and way of life, and also have Mass in English on Sundays at 11:00. Pace the peaceful cloister before heading back into the tourist mobs (free, €0.50 lights the frescoes; April-Oct daily 7:00-12:00 & 15:00-19:00; Nov-March Tue-Sun 7:00-12:00 & 15:00-18:00, Mon 16:00-18:00). Their fine little shop, with books on the church and its art, is worth a look.

Sights in San Gimignano

▲ **Civic Museum and Tower (Museo Civico and Torre Grossa)**—This small, fun museum, consisting of just three unfurnished rooms and a tower, is inside City Hall (Palazzo Comunale). The main room (across from the ticket desk), called the **Sala di Consiglio** (a.k.a. Dante Hall), is covered in festive frescoes, including the *Maestà* by Lippo Memmi. This virtual copy of Simone Martini's *Maestà* in Siena proves that Memmi didn't have quite the same talent as his famous brother-in-law.

Upstairs, the **Pinacoteca** displays a classy little painting collection of mostly altarpieces. The highlight is a 1422 altarpiece by Taddeo di Bartolo honoring St. Gimignano (far end of last room). You can see the saint, with the town—bristling with towers—in his hands, surrounded by events from his life.

Before going back downstairs, be sure to stop by the **Mayor's Room** (Camera del Podestà, across the stairwell from the

HILL TOWNS

Pinacoteca). Frescoed in 1310 by Memmo di Filippuccio, it offers an intimate and candid peek into the 14th century. The theme: profane love. As you enter, look to the left corner where a young man is ready to experience the world. He hits his parents up for a bag of money and is free. On the opposite wall (above the window), you'll see a series of bad decisions: Almost immediately he's entrapped by two prostitutes, who lead him into a tent where he loses his money, is turned out, and is beaten. Above the door, from left to right, you see a parade of better choices: marriage, the cradle of love, the bride led to the groom's house, and newlyweds bathing together and retiring happily to their bed.

The highlight for most visitors is a chance to climb the **Tower** (Torre Grossa, entrance halfway down the stairs from

the Pinacoteca). The city's tallest tower, 200 feet and 218 steps up, rewards those who climb it with a commanding view. See if you can count the town's 14 towers (yes, that includes the stubby little one just below this tower). It's a sturdy, modern staircase most of the way, but the last stretch is a steep, ladder-like climb.

Coming back down to earth, you leave the complex via a delightful stony loggia and courtyard out back.

Cost and Hours: €5 includes museum and tower, daily April-Sept 9:30-19:00, Oct-March 11:00-17:30, Piazza del Duomo, tel. 0577-990-310.

San Gimignano 1300—This small but interesting attraction, located inside the Palazzo Ficarelli on a quiet street a block over from the main street, is a trip back in time. When possible, attendants like to lead visitors on individual tours around the small exhibit. The highlight is a painstakingly rendered 1:100 scale clay model of San Gimignano at the turn of the 14th century. You can see the 72 original "tower houses," and marvel at how unchanged the street plan remains today. You'll peek into cross-sections of buildings, view scenes of medieval life both within and outside the city walls, and watch videos about town history and the making of the model. After walking through a gallery of modern Italian sculpture, your visit ends in the ceramics workshop next door, where models like this one are created from wet lumps of clay. (Conveniently, the "workshop" is one corner of a ceramics shop.) While cynics might view this as little more than a gimmick to sell more little ceramic buildings, the detail of the model is truly enchanting.

Cost and Hours: €5; April-Oct daily 9:00-19:00; Nov-March

Wed-Mon 10:00-17:00, Sat-Sun until 18:00, closed Tue; Via Berignano 23, tel. 0577-941-078, www.sangimignano1300.com.

Sleeping in San Gimignano

Although the town is a zoo during the daytime, locals outnumber tourists when evening comes, and San Gimignano becomes mellow and enjoyable. Drivers can unload near their hotels, then park outside the walls in recommended lots. Hotel websites provide instructions.

$$$ **Hotel l'Antico Pozzo** is an elegantly restored, 15th-century townhouse with 18 tranquil, comfortable rooms, a peaceful interior courtyard terrace, and an elite air (Sb-€100, small Db-€120, standard Db-€140, big Db-€180, includes breakfast, air-con, elevator, free Wi-Fi, near Porta San Matteo at Via San Matteo 87, tel. 0577-942-014, fax 0577-942-117, www.antico-pozzo.com, info@anticopozzo.com; Emanuele, Elisabetta, and Mariangela). If arriving by bus, save a crosstown walk by asking for the Porta San Matteo stop (rather than getting off at the main stop near Porta San Giovanni).

$$$ **Hotel la Cisterna,** right on Piazza della Cisterna, feels old and stately, with 49 predictable rooms, some with panoramic view terraces (Sb-€78, Db-€100, Db with view-€125, Db with view terrace-€140, 10 percent discount with this book when you book direct, includes buffet breakfast, air-con, elevator, cheap Wi-Fi, good restaurant with great view, closed Jan-Feb, Piazza della Cisterna 23, tel. 0577-940-328, fax 0577-942-080, www.hotelcisterna.it, info@hotelcisterna.it, Alessio).

$$$ **Ponte a Nappo,** run by enterprising Carla Rossi (who doesn't speak English) and her son Francesco (who does), has seven comfortable rooms and two apartments in a kid-friendly farmhouse. Located a long half-mile below town (best for drivers, but doable for hardy walkers), this place has killer views. A picnic dinner lounging on their comfy garden furniture as the sun sets is good Tuscan living (Db-€100-130, 2-6 person apartment-€130-250, price depends on season and length of stay, for best price book direct and mention Rick Steves, air-con mid-June-mid-Sept only, free Wi-Fi, free parking, pool, free loaner bikes, lunch and dinner available to guests, 15-minute walk or 5-minute drive from Porta San Giovanni, tel. 0577-907-282, mobile 349-882-1565, fax 0577-941-268, www.accommodation-sangimignano.com, info@rossicarla.it). About 100 yards below the monument square at Porta San Giovanni, find Via Vecchia (not left or right, but down a tiny road) and follow it down a dirt road for five minutes by car. They also rent a dozen or so rooms and apartments in town (including some in the Palazzo Tortoli, a stone tower right

Sleep Code

(€1 = about $1.40, country code: 39)

S = Single, **D** = Double/Twin, **T** = Triple, **Q** = Quad, **b** = bathroom, **s** = shower only. Unless otherwise noted, credit cards are accepted and breakfast is included (but usually optional). English is generally spoken, but I've noted exceptions. Many towns in Italy levy a hotel tax of about €2 per person, per night, which is generally not included in the rates I've quoted.

To help you sort easily through these listings, I've divided the accommodations into three categories based on the price for a standard double room with bath:

$$$ Higher Priced—Most rooms €100 or more.
  $$ Moderately Priced—Most rooms between €70-100.
    $ Lower Priced—Most rooms €70 or less.

Prices can change without notice; verify the hotel's current rates online or by email.

on the main square, for Db-€75-110; each one is described on their website).

$$ Palazzo al Torrione, on an untrampled side street just inside Porta San Giovanni, is quiet and handy, and generally better than most hotels (even though they don't have a full-time reception). Their 10 modern rooms are spacious and tastefully appointed (Db-€90, terrace Db-€110, Tb-€110, terrace Tb-€120, Qb-€120-130, 10 percent discount with this book when you book direct, breakfast-€7, communal kitchen, parking-€6/day, inside and left of gate at Via Berignano 76; operated from tobacco shop 2 blocks away, on the main drag at Via San Giovanni 59; tel. 0577-940-480, mobile 338-938-1656, fax 0577-955-605, www.palazzoal torrione.com, palazzoaltorrione@palazzoaltorrione.com, Vanna and Francesco).

$ Le Vecchie Mura Camere offers three good rooms above their restaurant in the old town (Db-€60, no breakfast, air-con, free Wi-Fi, Via Piandornella 15, tel. 0577-940-270, www.vecchie mura.it, info@vecchiemura.it, Bagnai family).

$ Locanda il Pino has just seven rooms and a big living room. It's dank but clean and quiet. Run by English-speaking Elena and her family, it sits above their elegant restaurant just inside Porta San Matteo (Db-€55, no breakfast, free Wi-Fi in lobby, easy parking just outside the gate, Via Cellolese 4, tel. 0577-940-415, locanda@ristoranteilpino.it). If you're arriving by bus, ask for the Porta San Matteo stop, rather than the main stop near Porta San Giovanni.

Eating in San Gimignano

My first two listings cling to quiet, rustic lanes overlooking the Tuscan hills (yet just a few steps off the main street); the rest are buried deep in the old center.

Dulcis in Fundo Ristorante, small and family-run, proudly serves modest portions of "revisited" Tuscan cuisine (with a modern twist and gourmet presentation) in a jazzy ambience. This enlightened place, whose menu identifies the sources of their ingredients, offers lots of vegetarian options and gladly caters to gluten-free diets—rare in Tuscany (€12 pastas, €13-16 *secondi,* meals served 12:30-14:30 & 19:15-21:30, closed Wed, Vicolo degli Innocenti 21, tel. 0577-941-919).

Le Vecchie Mura Ristorante has good and fast service, great prices, tasty if unexceptional home cooking, and the ultimate view. It's romantic indoors or out. They have a dressy, modern interior where you can dine with a view of the busy stainless-steel kitchen under rustic vaults, but the main reason to come is for the incredible cliffside garden terrace. Cliffside tables are worth reserving in advance by calling or dropping by: Ask for "front view" (€8-11 pastas, €12-15 *secondi,* open only for dinner from 18:00, last order at 22:00, closed Tue, Via Piandornella 15, tel. 0577-940-270, Bagnai family).

Trattoria Chiribiri, just inside Porta San Giovanni, serves homemade pastas and desserts at remarkably fair prices. While its petite size and tight seating make it hot in the summer, it's a good budget option—and as such, it's in all the guidebooks (€7 pastas, €9 *secondi,* daily 11:00-23:00, Piazza della Madonna 1, tel. 0577-941-948, Maria and Maurizio).

Locanda di Sant'Agostino spills out onto the peaceful square, facing Sant'Agostino Church. It's cheap and cheery, serving lunch and dinner daily—big portions of basic food in a restful setting. Dripping with wheat stalks and atmosphere on the inside, there's shady on-the-square seating outside (€8 pizzas, pastas, and *bruschette*; €9-14 *secondi,* daily 11:00-22:00, closed Tue off-season and Jan-Feb, Piazza Sant'Agostino 15, tel. 0577-943-141, Genziana and sons).

Enoteca: **diVinorum,** a cool wine bar with a small entrance right on Piazza Cisterna, has a contemporary cellar atmosphere and—best of all—a row of tables out back overlooking rolling Tuscan hills (just downhill and toward the main drag from Dulcis in Fundo, recommended above; at mealtimes, you'll have to order food to sit at the outdoor tables). They have local wines by the glass (€3-5) as well as snacks that can easily make a light meal (€10-15 *antipasti* plates, €7-8 *bruschette* and warm plates, daily 11:00-21:30, Nov-April until 20:00, Piazza Cisterna 30 or Via degli Innocenti 5, tel. 0577-907-192, Matteo).

Picnics: The big, modern **Co-op supermarket** sells all you need for a nice spread (Mon-Sat 8:30-20:00, Sun 8:30-12:30 except closed Sun Nov-March, at parking lot below Porta San Giovanni). Or browse the little shops guarded by boar heads within the town walls; they sell pricey boar meat *(cinghiale)*. Pick up 100 grams (about a quarter pound) of boar, cheese, bread, and wine and enjoy a picnic in the garden at the Rocca or the park outside Porta San Giovanni.

Gelato: To cap the evening and sweeten your late-night city stroll, stop by **Gelateria Pluripremiata "di Piazza"** on Piazza della Cisterna (at #4). Gelato-maker Sergio was a member of the Italian team that won the official Gelato World Cup—and his gelato really is a cut above (daily 8:00-24:00, tel. 0577-942-244, Dondoli family).

San Gimignano Connections

Bus tickets are sold at the bar just inside the town gate or at the TI. Many connections require a change at Poggibonsi (poh-jee-BOHN-see, with a soft "g"), which is also the nearest train station.

From San Gimignano by Bus to: Florence (hourly, less on Sun, 1.5-2 hours, change in Poggibonsi, €6.80), **Siena** (8/day direct, on Sun must change in Poggibonsi, 1.25 hours, €6), **Volterra** (4/day Mon-Sat; on Sun only 1/day—in the late afternoon and usually crowded—with no return to San Gimignano; 2 hours, change in Colle Val d'Elsa, €5.45). Note that the bus connection to Volterra is four times as long as the drive; if you're desperate to get there faster, you can pay about €70 for a taxi.

By Car: San Gimignano is an easy 45-minute drive from Florence (take the A-1 exit marked *Firenze Certosa*, then a right past tollbooth following *Siena per 4 corsie* sign; exit the freeway at Poggibonsi). From San Gimignano, it's a scenic and windy half-hour drive to Volterra.

Volterra

Encircled by impressive walls and topped with a grand fortress, Volterra sits high above the rich farmland surrounding it. More

than 2,000 years ago, Volterra was one of the most important Etruscan cities, and much larger than we see today. Greek-trained Etruscan artists worked here, leaving a significant stash of art, particularly funerary urns. Eventually Volterra was absorbed into the Roman Empire, and for centuries it was an independent city-state. Volterra fought bitterly against the Florentines, but like many Tuscan towns, it lost in the end and was given a fortress atop the city to "protect" its citizens.

Unlike other famous towns in Tuscany, Volterra feels neither cutesy nor touristy...but real, vibrant, and almost oblivious to the allure of the tourist dollar. This probably stems from the Volterrans' feisty resistance to change. (At a recent town meeting about whether to run high-speed Internet cable to the town, a local grumbled, "The Etruscans didn't need it—why do we?") This stubbornness helps make Volterra a refreshing change of pace from its more commercial neighbors. It also boasts some particularly fine sights for a small town, from a remarkably intact ancient Roman theater, to a finely decorated Pisan Romanesque cathedral, to an excellent museum of Etruscan artifacts. All in all, Volterra is my favorite small town in Tuscany.

Orientation to Volterra

Compact and walkable, the city stretches out from the pleasant Piazza dei Priori to the old city gates.

Tourist Information
The helpful TI is on the main square, at Piazza dei Priori 19 (daily 10:00-13:00 & 14:00-18:00, tel. 0588-87257, www.volterratur.it). The TI's excellent €5 audioguide narrates 20 stops (2-for-1 discount on audioguides with this book).

Arrival in Volterra
By Public Transport: Buses stop at Piazza Martiri della Libertà in the town center. Train travelers can reach the town with a short bus ride (see "Volterra Connections," later.)

Tuscan Hill Towns

To Florence & ... — S-2

To Florence & Pisa via Empoli

To Greve & Florence

CHIANTI

San Gimignano ●

Poggibonsi

Radda

T U S

Volterra ⑤ ●

Colle Val d'Elsa

SUPER-STRADA   S-222

Saline di Volterra ●

Monteriggione

To Pisa

Elsa R.

S-2

Siena Train Stn.

Siena ●   ①

②

═══ High-Speed Rail Line
═══ Scenic Drives

See Greater Siena detail map

S-73

③

San Galgano ■ Monastery

S-223

To Piombino

Ombrone R.

20 Kilometers
20 Miles

⑪

To Grosseto

HILL TOWNS

① Frances' Lodge Relais
② Borgo Argenina
③ Il Canto del Sole
④ To I Greppi di Silli
⑤ Podere Marcampo
⑥ Agriturismo Cretaiole
⑦ Le Casine di Castello & Casa Moricciani
⑧ Fonte Bertusi
⑨ La Crociona Agriturismo
⑩ Argiano Winery
⑪ Banfi Winery
⑫ Roberto Becchi's B&B
⑬ Alle Logge di Sotto
⑭ Casanova Agriturismo
⑮ Agriturismo il Molinello
⑯ La Porta & La Cantina Restaurants

By Car: Drivers will find the town ringed with easy numbered parking lots (#5, #6, and #8 are free; #3 is for locals only). The most central lots are the pay lots at Porta Fiorentina and underground at Piazza Martiri della Libertà (€1.50/hour, €11/24 hours).

Helpful Hints

Market Day: The market is on Saturday morning near the Roman Theater (8:00-13:00, at parking lot #5; in winter, it's right on Piazza dei Priori). The TI hands out a list of other market days in the area.

Festivals: Volterra's Medieval Festival takes place the third and fourth Sundays of August. Fall is a popular time for food festivals—check with the TI for dates and events planned.

Internet Access: Web & Wine has a few terminals, fine wine by the glass, and organic vegetarian food (€3/hour, no minimum, summer daily 9:30-1:00 in the morning, closed Thu in Sept-May, Via Porta all'Arco 11-15, tel. 0588-81531, www.weband wine.com, Lallo speaks English). **Enjoy Café Internet Point** has a couple of terminals in their basement (€3/hour, daily 6:30-1:00 in the morning, Piazza dei Martiri 3, tel. 0588-80530).

Laundry: The handy self-service **Lavanderia Azzurra** is just off

Vampire Volterra?

Fans of the *Twilight* books and films may recognize Volterra as the home of the powerful clan of vampires called the Volturi. For a while, a wave of *Twilight* interest swept the town—but most of that seems to have passed. Maybe that's because *Twilight* ties to Volterra were tenuous at best. Author Stephanie Meyer had never been to Volterra before setting part of her second novel, *New Moon,* in the town; she simply picked the name for its resemblance to the one she had already given to her characters, the "Volturi." Although the novel takes place in Volterra, most scenes in the *New Moon* film (2009) were filmed in Montepulciano.

And yet, although it was a random choice, it was serendipitous. Sitting on its stony main square at midnight, watching bats dart about as if they own the place, I realize there really is something supernatural about Volterra. The cliffs of Volterra inspired Dante's "cliffs of hell." In the winter, the town's vibrancy is smothered under a deadening cloak of clouds. The name Volterra means "land that floats"—referring to the clouds that often seem to cut it off from the rest of the world below.

The people of Volterra live in a cloud of mystery, too. Their favorite cookie, crunchy with almonds, is called Ossi di Morta ("bones of the dead"). Through the 1980s, Volterra was home to Italy's second-biggest psychiatric hospital. The town's first disco was named Catacombs. Volterra's top sight—the Etruscan Museum—is filled with hundreds of ancient caskets. And in the 1970s, when Volterra was the set of a wildly popular TV horror series called *Ritratto di Donna Velata (Portrait of a Veiled Woman),* all of Italy tuned in to Volterra every week for a good scare. Perhaps *Twilight* is just one more chapter in a long tale of a town that revels in being otherworldly.

the main square (€3 wash, €3-4 dry, daily 7:00-23:00, Via Roma 7, tel. 0588-80030).

Tours in Volterra

▲▲**Guided Volterra Walk**—Annie Adair (also listed individually, next) and her colleagues offer a great one-hour, English-only introductory walking tour of Volterra for €10. The walk touches on Volterra's Etruscan, Roman, and medieval history, as well as the contemporary cultural scene (April-July and Sept-Oct daily, rain or shine, at 18:00; meet in front of alabaster shop on Piazza Martiri della Libertà, no need to reserve—just show up, they need a minimum of 3 people, or €30—to make the tour go, www

.volterrawalkingtour.com or www.tuscantour.com, info@volterra
walkingtour.com). There's no better way to spend €10 and one hour
in this city.

Local Guide—American **Annie Adair** is an excellent city guide.
She and her husband Francesco, a sommelier, organize private food
and wine tours and even Tuscan weddings for Americans (€50/
hour, minimum 2 hours, tel. 0588-086-201, mobile 347-143-5004,
www.tuscantour.com, info@tuscantour.com). Francesco leads a
crash one-hour "Wine Tasting 101" class in sampling Tuscan
wines, held at a local wine bar (€50 per group plus cost of wine).

Sights in Volterra

I've arranged these sights as a handy little town walk, connected
by directions on foot. Not all the sights will interest everyone, so
skim the listings to decide which detours appeal to you.

· *Begin your visit of town at the Etruscan Arch. To find it, go all the
way down to the bottom of Via Porta all'Arco (you'll find the top of this
street between Piazza Martiri della Libertà, with the town bus stop,
and the main square, Piazza dei Priori).*

▲**Etruscan Arch (Porta all'Arco)**—Volterra's most famous
sight is its Etruscan arch, built of massive, volcanic tuff stones

in the fourth century B.C. (for
more information on tuff, see the
sidebar on page 644). Volterra's
original wall was four miles
around—twice the size of the
wall that encircles it today. With
25,000 people, Volterra was a key
trading center and one of 12 leading towns in the confederation of
Etruria Propria. The three seri-
ously eroded heads, dating from the first century B.C., show what
happens when you leave something outside for 2,000 years. The
newer stones are part of the 13th-century city wall, which incorporated parts of the much older Etruscan wall.

A plaque just outside remembers June 30, 1944. That night,
Nazi forces were planning to blow up the arch to slow the Allied
advance. To save their treasured landmark, Volterrans ripped up
the stones that pave Via Porta all'Arco and plugged the gate, managing to convince the Nazi commander that there was no need to
blow up the arch. Today, all the stones are back in their places, and
like silent heroes, they welcome you through the oldest standing
Etruscan gate into Volterra. Locals claim this as the only surviving
round arch of the Etruscan age; most experts believe this is where
the Romans got the idea for using a keystone in their arches.

HILL TOWNS

• *Go through the arch and head up Via Porta all'Arco, which I like to call...*

"Artisan Lane" (Via Porta all'Arco)—This steep and atmospheric strip is lined with interesting shops featuring the work of artisans and producers. Because of its alabaster heritage, Volterra attracted craftsmen and artists, who brought with them a rich variety of handiwork (shops generally open Mon-Sat 10:00-13:00 & 16:00-19:00, closed Sun; the TI produces a free booklet called *Handicraft in Volterra*).

From the Etruscan Arch, browse your way up the hill, checking out these shops and items (listed from bottom to top): La Mia Fattoria—a co-op of producers of cheese, salami, and olive oil lets you buy direct at farm prices (just up Via Laberinti near #52); alabaster shops (#57, #50, and #45); book bindery and papery (#26); jewelry (#25); etchings (#23); Web & Wine (Internet access; #11-15); and bronze work (#6).

• *Reaching the top of Via Porta all'Arco, turn left and walk a few steps into Volterra's main square, Piazza dei Priori. It's dominated by the...*

1 Hotel La Locanda
2 Albergo Etruria
3 Albergo Nazionale
4 To Park Hotel Le Fonti

5 To Albergo Villa Nencini & Old Etruscan Wall
6 La Primavera B&B
7 Seminario Vescovile Sant'Andrea
8 To Chiosco delle Monache Hostel & Hotel Foresteria
9 To Podere Marcampo
10 Ristorante Enoteca del Duca
11 Trattoria Don Beta
12 La Vecchia Lira
13 La Carabaccia
14 Ristorante il Sacco Fiorentino
15 La Vena di Vino Wine Bar
16 Ombra della Sera & Pizzeria Tavernetta
17 Despar Market
18 L'Isola di Gusto Gelato
19 Alab'Arte Alabaster Showroom
20 Alab'Arte Alabaster Workshop
21 "Artisan Lane"
22 Internet Cafés (2)
23 Launderette

HILL TOWNS

Palazzo dei Priori—Volterra's City Hall (c. 1209) claims to be the oldest of any Tuscan city-state. It clearly inspired the more famous Palazzo Vecchio in Florence. Town halls like this are emblematic of an era when city-states were powerful. They were architectural exclamation points declaring that, around here, no pope or emperor called the shots. Towns such as Volterra were truly city-states—proudly independent and relatively democratic. They had their own armies, taxes, and even weights and measures. Notice the horizontal "cane" cut into the City Hall wall (right of the door). For a thousand years, this square hosted a market, and the "cane" was the local yardstick. When not in use for meetings or weddings, the city council chambers—lavishly painted and lit with fun dragon lamps, as they have been for centuries of town meetings—are open to visitors.

Cost and Hours: €1.50, mid-March-Oct daily 10:30-17:30, Nov-mid-March Sat-Sun only 10:00-17:00.

• *Facing the City Hall, notice the black-and-white-striped wall to the right (set back from the square). The door in that wall leads into*

Italy Is Made of Tuff Stuff

Tuff (*tufo* in Italian) is a light-colored volcanic rock that is common in Italy. A part of Tuscany is even called the "Tuff Area." The seven hills of Rome are made of tuff, and quarried blocks of this stone can be seen in the Colosseum, Pantheon, and Castel Sant'Angelo. Just outside of Rome, the catacombs were carved from tuff. Sorrento rises above the sea on a tuff outcrop. Orvieto, Civita di Bagnoregio (pictured), and many other hill towns perch on bluffs of tuff.

Italy's early inhabitants, including the Etruscans and Romans, carved caves, tunnels, burial niches, and even roads out of tuff. Blocks of this rock were quarried to make houses and walls. Tuff is soft and easy to carve when it's first exposed to air, but hardens later, which makes it a good building stone.

Italy's tuff-producing volcanoes resulted from a lot of tectonic-plate bumping and grinding. This violent geologic history is reflected in Italy's volcanoes, like Vesuvius and Etna, and earthquakes such as the 2009 quake in the L'Aquila area northeast of Rome.

Tuff is actually just a big hardened pile of old volcanic ash. When volcanoes hold magma that contains a lot of water, they erupt explosively (think heat + water = steam = POW!). The exploded rock material gets blasted out as hot volcanic ash, which settles on the surrounding landscape, piles up, and over time welds together into the rock called tuff.

So when you're visiting an area in Italy of ancient caves or catacombs built out of this material, you'll know that at least once (and maybe more) upon a time, it was a site of a lot of volcanic activity.

Volterra's...

Duomo—This church is not as elaborate as its cousin in Pisa, but the simple 13th-century facade and the interior (rebuilt in the late 16th century), with its central nave flanked by monolithic stone columns, are beautiful examples of the Pisan Romanesque style.

Cost and Hours: Free, daily 8:00-12:30 & 15:00-18:00, Nov-March until 17:00.

Visiting the Church: Enter through the back door, and take a moment to let your eyes adjust to this dark, Romanesque space. (If you come through the main door around front, do this tour in reverse.) The interior was decorated mostly in the late 16th century, during Florentine rule under the Medici family. Their coat of arms, with its distinctive balls (called *palle*), is repeated multiple times throughout the building.

Head down into the nave to face the main altar. Up the stairs just to the right is a dreamy painted and gilded-wood *Deposition* (Jesus being taken down from the cross), restored to its original form. Carved in 1228, a generation before Giotto, it shows emotion and motion way ahead of its time (€1 buys some light).

The glowing **windows** in the transept and behind the altar are sheets of alabaster. These, along with the recorded Gregorian chants, add to the church's wonderful ambience.

The 12th-century marble **pulpit** is also beautifully carved. In the relief panel of the Last Supper, all the apostles are together except Judas, who's under the table with the evil dragon (his name is the only one not carved into the relief).

Just past the pulpit on the right (at the Rosary Chapel), check out the *Annunciation* by Fra Bartolomeo (who was a student of Fra Angelico and painted this in 1497). Bartolomeo delicately gives worshippers a way to see Mary "conceived by the Holy Spirit." Note the vibrant colors, exaggerated perspective, and Mary's *contrapposto* pose—all attributes of the Renaissance.

At the end of the nave, the **chapel** to the right of the doors has painted terra-cotta statue groups of the Nativity and the Adoration of the Magi, thought to be the work of master ceramists Luca and Andrea della Robbia. Luca is credited with inventing the glazing formula that makes his inventive sculptures shine even in poorly lit interiors.

Step outside the main door to see a classically Pisan space. A common arrangement in the Middle Ages was for the church to face the baptistery (you couldn't enter the church until you were baptized)...and for the hospital to face the cemetery (now the site of the local ambulance corps). These buildings all overlooked the same square. That's how it is in Pisa, and that's how it is here.

• *Exiting the cathedral out the front door, it's a short detour (to the right and around the corner) to the skippable Sacred Art Museum; otherwise, head back to the main square (either returning through the church to the back door, or looping around the block).*

Sacred Art Museum (Museo d'Arte Sacra)—This humble four-room museum collects sacred art and vestments from deconsecrated churches and small, unguarded churches from nearby villages. The museum may close in 2013, but if it does, you're not missing much.

Cost and Hours: Only possible with a €10 combo-ticket that includes the Etruscan Museum and Pinacoteca—no individual ticket, daily 9:00-13:00 & 15:00-18:00, morning only Nov-mid-March, well-explained in English, next to the Duomo at Via Roma 13, tel. 0588-86290.

HILL TOWNS

• *Head back to the main square. Facing the City Hall, go down the street to the left; after one short block, you're standing at the head (on the left) of...*

▲**Via Matteotti**—The town's main drag, named after the popular Socialist leader Giacomo Matteotti (killed by the Fascists in 1924), provides a good cultural scavenger hunt.

At #1 is a typical Italian bank security door. (Step in and say, "Beam me up, Scotty.") Back outside, stand at the corner, and look up and all around. Find the medieval griffin torch holder—symbol of Volterra—and imagine it holding a lit torch. The pharmacy sports the symbol of its medieval guild. Across the street from the bank, #2 is the base of what was a San Gimignano-style fortified Tuscan tower. Look up and imagine heavy beams cantilevered out, supporting extra wooden rooms and balconies crowding out over the street. Throughout Tuscany, today's stark and stony old building fronts once supported a tangle of wooden extensions.

As you head down Via Matteotti, notice how the doors show centuries of refitting work. Doors that once led to these extra rooms are now partially bricked up to make windows. Contemplate urban density in the 14th century, before the plague thinned out the population. Be careful: There's a wild boar (a local delicacy) at #10.

At #12, notice the line of doorbells: This typical palace, once the home of a single rich family, is now occupied by many middle-class families. After the social revolution in the 18th century and the rise of the middle class, former palaces were condominium-ized. Even so, like in *Dr. Zhivago,* the original family still lives here. Apartment #1 is the home of Count Guidi.

At #16, pop in to an alabaster showroom. Alabaster, mined nearby, has long been a big industry here. Volterra alabaster—softer and more porous than marble—was sliced thin to serve as windows for Italy's medieval churches.

At #19, the recommended La Vecchia Lira is a lively cafeteria. The Bar L'Incontro across the street is a favorite for pastries; in the summer, they sell homemade gelato, while in the winter they make chocolates.

Across the way, up Vicolo delle Prigioni, is a fun bakery *(panificio).* They're happy to sell small quantities if you want to try the local *cantuccini* (almond biscotti) or another treat (closed 14:00-17:30, Sat after 14:00, and all day Sun).

Continue to the end of the block. At #51, a bit of Etruscan wall is artfully used to display more alabaster art. And #56A is the alabaster art gallery of Paolo Sabatini.

Locals gather early each evening at Osteria dei Poeti (at #57) for some of the best cocktails in town—served with free munchies. The cinema is across the street. Movies in Italy are rarely in *versione originale*; Italians are used to getting their movies dubbed into Italian. To bring some culture to this little town, they also show live transmissions of operas and concerts (advertised in the window).

At #66, another Tuscan tower marks the end of the street. This noble house has a ground floor with no interior access to the safe upper floors. Rope ladders were used to get upstairs. The tiny door was wide enough to let in your skinny friends...but definitely not anyone wearing armor and carrying big weapons.

Across the street stands the ancient Church of St. Michael. After long years of barbarian chaos, the Lombards moved in from the north and asserted law and order in places like Volterra. That generally included building a Christian church on the old Roman forum to symbolically claim and tame the center of town. (Locals still call this San Michele in Foro—"in the forum.") The church standing here today is Romanesque, dating from the 12th century. Around the right side, find the crude little guy and the smiling octopus under its eaves—they've been making faces at the passing crowds for 800 years.

• *Two more sights—Palazzo Viti (fancy old palace) and the Pinacoteca (gallery of gilded altarpieces)—are a short stroll down Via dei Sarti: From the end of Via Matteotti, turn left. If you want to skip straight down to the Roman Theater, just head straight from the end of Via Matteotti onto Via Guarnacci, then turn left when you get to the Porta Fiorentina gate. To head directly to Volterra's top sight, the Etruscan Museum, just turn around, walk a block back up Via Matteotti, turn left on Via Gramsci, and follow it all the way through Piazza XX Settembre up Via Don Minzoni to the museum.*

Palazzo Viti—Go behind the rustic, heavy stone walls of the city and see how the nobility lived (in this case, rich from 19th-century alabaster wealth). One of the finest private residential buildings in Italy, with 12 rooms open to the public, Palazzo Viti feels remarkably lived in—because it is. You'll also find Signora Viti herself selling admission tickets. It's no wonder this time warp is so popular with Italian movie directors. Remember, you're helping keep a noble family in leotards.

Cost and Hours: €5, pick up the loaner English description, April-Oct daily 10:00-13:00 & 14:30-18:30, closed Nov-March, Via dei Sarti 41, tel. 0588-84047, www.palazzoviti.it.

• *A block past Palazzo Viti, also on Via dei Sarti, is the...*

Pinacoteca—This museum fills a 15th-century palace with fine paintings that feel more Florentine than Sienese—a reminder of whose domain this town was in. You'll see roomfuls of gilded altarpieces and saintly statues. Head upstairs to the first floor. If you go left, you'll circle all the way around and save the best for last—but to cut to the chase, turn right at the landing and go directly into the best room, with Luca Signorelli's beautifully lit *Annunciation* (1491), an example of classic High Renaissance (from the town cathedral), and (to the right) *Deposition from the Cross* (1521), the groundbreaking Mannerist work by Rosso Fiorentino (note the elongated bodies and harsh emotional lighting and colors). In the adjacent room, see Ghirlandaio's *Christ in Glory* (1492). The two devout-looking kneeling women are actually pagan, pre-Christian Etruscan demigoddesses, Attinea and Greciniana, but the church identified them as obscure saints to make the painting acceptable. Rather than attempt to get locals to stop venerating them (as their images were all over town), the church simply sainted them. Upstairs, the second floor has three more rooms of similar art. Before leaving, duck into the fine, tranquil, cloister-like courtyard.

Cost and Hours: €6, €10 combo-ticket includes Etruscan and (if it's open) Sacred Art museums, daily 9:00-18:45, Nov-mid-March until 13:45, Via dei Sarti 1, tel. 0588-87580.

• *Exiting the Pinacoteca, turn right, then right again down the Passo del Gualduccio passage into the parking-lot square; at the end of this square, turn right and walk along the wall, with fine views of the...*

Roman Theater—Built in about 40 B.C., this well-preserved theater has good acoustics. Because a fine aerial view is available from the city wall promenade, you may find it unnecessary to pay admission to enter. Belly up to the 13th-century wall and look down. The wall that you're standing on divided the theater from the town center...so, naturally, the theater became the town dump. Over time, the theater was forgotten—covered in the garbage of Volterra. Luckily, it was rediscovered in the 1950s, by an administrator (and armchair historian) at the local mental hospital. Since they couldn't secure government funding for the dig, the theater was first excavated by mental patients who found the activity therapeutic.

The stage wall was standard Roman design—with three levels from which actors would appear: one level for mortals, one for heroes, and the top one for gods. Parts of two levels still stand. Gods leaped out onto the third level for the last time around the third century A.D., which is when the town began to use the theater stones to build fancy baths instead. You can see the remains of the baths behind the theater, including the round sauna with brick supports that raise the heated floor.

From the vantage point on the city wall promenade, you can trace Volterra's vast Etruscan wall. Find the church in the distance, on the left, and notice the stones just below. They are from the Etruscan wall that followed the ridge into the valley and defined Volterra in the fourth century B.C.

Cost and Hours: €3.50, but you can view the theater free from

Via Lungo le Mure; the entrance is near the little parking lot just outside Porta Fiorentina—you can see the entry to the right as you survey the theater from above; mid-March-Oct daily 10:30-17:30, Nov-mid-March Sat-Sun only 10:00-16:00.

• *From the Roman Theater, make your way back to Via Matteotti (follow Via Guarnacci straight up from Porta Fiorentina). A block down Via Matteotti, you can't miss the wide, pedestrianized shopping street called Via Gramsci. Follow this up to Piazza XX Settembre, walk through that leafy square, and continue uphill on Via Don Minzoni. Watch on your left for the...*

▲▲**Etruscan Museum (Museo Etrusco Guarnacci)**—Filled top to bottom with rare Etruscan artifacts, this museum—even with few English explanations and its dusty, almost neglectful, old-school style—makes it easy to appreciate how advanced this pre-Roman culture was.

Cost and Hours: €8, €10 combo-ticket includes the Pinacoteca and (if it's open) Sacred Art Museum; daily mid-March-Oct 9:00-19:00, Nov-mid-March 8:30-13:45; ask at the ticket window for mildly interesting English pamphlet, audioguide-€3, Via Don Minzoni 15, tel. 0588-86347, www.comune.volterra.pi.it/english.

Visiting the Museum: The museum's three floors feel dusty and disorganized. As there are scarcely any English explanations, consider the serious but interesting €3 audioguide; the information below hits the highlights.

Ground Floor: The collection starts with a small gathering of pre-Etruscan Villanovian artifacts (c. 1500 B.C., to the left as you enter), but its highlight is straight ahead, sprawling through several rooms: a seemingly endless collection of Etruscan **funerary urns** (dating from the seventh to the first century B.C.). Designed to contain the ashes of cremated loved ones, each urn is tenderly carved with a unique scene, offering a peek into the still-mysterious Etruscan society. Etruscan urns have two parts: The casket on the bottom contained the remains (with elaborately carved panels), while the lid was decorated with a sculpture of the departed.

First pay attention to the people on top. While contemporaries of the Greeks, the Etruscans were more libertine. Their religion was less demanding, and their women were a respected part of both the social and public spheres. Women and men alike are depicted lounging on Etruscan urns. While they seem to be just hanging out, the lounging dead were actually offering the gods a banquet—in order to gain their favor in the transition to the next life. The banquet—where Etruscans really did lounge like this in front of a table—was the epitome of their social structure. But the outcome of this particular banquet had eternal consequences. The dearly departed are often depicted holding scrolls, blank wax tablets (symbolizing blank new lives in the next world), and containers

Under the Etruscan Sun
(c. 900 B.C.-A.D. 1)

Around 550 B.C.—just before the Golden Age of Greece—the Etruscan people of central Italy had their own Golden Age. Though their origins are mysterious, their mix of Greek-style art with Roman-style customs helped lay a civilized foundation for the rise of the Roman empire. As you travel through Italy—particularly in Tuscany (from "Etruscan"), you'll find traces of this long-lost people.

Etruscan tombs and artifacts are still being discovered, often by farmers in the countryside. Museums in Volterra and Cortona house fine collections of urns, pottery, and devotional figures. You can visit several domed tombs outside Cortona.

The Etruscans first appeared in the ninth century B.C., when a number of cities sprouted up in sparsely populated Tuscany and Umbria, including today's hill towns of Cortona, Chiusi, and Volterra. Possibly immigrants from Turkey, but more likely local farmers who moved to the city, they became traders and craftsmen, and welcomed new ideas from Greece.

More technologically advanced than their neighbors, the Etruscans mined metal, exporting it around the Mediterranean, both as crude ingots and as some of the finest-crafted jewelry in the known world. They drained and irrigated large tracts of land, creating the fertile farmland of central Italy's breadbasket. With their disciplined army, warships, merchant vessels, and (from the Greek perspective) pirate galleys, they ruled central Italy and the major ports along the Tyrrhenian Sea. For nearly two centuries (c. 700-500 B.C.), much of Italy lived a Golden Age of peace and prosperity under the Etruscan sun.

Judging from the frescoes and many luxury items that have survived, the Etruscans enjoyed the good life: They look healthy and vibrant as they play flutes, dance with birds, or play party games. Etruscan artists celebrated individual people, showing their wrinkles, crooked noses, silly smiles, and funny haircuts.

Thousands of surviving ceramic plates and cups attest to the importance of food. Men and women ate together, propped on their elbows on dining couches, surrounded by colorful decor. According to contemporary accounts, the Etruscans, even their slaves, were Europe's best-dressed people. The banqueters were entertained with music and dancing, and served by elegant and well-treated slaves.

Scholars today have deciphered the Etruscans' Greek-style alphabet and some individual words, but they have yet to fully crack the code. Much of what we know of the Etruscans comes from their tombs. The tomb was a home in the hereafter, complete with all of the deceased's belongings. The sarcophagus might have a statue on the lid of the deceased at a banquet—

lying across a dining couch, spooning with his wife, smiles on their faces, living the good life for all eternity.

Seven decades of wars with the Greeks (545-474 B.C.) disrupted their trade routes and drained the Etruscan League, just as a new Mediterranean power was emerging: Rome. In 509 B.C., the Romans overthrew their Etruscan king, and Rome expanded, capturing Etruscan cities one by one (the last in 264 B.C.). Etruscan resisters were killed, the survivors intermarried with Romans, and their kids grew up speaking Latin. By Julius Caesar's time, the only remnants of Etruscan culture were its priests, who became Rome's professional soothsayers. Interestingly, the Etruscan prophets had foreseen their own demise, having predicted that Etruscan civilization would last 10 centuries.

But Etruscan culture lived on in Roman religion (pantheon of gods, household gods, and divination rituals), art (realism), lifestyle (the banquet), and in a taste for Greek styles—the mix that became our "Western civilization."

that would generally be used at banquets, including libation cups for offering wine to the gods. The women in particular are finely dressed, sometimes holding a pomegranate (symbolizing fertility) or a mirror. Look at the faces, and imagine the lives they lived and the loved ones they left behind.

· Now tune into the reliefs carved into the fronts of the caskets. The motifs vary widely, from floral patterns to mystical animals (such as a Starbucks-like mermaid) to parades of magistrates. Most show journeys on horseback—appropriate for someone leaving this world and entering the next. The most evocative scenes show the fabled horseback-and-carriage ride to the underworld, where the dead are greeted by Charon, an underworld demon, with his hammer and pointy ears.

While the finer urns are carved of alabaster, most are made of limestone. Originally they were colorfully painted. Many lids are mismatched—casualties of reckless 18th- and 19th-century archaeological digs.

First Floor: You'll enter a room with a circular mosaic in the floor (a Roman original, found in Volterra and transplanted here). Turn left into a series of green rooms—the best presented (and most important) of the museum.

The first room, Sala XIV, collects scenes of Ulysses carved into the fronts of caskets. Turn left and head into Sala XV, with the museum's prize piece. Fans of Alberto Giacometti will be amazed at how the tall, skinny figure called *The Evening Shadow* (*L'Ombra della Sera*, third century B.C.) looks just like the modern Swiss sculptor's work—but is 2,500 years older. This is an exceptional example of the *ex-voto* bronze statues that the Etruscans created in thanks to the gods. With his supremely lanky frame, distinctive wavy hairdo, and inscrutable Mona Lisa smirk, this Etruscan lad captures the illusion of a shadow stretching long late in the day. Admire the sheer artistry of the statue; with its right foot shifted slightly forward, it even hints at the *contrapposto* pose that would become common in this same region during the Renaissance, two millennia later.

Continue circling clockwise, through Sala XVI (alabaster urns with more Greek myths), Sala XVII (ex-voto water-bearer statues, kraters—vases with handles, and bronze hand mirrors), and Sala XVIII (golden jewelry). Sala XIX shows off the museum's other top piece, the **Urn of the Spouses** (*Urna degli Sposi*, first century B.C.). It's unique for various reasons, including its material (it's in terra-cotta—a relatively rare material for these funerary urns) and its depiction of two people rather than one. Looking at this elderly couple, it's easy to imagine the long life they spent together and their desire to pass eternity lounging with each other at a banquet for the gods.

The rest of this floor has black glazed pottery; thousands of Etruscan, Greek, and Roman coins; and many more bronze ex-votos and jewelry.

Top Floor: From the top of the stairs, turn right, then immediately right again to find a re-created grave site, with several neatly aligned urns and artifacts that would have been buried with the deceased. Some of these were funeral dowries (called *corredo*) that the dead would pack along. You'll see artifacts such as mirrors, coins, hardware for vases, votive statues, pots, pans, and jewelry. On the landing are fragments from Volterra's acropolis—a site now occupied by the Medici Fortress.

• *After your visit, duck across the street to the alabaster showroom and the wine bar (both described next).*

▲Alabaster Workshop—Alab'Arte offers a fun peek into the art of alabaster. Their showroom is across from the Etruscan Museum,

but to find their powdery workshop, go a block downhill, in front of Porta Marcoli, where you can watch Roberto Chiti and Giorgio Finazzo at work. They are delighted to share their art with visitors. (Everything—including Roberto and Giorgio—is covered in a fine white dust.) Lighting shows off the translucent quality of the stone and the expertise of these artists. This is not a touristy guided visit, but something far more special: the chance to see busy artisans practicing their craft. For more such artisans in action, visit "Artisan Lane" (Via Porta all'Arco) described earlier, or ask the TI for their list of the town's many workshops open to the public.

Cost and Hours: Free, showroom—daily 10:30-13:00 & 15:30-19:00, Via Don Minzoni 18; workshop—March-Oct Mon-Sat 9:30-13:00 & 15:00-19:00, closed Sun, usually closed Nov-Feb—call ahead, Via Orti Sant'Agostino 28; tel. 0588-87968, www.alabarte.com.

▲La Vena di Vino (Wine-Tasting with Bruno and Lucio)—La Vena di Vino, also just across from the Etruscan Museum, is a fun *enoteca* where two guys who have devoted themselves to the wonders of wine share it with a fun-loving passion. Each day Bruno and Lucio open six or eight bottles, serve your choice by the glass, pair it with characteristic munchies, and offer fine music (guitars available for patrons) and an unusual decor (the place is strewn with bras). Hang out here with the local characters. This is your chance to try the Super Tuscan wine—a creative mix of international grapes grown in Tuscany. According to Bruno, the Brunello (€7/ glass) is just right with wild boar, and the Super Tuscan (€6) is perfect for meditation. Food is served all day, including some microwaved hot dishes or a plate of meats and cheeses. Although Volterra is famously quiet late at night, this place is full of action. Downstairs is a rustic cellar that doubles on weekend nights as a sort of disco.

Cost and Hours: Pay per glass, open Wed-Mon 11:30-1:00 in the morning, closed Tue, 3- to 5-glass wine tastings, shipping options available, Via Don Minzoni 30, tel. 0588-81491, www .lavenadivino.com.

• *Volterra's final sight is perched atop the hill just above the wine bar. Climb up one of the lanes nearby, then walk (to the right) along the formidable wall to find the park.*

Medici Fortress and Archaeological Park—The Parco Archeologico marks what was the acropolis of Volterra from 1500 B.C. until A.D. 1472, when Florence conquered the pesky city and burned its political and historic center, turning it into a grassy commons and building the adjacent Medici Fortezza. The old fortress—a symbol of Florentine dominance—now keeps people in rather than out. It's a maximum-security prison housing only about 100 special prisoners. (When you're driving from San Gimignano to Volterra, you pass another big, modern prison—almost surreal in the midst of all the Tuscan wonder.) Authorities prefer to keep organized crime figures locked up far away from their family ties in Sicily.

The park sprawling next to the fortress (toward the town center) is a rare, grassy meadow at the top of a rustic hill town—a favorite place for locals to relax and picnic on a sunny day. Nearby is an archaeological dig, which costs €3 to enter, but can be viewed through a fence for free.

Cost and Hours: Park—free to enter, closes at 20:00 in summer, 17:00 in winter.

Countryside Strolls—All the sights listed above are in a tight little zone of the old town, about a 10-minute walk from each other. But if you have time for a stroll, Volterra—perched on a ridge overlooking pristine Tuscan hills—has countryside galore to explore. Get some advice from the TI.

One popular walk is to head to the west end of town, out Porta San Francesco, into a workaday area (dubbed "Borgi," literally "neighborhoods") that sees few tourists. Continuing downhill (past the Church of San Giusto), you'll come to a cliff with a stretch of the original fourth-century B.C. Etruscan wall. Peering over the cliff from here, you can see that Volterra sits upon orange sandy topsoil packed onto clay cliffs, called Le Balze. At various points in its history, the town has been threatened by landslides, and parts of its hilltop have simply disappeared. The big church you see in the distance was abandoned in the late 1800s for fear that it would be swallowed up by the land. The distinctive cliffs surrounding Volterra are called *calanchi* (similar to the French *calanques* that slash the Mediterranean coast).

Sleeping in Volterra

(€1 = about $1.40, country code: 39)
Predictably for a small town, Volterra's accommodations are limited, and all have their quirks—but there are plenty of places offering a good night's sleep at a fair price. While it's convenient to stay inside the old town, the lodgings that are a short walk away are generally a bit cheaper (and much easier for drivers).

Inside Volterra's Old Town
$$$ Hotel La Locanda feels stately and old-fashioned. This well-located place (just inside Porta Fiorentina) rents 18 decent rooms with flowery decor and modern comforts (Db-€104, less off-season, 10 percent Rick Steves discount, includes breakfast, air-con, free Wi-Fi, Via Guarnacci 24/28, tel. 0588-81547, www .hotel-lalocanda.com, staff@hotel-lalocanda.com, Giulia, Stefania, and Irina).

$$ Albergo Etruria, on Volterra's main drag, rents 21 fresh, modern, and spacious rooms within an ancient stone structure. They have a welcoming TV lounge and a peaceful rooftop garden (Sb-€75, Db-€95, Tb-€115, 10 percent discount with cash and this book when you book direct, includes breakfast, fans, free but spotty Wi-Fi, Via Matteotti 32, tel. 0588-87377, fax 0588-92784, www .albergoetruria.it, info@albergoetruria.it, Lisa and Giuseppina are fine hosts).

$$ Albergo Nazionale, with 38 big rooms, is simple, a little musty, short on smiles, popular with school groups, and steps from the bus stop. While the place feels dated, it's an exceptionally handy location (Sb-€60-70, Db-€80-90, Tb-€105, 10 percent discount with cash and this book if you book direct, reception closes at midnight, includes breakfast, free Wi-Fi, Via dei Marchesi 11,

tel. 0588-86284, fax 0588-84097, www.hotelnazionale-volterra.it,
info@hotelnazionale-volterra.it).

Just Outside the Old Town

These accommodations are within a 5- to 15-minute walk of the
city walls.

$$$ Park Hotel Le Fonti, a dull 10-minute walk downhill
from Porta all'Arco, can't decide whether it's a business hotel or a
resort. The spacious, imposing building feels old and stately, and
has 67 rooms, many with views. While generally overpriced (the
management knows it's the only hotel of its kind in Volterra), it
can be a good value if you manage to snag a deal. In addition to the
swimming pool, guests can use a small spa with sauna, hot tub, and
an intriguing "emotional shower" (Db-€89-165, average is about
Db-€129 but prices vary wildly depending on season, "superior"
room is identical to others but has a view for €20 extra, "deluxe"
room with terrace costs €30 extra, includes breakfast, elevator,
pay Wi-Fi in lobby, on-site restaurant, wine bar, free parking, Via
di Fontecorrenti 5, tel. 0588-85219, fax 0588-92728, www.park
hotellefonti.com, info@parkhotellefonti.com).

$$ Albergo Villa Nencini, just outside of town, is big, professional, and older-feeling, with 36 cheaply furnished rooms. A few
rooms have terraces and many have views. Guests also enjoy the
large pool and free parking (Sb-€67, Db-€88, Tb-€115, 10 percent
discount with cash and this book, includes breakfast, pay Wi-Fi,
Borgo Santo Stefano 55, a 15-minute uphill walk to main square,
tel. 0588-86386, fax 0588-80601, www.villanencini.it, info@villa
nencini.it, Nencini family).

$ La Primavera B&B is a great value just a few minutes' walk
outside Porta Fiorentina (near the Roman Theater). Silvia rents
five charming, tidy rooms that share a cutesy-country, heavily per-
fumed lounge. The house is along a fairly busy road, but set back
along a pleasant courtyard (Db-€70, Tb-€90, includes breakfast,
free Wi-Fi, free parking, Via Porta Diana 15, tel. 0588-87295,
mobile 328-865-0390, www.affittacamere-laprimavera.com, info
@affittacamere-laprimavera.com).

$ Seminario Vescovile Sant'Andrea has been training priests
for more than 500 years. Today, the remaining eight priests still train
students, but when classes are over, their 16 rooms—separated by vast
and holy halls in an echoing old mansion—are rented very cheaply.
Look for the 15th-century Ascension ceramic by Andrea della
Robbia, tucked away in a corner upstairs (S-€17, Sb-€22, D-€32,
Db-€40, T-€48, Tb-€60, no breakfast, closed Oct-March, elevator, closes at 24:00, groups welcome, free parking, 10-minute walk
from Etruscan Museum, Viale Vittorio Veneto 2, tel. 0588-86028,
semvescovile@diocesivolterra.it; Alberto, Angela, and Sergio).

$ **Chiosco delle Monache,** Volterra's youth hostel, fills a wing of the restored Convent of San Girolamo with 68 beds in 23 rooms. It's modern, spacious, and very institutional, with lots of services and a tranquil cloister to wander. However, it's about a 20-minute hike out of town, in a boring area near deserted hospital buildings (bed in 6-bed dorm-€18, breakfast-€6 extra, lockers; Db-€69, includes breakfast; reception closed 13:00-15:00 and after 22:00, elevator, pay Wi-Fi, free parking, Via dell Teatro 4, look for hospital sign from main Volterra-San Gimignano road, tel. 0588-86613, www.ostellovolterra.it, info@ostellovolterra.it). Nearby and run by the same organization, $ **Hotel Foresteria** has 35 big, utilitarian, new-feeling rooms with great prices but the same location woes as the hostel; it's worth considering for budget travelers, families, and drivers (Sb-€44, Db-€62, Tb-€83, Qb-€102, 5b-€122, includes breakfast, air-con, elevator, pay Wi-Fi, restaurant, free parking, Borgo San Lazzaro, tel. 0588-80050, www.foresteriavolterra.it, info@foresteriavolterra.it).

Near Volterra

$$ **Podere Marcampo** is a newer *agriturismo* about 2.5 miles outside Volterra on the road to Pisa. Run by Genuino (owner of the recommended Ristorante Enoteca del Duca), his wife Ivana, and their English-speaking daughter Claudia, this peaceful spot has three well-appointed rooms and three apartments, plus a swimming pool with panoramic views. Genuino produces his award-winning Merlot on site and offers €20 wine-tastings with cheese and homemade salami. Cooking classes at their restaurant in town are also available (Db-€94, apartment-€118-145, more expensive mid-July-Aug, includes breakfast with this book, air-con, free Wi-Fi, free parking, tel. 0588-85393, Claudia's mobile 328-174-4605, www.agriturismo-marcampo.com, info@agriturismo-marcampo.com).

Eating in Volterra

Menus feature a Volterran take on regional dishes. *Zuppa alla Volterrana* is a fresh vegetable-and-bread soup, similar to *ribollita* (except that it isn't made from leftovers). *Torta di ceci*, also known as *cecina*, is a savory-pancake-like dish made with garbanzo beans. Those with more adventurous palates dive into *trippa* (tripe; comes in a bowl like stew), the traditional breakfast of the alabaster carvers. *Fegatelli* are meatballs made with liver.

Ristorante Enoteca del Duca, with a locally respected chef named Genuino, serves well-presented and creative Tuscan cuisine. You can dine under a medieval arch with walls lined with wine bottles, in a sedate, high-ceilinged dining room (with an

Etruscan statuette at each table), on a nice little patio out back, or in their little *enoteca* (wine cellar). It's a good place for truffles, and has a friendly staff and a fine wine list (which includes Genuino's own merlot, plus several much pricier options—choose carefully). The spacious seating, dressy clientele, and calm atmosphere make this a good choice for a romantic splurge (€42 food-sampler fixed-price meal, €10-15 pastas, €15-22 *secondi*, Wed-Mon 12:30-15:00 & 19:30-22:00, closed Tue, near City Hall at Via di Castello 2, tel. 0588-81510).

Don Beta is a family-run trattoria on the main drag, popular with travelers for its stylish home cooking. Mirko supervises the lively young team as they whisk out steaming plates of pasta and homemade desserts (€6-10 pastas, €12-18 *secondi*, daily 12:00-14:30 & 19:00-22:00, lighter menu available until 24:00, reservations smart, Via Matteotti 39, tel. 0588-86730).

La Vecchia Lira, bright and cheery, is a classy self-serve eatery that's a hit with locals as a quick and cheap lunch spot by day (with €5-10 meals), and a fancier restaurant at night (€9-10 pastas, €11-18 *secondi*; Fri-Wed 12:00-14:30 & 19:00-22:30, closed Thu, Via Matteotti 19, tel. 0588-86180, Lamberto and Massimo).

La Carabaccia feels like an old-school Italian eatery, with a 1950s turquoise color scheme, a deli up front, and a country-rustic dining room in back. They serve only two pastas and two *secondi* on any given night, so check the menu by the door to be sure you like the choices. Committed to tradition, on Fridays they serve only fish. They whip up €3-4 take-away sandwiches at the deli up front (€7-9 pastas and *secondi*, Tue-Sun 12:30-14:30 & 19:30-22:00, closed Mon, Piazza XX Settembre 4/5, tel. 0588-86239).

Ristorante il Sacco Fiorentino is a local favorite for traditional cuisine and seasonal seafood specials (€8-10 pastas, €10-15 *secondi*, Thu-Tue 12:00-15:00 & 19:00-22:00, closed Wed, Via Giusto Turazza 13, tel. 0588-88537).

La Vena di Vino is an *enoteca* serving up simple and traditional dishes and the best of Tuscan wine in a fun atmosphere. As their hot dishes are microwaved (there's no real kitchen), come here more for the wine and ambience than for the food (€8-12 meals, closed Tue, Via Don Minzoni 30, tel. 0588-81491). For more details, read the description on page 653.

Pizzerias: **Ombra della Sera** dishes out what local kids consider the best pizza in town. At €6-8 a pop, their pizzas make for a cheap date (Tue-Sun 12:00-15:00 & 19:00-22:00, closed Mon, Via Guarnacci 16, don't confuse this with their second, pricier location on Via Gramsci; tel. 0588-85274). **Pizzeria Tavernetta,** next door, is more romantic, with delightful indoor and on-the-street seating. Its romantically frescoed dining room upstairs is the classiest I've seen in a pizzeria. Marco, who looks like a younger Billy Joel, serves €5-8 pizzas (Thu-Tue 12:00-16:00 & 18:30-22:00, closed Wed, Via Guarnacci 14, tel. 0588-87630).

Picnic: You can assemble a picnic at the few *alimentari* around town (try Despar Market at Via Gramsci 12, Mon-Sat 7:30-13:00 & 16:00-20:00, Sun 8:00-13:00) and eat in the breezy Archaeological Park.

Gelato: Of the many ice-cream stands in the center,

I've found **L'Isola di Gusto** to be reliably high quality (Tue-Sun 11:00-late, closed Mon, Via Gramsci 3).

Volterra Connections

In Volterra, buses come and go from Piazza Martiri della Libertà (buy tickets at the tobacco shop on the main square, two short blocks away). Most connections—except to Pisa—are with the C.P.T. bus company through Colle Val d'Elsa ("koh-leh" for short), a workaday town in the valley (4/day Mon-Sat, 1/day Sun, 50 minutes, €2.75). Once in Colle, you must buy another ticket (from another bus company) at the newsstand near the bus stop, or from the blue automated machine at the bus stop (press "F" to toggle to English, then punch in the number for your destination). I've listed total journey fares below. The nearest train station is in Saline di Volterra, a 15-minute bus ride away (7/day, 4/day Sun); however, trains from Saline run only to the coast, not to the major bus destinations listed next.

From Volterra by Bus to: Florence (4/day Mon-Sat, 1/day Sun, 2 hours, change in Colle Val d'Elsa, €8.35), **Siena** (4/day Mon-Sat, no buses on Sun, 2 hours, change in Colle Val d'Elsa, €5.75), **San Gimignano** (4/day Mon-Sat, 1/day Sun, 2 hours, change in Colle Val d'Elsa, €5.45), **Pisa** (9/day, 2 hours, change in Pontedera, €5.50).

South of Siena

Just an hour south of Siena (or two hours south of Florence), you'll find a trio of inviting hill towns, with an emphasis on good wine and scenic country drives: The biggest and most interesting, Montepulciano, has an engaging medieval cityscape draped in a Renaissance coat, wine cellars that plunge deep down into the cliffs it sits upon, and a classic town square. Pienza is a tidily planned Renaissance town that once gave the world a pope. And mellow Montalcino is (even more than most towns around here) all about its wine: Brunello di Montalcino. All three are within about a half-hour drive of each other, making any one of them a good home base for the entire region. Just to the north are the rippling hills of the Crete Senese. Dressed in vibrant green in spring and parched brown in fall, this area is blessed with quintessential Tuscan scenery and dotted with worthwhile countryside accommodations. While my favorite home base for the region is the most interesting town, Montepulciano, you can't go wrong staying in the countryside or in Montalcino.

Montepulciano

Curving its way along a ridge, Montepulciano (mohn-teh-pull-chee-AH-noh) delights visitors with *vino* and views. Alternately under Sienese and Florentine rule, the city still retains its medieval *contrade* (districts), each with a mascot and flag. The neighborhoods compete the last Sunday of August in the Bravio delle Botti, where teams of men push large wine casks uphill from Piazza Marzocco to Piazza Grande, all hoping to win a banner and bragging rights. The entire last week of August is a festival: Each *contrada* arranges musical entertainment and serves food at outdoor eateries along with generous tastings of the local *vino*.

The city is a collage of architectural styles, but the elegant San Biagio Church, at the base of the hill, is its best Renaissance building. Most visitors ignore the architecture and focus more on the city's other creative accomplishment, the tasty Vino Nobile di Montepulciano red wine.

Orientation to Montepulciano

The commercial action in Montepulciano centers in the lower town, mostly along Via di Gracciano nel Corso (nicknamed "Corso"). This stretch begins at the town gate called Porta al Prato (near the TI, bus station, and some parking) and winds slowly up, up, up through town—narrated by my self-guided walk, later. Strolling here, you'll find eateries, gift shops, and tourist traps. The back streets are worth exploring. The main square, at the top of town (up a steep switchback lane from Corso), is Piazza Grande.

Standing proudly above all the touristy sales energy, it has a noble, Florentine feel.

Tourist Information

The TI is just outside the Porta al Prato city gate, directly underneath the small tree-lined parking lot. It offers a paltry town map for €0.50, books hotels and rooms for no fee, sells train tickets (€1 fee), has an Internet terminal (€3.50/hour), and can book one of the town's few taxis (Mon-Sat 9:30-12:30 & 15:00-18:00, Sun 9:30-12:30, daily until 20:00 in July-Aug, Piazza Don Minzoni, tel. 0578-757-341, www.prolocomontepulciano.it).

Note that on the main square there is an office that looks like a TI, but this is actually a privately run "Strada del Vino" (Wine Road) agency. They don't have city info, but they do provide wine-road maps, organize **wine tours** in the city, and lead minibus winery tours farther afield. They also offer other tours (olive oil, cheese, and slow food), cooking classes, and more, depending on season and demand (Mon-Fri 10:00-13:00 & 15:00-18:00, closed Sat-Sun but likely open Sat in summer, Piazza Grande 7, tel. 0578-717-484, www.stradavinonobile.it).

Arrival in Montepulciano

Buses leave passengers at the station on Piazza Nenni, steeply downhill from the Porta al Prato gate. From the station, cross the street and head inside the modern orange-brick structure burrowed into the hillside, where there's an elevator. Ride to level 1, walk straight ahead down the corridor (following signs for *centro storico*), and ride another elevator to level 1. You'll pop out at the Poggiofanti Gardens; walk to the end of this park and hook left to find the gate. From here, it's a 15-minute walk uphill along the Corso, the bustling main drag, to the main square, Piazza Grande (following my self-guided walk, described later). Alternatively, you can wait for the orange shuttle bus that takes you all the way up to Piazza Grande (2/hour, €1.10); it's a good strategy to take the bus up and walk back down.

Drivers arriving by car should park outside the walls. The city center is a "ZTL" zone—marked with a red circle—where you'll be fined if you drive; even if you were allowed, you wouldn't want to tackle the tiny roads inside the city. (If you're sleeping in town, your hotelier will give you a permit to park within the walls; be sure to get very specific instructions.) Well-signed pay-and-display parking lots ring the city center. To get the full Montepulciano experience of walking the full length of the town up the Corso, park just outside the Porta al Prato gate (#1 is handiest, but may be full; #2, #3, and #4 are nearby; #5 is near the bus station—you can ride up to the gate on the elevator described above). For a

HILL TOWNS

quick surgical strike, make a beeline to the lots up at the top end of town. Follow signs for *centro storico, duomo,* and *Piazza Grande,* and use the *Fortezza* or *San Donato* lots (flanking the fortress at the top of town). Drivers, be aware that Montepulciano is a very vertical town, and it's easy to get turned around. Mercifully, it's also a small town, so backtracking isn't too time-consuming. Just avoid the ZTL areas.

Helpful Hints

Market Day: It's on Thursday morning (8:00-13:00), near the bus station.

Services: There's no official **baggage storage** in town, but the TI might let you leave bags with them if they have space and you ask nicely. Public **WCs** are located at the TI, to the right of Palazzo Comunale, and at the Sant'Agostino Church.

Laundry: A self-service launderette is at Via del Paolino 2 (€4 wash, €4 dry, daily 8:00-22:00, tel. 0578-717-544).

Taxis: For a taxi, call any one of four local drivers direct: 335-617-7126, 330-173-2723, 348-286-8790, or 348-702-4124.

Self-Guided Walk

Welcome to Montepulciano

This two-part walk traces the spine of the town, from its main entrance up to its hilltop seat of power. Part 1 begins at Porta al Prato (where you'll enter if arriving at the bus station, parking at certain lots, or visiting the TI). Note that this part of the walk is uphill; if you'd rather skip straight to the more level part of town, ride the twice-hourly shuttle bus up, or park at one of the lots near the Fortezza. In that case, you can still do Part 1, backwards, on the way down.

Part 1: Up the Corso

This guided stroll takes you up through Montepulciano's commercial (and touristic) gamut, which curls ever so gradually from the bottom of town to the top. While the street is lined mostly with gift shops, you'll pass a few relics of an earlier, less commercial age.

Begin in front of the imposing Porta al Prato, one of the many stout city gates that once fortified this highly strategic town. Facing the gate, find the sign for the Porta di Bacco *"passagio secreto"* on the left. While Montepulciano did have secret passages tunneled through the rock beneath it for coming and going in case of siege, this particular passage—right next to the city's front door—was probably no *secreto*...though it works great for selling salami.

Walk directly below the entrance to the **Porta al Prato,** and

Montepulciano

To Siena via
Sinalunga & A-1
Autostrada
Freeway

SANT'
AGNESE

To Chiusi

VIA E. PERNABEI

VIA DEI CANNETI

Piazza
Don
Minzoni

Piazza
Marzocco

Poggio
Fanti
Gardens

BUS
STATION

200 Meters

200 Yards

PORTA AL
PRATO

SAN GALLO

WC

Piazza
Nenni

SANT'
AGOSTINO

PALAZZO
BUCELLI

VIA GRACCIANO NEL CORSO

COLONA
DELL'
MARZOCCO

SANTA
LUCIA

WC

VIA 1 MAGGIO

VIALE DELLE LETERE

VIALE DI LEBRE

POST

CLOCK
TOWER

SAN
FRANCESCO

PIANA
ARCHI

Piazza
S. Fran.

VIA POGGIOLO

VIA VOLTAIA NEL CORSO

RICCI

TALOSA

PALAZZO
COMUNALE

WC

Piazza
Grande

GESÙ

VIA DELL'OPIO

VIA D. ORIOLO

DUOMO

VIA FIOR VECCHIA

VIA DELL'OPIO NEL CORSO

#7

To
San Biagio
Church

VIA DI SAN BIAGIO

VIA SAN DONATO

PORTA DI
FARINE

To Pienza,
Montalcino

FORTEZZA

VIA COLLAZZI

V. POLIZIANO

VIA SAN PIETRO

VIA CIRCONVALLAZIONE

VIA DEL FILOSOFI

SANTA
MARIA

#8

FILOSOFI

1 Mueblè il Riccio
2 Albergo Duomo
3 Camere Bellavista
4 Vicolo dell'Oste B&B
5 Ai Quattro Venti
6 Ost. dell'Aquacheta
7 Osteria del Conte
8 Le Pentolaccia
9 Caffè Poliziano
10 Mazzetti Copper
11 Contucci Cantina
12 Ramaio Cesare
13 Civic Museum &
Cantine del Redi
14 Launderette

HILL TOWNS

look up to see the slot where the portcullis (heavily fortified gate) could slide down to seal things off. Notice that there are two gates, enabling defenders to trap would-be invaders in a no-man's land where they could be doused with hot tar (sticky and painful). Besides having a drop-down portcullis, each gate also had a hinged door—effectively putting four barriers between the town and its enemies.

Pass through the gate and head a block uphill to reach the **Colona dell' Marzocco.** This column, topped with a lion holding the Medici shield, is a reminder that Montepulciano existed under the auspices of Florence—but only for part of its history. Originally the column was crowned by a she-wolf suckling human twins, the civic symbol of Siena. At a strategic crossroads of mighty regional powers (Florence, Siena, and the papal states), Montepulciano often switched allegiances—and this column became a flagpole where the overlords du jour could tout their influence.

The column is also the starting point for Siena's masochistic local tradition, **Bravio delle Botti**, in which each local *contrada* (fiercely competitive neighborhood, like Siena's) selects its two stoutest young men to roll a 180-pound barrel up the hill through town. If the vertical climb through town wears you out, be glad you're only toting a camera.

A few steps up, on the right (at #91), is one of the many fine noble palaces that front Montepulciano's main strip. The town is fortunate to be graced with so many bold and noble palazzos— Florentine nobility favored Montepulciano as a breezy and relaxed place for a secondary residence. Grand as this palace is, with its stylized lion heads, it's small potatoes—the higher you go in Montepulciano, the closer you are to the town center...and the fancier the mansions.

Farther up on the right, at #75 (Palazzo Bucelli), take a moment to examine the **Etruscan and Roman fragments** embedded in the wall (left here by a 19th-century antiques dealer). You can quickly distinguish which pieces came from the Romans and those belonging to the earlier Etruscans by the differences in their alphabets: The "backwards" Etruscan letters (they read from right to left) look closer to Greek than the more modern Roman letters. Many of the fragments show a circle flanked by a pair of inward-facing semicircular designs. The circle represents the libation cup used for drinking at an Etruscan banquet. Banquets were at the center of Etruscan social life, and burial urns depict lounging nobles presenting a feast for the gods.

At the top of the block on the right, pass by the Baroque-style Church of Sant'Agostino. Huff up a few more steps (imagine pushing a barrel now), then take a breather to look back and see the **clock tower** in the middle of the street. The bell ringer at the top takes the form of the character Pulcinella, one of the wild and carefree revelers familiar from Italy's comedy theater *(commedia dell'arte)*.

Keep on going, bearing right (uphill) at the fork. At the *alimentari* on the right (at #23), notice the classic old sign advertising milk, butter, margarine, and olive and canola oil. Soon after, you'll pass under another sturdy **gateway**—indicating that this city grew in concentric circles. Passing through the gate and facing the loggia (with the Florentine Medici seal—a shield with balls), turn left and keep on going.

As you huff and puff, notice (on your right, and later on both sides) the steep, narrow, often covered lanes called *vicolo* ("little street"). You're getting a peek at the higgledy-piggledy medieval Montepulciano. Only when the rationality of Renaissance aesthetics took hold was the main street realigned, becoming symmetrical and pretty. Beneath its fancy suit, though, Montepulciano remains a rugged Gothic city.

On the left, watch for the hulking former palace (I told you they'd get bigger) that's now home to Banca Etruria. "Etruria"—a name you'll see everywhere around here—is a term for the Etruscan territory of today's Tuscany.

Just after is a fine spot for a coffee break (on the left, at #27): **Caffè Poliziano,** the town's most venerable watering hole (from 1868). Step inside to soak in the genteel atmosphere, with a busy espresso machine, newspapers on long sticks, and a little terrace with spectacular views (open long hours daily). It's named for a famous Montepulciano-born 15th-century poet who was a protégé of Lorenzo the Magnificent de Medici and tutored his two sons. So important is he to civic pride that townspeople are nicknamed *poliziani.*

A bit farther up and on the right, notice the precipitous Vicolo dello Sdrucciolo—literally "slippery lane." Any *vicolo* on the right can be used as a steep shortcut to the upper part of town, while those on the left generally lead to fine views. Many of these side lanes are spanned by brick arches, allowing the centuries-old buildings to lean on each other for support rather than toppling over—a fitting metaphor for the tight-knit communities that vitalize Italian small towns.

Soon the street levels out. Near the end, on the right (at #64), look for the **Mazzetti** copper shop, crammed full of both decorative and practical items. Because of copper's unmatched heat conductivity, it's a favored material in premium kitchens. The production of hand-hammered copper vessels like these is a dying art; in this shop, you can meet gregarious Cesare, who makes them in his workshop just up the street.

To get there, go up the covered lane just after the copper shop (Vicolo Benci, on the right). You'll emerge partway up the steep street just below the main square. Cesare's workshop and museum are across the street and a bit to the left (look for *Ramaio*; for details on him, see page 668). Steeply uphill, on the right just before reaching the square, Cesare's buddy Adamo loves to introduce travelers to Montepulciano's fine wines at the Contucci Cantina (described on page 667). Visit Cesare and Adamo now, or head up to the square for Part 2 of this walk before coming back down.

Either way, Montepulciano's main square is just ahead. You made it!

Part 2: Piazza Grande and Nearby

This pleasant, lively piazza is surrounded by a grab bag of architectural sights. If the medieval **Palazzo Comunale,** or town hall, reminds you of Palazzo Vecchio in Florence, it's because Florence dominated Montepulciano in the 15th and 16th centuries. The crenellations along the roof were never intended to hide soldiers—they're just meant to symbolize power. But the big, square central tower makes it clear that the city is keeping an eye out in all directions.

Take a moment to survey the square, where the town's four great powers stare each other down. Face the Palazzo Comunale, and keep turning to the right to see: the one-time building of the courts (Palazzo del Capitano); the noble Palazzo Tarugi, a Renaissance-arcaded confection; and the aristocratic Palazzo Contucci, with its 16th-century Renaissance facade. (The Contucci family still lives in their palace, producing and selling their own wine.) Continuing your spin, you see the unfinished Duomo looking glumly on, wishing the city hadn't run out of money for its facade. (Its interior, described later under "Sights and Experiences in Montepulciano," looks much better.)

A cistern system fed by rainwater draining from the roofs of surrounding palaces supplied the fine **well** in the corner. Check out its 19th-century pulleys, the grills to keep animals from contaminating the water supply, and the Medici coat of arms (with lions symbolizing the political power of Florence).

Climbing the town hall's **tower** rewards you with a windy but commanding view from the terrace below the clock. Go into the Palazzo Comunale, head up the stairs to your left, and pay on the second floor (€3, daily 10:00-18:00, closed in winter).

The street to the left as you face the tower leads to the **Fortezza**, or fortress. While you might expect the town to be huddled protectively around its fortress, in Montepulciano's case, it's built on a distant ledge at the very edge of town. That's because this fort wasn't meant to protect the townspeople—but to safeguard its rulers by keeping an eye on those townspeople.

Detour to the Church of San Francesco and Views: From the main square, it's a short, mostly level walk to a fine viewpoint. You could head down the wide street to the right as you face the tower. But for a more interesting look at Montepulciano behind its pretty Renaissance facades, go instead up the narrow lane between the two Renaissance palaces in the corner of the square. Within just a few steps, you'll be surrounded not by tidy columns and triangles, but by a mishmash of brick and stone. Pause at the Mueblè il Riccio B&B (with a fine courtyard—peek inside) and look high up across the street to see how centuries of structures have been stitched together, sometimes gracelessly.

Follow along this lane as it bends left, and eventually you'll pop out just below the main square, facing the recommended Cantine del Redi wine cellar (described later). Turn right and head down toward the church. At #21 (on the left), look for a red-and-gold shield, over a door, with the name *Talosa*. This marks the home of one of Montepulciano's *contrade*, or neighborhoods; birth and death announcements for the *contrada* are posted on the board next to the door.

Soon you'll come to a viewpoint (on the right) that illustrates Montepulciano's highly strategic position. The ancient town sitting on this high ridge was surrounded by powerful forces—everything you see in this direction was part of the Papal States, ruled from Rome. In the distance is Lake Trasimeno, once a notorious swampland that made it even harder to invade this town.

Continue a few steps farther to the big parking lot in front of the church. Head out to the terrace for a totally different view: the rolling hills that belonged to Siena. And keep in mind that Montepulciano itself belonged to Florence. For the first half of the 16th century, those three formidable powers—Florence, Siena, and Rome (the papacy)—vied to control this small area. Take in the view of Montepulciano's most impressive church, San Biagio—well worth a visit for drivers or hikers (described later).

From here, you can head back up to the main square, or drop into Cantine del Redi to spelunk its wine cellars.

Sights and Experiences in Montepulciano

These are listed in the order you'll reach them on the self-guided walk, above. For me, Montepulciano's best "experiences" are personal: dropping in on either Adamo, the winemaker at Contucci Cantina, or Cesare, the coppersmith at Ramaio Cesare. Either one will greet you with a torrent of cheerful Italian; just smile and nod, pick up what you can from gestures, and appreciate this rare opportunity to meet a true local character.

▲▲**Contucci Cantina**—Montepulciano's most popular attraction isn't made of stone... it's the famous wine, Vino Nobile. This robust red can be tasted in any of the cantinas lining Via Ricci and Via di Gracciano nel Corso, but the cantina in the basement of Palazzo Contucci is both historic and fun. Skip the palace's formal wine-tasting

HILL TOWNS

showroom facing the square, and instead head down the lane on the right to the actual cellars, where you'll meet lively Adamo (ah-DAH-moh), who has been making wine since 1953 and welcomes tourists into his cellar. While at the palace, you may meet Andrea Contucci, whose family has lived here since the 11th century. He loves to share his family's products with the public. Adamo and Signor Contucci usually have a dozen bottles open.

After sipping a little wine with Adamo, explore the palace basement, with its 13th-century vaults. Originally part of the town's wall, these chambers have been filled since the 1500s with huge barrels of wine. Dozens of barrels of Croatian, Italian, and French oak (1,000-2,500 liters each) cradle the wine through a two-year in-the-barrel aging process, while the wine picks up the personality of the wood. After about 35 years, an exhausted barrel has nothing left to offer its wine, so it's retired. Adamo explains that the French oak gives the wine "pure elegance," the Croatian is more masculine, and the Italian oak is a marriage of the two. Each barrel is labeled with the size in liters, the year the wine was barreled, and the percentage of alcohol (determined by how much sun shone in that year). "Nobile"-grade wine needs a minimum of 13 percent alcohol.

Cost and Hours: Free drop-in tasting, daily 8:30-12:30 & 14:30-18:30, Sat-Sun from 9:30, Piazza Grande 13, tel. 0578-757-006, www.contucci.it.

▲**Ramaio Cesare**—Cesare (CHEH-zah-ray) the coppersmith is an institution in Montepulciano, carrying on his father's and grandfather's trade by hammering into existence an immense selection of copper objects in his cavernous workshop. Though his English is limited, he's happy to show you photos of his work—including the copper top of the Duomo in Siena and the piece he designed and personally delivered to Pope Benedict. Next door, he has assembled a fine museum with items he and his relatives have made, as well as pieces from his personal collection. Cesare is evangelical about copper, and if he's not too busy, he'll create personalized mementoes for visitors—he loves meeting people from around the world who appreciate his handiwork (as his brimming photo album demonstrates). Cesare's justifiable pride in his vocation evokes the hardworking, highly skilled craft guilds that once dominated small-town Italy's commercial and civic life.

Cost and Hours: Demonstration and museum are free; Cesare is generally in his workshop Mon-Sat 8:00-12:30 & 14:30-18:30, Piazzetta del Teatro, tel. 0578-758-753, www.rameria.com. Cesare's shop *(negozio)* is on the main drag, just downhill at Corso #64—look for Rameria Mazzetti, open long hours daily.

Duomo—This church's unfinished facade—rough stonework left waiting for the final marble veneer—is not that unusual. Many

Tuscan churches were built just to the point where they had a functional interior, and then, for various practical reasons, the facades were left unfinished. But step inside and you'll be rewarded with some fine art. A beautiful Andrea della Robbia blue-and-white, glazed-terra-cotta *Altar of the Lilies* is behind the baptismal font (on the left as you enter). The high altar, with a top like a pine forest, features a luminous, early-Renaissance Assumption triptych by the Sienese artist Taddeo di Bartolo. Showing Mary in her dreamy eternal sleep as she ascends to be crowned by Jesus, it illustrates how Siena clung to the Gothic aesthetic—elaborate gold leaf and lacy pointed arches—to show heavenly grandeur at the expense of realism.

Cost and Hours: Free, daily 9:00-13:00 & 15:00-18:30.

▲**Cantine del Redi**—The most impressive wine cellars in Montepulciano sit below the Palazzo Ricci, just a few steps off the main square (toward the Church of San Francesco). Enter through the unassuming door and find your way down a spiral staircase—with rounded steps designed to go easy on fragile noble feet, and lined with rings held in place by finely crafted tiny wrought-iron goat heads. You'll wind up in the dramatic cellars, with gigantic barrels under even more gigantic vaults—several stories high. As you go deeper and deeper into the cellars, high up, natural stone seems to take over the brick. At the deepest point, the atmospheric cave, surrounding a filled-in well, a warren of corridors holds fine wine aging in bottles. Finally you wind up in the shop, where you're welcome to taste two or three Redi wines for free—or, if you show them this book, they'll offer you the free wines along with some light food in their spacious tasting room.

Cost and Hours: Free tasting, €7-20 bottles, affordable shipping, daily 10:30-19:00, next to Palazzo Ricci, tel. 0578-757-166, www.dericci.com.

Civic Museum (Museo Civico)—Eclectic and surprisingly modern, but small and ultimately forgettable, this museum collects bits and pieces of local history with virtually no English explanation. The ground floor and cellar hold ancient artifacts and vases, including some Etruscan items. The next two floors are the pinacoteca (art gallery), of which the highlight is the first-floor room filled with colorful Andrea della Robbia ceramic altarpieces. You'll find a similar della Robbia altarpiece in situ, in the Duomo, for free.

Cost and Hours: €5, Tue-Sun 10:00-13:00 & 15:00-18:00, closed Mon, Via Ricci 10, tel. 0578-717-300.

Just Outside Montepulciano

San Biagio Church—At the base of Montepulciano's hill, down a picturesque driveway lined with cypresses, this church—designed by Antonio da Sangallo and built of locally quarried travertine—is Renaissance perfection. The proportions of the Greek cross floor plan give the building a pleasing rhythmic quality. Bramante, who designed St. Peter's at the Vatican in 1516, was inspired by this dome. The lone tower was supposed to have a twin, but it was never built. The soaring interior, with a high dome and lantern, creates a fine Renaissance space. Walk around the building to study the freestanding towers, and consider a picnic or snooze on the grass in back. The street called Via di San Biagio, leading from the church up into town, makes for an enjoyable, if challenging, walk.

Cost and Hours: Free, normally open daily 8:30-18:30.

Sleeping in Montepulciano

(€1 = about $1.40, country code: 39)

$$$ Mueblè il Riccio ("Hedgehog") is medieval-elegant, with 10 modern and spotless rooms, an awesome roof terrace, and friendly owners. Five are new "superior" rooms with grand views across the Tuscan valleys (Sb-€80, Db-€100, view Db-€110, superior Db-€150, superior Db with balcony-€160, Tb-€116, superior Tb-€180, superior Qb-€200, breakfast-€8, air-con, Internet access and Wi-Fi, limited free parking—request when you reserve, a block below the main square at Via Talosa 21, tel. & fax 0578-757-713, www.ilriccio.net, info@ilriccio.net, Gió and Ivana speak English). Gió and his son Iacopo give tours of the countryside (€50/hour) in one of their classic Italian cars; for details, see their website. Ivana makes wonderful breakfast tarts.

$$ Albergo Duomo is big, modern, and nondescript, with 13 rooms (with small bathrooms) and a comfortable lounge downstairs (small Db-€75, standard Db-€95, Tb-€115, family deals, elevator, air-con in some rooms for €5 extra, free Wi-Fi, free parking nearby, Via di San Donato 14, tel. 0578-757-473, www.albergo duomo.it, albergoduomo@libero.it, Elisa and Saverio).

$$ Camere Bellavista has 10 charming, tidy rooms. True to its name, each room has a fine view—though some are better than others. Room 6 has a view terrace worth reserving (Db-€75, terrace Db-€100, cash only, optional €3-10 breakfast at a bar in the piazza, lots of stairs with no elevator, free Wi-Fi, Via Ricci 25, no reception—call before arriving or ring bell, mobile 347-823-2314, fax 0578-716-341, www.camerebellavista.it, bellavista@bccmp .com, Gabriella speaks only a smidgen of English).

$$ Vicolo dell'Oste B&B, just off the main drag halfway up through town, has five modern rooms with fully outfitted kitchenettes (Db-€95-100, Tb-€130, Qb-€140, includes breakfast at nearby café, free Wi-Fi, Via dell'Oste 1, tel. 0578-758-393, www.vicolodelloste.it, info@vicolodelloste.it, Luisa and Giuseppe).

Countryside Options near Montepulciano: If you'd rather be in the country than in town, don't miss the nearby options listed under "Sleeping near Pienza," later—about a 15-minute drive from Montepulciano.

Eating in Montepulciano

Ai Quattro Venti is fresh, flavorful, fun, and right on Piazza Grande, with a simple dining room and outdoor tables right on the square. It distinguishes itself by offering reasonable portions of tasty, unfussy Tuscan food in an unpretentious setting. Try their very own organic olive oil and wine (€8-9 pastas and *secondi*, Fri-Wed 12:30-14:30 & 19:30-22:30, closed Thu, next to City Hall on Piazza Grande, tel. 0578-717-231, Chiara).

Osteria dell'Aquacheta is a carnivore's dream come true, famous among locals for its excellent beef steaks. Its long, narrow room is jammed with shared tables and tight seating, with an open fire in back and a big hunk of red beef lying on the counter like a corpse on a gurney. Giulio, with a pen tucked into his ponytail, whacks off slabs with a cleaver, confirms the weight and price with the diner, and tosses the meat on the grill—seven minutes per side. Steaks are sold by weight (€3/100 grams, or *etto*, one kilo is about the smallest they serve, two can split it for €30). They also serve hearty €6 pastas and salads and a fine house wine. In

HILL TOWNS

the tradition of old trattorias, they serve one glass, which you use alternately for wine and water (Wed-Mon 12:30-15:00 & 19:30-22:30, closed Tue, Via del Teatro 22, tel. 0578-758-443).

Osteria del Conte, an attractive but humble family-run bistro, offers a €30 *menù del Conte*—a four-course dinner of local specialties including wine—as well as à la carte options and cooking like mom's. While the interior is very simple, they also have outdoor tables on a stony street at the edge of the historic center (€7-8 pastas, €9-14 *secondi*, Thu-Tue 12:30-14:30 & 19:30-21:30, closed Wed, Via San Donato 19, tel. 0578-756-062).

Le Pentolaccia is a small, family-run restaurant at the upper, relatively untouristy end of the main drag. With both indoor and outdoor seating, they serve traditional Tuscan dishes as well as daily fish specials (€8-10 pastas, €8-15 *secondi*, Fri-Wed 12:00-15:00 & 19:30-22:30, closed Thu, Corso 86, tel. 0578-757-582).

Near Montepulciano, in Monticchiello

If you'd enjoy getting out of town for dinner—but not too far—consider the 15-minute drive to the smaller, picturesque hill town of Monticchiello. Just inside the town's gate is the highly regarded **La Porta** restaurant, where Daria pleases diners either indoors or out with well-executed traditional Tuscan dishes (€9 pastas, €12-15 *secondi*, reservations smart; seatings at 12:30, 14:00, 19:30, and 21:30; closed Thu, Via del Piano 1, tel. 0578-755-163). If La Porta is closed or you want a bit more contemporary preparation in a modern atmosphere, continue 50 yards up into town and turn right to find **La Cantina**, run by daughter Deborah (similar prices, Tue-Thu 12:30-15:00 & 19:30-22:00, closed Wed, Via San Luigi 3, tel. 0578-755-280).

Getting There: It's a straight shot to Monticchiello, but finding the road is the hard part. At the base of Montepulciano, head toward Pienza. Shortly after passing the road to San Biagio Church (on the right), watch on the left for the Albergo San Biagio. Turn off and take the road that runs up past the left side of this big hotel, and follow it all the way to Monticchiello. This is a rough (gravel at times), middle-of-nowhere drive. As a bonus, right near Monticchiello is a twisty serpentine section lined with stoic cypress trees—one of those classic Tuscan images you'll see on calendars and postcards. It's also possible to reach Monticchiello more directly from Pienza (ask locals for directions).

Montepulciano Connections

Schedule information and bus tickets are available at the TI. All buses leave from Piazza Pietro Nenni. The bus station seems to double as the town hangout, with a lively bar and locals chatting inside. In fact, there's no real ticket window—you'll buy your tickets at the bar. Check www.sienamobilita.it for schedules.

From Montepulciano by Bus to: Florence (2/day with a change in Bettole, 2 hours, €8.70), **Siena** (8/day, none on Sun, 1.25 hours, €5.45), **Pienza** (8/day, 30 minutes, €2.05), **Montalcino** (4/day Mon-Fri, 3/day Sat, none Sun, change in Torrenieri, 1-1.25 hours total, €3.85). There are hourly bus connections to **Chiusi,** a town on the main Florence-Rome rail line (40 minutes, €2.70); Chiusi is a much better bet than the distant Montepulciano station (5 miles away), which is served only by milk-run trains. Buses connect Montepulciano's bus station and its train station (8/day, none on Sun).

To Montalcino: This connection is problematic by public transportation—consider asking at the TI for a **taxi**. Although expensive (about €60), a taxi could make sense for two or more people. Otherwise you can take a bus to Buonconvento, then change to get to Montalcino (2 hours). **Drivers** find route S-146 to Montalcino particularly scenic (see "The Crete Senese" on page 685).

Pienza

Set on a crest and surrounded by green, rolling hills, the small town of Pienza packs a lot of Renaissance punch. In the 1400s,

locally born Pope Pius II of the Piccolomini family decided to remodel his birthplace in the style that was all the rage: Renaissance. Propelled by papal clout, the town of Corsignano was transformed—in only five years' time—into a jewel of Renaissance architecture. It was renamed Pienza, after Pope Pius. The plan was to remodel the entire town, but work ended in 1464 when both the pope and his architect, Bernardo Rossellino, died. Their vision—what you see today— was completed a century later. The architectural focal point is the square, Piazza Pio II, surrounded by the Duomo and the pope's family residence, Palazzo Piccolomini. While Piazza Pio II is Pienza's pride and joy, the entire town—a mix of old stonework, potted plants, and grand views—is fun to explore, especially with a camera or sketchpad in hand. You can walk every lane in the tiny town in a few minutes.

Cute as the town is, it's far from undiscovered; tourists can flood Pienza in peak season, and boutiques selling gifty packages of pecorino cheese and local wine greatly outnumber local shops. While it offers fine views of the surrounding countryside, Pienza is situated on a relatively flat plateau rather than the steep pinnacle of more dramatic towns like Montepulciano and Montalcino. For these reasons, it's made to order as a stretch-your-legs break to enjoy the setting, and perhaps tour the palace, but it's not ideal for lingering overnight.

Nearly every shop sells the town's specialty: Pecorino cheese. This pungent sheep's cheese is available fresh (*fresco*) or aged (*secco*), and sometimes contains other ingredients, such as truffles or peppers. Look on menus for warm Pecorino (*al forno* or *alla griglia*), often topped with honey or pears and served with bread. Along with a glass of local wine, this just might lead you to a new understanding of *la dolce vita*.

HILL TOWNS

Orientation to Pienza

Tourist Information: The TI is 10 yards up the street from Piazza Pio II, inside the Diocesan Museum (Wed-Mon 10:00-13:00 & 15:00-18:00, closed Tue, Sat-Sun only in Nov-March, Corso il Rossellino 30, tel. 0578-749-905). Ignore the kiosk just outside the gate, labeled *Informaturista*, which is a private travel agency.

Arrival in Pienza: Buses drop you just a couple of blocks directly in front of the town's main entrance. If **driving**, read signs carefully—some parking spots are reserved for locals, other require the use of a cardboard clock, and others are pay-and-display. Parking is tight, so if you don't see anything quickly, head for the large lot at Piazza del Mercato near Largo Roma outside the old town: As you approach town and reach the "ZTL" cul-de-sac (marked with a red circle) surrounding the park right in front of the town gate, head up the left side of town and look for the turn-off on the left for parking (€1.50/hour, closed Fri morning during market).

Helpful Hints: Market day is Friday morning at Piazza del Mercato, just outside the town walls. A public **WC,** marked *gabinetti pubblici,* is on the right as you face the town gate from outside, on Piazza Dante Alighieri (down the lane next to the faux TI).

Sights in Pienza

▲Piazza Pio II—One of Italy's classic piazzas, this square is famous for its elegance and artistic unity. The square and the surrounding buildings were all designed by Rossellino to form an "outdoor room." Spinning around clockwise, you'll see City Hall (13th-century bell tower with a Renaissance facade and a fine loggia), the Bishop's Palace (now the Diocesan Museum), the Duomo, and the Piccolomini family palace. Just to the left of the church, a lane leads to the best viewpoint in town (described later).

Duomo—Its classic, symmetrical Renaissance facade—dated 1462 with the Piccolomini family coat of arms immodestly front and center—dominates Piazza Pio II. The interior is charming, with several Gothic altarpieces and painted arches. Windows feature the crest of Pius II, with five half-moons advertising the number of crusades that his family funded. The interior art is Sienese Gothic, on the cusp of the Renaissance. As the local clay and *tufo* stone did not make an ideal building foundation, the church is slouching. The church's cliff-hanging position bathes the interior in light, but also makes it feel as if the building could break in half if you jumped up and down. See the cracks in the apse walls, and get seasick behind the main altar.

Cost and Hours: Free, generally open daily 7:00-13:00 & 14:30-19:00.

▲**Palazzo Piccolomini**—The home of Pius II (see page 599) and the Piccolomini family (until 1962) can only be visited on an escorted audioguide tour (about 30 minutes total). You'll see six rooms (dining room, armory, bedroom, library, and so on), three galleries (art-strewn hallways), and the panoramic loggia before being allowed to linger in the beautiful hanging gardens. The drab interiors, faded paintings, coffered ceilings, and scuffed furniture have a mothballed elegance that makes historians wish they'd seen it in its heyday. The audioguide very dryly identifies each item in each room but (sadly) does little to muster enthusiasm for this small-town palace that once hosted a big-name player in European politics. While it's not quite the fascinating slice of 15th-century aristocratic life that it could be (I'd like to know more about the pope's toilet), this is still the best small-town palace experience I've found in Tuscany (it famously starred as the Capulets' home in Franco Zeffirelli's 1968 Academy Award-winning *Romeo and Juliet*). You can peek inside the door for free to check out the well-preserved, painted courtyard. In Renaissance times, most buildings were covered with elaborate paintings like these.

Cost and Hours: €7, Tue-Sun 10:00-13:00 & 14:00-18:30, first tour departs at 10:30, last tour at 18:00, closed Mon, Piazza Pio II 2, tel. 0578-748-392, www.palazzopiccolominipienza.it.

Diocesan Museum (Museo Diocesano)—This measly collection of religious paintings, ecclesiastical gear, altarpieces, and old giant hymnals from local churches fills one room of the cardinal's Renaissance palace. The art is provincial Sienese, displayed in chronological order from the 12th through 17th centuries (but with no English information).

Cost and Hours: €4.10, same hours as TI—which is where you'll buy the ticket, Corso il Rossellino 30.

View Terrace—As you face the church, the upper lane leading left brings you to the panoramic promenade. Views from the terrace include the Tuscan countryside and, in the distance, Monte Amiata, the largest mountain in southern Tuscany.

Sleeping near Pienza

While I wouldn't hang my hat in sleepy Pienza itself, some fine countryside options sit just outside town—including one of my favorite Italian *agriturismo* experiences, Cretaiole. Location-wise, this is an ideal home base: midway between Montepulciano and

HILL TOWNS

Montalcino, and immersed in Tuscan splendor. Three or four of *the* iconic Tuscan landscape vistas are within 10 or 15 minutes' drive of Pienza; you'll make your sightseeing commute along extremely scenic roads with plenty of strategically located pullouts.

$$$ Agriturismo Cretaiole, in pristine farmland just outside Pienza, is a terrific value if you want to call Tuscany home for a long stay. It's warmly run by reformed city-slicker Isabella, her country-boy husband Carlo, and their family. This family-friendly farm, deeply rooted in the culture, welcomes visitors for weeklong stays (generally Sat-Sat) in six comfortable apartments. Eager to share

their local traditions, they create a community of about 20 travelers who are looking for a rich cultural education. Carlo is a professional olive-oil taster. Carlo's father, Luciano, is in charge of the grappa and tends the vegetable garden (take your pick of the free veggies). And Isabella is a tireless Jill-of-all-trades, who prides herself on personally assisting each of her guests to find exactly the Tuscan experience they're dreaming of. Included in your stay are a pasta-making class hosted by Isabella followed by a Tuscan dinner, a visit to their family farm (with samples), a tour of their very own Etruscan-era hermitage, and an olive oil tasting lesson. You may also have the chance to go on a truffle hunt and/or help with grape and olive harvesting. While there's no swimming pool—for philosophical reasons—many thoughtful touches and extras, such as Wi-Fi, mountain bikes, and loaner mobile phones, are provided. Isabella also organizes fairly priced optional activities, such as tours to the studios of local artisans, side-trips to Siena, watercolor classes, dinner at a local monastery, and more (Db-€825/week, small Db apartment-€990/week, large Db apartment-€1,290/week, same apartment for four-€1,595/week, these prices promised with this book in 2013, fewer activities and lower prices mid-Nov-mid-March, tel. & fax 0578-748-083, Isabella's mobile 338-740-9245, www.cretaiole.it, info@cretaiole.it). It's on the Montalcino-Pienza road (S-146), about 11 miles out of Montalcino, and about 2.5 miles from Pienza. While they prefer weeklong stays, when things are slow they may accept guests for as few as three nights (for this you must book less than a month in advance, Db-€120, 3-night minimum). The same family runs two other properties, with the same activities and personal attention as the main *agriturismo:* **Le Casine di Castello** is a townhouse with two units and the same prices as Cretaiole, but guests have more independence. The more upscale **Casa Moricciani** is a swanky villa featuring dreamy views, plush interiors, loads of extras, and pure Tuscan luxury (€2,900/

HILL TOWNS

week upstairs or €3,900/week downstairs, each with 2 bedrooms and 2 bathrooms). Both properties are in the untouristy medieval village of Castelmuzio, five miles north of Pienza; for details, see www.buongiornotoscana.it.

$$$ Fonte Bertusi, nearly across the road from Cretaiole, is well-run by young couple Manuela and Andrea, Andrea's father Eduardo, and their attention-starved cats. This imaginative family has scattered vivid, whimsical bits and pieces of artwork around the grounds and in the rooms. The eight apartments are simple—mixing rustic decor with avant-garde creations—and a bit pricey, but the setting is sublime (nightly rate: 1-bedroom apartment-€130, 2-bedroom apartment-€260, includes breakfast; weekly rate: €710-1,010, €40 extra per person for breakfast all week; free Wi-Fi, laundry service, swimming pool, communal BBQ and outdoor kitchen, just outside Pienza toward San Quirico d'Orcia on the right—don't confuse it with the turnoff for "Il Fonte" just before, tel. 0578-748-077, www.fontebertusi.it, info@fontebertusi.it).

Pienza Connections

Bus tickets are sold at the bar/café (marked *Il Caffè*) just outside Pienza's town gate (or pay a little extra and buy tickets from the driver). Buses leave from a few blocks up the street, directly in front of the town entrance. Montepulciano is the nearest transportation hub to other points.

From Pienza by Bus to: Siena (6/day, none on Sun, 1.5 hours, €4.40), **Montepulciano** (8/day, 30 minutes, €2.05), **Montalcino** (4/day Mon-Fri, 3/day Sat, none sun, change in Torrenieri, 45-60 minutes total, €2.70).

Montalcino

On a hill overlooking vineyards and valleys, Montalcino—famous for its delicious and pricey Brunello di Montalcino red wines—is a must for wine lovers. It's a pleasant, low-impact town with a fine ambience but little sightseeing. Everyone touring this area seems to be relaxed and in an easy groove...as if enjoying a little wine buzz.

In the Middle Ages, Montalcino (mohn-tahl-CHEE-noh) was

considered Siena's biggest ally. Originally aligned with Florence, the town switched sides after the Sienese beat up Florence in the Battle of Montaperti in 1260. The Sienese persuaded the Montalcini to join their side by forcing them to sleep one night in the bloody Florentine-strewn battlefield.

Montalcino prospered under Siena, but like its ally, it waned after the Medici family took control of the region. The village became a humble place. Then, in the late 19th century, the Biondi Santi family created a fine, dark red wine, calling it "the brunette" (Brunello). Today's affluence is due to the town's much-sought-after wine.

If you're not a wine lover, you may find Montalcino a bit too focused on *vino,* but one sip of Brunello makes even wine skeptics believe that Bacchus was onto something. Note that Rosso di Montalcino (a younger version of Brunello) is also very good, at half the price. Those with a sweet tooth will enjoy crunching the Ossi di Morta ("bones of the dead") cookies popular in Tuscany.

Orientation to Montalcino

Sitting atop a hill amidst a sea of vineyards, Montalcino is surrounded by walls and dominated by the Fortezza (a.k.a. "La Rocca"). From here, roads lead down into the two main squares: Piazza Garibaldi and Piazza del Popolo.

Tourist Information: The helpful TI, just off Piazza Garibaldi in City Hall, can find you a room for no fee. They sell bus tickets; can call ahead to book a visit at a countryside winery (€1-per-person service fee); and have information on taxi service to nearby towns, abbeys, and monasteries (daily 10:00-13:00 & 14:00-17:30, closed Mon Nov-March, tel. & fax 0577-849-331, www.proloco montalcino.com).

Arrival in Montalcino: The **bus** station is on Piazza Cavour, about 300 yards from the town center. From here, simply follow Via Mazzini straight into town.

Drivers coming in for a short visit should drive right through the old gate under the fortress (follow signs to *Fortezza;* it looks almost forbidden) and grab a spot in the pay lot at the fortress (€1.50/hour, free 20:00-8:00). If you miss this lot—or if it's full—follow the town's western wall toward the Madonna del Socorrso church and a long pay lot with the same prices. Otherwise, park for free a short walk away.

Helpful Hints: Market day is Friday (7:00-13:00) on Viale della Libertà (near the Fortezza). Day-trippers be warned: Montalcino has **no baggage storage.**

Montalcino

HILL TOWNS

100 Meters
100 Yards

To Via Cassia,
Siena, Pienza &
Montepulciano

To Sant'Antimo & ⑤

1 Hotel Dei Capitani
2 Palazzina Cesira
3 Albergo Giardino
4 Affittacamere Mariuccia
5 To La Crociona Agriturismo
6 Re di Macchia
7 Taverna il Grappolo Blu

8 Ristorante-Pizzeria
  San Giorgio
9 Co-op Supermarket
10 Enoteca la Fortezza
   di Montalcino
11 Caffè Fiaschetteria Italiana
12 Enoteca di Piazza
13 To Banfi & Argiano Wineries

Sights in Montalcino

Fortezza—This 14th-century fort, built under the rule of Siena, is now little more than an empty shell. People visit for its wine bar (see page 617). You can climb the ramparts to enjoy a panoramic view of the Asso and Orcia valleys, or enjoy a picnic in the park surrounding the fort.

Cost and Hours: €4 for rampart walk—buy ticket and enter in the wine bar, €6 combo-ticket includes Civic Museum (sold only at museum), daily 9:00-20:00, until 18:00 Nov-March, last entry 30 minutes before closing.

Piazza del Popolo—All roads in tiny Montalcino seem to lead to the main square, Piazza del Popolo ("People's Square").

Since 1888, the recommended **Caffè Fiaschetteria Italiana** has been *the* elegant place to enjoy a drink. Its founder, inspired by Caffè Florian in Venice, brought fine coffee to this humble town of woodcutters.

City Hall was the fortified seat of government. It's decorated by the coats of arms of judges who, in the interest of fairness, were from outside of town. Like Siena, Montalcino was a republic in the Middle Ages. When Florentines took Siena in 1555, Siena's ruling class retreated here and held out for four more years. The Medici coat of arms (with the six pills), which supersedes all the others, is a reminder that in 1559 Florence finally took Montalcino.

The one-handed **clock** was the norm until 200 years ago. For five centuries the arcaded **loggia** hosted the town market. And, of course, it's fun to simply observe the *passeggiata*—these days mostly a parade of tourists here for the wine.

Montalcino Museums (Musei di Montalcino)—While it's technically three museums in one (archaeology, medieval art, and modern art), and it's surprisingly big and modern for this little town, Montalcino's lone museum ranks only as a decent bad-weather activity. The archaeology collection, filling the cellar, includes interesting artifacts from the area dating back as far as—gulp—200,000 B.C. With good English explanations, this section also displays a mannequin dressed as an Etruscan soldier and a model of the city walls in early Roman times. The ground, first, and second floors hold the medieval and modern art collections, with an emphasis on Gothic sacred art (with works from Montalcino's heyday, the 13th to 16th centuries). Most of the art was created by local artists. The ground floor is best, with a large collection of crucifixes and the museum's highlights, a glazed terra-cotta altarpiece and statue of St. Sebastian, both by Andrea della Robbia.

Cost and Hours: €4.50, €6 combo-ticket includes rampart walk at Fortezza, Tue-Sun 10:00-13:00 & 14:00-17:50, closed Mon,

Via Ricasoli 31, to the right of Sant'Agostino Church, tel. 0577-846-014.

Sleeping in Montalcino

(€1 = about $1.40, country code: 39)

$$$ Hotel Dei Capitani, at the end of town near the bus station, has plush public spaces, an inviting pool, and a cliffside terrace offering plenty of reasons for lounging. About half of the 29 rooms come with vast Tuscan views for the same price (request a view room when you reserve), the nonview rooms are bigger, and everyone has access to the terrace (Db-€138 with this book in 2013, extra bed-€40, air-con, elevator, free Internet access and Wi-Fi, limited free parking—first come, first served, Via Lapini 6, tel. 0577-847-227, www.deicapitani.it, info@deicapitani.it).

$$ Palazzina Cesira, right in the heart of the old town, is a gem renting five spacious and tastefully decorated rooms in a fine 13th-century residence with a palatial lounge and a pleasant garden. You'll enjoy a refined and tranquil ambience, a nice breakfast (with eggs), and the chance to get to know Lucilla and her American husband Roberto, who are generous with local advice (Db-€95, suites-€115, cash only, 2-night minimum, 3-night minimum on holiday weekends, air-con, free Internet access and Wi-Fi, free off-street parking, Via Soccorso Saloni 2, tel. & fax 0577-846-055, www.montalcinoitaly.com, p.cesira@tin.it).

$ Affittacamere Mariuccia has three small, colorful, good-value, Ikea-chic rooms on the main drag over a heaven-scented bakery (Sb-€35, Db-€50, no breakfast, check-in across the street at Enoteca Pierangioli before 20:00 or let them know arrival time, Piazza del Popolo 16, rooms at #28, tel. 0577-849-113, mobile 348-392-4780, www.affittacameremariuccia.it, enotecapierangioli@hotmail.com, Alessandro and Stefania speak English).

$ Albergo Giardino, old and basic, has nine big simple rooms, no public spaces, and a convenient location near the bus station (Db-€55-60, 10 percent discount with this book outside May and Sept, no breakfast, Piazza Cavour 4, tel. & fax 0577-848-257, mobile 338-684-3163, albergoilgiardino@virgilio.it; Roberto speaks English; dad Mario doesn't).

Near Montalcino

$$ La Crociona, an *agriturismo* farm and working vineyard, rents seven fully equipped apartments. Fiorella Vannoni and Roberto and Barbara Nannetti offer cooking classes and tastes of the Brunello wine grown and bottled on the premises (Db-€95, or €65 in Oct-mid-May; Qb-€130, or €95 in Oct-mid-May; lower weekly rates, metered gas heating, laundry-€8/load, pool, fitness

HILL TOWNS

room, La Croce 15, tel. 0577-847-133, fax 0577-846-994, www.la crociona.com, info@lacrociona.com). The farm is two miles south of Montalcino on the road to the Sant'Antimo Monastery; don't turn off at the first entrance to the village of La Croce—wait for the second one, following directions to Tenuta Crocedimezzo e Crociona). A good restaurant is next door.

Eating in Montalcino

Restaurants

Re di Macchia is an invitingly intimate restaurant where Antonio serves up the Tuscan fare Roberta cooks. Look for their seasonal menu and Montalcino-only wine list. Try the €25 fixed-price meal, and for €17 more, have it paired with local wines carefully selected to accompany each dish (€9-10 pastas, €16 *secondi*, Fri-Wed 12:00-14:00 & 19:00-21:00, closed Thu, reservations strongly recommended, Via Soccorso Saloni 21, tel. 0577-846-116).

Taverna il Grappolo Blu is unpretentious, friendly, and serious about its wine, serving local specialties and vegetarian options to an enthusiastic crowd (€8-9 pastas, €9-14 *secondi,* daily 12:00-15:00 & 19:00-22:00, reservations smart, near the main square, a few steps off Via Mazzini at Scale di Via Moglio 1, tel. 0577-847-150, Luciano).

Ristorante-Pizzeria San Giorgio is a homey trattoria/pizzeria with kitschy decor and reasonable prices. It's a reliable choice for a simple meal (€4-7 pizzas, €8 pastas, €8-12 *secondi*, daily 12:00-15:00 & 19:00-22:30, Via Soccorso Saloni 10-14, tel. 0577-848-507, Mara).

Picnic: Gather ingredients at the **Co-op supermarket** on Via Sant'Agostino (Mon-Sat 8:30-13:00 & 16:00-20:00, closed Sun, just off Via Ricasoli in front of Sant'Agostino Church), then enjoy your feast up at the Madonna del Soccorso Church, with vast territorial views.

Wine Bars: Note that two of the places listed under "Wine Bars *(Enoteche)* in Town," later, also serve light food.

Wine Tasting and Wineries

There are two basic approaches for sampling Montalcino's wines: at an *enoteca* in town, or at a countryside winery. Serious wine connoisseurs will enjoy a day of winery-hopping, sipping the wines right where they were created. But if you don't have the time, or want to try more than one producer's wines, you might prefer to simply visit a wine bar in town, where you can comfortably taste a variety of vintages before safely stumbling back to your hotel.

Wine Bars *(Enoteche)* in Town

Enoteca la Fortezza di Montalcino offers a chance to taste top-end wines by the glass, each with an English explanation. While wine snobs turn up their noses, the medieval setting inside Montalcino's fort is a hit for most visitors. Spoil yourself with Brunello in the cozy *enoteca* or at an outdoor table (€13 for 3 tastings, or €22 for 3 "top-end" tastings; €10-18 two-person sampler plates of cheeses, *salumi,* honeys, and olive oil; daily 9:00-20:00, closes at 18:00 Nov-March, inside the Fortezza, tel. 0577-849-211, www.enotecalafortezza.com).

Caffè Fiaschetteria Italiana, a classic, venerable café/wine bar, was founded by Ferruccio Biondi Santi, the creator of the famous Brunello wine. The wine library in the back of the café boasts many local choices. A meeting place since 1888, this grand café also serves light lunches and espresso to tourists and locals alike (€6-12 Brunellos by the glass, €3-5 light snacks, €8-12 plates; same prices inside, outside, or in back room; daily 7:30-23:00, closed Thu Nov-Easter, free Wi-Fi, Piazza del Popolo 6, tel. 0577-849-043). And if it's coffee you need, this place—with its classic 1961 espresso machine—is considered the best in town.

Enoteca di Piazza is one of a chain of wine shops with a system of mechanical dispensers. A "drink card" (like a debit card) keeps track of the samples you take, for which you'll pay from €1 to €9 for each 50-milliliter taste of the 100 different wines, including some whites—rare in this town. The only nibbles are saltine-type crackers. They hope you'll buy a bottle of the samples you like, and are happy to educate you in English. (Rule of thumb: A bottle costs about 10 times the cost of the sample. If you buy a bottle, the sample of that wine is free.) While the place feels a little formulaic, it can be fun—the wine is great, and the staff is casual and helpful (daily 9:00-20:00, near Piazza del Popolo at Via Matteotti 43, tel. 0577-848-104, www.enotecadipiazza.com). Confusingly, there are three similarly named places in this same area—this tasting room is a block below the main square.

Wineries in the Countryside

The surrounding countryside is littered with wineries, some of which offer tastings. A few require an appointment, but many are happy to serve a glass to potential buyers and show them around. The Montalcino TI can give you a list of more than 150 regional wineries and will call ahead for you (€1 fee per person). Or check with the vintners' consortium (tel. 0577-848-246, www.consorzio brunellodimontalcino.it, info@consorziobrunellodimontalcino.it). These two places listed below are big and capable of handling a steady flow of international visitors; they don't offer an "authentic"

Tuscan or cozy experience, but they are convenient and user-friendly.

Argiano claims to be one of the oldest working wineries in the region, dating back to 1580. About a 10-minute drive south of Montalcino at Sant'Angelo in Colle, their one-hour tour in English includes the vineyards, the exterior of a historic villa, and ancient moldy cellars full of wine casks. They also rent on-site apartments—handy for those who have oversampled (€20 tour includes six wine samples, reserve in advance, tel. 0577-844-037, www.argiano.net, coming by car the last two miles are along a rough-but-drivable track through vineyards).

Banfi, run by the Italian-American Mariani brothers, is huge and touristy. While it's not an intimate family winery, the grounds are impressive and they're well set up to introduce the passing hordes to their wines (€13 for 3 tastings, €3.50-25 per glass, daily 10:00-18:00, free tours Mon-Fri at 16:00—reserve in advance, 10-minute drive south of Montalcino in Sant'Angelo Scalo, tel. 0577-877-500, www.castellobanfi.com, reservations@banfi.it).

Bus Tour: If you lack a car (or don't want to drive), you can take a tour on the **Brunello Wine Bus,** which laces together a variety of wineries (€25, mid-June-Oct Tue, Thu, and Sat, departs at 9:00, returns at 20:00, tel. 0577-846-021, www.lecameredibacco .com, info@lecameredibacco.com).

Montalcino Connections

Montalcino is poorly connected to just about everywhere except Siena, but connections are generally workable. Montalcino's bus station is on Piazza Cavour, within the town walls. Bus tickets are sold at the bar on Piazza Cavour, at the TI, and at some tobacco shops, but not on board (except for the bus to Sant'Antimo). Check schedules at the TI, at the bus station, or at www.sienamobilita .it. The nearest train station is a 20-minute bus ride away, in Buonconvento (bus runs nearly hourly, €2.05).

From Montalcino by Bus: The handiest direct bus is to **Siena** (6/day Mon-Sat, 4/day Sun, 1.5 hours, €3.85). To reach **Pienza** or **Montepulciano,** ride the bus to Torrenieri (5/day Mon-Sat, none on Sun, 20 minutes), where you'll switch to line #114 for the rest of the way (from Torrenieri: 25 minutes and €2.70 total to Pienza; 45 minutes and €3.85 total to Montepulciano). A local bus runs to **Sant'Antimo** (3/day Mon-Fri, 2/day Sat, none on Sun, 15 minutes, €1.50, buy tickets on board). Anyone going to **Florence** by bus changes in Siena; since the bus arrives at Siena's train station, it's handier to go the rest of the way to Florence by train. Alternatively, you could take the bus to Buonconvento (described earlier), and catch the train there to Florence.

The Crete Senese

Between Siena and the trio of towns described above (Montepulciano, Pienza, Montalcino), the hilly area known as the "Sienese Clay Hills" is full of colorful fields and curvy, scenic roads. The Crete Senese (KRAY-teh seh-NAY-zeh) begins at Siena's doorstep and tumbles south through some of the most eye-pleasing scenery in Italy. You'll see an endless parade of classic Tuscan scenes, rolling hills topped with medieval towns, olive groves, rustic stone farmhouses, and a skyline punctuated with cypress trees. You won't find many wineries here, since the clay soil is better for wheat and sunflowers, but you will find the pristine, panoramic Tuscan countryside featured on countless calendars and postcards.

During the spring, the fields are painted in yellow and green with fava beans and broom, dotted by red poppies on the fringes. Sunflowers decorate the area during June and July, and expanses of windblown grass fill the landscape for much of the early spring and summer.

Most roads to the southeast of Siena will give you a taste of this area, but one of the most scenic stretches is the Lauretana road (Siena-Asciano-San Giovanni d'Asso, S-438, S-451, and SP-60a on road maps; the numbering changes as you drive, but it feels like the same road). To find the Lauretana road from Siena, follow signs for the A-1 expressway; you'll turn off onto S-438 (look for the sign for *Asciano*) well before you reach the expressway. You'll come across plenty of turnouts for panoramic photo opportunities on this road, as well as a few roadside picnic areas and several good accommodations (see "Sleeping in the Crete Senese," later).

For a break from the winding road, about 15 miles from Siena, you'll find the quaint and non-touristy village of **Asciano.** With a medieval town center and several interesting churches and museums, this town offers a rare look at everyday Tuscan living—and it's a great place for lunch (TI open Tue-Sun 10:30-13:00 & 15:00-18:00, Mon 10:00-13:00, at Corso Matteotti 18, tel. 0577-718-811). If you're in town on Saturday, gather a picnic at the outdoor market (Via Amendola, 8:00-13:00).

A bit farther along, in **Chiusure** (about 6 miles south of Asciano, on S-451), follow signs up a steep driveway to the *casa di reposo* (nursing home) for a fine viewpoint over the Crete Senese, including classic views of jagged *calanchi* cliffs. From that hilltop, you can also see the **Abbey of Monte Oliveto Maggiore.** Located 1.5 miles west of Chiursure, the abbey houses a famous fresco cycle of the life of St. Benedict, painted by Renaissance masters Il Sodoma and Luca Signorelli (free, daily 9:15-12:00 & 15:15-18:00, Nov-March until 17:00, Gregorian chanting Sun at 11:00 and

The Beauty of Tuscany's Geology (and Vice Versa)

While North Americans have romanticized notions of the "Tuscan" landscape, there's a surprisingly wide variety of land forms in the region. Never having been crushed by a glacier, Tuscany is anything but flat. The hills and mountains scattered around the area are made up of different substances, each of which is ideal for very different types of cultivation.

The Chianti region (between Florence and Siena) is rough and rocky, with an inhospitable soil that challenges grape vines to survive while coaxing them to produce excellent wine grapes.

Farther south, the soil switches from rock to clay, silt, and sand. The region called the Crete Senese is literally translated as the "Sienese Clay Hills"—a perfect description of the landscape. Seen from a breezy viewpoint, it's easy to imagine that these clay hills were once at the bottom of the sea floor. The soil here is the yin to Chianti's yang: not ideal for wine, but perfect for truffles and for vast fields of cereal crops such as wheat, fava beans, and sun-yellow rapeseed (for canola oil). In the spring and summer, the Crete Senese is blanketed with brightly colorful crops and flowers. But by the fall, after the harvest, it's a brown and dusty desolate wasteland punctuated with pointy cypress trees—still picturesque, but in a surface-of-the-moon way. Within the Crete Senese, you can distinguish two types of hills shaped by erosion: smooth, rounded *biancane* and pointy, jagged *calanchi*.

The area around Montepulciano and Montalcino is more varied, with rocky protuberances breaking up the undulating clay hills (and providing a suitable home for wine grapes). Even farther south is the Val d'Orcia, the valley of the Orcia River, with its own beauty that mixes clay hills and jutting rock.

You'll see many hot springs in this part of Tuscany, as well as town names with the word Terme (for "spa" or "hot spring"). These generally occur where clay meets rock: water moving through the clay encounters a barrier and gets trapped. Aside from hot water, another byproduct of this change in landscapes is travertine, explaining the quarries you may see in or near spa towns.

Mon-Sat at 18:15, call to confirm, tel. 0577-707-611, www.monte olivetomaggiore.it).

Once you reach the town of **San Giovanni d'Asso**—in the heart of the truffle region—it's a short drive southwest to Montalcino, or southeast to Pienza (each about 12 miles away).

Another scenic drive is the lovely stretch between Montalcino and Montepulciano. This route (S-146 on road maps) alternates between the grassy hills of the Crete Senese and sunbathed vineyards of the Orcia River valley. Stop by Pienza en route.

Sleeping in the Crete Senese

If pastoral landscapes and easy access to varied towns are your goals, you can't do much better than sleeping in the Crete Senese. These countryside options sit between Siena, Montepulciano, Pienza, and Montalcino (a 15- to 45-minute drive from any of them). These options line up on (or just off) the scenic roads (S-438 and S-451) south of Siena; I've listed them from north to south.

$$$ Recommended local guide **Roberto Bechi** (see page 586) has built a new house from scratch that's immersed in gorgeous Crete Sense scenery (about 15 minutes south of Siena). He plans to begin renting five spacious rooms there in late 2012; contact him to see if they're ready yet. The house (which Roberto designed and built himself) is entirely "green," with a zero-carbon footprint (likely Db-€100, mobile 328-425-5648, www.toursbyroberto.com, toursbyroberto@gmail.com). It's just off road S-438; take the turn off for Fontanelle.

$$$ **Alle Logge di Sotto,** right along route S-438 (with some road noise), is a pleasant country home with dramatic Crete Senese views, an immaculate garden, a swimming pool, and five tidy, nicely appointed rooms (Db-€110, includes breakfast, €700/week includes one dinner, cheaper in winter, €35/person for full dinner, Lauretana 14, Pievnia/Asciano, tel. 0577-717-199, mobile 338-969-6073, www.alleloggedisotto.it, contact@alleloggedisotto.it, Alessandro and Alessandra). They also offer cooking classes for their guests (€100/2 hours).

$ **Casanova Agriturismo** is for people who *really* want to stay on an authentic, working farm. This rustic place comes with tractors, plenty of farm smells and noises, and a barn full of priceless Chianina cows. If the five simple rooms and one apartment take a back seat to the farm workings, the lodgings are accordingly inexpensive, and you'll appreciate the results of their hard work when you dig into one of their fine farm-fresh dinners (€20/person). German Wiebke (who speaks great English and runs the accommodations), her Tuscan husband Bartolo (who works the fields), his mama Paola (who cooks), and the rest of the Conte clan make this a true *agriturismo* experience (Db-€60, apartment-€70 for 2 and €10 per additional person up to 4, breakfast-€5, free Wi-Fi in some areas, swimming pool, just outside Asciano on road S-451 toward Chiusure, tel. 0577-718-324, mobile 346-792-0859, www.agriturismo-casanova.it, info@agriturismo-casanova.it).

$$ **Agriturismo il Molinello** ("Little Mill") rents five apartments, two built over a medieval mill, on the grounds of a

working farm with organic produce, olives, and a truffle ground. Hardworking Alessandro and Elisa share their organic produce and offer weekly wine tastings for a minimum of four people; they also lead cooking classes on request. From May through October, they give free guided tours of Siena on Tuesday afternoons. More rustic than romantic, and lacking the dramatic views of some places, this is a nice mix of farm and style. With children, friendly dogs, toys, and a swimming pool, it's ideal for families (Db-€50-80, Qb-€70-100, apartment for up to 8-€80-200 depending on season and number of people, optional organic breakfast-€9.50, one-week stay required in July-Aug, discounts and no minimum stay off-season, free Internet access, free Wi-Fi in public areas, mountain-bike rentals, biking maps and guided bike tours, between Asciano and the village of Serre di Rapolano—on the road toward Rapolano, 30 minutes southeast of Siena, tel. 0577-704-791, mobile 335-692-5720, fax 0577-705-605, www.molinello.com, info@molinello.com).

Cortona

Cortona blankets a 1,700-foot hill surrounded by dramatic Tuscan and Umbrian views. Frances Mayes' book *Under the Tuscan Sun* placed this town in the touristic limelight, just as Peter Mayle's books popularized the Luberon region in France. But long before Mayes ever published a book, Cortona was popular with Romantics and considered one of the classic Tuscan hill towns. Although it's unquestionably touristy, unlike San Gimignano, Cortona maintains a rustic and gritty personality—even with its long history of foreigners who, enamored with its Tuscan charm, made this their adopted home.

The city began as one of the largest Etruscan settlements, the remains of which can be seen at the base of the city walls, as well as in the nearby tombs. It grew to its present size in the 13th to 16th centuries, when it was a colorful and crowded city, eventually allied with Florence. The farmland that fills almost every view from the city was marshy and uninhabitable until about 200 years ago, when it was drained and turned into some of Tuscany's most fertile land.

Art lovers know Cortona as the home of Renaissance painter Luca Signorelli, Baroque master Pietro da Cortona (Berretini), and the 20th-century Futurist artist Gino Severini. The city's museums and churches reveal many of the works of these native sons.

Orientation to Cortona

Most of the main sights, shops, and restaurants cluster around the level streets on the Piazza Garibaldi-Piazza del Duomo axis, but Cortona will have you huffing and puffing up some steep hills. From Piazza Garibaldi, it's a level five-minute walk down bustling shop-lined Via Nazionale to Piazza della Repubblica, the heart of the town, which is dominated by City Hall (Palazzo del Comune). From this square, a two-minute stroll leads you past the TI, the interesting Etruscan Museum, and the theater to Piazza del Duomo, where you'll find the recommended Diocesan Museum. These sights are along the more-or-less level spine that runs through the bottom of town; from here, Cortona sprawls upward. Steep streets, many of them stepped, go from Piazza della Repubblica up to the San Niccolò and Santa Margherita churches and the Medici Fortress (a 30-minute climb from Piazza della Repubblica). In this residential area, you'll see fewer tourists and get a better sense of the "real" Cortona.

In the flat valley below Cortona sprawls the modern, workaday town of Camucia (kah-moo-CHEE-ah), with the train station and other services (such as launderettes) that you won't find in the hill town itself.

Tourist Information

To reach the helpful TI, head to Piazza Signorelli, then walk through the courtyard of the Etruscan Museum and up a short flight of steps, at the back (Mon-Fri 9:00-13:00 & 15:00-18:00, Sat 9:00-13:00, closed Sun, possibly longer hours May-Sept, tel. 0575-637-223 or 0575-637-276, www.turismo.provincia.arezzo.it).

Arrival in Cortona

Cortona is challenging but doable by public transportation. There are few intercity buses, so your best bet for reaching the town is by train or by car.

By Train: Trains arrive at the unstaffed Camucia station, in the valley four miles below Cortona. Sporadic local buses connect the train station and Piazza Garibaldi in Cortona in about 10 minutes. (If you choose to walk, it's a long steep climb, and there are no sidewalks.) From the station, walk out the front door and look left to find the bus shelter (with schedules posted). Unfortunately, buses depart only about once per hour—and only twice daily on Sundays—and the schedule is not well-coordinated with train times (purchase €1.60 from driver; you want a bus marked for

Cortona rather than the opposite direction, Terontola). On the schedule, departures marked with *S* do not run during school vacations; those marked with *N* run only during school vacations. If you'd rather not wait, consider taking a taxi into town (€10, call for Dejan and his seven-seater cab, mobile 348-402-3501—Dejan also arranges day trips, see "Local Guides," later; or you can ask your hotel to arrange a taxi).

By Car: You'll find several lots ringing the walls; some are free (white lines), others require payment (blue lines), and still others are for local residents only (yellow lines), so check signs carefully. Your best bet is the large, free lot on Viale Cesare Battisti, just after the big Santo Spirito Church. From here, a series of stairs and escalators take you steeply up to Piazza Garibaldi. Piazza Garibaldi itself may have a handful of pay spots available (marked by blue lines, pay & display, free 20:00-8:00). The small town is actually very long, and it can be smart to drive to the top for sightseeing up there (free parking at Santa Margherita Basilica).

Helpful Hints

Market Day: The market is on Saturday on Piazza Signorelli (from early morning until 14:00).

Services: The town has **no baggage storage,** so try asking nicely at a hotel to leave your bag there. The best public **WC** is located in Piazza del Duomo, under Santa Margherita's statue.

Tuscan Cooking Classes: Husband-and-wife team **Romano and Agostina** hold morning hands-on cooking and cheesemaking classes, as well as wine-, cheese-, and oil-tasting courses three mornings a week in the kitchen of their recommended Ristorante La Bucaccia. In the five-hour class, you'll prepare two *antipasti,* two types of pasta, an entrée, and a dessert, which you then get to eat (roughly €90/person, price includes wine, 5 percent discount if you show this book, classes start at 9:30). A three-hour version starts at 11:00 (€70/person; try to book a few weeks in advance, evening and personalized classes available, Via Ghibellina 17, tel. 0575-606-039, www.labucaccia.it, info@labucaccia.it).

Local Guides: Giovanni Adreani exudes energy and a love of his city and Tuscan high culture. He is great at bringing the fine points of the city to life and can take visitors around in his car for no extra charge. As this region is speckled with underappreciated charms, having Giovanni for a day as your driver/guide promises to be a fascinating experience (€110/half-day, €200/day, tel. 0575-630-665, mobile 347-176-2830, www.adreanigiovanni.com, adreanigiovanni@libero.it). Reliable, English-speaking taxi driver **Dejan** (DAY-zhan) **Prvulovic** can also take you on full-day tours to Pienza, Montalcino,

Siena, Assisi, and Chianti—email him and devise your own itinerary (€220-250/day depending on number of passengers, mobile 348-402-3501, dejanprvi70@yahoo.it).

Self-Guided Walk

Welcome to Cortona

This introductory walking tour will take you from Piazza Garibaldi and up the main strip to the town center, its piazzas, and the Duomo.

• *Start at the bus stop in...*

Piazza Garibaldi: Many visits start and finish in this square, thanks to its bus stop. While the piazza, bulging out from the town fortifications like a big turret, looks like part of an old rampart, it's really a souvenir of those early French and English Romantics— the ones who first created the notion of a dreamy, idyllic Tuscany. During the Napoleonic Age, the French built this balcony (and the scenic little park behind the adjacent San Domenico Church) simply to enjoy a commanding view of the Tuscan countryside.

With Umbria about a mile away, Cortona marks the end of Tuscany. This is a major cultural divide, as Cortona was the last town in Charlemagne's empire and the last under Medici rule. Umbria, just to the south, was papal territory for centuries. These deep-seated cultural disparities were a great challenge for the visionaries who unified the fractured region to create the modern nation of Italy during the 1860s. An obelisk in the center of this square honors one of the heroes of the struggle for Italian unification—the brilliant revolutionary general, Giuseppe Garibaldi.

Enjoy the commanding view from here. Assisi is just over the ridge on the left. Lake Trasimeno peeks from behind the hill, looking quite normal today. But, according to legend, it was blood-red after Hannibal defeated the Romans here in 217 B.C., when 15,000 died in the battle. The only sizable town you can see, on the right, is Montepulciano. Cortona is still defined by its Etruscan walls— remnants of these walls, with stones laid 2,500 years ago, stretch from here in both directions.

Frances Mayes put Cortona on the map for many Americans with her book (and later movie) *Under the Tuscan Sun*. The book describes her real-life experience buying, fixing up, and living in a run-down villa in Cortona with her husband, Ed. The movie romanticized the story, turning Frances into a single,

HILL TOWNS

recently divorced writer who restores the villa and her peace of mind. Mayes' villa isn't "under the Tuscan sun" very often; it's named "Bramasole"—literally, "craving sun." On the wrong side of the hill, it's in the shade after 15:00. She and her husband still live there part of each year and are respected members of their adopted community (outside the walls, behind the hill on the left—a 20-minute walk away; ask at the TI for directions if you'd like to see it up close).

• *From this square, head into town along...*

Via Nazionale: The only level road in town, locals have nicknamed Via Nazionale the *ruga piana* (flat wrinkle). This is the main commercial street in this town of 2,500, and it's been that way for a long time. Every shop seems to have a medieval cellar or an Etruscan well. Notice the crumbling sandstone door frames. The entire town is constructed from this grainy, eroding rock.

• *Via Nazionale leads to...*

Piazza della Repubblica: City Hall faces Cortona's main

TUSCAN SUN

PORTA MONTANINA ← VIA PORTA MONTANINA

P

BAR

To Medici Fortress

SAN CRISTOFORO

VIA SANTA CROCE

SANTA MARGHERITA

SAN NICCOLÒ

VIA ORTO DELLA CERA

VIA SANTA MARGHERITA

← VIA SAN NICCOLÒ

VIA CANTUCCE

VIA DELLA SANTISSIMI TRINITÀ

SAN MARCO

PORTA BERADA

VIA SANTA MARGHERITA

CITY WALLS

VIA DEL CROCIFISSO

SAN DOMENICO

Public Gardens

VIA CESARE BATTISTI

VIALE DEI GIARDINI PUBBLICA

VIA SEVERINI

100 Meters

100 Yards

❶ Hotel San Luca
❷ Dolce Maria B&B & Locanda al Pozzo Antico
❸ Rugapiana Vacanze B&B
❹ San Marco Hostel
❺ Hotel Villa Marsili
❻ Casa Betania
❼ Istituto Santa Margherita
❽ Casa Kita
❾ Ristorante La Bucaccia
❿ Trattoria la Grotta
⓫ Ristorante La Loggetta & Despar Market Molesini
⓬ Fufluns Tavern Pizzeria
⓭ Osteria del Teatro
⓮ Enoteca la Saletta

HILL TOWNS

square. Note how City Hall is a clever hodgepodge of twin medieval towers, with a bell tower added to connect them, and a grand staircase to lend some gravitas. Notice also the fine wood balconies on the left. In the Middle Ages, wooden extensions like these were common features on the region's stone buildings. These balconies (not original, but rebuilt in the 19th century) would have fit right into the medieval cityscape. These days, you usually see only the holes that once supported the long-gone wooden beams.

This spot has been the town center since Etruscan times. Four centuries before Christ, an important street led from here up to the hill-capping temple. Later, the square became the Roman forum. Opposite City Hall is the handy, recommended Despar Market Molesini, good for cheap sandwiches. Above that is the loggia—once a fish market, now the recommended Ristorante La Loggetta.

• *The second half of the square, to the right of City Hall, is...*

Piazza Signorelli: Dominated by Casali Palace, this square was the headquarters of the Florentine captains who used to control the city. Peek into the palace entrance (under the MAEC sign) for a look at the coats of arms. Every six months, Florence would send a new captain to Cortona, who would help establish his rule by inserting his family coat of arms into the palace's wall. These date from the 15th to the 17th century, and were once painted with bright colors. Cortona's fine Etruscan Museum (described later, under "Sights in Cortona") is in the Casali Palace courtyard, which is lined with many more of these family coats of arms. The inviting Caffè del Teatro fills the loggia of the theater that is named for the town's most famous artist, Luca Signorelli.

• *Head down the street just to the right of the museum to...*

Piazza del Duomo: Here you'll find the Diocesan Museum (listed later, under "Sights in Cortona"), cathedral, and (closer to the top of the square) a statue of Santa Margherita. The cathedral's facade, though recently renovated, still seems a little underwhelming and tucked away. Cortona so loves its hometown saint, Margherita, that it put the energy it would otherwise have invested in its cathedral into the Santa Margherita Basilica, at the top of the hill (at the other end of town—not visible from here). Margherita was a 13th-century rich girl who took good care of the poor and was an early follower of St. Francis and St. Clare. Many locals believe that Margherita protected Cortona from WWII bombs.

The Piazza del Duomo terrace comes with a commanding view of the Tuscan countryside. Notice the town cemetery in the foreground. If you were standing here before the time of Napoleon, you'd be surrounded by tombstones. But Cortona's graveyards—like other urban graveyards throughout Napoleon's realm—were cleaned out in the early 1800s to reclaim land and improve hygiene.

• *Next, enter the...*

Duomo: The Cortona cathedral is not—strictly speaking—a cathedral, because it no longer has a bishop. The white-and-gray Florentine Renaissance-style interior is mucked up with lots of Baroque chapels filling once-spacious side niches. In the rear (on the right) is an altar cluttered with relics. Technically, any Catholic altar, in order to be consecrated, needs a relic embedded in it. Gently lift up the tablecloth (go ahead—the priest here doesn't mind), and you'll see a little marble patch that holds a bit of a saint (daily in summer 7:30-13:00 & 15:00-18:30, daily in winter 8:00-12:30 & 15:00-17:30, closed during Mass).

• *From here, you can visit the nearby Diocesan Museum, or head back toward Piazza della Repubblica to visit the Etruscan Museum in Piazza Signorelli (both listed next) or to get a bite to eat (see "Eating in Cortona," later).*

Sights in Cortona

▲**Etruscan Museum (Museo dell'Accademia Etrusca e della Città di Cortona)**—Located in the 13th-century Casali Palace and called MAEC for short, this fine gallery (established in 1727) is one of the first dedicated to artifacts from the Etruscan civilization. (In the logo, notice the E is backwards—in homage to the Etruscan alphabet.) This sprawling collection is nicely installed on four big floors with plenty of English information. The bottom two floors (underground) are officially the "Museum of the Etruscan and Roman City of Cortona." You'll see an exhibit on the Roman settlement and take a virtual tour of the Etruscan "Il Sodo" tombs (in the nearby countryside). The Cortona Tablet (*Tabula Cortonensis*, second century B.C.), a 200-word contract inscribed in bronze, contains dozens of Etruscan words archaeologists had never seen before its discovery in 1992. Along with lots of gold and jewelry, you'll find a seventh-century B.C. grater (for some *very* aged Parmesan cheese). The top two floors, called the "Accademia," display an even more eclectic collection, including more Etruscania, Egyptian artifacts, fine Roman mosaics, and a room dedicated to 20th-century abstract works by Severini, all lovingly described in English. A highlight is the magnificent fourth-century B.C. bronze oil lamp chandelier with 16 spouts. On the top floor, peek into the classic old library of the Etruscan Academy, founded in 1727 to promote an understanding of the city through the study of archaeology.

Cost and Hours: €10, €13 combo-ticket includes Diocesan Museum; April-Oct daily 10:00-19:00; Nov-March Tue-Sun 10:00-17:00, closed Mon; Casali Palace on Piazza Signorelli, tel. 0575-637-235, www.cortonamaec.org.

▲**Diocesan Museum (Museo Diocesano)**—This small collection contains some very choice artworks from the town's many churches, including works by Fra Angelico and Pietro Lorenzetti, and masterpieces by hometown hero and Renaissance master Luca Signorelli.

Cost and Hours: €5, €13 combo-ticket includes Etruscan Museum, helpful audioguide-€3; April-Oct daily 10:00-19:00; Nov-March Tue-Sun 10:00-17:00, closed Mon; Piazza del Duomo 1, tel. 0575-62-830.

Visiting the Museum: From the entrance, head straight into the Signorelli Room (Sala 4). Signorelli was a generation ahead of Michelangelo and, with his passion for painting ideas, was an inspiration for the younger artist (for more on Signorelli, visit the San Niccolò Church, described later). Take a slow stroll past his very colorful canvases, mostly relocated here from local churches. Among the most striking is *Lamentation over the Dead Christ*

HILL TOWNS

(*Compianto sul Cristo Morto*, 1502). Everything in Signorelli's painting has a meaning: The skull of Adam sits under the sacrifice of Jesus; the hammer represents the Passion (the Crucifixion leading to the Resurrection); the lake is blood; and so on. I don't understand all the medieval symbolism, but it is intense.

Then cut across the top of the stairwell into Sala 3, which was once the nave of the Gesù Church (look up at the beautiful wood-carved ceiling). In Fra Angelico's sumptuous *Annunciation* (c. 1430), Mary says "Yes," consenting to bear God's son. The angel's words are top and bottom, while Mary's answer is upside down (logically, since it's directed to God, who would be reading while looking down from heaven). Notice how the house sits on a pillow of flowers...the new Eden. The old Eden, featuring the expulsion of Adam and Eve from Paradise, is in the upper left. The bottom edge of the painting comes with comic strip-like narration of scenes from Mary's life. On the wall to the right, the crucifix (by Pietro Lorenzetti, c. 1325) is striking in its severity. Notice the gripping realism—even the tendons in Jesus' arms are pulled tight.

Now head back to the stairwell, which is lined with colorful Stations of the Cross scenes by another local but much later artist, the 20th-century's Gino Severini. These are actually "cartoons," models used to create permanent pieces for the approach up to the Santa Margherita Basilica. Downstairs, the lower refectory (Sala 6) has a vault with beautiful frescoes (1545) designed by Giorgio Vasari. Back up near the entrance, another staircase leads down to an important but dull collection of vestments and ecclesiastical gear.

San Francesco Church—Established by St. Francis' best friend, Brother Elias, this church dates from the 13th century. The wooden beams of the ceiling are original. While the place was redecorated in the Baroque age, some of the original frescoes that once wallpapered the church peek through the whitewash in the second chapel on the left. Francis fans visit for its precious Franciscan relics. To the left of the altar, you'll find one of Francis' tunics, his pillow (inside a fancy cover), and his gospel book. Notice how the entire high altar seems designed to frame its precious relic—a piece of the cross Elias brought back from his visit to the patriarch in Constantinople. You're welcome to climb the altar for a close-up look. In the humble choir area behind the main altar is Elias' very simple tomb (just a stone slab in the middle of the floor—on a nearby slab, see the *Frate Elia da Cortona* plaque).

Cost and Hours: Free, daily 9:00-17:30; Mass Mon-Sat at 17:00, Sun at 10:00.

San Niccolò Church—Signorelli enthusiasts will want to make the pilgrimage up to this tiny church, a steep 10-minute walk above the San Francesco Church. While it's not worth going out of the way for (the picturesque neighborhood surrounding it is, for many, more interesting), it's an easy detour if you're hiking up to Santa Margherita. The highlight of this humble church is an altarpiece painted on both sides by Signorelli, which is usually pulled halfway open so you can see both sides.

Cost and Hours: €1 donation, April-Oct Sat-Sun 11:00-13:00 & 15:00-18:00, likely daily in June-Sept, generally closed Nov-March, verify hours with TI before making the trip.

Santa Margherita Basilica—From San Niccolò Church, another steep path leads uphill 10 minutes to this basilica, which houses the remains of Margherita, the town's favorite saint. The red-and-white-striped interior boasts some colorfully painted vaults. Santa Margherita, an unwed mother from Montepulciano, found her calling with the Franciscans in Cortona, tending to the sick and poor. The well-preserved and remarkably emotional 13th-century crucifix on the right is the cross that, according to legend, talked to Margherita.

Cost and Hours: Free, daily 9:00-12:00 & 15:00-19:00 except closed Mon morning, tel. 0575-603-116.

Nearby: Still need more altitude? Head uphill five more minutes to the recently renovated **Medici Fortezza Girifalco** (€3, usually open daily late April-Sept 9:00-13:00 & 15:00-18:00, likely later in July-Aug, closed Oct-late April, sometimes closed for rehearsals by Italian rock legend Jovanotti, who lives in a villa beyond San Niccolò Church—check with TI). The views are stunning, stretching all the way to distant Lago Trasimeno.

Etruscan Tombs near Cortona—Guided tours to the tombs (called *melone* for their melon-like shape), in the locality of Sodo, are complicated to arrange. But the excavation site and bits of the ruins are easy to visit and can be seen from outside the fence in the morning. It's just a couple of miles northwest of Cortona on the Arezzo road (R-71), at the foot of the Cortona hill; ask anyone for "Il Sodo."

Sleeping in Cortona

(€1 = about $1.40, country code: 39)

Inside the Old Town

$$$ Hotel San Luca, perched on the side of a cliff, has 54 impersonal business-class rooms, half with stunning views of Lago Trasimeno. While the hotel feels tired and the rooms have seen better days, it's friendly and conveniently located, right at the bus stop on Piazza Garibaldi at the entrance to the Old Town (Sb-€70, Db-€100, Tb-€130, request a view room when you reserve for no extra charge, popular with Americans and groups, air-con, elevator, pay Wi-Fi, Piazza Garibaldi 2, tel. 0575-630-460, fax 0575-630-105, www.sanlucacortona.com, info@sanlucacortona.com). If driving, you might find a spot at the small public parking lot at the hotel; otherwise you can park at the big lot down below and ride the escalator up.

$$ Dolce Maria B&B is located in a 16th-century building with high-beamed ceilings. Though the breakfast area is small, the six rooms themselves are good-value, luminous, and spacious, with tasteful period furnishings and modern bathrooms. The B&B is run by warm and efficient Paola, who also runs the Antico Pozzo restaurant next door—the two businesses share a patio (Db-€80-100, air-con, free Wi-Fi, Via Ghini 12, tel. 0575-601-577, fax 057-560-4627, www.cortonastorica.com, info@cortonastorica.com).

$ San Marco Hostel, at the top of town, is housed in a remodeled 13th-century palace (bunk in 4- to 6-bed dorm-€17, in 2-bed room-€22, includes breakfast, lunch or dinner-€10.50, lockout 10:00-13:00; from Piazza Garibaldi head up steep Via Santa Margherita, then turn left to find Via Maffei 57; tel. & fax 0575-601-392, www.cortonahostel.com, ostellocortona@libero.it).

Outside the Old Town

These accommodations line up along the road that angles downhill from Piazza Garibaldi, within a 10-minute (uphill) walk to the entrance to the Old Town. Drivers may find these handier than the places in town.

$$$ Hotel Villa Marsili is a comfortable splurge just below town. It was originally a 15th-century church, then an elegant 18th-century home. Its 26 rooms and public areas have been recently redecorated and restored, and come with lots of thoughtful little touches. Guests can enjoy an evening aperitif with free snacks on the panoramic terrace. In general, the higher up the room, the fancier the decor and the higher the price. Diane Lane slept in one of the suites while filming *Under the Tuscan Sun* (Sb-€90, small standard Db-€150, superior Db-€180, deluxe Db-€230, Db suite-€350, extra bed-€25/child or €50/adult, Jacuzzi in deluxe room and suites, air-con, elevator, free Internet access and Wi-Fi, free street parking nearby—first come, first served, Viale Cesare Battisti 13, tel. 0575-605-252, fax 0575-605-618, www.villamarsili.net, info@villamarsili.net, Marina).

$ Casa Betania, a big, wistful convent with an inviting view terrace, rents 30 fine rooms (mostly twin beds) for the best price in town. While it's primarily for "thoughtful travelers," anyone looking for a peaceful place to call home will feel welcome in this pilgrims' resort. Marco, a big-city lawyer escaping from the rat race, has taken over this place and is turning it into an impressive retreat facility, with conference rooms, a chapel, wine cellar, cooking classes, and more (S-€32, D-€44, Db-€48, Tb-€66, extra bed-€20, breakfast-€4, free Wi-Fi, free parking, about a third of a mile out of town, a few minutes' walk below Piazza Garibaldi and through iron gates on the right at Via Gino Severini 50, tel. & fax 0575-630-423, www.casaperferiebetania.com, info@casaperferie betania.com).

$ Istituto Santa Margherita, run by the Serve di Maria Riparatrici sisters, rents 22 nicely renovated rooms in a smaller and more traditional-feeling convent just up the street from Casa Betania (Sb-€42, Db-€58, Tb-€75, Qb-€86, breakfast-€5, elevator, pay Wi-Fi, free parking, Viale Cesare Battisti 17, tel. 0575-178-7203 or 0575-630-336, fax 0575-630-549, www.santamargherita .smr.it, comunitacortona@smr.it).

$ Casa Kita, renting four slightly quirky rooms, is a homey place just below Piazza Garibaldi with fine views from its terrace. You'll really feel like you're staying in someone's home, but the prices are good (Db-€65, free Wi-Fi, 100 yards below Piazza Garibaldi at Vicolo degli Orti 7, tel. 389-557-9893, www.casakita .com, info@casakita.com, Lorenzini family).

Eating in Cortona

Ristorante La Bucaccia is a family-run eatery set in a rustic medieval wine cellar. It's dressy and romantic. Taking an evangelical pride in their Chianina beef dishes and homemade pastas, Romano hosts and his wife Agostina cooks. Reservations are required for dinner—and worth making (€8-9 pastas, €12-15 *secondi,* daily 12:00-15:30 & 19:00-24:00, show this book for a 5 percent discount and a small free appetizer, Via Ghibellina 17, tel. 0575-606-039).

Trattoria la Grotta, just off Piazza della Repubblica, is a traditional place serving daily specials to an enthusiastic clientele under grotto-like vaults (€7-9 pastas, €7-16 *secondi,* good wine by the glass, Wed-Mon 12:00-14:30 & 19:00-22:00, closed Tue, Piazza Baldelli 3, tel. 0575-630-271).

Locanda al Pozzo Antico offers an affordable menu of Tuscan fare, with a focus on fresh, quality produce, and using their own homemade olive oil. Eat in a classy, minimalist dining room or tucked away in a tranquil secret courtyard. Paola is a charming hostess (€6-9 pastas, €10-16 *secondi,* Fri-Wed 12:30-14:30 & 19:30-22:00, closed Thu, Via Ghini 12, tel. 0575-62091 or 0575-601-577; Paola, husband Franco, and son Gianni).

Ristorante La Loggetta serves up big portions of well-presented Tuscan cuisine on the loggia overlooking Piazza della Repubblica. While they have fine indoor seating under stone vaults, I'd eat here for the chance to gaze at the square over a meal

(€8-10 pastas, €8-15 *secondi*, Thu-Tue 12:30-15:00 & 19:30-23:00, closed Wed, Piazza Pescheria 3, tel. 0575-630-575).

Fufluns Tavern Pizzeria (that's the Etruscan name for Dionysus) is easy-going, friendly, and remarkably unpretentious for its location in the town center. It's popular with locals for its good, inexpensive Tuscan cooking, friendly staff, and stone-and-beam-cozy interior (€5-7 pizza and €6-10 pastas plus big salads, good house wine, Wed-Mon 12:15-14:30 & 19:15-22:30, closed Tue, a block below Piazza della Repubblica at Via Ghibellina 3, tel. 0575-604-140).

Osteria del Teatro tries very hard to create a romantic Old World atmosphere, and does it well. Chef and owner Emiliano serves nicely presented and tasty Italian and local cuisine (taking creative liberties with traditions). There's good outdoor seating, too. It feels upscale and a bit self-important (€8-9 pastas, €11-16 *secondi*, Thu-Tue 12:30-14:30 & 19:30-22:00, closed Wed, 2 blocks uphill from the main square at Via Maffei 2—look for the gnomes on the steps, tel. 0575-630-556).

Enoteca la Saletta, dark and classy with a nice mellow vibe, is good for fine wine and a light meal. You can sit inside surrounded by wine bottles or outside to people-watch on the town's main drag (€3-5 sandwiches and pizzas, €7-12 pastas and *secondi,* daily 7:30-24:00, meals served 12:00-24:00, closed Wed in winter, free Wi-Fi, Via Nazionale 26, tel. 0575-603-366).

Picnic: On the main square, the chic little **Despar Market Molesini** makes tasty sandwiches, served with a smile (see list on counter and order by number, or invent your own), and sells whatever else you might want for a picnic (Mon-Sat 7:00-13:30 & 16:00-20:00, Sun 9:00-13:00, Piazza della Repubblica 23). Munch your picnic across the square on the steps of City Hall, or just past Piazza Garibaldi in the public gardens behind San Domenico Church.

Cortona Connections

Cortona has good train connections with the rest of Italy through its Camucia-Cortona station. Arrive with small bills and coins, as the station is usually unstaffed, and its very basic ticket machine takes only cash—and for change gives only vouchers (which you can use to pay for a future journey). The machine will ask the following: *stazione di partenza* (departure station—select Camucia), *stazione di arrivo* (arrival station—key in the number of your destination from the posted list), *tipo di bilgietto* (select *solo andata,* one-way), *classe* (I go for *seconde*—second class), type of ticket (select *adulti*), and *quantità biglietti da emettere* (how many tickets you want). Then *premiere OK* (press OK) and insert the cash. After buying your ticket, immediately validate it in the yellow box next to the machine. It's possible to buy tickets on board the train for €5 extra—but you have to find the conductor before he finds you, or you'll pay a €40 fine.

To get to the train station at the foot of the hill, take a €10 taxi or hop the €1.20 bus (see "Arrival in Cortona," earlier; runs only about once hourly; buy tickets at newsstand, TI, or tobacco shop, or buy from driver for €0.40 more). Some buses from Piazza Garibaldi only take you as far as the newsstand that's 200 yards in front of the station.

From Camucia-Cortona by Train to: Rome (9/day, 2.5 hours, 4 direct, others with change), **Florence** (hourly, 1.5 hours), **Assisi** (every 2 hours, 70 minutes, change in Terontola), **Montepulciano** (9/day, 1.5-2 hours, change in Chiusi; because few buses serve Montepulciano's town center from its distant train station, it's better to go by train to Chiusi, then by hourly 40-minute bus to Montepulciano), **Chiusi** (9/day, 40 minutes).

Most trains stop at the Camucia-Cortona train station, but each day, two or three high-speed trains to/from Rome, Florence, and Assisi stop at **Terontola**, 10 miles away (buses go about hourly to Terontola, leaves from Piazza Garibaldi, 25-30 minutes, €2, check the schedule at the bus stop by the tree in the square or pick up printed bus schedule from the TI). Note that these trains require reservations, which you can't make on the spot; if taking one, reserve online in advance.

More Hill Towns and Sights

These are listed roughly from north to south.

▲Florence American Cemetery and Memorial

The compelling sight of endless rows of white marble crosses and Stars of David recalls the heroism of the young Americans who

fought so valiantly in World War II to free Italy (and ultimately Europe) from the grip of fascism. This particular cemetery is the final resting place of more than 4,000 Americans who died in the liberation of Italy. Climb the hill past the perfectly manicured lawn lined with grave markers, to the memorial, where maps and a history of the Italian campaign detail the Allied advance.

Cost and Hours: Free, daily 9:00-17:00; 7.5 miles south of Florence, off Via Cassia, which parallels the *superstrada* between Florence and Siena, 2 miles south of Florence Certosa exit on A-1 autostrada; buses from Florence stop just outside the cemetery; tel. 055-202-0020, www.abmc.gov.

▲San Galgano Monastery

Of southern Tuscany's several evocative monasteries, San Galgano is the best. Set in a forested area called the Montagnolo ("Medium-Size Mountains"), the isolated abbey and chapel are postcard-perfect, though you'll need a car to get here. Other, more accessible Tuscan monasteries worth visiting include Sant'Antimo (6 miles south of Montalcino) and Monte Oliveto Maggiore (15 miles south of Siena, mentioned in "The Crete Senese," earlier).

Cost and Hours: €2, June-Aug daily 9:00-20:00, shoulder season until 19:00, Nov-Feb daily 10:00-17:00, tel. 0577-756-738, www.prolocochiusdino.it; concerts sometimes held here in summer— info tel. 055-597-8309, www.festivalopera.it. For a quick snack, a small, touristy bar at the end of the driveway is your only option.

Getting There: Although a bus reportedly comes here from Siena, this sight is realistically accessible only for drivers. It's just outside Monticiano (not Montalcino), about an hour south of Siena. A warning to the queasy: These roads are curvy.

Visiting the Monastery: St. Galgano was a 12th-century saint who renounced his past as a knight to become a hermit. Lacking a cross to display, he created his own by miraculously burying his sword up to its hilt in a stone, à la King Arthur, but in reverse. After his death, a large Cistercian monastery complex grew. Today, all you'll see is the roofless, ruined abbey and, on a nearby hill, the Chapel of San Galgano with its fascinating dome and sword in the stone.

This picturesque Cistercian **abbey** was once a powerful institution in Tuscany. Known for their skill as builders, the Cistercians oversaw the construction of Siena's cathedral. But after losing most of its population in the plague of 1348, the abbey never really recovered and was eventually deconsecrated.

The Cistercian order was centered in France, and the architecture of the abbey shows a heavy French influence. Notice the large, high windows and the pointy, delicate arches. This is pure French Gothic, a style that never fully caught on in Italy (compare it with the chunky, elaborately decorated cathedral in Siena, built about the same time).

As you enter the church, look to the left to see a small section of the cloister wall. This used to surround the garden and was the only place where the monks were allowed to talk, for one hour each day. From inside the church, the empty windows frame the view of the chapel up on the hill.

In 2013, the upper floor of the actual monks' quarters (to the side of the abbey) may open to the public.

A path from the abbey leads up the hill to the **Chapel of San Galgano**. The unique, beehive-like interior houses St. Galgano's sword and stone, recently confirmed to date back to the 12th century. Don't try and pull the sword from the stone—the small chapel to the left displays the severed arms of the last guy who tried. The chapel also contains some deteriorated frescoes and more interesting *sinopie* (fresco sketches). The adjacent gift shop sells a little bit of everything, from wine to postcards to herbs, some of it monk-made.

▲Urbino

If you're driving through central Italy, Urbino is worth a stop for its sprawling, fascinating Ducal Palace. Although Urbino is the hometown of the artist Raphael and the architect Donato Bramante, it's better known for the Duke of Montefeltro, a mercenary general who built the palace and turned Urbino into an important Renaissance center. For my expanded coverage of Urbino, see www.ricksteves.com/urbino.

A classic hill town, Urbino has a medieval wall with four gates, and two main roads that crisscross at the town's main square, Piazza della Repubblica. The tiny **TI** is just across from the Ducal Palace (March-Oct Mon-Sat 9:00-19:00, Nov-Feb Mon-Sat 9:00-13:30 & 14:30-18:00, closed Sun year-round, Piazza Duca Federico 35, tel. 0722-2613, www.urbinoculturaturismo.it).

The **Ducal Palace** (Palazzo Ducale), which has more than 300 rooms, was built in the mid-1400s. While the rooms are fairly bare, the palace holds a few very special paintings, as well as exquisite inlaid-wood decorations. It's a monument to how one man—the Duke of Montefeltro—brought the Renaissance to his small town (€5, but sometimes €9 for special exhibits, Mon 8:30-14:00, Tue-Sun 8:30-19:15, last entry one hour before closing, tel. 072-232-2625). The highlights of the palace include great paintings such as Raphael's *Portrait of a Gentlewoman* (a.k.a. *La Muta*); the Renaissance courtyard patterned after the trendsetting Medici-Riccardi Palace in Florence; the richly paneled and inlaid-wood walls of the duke's study; and the vast cellars that include a giant stable with a clever horse-pie disposal system.

Stop by the **Oratory of St. John** to see its remarkable frescoed interior that tells the story of the life of St. John the Baptist (€2.50, Mon-Sat 10:00-12:30 & 15:00-17:30, Sun 10:00-12:30, 5-minute walk from main square—follow signs, Piazza Baricci 31; if no one's there, find attendant at the Oratory of San Giuseppe a few steps away; mobile 347-671-1181).

Finally, for the ultimate Urbino view, climb up to the grassy park surrounding the **fortress** (interior closed, but grounds open to the public). The Franciscan church spire, on the left, marks the main square.

Getting There: Urbino is easier for drivers, but public transportation is an option. Buses link Urbino with Pesaro, on the Ravenna-Pescara train line (buses run hourly, 1-hour trip). From Venice, Florence, or Rome, trains leave for Pesaro almost hourly (taking 3-5 hours). In Urbino, buses come and go from the Piazza Mercatale parking lot below the town, where an elevator lifts you up to the base of the Ducal Palace (or take a 5-minute steep walk up Via Mazzini to Piazza della Repubblica).

Sleeping in Urbino: The hotel scene is limited to a few comfortable, expensive places, including **Albergo San Domenico** (www.viphotels.it), **Hotel Raffaello** (www.albergoraffaello.com), and **Albergo Italia** (www.albergo-italia-urbino.it). The TI has a line on lots of families renting rooms.

Eating in Urbino: Try **Taverna degli Artisti** (Via Donato Bramante 52) and **Il Coppiere** (Via Santa Margherita 1), or **Ristorante/Pizzeria Le Tre Piante** (Via Voltaccia della Vecchia 1).

▲Chiusi

This small hill town (rated ▲▲ for Etruscan fans) was once one of the most important Etruscan cities. Today, it's a key train junction and a pleasant, workaday Italian village with an enjoyable historic center and few tourists. The hill upon which Chiusi sits is honeycombed with Etruscan tunnels, which you can see in a variety of ways.

Tourist Information: The well-organized TI faces the main square (daily April-Aug 9:00-13:00 & 15:00-18:00, Sept 10:00-13:00 & 15:00-18:00, Oct 9:00-13:00, Nov-March 9:30-12:30, Via Porsenna 79, tel. 0578-227-667, www.prolocochiusi.it).

Arrival in Chiusi: The region's **trains** (to Florence, Siena, and Rome—each of these is about an hour away) go through or change at this hub, making Chiusi an easy day trip. There's no luggage storage at the station, but the TI may be willing to take your bags for a short time. Buses link the train station with the town center two miles away (every 40 minutes, buy tickets at tobacco shop, bus doesn't run during a gap in the afternoon, taxi costs €10). All buses from the station drop off at a stop just below the center of town (follow well-marked pedestrian signs up to the TI and museums); about half continue on to a stop near the town theater, right downtown. **Drivers** follow signs for *centro storico*, then the TI. Easy and free parking lots are a five-minute walk from the center; pay spaces (marked with blue lines) are right downtown, next to the TI and museums. Hertz has a rental-car office near the train station (Via M. Buonarroti 21, tel. 057-822-3000).

Sights in Chiusi: All the town's sights are within a five-minute walk of each other and the TI.

The **Archaeological Museum** (Museo Archeologico Nazionale, a.k.a. the Etruscan Museum) thoughtfully presents a high-quality collection with plenty of explanations in English. The collection of funerary urns, some in painted terra-cotta and some in *pietra fetida* ("stinky stone"), are remarkably intact. You'll also see exhibits on two tombs in the nearby countryside: a model of the Tomba della Pellegrina, and small-scale reproductions of the frescoes from the Tomba della Scimmia—both mentioned below (€4, daily 9:00-20:00, in the stately Neoclassical-looking building just off the main square at Via Porsenna 93, tel. 0578-20177, www.archeotoscana.beniculturali.it).

The museum also arranges tours to visit the actual Pellegrina and Scimmia **tombs**; to take part, you'll need to have your own car and to join a guide (meet at the museum 15 minutes before the tour time). For the Tomba della Pellegrina (Tomb of the Pilgrim), from the Hellenistic period (4th century B.C.), tours depart daily at 11:00 and 16:00 (or 14:30 in winter). This is included in museum admission, and no reservations are necessary—just ask when you arrive. The other, the Tomba della Scimmia (Tomb of the Monkey), is a century earlier and has some well-preserved frescoes (€2; Mon, Tue, and Sat only; March-Oct at 11:00 and 16:00, Nov-Feb at 11:00 and 14:30; this tomb requires an advance reservation).

Troglodyte alert! The **Cathedral Museum** on the main square has a dark, underground labyrinth of Etruscan tunnels. The mandatory guided tour of the tunnels ends in a large Roman cistern, from which you can climb the church bell tower for an expansive view of the countryside (museum-€2, labyrinth-€3, combo-ticket-€4, daily June-mid-Oct 9:45-12:45 & 16:00-18:30, mid-Oct-May 9:45-12:45 only, 30-minute tunnel tours run every 40 minutes during museum hours, Piazza Duomo 1, tel. 0578-226-490).

Craving more underground fun? The **Museo Civico** provides hourly tours of the Etruscan water system, which includes an underground lake (€4; May-Oct Tue-Sun at 10:15, 11:30, 12:45, 15:15, 16:30, and 17:45; closed Mon, fewer tours and closed Mon-Wed off-season, call to confirm times, Via II Ciminia 1, tel. 0578-20530, mobile 334-626-6851).

▲Gubbio

This handsome town climbs Monte Ingino in northeast Umbria.
Tuesday is market day, when Piazza 40 Martiri (named for 40
local martyrs shot by Nazis) bus-
tles. Nearby are the ruins of the
Roman amphitheater, and a park
close by that's perfect for a picnic.
Head up Via della Repubblica to
the main square with the imposing Palazzo dei Consoli. Farther
up, Via San Gerolamo leads to the
funky lift that will carry you up

the hill, in two-person "baskets," for a stunning view from the top,
where the Basilica of San Ubaldo is worth a look. The **TI** is at Via
della Repubblica 15 (daily April-Sept 8:30-13:45 & 15:30-18:30,
Oct-March closes at 18:00 daily; tel. 075-922-0693, www.gubbio
-altochiascio.umbria2000.it). Buses from Gubbio run directly to
Rome and Perugia (where you can transfer to Florence).

▲Bevagna

This sleeper of a town south of Assisi has Roman ruins, interesting churches, and more. Locals offer their guiding services for free
(usually Italian-speaking only) and are excited to show visitors their
town. Get a map at the **TI** at Piazza Silvestri 1 (daily 9:30-12:30
& 15:30-19:30, tel. 074-236-1667) and wander. Highlights are the
Roman mosaics, remains of the arena, a paper-making workshop,
the Romanesque Church of San Silvestro, and a gem of a 19th-
century theater. Bevagna has all the elements of a hill town except
one: a hill. You can see the main sights easily in a couple of hours.

▲Spello

Umbrian hill town aficionados always include Spello on their
list. Just six miles south of Assisi, this town is much less touristy
than its neighbor to the north. Spello will give your legs a workout. Via Consolare goes up, up, up to the top of town. Views from
the terrace of the **Il Trombone** restaurant will have you singing
a tune (Via Fontanello 1, tel. 074-265-1069). The **TI** is on Piazza
Matteotti 3 (daily 9:30-12:30 & 16:00-18:00, afternoons 15:30-
17:30 in winter, tel. 074-230-1009, www.prospello.it). Spello is on
the Perugia-Assisi-Foligno train line.

ASSISI

Assisi is famous for its hometown boy, St. Francis, who made very good. While Francis the saint is interesting, Francesco Bernardone the man is even more so, and mementos of his days in Assisi are everywhere—where he was baptized, a shirt he wore, a hill he prayed on, and a church where a vision changed his life.

About the year 1200, this simple friar from Assisi countered the decadence of Church government and society in general with a powerful message of non-materialism and a "slow down and smell God's roses" lifestyle. Like Jesus, Francis taught by example, living without worldly goods and aiming to love all creation. A huge monastic order grew out of his teachings, which were gradually embraced (some would say co-opted) by the Church. Christianity's most popular saint and its purest example of simplicity is now glorified in beautiful churches, along with his female counterpart, St. Clare. In 1939, Italy made Francis one of its patron saints.

Francis' message of love, simplicity, and sensitivity to the environment has a broad and timeless appeal. But every pilgrimage site inevitably gets commercialized, and Francis' legacy is now Assisi's basic industry. In summer, this Umbrian town bursts with flash-in-the-pan Francis fans and Franciscan knickknacks. Those able to see past the glow-in-the-dark rosaries and bobblehead friars can actually have a "travel on purpose" experience. Even a block or two off the congested main drag, you'll find pockets of serenity that, it's easy to imagine, must have made Francis feel at peace.

Planning Your Time

Assisi is worth a day and a night. Its old town has a half-day of sightseeing and another half-day of wonder. The essential sight is the Basilica of St. Francis. For a good visit, take my self-guided "Welcome to Assisi" walk, ending at the Basilica of St. Francis. With more time, be sure to wander the back streets and linger on the main square, Piazza del Comune.

Most visitors are day-trippers. While the town's a zoo by day, it's a delight at night. Assisi after dark is closer to a place Francis could call home.

Orientation to Assisi

Crowned by a ruined castle, Assisi spills downhill to its famous Basilica of St. Francis. The town is beautifully preserved and rich in history. A 5.5-magnitude earthquake in 1997 did more damage to the tourist industry than to the town's buildings. Fortunately, tourists—whether art lovers, pilgrims, or both—have returned, drawn by Assisi's special allure.

The city sprawls across a ridge that rises from a flat plain. The Basilica of St. Francis sits at the low end of town; Piazza Matteotti (with bus station and parking lot) is at the high end; and the main square, Piazza del Comune, lies in between. The main drag (called Via San Francesco for most of its course) runs from Piazza del Comune to the basilica. Capping the hill above the town is a ruined castle called the Rocca Maggiore, and rising above that is Mount Subasio. The town is small, and slopes uphill from west to east. Walking uphill from the basilica to Piazza Matteotti takes 30 minutes, while the downhill journey takes about 15 minutes. Some Francis sights lie outside the city walls, in the valley beneath the ridge and in the hills above.

Tourist Information

The TI, which hands out free maps, is in the center of town on Piazza del Comune (Mon-Fri 8:00-14:00 & 15:00-18:00—until 18:30 June-mid-Oct, Sat-Sun 9:30-17:00—until 18:00 in April-Oct, tel. 075-813-8680). There's also a branch down in the valley, across the street from the big piazza in front of St. Mary of the Angels Basilica.

Arrival in Assisi

By Train and Bus: The train station is about two miles below Assisi, in Santa Maria degli Angeli, but orange city buses connect the station with the old town on the hilltop (2/hour, 15 minutes, €1). On the way up into town, buses stop at Piazza Giovanni Paolo II (near Basilica of St. Francis), then Largo Properzio (near Basilica of St. Clare), and finally Piazza Matteotti (top of old town). Buses usually leave from the train station at :16 and :46 past the hour (bus stop immediately to your left as you exit station; buy tickets at

ASSISI

the newsstand inside the train station for €1, or on board the bus for €1.50—exact change only, valid one hour after being stamped, good for any bus within the old town). You can check bags at the newsstand (€3/12 hours, daily 6:30-13:00 & 14:30-19:00), but not in the old town.

Going from the old town to the train station, the orange buses usually run from Piazza Matteotti at :10 and :40 past the hour (stopping outside Porta Nuova at Largo Properzio a couple of minutes later, and in Piazza Giovanni Paolo II a few minutes after that).

At Piazza Giovanni Paolo II (the big parking lot #A for cars and buses below the Basilica of St. Francis), there are two bus stops *(fermata bus):* one is for Linea #C, which goes to the train station (the sign reads *per f.s. S.M. Angeli, Linea C;* the orange bus headed for Piazza Matteotti also stops here—check the front of the bus for its destination); and the other is for Linea #B, a pale-yellow minibus that runs through the center of the old town to Piazza del Comune. Hop on a bus marked *Piazza Matteotti* if you're exhausted after your basilica visit and need a sweat-free five-minute return to the top of the old town (near many of my recommended hotels).

Taxis from the train station to the old town cost about €15. You can be charged extra for luggage, night service, additional people (four is customary)...and sometimes just for being a tourist. When departing the old town, you'll find taxi stands at Piazza Giovanni Paolo II, the Basilica of St. Francis, the Basilica of St. Clare, and Piazza del Comune (or have your hotel call for you, tel.

075-813-100). Expect to pay a minimum of €10 for any ride.

By Car: Drivers coming in for the day can follow the signs to several handy parking lots *(parcheggi)*. Piazza Matteotti's wonderful underground parking garage (#C) is at the top of the town and comes with bits of ancient Rome in the walls (daily 7:00-21:00, until 23:00 in summer). Another big lot, Parcheggio Giovanni Paolo II (#A), is at the bottom end of town, 200 yards below the Basilica of St. Francis. Between them is the unlettered Parcheggio Mojano; while outside the town wall, this comes with an escalator that transports you near the Basilica of St. Clare. At Parcheggio Porta Nuova (#B), an elevator delivers you to Porta Nuova near St. Clare's. The lots vary in price (€1.45-1.60/hour, most €10-12/day but Matteotti €17/day). For day-trippers, the best plan is to park at Piazza Matteotti, follow my self-guided town walk, tour the basilica, and then either catch a bus back to Piazza Matteotti or simply wander back up through town to your car.

Helpful Hints

Best Shopping: Tacky knickknacks line the streets leading to the Basilica of St. Francis. For better shops (with local handicrafts), head to Via San Rufino and Corso Mazzini (both just off Piazza del Comune, shops described later in the "Welcome to Assisi" self-guided walk). A Saturday-morning market fills Via Borgo San Pietro (along the bottom edge of town).

Festivals: Assisi annually hosts several interesting festivals commemorating St. Francis and life in the Middle Ages. **Festa di Calendimaggio** is a springtime medieval festival featuring costume parades, concerts, and competitions among Assisi's rival neighborhoods (www.calendimaggiodiassisi.it). Rustic medieval "taverns" pop up around the center offering *porchetta* (roasted pig) and *vino* (starts the first Thu-Sat in May; if one of these days is already a public holiday, it's held the following week). The **Settimana Francescana** commemorates the beginning of the end of Francis' life, when he made his way for the last time to the Porziuncola Chapel (Sept 28). This week-long celebration culminates in the **Festa di San Francesco,** which marks his death with religious processions, special services, and an arts, crafts, and folklore fair. The TI has a monthly *Assisi Informa* leaflet with details on upcoming festivals and celebrations; see also the event listings at www .assisi.regioneumbria.eu.

Internet Access: Facing the Cathedral of San Rufino, the recommended **Caffè Duomo** offers Internet access (€3/hour, daily 7:30-23:00, snacks, Piazza San Rufino 5, tel. 075-813-023).

Laundry: **3elleblu' Lavanderia** has a few machines; if they're not too busy, they can do it for you on the same day (€5/wash,

St. Francis of Assisi
(1181-1226)

In 1202, young Francesco Bernardone donned armor and rode out to battle the Perugians (residents of Umbria's capital city).

The battle went badly, and Francis was captured and imprisoned for a year. He returned a changed man. He avoided friends and his father's lucrative business, and spent more and more time outside the city walls fasting, praying, and searching for something.

In 1206, a vision changed his life, culminating in a dramatic confrontation. He stripped naked before the town leaders, threw his clothes at his father—turning his back on the comfortable material life—and declared his loyalty to God alone.

Idealistic young men flocked to Francis, and they wandered Italy like troubadours, spreading the joy of the Gospel to rich and poor. Francis became a cult figure, attracting huge crowds. They'd never seen anything like it—sermons preached outdoors, in the local language (not Church Latin), making God accessible to all. Francis' new order of monks was also extremely unmaterialistic, extolling poverty and simplicity. Despite their radicalism, the order eventually gained the pope's approval and spread through the world. Francis, who died in Assisi at the age of 45, left a legacy of humanism, equality, and love of nature that would eventually flower in the Renaissance.

In Francis' Sandal-Steps
1. Baptized in Assisi's **Cathedral of San Rufino** (then called St. George's).
2. Raised in the family home just off Piazza del Comune (now the **Chiesa Nuova**).
3. Heard call to "rebuild church" in **San Damiano.** (The crucifix of the church is now in the **Basilica of St. Clare.**)
4. Settled and established his order of monks at the **Porziuncola Chapel** (inside today's St. Mary of the Angels Basilica).
5. Met Clare. (Her tomb and possessions are at the **Basilica of St. Clare.**)
6. Received the pope's blessing for his order (1223 document in the reliquary chapel at the **Basilica of St. Francis**).
7. Had many visions and was associated with miracles during his life (depicted in **Giotto's frescoes** in the Basilica of St. Francis' upper level).
8. Died at the **Porziuncola,** his body later interred beneath the **Basilica of St. Francis.**

€4.50/dry, Mon-Fri 9:00-18:00, Sat 9:00-13:00, closed Sun, Via Borgo Aretino 6a, tel. 075-816-084).

Travel Agencies: You can purchase train and bus tickets at **Agenzia Viaggi Stoppini,** centrally located between Piazza del Comune and the Basilica of St. Clare. Manager Fabrizio is patient with tourists' needs (€1 surcharge for train tickets, Mon-Fri 9:00-12:30 & 15:30-18:30, Sat 9:00-12:30, closed Sun, Corso Mazzini 31, tel. 075-812-597). Depending on the bus company, either you'll buy tickets in advance at this agency (e.g., for Siena) or you'll pay the driver when you board the bus (e.g., for Rome or Sorrento). For more information, see "Assisi Connections," at the end of this chapter.

Local Guide: Giuseppe Karabotis is a good licensed guide (€130/2.5 hours, €260/6 hours, mobile 328-867-0567, iokarabot @libero.it); if he's busy, he can recommend other guides.

Local Guide with Car: Daniela Moretti is a hardworking young guide from Perugia who knows Assisi well. Besides touring in Assisi, she'll take you anywhere in Umbria with her car, which comfortably fits three travelers and jams in four (on foot: €120/half-day, €200/day; with car: €150/half-day, €250/day; mobile 335-829-9984, www.danyguide.com, danyguide @hotmail.com).

Getting Around Assisi

Cute, pale-yellow electrical minibuses, labeled *Linea A* and *Linea B*, connect the top of the town with the bottom. While it's only a 15-minute stroll down the hill, the climb back up can have you looking for a lift. Before boarding, confirm the destination (catch the bus below the Basilica of St. Francis at the Porta San Francisco). In the center of town, buses leave from Piazza del Comune and Piazza Matteotti. You can buy a bus ticket (good on any city bus) at a newsstand or kiosk for €1, or get a ticket from the driver for €1.50 (exact change only). After you've stamped your ticket on board the bus, it's valid for an hour.

Self-Guided Walk

▲▲Welcome to Assisi

There's much more to Assisi than just St. Francis and what the blitz tour groups see. This walk covers the town from top (Piazza Matteotti) to bottom (Basilica of St. Francis). To get to Piazza Matteotti, ride the bus from the train station (or from Piazza Giovanni Paolo II) to the last stop; drive (underground parking); or hike five minutes uphill from Piazza del Comune.

You can download a free Rick Steves audio tour of this walk; see page 1101.

• *Start 50 yards beyond Piazza Matteotti (away from city center—see map).*

❶ The Roman Amphitheater (Anfiteatro Romano)

A lane named Via Anfiteatro Romano skirts the cozy neighborhood built around a Roman amphitheater—a reminder that Assisi was once an important Roman town. Circle the amphitheater counterclockwise. Imagine how colorful the town laundry basin (on the right) must have been in previous generations, when the women of Assisi gathered here to do their wash. Just beyond the basin is a small rectangular pool; above it are the coats of arms of Assisi's leading families. A few steps farther, leave the amphitheater, hiking up the stairs on the right to the top of the hill, for an aerial view of the ancient oval. The Roman stones have long been absorbed into the medieval architecture. It was Roman tradition to locate the amphitheater outside of town, which this used to be. While the amphitheater dates from the first century A.D., the buildings filling it today were built in the 13th and 14th centuries.

• *Continue on, enjoying the grand view of the fortress in the distance. The lane leads down to a city gate and an...*

❷ Umbrian View

Step outside of Assisi at the Porta Perlici for a commanding view. Umbria, called the "green heart of Italy," is the country's geographical center and only landlocked region. Enjoy the various shades of green: silver green on the valley floor (olives), emerald green (grapevines), and deep green on the hillsides (evergreen oak trees). Also notice Rocca Maggiore ("big fortress"), which provided townsfolk a refuge in times of attack, and, behind you atop the nearer hill, Rocca Minore ("little fortress"), which gives the town's young lovers a little privacy. The quarry (under the Rocca Maggiore) was a handy source for Assisi's characteristic pink limestone.

• *Go back through the gate and follow Via Porta Perlici—it's immediately on your right—downhill into town (toward Hotel La Rocca). Enjoy the higgledy-piggledy architecture (this neighborhood has some of*

the most photogenic back lanes in town). You'll pass a wall containing an aqueduct (on the left, at the arch before #52) that goes back to Roman times. It still brings water from a mountain spring into the city (push the brass tap for a taste). After another 50 yards, turn left through a medieval town gate (with Hotel La Rocca on your right). Just after the hotel, you'll pass a second gate dating from

Welcome to Assisi Walk

Roman times. Follow Via Porta Perlici downhill until you hit a fine square facing a big church.

❸ Cathedral of San Rufino (Cattedrale San Rufino)

Trick question: Who's Assisi's patron saint? While Francis is one of Italy's patron saints, Rufino (the town's first bishop, martyred and buried here in the third century) is Assisi's. The cathedral (seat of the local bishop) is 11th-century Romanesque with a Neoclassical interior. Although it has what is considered to be one of the best and purest Romanesque facades in all of Umbria, the big triangular top of it (just a decorative wall) was added in Gothic times. Study the lions at the

100 Meters
100 Yards

CITY WALLS

SAN LORENZO

HOTEL LA ROCCA

PORTA PERLICI ❷

ROMAN AMPHITHEATER

ROCCA MINORE

WALK BEGINS

SAN RUFINO ❸ ❹

Piazza Matteotti P

B Bus Station

To Porta Cappuccini

To Porta Nuova

❶ Roman Amphitheater
❷ Umbrian View
❸ Cathedral of San Rufino
❹ Medieval Architecture
❺ Basilica of St. Clare & Another Umbrian View
❻ Arches & Artisans
❼ Temple of Minerva/ Christian Church
❽ Church of Santo Stefano
❾ To Via San Francesco

ASSISI

base of the facade, flanking each door. One is eating a Christian martyr, reminding worshippers of the courage of early Christians.

Enter the church. While the front of the church is an unremarkable mix of 17th- and 18th-century Baroque and Neoclassical, the rear (near where you enter) has several points of interest. Notice first the two fine statues: *St. Francis* and *St. Clare* (by Giovanni Dupré, 1888). To your right is an old baptismal font (in the corner with the semicircular black iron grate). In about 1181, a baby boy was baptized in this font. His parents were upwardly mobile Francophiles who called him Francesco ("Frenchy"). In 1194, a nobleman baptized his daughter Clare here. Eighteen years later, their paths crossed in this same church, when Clare attended a class and became mesmerized by the teacher—Francis. Traditionally, the children of Assisi are still baptized here.

The striking glass panels in the floor reveal foundations preserved from the ninth-century church that once stood here. You're walking on history. After the 1997 earthquake, structural inspectors checked the church from ceiling to floor. When they looked under the paving stones, they discovered graves (until Napoleon decreed otherwise, it was common practice to bury people in churches). Underneath that level, they found Roman foundations and some animal bones (suggesting the possibility of animal sacrifice). There might have been a Roman temple here; churches were often built upon temple ruins. Stand at the back of the church facing the altar, and look left to the Roman cistern (inside the great stone archway, next to where you entered). Take the three steps down (to trigger the light) and marvel at the fine stonework and Roman engineering. In the Middle Ages, this was the town's emergency water source when under attack.

Underneath the church, incorporated into the Roman ruins, are the foundations of an earlier Church of San Rufino, now the crypt and **Diocesan museum**. When it's open, you can go below to see the saint's sarcophagus and the small museum featuring the cathedral's art from centuries past.

Cost and Hours: Cathedral—free, daily 7:00-19:00, Nov-mid-March closed Mon-Fri 12:30-14:30, tel. 075-812-283; crypt/museum—€3.50, March-Oct Thu-Tue 10:00-13:00 & 15:00-18:00, longer hours in Aug, shorter hours Nov-Feb, closed Wed except in Aug, tel. 075-812-712, www.assisimuseodiocesano.com.

• *Leaving the church, take a sharp left (at the pizza-by-the-slice joint, on Via Dono Doni). After 20 yards, take a right and go all the way down the stairway to see some...*

❹ Medieval Architecture

At the bottom of the stairs, notice the pink limestone pavement, part of the surviving medieval town. The arches built over doorways indicate that the buildings date from the 12th through the 14th centuries, when Assisi was booming. Italian cities such as Assisi—thriving on the north-south trade between northern Europe and Rome—were in the process of inventing free-market capitalism, dabbling in democratic self-rule, and creating the modern urban lifestyle. The vaults you see that turn lanes into tunnels are reminders of medieval urban expansion—creating more living space (mostly 15th century). While the population grew, people wanted to live within the town's protective walls. Medieval Assisi had several times the population density of modern Assisi.

Notice the blooming balconies; Assisi holds a flower competition each June.

• *From the bottom of the stairs, head to the left and continue downhill. When you arrive at a street, turn left, going slightly uphill for a long block, then take the low road (right) at the Y, and head down Via Sermei. Continue ahead, following the S. Chiara sign downhill to the*

St. Clare
(1194-1253)

The 18-year-old rich girl of Assisi fell in love with Francis' message, and made secret arrangements to meet him. The night of Palm Sunday, 1212, she slipped out of her father's mansion in town and escaped to the valley below. A procession of friars with torches met her and took her to (what is today) St. Mary of the Angels Basilica. There, Francis cut her hair, clothed her in a simple brown tunic, and welcomed her into a life of voluntary poverty. Clare's father begged, ordered, and physically threatened her to return, but she would not budge.

Clare was joined by other women who banded together as the Poor Clares. She spent the next 40 years of her life within the confines of the convent of San Damiano: barefoot, vegetarian, and largely silent. Her regimen of prayer, meditation, and simple manual labor—especially knitting—impressed commoners and popes, leading to her canonization almost immediately after her death. St. Clare is often depicted carrying a monstrance (a little temple holding the Eucharist wafer).

---

big church. Cross the street and walk under the three massive buttresses to Piazza Santa Chiara and the front of the church.

❺ Basilica of St. Clare (Basilica di Santa Chiara)

Dedicated to the founder of the Order of the Poor Clares, this Umbrian Gothic church is simple, in keeping with the nuns' dedication to a life of contemplation. In Clare's lifetime, the order was located in the humble Church of San Damiano, in the valley below, but after Clare's death, they needed a bigger and more glorious building. The church was built in 1265, and the huge buttresses were added in the next century.

The interior's fine frescoes were whitewashed in Baroque times. The battered remains of one on the left shows how the fresco surface was hacked up so whitewash would stick. Imagine all the pristine frescoes hiding behind the whitewash (here and all over Europe).

The Chapel of the Crucifix of San Damiano, on the right, has the wooden crucifix that changed Francis' life. In 1206, an emaciated, soul-searching, stark-raving Francis knelt before this crucifix (then located in the Church of San Damiano) and asked for guidance. The crucifix spoke: "Go and rebuild my Church, which you can see has fallen into ruin." Francis followed the call.

Stairs lead from the nave down to the tomb of St. Clare. Her tomb is at the far end (the image is wax; her bones lie underneath).

As you circulate with the crowd of pilgrims, notice the paintings on the walls depicting spiritual lessons from Clare's life and death. At the opposite end of the crypt (back between the stairs, in a large glassed-in area) are important relics: the saint's robes, hair (in a silver box), and an enormous tunic she made—along with relics of St. Francis (including a blood-stained stocking he wore after receiving the stigmata). The attached cloistered community of the Poor Clares has flourished for 700 years.

Cost and Hours: Free, daily 6:30-12:00 & 14:00-19:00, until 18:00 in winter.

• *Leave the church and belly up to the viewpoint at the edge of the square for...*

Another Umbrian View: On the left is the convent of St. Clare (global headquarters of all the Poor Clares). Below you lies the olive grove of the Poor Clares, which has been there since the 13th century. In the distance is a grand Umbrian view. Assisi overlooks the richest and biggest valley in otherwise hilly and mountainous Umbria. The municipality of Assisi has a population of 25,000, but only 3,500 people live in the old town. The lower town grew up with the coming of the railway in the 19th century. In the haze, the blue-domed church is St. Mary of the Angels (Santa Maria degli Angeli, described later), the cradle of the Franciscan order. A popular pilgrimage site today, it marks the place where St. Francis lived and worked.

Spanish-speaking Franciscans settled in California. Three of their missions grew into major cities: Los Angeles (named after this church), San Francisco (named after St. Francis), and Santa Clara (named after St. Clare).

• *From the church square, step out into Via Santa Chiara.*

❻ Arches and Artisans

Notice the three medieval town gates (two behind the church, and one uphill toward the town center). The gate over the road behind the church dates from 1265. (Farther on, you can just see the crenellations of the 1316 Porta Nuova, which marks the final medieval expansion of Assisi.) Toward the city center (on Via Santa Chiara, the high road), an arch marks the site of the Roman wall. These three gates represent the town's three walls, illustrating how much the city has grown since ancient times.

Walk uphill along Via Santa Chiara (which becomes Corso Mazzini) to the city's main square. The street is lined with interesting shops selling traditional embroidery, religious souvenirs, and gifty local edibles. The shops on Corso Mazzini, on the stretch between the gate and the Piazza del Comune, show off many local crafts. As you browse, watch for the following shops: Galleria d'Arte Perna (on the left, #20) sells the medieval fantasy townscapes of Paolo Grimaldi, a local painter who runs this shop with his brother, Alessandro. A helpful travel agency is across the street and a few steps up (at #31, Agenzia Viaggi Stoppini; see "Helpful Hints," earlier). Next, the shop L'Ulivo Sculture (on the left at #14D) sells olive-wood carvings, as does Poiesis, across the street at #23. It's said that St. Francis made the first nativity scene to help humanize and, therefore, teach the Christmas message. That's why you'll see so many crèches in Assisi. (Even today, nearby villages are enthusiastic about their "living" manger scenes, and Italians everywhere enjoy setting up elaborate crèches in churches for Christmas.) Adjacent to #14 is a bakery, Bar Sensi, selling the traditional raisin-and-apple strudel called *rocciata* (roh-CHAH-tah, €3.50 each). Farther along on the left (at #2) is Il Duomo, selling religious art, manger scenes, and crucifixion figurines. Across the street, on the right, is Centro Ricami, a respected embroidery shop. And on the square (at #34, opposite the flags), the recommended La Bottega dei Sapori is worth a visit for edible and drinkable souvenirs.

You've walked up what was, in ancient times, the main drag into town. Ahead of you, the six fluted Corinthian columns of the Temple of Minerva marked the forum (today's Piazza del Comune). Sit at the fountain on the piazza for a few minutes of people-watching—don't you just love Italy? Within a few hundred yards of this square, on either side, were the medieval walls. Imagine the commotion of 5,000 people confined within these walls. No wonder St. Francis needed an escape for some peace and quiet.

• *Now, head over to the temple on the square.*

❼ Temple of Minerva/Christian Church

Assisi has always been a spiritual center. The Romans went to great lengths to make this first-century B.C. Temple of Minerva a centerpiece of their city. Notice the columns that cut into the stair-

way. It was a tight fit here on the hilltop. In ancient times, the stairs went down—about twice as far as they do now—to the main drag, which has gradually been filled in over time. The Church of Santa Maria sopra ("over") Minerva was added in the ninth century. The bell tower is from the 13th century.

Pop inside the temple/church. Today's interior is 17th-century Baroque. Walk to the front. Flanking the altar are the original Roman temple floor stones. You can even see the drains for the bloody sacrifices that took place here. Behind the statues of Peter and Paul, the original Roman embankment peeks through.

Cost and Hours: Free, Mon-Sat 7:15-19:30, Sun 8:00-19:30, in winter closes at sunset and midday.

• *Across the square at #11, step into the 16th-century frescoed vaults of the...*

Old Market: Notice the Italian flair for design. Even this smelly market was once finely decorated. The art style is called "grotesque"—literally from a cave (grotto-esque), named for the fanciful Roman paintings found on the walls of Italian caves. This scene was indisputably painted after 1492. How do they know? Because it features turkeys—first seen in Europe after Columbus returned from the Americas with his bag of exotic souvenirs. The turkeys painted here may have been that bird's European debut.

• *From the main square, hike past the temple up the high road, Via San Paolo. After 200 yards (across from #24), a sign directs you down a stepped lane to the...*

❽ Church of Santo Stefano (Chiesa di Santo Stefano)

Surrounded by cypress, fig, and walnut trees, Santo Stefano—which used to be outside the town walls in the days of St. Francis—is a delightful bit of offbeat Assisi. Legend has it that Santo Stefano's bells miraculously rang on October 3, 1226, the day St. Francis died. Step inside. This is the typical rural Italian Romanesque church—no architect, just built by simple stone-masons who put together the most basic design. Hundreds of years later, it still stands.

Cost and Hours: Free, daily 8:30-21:30, Sept-May until 18:30.

• *The lane zigzags down to Via San Francesco. Turn right and walk under the arch toward the Basilica of St. Francis.*

❾ Via San Francesco

This main drag leads from the town to the basilica holding the body of St. Francis. Francis was a big deal even in his own day. He was made a saint in 1228—the same year that the basilica's foundations were laid—and his body was moved here by 1230. Assisi was a big-time pilgrimage center, and this street was its booming hub. The arch marks the end of what was Assisi in St. Francis' day. Notice the fine medieval balcony immediately past the arch. About 30 yards farther down (on the left), cool yourself at the fountain, as medieval pilgrims might have. The hospice next door was built in 1237 to house pilgrims. Notice the three surviving faces of its fresco: Jesus, Francis, and Clare. Farther down, across from #12a (on the left), is the Oratorio dei

Pellegrini, dating from the 1450s. A brotherhood ran a hostel here for travelers passing through to pay homage to St. Francis. The chapel offers a richly frescoed space in which to contemplate the saint's message.

• *Continuing on, you'll eventually reach Assisi's main sight, the Basilica of St. Francis.*

Self-Guided Tour

▲▲▲Basilica of St. Francis (Basilica di San Francesco)

The basilica is one of the artistic and religious highlights of Europe. It rises where, in 1226, St. Francis was buried (with the outcasts he

 had stood by) outside of his town on the "Hill of the Damned"— now called the "Hill of Paradise." The basilica is frescoed from top to bottom with scenes by the leading artists of the day: Cimabue, Giotto, Simone Martini, and Pietro Lorenzetti. A 13th-century historian wrote, "No more exquisite monument to the Lord has been built."

From a distance, you see the huge arcades "supporting" the basilica. These were 15th-century quarters for the monks. The arcades that line the square and lead to the church housed medieval pilgrims.

Cost and Hours: Free entry; lower basilica daily 6:00-18:45, until 17:45 in Nov-March; reliquary chapel in lower basilica generally open Mon-Fri 9:00-18:00, often closed Sat-Sun and occasionally at other times for religious services; upper basilica daily 8:30-18:45, until 17:45 in Nov-March. Modest dress is required to enter the church—no sleeveless tops or shorts for men, women, or children.

Information: The church courtyard at the entrance of the lower basilica has an info office (Mon-Sat 9:15-12:00 & 14:15-17:30, closed Sun, tel. 075-819-001, www.sanfrancescoassisi.org). To find out about upcoming concerts at the basilica, try tel. 075-819-0084.

Tours: Audioguides (boring and old-school) are available at the kiosk located outside the entrance of the upper basilica (€6 donation requested, daily 9:00-17:00, 40 minutes). You can download a free Rick Steves audio version of this chapter's tour of the basilica; see page 1101. You can also take an English tour, offered daily except Sunday (€10 donation requested, call or email to reserve, tel. 075-819-0084, www.sanfrancescoassisi.org, assisisan francesco@libero.it).

1 Lower Basilica Entrance
2 Upper Basilica Entrance
3 Pinacoteca (Art Museum)
4 To Ostello della Pace
5 To Le Mandrie di
   San Paolo Agriturismo
6 Locanda del Podestà
   Restaurant
7 Ristorante Metastasio
8 Launderette

Services: The church bookshop is in the inner courtyard behind the upper and lower basilica. It sells the excellent guidebook *The Basilica of Saint Francis: A Spiritual Pilgrimage* (€3, by Goulet, McInally, and Wood; I used this book, and a tour with Brother Michael, as sources for this self-guided tour). There are two different pay WCs within a half-block of the lower entrance—up the road in a squat building, and halfway down the big piazza on the left.

Attending Mass: To worship in the basilica, consider joining the Franciscan brothers in the lower basilica in the morning at 7:15 or 11:00, or experience a Mass sung by the basilica choir many Sundays at 10:30. On Sundays in summer (Easter-Oct), there's an English Mass in the Upper Basilica at 8:30. Additional English and sung Masses don't follow a set schedule. Call the basilica to find out when English-speaking pilgrimage groups or choirs have reserved Masses, and attend with them (tel. 075-819-0084).

The Franciscan Message

Francis' message caused a stir. Not only did he follow Christ's teachings, he followed Christ's lifestyle, living as a poor, wandering preacher. He traded a life of power and riches for one of obedience, poverty, and chastity. He was never ordained as a priest, but his influence on Christianity was monumental.

The Franciscan realm (Brother Sun, Sister Moon, and so on) is a space where God, man, and the natural world frolic harmoniously. Francis treated every creature—animal, peasant, pope—with equal respect. He and his "brothers" (*fratelli,* or friars) slept in fields, begged for food, and exuded the joy of non-materialism. Franciscan friars were known as the "Jugglers of God," modeling themselves on French troubadours (*jongleurs,* or jugglers) who roved the countryside singing, telling stories, and cracking jokes.

In an Italy torn by conflict between towns and families, Francis promoted peace and the restoration of order. (He set an example by reconstructing the crumbled San Damiano chapel.) While the Church was waging bloody Crusades, Francis pushed ecumenism and understanding. And the Franciscan message had an impact. In 1288, just 62 years after Francis died, a Franciscan became pope (Nicholas IV). Francis' message also led to Church reforms that many believe delayed the Protestant Reformation by a century.

This richly decorated basilica seems to contradict the teachings of the poor monk it honors, but it was built as an act of religious and civic pride to remember the hometown saint. It was

Overview

The Basilica of St. Francis, a theological work of genius, can be difficult for the 21st-century tourist/pilgrim to appreciate.

Since the basilica is the reason that most people visit Assisi, and the message of St. Francis has even the least devout sightseers blessing the town Vespas, I've designed this self-guided tour with an emphasis on the place's theology (rather than art history).

A disclaimer before we start: Just as Francis used many biblical legends to help teach the Christian message, legends from the life of Francis were told in later ages to teach the same message. Are they true? In general, probably not. Are they in keeping with Francis' message? Yes. Do I share legends here as if they are historic? Sure.

The church has three parts: the upper basilica, the lower basilica, and the saint's tomb (below the lower basilica). To get oriented, stand at the lower entrance in the courtyard. While empty today, centuries ago this main plaza was cluttered with pilgrim services and the medieval equivalent of souvenir shops. Opposite the entry to the lower basilica is the information center.

also designed—and still functions—as a pilgrimage center and a splendid classroom. Though monks in robes may not give off an "easy-to-approach" vibe, the Franciscans of today are still God's jugglers (and many of them speak English).

Here is Francis' message, in his own words:

The Canticle of the Sun

Good Lord, all your creations bring praise to you!

Praise for Brother Sun, who brings the day. His radiance reminds us of you!

Praise for Sister Moon and the stars, precious and beautiful.

Praise for Brother Wind, and for clouds and storms and rain that sustain us.

Praise for Sister Water. She is useful and humble, precious and pure.

Praise for Brother Fire who cheers us at night.

Praise for our sister, Mother Earth, who feeds us and rules us.

Praise for all those who forgive because you have forgiven them.

Praise for our sister, Bodily Death, from whose embrace none can escape.

Praise and bless the Lord, and give thanks, and, with humility, serve him.

Enter through the grand doorway of the lower basilica. Just inside, decorating the top of the first arch, look up and see St. Francis, who greets you with a Latin inscription. Sounding a bit like John Wayne, he says the equivalent of, "Slow down and be joyful, pilgrim. You've reached the Hill of Paradise. And, if you're observant and thoughtful, this church will knock your spiritual socks off."

• *Start with the tomb. To get there, turn left into the nave. Midway down, follow the signs and go right, to the tomb downstairs.*

The Tomb

The saint's remains are above the altar in the stone box with the iron ties. In medieval times, pilgrims came to Assisi because St. Francis was buried here. Holy relics were the "ruby slippers" of medieval Europe. Relics gave you power—they answered your prayers and won your wars—and ultimately helped you get back to your eternal Kansas. Assisi made no bones about promoting the saint's relics, but hid his tomb for obvious reasons of security. His body was buried secretly while the basilica was under construction, and over the next 600 years, the exact location was forgotten. When the tomb was to be opened to the public in 1818, it took more than a month to find his actual remains.

Francis' four closest friends and first followers are memorialized in the corners of the room. Opposite the altar, up four steps between the entrance and exit, notice the small copper box behind the metal grill. This contains the remains of Francis' rich Roman patron, Jacopa dei Settesoli. She traveled to see him on his deathbed, but was turned away because she was female. Francis waived the rule and welcomed "Brother Jacopa" to his side. These five tombs—in the Franciscan spirit of being with your friends—were added in the 19th century.

The candles you see are the only real candles in the church (others are electric). Pilgrims pay a coin, pick up a candle, and place it in the small box on the side. Franciscans will light it later.

• *Climb back up to the lower nave.*

Lower Basilica

Appropriately Franciscan—subdued and Romanesque—this nave is frescoed with parallel scenes from the lives of Christ (right) and Francis (left), connected by a ceiling of stars. The Passion of Christ and the Compassion of Francis lead to the altar built over Francis' tomb. After the church was built and decorated, side chapels were erected to provide mausoleums for the rich families that patronized the work of the order. Unfortunately, in the process, huge arches were cut out of some frescoed scenes, but others survive. In the fresco directly above the entry to the tomb, Christ is being taken down from the cross (just the bottom half of his body can be seen, on the left), and it looks like the story is over. Defeat. But in the opposite fresco (above the tomb's exit), we see Francis preaching to the birds, reminding the faithful that the message of the Gospel survives.

These stories directed the attention of the medieval pilgrim to the altar, where he could meet God through the sacraments. The church was thought of as a community of believers sailing toward God. The prayers coming out of the nave (*navis,* or ship) fill the triangular sections of the ceiling—called *vele,* or sails—with spiritual wind. With a priest for a navigator and the altar for a helm, faith propels the ship.

Stand behind the altar (toes to the bottom step, facing the entrance) and look up. The three scenes above you represent the creed of the Franciscans: Directly above the tomb of St. Francis, to the right, **Obedience** (Francis appears twice, wearing a rope harness and kneeling in front of Lady Obedience); to the left, **Chastity** (in her tower of purity held up by two angels); and straight ahead, **Poverty**. Here Jesus blesses the marriage as Francis slips a ring on

ASSISI

Basilica of St. Francis—Lower Level

EXIT
To Upper
Basilica
& Bookshop

RELIQUARY
CHAPEL

6
3 **4**
ALTAR
5
7

9 **8**

N
A
V
E

Not to Scale

2

INFO

1

ENTRANCE

Lower
Piazza
To
Porta
San Francesco

Outside stairs
to upper basilica

WC

Upper Piazza

ASSISI

1 St. Francis (on Ceiling)
2 Stairs to Tomb Entrance
3 Obedience (on Ceiling)
4 Chastity (on Ceiling)
5 Poverty (on Ceiling)

6 Francis on a Heavenly Throne
7 Reliquary Chapel Entrance
8 GIOTTO – Crucifixion
9 CIMABUE – St. Francis

Lady Poverty. In the foreground, two "self-sufficient" yet pint-size merchants (the new rich of a thriving northern Italy) are throwing sticks and stones at the bride. But Poverty, in her patched wedding dress, is fertile and strong, and even bare brambles blossom into a rosebush crown.

The three knots in the rope that ties the Franciscan robe symbolize the monks' vows of obedience, chastity, and poverty. St. Francis called money the "devil's dung." The jeweled belt of a rich person was all about material wealth. A bag of coins hung from it, as did a weapon to protect that person's wealth. Franciscans instead bound their tunics with a simple rope, its three knots a constant reminder of their vows.

Now put your heels to the altar and—bending back like a drum major—look up for a peek at the reward for a life of obedience, chastity, and poverty: **Francis on a heavenly throne** in a rich, golden robe. He traded a life of earthly simplicity for glory in heaven.

• *Turn to the right and march to the corner, where steps lead down into the...*

Reliquary Chapel

This chapel is filled with fascinating relics (which a €0.50 flier explains in detailed English; often closed Sat-Sun). Step in and circle the room clockwise. You'll see the silver chalice and plate that Francis used for the bread and wine of the Eucharist (in a small, dark, windowed case set into wall, marked *Calice e Patena*). Francis believed that his personal possessions should be simple, but the items used for worship should be made of the finest materials. Next, the Veli di Lino is a cloth Jacopa wiped her friend's brow with on his deathbed. In the corner display case is a small section of the itchy haircloth *(cilizio)*—not sheep's wool, but cloth made from scratchy horse or goat hair—worn by Francis as penance (the cloth he chose was the opposite of the fine fabric his father sold). In the next corner are the tunic and slippers that Francis donned during his last days. Next, find a prayer (in a fancy silver stand) that St. Francis wrote for Brother Leo and signed with a T-shaped character—his tau cross. The last letter in the Hebrew alphabet, tav ("tau" in Greek) is symbolic of faithfulness to the end, and Francis adopted it for his signature. Next is a papal document (1223) legitimizing the Franciscan order and assuring his followers that they were not risking a (deadly) heresy charge. Finally, just past the altar, see the tunic that was lovingly patched and stitched by followers of the five-foot, four-inch-tall St. Francis.

Before leaving the chapel, notice the modern paintings done in the last year or so by local artists. Over the entrance, Francis is shown being born in a stable like Jesus (by Capitini). Scenes from the life of Clare and Padre Pio (a Capuchin priest, very popular in Italy, who was sainted in 2002) were painted by Stefanelli and Antonio.

• *Return up the stairs, stepping into the...*

Lower Basilica's Transept

The decoration of this church brought together the greatest Sienese (Lorenzetti and Simone Martini) and Florentine (Cimabue and Giotto) artists of the day. Look around at the painted scenes. In 1300, this was radical art—believable homespun scenes, landscapes, trees, real people. Directly opposite the reliquary chapel, study **Giotto's painting of the Crucifixion,** with the eight sparrow-like angels. For the first time, holy people are expressing emotion: One angel turns her head sadly at the sight of Jesus, and another scratches her hands down her cheeks, drawing blood. Mary (lower left), previously in control, has fainted in despair. The Franciscans, with their goal of bringing God to the people, found a natural partner in Europe's first naturalist (and therefore modern) painter, Giotto.

To grasp Giotto's artistic leap, compare his work with the painting to the right, by Cimabue. It's Gothic, without the 3-D

architecture, natural backdrop, and slice-of-life reality of Giotto's work. **Cimabue's St. Francis** (far right) shows the saint with the stigmata—Christ's marks of the Crucifixion. Contemporaries described Francis as being short, with a graceful build, dark hair, and sparse beard. (This is considered the most accurate portrait of Francis—done according to the description of one who knew him.) The sunroof haircut (tonsure) was standard for monks of the day. According to legend, the brown robe and rope belt were inventions of necessity. When Francis stripped naked and ran away from Assisi, he grabbed the first clothes he could, a rough wool peasant's tunic and a piece of rope, which became the uniform of the Franciscan order. To the left, at eye level under the sparrow-like angels, are paintings of saints and their exquisite halos (by Simone Martini or his school). To the right of the door at the same level, see five of Francis' closest followers—clearly just simple folk.

Francis' friend, "Sister Bodily Death," was really not all that terrible. In fact, Francis would like to introduce you to her now (above and to the right of the door leading into the reliquary chapel). Go ahead, block the light from the door with this book and meet her. Before his death, Francis added a line to *The Canticle of the Sun:* "Praise for our sister, Bodily Death, from whose embrace none can escape."

• *Now cross the transept to the other side of the altar (enjoying some of the oldest surviving bits of the inlaid local-limestone flooring—c. 13th century), and find the staircase going up. Immediately above the stairs is Pietro Lorenzetti's* Francis Receiving the Stigmata. *(Francis is considered the first person ever to earn the marks of the cross through his great faith and love of the Church.) Make your way to the...*

Courtyard

The courtyard overlooks the 15th-century cloister, the heart of this monastic complex. Pope Sixtus IV (of Sistine Chapel fame) had it built as a secure retreat for himself. Balanced and peaceful by design, the courtyard also functioned as a cistern to collect rainwater, supplying enough for 200 monks (today, there are about 40). The Franciscan order emphasizes teaching. This place functioned as a kind of theological center of higher learning, which rotated monks in for a six-month stint, then sent them back home more prepared and better inspired to preach effectively. That explains the complex narrative of the frescoes wallpapering the walls and halls here.

The **treasury** *(Museo del Tesoro)* to the left of the bookstore features ornately decorated chalices, reliquaries, vestments, and altarpieces (free but donation requested, Mon-Sat 10:30-13:00 & 14:00-17:30, Sun 10:00-17:30, shorter hours Nov-March).

• *From the courtyard, climb the stairs (next to the bookshop) to the...*

Upper Basilica

Built later than its counterpart below, the brighter upper basilica is considered the first Gothic church in Italy (started in 1228). You've followed the intended pilgrims' route, entering the lower church and finishing here. Notice how the pulpit (embedded in the corner pillar) can be seen and heard from every spot in the packed church. The spirit of the order was to fill the church and preach. See also the design in the round window in the west end (high above the entry). The tiny centerpiece reads "IHS" (the first three letters of Jesus' name in Greek). And, as you can see, this trippy kaleidoscope seems to declare that all light radiates from Jesus. The windows here are treasures from the 13th and 14th centuries. Those behind the apse are among the oldest and most precious in Italy. Imagine illiterate medieval peasants entranced by these windows,

Basilica of St. Francis—Upper Level

ALTAR

1 A common man spreads his cape before Francis

2 Francis offers his cape to a needy stranger

3 Francis is visited by the Lord in a dream

4 Francis prays to the crucifix

5 Francis relinquishes his possessions

6 The pope has a dream

7 The pope confirms the Franciscan order

8 A vision of the flaming chariot

9 A vision of thrones

10 Exorcism of demons in Arezzo

11 St. Francis before the sultan

12 Ecstasy of St. Francis

13 The crèche at Greccio

14 Miracle of the spring

21 Three "post mortem miracles" associated with St. Francis

20 Francis' death, funeral, and canonization

Not to Scale

SOUTH WALL

NAVE

NORTH WALL

19 Francis receives the stigmata

18 The apparition at Arles

17 Preaching for Pope Honorius III

16 The Knight of Celano invites Francis to his deathbed

15 Sermon to the birds

22 Tan patches on ceiling

MAIN ENTRANCE

Stairs down to lower basilica

Lawn
WITH TAU CROSS & "PAX"

To Piazza Comune & the rest of Assisi

ASSISI

so full of meaning that they were nicknamed "Bibles of the Poor." But for art lovers, the basilica's draw is that Giotto and his assistants practically wallpapered it circa 1297-1300. Or perhaps the job was subcontracted to other artists—scholars debate it (for more on Giotto, see page 154). Whatever the case, the anatomy, architectural depth, and drama of these frescoes helped to kick off the Renaissance. The gallery of frescoes shows 28 scenes from the life of St. Francis. The events are a mix of documented history and folk legend.

• *Get oriented by facing the basilica's main altar. Working clockwise, start on the right-hand (north) wall, and follow along with the help of the numbered map key. The subtitles in the black strip below the frescoes describe each scene in clear Latin—and affirm my interpretation.*

❶ **A common man spreads his cape before Francis** in front of the Temple of Minerva on Piazza del Comune. Before his conversion, young Francis was the model of Assisian manhood—handsome, intelligent, and well dressed, befitting the son of a wealthy cloth dealer. Above all, he was liked by everyone, a natural charmer who led his fellow teens in nights of wine, women, and song. Medieval pilgrims understood the deeper meaning of this scene: The "eye" of God (symbolized by the rose window in the Temple of Minerva) looks over the young Francis, a dandy "imprisoned" in his own selfishness (the Temple—with barred windows—was once a prison).

❷ **Francis offers his cape to a needy stranger**. Francis was always generous of spirit. He became more so after being captured in battle and held for a year as a prisoner of war, then suffering from illness. Charity was a Franciscan forte.

❸ **Francis is visited by the Lord in a dream.** Still unsure of his calling, Francis rode off to the Crusades. One night, he dreams of a palace filled with armor marked with crosses. Christ tells him to leave the army—to become what you might consider the first "conscientious objector"—and go home to wait for a non-military assignment in a new kind of knighthood. He returned to Assisi and, though reviled as a coward, would end up fighting for spiritual wealth, not earthly power and riches.

❹ **Francis prays to the crucifix** in the Church of San Damiano. After months of living in a cave, fasting, and meditating, Francis kneels in the run-down church and prays. The crucifix speaks, telling him: "Go and rebuild my Church, which you can see has fallen into ruin." Francis hurried home and sold his father's cloth to pay for God's work. His furious father dragged him before the bishop.

❺ **Francis relinquishes his possessions.** In front of the bishop and the whole town, Francis strips naked and gives his dad his clothes, credit cards, and time-share on Capri. Francis raises his hand and says, "Until now, I called you father. From now on, my only father is my Father in Heaven." Notice God's hand blessing the action from above. Francis then ran off into the hills, naked and singing. In this version, Francis is covered by the bishop, symbolizing his transition from a man of the world to a man of the Church. Notice the disbelief and concern on the bishop's advisors' faces; subtle expressions like these wouldn't have made it into other medieval frescoes of the day.

❻ **The pope has a dream.** Francis headed to Rome, seeking the pope's blessing on his fledgling movement. Initially rebuffing Francis, the pope then dreams of a simple, barefooted man propping up his teetering Church, and then...

❼ **The pope confirms the Franciscan order,** handing Francis and his gang the document now displayed in the reliquary chapel.

Francis' life was peppered with visions and miracles, shown in three panels in a row: ❽ **vision of the flaming chariot,** ❾ **vision of thrones,** and ❿ **exorcism of demons in Arezzo.**
• *Next see...*

⓫ **St. Francis before the sultan.** Francis' wandering ministry took him to Egypt during the Crusades (1219). He walked unarmed into the Muslim army camp. They captured him, but the sultan was impressed with Francis' manner and let him go, reportedly whispering, "I'd convert to your faith, but they'd kill us both." Here the sultan gestures from his throne.

⓬ **Ecstasy of St. Francis.** This oft-painted scene shows the mystic communing with Christ.

⓭ **The crèche at Greccio.** A creative teacher, Francis invents the tradition of manger scenes.
• *Around the corner, see the...*

⓮ **Miracle of the spring.** Shown here getting water out of a rock to quench a stranger's thirst, Francis felt closest to God when in the hills around Assisi, seeing the Creator in the creation.
• *Cross over to the far side of the entrance door.*

⓯ **Sermon to the birds.** In his best-known miracle, Francis is surrounded by birds as they listen to him teach. Francis embraces all levels of creation. One interpretation of this scene is that the birds, which are of different species, represent the diverse flock of humanity and nature, all created and beloved by God and worthy of one another's love.

This image of well-fed birds is an appropriate one to take with you. It's designed to remind pilgrims that, like the birds, God gave us life, plenty of food, feathers, wings, and a world to fly around in. Francis, patron saint of the environment and animals, taught his followers to count their blessings. A monk here reminded me that even a student backpacker today eats as well as the wealthiest nobleman in the days of Francis.

ASSISI

• *Continue to the south wall for the rest of the panels.*

Despite the hierarchical society of his day, Francis was welcomed by all classes, shown in these three panels: ❶ **the knight of Celano invites Francis to his deathbed;** ❷ **preaching for Pope Honorius III,** who listens intently; and ❸ **the apparition at Arles,** which illustrates how Francis could be in two places at once (something only Jesus and saints can pull off). The proponents of Francis, who believed he was destined for sainthood, show him performing the necessary miracles.

❹ **Francis receives the stigmata.** It's September 17, 1224, and Francis is fasting and praying on nearby Mount Alverna when a six-winged angel (called a seraph) appears with holy laser-like powers to burn in the marks of the Crucifixion, the stigmata. For the strength of his faith, Francis is given the marks of his master, the "battle scars of love." These five wounds suffered by Christ (nails in palms and feet, lance in side) marked Francis' body for the rest of his life.

The next panels deal with ❺ **Francis' death, funeral, and canonization.** The last panels show ❻ **miracles** associated with the saint after his death, proving that he's in heaven and bolstering his eligibility for sainthood.

Francis died thanking God and singing his *Canticle of the Sun.* Just as he referred to the sun as his brother and the moon as his sister, Francis called his body "brother." On his deathbed he conceded, "Maybe I was a bit tough on brother ass." Ravaged by an aestheticism extreme enough to earn him the stigmata and tuberculosis, Francis died in 1226.

Before leaving through the front entrance, look up at the ceiling and the walls near the rose window to see ❼ **large tan patches.** In 1997, when a 5.5-magnitude quake hit Assisi, it shattered the upper basilica's frescoes into 300,000 fragments, which were meticulously picked up and pieced back together. Shortly after the quake, an aftershock shook the ceiling frescoes down, killing two monks and two art scholars standing here.

Outside, on the lawn, the Latin word *pax* (peace) and the Franciscan tau cross are sculpted from shrubbery. For a drink or snack, the Bar San Francisco (facing the upper basilica) is handy. For *pax,* take the high lane back to town, up to the castle, or into the countryside.

More Sights in Assisi

▲**Roman Forum (Foro Romano)**—For a look at Assisi's Roman roots, tour the Roman Forum, which is underneath Piazza del Comune. The floor plan is clearly explained in English, as are the surviving odd bits and obscure pieces. During your visit, you'll walk on an ancient Roman road.

Cost and Hours: €4, included in €8 combo-ticket that also covers next two sights, daily 10:00-13:00 & 14:30-18:00, until 19:00 in June-Aug, until 17:00 in Nov-Feb; from Piazza del Comune, go a half-block down Via Portica—it's on your right; tel. 075-815-5077.

Pinacoteca—This small, unexciting museum attractively displays its 13th- to 17th-century art (mainly frescoes), with general English information in nearly every room. There's a damaged Giotto Madonna and a rare secular fresco (to the right of the Giotto art), but it's mainly a peaceful walk through a pastel world—best for art lovers.

Cost and Hours: €3, included in €8 combo-ticket, same hours as Roman Forum, Via San Francesco, across from #13C—look for banner above entryway, on main drag between Piazza del Comune and Basilica of St. Francis, tel. 075-815-5077.

▲Rocca Maggiore—The "big castle" offers a good look at a 14th-century fortification and a fine view of Assisi and the Umbrian countryside. If you're pinching your euros, skip it—the view is just as good from outside the castle. There's talk of restoring some rooms in their original medieval style, possibly in time for your visit.

Cost and Hours: €5, included in €8 combo-ticket, daily from 10:00 until an hour before sunset—about 19:15 in summer, tel. 075-815-5077.

Church of San Damiano (Chiesa di San Damiano)—Located on the slope steeply below the Basilica of St. Clare, this church and convent was where Francis received his call and where Clare spent her days as mother superior of the Poor Clares. Today, there's not much to see, but it's a relatively peaceful escape from touristy Assisi. Drivers can zip right there (watch for the turnoff on the road up to Piazza Matteotti), while walkers descend pleasantly from Assisi for 15 minutes through an olive grove.

In 1206, Francis was inside the church when he heard the wooden crucifix order him to rebuild the church. (The crucifix in San Damiano is a copy; the original is now displayed in the Basilica of St. Clare.) Francis initially interpreted these miraculous words as a call to rebuild crumbling San Damiano. He sold his father's cloth for money to fix the church. (The church we see today, however, was rebuilt later by others.) Eventually, Francis realized his charge was to revitalize the Christian Church at large.

As he approached the end of his life, Francis came to San Damiano to visit his old friend Clare. She set him up in a simple reed hut in the olive grove, where he was inspired to write his poem *The Canticle of the Sun* (see page 725).

Cost and Hours: Free, daily, convent open 10:00-12:00 &

ASSISI

14:00-18:00, closes at 16:30 in winter, church opens at 6:30, start walking from the Porta Nuova parking lot at the south end of Assisi and follow the signs, tel. 075-812-273, www.assisiofm.it.

Commune with Nature—For a picnic with the same birdsong and views that inspired St. Francis, leave the tourists behind and hike to the Rocca Minore (small private castle, not tourable) above Piazza Matteotti.

In Santa Maria degli Angeli

This modern part of Assisi sits in the flat valley below the hill town (see "Assisi Area" map, earlier). Whether you're arriving by car or by train, it's practical to visit these sights on the way into or out of Assisi (they're an easy walk from the train station—which has baggage storage—and there's ample, well-marked parking).

▲▲**St. Mary of the Angels Basilica (Basilica Patriarcale di Santa Maria degli Angeli in Porziuncola)**—This huge basilica, towering above the buildings below Assisi, marks the spot where Francis lived, worked, and died.
It's a grandiose church built around a humble chapel—reflecting the monumental impact of this simple saint on his town and the world.

Cost and Hours: The basilica is free to enter and open Mon-Sat 6:15-12:50 & 14:30-19:30; it opens 30 minutes later on Sun (tel. 075-805-11). A little TI kiosk is across the street from the souvenir stands (generally daily 9:30-12:30 & 15:30-18:30 but hours a bit erratic, tel. 075-804-4554). As you face the church, the best WC is on your right (€0.50).

Getting There: From Assisi's train station, it's a five-minute walk to the basilica (exit station left, after 50 yards take the underground pedestrian walkway—*sottopassaggio*—on your left, then look for the dome in the distance). When you leave the basilica, you can catch an orange bus that goes to the station and on to Assisi's old town (leaving the church, the stop is on your right, by the side of the church). These orange city buses run twice hourly (buses to the old town depart the basilica at :10 and :40 after the hour; tickets cost €1 if you buy at a tobacco shop or the newsstand near the TI, €1.50 if you buy from driver—have exact change ready, stamp your ticket on board; 20-minute ride up to old town).

Visiting the Basilica: This grand church was built in the 16th century around the tiny but historic **Porziuncola Chapel** (now directly under the dome). The last part of the church's Italian name ("in Porziuncola") means literally "over the Porziuncola Chapel."

After Francis' conversion, some local monks gave him this *porziuncola*, or "small portion"—a little land with a fixer-upper chapel. Francis lived here after he founded the Franciscan Order, and this was where he consecrated St. Clare as a Bride of Christ. What would humble Francis think of the huge church—Christianity's 10th largest—built over his tiny chapel?

Behind the chapel on the right, find the **Cappella del Transito,** which marks the site of Francis' death on October 3, 1226. Francis died as he'd lived—simply, in a small hut located here. On his last night on earth, he invited some friars to join him in a Last Supper-style breaking of bread. Then he undressed, lay down on the bare ground, and began to recite Psalm 141, "Lord, I cry unto thee." He spoke the last line, "Let the wicked fall into their own traps, while I escape"...and he passed on.

From the right transept, follow *Roseto* signs to the rose garden. You'll walk down a passage with gardens on either side (viewable through the windows)—on the left, a tranquil park with a statue of Francis petting a sheep, and on the right, the **rose garden**. Francis, fighting a temptation that he never named, once threw himself onto the roses. As the story goes, the thorns immediately dropped off. Thornless roses have grown here ever since.

Exiting the passage, turn right to find the **Rose Chapel** (Cappella delle Rose), built over the place where Francis lived.

In the autumn, a room in the next **hallway** displays a giant animated nativity scene (a reminder to pilgrims that Francis first established the tradition of manger scenes as a teaching aid). You'll pass a free 10-minute video (in English, daily 10:00-12:30 & 16:00-18:00). The bookshop has some works in English and an "old pharmacy" selling herbal cures. Exiting the building, you'll pass the **Porziuncola Museum,** featuring a few monastic cells of interest to pilgrims, a model of Assisi during Francis' lifetime, and religious art and objects from the basilica. Upstairs are some monks' cells, which provide intriguing insight into the spartan lifestyles of the pious and tonsured (€2.50, no English information, museum open April-Oct Tue-Sun 9:30-12:30 & 15:30-19:00, Nov-March until 18:00, closed Mon, tel. 075-805-1419, www.porziuncola.org).

Museo Pericle Fazzini—This small museum, housed in the arcaded building opposite St. Mary of the Angels Basilica, features works by the contemporary Italian sculptor Pericle Fazzini. His works feature elongated, wildly distorted, and very expressive figures. The permanent collection, on the first floor, includes bronzes, wooden sculptures (including one of St. Francis), and the original bronze casting of *The Risen Christ*—a miniature of Fazzini's famous bronze of Jesus rising from a nuclear-bomb crater, commissioned by the pope for the Sala Nervi audience hall of the Vatican. Biographical information on the sculptor is provided in English. Upstairs on the second floor are temporary exhibits.

Cost and Hours: €5, Tue-Sun 10:00-13:00 & 16:00-19:00, closed Mon, tel. 075-804-4586, www.museo.periclefazzini.it.

Outside of Assisi

Hermitage (Eremo delle Carceri)—If you want to follow further in St. Francis' footsteps, take a trip up the rugged slopes of nearby Mount Subasio to the humble hermitage where Francis and his followers retreated for solitude. Today the spot is marked by a 14th-century convent. The highlight is a look at the tiny, dank cave where Francis would retire for private prayer.

Cost and Hours: Free, daily 6:30-19:00, until 18:00 off-season, last entry 30 minutes before closing, tel. 075-812-301, www.eremocarceri.it.

Getting There: There is no public transportation; either drive, take a taxi, or hike. Starting from Assisi's Porta Cappuccini gate, it's a stiff three-mile, 1.5-hour hike with an elevation gain of about 1,000 feet. You'll walk along a narrow, switchbacked, paved road enjoying brisk air and sporadic views. A souvenir kiosk at the entrance sells drinks and sandwiches.

Sleeping in Assisi

Assisi accommodates large numbers of pilgrims on religious holidays (see list on page 1106). Finding a room at any other time should be easy. Few hotels are air-conditioned. Locals suggest that you keep your windows closed through the middle of the day so that your room will be as cool as possible in the evening.

Hotels and Rooms

$$$ Hotel Umbra, a quiet villa in the middle of town, has 24 spacious but overpriced rooms with great views, thinning carpets, and dated decor (Sb-€75, standard Db-€110, bigger "superior" Db with better views-€125, Tb-€155, 10 percent cash discount for 2 or more nights with this book, air-con, elevator, Wi-Fi, peaceful garden and view sun terrace, most rooms have views—request when you reserve, closed Dec-March, just off Piazza del Comune under the arch at Via degli Archi 6, tel. 075-812-240, fax 075-813-653, www.hotelumbra.it, info@hotelumbra.it, family Laudenzi).

$$ Hotel Ideale, on a ridge overlooking the valley, offers 14 airy, basic, modern rooms (all with views, 12 with balconies), a

---

Sleep Code

(€1 = about $1.40, country code: 39)

S = Single, **D** = Double/Twin, **T** = Triple, **Q** = Quad, **b** = bathroom, **s** = shower only. Unless otherwise noted, credit cards are accepted, English is spoken, and breakfast is included.

To help you sort easily through these listings, I've divided the accommodations into three categories based on the price for a standard double room with bath:

$$$ Higher Priced—Most rooms €100 or more.
$$ Moderately Priced—Most rooms between €55-100.
$ Lower Priced—Most rooms €55 or less.

Prices can change without notice; verify the hotel's current rates online or by email.

---

tranquil garden setting, and free parking (Sb-€50, Db-€90, prices good with this book through 2013, 10 percent discount for stays of 3 or more nights, may be cheaper off-season, air-con, free Wi-Fi, confirm your arrival time especially if it's after 17:00, Piazza Matteotti 1, tel. 075-813-570, fax 075-813-020, www.hotelideale .it, info@hotelideale.it, friendly sisters Lara and Ilaria and their monolingual family). The hotel is close to the bus stop (and parking lot) at Piazza Matteotti at the top end of town.

$$ Hotel Belvedere, a great value, is a modern building with 12 spacious, classic-feeling rooms; eight come with sweeping views (Sb-€45, Db-€65, breakfast-€5, elevator, free Wi-Fi in lobby, large communal view terrace, 2 blocks past Basilica of St. Clare at Via Borgo Aretino 13, tel. 075-812-460, fax 075-816-812, www.assisi hotelbelvedere.it, info@assisihotelbelvedere.it, run by Enrico and Mary from New Jersey).

$$ La Pallotta offers seven clean, bright, small rooms and a communal view room on the top floor. They provide guests with a loaner Assisi guidebook, map, and audioguide, as well as a bus ticket and English helpline number (Sb-€45, Db-€79, free Internet access and Wi-Fi, free use of washer and clothesline, free hot drinks and cake at teatime; a block off Piazza del Comune at Via San Rufino 6—go up a short flight of stairs outside building, above the arch, to reach entrance; tel. & fax 075-812-307, www .pallottaassisi.it, pallotta@pallottaassisi.it, helpful Stefano, Serena, and family). If you're driving, head to Piazza San Rufino, where they'll meet you (call ahead). They also have a good restaurant (see "Eating in Assisi," later).

$$ Hotel San Rufino offers a great locale, solid stone quality, and 11 comfortable rooms (Sb-€46, Db-€57, Tb-€78, Qb-€92,

ASSISI

Assisi Hotels & Restaurants

breakfast-€5, elevator; from Cathedral of San Rufino, follow sign to Via Porta Perlici 7; tel. & fax 075-812-803, www.hotelsanrufino .it, info@hotelsanrufino.it). Their nine-room annex, Albergo Il Duomo (listed later), saves you about €5 a night for a double with no loss in comfort.

$$ Hotel La Rocca, on the peaceful top end of town, has 32 solid and modern rooms in a medieval shell (Sb-€46, Db-€59, Tb-€79, breakfast-€5, air-con, elevator, pay Wi-Fi, parking-€7, sunny rooftop terrace, decent restaurant upstairs, 3-minute walk from Piazza Matteotti at Via Porta Perlici 27, tel. 075-812-284, fax 075-816-467, www.hotelarocca.it, info@hotelarocca.it).

$$ Hotel Sole, renting 38 rooms in a 15th-century building, is well-worn and forgettable, but the location is central. Half of its rooms are in a newer annex across the street (Sb-€50, Db-€70, Tb-€90, ask for a discount, breakfast-€5, air-con-€5 extra, pay Wi-Fi, public parking nearby, 100 yards before Basilica of St.

Clare at Corso Mazzini 35, tel. 075-812-373, fax 075-813-706, www.assisihotelsole.com, info@assisihotelsole.com).

$ Camere Carli has six shiny, spacious, new rooms in a solid, minimalist place above a shop (Sb-€37, Db-€48, Tb-€60, Qb-€70, show this book to get these prices, family lofts, lots of stairs and no elevator, free Wi-Fi, free parking 100 yards away, facing the Duomo at Via Porta Perlici 1, tel. 075-812-490, mobile 339-531-1366, www.camerecarli.it, carliarte@live.it, pleasant Carli speaks limited English).

$ Albergo Il Duomo's nine rooms are tidy and *tranquillo*. Located on a stair-stepped lane one block up from Hotel San Rufino, it's more atmospheric and has nicer bathrooms than its parent hotel (Sb-€42, Db-€53, Tb-€68, breakfast-€5, Vicolo San Lorenzo 2 but check in at Hotel San Rufino—see earlier, tel. & fax 075-812-742, www.hotelsanrufino.it, info@hotelsan rufino.it).

$ Camere Annalisa Martini is a cheery home in the town's medieval core that swims in vines and roses. Annalisa enthusiastically accommodates her guests with a picnic garden, a washing machine (€7/small load, includes line drying), a communal refrigerator, and six homey rooms (S-€27, Sb-€30, D-€38, Db-€42, Tb-€58, Qb-€68, rates soft for last-minute bookings, cash only, 3 rooms share 2 bathrooms, no breakfast; 1 block from Piazza del Comune—go downhill toward basilica, turn left on Via San Gregorio to #6; tel. & fax 075-813-536, cameremartini@libero.it, Mamma Rosignoli—"roh-sin-YOH-lee"—doesn't speak English, but Annalisa does).

Hostel: Francis probably would have bunked with the peasants in Assisi's **$ Ostello della Pace** (€17 beds in 4- to 8-bed rooms, €20/person in private 2- to 4-person rooms with bath, dinner-€10.50, laundry service-€4, lockout 10:00-16:00, midnight curfew; take orange shuttle bus from station to Piazza Giovanni Paolo II, then walk 15 minutes downhill to Via di Valecchie 177—see map on page 722; tel. & fax 075-816-767, www.assisihostel.com, info@assisihostel.com).

Sweet Dreams in a Convent

Assisi is filled with convents, most of which rent rooms to pilgrims and travelers. While you don't need to be a pilgrim or even a Christian to be welcome, it's just common sense to stay in a convent *only* if you're approaching Assisi with a contemplative mindset. Convents feel institutional, house many groups, and are not particularly cheap—but they come with all the facilities you might need to enjoy a spirit-filled visit to Assisi.

$$ St. Anthony's Guest House is where the Franciscan Sisters of the Atonement (including several Americans and Canadians) offer a very warm and tranquil welcome. Their oasis of peace is just above the Basilica of St. Clare. With only 35 beds in 19 rooms (some with great views—request when you reserve) at a reasonable price, they book up literally months in advance (Sb-€40-45, Db-€60-65, Tb-€80-85, 2-night minimum, cash only for short stays, no problem if couples want to share a bed, elevator, no air-con but fans, 23:00 curfew, closed mid-Nov-Feb, library, views, picnic garden, parking-€3 donation, just below Piazza Matteotti at Via Galeazzo Alessi 10, tel. 075-812-542, fax 075-813-723, atone assisi@tiscali.it).

Agriturismo near Assisi

$$ Le Mandrie di San Paolo ("The Herd of St. Paul") is a meticulously restored 1,000-year-old stone house renting 12 rustic but comfortable rooms. Soulful Alex and the Damiani family are justifiably proud of their fine craftsmanship, passion for hospitality, and connection to the land. They also have an olive grove (ask Alex if he'll give you a tour of their modern mill in the valley), lots of animals, a beautiful swimming pool, sauna/steam room, fine restaurant, and spectacular views over Assisi and the valleys of Umbria (Db-€90; 2-bedroom apartments: Db-€120, Qb-€150; family deals, 3-night minimum in June-mid-Sept, pay Wi-Fi, mobile 349-821-7867, tel. 075-806-4070, www.agriturismo mandriesanpaolo.it). Their restaurant is a great choice, and worth considering for non-guests who just want to get out of town (€25-30 for 4-course meal, daily 19:30-22:00, in winter available weekends only, reservations smart). It's about a 10-minute drive from Assisi, on the hill high above the village of Viole (a.k.a. San Vitale). Just head southeast of Assisi following signs for *Viole*; when you enter town, before you reach the arch, turn left and follow signs up the hill.

Eating in Assisi

I've listed decent, central, good-value restaurants. Assisi's food is heavy and rustic. Locals brag about their sausage and love to grate truffles on pasta. To bump up any meal, consider a glass or bottle of the favorite homegrown red wine, Sagrantino de Montefalco. Sagrantino is Umbria's answer to Brunello (although many wine lovers around here would say that it's vice versa). Before or after dinner, enjoy a drink on the main square facing the Roman temple...or hang out with the local teens with a take-away beer under the temple's columns.

Fine Dining

Ristorante Medioevo is my vote for your best splurge. With heavy but spacious cellar vaults, William Ventura's restaurant is an elegant, accessible playground of gastronomy. Maître d' Massimo will guide you to the best of Umbrian cuisine. He features traditional cuisine with a modern twist, dictated by what's in season. While his first passion is cooking, his second is music—mellow jazz and bossa nova give a twinkle to the medieval atmosphere. Dishes are well-presented; beef and game dishes are the specialties, and the wonderful Sagrantino wine is served by the glass. As a special treat for readers of this book, when you order a glass of Sagrantino, you'll receive a small slice of just the right strong pecorino cheese—to better understand the Italian fascination with "a good marriage" between food and wine (€9-13 pastas, €12-16 *secondi*, Tue-Sun 12:30-15:00 & 19:30-22:45, closed Mon, in winter open weekends only; from the fountain on Piazza del Comune, hike downhill two blocks to Via Arco dei Priori 4; tel. 075-813-068).

La Pallotta, a local favorite run by a friendly and hardworking family—with Margarita in charge of the kitchen—offers delicious, well-presented regional specialties, such as *piccione* (squab, a.k.a. pigeon) and *coniglio* (rabbit). And they like to serve split courses *(bis)* featuring the two local pastas. Reservations are smart (€7-9 pastas, €8-15 *secondi,* good €27 fixed-price sampler of local specialties, Wed-Mon 12:15-14:30 & 19:15-23:00, last orders at 21:30, closed Tue, vegetarian options, a few steps off Piazza del Comune across from temple/church at Vicolo della Volta Pinta 2, tel. 075-812-649).

Casual Eateries

At **Locanda del Podestà,** chef Stelvio cooks up tasty grilled Umbrian sausages, *gnocchi alla locanda,* and all manner of truffles, while Romina graciously serves happy diners who know a good value. Try the tasty *scottaditto* ("scorch your fingers") lamb chops (€5-7 pastas, €11-14 *secondi,* Thu-Tue 12:00-14:30 & 19:00-21:30, closed Wed and Jan, 5-minute walk uphill along Via Cardinale Merry del Val from basilica, San Giacomo 6c—see map on page 722, tel. 075-816-553).

Ristorante Metastasio, just up the street from Podestà, offers a pricey, traditional menu and Assisi's best view terrace for dining (€9-12 pastas, €10-18 *secondi,* Thu-Tue 12:00-14:30 & 19:00-21:30, closed Wed, terrace closed in bad weather, Via Metastasio 9, tel. 075-816-525).

Trattoria da Erminio has peaceful tables on a tiny square, and indoor seating under a big, medieval (but air-conditioned) brick vault. Run by Federico and his family for three generations, it specializes in local meat cooked on an open-fire grill. They have good Umbrian wines—before you order, ask Federico or Giuliana for a taste of the Petranera wine (€8-11 pastas, €9-13 grilled meats, €18 tourist fixed-price meal featuring local recipes based on seasonal produce—changes weekly, Fri-Wed 12:00-14:30 & 19:00-21:00, closed Thu; from Piazza San Rufino, go a block up Via Porta Perlici and turn right to Via Montacavallo 19; tel. 075-812-506).

Picnic on the Main Square

There are many little grocery stores *(alimentari)* nearby.

Try **La Bottega dei Sapori** for a picnic of Umbrian treats: good prosciutto sandwiches and specialty items, including truffle paste and olive oil. Friendly Fabrizio, who is a slow-food enthusiast, may give you a taste. He also stocks the best Umbrian wines at good-to-go prices—nice if you have an appointment with your terrace for sunset (€3-4 sandwiches, daily 9:00-20:00, until 21:00 in summer, closed Jan-Feb, Piazza del Comune 34, tel. 075-812-294).

ASSISI

Assisi Connections

From Assisi by Train to: Rome (nearly hourly, 2-3.5 hours, 5 direct, €20, most others change in Foligno, €9.70; train timetables change frequently—double-check details), **Florence** (8/day direct, 2-3 hours, €12-19 depending on speed), **Orvieto** (roughly hourly, 2-2.5 hours, with transfer in Terantola or Orte, €8.30), **Siena** (hourly, 3.25-4.25 hours, most involve 2 transfers, €11.05; bus is faster), **Cortona** (every 2 hours, 70 minutes to Camucia-Cortona station, €5.25). The train station's ticket office is often open only Mon-Fri 12:35-19:25, closed Sat-Sun; when the office is closed, use the ticket machine (may only accept credit cards; newsstands sell only regional tickets and accept cash). You can get train information and tickets from Agenzia Viaggi Stoppini in the middle of town (see "Helpful Hints" on page 710). Train station tel. 075-804-0272 (generally unresponsive; you're better off asking at Agenzia Viaggi Stoppini or checking online at www.trenitalia.com).

By Bus: Service to **Rome** is operated by Sulga bus company (2/day, 3 hours, €16, pay driver, departs from Piazza San Pietro, arrives at Rome's Tiburtina station where you can connect with the train to Fiumicino airport, tel. 800-099-661, www.sulga.it). A bus for **Siena** (1/day at 10:20, 2 hours, €13) usually departs from St. Mary of the Angels (at Piazza Garibaldi, near the basilica); you can't buy Siena tickets from the driver—you must buy them at Assisi's Agenzia Viaggi Stoppini (see "Helpful Hints" on page 710). A bus operated by Curreri leaves twice a week to **Sorrento** (6 hours, book online but pay driver, www.curreriviaggi.it).

Don't take the bus to **Florence;** the train is better. To see either **Gubbio** (described on page 706) or **Todi** as a side-trip from Assisi, you'll need a car—bus schedules don't accommodate day-trippers. Day trips to **Spello** (described on page 706) and **Lake Trasimeno** work by train, but not by bus. A day trip to **Perugia** is possible with buses operated by Umbria Mobilità (www.umbria mobilita.it). For nearby day-trip options like these, you could also consider taking a tour; the recommended Agenzia Viaggi Stoppini offers several (see page 712, www.viaggistoppiniassisi.it).

By Plane: Perugia/Assisi Airport, about 10 miles from Assisi, has daily connections to London Stansted airport (on Ryanair), Milan, and—seasonally—to Barcelona and Trapani in Sicily. Only a very sporadic bus runs between Assisi and the airport (just a few times a day); a taxi costs about €30 (airport code: PEG, tel. 075-592-141, www.airport.umbria.it).

ASSISI

ORVIETO and CIVITA

While Tuscany is justifiably famous for its many fine hill towns, Umbria, just to the south, has some stellar offerings of its own. Assisi (covered in its own chapter) is a must for nature lovers and Franciscan pilgrims, but if you're after views, wine, and charming villages, you'll find Umbria's best in Orvieto and Civita de Bagnoregio. About a 30-minute drive apart, these hill towns—one big, one small—perch high above scenic plains. Pleasant Orvieto is best known for its colorful-inside-and-out cathedral and its fine Orvieto Classico wine. Tiny Civita de Bagnoregio, my favorite hill town, is an improbable pinnacle of traditional Italian village culture, just accessible enough that modern tourists are keeping it going. Taken together, Orvieto and Civita make a perfect duet for experiencing what the hill-town fuss is all about.

Planning Your Time

This pair of towns deserves at least an overnight, although even a few hours in each is enough to sample what it has to offer. Both are also great places to slow down and relax. Stay in one, and side-trip to the other (Orvieto has more restaurants and other amenities and is easier to reach, while Civita really lets you get away from it all). The two towns are connected by a 30-minute drive or a 45-minute bus ride, and Orvieto is conveniently close to Rome (about an hour away by train or expressway).

Orvieto

Just off the freeway and the main train line, Umbria's grand hill town entices those heading to and from Rome. While no secret,

it's well worth a visit. The town sits majestically on its *tufo* throne a thousand feet above the valley floor (for more on volcanic tuff, see the sidebar on page 644). Orvieto became a regional power in

the Middle Ages, and even earlier, a few centuries before Christ, it was one of a dozen major Etruscan cities. Some historians believe Orvieto may have been a religious center—a kind of Etruscan Mecca (locals are looking for archaeological proof—the town and surrounding countryside are dotted with Etruscan ruins).

Orvieto, which has three popular claims to fame (cathedral, Classico wine, and ceramics), is loaded with tourists by day and quiet by night. Drinking a shot of the local white wine in a ceramic cup as you gaze up at the cathedral lets you experience Orvieto's three C's all at once. (Is the cathedral best in the afternoon, when the facade basks in golden light, or early in the morning, when it rises above the hilltop mist? You decide.) And a visit to Orvieto comes with a wonderful bonus: an easy bus connection with Civita di Bagnoregio (covered later in this chapter).

Orientation to Orvieto

Orvieto has two distinct parts: the old-town hilltop and the dreary new town below (called Orvieto Scavi). Whether coming by train or car, you first arrive in the forgettable, modern lower part of town. From there you can drive or take the funicular, elevator, or escalator up to the medieval upper town, an atmospheric labyrinth of streets and squares where all the sightseeing action is.

Tourist Information

A **seasonal TI** is at the top of the funicular, to your right as you exit into Piazza Cahen, the start of the upper town (March-Sept daily 10:00-18:00, closed Oct-Feb). The **main TI** is on the cathedral square at Piazza del Duomo 24 (Mon-Fri 8:15-13:50 & 16:00-19:00, Sat-Sun 10:00-13:00 & 15:00-18:00, tel. 0763-341-772). Pick up the free city map and their green city guide, and ask about train and bus schedules. The ticket office (next to the main TI) sells combo-tickets and books reservations for the underground tours (tel. 0763-340-688).

Orvieto

200 Meters
200 Yards

To Train Station

STR. DEL RIORGO

STRADA DELLA STAZIONE

STRADA DELLA STAZIONE

LA RUPE WALK

VIALE CARDUCCI

VIA PACE

VIA CORSO

VIA D.

LA RUPE WALK

ETRUSCAN NECROPOLIS

Cliffs

Park

Piazza Corsica

VIA DEL POPOLO

PALAZZO DEL POPOLO

Piazza del Popolo

TORRE DEL MORO

WALK ENDS

SAN GIOVENALE

Piazza S. Giovenale

V. MALABRANCA

V. MAGALOTTI

VIA PECORELLI

Piazza Vittozzi

Piazza Repubblica

STRADA DELLE CONC.

V. CAGNA

WELL OF THE CAVE

VIA DELLA CAVA

FILIPPESCHI

VIA DEL DUOMO

MICHELANGELI

VIA ANGELICO

CITY HALL

VIA GARIBALDI

V. COZZA

RAMPARTS WALK

PORTA MAGGIORE

V. RANIERI

SAN GIOVANNI EVANGELISTA

VIA RIPA MEDICI

VIA DEGLI ALBERICI

LIPICINI

VIA MAITANI

ARCHAEO-LOGICAL MUSEUM

Piazza Febei

To Bolsena & Viterbo

STRADA DI PORTA ROMANA

VIA DI VOLSINIA

V. CLEMENTINI

ELEVATOR & ESCALATOR

Campo della Fiera

PORTA ROMANA

VIA DELLA SEGHERIA

- - - WELCOME TO ORVIETO WALK
- - - LA RUPE VIEW WALK
· · · · · RAMPARTS WALK

① Hotel Duomo
② Grand Hotel Italia
③ Hotel Corso
④ Hotel Posta
⑤ Villa Mercede
⑥ Istituto S.S. Salvatore
⑦ Valentina's Rooms
⑧ La Magnolia B&B
⑨ B&B Michelangeli
⑩ Casa Sèlita B&B
⑪ La Palomba Restaurant
⑫ Antico Bucchero
⑬ L'Antica Trattoria dell'Orso

⑭ Trattoria la Grotta &
 Sidis Supermarket

⑮ Trattoria del Moro Aronne

⑯ Trattoria da Carlo

⑰ Pizzeria & Rest. Charlie

⑱ Enoteca al Duomo &
 Pasqualetti Gelateria

⑲ L'Oste del Re

⑳ Il Vincaffè Bar

㉑ Internet Access (2)

㉒ Tobacco Shop (Bus Tickets)

㉓ La Rupe View Walk Access (5)

㉔ Romantic Rampart Stroll

㉕ MoDo Art Galleries &
 National Arch. Museum

Combo-Ticket: The €18 **Carta Unica** combo-ticket covers Orvieto's top sights (virtually every sight recommended here, including Underground Orvieto Tours) and includes one round-trip on the bus and/or funicular (www.cartaunica.it). To cover your funicular ride, you can buy the combo-ticket at the bar at the train station upon arrival (if they haven't run out), or at a seasonal ticket office in the train station parking lot (behind the station, Easter-Sept daily 9:00-16:00, closed Oct-Easter, tel. 0763-302-378). It's also available at the ticket office next to the TI on Piazza del Duomo, as well as at most of the sights it covers.

Arrival in Orvieto

By Train: From the train station at the foot of the hill town, a **funicular** carries you to the top. Buy your ticket at the entrance to the *funiculare;* look for the *biglietteria* sign (€1, €0.80 with same-day train ticket, good for 70 minutes, includes minibus from Piazza Cahen to Piazza del Duomo, Mon-Sat 7:20-20:30, Sun 8:00-20:30, every 10 minutes, or every 15 minutes on Sun). Or buy a Carta Unica combo-ticket (described earlier) to cover your funicular ride. If you arrive outside the funicular's operating hours, you can take a taxi (figure about €12) or bus to the upper town's Piazza della Repubblica (buses run roughly 2/hour until midnight, buy €1.50 ticket from driver). There's no baggage storage at the train station (the nearest place for day-trippers to store bags is Hotel Picchio, €4/bag, 300 yards from the station at Via G. Salvatori 17).

As you exit the funicular at the top, you're in Piazza Cahen, located at the east end of the upper town. To your left is a ruined fortress with a garden and a commanding view. To your right is the seasonal TI (closed Oct-Feb) and, down a steep path, St. Patrick's Well. Farther to the right is a park with Etruscan ruins and another sweeping view. Just in front of you is the orange shuttle bus, waiting to take you to Piazza del Duomo. The bus fills up fast, but the views from the ruined fortress are worth pausing for—if you miss the bus, you can wait for the next one, or just walk to the cathedral (head uphill on Corso Cavour; after about 10 minutes take a left onto Via del Duomo). The bus drops you in Piazza del Duomo, just steps from the main TI and within easy walking distance of most of my recommended sights. If you forgot to check at the station for the train schedule to your next destination, no problem—the schedule is posted at the top of the funicular and is also available at the TI.

By Car: For free parking, use the huge lot behind the train station, at the base of the hill, then ride the funicular up (5 minutes off the autostrada, follow the *P funiculare* signs, then see "By Train," above). Up top, there's also some free parking in the north half (white lines) of Piazza Cahen (at the top end of the funicular). There are several pay options: the small lot in Piazza Marconi, near Orvieto's cathedral (€1.50 for first hour, €1/hour thereafter); the south half (blue lines) of Piazza Cahen (€1.20/hour); and the Campo della Fiera lot just below the west end of town (€1/hour; from top level of lot, walk up into town or take escalator—7:00-21:00—or elevator—7:00-24:00; both free). Generally, white lines indicate free parking, and blue lines require you to buy a "pay and display" slip from a nearby machine. While you can drive up Via Postierla and Via Roma to get to central parking lots, Corso Cavour and other streets in the old center are closed to traffic and monitored by cameras (look for red lights, and avoid streets marked by a red circle).

By Taxi: Taxis line up in front of the train station and charge about €12 for a ride to the cathedral (a ridiculous price considering the fun and ease of the €1 funicular/shuttle-bus ride to the cathedral square; tel. 360-433-057).

Helpful Hints

Market Days: On Thursday and Saturday mornings, Piazza del Popolo becomes a busy farmers' market.

Internet Access: Caffè Montanucci has four terminals (€2.50/30 minutes, Corso Cavour 21, daily 7:00-24:00), and **Copisteria ESPA** has three (€3/30 minutes, Via Felice Cavallotti 9, Mon-Fri 9:00-13:00 & 16:00-19:40, Sat 9:00-13:00, closed Sun).

Driver: For a private car hire, consider **Giuliotaxi**, enthusiastically run by charming, English-speaking Giulio and his sister Maria Serena. They charge about €50 for a ride to Bagnoregio, and provide a good way to explore the region (mobile 360-433-057, www.italy-driver.com, giuliotaxi@libero.it).

Local Guide: Manuela del Turco is good (€120/2.5-hour tour, mobile 333-221-9879, manueladel@virgilio.it).

After Dark: In the evening, there's little going on other than strolling and eating. The big *passeggiata* scene is down Via del Duomo and Corso Cavour. **Il Vincaffè** is *the* place for the classy young crowd late at night, with lots of good wines by the glass (Via Filippeschi 39).

Self-Guided Walk

Welcome to Orvieto

A quickie L-shaped walk takes you through Orvieto's historic center. Each evening, this route is the scene of the local *passeggiata*. Facing the cathedral, head left. Stroll past the clock tower (first put here in 1347 for the workers building the cathedral), which marks the start of Via del Duomo, lined with shops selling ceramics. **Via dei Magoni** (second left) has several artisan shops and the crazy little Il Mago di Oz ("Wizard of Oz") shop, a wondrous

ORVIETO AND CIVITA

toyland created by eccentric Giuseppe Rosella (Via dei Magoni 4, tel. 0763-342-063; he runs another store nearby at Via Pedota 9). Have Giuseppe push a few buttons, and you're far from Kansas (no photos allowed).

Via del Duomo continues to Orvieto's main intersection, where it meets Corso Cavour and a tall, stark tower—the **Torre del Moro**. The tower marks the center of town, serves as a handy orientation tool, and is decorated by the coats of arms of past governors. The elevator leaves you with 173 steps still to go to earn a commanding view (€2.80, daily March-Oct 10:00-19:00, May-Aug until 20:00, Nov-Feb 10:30-16:30).

This crossroads divides the town into **four quarters** (notice the *Quartiere* signs on the corners). Residents of these four districts compete in a lively equestrian competition on Piazza del Popolo during the annual Corpus Christi celebration. Historically, the four streets led from here to the market and the fine palazzo on Piazza del Popolo, the well, the Duomo, and City Hall.

Before heading left down Corso Cavour, side-trip a block farther ahead, behind the tower, for a look at the striking **Palazzo del Popolo.** Built of local *tufo,* this is a textbook example of a fortified medieval public palace: a fortress designed to house the city's leadership and military, with a market at its base, fancy meeting rooms upstairs, and aristocratic living quarters on the top level.

Return to the tower and head down Corso Cavour (turning right) past classic storefronts to **Piazza della Repubblica** and City Hall. The original vision—though it never came to fruition—was for City Hall to have five arches flanking the main central arch (marked by the flags today). The Church of Sant'Andrea (left of City Hall) sits atop an Etruscan temple that was likely the birthplace of Orvieto centuries before Christ. Inside is an interesting architectural progression: Romanesque (with few frescoes surviving), Gothic (the pointy vaults over the altar), and a Renaissance barrel vault in the apse (behind the altar)—all lit by fine alabaster windows.

From City Hall, you can continue to the far end of town to the **Church of San Giovenale**—where, if you have the MoDo ticket (see page 758), you can see the statues of the apostles that once stood in the Duomo (though it's possible these statues may someday be moved back inside the Duomo). From here you can take a left and walk the cliffside ramparts (see "View Walks," later).

Sights in Orvieto

▲▲Duomo

The cathedral has Italy's liveliest facade (from 1330, by Lorenzo Maitani and others). This colorful, prickly Gothic facade, divided by four pillars, has been compared to a medieval altarpiece. The optical-illusion interior features some fine art, including Luca Signorelli's lavishly frescoed Chapel of San Brizio.

Cost and Hours: €3; April-Sept Mon-Sat 9:30-19:00, Sun 13:00-17:30 or until 18:30 July-Sept; March and Oct Mon-Sat 9:30-18:00, Sun 13:00-17:30; Nov-Feb Mon-Sat 9:30-13:00 & 14:30-17:00, Sun 14:30-17:30; last entry 30 minutes before closing. A €5 combo-ticket includes the Duomo, the chapel, and the Museo dell'Opera del Duomo, called the "MoDo" (available at the chapel; MoDo alone costs €4). Admission is also covered by the €18 Carta Unica combo-ticket.

❷ Self-Guided Tour: Begin by viewing the **exterior facade**. Grab a gelato (buy it to the left of the church) and study this gleaming mass of mosaics, stained glass, and sculpture.

At the base of the cathedral, the four broad **marble pillars** carved with biblical scenes tell the story of the world in four acts, from left to right. The relief on the far left shows the Creation (see God performing surgery as he extracts Adam's rib, and the snake tempting Eve). Next is the Tree of Jesse (Jesus' family tree—with Mary, then Jesus on top) flanked by Old Testament stories, then the New Testament (look for the unique manger scene and other famous episodes from the life of Christ). On the far right is the Last Judgment (Christ judging on top, with a commotion of sarcophagi popping open and all hell breaking loose at the bottom).

Each pillar is topped by a bronze symbol of one of the Evangelists: angel (Matthew), lion (Mark), eagle (John), and ox (Luke). The bronze doors are modern, by the Sicilian sculptor Emilio Greco. (A gallery devoted to Greco's work is to the immediate right of the church; see page 758.) In the mosaic below the rose window, Mary is transported to heaven. In the uppermost mosaic, Mary is crowned.

Now step inside. (You can peek down the nave from the back of the church for free, but it's worth paying admission to go all the way in.) The **nave** feels spacious and less cluttered than most Italian churches. Until 1877 it was much busier, with statues of the apostles at each column and fancy chapels. Then the people decided they wanted to "un-Baroque" their church. (More recently, however, there's been talk of returning the apostles to their original locations.)

The interior is warmly lit by **alabaster windows**, highlighting the black-and-white striped stonework. Why such a big and impressive church in such a little town? First of all, it's not as big

Orvieto's Duomo

25 Meters

25 Yards

HIGH ALTAR

7

5 CHAPEL OF THE CORPORAL

6

To Gelato & WC

9 **13**

10 CHAPEL OF SAN BRIZIO **12**

11 **14**

8

N A V E

DISABLED EXIT

EXIT

1 **2** **3** ENTER **4**

To Museo Emilio Greco & Palazzi Papali

FACADE

Piazza del Duomo

VIA DEL DUOMO

VIEW

To Corso Cavour

ARCHAEOLOGICAL MUSEUM

VIA MAITANI

ORVIETO AND CIVITA

1 Creation
2 Tree of Jesse & Old Testament Stories
3 New Testament Stories
4 Last Judgment
5 "Corporal" (Linen Cloth)
6 Reliquary
7 Miracle of Bolsena Fresco

8 Pietà
9 Sermon of the Antichrist
10 End of the World (above doorway)
11 Resurrection of the Bodies
12 Last Judgment
13 Elect in Heaven
14 Damned in Hell

as it looks. The architect created an illusion—with the nave wider at the back and narrower at the altar, the space seems longer than it is. Still, it's a big and rich church. That's because of a famous blood-stained cloth, kept in a silver-gilt reliquary in the **Chapel of the Corporal**.

Find the chapel in the north transept, left of the altar. In 1263, or so the story goes, a skeptical priest named Peter of Prague passed through Bolsena (a few miles from Orvieto) while on a pilgrimage to Rome. He had doubts that the bread used in Communion could really be transformed into the body of Christ. But during Mass, as he held the host aloft and blessed it, the bread began to bleed, running down his arms and dripping onto a linen cloth (a "corporal") on the altar. The bloody cloth (in the turquoise frame above the main altar) was brought to Orvieto, where Pope Urban IV happened to be visiting. The amazed pope proclaimed a new holiday, Corpus Christi (Body of Christ), and the Orvieto cathedral was built (begun in 1290) to display the miraculous relic. Find the fine **reliquary** (which no longer holds the blood-stained relic) in a glass case on the left. Until the 1970s, this silver-and-blue enamel reliquary (c. 1358)—considered one of the finest medieval jewels in Italy—held the linen relic as if in a frame. Notice how it evokes the facade of this cathedral. For centuries, the precious linen was paraded through the streets of Orvieto in this ornate reliquary.

The room was frescoed in the 14th century with scenes attesting to Christ's presence in the communion wafer (for example, the panel above the glass case to the left illustrates how the wafer bleeds if you cook it). You can see the **Miracle of Bolsena** depicted in the fresco on the chapel's right wall.

The new cathedral put Orvieto (then known as "Urbs Vetus") on the map, and with lots of pilgrims came lots of wealth. Two future popes used the town as a refuge when their enemies forced them to flee Rome. Later, as the Roman Catholic Church countered the Reformation, it made reforms of its own. For instance, altars were moved back to let people get closer to the religious action. The confused patching on the marble floor in the middle of the nave is evidence that, prior to the Counter-Reformation, the altar stood here.

Now leave the Chapel of the Corporal and walk to the middle front of the church, where you'll see a patch in the marble floor, a fine marble statue, and the highly decorated **high altar.** The brilliant stained glass from the 14th century is original and painstakingly restored. The fine organ, high on the left, has more than 5,000 pipes. The marble *pietà* (statue of Mary holding Jesus' just-crucified body, near the pillar on the left) was carved in 1579 by local artist Ippolito Scalza. Clearly inspired by Michelangelo's *Pietà*, this exceptional piece with four figures was sculpted from

ORVIETO AND CIVITA

756   Rick Steves' Italy

one piece of marble. Notice the texture Scalza gave this wonderful work. Look high up in the right transept at the alabaster rose window. Also note how the architect's trick, making the church look bigger from the rear, works in reverse from here. If you look to the back, the church feels stubbier than it actually is.

To the right of the altar is Orvieto's one must-see artistic sight, the **Chapel of San Brizio**. It features Luca Signorelli's brilliantly lit frescoes of the Day of Judgment and Life after Death (painted 1499-1504). Step into the chapel and you're surrounded by vivid scenes crammed with figures. Although the frescoes refer to themes of resurrection and salvation, they also reflect the turbulent political and religious atmosphere of late 15th-century Italy.

The chapel is decorated in one big and cohesive story. Start with the wall to your left as you enter, and do a quick counterclockwise spin to get oriented to the basic plot: Antichrist (a false prophet), end of the world (above the arch leading to the nave), Resurrection, hell, Judgment Day (Fra Angelico painted Jesus above the window), and finally heaven.

Now do a slower turn to take in the full story: In the **Sermon of the Antichrist** (left wall), a crowd gathers around a man preaching from a pedestal. It's the Antichrist, who comes posing as Jesus to mislead the faithful. This befuddled Antichrist forgets his lines mid-speech, but the Devil is on hand to whisper what to say next. His words sow wickedness through the world, including executions (upper right). The worried woman in red and white (foreground, left of pedestal) gets money from a man for something she's not proud of (perhaps receiving funds from a Jewish moneylender—notice the Stars of David on his purse).

Most likely, the Antichrist himself is a veiled reference to Savonarola (1452-1498), the charismatic Florentine monk who defied the pope, drove the Medici family from power, and riled the populace with apocalyptic sermons. Many Italians—including the painter Signorelli—viewed Savonarola as a tyrant and heretic, the Antichrist who was ushering in the Last Days.

In the upper left, notice the hardworking angel. He looks as if he's at batting practice, hitting followers of the Antichrist back to earth as they try to get through the pearly gates. In the bottom left is a self-portrait of the artist, **Luca Signorelli** (c. 1450-1523), well-dressed in black with long golden hair. Signorelli, from nearby Cortona, was at the peak of his powers, and this chapel was his masterpiece. He looks out proudly as if to say, "I did all this in just five years, on time and on budget," confirming his reputation as a speedy, businesslike painter. Next to him is the artist Fra Angelico, who started the chapel decoration five decades earlier, but completed only a small part of it.

Around the arch, opposite the windows, are signs of the **end of the world:** eclipse, tsunami, falling stars, earthquakes, violence in the streets, and a laser-wielding gray angel.

On the right wall (opposite the Antichrist) is the **Resurrection of the Bodies.** Trumpeting angels blow a wake-up call, and the dead climb dreamily out of the earth to be clothed with new bodies. On the same wall (below the action, at eye level) is a gripping *pietà*. Also by Signorelli, this *pietà* gives an insight into the genius and personality of the artist. Look at the emotion in the faces of the two Marys and consider that Signorelli's son had just died. The Deposition scene (behind Jesus' leg) seems inspired by ancient Greek scenes of a pre-Christian hero's death. In the confident spirit of the Renaissance, the artist incorporates a pagan scene to support a Christian story. This 3-D realism in a 2-D sketch shows the work of a talented master.

The altar wall (with the windows) features the **Last Judgment.** To the left of the altar (and continuing on the left wall) are the **Elect in Heaven.** They spend eternity posing like bodybuilders while listening to celestial Muzak. To the right (and continuing on the right wall) are the **Damned in Hell,** in the scariest mosh pit ever. Devils torment sinners in graphic detail, while winged demons control the airspace overhead. In the center, one lusty demon turns to tell the frightened woman on his back exactly what he's got planned for their date. (According to legend, this was Signorelli's lover, who betrayed him...and ended up here. You'll see this couple all over town.) Signorelli's ability to tell a story through human actions and gestures, rather than symbols, inspired his younger contemporary, Michelangelo, who meticulously studied the elder artist's nudes.

In this chapel, Christian theology sits physically and figuratively upon a foundation of classical logic. Below everything are Greek and Latin philosophers, plus Dante, struggling to reconcile Classic truth with Church doctrine. You can see the intellectual challenge on their faces as they ponder this puzzle. They're immersed in fanciful Grotesque (i.e., grotto-esque) decor. Dating from 1499, this is one of the first uses of the frilly, nubile, and even sexy "wallpaper pattern" so popular in the Renaissance. (It was inspired by the decorations found in Nero's Golden House in Rome, which had been discovered under street level just a few years earlier and was mistaken for an underground grotto.)

During the Renaissance, nakedness symbolized purity. When attitudes changed during the Counter-Reformation, the male figures in Signorelli's frescoes were given penis-covering sashes. During a 1982 restoration, most—but not all—of the sashes were removed. A little of that prudishness survives to this day, as those in heaven were left with their sashes modestly in place.

In the future, you may be able to connect directly from the cathedral interior to the adjacent MoDo City Museum (described next), through a passage with a beautiful old library. Otherwise, you'll have to exit the church and turn left to find the museum. Either way, when you're done sightseeing here, if you want to visit a **viewpoint park,** exit left from the Duomo and pass the small parking lot and WC.

Near the Duomo: MoDo and Other Museums

▲▲**MoDo City Museum (Museo dell'Opera del Duomo)**— This museum is a confusing ensemble of several different sights scattered around town: the cathedral art collections split between two small galleries behind the cathedral; the Emilio Greco collection (next to the cathedral, in Palazzo Soliano); and, at the far end of town, the Church of San Giovenale, which has statues of the 12 apostles that were added to the Duomo in the Baroque Age (c. 1700) and removed in the late 1800s.

Cost and Hours: €4 MoDo ticket covers all MoDo sights (or get the €5 combo-ticket that includes the Duomo); April-Sept daily 9:30-19:00; March and Oct Wed-Mon 10:00-17:00, closed Tue; Nov-Feb Wed-Mon 10:00-13:00 & 14:00-17:00, closed Tue; last entry 30 minutes before closing, Piazza Duomo, tel. 0763-343-592, www.operadelduomo.it.

Cathedral Art Collections: Behind the Duomo, a complex of medieval palaces called Palazzi Papali shows off the city's best devotional art. The highlight is just inside the door: a marble Mary and Child who sit beneath a bronze canopy, attended by exquisite angels. This proto-Renaissance ensemble, dating from around 1300, once filled the niche in the center of the cathedral's facade.

Buy your ticket, then head upstairs. From here, turn left and progress through the collection. The first room displays paintings from the late 1500s that decorated the side chapels with a harsh Counter-Reformation message. In the next room, look for a *Madonna and Child* from 1322 by Sienese great Simone Martini, who worked in Orvieto, as well as other saintly statues and fine inlaid woodwork from the original choir. Circling back into the lobby, find the final room, packed with church art surrounded by sinopias (preliminary drawings for frescoes, with a roughed-up surface so the wet plaster would stick).

Museo Emilio Greco: This collection occupies the front part of the long museum building. Emilio Greco (1913-1995) was a Sicilian artist who designed the modern doors of Orvieto's cathedral. His sketches and about 30 of his bronze statues are on display here, showing his absorption with gently twisting and turning nudes. Greco's sketchy outlines of women are simply beautiful. The artful installation of his work in this palazzo, with walkways and even a spiral staircase up to the ceiling, allows you to view his sculptures from different angles.

National Archaeological Museum of Orvieto (Museo Archeologico Statale di Orvieto)—This small five-room collection, immediately behind the cathedral in the ground floor of Palazzi Papali (under MoDo), beautifully shows off a trove of well-preserved Etruscan bronzes, terra-cotta objects, and ceramics—some with painted colors surviving from 500 B.C. Hiding at the end of the hall are the reconstructed sixth-century Golini tombs (named after the man who discovered them in 1836), frescoed with scenes from an Etruscan banquet in the afterlife.

Cost and Hours: €3, daily 8:30-19:30, tel. 0763-341-039, www.archeopg.arti.beniculturali.it ("Museums" tab). The overpriced audioguide gives a virtual visit to the necropolis sites near Orvieto (€5, 30 minutes). For background on the Etruscans, see page 650.

Archaeological/Etruscan Museum (Museo Claudio Faina e Museo Civico)—A former palace across from the entrance to the cathedral holds an Etruscan collection. The ground floor features the "Museo Civico," with fragments of Roman and Etruscan sculpture. On the first floor is the "Collezione Conti Fiana," with Etruscan jewelry and an extensive array of Roman coins (push the brass buttons and they rotate so you can see both sides). The top floor features the best of the Etruscan vases and bronzes, lots of votives found buried in tombs, and fine views of the Duomo.

Cost and Hours: €4.50; April-Sept daily 9:30-18:00; Oct-March Tue-Sun 10:00-17:00, closed Mon; English descriptions throughout, tel. 0763-341-511, www.museofaina.it.

Underground Orvieto

If you're short on time and have to choose one means of going underground in Orvieto, I'd recommend Well of the Cave or St. Patrick's Well over Underground Orvieto Tours.

▲**St. Patrick's Well (Pozzo di San Patrizio)**—Modern engineers are impressed by this deep well—175 feet deep and 45 feet wide—designed in the 16th century with a double-helix pattern. The two spiral stairways allow an efficient one-way traffic flow: intriguing now, but critical then. Imagine if donkeys and people, balancing jugs of water, had to go up and down the same stairway. At the bottom is a bridge that people could walk on to scoop up water.

The well was built because a pope got nervous. After Rome was sacked in 1527 by renegade troops of the Holy Roman Empire, the pope fled to Orvieto. He feared that even this little town (with no water source on top) would be besieged. He commissioned a well, which was started in 1527 and finished 10 years later. It was a huge project. (As it turns out, the town was never besieged, but supporters believe that the well was worth the cost and labor because of its deterrence value—attackers would think twice about besieging a town with a water source.) Even today, when a local is faced with a difficult task, people say, "It's like digging St. Patrick's Well." It's a total of 496 steps up and down—lots of exercise and not much to see other than some amazing 16th-century engineering.

Cost and Hours: €5; interesting €1 audioguide, ID required; daily May-Aug 9:00-19:45, until 18:45 in March-April and Sept-Oct, shorter hours Nov-Feb; the well is to your right as you exit the funicular, Viale Sangallo, tel. 0763-343-768. Bring a sweater if you plan to descend to the chilly depths.

Well of the Cave (Pozzo della Cava)—While renovating its trattoria, an Orvieto family discovered a vast underground network of Etruscan-era caves, wells, and tunnels. The excavation started in 1984 and continues to this day. It's well-explained in English and makes for a fun subterranean wander.

Cost and Hours: €3, €2 if you have a funicular ticket, Tue-Sun 9:00-20:00, closed Mon, Via della Cava 28, tel. 0763-342-373, www.pozzodellacava.it.

Underground Orvieto Tours (Parco delle Grotte)—Guides weave archaeological history into a good look at about 100 yards of Etruscan and medieval caves. You'll see the remains of an old olive press, an impressive 130-foot-deep Etruscan well shaft, what's left of a primitive cement quarry, and an extensive dovecote (pigeon coop) where the birds were reared for roasting (pigeon dishes are still featured on many Orvieto menus; look for—or avoid—*piccione*).

Cost and Hours: €6; 45-minute English tours depart at 11:15, 12:30, 16:15, and 17:30; more often with demand, book tour and depart from ticket office at Piazza Duomo 23 (next to main TI); confirm times at TI or by calling 0763-340-688, www.orvieto underground.it.

Etruscan Necropolis (Necropoli Etrusca di Crocifisso del Tufo)—Below town, at the base of the cliff, is a remarkable "city of the dead" that dates back to the sixth to third century B.C. The tombs, which are laid out in a kind of street grid, are empty, and there's precious little to see here other than the basic stony construction. But it is both eerie and fascinating to wander the streets of an Etruscan cemetery.

Cost and Hours: €3, daily April-Sept 8:30-19:00, Oct-March 8:30-17:00, www.archeopg.arti.beniculturali.it ("Archaeological Areas" tab).

View Walks

▲Hike Around the City on the Rupe—Orvieto's Rupe is a peaceful paved path that completely circles the town at the base of

the cliff upon which it sits. With the help of the TI's *Anello delle Rupe* map, you'll see there are five access points from the town for the three-mile walk (allow about two hours round-trip). Once on the trail, it's fairly level and easy to follow. On one side you have the cliff, with the town high above. On the other side you have Umbrian views stretching into the distance. I'd leave Orvieto at Piazza Marconi and walk left (counterclockwise) three-quarters of the way around the town (there's a fine view down onto the Etruscan Necropolis midway), and ride the escalator and elevator back up to the town from the big Campo della Fiera parking lot. If you're ever confused about the path, follow the *la Rupe* signs.

▲Shorter Romantic Rampart Stroll—Thanks to its dramatic hilltop setting, several fine little walks wind around the edges of Orvieto. My favorite after dark, when it's lamplit and romantic, is along the ramparts at the far west end of town. Start at the Church of San Giovenale. With your back to the church, go a block to the right to the end of town. Then head left along the ramparts, with cypress-dotted Umbria to your right, and follow Vicolo Volsinia to the Church of San Giovanni Evangelista.

Near Orvieto

Wine-Tasting—Orvieto Classico wine is justly famous. Two inviting wineries sit just outside Orvieto on the scenic Canale route to Bagnoregio; if you're side-tripping to Civita, it's easy to stop at either or both for a tasting (but call ahead).

For a short tour of a winery with Etruscan cellars, visit **Tenuta Le Velette,** where English-speaking Corrado and Cecilia (cheh-CHEEL-yah) Bottai will welcome you if you've set up an appointment (€8-21 for tour and tasting, price varies depending on wines and number of people, Mon-Fri 8:30-12:00 & 14:00-17:00, Sat 8:30-12:00, closed Sun, also has accommodations—see listing on page 765, tel. 0763-29090, mobile 348-300-2002, www .levelette.it). From their sign (5-minute drive past Orvieto at top of switchbacks just before Canale, on road to Bagnoregio), cruise down a long tree-lined drive, then park at the striped gate (must call ahead; no drop-ins).

Custodi is another respected family-run winery that produces Orvieto Classico, grappa, and olive oil on their 140-acre estate. Stop by for a tour of their cantina, an explanation of the winemaking process, and a tasting of four of their wines. Reserve ahead. An assortment of *salumi* and local cheeses to go with your wine-tasting is possible on request (€7/person for wines only, €16/person with light lunch, daily 8:30-12:30 & 15:30-18:30 except closed Sun afternoons, Viale Venere S.N.C. Loc. Canale; on the road from Orvieto to Civita, a half-mile after Le Velette, it's the first building before Canale; tel. 0763-29053, mobile 392-161-9334, www .cantinacustodi.com, info@cantinacustodi.com). Helpful Chiara and Laura Custodi speak English.

Sleeping in Orvieto

In the Town Center

$$$ Hotel Duomo is centrally located and modern, with splashy art and 17 sleek rooms. Double-paned windows keep the sound of the church bells well-muffled (Sb-€80, Db-€120, Db suite-€140, Tb-€150, extra bed-€10, 10 percent cash discount with this book, air-con, elevator, free Internet access and Wi-Fi, private parking-€10, sunny terrace, a block from Duomo behind *gelateria* at Vicolo di Maurizio 7, tel. 0763-341-887, fax 0763-394-973, www .orvietohotelduomo.com, info@orvietohotelduomo.com, Gianni and Maura Massaccesi don't speak English, daughter Elisa does). The Massaccesi family also owns a three-room B&B 50 yards from the hotel (Sb-€70, Db-€90, Tb-€110, breakfast at the main hotel).

$$$ Grand Hotel Italia feels businesslike, bringing predictable modern class to this small town. The 46 rooms are spacious and well-located in the heart of Orvieto (Sb-€80, Db-€140, extra bed-€30, air-con, elevator, stay-awhile lobby and terrace, free Internet access and Wi-Fi, parking-€10—reserve ahead, Via di Piazza del Popolo 13, tel. 0763-342-065, www.grandhotelitalia.it, hotelita@libero.it).

$$ Hotel Corso is friendly, with 18 frilly and flowery rooms—some with balconies and views. Their sunlit little terrace is enjoyable, but the location—halfway between the center of town and

Sleep Code

(€1 = about $1.40, country code: 39)
S = Single, **D** = Double/Twin, **T** = Triple, **Q** = Quad, **b** = bathroom,
s = shower only. Unless otherwise noted, credit cards are
accepted and breakfast is included (but usually optional).
English is generally spoken, but I've noted exceptions. Many
towns in Italy levy a hotel tax of about €2 per person, per
night, which is generally not included in the rates I've quoted.

To help you sort easily through these listings, I've divided
the accommodations into three categories based on the price
for a standard double room with bath:

$$$ Higher Priced—Most rooms €100 or more.
 $$ Moderately Priced—Most rooms between €70-100.
  $ Lower Priced—Most rooms €70 or less.

Prices can change without notice; verify the hotel's
current rates online or by email.

the funicular—feels less convenient than others (Sb-€70, Db-€95,
Tb-€115, 10 percent discount with this book, buffet break-
fast-€6.50, ask for quieter room off street, air-con, elevator, free
Wi-Fi, free public parking nearby and on main street, reserved
parking-€7, up from funicular toward Duomo at Corso Cavour
339, tel. 0763-342-020, fax 0763-340-648, www.hotelcorso.net,
info@hotelcorso.net, Carla).

$ Hotel Posta is a dumpy, long-ago-elegant palazzo renting
20 quirky rooms with vintage furniture—among the cheapest in
town. It's clean, relatively well-maintained, and centrally located
(S-€31, Sb-€37, D-€44, Db-€57, breakfast-€6, cash only, elevator,
Via Luca Signorelli 18, tel. & fax 0763-341-909, www.orvietohotels
.it, hotelposta@orvietohotels.it, little English spoken, Alessia).

$ Villa Mercede, a wonderful value, is a religious institu-
tion offering 23 cheap, simple twin-bedded rooms, each with a
big modern bathroom and many with glorious Umbrian views
(Sb-€50, Db-€70, Tb-€90, elevator, free Wi-Fi, free parking, a
half-block from Duomo at Via Soliana 2, tel. 0763-341-766, fax
0763-340-119, www.villamercede.it, info@villamercede.it).

$ Istituto S.S. Salvatore rents nine spotless twin rooms and
five singles in their convent, which comes with a peaceful terrace
and garden, great views, and a 22:30 curfew. Though the nuns
don't speak English, tech-savvy Sister Maria Stella has mastered
Google Translator, and will happily use it to answer your questions (Sb-€38, Db-€58, €5 less per person Oct-March, cash only,
no breakfast, elevator, free parking, just off Piazza del Popolo at

Via del Popolo 1, tel. & fax 0763-342-910, istitutosansalvatore @tiscali.it).

$ Valentina's Rooms include six clean, airy, well-appointed rooms and two apartments, all with big beds and antique furniture. Her place is located in the heart of Orvieto, behind the palace on Piazza del Popolo (Db-€58/€65, Tb-€75/€85, studio with kitchen-€80/€90, lower room rates are cash only and good with this book for stays of two or more nights; bright, spacious family apartment for up to 5 people-€170/night or €150/night for stays of three or more nights; breakfast-€5, air-con-€5, free Wi-Fi, Via Vivaria 7, tel. 0763-341-607, mobile 393-970-5868, www.bandb valentina.com, valentina.z@tiscalinet.it). Valentina also rents three rooms across the square that share a kitchen (D-€50, private bathroom down the hall, no air-con).

$ La Magnolia B&B has lots of fancy terra-cotta tiles, a couple of rooms with frescoed ceilings, terraces, and other welcoming touches. Its seven unique rooms, some like mini-apartments with kitchens, are cheerfully decorated and on the town's main drag. The three units facing the busy street are air-conditioned and have good double-paned windows (Db-€65, plush Db apartment-€75, extra person-€15, family deals, book direct and stay at least two nights to get a 10 percent Rick Steves discount, no elevator, free Wi-Fi, use of washer-€3.50, Via Duomo 29, tel. 0763-342-808, mobile 349-462-0733, www.bblamagnolia.it, info@bblamagnolia .it, Serena and Loredana).

$ B&B Michelangeli, hiding along a residential lane a few blocks from the tourist scene, is run by eager-to-please Francesca, who speaks limited English but provides homey touches and free tea, coffee, and breakfast supplies in her two comfortable and well-appointed apartments (Db-€70, kids-€10 extra, fully equipped kitchen, free Wi-Fi, washing machine, underground parking-€5, Via Saracinelli 20, tel. 0763-393-862, mobile 347-089-0349, www .bbmichelangeli.com, f_michelangeli@alice.it).

Just Outside the Town Center: **$$ Casa Sèlita B&B,** a peaceful country house, offers easy access to Orvieto (best for drivers, but workable for adventurous train travelers). It's nestled in an orchard just below the town cliffs; to get to town, you'll climb a path steeply through their fields to reach the big Campo della Fiera parking lot, with its handy escalator taking you the rest of the way up into Orvieto. Its five rooms with terraces are airy and fresh, with dark hardwood floors, fluffy down comforters, and modern baths. Enjoy the views from the relaxing garden. Conscientious Sèlita, her husband Ennio, and daughter Elena are gracious hosts (Sb-€55, Db-€80, Tb-€90, €5 less with stays of two or more nights, €5 more off-season for heat, these prices promised to my readers through 2013 if you book direct, cash preferred, fans, free

Internet access and Wi-Fi, free parking, Strada di Porta Romana 8, don't use GPS—sends you to the wrong location, mobile 339-225-4000 or 328-611-2052, tel. 0763-344-218, www.casaselita.com, info @casaselita.com).

Near Orvieto

All of these (except the last one) are within a 20-minute drive of Orvieto, in different directions, and require a car.

$$$ La Rocca Orvieto, run by Emiliano and Sabrina, is a fancy spa-type "country resort," located 15 minutes north of Orvieto by car. They produce their own olive oil and wine and have nine rooms and 10 apartments—all with air-conditioning and Wi-Fi (Db-€110-150, 10 percent discount with this book—mention when you reserve, pool, panoramic view restaurant, wellness center with Jacuzzi and steam room, gym, mountain bikes, bocce court, hiking paths, tel. 0763-344-210 or 0763-393-437, fax 0763-395-155, mobile 348-640-0845, www.laroccaorvieto.com, info @laroccaorvieto.com).

At **$$$ Agriturismo Locanda Rosati,** you'll be greeted by friendly hosts Giampiero Rosati and niece Cristiana, who rent 10 tastefully decorated rooms in a pleasant, homey atmosphere (Db-€110-140, Tb-€140-160, full traditional dinners for €35 on request with this book, air-con, swimming pool, 5 miles from Orvieto on the road to Viterbo, tel. 0763-217-314, www.locandarosati.it, info @locandarosati.it).

$$$ Borgo Fontanile is a vacation home with a swimming pool, terrace, and kids' play area. Its five new apartments with rustic wood beams and terra-cotta tile floors sleep up to four people (€40-50/night per person, discounts for longer stays, €400-800/apartment per week, air-con, Vocabolo Fornace 159, Loc. Baschi, tel. & fax 074-495-7342, www.borgofontanile.com, info@borgo fontanile.com).

$$ Tenuta le Velette is a sprawling, family-run farmhouse. Cecilia and Corrado Bottai rent six fully furnished apartments and villas scattered over their expansive and scenic grounds. They range wildly in size—accommodating from 2 to 14 people—but they all nestle in perfect Umbrian rural peace and tranquility (Db apartment-€90-110, see website for details on various villas, 2-night minimum, 10 percent discount for weekly stay, free Wi-Fi, pool, bocce court, 5 minutes from Orvieto—drive toward Bagnoregio-Canale and follow *Tenuta le Velette* signs, tel. 0763-29090, mobile 348-300-2002, fax 0763-29114, www.levelette.it, cecilialevelette @libero.it). They also offer wine-tastings (see listing on page 761).

$$ Agriturismo Cioccoleta ("Little Stone") has eight rooms with cozy country decor, each named after one of the grapes grown in the *agriturismo*'s vineyards. It's family-run and offers sweeping views of Orvieto and the pastoral countryside (Db-€70, Tb-€90, Qb-€110, 10 percent discount with this book—mention when you reserve, includes breakfast, free Wi-Fi, 3 miles north of Orvieto at Località Bardano 34 in Bardano, tel. 0763-316-011, mobile 349-860-9780, www.cioccoleta.it, info@cioccoleta.it, Angela Zucconi).

$$ Agriturismo Poggio della Volara, 12 miles southeast of Orvieto, has seven apartments (sleeping from two to five people) and seven rooms in two buildings overlooking a swimming pool (Db-€90, Tb-€120, smaller apartment-€100, larger apartment-€170, room rates include breakfast but costs €8 extra in apartments, air-con in all but four rooms, free Wi-Fi, tel. 0744-951-820, mobile 347-335-2523, www.poggiodellavolara.it, info @poggiodellavolara.it, Marco).

Farther Out, Northwest of Todi: **$$$ Agriturismo Fattoria di Vibio** produces olive oil and honey, sells organic products, and offers classes and spa services. In August, its 14 rooms rent at peak prices (and for one week during the month they require a minimum seven-night stay, with arrivals and departures on Saturdays). The rest of the year, no minimum stay is required, although rates drop dramatically for longer visits (Db-€210-340, includes breakfast and dinner). Its three cottages sleep from four to seven people and rent only by the week (€1,260-2,100/week depending on amenities, see complicated rate table on website, farthest cottage is 20 miles northeast of Orvieto, tel. 075-874-9607, fax 075-878-0014, www.fattoriadivibio.com, info@fattoriadivibio.com).

Eating in Orvieto

La Palomba features game and truffle specialties in a wood-paneled dining room. Gianpiero, Enrica, and the Cinti family take care of their regulars and visiting travelers alike, offering both a fine value and a classy conviviality. Seating is comfortable and not too crowded. Truffles are ground right at your table—try the *ombricelli al tartufo* (homemade pasta with truffles), then follow that up with some *piccione* (pigeon). As firm believers in the slow-food movement, they use ingredients that are mostly organic and locally produced (€8-12 pastas, €9-15 *secondi*, Thu-Tue 12:30-14:15 & 19:30-22:00, closed Wed and July, reservations smart, just off Piazza della Repubblica at Via Cipriano Manente 16, tel. 0763-343-395).

Antico Bucchero, a bit mod under a big white vault, makes a nice splurge with its candlelit ambience and delicious food (€7-8 pastas, €12-13 *secondi*, Thu-Tue 12:00-15:00 & 19:00-23:00, closed Wed, indoor/outdoor seating, a half-block south of Corso Cavour, between Torre del Moro and Piazza della Repubblica at Via de Cartari 4, tel. 0763-341-725, Piero and Silvana).

L'Antica Trattoria dell'Orso offers well-prepared Umbrian cuisine paired with fine wines in a homey and peaceful atmosphere. Ciro and chef Gabriele enjoy getting to know their diners, and will steer you toward the freshest seasonal plates of their famous pastas and passionately prepared vegetables. Or just trust Gabriele, and go for their €30 complete tasting meal, which includes wine (€8-12 pastas, €9-16 *secondi*, Wed-Sat 12:00-14:00 & 19:30-22:00, Sun 12:00-14:00, closed Mon-Tue, just off Piazza della Repubblica at Via della Misericordia 18/20, tel. 0763-341-642).

Trattoria la Grotta, pricey and chic, prides itself on serving only the freshest food and finest wine. The decor is Signorelli mod and the ambience is quiet, with courteous service. Owner-chef Franco has been at it for 50 years, and promises diners a free coffee, grappa, *limoncello*, or *vin santo* with this book (€7-9 pastas, €14-18 *secondi*, Wed-Mon opens at 12:00 for lunch and at 19:00 for dinner, closed Tue, Via Luca Signorelli 5, tel. 0763-341-348).

Trattoria del Moro Aronne is a long-established family bistro run by Cristian and his mother Rolanda, who lovingly prepare homemade pasta and market-fresh meats and produce for their typical Umbrian specialties. Be sure to sample the *nidi*—folds of fresh pasta enveloping warm, gooey Pecorino cheese sweetened with honey. The crème brûlée is a winner for dessert. Three small and separate dining areas make the interior feel intimate. This place is known locally as a good value (€7-10 pastas, €9-14 *secondi*, Wed-Mon 12:30-15:00 & 19:30-22:00, closed Tue, Via San Leonardo 7, tel. 0763-342-763).

Trattoria da Carlo, hiding on its own little piazzetta between Via Corso Cavour and Piazza del Popolo, is a cozy spot with white tile inside and inviting tables outside. Animated and opinionated Carlo—a likeable loudmouth—holds court, chatting up his diners as much as he cooks, while his mama scuttles about taking orders, bussing dishes, and lovingly rolling her eyes at her son's big personality. The short, pricey menu changes constantly (€9 pastas, €12-18 *secondi*, daily 12:00-15:00 & 19:00-24:00, Vicolo del Popolo 1/9, tel. 0763-343-916).

Pizzeria & Restaurant Charlie is a local favorite. It's popular with families and students for casual dinners of wood-fired €6-8 pizzas, big salads, homemade €7-9 pastas, or €12-15 grilled meat dishes. In a quiet courtyard guarded by a medieval tower, it's centrally located a block southwest of Piazza della Repubblica (Wed-Mon 12:30-14:30 & 19:00-23:30, closed Tue, dinner only Nov-Feb, Via Loggia dei Mercanti 14, tel. 0763-344-766).

Enoteca al Duomo, to the left of the Duomo with pleasant outdoor seating, is run by Roman transplants Emilano and Ilaria. They serve rustic *panini* (€6 to eat in, €4 to go), wines by the glass, and a full menu of local dishes in a wine-bar atmosphere (€9-11 pastas and meal-size salads, €10-19 *secondi,* daily 10:00-24:00, Piazza del Duomo 13, mobile 676-334-4607).

L'Oste del Re, a simple trattoria on Corso Cavour, serves lunch with a focus on local cheeses and meats, and pizza in the evenings (Thu-Tue 11:00-15:30 & 19:00-22:30, closed Wed, Corso Cavour 58, tel. 0763-343-846).

Supermarket: Sidis, tucked away two minutes from the Duomo, has what you need to put together a functional picnic or stock your hotel room pantry (Mon-Sat 8:00-13:30 & 16:30-19:30, closed Sun, just past recommended Trattoria la Grotta at Via Luca Signorelli 23).

Gelato: For dessert, try the deservedly popular *gelateria* **Pasqualetti** (daily 11:30-21:00, open later June-Aug, closed in winter, next to left transept of church, Piazza del Duomo 14; another branch is at Corso Cavour 56, open daily 11:00-23:00, closes at 19:00 in winter).

Orvieto Connections

From Orvieto by Train to: Rome (roughly hourly, 1-1.5 hours), **Florence** (hourly, 2 hours, use Firenze S.M.N. train station—see page 458), **Siena** (12/day, 2.5 hours, change in Chiusi, all Florence-bound trains stop in Chiusi), **Assisi** (roughly hourly, 2.5 hours, 1 or 2 transfers). The train station's Buffet della Stazione is surprisingly good if you need a quick *focaccia* sandwich or pizza picnic for the train ride.

Tip for Drivers: If you're thinking of driving to Rome, consider stashing your car in Orvieto instead. You can easily park the car, safe and free, behind the Orvieto train station (for up to a week or more), and zip effortlessly into Rome by train (1.25 hours).

Getting to Civita di Bagnoregio: To reach Civita, you'll first head for the adjacent town of Bagnoregio. From there, it's a 30-minute walk, quick shuttle bus ride, or five-minute drive to Civita.

By Bus to Bagnoregio: The trip from Orvieto to Bagnoregio takes about 45 minutes (€2 one-way if bought in advance from bar or tobacco shop, €7 one-way if purchased from driver—this includes a €5 fine for not buying your ticket in advance). Here are likely departure times (but confirm) from Orvieto's Piazza Cahen on the blue Cotral bus, daily except Sunday (when this bus does not run at all): 6:20, *7:25, *7:50, 12:45, 15:45, and 18:20; slower buses depart at *13:55 and *17:40. Departures marked with an asterisk (*) run only during the school year (roughly Sept-June). Buy your ticket at the tobacco shop on Corso Cavour, a block up from the funicular (daily 8:00-13:00 & 16:00-20:00)—otherwise you'll pay the premium ticket price on board the bus. If you'll be

Orvieto & Civita Area

To Florence

TRAIN STATION & FUNICULAR TO UPPER TOWN

A-1

S-79 bis

To Siena

To Todi & Assisi

• Acquapendente

❻

Lake Corbara

S-2 (VIA CASSIA)

❸

Orvieto
See detail map

ORVIETO EXIT

S-448

S-74

❹

Porano

❷

❶

❺

Canale

❼

• Bolsena

Baschi

Lubriano

Civita di Bagnoregio

Bagnoregio

Lake Bolsena

❾

BRIDGE (FOR PEDESTRIANS & VESPAS)

Tiber River

A-1

S-71

• Capodimonte

• Montefiascone

N

5 Kilometers

5 Miles

S-2 (VIA CASSIA)

To Viterbo & Rome

To Rome

❶ Tenuta le Velette Winery & Accommodations
❷ Custodi Winery
❸ La Rocca Orvieto
❹ Agriturismo Locanda Rosati
❺ Borgo Fontanile Vacation Rental
❻ Agriturismo Cioccoleta
❼ Agriturismo Poggio della Volara
❽ Agriturismo Fattoria di Vibio
❾ Agriturismo Le Corone

ORVIETO AND CIVITA

returning to Orvieto by bus, it's also simpler to get a return ticket now rather than in Bagnoregio. The bus stop is at the far left end of Piazza Cahen (across the street from the bus parking lot; see map on page 749). The schedule is posted at the stop—look for the *A.co.tra.l. Capolinea* sign. The bus you want says *Bagnoregio* in the window. Buses stop five minutes later at Orvieto's train station— to catch the bus there, wait to the left of the funicular station (as you're facing it); schedule and tickets are available in the tobacco shop/bar in the train station. The last bus back from Bagnoregio usually leaves at 17:25. For more information, call 0761-760-049 (may be Italian-only), or see www.cotralspa.it (though this site's timetables are often out of date).

To reach Civita from Bagnoregio, follow the directions under "Arrival in Bagnoregio, near Civita," later.

By Car to Bagnoregio and Civita: Orvieto overlooks the autostrada (and has its own exit). From the Orvieto exit, the shortest way to Civita is to turn left (below Orvieto) and then simply follow the signs to *Lubriano* and *Bagnoregio.*

A more winding and scenic route takes about 10 to 15 minutes longer: From the freeway, pass under hill-capping Orvieto (on your right, signs to *Lago di Bolsena,* on Viale I Maggio), then take the first left (direction: Bagnoregio), winding up past great Orvieto views and the recommended Tenuta Le Velette and Custodi wineries (reservations required) en route to Canale, and through farms and fields of giant shredded wheat to Bagnoregio.

Either way, just before Bagnoregio, follow the signs left to *Lubriano,* head into that village, turn right as you enter town, and pull into the first little square by the yellow church (on the left) for a breathtaking view of Civita. You'll find an even better view farther inside the town, from the tiny square at the next church (San Giovanni Battista). Then return to the Bagnoregio road.

Drive through the town of Bagnoregio (following yellow *Civita* signs) and park in the lot at the base of the steep pedestrian bridge; pay for parking at the automated machine next to the bridge entrance (€2/first hour, €1/each additional hour, free 20:00-8:00). The bridge at this parking lot leads up to the traffic-free 2,500-year-old canyon-swamped pinnacle town of Civita di Bagnoregio.

Civita di Bagnoregio

Perched on a pinnacle in a grand canyon, the traffic-free village of Civita di Bagnoregio is Italy's ultimate hill town. In the last decade, the real Civita (CHEE-vee-tah) has died—the last of its lifelong residents have moved away. But relatives and newcomers are moving in and revitalizing the village, and it remains an amazing place to visit. (It's even become popular as a backdrop for movies, soap operas, and advertising campaigns.) Civita is connected to the world and the town of Bagnoregio by a long pedestrian bridge—and a website (www.civitadibagnoregio.it, run by B&B owner Franco).

Civita's history goes back to Etruscan and ancient Roman times. In the early Middle Ages, Bagnoregio was a suburb of Civita, which had a population of about 4,000. Later, Bagnoregio surpassed Civita in size—especially following a 1695 earthquake, after which many residents fled Civita to live in Bagnoregio, fearing their houses would be shaken off the edge into the valley below. You'll notice Bagnoregio is dominated by Renaissance-style build-

Civita di Bagnoregio

NOTE: MAP NOT TO SCALE; A WALK ACROSS CIVITA TAKES APPROX. 5 MINUTES— BUT DON'T RUSH IT!

To Lubriano Town

Cliffs

Cliffs

OSTERIA AL FORNO DI AGNESE

ANTICO FORNO TRATTORIA & CIVITA B&B

LOCANDA DELLA BUONA VENTURA

CAMPANILE (BELL TOWER)

MARIA'S GARDEN

OLIVE PRESS & BRUSCHETTERIA

OLD LAUNDRY & WC

Piazza

CHURCH

ALMA CIVITA

ARCH

MAIN STRADA

ETRUSCAN COLUMNS

FOOTBRIDGE

To Bagnoregio

PALACE

SNACK BAR

WINE CELLAR & BRUSCHETTE

ANTICA CIVITA MUSEUM

WINE BAR PEPPONE

CAVES & CHAPEL CARVED IN ROCK

Cliffs

Trail to Etruscan tunnel under Civita

RUINS OF HOUSE OF ST. BONAVENTURE

ings while, architecturally, Civita remains stuck in the Middle Ages.

While Bagnoregio lacks the pinnacle-town romance of Civita, it's actually a healthy, vibrant community (unlike Civita, the suburb now nicknamed "the dead city"). In Bagnoregio, get a haircut, sip a coffee on the square, and walk down to the old laundry (ask, *"Dov'è la lavanderia vecchia?"*). Off-season, when Civita and Bagnoregio are deadly quiet—and cold—I'd side-trip in quickly from Orvieto rather than spend the night.

Orientation to Civita

Arrival in Bagnoregio, near Civita

If you're taking the **bus** from Orvieto, you'll get off at the bus stop in Bagnoregio. Look at the posted bus schedule and write down the return times to Orvieto, or check with the driver.

From Bagnoregio to Civita: Civita sits at the opposite end of Bagnoregio, about a mile away from the bus stop. From Bagnoregio, you can walk (allow around 30 minutes—see next paragraph) or take the **shuttle bus** to the base of the bridge to Civita (usually 1-2/hour but no buses 13:15-15:30, 10-minute ride, €0.70 one-way, €1 round-trip, pay driver, first bus runs Mon-Sat at about 7:30, Sun at 8:50, last at 18:15). Catch the shuttle at the bus stop marked *Bus to Civita* across the street from the gas station. From the base of the bridge, you have to walk the rest of the way (a 10-minute uphill hike across a pedestrian bridge). To return to

ORVIETO AND CIVITA

Bagnoregio by bus, check the schedule posted near the bridge (at edge of parking lot, where the bus let you off) before heading up to Civita, or ask at the recommended Trattoria Antico Forno.

To **walk** from the Bagnoregio bus stop to the base of Civita's bridge (at least 20 minutes, fairly level, leave heavy bags with Mauro—see "Helpful Hints," below), take the road going uphill, Via Garibaldi (overlooking the big parking lot). Once on the road, take the first right and an immediate left onto the main drag, Via Roma. Follow this straight out to the belvedere for a superb viewpoint. From the viewpoint, backtrack a few steps (staircase at end of viewpoint is a dead end) and take the stairs down to the road leading to the bridge.

A **taxi** from Orvieto to the base of the pedestrian bridge costs around €50 (see page 751).

Drivers coming from Orvieto or elsewhere can avoid a long walk by driving through Bagnoregio and parking under the bridge at the base of Civita (for more driving tips, see "Orvieto Connections," earlier).

Helpful Hints

Market Day: A lively market fills the Bagnoregio bus-station parking lot each Monday.

Baggage Storage: While there's no official baggage-check service in Bagnoregio, I've arranged with Mauro Laurenti, who runs the **Bar/Enoteca/Caffè Gianfu** and **Cinema Alberto Sordi,** to let you leave your bags there (€1/bag, Fri-Wed 6:00-13:00 & 13:30-24:00, closed Thu). As you get off the bus, go back 50 yards or so in the direction that the Orvieto bus just came from, and go right around corner.

Food near Bagnoregio Bus Stop: About 100 yards from the bus stop, within a few steps of the Porta Albana (old gate to the town), you'll find both a small grocery store and a great little bakery, **L'Arte del Pane,** with fresh pizza by the slice (Via Matteotti 5, opposite the cinema).

Orvieto Bus Tickets: To save money on bus fare to Orvieto, buy a ticket before boarding from the newsstand (with the awning marked *art.regalo edicola cartoleria*) near the Bagnoregio bus stop, across from the gas station (€2 one-way in advance; €7 from driver).

Self-Guided Walk

Welcome to Civita

Civita was once connected to Bagnoregio, before the saddle between the separate towns eroded away. Photographs around town show the old donkey path, the original bridge. It was bombed in World War II and replaced in 1966 with the new footbridge that you're climbing today. The town's hearty old folks hang on to the bridge's handrail when fierce winter weather rolls through.

• *Entering the town, you'll pass through a cut in the rock and a 12th-century Romanesque...*

Arch: This was the main Etruscan road leading to the Tiber Valley and Rome. The stone passageway was cut by the Etruscans 2,500 years ago.

• *Inside the town gate, to the left (just beyond the Bottega souvenir store), is an unmarked and less-than-pristine WC. It faces the town's old laundry, which dates from just after World War II, when water was finally piped into the town. Until recently, this was a lively village gossip center.*

Inside the entry arch and on the right are the remains of a...

Renaissance Palace: The wooden door and windows (above the door) lead only to thin air. They were part of the facade of one of five palaces that once graced Civita. Much of the palace fell into the valley, riding a chunk of the ever-eroding rock pinnacle. Today, the door leads to a remaining section of the palace—complete with Civita's first hot tub, as it was once owned by the "Marchesa," a countess who married into Italy's biggest industrialist family.

Check out the canyon viewpoint a few steps to the left of the palace. Walk a few steps up along the terrace for grand vistas. Lean over the banister and listen to the sounds of the birds and the bees. Just beyond that is the site of the long-gone home of Civita's one famous son, St. Bonaventure, known as the "second founder of the Franciscans" (look for the small plaque on the wall higher up, at the fence).

• *Now wander to the main square and Civita's church.*

Piazza: Here in the town square you'll find Wine Bar da Peppone (if it's chilly, go inside for the inviting fire), two restaurants, and wild donkey races on the first Sunday of June and the second Sunday of September. At Christmastime, a living nativity scene is enacted in this square, and if you're visiting at the end of July or beginning of August, you might catch a

play here. The pillars that stand like giants' bar stools are ancient Etruscan. The church with its *campanile* (bell tower) marks the spot

where an Etruscan temple, and then a Roman temple, once stood.
• *Go into the church.*

Church: A cathedral until 1699, the church houses records of about 60 bishops that date back to the seventh century (church open daily 9:30-13:00 & 15:00-18:00). Inside you'll see frescoes and statues from "the school of Donatello." The central altar is built upon the relics of the Roman martyr St. Victoria, who once was the patron saint of the town. St. Marlonbrando served as a bishop here in the ninth century; an altar dedicated to him is on the right. The fine crucifix over this altar, carved out of pear wood in the 15th century, is from the school of Donatello. It's remarkably expressive and greatly venerated by locals. Jesus' gaze is almost haunting. Some say his appearance changes based on what angle you view him from: looking alive from the front, in agony from the left, and dead from the right. Regardless, his eyes follow you from side to side. On Good Friday, this crucifix goes out and is the focus of the midnight procession.

On the left side of the nave above an altar is an intimate fresco of the *Madonna of the Earthquake,* given this name because—in the shake of 1695—the whitewash fell off and revealed this tender fresco of Mary and her child. (During the Baroque era, a white-and-bright interior was in vogue, and churches such as these—which were covered with precious and historic frescoes— were simply whitewashed over.) On the same wall—just toward the front from the *Madonna*—find the faded portrait of Santa Apollonia, the patron saint of your teeth; notice the scary-looking pincers. Say hello to Annarita, the church attendant. Drop a coin into the offering box.

• *Just around the corner from the church, on the main street, are several...*

Eateries: At Rossana and Antonio's cool **Bruschette con Prodotti Locali,** pull up a chair and let them or their daughters, Arianna and Antonella, serve you *panini* (sandwiches), bruschetta (garlic toast with optional tomato topping), *salumi,* grilled sausages, wine, and a local cake called *ciambella*. After eating, wander down to see their cellar with its traditional winemaking gear and provisions for rolling huge kegs up the stairs. Tap on the kegs in the bottom level to see which are full (daily 11:00-17:00, in summer until 20:00, tel. 0761-793-270). The rock below Civita is honeycombed with ancient cellars like this (for keeping wine at the same temperature all year) and cisterns (for collecting rainwater, since there was no well in town). Many date from Etruscan times.

Farther down, you'll pass two places (both on the left) operated by rival grandsons of Civita native Vittoria. First comes Maurizio's **Alma Civita,** a surprisingly trendy and upscale-feeling restaurant with tables outside, inside, and in a cozy room carved deep into the rock (for more, see "Eating in Civita," later). A bit farther along you reach his cousin Fabrizio's vastly different **Antico Frantoio Bruschetteria,** a rustic, super-atmospheric place for a bite to eat. The specialty here: delicious bruschetta toasted over hot coals. Peruse the menu, choose your topping (chopped tomato is super), and get a glass of wine for a fun, affordable snack (roughly 10:00-20:00 in summer, off-season open weekends only 10:00-19:00, mobile 328-689-9375).

While waiting for your bruschetta, take a look around to see Vittoria's mill *(mulino),* an interesting collection of old olive presses. The huge **olive press** in the entry is about 1,500 years old. Until

the 1960s, blindfolded donkeys trudged in the circle here, crushing olives and creating paste that filled the circular filters and was put into a second press. Notice the 2,500-year-old sarcophagus niche. The hole in the floor (with the glass top) was a garbage hole. In ancient times, residents would toss their jewels down when under attack; excavations uncovered a windfall of treasures (if you're not eating here, a €1 donation is requested).

• *Across the street and down a tiny lane, find...*

Antica Civita: This is the closest thing the town has to a museum. The humble collection is the brainchild of Felice, Vittoria's son, who has hung old black-and-white photos, farm tools, olive presses, and local artifacts in a series of old caves. Felice wants to give visitors a feeling for life in Civita when its traditional economy was strong (€1, daily 9:30-19:00, some English explanations).

• *On the left 20 yards farther down is...*

Maria's Garden (Maria's Giardino): Maria is too frail to live in Civita these days, but you may be able to peek into her garden and enjoy her view. She and her husband, Peppone (who passed away in 2009), used to carry goods on a donkey back and forth 40 times a day on the path between the old town and Bagnoregio. She's now the last native Civita resident still living. As you view the canyon in which Civita is stranded, imagine the work the two rivers did—in the same style as the Colorado River—to carve all this. Listen to the roosters and voices from distant farms.

• *At the end of town, the main drag winds downhill. On your right are small...*

Etruscan Caves: The first two caves were used as stables until a few years ago. The third cave is an unusual chapel, cut deep into the rock, with a barred door; this is the **Chapel of the**

Incarcerated (Cappella del Carcere). In Etruscan times, the chapel—with a painted tile depicting the Madonna and child—may have originally been a tomb, and in medieval times, it was used as a jail. When Civita's few residents have a religious procession, they come here in honor of the Madonna of the Incarcerated.

• *After the chapel, the paving-stone path peters out into a dirt trail leading down and around to the right to an...*

Etruscan Tunnel: This tunnel dates from pre-Roman times. Tall enough for a woman with a jug on her head to pass through, it may have served as a shortcut to the river below. It was widened in the 1930s so that farmers could get between their scattered fields more easily. Think of the scared villagers who huddled here for refuge during WWII bombing raids.

• *Backtrack to return to the...*

Piazza: Evenings on Civita's town square are a bite of Italy. The same people sit on the same church steps under the same moon, night after night, year after year. I love my cool, late evenings in Civita. If you visit in the morning, have cappuccino and rolls at the small café/wine bar on the town square.

Whenever you visit, stop halfway up the donkey path and listen to the sounds of rural Italy. Reach out and touch one of the Monopoly houses. If you know how to turn the volume up on the crickets, do so.

Sleeping in Civita or Bagnoregio

(€1 = about $1.40, country code: 39)

In Civita and Bagnoregio, there are 14 B&B rooms up for grabs, and one bigger hotel. Outside the town there are plenty of *agriturismi;* otherwise, there's always Orvieto.

In Civita

$$$ Locanda della Buona Ventura has four rooms decorated in medieval rustic-chic, filling the old mayor's house and overlooking Civita's piazza. The local-products shop just across the square functions as the reception, and has an old well down steep stairs worth checking out (Db-€120, breakfast at nearby restaurant, mobile 347-627-5628, raffaele_rocchi@libero.it, Lara).

$$ Alma Civita is a classic old stone house that was recently renovated by a sister-and-brother team, Alessandra and Maurizio (hence the name: Al-Ma), to provide Civita's two most comfortable and modern rooms (Db-€90, tel. 0761-792-415, mobile 347-449-8892, www.almacivita.com, prenotazione@almacivita.com). They also have a restaurant (see later).

$ Civita B&B, run by gregarious Franco Sala, has three fine little rooms above Trattoria Antico Forno, each overlooking Civita's main square (S-€50, Sb-€55, D-€70, Db-€75, T-€95, continental breakfast, free Wi-Fi, Piazza del Duomo Vecchio, tel. 076-176-0016, mobile 347-611-5426, www.civitadibagnoregio.it, fsala@pelagus.it).

In Bagnoregio

$$ Romantica Pucci B&B is a haven for city-weary travelers. Its five spacious rooms are indeed romantic, with canopied beds and flowing veils. Both homey and elegant, it's like sleeping at Katharine Hepburn's place (Db-€80, air-con, free time-limited Internet access, free parking, "Pucci Speciality" €20 family-style dinner is popular with guests—non-guests are also welcome for dinner, free Wi-Fi in lobby, Piazza Cavour 1, tel. 076-179-2121, www.hotelromanticapucci.it, hotelromanticapucci@libero.it). It's just above the parking lot you see when you arrive in Bagnoregio— look for a sign marking its private parking place. From the bus stop, take Via Garibaldi uphill above the parking lot, bear right at the tobacco shop onto Via Roma, then look for the hotel sign straight ahead.

$ Hotel Divino Amore has 23 bright, modern rooms, some with perfect views of a miniature Civita (Sb-€50, Db-€70, Tb-€80, Qb-€90, Via Fidanza 25-27, tel. & fax 076-178-0882, mobile 329-344-8950, www.hoteldivinoamore.com, info@hoteldivinoamore .com). From the bus stop, follow Via Garibaldi uphill above the parking lot, where it becomes Via Fidanza, and continue straight along for about 200 yards; #25 is on the left.

Outside of Town

$ Agriturismo Le Corone, in the valley below Civita, is an economical answer if you dream of a lazy few days relaxing among the olive trees. Flexible Fabrizio of Antico Frantoio Bruschetteria will pick you up from Bagnoregio, then drive you 10 minutes along a winding road to a simple but cozy home with a kitchen/living room, two bedrooms, and small garden. Civita is a steep but picturesque 45-minute uphill hike away (or persuade Fabrizio to give you a ride), and firewood is provided for romantic evenings (€35/ night per person, maximum 6 people, no minimum occupancy, home-cooked pasta dinner-€10, Strade della Valle—see map on page 769, mobile 328-689-9375, www.corone-civita.com, info @corone-civita.com).

Eating in Civita or Bagnoregio

In Civita

In my self-guided walk, I've listed a pair of *bruschette* places that are handy for a snack as you explore town. For a full meal, consider one of these three options.

Osteria Al Forno di Agnese is a delightful spot where Manuela and her friends serve visitors simple yet delicious meals on a covered patio just off Civita's main square (€8-9 pastas including gluten-free options, €7-12 *secondi*, opens daily at 12:00 for lunch and at 19:00 for dinner, sometimes closed Tue in bad weather, tel. 0761-792-571, mobile 340-1259-721).

Trattoria Antico Forno cooks up rustic dishes, homemade pasta, and salads at affordable prices. Try their homemade pasta with truffles (€6-8 pastas, €7-11 *secondi*, daily for lunch 12:30-15:30 and dinner 19:00-22:00, on main square, also rents rooms—see Civita B&B listing on previous page, tel. 076-176-0016, Franco and his assistants Nina and Fiorella).

Alma Civita feels like a fresh new take on old Civita, created by two of its longtime residents: Alessandra (an architect) and her brother Maurizio (who runs the restaurant). Choose from one of three different seating areas: outside on a stony lane, in the modern and trendy-feeling main-floor dining room, or in the equally modern but atmospheric cellar. Even deeper is an old Etruscan tomb that's now a wine cellar (€3-5 *bruschette* and *antipasti*, €6-8 pastas, €6-10 *secondi*; May-Oct Wed-Mon 10:30-18:00, closed Tue, dinner served on Sat only; Nov-April Fri-Sun 10:30-18:00, closed Mon-Thu; tel. 0761-792-415).

In Bagnoregio

Hostaria del Ponte offers creative, light, and traditional cuisine with a great view terrace at the parking lot at the base of the bridge to Civita. Big space heaters make it comfortable to enjoy the wonderful view as you dine from their rooftop terrace, even in spring and fall (€9 pastas, €12-14 *secondi*, reservations often essential, Tue-Sun 12:30-14:30 & 19:30-21:30, closed Mon; Nov-April also closed Sun eve, tel. 076-179-3565, Lorena).

Bagnoregio Connections

From Bagnoregio to Orvieto: Public buses (45 minutes, €2 one-way if purchased in advance, €7 one-way from driver) connect Bagnoregio to the rest of the world via Orvieto. Departures from Bagnoregio—daily except Sunday and some holidays—are likely to be (but confirm): 5:30, *6:35, 6:50, 9:55, 10:10 or *10:25, 13:00, *13:35, 14:25, and 17:25. Departures marked with an asterisk (*) operate only during the school year (roughly Sept-June; for info on coming from Orvieto, see "Orvieto Connections," page 768).

Remember to save money by buying your ticket in Bagnoregio before boarding the bus—purchase one from the newsstand near the bus stop, across from the gas station. Better yet, if you're side-tripping from Orvieto, buy two tickets in Orvieto so you already have one when you're ready to come back.

From Bagnoregio to Points South: Public buses run to **Viterbo,** which has a good train connection to Rome (buses go weekdays at 5:10, 6:30, 7:15, 7:40, 10:00, 13:00, 13:45, 14:20, 14:50, and 18:05; less frequent Sat-Sun, 35 minutes).

ROME

Roma

Rome is magnificent and brutal at the same time. It's a showcase of Western civilization, with astonishingly ancient sights and a modern vibrancy. But if you're careless, you'll be run down or pickpocketed. And with the wrong attitude, you'll be frustrated by the kind of chaos that only an Italian can understand. On my last visit, a cabbie struggling with the traffic said, *"Roma chaos."* I responded, *"Bella chaos."* He agreed.

While Paris is an urban garden, Rome is a magnificent tangled forest. If your hotel provides a comfortable refuge; if you pace yourself; if you accept—and even partake in—the siesta plan; if you're well-organized for sightseeing; and if you protect yourself and your valuables with extra caution and discretion, you'll love it. (And Rome is much easier to live with if you can avoid the midsummer heat.)

For me, Rome is in a three-way tie with Paris and London as Europe's greatest city. Two thousand years ago, the word "Rome" meant civilization itself. Everything was either civilized (part of the Roman Empire, Latin- or Greek-speaking) or barbarian. Today, Rome is Italy's political capital, the capital of Catholicism, and the center of the ancient world, littered with evocative remains. As you peel through its fascinating and jumbled layers, you'll find Rome's buildings, cats, laundry, traffic, and 2.7 million people endlessly entertaining. And then, of course, there are its stupendous sights.

Visit St. Peter's, the greatest church on earth, and scale Michelangelo's 448-foot-tall dome, the world's tallest. Learn something about eternity by touring the huge Vatican Museum. You'll find the story of creation—bright as the day it was painted—in the restored Sistine Chapel. Do the "Caesar Shuffle" through ancient

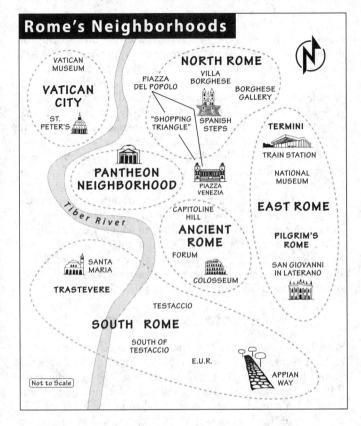

Rome's Neighborhoods

VATICAN MUSEUM

VATICAN CITY

ST. PETER'S

NORTH ROME

VILLA BORGHESE

PIAZZA DEL POPOLO

BORGHESE GALLERY

"SHOPPING TRIANGLE"

SPANISH STEPS

TERMINI

TRAIN STATION

NATIONAL MUSEUM

PANTHEON NEIGHBORHOOD

PIAZZA VENEZIA

Tiber River

CAPITOLINE HILL

EAST ROME

ANCIENT ROME

FORUM

PILGRIM'S ROME

SAN GIOVANNI IN LATERANO

COLOSSEUM

SANTA MARIA

TRASTEVERE

TESTACCIO

SOUTH ROME

SOUTH OF TESTACCIO

E.U.R.

APPIAN WAY

Not to Scale

Rome's Forum and Colosseum. Savor Europe's most sumptuous building, the Borghese Gallery, and take an early evening "Dolce Vita Stroll" down Via del Corso with Rome's beautiful people. Enjoy an after-dark walk from Campo de' Fiori to the Spanish Steps, lacing together Rome's Baroque and bubbly nightspots. Dine well at least once.

Planning Your Time

Rome is wonderful, but it's huge and exhausting. On a first-time visit, many travelers find that Rome is best done quickly—Italy is more charming elsewhere. But whether you're here for a day or a week, you won't be able to see all of these sights, so don't try—you'll keep coming back to Rome. After several dozen visits, I still have a healthy list of excuses to return.

Rome in a Day: Some people actually try to "do" Rome in a day. Crazy as that sounds, if all you have is a day, it's one of the most exciting days Europe has to offer. Start at 8:30 at the Colosseum. Then explore the Forum, hike over Capitoline Hill, and cap your "Caesar Shuffle" with a visit to the Pantheon. After a quick lunch, taxi to the Vatican Museum (the lines usually die down mid-afternoon, or you can reserve a visit online in advance). See the Vatican Museum, then St. Peter's Basilica (open until 19:00 April-Sept). Taxi back to Campo de' Fiori to find dinner. Finish your day lacing together all the famous floodlit spots (follow my self-guided Heart of Rome Walk). If you only want a day in Rome, consider side-tripping from Orvieto or Florence, or fit it in before taking the night train to Venice (via Milan).

Rome in Two to Three Days: On the first day, do the "Caesar Shuffle" from the Colosseum to the Forum, then over Capitoline Hill to the Pantheon. After a siesta, join the locals strolling from Piazza del Popolo to the Spanish Steps (follow my self-guided "Dolce Vita Stroll"). On the second day, see Vatican City (St. Peter's, climb the dome, tour the Vatican Museum). Have dinner on the atmospheric Campo de' Fiori, and then walk to the Trevi Fountain and Spanish Steps (following my Heart of Rome Walk). With a third day, add the Borghese Gallery (reservations required) and the National Museum of Rome.

Orientation to Rome

Sprawling Rome actually feels manageable once you get to know it. The old core, with most of the tourist sights, sits in a diamond formed by Termini train station (in the east), the Vatican (west), Villa Borghese Gardens (north), and the Colosseum (south). The Tiber River runs through the diamond from north to south. In the center of the diamond sits Piazza Venezia, a busy square and traffic hub. It takes about an hour to walk from Termini Station to the Vatican.

Think of Rome as a series of neighborhoods, huddling around major landmarks.

Ancient Rome: In ancient times, this was home for the grandest buildings of a city of a million people. Today, the best of the classical sights stand in a line from the Colosseum to the Forum to the Pantheon.

Pantheon Neighborhood: The Pantheon anchors the neighborhood I like to call the heart of Rome. It stretches eastward from the Tiber River through Campo de' Fiori and Piazza Navona, past the Pantheon to the Trevi Fountain.

Vatican City: Located west of the Tiber, it's a compact world of its own, with two great, huge sights: St. Peter's Basilica and the Vatican Museum.

North Rome: With the Spanish Steps, Villa Borghese Gardens, and trendy shopping streets (Via Veneto and the "shopping triangle"), this is a more modern, classy area.

ROME

East Rome: This includes the area around Termini Station, with its many recommended hotels and public-transportation connections. Nearby is the neighborhood I call "Pilgrim's Rome," with several prominent churches dotting the area south of the station.

South Rome: South of Vatican City is Trastevere, the seedy, colorful wrong-side-of-the-river neighborhood that provides a look at village Rome. It's the city at its crustiest—and perhaps most "Roman." Across the Tiber River, directly south of the city center, are the gritty/colorful Testaccio neighborhood, the 1930s suburb of E.U.R., and the Appian Way, home of the catacombs.

Within each of these neighborhoods, you'll find elements from the many layers of Rome's 2,000-year history: the marble ruins of ancient times; tangled streets of the medieval world; early Christian churches; grand Renaissance buildings and statues; Baroque fountains and church facades; 19th-century apartments; and 20th-century boulevards choked with traffic.

Since no one is allowed to build taller than St. Peter's dome, and virtually no buildings have been constructed in the city center since Mussolini got distracted in 1938, Rome has no modern skyline. The Tiber River is basically ignored—after the last floods (1870), the banks were built up very high, and Rome turned its back on its naughty river.

Tourist Information

Rome has two tourist information offices and several TI kiosks. The TI offices are at the airport (Terminal 3, daily 9:00-18:30) and Termini train station (daily 8:00-21:00, 100 yards down track 24, look for signs). Little kiosks (generally open daily 9:30-19:00) are near the Forum (on Piazza del Tempio della Pace), on Via Nazionale (at Palazzo delle Esposizioni), near Castel Sant'Angelo (at Piazza Pia), near Piazza Navona (at Piazza delle Cinque Lune), and near the Trevi Fountain (at Via del Corso and Via Minghetti). The TI's website is http://en.turismoroma.it. The TIs don't offer room-booking services. If a commercial info-center offers to book you a room, just say no—you'll save money by booking direct.

At any TI, ask for a city map and a listing of sights and hours (in the free *Evento* booklet with English-language pages listing the month's cultural events). Your hotel will have a freebie map and may also have the free *Evento* booklet, saving you a trip to the TI if that's all you need. The best map I found is published by Rough Guide (€9 in bookstores).

Rome's single best source of up-to-date tourist information is its **call center,** with English-speakers on staff. Dial 06-0608 (answered daily 9:00-21:00, press 2 for English, www.060608.it).

Several English-oriented **websites** provide insight into events and daily life in the city: www.inromenow.com (light tourist info

ROME

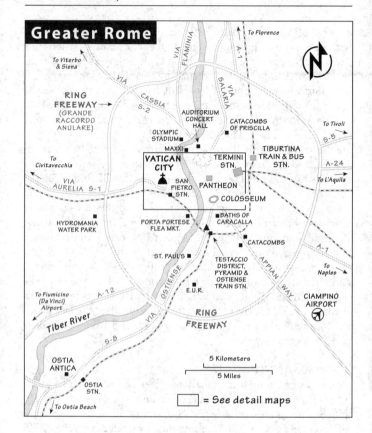

on lots of topics), www.wantedinrome.com (events and accommodations), and http://rome.angloinfo.com (on living in and moving to Rome).

Arrival in Rome

By Train at Termini Station

Termini, Rome's main train station, is a buffet of tourist services. While information desks are jammed with travelers, very handy red info kiosks at the head of the tracks can answer your simple questions. The Customer Care window near the main entrance and ticket booths can also be helpful for schedule questions.

Along track 24, about 100 yards down, you'll find the **TI** (daily 8:00-21:00), a **post office** (Mon-Fri 8:30-14:00, Sat 8:30-13:00, closed Sun), a **hotel booking** office, and **car rental** desks. The **baggage storage** *(deposito bagagli)* is downstairs (€5/5 hours, then cheaper, daily 6:00-24:00).

The **"Leonardo Express" train** to Fiumicino Airport runs from track 24 (see page 925). A good self-service **cafeteria,** Ciao, is near the head of track 24, upstairs, with fine views (daily 11:00-22:30). For **sandwiches** to go, try VyTA in the atrium across from track 1.

Near track 1, you'll find a **pharmacy** (daily 7:30-22:00); along the same track is a **waiting room** and **Despar Express**, selling everything from groceries to electronics (daily 7:00-21:30). If you can't find what you're looking for there, try downstairs at **Conad** (daily 6:00-24:00) or one of the many other specialty shops.

Elsewhere in the station are **ATMs,** late-hours banks, and 24-hour thievery. In the station's main entrance lobby, **Borri Books** sells books in English, including popular fiction, Italian history and culture, and kids' books, plus maps upstairs (daily 7:00-23:00).

Termini is also a local transportation hub. The city's two Metro lines (A and B) intersect downstairs at Termini Metro station. Buses (including Rome's hop-on, hop-off bus tours—see "Tours in Rome," later) leave across the square directly in front of the main station hall. The Metro and bus areas are under construction until sometime in 2013—look for signs directing you to the Metro platform or bus stop. Taxis queue in front; avoid con men hawking "express taxi" services in unmarked cars (only use cars marked with the word *taxi* and a phone number). To avoid the long taxi line, simply hike out past the buses to the main street and hail one.

From Termini, most of my recommended hotels are easily accessible by foot (for those near this train station) or by Metro (for those in the Colosseum and Vatican neighborhoods).

The station has some sleazy sharks with official-looking business cards; avoid anybody selling anything unless they're in a legitimate shop at the station.

By Train or Bus at Tiburtina Station

Tiburtina, Rome's second-largest train station, is located in the city's northeast corner. In general, slower trains (from Milan, Bolzano, Bologna, Udine, and Reggio di Calabria) and some night trains (from Munich, Milan, Venice, Innsbruck, and Udine) use Tiburtina, as does the night bus to Fiumicino Airport. Direct night trains from Paris and Vienna use Termini train station instead.

Tiburtina has been newly redeveloped for high-speed rail, including some Eurostar Italia trains and the new Italo service (run by a private operator, see page 1086). Some Italo trains may also stop at Ostiense Station. A separate "Casa Italo" area in each station has dedicated service counters, red ticket machines, and waiting areas. You can also book Italo tickets by phone (tel. 06-0708) or online (www.italotreno.it). Because this is a new company, it's hard to predict the level of service or even its long-term survival.

ROME

Tiburtina is also known as a hub for bus service to destinations all across Italy. Buses depart from the piazza in front of the station. Ticket offices are located in the piazza and around the corner on Circonvallazione Nomentana (just beyond the elevated freeway).

The Tiburtina Station is on Metro line B, with easy connections to Termini (a straight shot, four stops away) and the entire Metro system. Or take bus #492 from Tiburtina to various city-center stops (such as Piazza Barberini, Piazza Venezia, and Piazza Cavour) and the Vatican neighborhood.

By Car

The Grande Raccordo Anulare circles greater Rome. This ring road has spokes that lead you into the center. Entering from the north, leave the autostrada at the Settebagni exit. Following the ancient Via Salaria (and the black-and-white *Centro* signs), work your way doggedly into the Roman thick of things. This will take you along the Villa Borghese Gardens and dump you right on Via Veneto in downtown Rome. Avoid rush hour and drive defensively: Roman cars stay in their lanes like rocks in an avalanche.

Parking in Rome is dangerous. Park near a police station or get advice at your hotel. The Villa Borghese underground garage is handy (Metro: Spagna). Garages charge about €24 per day.

Consider this: Your car is a worthless headache in Rome. Avoid a pile of stress and save money by parking at the huge, easy, and relatively safe lot behind the train station in the hill town of Orvieto (follow *P* signs from autostrada) and catching the train to Rome (hourly, 1-1.5 hours).

If you absolutely must drive and park a car in Rome, try to avoid commuter traffic by arriving Friday evening, or anytime during the weekend, and by leaving town during the weekend. Park your car at Tiburtina Station (€1/hour, www.atac.roma.it) and take a 10-minute ride on the Metro line B into the center.

By Plane or Cruise Ship

For information on Rome's airports and Civitavecchia's cruise ship terminal, see the end of this chapter.

Helpful Hints

Sightseeing Tips: Avid sightseers can save money by buying the Roma Pass (see "Tips on Sightseeing in Rome" sidebar, later), available at TIs and participating sights—buy one before visiting the Colosseum or Forum, and you can skip the long lines there. If you want to see the Borghese Gallery, remember to reserve ahead (see page 862). To bypass the long Vatican Museum line, reserve an entry time online (see page 852 for details).

ROME

Daily Reminder

Sunday: These sights are closed: the Vatican Museum (except for the last Sunday of the month, when it's free and even more crowded), Villa Farnesina, and Catacombs of San Sebastiano. In the morning, the Porta Portese flea market hops, and the old center is delightfully quiet. Via dei Fori Imperiali is closed to traffic (9:00-17:00) and fun to stroll.

Monday: Many sights are closed, including the National Museum of Rome, Borghese Gallery, Capitoline Museums, Catacombs of Priscilla, Museum of the Imperial Forums (includes Trajan's Market and Trajan's Forum), Castel Sant'Angelo, Ara Pacis, Montemartini Museum, E.U.R.'s Museum of Roman Civilization, Etruscan Museum, Museum of the Liberation of Rome, MAXXI, some Appian Way sights (Tomb of Cecilia Metella; Circus and Villa of Maxentius; and the San Sebastiano Gate and Museum of the Walls), and Ostia Antica.

Major sights that are open include the Colosseum, Forum, and Vatican Museum, among others. Churches are open as usual. The Baths of Caracalla close early in the afternoon.

Tuesday: All sights are open in Rome. This isn't a good day to side-trip to Naples, because its Archaeological Museum is closed.

Wednesday: All sights are open, except the Catacombs of San Callisto. St. Peter's Basilica may be closed in the morning for a papal audience.

Thursday/Friday: All sights are open.

Saturday: Most sights are open in Rome, except for the Synagogue and Jewish Museum.

Internet Access: If your hotel doesn't offer free or cheap Internet access, your hotelier can point you to the nearest Internet café.

Bookstores: These stores (all open daily except Anglo American and Open Door) sell travel guidebooks, including mine. The first two are chains, while the others have a more personal touch. **Borri Books** is at Termini Station, and **Feltrinelli International** has two branches (at Largo Argentina, and just off Piazza della Repubblica at Via Vittorio Emanuele Orlando 84, tel. 06-482-7878). **Anglo American Bookshop** has great art and history sections (closed all day Sun and Mon morning, a few blocks south of Spanish Steps at Via della Vite 102, tel. 06-679-5222). **Libreria Fanucci** has a small selection but is centrally located (a block toward the Pantheon from Piazza Navona at Piazza Madama 8, tel. 06-686-1141). In Trastevere, Irishman Dermot at the **Almost Corner Bookshop** stocks an

ROME

Tips on Sightseeing in Rome

These tips will help you use your time and money efficiently, making the Eternal City seem less eternal and more entertaining. For general advice on sightseeing, see page 18.

Passes

Roma Pass: Rome offers several sightseeing passes to help you save money. For most visitors, the Roma Pass (www.roma

pass.it) is the clear winner. The Roma Pass costs €30 and is valid for three days, covering public transportation and free or discounted entry to Roman sights. You get free admission to your first two sights (where you also get to skip the ticket line) and then a discount on the rest within the three-day window. Sights covered (or dis-
counted) by the pass include the following: Colosseum/Palatine Hill/Roman Forum, Borghese Gallery (though you still must make a reservation), Capitoline Museums, Castel Sant'Angelo, Montemartini Museum, Ara Pacis, Museum of Roman Civilization, Etruscan Museum, Baths of Caracalla, Trajan's Market, and some of the Appian Way sights. The pass also covers four branches of the National Museum of Rome, considered as a single "sight": Palazzo Massimo (the most important of the lot), Crypta Balbi (medieval art), Palazzo Altemps (sculpture collection), and Museum of the Bath (ancient inscriptions).

If you'll be visiting any two of the major sights in a three-day period, get the pass. It's sold at participating sights, TIs, and many tobacco shops or newsstands (look for a *Roma Pass* sign; all should offer the same price). Try to buy it at a less crowded TI or sight (you can buy it at a sight even if you don't intend to use it there). Don't bother to order it online—you have to physically pick up the pass in Rome, which negates any time-saving advantage.

Validate your Roma Pass by writing your name and validation date on the card. Then insert it directly into the turnstile at your first two (free) sights. At other sights, show it at the ticket office to get your reduced *(ridotto)* price—about 30 percent off.

To get the most of your pass, visit the two most expensive sights first—for example, the Colosseum (€12) and the National Museum (€10). Definitely use it to bypass the long ticket-buying line at the Colosseum. For sights that normally sell a combined ticket (such as the Colosseum/Palatine Hill/Roman Forum or the National Museum branches), visiting the combined sight counts as a single entry.

The Roma Pass comes with a three-day transit pass. Write your name and birth date on the transit pass, validate it on your first bus or Metro ride by passing it over a sensor at a turnstile or validation machine (look for a yellow circle), and you can take unlimited rides within Rome's city limits until midnight of the third day.

The TI's other passes—Roma & Più Pass ("Rome & More") and the Archeologia Card—are generally not worth the trouble for most tourists.

Combo-Ticket for Colosseum, Forum, and Palatine Hill: A €12 combo-ticket covers these three adjacent sights (no individual tickets are sold per sight). The combo-ticket allows one entry per sight and is valid for two days. Note that these sights are also covered by the Roma Pass. To avoid ticket-buying lines at the Colosseum and Forum, purchase your combo-ticket or Roma Pass at the lesser-visited Palatine Hill. Between the combo-ticket or Roma Pass, the pass is the better deal, unless you're planning on seeing only the sights covered by the combo-ticket.

Top Tips

Museum Reservations: The marvelous Borghese Gallery requires reservations in advance (for specifics, see page 862). You can reserve online to avoid long lines at the Vatican Museum (see page 852).

Opening Hours: Rome's sights have notoriously variable hours from season to season. Get a current listing of opening times—ask for the free booklet *Evento* at a TI or your hotel. Or check online at www.060608.it/en (find "Cultural Heritage" in the menu under "Culture and Leisure"; search by using the Italian names of sights). On holidays, expect shorter hours or closures.

Churches: Many churches, which have divine art and free entry, open early (around 7:00-7:30), close for lunch (roughly 12:00-15:00), and close late (about 19:00). Kamikaze tourists maximize their sightseeing hours by visiting churches before 9:00 or late in the day and, during the siesta, seeing major sights that stay open all day (St. Peter's, Colosseum, Forum, Capitoline Museums, Pantheon, and National Museum of Rome). Dress modestly for church visits.

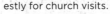

Picnic Discreetly: Public drinking and eating is not allowed at major sights, though the ban has proven difficult to enforce. To avoid the risk of being fined, choose an empty piazza for your picnic, or keep a low profile.

Miscellaneous Tips: I carry a plastic water bottle and refill it at Rome's many public drinking spouts. Because public restrooms are scarce, use toilets at museums, restaurants, and bars.

ROME

Italian-interest section (Via del Moro 45, tel. 06-583-6942), and the **Open Door Bookshop** carries the only used books in English in town (closed Sun, Via della Lungaretta 23, tel. 06-589-6478).

Laundry: Your hotelier can direct you to the nearest launderette. The **ondablu** chain usually comes with Internet access; one of their more central locations is near Termini Station (€2/hour, about €8 to wash and dry a 15-pound load, usually open daily 8:00-22:00, Via Principe Amedeo 70b, tel. 06-474-4647).

Travel Agencies: You can get train tickets and railpass-related reservations and supplements at travel agencies (at little or no additional cost), avoiding a trip to a train station. Your hotelier will know of a convenient agency nearby.

Updates to this Book: Check www.ricksteves.com/update for any significant changes that have occurred since this book was printed.

Dealing with (and Avoiding) Problems

Theft Alert: While violent crime is rare in the city center, petty theft is rampant. With sweet-talking con artists meeting you at the station, well-dressed pickpockets on buses, and thieving gangs of children at the ancient sites, Rome is a gauntlet of rip-offs. Although it's not as bad as it was a few years ago, and pickpockets don't want to hurt you—they usually just want your money—green or sloppy tourists will be scammed. Thieves strike when you're distracted. Don't trust kind strangers. Keep nothing important in your pockets. Be most on guard while boarding and leaving buses and subways. Thieves crowd the door, then stop and turn while others crowd and push from behind. You'll find less crowding and commotion—and less risk—waiting for the end cars of a subway rather than the middle cars. The sneakiest thieves pretend to be well-dressed businessmen (generally with something in their hands), or tourists wearing fanny packs and toting cameras and even Rick Steves guidebooks.

Scams abound: Don't give your wallet to self-proclaimed "police" who stop you on the street, warn you about counterfeit (or drug) money, and ask to see your cash. If a bank machine eats your ATM card, see if there's a thin plastic insert with a tongue hanging out that thieves use to extract it.

If you know what to look out for, fast-fingered moms with babies and gangs of children picking the pockets and handbags of naive tourists are not a threat, but an interesting, albeit sad, spectacle. Pickpockets troll through the tourist crowds around the Colosseum, Forum, Vatican, and train and Metro stations. Watch them target tourists who are overloaded with bags or distracted with a camera. The kids look like beggars and hold up newspapers or cardboard signs to confuse their victims. They scram like stray cats if you're on to them.

Reporting Losses: To report lost or stolen items, file a police report (at Termini Station, with *polizia* at track 11 or with Carabinieri at track 20; offices are also at Piazza Venezia). You'll need the report to file an insurance claim for lost gear, and it can help with replacing your passport—first file the police report, then call your embassy to make an appointment (US embassy: tel. 06-46741, Via Vittorio Veneto 121, www .usembassy.it). For information on how to report lost or stolen credit cards, see page 15.

Emergency Numbers: Police—tel. 113. Ambulance—tel. 118.

Pedestrian Safety: Your main safety concern in Rome is crossing streets safely. Use extreme caution. Scooters don't need to stop at red lights, and even cars exercise what drivers call the "logical option" of not stopping if they see no oncoming traffic. Each year, as noisy gasoline-powered scooters are replaced by electric ones, the streets get quieter (hooray), but more dangerous for pedestrians. Follow locals like a shadow when you cross a street (or spend a good part of your visit stranded on curbs). When you do cross alone, don't be a deer in the headlights. Find a gap in the traffic and walk with confidence while making eye contact with approaching drivers—they won't hit you if they can tell where you intend to go.

Staying/Getting Healthy: The siesta is a key to survival in summertime Rome. Lie down and contemplate the extraordinary power of gravity in the Eternal City. I drink lots of cold, refreshing water from Rome's many drinking fountains (the Forum has three).

There's a pharmacy (marked by a green cross) in every neighborhood. Pharmacies stay open late in Termini Station (daily 7:30-22:00) and at Piazza dei Cinquecento 51 (open 24 hours daily, next to Termini Station on the corner of Via Cavour, tel. 06-488-0019).

Embassies can recommend English-speaking doctors. Consider MEDline, a 24-hour home-medical service; doctors speak English and make calls at hotels for €150 (tel. 06-808-0995). Anyone is entitled to free emergency treatment at public hospitals. The hospital closest to Termini Station is Policlinico Umberto 1 (entrance for emergency treatment on Via Lancisi, translators available, Metro: Policlinico). Readers report that the staff at Santa Susanna Church, home of the American Catholic Church in Rome, offers useful advice and medical referrals (see page 872).

ROME

Rome's Public Transportation

1/4 Kilometer
1/4 Mile

Tiber River

25 · Lepanto · M

492 · Ottaviano · M · 280

Cipro · M · 492 · CASTEL SANT' ANGELO

Valle Aurelia · M · VATICAN MUSEUM · 23

To M Battistini ·

ST. PETER'S

B · 40

25 · 280 · PIAZZA NAVONA

64 · 116

GIANICOLO TERMINAL · 64

64 · 40 · 62

23 · 280

To Civitavecchia

SAN PIETRO STATION · 23 · 280 · 116

CAMPO DE' FIORI

Legend:

- M— Metro Line A
- M— Metro Line B
- 64 ---- Bus Routes
- 117 ──── Elettrico Minibus Routes
- 116 ·······
- ⊢─┤ 8 Tram
- ─ ─ ─ ─ Rail

SANTA MARIA IN TRASTEVERE · B

Piazza Mastai · T · Piazza Belli · 8

23 · 280

To Ostiense & Termini Stations

PORTA PORTESE

Getting Around Rome

Sightsee on foot, by city bus, by Metro, or by taxi. I've grouped your sightseeing into walkable neighborhoods. Make it a point to visit sights in a logical order. Needless backtracking wastes precious time.

The public transportation system, which is cheap and efficient, consists primarily of buses, a few trams, and the two underground subway (Metro) lines. Consider it part of your Roman experience.

The walking-tour company, Rome Walks, has produced an orientation video to Rome's transportation system; find it on You Tube by searching for "Understanding Rome's Public Transport."

For information, visit www.atac.roma.it, which has a useful route planner in English, or call 06-57003.

ROME

Buying Tickets

All public transportation uses the same ticket. It costs €1.50 and is valid for one Metro ride—including transfers underground—plus unlimited city buses and *elettrico* buses during a 100-minute period. Passes good on buses and the Metro are sold in increments of one day (€6, good until midnight), three days (€16.50), one week (€24, about the cost of three taxi rides), and one month (€35, valid for a calendar month).

You can purchase tickets and passes at some newsstands, tobacco shops (*tabacchi*, marked by a black-and-white *T* sign), and major Metro stations and bus stops, but not on board. It's smart to stock up on tickets early, or to buy a pass or a Roma Pass (which includes a three-day transit pass—see page 788). That way, you don't have to run around searching for an open tobacco shop when you spot your bus approaching. Metro stations rarely have human ticket-sellers, and the machines are often either broken or require exact change (it helps to insert your smallest coin first).

Rome's Metro

VILLA BORGHESE

Lepanto — Flaminio

Ottaviano

Line A

PIAZZA DEL POPOLO

Cipro

Valle Aurelia

VATICAN MUSEUM & ST. PETER'S

SPANISH STEPS

Spagna

CAPUCHIN CRYPT

Baldo degli Ubaldi

Barberini

BATHS OF DIOCLETIAN

Cornelia

TREVI FOUNTAIN

Battistini

Repubblica

Cavour

FORUM

Line B

ST. PETER IN CHAINS

COLOSSEUM

Colosseo

	Metro Line A
	Metro Line B
	Rail
	Bus
FORUM	Sights Near Metro Stations

Circo Massimo

BATHS OF CARACALLA

TESTACCIO

Piramide

Ostiense Station

Garbatella

San Paolo Basilica

Tiber River

Marconi

E.U.R.

E.U.R. Magliana

E.U.R. Fermi

E.U.R. Palasport

To Ostia Antica

Laurentina

ROME

Validate your ticket by sticking it in the Metro turnstile (magnetic-strip-side up, arrow-side first) or in the machine when you board the bus (magnetic-strip-side down, arrow-side first)—watch others and imitate. It'll return your ticket with your expiration time printed. To get through a Metro turnstile with a transit pass or Roma Pass, use it just like a ticket (on buses, however, you need to validate your pass only if that's your first time using it).

By Metro

The Roman subway system (Metropolitana, or "Metro") is simple, with two clean, cheap, fast lines—A and B—that intersect at Termini Station. The Metro runs from 5:30 to 23:30 (Fri-Sat until 1:30 in the morning). The subway's first and last compartments are generally the least crowded (and the least likely to harbor pickpockets).

ROME

You'll notice lots of big holes in the city as a new line is built. Line C, from the Colosseum to Largo Argentina, will likely be done in 2020. Because of this construction, you may find the system closed at 21:00 on some nights.

While much of Rome is not served by its skimpy subway, the following stops are helpful:

Termini (intersection of lines A and B): Termini Station, shuttle train to airport, National Museum of Rome, and recommended hotels

Repubblica (line A): Baths of Diocletian, Via Nazionale, and recommended hotels

Barberini (line A): Capuchin Crypt, Trevi Fountain, and Villa Borghese

Spagna (line A): Spanish Steps and classy shopping area

Flaminio (line A): Piazza del Popolo, start of recommended "Dolce Vita Stroll" down Via del Corso

Ottaviano (line A): St. Peter's Basilica, Vatican Museum, and recommended hotels

Tiburtina (line B): Tiburtina train and bus station

Colosseo (line B): Colosseum, Roman Forum, bike rental, and recommended hotels

Piramide (line B): Protestant Cemetery, Testaccio, and trains to Ostia Antica

E.U.R. (line B): Mussolini's futuristic suburb

By Bus

The Metro is handy, but it won't get you everywhere—take the bus. Bus routes are clearly listed at the stops. TIs usually don't have bus maps, but with some knowledge of major stops, you won't necessarily need one (though if you do want a route map, find one printed inside the free-at-hotels *Evento* magazine, or buy it from tobacco shops).

Buses—especially the touristy #40 and #64—are havens

for thieves and pickpockets. Assume any commotion is a thief-created distraction. If one bus is packed, there's likely a second one on its tail with far fewer crowds and thieves. Once you know the bus system, you'll find it's easier than searching for a cab.

ROME

Tickets have a barcode and must be stamped on the bus in the yellow box with the digital readout (be sure to retrieve your ticket).

 Validate your ticket as you board (magnetic-strip-side down, arrow-side first), otherwise you're cheating. While relatively safe, riding without a stamped ticket on the bus is stressful. Inspectors fine even innocent-looking tourists €50. There's no need to validate a transit pass or Roma Pass on the bus, unless your pass is new and hasn't yet been stamped elsewhere in the transit system. Bus etiquette (not always followed) is to board at the front or rear doors and exit at the middle.

Regular bus lines start running at about 5:30, and during the day they run every 5-10 minutes. After 23:30, and sometimes earlier (such as on Sundays), buses are less frequent but still dependable. Night buses are also reliable, and are marked with an *N* and an owl symbol on the bus-stop signs.

These are the major bus routes:

Bus #64: This bus cuts across the city, linking Termini Station with the Vatican, stopping at Piazza della Repubblica (sights), Via Nazionale (recommended hotels), Piazza Venezia (near Forum), Largo Argentina (near Pantheon), St. Peter's Basilica (get off just past the tunnel), and San Pietro Station. Ride it for a city overview and to watch pickpockets in action. The #64 can get horribly crowded.

Bus #40: This express bus, which mostly follows the #64 route (but branches off on the Vatican side of the river), is especially helpful—fewer stops and crowds.

The following three routes conveniently connect Trastevere with other parts of Rome:

Bus #H: This express bus, linking Termini Station and Trastevere, makes a few stops on Via Nazionale (for Trastevere, get off at Piazza Belli, just after crossing the Tiber River).

Bus #8: This tram connects Largo Argentina with Trastevere (get off at Piazza Belli).

Buses #23 and #280: These link the Vatican with Trastevere and Testaccio, stopping at the Vatican Museum (nearest stop is Via Leone IV), Castel Sant'Angelo, Trastevere (Piazza Belli), Porta Portese (Sunday flea market), and Piramide (Metro and gateway to Testaccio).

Other useful routes include:

Bus #62: Largo Argentina to St. Peter's Square.

Bus #81: San Giovanni in Laterano, Largo Argentina, and Piazza Risorgimento (Vatican).

ROME

Buses #85 and #87: Piazza Venezia, Colosseum, San Clemente, and San Giovanni in Laterano.

Bus #492: Travels east-west across the city, connecting Tiburtina (train and bus stations), Largo Santa Susanna (near Piazza della Repubblica), Piazza Barberini, Piazza Venezia, Largo Argentina, Piazza Cavour (Castel Sant'Angelo), and Piazza Risorgimento (St. Peter's Basilica and Vatican).

Bus #714: Termini Station, Santa Maria Maggiore, San Giovanni in Laterano, Terme di Caracalla (Baths of Caracalla), and on to E.U.R.

***Elettrico* Minibuses:** Two cute *elettrico* minibuses that wind through the narrow streets of old and interesting neighborhoods are great for transport or simple joyriding. ***Elettrico* #116** runs through the medieval core of Rome: Ponte Vittorio Emanuele II (near Castel Sant'Angelo) to Campo de' Fiori, Pantheon, Piazza Barberini, and the southern edge of the scenic Villa Borghese Gardens. ***Elettrico* #117** connects San Giovanni in Laterano, Colosseo, Via dei Serpenti, Trevi Fountain, Piazza di Spagna, and Piazza del Popolo—and vice versa. Where Via del Corso hits Piazza del Popolo, a #117 is usually parked and ready to go. Riding it from here to the end of the line, San Giovanni in Laterano, makes for a fine joyride that leaves you, conveniently, at a great sight.

By Taxi

I use taxis in Rome more often than in other cities. They're reasonable and useful for efficient sightseeing in this big, hot metropolis.

Taxis start at €3, then charge about €1.30 per kilometer (surcharges: €1.50 on Sun, €3.50 for nighttime hours of 22:00-7:00, one regular suitcase or bag rides free, tip by rounding up to the nearest euro). Sample fares: Termini Station to Vatican-€10; Termini Station to Colosseum-€6; Colosseum to Trastevere-€7 (or look up your route at www.worldtaximeter.com). Three or four companions with more money than time should taxi almost everywhere.

It's tough to wave down a taxi in Rome, especially at night. Find the nearest taxi stand by asking a passerby or a clerk in a shop, *"Dov'è una fermata dei taxi?"* (doh-VEH OO-nah fehr-MAH-tah DEHee TAHK-see). Some taxi stands are listed on my maps. To save time and energy, have your hotel or restaurant call a taxi for you; the meter starts when the call is received (generally adding a euro or two to the bill). To call a cab on your own, dial 06-4994 or 06-6645. It's routine for Romans to ask the waiter in a restaurant to call a taxi when they ask for the bill. The waiter will tell you how many minutes you have to enjoy your coffee.

Beware of corrupt taxis. A common cabbie scam is to take your €20 note, drop it, and pick up a €5 note (similar color), claiming that's what you gave him. To avoid this scam, pay in small bills; if you only have a large bill, show it to the cabbie as you state its face value. Keep an eye on the meter, if the cabbie turns it off abruptly when he stops and announces a too-high fare, you'll know what you owe.

If hailing a cab on the street, be sure the meter is restarted when you get in (should be around €3, or around €5 if you or your hotelier phoned for the taxi). Many meters show both the fare and the time elapsed during the ride—and some tourists pay €10 for an eight-minute trip (more than the fair meter rate).

When you arrive at the train station or airport, beware of hustlers conning naive visitors into unmarked, rip-off "express taxis." Only use official taxis, with a *taxi* sign and phone number marked on the door. By law, they must display a multilingual official price chart. If you have any problems with a taxi, point to the chart and ask the cabbie to explain it to you. Making a show of writing down the taxi number (to file a complaint) can motivate a driver to quickly settle the matter.

If you take a Rome city cab from Fiumicino Airport to anywhere in central Rome within the old city walls, the cost should be €48 (covering up to four people and their bags); however, every year some readers report being ripped off. The catch is that cabbies *not* based in Rome or Fiumicino can charge €70. At the airport, look specifically for a Rome city cab, with the "SPQR" shield on the door. By law, they can charge only €48 for the ride (still, be sure to establish the price before you get in).

Tired travelers arriving at the airport will likely find it less stressful to take an airport shuttle van to their hotel, or catch the train to Termini Station and take the Metro or a cheaper taxi from there (see page 926 for details on getting from the airport to downtown Rome via taxi, shuttle, or train).

By Bike

Biking in the big city of Rome can speed up sightseeing or simply be an enjoyable way to explore. Though Roman traffic can be stressful, Roman drivers are respectful of cyclists. Still, use caution and never assume the right of way. The best rides are on small streets in the city center. A bike path along the banks of the Tiber River makes a good 20-minute ride (easily accessed from the ramps at Porta Portese and Ponte Regina Margherita near Piazza del Popolo). Get a bike with a well-padded seat—the little stones that pave Roman streets are unforgiving.

ROME

Top Bike Rental and Tours is professionally run by Roman bike enthusiasts who want to show off their city. Your rental comes with a handy map that suggests a route and indicates less-trafficked streets. Owner Ciro also offers four-hour-long English-only guided tours around the city and the Ancient Appian Way; check his website for days and times (rental: €15/day, 10 percent discount with this book, best to reserve in advance via email; bike tours: start at €35, reservations required; daily 10:00-19:00, leave ID for deposit, from Santa Maria Maggiore go up Via dell'Olmata and turn left at the end of the block, Via dei Quattro Cantoni 40, tel. 06-488-2893, www.topbikerental.com, info@topbikerental.com).

Cool Rent, near the Colosseo Metro stop, is cheaper but less helpful (€3/hour, €10/day, 3-person bike cart €10/hour, daily 9:30-20:00, driver's license or other ID for deposit, 10 yards to the right as you exit the Metro). A second outlet is just off Via del Corso (on Largo di Lombardi, near corner of Via del Corso and Via della Croce, mobile 388-695-9303, Sasin).

Tours in Rome

Walking Tours

Finding the best guided tours in Rome is challenging. Local guides are good but pricey. Tour companies are cheaper, but quality and organization are unreliable. To sightsee on your own, download my series of free audio tours that illuminate some of Rome's top sights and neighborhoods (see sidebar on page 1101 for details).

If you do hire a private Italian guide, consider organizing a group of four to six people from your hotel to split the cost (€180 for a half-day tour); this ends up costing about the same per person as going on a scheduled tour from one of the walking-tour companies listed below (about €25, generally expat guides).

Local Guides—I've worked with each of these licensed independent local guides. They're worth every euro. They speak excellent English and enjoy tailoring tours to your interests. Their prices (roughly €50/hour) flex with the day, season, and demand. Arrange your date and price by email.

Francesca Caruso loves to teach and share her appreciation of her city, and has contributed generously to this chapter (francescainroma@gmail.com). Popular with my readers, Francesca understandably books up quickly; if she's busy, she'll recommend one of her colleagues. **Carla Zaia** is an engaging expert on all things Roman (mobile 349-759-0723, carlaromeguide@gmail.com). **Cristina Giannicchi** has an archaeology background (mobile 338-111-4573, www.crisacross.com, crisgiannicchi@gmail.com). **Sara Magister** is a Roman with a doctorate in art history and author of a book on Renaissance Rome (mobile 339-379-3813, a.magister

ROME

@iol.it). **Giovanna Terzulli** is a personable, knowledgeable art historian (terzulli@tiscali.it). **Alessandra Mazzoccoli** is experienced, easygoing, and good with all ages (alemazzoccoli@gmail.com). Italian-American **Sean Finelli,** known as "The Roman Guy," offers several walking tours and a trip-planning service (www.theromanguy.com).

Walking-Tour Companies—Rome has many highly competitive tour companies, each offering a series of themed walks through various slices of Rome. Three-hour guided walks generally cost €25-30 per person. Guides are usually native English speakers, often American expats. Tours are limited to small groups, geared to American tourists, and given in English only. I've listed some here, but without a lot of details on their offerings. Before your trip, spend some time on these companies' websites to get to know your options, as each company has a particular teaching and guiding personality. Some are highbrow, and others are less scholarly. It's sometimes required, and always smart, to book a spot in advance (easy online). I must add that we get a lot of negative feedback on some of these tour companies. Readers report that their advertising can be misleading, and scheduling mishaps are common.

Context Rome's walking tours are more intellectual than most, designed for travelers with longer-than-average attention spans. They are more expensive than others and are led by "docents" rather than guides (tel. 06-9672-7371, US tel. 800-691-6036, www.contextrome.com). **Enjoy Rome** offers a number of different walks and a website filled with helpful information (Via Marghera 8a, tel. 06-445-1843, www.enjoyrome.com, info@enjoyrome.com). **Rome Walks** has put together several particularly creative itineraries (mobile 347-795-5175, www.romewalks.com, info@romewalks.com, Annie). **Roman Odyssey** gives readers of this book a 10 percent discount on their walks (tel. 06-580-9902, mobile 328-912-3720, www.romanodyssey.com, Rahul). **Through Eternity** offers travelers with this book a 10 percent discount on most tours and a 20 percent discount on its Underground Rome; book through their website for the best discount (tel. 06-700-9336, mobile 347-336-5298, www.throetheternity.com, office@througheternity.com, Rob). **Walks of Italy** has fun guides who lead a variety of good walks for groups no bigger than 12 people at a time (10 percent discount for readers of this book, US tel. 202/684-6916, Italian mobile 334-974-4274, www.walksofitaly.com, Jason Spiehler).

Hop-on, Hop-off Bus Tours

Several different agencies, including the ATAC public bus company, run hop-on, hop-off tours around Rome. These tours are constantly evolving and offer varying combinations of sights. You can grab one (and pay as you board) at any stop; Termini Station

ROME

and Piazza Venezia are handy hubs. Although the city is perfectly walkable and traffic jams can make the bus dreadfully slow, these open-top bus tours remain popular.

Trambus 110 seems to be the best. Operated by the ATAC city-bus lines, it offers an orientation tour on big red double-

decker buses with an open-air upper deck. In less than two hours, you'll have 80 sights pointed out to you (with a next-to-worthless recorded narration). While you can hop on and off, the service can be erratic (mobbed midday, not ideal in bad weather), and it can be very slow in heavy traffic. It's best to think of this as a two-hour quickie orientation with scant information and lots of images. Stops include Ara Pacis, Piazza Cavour, St. Peter's Square, Corso Vittorio Emanuele (for Piazza Navona), Piazza Venezia, Colosseum, and Via Nazionale. Bus #110 departs every 20 minutes. You can catch it at any stop, including Termini Station. Buy the ticket as you board (runs daily April-Oct 8:30-20:30, shorter hours off-season, single tour-€12, 48-hour ticket-€18, tel. 800-281-281, www.trambusopen.com).

Archeobus is an open-top bus, also operated by ATAC, that runs twice hourly from Termini Station out to the ancient

Appian Way (with stops at the Colosseum, Baths of Caracalla, San Callisto, San Sebastiano, and the Tomb of Cecilia Metella). This is a handy way to see the sights down this ancient Roman road, but it can be frustrating for various reasons—sparse narration, sporadic service, and not ideal for hopping on and off (€15, €25 combo-ticket with Trambus 110, ticket valid 48 hours, 1.5-hour loop, daily 9:00-16:30, less frequent off-season, from Termini Station and Piazza Venezia, tel. 800-281-281, www.trambusopen.com). A similar bus laces together all the Christian sights.

Car and Minibus Tours

Autoservizi Monti Concezio, run by gentle, capable, and English-speaking Ezio, offers private cars or minibuses with driver/guides (car-€40/hour, minibus-€45/hour, 3-hour minimum for city sightseeing, long rides outside Rome are more expensive, mobile 335-636-5907 or 349-674-5643, www.tourservicemonti.it, info@tourservicemonti.it).

ROME

Miles & Miles Private Tours is a family-run company offering a number of tours (all explained on their website) in Mercedes minibuses and cars, all with good English-speaking driver/guides (€60/hour for up to 8 people, 5-hour minimum, Rick Steves readers booking direct get a 10 percent discount off any web prices they offer, mobile 331-466-4900, www.milesandmiles.net, info @milesandmiles.net, Francesco answers the mobile phone, while Kimberly—an American—runs their office). They can also provide unguided long-distance transportation; if traveling with a small group or a family from Rome to Florence or the Amalfi Coast, consider paying extra to turn the trip into a memorable day tour with door-to-door service.

Weekend Tour Packages for Students in Rome

Andy Steves (Rick's son) runs Weekend Student Adventures, offering experimental three-day weekend tours for €200-300, designed for American students studying abroad; see www.wsaeurope.com for details on tours of Rome and other great cities.

Self-Guided Walks in Rome

Here are three walks that give you a moving picture of Rome, an ancient yet modern city. You'll walk through history (Roman Forum Walk), take a refreshing early-evening walk (Dolce Vita Stroll), and enjoy the thriving local scene, best at night (Heart of Rome Walk).

Roman Forum Walk

The Forum was the political, religious, and commercial center of the city. Rome's most important temples and halls of justice were

here. This was the place for religious processions, political demonstrations, elections, important speeches, and parades by conquering generals. As Rome's empire expanded, these few acres of land became the center of the civilized world.

ROME

Cost: €12 combo-ticket covers both the Roman Forum/Palatine Hill (grouped as one sight for the purposes of the ticket) and the Colosseum; also covered by the Roma Pass. The combo-ticket is valid two consecutive days, but once your ticket is scanned for either the Forum/Palatine Hill or the Colosseum, you can't re-enter that sight (even the next day).

Hours: The Roman Forum, Colosseum, and Palatine Hill are all open daily 8:30 until one hour before sunset: April-Sept until 19:15, Oct until 18:30, Nov-mid-Feb until 16:30, mid-Feb-mid-March until 17:00, mid-March-late March until 17:30; last entry one hour before closing.

Avoiding Lines: See "Avoiding Lines" on page 827.

Getting There: The closest Metro stop is Colosseo. The Forum has two entrances. The main entrance is on Via dei Fori Imperiali ("Road of the Imperial Forums"). From the Colosseo Metro stop, walk away from the Colosseum on Via dei Fori Imperiali to find the low-profile Forum ticket office (look closely), located where Via Cavour spills into Via dei Fori Imperiali.

The other entrance is at the Palatine Hill ticket office on Via di San Gregorio—after buying your ticket, take the path to the right (not up the hill), and wind around to enter the Forum at the Arch of Titus.

Information: A free visitors center (called I Fori di Roma), located across Via dei Fori Imperiali from the Forum's main entrance, has a TI (which sells the Roma Pass), bookshop, small café, WCs, and a film (daily 9:30-18:30). A bookstore is at the Forum entrance. Vendors at outside sell *Rome: Past and Present* books with plastic overlays that restore the ruins (includes DVD, smaller book marked €15, prices soft, so offer €10). Info office tel. 06-3996-7700, http://archeoroma.beniculturali.it/en.

Tours: An unexciting yet informative **audioguide** helps decipher the rubble (€5/2 hours, €7 version includes Palatine Hill and lasts 3 hours, must leave ID), but you'll have to return it to one of the Forum entrances instead of being able to exit directly to Capitoline Hill or the Colosseum. Official **guided tours** in English might be available (inquire at ticket office). You can download this walk as a free Rick Steves **audio tour** (see page 1101).

With Limited Time: Walk from the Arch of Titus to the Arch of Septimius Severus. Don't miss the Basilica of Constantine hiding behind the trees.

Services: WCs are at the main entrance and in the middle of the Forum, near #8 on the map.

Plan Ahead: The ancient paving at the Forum is uneven; wear sturdy shoes. I carry a water bottle and refill it at the Forum's public drinking fountains.

• *Start at the Arch of Titus (Arco di Tito). It's the white triumphal arch that rises above the rubble on the east end of the Forum (closest to the Colosseum). Stand at the viewpoint alongside the arch and gaze over the valley known as the Forum.*

❶ **Arch of Titus (Arco di Tito):** The Arch of Titus commemorated the Roman victory over the province of Judaea (Israel) in A.D. 70. The Romans had a reputation as benevolent conquerors who tolerated the local customs and rulers. All they required was

Roman Forum

Not to Scale

CAPITOLINE HILL

VICTOR EMMANUEL MONUMENT

To Piazza Venezia

To Gaul

STEPS TO CAPITOLINE HILL

EXIT

CAESAR'S FORUM

TRAJAN'S FORUM

VIA DEI FORI IMPERIALI

FORUM SQUARE

WC

PALATINE HILL

CIRCUS MAXIMUS

VIA SACRA

MAIN ENTRANCE

I FORI DI ROMA VISITORS CENTER

TICKET OFFICE & WC

"WATCH ROME GROW" MAPS

ROMAN FORUM

ACCESS BETWEEN FORUM & PALATINE HILL

TO CLIMB PALATINE HILL

DIRECT TO FORUM

PALATINE HILL TICKET OFFICE

S. FRANCESCA ROMANA

TOUR BEGINS

TEMPLE OF VENUS & ROME

EXIT

VIA DI SAN GREGORIO

To Carthage

ARCH OF CONSTANTINE

COLOSSEUM

Colosseo M

① Arch of Titus
② Basilica of Constantine
③ The Forum's Main Square
④ Temple of Julius Caesar
⑤ Temple of Antoninus Pius & Faustina
⑥ Basilica Aemilia
⑦ Caligula's Palace
⑧ Temple of Vesta
⑨ House of the Vestal Virgins
⑩ The Curia
⑪ Rostrum
⑫ Arch of Septimius Severus
⑬ Temple of Saturn
⑭ Column of Phocas

ROME

allegiance to the empire, shown by worshipping the emperor as a god. No problem for most conquered people, who already had half a dozen gods on their prayer lists anyway. But Israelites believed in only one god, and it wasn't the emperor. Israel revolted. After a short but bitter war, the Romans defeated the rebels, took Jerusalem, destroyed their temple (leaving only the foundation wall—today's revered "Wailing Wall"), and brought home 50,000 Jewish slaves... who were forced to build this arch (and the Colosseum).

• *Walk down the Via Sacra into the Forum. After about 50 yards, turn right and follow a path uphill to the three huge arches of the...*

❷ Basilica of Constantine (a.k.a. Basilica Maxentius): Yes, these are big arches. But they represent only one-third of the original Basilica of Constantine, a mammoth hall of justice. The arches were matched by a similar set along the Via Sacra side (only a few squat brick piers remain). Between them ran the central hall, which was spanned by a roof 130 feet high—about 55 feet higher than the side arches you see. (The stub of brick you see sticking up began an arch that once spanned the central hall.) The hall itself was as long as a football field, lavishly furnished with colorful inlaid marble, a gilded bronze ceiling, and statues, and filled with strolling Romans. At the far (west) end was an enormous marble statue of Emperor Constantine on a throne. (Pieces of this statue, including a hand the size of a man, are on display in Rome's Capitoline Museums.)

The basilica was begun by the emperor Maxentius, but after he was trounced in battle (see page 830), the victor Constantine completed the massive building. No doubt about it, the Romans built monuments on a more epic scale than any previous Europeans, wowing their "barbarian" neighbors.

• *Now stroll deeper into the Forum, downhill along the Via Sacra, through the trees. Many of the large basalt stones under your feet were walked on by Caesar Augustus 2,000 years ago. Pass by the only original bronze door still swinging on its ancient hinges (the green door at the Tempio di Romolo, on the right—if it happens to be open, peek in), and continue between ruined buildings until the Via Sacra opens up to a flat, grassy area.*

❸ The Forum's Main Square: The original Forum, or main square, was this flat patch about the size of a football field, stretching to the foot of Capitoline Hill. Surrounding it were temples, law courts, government buildings, and triumphal arches.

Rome was born right here. According to legend, twin brothers Romulus (Rome) and Remus were orphaned in infancy and raised by a she-wolf on top of Palatine Hill. Growing up, they found it hard to get dates. So they and their cohorts attacked the nearby Sabine tribe and kidnapped their women. After they made peace, this marshy valley became the meeting place and then the trading center for the scattered tribes on the surrounding hillsides.

ROME

Rome: Republic and Empire
(500 B.C.-A.D. 500)

Ancient Rome spanned a thousand years, from about 500 B.C. to A.D. 500. During that time, Rome expanded from a small tribe of barbarians to a vast empire, then dwindled slowly to city size again. For the first 500 years, when Rome's armies made her ruler of the Italian peninsula and beyond, Rome was a republic governed by elected senators. Over the next 500 years, a time of world conquest and eventual decline, Rome was an empire ruled by a military-backed dictator.

Julius Caesar bridged the gap between republic and empire. This ambitious general and politician, popular with the people because of his military victories and charisma, suspended the Roman constitution and assumed dictatorial powers in about 50 B.C. A few years later, he was assassinated by a conspiracy of senators. His adopted son, Augustus, succeeded him, and soon "Caesar" was not just a name but a title.

Emperor Augustus ushered in the Pax Romana, or Roman peace (A.D. 1-200), a time when Rome reached her peak and controlled an empire that stretched even beyond Eurail—from England to Egypt, Turkey to Morocco.

The square was the busiest and most crowded—and often the seediest—section of town. Besides the senators, politicians, and currency exchangers, there were even sleazier types—souvenir hawkers, pickpockets, fortune-tellers, gamblers, slave marketers, drunks, hookers, lawyers, and tour guides.

The Forum is now rubble, but imagine it in its prime: blindingly brilliant marble buildings with 40-foot-high columns and shining metal roofs; rows of statues painted in realistic colors; processional chariots rattling down the Via Sacra. Mentally replace tourists in T-shirts with tribunes in togas. Imagine the buildings towering and the people buzzing around you while an orator gives a rabble-rousing speech from the Rostrum. If things still look like just a pile of rocks, at least tell yourself, "But Julius Caesar once leaned against these rocks."

• *At the near (east) end of the main square (the Colosseum is to the east) are the foundations of a temple now capped with a peaked wood-and-metal roof.*

❹ **Temple of Julius Caesar (Tempio del Divo Giulio, or Ara di Cesare):** Julius Caesar's body was burned on this spot (under the metal roof) after his assassination. Peek behind the wall into the small apse area, where a mound of dirt usually has fresh flowers—given to remember the man who, more than any other, personified the greatness of Rome.

Caesar (100-44 B.C.) changed Rome—and the Forum—dramatically. He cleared out many of the wooden market stalls and began to ring the square with even grander buildings. Caesar's house was located behind the temple, near that clump of trees. He walked right by here on the day he was assassinated ("Beware the Ides of March!" warned a street-corner Etruscan preacher).

Though he was popular with the masses, not everyone liked Caesar's urban design or his politics. When he assumed dictatorial powers, he was ambushed and stabbed to death by a conspiracy of senators, including his adopted son, Brutus *("Et tu, Brute?")*.

The funeral was held here, facing the main square. The citizens gathered, and speeches were made. Mark Antony stood up to say (in Shakespeare's words), "Friends, Romans, countrymen, lend me your ears. I come to bury Caesar, not to praise him." When Caesar's body was burned, the citizens who still loved him threw anything at hand on the fire, requiring the fire department to come put it out. Later, Emperor Augustus dedicated this temple in his name, making Caesar the first Roman to become a god.

• *Behind and to the left of the Temple of Julius Caesar are 10 tall columns. These belong to the...*

❺ **Temple of Antoninus Pius and Faustina:** The Senate built this temple to honor Emperor Antoninus Pius (A.D. 138-161) and his deified wife, Faustina. The 50-foot-tall Corinthian (leafy) columns must have been awe-inspiring to out-of-towners who grew up in thatched huts. Although the temple has been inhabited by a church, you can still see the basic layout—a staircase led to a shaded porch (the columns), which admitted you to the main building (now a church), where the statue of the god sat. Originally, these columns supported a triangular pediment decorated with sculptures.

Picture these columns, with gilded capitals, supporting brightly painted statues in the pediment, and the whole building capped with a gleaming bronze roof. The stately gray rubble of today's Forum is a faded black-and-white photograph of a 3-D Technicolor era.

The building is a microcosm of many changes that occurred after Rome fell. In medieval times, the temple was pillaged. Note the diagonal cuts high on the marble columns—a failed attempt by scavengers to cut through the pillars to pull them down for their precious stone. (They used vinegar and rope to cut the marble... but because vinegar also eats through rope, they abandoned the attempt.) In 1550, a church was housed inside the ancient temple. The green door shows the street level at the time of Michelangelo. The long staircase was underground until excavated in the 1800s.

• *There's a ramp next to the Temple of A. and F. Walk halfway up it and look to the left to view the...*

❻ **Basilica Aemilia:** A basilica was a covered public forum, often serving as a Roman hall of justice. In a society that was as legal-minded as America is today, you needed a lot of lawyers—and a big place to put them. Citizens came here to work out matters such as inheritances and building permits, or to sue somebody.

Notice the layout. It was a long, rectangular building. The stubby columns all in a row form one long, central hall flanked by two side aisles. Medieval Christians required a larger meeting hall for their worship services than Roman temples provided, so they used the spacious Roman basilica as the model for their churches. Cathedrals from France to Spain to England, from Romanesque to Gothic to Renaissance, all have the same basic floor plan as a Roman basilica.

• *Return again to the Temple of Julius Caesar. To the right of the temple are the three tall Corinthian columns of the Temple of Castor and Pollux. Beyond that is Palatine Hill—the corner of which may have been...*

❼ **Caligula's Palace (a.k.a. the Palace of Tiberius):** Emperor Caligula (ruled A.D. 37-41) had a huge palace on Palatine Hill overlooking the Forum. It actually sprawled down the hill into the Forum (some supporting arches remain in the hillside).

Caligula was not a nice person. He tortured enemies, stole senators' wives, and parked his chariot in handicap spaces. But Rome's luxury-loving emperors only added to the glory of the Forum, with each one trying to make his mark on history.

• *To the left of the Temple of Castor and Pollux, find the remains of a small white circular temple.*

❽ **Temple of Vesta:** This is perhaps Rome's most sacred spot. Rome considered itself one big family, and this temple represented a circular hut, like the kind that Rome's first families lived in. Inside, a fire burned, just as in a Roman home. And back in the days before lighters and butane, you never wanted your fire to go out. As long as the sacred flame burned, Rome would stand. The flame was tended by priestesses known as Vestal Virgins.

• *Around the back of the Temple of Vesta, you'll find two rectangular brick pools. These stood in the courtyard of the...*

❾ **House of the Vestal Virgins:** The Vestal Virgins lived in a two-story building surrounding a long central courtyard with these two pools at one end. Rows of statues depicting leading Vestal Virgins flanked the courtyard. This place was the model—both architecturally and sexually—for medieval convents and monasteries.

Chosen from noble families before they reached the age of 10, the six Vestal Virgins served a 30-year term. Honored and revered by the Romans, the Vestals even had their own box opposite the emperor in the Colosseum. The statues that line the courtyard honor dutiful Vestals.

ROME

As the name implies, a Vestal took a vow of chastity. If she served her term faithfully—abstaining for 30 years—she was given a huge dowry and allowed to marry. But if they found any Virgin who wasn't, she was strapped to a funeral car, paraded through the streets of the Forum, taken to a crypt, given a loaf of bread and a lamp...and buried alive. Many women suffered the latter fate.

• *Return to the Temple of Julius Caesar and head to the Forum's west end (opposite the Colosseum). As you pass alongside the big open space of the Forum's main square, consider how the piazza is still a standard part of any Italian town. It has reflected and accommodated the gregarious and outgoing nature of the Italian people since Roman times.*

Stop at the big, well-preserved brick building (on right) with the triangular roof. Look in at...

❿ The Curia (Senate House): The Curia was the most important political building in the Forum. While the present building dates from A.D. 283, this was the site of Rome's official center of government since the birth of the republic. (Ongoing archaeological work may restrict access to the Curia, as well as the Arch of Septimius Severus—described later—and the exit to Capitoline Hill.) Three hundred senators, elected by the citizens of Rome, met here to debate and create the laws of the land. Their wooden seats once circled the building in three tiers; the Senate president's podium sat at the far end. The marble floor is from ancient times. Listen to the echoes in this vast room—the acoustics are great.

Rome prided itself on being a republic. Early in the city's history, its people threw out the king and established rule by elected representatives. Each Roman citizen was free to speak his mind and have a say in public policy. Even when emperors became the supreme authority, the Senate was a power to be reckoned with. The Curia building is well-preserved, having been used as a church since early Christian times. In the 1930s, it was restored and opened to the public as a historic site. (Note: Although Julius Caesar was assassinated in "the Senate," it wasn't here—the Senate was temporarily meeting across town.)

A statue and two reliefs inside the Curia help build our mental image of the Forum. The statue, made of porphyry marble in about A.D. 100 (with its head, arms, and feet now missing), was a tribute to an emperor, probably Hadrian or Trajan. The two relief panels may have decorated the Rostrum. Those on the left show people (with big stone tablets) standing in line to burn their debt records following a government amnesty. The other shows the distribution of grain (Rome's welfare system), some buildings in the background, and the latest fashion in togas.

• *Go back down the Senate steps and find the 10-foot-high wall just to the left of the big arch, marked...*

Rome Falls

Remember that Rome lasted 1,000 years—500 years of growth, 200 years of peak power, and 300 years of gradual decay. The fall had many causes, among them the barbarians who pecked away at Rome's borders. Christians blamed the fall on moral decay. Pagans blamed it on Christians. Socialists blamed it on a shallow economy based on the spoils of war. (Republicans blamed it on Democrats.) Whatever the reasons, the far-flung empire could no longer keep its grip on conquered lands, and it pulled back. Barbarian tribes from Germany and Asia attacked the Italian peninsula and even looted Rome itself in A.D. 410, leveling many of the buildings in the Forum. In 476, when the last emperor checked out and switched off the lights, Europe plunged into centuries of ignorance, poverty, and weak government—the Dark Ages.

But Rome lived on in the Catholic Church. Christianity was the state religion of Rome's last generations. Emperors became popes (both called themselves "Pontifex Maximus"), senators became bishops, orators became priests, and basilicas became churches. The glory of Rome remains eternal.

❶ Rostrum (Rostri): Nowhere was Roman freedom more apparent than at this "Speaker's Corner." The Rostrum was a raised platform, 10 feet high and 80 feet long, decorated with statues, columns, and the prows of ships (rostra).

On a stage like this, Rome's orators, great and small, tried to draw a crowd and sway public opinion. Mark Antony rose to offer Caesar the laurel-leaf crown of kingship, which Caesar publicly (and hypocritically) refused while privately becoming a dictator. Men such as Cicero railed against the corruption and decadence that came with the city's newfound wealth. In later years, daring citizens even spoke out against the emperors, reminding them that Rome was once free. Picture the backdrop these speakers would have had—a mountain of marble buildings piling up on Capitoline Hill.

In front of the Rostrum are trees bearing fruits that were sacred to the ancient Romans: olives (provided food, light, and preservatives), figs (tasty), and wine grapes (made a popular export product).

• *The big arch to the right of the Rostrum is the...*

⑫ Arch of Septimius Severus: In imperial times, the Rostrum's voices of democracy would have been dwarfed by images of the empire, such as the huge six-story-high Arch of Septimius Severus (A.D. 203). The reliefs commemorate the African-born emperor's battles in Mesopotamia. Near ground level, see soldiers marching captured barbarians back to Rome for the victory parade. Despite Severus' efficient rule, Rome's empire was crumbling under the weight of its own corruption, disease, decaying infrastructure, and the constant attacks by foreign "barbarians."

• *Pass underneath the Arch of Septimius Severus and turn left. If the path is blocked, backtrack toward the Temple of Julius Caesar and around the square. On the slope of Capitoline Hill are the eight remaining columns of the...*

⑬ Temple of Saturn: These columns framed the entrance to the Forum's oldest temple (497 B.C.). Inside was a humble, very old wooden statue of the god Saturn. But the statue's pedestal held the gold bars, coins, and jewels of Rome's state treasury, the booty collected by conquering generals.

• *Standing here, at one of the Forum's first buildings, look east at the lone, tall...*

⑭ Column of Phocas—Rome's Fall: This is the Forum's last monument (A.D. 608), a gift from the powerful Byzantine Empire to a fallen empire—Rome. Given to commemorate the pagan Pantheon's becoming a Christian church, it's like a symbolic last nail in ancient Rome's coffin. After Rome's 1,000-year reign, the city was looted by Vandals, the population of a million-plus shrank to about 10,000, and the once-grand city center—the Forum—was abandoned, slowly covered up by centuries of silt and dirt. In the 1700s, an English historian named Edward Gibbon overlooked this spot from Capitoline Hill.

Hearing Christian monks singing at these pagan ruins, he looked out at the few columns poking up from the ground, pondered the decline and fall of the Roman Empire, and thought, "Hmm, that's a catchy title...."

• *From here, you have several options:*

1. *Exiting past the Arch of Titus lands you at the Colosseum (page 825).*
2. *Exiting past the Arch of Septimius Severus leads you to the stairs up to Capitoline Hill (page 835).*
3. *The Forum's main entrance spills you back out onto Via dei Fori Imperiali (for Trajan's Column, Market, and Museum of the Imperial Forums, page 834).*
4. *From the Arch of Titus, you can climb Palatine Hill (page 832).*

ROME

▲▲Dolce Vita Stroll

This is the city's chic stroll, from Piazza del Popolo (Metro: Flaminio) down a wonderfully traffic-free section of Via del Corso, and up Via Condotti to the Spanish Steps. It takes place from around 17:00 to 19:00 each evening (Fri and Sat are best), except on Sunday, when it occurs earlier in the afternoon. Leave before 18:00 if you plan to visit the Ara Pacis (Altar of Peace), which closes at 19:00 and is closed Monday.

As you stroll, you'll see shoppers, people-watchers, and flirts on the prowl filling this neighborhood of some of Rome's most fashionable stores (some open after siesta 16:30-19:30). While both the crowds and the shops along Via del Corso have gone downhill recently, elegance survives in the grid of streets between here and the Spanish Steps. If you get hungry during your stroll, see page 918 for descriptions of neighborhood wine bars and restaurants.

To reach **Piazza del Popolo,** where the stroll starts, take Metro line A to Flaminio and walk south to the square. Delightfully car-free, Piazza del Popolo is marked by an obelisk that was brought to Rome by Augustus after he conquered Egypt. (It used to stand in the Circus Maximus.) In medieval times, this area was just inside Rome's main entry (for more background on the square, see page 865).

If starting your stroll early enough, the Baroque church of **Santa Maria del Popolo** is worth popping into (Mon-Sat until 18:30, Sun until 19:30, next to gate in old wall on north side of

---

The *Passeggiata*

Throughout Italy, early evening is time to stroll. While elsewhere in Italy this is called the *passeggiata,* in Rome it's a cruder, big-city version called the *struscio* (meaning "to rub").

Unemployment among Italy's youth is very high; many stay with their parents even into their thirties. They spend a lot of time being trendy and hanging out. Like American kids gathering at the mall, working-class suburban youth *(coatto)* converge on the old center, as there's little to keep them occupied in Rome's dreary outskirts (which lack public spaces). The hot *vroom-vroom* motor scooter is their symbol; haircuts and fashion are follow-the-leader.

In a more genteel small town, the *passeggiata* comes with sweet whispers of *"bella"* and *"bello"* ("pretty" and "handsome"). In Rome, the admiration is stronger, oriented toward consumption—they say *"buona"* and *"buono"*—meaning, roughly, "tasty." But despite how lusty this all sounds, you'll see just as many chunky, middle-aged Italians out and about as hormone-charged youth.

Dolce Vita Stroll

Piazza Flaminio — M Flaminio
SANTA MARIA DEL POPOLO
Piazza del Popolo
WALK BEGINS
Villa Borghese
Galoppatoio
V. L. SAVOIA
FERD. SAVOIA
VIA DI RIPETTA
VIA DEL CORSO
VIA DEL BABUINO
MARGUTTA
VILLA MEDICI
LUNGOTEVERE IN AUGUSTA
Tiber River
ARA PACIS
FREZZA ❷ PONTE
MAUSOLEUM OF AUGUSTUS
Piazza Imperatore
PONTE CAVOUR
VIA VITTORIA ❶
❸ VIA CROCE
Piazza di Spagna — WC M Spagna
VIA CAROZZE
TRINITÀ DEI MONTI
SPANISH STEPS
WALK ENDS FOR (WINDOW) SHOPPERS
VIA SISTINA
McDonald's
PROPA.
T
VIA CONDOTTI
TOMACELLI
VIA BORGOGNONA
VIA FRATTINA ❹
VIA DUE MACELLI
Piazza Barghese
VIA DELLA SCROFA
VIA FONT BORGHESE
Piazza S. Lorenzo
VIA VITE
POST
V. MERCEDE
To Barberini M
Piazza Parlamento
PREFETTI VALD. ❺
CAMPO MARZIO
V. CON
VIA DEL TRITONE
T
PARLIAMENT
Piazza di Montecitorio
Piazza Colonna
T B
SABINA
TREVI FOUNTAIN
PALAZZO DEL QUIRINALE
Piazza di Pietra
MURATTE
UMILTA
DATARIA
Piazza del Quirinale
Piazza Rotonda
CARAVITA
VIA DELLA SCROFA
SAN IGNAZIO
PANTHEON
SANTA MARIA SOPRA MINERVA
Piazza del Collegio Romano
GALLERIA DORIA PAMPHLIJ
VIA DEL CORSO
CORSO VITT. EMANUELE II
Largo Argentina
PLEBISCITO
BATT.
V. N. NOV.
Piazza Venezia
B
TRAJAN'S COLUMN
T
TRAJAN'S MARKET
VIA D'ARA COELI
SAN MARCO
VICTOR EMMANUEL MONUMENT
VIA DEI FORI IMPERIALI
To Colosseum M
200 Meters
200 Yards
CAPITOLINE HILL
GRAND STAIRCASE
WALK ENDS FOR HISTORIANS
Piazza del Campodoglio
FORUM

❶ Ristorante il Gabriello
❷ Osteria Gusto
❸ L'EnotecAntica
❹ Palatium Enoteca Regionale
❺ Trattoria dal Cav. Gino

ROME

square). Inside, look for Raphael's Chigi Chapel (KEE-gee, second chapel on left) and two paintings by Caravaggio (in the Cerasi Chapel, left of altar; see listing on page 866).

From Piazza del Popolo, shop your way down **Via del Corso.** With the proliferation of shopping malls, many chain stores lining Via del Corso are losing customers and facing hard times. Still, this remains a fine place to feel the pulse of Rome at twilight.

Historians side-trip right down Via Pontefici past the fascist architecture to see the massive, rotting, round-brick **Mausoleum of Augustus,** topped with overgrown cypress trees. Beyond it, next to the river, is Augustus' **Ara Pacis,** enclosed within a protective glass-walled museum (described on page 868). From the mausoleum, walk down Via Tomacelli to return to Via del Corso and the 21st century.

From Via del Corso, window-shoppers should take a left down **Via Condotti** to join the parade to the **Spanish Steps.** The streets that parallel Via Condotti to the south (Borgognona and Frattina) are more elegant and filled with high-end boutiques. A few streets to the north hides the narrow Via Margutta. This is where Gregory Peck's *Roman Holiday* character lived (at #51); today it has a leafy tranquility and is filled with pricey artisan shops.

Historians: Ignore Via Condotti and forget the Spanish Steps. Stay on Via del Corso, which has been straight since Roman times, and walk a half-mile down to the Victor Emmanuel Monument. Climb Michelangelo's stairway to his glorious (especially when floodlit) square atop Capitoline Hill. Stand on the balcony (just past the mayor's palace on the right), which overlooks the Forum. As the horizon reddens and cats prowl the unclaimed rubble of ancient Rome, it's one of the finest views in the city.

Heart of Rome Walk

Rome's most colorful neighborhood features narrow lanes, intimate piazzas, fanciful fountains, and some of Europe's best people-watching. During the day, this walk shows off the colorful Campo de' Fiori market and trendy fashion boutiques as it meanders past major monuments such as the Pantheon and the Spanish Steps.

But, when the sun sets, unexpected magic happens. A stroll in the cool of the evening brings out all the romance of the Eternal City. Sit so close to a bubbling fountain that traffic noise evaporates. Jostle with kids to see the gelato flavors. Watch lovers straddling more than the bench. Jaywalk past *polizia* in flak-proof vests. And marvel at the ramshackle elegance that softens this brutal city for those who were born here and can't imagine living anywhere else. These are the flavors of Rome, best tasted after dark.

This walk is equally pleasant in reverse order. You could ride the Metro to the Spanish Steps and finish at Campo de' Fiori, near

Heart of Rome Walk

V. PONT

ARA PACIS

MAUSOLEUM OF AUGUSTUS

N

Piazza Cavour

PONTE CAVOUR

VIA DI RIPETTA

Piazza Augusto Imperatore

FORMER HALL OF JUSTICE

Tiber River

LUNGOTEVERE MARZIO

Piazza Borghese

CLEMENTINO

VIA DELLA SCROFA

PREFETTI

PONTE UMBERTO

Piazza Ponte Umbertol

MONTE BRIANZO

STELLETTA

CAMPO

UFFICI

To Ponte Sant'Angelo

VIA DEI CORONARI

VOLPE

ANCIENT STADIUM ENTRANCE T

GIOLITTI'S GELATO

VIA DELLE COPPELLE

LA MADDELENA

SAN LUIGI

VIA IN AQUIRO

Piazza Fico

FOUR RIVERS FOUNTAIN TRE SCALINI

SALVATORE ITALY'S SENATE

GIUSTINIANI

CHIESA NUOVA

SANT' AGNESE

T

SANT' EUSTACHIO

Piazza Rotunda

PANTHEON

Piazza della Chiesa Nuova

Piazza Navona

SANT' IVO

Piazza Sant'Eustachio

CORSO DEL RINASCIMENTO

Piazza Pasquino

PASQUINO STATUE

CITY MUSEUM

ARGENTINA

VIA DE CESTARI

CORSO VITTORIO EMANUELE II II

B

CORSO VITTORIO EMANUELE II

WALK BEGINS

BRUNO STATUE

Campo de' Fiori

VIA D. BAULLARI

SANT' ANDREA DELLA VALLE

V. CHIAVARI

Largo Argentina

B T

LARGO ARGENTINA RUINS

Piazza Farnese

To Trastevera

PALAZZO FARNESE

Largo Pallaro

150 Meters

150 Yards

ROME

many recommended restaurants. To lengthen this walk, you could start in Trastevere; see directions on page 875.

• *Start this walk at Campo de' Fiori, my favorite outdoor dining room (especially after dark—see "Eating in Rome," page 908). It's a few blocks east of Largo Argentina, a major transportation hub. Buses #40, #64, and #492 stop at both Largo Argentina and along Corso Vittorio Emanuele II, a long block north of Campo de' Fiori. A taxi from Termini Station costs about €8.*

Campo de' Fiori: One of Rome's most colorful spots, this bohemian piazza hosts a fruit and vegetable **market** in the morning, cafés in the evening, and pub-crawlers at night. In ancient

times, the "Field of Flowers" was an open meadow. Later, Christian pilgrims passed through on their way to the Vatican, and a thriving market developed.

Lording over the center of the square is a statue of **Giordano Bruno,** an intellectual heretic who was burned on this spot in 1600. When the statue of Bruno was erected in 1889, riots overcame Vatican protests against honoring a heretic. Bruno faces his nemesis, the Vatican Chancellory (the big white building just outside the far-right corner of the square), while his pedestal reads, "And the flames rose up." Check out the reliefs on the pedestal for scenes from Bruno's trial and execution. Even today, this neighborhood is known for its free spirit and occasional demonstrations.

Campo de' Fiori is the product of centuries of unplanned urban development. At the east end of the square (behind Bruno), the ramshackle apartments are built right into the old outer wall of ancient Rome's mammoth Theater of Pompey. This entertainment complex covered several city blocks, stretching from here to Largo Argentina. Julius Caesar was assassinated in the Theater of Pompey, where the Senate was renting space.

The square is lined with and surrounded by fun eateries. Bruno faces the **Forno** (in the left corner of the square). Step in, at least to observe the frenzy as pizza is sold hot out of the oven. You can order *un etto* (100 grams, an average serving) by pointing, then take your snack to the counter to pay. The many bars lining the square are fine for drinks and watching the scene. On weekend nights, when the Campo is packed with beer-drinking kids, this medieval square is transformed into one vast Roman street party.

• *If Bruno did a hop, step, and jump forward, then turned right on Via dei Baullari and marched 200 yards, he'd cross the busy Corso Vittorio*

Emanuele; then, continuing another 150 yards on Via Cuccagna, he'd find...

Piazza Navona: This oblong square retains the shape of the original racetrack that was built around A.D. 80 by the emperor Domitian. (To see the ruins of the original entrance, exit the square at the far—or north—end, then take an immediate left, and look down to the left 25 feet below the current street level.) Since ancient times, the square has been a center of Roman life. In the 1800s, the city would flood the square to cool off the neighborhood.

The **Four Rivers Fountain** in the center is the most famous fountain by the man who remade Rome in Baroque style, Gian

Lorenzo Bernini. Four burly river gods (representing the four continents that were known in 1650) support an Egyptian obelisk. The water of the world gushes everywhere. The Nile has his head covered, since the headwaters were unknown then. The Ganges holds an oar. The Danube turns to admire the obelisk, which Bernini had moved here from a stadium on the Appian Way. And Uruguay's Río de la Plata tumbles backward in shock, wondering how he ever made the top four. Bernini enlivens the fountain with horses plunging through the rocks and exotic flora and fauna from these newly discovered lands. Homesick Texans may want to find the armadillo. (It's the big, weird, armor-plated creature behind the Plata river statue.)

The Plata river god is gazing upward at the **Church of St. Agnes,** worked on by Bernini's former student-turned-rival, Francesco Borromini. Borromini's concave facade helps reveal the dome and epitomizes the curved symmetry of Baroque. Tour guides say that Bernini designed his river god to look horrified at Borromini's work. Or maybe he's shielding his eyes from St. Agnes' nakedness, as she was stripped before being martyred. But either explanation is unlikely, since the fountain was completed two years before Borromini even started work on the church.

Piazza Navona is Rome's most interesting night scene, with street music, artists, fire-eaters, local Casanovas, ice cream, and outdoor cafés that are worthy of a splurge if you've got time to sit and enjoy Italy's human river.

• *Leave Piazza Navona directly across from Tre Scalini (famous for its rich chocolate ice cream), and go east down Corsia Agonale, past rose peddlers and palm readers. Jog left around the guarded building (where*

ROME

Italy's senate meets), and follow the brown sign to the Pantheon, which is straight down Via del Salvatore.

The Pantheon: Sit for a while under the portico of the Pantheon (romantically floodlit and moonlit at night).

The 40-foot, single-piece granite columns of the Pantheon's entrance show the scale the ancient Romans built on. The columns support a triangular Greek-style roof with an inscription that says

"M. Agrippa" built it. In fact, it was built *(fecit)* by Emperor Hadrian (A.D. 120), who gave credit to the builder of an earlier structure. This impressive entranceway gives no clue that the greatest wonder of the building is inside—a domed room that inspired later domes, including Michelangelo's St. Peter's and Brunelleschi's Duomo (in Florence).

If it's open, pop into the Pantheon for a look around (interior described on page 841). If you have extra time, consider detouring to several interesting churches near the Pantheon (listed on page 843).

• *With your back to the Pantheon, veer to the right, uphill toward the yellow sign that reads* Casa del Caffè *at the Tazza d'Oro coffee shop on Via Orfani.*

From the Pantheon to the Trevi Fountain: Tazza d'Oro Casa del Caffè, one of Rome's top coffee shops, dates back to the days when this area was licensed to roast coffee beans. Locals come here for a shot of espresso or, when it's hot, a refreshing *granita di caffè con panna* (coffee slush with cream).

• *Continue up Via Orfani to...*

Piazza Capranica is home to the big, plain Florentine Renaissance-style Palazzo Capranica (directly opposite as you enter the square). Big shots, like the Capranica family, built towers on their palaces—not for any military use, but just to show off.

• *Leave the piazza to the right of the palace, heading down Via in Aquiro.*

The street Via in Aquiro leads to a sixth-century B.C. **Egyptian obelisk** taken as a trophy by Augustus after his victory in Egypt over Mark Antony and Cleopatra. The obelisk was set up as a sundial. Follow the zodiac markings to the well-guarded front door. This is Italy's **parliament building,** where the lower house meets; you may see politicians, political demonstrations, and TV cameras.

• *To your right is Piazza Colonna, where we're heading next—unless you like gelato...*

A one-block detour to the left (past Albergo Nazionale) brings you to Rome's most famous *gelateria*. **Giolitti's** is cheap for takeout or elegant and splurge-worthy for a sit among classy locals (open daily until past midnight, Via Uffici del Vicario 40); get your gelato in a cone *(cono)* or cup *(coppetta)*.

Piazza Colonna features a huge second-century column. Its reliefs depict the victories of Emperor Marcus Aurelius over the barbarians. When Marcus died in A.D. 180, the barbarians began to get the upper hand, beginning Rome's long three-century fall. The big, important-looking palace houses the headquarters for the prime minister's cabinet.

Noisy **Via del Corso** is Rome's main north-south boulevard. It's named for the Berber horse races—without riders—that took place here during Carnevale. This wild tradition continued until the late 1800s, when a series of fatal accidents (including, reportedly, one in front of Queen Margherita) led to its cancellation. Historically the street was filled with meat shops. When it became one of Rome's first gas-lit streets in 1854, these butcher shops were banned and replaced by classier boutiques, jewelers, and antiques dealers. Nowadays the northern part of Via del Corso is closed to traffic, and for a few hours every evening it becomes a wonderful parade of Romans out for a stroll (see the "Dolce Vita Stroll," earlier).

• *Cross Via del Corso to enter a big palatial building with columns, which houses the Galleria Alberto Sordi shopping mall (with convenient WCs). Inside, take the fork to the right and exit at the back. (If you're here after 22:00, when the mall is closed, circle around the right side of the Galleria on Via dei Sabini.) Once out the back, head up Via de Crociferi, to the roar of the water, lights, and people at the...*

Trevi Fountain: The Trevi Fountain shows how Rome took full advantage of the abundance of water brought into the city by its great aqueducts. This watery Baroque avalanche by Nicola Salvi was com-pleted in 1762. Salvi used the palace behind the fountain as a theatrical backdrop for the figure of "Ocean," who represents water in every form. The statue surfs through his wet kingdom—with water gushing from 24 spouts and tumbling over 30 different kinds of plants—while Triton blows his conch shell.

The magic of the square is enhanced by the fact that no streets

Rome at a Glance

▲▲▲**Colosseum** Huge stadium where gladiators fought. **Hours:** Daily 8:30 until one hour before sunset: April-Sept until 19:15, Oct until 18:30, off-season closes as early as 16:30. See page 825.

▲▲▲**Roman Forum** Ancient Rome's main square, with ruins and grand arches. **Hours:** Same hours as Colosseum. See page 831.

▲▲▲**Pantheon** The defining domed temple. **Hours:** Mon-Sat 8:30-19:30, Sun 9:00-18:00, holidays 9:00-13:00, closed for Mass Sat at 17:00 and Sun at 10:30. See page 841.

▲▲▲**St. Peter's Basilica** Most impressive church on earth, with Michelangelo's *Pietà* and dome. **Hours:** Church—daily April-Sept 7:00-19:00, Oct-March 7:00-18:00, often closed Wed mornings; dome—daily April-Sept 8:00-18:00, Oct-March 8:00-17:00. See page 845.

▲▲▲**Vatican Museum** Four miles of the finest art of Western civilization, culminating in Michelangelo's glorious Sistine Chapel. **Hours:** Mon-Sat 9:00-18:00. Closed on religious holidays and Sun, except last Sun of the month (open 9:00-14:00). May be open some Fri nights by online reservation only. Hours are subject to change. See page 851.

▲▲▲**Borghese Gallery** Bernini sculptures and paintings by Caravaggio, Raphael, and Titian in a Baroque palazzo. Reservations mandatory. **Hours:** Tue-Sun 9:00-19:00, closed Mon. See page 861.

▲▲▲**National Museum of Rome** Greatest collection of Roman sculpture anywhere. **Hours:** Tue-Sun 9:00-19:45, closed Mon. See page 870.

▲▲**Palatine Hill** Ruins of emperors' palaces, Circus Maximus view, and museum. **Hours:** Same as Colosseum. See page 832.

▲▲**Capitoline Museums** Ancient statues, mosaics, and expansive view of Forum. **Hours:** Tue-Sun 9:00-20:00, closed Mon. See page 837.

▲▲**Ara Pacis** Shrine marking the beginning of Rome's Golden Age. **Hours:** Tue-Sun 9:00-19:00, closed Mon. See page 868.

▲▲**Dolce Vita Stroll** Evening *passeggiata,* where Romans strut their stuff. **Hours:** Roughly Mon-Sat 17:00-19:00 and Sun afternoons. See page 813.

▲▲**Catacombs** Underground tombs, mainly Christian, some outside the city. **Hours:** Generally open 10:00-12:00 & 14:00-17:00. See pages 867 and 886.

▲**Arch of Constantine** Honors the emperor who legalized Christianity. **Hours:** Always viewable. See page 830.

▲**St. Peter-in-Chains Church** with Michelangelo's *Moses*. **Hours:** Daily 8:00-12:30 & 15:00-19:00, until 18:00 in winter. See page 831.

▲**Trajan's Column, Market, and Museum of the Imperial Forums** Tall column with narrative relief, and museum with entry to Trajan's Market. **Hours:** Column always viewable; museum open Tue-Sun 9:00-19:00, closed Mon. See page 834.

▲ **Piazza del Campidoglio** Square atop Capitoline Hill, designed by Michelangelo, with a museum, grand stairway, and Forum overlooks. **Hours:** Always open. See page 835.

▲**Victor Emmanuel Monument** Gigantic edifice celebrating Italian unity, with Rome from the Sky elevator ride up to 360-degree city view. **Hours:** Monument open daily 9:30-18:30; elevator open Mon-Thu 9:30-18:30, Fri-Sun 9:30-19:30. See page 840.

▲**Trevi Fountain** Baroque hot spot into which tourists throw coins to ensure a return trip to Rome. **Hours:** Always flowing. See page 844.

▲**Castel Sant'Angelo** Hadrian's Tomb turned castle, prison, papal refuge, now museum. **Hours:** Tue-Sun 9:00-19:30, closed Mon. See page 859.

▲**Capuchin Crypt** Decorated with the bones of 4,000 Franciscan friars. **Hours:** Daily 9:00-19:00. See page 864.

▲**Baths of Diocletian** Once ancient Rome's immense public baths, now a Michelangelo church. **Hours:** Mon-Sat 7:00-18:30, Sun 7:00-19:30, closed to sightseers during Mass. See page 871.

▲**Santa Maria della Vittoria** Church with Bernini's swooning *St. Teresa in Ecstasy*. **Hours:** Mon-Sat 8:30-12:00 & 15:30-18:00, Sun 15:30-18:00. See page 871.

ROME

directly approach it. You can hear the excitement as you draw near, and then—*bam!*—you're there. The scene is always lively, with lucky Romeos clutching dates while unlucky ones clutch beers. Romantics toss a coin over their shoulder, thinking it will give them a wish and assure their return to Rome. That may sound silly, but every year I go through this tourist ritual...and it actually seems to work.

Take some time to people-watch (whisper a few breathy *bellos* or *bellas*) before leaving. There's a peaceful zone at water level on the far right.

• *From the Trevi Fountain, we're 10 minutes from our next stop, the Spanish Steps. Just use a map to get there, or follow these directions: Facing the Trevi Fountain, go forward, walking along the right side of the fountain on Via della Stamperia. Cross busy Via del Tritone. Continue 100 yards and veer right at Via delle Fratte, a street that changes its name to Via Propaganda before ending at the...*

Spanish Steps: Piazza di Spagna, with the very popular Spanish Steps, is named for the Spanish Embassy to the Vatican, which has been here for 300 years. It's been the hangout of many Romantics over the years (Keats, Wagner, Openshaw, Goethe, and others). In the 1700s, British aristocrats on the "Grand Tour" of Europe came here to ponder Rome's decay. The British poet John Keats pondered his mortality, then died of tuberculosis at age 25 in the pink building on the right side of the steps. Fellow Romantic Lord Byron lived across the square at #66.

The **Sinking Boat Fountain** at the foot of the steps, built by Bernini or his father, Pietro, is powered by an aqueduct. Actually, all of Rome's fountains are aqueduct-powered; their spurts are determined by the water pressure provided by the various aqueducts. This one, for instance, is much weaker than Trevi's gush.

The piazza is a thriving scene at night. Window-shop along Via Condotti, which stretches away from the steps. This is where Gucci and other big names cater to the trendsetting jet set. It's clear that the main sight around here is not the famous steps, but the people who sit on them.

• *Our walk is finished. If you'd like to reach the top of the steps sweat-free, take the free elevator just outside the Spagna Metro stop (to the left, as you face the steps; elevator closes at 21:00). A free WC is underground in the piazza near the Metro entrance, by the middle palm tree (10:00-19:30). The nearby McDonald's (as you face the Spanish Steps, go right one block) is big and lavish, with a salad bar and WC. When you're ready to leave, you can zip home on the Metro (usually open until 23:30, Fri-Sat until 1:30 in the morning) or grab a taxi at either the north or south side of the piazza.*

Sights in Rome

I've clustered Rome's sights into walkable neighborhoods, some quite close together (see the "Rome's Neighborhoods" map on page 781). Save transit time by grouping your sightseeing according to location. For example, the Colosseum and the Forum are a few minutes' walk from Capitoline Hill; a 15-minute walk beyond that is the Pantheon. I like to tour these sights in one great day, starting at the Colosseum and ending at the Pantheon.

Ancient Rome

The core of ancient Rome, where the grandest monuments were built, is between the Colosseum and Capitoline Hill. Among the ancient forums, a few modern sights have popped up.

The Colosseum and Nearby

▲▲▲**Colosseum (Colosseo)**—Built when the Roman Empire was at its peak in A.D. 80, the Colosseum represents Rome at its

grandest. The Flavian Amphitheater (the Colosseum's real name) was an arena for gladiator contests and public spectacles. When killing became a spectator sport, the Romans wanted to share the fun with as many people as possible, so they stuck two semicircular theaters together to create a freestanding amphitheater. The outside (where slender cypress trees stand today) was decorated with a 100-foot-tall bronze statue of Nero that gleamed in the sunlight. In a later age, the colossal structure was nicknamed a "coloss-eum," the wonder of its age. It could accommodate 50,000 roaring fans (100,000 thumbs).

This 2,000-year-old building is the classic example of Roman engineering. The Romans pioneered the use of concrete and the rounded arch, which enabled them to build on this tremendous scale. The exterior is a skeleton of 3.5 million cubic feet of travertine stone. (Each of the pillars flanking the ground-level arches weighs five tons.) It took 200 ox-drawn wagons shuttling back and forth every day for four years just to bring the stone here from Tivoli. The Romans stacked stone blocks (without mortar) into the shape of an arch, supported temporarily by wooden scaffolding. Finally, they wedged a keystone into the top of the arch—it not only kept the arch from falling, it could bear even more weight above. Iron pegs held the larger stones together—notice the small holes that pockmark the sides.

While the essential structure of the Colosseum is Roman, the four-story facade is decorated with mostly Greek columns—Doric-like Tuscan columns on the ground level, Ionic on the second story, Corinthian on the next level, and at the top, half-columns with a mix of all three. Originally, copies of Greek statues stood in the arches of the middle two stories, giving a veneer of sophistication to this arena of death.

This was where ancient Romans—whose taste for violence was the equal of modern America's—enjoyed their *Dirty Harry*s and *Terminator*s. Gladiators, criminals, and wild animals fought to the death in every conceivable scenario. The bit of reconstructed Colosseum floor gives you an accurate sense of the original floor and the subterranean warren where animals were held, then lifted up in elevators. Released at floor level, animals would pop out from

ROME

behind blinds into the arena—the gladiator didn't know where, when, or by what he'd be attacked.

Only a third of the original Colosseum remains. Earthquakes destroyed some of it, but most was carted off as easy pre-cut stones for other buildings during the Middle Ages and Renaissance.

Cost and Hours: €12 combo-ticket includes Roman Forum and Palatine Hill—see page 789, open daily 8:30 until one hour before sunset, last entry one hour before closing—for specifics, see "Hours" on page 803, audioguide-€5.50, Metro: Colosseo, tel. 06-3996-7700, http://archeoroma.beniculturali.it/en.

Avoiding Lines: Crowds tend to be thinner (and lines shorter) in the afternoon (especially after 15:00 in summer); this is also true at the Forum.

You can save lots of time by buying your combo-ticket in advance, having the Roma Pass, booking a guided tour, or renting an audioguide or videoguide. Here are the options:

1. Buy your combo-ticket (or Roma Pass) at the less-crowded Palatine Hill entrance, 150 yards away on Via di San Gregorio (facing the Forum, with Colosseum at your back, go left down the street). You can also buy a Roma Pass at the tobacco shop in the Colosseo Metro station, the I Fori di Roma visitors center on Via dei Fori Imperiali (see page 804), or other sights around town. It should cost the same no matter where you buy it. (Avoid buying your ticket or Roma Pass at the Forum, which also tends to have lines.)

2. Buy a combo-ticket online at www.ticketclic.it (€1.50 booking fee, not changeable). The "free tickets" you'll see listed are valid only for EU citizens with ID.

3. Pay to join an official guided tour, or rent an audioguide or videoguide (see "Tours," page 829). This lets you march right up to the Colosseum's guided visits *(Visite Guidate)* desk, thus bypassing the ticket lines. Even if you don't use the device or accompany the guided tour, the extra cost might be worth it just to skip the ticket line.

4. Hire a private walking-tour guide. Guides of varying quality linger outside the Colosseum, offering tours that allow you to skip the line. Be aware that these private guides may try to mislead you into thinking the Colosseum lines are longer than they really are. For more on this option, see "Tours" on page 829.

Restoration: The arena is being cleaned from top to bottom, given permanent lighting, and outfitted with new shops and services. Long-range plans include building a free-standing ticket booth outside the Colosseum. These ongoing renovations, scheduled to last several years, may affect your visit.

Warning: Beware of the **greedy gladiators.** For a fee, the incredibly crude, modern-day gladiators snuff out their cigarettes

ROME

and pose for photos. They're officially banned from panhandling in this area, but you may still see them, hoping to intimidate easy-to-swindle tourists into paying too much money for a photo op. (If you go for it, €4-5 for one photo usually keeps them appeased.) Also, look out for **pickpockets** and con artists in this prime tourist spot.

Getting There: The Colosseo Metro stop on line B is just across the street from the monument. Bus #60 is handy for hotels near Via Firenze and Via Nazionale. Bus #87 links Largo

Argentina with the Colosseum.

Getting In: If you need to buy a ticket or sign up for a guided tour, follow the signs for the appropriate line. With a combo-ticket or Roma Pass in hand, look for signs for *ticket holders* or *Roma Pass*, allowing you to bypass the long lines.

Tours: A dry but fact-filled **audioguide** is available just past the turnstiles (€5.50/2 hours). A handheld **videoguide** senses where you are in the site and plays related video clips (€6).

Official **guided tours** in English depart nearly hourly between 10:00 and 17:00, and last 45-60 minutes (€5 plus Colosseum ticket, purchase inside the Colosseum near the ticket booth marked *Visite Guidate;* if you're lost, ask a guard to direct you to the desk).

Private guides stand outside the Colosseum, looking for business (€25-30/2-hour tour of the Colosseum, Palatine Hill, and Forum). If booking a private guide, make sure that your tour will start right away and that the ticket you receive covers all three sights: the Colosseum, Forum, and Palatine Hill.

You can also download a free Rick Steves **audio tour** of the Colosseum to your mobile device; see page 1101.

A 1.5-hour **behind-the-scenes tour** takes you through restricted areas, including underground passageways and the third floor, which are off-limits to regular Colosseum visitors. It's generally offered April-Nov only, and closes during and after bad weather, as the underground passageways flood easily. While interesting, this tour certainly isn't essential to appreciating the Colosseum. It's operated by Pierreci, a private company; to book, contact them at least a day in advance (€8 plus Colosseum ticket, www.pierreci.it, call 06-3996-7700 during business hours: Mon-Fri 9:00-18:00, Sat 9:00-14:00, closed Sun, no same-day reservations). After dialing, wait for English instructions on how to reach a live operator, then reserve a time and pre-pay with a credit card. Without a reservation, you can try to join the next available tour (may be in Italian): Once you have your Colosseum entrance ticket and are at the turnstiles, look for the tour meeting point just past the ticket desk; pay the guide directly.

With Limited Time: With a single glance, you can basically see the entire interior. It's not necessary to go upstairs or circle the place.

▲**Arch of Constantine**—If you are a Christian, were raised a Christian, or simply belong to a so-called "Christian nation," ponder this arch. It marks one of the great turning points in history: the military coup that made Christianity mainstream. In A.D. 312, Emperor Constantine defeated his rival Maxentius in the crucial Battle of the Milvian Bridge. The night before, he had seen a vision of a cross in the sky. Constantine—

whose mother and sister had already become Christians—became sole emperor and legalized Christianity. With this one battle, a once-obscure Jewish sect with a handful of followers became the state religion of the entire Western world. In A.D. 300, you could be killed for being a Christian; a century later, you could be killed for not being one. Church enrollment boomed.

The restored arch is like an ancient museum. It's decorated entirely with recycled carvings originally made for other buildings. By covering it with exquisite carvings of high Roman art—works that glorified previous emperors—Constantine put himself in their league. Hadrian is featured in the round reliefs, with Marcus Aurelius in the square reliefs higher up. The big statues on top are of Trajan and Augustus. Originally, Augustus drove a chariot similar to the one topping the modern Victor Emmanuel II Monument. Fourth-century Rome may have been in decline, but Constantine clung to its glorious past.

▲**St. Peter-in-Chains Church (San Pietro in Vincoli)**—Built in the fifth century to house the chains that held St. Peter, this church is most famous for its Michelangelo statue. Check out the much-venerated chains under the high altar, then focus on mighty Moses. (Note that this isn't the famous St. Peter's Basilica, which is at Vatican City.)

Pope Julius II commissioned Michelangelo to build a massive tomb, with 48 huge statues, topped with a grand statue of this egomaniacal pope. The pope had planned to have his tomb placed in the center of St. Peter's Basilica. When Julius died, the work had barely been started, and no one had the money or necessary commitment to Julius to finish the project.

In 1542, some of the remnants of the tomb project were brought to St. Peter-in-Chains and pieced together by Michelangelo's assistants. Some of the best statues ended up elsewhere, such as the *Prisoners* in Florence and the *Slaves* in the Louvre. *Moses* and the Louvre's *Slaves* are the only statues Michelangelo personally completed for the project. Flanking *Moses* are the Old Testament sister-wives of Jacob, Leah (to our right) and Rachel, both begun by Michelangelo but probably finished by pupils.

This powerful statue of Moses—mature Michelangelo—is worth studying. The artist worked on it in fits and starts for 30 years. Moses has received the Ten Commandments. As he holds the stone tablets, his eyes show a man determined to stop his tribe from worshipping the golden calf and idols...a man determined to win salvation for the people of Israel. Why the horns? Centuries ago, the Hebrew word for "rays" was mistranslated as "horns."

Cost and Hours: Free, daily April-Sept 8:00-12:30 & 15:00-19:00, Oct-March 8:00-12:30 & 15:00-18:00, modest dress required; the church is a 10-minute uphill walk from the Colosseum, or a shorter, simpler walk from the Cavour Metro stop.

The Roman Forum and Nearby

▲▲▲**Roman Forum (Foro Romano)**—This is ancient Rome's birthplace and civic center, and the common ground between

ROME

Rome's famous seven hills. As just about anything important that happened in ancient Rome happened here, it's arguably the most important piece of real estate in Western civilization. While only a few fragments of that glorious past remain, history-seekers find plenty to ignite their imaginations amid the half-broken columns and arches.

Cost and Hours: €12 combo-ticket includes Colosseum and Palatine Hill—see page 789, open daily 8:30 until one hour before sunset, last entry one hour before closing, audioguide-€5, Metro: Colosseo, tel. 06-3996-7700, http://archeoroma.beniculturali .it/en.

See my self-guided walk on page 803.

▲▲**Palatine Hill (Monte Palatino)**—The hill overlooking the Forum is jam-packed with history—"the huts of Romulus," the

huge Imperial Palace, a view of the Circus Maximus—but there's only the barest skeleton of rubble left to tell the story.

We get our word "palace" from this hill, where the emperors chose to live. The Palatine Hill was once so filled with palaces that later emperors had to build out. (Looking up at it from the Forum, you see the substructure that supported these long-gone palaces.)

The Palatine museum contains statues and frescoes that help you imagine the luxury of the imperial Palatine. From the pleasant garden, you'll get an overview of the Forum. On the far side, look down into an emperor's private stadium and then beyond at the grassy Circus Maximus, once a chariot course. Imagine the cheers, jeers, and furious betting.

While many tourists consider the Palatine Hill just extra credit after the Forum, it offers an insight into the greatness of Rome. (And, if you're visiting the Colosseum or Forum, you've got a ticket whether you like it or not.)

Cost and Hours: €12 combo-ticket covers both the Roman Forum/Palatine Hill (grouped as one sight for the purposes of the ticket) and the Colosseum. The combo-ticket is valid two consecutive days, but once your ticket is scanned for either the Forum/Palatine Hill or the Colosseum, you can't re-enter that sight (even the next day)—see page 789; open same hours as Roman Forum and Colosseum.

ROME

The closest Metro stop is Colosseo. The entrance is on Via di San Gregorio (facing the Forum with the Colosseum at your back, it's down the street to your left). You can also enter the Palatine from within the Roman Forum—just climb the hill from the Arch of Titus.

Audioguides cost €5/2 hours (€7 version includes Roman Forum and lasts 3 hours, must leave ID). Guided tours in English might be available (inquire at the ticket booth). WCs are at the ticket office when you enter, up the hill near the stadium, at the museum in the center of the site, and hiding among the orange trees in the Farnese Gardens.

Mamertine Prison—This 2,500-year-old cistern-like prison is where, according to Christian tradition, the Romans imprisoned Saints Peter and Paul. Though it was long a charming and historic sight, its artifacts have been removed, and today it's run by a commercial tour-bus company charging €10 for a cheesy

ROME

"multimedia" walk-through. Don't go in. Instead, stand outside and imagine how this dank cistern once housed prisoners of the emperor. Amid fat rats and rotting corpses, unfortunate humans awaited slow deaths. It's said that a miraculous fountain sprang up inside so Peter could convert and baptize his jailers, who were also subsequently martyred. Before the commercial ruination of this sacred and ancient site, on the walls you could read lists of notable prisoners (Christian and non-Christian) and the ways they were executed: *strangolati, decapitato, morto per fame* (died of hunger). The sign by the Christian names read, "Here suffered, victorious for the triumph of Christ, these martyr saints." Today this sight itself has been martyred by a city apparently desperate to monetize its heritage.

▲**Trajan's Column, Market, and Museum of the Imperial Forums**—This grand column is the best example of "continuous narration" that we have from antiquity. More than 2,500 figures spiral around the 140-foot-high column, telling of Trajan's victorious Dacian campaign (circa A.D. 103, in present-day Romania), from the assembling of the army at the bottom to the victory sacrifice at the top. At one point, the ashes of Trajan and his wife were held in the base, and the sun glinted off a polished bronze statue of Trajan at the top. (Today, St. Peter is on top.) Study the propaganda that winds up the column like a scroll, trumpeting Trajan's wonderful military exploits (for a rolled-out version of the column's story, visit the E.U.R.'s Museum of Roman Civilization). This column marked "Trajan's Forum," which was built to handle the shopping needs of a wealthy city of more than a million people. Commercial, political, religious, and social activities all mixed in the forum.

Nestled into the cutaway curve of Quirinal Hill is the semi-circular brick complex of Trajan's Market. It was likely part shopping mall, part warehouse, and part administration building. Or, as some archaeologists have recently suggested, it may have contained mostly government offices.

Paying the admission fee gets you inside Trajan's Market, Trajan's Forum, and the **Museum of the Imperial Forums**. The museum features discoveries from the forums of emperors Julius Caesar, Augustus, Nerva, and Trajan, with fragments of statues and a slideshow that reconstructs how the forum looked in each emperor's time.

Cost and Hours: Museum—€11, includes entry to the market ruins—also viewable for free from Via dei Fori Imperiali, Tue-Sun 9:00-19:00, closed Mon, last entry one hour before closing, audioguide-€3.50, entrance is uphill from the column on Via IV Novembre 94, tel. 06-0608, www.mercatiditraiano.it.

Getting There: Trajan's Column is just a few steps off Piazza

Venezia (a hub for major bus routes #40, #64, #85, and #87) on Via dei Fori Imperiali, across the street from the Victor Emmanuel Monument. Trajan's Market can be entered only through the Museum of the Imperial Forums at Via IV Novembre 94 (up the staircase from Trajan's Column). Trajan's Forum stretches southeast of the column toward the Colosseo Metro stop and the Colosseum itself.

Bocca della Verità—The legendary "Mouth of Truth" at the Church of Santa Maria in Cosmedin draws a playful crowd. Stick

your hand in the mouth of the gaping stone face in the porch wall. As the legend goes (and was popularized by the 1953 film *Roman Holiday*, starring Gregory Peck and Audrey Hepburn), if you're a liar, your hand will be gobbled up. The mouth is only accessible when the church gate is open, but it's always (partially) visible through the gate, even when closed. If the church itself is open, step inside to see one of the few unaltered medieval church interiors in Rome. Notice the mismatched ancient columns and beautiful *cosmatesque* floor—a centuries-old example of recycling.

Cost and Hours: €0.50, daily 9:30-17:50, closes earlier off-season, Piazza Bocca della Verità, near the north end of Circus Maximus.

Capitoline Hill

Of Rome's famous seven hills, this is the smallest, tallest, and most famous—home of the ancient Temple of Jupiter and the center of

city government for 2,500 years. There are several ways to get to the top of Capitoline Hill. If you're coming from the north (from Piazza Venezia), take Michelangelo's impressive stairway to the right of the big, white Victor Emmanuel Monument. Coming from the southeast (the Forum),

take the steep staircase near the Arch of Septimius Severus. From near Trajan's Forum along Via dei Fori Imperiali, take the winding road. All three converge at the top, in the square called Campidoglio (kahm-pee-DOHL-yoh).

▲Piazza del Campidoglio (Capitoline Hill Square)—This square atop the hill, once the religious and political center of

Capitoline Hill & Piazza Venezia

GALLERIA DORIA PAMPHILJ

To Piazza del Popolo

VIA DEL CORSO

VIA BATTISTI
#64, 40

VIA 4 NOVEMBRE

VIA 4 NOVEMBRE

Largo Magnanapoli

VIA DEL PLEBISCITO

Piazza Venezia

VIA NAZIONALE

PALAZZO VENEZIA
#64, 85

To Gesù & Pantheon

S. MARCO

TRAJAN'S COLUMN

TRAJAN'S FORUM

MUSEUM OF IMPERIAL FORUMS & TRAJAN'S MARKET

VIA ALESSANDRINA

VIA D'ARACOELI
#64
#110

VICTOR EMMANUEL MONUMENT
CAFÉ

STA. MARIA ARACOELI

CAESAR'S FORUM

VIA DEI FORI IMPERIALI

GRAND STAIRCASE

PALAZZO NUOVO

STATUE

PALAZZO SENATORIO

MAMERTINE PRISON

SANTI LUCA E MARTINA

To Colosseum & M

Piazza Caffarelli

PUBLIC CAFÉ ENTRANCE

CAPITOLINE MUSEUMS

TABULARIUM

EXIT

VIA TEATRO MARCELLO

To

CAFÉ

PALAZZO DEI CONSERVATORI

FORO ROMANO

ARCH OF SEPTIMIUS SEVERUS

ROMAN FORUM

100 Meters
100 Yards

1. Piazza del Campidoglio
2. Capitoline Museums Entrance
3. Copy of She-Wolf Statue
4. "Il Nasone" Water Fountain
5. Views of Forum
6. Shortcut to Santa Maria in Aracoeli Church
7. Shortcut to Victor Emmanuel Monument
8. Mussolini's Balcony
9. Michelangelo's Grand Staircase
10. To Teatro di Marcello Ruins
11. Rome from the Sky

ROME

ancient Rome, is still the home of the city's government. In the 1530s, the pope called on Michelangelo to re-establish this square as a grand center. Michelangelo placed the ancient equestrian statue of Marcus Aurelius as the square's focal point. Effective. (The original statue is now in the adjacent museum.) The twin buildings on either side are the Capitoline Museums. Behind the replica of the statue is the mayoral palace (Palazzo Senatorio).

Shortcut to the Victor Emmanuel Monument and Aracoeli Church

A clever shortcut lets you go directly from Piazza del Campidoglio, the square atop Capitoline Hill, to Santa Maria in Aracoeli Church and an upper level of the Victor Emmanuel Monument, avoiding long flights of stairs. Facing the square's equestrian statue, head to the left, climbing the wide set of stairs near the she-wolf statue. Midway up the stairs (at the column), turn left to reach the back entrance to the Aracoeli Church. To reach the Victor Emmanuel Monument, pass the column and continue to the top of the steps, pass through the iron gate, and enter the small unmarked door at #13 on the right. You'll soon emerge on a café terrace that leads to the monument and the Rome from the Sky elevator.

Michelangelo intended that people approach the square from his grand stairway off Piazza Venezia. From the top of the stairway, you see the new Renaissance face of Rome, with its back to the Forum. Michelangelo gave the buildings the "giant order"— huge pilasters make the existing two-story buildings feel one-storied and more harmonious with the new square. Notice how the statues atop these buildings welcome you and then draw you in.

The terraces just downhill (past either side of the mayor's palace) offer grand views of the Forum. To the left of the mayor's palace is a copy of the famous she-wolf statue on a column. Farther down is *il nasone* ("the big nose"), a refreshing water fountain (see photo). Block the spout with your fingers, and water spurts up for drinking. Romans joke that a cheap Roman boy takes his date out for a drink at *il nasone*. Near the she-wolf statue is the staircase leading to a shortcut to the Victor Emmanuel Monument (see sidebar).

▲▲**Capitoline Museums (Musei Capitolini)**—Some of ancient Rome's most famous statues and art are housed in the two palaces (Palazzo dei Conservatori and Palazzo Nuovo) that flank the equestrian statue in Piazza del Campidoglio. They're connected by an underground passage that leads to the vacant Tabularium and panoramic views of the Roman Forum.

Cost and Hours: €12, €14 combo-ticket includes Montemartini Museum, Tue-Sun 9:00-20:00, closed Mon, last entry one hour before closing, audioguide-€5, tel. 06-8205-9127 or 06-0608, www.museicapitolini.org.

Visiting the Museums: The museum's layout—with two different buildings connected by an underground passage—can be confusing, but you're likely to happen upon all of the highlights. You'll enter at the Palazzo dei Conservatori (on your right as you face the equestrian statue), cross underneath the square (beneath the Palazzo Senatorio, the mayoral palace, not open to public), and exit from the Palazzo Nuovo (on your left).

The **Palazzo dei Conservatori** claims to be one of the world's oldest museums, founded in 1471 when a pope gave ancient statues to the citizens of Rome. In the courtyard, enjoy the massive chunks of Constantine: his head, hand, and foot. When intact, this giant held the place of honor in the Basilica of Constantine in the Forum.

The museum is worthwhile, with lavish rooms and several great statues, including the *Boy Extracting a Thorn*. In one grand room, you'll see the 13th-century *Capitoline She-Wolf* (the little statues of Romulus and Remus were added in the Renaissance), the enchanting *Commodus as Hercules*, and a marvelous statue of Marcus Aurelius (the father of Commodus) on a horse. The greatest surviving equestrian statue of antiquity, this was the original centerpiece of the square (where a copy stands today).

Christians in the Dark Ages thought that the statue's hand was raised in blessing, which probably led to their misidentifying him as Constantine, the first Christian emperor. While most pagan statues were destroyed by Christians, "Constantine" was spared.

The second-floor café, **Caffè Capitolino,** has a splendid patio offering city views. It's lovely at sunset (public entrance for non-museum-goers off Piazza Caffarelli and through door #4).

Go downstairs to the **Tabularium.** Built in the first century B.C., these sturdy vacant rooms once held the archives of ancient Rome. The word Tabularium comes from "tablet," on which Romans wrote their laws. You won't see any tablets, but you will see a stunning head-on view of the Forum from the windows.

Leave the Tabularium and enter the **Palazzo Nuovo,** which houses mostly portrait busts of forgotten emperors. But it also has two must-see statues: the *Dying Gaul* and the *Capitoline Venus* (both on the first floor up).

Santa Maria in Aracoeli Church—The church atop Capitoline Hill is old and dear to the hearts of Romans. It stands on the site where Emperor Augustus (supposedly) had a premonition of the com-
ing of Mary and Christ standing on an
"altar in the sky" *(ara coeli)*. The church
is Rome in a nutshell, where you can
time-travel across 2,000 years by standing in one spot.

Cost and Hours: Free, daily
April-Oct 9:00-12:30 & 15:00-18:30,
Nov-March 9:00-12:30 & 14:30-17:30.
While dedicated pilgrims climb up the
long, steep staircase from street level
(the right side of Victor Emmanuel
Monument, as you face it), savvy sightseers prefer to enter through
the shortcut atop Capitoline Hill (see sidebar).

Piazza Venezia

This vast square, dominated by the big, white Victor Emmanuel
Monument, is a major transportation hub and the focal point of
modern Rome. (The square has been dug up for years—Metro
line C is under construction, and when anything of archaeological
importance is uncovered, progress is interrupted, hence the canopied site on the square today.) With your back to the monument
(you'll get the best views from the terrace by the guards and eternal flame), look down Via del Corso, the city's axis, surrounded by
Rome's classiest shopping district. In the 1930s, Benito Mussolini
whipped up Italy's nationalistic fervor from a balcony above the
square (it's the less-grand balcony on the left). Fascist masses
filled the square screaming, "Four more years!"—or something
like that. Mussolini created the boulevard Via dei Fori Imperiali
(to your right) to open up views of the Colosseum in the distance
to impress his visiting friend Adolf Hitler. Mussolini lied to his
people, mixing fear and patriotism to push his country to the right
and embroil the Italians in expensive and regrettable wars. In 1945,
they shot Mussolini and hung him from a meat hook in Milan.
(Former Prime Minister Silvio Berlusconi's headquarters are still
located—thought-provokingly—just behind Mussolini's. That
explains all the security on Via del Plebiscito.)

With your back still to the monument, circle around the left
side, and look down into the ditch on your left to see the ruins of
an ancient apartment building from the first century A.D.; part of it
was transformed into a tiny church (faded frescoes and bell tower).
Rome was built in layers—almost everywhere you go, there's an

earlier version beneath your feet. (The hop-on, hop-off Trambus 110 stops just across the busy intersection from here.)

Continuing on, you reach two staircases leading up Capitoline Hill. One is Michelangelo's grand staircase up to the Campidoglio. The longer of the two leads to the Santa Maria in Aracoeli Church, a good example of the earliest style of Christian churches (described earlier). The contrast between this climb-on-your-knees ramp to God's house and Michelangelo's elegant stairs illustrates the changes Renaissance humanism brought civilization.

From the bottom of Michelangelo's stairs, look right several blocks down the street to see a condominium actually built upon the surviving ancient pillars and arches of Teatro di Marcello.

▲Victor Emmanuel Monument—This oversize monument to Italy's first king, built to celebrate the 50th anniversary of the country's unification in 1861, was part of Italy's push to overcome the new country's strong regionalism and create a national identity. At the base of this statue, Italy's Tomb of the Unknown Soldier—flanked by Italian flags and armed guards—is watched over by the goddess Roma (with the gold mosaic background).

The scale of the monument is over-the-top: 200 feet high, 500 feet wide. The 43-foot-long statue of the king on the horse is one of the biggest equestrian statues in the world. The king's moustache forms an arc five feet long, and a person could sit within the horse's hoof. With its gleaming white sheen (from a recent scrubbing) and enormous scale, the monument provides a vivid sense of what Ancient Rome looked like at its peak—imagine the Forum filled with shiny, grandiose buildings like this one.

The "Vittoriano" (as locals call it) is open and free to the public. You can simply climb the front stairs, or go inside from one of several entrances: midway up the monument through doorways flanking the central statue, on either side at street level, and at the base of the colonnade (two-thirds of the way up, near the shortcut from Capitoline Hill). The little-visited **Museum of the Risorgimento** fills several floors with displays (free, well-described in English) on the movement and war that led to the unification of Italy in 1870. A section on the lower east side hosts temporary exhibits of minor works by major artists (free to enter museum, exhibits around €10, tel. 06-322-5380, www.comunicare organizzando.it/home.asp). A café is at the base of the top colonnade, on the monument's east side.

You can climb the stairs to the midway point for a decent

view, keep climbing to the base of the colonnade for a better view, or, for the best view, ride the **Rome from the Sky** elevator, which zips you from the top of the stair climb (at the back of the monument) to the rooftop for the grandest, 360-degree view of the center of Rome—even better than from the top of St. Peter's dome. Helpful panoramic diagrams describe the skyline, with powerful binoculars available for zooming in on particular sights. It's best in late afternoon, when it's beginning to cool off and Rome glows.

Cost and Hours: Monument—Free, daily 9:30-18:30, a few WCs scattered throughout, tel. 06-679-3598. Elevator—€7, Mon-Thu 9:30-18:30, Fri-Sun 9:30-19:30, ticket office closes 45 minutes earlier, WC at entrance, tel. 06-6920-2049; follow *ascensori panoramici* signs inside the Victor Emmanuel Monument or take the shortcut from Capitoline Hill (no elevator access from street level).

Pantheon Neighborhood

Besides being home to ancient sights and historic churches, this neighborhood gives Rome its urban-village feel. Wander narrow streets, sample the many shops and eateries, and gather with the locals in squares marked by bubbling fountains. Exploring is especially good in the evening, when the restaurants bustle and streets are jammed with foot traffic. For a self-guided walk of this neighborhood, from Campo de' Fiori to the Trevi Fountain, see my "Heart of Rome Walk" on page 815.

Getting There: To reach the Pantheon neighborhood, you can walk (it's a 15-minute walk from Capitoline Hill), take a taxi, or catch a bus. Buses stop at a chaotic square called Largo Argentina, a few blocks south of the Pantheon—from here you can walk north on either Via dei Cestari or Via di Torre Argentina to the Pantheon. Buses #40 and #64 carry tourists and pickpockets frequently between the Termini train station and Vatican City (#492 serves the same areas via a different route). Bus #87 connects to the Colosseum. The *elettrico* minibus #116 runs between Campo de' Fiori and Piazza Barberini via the Pantheon. The most dramatic approach is on foot coming from Piazza Navona along Via Giustiniani, which spills directly into Piazza della Rotonda, offering the classic Pantheon view.

▲▲▲**Pantheon**—For the greatest look at the splendor of Rome, antiquity's best-preserved interior is a must. Built two millennia ago, this influential domed temple served as the model for

ROME

Pantheon Neighborhood

Michelangelo's dome of St. Peter's and many others.

Because the Pantheon became a church dedicated to the martyrs just after the fall of Rome, the barbarians left it alone, and the locals didn't use it as a quarry. The portico is called "Rome's umbrella"—a fun local gathering in a rainstorm. Walk past its one-piece granite columns (biggest in Italy, shipped from Egypt) and through the original bronze doors. Sit inside under the glorious skylight and enjoy classical architecture at its best.

The dome, 142 feet high and wide, was Europe's biggest until the Renaissance. Michelangelo's dome at St. Peter's, while much higher, is about three feet narrower. The brilliance of this dome's construction astounded architects through the ages. During the Renaissance, Brunelleschi was given permission to cut into the dome (see the little square hole above and to the right of the entrance) to analyze the material. The concrete dome gets thinner and lighter with height—the highest part is volcanic pumice.

This wonderfully harmonious architecture greatly inspired Raphael and other artists of the Renaissance. Raphael, along with Italy's first two kings, chose to be buried here.

The Pantheon is the only ancient building in Rome continuously used since its construction. When you leave, notice that the building is sunken below current street level, showing how the rest of the city has risen on 20 centuries of rubble.

The nearest WCs are at bars and cafés on the Pantheon's square. Several reasonable eateries are a block or two north up Via del Pantheon. Some of Rome's best gelato is nearby.

Cost and Hours: Free, Mon-Sat 8:30-19:30, Sun 9:00-18:00, holidays 9:00-13:00, closed for Mass Sat at 17:00 and Sun at 10:30, audioguide-€5, tel. 06-6830-0230. You can download a free Rick Steves audio tour of the Pantheon to your mobile device; see page 1101.

When to Go: Try to get to the Pantheon first thing in the morning: While it's jammed with people midday, you'll have it all to yourself before 9:00.

▲▲**Churches near the Pantheon**—The **Church of San Luigi dei Francesi** has a magnificent chapel painted by Caravaggio (free, daily 10:00-12:30 & 15:00-19:00 except closed Thu afternoon, between the Pantheon and the north end of Piazza Navona). The only Gothic church in Rome is the **Church of Santa Maria sopra Minerva,** with a little-known Michelangelo statue, *Christ Bearing the Cross* (free, Mon-Fri 7:00-19:00, Sat-Sun 8:00-12:30 & 15:30-19:00, on a little square behind Pantheon, to the east). The **Church of San Ignazio,** several blocks east of the Pantheon, is a riot of Baroque illusions with a false dome (free, Mon-Sat 7:30-19:00, Sun 9:00-19:00). A few blocks away, across Corso Vittorio Emanuele, is the rich and Baroque **Gesù Church,** headquarters of the Jesuits in Rome (free, daily 7:00-12:30 & 16:00-19:45, interesting daily service at 17:30).

▲**Galleria Doria Pamphilj**—This underappreciated gallery, in the heart of the old city, offers a rare chance to wander through a noble family's lavish rooms with the prince who calls this downtown mansion home. Well, almost. Through an audioguide, the prince lovingly narrates his family's story as you tour the palace and its world-class art. Don't miss Velázquez's intense, majestic, ultra-realistic portrait of Pope Innocent X (1574-1655), patriarch of the Pamphilj (pahm-FEEL-yee) family. It stands alongside an equally impressive bust of the pope by Bernini. Stroll through a mini-Versailles-like hall of mirrors to more paintings, including works by Titian and Raphael. Finally, relax along with Mary, Joseph, and Jesus, and let the angel serenade you in Caravaggio's *Rest on the Flight to Egypt.*

Cost and Hours: €10.50, includes worthwhile 1.5-hour audioguide, daily 10:00-17:00, last entry 45 minutes before closing, elegant café, from Piazza Venezia walk 2 blocks up Via del Corso to #305, tel. 06-679-7323, www.dopart.it/roma.

ROME

Piazza di Pietra (Piazza of Stone)—The square was actually a quarry set up to chew away at the abandoned Temple of Hadrian, dedicated to the emperor responsible for building the Pantheon (look for his bust and a model of the temple in a window on the square). You can still see the holes that hungry medieval scavengers chipped into the columns to steal the metal pins that held the slabs together. Look over the railing to see ground level 1,900 years ago (two blocks toward Via del Corso from Pantheon).

▲**Trevi Fountain**—The bubbly Baroque fountain, worth ▲▲ by night, is a minor sight to art scholars...but a major nighttime gathering spot for teens on the make and tourists tossing coins. The coins tourists deposit daily are collected to feed Rome's poor (for more on the fountain, see page 821).

Palazzo del Quirinale—This presidential palace, the former home of several popes and the Italian royal family, feels like a combination the White House and the Palace of Versailles. Guided tours—on Sundays only—take you through its opulent public rooms. Named after the highest of Rome's seven hills, the square in front offers fine views of St. Peter's Basilica.

Cost and Hours: €5, Sun 8:30-12:00 only—closed rest of the week, expect a line, square always open, 200 yards east and up the hill from Trevi Fountain on Piazza del Quirinale, tel. 06-46991, www.quirinale.it.

Vatican City

Vatican City, the world's smallest country, contains St. Peter's Basilica (with Michelangelo's exquisite *Pietà*) and the Vatican

Museum (with Michelangelo's Sistine Chapel). A helpful **TI** is just to the left of St. Peter's Basilica as you're facing it (Mon-Sat 8:30-18:15, closed Sun, tel. 06-6988-1662, Vatican switchboard tel. 06-6982, www.vatican.va). The entrances to St. Peter's and to the Vatican Museum are a 15-minute walk apart (follow the outside of the Vatican wall, which links the two sights). The nearest Metro stop—Ottaviano—still involves a 10-minute walk to either sight.

Modest dress is required of men, women, and children

Vatican City

Piazzale degli Eroi

Cipro M

MARKET

VIA ANDREA DORIA

VIA CANDIA

VIA JUNIS

VIA LEONE IV

VIA SEBASTIANO VENIERO

VIA CIPRO

#492 B

VIA-ANGELO EMO

VIALE VATICANO

WALL

VATICAN MUSEUM

VATICAN CITY

Gardens

SISTINE CHAPEL

PAPAL APT. 2

RADIO VATICAN

ST. PETER'S

2

OBELISK

St. Peter's Square T

AUDIENCE HALL

WALL

#64 B

VIA PORTA CAVALLEGGERI

To Civitavecchia

VIA D. STAZIONE

200 Meters

200 Yards

VIALE DELLE MILIZIE

TRIONFALE

VIALE GIULIO CESARE

Piazza dei Quiriti

Ottaviano M

VIA DEGLI SCIPIONI

VIA BARLETTA

VIA OTTAVIANO

Piazza del Risorgimento

#49 B T

VIA COLA DI RIENZO

VIA CRESCENZIO

ITALIAN POST

BORGO VITTORIO

BORGO PIO

VIA CORRIDORI

To Castel Sant'Angelo & Bus #40

WALL

VIA DELLA CONCILIAZIONE

BORGO SANTO SPIRITO

PONTE VITTORIO EMANUELE II

Tiber River

PONTE PRINCIPE AMEDEO

TUNNEL

To San Pietro Train Station

To Trastevere

1 Entrance to Vatican Museum   **2** Post Office & WC

---

throughout Vatican City, even outdoors. Otherwise the Swiss Guard can turn you away. Cover your shoulders; bring a light jacket or cover-up if you're wearing a tank top. Wear long pants instead of shorts. Skirts or dresses should extend below your knee.

▲▲▲St. Peter's Basilica (Basilica San Pietro)

There is no doubt: This is the richest and grandest church on earth. To call it vast is like calling Einstein smart. Plaques on the floor show where other, smaller churches would end if they were placed inside. The ornamental cherubs would dwarf a large man. Birds roost inside, and thousands of people wander about,

ROME

heads craned heavenward, hardly noticing each other. Don't miss Michelangelo's *Pietà* (behind bulletproof glass) to the right of the entrance. Bernini's altar work and twisting, towering canopy are brilliant.

Cost: Free entry to basilica and crypt. Dome climb-€6 if you take the stairs all the way up, or €7 to ride an elevator partway (to the roof), then climb to the top of the dome (for details, see "Dome Climb," later). Museum-Treasury-€6.

Hours: The **church** is open daily April-Sept 7:00-19:00, Oct-March 7:00-18:00. It closes on Wednesday mornings during papal audiences. **Mass** is held daily, generally in Italian and in the south (left) transept, though other possible locations are the apse and the Blessed Sacrament Chapel (on right side of nave). Mass is typically scheduled on Mon-Sat at 8:30, 9:00, 10:00, 11:00, 12:00, and 17:00 (in Latin, in the apse); and on Sun and holidays at 9:00, 10:30 (in Latin), 11:30, 12:15, 13:00, 16:00, and 17:45. Confirm the schedule and location on site, or go to www.vatican.va (click on "Basilicas and Papal Chapels" link).

The **Museum-Treasury** is open daily April-Sept 9:00-18:15, Oct-March 9:00-17:15. The **crypt** is open daily 9:00-16:00. The **dome** is open to climbers daily April-Sept 8:00-18:00, Oct-March 8:00-17:00, last entry 30 minutes before closing.

When to Go: The best time to visit the church is early (before 10:00) or late; at 17:00, when the church is fairly empty, sunbeams can work their magic, and the late-afternoon Mass fills the place with spiritual music. The downside to visiting late is that the area around the altar and beyond is often roped off from around 16:00 to prepare for Mass. Still, the shorter line, smaller crowds, and ambience might make it worthwhile.

Avoiding Lines: The security-checkpoint lines can get quite long and there's no reliable way to avoid them (thankfully, they move relatively quickly). Occasionally, St. Peter's is accessible from the Vatican Museum (though the museum comes with its own long lines, which can be avoided if you reserve your entry time). If you visit the Vatican Museum first, pray that the shortcut from the Sistine Chapel directly to St. Peter's is open (depends on crowd levels—see page 859 for specifics.)

Dress Code: No shorts, above-the-knee skirts, or bare shoulders (this applies to men, women, and children). Attendants strictly enforce this dress code, even in hot weather.

Getting There: Take the Metro to Ottaviano, then walk 10 minutes south on Via Ottaviano. There are several good bus options: The #40 express bus drops off at Piazza Pio, next to Castel Sant'Angelo—a 10-minute walk to St. Peter's. The more crowded bus #64 is convenient for pickpockets and stops just outside St. Peter's Square to the south (get off the bus after it crosses the Tiber, at the first stop past the tunnel; backtrack toward the tunnel and turn left when you see the rows of columns). Bus #492 heads through the center of town, stopping at Largo Argentina, and gets you near Piazza Risorgimento (get off when you see the Vatican walls). A taxi from Termini train station to St. Peter's costs about €11.

Tours: The Vatican TI conducts free 1.5-hour tours of **St. Peter's** (depart from TI Mon-Fri 14:15, plus Tue and Thu 9:45, confirm schedule at TI, tel. 06-6988-1662). Audioguides can be rented near the checkroom (€5 plus ID, for church only, daily 9:00-17:00). You can download a free Rick Steves audio tour of St. Peter's Basilica to your mobile device; see page 1101.

To see St. Peter's original grave, you can take a **Scavi "Excavations"** tour into the Necropolis (€12, 1.5 hours, ages 15 and older only, no photos). Book at least two months in advance by phone (tel. 06-6988-5318), email (scavi@fsp.va), or fax (06-6987-3017), following the detailed instructions at www.vatican.va (search on "Excavations Office"); no response means they're booked up.

Dome Climb (Cupola): To get to the roof (which is about the halfway point to the dome), you can either take the elevator (€7) or stairs (€6, 231 steps); from the roof, you'll have to climb 323 steps to the top of the dome. Allow an hour to go up and down. The entry to the elevator is just outside the basilica on the north side of St. Peter's (near the secret exit from the Sistine Chapel). Look for signs to the cupola.

Vatican Gardens: If you want to walk through the Vatican Gardens, you must book a tour online at least two days in advance at http://biglietteriamusei.vatican.va. No response means they're booked up (€31, 2 hours, usually daily except Wed and Sun, includes entry to Vatican Museum; tours start at 9:30 or 10:00 at Vatican Museum tour desk). Roma Cristiana's open-bus tours of the gardens can usually be booked on short notice (€15, 1 hour, 2/hour Mon-Tue and Thu-Sat 8:00-13:00, best to reserve a couple days in advance but same-day availability possible, Opera Romana Pellegrinaggi office in front of St. Peter's Square, Piazza Pio XII 9, tel. 06-6989-6380 or 06-698-961).

With Limited Time: Stroll the nave, glance up at the dome and down at the marker of St. Peter's tomb. Don't miss the Pietà. Skip the crypt and the dome climb.

Baggage Check: The free bag check (mandatory for bags larger than a purse or daypack) is outside the basilica (to the right as you face the entrance) and just inside the security checkpoint.

Services: WCs are to the right and left on St. Peter's Square (just outside the security checkpoint and exit), near baggage storage down the steps on the right side of the entrance, and on the roof.

⊙ Self-Guided Tour: For a quick walk through the basilica, follow these points:

❶ The atrium is itself bigger than most churches. The huge white columns on the portico date from the first church (fourth century). Notice the historic doors (the Holy Door, on the right, won't be opened until the next Jubilee Year, in 2025).

❷ The purple, circular porphyry stone marks the site of Charlemagne's coronation in A.D. 800 (in the first St. Peter's church that stood on this site). From here, get a sense of the immensity of the church, which can accommodate 60,000 worshippers standing on its six acres.

❸ Michelangelo planned a Greek-cross floor plan, rather than the Latin-cross standard in medieval churches. A Greek cross, symbolizing the perfection of God, and by association the goodness of man, was important to the humanist Michelangelo. But accommodating—and impressing—large crowds was important to the Church in the fancy Baroque age, which followed Michelangelo, so the original nave length was doubled. Stand halfway up the nave and imagine the stubbier design that Michelangelo had in mind.

❹ View the magnificent dome from the statue of St. Andrew. See the vision of heaven above the windows: Jesus, Mary, a ring of saints, rings of angels, and, on the very top, God the Father.

Visitors can go down to the crypt (labeled as the *Grotte* or *Tombe*) within the foundations of Old St. Peter's, containing tombs of popes and memorial chapels. The crypt entrance is usually beside the statue of St. Andrew, to the left of the main altar. Stairs lead you down to the floor level of the previous church, where you'll pass the sepulcher of Peter. This lighted niche with an icon is not Peter's actual tomb, but part of a shrine that stands atop Peter's tomb. The walk through the crypt is free and quick (15 minutes)—but you won't see St. Peter's original grave unless you take a Scavi "Excavations" tour (explained earlier).

❺ The statue of St. Peter, with an irresistibly kissable toe, is one of the few pieces of art that predate this church. It adorned the first St. Peter's church.

❻ Circle to the right around the statue of Peter to find the lighted glass niche with the red-robed body of Pope John XXIII (r. 1958-1963), who presided over the landmark Vatican II Council that instituted major reforms and brought the Church into the modern age.

❼ The main altar sits directly over St. Peter's tomb and under Bernini's seven-story bronze canopy.

❽ St. Peter's throne and Bernini's starburst dove window is the site of a daily Mass (check the schedule on site, or go to www .vatican.va—click on "Basilicas and Papal Chapels" link; for Mass times in other locations, see "Hours" on page 846).

St. Peter's Basilica

Not to Scale

APSE

MAIN ALTAR

DOME ENTRANCE

NAVE

Court-yard

EXIT FROM SISTINE CHAPEL

ATRIUM

SWISS GUARDS

ENTER

AUDIOGUIDES, WC & BAGGAGE STORAGE

STEPS

St. Peter's Square

1. Holy Door
2. Charlemagne's Coronation Site
3. Extent of Original "Greek Cross" Plan
4. St. Andrew Statue; View of Dome; Crypt Entrance
5. St. Peter Statue (with Kissable Toe)
6. Pope John XXIII
7. Main Altar (over Peter's Tomb)
8. BERNINI – Dove Window & Throne of Peter
9. Peter's Crucifixion Site
10. RAPHAEL – Mosaic Copy of The Transfiguration
11. MICHELANGELO – Pietà
12. Tomb of Pope John Paul II
13. Museum-Treasury
14. Blessed Sacrament Chapel
15. Dome Entrance

ROME

9. St. Peter was crucified on this spot when this location was simply "the Vatican Hill." The obelisk now standing in the center of St. Peter's square marked the center of a Roman racecourse long before a church stood here.

10. The church is filled with mosaics, not paintings. Notice the mosaic copy of Raphael's *Transfiguration*.

11. Michelangelo sculpted his *Pietà* when he was 24 years old.

Benedict XVI

When Josef Ratzinger became the 265th pope, he introduced himself as "a simple, humble worker in the vineyard of the Lord." But the man has a complex history, a reputation for intellectual brilliance, a flair for the piano, and a penchant for controversy for his unbending devotion to traditional Catholic doctrine.

Born in small-town Bavaria in 1927, he lived under Nazi rule as many Germans did—outwardly obeying leaders while inwardly conflicted. Like all 14-year-old boys, he joined the Hitler Youth and, like most German men, was drafted into the army. During World War II, he trained to spray flak from anti-aircraft guns, saw Jews transported to death camps, and, like many Germans in the final days of the war, deserted his post.

After the war, he completed his studies in theology and became a rising voice of liberal Catholicism, serving as an advisor at the Second Vatican Council (1962-1965). But after the May 1968 student revolts rocked Europe's Establishment, he became increasingly convinced that Church tradition was needed to offset the growing chaos of the world.

Pope John Paul II appointed him to several positions, and Ratzinger became the pope's closest advisor and good friend. Every Friday afternoon for two decades, they met for lunch, intellectual sparring, and friendly conversation.

Under John Paul II, Ratzinger served as the "enforcer" of Church doctrine, earning the nickname "God's Rottweiler." He spoke out against ordaining women, chastised Latin American priests for fomenting class warfare (Liberation theology), reassigned bishops who were soft on homosexuality, reaffirmed opposition to birth control, and wrote thoughtful papers challenging the secular world's moral relativism. He also punished pedophile priests, though critics charged him with being too focused on preserving the Church's image. In 2010, he was again criticized, now as pope, for not dealing forcefully enough with sex abusers.

Ratzinger chose the name of "Benedict" to recall both Pope Benedict XV (who tried to bring Europeans together after World War I) and the original St. Benedict (c. 480-543), the monk who symbolizes Europe's Christian roots. A true pan-European who speaks many languages, Ratzinger heads a Church that thrives everywhere except Europe, which is becoming increasingly secular (with the notable exception of an increasing Muslim population). Benedict XVI has continued John Paul II's two priorities: defending Catholic doctrine in a changing world and building bridges with fellow Christians.

(A *pietà* is a work that represents Mary with the body of Christ taken down from the cross.) Michelangelo's mastery of the body is obvious in this powerfully beautiful masterpiece. Jesus is believably dead, and Mary, the eternally youthful "handmaiden" of the Lord, accepts God's will...even if it means giving up her son.

⓬ The tomb of Pope John Paul II was moved to the chapel of San Sebastian in 2011, after he was beatified by Pope Benedict XVI (a step on the road to sainthood). He lies beneath a painting of the steadfast St. Sebastian, his favorite saint.

⓭ Outside on the north side of St. Peter's, an elevator leads to the roof and the stairway up the dome. The dome, Michelangelo's last work, is (you guessed it) the biggest anywhere. Taller than a football field is long, it's well worth the sweaty climb for a great view of Rome, the Vatican grounds, and the inside of the basilica—particularly heavenly while there is singing. Look around—Rome has no modern skyline. No building in Rome is allowed to exceed the height of St. Peter's. The elevator takes you to the rooftop of the nave. From there, a few steps take you to a balcony at the base of the dome looking down into the church interior. After that, the one-way, 323-step climb (for some people, it's claustrophobic) to the cupola begins. The rooftop level (below the dome) has a gift shop, WC, drinking fountain, and a commanding view.

⓮ For most, the museum-treasury (on the left side of the nave, near the altar) is not worth the admission.

⓯ You're welcome to step through the metalwork gates into the Blessed Sacrament Chapel, an oasis of peace reserved for prayer and meditation (on the right-hand side of the church, about midway to the altar).

▲▲▲Vatican Museum (Musei Vaticani)

The four miles of displays in this immense museum—from ancient statues to Christian frescoes to modern paintings—culminate in the Raphael Rooms and Michelangelo's glorious Sistine Chapel. This is one of Europe's top three or four houses of art. It can be exhausting, so plan your visit carefully, focusing on a few themes. Allow two hours for a quick visit, three or four hours for enough time to enjoy it.

Cost and Hours: €15 plus optional €4 reservation fee, Mon-Sat 9:00-18:00, last entry at 16:00 (though the official closing time is 18:00, the staff starts ushering you out at 17:30), closed on religious holidays and Sun except last Sun of the month (when it's free, more crowded, and open 9:00-14:00, last entry at 12:30); may be open Fri nights May-July and Sept-Oct 19:00-23:00 (last entry at 21:30) by online reservation only. Hours are subject to constant change and frequent holidays; check http://mv.vatican.va for current times. Lines are extremely long in the morning—go in the afternoon, or skip the ticket-buying line altogether by reserving an entry time on their website. A €7 audioguide is available (ID required).

The museum is closed on many holidays (mainly religious ones), including, for 2013: Jan 1 (New Year's), Jan 6 (Epiphany), Feb 11 (Vatican City established), March 19 (St. Joseph), April 1 (Easter Monday), May 1 (Labor Day), June 29 (Saints Peter and Paul), Aug 15 plus either Aug 14 or 16—it varies year to year (Assumption of the Virgin), Nov 1 (All Saints' Day), Dec 8 (Immaculate Conception), and Dec 25 and 26 (Christmas).

Individual rooms may close at odd hours, especially in the afternoon. The rooms described here are usually open.

Reservations: Bypass the long ticket lines by reserving an entry time online at http://mv.vatican.va. It costs €19 (€15 ticket plus €4 booking fee, pay with credit card). It's easy. You choose your day and time, they email you a confirmation immediately, and you print out the voucher with its reservation bar code. At the Vatican Museum, bypass the ticket-buying line and queue up at the "Entrance with Reservations"

line (to the right). Show your voucher to the guard, who will scan it and let you in. Once inside the museum, go to a ticket window *(a cassa),* either in the lobby or upstairs, present your voucher and ID, and they'll issue your ticket.

When to Go: The museum is generally hot and crowded, with waits of up to two hours to buy tickets (figure about a 10-minute wait for every 100 yards in line). The worst days are Saturdays, the last Sunday of the month (when it's free), Mondays, rainy days, and any day before or after a holiday closure. Mornings are most crowded. To see the Sistine Chapel with fewer crowds, visit at the end of the day.

Avoiding Lines: The best way to skip the long lines is to **reserve tickets** in advance (described above). If you book a **guided tour** (see "Tours," next page), you can approach the guard with your voucher and go right in. If you book with a private tour company, you may still have a short wait at crowded times.

You can often buy **same-day, skip-the-line tickets** through the TI in St. Peter's Square (to the left, as you face the basilica). You pay the same price (€15 ticket plus €4 reservation fee) that you would online. If the TI doesn't have tickets, you could try the tour company called Roma Cristiana, which sells higher-priced, same-day tickets from their kiosk at St. Peter's Square (€15 ticket plus €11 booking fee, entrances almost hourly, tel. 06-6980-6380, www.operaromanapellegrinaggi.org).

If you don't have a reservation, **try arriving after 14:00,** when crowds subside somewhat. Another good time is during the papal audience, on Wednesday at 10:30, when many tourists are at St. Peter's Basilica.

Make sure you get in the right line. Generally, individuals without tickets line up against the Vatican City wall (to the left of the entrance as you face it), and reservation holders (both individuals and groups) enter on the right.

Dress Code: Remember, modest dress is required (no shorts, above-knee skirts, or bare shoulders).

Getting There: The Ottaviano Metro stop is a 10-minute walk from the entrance. Bus #49 from Piazza Cavour stops right at the entrance. Bus #23 from Trastevere hugs the west bank of the Tiber and stops on Via Leone IV, just downhill from the entrance. Bus #492 heads from the city center past Piazza Risorgimento and the Vatican walls, and also stops on Via Leone IV. Bus #64 stops on the other side of St. Peter's Square, a 15- to 20-minute walk (facing the church from the obelisk, take a right through the colonnade and follow the Vatican Wall). Taxis are reasonable (hop in and say, "moo-ZAY-ee vah-tee-KAH-nee").

Tours: A €7 **audioguide** is available at the top of the spiral ramp/escalator (ID required). If you rent an audioguide, you lose the option of taking the shortcut from the Sistine Chapel to St. Peter's (described later, under "Museum Strategies"), since audioguides must be returned to the museum entrance/exit.

You can download a free Rick Steves **audio tour** of the Sistine Chapel to your mobile device; see page 1101.

The Vatican offers **English tours** that are easy to book online (€31, includes admission, http://mv.vatican.va). As with individual ticket reservations, present your confirmation voucher to a guard to the right of the entrance; then, once inside, go to the Guided Tours desk (in the lobby, up a few stairs).

Both **private tour** companies and private guides offer English tours of the museum, usually allowing you to skip the long ticket-buying line. For a listing of several companies, see page 800.

With Limited Time: See the octagonal courtyard *(Laocoön),* then follow the crowd flow directly to the Sistine Chapel, sightseeing along the way. Skip the Etruscan Wing and the Pinacoteca. From the Sistine Chapel, head straight to St. Peter's via the shortcut, if open (see "Museum Strategies," below).

Security and Baggage Check: To enter the museum, you pass through a metal detector (no pocket knives allowed). The baggage check (to the right after security) takes only bigger bags; you'll need to carry your day bag with you.

Museum Strategies: The museum has two exits, and you'll

ROME

Vatican City

This tiny independent country of little more than 100 acres, contained entirely within Rome, has its own postal system, armed guards, helipad, mini-train station, and radio station (KPOP). It also has two huge sights: St. Peter's Basilica (with Michelangelo's *Pietà*) and the Vatican Museum (with the Sistine Chapel). Politically powerful, the Vatican is the religious capital of 1.1 billion Roman Catholics. If you're not a Catholic, become one for your visit.

The pope is both the religious and secular leader of Vatican City. For centuries, locals referred to him as "King Pope." Italy and the Vatican didn't always have good relations. In fact, after unification (in 1870), when Rome's modern grid plan was built around the miniscule Vatican, it seemed as if the new buildings were designed to be just high enough so no one could see the dome of St. Peter's from street level. Modern Italy was created in 1870, but the Holy See didn't recognize it as a country until 1929, when the pope and Mussolini signed the Lateran Pact, giving sovereignty and a few nearby churches to the Vatican.

Like every European country, Vatican City has its own versions of the euro coin (with a portrait of Pope Benedict XVI and, before him, of Pope John Paul II). You're unlikely to find one in your pocket, though, as they are snatched up by collectors before falling into circulation.

Post Offices: The Vatican postal service is famous for its stamps, which you can get from offices on St. Peter's Square (next to TI or between the columns just before the security checkpoint) or in the Vatican Museum (Mon-Sat 8:30-18:30, closed Sun). Vatican stamps are good throughout Rome, but to use the Vatican's mail service, you need to mail your cards from the Vatican; write your postcards ahead of time. (Note that the Vatican won't mail cards with Italian stamps.)

Seeing the Pope: Your best chances for a sighting are on Sunday or Wednesday. The pope usually gives a blessing at noon on Sunday from his apartment on St. Peter's Square (except in July and August, when he speaks at his summer residence at Castel Gandolfo, 25 miles from Rome, reachable by train from

want to decide which you'll take before you enter. The **main exit** is right near the entrance. Use this one if you want to rent an audio-guide (which you must return at the entrance) or if you plan on following this self-guided tour exactly as laid out, visiting the Pinacoteca (painting gallery) at the end.

The other exit is a handy but sometimes closed) **shortcut** that leads from the Sistine Chapel directly to St. Peter's Basilica (spilling out alongside the church; see map on page 857). This route saves you a 30-minute walk (15 minutes back to the Vatican Museum entry/exit, then 15 minutes to St. Peter's) and lets you

Rome's Termini train station). St. Peter's is easiest (just show up) and, for most, enough of a "visit." Those interested in a more formal appearance (though not more intimate) can get a ticket for the Wednesday general audience (at 10:30) when the pope, arriving in his Popemobile, greets and blesses the crowds at St. Peter's from a canopied platform on the square (except in winter, when he speaks at 10:30 in the 7,000-seat Paolo VI Auditorium, next to St. Peter's Basilica). If you only want to see St. Peter's—but not the pope—avoid these times (the basilica closes during papal audiences and crowds are substantial).

For the Wednesday audience, while anyone can observe from a distance, you need a (free) ticket to get close to the papal action (and get a seat). To find out the pope's schedule and request a ticket, see www.vatican.va (click on the "Prefecture of the Papal Household" link) or call 06-6988-3114.

The American Catholic Church in Rome, Santa Susanna, lets you order tickets online (free, no booking fee but donations appreciated) for the Wednesday general audience. Pick up your reserved tickets, or check for last-minute availability, at the church the Tuesday before the audience between 17:00 and 18:45 (consider staying for the 18:00 English Mass) or Wednesday morning between 7:00 and 8:30 (Via XX Settembre 15, near recommended Via Firenze hotels, Metro: Repubblica, tel. 06-4201-4554—charming Rosanna speaks English, details at www.santasusanna.org).

Probably less convenient—unless you're already at the basilica—is getting a ticket at St. Peter's Square from the Vatican guard at their station at the bronze doors (open Tue 12:00-19:30; last-minute tickets may be available Wed morning—just join the line). It's under the "elbow" of Bernini's colonnade, on the right side of the square as you face the basilica (see map on page 857).

While many visitors come hoping for a more intimate audience, private audiences ended with the death of Pope John Paul II. Pope Benedict doesn't do them.

ROME

avoid the often-long security line at the basilica's main entrance. If you take this route, you'll have to forgo an audioguide and skip the Pinacoteca (or tour it earlier). Officially, this exit is for Vatican guides and their groups only. However, it's often open to anyone (depending on how crowded the chapel is and how the guards feel). It's worth a shot (try blending in with a group that's leaving), but be prepared for the possibility that you won't get through.

Photography: No photos are allowed in the Sistine Chapel. Elsewhere in the museum, photos without a flash are permitted.

○ **Self-Guided Tour:** Start, as civilization did, in **Egypt and Mesopotamia.** Decorating the museum's courtyard are some of the best **Greek and Roman statues** in captivity, including the *Laocoön* group (first century B.C., Hellenistic) and the *Apollo Belvedere* (a second-century Roman copy of a Greek original). The centerpiece of the next hall is the *Belvedere Torso* (just a 2,000-year-old torso, but one that had a great impact on the art of Michelangelo). Finishing off the classical statuary are two fine fourth-century porphyry sarcophagi. These royal purple tombs were made (though not used) for the Roman emperor Constantine's mother and daughter. They were Christians—and therefore outlaws—until Constantine made Christianity legal in A.D. 312, and they became saints. Both sarcophagi were quarried and worked in Egypt. The technique for working this extremely hard stone (a special tempering of metal was required) was lost after this, and porphyry marble was not chiseled again until Renaissance times in Florence.

After long halls of tapestries, old maps, broken penises, and fig leaves, you'll come to what most people are looking for: the Raphael Rooms and Michelangelo's Sistine Chapel.

After fancy rooms illustrating the "Immaculate Conception of Mary" (in the 19th century, the Vatican codified this hard-to-sell doctrine, making it a formal part of the Catholic faith) and the triumph of Constantine (with divine guidance, which led to his conversion to Christianity), you enter rooms frescoed by **Raphael** and his assistants. The highlight is the restored *School of Athens*. This is remarkable for its blatant pre-Christian classical orientation, especially since it originally wallpapered the apartments of Pope Julius II. Raphael honors the great pre-Christian thinkers—Aristotle, Plato, and company—who are portrayed as the leading artists of Raphael's day. There's Leonardo da Vinci, whom Raphael worshipped, in the role of Plato. Michelangelo broods in the foreground, added later. When Raphael snuck a peek at the Sistine Chapel, he decided that his arch-competitor was so good that he had to put their personal differences aside and include him in this tribute to the artists of his generation. Today's St. Peter's was under construction as Raphael was working. In the *School of Athens*, he gives us a sneak preview of the unfinished church.

Next is the brilliantly restored **Sistine Chapel.** This is the pope's personal chapel and also the place where, upon the death of the ruling pope, a new pope is elected (as in April 2005).

The Sistine Chapel is famous for Michelangelo's pictorial culmination of the Renaissance, showing the story of creation, with a powerful God weaving in and out of each scene through that busy first week. This is an optimistic and positive expression of the High Renaissance and a stirring example of the artistic and theological maturity of the 33-year-old Michelangelo, who spent four

Vatican Museum Overview

To Cipro Ⓜ ← VIALE VATICANO Bus #49 ⒷⓉ

To Ottaviano Ⓜ

VIA SEBASTIANO VENIERO

VIA LEONE IV

VIA OTTAVIANO

① MUSEUM ENTRANCE & EXIT

Ⓑ Bus #23 & Bus #492

WALL

② **④** **⑤** **③**

⑩

CAFETERIA

⑥

VATICAN MUSEUM

⑦

VATICAN CITY

Piazza del Risorgimento

ITALIAN POST

VIA DI PORTA ANGELICA

BORGO VITTORIO

BORGO PIO

Gardens

⑧

PAPAL APARTMENTS

SISTINE CHAPEL

ELEVATOR

⑨ CAFÉ

EXIT ATRIUM

PAPAL TICKET PICKUP

ST. PETER'S BASILICA

OBELISK

Piazza Pio XII Ⓣ

VIA DELLA CONCILIAZIONE

ℹ St. Peter's Square

100 Meters
100 Yards

AUDIENCE HALL

WALL

Ⓑ Bus #64

TUNNEL

VIA PORTA CAVALLEGGERI

To Civitavecchia

VIA D. FORNACI

VIA INNOCENZO III

VIA D. STAZIONE DI SAN PIETRO

VIA D. ALCIDE DE GASPERI

SAN PIETRO TRAIN STATION

To Termini Station

ROME

① Main Entrance & Exit
② Egyptian Rooms
③ Cortile della Pigna
④ Octagonal Courtyard
⑤ Etruscan Wing
⑥ Tapestries
⑦ Map Gallery & View of Vatican City
⑧ Raphael Rooms
⑨ Sistine Chapel & Exit to St. Peter's
⑩ Pinacoteca

From obelisk to museum entry via road is a 15-minute walk

years on this work.

The ceiling shows the history of the world before the birth of Jesus. We see God creating the world, creating man and woman, destroying the earth by flood, and so on. God himself, in his purple robe, actually appears in the first five scenes. Along the sides (where the ceiling starts to curve), we see the Old Testament prophets and pagan Greek prophetesses who foretold the coming of Christ. Dividing these scenes and figures are fake niches (a painted 3-D illusion) decorated with nude statue-like figures with symbolic meaning.

When the ceiling was finished and revealed to the public, it simply blew 'em away—it was unlike anything seen before. It both caps the Renaissance and turns it in a new direction. In perfect Renaissance spirit, it mixes Old Testament prophets with classical figures. But the style is more dramatic, shocking, and emotional than the balanced Renaissance works before it. This is a very personal work—the Gospel according to Michelangelo—but its themes and subject matter are universal. Many art scholars contend that the Sistine ceiling is the single greatest work of art by any one human being.

Later, after the Reformation wars had begun and after the Catholic army of Spain had sacked the Vatican, the reeling Church began to fight back. As part of its Counter-Reformation, a much older Michelangelo was commissioned to paint the *Last Judgment* (behind the altar).

It's Judgment Day, and Christ—the powerful figure in the center, raising his arm to spank the wicked—has come to find out who's naughty and who's nice. Beneath him, a band of angels blows its trumpets Dizzy Gillespie-style, giving a wake-up call to the sleeping dead. The dead at lower left leave their graves and prepare to be judged. The righteous, on Christ's right hand (the left side of the picture), are carried up to the glories of heaven. The wicked on the other side are hurled down to hell, where demons wait to torture them. Charon, from the underworld of Greek mythology, waits below to ferry the souls of the damned to hell.

When *The Last Judgment* was unveiled to the public in 1541, it caused a sensation. The pope is said to have dropped to his knees and cried, "Lord, charge me not with my sins when thou shalt come on the Day of Judgment."

And it changed the course of art. The complex composition, with more than 300 figures swirling around the figure of Christ, went far beyond traditional Renaissance balance. The twisted figures shown from every imaginable angle challenged other painters to try and top this master of 3-D illusion. And the sheer terror and drama of the scene was a striking contrast to the placid optimism of, say, Raphael's *School of Athens*. Michelangelo had Baroque-en all the rules of the Renaissance, signaling a new era of art.

For a **shortcut directly to St. Peter's Basilica** (see "Museum Strategies," earlier), you'll exit at the far-right corner of the Sistine Chapel (with your back to the altar). This route saves you a 30-minute walk and the wait in the St. Peter's security line, but if you exit here, you're done with the museum—you can't get back to the main entrance/exit (where audioguides need to be returned) or the **Pinacoteca** (the Vatican's small but fine collection of paintings, with Raphael's *Transfiguration*, Leonardo's unfinished *St. Jerome*, and Caravaggio's *Deposition*).

If you skip the shortcut and take the long march back, you'll find, along with the Pinacoteca, a cafeteria (long lines, uninspired food), the underrated early-Christian art section, and the exit via the souvenir shop.

Near Vatican City

▲**Castel Sant'Angelo**—Built as a tomb for the emperor, used through the Middle Ages as a castle, prison, and place of last ref-

uge for popes under attack, and today a museum, this giant pile of ancient bricks is packed with history.

Cost and Hours: €8.50, Tue-Sun 9:00-19:30, closed Mon, last entry one hour before closing, near Vatican City, Metro: Lepanto or bus #40 or #64, tel. 06-681-9111, www.castelsantangelo.beniculturali.it.

Background: Ancient Rome allowed no tombs—not even the emperor's—within its walls. So Emperor Hadrian grabbed the most commanding position just outside the walls and across the river and built a towering tomb (c. A.D. 139) well within view of the city. His mausoleum was a huge cylinder (210 by 70 feet) topped by a cypress grove and crowned by a huge statue of Hadrian himself riding a chariot. For nearly a hundred years, Roman emperors (from Hadrian to Caracalla, in A.D. 217) were buried here.

In the year 590, the archangel Michael appeared above the mausoleum to Pope Gregory the Great. Sheathing his sword, the angel signaled the end of a plague. The fortress that was Hadrian's mausoleum eventually became a fortified palace, renamed for the "holy angel."

Castel Sant'Angelo spent centuries of the Dark Ages as a fortress and prison, but was eventually connected to the Vatican via an elevated corridor at the pope's request (1277). Since Rome was repeatedly plundered by invaders, Castel Sant'Angelo was a handy place of last refuge for threatened popes. In anticipation of long sieges, rooms were decorated with papal splendor (you'll see paintings by Carlo Crivelli, Luca Signorelli, and Andrea Mantegna). In 1527, during a sack of Rome by troops of Charles V of Spain, the pope lived inside the castle for months with his entourage of hundreds (an unimaginable ordeal, considering the food service at the top-floor bar).

Visiting the Castle: Touring the place is a stair-stepping workout. After you walk around the entire base of the castle, take the small staircase down to the original Roman floor (following the route of Hadrian's funeral procession). In the atrium, study the model of the mausoleum as it was in Roman times. Imagine being surrounded by a veneer of marble, and the niche in the wall filled with a towering "welcome to my tomb" statue of Hadrian. From here, a ramp leads to the right, spiraling 400 feet. While some of the fine original brickwork and bits of mosaic survive, the marble veneer is long gone (notice the holes in the wall that held it in place).

At the end of the ramp, a bridge crosses over the room where the ashes of the emperors were kept. From here, the stairs continue out of the ancient section and into the medieval structure (built atop the mausoleum) that housed the papal apartments. Don't miss the Sala del Tesoro (Treasury), where the wealth of the Vatican was locked up in a huge chest. (*Do* miss the 58 rooms of the military museum.) From the pope's piggy bank, a narrow flight of stairs leads to the rooftop and perhaps the finest view of Rome anywhere (pick out landmarks as you stroll around). From the safety of this dramatic vantage point, the pope surveyed the city in times of siege. Look down at the bend of the Tiber, which for 2,700 years has cradled the Eternal City.

Ponte Sant'Angelo—The bridge leading to Castel Sant'Angelo was built by Hadrian for quick and regal access from downtown

to his tomb. The three middle arches are actually Roman originals and a fine example of the empire's engineering expertise. The statues of angels (each bearing a symbol of the passion of Christ—nail, sponge, shroud, and so on) are Bernini-designed and textbook Baroque. In the Middle Ages, this was the only bridge in the area that connected St. Peter's and the Vatican with downtown Rome. Nearly all pilgrims passed this bridge to and from the church. Its shoulder-high banisters recall a tragedy: During a Jubilee Year festival in 1450, the crowd got so huge that the mob pushed out the original banisters, causing nearly 200 to fall to their deaths.

North Rome
Borghese Gardens and Via Veneto

▲**Villa Borghese Gardens**—Rome's semi-scruffy three-square-mile "Central Park" is great for its shade and for people-watching

plenty of modern-day Romeos and Juliets. The best entrance is at the head of Via Veneto (Metro: Barberini, then 10-minute walk up Via Veneto and through the old Roman wall at Porta Pinciana, or catch a cab to Via Veneto—Porta Pinciana). There you'll find a cluster of buildings with a café, a kiddie arcade, and bike rental (€4/hour). Rent a bike or, for roman-

tics, a pedaled rickshaw *(riscio)*. Bikes come with locks to allow you to make sightseeing stops. Follow signs to discover the park's cafés, fountains, statues, lake, great viewpoint over Piazza del Popolo, and prime picnic spots. Some sights require paid admission, including Rome's zoo, the National Gallery of Modern Art (which holds 19th-century art; not to be confused with MAXXI, described later), and the Etruscan Museum (also described later).

▲▲▲**Borghese Gallery (Galleria Borghese)**—This plush museum, filling a cardinal's mansion in the park, offers one of Europe's most sumptuous art experiences. You'll enjoy a collection of world-class Baroque sculpture, including Bernini's *David* and his excited statue of Apollo chasing Daphne, as well as paintings by Caravaggio, Raphael, Titian, and Rubens. The museum's slick, mandatory reservation system keeps crowds to a manageable size.

The essence of the collection is the connection of the Renaissance with the classical world. As you enter, notice the second-century Roman reliefs with Michelangelo-designed panels above either end of the portico. The villa was built in the early 17th century by the great art collector Cardinal Scipione Borghese, who wanted to prove that the glories of ancient Rome were matched by the Renaissance.

In the main entry hall, high up on the wall, is a thrilling first-century Greek sculpture of a horse falling. The Renaissance-era rider was added by Pietro Bernini, father of the famous Gian Lorenzo Bernini.

Each room seems to feature a Baroque masterpiece. The best of all is in Room III: Bernini's ***Apollo and Daphne.*** It's the perfect Baroque subject—capturing a thrilling, action-filled moment. In the mythological story, Apollo—made stupid by Cupid's arrow of love—chases after Daphne, who has been turned off by the "arrow of disgust." Just as he's about to catch her, she calls to her father

Borghese Gallery—Ground Floor

ROOM VI | ROOM V | ROOM IV | ⑨ | ROOM III
⑥ | | ④ | | ③
| | | CHAPEL
| | ⑤ | ROOM II
ROOM VII | MAIN ENTRY HALL | | ②
⑦ | |
| | | ROOM I
ROOM VIII | | START | ①
⑧ | | PORTICO
Not to Scale | | ⑩
To Basement

- ① CANOVA – Pauline Borghese as Venus
- ② BERNINI – David
- ③ BERNINI – Apollo and Daphne
- ④ BERNINI – The Rape of Proserpina
- ⑤ UNKNOWN – Diana the Hunter; other marbles
- ⑥ BERNINI – Aeneas, Anchises, and Ascanius
- ⑦ "Theater of the Universe"
- ⑧ CARAVAGGIO – Various
- ⑨ Stairs up to Pinacoteca
- ⑩ To Basement (Tickets, Info, Shop, WC)

to save her. Magically, her fingers begin to sprout leaves, her toes become roots, her skin turns to bark, and she transforms into a tree. Frustrated Apollo will end up with a handful of leaves. Walk slowly around the statue. It's more air than stone.

Cost and Hours: €12.50; drops to €8.50 when there's no temporary exhibit, both prices include basic €2 reservation fee, credit cards accepted, Tue-Sun 9:00-19:00, closed Mon, ticket office closes one hour before museum, no photos, all bags and cameras must be checked (free).

Reservations: Reservations are mandatory and simple to get. It's easiest by booking online (www.ticketeria.it, €1 extra booking fee, user-friendly website). You can also reserve by telephone (tel. 06-32810, press 2 for English, pay for tickets on arrival). Call during Italian office hours: Mon-Fri 9:00-18:00, Sat 9:00-13:00, office closed Sat in Aug and Sun year-round.

Every two hours, 360 people are allowed to enter the museum. Entry times are 9:00, 11:00, 13:00, 15:00, and 17:00. Reserve a *minimum* of several days in advance for a weekday visit, and at least a week ahead for weekends. Reservations are tightest at 11:00 and 15:00, on Tuesdays, and on weekends. For off-season weekdays (but not weekends), your chances of getting a same-day reservation are fairly high if you're flexible about the entry time (but you must go in person—you can't call to reserve same-day tickets).

After you reserve a day and time, you'll get a claim number. Be at the Borghese Gallery 30 minutes before your appointed time to pick up your ticket in the lobby on the lower level. Punctuality is critical (arriving late can mean forfeiting your reservation). You can try skipping the ticket pickup line by paying with a credit card at one of the computer kiosks (but they don't always work).

You can use a Roma Pass for entry, but you still need to make a reservation (by phone only—not online; specify that you have the Roma Pass). If you don't have a reservation, try arriving near the top of the hour, when the museum sells unclaimed tickets to those standing by. Generally, out of 360 reservations, a few will fail to show (but more than a few may be waiting to grab them). You're most likely to land a stand-by ticket at 9:00.

Getting There: The museum is set idyllically but inconveniently in the vast Villa Borghese Gardens. To avoid missing

your appointment, allow yourself plenty of time to find the place. A taxi drops you 100 yards from the museum. Your destination is the Galleria Borghese (gah-leh-REE-ah bor-GAY-zay). Be sure *not* to tell the cabbie "Villa Borghese"—which is the park, not the museum.

Bus #910 goes from Termini train station to the Via Pinciana stop (a few steps from the villa). Coming from Campo de' Fiori or Via del Corso (at Via Minghetti), bus #116 drops you off at the southern edge of the park. From Largo Argentina, bus #63 takes you to the US Embassy on Via Veneto; walk uphill on Via Veneto to the southern edge of the park.

By Metro, from the Barberini Metro stop, walk 10 minutes up Via Veneto, enter the park, and turn right, following signs another 10 minutes to the Borghese Gallery.

Tours: Guided English tours are offered at 9:10 and 11:10 (€6.50; may also be offered on busy weekends at 13:10 and 15:10). You can't book a tour when you make your museum reservation— sign up as soon as you arrive. Or consider the excellent 1.5-hour audioguide tour (€5).

With Limited Time: Focus on the ground-floor sculptures, especially Bernini.

Museum Strategy: Visits are strictly limited to two hours.

ROME

Budget most of your time for the more interesting ground floor, but set aside 30 minutes for the paintings of the Pinacoteca upstairs (highlights are marked by the audioguide icons). Avoid the crowds by seeing the Pinacoteca first. The fine bookshop and cafeteria are best visited outside your two-hour entry window (the bookshop closes 30 minutes before the gallery).

Etruscan Museum (Villa Giulia Museo Nazionale Etrusco)—The fascinating Etruscan civilization thrived in Italy around 600 B.C., when Rome was an Etruscan town. The Villa Giulia (a fine Renaissance palace in the Villa Borghese Gardens) hosts a museum that tells the story. The displays are clean and bright, with good English information.

The star of the museum is the famous "husband and wife sarcophagus"—a dead couple seeming to enjoy an everlasting banquet from atop their tomb (sixth century B.C. from Cerveteri). Historians also dig the gold sheets from Pyrgi, with inscriptions in two languages—the "Etruscan Rosetta Stone" that has helped scholars decipher their odd language, and the Apollo of Veio, which stood atop Apollo's temple. The smiling god welcomes Hercules, while his mother Latona stands nearby cradling baby Apollo. For more on the Etruscans, see the sidebar on page 650.

Cost and Hours: €8, Tue-Sun 8:30-19:30, closed Mon, last entry one hour before closing, good English information, 20-minute walk from Borghese Gallery, Piazzale di Villa Giulia 9, tel. 06-322-6571.

Via Veneto—In the 1960s, movie stars from around the world paraded down curvy Via Veneto, one of Rome's glitziest nightspots. Today it's still lined with the city's poshest hotels and the US Embassy, but any hint of local color has faded to bland.

▲Capuchin Crypt—If you want to see artistically arranged bones, this is the place. The crypt is below the Church of Santa Maria della Immacolata Concezione at Via Veneto 27, just up from Piazza Barberini. In 2012, church officials added a new six-room museum, which shows the clothing, footwear, books, and other religious artifacts used by members of the order. For most travelers, however, the morbid attraction remains the crypt.

The bones of more than 4,000 friars who died between 1528 and 1870 are in the basement, all lined up in a series of six crypts for the delight—or disgust—of the always-wide-eyed visitor. The monastic message on the wall explains that this is more than just a macabre exercise: "We were what you are...you will become what we are now."

ROME

As you leave (humming "the foot bone's connected to the..."), pick up a few of Rome's most interesting postcards—the proceeds support Capuchin mission work. Head back outside, where it's not just the bright light that provides contrast with the crypt. Within a few steps are: the US Embassy, Hard Rock Cafe, and fancy Via Veneto cafés, filled with the poor and envious keeping an eye out for the rich and famous.

Cost and Hours: €6, daily 9:00-19:00, last entry 30 minutes before closing, modest dress required, no photos, turn off mobile phones, Metro: Barberini, tel. 06-487-1185.

Piazza del Popolo—This vast oval square marks the traditional north entrance to Rome. From ancient times until the advent of trains and airplanes, this was just about any visitor's first look at Rome. Today the square, known for its symmetrical design and its art-filled churches, is the starting point for the city's evening *passeggiata* (see my "Dolce Vita Stroll" on page 813).

From the Flaminio Metro stop, pass through the third-century Aurelian Wall via the Porta del Popolo, and look south. The 10-story obelisk in the center of the square once graced the temple of Ramses II in Egypt and the Roman Circus Maximus racetrack. The obelisk was brought here in 1589 as one of the square's beautification projects. (The piazza's oval shape dates from the early 19th century.) At the south side of the square, twin domed churches mark the spot where three main boulevards exit the square and form a trident. The central boulevard (running between the churches) is Via del Corso, which since ancient times has been the main north-south drag through town, running to Capitoline Hill (the governing center) and the Forum.

Along the north side of the square (flanking the Porta del Popolo) are two 19th-century buildings that give the square its pleasant symmetry: the Carabinieri station and the Church of Santa Maria del Popolo.

Two large fountains grace the sides of the square—Neptune to the west and Roma to the east (marking the base of Pincio Hill). Though the name Piazza del Popolo means "Square of the People" (and it is a popular hangout), the word was probably derived from the Latin *populus*, after the poplar trees which once stood here.

Church of Santa Maria del Popolo—One of Rome's most overlooked churches, this features two chapels with top-notch art

and a facade built of travertine scavenged from the Colosseum. The church is brought to you by the Rovere family, which produced two popes, and you'll see their symbol—the oak tree and acorns—throughout.

Go inside. The Chigi Chapel (second on the left) was designed by Raphael and inspired (as Raphael was) by the Pantheon. Notice the Pantheon-like dome, pilasters, and capitals. Above in the oculus, God looks in, aided by angels who power the eight known planets. Raphael built the chapel for his wealthy banker friend Agostino Chigi, buried in the pyramid-shaped tomb in the wall to the right of the altar. Later, Chigi's great-grandson hired Bernini to make two of the four statues, and Bernini delivered a theatrical episode. In one corner, Daniel straddles a lion and raises his praying hands to God for help. Kitty-corner across the chapel, an angel grabs Habbakuk's hair and tells him to go take some food to poor Daniel.

In the Cerasi Chapel (left of altar), Caravaggio's *The Conversion on the Way to Damascus* shows Paul sprawled on his back beside his horse while his servant looks on. The startled future saint is blinded by the harsh light as Jesus' voice asks him, "Why do you persecute me?" In the style of the Counter-Reformation, Paul receives his new faith with open arms.

In the same chapel, Caravaggio's *Crucifixion of St. Peter* is shown as a banal chore; the workers toil like faceless animals. The light and dark are in high contrast. Caravaggio liked to say, "Where light falls, I will paint it."

Cost and Hours: Free, Mon-Sat 7:00-12:00 & 16:00-18:30, Sun 8:00-13:30 & 16:30-19:30, often partially closed to accommodate its busy schedule of Masses, on north side of Piazza del Popolo—as you face the gate in the old wall from the square, the church entrance is to your right.

▲▲**Catacombs of Priscilla (Catacombe di Priscilla)**— While most tourists and nearly all tour groups go out to the ancient Appian Way to see the famous catacombs of San Sebastiano and San Callisto, the Catacombs of Priscilla (on the other side of town) are less commercialized and crowded, and just feel more intimate, as catacombs should.

You enter from a convent and explore the result of 250 years

of tunneling that occurred from the second to the fifth centuries. Visits are by 30-minute guided tour only (English-language tours go whenever a small group gathers—generally every 20 minutes or so). You'll see a few thousand of the 40,000 niches carved here, along with some

beautiful frescoes, including what is considered the first depiction of Mary nursing the Baby Jesus.

Cost and Hours: €8, Tue-Sun 8:30-12:00 & 14:30-17:00, closed Mon, last entry 30 minutes before closing, closed one random month a year—check website or call first, tel. 06-8620-6272, www.catacombepriscilla.com.

Getting There: The catacombs are northeast of Termini train station (at Via Salaria 430), far from the center (a €15 taxi ride) but well-served by buses (20-30 minutes). From Termini, take bus #92 or #86 from Piazza Cinquecento. From Piazza Venezia and along Via del Corso, take bus #63 or #630. Tell the driver "Piazza Crati" and "kah-tah-KOHM-bay" and he'll let you off near Piazza Crati (at the Nemorense/Crati stop). From there, walk through the little market in Piazza Crati, then down Via di Priscilla (about 5 minutes). The entrance is in the orange building on the left at the top of the hill.

For more information see "Catacombs" on page 890.

MAXXI—Rome's "National Museum of Art of the 21st Century" is the big news on the museum scene here—as you can imagine it would be, after the 10 years and €150 million it took to make it happen. Like many contemporary art museums, it's notable more for the building than the art inside. To me, it comes off as a second-rate Pompidou Center. While not to my taste, it's one of the few places in the city where fans of contemporary architecture can see the latest trends.

Cost and Hours: €11, Tue-Sun 11:00-19:00, Thu and Sat until 22:00, closed Mon, last entry one hour before closing; no permanent collection, several rotating exhibits throughout the year—preview on their site; tram #2 from Piazza del Popolo to Piazza Apollo Doro, Via Guido Reni 4a, tel. 06-322-5178, www.fondazionemaxxi.it.

From the Spanish Steps to the Ara Pacis

▲**Spanish Steps**—The wide, curving staircase, culminating with an obelisk between two Baroque church towers, makes for one of Rome's iconic sights. Beyond that, it's a people-gathering place. By day, the area hosts shoppers looking for high-end fashions; on warm evenings, it attracts young people in love with the city. For more, see the "Heart of Rome Walk" on page 815.

"Shopping Triangle"—The triangular-shaped area between the Spanish Steps, Piazza Venezia, and Piazza del Popolo (along Via del Corso, see map on page 865) contains Rome's highest concentration of upscale boutiques and fashion stores.

▲▲**Ara Pacis (Altar of Peace)**—On January 30, 9 B.C., soon-to-be-emperor Augustus led a procession of priests up the steps and into this newly built "Altar of Peace." They sacrificed an animal on the altar and poured an offering of wine, thanking the gods for helping Augustus pacify barbarians abroad and rivals at home. This marked the dawn of the Pax Romana (c. A.D. 1-200), a Golden Age of good living, stability, dominance, and peace (pax). The Ara Pacis (AH-rah PAH-chees) hosted annual sacrifices by the emperor until the area was flooded by the Tiber River. Buried

ROME

under silt, it was abandoned and forgotten until the 16th century, when various parts were discovered and excavated. Mussolini gathered the altar's scattered parts and reconstructed them here in 1938. In 2006, the Altar of Peace reopened to the public in a striking modern building. As the first new building allowed to be built in the old center since 1938, it's been controversial, but its quiet, air-conditioned interior may have signaled the dawn of another new age in Rome.

The Altar of Peace was originally located east of here, along today's Via del Corso. The model shows where it stood in relation to the Mausoleum of Augustus (now next door) and the Pantheon. Approach the Ara Pacis and look through the doorway to see the raised altar. This simple structure has just the basics of a Roman temple: an altar for sacrifices surrounded by cubicle-like walls that enclose a consecrated space.

The reliefs on the north and south sides probably depict the parade of dignitaries who consecrated the altar, while the reliefs on the west side (near the altar's back door) celebrate the two things Augustus brought to Rome: peace (goddess Roma as a conquering Amazon, right side) and prosperity (fertility goddess surrounded by children, plants, and animals).

Cost and Hours: €7.50, tightwads can look in through huge windows for free; Tue-Sun 9:00-19:00, closed Mon, last entry one hour before closing; €3.50 audioguide available as free download at www.arapacis.it, good WC downstairs. The Ara Pacis is a long block west of Via del Corso on Via di Ara Pacis, on the east bank of the Tiber near Ponte Cavour, Metro: Spagna; a 10-minute walk down Via dei Condotti, tel. 06-0608.

▲**Fausto delle Chiaie (Fausto of the Beach)**—This eccentric fellow (who's likely more sane than the rest of us) is a self-appointed part of the Ara Pacis. Fausto's installation art, usually strewn along the curb that runs between the Ara Pacis and Mausoleum of Augustus, aims to take you to a different dimension. Though he sits next to the local art academy, he stresses that the proximity is merely a coincidence. Charming Fausto speaks English and reminds you that his "plastic secretary" (a tip box) is at the end of the curb. He may be mini compared to the nearby museum, but for me he's more entertaining than the MAXXI.

East Rome
Near Termini Train Station
These sights are within a 10-minute walk of the train station. By

Near Termini Station

Metro, use the Termini stop for the National Museum and the Repubblica stop for the rest.

▲▲▲**National Museum of Rome (Museo Nazionale Romano Palazzo Massimo alle Terme)**—The National Museum's main branch, at Palazzo Massimo, houses the greatest collection of ancient Roman art anywhere. It's a historic yearbook of Roman marble statues with some rare Greek originals. On the ground floor alone, you can look eye-to-eye with Julius and Augustus Caesar, Alexander the Great, and Socrates.

On the first floor, along with statues and busts showing such emperors as Trajan and Hadrian, you'll see the best-preserved Roman copy of the Greek *Discus Thrower*. Statues of athletes like this commonly stood in the baths, where Romans cultivated healthy bodies, minds, and social skills, hoping to lead well-rounded lives. Other statues on this floor originally stood in the pleasure gardens of the Roman rich—surrounded by greenery with the splashing sound of fountains, all painted in bright, lifelike colors. Though executed by Romans, the themes are mostly Greek, with godlike humans and human-looking gods.

The second floor contains frescoes and mosaics that once decorated the walls and floors of Roman villas. They're remarkably realistic and unstuffy, featuring everyday people, animals, flowery patterns, and geometrical designs. The Villa Farnesina frescoes—in black, red, yellow, and blue—are mostly architectural designs, with fake columns, friezes, and garlands. The Villa di Livia frescoes, owned by the wily wife of Augustus, immerse you in a leafy green garden full of birds and fruit trees, symbolizing the gods.

Finally, descend into the basement to see fine gold jewelry, dice, an abacus, and vault doors leading into the best coin collection in Europe, with fancy magnifying glasses maneuvering you through cases of coins from ancient Rome to modern times.

Cost and Hours: €10 combo-ticket covers three other branches—all skippable, Tue-Sun 9:00-19:45, closed Mon, last entry 45 minutes before closing, audioguide-€5, about 100 yards from train station, Metro: Repubblica or Termini, tel. 06-3996-7700, http://archeoroma.beniculturali.it/en. The museum is about 100 yards from Termini train station—as you leave the station, it's the sandstone-brick building on your left. Enter at the far end, at Largo di Villa Peretti.

▲**Baths of Diocletian (Terme di Diocleziano)**—Around A.D. 300, Emperor Diocletian built the largest baths in Rome. This sprawling meeting place—with baths and schmoozing spaces to accommodate 3,000 bathers at a time—was a big deal in ancient times.

While much of it is still closed, the best part is open: the Church of Santa Maria degli Angeli. From noisy Piazza della Repubblica, step into the vast and cool church built upon the remains of a vast and steamy Roman bath complex. The church we see today was (at least partly) designed by Michelangelo (1561), who used the baths' main hall as the nave. Later, when Piazza della Repubblica became an important Roman intersection, another architect renovated the church. To allow people to enter from the grand new piazza, he spun it 90 degrees, turning Michelangelo's nave into a long transept. The eight red granite columns are original, from ancient Rome—stand next to one and feel its five-foot girth. (Only the eight in the transept proper are original. The others are made of plastered-over brick.) In Roman times, this hall was covered with mosaics, marble, and gold, and lined with statues.

Cost and Hours: Free, Mon-Sat 7:00-18:30, Sun 7:00-19:30, closed to sightseers during Mass, faces Piazza della Repubblica.

▲**Church of Santa Maria della Vittoria**—This church houses Bernini's statue, the swooning *St. Teresa in Ecstasy*. Inside the church, you'll find St. Teresa to the left of the altar. Teresa has just been stabbed with God's arrow of fire. Now, the angel pulls it out and watches her reaction. Teresa swoons, her eyes roll up, her hand goes limp, she parts her lips...and moans. The smiling, cherubic angel understands just how she feels. Teresa, a 16th-century

ROME

Spanish nun, later talked of the "sweet-ness" of "this intense pain," describing her oneness with God in ecstatic, even erotic, terms.

Bernini, the master of multimedia, pulls out all the stops to make this mystical vision real. Actual sunlight pours through the alabaster windows, bronze sunbeams shine on a marble angel holding a golden arrow. Teresa leans back on a cloud and her robe ripples from within, charged with her spiritual arousal. Bernini has created a lit-tle stage-setting of heaven. And watching from the "theater boxes" on either side are members of the family who commissioned the work.

Cost and Hours: Free, pay €0.50 for light, Mon-Sat 8:30-12:00 & 15:30-18:00, Sun 15:30-18:00, about 5 blocks northwest of Termini train station on Largo Susanna, Metro: Repubblica.

Santa Susanna Church—The home of the American Catholic Church in Rome, Santa Susanna holds Mass in English daily at 18:00 and on Sunday at 9:00 and 10:30. They arrange papal audi-ence tickets (see page 854), and their excellent website contains tips for travelers and a list of convents that rent out rooms.

Cost and Hours: Free, daily 9:00-12:00 & 16:00-18:00, Via XX Settembre 15, near recommended Via Firenze hotels, Metro: Repubblica, tel. 06-4201-4554, www.santasusanna.org.

Pilgrim's Rome

East of the Colosseum (and south of Termini train station) are several venerable churches that Catholic pilgrims make a point of visiting. Near one of the churches is a small WWII museum.

Church of San Giovanni in Laterano—Built by Constantine, the first Christian emperor, this was Rome's most important church through medieval times. A building alongside the church houses the Holy Stairs (Scala Santa) said to have been walked up by Jesus, which today are ascended by pilgrims on their knees.

Cost and Hours: Free, church—daily 7:00-18:30; Holy Stairs—daily April-Sept 6:15-12:00 & 15:30-18:45, Oct-March 6:15-12:00 & 15:00-18:15; audioguide-€5; Piazza di San Giovanni in Laterano, Metro: San Giovanni, or bus #85 or #87; tel. 06-6988-6409.

Museum of the Liberation of Rome (Museo Storico della Liberazione di Roma)—This small memorial museum, near the Church of San Giovanni in Laterano, is housed in the prison wing of the former Nazi police headquarters of occupied Rome. Other than a single printed sheet to help, there's little in English. Still,

Pilgrim's Rome

Piazza Cinquecento

Termini Ⓜ TERMINI STATION

VIA NAZIONALE

VIA DEPRETIS

VIA TORINO

VIA GIO. GIOLITTI

VIA MARSALA

VIALE PRETORIANO

VIA MILANO

SANTA MARIA MAGGIORE

MANIN

GIOBERTI

VIA FILIPPO TURATI

Piazzale Sisto V

VIA PANISPERNA

VIA URBANA

VIA CAVOUR

NAPOLEONE III

VIA MERULANA

SANTA PRASSEDE

Piazza Vittorio Emanuele II

Cavour Ⓜ VIA G. LANZA

VIA C. ALBERTO

VIA CAVOUR

ANNIBALDI

ST. PETER-IN-CHAINS

MUSEUM OF ASIAN ART

Vittorio Emanuele Ⓜ

VIA - PRINCIPE - EUGENIO

VIA CONTE VERDE

VIALE MANZONI

Colosseo Ⓜ

To Forum

V. DEL MONTE OPPIO

Parco di Traiano

VIA LABICANA

SAN CLEMENTE

Manzoni Ⓜ SAN QUINTINO

VIA STATILIA

COLOSSEUM

S. QUATTRO

VIA SS. GIOVANNI LAT.

VIALE MANZONI

VIA TASSO

Villa Wolkonski

VIA CLAUDIA

CAPO - D'AFRICA

MUSEUM OF THE LIBERATION OF ROME

HOLY STAIRS

SANTI GIOVANNI E PAOLO

Piazza San Giovanni in Laterano

Piazza di Porta San Giovanni

CITY WALLS

Piazza Celimontana

V. CARLO FELICE

Villa Celimontana

SAN GIOVANNI IN LATERANO

Piazzale di Appio

VIA APPIA NUOVA

San Giovanni Ⓜ

250 Meters

250 Yards

Piazza Celimontana

V. DELL'AMBA ARADAM

MARKET

VIA S. ANNIO

for those interested in resistance movements and the Nazi occupation, it's a stirring visit. You'll see a few artifacts, many photos of heroes, and a couple of cells preserved as they were found on June 4, 1944, when the city was liberated.

Cost and Hours: Free, Tue-Sun 9:30-12:30, Tue and Thu-Fri also 15:30-19:30, closed Mon and Aug, just behind the Holy Stairs at Via Tasso 145; tel. 06-700-3866.

Church of Santa Maria Maggiore—Some of Rome's best-surviving mosaics line the nave of this church built as Rome was falling. The nearby Church of Santa Prassede has still more early mosaics.

Cost and Hours: Free, daily 7:00-19:00, audioguide-€5, Piazza Santa Maria Maggiore, Metro: Termini or Vittorio Emanuele, tel. 06-6988-6802.

▲**Church of San Clemente**—Besides visiting the church itself, with frescoes by Masolino, you can also descend into the ruins of

ROME

Trastevere

1. Hotel Santa Maria
2. Residenza Arco dei Tolomei & Arco del Lauro B&B
3. Casa San Giuseppe
4. To Hotel San Francesco
5. Taverna Trilussa
6. Trattoria da Lucia
7. Trattoria da Olindo
8. Dar Poeta Pizzeria
9. Osteria Ponte Sisto da Oliviero
10. Ristorante & Gelateria Checco er Carettiere
11. Pizzeria "Ai Marmi"
12. Cantina Paradiso Wine & Cocktail Bar

an earlier church. Descend yet one more level and enter the eerie remains of a pagan temple to Mithras.

Cost and Hours: Upper church—free, lower church—€5, both open Mon-Sat 9:00-12:30 & 15:00-18:00, Sun 12:00-18:00, last entry to lower church 20 minutes before closing; Via di San Giovanni in Laterano, Metro: Colosseo, or bus #85 or #87; tel. 06-774-0021, www.basilicasanclemente.com.

South Rome

The area south of the center contains some interesting but widely scattered areas, from Trastevere to the Jewish Quarter to Testaccio to E.U.R.

Trastevere and Nearby

Trastevere is the colorful neighborhood across *(tras)* the Tiber

(Tevere) River. Trastevere (trahs-TAY-veh-ray) offers the best look at medieval-village Rome. The action unwinds to the chime of the church bells. Go there and wander. Wonder. Be a poet. This is Rome's Left Bank. (You can download a free Rick Steves audio tour of this neighborhood to your mobile device; see page 1101.)

Soccer: The National Obsession

One of Rome's most local "sights" is a soccer match. Winston Churchill said that Italians lose wars like soccer matches and soccer matches like wars. Soccer
(calcio) is the national obsession: Everyone, regardless of age or social class, is an expert, quick with an opinion on a coach's lousy decision or a referee's unprofessional conduct. Fans love to insult officials: A favorite is *"arbitro cornuto!"*—the referee is a cuckold (i.e., his wife sleeps around). The country's obsession turned into jubilation on July 9, 2006, when Italy won the World Cup, and Rome—along with every other city, town, and village in Italy—went crazy with joy.

Rome has a special passion for soccer. It has two teams, Roma (representing the city) and Lazio (the region), and the rivalry is fanatic. When Romans are introduced, they ask each other, *"Laziale o romanista?"* The answer can compromise a relationship. Both Roma (jersey: yellow and red; symbol: she-wolf) and Lazio (jersey: light blue and white; symbol: imperial eagle) claim to be truly Roman. Lazio is older (founded in 1900), but Roma has more supporters. Lazio is supposed to be more upper-class, Roma more popular, but the social division is blurred.

This proud neighborhood was long a working-class area. Now that it's becoming trendy, high rents are driving out the source of so much color. Still, it's a great people scene, especially at night. Stroll the back streets (for restaurant recommendations, see page 908).

To reach Trastevere by foot from Capitoline Hill, cross the Tiber on Ponte Fabricio to Isola Tiberina; from there, Ponte Cestio takes you to Trastevere. You can also take tram #8 from Largo Argentina, or bus #H from Termini and Via Nazionale (get off at Piazza Belli). From the Vatican (Piazza Risorgimento), it's bus #23 or #271.

Linking Trastevere with the Heart of Rome Walk: You can walk from Trastevere to Campo de' Fiori to link up with the beginning of my Heart of Rome Walk (see page 815): From Trastevere's church square (Piazza di Santa Maria), take Via del Moro to the river and cross at Ponte Sisto, a pedestrian bridge that has a good view of St. Peter's dome. Continue straight ahead for one block. Take the first left, which leads down Via di Capo di Ferro through the scary and narrow darkness to Piazza Farnese, with the impos-

The most eagerly awaited sporting event of the year is the derby, when the two teams fight it out at the Olympic Stadium (Stadio Olimpico). All of Italy acknowledges that team spirit is most fervent in Rome. Fans prepare months in advance, and on the day of the match they fill the entire stadium with team colors, flags, banners, and smoke candles.

Witty slogans on banners work like dialogues: A Roma banner proclaimed, "Roma: Only the sky is higher than you." The Lazio banner replied, "In fact, the sky is blue and white" (like its team colors). The exchange revealed that there had been a Lazio informer on the Roma side, which traumatized Roma fans for weeks. Tourists go to a match more for the action in the stands than the action on the field—for some, it's the most Roman of all experiences.

Both teams call the Olympic Stadium home, so you can catch a game most weekends from September to May (Metro line A to Flaminio, then catch tram #2 to the end of the line, Piazza Mancini, and cross the bridge to the stadium). If you're coming from Termini train station, take bus #910; from the Vatican, take bus #32 from Piazza Risorgimento. It's best to buy tickets in advance at www.listicket.it or in town at a team store.

ing Palazzo Farnese. Michelangelo contributed to the facade of this palace, now the French Embassy. The fountains on the square feature huge one-piece granite hot tubs from the ancient Roman Baths of Caracalla. One block from there (opposite the palace) is the atmospheric square, Campo de' Fiori.

▲**Church of Santa Maria in Trastevere**—One of Rome's old-est church sites, a basilica was erected here in the fourth century, when Christianity was legalized. It is said to have been the first church in Rome dedicated to the Virgin Mary. The structure you see today dates mainly from the 12th century. Its portico (covered area just outside the door) is decorated with fascinating fragments of stone—many of them lids from catacomb burial niches—and filled with early Christian symbolism. The church is on Piazza di Santa Maria, the Trastevere neighborhood's most important meeting place. With its broad and inviting steps, the 17th-century fountain was actually designed to be the "sofa" of the neighborhood. During major soccer games, a large screen is set up here so that everybody can share in the tension and excitement. At other times, children gather here with a ball and improvise matches of their own. For more on soccer, see the sidebar on the previous page.

Cost and Hours: Free, daily 7:30-21:00.

▲**Villa Farnesina**—Here's a unique opportunity to see a sumptuous Renaissance villa in Rome decorated with Raphael paintings. It was built in the early 1500s for the richest man in Renaissance Europe, Siennese banker Agostino Chigi. Architect Baldassare Peruzzi's design—a U-shaped building with wings enfolding what used to be a vast garden—successfully blended architecture and nature in a way that both ancient and Renaissance Romans loved. Orchards and flower beds flowed down in terraces from the palace to the riverbanks. Later construction of modern embankments and avenues robbed the garden of its grandeur, leaving it with a more melancholy charm.

In the Loggia of Galatea, find Raphael's painting of the nymph Galatea (on the wall by the entrance door). Galatea is considered Raphael's vision of female perfection—not a portrait of an individual woman, but a composite of his many lovers in an idealized vision. Raphael and his assistants also painted the subtly erotic Loggia of Psyche.

Cost and Hours: €5; Mon and Sat 9:00-17:00, Tue-Fri 9:00-14:00, closed Sun, last entry 20 minutes before closing; across the river from Campo de' Fiori, a short walk from Ponte Sisto and a block behind the river at 230 Via della Lungara; tel. 06-6802-7268, www.villafarnesina.it.

Gianicolo Hill Viewpoint—From this park atop a hill, the city views are superb, and the walk to the top holds a treat for architecture buffs. Start at Trastevere's Piazza di San Cosimato, and follow Via Luciano Manara to Via Garibaldi, at the base of the hill. Via Garibaldi winds its way up the side of the hill to the Church of San Pietro in Montorio. To the right of the church, in a small courtyard, is the Tempietto by Donato Bramante. This tiny church, built to commemorate the martyrdom of St. Peter, is considered a jewel of Italian Renaissance architecture.

Continuing up the hill, Via Garibaldi connects to Passeggiata del Gianicolo. From here, you'll find a pleasant park with panoramic city views. Ponder the many Victorian-era statues, including that of baby-carrying, gun-wielding, horse-riding Anita Garibaldi. She was the Brazilian wife of the revolutionary General Giuseppe Garibaldi, who helped forge a united Italy in the late 19th century.

Near Trastevere: Jewish Quarter

From the 16th through the 19th centuries, Rome's Jewish population was forced to live in a cramped ghetto at an often-flooded bend of the Tiber River. While the medieval Jewish ghetto is long gone, this area—just across the river and toward Capitoline Hill from Trastevere—is still home to Rome's synagogue and fragments of its Jewish heritage.

You can download a free Rick Steves audio tour of this neighborhood to your mobile device; see page 1101.

Synagogue (Sinagoga) and Jewish Museum (Museo Ebraico)—Rome's modern synagogue stands proudly on the spot where the medieval Jewish community was sequestered for more than 300 years. The site of a historic visit by Pope John Paul II, this synagogue features a fine interior and a museum filled with artifacts of Rome's Jewish community. Modest dress is required. The only way to visit the synagogue—unless you're here for daily prayer service—is with a tour.

Cost and Hours: €10 ticket includes museum and guided hourly tour of synagogue; mid-June-mid-Sept Sun-Thu 10:00-19:00, Fri 10:00-16:00, closed Sat; mid-Sept-mid-June Sun-Thu 10:00-17:00, Fri 9:00-14:00, closed Sat; last entry 45 minutes before closing, English tours usually at :15 past the hour, 30 minutes, check schedule at ticket counter; on Lungotevere dei Cenci, tel. 06-6840-0661, www.museoebraico.roma.it. Walking tours of the Jewish Ghetto are conducted at least once a day except Saturday.

Testaccio

In the gritty Testaccio neighborhood, several fascinating but lesser sights cluster at the Piramide Metro stop between the Colosseum and E.U.R. (This is a quick and easy stop as you return from E.U.R., or when changing trains en route to Ostia Antica.)

Working-class since ancient times, the Testaccio neighborhood has recently gone trendy-bohemian. Visitors wander through an awkward mix of yuppie and proletarian worlds, not noticing—but perhaps sensing—the "Keep Testaccio for the Testaccians" graffiti.

Pyramid of Gaius Cestius—An Egyptian-style pyramid from ancient Rome stands next to the Piramide Metro stop. The Mark Antony/Cleopatra scandal (c. 30 B.C.) brought exotic Egyptian styles into vogue. A rich Roman magistrate, Gaius Cestius, had

ROME

this pyramid built as his tomb, complete with a burial chamber inside. Made of brick covered in marble, the 90-foot structure was completed in just 330 days (as stated in its Latin inscription). While smaller than actual Egyptian pyramids, its proportions are correct. It was later incorporated into the Aurelian Wall, and it now stands as a marker to the entrance of Testaccio.

Porta San Paolo and Museo della Via Ostiense—This formidable gate (also next to the Piramide Metro stop) is from the Aurelian Wall, begun in the third century under Emperor Aurelian. The wall, which encircled the city, was 12 miles long and averaged about 26 feet high, with 14 main gates and 380 72-foot-tall towers. Most of what you'll see today is circa A.D. 400, but the barbarians reconstructed the gate later, in the sixth century.

Inside the gate is a tiny free museum (find entrance near pyramid; open Tue and Thu 9:00-13:30 & 14:30-16:30, Wed and Fri-Sat 9:00-13:30, some Sun 9:00-13:30, closed Mon). The museum offers

ROME

a free ramble along the ramparts, plus exhibits on Ostia Antica, Rome's ancient port (for more information, see page 891). You'll see models of the ancient city and its famed hexagonal harbor, and of the Ostian Way—the straight Roman road that paralleled the curvy Tiber for 15 miles from Rome to the sea. (For more on the Aurelian Wall, visit the San Sebastiano Gate and Museum of the Walls, described on page 888.)

Protestant Cemetery—The Cemetery for the Burial of Non-Catholic Foreigners (Cimitero Acattolico per gli Stranieri al

Testaccio) is a tomb-filled park, running along the wall just beyond the pyramid. The cemetery is also the only English-style landscape (rolling hills, calculated vistas) in Rome, and a favorite spot for a quiet stroll. From the Piramide Metro stop, walk between the pyramid and the Roman gate on Via Persichetti/Via Marmorata.

Then go left on Caio Cestio to the gate of the cemetery. Originally, none of the Protestant epitaphs were allowed to make any mention of heaven. Signs direct visitors to the graves of notable non-Catholics who died in Rome since 1738. Many of the buried were diplomats. And many, such as the poets Percy Shelley (1792-1822) and John Keats (1795-1821), were from the Romantic Age. They came on the Grand Tour and—"captivated by the fatal charms of Rome," as Shelley wrote—never left.

Head 90 degrees left to find Keats' tomb, in the far corner. Keats died in his twenties, unrecognized. He wanted to be unnamed on a tomb that read, "Young English Poet, 1821. Here lies one whose name was writ in water." (To see Keats' tomb when the cemetery is closed, look through the tiny peephole on Via Caio Cestio, 10 yards off Via Marmarata.) Shelley's tomb is straight ahead from the entrance, up the hill, at the base of the stubby tower.

Cost and Hours: €3 suggested donation—leave in box by entrance, Mon-Sat 9:00-17:00, Sun 9:00-13:00, last entry 30 minutes before closing, staff at info office can help you find specific graves, www.cemeteryrome.it.

Monte Testaccio—The area surrounding this small hill is a popular nightlife spot (as you leave the cemetery, turn left and continue two blocks down Caio Cestio). The hill, actually a 115-foot-tall ancient trash pile, is made of broken *testae*—earthenware jars mostly used to haul oil 2,000 years ago, when this was a gritty port warehouse district. For 500 years, rancid oil vessels were discarded here. Slowly, Rome's lowly eighth hill was built. Because the caves dug into the hill stay cool, trendy bars, clubs, and restaurants compete with gritty car-repair places for a spot. The neighborhood was once known for a huge slaughterhouse and a Roma (Gypsy) camp that squatted inside an old military base. Now it's home to the Testaccio Village (a site for summer concerts and techno raves—dead until late at night, when it thrives), a weekend farmers' market, and branch of the MACRO contemporary art gallery (Metro: Piramide).

Testaccio Market and Neighborhood—The covered and colorful Mercato di Testaccio is a focal point of the neighborhood. It recently moved to a more modern and "hygienic" location—many fear that it's lost some of its edgy charm. Still, it's a good look at one of the many neighborhood markets where locals do their daily shopping (Mon-Sat until 13:00, across from Monte Testaccio on Via Galvani). Testaccio has long been the neighborhood of slaughterhouses, and its restaurants are renowned for their ability to cook up the least palatable part of the animals...the "fifth quarter." The rest of the neighborhood is slowing gentrifying, with high-end shoe and clothing boutiques appearing alongside the traditional merchants.

South of Testaccio

▲Montemartini Museum (Musei Capitolini Centrale Montemartini)—This museum houses a dreamy collection of 400 ancient statues, set evocatively in a classic 1932 electric power plant, among generators and *Metropolis*-type cast-iron machinery. While the art is not as famous as the collections you'll see downtown, the effect is fun and memorable—and you'll encounter absolutely no tourists. If you're tackling Rome with kids, this museum is ideal: It's uncrowded and cool, immersed in an old power plant, with art placed at kid-level.

Cost and Hours: €7.50, €14 combo-ticket with Capitoline Museums, Tue-Sun 9:00-19:00, closed Mon, last entry 30 minutes before closing, look for red banner marking Via Ostiense 106, a short walk from Metro: Garbatella, tel. 06-574-8030, www.centrale montemartini.org.

▲St. Paul's Outside the Walls (Basilica San Paolo Fuori le Mura)—This was the last major construction project of Imperial Rome (c. A.D. 380) and the largest church in Christendom until St. Peter's.

Cost and Hours: Free, daily 7:00-18:30, modest dress code enforced, dry audioguide-€5 plus

South of Testaccio

To Trastevere

Tiber River

To Civitavecchia

VIALE AVENTINO

To Colosseum & Termini Station

See Testaccio map

PYRAMID
Protestant Cemetery

PORTA SAN PAOLO & MUSEUM

Monte Testaccio

Piramide

PORTA SAN PAOLO STATION (TRAINS TO OSTIA ANTICA)

OSTIENSE STATION

VIA DEL PORTO FLUVIALE

VIA P. MATTEUCCI

To Termini Station

PONTE DELL' INDUSTRIA

VIA GUGLIELMO MARCONI

FORMER MERCATO CENTRALE

MONTEMARTINI MUSEUM

VIA OSTIENSE

VIA GIROLAMO BENZONI

VIA IGNAZIO PERSICO

Garbatella

Tiber River

LUNGOTEVERE DI SAN PAOLO

Metro Line B

N

300 Meters

300 Yards

ST. PAUL'S OUTSIDE THE WALLS

To E.U.R. by Metro

VIALE F. BALDELLI

To Ostia Antica by road

San Paolo

ID, Via Ostiense 186, Metro: San Paolo, exit the Metro station following *via Ostiense* sign, and look for the church's round tower, www.basilicasanpaolo.org.

❍ **Self-Guided Tour:** After a tragic 19th-century fire, St. Paul's was rebuilt in the same general style and size as the original. The column-lined courtyard leading up to the church is typical of early Christian churches—the first version of St. Peter's Basilica also had this kind of welcoming zone.

Step inside and feel as close as you'll get in the 21st century to experiencing a monumental Roman basilica. Marvel at the ceiling, and imagine building it with those massive wood beams in A.D. 380.

Alabaster windows light the vast interior. It feels sterile, but in a good way—as if you're already in heaven. Along with St. Peter's Basilica, San Giovanni in Laterano, and Santa Maria Maggiore, this church is, legally speaking, part of the Vatican rather than Italy. The triumphal arch leading to the altar has a fifth-century mosaic of Christ raising his hand in blessing. The church is built upon the supposed grave of St. Paul. According to tradition,

Paul was decapitated two miles from this spot. His head was preserved at San Giovanni in Laterano, and his body was buried here under the altar. In 2006, archaeologists unearthed a sarcophagus with early inscriptions identifying it as Paul's.

Ringing the upper part of the church are round mosaic portraits of 265 popes, from St. Peter (the first one in the right transept) to the present. Find the recent popes to the right of the altar—not in the nave, but farther to the right, under the arches of the dim right aisle. You'll see globetrotting John Paul II *(Jo Paulus II)* and progressive John XXIII, who oversaw the Vatican II changes of the 1960s. A portrait of Pope #265—Benedict XVI—was recently installed, alongside blank medallions for future popes.

The peaceful 13th-century cloister (€4) has elegant Romanesque columns and arches, and fragments of early Christian/Roman sarcophagi.

E.U.R.

In the late 1930s, Italy's dictator, Benito Mussolini, planned an international exhibition to show off the wonders of his fascist society. But these wonders brought us World War II, and Il Duce's

celebration never happened. The unfinished mega-project was completed in the 1950s, and today it houses government offices and big, obscure museums filled with important, rarely visited relics.

If Hitler and Mussolini had won the war, our world might look like E.U.R. (AY-oor). Hike down E.U.R.'s wide, pedestrian-mean boulevards. Patriotic murals, aren't-you-proud-to-be-an-extreme-right-winger pillars, and stern squares decorate the soulless planned grid and stark office blocks. Boulevards named for Astronomy, Electronics, Social Security, and Beethoven are more exhausting than inspirational.

Despite its grim past, E.U.R. is now an up-and-coming place with young people and trendy cafés. It's worth a trip for its Museum of Roman Civilization (described later). And because a few landmark buildings of Italian modernism are located here and there, E.U.R. has become an important destination for architecture buffs.

The Metro skirts E.U.R. with three stops (10 minutes from the Colosseum). Use E.U.R. Magliana for the "Square Colosseum" and E.U.R. Fermi for the Museum of Roman Civilization. Consider walking 30 minutes from the palace to the museum through the center of E.U.R.

Palace of the Civilization of Labor (Palazzo della Civiltà del Lavoro)—From the Magliana Metro stop, stairs lead uphill to this epitome of fascist architecture. With its giant no-questions-asked patriotic statues and its black-and-white simplicity, this is

E.U.R.'s tallest building and key landmark. It's understandably nicknamed the "Square Colosseum." Closed to the public while they decide how to use it, it's still interesting to walk around. Downhill, in front of the palace, Caffè Palombini is a popular institution for lunch or a drink (daily 7:00-22:00; good gelato, pastries, and snacks; Piazzale Adenauer 12, tel. 06-591-1700).

▲**Museum of Roman Civilization (Museo della Civiltà Romana)**—With dozens of rooms of plaster casts and models illustrating the greatness of classical Rome, this vast and heavy museum gives a strangely lifeless, close-up look at Rome. Each room has a theme, from military tricks to musical instruments. One long hall is filled with casts of the reliefs of Trajan's Column. The highlight is the huge scale model of Constantine's Rome, circa A.D. 300. The Planetarium and Astronomical Museum are mostly of interest to children—so don't bother with the €9.50 combo-ticket unless you have kids.

Cost and Hours: €7.50, sometimes €9 with special exhibits, Tue-Sun 9:00-14:00, closed Mon, last entry one hour before closing, Piazza G. Agnelli; leave the E.U.R. Fermi Metro station on Via America, head toward McDonald's, and at T-intersection, turn left and go uphill three blocks to Via dell'Arte—you'll see its colonnade on the right; to return to the city center, access the Metro entrance across the street, tel. 06-5422-0919, www.museociviltaromana.it.

Ancient Appian Way

Southeast of the city center lie several ancient sights that make the trek here worthwhile.

Baths of Caracalla (Terme di Caracalla)—Inaugurated by Emperor Caracalla in A.D. 216, this massive bath complex could

accommodate 1,600 visitors at a time. Today it's just a shell—a huge shell—with all of its sculptures and most of its mosaics moved to museums. You'll see a two-story roofless brick building surrounded by a garden, bordered by ruined walls. The two large rooms at either end of the building were used for exercise. In between the exercise rooms was a pool flanked by two small mosaic-floored dressing rooms. Niches in the walls once held statues. The baths' statues are displayed elsewhere: For example, the immense *Toro Farnese* (a marble sculpture of a bull surrounded by people) snorts in Naples' Archaeological Museum.

In its day, this was a remarkable place to hang out. For ancient Romans, bathing was a social experience. The Baths of Caracalla functioned until Goths severed the aqueducts in the sixth century. In modern times, grand operas are performed here.

Cost and Hours: €6, includes the Tomb of Cecilia Metella and the Villa dei Quintili on the Appian Way, Mon 9:00-14:00, Tue-Sun 9:00 until one hour before sunset (19:00 in summer, 16:30 in winter), last entry one hour before closing, audioguide-€5, good €8 guidebook; Metro: Circus Maximus, plus a 5-minute walk south along Via delle Terme di Caracalla; bus #714 from Termini train station or bus #118 from the Appian Way—see "Getting There" on page 889; tel. 06-3996-7700.

▲**Appian Way**—For a taste of the countryside around Rome and more wonders of Roman engineering, take the four-mile trip from the Colosseum out past the wall to a stretch of the ancient Appian Way, where the original pavement stones are lined by several interesting sights. Ancient Rome's first and greatest highway, the Appian Way once ran from Rome to the Adriatic port of Brindisi, the gateway to Greece. Today you can walk (or bike) some stretches of the road, rattling over original paving stones, past crumbling monuments that once lined the sides.

The wonder of its day, the Appian Way was the largest, widest, fastest road ever, called the "Queen of Roads." Built in 312 B.C. and named after Appius Claudius Caecus (a Roman official), it connected Rome with Capua (near Naples), running in a straight line for much of the way, ignoring the natural contour of the land. Eventually, this most important of Roman roads stretched 430 miles to the port of Brindisi—the gateway to the East—where boats sailed for Greece and Egypt. Twenty-nine such roads fanned out from Rome. Just as Hitler built the Autobahn system in anticipation of empire maintenance, the expansion-minded Roman government realized the military and political value of a good road system. Today the road and the landscape around it are preserved as a cultural park.

For the tourist, the ancient Appian Way offers three attractions: the road itself, with its ruined monuments; the two major Christian catacombs open to visitors; and the peaceful atmosphere, which provides a respite from the city. Be aware, however, that the road today is busy with traffic—and actually quite treacherous in spots.

ROME

Ancient Appian Way

To
San Sebastiano Gate,
Museum of the Walls &
Central Rome

DOMINE
QUO VADIS
CHURCH

VIA LATINA

500 Meters

500 Yards

VIA DELLA CAFFARELLA

VIA ARDEATINA

PEDESTRIAN WALKWAY (CLOSED WEDS.)

COLUMBARIUM

SECOND MILESTONE

CATACOMBS OF
SAN CALLISTO

V. D. SETTE CHIESE

VIA APPIA

FOSSE
ARDEATINE

VIA APPIA PIGNATELLI

CATACOMBS OF
SAN SEBASTIANO
& WC

VILLA OF
MAXENTIUS

CIRCUS OF
MAXENTIUS

BASILICA

VIA ARDEATINA

VIA DI SAN SEBASTIANO

APPIA ANTICA

TOMB OF
CECILIA
METELLA

THIRD
MILESTONE

VIA CECILIA METELLA

APPIA ANTICA CAFFÈ
& BIKE RENTAL

VIA APPIA ANTICA

To
Aqueduct
Park

ALIMENTARI

TORRE DI
CAPO DI
BOVE

CAPO DI BOVE

SCENIC
SECTION

To 4th through 11th
Milestones & Brindisi

A Bus #660 Stop
B Bus #118 Stops
C Bus #118
(Southbound Stop Only)
D Bus #218 Stop
E Archeobus Stops

ROME

The road starts at the massive **San Sebastiano Gate and Museum of the Walls,** about two miles south of the Colosseum. The stretch that's of most interest to tourists starts another two miles south of the gate. I like to begin near the Tomb of Cecilia Metella, at the far (southern) end of the key sights, and work northward (mostly downhill) toward central Rome.

Cost and Hours: San Sebastiano Gate and Museum of the Walls—€4, Tue-Sun 9:00-14:00, closed Mon, last entry 30 minutes before closing, tel. 06-7047-5284.

When to Go: Visit in the morning or late afternoon, since many of the sights—including the Catacombs of San Callisto—

shut down from 12:00 to 14:00. All the recommended sights are open on Tuesday, Thursday, Friday, and Saturday. On Monday, several sights are closed, including the Tomb of Cecilia Metella, the Circus and Villa of Maxentius, and the San Sebastiano Gate and Museum of the Walls. On Wednesday, the Catacombs of San Callisto and the pedestrian path through the park are closed. On Sunday, the Catacombs of San Sebastiano are closed; however, the Appian Way is closed to car traffic, making it a great day for walking or biking (although the old stones are bumpy).

Getting There: Bus #660 drops you off at the Tomb of Cecilia Metella. In Rome, take Metro line A to the Colli Albani stop, where you catch bus #660 (2/hour, along Via Appia Nuova) and ride 10 minutes to the last stop—Cecilia Metella/Via Appia Antica (at the intersection of Via Cecilia Metella and Via Appia Antica). As it can be frustrating to buy a bus ticket on the Appian Way, have one in hand for your return trip.

A **taxi** will get you from Rome to the Tomb of Cecilia Metella for about €20. However, to return by taxi, you'll have to phone for one; there are no taxi stands on the Appian Way (or just take handy bus #118 back to Rome).

If you want to visit just a few sights, consider **bus #118.** In Rome, catch #118 from either the Piramide or Circo Massimo Metro stops; going away from the city center, it stops at the San Sebastiano Gate, Domine Quo Vadis Church, Catacombs of San Callisto, and Catacombs of San Sebastiano. Although bus #118 does not stop at the Tomb of Cecilia Metella, the tomb is only 500 yards away from the San Sebastiano bus stop. Going back to Rome, bus #118 takes a somewhat different route (skipping the Catacombs of San Sebastiano); catch this northbound bus just up the road at the Catacombs of San Callisto.

Bus #218 goes from San Giovanni in Laterano to Domine Quo Vadis Church and the west entrance of the Catacombs of San Callisto, but isn't that useful for other Appian Way sights.

The handy, but much more expensive, **Archeobus** runs from Termini train station to the major Appian Way sights (see "Tours," page 802). It stops at all the key attractions—you can hop off, tour the sights, and pick up a later bus (officially runs twice hourly, but service can be spotty).

Getting Back: No matter how you arrive at the Appian Way, **bus #118** is an easy, cheap way to return to Rome (get off at the end of the line, the Piramide Metro stop).

Information: The **Via Appia Antica TI** near Domine Quo Vadis Church gives out maps and information on the entire park, which stretches east and south of the visit outlined here (daily April-Oct 9:30-17:30, Nov-March 9:30-16:30, rents bikes, Via Appia Antica 58/60, tel. 06-513-5316, www.parcoappiaantica).

ROME

Catacombs

The catacombs are burial places for (mostly) Christians who died in ancient Roman times. By law, no one was allowed to be buried within the walls of Rome. While pagan Romans were into cremation, Christians preferred to be buried (so that they could be resurrected when the time came). But land was expensive, and most Christians were poor. A few wealthy, landowning Christians allowed their properties to be used as burial places.

The 40 or so known catacombs are scattered outside the ancient walls of Rome. From the first through the fifth centuries, Christians dug an estimated 375 miles of tomb-lined tunnels, with networks of galleries as many as five layers deep. The volcanic tuff that Rome sits atop—which is soft and easy to cut, but hardens when exposed to air—was perfect for the job. The Christians burrowed many layers deep for two reasons: to get more mileage out of the donated land, and to be near martyrs and saints already buried there. Bodies were wrapped in linen (like Christ's). Since they figured the Second Coming was imminent, there was no interest in embalming the body.

When Emperor Constantine legalized Christianity in A.D. 313, Christians had a new, interesting problem: There would be no more recently persecuted martyrs to bind them together and inspire them. Instead, the early martyrs and popes assumed more importance, and Christians began making pilgrimages to their burial places in the catacombs.

In the 800s, when barbarian invaders started ransacking the tombs, Christians moved the relics of saints and martyrs to the safety of churches in the city center. For a thousand years, the catacombs were forgotten. In early modern times, they were

Capo di Bove has a small info center with a good €4 map/guide, active excavations, and a relaxing garden (Mon-Sat 10:00-16:00, Sun 10:00-18:00, great place for discreet picnic, clean WCs, Via Appia Antica 222, tel. 06-3996-7700); it's 100 yards uphill from **Appia Antica Caffè,** which also has maps and rents bikes (mobile 340-319-8060).

Services: Free WCs are at the San Sebastiano and San Callisto catacombs and at Capo di Bove, and WCs for paying customers are at the Tomb of Cecilia Metella and the Appia Antica Caffè. There are several water fountains along the way to refill water bottles.

▲▲**Catacombs of San Sebastiano**—A guide leads you underground through the tunnels where early Christians were buried. You'll see faded frescoes and graffiti by early-Christian tag artists. Besides the catacombs themselves, there's a historic fourth-century basilica with holy relics. See the "Catacombs" sidebar for more information.

excavated and became part of the Romantic Age's Grand Tour of Europe.

When abandoned plates and utensils from ritual meals were found, 18th- and 19th-century Romantics guessed that persecuted Christians hid out in these candlelit galleries. The popularity of this legend grew, even though it was untrue: By the second century, more than a million people lived in Rome, and the 10,000 early Christians didn't need to camp out in the catacombs. They hid in plain view, melting into obscurity within the city itself.

The underground tunnels, while empty of bones, are rich in early Christian symbolism, which functioned as a secret language. The dove represented the soul. You'll see it quenching its thirst (worshipping), with an olive branch (at rest), or happily perched (in paradise). Peacocks, known for their purportedly "incorruptible flesh," embodied immortality. The shepherd with a lamb on his shoulders was the "good shepherd," the first portrayal of Christ as a kindly leader of his flock. The fish was used because the first letters of these words ("Jesus Christ, Son of God, Savior") spelled "fish" in Greek. And the anchor is a cross in disguise. A second-century bishop had written on his tomb, "All who understand these things, pray for me." You'll see pictures of people praying with their hands raised—the custom at the time.

Cost and Hours: €8, includes 35-minute tour, 2/hour, Mon-Sat 10:00-17:00, closed Sun and mid-Nov–mid-Dec, last entry 30 minutes before closing, Via Appia Antica 136, tel. 06-785-0350, www.catacombe.org.

▲▲**Catacombs of San Callisto**—The larger of the two sets of catacombs, San Callisto also is the more prestigious, having been the burial site for several early popes.

Cost and Hours: €8, includes 30-minute tour, at least 2/hour, Thu-Tue 9:00-12:00 & 14:00-17:00, closed Wed and Feb, Via Appia Antica 110, tel. 06-5130-1580 or 06-513-0151, www.catacombe.roma.it.

Near Rome

▲▲**Ostia Antica**—For an exciting day trip, pop down to the Roman port of Ostia, which is similar to Pompeii but a lot closer and, in some ways, more interesting. Because Ostia was a working port town, it shows a more complete and gritty look at Roman life

ROME

than wealthier Pompeii. Wandering around today, you'll see warehouses, apartment flats, mansions, shopping arcades, and baths that served a once-thriving port of 60,000 people. Later, Ostia became a ghost town, and it's now excavated. Buy a map, then explore the town, including the 2,000-year-old theater. Finish with its fine little museum.

Cost and Hours: €8.50 for the site and museum, April-Oct Tue-Sun 8:30-19:00, Nov-Feb Tue-Sun 8:30-17:00, March Tue-Sun 8:30-18:00, closed Mon year-round, last entry one hour before closing. The museum closes from 13:30 to 14:30 for lunch. Tel. 06-5635-0215. Helpful websites include www.ostia-antica.org and http://archeoroma.beniculturali.it/en. A map of the site with suggested itineraries is available for €2 from the ticket office. Although you'll see little audioguide markers throughout the site, there are no audioguides for rent. But you can download a free Rick Steves audio tour of Ostia Antica to your mobile device; see page 1101.

Getting There: Getting to Ostia Antica from downtown Rome is a snap—it's a 45-minute combination Metro/train ride. (Since the train is part of the Metro system, it only costs one Metro ticket each way—€3 total round-trip.)

From Rome, take Metro line B to the Piramide stop, which is also the Roma Porta San Paolo train station. The train tracks are just a few steps from the Metro tracks: Follow signs to *Lido*—go up the escalator, turn left, and go down the steps into the Roma-Lido station. All trains depart in the direction of Lido, leave every 15 minutes, and stop at Ostia Antica along the way. The lighted schedule reads something like, "*Prossima partenza alle ore 13.25, bin 3,*" meaning, "Next departure at 13:25 from track 3." Look for the next train, hop on, ride for about 30 minutes (no need to stamp your Metro ticket again, but keep it handy in case they decide to check), and get off at the Ostia Antica stop.

Leaving the train station in Ostia Antica, cross the road via the blue skybridge and walk straight down Via della Stazione di Ostia Antica, continuing straight until you reach the parking lot. The entrance is to your left. (If you don't have a ticket to get back, purchase one at the ticket window at the station, or from the nearby snack bar.)

Tip: If you're using the Metro and want to maximize sightseeing efficiency on your Ostia day trip, consider visiting the sights in south Rome on your return. The Piramide Metro stop—where you'll change trains—really *is* next to a pyramid, and is on the edge of the Testaccio neighborhood, which has several interesting sights. Other south Rome sights include St. Paul's Outside the Walls, E.U.R., and the Montemartini Museum (for more on all of these, see page 882).

ROME

Sleeping in Rome

Double rooms listed in this chapter range from about €65 (very simple, toilet and shower down the hall) to €400 (maximum plumbing and more), with most clustering around €150 (with private bathrooms). I've favored these pricier options, because intense Rome is easier to enjoy with a welcoming oasis to call home.

Haggle if you arrive late in the day during off-season (roughly mid-July through August and November through mid-March). It's common for hotels in Rome to lower their prices 10-50 percent in the off-season, although prices at hostels and the cheaper hotels won't fluctuate much. Room rates are lowest in sweltering August.

Traffic in Rome roars. Thanks to double-paned windows and air-conditioning, night noise is not the problem it once was. Even so, light sleepers who ask for a *tranquillo* room will likely get a room in the back...and sleep better. Once you actually see your room, consider the potential problem of night noise. If necessary, don't hesitate to ask for a quieter room.

Almost no hotels have parking, but nearly all have a line on spots in a nearby garage (about €24/day).

Convents: Although I list just a few, Rome has many convents that rent out rooms. See the Church of Santa Susanna's website for a list (www.santasusanna.org, select "Coming to Rome"). At convents, the beds are twins and English is often in short supply, but the price is right. Consider these nun-run places, all listed

---

Sleep Code

(€1 = about $1.40)

S = Single, **D** = Double/Twin, **T** = Triple, **Q** = Quad, **b** = bathroom, **s** = shower only. Unless otherwise noted, breakfast is included, hotel staff speak basic English, and credit cards are accepted.

To help you easily sort through these listings, I've divided the accommodations into three categories based on the price for a double room with bath during high season:

  $$$ Higher Priced—Most rooms €180 or more.
   $$ Moderately Priced—Most rooms between €130-180.
    $ Lower Priced—Most rooms €130 or less.

Rome charges a hotel tax of €2-3 per person, per night that must be paid in cash at checkout. This tax is typically not included in the prices I've listed here.

Prices can change without notice; verify the hotel's current rates online or by email.

ROME

in this chapter: the expensive but divine **Casa di Santa Brigida** (near Campo de' Fiori), **Suore di Santa Elisabetta** (near Santa Maria Maggiore), **Casa Sant'Anna** (near the Colosseum), **Casa Il Rosario** (near Piazza Venezia), and **Casa per Ferie Santa Maria alle Fornaci** (near the Vatican).

Hostels: If going the hostel route, consider the ones I list in this chapter (within a 10-minute walk of Termini train station), or check www.backpackers.it for more listings.

Near Termini Train Station

While not as atmospheric as other areas of Rome, the hotels near Termini train station are less expensive, and public-transportation options link these places easily with the entire city. The city's two Metro lines intersect at the station, and most buses leave from here. Piazza Venezia is a 20-minute walk down Via Nazionale.

West of the Station

Most of these hotels are on or near Via Firenze, a safe, handy, central, and relatively quiet street that's a 10-minute walk from Termini train station and the airport train, and two blocks beyond Piazza della Repubblica. The Defense Ministry is nearby, so you've got heavily armed guards watching over you all night.

The neighborhood is well-connected by public transportation (with the Repubblica Metro stop nearby). Virtually all the city buses that rumble down Via Nazionale (#64, #70, #115, #640, #492, and the #40 express) take you to Piazza Venezia (Forum) and Largo Argentina (Pantheon). From Largo Argentina, bus #64 (jammed with people and thieves), the #40 express bus, and bus #492 continue to the Vatican. Or, at Largo Argentina, you can transfer to electric trolley #8 to Trastevere (get off at first stop after crossing the river).

To stock your closet pantry, pop over to **Despar Supermarket** (daily 8:00-21:00, Via Nazionale 213, at the corner of Via Venezia). A 24-hour **pharmacy** near the recommended hotels is Farmacia Piram (Via Nazionale 228, tel. 06-488-4437).

$$$ Residenza Cellini feels like the guest wing of a gorgeous Neoclassical palace. It offers 11 rooms, "ortho/anti-allergy beds," four-star comforts and service, and a breezy breakfast terrace (Db-€190, larger Db-€210, extra bed-€25, prices good through 2013 with this book and cash, air-con, elevator, Internet access and Wi-Fi, Via Modena 5, tel. 06-4782-5204, fax 06-4788-1806, www.residenzacellini.it, residenzacellini@tin.it, Barbara, Gaetano, and Donato).

$$$ Hotel Modigliani, a delightful 23-room place, is energetically run in a clean, bright, minimalist yet in-love-with-life style that its artist namesake would appreciate. It has a vast and

Hotels near Termini Station

1 Residenza Cellini, Target Inn, Bellesuite Rome & Hotel Adler
2 Hotel Modigliani
3 IQ Hotel & Hotel Opera Roma
4 Hotels Oceania & Nardizzi Americana
5 Hotel Aberdeen
6 Hotel Sonya
7 Hotel Selene Roma
8 Hotel Italia Roma
9 Hotel Margaret
10 Hotel Montreal
11 Suore di Sta. Elisabetta
12 Gulliver's Lodge B&B
13 The Beehive
14 Hotel Select Garden
15 Hotel Sileo
16 Hotel Robinson
17 Funny Palace Hostel & Launderette/Internet Café
18 Yellow Hostel
19 Despar Supermarket

ROME

plush lounge, a garden, and a newsletter introducing you to each of the staff (Db-€195, but check website for deals and ask for a 10 percent Rick Steves discount; air-con, Wi-Fi; northwest of Via Firenze—from Tritone Fountain on Piazza Barberini, go 2 blocks up Via della Purificazione to #42; tel. 06-4281-5226, www.hotel modigliani.com, info@hotelmodigliani.com, Giulia and Marco).

\$\$\$ IQ Hotel, facing the Opera House, opened in 2010 and feels almost Scandinavian in its efficiency, without a hint of the

Old World. Its 88 rooms are fresh and spacious, the roof garden comes with a swing set, and vending machines dispense bottles of wine (Db-€100-220 depending on room size and season—likely €200 in peak season, €40 extra for 3rd and 4th person, 10 percent discount off best Web price for Rick Steves readers—must book direct and request at time of booking, breakfast-€10, air-con, elevator, Internet access and Wi-Fi, cheap self-service laundry, gym, Via Firenze 8, tel. 06-488-0465, fax 06-4893-0442, www.iqhotel roma.it, info@iqhotelroma.it, manager Diego).

$$ Hotel Oceania is a peaceful slice of air-conditioned heaven. This 24-room manor house-type hotel is spacious and quiet, with tastefully decorated rooms. Stefano runs a fine staff, serves wonderful coffee, provides lots of thoughtful extra touches, and works hard to maintain a caring family atmosphere (Sb-€135, Db-€168, Tb-€198, Qb-€220, these prices good through 2013 with this book, 5 percent less with cash, deep discounts summer and winter, roof terrace, family suite, Internet access and Wi-Fi, videos in the TV lounge, Via Firenze 38, third floor, tel. 06-482-4696, fax 06-488-5586, www.hoteloceania.it, info@hoteloceania .it; Anna and Radu round out the staff).

$$ Hotel Aberdeen, which perfectly combines high quality and friendliness, is warmly run by Annamaria, with support from sister Laura and cousin Cinzia, and staff members Mariano and Costel. The 37 comfy, modern rooms are a good value (Sb-€102, Db-€170, Tb-€180, Qb-€200, for these rates—or better—book direct via email or use the "Rick Steves reader reservations" link on their website, much cheaper rates off-season, air-con, Internet access and Wi-Fi, Via Firenze 48, tel. 06-482-3920, fax 06-482-1092, www.hotelaberdeen.it, info@hotelaberdeen.it).

$$ Hotel Opera Roma, with contemporary furnishings and marble accents, boasts 15 spacious, modern, and thoughtfully appointed rooms. It's quiet and just a stone's throw from the Opera House (Db-€165, Tb-€190, these prices good through 2013 with this book, 5 percent less with cash, air-con, elevator, Internet access and loaner laptop on request, Via Firenze 11, tel. 06-487-1787, www.hoteloperaroma.com, info@hoteloperaroma .com, Rezza, Litu, and Federica).

$$ Hotel Sonya offers 34 well-equipped rooms, a hearty breakfast, a central location, and decent prices (Sb-€90, Db-€150, Tb-€165, Qb-€185, Quint/b-€200, 5 percent discount with this book and cash, air-con, elevator, loaner laptops in room and Wi-Fi, faces the Opera House at Via Viminale 58, Metro: Repubblica or Termini, tel. 06-481-9911, fax 06-488-5678, www.hotelsonya.it, info@hotelsonya.it, Francesca and Ivan).

$$ Hotel Selene Roma spreads its 40 rooms out on a few floors of a big palazzo. With elegant furnishings and room to breathe, it's a fine value (Db-€150, Tb-€165, email direct for 10 percent discount, air-con, elevator, Wi-Fi, Via del Viminale 8, tel. 06-474-4781, www.hotelseleneroma.it, reception@hotelselene roma.it).

$$ Bellesuite Rome offers six bright, modern rooms with all the comforts in a quiet building (Db-€150, Tb-€190, Qb-€215, air-con, elevator, Wi-Fi, Via Modena 5, tel. 06-9521-3049, www .bellesuiterome.com, mail@bellesuiterome.com).

$$ Target Inn is a sleek, practical-but-forgettable six-room place next to Residenza Cellini (listed earlier). It's owned by the same people who run the recommended Target Restaurant nearby (Db-€150, air-con, elevator, Wi-Fi, Via Modena 5, tel. 06-474-5399, www.targetinn.com, info@targetinn.com).

$ Hotel Adler evokes a more genteel age of travel, with a small garden patio and eight basic rooms on a wide and elegant hall (Db-€125, Tb-€165, Qb-€190, Quint/b-€210, 5 percent off these prices with this book, additional 5 percent discount if you pay cash, air-con, elevator, Internet access and Wi-Fi, Via Modena 5, second floor, tel. 06-484-466, fax 06-488-0940, www.hotel adler-roma.com, info@hoteladler-roma.com).

$ Hotel Nardizzi Americana, with 33 decent rooms and a delightful rooftop terrace, is another solid value (Sb-€95, Db-€125, Tb-€155, Qb-€175; to get the best rates, check their "Rick Steves readers reservations" link along with the rest of their website; additional 10 percent off any price with cash, air-con, elevator, Internet access and Wi-Fi, Via Firenze 38, fourth floor, tel. 06-488-0035, fax 06-488-0368, www.hotelnardizzi.it, info@hotelnardizzi.it; friendly Stefano, Fabrizio, Mario, and Giancarlo).

$ Hotel Italia Roma, in a busy and handy locale, is located safely on a quiet street next to the Ministry of the Interior. Thoughtfully run by Andrea, Sabrina, Abdul, and Gabriel, it has 35 modest but comfortable rooms (Sb-€90, Db-€130, Tb-€180, Qb-€200, 30 percent cheaper July-Aug, air-con-€10 extra per day, elevator, Internet access and Wi-Fi, Via Venezia 18, just off Via Nazionale, Metro: Repubblica, tel. 06-482-8355, fax 06-474-5550, www.hotelitaliaroma.it, info@hotelitaliaroma.it). The four "residenza" rooms upstairs on the third floor are newer and a bit more expensive. They also have eight similar annex rooms across the street.

$ Hotel Margaret fills its walls with Impressionist prints and offers 12 decent rooms at a fair price (Db-€110, Tb-€150, Qb-€170, mention this book for best rates, air-con, elevator, Wi-Fi, north of Piazza Repubblica at Via Antonio Salandra 6, fourth floor, tel. 06-482-4285, fax 06-482-4277, www.hotelmargaret.net, info @hotelmargaret.net, Emanuela).

Southwest of the Station

These good-value places cluster around the basilica of Santa Maria Maggiore, on the edge of Rome's international district.

$ Hotel Montreal is a basic three-star place with 27 small rooms on a big street a block southeast of Santa Maria Maggiore (Sb-€90, Db-€110, Tb-€135, may be less if you email direct and ask for a Rick Steves discount, air-con, elevator, Internet access and Wi-Fi, small garden terrace, good security, Via Carlo Alberto 4, 1 block from Metro: Vittorio Emanuele, 3 blocks from Termini train station, tel. 06-445-7797, fax 06-446-5522, www.hotel montrealroma.com, info@hotelmontrealroma.com, Pasquale).

$ Suore di Santa Elisabetta is a heavenly Polish-run convent with a serene garden and 70 beds in tidy twin-bedded (only) rooms. Often booked long in advance, with such tranquility it's a super value (S-€40, Sb-€48, D-€66, Db-€85, Tb-€106, Qb-€128, Quint/b-€142, no air-con, elevator serves top floors only, fine view roof terrace and breakfast hall, 23:00 curfew, a block southwest of Santa Maria Maggiore at Via dell'Olmata 9, Metro: Termini or Vittorio Emanuele, tel. 06-488-8271, fax 06-488-4066, www.csse -roma.eu, ist.it.s.elisabetta@libero.it).

$ Gulliver's Lodge B&B has four fun, colorful rooms on the ground floor of a large, secure building. While on a busy street, the rooms are quiet. Although the public spaces are few, in-room extras like DVD players (and DVDs, including my Italy shows) make it a fine home base (Db-€120, Tb-€135, mention the book for these prices, cash only, air-con, Internet access and Wi-Fi, a 15-minute walk southwest of Termini train station at Via Cavour 101, Metro: Cavour, tel. 06-9727-3787, www.gulliverslodge.com, info@gulliverslodge.com, Sara and Mary).

Sleeping Cheaply, Northeast of Termini Train Station

The cheapest places in town are northeast of Termini train station (Metro: Termini). Some travelers feel this area is weird and spooky after dark, but these hotels feel plenty safe. With your back to the train tracks, turn right and walk two blocks out of the station. **Splashnet** launderette/Internet café is handy (€8 full-serve wash and dry, Internet access-€1.50/hour, €2 luggage storage per day—or free if you wash and go online, daily 8:30-23:00, just off Via Milazzo at Via Varese 33, tel. 06-4470-3523).

$ The Beehive gives vagabonds—old and young—a cheap, clean, and comfy home in Rome, thoughtfully and creatively run by Steve and Linda, a friendly American couple, and their hardworking staff. They offer six great-value artsy-mod double rooms (D-€80, T-€105) and an eight-bed dorm (€30 bunks). Their nearby

ROME

annex, The Sweets, has similar style and several rooms with private baths (Sb-€60, Db-€100, air-con-€10, Internet access and Wi-Fi, private garden terrace, 2 blocks from Termini train station at Via Marghera 8, tel. 06-4470-4553, www.the-beehive.com, info@the-beehive.com). They also run **Cross-Pollinate,** a good resource for B&Bs and apartments across Rome, Florence, and Venice (www.cross-pollinate.com; see page 27).

$ Hotel Select Garden, a modern and comfortable 21-room hotel run by the cheery Picca family, boasts lively modern art adorning the walls and a beautiful lemon-tree garden. It's a safe, tranquil, and welcoming refuge just a couple of blocks from the train station (Sb-€95, Db-€120, Tb-€140, these prices good through 2013 with this book, air-con, Wi-Fi, Via V. Bachelet 6, tel. 06-445-6383, fax 06-444-1086, www.hotelselectgarden.com, info@hotelselectgarden.com, Armando).

$ Hotel Sileo, with shiny chandeliers in dim rooms, is a homely little place renting 10 basic rooms (Db-€75, Tb-€90, air-con, elevator, Wi-Fi, Via Magenta 39, fourth floor, tel. & fax 06-445-0246, www.hotelsileo.com, info@hotelsileo.com). Friendly Alessandro and Maria Savioli don't speak English, but daughter Anna does.

$ Hotel Robinson is just a few steps from the station, but tucked away from the commotion. Set on an interior courtyard, it has 20 simple rooms that are a fine value (Sb-€65, Db-€85, Tb-€120, mention this book for these rates and a small breakfast, air-con-€10, Wi-Fi, Via Milazzo 3, tel. 06-491-423, fax 06-8968-5644, www.hotelrobinsonrome.com, info@hotelrobinsonrome.com).

$ Funny Palace Hostel, adjacent to Splashnet and run by its entrepreneurial owner Mabri, rents dorm beds in quiet four-person rooms and 18 stark-but-clean private rooms (dorm beds-€25, Db-€100, cash only, reception in the launderette—described earlier, Via Varese 33/31, tel. 06-4470-3523, www.hostelfunny.com).

$ Yellow Hostel rents 130 beds in 4-, 6-, and 12-bed coed dorms to 18- through 39-year-olds only (they also have 11 private rooms). Hip yet sane, it's well-run with fine facilities, including lockers. There's no curfew, and its café/late-night bar is next door (€18-35/bed depending on plumbing, size, and season; reserve via email—no telephone reservations accepted, Wi-Fi and iPad rental available, 6 blocks from station, just past Via Vicenza at Via Palestro 40/44, tel. 06-493-82682, www.yellowhostel.com).

Near Ancient Rome

Stretching from the Colosseum to Piazza Venezia, this area is central. Sightseers are a short walk from the Colosseum, Roman Forum, and Trajan's Column.

Hotels & Restaurants near Ancient Rome

1. Hotel Lancelot
2. Hotel Paba
3. Nicolas Inn B&B, Hotel Pensione Rosetta & Enoteca Cavour 313
4. Casa Sant'Anna
5. Hotel Nerva
6. Casa Il Rosario
7. Hotel Giardino
8. Caffè dello Studente & Hostaria da Nerone Rest.
9. Trattoria Luzzi
10. La Taverna dei Quaranta

ROME

Near the Colosseum

$$$ Hotel Lancelot is a comfortable yet elegant refuge—a 60-room hotel with the ambience of a B&B. It's quiet and safe, with a shady courtyard, restaurant, bar, and tiny communal sixth-floor terrace. It's well-run by Faris and Lubna Khan, who serve a good €25 dinner—a chance to connect with your hotel neighbors and the staff. No wonder it's popular with returning guests (Sb-€126, Db-€194, Tb-€224, Qb-€264, €20 extra for sixth-floor terrace room with a Colosseum view, 5 percent off these rates with this book, air-con, elevator, wheelchair-accessible, Wi-Fi, parking-€10/day, 10-minute walk behind Colosseum near San Clemente Church at Via Capo d'Africa 47, tel. 06-7045-0615, fax 06-7045-0640, www.lancelothotel.com, info@lancelothotel.com). Faris and Lubna speak the Queen's English.

$$ Hotel Paba has seven fresh rooms, chocolate-box-tidy and lovingly cared for by Alberta Castelli. Though it overlooks busy Via Cavour just two blocks from the Colosseum, it's quiet enough (Db-€135, extra bed-€40, 5 percent cash discount, big beds, breakfast served in room, air-con, elevator, Wi-Fi, Via Cavour 266, Metro: Cavour, tel. 06-4782-4902, fax 06-4788-1225, www.hotel paba.com, info@hotelpaba.com).

$$ Nicolas Inn Bed & Breakfast, a delightful little four-room place with thoughtful touches, is spacious and bright. It's run by François and American expat Melissa, who make you feel like you have caring friends in Rome (Db-€150-170, 10 percent Rick Steves discount with this book, cash only, included breakfast served at neighboring bar, air-con, Wi-Fi, Via Cavour 295, tel. 06-9761-8483, www.nicolasinn.com, info@nicolasinn.com).

$ Hotel Pensione Rosetta, homey and family-run, rents 18 rooms. It's pretty minimal, with no lounge and no breakfast, but has a good location and reasonable prices (Sb-€70, Db-€95, Tb-€110, air-con, Wi-Fi, Via Cavour 295, tel. 06-478-23069, www.rosettahotel.com, info@rosettahotel.com, Antonietta and Francesca).

$ Casa Sant'Anna, while stern and sterile, is still a welcoming and cozy convent that rents 60 rooms to travelers. Built for Russian and Brazilian pilgrims, it's well-run and situated on a characteristic square near a Metro stop and the Roman Forum (Sb-€50, Db-€80, dinner-€20, Piazza della Madonna dei Monti 3, Metro: Cavour, tel. 06-485-778, www.casasantanna.it, info @casasantanna.it).

Near Piazza Venezia

$$$ Hotel Nerva is a three-star slice of tranquility with 19 small, overpriced (but often discounted) rooms on a surprisingly quiet back street just steps away from the Roman Forum (Sb-€130, Db-€190, extra bed-€40, ask for Rick Steves discount, rates very soft—especially off-season, air-con, elevator, Wi-Fi, Via Tor de' Conti 3, tel. 06-678-1835, fax 06-6992-2204, www.hotelnerva .com, info@hotelnerva.com, Antonio, Paolo, Anna).

$ Casa Il Rosario is a peaceful, well-run Dominican convent renting 40 rooms with monastic simplicity to both pilgrims and tourists in a good neighborhood (reserve several months in advance, S-€42, Sb-€56, Db-€94, Tb-€120, single beds only, fans, free Internet access, roof-terrace picnics welcome, 23:00 curfew, midway between Quirinale and Colosseum near bottom of Via Nazionale at Via Sant'Agata dei Goti 10, bus #40 or #170 from Termini, tel. 06-679-2346, fax 06-6994-1106, irodopre@tin.it).

$ Hotel Giardino offers 11 basic rooms in a central location three blocks northeast of Piazza Venezia. With a tiny central lobby and a small breakfast room, it suits travelers who prize location over big-hotel amenities (Sb-€85, Db-€130, one smaller Db for 15 percent less, these prices with cash and this book, air-con, Wi-Fi, effective double-paned windows, on a busy street off Piazza di Quirinale at Via XXIV Maggio 51, tel. 06-679-4584, fax 06-8928-1175, www.hotel-giardino-roma.com, info@hotel-giardino-roma.com, helpful Gianluca).

In the Pantheon Neighborhood

Winding, narrow lanes filled with foot traffic and lined with boutique shops and tiny trattorias...this is village Rome at its best. The atmosphere isn't cheap, but this is where you want to be—especially at night, when Romans and tourists gather in the floodlit piazzas for the evening stroll, the *passeggiata*.

Near Campo de' Fiori

You'll pay a premium (and endure a little extra night noise) to stay in the old center. But each of these places is romantically set deep in the tangled back streets near the idyllic Campo de' Fiori and, for many, worth the extra money.

$$$ Casa di Santa Brigida overlooks the elegant Piazza Farnese. With soft-spoken sisters gliding down polished hallways and pearly gates instead of doors, this lavish 20-room convent makes exhaust-stained Roman tourists feel like they've died and gone to heaven. If you don't need a double bed or a TV in your room, it's worth the splurge—especially if you luxuriate in its ample public spaces or on its lovely roof terrace (Sb-€120, twin Db-€200, book well in advance, air-con, elevator, Internet access and Wi-Fi, tasty €25 dinners, roof garden, plush library, Monserrato 54, tel. 06-6889-2596, fax 06-6889-1573, piazzafarnese@brigidine.org, many of the sisters are from India and speak English—pray you get to work with wonderful sister Gertrude).

$$$ Relais Teatro Argentina, a six-room gem, is steeped in tasteful old-Rome elegance, but has all the modern comforts. It's cozy and quiet like a B&B and couldn't be more centrally located (Db-€210, Tb-€240, discounts for cash and for stays of 3 days or more, air-con, no elevator, 3 flights of stairs, Internet access and Wi-Fi, Via del Sudario 35, tel. 06-9893-1617, www.relaisteatroargentina.com, info@relaisteatroargentina.com, Carlotta).

$$ Hotel Smeraldo, with 50 rooms, is strictly run by an impersonal staff, but it's clean and a reasonable deal (Sb-€110,

Db-€140, Tb-€170, buffet breakfast free with this book in 2013, air-con, elevator, Internet access and Wi-Fi, flowery roof terrace, midway between Campo de' Fiori and Largo Argentina at Vicolo dei Chiodaroli 9, tel. 06-687-5929, fax 06-6880-5495, www .smeraldoroma.com, info@smeraldoroma.com, Massimo and Walter). Their **Dipendenza Smeraldo,** 10 yards around the corner at Via dei Chiavari 32, has 16 similar rooms (same price and free breakfast, same reception and contact info).

In the Jewish Ghetto
$$ Hotel Arenula, with 50 decent rooms, is the only hotel in Rome's old Jewish ghetto. Though it has the ambience of a gym and attracts lots of students, it is in the thick of old Rome (Sb-€75-98, Db-€133, 5 percent off with this book in high season of 2013, extra bed-€21, air-con, no elevator, Wi-Fi, opposite the fountain in the park on Via Arenula at Via Santa Maria de' Calderari 47, tel. 06-687-9454, fax 06-689-6188, www.hotelarenula.com, info @hotelarenula.com).

Close to the Pantheon
These places are buried in the pedestrian-friendly heart of ancient Rome, each within about a five-minute walk of the Pantheon. You'll pay more here—but you'll save time and money by being exactly where you want to be for your early and late wandering.

$$$ Hotel Nazionale, a four-star landmark, is a 16th-century palace that shares a well-policed square with the Parliament building. Its 100 rooms are accentuated by lush public spaces, fancy bars, a uniformed staff, and a marble-floored restaurant. It's a big, stuffy hotel with a revolving front door, but it's a worthy splurge if you want security, comfort, and the heart of Rome at your doorstep (Sb-€220, Db-€350, giant deluxe Db-€480, extra person-€70, check online for summer and weekend discounts—you'll typically save 30 percent off their sky-high rack rates, air-con, elevator, Wi-Fi, Piazza Montecitorio 131, tel. 06-695-001, fax 06-678-6677, www.hotelnazionale.it, info@hotelnazionale.it).

$$$ Albergo Santa Chiara, in the old center, is big, solid, and hotelesque. Flavia, Silvio, and their fine staff offer marbled elegance (but basic furniture) and all the hotel services. Its ample public lounges are dressy and professional, and its 99 rooms are quiet and spacious (Sb-€138, Db-€190, Db-€215 April-June and Oct, Tb-€260, check website for discounts, book online direct and request special Rick Steves rates, elevator, air-con, Wi-Fi, behind Pantheon at Via di Santa Chiara 21, tel. 06-687-2979, fax 06-687-3144, www.albergosantachiara.com, info@albergosantachiara.com).

$$$ Hotel Portoghesi is a classic hotel with 28 rooms in the medieval heart of Rome. It's peaceful, quiet, and calmly run,

Hotels in the Pantheon Neighborhood

1. Casa di Santa Brigida
2. Relais Teatro Argentina
3. Hotel Smeraldo
4. Dipendenza Smeraldo
5. Hotel Arenula
6. Hotel Nazionale
7. Albergo Santa Chiara
8. Hotel Portoghesi
9. Hotel Due Torri

and comes with a delightful roof terrace—though you pay for the location (Sb-€130-160, Db-€160-200, price range reflects low and high season, breakfast on roof, air-con, elevator, Wi-Fi, Via dei Portoghesi 1, tel. 06-686-4231, fax 06-687-6976, www.hotel portoghesiroma.it, info@hotelportoghesiroma.it).

$$$ Hotel Due Torri, hiding out on a tiny quiet street, is beautifully located. It feels professional yet homey, with an accommodating staff, generous public spaces, and 26 small rooms. While the location and lounge are great, the rooms are overpriced (Sb-€125, Db-€195, family apartment-€240 for 3 and €260 for 4, check website for frequent discounts, air-con, elevator, Wi-Fi, a block off Via della Scrofa at Vicolo del Leonetto 23, tel. 06-6880-6956, fax 06-686-5442, www.hotelduetorriroma.com, info@hoteldue torriroma.com, Cinzia).

In Trastevere

Colorful and genuine in a gritty sort of way, Trastevere is a treat for travelers looking for a less touristy and more bohemian atmosphere. Choices are few here, but by trekking across the Tiber, you can have the experience of being comfortably immersed in old Rome. To locate the following places, see the map on page 874.

$$$ Hotel Santa Maria sits like a lazy hacienda in the midst of Trastevere. Surrounded by a medieval skyline, you'll feel as if you're on some romantic stage set. Its 20 small but well-equipped, air-conditioned rooms—former cells in a cloister—are all on the ground floor, as are a few suites for up to six people. The rooms circle a gravelly courtyard of orange trees and stay-awhile patio furniture (Db-€180, Tb-€220; prices good through 2013 with this book, cash, and minimum stay of three nights; family rooms, free loaner bikes, Internet access and Wi-Fi, face church on Piazza Maria Trastevere and go right down Via della Fonte d'Olio 50 yards to Vicolo del Piede 2, tel. 06-589-4626, fax 06-589-4815, www.hotelsantamaria.info, info@hotelsantamaria.info). Some rooms come with family-friendly fold-down bunks for €30 extra per person. Their freshly renovated six-room **Residenza Santa Maria** is a couple of blocks away (same prices and contact info).

$$$ Residenza Arco dei Tolomei is your most poetic Trastevere experience imaginable, with six small, unique, antique-filled rooms boasting fragrant balconies. With its quiet and elegant setting, you can pretend you're visiting aristocratic relatives (Db-€200, discounts for cash and for stays of three days or more, reserve well in advance, Internet access and Wi-Fi, from Piazza Piscinula a block up Via dell'Arco de' Tolomei at #27, tel. 06-5832-0819, fax 06-6456-1375, www.bbarcodeitolomei.com, info@bb arcodeitolomei.com; Marco, Gianna Paola, and dog Pixel).

$$ Casa San Giuseppe is down a characteristic laundry-strewn lane with a sunny roof terrace and views of Aurelian Walls. While convent-owned, it's a secular place renting 29 plain but peaceful, spacious, and spotless rooms (Sb-€115, Db-€155, Tb-€185, Qb-€215, garden-facing rooms are quiet, air-con, elevator, Internet access, parking-€15, just north of Piazza Trilussa at Vicolo Moroni 22, tel. 06-5833-3490, fax 06-5833-5754, www .casasangiuseppe.it, info@casasangiuseppe.it, Andrea).

$$ Arco del Lauro B&B rents six white, minimalist rooms in a good location. Facing a courtyard (no views but little noise), the friendly welcome and good value make up for the lack of public spaces (Db-€135, Qb-€185, prices good if booked direct, cash only, includes breakfast served in a café, air-con, Internet access and

Wi-Fi, from Piazza Piscinula a block up Via dell'Arco de' Tolomei at #29, tel. 06-9784-0350, mobile 346-244-3212, fax 06-9725-6541, www.arcodellauro.it, info@arcodellauro.it, Lorenza and Daniela).

$$ Hotel San Francesco, big and blocky yet welcoming, stands like a practical and efficient oasis at the edge of all the Trastevere action. Renting 24 trim rooms in this authentic district, it comes with an inviting roof terrace and a helpful staff. Handy trams to Largo Argentina are just a block away (Db-€90-180, prices vary wildly, email direct and mention this book for best rates, air-con, elevator, Wi-Fi, Via Jacopa de' Settesoli 7, tel. 06-5830-0051, www.hotelsanfrancesco.net, info@hotelsanfrancesco.net).

Near Vatican City

Sleeping near the Vatican is expensive, but some enjoy calling this more relaxed, residential neighborhood home. Even though it's handy to the Vatican (when the rapture hits, you're right there), everything else is a long way away. Fortunately, it's well-served by public transit—use the Metro (line A) and bus (ask your hotel for the most convenient routes) to easily connect with the center.

$$$ Hotel Alimandi Vaticano, facing the Vatican Museum, is beautifully designed. Run by the Alimandi family (Enrico, Irene, and Germano), it features four stars, 24 spacious rooms, and all the modern comforts you can imagine (Sb-€170, standard Db-€170-200, big Db with 2 double beds-€240-260, Tb-€230-260, 5 percent less with cash, air-con, elevator, Internet access and Wi-Fi, Viale Vaticano 99, Metro: Ottaviano, tel. 06-397-45562, fax 06-397-30132, www.alimandivaticanohotel.com, alimandi vaticano@alimandi.com).

$$ Hotel Alimandi Tunisi is a good value, run by other members of the friendly and entrepreneurial Alimandi family—Paolo, Luigi, Marta, and Barbara. They have 27 modest but comfortable rooms and vast public spaces, including a piano lounge, pool table, and rooftop terrace where the grand buffet breakfast is served (Sb-€90, Db-€130-175, 5 percent less with cash, elevator, air-con, Internet access and Wi-Fi, down the stairs directly in front of Vatican Museum, Via Tunisi 8, Metro: Ottaviano, tel. 06-3972-3941, fax 06-3972-3943, www.alimanditunisi.com, alimandi@tin.it).

$$ Hotel Gerber, set in a quiet residential area, is family-run with 27 well-polished, businesslike rooms (Sb-€140, Db-€180, Tb-€200, Qb-€220, 10 percent high-season discount and 15 percent low-season discount off these prices with this book in 2013 when you book direct, air-con, elevator, Wi-Fi, leafy terrace; from Lepanto Metro station, go one block down Via M. Colonna and turn right to Via degli Scipioni 241; tel. 06-321-6485, fax 06-321-7048, www.hotelgerber.it, info@hotelgerber.it; Peter, Simonetta, and friendly dog Kira).

Hotels & Restaurants near Vatican City

1. Hotel Alimandi Vaticano
2. Hotel Alimandi Tunisi
3. To Hotel Gerber & Casa Valdese
4. To Casa per Ferie Rooms
5. Hostaria dei Bastioni Restaurant
6. L'Insalata Ricca, Duecento Gradi & Gelateria Old Bridge
7. La Rustichella & Gelateria Millennium
8. Tre Pupazzi & Vecchio Borgo Rest.
9. Mercato Trionfale
10. Supermarket

ROME

$ Casa Valdese is an efficient, well-managed, church-run hotel that's popular with Germans. Its 33 big, quiet rooms are located just over the Tiber River and near the Vatican. It feels safe if a bit institutional, with the bonus of two breezy, communal roof terraces with incredible views (two external Sb-€58, Db-€130, Tb-€180, Qb-€210, discounts for 3-night stays, air-con, Internet access and Wi-Fi; from Lepanto Metro station, go one block down Via M. Colonna, turn left on Via degli Scipioni, then continue for a block to the intersection with Via Alessandro Farnese 18; tel.

06-321-5362, fax 06-321-1843, www.casavaldeseroma.it, reception @casavaldeseroma.it, Matteo).

$ Casa per Ferie Santa Maria alle Fornaci is simple and efficient, housing pilgrims and secular tourists just a short walk south of the Vatican in 54 identical, stark, utilitarian, mostly twin-bedded rooms. Reserve at least three months in advance (Sb-€70, Db-€100, Tb-€135, air-con, elevator; take bus #64 from Termini train station to San Pietro train station, then walk 100 yards north along Via della Stazione di San Pietro to Piazza Santa Maria alle Fornaci 27; tel. 06-393-67632, fax 06-393-66795, www.trinitari demathai.it, cffornaci@tin.it, Carmine).

Eating in Rome

I've listed a number of restaurants I enjoy. While most are in quaint and therefore pricey and touristy areas (Piazza Navona, the Pantheon neighborhood, Campo de' Fiori, and Trastevere), many are tucked away just off the tourist crush.

I'm impressed by how small the price difference can be between a mediocre Roman restaurant and a fine one. You can pay about 20 percent more for double the quality. If I had $90 for three meals in Rome, I'd spend $50 for one and $20 each for the other two, rather than $30 on all three. For splurge meals, I'd consider Gabriello, Fortunato, and Taverna Trilussa (in that order).

Rome's fabled nightspots (most notably Piazza Navona, near the Pantheon, and Campo de' Fiori) are lined with the outdoor tables of touristy restaurants with enticing menus and formal-vested waiters. The atmosphere is super-romantic: I, too, like the idea of dining under floodlit monuments, amid a constantly flowing parade of people. But you'll likely be surrounded by tourists, and noisy English-speakers can kill the ambience of the spot...leaving you with just a forgettable and overpriced meal. Restaurants in these areas are notorious for surprise charges, forgettable food, microwaved ravioli, and bad service.

I enjoy the view by savoring just a drink or dessert on a famous square, but I dine with locals on nearby low-rent streets, where the proprietor needs to serve a good-value meal and nurture a local following to stay in business. If you're set on eating—or just drinking and snacking—on a famous piazza, you don't need a guidebook listing to choose a spot; enjoy the ritual of slowly circling the square, observing both the food and the people eating it, and sit where the view and menu appeal to you.

In Trastevere

Colorful Trastevere is now pretty touristy. Still, Romans join the tourists to eat on the rustic side of the Tiber River. Start at the central square, Piazza di Santa Maria. This is where the tourists dine, while others wander the back streets in search of mom-and-pop places with barely a menu. My recommendations are within a few minutes' walk of each other (between Piazza di Santa Maria in Trastevere and Ponte Sisto; see map on page 874).

Taverna Trilussa is your best bet for dining well in Trastevere. Brothers Massimo and Maurizio offer quality and value without pretense. With a proud 100-year-old tradition, this place has the right mix of style and informality. The service is fun-loving (they're happy to let you split plates into smaller portions to enjoy a family-style meal), yet professional. The menu celebrates local classics and seasonal specials, and comes with a big wine selection. The spacious dining hall is strewn with eclectic Roman souvenirs. For those who'd rather eat outdoors, Trilussa has an actual terrace rather than just tables jumbled together on the sidewalk (€15 pastas, €20 *secondi,* Mon-Sat from 19:30 for dinner, closed Sun, reservations very smart, Via del Politeama 23, tel. 06-581-8918).

Trattoria da Lucia lets you enjoy simple, traditional food at a good price. It's your basic old-school, Trastevere dining experience, and has been family-run since World War II. You'll meet four generations of the family, including Giuliano and Renato, their uncle Ennio, and Ennio's mom—pictured on the menu in the 1950s. The family specialty is *spaghetti alla Gricia,* with pancetta (€9 pastas, €11 *secondi,* Tue-Sun 12:30-15:00 & 19:30-23:00, closed Mon, cash only, evocative outdoor or comfy indoor seating—but avoid back room, just off Via del Mattonato at Vicolo del Mattonato 2, tel. 06-580-3601).

Trattoria da Olindo takes homey to extremes. You really feel like you dropped in on a family that cooks for the neighborhood to supplement their income. Don't expect any smiles here (€8 pastas, €10 *secondi,* Mon-Sat dinner served 20:00-22:30, closed Sun, cash only, indoor and funky outdoor seating, on the corner of Vicolo della Scala and Via del Mattonato at #8, tel. 06-581-8835).

Dar Poeta Pizzeria, tucked in a back alley and a hit with local students, cranks out some of the best wood-fired pizza I've had in Rome. It's run by three friends—Marco, Paolo, and another Marco—who welcome you into the informal restaurant beneath exposed brick arches. If you're in a spicy mood, order *lingua di fuoco* (tongue of fire). If you're extra hungry, pay an extra euro for *pizza alto* (thicker crust). Choose between their classic, cramped interior and lively tables outside on the cobblestones. Their chocolate dessert calzone is a favorite (€6-9 pizzas, daily 12:00-24:00, Vicolo del Bologna 45, tel. 06-588-0516).

Osteria Ponte Sisto da Oliviero, small and Mediterranean, specializes in traditional Roman cuisine, but has frequent Neapolitan specials as well. Just outside the tourist zone, it caters mostly to Romans and offers beautiful desserts and a fine value (€9 pastas, €12 *secondi*, Thu-Tue 12:30-15:30 & 19:30-24:00, closed Wed, Via Ponte Sisto 80, tel. 06-588-3411, reservations smart, Oliviero). If you're coming from the city center, cross Ponte Sisto (pedestrian bridge), continue across the little square (Piazza Trilussa), and you'll see it on the right.

Ristorante Checco er Carettiere is a big, family-run place that's been a Trastevere fixture for four generations—as the photos on the wall attest. With white tablecloths, well-presented food, and dressy local diners, this is a popular place for a special meal in Trastevere. While it's overpriced, you'll eat well amid lots of fun commotion (€18 pastas, €22 *secondi*, daily 12:30-15:00 & 19:30-23:15, Via Benedetta 10, tel. 06-580-0985). Their *osteria* next door (at #13) shares the same kitchen and offers less ambience, lower prices, and a more basic menu (€11 pastas, €15 *secondi*). Many Romans consider their *gelateria* (next door at #7) to be among the best on this side of the river.

Pizzeria "Ai Marmi" is a bright and noisy festival of pizza, where the oven and pizza-assembly line are surrounded by marble-slab tables (hence the nickname "the Morgue"). It's a classic Roman scene, whether you enjoy the chaos inside or sit at a sidewalk table, with famously good €8 pizzas and very tight seating. Expect a long line between 20:00 and 22:00 (Thu-Tue 19:00-24:00, closed Wed, cash only, tram #8 from Largo Argentina to first stop over bridge, just beyond Piazza Sonnino at Viale di Trastevere 53, tel. 06-580-0919).

Cantina Paradiso Wine and Cocktail Bar, a block over Viale di Trastevere from the touristy action, has a funky romantic charm. During happy hour (18:00-21:00), the €8 drinks come with a well-made little buffet that can turn into a cheap, light dinner (€8 pastas, daily 12:00-24:00, Via San Francesco a Ripa 73, tel. 06-589-9799, Weronika).

And for Dessert: **Gelateria alla Checco er Carettiere,** run by and next door to the famous, recommended restaurant of the same name, is many locals' favorite spot for gelato in Trastevere (daily 12:00-24:00, Via Benedetta 7).

In the Jewish Ghetto

The Jewish Ghetto sits just across the river from Trastevere (see map on page 875).

Sora Margherita, hiding without a sign on a cluttered square, has been a rustic neighborhood favorite since 1927. Amid a pictur-esque commotion, families chow down on old-time Roman and Jewish dishes for a decent price. It's technically not a real restau-rant (it avoids red tape by officially registering itself an *associazione culturale*)—you can even sign a card to join the "cultural association" (don't worry; membership has no obligations except that you enjoy your meal). The menu's crude term for the fettuccini gives you some idea of the mood of this place: *nazzica culo* ("shaky ass"— what happens while it's made). Reservations are almost always necessary (€10 pastas, €12 *secondi*; Sept-May Mon-Sat 12:30-15:00, dinner seatings on Mon, Wed, Fri, and Sat at 20:00 and 21:30, closed Sun; June-July same hours except closed Sat, closed in Aug, just south of Via del Portico d'Ottavia at Piazza delle Cinque Scole 30—look for the red curtain, tel. 06-687-4216).

In the Pantheon Neighborhood

For the restaurants in this central area, I've listed them based on which landmark they're closest to: Campo de' Fiori, Piazza Navona, the Trevi Fountain, or the Pantheon itself.

On and near Campo de' Fiori

While it is touristy, Campo de' Fiori offers a sublimely romantic setting. And, since it's so close to the heart of the Roman people, it remains popular with locals, even though its restaurants offer greater atmosphere than food value. The square is lined with popular and interesting bars, pizzerias, and small restaurants—all great for people-watching over a glass of wine. Later at night it's taken over by a younger clubbing crowd.

Osteria da Giovanni ar Galletto is nearby, on the more elegant and peaceful Piazza Farnese. Angelo entertains an upscale Roman clientele and has magical outdoor seating. Regrettably, service can be horrible, you need to double-check the bill, and single diners aren't treated very well. Still, if you're in no hurry and ready to savor my favorite al fresco setting in Rome (while humoring the waiters), this can be a good bet (€12 pastas, €15-20 *secondi*, Mon-Sat 12:15-15:00 & 19:30-23:00, closed Sun, reservations smart for outdoor seating, tucked in corner of Piazza Farnese at #104, tel. 06-686-1714).

Osteria Enoteca al Bric is a mod bistro run by helpful Roberto and Barbara, who love to cook, serve fine wine, and listen to jazz. Wine-case lids decorate the wall like happy memories. They offer a fun, €22 happy-hour deal for two from 19:30 to 20:30 that includes a plate of cheeses and meats, two glasses of good wine, water, and bread (Tue-Sun from 19:30 for dinner, closed Mon, reserve if dining after 20:30, can be pricey, 100 yards off Campo de' Fiori at Via del Pellegrino 51, tel. 06-687-9533).

Vineria Salumeria Roscioli is an elegant *enoteca* that's a hit with local foodies, so reservations are a must. While it's just a salami toss away from touristy Campo de' Fiori, you'll dine with classy locals, and feel like you're sitting in a romantic (and expensive) deli after hours. They have a good selection of fine cheeses,

ROME

Restaurants in the Pantheon Neighborhood

① Osteria da Giovanni ar Galletto
② Osteria Enoteca al Bric
③ To Vineria Salumeria Roscioli
④ Filetti di Baccalà
⑤ Trattoria der Pallaro
⑥ Pizzeria da Baffetto 2
⑦ Pizzeria da Baffetto
⑧ Ciccia Bomba
⑨ Cul de Sac & L'Insalata Ricca
⑩ L'Insalata Ricca
⑪ Rist. Pizzeria "da Francesco"
⑫ L'Antica Birreria Peroni
⑬ Rist. Pizzeria Sacro e Profano

14 Ristorante da Fortunato
15 Ristorante Enoteca Corsi
16 Trattoria dal Cav. Gino
17 Miscellanea
18 Osteria da Mario
19 Taverna le Coppelle
20 Pizzeria Florida

21 Antica Salumeria
22 Super Market Carrefour Express
23 Supermercato Despar
24 Gelateria Caffè Pasticceria Giolitti
25 Crèmeria Monteforte
26 Gelateria San Crispino
27 Bar Pascucci

ROME

meats, local dishes, and top-end wines by the glass (€15-25 plates, Mon-Sat 12:30-16:00 & 19:00-24:00, closed Sun, 3 blocks east of Campo de' Fiori at Via dei Giubbonari 21, tel. 06-687-5287).

Filetti di Baccalà is a cheap and basic Roman classic, where nostalgic regulars cram into wooden tables and savor their old-school favorites—fried cod finger-food fillets (€5 each) and raw *puntarelle* greens (slathered with anchovy sauce in spring and winter). Study what others are eating, and order from your grease-stained server by pointing at what you want. Sit in the fluorescently lit interior or try to grab a seat out on the little square, a quiet haven a block east of Campo de' Fiori (Mon-Sat 17:30-23:00, closed Sun, cash only, Largo dei Librari 88, tel. 06-686-4018). If you're not into greasy spoons, avoid this place.

Trattoria der Pallaro, an eccentric and well-worn eatery that has no menu, has a slogan: "Here, you'll eat what we want to feed you." Paola Fazi—with a towel wrapped around her head turban-style—and her gang dish up a five-course meal of homey Roman food. You have three menu choices: €25 for the works; €20 for appetizers, *secondi*, and dessert; or €15 for appetizers and pasta. Any option is filling, includes wine and coffee, and is capped with a thimble of mandarin juice. While the service can be odd and the food is rustic, the experience is fun (daily 12:00-16:00 & 19:00-24:00, reserve if dining after 20:00, cash only, indoor/outdoor seating on quiet square, a block south of Corso Vittorio Emanuele, down Largo del Chiavari to Largo del Pallaro 15, tel. 06-6880-1488).

Pizzeria da Baffetto 2 makes pizza Roman-style: thin crust, crispy, and wood-fired. Eat in the cramped informal interior, or outside on the busy square (€7-9 pizzas, daily 18:30-24:00, Sat-Sun also open for lunch 12:30-15:30, a block north of Campo de' Fiori at Piazza del Teatro di Pompeo 18, tel. 06-6821-0807).

Near Piazza Navona

Piazza Navona is the quintessential setting for dining on a Roman square. Whether you eat here or not, you'll want to stroll the piazza before or after your evening meal. This is where many people fall in love with Rome. The tangled streets just to the west are lined with popular eateries of many stripes.

Ciccia Bomba is a traditional trattoria where Gianpaolo, Gianluca, and their crew serve up tasty homemade pasta, wood-fired pizza, and other Roman specialties (consider their daily-special sheet)—all at a good price. While you can sit at a table on ancient pavement next to your own column, I like the ambience upstairs (€7 pastas, €9 *secondi*, Thu-Tue 12:30-15:00 & 19:00-24:00, closed Wed, Via del Governo Vecchio 76, a block west of Piazza Navona, just north from Piazza Pasquino, tel. 06-6880-2108).

Cul de Sac, a corridor-wide trattoria lined with wine bottles, is packed with an enthusiastic crowd enjoying a wide-ranging menu, from pasta to homemade pâté. They have fun tasting-plates of *salumi* and cheese, more than a thousand different wines, and fine outdoor seating. It's small, and they don't take reservations—come early to avoid a wait (€7-15 plates, daily 12:00-16:00 & 18:00-24:00, a block off Piazza Navona on Piazza Pasquino, tel. 06-6880-1094).

Ristorante Pizzeria "da Francesco," bustling and authentic, has a 50-year-old tradition, a hardworking young waitstaff, great indoor seating, and classic outdoor seating on a cluttered little square that makes you want to break out a sketchpad. Their blackboard explains the daily specials (€9 pizzas and pastas, €15 *secondi*, open daily 12:00-15:00 & 19:00-24:00 except closed Tue at lunch, 3 blocks west of Piazza Navona at Piazza del Fico 29, tel. 06-686-4009).

Pizzeria da Baffetto, buried deep in the old quarter behind Piazza Navona, is a Roman favorite, offering tasty pizza but rude service. Its tables are tightly arranged amid the mishmash of photos and sketches littering the walls. The pizza-assembly kitchen keeps things energetic, and the pizza oven keeps the main room warm (you can opt for a table on the cobbled street). Come early or late, or be prepared to wait (€7 pizzas, daily from 18:30, cash only; order "P," "M," or "D"—small, medium, or large; west of Piazza Navona on the corner of Via Sora at Via del Governo Vecchio 114, tel. 06-686-1617).

L'Insalata Ricca is a popular local chain that specializes in healthy, filling €8 salads and less-healthy pastas and main courses (daily 12:00-15:45 & 18:45-24:00). They have a handy branch on Piazza Pasquino (next to the recommended Cul de Sac, tel. 06-6830-7881) and a more spacious and enjoyable location a few blocks away, on a bigger square next to busy Corso Vittorio Emanuele (near Campo de' Fiori at Largo dei Chiavari 85, tel. 06-6880-3656).

Near the Trevi Fountain

L'Antica Birreria Peroni is Rome's answer to a German beer hall. Serving hearty mugs of the local Peroni beer and lots of just plain fun beer-hall food and Italian classics, the place is a hit with Romans for a cheap night out (Mon-Sat 12:00-24:00, closed Sun, midway between Trevi Fountain and Capitoline Hill, a block off Via del Corso at Via di San Marcello 19, tel. 06-679-5310).

Ristorante Pizzeria Sacro e Profano fills an old church with spicy southern Italian (Calabrian) cuisine and satisfied tourists. Run with enthusiasm by Emiliano and friends, this is just far enough away from the Trevi mobs. Their pizza oven is wood-fired, and their hearty €15 *antipasti* plate is a filling montage of

ROME

Calabrian taste treats (Mon-Sat 12:00-15:00 & 18:00-23:00, closed Sun, a block off Via del Tritone at Via dei Maroniti 29, tel. 06-679-1836).

Close to the Pantheon

Eating on the square facing the Pantheon is a temptation, and I'd consider it just to relax and enjoy the Roman scene. But if you walk a block or two away, you'll get less view and better value. Here are some suggestions.

Ristorante da Fortunato is an Italian classic, with fresh flowers on the tables and white-coated, black-tie career waiters politely serving good meat and fish to politicians, foreign dignitaries, and tourists with good taste. Don't leave without perusing the photos of their famous visitors—everyone from former Iraqi Foreign Minister Tariq Aziz to Bill Clinton seems to have eaten here. All are pictured with the boss, Fortunato, who, since 1975, has been a master of simple edible elegance. (His son Jason is now on the team.) The outdoor seating is fine for watching the river of Roman street life flow by, but the real atmosphere is inside. For a dressy night out, this is a reliable and surprisingly reasonable choice—but be sure to reserve ahead (plan to spend €45 per person, daily 12:30-15:30 & 19:30-23:30, a block in front of the Pantheon at Via del Pantheon 55, tel. 06-679-2788).

Ristorante Enoteca Corsi is a wine shop that grew into a thriving lunch-only restaurant. The Paiella family serves straightforward, traditional cuisine at great prices to an appreciative crowd of office workers. Check the blackboard for daily specials (gnocchi on Thursday, fish on Friday, and so on). Friendly Giuliana, Claudia, Sara, and Manuela welcome eaters to step into their wine shop and pick out a bottle. For the cheap take-away price, plus €2-4 (depending on the wine), they'll uncork it at your table. With €9 pastas, €13 main dishes, and fine wine at a third of the price you'd pay in normal restaurants, this can be a good value. And guests with this book finish their meal with a free glass of homemade *limoncello* (Mon-Sat 12:00-15:30, closed Sun, no reservations possible, a block toward the Pantheon from the Gesù Church at Via del Gesù 87, tel. 06-679-0821).

Trattoria dal Cav. Gino, tucked away on a tiny street behind the Parliament, has been a favorite since 1963. Photos on the wall recall the days when it was the haunt of big-time politicians. Grandpa Gino shuffles around grating the parmesan cheese while his English-speaking children Carla and Fabrizio serve up traditional Roman favorites and make sure things run smoothly. Reserve ahead, even for lunch, as you'll be packed in with savvy locals (€8 pastas, €11 *secondi,* cash only, Mon-Sat 13:00-14:45 & 20:00-22:30, closed Sun, fish on Friday, behind Piazza del Parlamento and just

ROME

off Via di Campo Marzio at Vicolo Rosini 4, tel. 06-687-3434).

Miscellanea is run by much-loved Mikki, who's on a mission to keep foreign students well-fed. Welcoming travelers as well as locals, he offers hearty €4 sandwiches and a long list of €7 salads, along with pasta and other staples. Mikki (and his son Romeo) often tosses in a fun little extra, including—if you have this book on the table—a free glass of Mikki's "sexy wine" (from *fragoline*, strawberry-flavored grapes). While basic, it's convenient and inexpensive (daily 8:00-24:00, indoor/outdoor seating, facing the rear of the Pantheon at Via della Palombella 34, tel. 06-6813-5318).

Osteria da Mario, a homey little mom-and-pop joint with a no-stress menu, serves traditional favorites in a fun dining room or on tables spilling out onto a picturesque old Roman square (€8 pastas, €10 *secondi,* Mon-Sat 13:00-15:30 & 19:00-23:00, closed Sun; from the Pantheon walk 2 blocks up Via del Pantheon, go left on Via delle Coppelle, and take first right to Piazza delle Coppelle 51; tel. 06-6880-6349, Marco).

Taverna le Coppelle is simple, basic, family-friendly, and inexpensive—especially for pizza—with a checkered-tablecloth ambience (€9 pizzas, daily 12:30-15:00 & 19:30-23:30, Via delle Coppelle 39, tel. 06-6880-6557, Alfonso).

Pizzeria Florida, about four blocks south of the Pantheon, offers cheap pizza slices and sandwiches to go (daily 10:00-22:00, Via Florida 25, across from cat sanctuary, tel. 06-6880-3236).

Picnicking Close to the Pantheon

It's fun to munch a picnic with a view of the Pantheon. (Remember to be discreet.) Here are some options.

Antica Salumeria is an old-time *alimentari* (grocery store) on the Pantheon square. While they hustle most tourists into pre-made €5 sandwiches, you can make your own picnic. Find your way to the back to buy artichokes, mixed olives, bread, cheese, and meat (daily 8:00-21:00, mobile 334-340-9014).

Supermarkets near the Pantheon: Food is relatively cheap at Italian supermarkets. **Super Market Carrefour Express** is a convenient place for groceries a block from the Gesù Church (Mon-Sat 8:00-21:00, Sun 9:00-19:30, 50 yards off Via del Plebiscito at Via del Gesù 59). Another place, **Supermercato Despar,** is half a block from the Pantheon toward Piazza Navona (daily 8:30-22:00, Via Giustiniani 18).

Gelato Close to the Pantheon

Three fine *gelaterie* and bars specializing in fresh-fruit smoothies are within a five-minute walk of the Pantheon.

Gelateria Caffè Pasticceria Giolitti, Rome's most famous and venerable ice-cream joint, has reasonable take-away prices

ROME

and elegant Old World seating (daily 7:00-24:00, just off Piazza Colonna and Piazza Monte Citorio at Via Uffici del Vicario 40, tel. 06-699-1243).

Crèmeria Monteforte is known for its traditional, quality gelato and super-creamy sorbets *(cremolati)*. The fruit flavors are especially refreshing—think gourmet slushies (Tue-Sun 10:00-24:00, off-season closes earlier, closed Mon and Dec-Jan, faces the west side of the Pantheon at Via della Rotonda 22, tel. 06-686-7720).

Gelateria San Crispino serves small portions of particularly tasty gourmet gelato using creative ingredients. Because of their commitment to natural ingredients, the colors are muted; gelato purists consider bright colors a sign of unnatural chemicals, used to attract children. They serve cups, but no cones (daily 12:00-24:00, a block in front of the Pantheon on Piazza della Maddalena, tel. 06-6889-1310).

Bar Pascucci is a hole in the wall that's been making refreshing fruit *frullati* and frappés (like smoothies and shakes) for more than 75 years. Add a sandwich or fruit salad to make a healthy light meal (Mon-Sat 6:00-23:00, closed Sun, near Largo Argentina at Via di Torre Argentina 20, tel. 06-686-4816).

In North Rome:
Near the Ara Pacis and Spanish Steps

To locate these restaurants, see the "Dolce Vita Stroll" map on page 814.

Ristorante il Gabriello is inviting and small—modern under medieval arches—and provides a peaceful and local-feeling respite from all the top-end fashion shops in the area. Claudio serves with charisma, while his brother Gabriello cooks creative Roman cuisine using fresh, organic products from his wife's farm. Italians normally just trust their waiter and say, "Bring it on." Tourists are understandably more cautious, but you can be trusting here. Simply close your eyes and point to anything on the menu. Or invest €45 in "Claudio's Extravaganza" (not including wine), and he'll shower you with edible kindness. Specify whether you'd prefer fish, meat, or both. (Romans think raw shellfish is the ultimate in fine dining. If you differ, make that clear.) When finished, I stand up, hold my belly, and say, *"Ahhh, la vita è bella"* (€10 pastas, €15 *secondi*, dinner only, Mon-Sat 19:00-23:00, closed Sun, reservations smart, air-con, dress respectfully—no shorts please, 3 blocks from Spanish Steps at Via Vittoria 51, tel. 06-6994-0810).

Osteria Gusto is thriving with trendy locals. While pricey, it's untouristy, gives a glimpse of today's Roman scene, and is fine for a glass of good wine over an artisanal cheese plate or a complete dinner (€13 pastas, €18 *secondi*, daily 12:30-15:30 & 19:00-24:00, opens at 18:30 for drinks and appetizers only, reservations recommended after 20:00 and on weekends, on the corner of Via Soderini at Via della Frezza 16, tel. 06-3211-1482). Their more expensive *ristorante* and more casual wine bar (which offers lighter bites) are directly adjacent.

L'EnotecAntica, an upbeat, atmospheric 200-plus-year-old *enoteca,* has around 60 Italian-only wines by the glass (€4-10, listed on a big blackboard) and a fresh €14 *antipasti* plate of veggies, *salumi,* and cheese. Very crowded on summer evenings, it comes with wonderful ambience both inside and out; its outside tables are set on a quiet cobbled street (daily 12:00-24:00, Via della Croce 76b, tel. 06-679-0896).

Palatium Enoteca Regionale is a crisp, modern restaurant funded by the region of Lazio (home to Rome) to show off its finest agricultural fare. Surrounded by locals, you'll enjoy generous, shareable plates of cheeses and *salumi,* a limited menu of pasta and meat, and a huge selection of local wine (€12-16 dishes, Mon-Sat 12:30-15:30 & 19:30-23:00, closed Sun, 5 blocks in front of the Spanish Steps at Via Frattina 94, tel. 06-6920-2132).

In Ancient Rome:
Near the Colosseum and Forum

You'll find good views but poor value at the restaurants directly behind the Colosseum. To get your money's worth, eat at least a block away. Here are several handy eateries, all shown on the map on page 900: one at the foot of Via Cavour, two at the top of Terme di Tito (a long block uphill from the Colosseum, near St. Peter-in-Chains church—of Michelangelo's *Moses* fame; for directions, see page 831), and two a couple of blocks to the east.

Enoteca Cavour 313 is a wine bar with a mission: to offer good wine and quality food with an old-fashioned commitment to value and friendly service. It's also a convenient place for a good lunch near the Forum and Colosseum. Angelo and his three partners enjoy creating a mellow ambience under lofts of wine bottles (limited menu of daily specials and fine wines by the glass, daily 12:30-14:45 & 19:00-24:00, 100 yards off Via dei Fori Imperiali at Via Cavour 313, tel. 06-678-5496).

Hostaria da Nerone is a traditional place serving hearty classics, including tasty homemade pasta dishes. Their *antipasti* plate—with a variety of veggies, fish, and meat—is a good value for a quick lunch. While the *antipasti* menu indicates specifics, you can have a plate of whatever's out—just direct the waiter to assemble the €9 *antipasti* plate of your lunchtime dreams (€10 pastas, €12 *secondi,* Mon-Sat 12:00-15:00 & 19:00-23:00, closed Sun, indoor/outdoor seating, Via delle Terme di Tito 96, tel. 06-481-7952, run by Teo and Eugenio).

ROME

Caffè dello Studente, next door to Hostaria da Nerone, is popular with engineering students attending the nearby University of Rome. Pina, Mauro, and their perky daughter Simona (who speaks English) give my readers a royal welcome and serve average, microwaved *bar gastronomia* fare—toasted sandwiches, salads, and mixed bruschetta. If it's not busy, show this book when you order at the bar and sit without paying extra at a table (Mon-Sat 7:30-22:30, April-Oct Sun 9:00-22:30, Nov-March closed Sun, Via delle Terme di Tito, tel. 06-488-3240).

Trattoria Luzzi is a well-worn, no-frills eatery serving simple food in a high-energy environment (as they've done since 1945). With good prices, big portions, and proximity to the Colosseum, it draws a crowd—reserve or expect a short wait at lunch and after 19:30 (€6 pastas, €7 pizzas, €9 *secondi*, Thu-Tue 12:00-24:00, closed Wed, Via San Giovanni in Laterano 88, tel. 06-709-6332).

La Taverna dei Quaranta, a casual neighborhood favorite, is a bit more refined than nearby Luzzi, but still far from pretentious. In the evening, they fire up the wood oven for pizza, to go along with a basic menu of Roman classics and seasonal specialties. As the place caters mostly to locals, service can be a bit slow and straightforward—but it's a good bet in this touristy area (€8 pastas, €13 *secondi*, daily 12:00-15:30 & 19:00-24:00, Via Claudia 24, tel. 06-700-0550).

Near Termini Station

These restaurants are near my recommended hotels on Via Firenze. Several are clustered on Via Flavia, others are nearby (Target, etc.), and a few, such as Bar Tavola Calda, are good options for quick meals.

On (or near) Via Flavia

To easily check out a fun and varied selection of eateries within a block of each other, walk to Via Flavia (a block behind the Church of Santa Maria della Vittoria of *St. Teresa in Ecstasy* fame) and survey these choices—an old-time restaurant, a good pizzeria, a small romantic place, and a friendly wine bar.

Ristorante da Giovanni, well-worn and old-fashioned, makes no concessions to tourism or the modern world—just hardworking cooks and waiters serving standard dishes at great prices to a committed clientele. It's simply fun to eat in the middle of this high-energy, Roman time warp (€6-10 pastas and *secondi*, daily specials, Mon-Sat 12:00-15:00 & 19:00-22:00, closed Sun and Aug, corner of Via XX Settembre at Via Antonio Salandra 1, tel. 06-485-950).

Annicinquanta Pizzeria, big and classic, serves the neighborhood's favorite pizzas in a calm ambience with outdoor seating (€8 Neapolitan-style pizzas, daily 12:15-15:30 & 19:30-24:00 except

Restaurants near Termini Station

1. Ristorante da Giovanni
2. Annincinquanta Pizzeria, Ristorante la Pentolaccia & I Colori del Vino Enoteca
3. Target Restaurant
4. Hostaria Romana
5. Ricci Est Est Est Pizzeria
6. Bar Tavola Calda
7. Snack Bar
8. Panificio Firenze & Bufala e Pachino Pizza
9. Flann O'Brien Irish Pub

no lunch on Sat, Via Flavia 3, tel. 06-4201-0460).

Ristorante la Pentolaccia, pricier and more romantic than the nearby Da Giovanni, is a dressy, tourist-friendly place with tight seating and traditional Roman cooking—consider their daily specials. This is a local hangout, and reservations are smart (daily 12:00-15:00 & 17:30-23:00, a block off Via XX Settembre at Via Flavia 38, tel. 06-483-477). To start things off with a free bruschetta, leave this book on the table.

I Colori del Vino Enoteca is a modern wine bar that feels like a laboratory of wine appreciation. It has woody walls of bottles, a creative menu of meats and cheeses with different regional themes, and a great list of fine wines by the glass. Helpful, English-speaking Marco carries on a long family tradition of celebrating the fundamentals of good nutrition: fine wine, cheese, meat, and bread (Mon-Fri 12:00-15:00 & 17:30-23:00, closed Sat-Sun because Marco doesn't cater to noisy weekend drinkers, corner of Via Flavia and Via Aureliana, tel. 06-474-1745). Remember Shakespeare's sage warning about drinking: "It provokes the desire, but it takes away the performance."

More Eateries near the Station

Target Restaurant seems to be the favorite recommendation of every hotel receptionist and tour guide for this neighborhood. It has reliably good food, a sleek look, capable service, and practical prices (€8-12 salads, pastas, and pizzas; €20 *secondi*, daily 12:00-15:00 & 19:00-24:00 except no lunch on Sun, reserve to specify seating outside or inside—avoid getting seated in basement, Via Torino 33, tel. 06-474-0066).

Hostaria Romana is a busy bistro with a hustling and fun-loving gang of waiters, and noisy walls graffitied by happy eaters. As its menu specializes in traditional Roman dishes, it's a good place to try *saltimbocca alla romana* or *bucatini all'amatriciana*. Their €10 *antipasti* plate, with a variety of vegetables and cheeses, makes a hearty start to your meal (€9 pastas, €14 *secondi*, Mon-Sat 12:15-15:00 & 19:15-23:00, closed Sun, reservations smart, a block up the lane just past the entrance to the big tunnel near the Trevi Fountain at Via del Boccaccio 1, tel. 06-474-5284).

Ricci Est Est Est Pizzeria, a venerable family-run pizzeria, has plenty of historical ambience, good €8 pizzas, and danger-ously tasty *fritti*, such as fried *baccalà* (cod) and zucchini flowers (Tue-Sun 19:00-24:00, closed Mon and Aug, Via Genova 32, tel. 06-488-1107).

Fast, Simple Meals near the Station

Bar Tavola Calda is a workers' favorite for a quick, cheap lunch. They have good, fresh, hot dishes ready to go for a fine price. Head back past the bar to peruse their enticing display, point at what you want, then grab a seat and the young waitstaff will serve you (Mon-Sat 6:00-18:00, closed Sun, Via Torino 40).

Snack Bar puts out a lunchtime display of inexpensive pastas, colorful sandwiches, fresh fruit, and salad. Their loyal custom-ers appreciate the fruit salad with yogurt (daily 6:00-24:00, Via Firenze 33, mobile 339-393-1356, Enrica).

Panificio Firenze makes hearty sandwiches, has a selection of well-priced wine, and stocks other goodies for a picnic to go (sandwiches priced by weight, Mon-Fri 7:00-19:00, Sat 7:00-14:00, closed Sun, Via Firenze 51-52, tel. 06-488-5035, Giovanni).

Bufala e Pachino Pizza is a convenient place for pizza by the slice *(al taglio)* and priced by weight—just point and tell them how much you'd like. Their *supplí* (fried rice balls filled with mozzarella), at just €1 each, make for cheap, filling snacks (daily 10:00-23:00, Via Firenze 54).

Flann O'Brien Irish Pub is an entertaining place for a light meal of pasta...or something *other* than pasta, such as grilled meats and giant salads, served early and late, when other places are closed. They have Irish beer, live sporting events on TV, and perhaps the most Italian crowd of all. Walk way back before choosing a table. Live bands often play on Friday evenings (daily 7:00-24:00, Via Nazionale 17, at intersection with Via Napoli, tel. 06-488-0418).

Near Vatican City

Avoid the restaurant-pushers handing out fliers near the Vatican: They're hawking places with bad food and expensive menu tricks. Try any of these instead (see map on page 907).

Handy Lunch Places near Piazza Risorgimento

These are a stone's throw from the Vatican wall, located halfway between St. Peter's Basilica and the Vatican Museum. They're all fast and cheap, with a good *gelateria* next door.

Hostaria dei Bastioni, run by Antonio while Emilio cooks, has noisy street-side seating and a quiet interior (€8 pastas, €12 *secondi*, Mon-Sat 12:00-15:30 & 18:30-23:00, closed Sun, at corner of Vatican wall at Via Leone IV 29, tel. 06-3972-3034).

L'Insalata Ricca is another branch of the popular chain that serves salads and pastas (daily 12:30-15:30 & 18:30-23:45, across from Vatican walls at Piazza Risorgimento 5, tel. 06-3973-0387).

Duecento Gradi is a good bet for fresh and creative €5 sandwiches. Munch your lunch on a stool or take it away (daily 11:00-24:00, Piazza Risorgimento 3, tel. 06-3975-4239).

Gelato: **Gelateria Old Bridge** scoops up hearty portions of fresh gelato for tourists and nuns alike—join the line (daily 10:00-23:00, just off Piazza Risorgimento across from Vatican walls at Via Bastioni 3).

Other Good Options in the Vatican Area

The first three listings—the restaurant, the streets with pizza shops, and the covered market—are near the Vatican Museum. The Borgo Pio eateries are near St. Peter's Basilica.

La Rustichella serves tasty wood-fired pizza and the usual pasta in addition to their sprawling *antipasti* buffet (€8 for a single plate). Arrive when it opens at 19:00 to avoid a line and have the pristine buffet to yourself. Do like the Romans do—take a moderate amount and make one trip only (Tue-Sun 12:30-15:00

ROME

& 19:00-24:00, closed Mon, near Metro: Cipro, opposite church at end of Via Candia, Via Angelo Emo 1, tel. 06-3972-0649). Consider the fun and fruity **Gelateria Millennium** next door.

Viale Giulio Cesare and *Via Candia:* These streets are lined with cheap *pizza rustica* shops, self-serve places, and basic eateries.

Covered Market: As you collect picnic supplies, turn your nose loose in the wonderful **Mercato Trionfale** covered market. It's one of the best in the city, located three blocks north of the Vatican Museum (Mon-Sat roughly 7:00-14:00, Tue and Fri some stalls stay open until 19:00, closed Sun, corner of Via Tunisi and Via Andrea Doria). If the market is closed, try several nearby supermarkets; the most convenient is **Carrefour Express** (Mon-Sat 8:00-20:00, Sun 9:00-20:00, Via Sebastiano Veniero 16).

Along Borgo Pio: The pedestrians-only Borgo Pio—a block from Piazza San Pietro—has restaurants worth a look, such as **Tre Pupazzi** (Mon-Sat 12:00-15:00 & 19:00-23:00, closed Sun, at corner of Via Tre Pupazzi and Borgo Pio, tel. 06-686-8371). At **Vecchio Borgo,** across the street, you can get pasta, pizza slices, and veggies to go (Mon-Sat 9:00-21:00, closed Sun, Borgo Pio 27a, tel. 06-8117-3585).

Rome Connections

Rome is well-connected with the rest of the planet: by train, bus, plane, car, and cruise ship. This section addresses your arrival and departure from the city. It explains the various options and gives a rundown on their points of departure.

By Train

Rome's main train station is the centrally located **Termini** train station, which has connections to the airport. Rome's other major station is the **Tiburtina** bus/train station, which is starting to get some high-speed rail connections. For in-depth descriptions of both Termini and Tiburtina stations, see page 796. Smaller stations include **Ostiense** (useful for going to South Rome and Testaccio, also may have some high-speed rail) and its neighbor, **Porta San Paolo** (with connections to Ostia Antica). If you're staying near the Vatican and taking a regional train, it saves time to get off at the **San Pietro** train station rather than at Termini. Cruise-ship passengers coming from Civitavecchia on a day trip usually use Ostiense or San Pietro.

Nearly all of the most convenient connections for travelers depart from Termini, but as a precaution, it's always smart to confirm whether your train departs from Termini or Tiburtina.

From Rome's Termini Station by Train to: Venice (roughly hourly, 3.75 hours, overnight possible with transfer in Milan),

Florence (at least hourly, 1.5 hours, some stop at Orvieto en route), **Siena** (1-2/hour, 1 change, 3-4 hours), **Orvieto** (hourly, 1.25 hours), **Assisi** (hourly, 2-3.5 hours, 5 direct, most others change in Foligno), **Pisa** (hourly, 3-4 hours, many change in Florence), **La Spezia** (8/day direct, more with transfers in Pisa, 3-4.5 hours), **Milan** (hourly, 3-8 hours, overnight possible), **Milan's Malpensa Airport** (1 direct express/day, 4.5 hours), **Naples** (at least hourly, 1.25 hours on Frecciarossa trains, otherwise 2 hours), **Civitavecchia** cruise-ship port (2-3/hour, 1-1.5 hours), **Brindisi** (6/day, 3 direct, 6-9 hours, overnight possible), **Amsterdam** (6/day, 20 hours), **Interlaken** (5/day, 6.5-8 hours), **Frankfurt** (6/day, 11-12 hours), **Munich** (5/day, 10-11.5 hours, 1 direct night train, 11.5 hours), **Nice** (7/day, 8.75-10.5 hours,), **Paris** (4/day, 10.75-12.75 hours; 1 night train, 14 hours, transfer in Milan, important to reserve ahead at www.thello.com), **Vienna** (2/day, 11.75 hours, 1 direct night train, 12 hours).

From Rome's Tiburtina Station by Train to: **Florence** (8/day, 1.5 hours), **Milan** (8/day, 3.5 hours), **Naples** (5/day, 1.25 hours).

By Bus

Long-distance buses (such as from Siena and Assisi) arrive at Rome's **Tiburtina Station** (described on page 796).

From Rome by Bus to: **Assisi** (2/day, 3 hours—the train makes much more sense), **Siena** (8/day, 3 hours), **Sorrento** (1-2/day, 4 hours; this is a cheap and easy way to go straight to Sorrento).

By Plane

Rome's two airports—**Fiumicino** (a.k.a. Leonardo da Vinci, airport code: FCO) and the small **Ciampino** (airport code: CIA)—share the same website (www.adr.it).

Fiumicino Airport

Rome's major airport has a TI (in Terminal 3, daily 9:00-18:30), ATMs, banks, luggage storage, shops, and bars. The Rome Walks website (www.romewalks.com) has a useful video on options for getting into the city from the airport.

The slick, direct **"Leonardo Express" train** connects the airport and Rome's central Termini train station in 30 minutes for €14. Trains run twice hourly in both directions from roughly 6:00 to 23:00 (leaving the airport at :07 and :37). From the airport's arrival gate, follow signs to the train car icon or *Stazione/Railway Station*. Buy your ticket from a machine, the Biglietteria office, or a newsstand at the platform; then validate it in a yellow machine near the track. Make sure the train you board is going to the central "Roma Termini" station, not "Roma Orte" or others.

Going from Termini train station to the airport, trains depart at about :22 and :52 past the hour, from track 24. Check the

ROME

departure boards for "Fiumicino Aeroporto"—the local name for the airport—and confirm with an official or a local on the platform that the train is indeed going to the airport (€14, buy ticket from any tobacco shop or a newsstand in the station, or at the self-service machines, Termini-Fiumicino trains run 5:52-22:52). Read your ticket: If it requires validation, stamp it in the yellow machine near the platform before boarding. From the train station at the airport, you can access most of the terminals. American airlines flying direct to the US depart from Terminal 5, which is a separate building not connected to the rest of the terminals. If you arrive by train, catch the T5 shuttle bus *(navetta)* on the sidewalk in front of Terminal 3—it's too far to walk with luggage.

Allow lots of time going in either direction; there's a fair amount of transportation involved, including moving walkways, escalators, and walking (e.g., getting from your hotel to Termini, from Termini to the train platform, the ride to the airport, getting from the airport train station to check-in, etc.). Flying to the US involves an extra level of security—plan on getting to the airport even earlier than normal (I like to arrive 2.5 hours ahead of my flight).

The **Terravision Express bus** connects Fiumicino and Termini train station, departing every 40 minutes (€6 one-way, €11 round-trip; leaves the airport from Terminal 3, leaves Termini Station from Via Marsala—just outside the exit closest to track 1; one hour, www.terravision.eu). The **SIT Bus Shuttle** also connects Fiumicino and Termini (€8 one-way, €15 round-trip, similar schedule and info to Terravision, tel. 06-592-3507, www.sitbusshuttle .com). While cheaper than the train, the buses take twice as long and can potentially fill up (allow plenty of extra time).

Shuttle van services run to and from the airport and can be economical for one or two people. It's cheaper from the airport to downtown, as several companies compete for this route; by surveying the latest deals, you should be able to snare a ride into town for around €10. To get from your hotel to the airport, consider Rome Airport Shuttle (€25/1 person, extra people-€6 each, by reservation only, tel. 06-4201-4507 or 06-4201-3469, www.airport shuttle.it).

A **taxi** between Fiumicino and downtown Rome takes 45 minutes in normal traffic (for tips on taxis, see page 798). If you're catching a taxi at the airport, be sure to wait at the taxi stand. Avoid unmarked, unmetered taxis; these guys will try to tempt you away from the taxi-stand lineup by offering an immediate (rip-off) ride. Rome's and Fiumicino's official taxis have a fixed rate to and from the airport (€48 for up to four people with bags).

Cabbies not based in Rome or Fiumicino are allowed to charge €70 for the ride. That sign is posted next to the €48-fare sign—confusing many tourists and allowing dishonest cabbies to overcharge. It's best to use a Rome city cab, with the "SPQR" shield on the door. They can only charge €48 for the ride to anywhere in the historic center (within the old city walls, where most of my recommended hotels are located).

If your cab driver tries to charge you more than €48 from the airport into town, say, *"Quarant'otto euro—è la legge"* (kwah-rahnt-OH-toh AY-oo-roh—ay lah LEJ-jay; which means, "Forty-eight euros—it's the law"), and they should back off.

To get from the airport into town cheaply by taxi, try teaming up with any tourist also just arriving (most are heading for hotels near yours in the center). When you're departing Rome, your hotel can arrange a taxi to the airport at any hour.

For **airport information,** call 06-65951. To inquire about flights, call 06-6595-3640.

Ciampino Airport

Rome's smaller airport (tel. 06-6595-9515) handles charter flights and some budget airlines (including all Ryanair and some easyJet flights).

To get to downtown Rome from the airport, you can take the Cotral bus, which leaves every 40 minutes (€5, 20-minute ride, toll-free tel. 800-174-471, www.cotralspa.it), to the Anagnina Metro stop, where you can connect by Metro to the stop nearest your hotel. Rome Airport Shuttle also offers service to and from Ciampino (€25/1 person, listed earlier). The Terravision Express Shuttle connects Ciampino and Termini train station, leaving every 20 minutes (€4 one-way, €8 round-trip, www.terravision .eu). The SIT Bus Shuttle also connects Termini to Ciampino (€4, about 2/hour, 45 minutes, runs 7:45-23:15 Ciampino to Termini, 4:30-21:30 Termini to Ciampino, pickup on Via Marsala just outside the train exit closest to track 1, tel. 06-592-3507, www.sit busshuttle.it). A taxi should cost €30 to downtown (within the old city walls, including most of my recommended hotels).

By Cruise Ship

Hundreds of cruise ships—including Carnival, Royal Caribbean, Princess, and Celebrity lines—dock each year at the port of **Civitavecchia,** about 45 miles northwest of Rome. If your trip includes cruising beyond Rome, consider my new guidebook, *Rick Steves' Mediterranean Cruise Ports.* Port facilities include a TI (tel. 0766-1892-667), ATMs, Internet access, bag storage, and cafés.

To get from your ship to Civitavecchia's train station, take the free shuttle bus to the port entrance (some shuttles may take you all the way to the station—ask). From the shuttle-bus stop, walk through the security checkpoint at the port gate, and then

ROME

walk about 10 minutes straight ahead up the main road with the sea on your right-hand side. After about three blocks, at Hotel de La Ville, bear left and uphill through a long parking lot to the pale-orange train station (marked *Civitavecchia*); if you get turned around, look for signs to *Stazione FF. SS.*

Taxis also wait at the port gate, attempting to extort €15 for the very short ride to the train station (tel. 076-626-121). A local bus to the train station only saves you a few minutes of walking; take one only if you're carrying heavy bags or have limited mobility. **Buses** #B, #C, and #D go from just above the port gate on Largo Plebiscito (Viale Garibaldi stop) one stop to the train station (Stazione FF. SS. stop; €1, 3-4/hour, 5 minutes, buy ticket at a tobacco shop before you board).

Getting Between Civitavecchia and Downtown Rome

The traffic between Civitavecchia and Rome is terrible, making trains faster and more economical than a taxi (which can run €110-150 one-way). Recommended driver Ezio of Autoservizi Monti Concezio takes cruise travelers to Rome in a private car (€130/2 people, €20 for each additional person) and offers full-day tours of the city (€380/2 people, €30 for each additional person; see "Car and Minibus Tours" on page 802). Beware of unlicensed taxis offering a huge price break; local police sometimes follow these "gypsy" cabs in a scam that imposes hefty fines on both the driver and the passengers (the driver later gets a kickback from the cop).

Keep in mind that it takes approximately 1.5 hours each way to get between your ship and downtown Rome—so you'll need to mentally subtract at least three hours from the time you have in port.

Frequent trains (2-3/hour) connect Civitavecchia with several stations in Rome. Depending on your sightseeing plans, you'll likely be best off heading either to **Ostiense Station** (with a handy Metro station, just two stops from the Colosseum) or **San Pietro Station** (15 minute walk or a couple stops on bus #64 to get to St. Peter's Basilica). **Termini Station,** the main hub for the city's transit and for shuttle trains to the airport, overshoots the key city-center sights a bit.

Regional trains (marked *REG*) head into Rome roughly twice an hour, stopping at San Pietro and Ostiense stations on their way to Termini (40-55 minutes to San Pietro, 55-70 minutes to Ostiense, 80 minutes to Termini). The **Intercity train** (marked *IC*) is somewhat faster (50 minutes to Ostiense, 60 minutes to Termini), but doesn't stop at San Pietro Station, and isn't covered by the good-value BIRG ticket (described next). When there are enough ships in port to justify it, there's also a special **express**

"**Seatrain**" to San Pietro Station, offering one daily round-trip designed for cruise travelers.

If you're taking a regional train, save money by getting the wonderful BIRG ticket: a €12 day pass covering second-class, round-trip train travel between Civitavecchia and Rome as well as unlimited travel on Rome's buses, Metro, and trams—a great convenience (not valid on fast Intercity trains or the express Seatrain). Otherwise, expect to pay about €4.50 each way for regional trains or €9.50 on the Intercity. All train tickets must be validated in the yellow box before getting on the train.

The Civitavecchia train station has five main platforms (*binario*, or *bin*; numbered 1 through 5), connected by an underground tunnel. There are also two "short" *(tronco)* platforms, 1T and 2T, at the far-right end of the station as you face the tracks; these are *not* the same as tracks 1 and 2. Be sure you're waiting at the correct platform. For a useful video on taking the train from the port into the city, check out the Rome Walks website (www.romewalks .com).

Getting Between Civitavecchia and Fiumicino Airport

You'll need to take two **trains** to link Civitavecchia and Fiumicino Airport: one between Civitavecchia and Rome's Termini train station, and another between Termini and the airport. See "By Plane," earlier.

Shuttle van services run between the port and Rome's Fiumicino Airport. Try **Rome Airport Shuttle** (€90/1-2 people, €15 each additional person up to 8, share with others and save, much more for pickup between 21:00 and 7:00, tel. 06-4201-4507 or 06-4201-3469, www.airportshuttle.it). A **taxi** costs about €120 one-way between Civitavecchia and Fiumicino Airport.

NAPLES

Napoli

If you like Italy as far south as Rome, go farther south—it gets better. If Italy is getting
on your nerves, don't go farther. Italy inten-
sifies as you plunge deeper. Naples is Italy
in the extreme—its best (birthplace of pizza
and Sophia Loren) and its worst (home of
the Camorra, Naples' "family" of organized
crime). Just beyond Naples you'll find the remarkable ruins of
Pompeii and Herculaneum...and the brooding volcano that did
them both in, Mount Vesuvius.

Neapolis ("new city") was a thriving Greek commercial center
2,500 years ago. Today, it remains southern Italy's leading city.
Naples impresses visitors with one of Europe's top archaeological museums (with artifacts from Pompeii and other nearby sites),
fascinating churches that convey the city's unique personality and
powerful devotion, an underground warren of Greek and Roman
ruins, fine works of art (including pieces by Caravaggio, who lived
here for a time), and evocative nativity scenes (called *presepi*).
Naples, of course, makes the best pizza you'll find anywhere, and
tasty pastries as well (try the crispy, ricotta-stuffed *sfogliatella*). But
more than anything, Naples has a brash and vibrant street life—"in
your face" in ways both good and bad. Walking through its colorful old town is one of my favorite experiences anywhere in Italy.
For a grand overlook, head to the hilltop viewpoint (San Martino)
for sweeping views of the city and its bay.

Naples—Italy's third-largest city, with more than one million people—has almost no open spaces or parks, which makes its
position as Europe's most densely populated city plenty evident.
Watching the police try to enforce traffic sanity is almost comical

in Italy's grittiest, most polluted, and most crime-ridden city. But Naples surprises the observant traveler with its impressive knack for living, eating, and raising children in the streets with good humor and decency. Overcome your fear of being run down or ripped off long enough to talk with people. Enjoy a few smiles and jokes with the man running the neighborhood tripe shop, or the woman taking her day-care class on a walk through the traffic.

The pulse of Italy throbs in Naples. Like Cairo or Mumbai, it's appalling and captivating at the same time, the closest thing to "reality travel" that you'll find in Western Europe. But this tangled mess still somehow manages to breathe, laugh, and sing—with a joyful Italian accent.

Planning Your Time

Naples makes an ideal day trip either from Rome or from the comfortable home base of Sorrento, located an hour south (see Sorrento chapter). Or stow your bag at the station and see Naples in a few hours when you change trains here on the way between Rome and Sorrento. A little Naples goes a long way; if you're not comfortable in chaotic and congested cities, think twice before spending the night here. But those who are intrigued by the city's sights and street life enjoy overnighting in Naples.

On a quick visit, start with the Archaeological Museum (closed Tue), follow my "A Slice of Neapolitan Life" self-guided walk, and celebrate your survival with pizza. With more time, dip into more churches, go underground to see Greek and Roman ruins, and consider ascending San Martino for the view. Of course, Naples is huge. But even with limited time, if you stick to the prescribed route and grab a cab when you're lost or tired, it's fun. Treat yourself well in Naples; the city is cheap by Italian standards. This is a place where splurging on a sane and comfortable hotel is a particularly worthwhile investment.

For a blitz tour from Rome, you could have breakfast on an early Rome-Naples express train (for example, Mon-Fri 7:35-8:45), do Naples and Pompeii in a day, and be back in Rome in time for *Letterman*. That's exhausting, but more memorable than a fourth day in Rome.

Remember that in the afternoon, Naples' street life slows and many churches and museums close as the temperature soars. The city comes back to life in the early evening.

Orientation to Naples

Naples is set deep inside the large and curving Bay of Naples, with Mount Vesuvius looming just five miles away. Although Naples is a sprawling city, its fairly compact core contains the most interesting sights. The tourist's Naples is a triangular shape, from the Centrale train station to the east, the Archaeological Museum to the west, and the Piazza del Plebiscito (with the Royal Palace) and the port to the south. Within this triangle are unusual churches and a very straight street. Rising above this historic core are hills and mountains, some capped with mighty fortresses (such as San Martino).

Tourist Information

Naples has three autonomous TI organizations, which are equally incapable of dispensing reliable advice. The most convenient—but least helpful—is in the **Centrale train station** (daily 9:00-19:00, near track 23, operated by a private agency, tel. 081-268-779).

The regional TI has two branches: one at the **Galleria Umberto I shopping mall** (across from the entrance to the Teatro di San Carlo; Mon-Sat 9:00-19:00, Sun 9:00-14:00, tel. 081-402-394) and another across from the **Church of Gesù Nuovo** (same hours, tel. 081-551-2701).

The city of Naples operates a main TI on **Piazza del Plebiscito** (at #14, to right of church entrance, Mon-Fri 9:00-19:00, closed Sat-Sun, tel. 081-795-6162), plus two kiosks with limited hours: one near the Museo Metro stop in the park next to the **Archaeological Museum**, and another at **Piazza de Nicola** a few blocks in front of the train station (both Mon-Fri 10:30-14:00, closed Sat-Sun).

Cruise-ship passengers exiting the **cruise terminal** complex pass through a little checkpoint (marked *Molo Angioimo*) that has a small TI.

At any TI, pick up a map and ask for the *Qui Napoli* booklet, which lists the latest museum hours, events, and transportation info (due to funding cuts, the booklet is often out of print; if so, ask if they have an old one). The best overall website is www.inaples.it.

Arrival in Naples

By Train: There are several Naples train stations, but all trains coming into town stop at either Napoli Centrale or Garibaldi—essentially the same place, with Centrale on top of Garibaldi.

Centrale is the busiest station, facing the vast and gritty Piazza Garibaldi. You'll find all the administrative facilities in Centrale, including a TI (near track 23), an ATM (at Banco di Napoli near track 24), and a baggage check (€5/5 hours, then €0.70/hour, daily

Naples

Cavour
To 5
Piazza
Cavour M
VIA FORIA CARBONARA
Piazza
Capuana
CASANOVA
NOV.
Airport 1
Bus
FIRENZE B

ARCHAEO-
LOGICAL
MUSEUM
B i
Museo M
VIA DUOMO
S. APOST.
S. PAOLO
DUOMO
VIA TRIBUNALI
Piazza
Garibaldi B
2 M i
CAPPELLA
SANSEVERO
4
FISH
MKT.
CENTRALE
STATION
(F.S.)
To
Pompei
Town

Monte-
santo Metro &
Funicular
Piazza
Dante
Dante M
SAN
DOM.
GESÙ
NUOVO
VIA S.
BIAGIO
FORCELLA
Porta
Nolana
CIRCUM-
VESUVIANA
TERMINUS
STATION
(TO POMPEII
RUINS)

VIA TARSIA
VIA P. SCURA
VIA TOLEDO
VIA D. CROCE
"SPACCANAPOLI"
CORSO UMBERTO I

SANTA
CHIARA

VIA P. IGNASECCA
Piazza
Carità
VIA ROMA
VIA MORGANTINA
VIA DIAZ
Piazza
Bovio
CORSO VIT. EMAN.
DEPRETIS
VIA C. COLOMBO
NUOVA MARINA
Port

SPANISH
QUARTER
Centrale
Funicular

GALLERIA
UMBERTO I
Piazza
Municipio
B
Bus to
Airport
T Tram to
Train Station

STAZIONE
MARITTIMA
Car Ferries to
Sicily & Sardinia

TEATRO DI
SANCARLO
i
CASTEL
NUOVO
To 3
i
Piazza del Plebiscito
ROYAL
PALACE
BEVERELLO
PORT
To Sorrento,
Capri, Ischia,
& Procida

S. FRAN.
DI PAOLA

See "Slice of Neopolitan Life Walk" detail map

VITTORIO TUNNEL
VIA NAZARIO SAURO
Bay of Naples
N

VIA PARTENOPE
To Lungomare
CASTEL
DELL'OVO
BORGO
MARINARO
500 Meters
500 Yards

1 Grand Hotel Europa
2 Hotel Potenza, La Cantina
dei Mille & Iris Ristorante
3 To Pinto-Storey Hotel

4 Pio Monte della
Misericordia Church
5 To Museo di Capodimonte

7:00-23:00, marked *deposito bagagli*, near track 5).

Garibaldi is a subway station used by trains to make a quick stop as they barrel through. It's connected to the Centrale Station by escalators. The Circumvesuviana stop, where you can catch a commuter train to Sorrento or Pompeii, is also on this level. (But note that this is not technically the terminus for the Circumvesuviana—there's one more stop deeper in the city, called "Napoli P. Nolana," across from the Porta Nolana Fish Market.) For more on the Circumvesuviana, see "Getting Around the

Planning Your Time in the Region

On a quick trip, give the entire area—including Sorrento and Naples—a minimum of three days. With Sorrento as your sunny springboard (see Sorrento chapter), spend a day in Naples, a day exploring the Amalfi Coast, and a day split between Pompeii and the town of Sorrento. While Paestum (Greek temples), Mount Vesuvius, Herculaneum (an ancient Roman site like Pompeii), and the island of Capri are decent destinations, they are worthwhile only if you have more time. For a map, see page 933.

The **Campania ArteCard** regional pass may save you a few euros if you're here for a quick trip, using public transportation, and plan on going to Pompeii (€11), Herculaneum (€11), or Naples' Archaeological Museum (€6.50). There are several versions, which generally cover most sights and the public transportation in the area. The three-day Tutta la Regione version makes the most sense, including free entry to two sights (50 percent off others) and transportation within Naples, on the Circumvesuviana train, and on Amalfi Coast buses (€27, sold at Naples TIs and participating sights, activates on first use, expires three days later at midnight, www.campaniarte card.it).

Region," later.

By Ferry or Cruise Ship: Naples is a ferry hub with great boat connections to Sorrento, Capri, and other nearby destinations. Ferries use the smaller Port Beverello dock (called Molo Beverello), while cruise ships use the Stazione Marittima cruise terminal. The two docks are side-by-side at the port on the southeast edge of downtown Naples, near Castel Nuovo and the grand square called Piazza del Plebiscito. In the covered area between the cruise-terminal buildings, you'll find cafés and various shops, including a tobacco shop (where you can buy bus tickets). Out by the street is the recommended Ontano Tours travel agency (see "Helpful Hints," later).

Whether arriving by ferry or cruise ship, you can get to the city center by taxi, bus, or on foot; the Alibus shuttle bus runs to the airport (see "By Plane," next; the stop is a couple of blocks inland from the port, between Castel Nuovo and Teatro di San Carlo). The **taxi** stand is in front of the port area; figure €12-15 to get to the train station or to the Archaeological Museum (see "Getting Around Naples—By Taxi" on page 937). **Tram #1** stops at the busy road directly in front of the cruise terminal and heads to Piazza Garibaldi and the train station, where you can connect to trains to sights outside of town (6/hour, 15 minutes, buy €1.20 ticket at tobacco shop, validate ticket in yellow box on the bus as

NAPLES

you board). Straight ahead across the road (on the right side of the big fortress) is a drab square called Piazza Municipio; from here, a **bus** stop to Naples' Archaeological Museum is a half-block down on Via Agostino Depretis (#R4, departs every 10-15 minutes, ride six stops to Piazza Museo).

On foot, it's a seven-minute **walk**—past the gigantic Castel Nuovo—to Piazza del Plebiscito and the old city center: After crossing the busy street in front of the port, head up the ramp just to the right of the castle. At the top, angle left, past Teatro di San Carlo, to Piazza del Plebiscito. From this square, you could do a truncated version of my self-guided walk (begin near the end of "Part 2," do that stretch backwards up the hill, then launch right into "Part 3").

By Plane: Naples International Airport (a.k.a. Capodichino, code: NAP) is located four miles northeast of the city center (tel. 081-789-6111 for operator, tel. 848-888-777 for info, www.gesac.it). Alibus shuttle buses zip you from the airport to Naples' Centrale train station/Piazza Garibaldi in 15 minutes, and then head to the port for boats to Capri and Sorrento (daily 6:30-24:00, 3/hour, less frequent early and late, 30 minutes to the port, €3, turn right as you exit and find platform #2 at the bus stop, pay driver, stops at train station and port only). It's tough to get a cabbie to use the meter from the airport, but a taxi ride should cost about €20 (see "Getting Around Naples—By Taxi" on page 937).

To reach **Sorrento** from Naples Airport, take the direct Curreri bus (daily at 9:00, 11:00, 13:00, 14:30, 16:30, and 19:30; likely 2 additional departures May-Oct, 1.5 hours, €10, pay driver, tel. 081-801-5420, www.curreriviaggi.it).

Helpful Hints

Theft Alert: Err on the side of caution. Don't venture into neighborhoods that make you uncomfortable. Walk with confidence, as if you know where you're going and what you're doing. Assume able-bodied beggars are thieves.

Stick to busy streets and beware of gangs of hoodlums. A third of the city is unemployed, and past local governments have set an example that the Mafia would be proud of. Assume con artists are more clever than you. Any jostle or commotion is probably a thief-team smokescreen. To keep bags safe, it's probably best to store them at Centrale Station or keep them at your hotel.

Always walk on the sidewalk (even if the locals don't) and carry your bag on the side away from the street—thieves on scooters have been known to snatch bags as they swoop by. The less you have dangling from you (including cameras and necklaces), the better.

Perhaps your biggest risk of theft is while catching or riding the Circumvesuviana commuter train. If you're connecting from a major train, you'll be stepping from a relatively secure compartment into a crowded Naples subway filled with thieves hunting disoriented tourists with luggage. While I ride the Circumvesuviana comfortably and safely, each year I hear of many who get ripped off on this ride. You won't be mugged—but you may be conned or pickpocketed. Especially late at night, the Circumvesuviana train is plagued by intimidating ruffians. For maximum safety and peace of mind, sit in the front car, where the driver will double as your protector.

Con artists may say you need to "transfer" by taxi to catch the Circumvesuviana; you don't. Anyone offering to help you with your bags is likely a thief, despite displayed credentials. There are no porters at Centrale Station or in the lower level where the Circumvesuviana station is located. Wear your money belt, hang on to your bag, and don't display any valuables.

Traffic Safety: In Naples, red lights are discretionary, and pedestrians need to be wary, particularly of motor scooters. Smart tourists jaywalk in the shadow of bold and confident locals, who generally ignore crosswalks. Wait for a break in traffic, cross with confidence, and make eye contact with approaching drivers. The traffic will stop. Even on "pedestrian" streets, stay alert to avoid being sideswiped by scooters that nudge their way through the crowds.

Travel Agency: Ontano Tours books train and boat tickets from a small office next to the busy street directly in front of the cruise terminal (Mon-Sat 8:30-20:00, closed Sun, tel. 081-580-0340, www.ontanotour.it).

Getting Around Naples

By Subway: Naples' ragged and slow-moving subway, the Metropolitana, has two lines. The handiest is line 2, which runs from Centrale Station (catch it downstairs at the Garibaldi stop) through the center of town (direction: Pozzuoli), stopping at Piazza Cavour (a five-minute walk from the Archaeological Museum) and Montesanto (top of Spanish Quarter and Spaccanapoli street, and base of funicular up to San Martino). Line 1 runs from the central Dante stop, stopping at the Museo station (near the Archaeological Museum and next to line 2's Piazza Cavour stop), then looping through town out to Piscinola/Scampia (suburbs). While the Piazza Cavour and Museo subway stops are near each other, they aren't connected (but are at opposite ends of the same park, about a five-minute walk). Tickets cost €1.20 and are good for 1.5 hours. All-day tickets cost €3.60 (or €3 on weekends). Validate tickets in

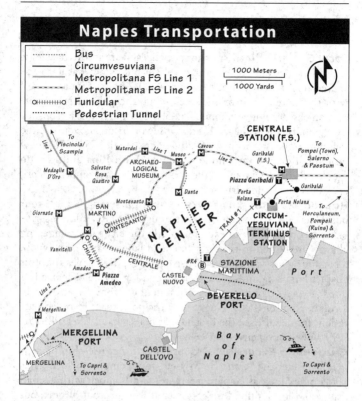

the small yellow boxes you'll see before you reach the track.

By Funicular: Naples' network of funiculars *(funicolare),* which carry commuters and sightseers into the hilly neighborhoods above downtown, are covered by the same tickets as the Metro. Three handy Metro lines converge at the location that's of most interest to tourists, the San Martino hilltop (with its fortress and monastery/museum): the Centrale line (from the Spanish Quarter, just above Piazza del Plebiscito), the Montesanto line (from the Montesanto Metro stop and Via Pignasecca market zone), and the Chiaia line (from near the Piazza Amadeo Metro stop).

By Bus or Tram: Buses and trams can be handy for certain trips, such as getting from the port to the train station or the Archaeological Museum. If you need to curtail my self-guided walk, you can hop a bus to the station. Tickets cost €1.20 at tobacco shops; validate the ticket in the yellow box on the bus as you board.

By Taxi: Taxi drivers in Naples are notorious for overcharging. A short ride in town should cost €10-12. Ask for the *tariffa predeterminata* (a fixed rate). There are some legitimate extra charges (baggage fees, €2.50 supplement after 22:00 or all day Sun and holidays).

Tours in Naples

Local Guides—**Pina Esposito** specializes in art and archaeology, and does fine tours of Naples' excellent but somewhat hard-to-appreciate Archaeological Museum (€120/2 hours, 10 percent off with this book, confirm one week in advance, sometimes available on shorter notice, mobile 349-596-8251, annamariaesposito1 @virgilio.it). The team at **Mondo Guide** offers private tours of the museum and city (€50/hour, €320/4 hours, tel. 081-751-3290, www .mondoguide.it, info@mondoguide.it). Both Pina and Mondo Guide can also lead tours of the surrounding area (Pompeii, Capri, etc.) and can provide drivers.

Hop-on, Hop-off Bus Tours—**CitySightseeing Napoli** tour buses make four different loops through the city, allowing riders to get on and off to explore. While the city's most engaging charms are buried in the tight tangle of lanes near Spaccanapoli, a bus tour gives you a better sense of the greater Naples that this chapter largely ignores (€22, tickets good for 24 hours, sparse frequency—4-11/day depending on route, buy from driver or from kiosk in front of Castel Nuovo near the port, scant recorded narration; for details, see the brochure at hotels and TI, tel. 081-551-7279, www.napoli.city-sightseeing.it).

Cruise-Ship Excursions—Convenient for cruise-ship passengers, consider the "Can't Be Missed" tour company, which gives you a quick look at Naples, Sorrento, and Pompeii with a small group and local guide for €65 (meet at 8:30 in front of port, bus leaves at 9:00, returns at 17:15, Pompeii ticket extra, mobile 329-129-8182, www.cantbemissedtours.com).

Self-Guided Tour

▲▲▲Archaeological Museum (Museo Archeologico)

For lovers of antiquity, this museum alone makes Naples a worthwhile stop. Considering its popularity and the importance of the collection, it's remarkable how ramshackle, unkempt, and dumpy its displays are. Still, if you can overlook the dust bunnies, this museum offers the best possible peek into the artistic jewelry boxes of Pompeii and Herculaneum. When Pompeii was excavated in the early 1800s, Naples' Bourbon king bellowed, "Bring me the best of what you find!" The actual sites are impressive but barren; the fin-

NAPLES

est art and artifacts ended up here.

Cost and Hours: €6.50, but often €10 with mandatory special exhibits, cash only, Wed-Mon 9:00-19:30, closed Tue, last entry 30 minutes before closing. A few less-important collections close early (generally around 12:30)—but none of the items on my self-guided tour are affected. Early and temporary closures are noted on a board near the ticket office.

Getting There: To take the subway from Centrale Station, follow signs to the Metro, called *Metropolitana*, located downstairs at the Garibaldi subway station (across from track 13). Buy your ticket at the newsstand or a tobacco shop, and validate it in the small yellow boxes near the escalator going down to the tracks. You're looking for trains heading in the direction of Pozzuoli (generally depart from track 4). Hop on any train that comes through (confirm by its sign or with a local that it's going to Pozzuoli), and ride the subway one stop. As you leave the Metro, exit and hike five minutes uphill through the park along the busy street. Look for a grand old red building located up a flight of stairs at the top of the block.

If taking the Metro back to Centrale Station, exit the museum to the left, and continue downhill to the Cavour stop, passing the Museo subway station (which is on a different line).

Figure on €12 for a taxi from the train station to the museum.

Information: The shop sells a worthwhile *National Archaeological Museum of Naples* guidebook—at €12, it's still a better value than the audioguide. Tel. 081-442-2149.

Tours: For the basics, you can follow my self-guided tour (below). If you want a **guided tour,** book Pina Esposito in advance (see "Tours in Naples," earlier; €120/2-hour tour, 10 percent less with this book; if you haven't booked ahead and see that she's available at the museum, help her assemble a group of up to 10 to split the fee). **Audioguides,** which haven't been updated for years, cost €5 (at ticket desk).

Baggage Check: Bag check is obligatory and free.

Photography: Photos are allowed without a flash.

Renovations: The museum seems to be in constant chaos due to ongoing renovations. If you can't find a particular work, ask a museum custodian, *"Dov'è?"* (DOH-vay, meaning "Where is?"), followed by the item's name.

Eating: For ideas on where to grab a meal near the museum, see page 964.

Self-Guided Tour: Overview

Entering the museum, stand at the base of the grand staircase. To your right, on the ground floor, are larger-than-life statues from the Farnese Collection, starring the *Toro Farnese* and the

Farnese Hercules. Up the stairs on the mezzanine level (turn left at the lion) are mosaics and frescoes from Pompeii, including the *Battle of Alexander* and the Secret Room of erotic art. On the top floor is a scale model of Pompeii and bronze statues from Herculaneum (a nearby town destroyed in the same eruption that devastated Pompeii). You'll find WCs by circling behind the staircase.

• *From the base of the grand staircase, turn right and head to the far end, angling a bit to reach the farthest room.*

Ground Floor: The Farnese Collection

The museum's ground floor alone has enough Greek and Roman art to put any museum on the map. Its highlight is the Farnese Collection, a grand hall of huge, bright, and wonderfully restored statues excavated from Rome's Baths of Caracalla.

The tangled *Toro Farnese* depicts a woman being tied to a bull. At 13 feet, it's the tallest ancient marble group ever found, and the largest intact statue from antiquity. A third-century A.D. copy of a lost bronze Hellenistic original, it was carved out of one piece of marble. Michelangelo and others "restored" it at the pope's request— meaning that they integrated surviving bits into a new work. Panels on the wall show which pieces were actually carved by Michelangelo (in blue on the chart): the head of the woman in back, the torso of the aunt under the bull, and the dog. (Imagine how the statue would stand out if it was thoughtfully lit and not surrounded by white walls.)

Here's the story behind the statue: Once upon an ancient Greek time, King Lycus was bewitched by Dirce. He abandoned his pregnant wife, Antiope (standing regally in the background). The single mom gave birth to twin boys (shown here). When they grew up, they killed their deadbeat dad and tied Dirce to the horns of a bull to be bashed against a mountain. Captured in marble, the action is thrilling: cape flailing, dog snarling, hooves in the air. You can almost hear the bull snorting. And in the back, Antiope oversees this harsh ancient justice with satisfaction.

NAPLES

At the far end of the hall stands the *Farnese Hercules*. The great Greek hero is exhausted. He leans wearily on his club (draped with his lion skin) and bows his head. He's just finished the daunting Eleventh Labor, having traveled the world, fought men and gods, freed Prometheus from his rock, and carried Atlas' weight of the world on his shoulders. Now he's returned with the prize: the golden apples of the gods, which he cups behind his back. But, after all that, he's just been told he has to return the stolen apples and do one final labor: descend into Hell itself.

The 10-foot colossus is a third-century A.D. Roman marble copy (signed by "Glykon") of a fourth-century B.C. Greek bronze original (probably by Lysippos). The statue was enormously famous in its day. Dozens of copies—some marble, some bronze—have been found in Roman villas and baths. This version was unearthed in Rome's Baths of Caracalla in 1546, along with the *Toro Farnese*.

The *Farnese Hercules* was equally famous in the 16th-18th centuries. Tourists flocked to admire it, art students studied it from afar in prints, Louis XIV made a copy for Versailles, and petty nobles everywhere put small-scale knock-offs in their gardens. This curly-haired version of Hercules became the modern world's image of the Greek hero.

Behind Hercules is a series of small rooms lined with precious stones. In the farthest one, in a freestanding glass case, is the sumptuous **Farnese Cup** (*Tazza Farnese*, second century B.C., from Egypt). This large, ancient cameo made of agates looks more like a cereal bowl than a cup. Its decorations are both Egyptian (the Nile toting a lush cornucopia) and, on the flip side, Greek (Medusa's head).

• *Backtrack to the main entry hall, then head up to the mezzanine level (turning left at the lion).*

Mezzanine: Pompeiian Mosaics and the Secret Room

Most of these mosaics—of animals, musicians, and geometric designs—were taken from Pompeii's House of the Faun (see page 979). Walk through several rooms and look for the 20-inch-high statue in a freestanding glass case: the house's delightful centerpiece, the *Dancing Faun*. This rare surviving Greek bronze statue (from the fourth century B.C.) is surrounded by some of the best mosaics of that age.

NAPLES

A museum highlight, just beyond the statue, is the grand **Battle of Alexander,** a second-century B.C. copy of the original Greek fresco, done a century earlier. It decorated a floor in the House of the Faun and was found intact; the damage you see occurred as this treasure was moved from Pompeii to the king's collection here. Alexander (left side of the

scene, with curly hair and sideburns) is about to defeat the Persians under Darius (central figure, in chariot with turban and beard).

This pivotal victory allowed Alexander to quickly over-run much of Asia (331 B.C.). Alexander is the only one without a helmet...a confident master of the battlefield while everyone else is fighting for their lives, eyes bulging with fear. Notice how the horses, already in retreat, add to the scene's propaganda value. Notice also the shading and perspective, which Renaissance artists would later work so hard to accomplish. (A modern reproduction of the mosaic is now back in the House of the Faun.)

The **Secret Room** *(Gabinetto Segreto)* contains a sizable assortment of erotic frescoes, well-hung pottery, and perky statues that once decorated bedrooms, meeting rooms, brothels, and even shops at Pompeii and Herculaneum. These bawdy statues and frescoes—many of them once displayed in Pompeii's grandest houses—were entertainment for guests. (By the time they made it to this museum, in 1819, the frescoes could be viewed only with permission from the king—see the letters in the glass case just outside the door.) The Roman nobles commissioned the wildest scenes imaginable. Think of them as ancient dirty jokes.

At the entrance, you're enthusiastically greeted by big stone penises that once projected over Pompeii's doorways. A massive phallus was not necessarily a sexual symbol, but a magical amulet used against the "evil eye." It symbolized fertility, happiness, good luck, riches, straight A's, and general well-being.

Circulating counterclockwise through this section, look for: a faun playfully pulling the sheet off a beautiful woman, only to be grossed out by a hermaphrodite's plumbing (perhaps the original *"Mamma mia!"*; #12); horny pygmies from Africa in action (#27); a toga with an embarrassing bulge (#34); a particularly high-quality statue of a goat and a satyr illustrating the act of sodomy (#36); and, watching over it all with remarkable aplomb, Venus, the patron goddess of Pompeii (#39).

The next room is furnished and decorated the way an ancient brothel might have been. The 10 frescoes on the wall functioned as both a menu of services offered and as a kind of *Kama Sutra* of sex positions. The glass cases contain more phallic art.

• *So, now that your travel buddy is finally showing a little interest in art...finish up your visit by climbing the stairs to the top floor.*

Top Floor: Statues, Artifacts, and a Model of Pompeii

At the top of the stairs, go through the center door to enter a grand, empty hall. This was the **great hall** of the university (17th and 18th centuries) until the building became the royal museum in 1777. The sundial (from 1791) still works. At noon, a sunray strikes the spot, indicating today's date...if you know your zodiac.

To your right (look for the *La Villa dei Papiri* sign) is an exhibit of **bronze statues** that once decorated the Herculaneum holiday home of Julius Caesar's father-in-law. The statues depict racers, dancers, fauns, and lots of disembodied heads (first-century B.C. copies of fourth-century B.C.

originals). In the second room (labeled *tablinum*), look into the lifelike blue eyes of the intense *Corridore* (athletes), bent on doing their best. The *Five Dancers*, with their inlaid-ivory eyes and graceful poses, decorated a portico. The next room (marked *rectangular peristyle*) has more fine works: *Resting Hermes* (with his tired little heel wings) is taking a break. Nearby, the *Drunken Faun* (singing and snapping his fingers to the beat, a wineskin at his side) is clearly living for today—true to the *carpe diem* preaching of the Epicurean philosophy. Caesar's father-in-law was an Epicurean philosopher, and his library—containing 2,000 papyrus scrolls—supported his outlook.

Return to the grand hall and continue to the other side, passing through several rooms of vases, statuettes, spoons, glassware, and other objects found at Pompeii. Keep going to the far end, where you'll find a **scale model** of the archaeological site of Pompeii, circa 1879 *(plastico di Pompeii)*. Belly up to the railing and find the Porta Marina entrance and the large rectangle of the town's Forum. Another model on the wall shows the site in 2004, after more excavations.

The Rest of the Museum

After years in restoration, the museum's large collection of **frescoes** taken from the walls of Pompeii villas is back (in Rooms LXVI to LXXVIII—at the end of the great hall and on the left). Pompeiians loved to decorate their homes with scenes from mythology (Hercules' Labors, Venus and Mars in love), landscapes, everyday market scenes, and faux architecture. The display is roughly chronological.

For extra credit, visit *Doriforo*. (Ask a guard, *"Dov'è il Doriforo?"* He was last spotted on the ground floor, in the hall to the left, as you face the staircase—on the way to the exit.) This seven-foot-tall "spear-carrier" (the literal translation of *doriforo*) just stands there, as if holding a spear. What's the big deal about this statue, which looks like so many others? It's a marble replica made by the Romans of one of the most-copied statues of antiquity, a fifth-century B.C. bronze Greek original by Polyclitus. This copy once stood in a Pompeii gym, where it inspired ancient athletes by showing the ideal proportions of Greek beauty. So full of motion, and so realistic in its *contrapposto* pose (weight on one foot), the *Doriforo* would later inspire Donatello and Michelangelo, triggering the Renaissance. And so the glories of ancient Pompeii, once buried and forgotten, live on today.

Self-Guided Walk

▲▲▲A Slice of Neapolitan Life

Walk from the Archaeological Museum through the heart of town and back to the Centrale train station. Allow at least three hours, plus time for pizza and sightseeing stops. If you have limited time, do a shorter, 1.5-hour-long version by walking briskly and skipping Part 2.

Naples, a living medieval city, is its own best sight. Couples artfully make love on Vespas surrounded by more fights and smiles per cobblestone than anywhere else in Italy. Rather than seeing Naples as a list of sights, visit its one great museum and then capture its essence by taking this walk through the core of the city. Should you become overwhelmed or lost, step into a store and ask for directions: "Where is Centrale Station?" in Italian is *"Dov'è la stazione Centrale?"* (DOH-vay lah staht-zee-OH-nay chen-TRAH-lay). Or point to the next sight in this book.

Part 1: Piazza Dante and Via Pessina

The first two parts of this walk are a straight one-mile ramble

"A Slice of Neapolitan Life" Walk

To Museo di Capodimonte

VIA STA. TERESA

VIA FORIA

ARCHAEOLOGICAL MUSEUM

Piazza Cavour

M Cavour

UNDERGROUND PASSAGE

S. APOST.

One stop on Metro to Piazza Garibaldi & Centrale Station

M Museo

WALK BEGINS

GALLERIA PRINCIPE

NAPOLI SOTTERRANEA

S. PAOLO

DUOMO

VIA SAPIENZA

VIA ATRI

VIA DEI TRIBUNALI

S. GREG. ARMENO

S. LORENZO MAGGIORE

VIA DUOMO

VIA VICARIA VECCHIA

PACE

FORCELLA

COLLETTA

Piazza Bellini

CAFFÈ MEXICO

VIA PORT' ALBA

CAPPELLA SANSEVERO

SAN DOM.

VIA S. BIAGIO

POLO NORD GELATERIA

PIZZA

Piazza Dante

Dante M

GESÙ NUOVO

VIA B. CROCE

CHAPEL OF MARADONA

"SPACCANAPOLI"

PIZZA

To M Montesanto (& funicular)

VIA TOLEDO

Piazza Gesù Nuovo

VIA S. SEBASTIANO

WALK ENDS

To Piazza Garibaldi & Centrale Station (10 min. walk)

Piazza Sette Settembre

VIA MADDALONI

SANTA' CHIARA

SCATURCHIO PASTICCERIA

VIA MEZZOCANNONE

CORSO UMBERTO I

VIA MORG.

CALATA TRINITÀ MAGGIORE

VIA NUOVA MARINA

Piazza Carità

FASCIST BLDG.

POST

V. DONNALBINA

Piazza Bovio

SPANISH QUARTER

BNL BANK

VIA BATT.

Piazza Matteotti

VIA A. DIAZ

VIA S. FELICE

VIA AGOSTINO DEPRETIS

VIA ALCIDE D. GASPERI

VIA CRISTOFORO COLOMBO

Port

VIA PORTA DI TAPPIA

BANCO DI NAPOLI

B

BANCA INTESA SANPAOLO

GALLERIA UMBERTO I

Piazza Municipio

Alibus Bus To Airport

B

Tram to Train Station

STAZIONE MARITTIMA (CRUISE TERMINAL)

Centrale Funicular

CASTEL NUOVO

GRAN CAFFÈ GAMBRINUS

TEATRO DI SAN CARLO

ROYAL PALACE

PORT BEVERELLO (BOATS TO SORRENTO & CAPRI)

V. AM. FERDINANDO AG.ON

Piazza del Plebiscito

SAN FRANCESCO DI PAOLA

V. AM. FERDINANDO AG.ON

CONSOLE

TUNNEL

VIA NAZARIO SAURO

To Castel dell'Ovo

Bay of Naples

300 Meters

300 Yards

NAPLES

down a boulevard to Piazza del Plebiscito. Ideally, begin by touring the Archaeological Museum (at the top of Piazza Cavour, Metro: Cavour or Museo; for a self-guided tour, see earlier).

• *Leaving the Archaeological Museum, turn right and go one block, to the head of Via Pessina. Follow this busy street downhill to Piazza Dante—see his statue in the distance. (Alternatively, to avoid the traffic-clogged Via Pessina, when you leave the museum, you can cross the street, cut through the fancy Galleria Principe mall—only the second-most-impressive gallery we'll see on this walk—then continue out the bottom end and two more blocks, jogging right to reach Piazza Dante.)*

Piazza Dante: This square is marked by a statue of Dante, the medieval poet. Here you can feel Italy...but many Neapolitans merely feel the repression of the central state. When Napoleon was defeated, Naples became its own independent kingdom. But with Italian unification in 1861, Naples went from being a thriving cultural and political capital to a provincial town, its money used to help establish the industrial strength of the north. Originally, a statue of a Spanish Bourbon king stood here. The grand red-and-gray building is typical of Bourbon structures from that period. With the unification of Italy, the king, symbolic of Italy's colonial subjugation, was replaced by Dante—considered the father of the Italian language and a strong symbol of nationalism.

Old Dante looks out over an urban area that was once grand, then chaotic, and is now slowly becoming grand again. Behind Dante's right shoulder is the Port'Alba, part of Naples' old wall and the entrance to a small street lined with book vendors. Via Pessina, the long, straight street that you're walking, originated as a military road built by Spain in the 16th century. It skirted the old town wall to connect the Spanish military headquarters (now the museum) with the Royal Palace (down by the bay). A subway station called Dante (with a modern-art flair) was recently built here on Piazza Dante. Construction was slowed by the city's rich underground history: 13 feet down—Roman ruins; 23 feet down—Greek ruins; and every inch of the way—big headaches for construction workers.

Across the street, **Caffè Mexico** (at #86) is an institution known for its espresso, which is served already sweetened—ask for *senza zucchero* if you don't want sugar (pay first, then take receipt to the counter and hand it over with a €0.10 coin as a tip). Most Italians agree that Neapolitan coffee is the best anywhere.

• *Continue walking downhill on...*

Via Pessina: As you stroll, remember that here in Naples, red traffic lights are considered "decorations." When crossing a street, try to tag along with a native. The people here are survivors: A long history of corrupt and greedy colonial overlords has taught Neapolitans to deal creatively with authority. Many credit this aspect of Naples' past for the advent of organized crime here.

Via Pessina becomes Via Toledo (another reminder of Spanish rule), Naples' principal shopping street. In 1860, from the white marble balcony of the Neoclassical building overlooking Piazza Sette Settembre, the famous revolutionary Giuseppe Garibaldi declared Italy united and Victor Emmanuel II its first king. Not until 1870, when Rome fell to the unification forces, was the dream of Italian unity fully realized.

• *Continue straight on Via Toledo. About three blocks below Piazza Dante and a block past Piazza Sette Settembre, you'll come to the long, straight, narrow street called...*

Spaccanapoli: Before crossing the street—whose name translates as "split Naples"—look left. Look right. Since ancient times, this thin street has bisected the city. It changes names several times: Via Maddaloni (as it's called here), Via B. Croce, Via S. Biagio dei Librai, Forecella, and Vicaria. We'll return to this intersection later.

• *If you want to abbreviate this walk, turn left here and skip ahead to "Part 3."*

Part 2—described next—is a bit of a detour, and requires backtracking uphill later. But if you have time, it's worth the effort.

Part 2: Via Toledo, the Spanish Quarter, and Piazza del Plebiscito

• *Stay on Via Toledo, which runs through...*

Piazza Carità: Surrounded by fascist architecture from 1938, this square is full of stern, straight, obedient lines. (For the best fascist architecture in town, take a slight detour from here: With your back to Via Toledo, leave Piazza Carità downhill on the right-hand corner and walk a block to the Poste e Telegrafi building. There you'll see several government buildings with stirring reliefs singing the praises of a totalitarian society.)

If you're feeling adventurous, head up one of Naples' most colorful open-air market streets: **Via Pignasecca.** It's the first street you pass on the right as you enter Piazza Carità (angling sharply back the way you came). Strolling this chaotic strip, you'll pass meat and fish stalls, produce stands, street-food vendors, and much more. The action continues for several blocks, all the way up to the Montesanto station, where you can access the Metro or the **Montesanto funicular** up to the sights on San Martino (described later).

• *From Piazza Carità, continue south down Via Toledo for a few blocks, looking to your left for more...*

Fascist Architecture (Banks): You can't miss the two big, blocky bank buildings. First comes the chalky-white BNL Bank. A bit farther down, try robbing the Banco di Napoli (Via Toledo 178). Step across the street and check out its architecture: typical fascist arches and reliefs, built to celebrate the bank's 400th anniversary (est. 1539—how old is *your* bank?).

• *On the next block (marked* Banca Prossima*) is the...*

Banca Intesa Sanpaolo: This fills an older palace—take a free peek at the opulent interior. In the lobby, you can buy a ticket for the **Galleria d'Italia Palazzo Zevallos Stigliano,** a small collection located in the upper two floors. The gallery's only piece worth seeing—on the second floor—is a great late Caravaggio painting. *The Martyrdom of Saint Ursula* shows a terrible scene: His marriage proposal rejected, the king of the Huns shoots an arrow into Ursula's chest. Blood spurts, Ursula is stunned but accepts her destiny sweetly, and Caravaggio himself—far right, his last self-portrait—screams to symbolize the rejection of evil. The rest of the second floor holds opulent chandeliered apartments, a few Neapolitan landscapes, and little else. The first floor has fine temporary exhibits (€4, Tue-Sun 10:00-18:00, closed Mon; entry includes 40-minute audioguide, a look at old Naples paintings, and a fine WC; Via Toledo 185, tel. 800-1605-2007, www.palazzo zevallos.com).

• *Feeling bold? From here, side-trip uphill a couple of blocks into the...*

Spanish Quarter: This is a classic world of *basso* (low) living. In such tight quarters, families generally do it in the road. This

is *the* cliché of life in Naples, as shown in so many movies. The Spanish Quarter is Naples at its rawest, poorest, and most characteristic. The only predictable things about this Neapolitan tide pool are the ancient grid plan of its streets (which survives from Greek times), the friendliness of its shopkeepers, and the boldness of its mopeds. Concerned locals will tug on their lower eyelids, warning you to be wary. Hungry? Pop into a grocery shop and ask the man to make you his best prosciutto-and-mozzarella sandwich (the price should be about €4).

• *Return to Via Toledo (clogged with more people than cars) and work your way down. Near the bottom of the street, on the right, notice the station for the* **Centrale funicular.** *If you have extra time and enjoy city views, this can take you sweat-free up to the top of San Martino, the hill with a fortress and a monastery/museum looming over town (covered* *by regular €1.20 transit ticket; see page 958 for details on fortress and museum).*

But for now, keep heading down the main drag to the immense...

Piazza del Plebiscito: This square celebrates the 1861 vote (*plebiscito*, plebiscite), when Naples chose to join Italy. Dominating the top of the square is the **Church of San Francesco di Paola,** with its Pantheon-inspired dome and broad, arcing colonnades. If it's open, step inside to ogle the vast interior—a Neoclassical recreation of one of ancient Rome's finest buildings (free, daily 8:30-12:00 & 16:00-19:00).

• *Opposite is the...*

Royal Palace *(Palazzo Reale):* Having housed Spanish, French, and even Italian royalty, this building displays statues of all those who stayed here. Look for eight kings in the niches, each from a different dynasty (left to right): Norman, German, French, Spanish, Spanish, Spanish, French (Napoleon's brother-in-law), and, finally, Italian—Victor Emmanuel II, King of Savoy. The statues were done at the request of V. E. II's son, so his dad is the most dashing of the group. While you could consider touring the interior, it's relatively unimpressive (described under "Sights in Naples," later).

The **Gran Caffè Gambrinus,** facing the piazza, takes you back to the elegance of 1860. It's a classic place to sample a unique Neapolitan treat called *sfogliatella* (crispy scallop shell-shaped pastry filled with sweet ricotta cheese). Or you might prefer the mushroom-shaped, rum-soaked bread-like cakes called *babà*, which come in a huge variety. Stand at the bar *(banco)*, pay double to sit *(tavola)*, or just wander around as you imagine the café buzzing with the ritzy intellectuals, journalists, and artsy bohemian types who munched on *babà* here during Naples' 19th-century heyday (daily 7:00-24:00, Piazza del Plebiscito 1, tel. 081-417-582).

• *Continue 50 yards past the Royal Palace (toward the trees) to enjoy a...*

Fine Harbor View: While boats busily serve Capri and Sorrento, Mount Vesuvius smolders ominously in the distance. Look back to see the vast "Bourbon red" palace—its color inspired by Pompeii. The hilltop above Piazza del Plebiscito is San Martino, with its Carthusian monastery-turned-museum and Castle of St. Elmo (we've already passed two funiculars that can take you up to enjoy the view). This street continues to Naples' romantic harborfront—the fishermen's quarter (Borgo Marinaro)—a fortified island connected to the mainland by a stout causeway, with its fanciful Castel dell'Ovo (castle of the egg) and trendy harborside restaurants. Farther along the harborfront stretches the Lungomare promenade and Santa Lucia district. (The long harborfront promenade, Via Francesco Caracciolo, is a delightful people-watching scene on balmy nights.)

• *Head back to the piazza and go behind the palace, where you can peek inside the Neoclassical...*

Teatro di San Carlo: Built in 1737, 41 years before Milan's La Scala, this is Europe's oldest opera house and Italy's second-most-respected (after La Scala). The theater burned down in 1816, and was rebuilt within the year. Guided 35-minute visits basically just show you the fine auditorium with its 184 boxes—each with a big mirror to reflect the candlelight (€5, tours every 40 minutes, Mon-Sat 10:00-16:00, closed Sun, tel. 081-797-2111, www.teatrosan carlo.it).

Beyond Teatro di San Carlo and the Royal Palace is the huge, harborfront **Castel Nuovo,** which houses government bureaucrats and the **Civic Museum.** It feels like a mostly empty shell, with a couple of dusty halls of Neapolitan art, but the views over the bay from the upper terraces are impressive (€6, Mon-Sat 9:00-19:00, closed Sun, last entry one hour before closing, tel. 081-795-7722).

Across the street from Teatro di San Carlo, go through the tall yellow arch into the Victorian iron and glass of the 100-year-old shopping mall, **Galleria Umberto I.** It was built in 1892 to reinvigorate the district after a devastating cholera epidemic occurred here. Gawk up.

• *For Part 3 of this walk, double back up Via Toledo to Piazza Carità, veering right (just above the first big fascist-style building we saw earlier) on Via Morgantini through Piazza Monteoliveto. Cross the busy street, then angle up Calata Trinità Maggiore to the fancy column at the top of the hill. (To avoid the backtracking and uphill walk, catch a €10 taxi to the Church of Gesù Nuovo—JAY-zoo noo-OH-voh.)*

Part 3: Spaccanapoli Back to the Station

You're back at the straight-as-a-Greek-arrow Spaccanapoli, formerly the main thoroughfare of the Greek city of Neapolis.

• *Stop at...*

Piazza Gesù Nuovo: This square is marked by a towering 18th-century Baroque monument to the Counter-Reformation. Although the Jesuit order was powerful in Naples because of its Spanish heritage, locals never attacked Protestants here with the full fury of the Spanish Inquisition.

If you'd like, you can visit two bulky old churches, starting with the austere, fortress-like, 17th-century **Church of Gesù Nuovo,** followed by the simpler **Church of Santa Chiara** (across the street). Both are described in more detail later, under "Sights in Naples."

• *After touring the churches, continue along the main drag. Since this is a university district, you'll see lots of students and bookstores. This neighborhood is also extremely superstitious. Look for incense-burning women with carts full of good-luck charms for sale.*

Farther down Spaccanapoli, you'll see the next square...

Piazza San Domenico Maggiore: This square is marked by an ornate 17th-century monument built to thank God for ending the plague. But more important is the well-loved **Scaturchio Pasticceria,** another good place to try *sfogliatella* (€1.70 to go, costs double at a table in the square, daily 7:20-20:40, tel. 081-551-7031).

From this square, detour left along the right side of the castle-like church, then follow yellow signs, taking the first right and walking one block to the remarkable **Capella Sansevero.** This Baroque chapel is well worth visiting (described later, under "Sights in Naples").

• *After touring the chapel, return to Via B. Croce (a.k.a. Spaccanapoli), turn left, and continue your cultural scavenger hunt. At the intersection of Via Nilo, find the...*

Statue of the Nile (on the left): A reminder of the multiethnic make-up of Greek Neapolis, this statue is in what was the Egyptian quarter. Locals like to call this statue *The Body of Naples,* with the overflowing cornucopia symbolizing the abundance of their fine city. (I once asked a Neapolitan man to describe the local women, who are famous for their beauty, in one word. He replied simply, "Abundant.") This intersection is considered the center of old Naples.

• *Directly opposite the statue, between the two doors of Bar Nilo, is the...*

"Chapel of Maradona": The small "chapel" on the wall is dedicated to Diego Maradona, a soccer star who played for Naples in the 1980s. Locals consider soccer almost a religion, and this guy was practically a deity. You can even see a "hair of Diego" and a teardrop from the city when he went to another team for more money. Unfortunately, his reputation has since been sullied by problems he's had with organized crime, drugs, and police. Perhaps inspired by Maradona's example, the coffee bar has posted a quadrilingual sign (though strangely, not in English) threatening that those who take a picture without buying a cup of coffee may find their camera damaged...*Capisce?* (Note that this "chapel" is removable—if it's raining or they're just feeling grumpy, it may be gone.)

• *As you continue, you'll begin to see shops selling...*

Presepi (Nativity Scenes): A few blocks farther along Spaccanapoli, at the tiny square, Via San Gregorio Armeno leads left into a colorful district (and also to the underground Napoli

Sotterranea archaeological site—described later, under "Sights in Naples"). This has the highest concentration of shops that sell tiny components of fantastic *presepi*, including figurines caricaturing local politicians and celebrities. Just as many Americans keep an eye out year-round for Christmas-tree ornaments, Italians regularly add pieces to the family *presepe*, the centerpiece of their holiday celebrations.

• *Back on Spaccanapoli, as Via B. Croce becomes Via S. Biagio dei Librai, notice the...*

Gold and Silver Shops: Some say stolen jewelry ends up here, is melted down immediately, and gets resold in some other form as soon as it cools. The inimitable Sr. Grassi runs the Ospedale delle Bambole (doll hospital) at #81.

• *Cross busy Via Duomo. If you have time and aren't churched out, consider detouring five minutes north (left) up Via Duomo to visit Naples'* **Duomo**; *just around the corner is the* **Pio Monte della Misericordia Church**, *with a fine Caravaggio painting (both described later, under "Sights in Naples"). Afterwards, continue straight along Via Vicaria. As you stroll, ponder Naples' vibrant...*

Street Life, Past and Present: Here, the street and side-street scenes along Via Vicaria intensify. This is known as a center of the Camorra (organized crime). Paint a picture with these thoughts: Naples has the most intact street plan of any ancient Roman city. Imagine this city during those times (and retain these images as you visit Pompeii), with streetside shop fronts that close up after dark, turning into private homes. Today, it's just one more page in a 2,000-year-old story of a city: all kinds of meetings, beatings, and cheatings; kisses, near misses, and little-boy pisses.

You name it, it occurs right on the streets today, as it has since ancient times. People ooze from crusty corners. Black-and-white death announcements add to the clutter on the walls. Widows sell cigarettes from buckets. For a peek behind the scenes in the shade of wet laundry, venture down a few side streets. Buy two carrots as a gift for the woman on the fifth floor if she'll lower her bucket to pick them up. The neighborhood action seems best at about 18:00.

A few blocks on, at the tiny fenced-in triangle of greenery, hang out for a few minutes to just observe the crazy motorbike action and teen scene.

• *From here, veer right onto Via Forcella (which leads to the busy boulevard that takes you to the Centrale station). A block down, a tiny, fenced-in traffic island protects a chunk of the ancient Greek wall of*

Neapolis (fourth century B.C.). Turn right here on Via Pietro Colletta, walk 40 yards, and step into the North Pole, at the...

Polo Nord Gelateria: The oldest *gelateria* in Naples has had four generations of family working here since 1931. Before you order, sample a few flavors, including their *bacio* or "kiss" flavor (chocolate and hazelnut)—all are made fresh daily (Mon-Sat 10:00-23:00, Sun 10:00-14:00 & 17:00-23:00, Via Pietro Colletta 41, tel. 081-205-431). Via Pietro Colletta leads past two of Napoli's most competitive **pizzerias** (see "Eating in Naples," later) to Corso Umberto I.

• *Turn left on the grand boulevard-like Corso Umberto I. From here to the Centrale Station, it's at least a 10-minute walk (if you're tired, hop on a bus; they all go to the station). To finish the walk, continue on Corso Umberto I—past a gauntlet of purse/CD/sunglasses salesmen and shady characters hawking stolen mobile phones—to the vast, ugly Piazza Garibaldi. On the far side is the station. You made it.*

Sights in Naples

Churches on or near Spaccanapoli

These churches are linked—in this order—on "Part 3" of my self-guided walk, earlier.

▲**Church of Gesù Nuovo**—This church's unique pyramid-grill facade survives from a fortified 15th-century noble palace. Step inside for a brilliant Neapolitan Baroque interior. The second chapel on the right features a much-adored **statue of Giuseppe Moscati** (1880-1927), a Christian doctor famous for helping the poor. In 1987, Moscati became the first modern doctor to be canonized. Sit and watch a steady stream of Neapolitans taking turns to kiss and touch the altar, then hold the good doctor's highly polished hand.

Continue on to the third chapel and enter the **Sale Moscati.** Look high on the walls of this long room to see hundreds of "Ex Votos"—tiny red-and-silver plaques of thanksgiving for prayers answered with the help of St. Moscati (each has a symbol of the ailment cured). Naples' practice of using Ex Votos, while incorporated into its Catholic rituals, goes back to its pagan Greek roots. Rooms from Moscati's nearby apartment are on display, and a glass case shows possessions and photos of the great doctor. As you leave the Sale Moscati, notice the big bomb casing that hangs in the left corner. It fell through the church's dome in 1943, but caused almost no damage...yet another miracle.

Cost and Hours: Free, daily 7:00-13:00 & 16:00-19:30, Piazza del Gesù.

Church of Santa Chiara—Dating from the 14th century, this church is from a period of French royal rule under the Angevin dynasty. Consider the stark contrast between this church (Gothic) and the Gesù Nuovo (Baroque), across the street. Inside, notice the huge inlaid-marble Angevin coat of arms on the floor. The faded Trinity on the back wall (on the right as you face the door), shows a dove representing the Holy Spirit between the heads of God the Father and Christ (c. 1414). This is an example of the fine frescoes that once covered the walls. Most were stuccoed over during Baroque times or destroyed in 1943 by WWII bombs. The altar is adorned with four finely carved Gothic tombs of Angevin kings. A chapel stacked with Bourbon royalty is just to the right.

Cost and Hours: Free, daily 7:00-13:00 & 16:30-20:00, Via Santa Chiara.

Nearby: The church's tranquil **cloistered courtyard**, colorfully decorated with vivid frescoes and cheery majolica-tiled pillars, is relaxing but overpriced at €5, and its museum is skippable. (If you'd like to visit it, leave the church, taking a right and heading to the back of the building. Continue through the archway straight ahead, and pass all the parked cars to reach the farthest door on the right.)

▲▲Cappella Sansevero—This small chapel is a Baroque explosion mourning the body of Christ, who lies on a soft pillow under an incredibly realistic veil. It's also the personal chapel of Raimondo de Sangro, an eccentric Freemason, containing his tomb and the tombs of his family. Raimondo was a grand master of the Freemasons of the Kingdom of Naples. His chapel—filled with Freemason symbolism—is a complex ensemble, with statues representing virtues such as self-control, religious zeal, and the Freemason philosophy of freedom through enlightenment. Though it's a pricey private enterprise, the chapel is worth a visit.

Cost and Hours: €7, buy tickets at office at the corner, Mon and Wed-Sat 10:00-18:00, Sun 10:00-13:30, closed Tue, last entry 20 minutes before closing, no photos but postcards sold in gift shop, Via de Sanctis 19, tel. 081-551-8470, www.museosansevero.it. Good English explanations are posted throughout; when you buy your ticket, pick up the floor plan, which identifies each of the statues lining the nave.

Visiting the Chapel: Study the incredible *Veiled Christ* in the center. Carved out of marble, it's like no other statue I've seen (by Giuseppe "Howdeedoodat" Sammartino, 1753). The Christian message (Jesus died for our salvation) is accompanied by a Freemason message (the veil represents how the body and ego are obstacles to real spiritual freedom). As you walk from Christ's feet to his head, notice how the expression on Jesus' face goes from suffering to peace.

Raimondo's mom and dad are buried on either side of the **main altar.** To the right of the altar, marking his father's tomb, a statue representing *Despair* or *Disillusion* struggles with a marble rope net (carved out of a single piece of stone), symbolic of a troubled mind. The flames on the head of the winged boy represent human intellect—more Freemason symbolism, showing how knowledge frees the human mind. To the left of the main altar is a statue of *Modesty*, marking the tomb of Raimondo's mother (who died young, at 20). The veiled woman fingers a broken tablet, symbolizing an interrupted life.

Raimondo de Sangro lies buried in a side altar (on the right). An inventor, he created the deep-green pigment used on the ceiling fresco. The inlaid M. C. Escher-esque maze on the floor around de Sangro's tomb is another Freemason reminder of how the quest for knowledge gets you out of the maze of life. This tilework once covered the floor of the entire chapel.

Your Sansevero finale is downstairs: two mysterious...**skeletons.** Perhaps another of the mad inventor's fancies: Inject a corpse with a fluid to fossilize the veins so that they'll survive the body's decomposition. While that's the legend, it was most likely created to illustrate how the circulatory system works.

▲**Duomo**—Naples' historic cathedral, built by imported French Anjou kings in the 14th century, boasts a breathtaking Neo-Gothic facade. Step into the vast interior to see the mix of styles along the side chapels—from pointy Gothic arches to rounded Renaissance ones to gilded Baroque decor.

Cost and Hours: Free, Mon-Sat 8:30-13:30 & 14:30-20:00, Sun 8:30-13:30 & 16:30-19:30, Via Duomo.

Visiting the Church: Explore the two largest side-chapels—each practically a church in its own right. On the left, the Chapel of St. Restituta stands on the site of the original, early-Christian church that predated the cathedral (at the far end, you can pay €1.50 to see its sixth-century baptismal font under mosaics, and go downstairs to see its even earlier foundations). On the right is the Chapel of San Genarro—dedicated to the beloved patron saint of Naples—decorated with silver busts of centuries of bishops, and seven paintings done on bronze.

Back out in the main nave, the altar at the front is ringed by carved wooden seats, filled three times a year by clergy to witness the Miracle of the Blood. Thousands of Neapolitans cram into this church for a peek at two tiny vials with the dried blood of St. Genarro. As the clergy roots—or even jeers—for the miracle to occur, the blood temporarily liquefies. Neapolitans take this ritual with deadly seriousness, and believe that if the blood remains solid, it's terrible luck for the city. Sure enough, on the rare occasion that the miracle fails, locals can point to a terrible event soon after—such as an earthquake or an eruption of Mount Vesuvius.

The stairs beneath the altar take you to a crypt with the relics of St. Genarro and (across the room) a statue of the bishop who rescued the relics from a rival town and returned them to Naples.

Pio Monte della Misericordia—Art lovers come to this small church (near the Duomo) to appreciate one of the best works by Caravaggio, *The Seven Works of Mercy*, which hangs over the main altar. In one crowded canvas, the great early-Baroque artist illustrates seven virtues: burying the dead (the man carrying a corpse by the ankles), visiting the imprisoned and feeding the hungry (the woman breastfeeding the man), sheltering the homeless (a pilgrim on the Camino de Santiago, with his floppy hat, negotiates with an innkeeper), caring for the sick and clothing the naked (St. Martin offers part of his cloak to the injured man in the foreground), and giving drink to the thirsty (Samson chugs from a jawbone in the background)—all of them set in a chaotic Neapolitan alley, and watched over by Mary, Jesus, and a pair of angels.

Cost and Hours: €5, Thu-Tue 9:00-14:30, closed Wed, Via dei Tribunali 253, tel. 081-446-944.

In the City Center

Royal Palace (Palazzo Reale)—Facing Piazza del Plebiscito, this huge, lavish palace welcomes the public. The palace's grand Neoclassical staircase leads up to a floor with 30 plush rooms. You'll follow a one-way route (with some English descriptions) featuring the palace theater, paintings by "the Caravaggio Imitators," Neapolitan tapestries, fine inlaid-stone tabletops, chandeliers, gilded woodwork, and more. The rooms do feel quite grand, but lack the personality and sense of importance of Europe's best palaces. Don't miss the huge, tapestry-laden Hercules Hall. On the way out, stop into the chapel, with a fantastic nativity scene—a commotion of 18th-century ceramic figurines.

Cost and Hours: €4, more with special exhibits, includes painfully dry audioguide, Thu-Tue 9:00-20:00, closed Wed, last entry one hour before closing, tel. 848-800-288.

▲▲Napoli Sotterranea—This archaeological site, a manmade underground maze of passageways and ruins from Greek and Roman times, can only be toured with a guide. You'll descend 121 steps under the modern city to explore two different underground areas. One is the old Greek tuff quarry used to build the city of Neapolis, which was later converted into an immense cistern by the Romans. The other is an excavated portion of the Greco-Roman theater that once seated 6,000 people. It's clear that this space has been encroached upon by modern development—some people's windows literally look down into the theater ruins. The tour involves a lot of stairs, as well as a long, narrow 20-inch-wide walkway—lit only by candlelight—that uses an ancient water channel (a heavyset person could not comfortably fit through this, and claustrophobes will be miserable). Although there's not much to actually see, the experience is fascinating, and includes a little history from World War II—when the quarry/cistern was turned into a shelter to protect locals for American bombs.

Cost and Hours: €9.30; includes 1.25-hour tour. Visits in English are offered daily at 10:00, 12:00, 14:00, 16:00, and 18:00. Bring a light sweater. Tel. 081-296-944, www.napolisotterranea .org.

Getting There: The site is a 10-minute walk from the Archaeological Museum, and just a couple of blocks uphill from Spaccanapoli's statue of the Nile. Meet at the office immediately to the left of the Church of San Paolo Maggiore (Piazza San Gaetano 68, just off Via dei Tribunali, look for the *Sotterranea* signs); don't confuse this office with the similarly marked coffee bar on the nearby square.

Porta Nolana Open-Air Fish Market—Naples' fish market squirts and stinks as it has for centuries under the Porta Nolana

(gate in the city wall), immediately in front of the Napoli P. Nolana Circumvesuviana station and four long blocks from Centrale Station. Of the town's many boisterous outdoor markets, this will net you the most photos and memories. From Piazza Nolana, wander under the medieval gate and take your first left down Vico Sopramuro, enjoying this wild and entirely edible cultural scavenger hunt (Tue-Sun 8:00-14:00, closed Mon).

Two other markets with more clothing and fewer fish are at Piazza Capuana (several blocks northwest of the Centrale station and tumbling down Via Sant'Antonio Abate, Mon-Sat 8:00-18:00, Sun 9:00-13:00) and a similar cobbled shopping zone along Via Pignasecca (just off Via Toledo, west of Piazza Carità, described on page 947).

Lungomare *Passeggiata*—Each evening, relaxed and romantic Neapolitans in the mood for a scenic harborside stroll do their *vasche* (laps) along the inviting Lungomare promenade. To join in this elegant people-watching scene (best after 19:00), stroll about 15 minutes from Piazza del Plebiscito along Via Nazario Sauro.

Detour out along the fortified causeway to poke around Borgo Marinaro ("fishermen's quarter"), with its striking Castel dell'Ovo and a trendy restaurant scene where you can dine amidst yachts with a view of Vesuvius. This is known as the Santa Lucia district because this is where the song "Santa Lucia" was first performed. (The song is probably so famous in America because immigrants from Naples sang it to remember the old country.) Beyond that stretches the Lungomare, along Via Francesco Caracciolo. Taxi home or retrace your steps back to the old center.

On San Martino

The ultimate view overlooking Naples, its bay, and the volcano is from the hill called San Martino, just above (and west of) the city center. Up top you'll find a mighty fortress (offering the best views from its ramparts) and the adjacent monastery-turned-museum. While neither of these sights is exciting in its own right, the views are. And the surrounding neighborhood (especially Piazza Fuga) has a classy "uptown" vibe compared to the gritty city-center streets below.

Getting There: From Via Toledo, the Spanish Quarter gradually climbs up San Martino's lower slopes, before steep paths take you up the rest of the way. But the easiest way to ascend San Martino is by funicular. Three different funicular lines lead from lower Naples to the hilltop: the Centrale line from near the bottom of Via Toledo, the Montesanto line from the Metro stop of the same name (near the top end of Via Toledo), and the Chiaia line from the other side of the hill, near Piazza Amadeo (all three are covered by the €1.20 local transit ticket). Ride any of these three up to the end of the line. All three lines converge within a few blocks at the top of the hill—Centrale and Chiaia wind up at opposite ends of the charming Piazza Fuga, while Montesanto terminates a bit closer to the fortress and museum. Leaving any of the funiculars, head uphill, carefully tracking signs for *Castel S. Elmo* and *Museo di San Martino* (strategically placed escalators make the climb easier). You'll reach the castle first, and then the monastery/museum.

Castel Sant'Elmo—While it's little more than an empty husk with a decent modern art museum, this 16th-century, Spanish-built, star-shaped fortress boasts ▲▲ views over the city and the entire Bay of Naples. Buy your ticket at the booth, then ride the elevator up to the upper courtyard and climb up to the ramparts for a slow circle to enjoy the 360-degree views. In the middle of the yard is the likeable little Museo del Novecento, a gallery of works by 20th-century Neapolitan artists (last entry at 18:00); the castle also hosts temporary exhibits.

Cost and Hours: €5, may be free before 10:00 and after 16:00, open Wed-Mon 8:30-19:30, closed Tue, last entry one hour before closing, hours can fluctuate depending on season and due to funding cuts, Via Tito Angelini 22, tel. 081-229-4401.

▲San Martino Carthusian Monastery and Museum (Certosa e Museo di San Martino)—The monastery, founded in 1325 and dissolved in the early 1800s, is now a sprawling museum with several parts. The terrace out front—popular with budding soccer stars—has city views nearly as good as the ones you'll pay to see from inside. If you want to tour the place, buy your ticket and head into the complex (which has some English information). Step into the church, a Baroque explosion with beautifully decorated chapels. Around the humble cloister are a variety of museum exhibits. The Naval Museum has nautical paintings, model boats, and giant ceremonial gondolas. In an adjacent hall is an excellent collection of *presepi* nativity scenes, both life-size and miniature, including a spectacular one by Michele Cucinello—the best I've seen in this *presepi*-crazy city. Beyond that is the larger garden cloister, ringed with a painting gallery (with lots of antique maps and artifacts of old Naples), and an entrance to a pretty view terrace.

Cost and Hours: €6, audioguide-€5, Thu-Tue 8:30-19:30, closed Wed, last entry one hour before closing, Largo San Martino 8, tel. 081-578-1769, http://museosanmartino.campania beniculturali.it.

On Capodimonte

Another hilltop, about a mile due north from the Archaeological Museum, is home to Naples' top art museum—the **Museo di Capodimonte**. Its three floors of art include works by Raphael, Titian, Caravaggio, and Bellini. While most visitors to Naples prefer to focus on the city's uniquely vibrant street life, characteristic churches, and remarkable ancient artifacts—and there are far better art museums elsewhere in Italy—art lovers with some time to spare may find a visit to Capodimonte worth the trip. While sporadic buses run from near the Archaeological Museum to Capodimonte, it's easier to take a taxi (about €8-10 from downtown).

Cost and Hours: €7.50, Thu-Tue 8:30-19:30, closed Wed, last entry one hour before closing, Via Miano 2, tel. 081-749-9111.

Sleeping in Naples

As an alternative to intense Naples, most travelers prefer to sleep in mellow Sorrento, just over an hour away (see Sorrento chapter). But, if needed, here are a few options. In this business-oriented (rather than tourist-oriented) city, summer (July-Sept) is low season, when prices are particularly soft.

In the Town Center

$$$ Decumani Hotel de Charme is a classy oasis tucked away on a residential lane in the very heart of the city, just off Spaccanapoli. While the neighborhood is Naples-dingy, the 22 rooms—filling an elegant 18th-century palace with a gorgeous breakfast room—

Sleep Code

(€1 = about $1.40, country code: 39)
S = Single, **D** = Double/Twin, **T** = Triple, **Q** = Quad, **b** = bathroom, **s** = shower only. Unless otherwise noted, credit cards are accepted, English is spoken, and breakfast is included. Many cities in Italy levy a hotel tax of about €2 per person, per night, which must be paid in cash (not included in the rates I've quoted).

To help you sort easily through these listings, I've divided the accommodations into three categories based on the price for a standard double room with bath:

$$$ Higher Priced—Most rooms €130 or more.
 $$ Moderately Priced—Most rooms between €90-130.
  $ Lower Priced—Most rooms €90 or less.

Prices can change without notice; verify the hotel's current rates online or by email.

are an inviting retreat (standard Db-€134, bigger deluxe Db with Jacuzzi-€15 more, rates soft—check website for deals, air-con, elevator, free Wi-Fi, Via San Giovanni Maggiore Pignatelli 15—this lane is roughly across the street from the entrance to the Santa Chiara cloister, second floor, tel. 081-551-8188, www.decumani .com, info@decumani.com). The same company has a second branch, **Chiaja Hotel de Charme**. Renting 33 rooms, it's on the upscale Via Chiaia pedestrian shopping drag near Piazza del Plebiscito (smaller standard Db with interior view-€145, bigger streetview Db with tub-€165, air-con, elevator, free Wi-Fi, Via Chiaia 216, tel. 081-415-555, www.hotelchiaia.it, info@hotelchiaia.it).

$$$ Hotel Piazza Bellini is a newish hotel with 48 stripped-down-minimalist but comfy rooms surrounding a quiet courtyard. Situated next to a busy square on a gloomy street two blocks below the Archaeological Museum, it offers modern sanity in the city center (Sb-€130-140, Db-€140-150, bi-level "superior" Db-€20 more, extra bed-€20, air-con, elevator, free Internet access and Wi-Fi, Via Santa Maria di Constantinopoli 101, Metro: Cavour, tel. 081-451-732, www.hotelpiazzabellini.com, info@hotelpiazza bellini.com).

$$ Art Resort Galleria Umberto has 10 rooms and five suites in two different buildings inside the Umberto shopping gallery just off Piazza del Plebiscito. This genteel-feeling place gilds the lily, but has older bathrooms. For a unique view, consider paying €20 extra for a room overlooking the gallery (non-view Db-€120, elevator, air-con, free Wi-Fi, Galleria Umberto 83, 4th floor, tel. 081-497-6224, www.artresortgalleriaumberto.it, info@artresort galleriaumberto.it).

NAPLES

$$ Hotel Il Convento, with 14 small but comfortable rooms with balconies, is a good choice for those who want to sleep in the gnarly, tight tangle of lanes called the Spanish Quarter—quintessential Naples. While the neighborhood can feel sketchy after dark, you're only a couple of short blocks off the main Via Toledo drag, and heavy-duty windows help block out some of the scooter noise. As this pricey refuge is a rare haven in this character-istic corner of town, it's in all the guidebooks (Sb-€80, Db-€120, Tb-€130, Qb-€160, elevator, air-con, free Wi-Fi, Via Speranzella 137A, tel. 081-403-977, www.hotelilconvento.com, info@hotelil convento.com).

Near the Train Station

Although rates here are cheaper and it's very handy to the station, this area is relatively inconvenient for sightseeing, less characteris-tic than the areas described above, and can feel unnerving—espe-cially after dark.

$ Grand Hotel Europa, a gem set in the seedy neighborhood around the station, has 89 decent rooms whimsically decorated with not-quite-right reproductions of famous paintings (Sb-€65, Db-€85, Tb-€109, book direct and ask for 15 percent Rick Steves discount off these prices or check website for special deals, air-con, elevator, free Internet access, free Wi-Fi in reception, restaurant; from the station, walk 30 yards past track 5, turn left, make a quick right around the green *Polfer* sign, and go out the gate to Corso Meridionale 14; tel. 081-267-511, www.grandhoteleuropa.com, info@grandhoteleuropa.com, well-run by Claudio).

$ Hotel Suite Esedra, with 17 small but tasteful rooms, is a four-star charmer on a tiny square off busy Corso Umberto I, located just outside of the station-neighborhood sleaze (Sb-€60, Db-€80, these prices if you book direct and mention this book, air-con, elevator, free Wi-Fi, 10-minute walk from the station at Via Arnaldo Cantani 12, tel. 081-287-451, fax 081-553-7087, www.hotelsuiteesedranapoli.it, info@hotelsuiteesedranapoli.it, Alessandro).

$ Hotel Potenza offers 26 nicely decorated rooms, along with a rare bit of security and peace on Piazza Garibaldi, with good windows that help block out the bustle (Sb-€55, Db-€70, Tb-€80, air-con, no elevator, free Wi-Fi, 100 yards in front of the station at Piazza Garibaldi 120, tel. 081-286-330, www.hotelpotenza.com, info@hotelpotenza.com, Valenzano family).

Farther Out

$$ Pinto-Storey Hotel seems a world away from the bustle of the rest of the city. With 16 straightforward rooms in a relatively upscale neighborhood (three Metro stops from the train station),

Naples Hotels & Restaurants

To Museo di Capodimonte

VIA STA. TERESA

VIA FORIA

Cavour

Piazza Cavour

UNDERGROUND PASSAGE

ARCHAEOLOGICAL MUSEUM

14

S. AFOST

One stop on Metro to Piazza Garibaldi & Centrale Station

Museo

VIA PESSINA

GALLERIA PRINCIPE

NAPOLI SOTTERRANEA

S. PAOLO

9

DUOMO

16

VIA DUOMO

VIA VICARIA VECCHIA

COLLETTA

13

VIA SAPIENZA

VIA DEI TRIBUNALI

S. LORENZO MAGGIORE

FORCELLA

3

8

S. GREG ARMENO

15

Piazza Bellini

CAPPELLA SANSEVERO

VIA S. BIAGIO

7

CAFFÈ MEXICO

VIA PORT' ALBA

SAN DOM

CHAPEL OF MARADONA

To Piazza Garibaldi & Centrale Station (10 min. walk)

Piazza Dante

Dante

VIA SAN SEBASTIANO

VIA B. CROCE

"SPACCANAPOLI"

GESÙ NUOVO

6

To Montesanto (& funicular)

Piazza Gesù Nuovo

VIA TOLEDO

1

SCATURCHIO PASTICCERIA

VIA MEZZOCANNONE

CORSO UMBERTO I

Piazza Sette Settembre

VIA MADDALONI

SANTA CHIARA

10

CALATA TRINITÀ MAGGIORE

VIA NUOVA MARINA

11

VIA MORG.

MONTEOLIVETO

V. DONNALBINA

Piazza Carità

FASCIST BLDG.

POST

VIA BATT.

VIA S. FELICE

Piazza Bovio

PIGNA SECCA

BNL BANK

Piazza Matteotti

VIA A. DIAZ

VIA AGOSTINO DEPRETIS

VIA ALCIDE D. GASPERI

SPANISH QUARTER

VIA PORTA DI TAPPIA

B

VIA CRISTOFORO COLOMBO

Port

5

12

BANCO DI NAPOLI

BANCA INTESA SANPAOL

GALLERIA UMBERTO I

Piazza Municipio

T Tram to Train Station

STAZIONE MARITTIMA (CRUISE TERMINAL)

Centrale Funicular

Alibus Bus To Airport

B

4

CASTEL NUOVO

VIA TOLEDO

TEATRO DI SAN CARLO

2

GRAN CAFFÈ GAMBRINUS

ROYAL PALACE

V. AM. FERDINANDO ACTON

PORT BEVERELLO (BOATS TO SORRENTO & CAPRI)

Piazza del Plebiscito

SAN FRANCESCO DI PAOLA

CONSOLE

TUNNEL

VIA NAZARIO SAURO

Bay of Naples

300 Meters

300 Yards

To Castel dell'Ovo

Naples Hotels & Restaurants Key

① Decumani Hotel de Charme
② Chiaja Hotel de Charme
③ Hotel Piazza Bellini &
   La Santaza del Gusto
④ Art Resort Galleria Umberto
⑤ Hotel Il Convento
⑥ Hotel Suite Esedra
⑦ Antica Pizzeria da Michele
   & Pizzeria Trianon
⑧ Gino Sorbillo Pizzeria

⑨ Pizzeria di Matteo
⑩ Ecomesarà
⑪ Osteria il Garum
⑫ Valù
⑬ Caffetteria Angela
⑭ Salumeria Pasquale Carrino
⑮ Polo Nord Gelateria
⑯ Pio Monte della
   Misericordia Church

the hotel has an old-time charm (Sb-€78, Db-€98, Tb-€139, these prices if you book direct and mention this book, air-con-€9, elevator, pay Wi-Fi, across the square from Metro line 2's Amedeo stop at Via Martucci 72, tel. 081-681-260, fax 081-667-536, www.pinto storey.it, info@pintostorey.it).

Eating in Naples

Cheap and Famous Pizza

Naples—whose pizzerias bake just the right combination of fresh dough, mozzarella, and tomatoes in traditional wood-burning ovens—is the birthplace of pizza. Drop by one of the most venerable pizzerias in town. The first two—my favorites—are both a few long blocks from the station (at the end of my "A Slice of Neapolitan Life" self-guided walk). If you don't care to wait, grabbing a slice from a random Neapolitan street vendor can be better than one from the finest pizzeria in many Italian towns.

Antica Pizzeria da Michele is for pizza purists. Filled with locals (and tourists), it serves just two varieties: *margherita* (tomato sauce and mozzarella) and *marinara* (tomato sauce, oregano, and garlic, no cheese). Come early to sit and watch the pizza artists in action. A pizza with beer costs €6-7. As this place is often jammed with a long line, arrive early or late to get a seat. If there's a mob, head inside to get a number. If it's just too crowded to wait, the less-exceptional Pizzeria Trianon (described next) generally has room (Mon-Sat 10:30-24:00, closed Sun; look for the vertical red *Antica Pizzeria* sign at the intersection of Via Pietro Colletta and Via Cesare Sersale at #1; tel. 081-553-9204).

Pizzeria Trianon, across the street, has been da Michele's archrival since 1923. It offers more choices, slightly higher prices (€5-7), air-conditioning, and a cozier atmosphere. For less chaos, head upstairs. While waiting for your meal, you can survey the transformation of a humble wad of dough into a smoldering bubbly feast in their entryway pizza kitchen (daily 11:00-15:30 &

19:00-23:00, Via Pietro Colletta 42, tel. 081-553-9426, Giuseppe).

On Via dei Tribunali: This street, which runs a couple of blocks north of Spaccanapoli, is home to several pizzerias that are more convenient to downtown sightseeing. Two in particular are always mentioned on all the "best pizza in Naples" lists...as you'll learn the hard way if you show up at peak mealtimes, when huge mobs crowd outside the front door waiting for a table (both have €4-6 pizzas and are closed on Sun). **Gino Sorbillo** is a local favorite; while his relatives' similar, nearby places are fine, for the real deal, connoisseurs want Gino's at #32 (Via dei Tribunali, tel. 081-446-643). At **Pizzeria di Matteo,** people waiting out front snack on €0.50 croquettes *(crocchè),* sold at the little window (Via dei Tribunali 94, tel. 081-455-262).

Near Spaccanapoli and Via Toledo

Ecomesarà serves up Neapolitan and *meridionale* (southern Italian) dishes in a modern setting just below the Santa Chiara cloister, a long block south of Spaccanapoli. The atmosphere is mellow and international, and Christiano and his staff are happy to explain the menu of small and big plates. The food is presented with modern class but without pretense (€8-13 dishes, Tue-Sun 11:30-15:00 & 19:30-23:00, closed Mon, Via Santa Chiara 49, tel. 081-1925-9353).

Osteria il Garum is named for the ancient fish sauce that was widely used in Roman cooking. These days, mild-mannered Luigi and his staff inject their pricey local cuisine with centuries of tradition, served in a cozy split-level cellar or outside on a covered terrace facing a neighborhood church. It's just between Via Toledo and Spaccanapoli, a short walk from the Church of Gesù Nuovo (€9-13 pastas, €14-17 *secondi,* daily 12:00-15:30 & 19:00-23:30, Piazza Monteoliveto 2A, tel. 081-542-3228).

Valù, with a modern red-and-black color scheme and a wine-bar vibe, sits in the colorful and rowdy Spanish Quarter just a block off Via Toledo. This *risotteria* specializes in risotto, serving 20 different variations. Choose between the interior or a few outdoor tables along a tight alley (€10-12 risottos, €8-12 meat dishes, Mon-Sat 12:30-15:00 & 19:00-24:00, closed Sun, Vico Lungo del Gelso 80, tel. 081-038-1139).

Near the Archaeological Museum

La Santaza del Gusto, two blocks downhill from the museum, tackles food creatively in two different settings: The downstairs cheese bar/*osteria* is casual, trendy, and playful, with €5-8 panini and €10-15 meals listed on the chalkboard. Upstairs is the more refined yet still polka-dotted restaurant, with pricier €12-18 main dishes and €35-65 set-price meals. Either option injects crusty Naples with a little modern color and irreverence (Tue-Sat 12:00-

15:30 & 19:30-23:30, in summer open Sun lunch but closed Sun dinner and all day Mon, in winter open Mon dinner but closed Mon lunch and all day Sun, Via Constantinopoli 100, tel. 081-401-578).

Caffetteria Angela is a fun little eating complex: coffee bar; *tavola calda* with hot ready-to-eat dishes (€3-4); and a tiny meat, cheese, and bread shop with all you need for a cheap meal to go. It offers honest pricing and simple, peaceful, air-conditioned indoor seating (no cover, open Mon-Sat 7:00-21:00, Sun 9:00-14:00, just off Via Pessina, 3 blocks below museum at Via Conte di Ruvo 21, tel. 081-549-9660).

Salumeria Pasquale Carrino is a tiny *salumi* shop with an exuberant owner—the fun-loving and flamboyant Pasquale—who turns sandwich-making into a show (€3-7 sandwiches good for two people, Mon-Sat 8:00-15:00 & 17:00-20:00, closed Sun, 100 yards from museum—as you leave take two rights and a left to Via Salvator Rosa 10, tel. 081-564-0889).

Near the Station

While far from high cuisine, these functional options are worth considering if you're on the way back to catch your train, or if you're sleeping in this neighborhood and don't want to venture far: **La Cantina dei Mille,** a block in front of the train station, is a traditional family-style place serving good, basic Neapolitan food to good, basic Neapolitans (€4-6 pizza and pasta, daily 12:00-16:00 & 17:00-24:00; with your back to the station, it's about halfway up the left side of Piazza Garibaldi at #126; tel. 081-283-448). Next door, **Iris** is another decent choice. The recommended **Grand Hotel Europa** has a restaurant peacefully buried in its basement, offering friendly service and a fine value (€6-8 pastas and *secondi,* daily, light lunches anytime, dinner served 19:00-22:30).

Naples Connections

From Naples by Boat to: Sorrento (6/day, more in summer, departs roughly every 2 hours starting at 9:00, 35 minutes, €11), **Capri** (roughly 2/hour, 45 minutes, €17). Seasonal boats to **Positano** (summer only, 4/day, 1.25-1.5 hours, €17) continue on to **Amalfi** (1.5-2 hours, €18). For a map showing boat connections, see page 1023.

By Train to: Rome (at least hourly, 1.25 hours on Frecciarossa express trains, €45; otherwise 2 hours, €11-22), **Florence** (3/day direct, 3 hours, €72; otherwise about hourly with change in Rome, 4.25 hours, €56-59), **Salerno** (2/hour, 30-75 minutes, €7.50-17, avoid slow *diretto* train), **Paestum** (almost hourly, 1.5 hours, direction: Sapri), **Brindisi** (8/day, 4.75-7 hours, overnight possible,

Getting Around the Region

To connect Naples, Sorrento, and the Amalfi Coast, you can travel on land by train, bus, and taxi. Whenever possible, consider taking a boat—it's faster, cooler, and more scenic, and you can take coastline photos that you can't get from land. For specifics, check the "Connections" sections of the Naples, Sorrento, and Amalfi Coast chapters. Confirm times and prices locally.

By Circumvesuviana Train: This useful commuter train—popular with locals, tourists, and pickpockets—links Naples, Herculaneum, Pompeii, and Sorrento. At Naples' Centrale train station, follow the signs to the Circumvesuviana (across from track 13, downstairs, and down the corridor to the left), where you'll find the ticket office and info booth. When you buy your ticket, ask which track your train will depart from (**"Quale binario?"**; KWAH-lay bee-NAH-ree-oh). Just beyond, you'll find the gate where you insert your ticket. The train platforms are downstairs. The Circumvesuviana also has its own terminal (called Napoli P. Nolana, across from the Porta Nolana fish market), but there's no reason to use it unless you happen to be nearby.

Trains marked *Sorrento,* which depart twice hourly, take you to Herculaneum/Ercolano (about 20 minutes, €2.10 one-way), Pompeii (about 40 minutes, €2.80 one-way), and Sorrento, the end of the line (70 minutes, €4 one-way). Though not covered by railpasses, Circumvesuviana tickets are covered by the Campania ArteCard (see page 934). All-day Circumvesuviana tickets are available, but—unless you're making several stops on a long round-trip—aren't worth considering, except on weekends, when they're nearly half-price (€12 Mon-Fri, €6.30 "weekend pass" available Sat-Sun). Not all of the trains go as far as Sorrento; check the schedule or confirm with a local before boarding to make sure the train goes where you want. Express trains marked *DD* (6/day) get you to Sorrento 20 minutes sooner (and also stop at Herculaneum and Pompeii). If you're heading to Pompeii or Herculaneum, take any train headed for Sorrento—they all stop at both places. When returning to Naples' Centrale station on the Circumvesuviana, get off at Garibaldi—the next-to-the-last stop (the Centrale station is just up the escalator). When returning from Sorrento to Naples, you can use your Circumvesuviana ticket to cover all public transit within three hours of validation (no need to validate again). Be on guard: Many readers report being ripped off on the Circumvesuviana (see "Theft Alert," page 935). For information, see www.vesuviana.it.

If you're coming **from Rome,** note that a different (non-Circumvesuviana) train—run by the national rail company—goes from Rome to Naples, then continues to the ugly modern city of Pompei. There is almost no reason to go to Pompei city, where you'll face a long walk to the actual site. Therefore, from Rome, it's better to simply get off at Naples' Centrale station and transfer to the Circumvesuviana (to the Pompei Scavi stop). The Pompei city train station is useful only for connecting to Salerno or Paestum (not quite hourly, 30 minutes to Salerno, 1 hour to

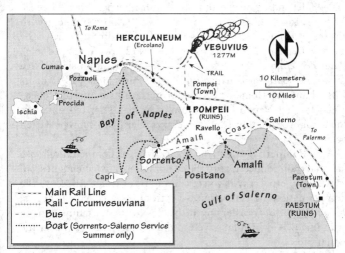

Paestum, direction: Sapri).

By Bus: SITA buses (often blue or green-and-white) connect the towns. Buses that travel along the highly touristed Amalfi Coast can be crowded; for tips, see "Getting Around the Amalfi Coast—By Bus" on page 1024.

By Taxi: For €100, you can take a 30-mile taxi ride from Naples directly to your Sorrento hotel; agree on a set price without the meter and pay upon arrival. You can hire a cab on Capri for about €70/hour. Taxis in the Amalfi Coast are generally expensive, and more than willing to overcharge you, but they can be convenient, especially with a larger group. See "Getting Around the Amalfi Coast—By Taxi" on page 1025.

By Boat: Several ferry companies service the Naples, Sorrento, and Amalfi Coast areas. While these can change from year to year, major companies include Caremar (www.caremar .it), SNAV (www.snav.it), Gescab (a.k.a. NLG Jet, www.gescab .it), Metrò del Mare (www.metrodelmare.net), and Alilauro (www .alilauro.it). Each company has different destinations and prices; some compete for the same trips. The quicker the trip, the higher the price. A hydrofoil, called a "jet boat," skims between Naples and Sorrento—it's faster, safer from pickpockets, more scenic, and more expensive than the train (6/day, more in summer, departs roughly every 2 hours starting at 9:00, 35 minutes, €11). A taxi from Naples' Centrale train station to its port costs about €12-15.

For schedules to Capri, you can check online (www.capri tourism.com; click "Shipping Timetable"), at any TI, or at Naples' Port Beverello boat dock. Ticket windows clearly display the next available departure. The number of boats that run per day depends on the season. Trips are canceled in bad weather. Most boats charge an extra fee for luggage (about €2).

If you plan to arrive at and leave a destination by boat, make note upon your arrival of the return times—the last boat usually leaves before 19:00.

NAPLES

€20-48 depending on speed; from Brindisi, ferries sail to Greece), **Milan** (direct trains hourly, 5 hours, €100, more frequent with change in Rome, overnight possible), **Venice** (almost hourly, 5.5-7 hours with changes in Bologna or Rome, €121, overnight possible), **Palermo** (2/day direct, 9-9.5 hours, €53, overnight possible), **Nice** (2/day, 12 hours with change in Genoa), **Paris** (3/day, 13-15 hours with change in Rome or Milan). Any train listed on the schedule as leaving Napoli PG or Napoli-Garibaldi departs not from the actual station, but from the Piazza Garibaldi subway station below.

To Pompeii: To visit the ancient site of Pompeii, don't use national train connections to the city of Pompei (which might seem convenient, especially if you're coming from Rome). Because the Pompei national train station is far from the archaeological site, you're better off transferring in Naples to the Circumvesuviana train (below)—which takes you to the Pompei Scavi stop near the actual site.

By Circumvesuviana Train: See the "Getting Around the Region" sidebar for information on getting to Herculaneum, Pompeii, and Sorrento.

Pompeii, Herculaneum & Vesuvius

Stopped in their tracks by the eruption of Mount Vesuvius in A.D. 79, Pompeii and Herculaneum offer the best look anywhere at what life in Rome must have been like around 2,000 years ago. These two cities of well-preserved ruins are yours to explore. Of the two sites, Pompeii is grander, while Herculaneum is smaller and more intimate. Vesuvius, still smoldering ominously, rises up on the horizon. It last erupted in 1944, and is still an active volcano. Buses drop you a steep half-hour hike from the summit.

Pompeii

A once-thriving commercial port of 20,000, Pompeii (worth ▲▲▲) grew from Greek and Etruscan roots to become an important Roman city. Then, on August 24, A.D. 79, everything changed.

Vesuvius erupted and began to bury the city under 30 feet of hot volcanic ash. For the archaeologists who excavated it centuries later, this was a shake-and-bake windfall, teaching them volumes about daily Roman life. Pompeii was accidentally rediscovered in 1599; excavations began in 1748.

Orientation to Pompeii

Cost: €11, cash only.

Hours: Daily April-Oct 8:30-19:30, Nov-March 8:30-17:00 (last entry 1.5 hours before closing).

Closures: Be warned that some buildings and streets are bound to be closed for restoration when you visit.

Crowd-Beating Tips: On busy days, there can be a line of up to 30 minutes to buy a ticket. If you anticipate lines, buy your ticket at the "info point" kiosk at the train station (same price as at the site, credit cards accepted).

Getting There: Pompeii is roughly midway between Naples and Sorrento on the Circumvesuviana train line (2/hour, €2.80 and 40 minutes from Naples, one-way, not covered by railpasses. Get off at the Pompei Scavi, Villa dei Misteri stop; from Naples, it's the stop after Torre Annunziata. The DD express trains bypass several of the suburban stations but stop at the site, making the trip slightly faster. The "info point" kiosk at the station is a private agency selling tours (not a real TI), but they can provide some information and sell tickets for the site. From the Pompei Scavi train station, it's just a short five-minute walk to the site entrance: Turn right and walk down the road about a block to the entrance (first left turn). Parking is available at Camping Zeus near the Circumvesuviana train station (€2.50/hour); several other campgrounds/parking lots are nearby.

Information: To cope with ongoing renovation and various site closures, be sure to pick up the free, helpful map at the entrance (ask for it when you buy your ticket, also check at the info window to the left of the WCs—the maps aren't available within the walls of Pompeii). Tel. 081-857-5347, www.pompeiisites.org.

The bookshop sells the small Pompeii and Herculaneum *Past and Present* book. Its plastic overlays allow you to re-create the ruins (€13 in bookstores, pay no more than that if you buy from a street vendor; look for the current year's edition).

Tours: My self-guided tour in this chapter covers the basics and provides a good framework for exploring the site on your own. You can download this chapter as a free Rick Steves **audio tour**; see page 1101.

NAPLES

Live guides (around €110/2 hours) of varying quality—there really is no guarantee of what you're getting—cluster near the ticket booth and may try to herd you into a group with other travelers, which makes the price more reasonable for you. For a private two-hour tour, consider **Gaetano Manfredi** who is pricey but brings energy and theatricality to his tours (€120-220 for 8-10 people, book in advance by email, mobile 338-725-5620, www.pompeiitourguide.com, gaetanoguide@hotmail.it). **Antonio Somma** also specializes in the site and does tours of the surrounding region (€115 for up to 8 people, book in advance, mobile 393-406-3824 or 339-891-9489, www.pompeitour.com, info@pompeitour.com). The Naples-based guides recommended on page 938 can also guide you at Pompeii. Parents, note that the ancient brothel and its sexually explicit frescoes are included on tours; let your guide know if you'd rather skip that stop.

Audioguides are available from a kiosk near the ticket booth at the Porta Marina entrance (€6.50, €10/2 people, ID required), but they offer basically the same info as your free booklet.

Length of This Tour: Allow two hours, or three if you visit the theater and amphitheater.

With Limited Time: If you're short on time, focus on the Forum, Baths of the Forum, House of the Faun, House of the Vettii (if it's open), and brothel.

Baggage Check: A free baggage check is near the turnstiles at the site entrance.

Services: The site has two WCs—one near the entrance and another in the cafeteria.

Eating: The Ciao cafeteria within the site serves good sandwiches, pizza, and pasta at a reasonable price. A few mediocre restaurants cluster between the entrance and the train station. Your cheapest bet may be to bring your own food for a discreet picnic.

Starring: Roofless (collapsed) but otherwise intact Roman buildings, plaster casts of hapless victims, a few erotic frescoes, and the dawning realization that these ancient people were no different from us.

Background

Pompeii, founded in 600 B.C., eventually became a booming Roman trading city. Not rich, not poor, it was middle class—a

perfect example of typical Roman life. Most streets would have been lined with stalls and jammed with customers from sunup to sundown. Chariots vied with shoppers for street space. Two thousand years ago, Rome controlled the entire Mediterranean—making it a kind of free-trade zone—and Pompeii was a central and bustling port.

There were no posh neighborhoods in Pompeii. Rich and poor mixed it up as elegant houses existed side by side with simple homes. While nearby Herculaneum would have been a classier place to live (traffic-free streets, fancier houses, far better drainage), Pompeii was the place for action and shopping. It served an estimated 20,000 residents with more than 40 bakeries, 30 brothels, and 130 bars, restaurants, and hotels. With most of its buildings covered by brilliant white ground-marble stucco, Pompeii in A.D. 79 was an impressive town.

As you tour Pompeii, remember that its best art is in the Archaeological Museum in Naples (described earlier in this chapter).

Self-Guided Tour

• *Just past the ticket-taker, start your approach up to the...*

❶ Porta Marina

The city of Pompeii was born on the hill ahead of you. This was the

original town gate. Before Vesuvius blew and filled in the harbor, the sea came nearly to here. Look to the left (near the tall cypress tree) to see the stone rings where ships tied up to the dock. Also notice the two openings in the gate (ahead, up the ramp). Both were left open by day to admit major traffic. At night, the larger one was closed for better security.

• *Pass through the Porta Marina and continue up to the top of the street, pausing at the three large stepping-stones in the middle.*

Pompeii Tour

VESUVIUS (IN DISTANCE)

PATH

CITY WALLS

PORTA DEL VESUVIO

UNEXCAVATED AREA

PORTA DI ERCOLANO

HOUSE OF THE VETTII (MAY BE CLOSED)

HOUSE OF THE FAUN

VIC. VETTII

VIA VESUVIO

VIA NOLA

VIA MERCURIO

VIA CONSOLARE

CITY WALLS

VIA FORTUNA

TABERNA HEDONES

VIA STABIANA

To 18

VIA AUGUSTALI

CAFETERIA & WC

TEMPLE OF JUPITER

FORUM

VIA TEATRI

VIA ABBONDANZA

TEATRO PICCOLO

PORTA MARINA ENTRANCE

THEATER

WALK ENDS

TICKETS

CIRCUM-VESUVIANA TRAIN STATION

WALK BEGINS

EXIT

CITY WALLS

Piazza Esedra

VIA DEI TEATRI

SS-18

VIA PLINIO

200 Meters
200 Yards

① Porta Marina
② Pompeii's Streets
③ Forum
④ Basilica
⑤ Via Abbondanza
⑥ Fish & Produce Market; Plaster Casts of Victims
⑦ Baths of the Forum
⑧ Fast-Food Joint
⑨ House of the Tragic Poet
⑩ Aqueduct Arch
⑪ House of the Faun
⑫ Original Lead Pipes
⑬ House of the Vettii
⑭ Bakery & Mill
⑮ Brothel
⑯ Temple of Isis
⑰ Theater & Piccolo Theater
⑱ To Amphitheater

❷ Pompeii's Streets

Every day, Pompeiians flooded the streets with gushing water to clean them. These stepping-stones let pedestrians cross with-

out getting their sandals wet. Chariots traveling in either direction could straddle the stones (all had standard-size axles). A single stepping-stone in a road means it was a one-way street, a pair indicates an ordinary two-way, and three (like this) signifies a major

thoroughfare. The basalt stones are the original Roman pavement. The sidewalks (elevated to hide the plumbing) were paved with bits of broken pots (an ancient form of recycling) and studded with reflective bits of white marble. These "cats' eyes" helped people get around after dark, either by moonlight or with the help of lamps.

• *Continue straight ahead, don your mental toga, and enter the city as the Romans once did. The road opens up into the spacious main square: the Forum. Stand at the near end of this rectangular space and look toward Mount Vesuvius.*

❸ The Forum (Foro)

Pompeii's commercial, religious, and political center stands at the intersection of the city's two main streets. While it's the most

ruined part of Pompeii, it's grand nonetheless. Picture the piazza surrounded by two-story buildings on all sides. The pedestals that line the square once held statues (now safely displayed in the museum in Naples). In

its heyday, Pompeii's citizens gathered here in the main square to shop, talk politics, and socialize. Business took place in the important buildings that lined the piazza.

The Forum was dominated by the **Temple of Jupiter,** at the far end (marked by a half-dozen ruined columns atop a stair-step base). Jupiter was the supreme god of the Roman pantheon—you might be able to make out his little white marble head at the center-rear of the temple.

At the near end of the Forum (behind where you're standing) is the **curia,** or city hall. Like many Roman buildings, it was built with brick and mortar, then covered with marble walls and floors. To your left (as you face Vesuvius and the Temple of Jupiter) is the **basilica,** or courthouse.

Since Pompeii was a pretty typical Roman town, it has the same layout and components that you'll find in any Roman city—main square, curia, basilica, temples, axis of roads, and so on. All power converged at the Forum: religious (the temple), political (the curia), judicial (the basilica), and commercial (this piazza was the main marketplace). Even the power of the people was expressed here, since this where they gathered to vote. Imagine the hubbub of this town square in its heyday.

Look beyond the Temple of Jupiter. Five miles to the north looms the ominous backstory to this site: **Mount Vesuvius.** Mentally draw a triangle up from the two remaining peaks to reconstruct the mountain before the eruption. When it blew, Pompeiians had no idea that they were living under a volcano, since Vesuvius hadn't erupted for 1,200 years. Imagine the wonder—then the horror—as a column of pulverized rock roared upward, and then ash began to fall. The weight of the ash and small rocks collapsed Pompeii's roofs later that day, crushing people who had taken refuge inside buildings instead of fleeing the city.

• *As you face Vesuvius, the basilica is to your left, lined with stumps of columns. Step inside and see the layout.*

❹ Basilica

Pompeii's basilica was a first-century palace of justice. This ancient law court has the same floor plan later adopted by many Christian churches (which are also called basilicas). The big central hall (or nave) is flanked by rows of columns marking off narrower side aisles. Along the side walls are traces of the original marble.

The columns—now stumps all about the same height—were not ruined by the volcano. Rather, they were left unfinished when

Vesuvius blew. Pompeii had been devastated by an earthquake in A.D. 62, and was just in the process of rebuilding the basilica when Vesuvius erupted 17 years later. The half-built columns show off the technology of the day. Uniform bricks were stacked around a cylindrical core. Once finished, they would have been coated with marble dust stucco to simulate marble columns—an economical construction method found throughout Pompeii (and the Roman Empire).

Besides the earthquake and the eruption, Pompeii's buildings have suffered other ravages over the years, including Spanish plunderers (c. 1800), 19th-century souvenir hunters, WWII bombs, wild vegetation, another earthquake in 1980, and modern neglect.

The fact that the entire city was covered by the eruption of A.D. 79 actually helped preserve it, saving it from the sixth-century barbarians who plundered many other towns into oblivion.

• *Exit the basilica and cross the short side of the square, where the city's main street hits the Forum.*

❺ Via Abbondanza

Glance down Via Abbondanza, Pompeii's main street. Lined with shops, bars, and restaurants, it was a lively, pedestrian-only zone. The three "beaver-teeth" stones are traffic barriers that kept chariots out. On the corner (just to the left), take a close look at the dark travertine column standing next to the white one. Notice that the marble drums of the white column are not chiseled entirely round—another construction project left unfinished when Vesuvius erupted.

• *Head toward Vesuvius, walking along the right side of the Forum. Immediately to the right of the Temple of Jupiter (just before the four round arches), a door leads into the market hall, where you'll find two glass cases.*

❻ Fish and Produce Market— Plaster Casts of Victims

As the frescoes on the wall (just inside on the left) indicate, this is where Pompeiians came to buy their food—fish, bread, chickens, and so on. These fine examples of Roman art—with their glimpses of everyday life and their mastery of depth and illusion—would not be matched until the Renaissance, a thousand years after the fall of Rome.

The glass cases hold casts of Pompeiians, eerily captured in their last moments. They were quickly suffocated by a superheated avalanche of gas and ash, and their bodies were encased in volcanic debris. While excavating, modern archaeologists detected hollow spaces underfoot, created when the victims' bodies decomposed. By gently filling the holes with plaster, the archaeologists were able to create molds of the Pompeiians who were caught in the disaster.

• *Continue on, leaving the Forum through an arch behind the Temple of Jupiter. Here you'll find a pedestrian-only road sign (ahead on the right corner, above the* REG VII INS IV *sign) and more "beaver-teeth" traffic blocks. The modern cafeteria is the only eatery inside the*

The Eruption of Vesuvius

At about 1:00 in the afternoon on August 24, A.D. 79, Mount Vesuvius erupted, sending a mushroom cloud of ash, dust, and rocks 12 miles into the air. It spewed for 18 hours straight, as winds blew the cloud southward. The white-gray ash settled like a heavy snow on Pompeii, its weight eventually collapsing roofs and floors, but leaving the walls intact. While most of Pompeii's 20,000 residents fled that day, about two thousand stayed behind.

Although the city of Herculaneum was closer to the volcano—about four miles away—it had largely escaped the rain of ash, due to the direction of the wind. However, 12 hours after Vesuvius awoke, the type of eruption suddenly changed. The column of hot gas and rock collapsed, creating a superheated avalanche of ash, pumice, and gas. This red-hot "pyroclastic flow" sped down the side of the mountain at nearly 100 miles per hour, engulfing Herculaneum. Several more flows over the next few hours further entombed Herculaneum, burying it in nearly 60 feet of hot material that later cooled into rock, freezing the city in time. Then around 7:30 in the morning, another pyroclastic flow headed south and struck Pompeii, dealing a fatal blow to those who'd remained behind.

archaeological site (with a coffee bar and WC). Twenty yards past the cafeteria, on the left-hand side at #24, is the entrance to the...

❼ Baths of the Forum (Terme del Foro)

Pompeii had six public baths, each with a men's and a women's section. You're in the men's zone. The leafy courtyard at the entrance was the gymnasium. After working out, clients could relax with a hot bath *(caldarium),* warm bath *(tepidarium),* or cold plunge *(frigidarium).*

The first big, plain room you enter served as the **dressing room.** Holes on the walls were for pegs to hang clothing. High up, the window (with a faded Neptune underneath) was originally covered with a less-translucent Roman glass. Walk over the non-slip mosaics into the next room.

The *tepidarium* is ringed by mini-statues or *telamones* (male caryatids, figures used as supporting pillars), which divided the lockers. Clients would undress and warm up here, perhaps stretching out on one of the bronze benches near the bronze heater for a massage. Look at the ceiling—half crushed by the eruption and half intact, with its fine blue-and-white stucco work.

Next, admire the engineering in the steam-bath room, or *caldarium.* The double floor was heated from below—so nice with bare feet (look into the grate to see the brick support towers). The double walls with brown terra-cotta tiles held the heat. Romans soaked in the big tub, which was filled with hot water. Opposite the big tub is a fountain, which spouted water onto the hot floor, creating steam. The lettering on the fountain reminded those enjoying the room which two politicians paid for it...and how much it cost them (5,250 *sestertii*). To keep condensation from dripping annoyingly from the ceiling, fluting (ribbing) was added to carry water down the walls.

• *Today's visitors exit the baths through the original entry. If you're a bit hungry, immediately across the street is an ancient...*

❽ Fast-Food Joint

After a bath, it was only natural to want a little snack. So, just across the street is a fast-food joint, marked by a series of rectangular marble counters. Most ancient Romans didn't cook for themselves in their tiny apartments, so to-go places like this were commonplace. The holes in the counters held the pots for food. Each container was like a thermos, with a wooden lid to keep the soup hot, the wine cool, and so on. Notice the groove in the front doorstep and the holes out on the curb. The holes likely accommodated cords for stretching awnings over the sidewalk to shield the clientele from the hot sun, while the grooves were for the shop's folding accordion doors. Look at the wheel grooves in the pavement, worn down through centuries of use. Nearby are more stepping-stones for pedestrians to cross the flooded streets.

• *Just a few steps uphill from the fast-food joint, at #5 (with a locked gate), is the...*

❾ House of the Tragic Poet (Casa de Poeta Tragico)

This house is typical Roman style. The entry is flanked by two family-owned shops (each with a track for a collapsing accordion door). The home is like a train running straight away from the street: atrium (with skylight and pool to catch the rain), den (where deals were made by the shopkeeper), and garden (with rooms facing it and a shrine to remember both the gods and family ancestors). In the entryway is the famous "Beware of Dog" *(Cave Canem)* mosaic.

Today's visitors enter the home by the back door (circle around to the left). On your way there, look for the modern exposed pipe on the left side of the lane; this is the same as ones used in the ancient plumbing system, hidden beneath the raised sidewalk. Inside the house, the grooves on the marble well-head in the entry hall (possibly closed) were formed by generations of inhabitants dragging the bucket up by rope. The richly frescoed dining room is off the garden. Diners lounged on their couches (the Roman custom) and enjoyed frescoes with fake "windows," giving the illusion of a bigger and airier room. Next to the dining room is a humble BBQ-style kitchen with a little closet for the toilet (the kitchen and bathroom shared the same plumbing).

• *Return to the fast-food place and continue about 10 yards downhill to the big intersection. From the center of the intersection, look left to see a giant arch, framing a nice view of Mount Vesuvius.*

⑩ Aqueduct Arch—Running Water

Water was critical for this city of 20,000 people, and this arch was part of Pompeii's water-delivery system. A 100-mile-long aqueduct carried fresh water down from the hillsides to a big reservoir perched at the highest point of the city wall. Since overall water pressure was disappointing, Pompeiians built arches like the brick one you see here (originally covered in marble) with hidden water tanks at the top. Located just below the altitude of the main tank, these smaller tanks were filled by gravity, and provided each neighborhood with reliable pressure.

• *If you're thirsty, fill your water bottle from the modern fountain. Then continue straight downhill one block (50 yards) to #2 on the left.*

⑪ House of the Faun (Casa del Founo)

Stand across the street and marvel at the grand entry with *"HAVE"* (hail to you) as a welcome mat. Go in. Notice the two shrines above the entryway—one dedicated to the gods, the other to this wealthy family's ancestors.

You are standing in Pompeii's largest home, where you're greeted by the delightful small bronze statue of the *Dancing Faun,* famed for its realistic movement and fine proportion. (The original, described on page 941, is in Naples' Archaeological Museum.) With 40 rooms and 27,000 square feet, the House of the Faun covers an entire city block. The next floor mosaic, with an intricate diamond-like design, decorates the homeowner's office. Beyond that is the famous floor mosaic of the *Battle of Alexander.* (The original is also at the museum in Naples.) In 333 B.C., Alexander the Great beat Darius and the Persians. Romans had great respect for Alexander, the first great emperor before Rome's.

While most of Pompeii's nouveau riche had notoriously bad taste and stuffed their palaces with over-the-top, mismatched decor, this guy had class. Both the faun (an ancient copy of a famous Greek statue) and the Alexander mosaic show an appreciation for history.

The house's back courtyard leads to the exit in the far-right corner. It's lined with pillars rebuilt after the A.D. 62 earthquake. Take a close look at the brick, mortar, and fake marble stucco veneer.

• *Sneak out of the House of the Faun through its back door and turn right. (If this exit is closed, return to the entrance and make a U-turn left, around to the back of the house.) Thirty yards down, along the right-hand side of the street are metal cages protecting...*

⑫ Original Lead Pipes

These 2,000-year-old pipes (made of lead imported from Britannia) were part of the city's elaborate water system. From the aqueduct-fed water tank at the high end of town, three independent pipe systems supplied water to the city: one for baths, one for private homes, and one for public water fountains. If there was a water shortage, democratic priorities prevailed: First the baths were cut off, then the private homes. The last water supply to go was the public fountains, where all citizens could get drinking and cooking water.

• *If the street's not closed off, take your first left (on Vicolo dei Vettii), walk about 20 yards, and find the entrance (on the left) to the next stop. (If the street is closed, turn right down the street marked* REG VI INS XIV *and skip down to the next set of directions.)*

⑬ House of the Vettii (Casa dei Vettii)

Pompeii's best-preserved home has been completely blocked off for years; unfortunately it's unlikely to reopen in time for your visit. The House of the Vettii was the bachelor pad of two wealthy merchant brothers. If you can see the entryway, you may spot the huge erection. This is not pornography. There's a meaning here: The penis and the sack of money balance each other on the gold-smith scale above a fine bowl of fruit. Translation: Only with a balance of fer-tility and money can you have abundance.

If it's open, step into the atrium with its ceiling open to the sky to collect light and rainwater. The pool, while decorative, was a functional water-supply tank. It's flanked by large money boxes anchored to the floor. The brothers were certainly successful merchants, and possibly moneylenders, too.

Exit on the right, passing the tight servant quarters, and go into the kitchen, with its bronze cooking pots (and an exposed lead pipe on the back wall). The passage dead-ends in the little Venus Room, which features erotic frescoes behind glass.

Return to the atrium and pass into the big colonnaded garden. It was replanted according to the plan indicated by the traces of roots that were excavated from the volcanic ash. Richly frescoed entertainment rooms ring this courtyard. Circle counterclockwise. The dining room is finely decorated in black and "Pompeiian red" (from iron rust). Study the detail. Notice the lead humidity seal between the wall and the floor, designed to keep the moisture-sensitive frescoes dry. (Had Leonardo da Vinci taken this clever step, his *Last Supper* in Milan might be in better shape today.) Continuing around, you'll see more of the square white stones inlaid in the floor. Imagine them reflecting like cats' eyes as the brothers and their friends wandered around by oil lamp late at night. Frescoes in the Yellow Room (near the exit) show off the ancient mastery of perspective, which would not be matched elsewhere in Europe for nearly 1,500 years.

• *Facing the entrance to the House of the Vettii, turn left and walk downhill one long block (along Vicolo dei Vettii) to a T-intersection (Via della Fortuna), marked by a stone fountain with a bull's head for a spout. Intersections like this were busy neighborhood centers, where the rent was highest and people gathered. With the fountain at your back, turn left, then immediately right, walking along a gently curving road (Vicolo Storto). On the left side of the street, at #22, find four big stone cylinders.*

⓮ Bakery and Mill (Forno e Mulini)

The brick oven looks like a modern-day pizza oven. The stubby stone towers are flour grinders. Grain was poured into the top, and

donkeys or slaves pushed wooden bars that turned the stones. The powdered grain dropped out of the bottom as flour—flavored with tiny bits of rock. Each neighborhood had a bakery like this.

Continue to the next intersection (Via degli Augustali, where there's another fast-food joint, at #32) and turn left. As you walk, look at the destructive power of all the vines, and notice how deeply the chariot grooves have worn into the pavement. Deep grooves could break wagon wheels. The suddenly ungroovy stretch indicates that this road was in the process of being repaved when the eruption shut everything down.

• *Head about 50 yards down this (obviously one-way) street to #44 (on the left). Here you'll find the Taberna Hedones (with a small atrium, den, and garden). This bar still has its original floor and, deeper in, the mosaic arch of a grotto fountain. Just past the tavern, turn right and walk downhill to #18, on the right.*

Possible detour: If the road past the tavern is blocked off, here's another way to reach the next stop: First, backtrack to the Forum—go back the way you came, turn left at the bull's-head fountain, then turn left again at the aqueduct arch. Back in the Forum, head down to the far end and turn left onto the main street, Via dell'Abbondanza (which we looked down earlier—remember the beaver teeth?). Follow this, turning left up the second street (after the fountain, marked REG VII INS I, *with a small* Vicolo del Lupanare *sign). This leads to the entrance of the...*

⓯ Brothel (Lupanare)

You'll find the biggest crowds in Pompeii at a place that was likely popular 2,000 ago, too—the brothel. Prostitutes were nicknamed *lupe* (she-wolves), alluding to the call they made when trying to attract business. The brothel was a simple place, with beds and pillows made of stone. The ancient graffiti includes tallies and exotic names of the women, indicating the prostitutes came from all corners of the Mediterranean (it also served as feedback from satisfied customers). The faded frescoes above the cells may have been a kind of menu for services offered. Note the idealized women (white, which was considered beautiful; one wears an early bra) and the rougher men (dark, considered horny). The bed legs came with little disk-like barriers to keep critters from crawling up.

• *Leaving the brothel, go right, then take the first left, and continue going downhill two blocks to the intersection with Pompeii's main drag, Via dell'Abbondanza. The Forum—and exit—are to the right, for those who may wish to opt out from here.*

The huge amphitheater—which is certainly skippable—is 10 minutes to your left. But for now, go left for 60 yards, then turn right just beyond the fountain, and walk down Via dei Teatri. Turn left before the columns, and head downhill another 60 yards to #28, which marks the...

⑯ Temple of Isis

This Egyptian temple served Pompeii's Egyptian community. The little white stucco shrine with the modern plastic roof housed holy water from the Nile. Isis, from Egyptian myth, was one of many foreign gods adopted by the eclectic Romans. Pompeii must have had a synagogue, too, but it has yet to be excavated.

• *Exit the temple where you entered, and go right. At the next intersection, turn right again, and head downhill to the adjacent theaters. Your goal is the large theater down the corridor at #20, but if it's closed, look at the smaller but similar theater (Teatro Piccolo) just beyond at #19.*

⑰ Theater

Originally a Greek theater (Greeks built theirs with the help of a hillside), this was the birthplace of the Greek port here in 470 B.C. During Roman times, the theater sat 5,000 people in three sets of seats, all with different prices: the five marble terraces up close (filled with romantic wooden seats for two), the main section, and the cheap nosebleed section (surviving only on the high end, near the trees). The square stones above the cheap seats once supported a canvas rooftop. Take note of the high-profile boxes, flanking the stage, for guests of honor. From this perch, you can see the gladiator barracks—the colonnaded courtyard beyond the theater. They lived in tiny rooms, trained in the courtyard, and fought in the nearby amphitheater.

• *You've seen Pompeii's highlights. When you're ready to leave, backtrack to the main road and turn left, going uphill to the Forum, where you'll find the main entrance/exit.*

However, there's much more to see—three-quarters of Pompeii's 164 acres have been excavated, but this tour has covered only a third of the site. *After the theater—if you still have energy to see more—go back to the main road, and take a right toward the eastern part of the site, where the crowds thin out. Go straight for about 10 minutes, likely jogging right after a bit (just follow the posted maps). You'll wind up passing through a pretty, forested area. At the far end is the...*

⑱ Amphitheater

If you can, climb to the upper level of the amphitheater (though the stairs are often blocked). With Vesuvius looming in the background, mentally replace the tourists below with gladiators and wild animals locked in combat. Walk along the top of the amphitheater and look down into the grassy rectangular area surrounded by columns. This is the **Palaestra,** an area once used for athletic training. (If you can't get to the top of the amphitheater, you can see the Palaestra from outside—in fact, you can't miss it, as it's right next door.) Facing the other way, look for the bell tower that tops the roofline of the modern city of Pompei, where locals go about their daily lives in the shadow of the volcano, just as their ancestors did 2,000 years ago. *HAVE!*

• *If it's too crowded to bear hiking back along uneven lanes to the entrance, you can slip out the site's "back door," which is next to the amphitheater. Exiting, turn right and follow the site's wall through nondescript neighborhoods all the way back to the entrance.*

Herculaneum (Ercolano)

Smaller, less crowded, and not as ruined as its famous big sister, Herculaneum (worth ▲▲) offers a closer, more intimate peek into ancient Roman life but lacks the grandeur of Pompeii (there's barely a colonnade).

Cost and Hours: €11, €20 combo-ticket includes Pompeii and three lesser sites (valid 3 consecutive days). Open daily April-Oct 8:30-19:30, Nov-March 8:30-17:00, ticket office closes 1.5 hours earlier (tel. 081-777-7008, www.pompeiisites.org).

Getting There: Herculaneum (Ercolano) is about 20 minutes from Naples and 50 minutes from Sorrento on the same Circumvesuviana train that goes to Pompeii. For details on the Circumvesuviana, see page 966. Get off at the Ercolano Scavi train stop. To walk to the ruins, leave the Ercolano station and turn right, then left; go eight blocks straight downhill from the station to the end of the road, where you'll see the entrance marked by a grand arch. (Skip Museo MAV.) Pass through the arch and continue down the path, taking in the bird's-eye first impression of the site. The ticket office, baggage storage (pick up bags 30 minutes prior to site closing), and WCs are located in the modern building, 200 yards ahead.

Information: Pick up a free detailed map and excellent booklet (with numbered explanations of each building) at the info desk next to the ticket window. The site also has a bookstore.

Audioguide: The informative and interesting audioguide sheds light on the ruins and life in Herculaneum in the first century A.D. (€6.50, €10/2 people, ID required, pick up 100 yards after the ticket turnstiles).

Length of This Tour: Allow one hour.

◆ Self-Guided Tour: Caked and baked by the same A.D. 79 eruption that pummeled Pompeii (see sidebar on page 977), Herculaneum is a small community of intact buildings with plenty of surviving detail. While Pompeii was initially smothered in ash, Herculaneum was spared at first—due to the direction of the wind—but got slammed about 12 hours after the eruption started by a superheated avalanche of ash and hot gases roaring off the volcano. The city was eventually buried under nearly 60 feet of super-heated ash, which hardened into tuff, perfectly preserving the city until excavations began in 1748.

After leaving the ticket window, walk the long path around the site to the entrance. From here, you can get a sense of just how much volcanic material piled up. The present-day city of Ercolano looms just above, and the modern buildings don't look much different from their ancient counterparts.

After crossing the modern bridge into the excavation site, stroll straight to the end of the street and find the **Seat of the Augustali** (Sede degli Augustali). Decorated with frescoes of Hercules (for whom this city was named), it was a forum for freed slaves climbing their way up the ladder of Roman society.

Leave the building through the back and go to the right, down the lane. The adjacent *thermopolium* (at #19) was the Roman equivalent to a fast-food joint, with giant jars for wine, oil, and snacks. Most of the buildings along here were shops, with apartments above. Look around doorways for ancient bits of wood charred by the pyroclastic flows. Most buildings were made of stone, but the floors and beams were wood (which doesn't survive at any other ancient site).

A few steps on, at #14, the **Bottega ad Cucumas** wine shop still has charred remains of beams, and its drink list remains frescoed on the outside wall.

Take the next right, go halfway down, and on the left find the **House of Neptune and Amphitrite** (Casa di Nettuno e Anfitrite). Outside, notice the intact upper floor and imagine it going even higher. Inside, you'll see colorful mosaics and a unique "frame" made of shells.

Back outside, continue downhill to the intersection, then head left to the far end of the site and the don't-miss-it **gymnasium** *(palestra)* complex. The highlight is the Hydra of Lerna, a sculpted bronze fountain that features the seven-headed monster defeated by Hercules as one of his 12 labors. Find the Hydra by walking through the triangular-shaped entrances carved in the tuff wall. To light up this cavernous space, go to the second doorway on the left wall and press the switch. Just outside, take a close look at the "marble" columns, which are actually made of rounded bricks covered with a thick layer of plaster, shaped to look like carved marble. While important buildings in Rome had solid marble columns, these are typical of ordinary buildings.

Downhill at #21, the **House of the Deer** (Casa dei Cervi) is also worth seeking out. It's named for the statues of deer being attacked by dogs in the garden courtyard (these are copies; the originals are in the Archaeological Museum in Naples). As you wander through the rooms, notice the colorfully frescoed walls. Ancient Herculaneum, like all Roman cities of that age, was filled with color, rather than the stark white we often imagine (even the statues were painted).

Continuing downhill, the **baths** (Terme Suburbane, enter near the side of the statue, sometimes closed) illustrate the city's devastation. After you descend into the baths, look back at the steps. You'll see the original wood charred in the disaster, protected by the wooden planks you just walked on. At the bottom of the stairs, in the waiting room to the right, notice where the floor collapsed under the sheer weight of the volcanic debris. (The sunken pavement reveals the baths' heating system: hot air generated by wood-burning furnaces and circulated between the different levels of the floor.) A doorway in front of the stairs is still filled with solidified ash. Despite the damage, elements of refinement remain intact, such as the delicate stuccoes in the *caldarium* (hot bath).

Back outside, make your way down the steps to the sunken area just below. As you descend, you're walking across what was formerly Herculaneum's beach (the shoreline was extended outward by material from the volcano). Looking back, you'll see **arches** that were part of boat storage areas. Archaeologists used to wonder why so few victims were found in Herculaneum. But during excavations in 1981, hundreds of skeletons were discovered here, between the wall of volcanic stone behind you and the city in front of you. Some of Herculaneum's 4,000 citizens tried to escape by sea, but were overtaken by the pyroclastic flows.

Thankfully, your escape is easier. Either follow the sounds of the water and continue through the tunnel; or, more scenically, backtrack and exit the same way you entered.

Vesuvius

The 4,000-foot-high Vesuvius, mainland Europe's only active volcano, has been sleeping restlessly since 1944. Up here, it's desolate and lunar-like, and the rocks are newly created. Walk the entire accessible part of the crater lip for the most interesting views; the far end overlooks Pompeii. Be still. Listen to the wind and the occasional cascades of rocks tumbling into the crater. Any steam? Vesuvius is closed to visitors when erupting.

Cost and Hours: €8, which includes a mandatory guide who provides a brief introduction, then sets you free (daily April-Oct 9:00-17:00, until 18:00 in summer, Nov-March 9:00-15:00, no WC, tel. 081-865-3911, www .parconazionaledelvesuvio.it).

Getting to Vesuvius: The summit is accessible year-round by car (just drive to the end of the road and pay €2.50 to park), by taxi (€90 round-trip from Naples including a 2-hour wait, cheaper from Pompeii), or by bus. From the parking lot, it's a steep 30-minute hike to the top for a sweeping view of the Bay of Naples. Bring a coat; it's often cold and windy (especially Oct-April).

From **Pompeii,** you have three bus services to choose from, each taking about three hours (including 1.25 hours at the top). Various local tour operators and travel agencies sell tickets for one of these three trips.

The **UnicoCampania** bus—marked *EAVBUS* or *City Sightseeing Napoli*—goes up the main road and lets you return on any scheduled departure (€10 round-trip plus €8 summit admission, 12/day, weather permitting in winter, departs from Piazza Anfiteatro, Piazza Esedra in front of TI, and Pompei Scavi Circumvesuviana station, tel. 081-551-3109, www.unicocampania.it).

Busvia del Vesuvio winds you up a bumpy private road through the back of the national park in a cross between a shuttle bus and a monster truck. It's a fun, more scenic way to go, but not for the easily queasy (€20 includes summit admission, runs hourly April-Oct daily 9:00-16:00, also at 17:00 June-Aug, rarely runs Nov-March—call for schedule, departs from in front of Pompei Scavi Circumvesuviana station, mobile 340-935-2616, www.bus viadelvesuvio.com).

The old-fashioned **Vesuvius Trolley Tram** (Tramvia del Vesuvio) uses the main road that the UnicoCampania bus does (€12 round-trip plus €8 summit admission, 6/day, departs from in front of Pompeii Scavi Circumvesuviana station, tickets sold at various agencies near the Pompeii entrance).

From **Herculaneum,** your best bet is the Vesuvio Express, which makes the trip in small vans from Herculaneum's Ercolano Scavi Circumvesuviana station (€10 round-trip plus €8 summit admission, daily from 9:00, runs every 45 minutes based on demand, about 2.5 hours, tel. 081-739-3666, www.vesuvio express.it).

NAPLES

SORRENTO and CAPRI

Without a hint of big-city Naples and just an hour to the south, serene Sorrento makes an ideal home base for exploring this fascinating region, from Naples to the Amalfi Coast to Paestum. And the jet-setting island of Capri is just a short cruise from Sorrento, offering more charm and fun (outside of the crowded months of July and August) than its glitzy reputation would lead you to believe.

Sorrento

Wedged on a ledge under the mountains and over the Mediterranean, spritzed by lemon and olive groves, Sorrento is an attractive resort of 20,000 residents and, in summer, just as many tourists. It's as well-located for regional sightseeing as it is a fine place to stay and stroll. The Sorrentines have gone out of their way to create a completely safe and relaxed place for tourists to come and spend money. Everyone seems to speak fluent English and work for the Chamber of Commerce. This gateway to the Amalfi Coast has an unspoiled old quarter, a lively main shopping street, and a spectacular cliffside setting. Residents are proud of the many world-class romantics who've vacationed here, such as the famed tenor Enrico Caruso, who chose Sorrento as the place to spend his last weeks in 1921.

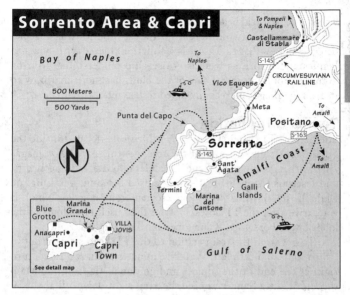

Sorrento Area & Capri

Bay of Naples

To Pompeii & Naples

Castellammare di Stabia

To Naples

S-145

CIRCUMVESUVIANA RAIL LINE

500 Meters

500 Yards

Vico Equense

Meta

To Amalfi

Punta del Capo

Positano

S-163

N

Sorrento

S-145

To Amalfi

Sant' Agata

Amalfi Coast

Termini

Marina del Cantone

Galli Islands

Gulf of Salerno

Marina Grande

Blue Grotto

VILLA JOVIS

Anacapri

Capri

Capri Town

See detail map

Planning Your Time

With Sorrento as your home base, spend a minimum of three days and nights in the region. On your way to or from Sorrento, you could stop off for a quick visit in Naples. After settling in Sorrento, spend a day touring the Amalfi Coast by bus, and another day split between Sorrento and Pompeii (accessible by Circumvesuviana train—see page 966). With more time, catch a quick boat ride to the nearby island of Capri or linger on the Amalfi Coast (see next chapter), heading as far south as Paestum's Greek temples.

Sorrento hibernates in January and February, when many places close down.

Orientation to Sorrento

Sorrento is long and narrow. The main drag, Corso Italia (50 yards in front of the Circumvesuviana train station), runs parallel to the sea from the station through the town center and out to the cape,

where the road's name becomes Via Capo. Piazza Tasso marks the town's center. Nearly everything mentioned here (except Meta beach and the hotels on Via Capo) is within a 10-minute walk of the train station. The town is perched on a cliff (some hotels have elevators down to sundecks on the water); the best real beach is at Meta, two miles away.

Sorrento has two different port areas: The Marina Piccola, directly below Piazza Tasso, is a functional jetty with boats to Naples and Capri, as well as cruise-ship tenders. The Marina Grande, around the west side of the bluff, has more charm, with its fishing village and recommended restaurants.

Tourist Information

The helpful TI (labeled *Soggiorno e Turismo*)—located inside the Foreigners' Club—hands out the free monthly *Surrentum* magazine, with a great city map and schedules of boats, buses, concerts, and festivals (Mon-Fri 8:30-16:15, closed Sat-Sun, Via Luigi de Maio 35, tel. 081-807-4033, www.sorrentotourism.com, Nino). If you arrive after the TI closes, look for their useful handouts in the lobby of the Foreigners' Club (open until midnight).

To get from the train station to the TI, head straight out to Corso Italia and turn left. Walk five minutes to Piazza Tasso, turn right at the end of the square, and go down Via Luigi de Maio through Piazza Sant'Antonino, bearing right downhill about 30 yards to the Foreigners' Club mansion at #35.

If you just need quick advice, the fake tourist office—located in a green caboose just outside the train station—can be of help. While they're a private business with hopes that you'll purchase one of their overpriced excursions, they're willing to give basic information on directions, buses, and ferries.

Arrival in Sorrento

By Train: Those arriving by train (Sorrento is the last stop on the Circumvesuviana train line) will see the Amalfi bus stop, as well as taxis waiting to overcharge them. All recommended hotels—except those on Via Capo—are within a 10-minute walk (a much cheaper mode of transport than the €15 fare taxi drivers will gouge you). For details on taking the bus to hotels on Via Capo, see page 1004.

By Boat: Passenger boats dock at Marina Piccola, Sorrento's little harbor. To get to Piazza Tasso, it's a 15-minute uphill hike or a short ride on a small blue bus (4/hour, €1, buy ticket from driver, day passes not valid) or red-and-white bus #B or #C (3/hour, buy €1 tickets at the tobacco shop or adjacent kiosk).

By Car: The Achille Lauro underground parking garage is centrally located, just a couple of blocks in front of the train station (€2/hour, on Via Correale).

Helpful Hints

Church Services: The **cathedral** hosts an English-language Anglican service at 17:00 most Sundays mid-April-July and

Sept-Oct. At **Santa Maria delle Grazie** (perhaps the most beautiful Baroque church in town), cloistered nuns sing from above and out of sight during a Mass each morning at 7:30 (on Via delle Grazie).

Bookstore: Libreria Tasso has a decent selection of books in English, including this one (June-Sept daily 10:00-22:00; Oct-May Mon-Sat 9:45-13:00 & 16:00-20:30, Sun 11:00-13:00 & 17:00-20:00; Via San Cesareo 96, one block north of cathedral, near Sorrento Men's Club; tel. 081-807-1639).

Laundry: Sorrento has two handy self-service launderettes (both charge about €8/load wash and dry, includes soap). One launderette is just down the alley next to Corso Italia 30 (daily May-Sept 7:00-24:00, Oct-April 8:00-23:00, tel. 081-878-1185). The other is at the Via Capo end of town, at the corner of Corso Italia and Via degli Aranci (daily 8:00-22:00).

Travel Agency: Top Level Travel books train tickets, flights, and more (Mon-Sat 9:00-13:00 & 16:00-20:00, closed Sun, Via degli Aranci 67, tel. 081-877-4742). Exiting the train station, go left around the station and go up the stairs—it's on the first floor next to Bar Paradise.

Local Guides: Giovanna Donadio is a good tour guide for Sorrento, Amalfi, and Capri (€100/half-day, €160/day, same price for any size of group, mobile 338-466-0114, giovanna _dona@hotmail.com). **Giovanni Visetti** is a nature lover who organizes hikes (mobile 339-694-2911, www.giovis.com, giovis@giovis.com).

Where It's At: The **Foreigners' Club** provides reasonably priced snacks and drinks, music, dancing, and magnificent vistas from its cliffside terrace—drop in for the view overlooking the harbor and the Bay of Naples (daily 9:30-24:00, behind TI, public WC, Via Luigi de Maio 35, tel. 081-877-3263). Also see "Nightlife in Sorrento" and "Eating in Sorrento," later.

Getting Around Sorrento

By Bus: City buses (either orange or red-and-white) all stop near the main square, Piazza Tasso. Bus #A runs east to Meta beach or west to the hotels on Via Capo and beyond; buses #B and #C go to the port (Marina Piccola); and bus #D heads to the fishing village (Marina Grande). Buses #A and #D stop at the beginning of Corso Italia (west side of Piazza Tasso for Via Capo or Marina Grande, east side for Meta); #B and #C stop at the corner of Piazza Sant'Antonino, just down the hill towards the water. The trip between Piazza Tasso and Marina Piccola costs just €1; for other trips, tickets cost €2.40 and are good for 45 minutes (purchase at tobacco shops and newsstands). Stamp your ticket upon entering the bus. The one-day pass (€7.20) and three-day pass (€18)

Sorrento

SORRENTO AND CAPRI

1. Hotel Antiche Mura & Plaza Sorrento
2. Casa Astarita B&B
3. Hotel Mignon
4. Hotel del Corso & Gelateria Primavera
5. Il Palazzo Starace B&B
6. Ulisse Deluxe Hostel
7. Hotel Nice & Penisola Rent
8. Hostel Le Sirene
9. Grand Hotel Ambasciatori
10. Hotel La Meridiana Sorrento
11. Hotel Minerva
12. Hotel La Tonnarella & Hotel Désirée
13. Albergo Settimo Cielo
14. Hotel Elios
15. Ristorante il Buco & Teatro Tasso
16. L'Antica Trattoria

are also valid for the entire Amalfi Coast.

A different, blue bus (operated by a separate company) runs only between the port and Piazza Tasso (4/hour, €1, buy ticket from driver); it's not covered by other bus tickets or passes.

By Rental Wheels: Many places rent motor scooters for about €35 per day, including **Europcar** (Mon-Sat 9:00-13:00 & 16:00-19:30, closed Sun, Corso Italia 210p, tel. 081-878-1386,

⑰ Inn Bufalito	㉖ Trattoria da Emilia
⑱ Photo Ristorante	㉗ Foreigners' Club Rest.
⑲ Rist. Pizzeria da Gigino	㉘ Verde Mare
⑳ Ristorante Pizzeria Lanterna Due	㉙ Sorrento Men's Club
	㉚ The English Inn
㉑ Meating	㉛ Launderettes (2)
㉒ Pizzeria da Franco	㉜ Europcar
㉓ Decò Supermarket	㉝ Top Level Travel
㉔ Gelateria David	㉞ City Bus Stop
㉕ Ristorante Delfino	㉟ SITA Bus Stop

www.sorrento.it) and **Penisola Rent,** a half-block away (Mon-Sat 9:00-13:00 & 16:00-20:30, Sun 9:00-13:00 only, located in Hotel Nice, tel. 081-877-4664, www.penisolarent.com). Don't rent a car in summer unless you enjoy traffic jams.

By Taxi: Taxis are expensive, charging an outrageous €15 (or more) for the short ride from the station to hotels. Because of heavy traffic and the complex one-way road system, you can often walk faster than you can ride. If you do use a taxi, even if you agree to a set price, be sure it has a meter (all official taxis have one). I think taxis are a huge rip-off, since city officials don't have the nerve to regulate them, and hotels are afraid to alienate them. Walk or take the bus instead.

By Bus Tour: If you'd like to get out of town to see more of the Sorrentine Peninsula, consider **CitySightseeing Sorrento**'s hop-on, hop-off bus tours, with headphone commentary about the two bays flanking this scenic spit of land (€12, 4/day, April-Oct daily, full loop is 1.75 hours, first bus departs from train station at 9:30, buy tickets on board). The pointless **tourist train** you'll see departing from Piazza Tasso loops only through the town itself— all easily reachable by foot (€6, 30-minute tour).

Self-Guided Walk

Welcome to Sorrento

Get to know Sorrento with this lazy self-guided town stroll.

• *Begin on the main square. Stand under the flags with your back to the sea, and face...*

Piazza Tasso: As in any southern Italian town, this "piazza" is Sorrento's living room. It may be noisy and congested, but locals want to be where the action is...and be part of the scene. The most expensive apartments and top cafés are on or near this square. Buses stop near here on their way to Marina Piccola (where boats depart from the harbor for Naples and Capri, a 10-minute hike below you), to the train station (left), and to Via Capo (right).

This square spans a gorge that divided the town until the 19th century. The old town (on your right) still has some surviving ancient Greek streets. The new town (to your left) was farm country just two centuries ago. A statue of St. Anthony, patron of Sorrento, faces north as if greeting those coming from Naples (often equipped with an armload of fresh lemons and oranges). If you walk a block inland, go right up to the green railing, and look down, you'll see steps that were carved in the fifth century B.C.

Sorrento's name came from the Greek word for "siren," the legendary half-bird, half-woman who sang an intoxicating lullaby. According to Homer, the sirens lived on an island near here. No one had ever sailed by the sirens without succumbing to their incredible musical charms...and to death. But Homer's hero Ulysses was determined to hear the song. He put wax in his oarsmen's ears and had himself lashed to the mast of his ship. Oh, it was nice. The sirens, thinking they had lost their powers, threw themselves into the sea, and the place became safe to inhabit. Ulysses' odyssey was all about the westward expansion of Greek culture, and to the ancient Greeks, places like Sorrento were the wild, wild west.

• *With your back still to the sea, head to the far-right corner of the square, behind the statue of Torquato Tasso, the square's namesake. (A Sorrento native, he was a lively Renaissance poet.) Peek into the big courtyard of Palazzo Correale (#18, behind the statue in the right corner) to get a feel for an 18th-century aristocratic palace's courtyard, lined with characteristic tiles. In the passage, a fun shop sells regional products and offers free biscuits and tastes of liqueurs. As you're leaving the courtyard, on your immediate left you'll see the narrow...*

Via Santa Maria della Pietà: Here, just a few yards off the noisy main drag, is a street that goes back centuries before Christ. About 100 yards down the lane, at #24 (on the left), find a 13th-century palace (no balconies back then...for security reasons), now an elementary school. A few steps farther on, you'll see a tiny shrine across the street. Typical of southern Italy, it's where the faithful pray to their saint, who contacts Mary, who contacts Jesus, who contacts God. This shrine is a bit more direct—it starts right with Mary.

• *Continue down the lane, which ends at the...*

Cathedral: This is the seat of the local bishop. Pop in for a cool stroll around the ambulatory, checking out the impressive *intarsio* (inlaid-wood) doors. Two sets, inlaid on both sides, show many scenes of the town and its industry. The doors facing the main street include an old town map. These were made to celebrate the pope's visit in 1992. Also notice the intricate inlaid Stations of the Cross (free, daily 8:30-18:00, closed 11:00-12:15 on Sun).

• *Backtrack 10 yards down Via Santa Maria della Pietà, turn left, cross busy Corso Italia (look back at the bell tower, with its ancient Roman columns at the base), and go straight on Via P. Reginaldo Giuliani, following the...*

Old Greek Street Plan: Notice here how streets are laid out—east-west for the most sunlight and north-south for the prevailing and cooling breeze.

• *One block ahead is a fine old portico, the...*

Sorrento Men's Club: Once the meeting place of the town's nobles, this club has been a retreat for retired working-class men for generations. Strictly no women—and no phones.

Italian men venerate their mothers. (Italians joke that Jesus must have been a southern Italian because his mother believed her son was God, he believed his mom was a virgin, and he lived at home with her until he was 30.) But Italian men have also built into their culture ways to be on their own. Here, men play cards and gossip under a historic emblem of the city and a finely frescoed 16th-century dome, with its marvelous 3-D scenes.

• *At the Men's Club, turn right onto...*

Via San Cesareo: This touristy pedestrian-only shopping street leads four or five blocks back to Piazza Tasso. All along the way, you can peruse (and sample) lemon products in the very competitive shops. Notice the huge ancient doorways with their tiny doors—to let the right people in, carefully, during a more-dangerous age.

• *At the noisy street on the edge of Piazza Tasso, turn left and fight the traffic downhill to the next square, with another...*

Statue of St. Anthony (Antonino): Sorrento's town saint humbly looms among the palms, facing the basilica where his reliquary lies (under the altar in the crypt, surrounded by lots of votives). From here, you can quit the walk and stay in the city center, or continue to the village-like waterfront (if it's before 20:00, you can catch a bus to get back).

• *Exit the square diagonally to the left and gradually wind your way downhill toward Marina Grande (not down the street that leads to the Foreigners' Club and port). After a block or so, on the right you'll see the trees in front of the Imperial Hotel Tramontano, and to their right a path leading to a...*

Cliffside Square: This fine public square, the Villa Comunale, overlooks the harbor. Belly up to the banister to enjoy the view of the little harbor and the Bay of Naples. From here, steps zigzag down to Marina Piccola, where lounge chairs, filled by vacationers working on tans, line the sundecks. The Franciscan church fronting this square has a great little cloister (pop in to see Sicilian Gothic—a 13th-century mix of Norman, Gothic, and Arabic styles).

• *Return to the road and continue downhill, walking through the next square (Piazza della Vittoria), which offers another grand view. Stay on the road closest to the water—it eventually leads to stairs that zigzag down to Marina Grande, Sorrento's big harbor. Just before reaching the harbor, you pass under an...*

Ancient Greek Gate: This gate is a reminder that Marina Grande is a separate town from Sorrento, with its own proud residents. It's said that even their cats look different. Because Marina Grande dwellers lived outside the wall and were more susceptible to rape, pillage, and plunder, Sorrentines believe that they come from Saracen (Turkish pirate) stock. Sorrentines still scare their children by saying, "Behave—or the Turks will take you away."

Marina Grande's economy is still based on its fishing fleet. People respect old traditions. Women wear black when a relative dies (1 year for an uncle, aunt, or sibling; 2-3 years for a husband or parent). Men get off easy, just wearing a black button if their loved one dies.

There are two recommended restaurants on the harbor. **Trattoria da Emilia** has an old newspaper clipping, tacked near the door, about Sophia Loren filming here. On the far side of the harbor, **Ristorante Delfino** boasts a sundeck for a lazy drink before or after lunch.

From here, buses return to the center at Piazza Tasso every hour (€2.40, buy ticket at tobacco shop).

Sights in Sorrento

▲▲**Strolling**—Take time to explore the surprisingly pleasant old city between Corso Italia and the sea. Views from the pub-

lic park next to Imperial Hotel Tramontano are worth the detour. Each night in summer (May-Oct at 19:30; Nov-April weekends only), the police close off the Corso Italia to traffic, and Sorrento's main drag becomes a thriving people scene. The *passeggiata* peaks at about 22:00. (When Piazza Tasso and the main thoroughfare are closed to traffic, buses for Via Capo leave from up on Via degli Aranci, a short walk from Piazza Tasso along Via Fuorimura.)

Lemon Products Galore—Via San Cesareo is lined with hard-working rival shops selling a mind-boggling array of lemon products and offering samples of lots of sour goodies. Poke around for a pungent experience.

▲**Lemon Grove Garden (Giardini di Cataldo)**—This small park consists of an inviting organic lemon and orange grove lined with shady, welcoming paths. The owners of the grove are seasoned green thumbs, having worked the orchard through many generations. You'll see that they've even grafted orange-tree branches onto a lemon tree so that both fruits now grow on the same tree. The garden is dotted with benches, tables, and an inviting little tasting (and buying) stand. You'll get a chance to sniff and taste the varieties of lemons, and enjoy free samples of chilled *limoncello* along with various other homemade liqueurs made from basil, mandarins, or fennel (enthusiastically free, daily April-Sept 9:30-20:00 or 21:00, Oct-March 10:00-sunset, closed in rainy weather, tel. 081-807-4040). The main shop selling their organic homemade products and tasty gelato is across from the Corso Italia entrance at #267; a smaller stand is inside. Enter the garden either on Corso Italia (100 yards north of the train station—where painted tiles

Lemons

Around here, *limoni* are ubiquitous: screaming yellow painted on ceramics, dainty bottles of *limoncello*, and lemons the size of softballs at the fruit stand. The Amalfi Coast and Sorrento area produces several different kinds of lemons.

The gigantic bumpy lemons are actually citrons, called *cedri*, and are more for show—they're pulpier than they are juicy, and make a good marmalade. The juicy *sfusato sorrentino*, grown only in Sorrento, is shaped like an American football, while the *sfusato amalfitano*, with knobby points on both ends, is less juicy but equally aromatic. These two kinds of luscious lemons are used in sweets such as *granita* (shaved ice doused in lemonade), *limoncello* (a candy-like liqueur with a big kick, called *limoncino* on the Cinque Terre), *delizia* (a dome of fluffy cake filled and slathered with a thick whipped lemon cream), *spremuta di limone* (fresh-squeezed lemon juice), and, of course, gelato or *sorbetto alla limone*.

show lemon fantasies), or at the intersection of Via Capasso and Via Rota (next to the Hotel La Meridiana Sorrento).

▲**Swimming near Sorrento**—If you require immediate tanning, you can rent a chair on the pier by the port. There are no great beaches in Sorrento—the gravelly, jam-packed private beaches of **Marina Piccola** are more for partying than pampering, and there's just a tiny spot for public use.

A sandy beach is two miles away at **Meta.** While the Meta Circumvesuviana stop is a very long walk from the beach (or a €25 cab ride), the red-and-white bus #A goes directly from Piazza Tasso to the Meta beach (last stop, schedule posted for hourly returns). At Meta, you'll find pizzerias, snack bars, and a little free section of beach, but the place is mostly dominated by several sprawling private-beach complexes—if you go, pay for a spot in one of these. Lido Metamare seems best (open May-Sept, €2.50 entry; lockable changing cabins, lounge chairs, and more available for an extra fee; tel. 081-532-2505). It's a very Italian scene—locals complain that it's "too local" (i.e., inundated with Naples' riffraff)—with light lunches, a playground, a manicured beach, loud pop music...and no international tourists.

Tarzan might take Jane to the wild and stony beach at **Punta del Capo,** a 15-minute bus ride from Piazza Tasso (the same bus #A explained above, but in the opposite direction from Meta; 2/

hour, get off at stop in front of the American Bar, then walk 10 minutes past ruined Roman Villa di Pollio). Another good choice is **Marina di Puolo,** a tiny fishing town popular in the summer for its sandy beach, surfside restaurants, and beachfront disco (to get here, stay on bus #A a bit farther—ask driver to let you off at Marina di Puolo—then follow signs and hike down about 15 minutes).

Tennis—The Sorrento Sport Snack Bar has two fine courts open to the public (daily 9:30-23:00, until 20:00 in winter, €12/hour including rackets and balls for two people, call for reservation, across from recommended Grand Hotel Ambasciatori at Via Califano 5, tel. 081-807-1616).

Scuba Diving—To escape the shops, dive deep into the Mediterranean. PADI-certified Futuro Mare offers a one-hour boat ride out to the protected marine zone that lies between Sorrento and Capri, where you can try the beginners' dive (€90, includes instruction and complete supervision, April-Oct usually daily at 9:30). The boat also takes experienced certified divers (1 dive-€60, 2 dives-€95, April-Oct daily at 9:30 and 14:00). The whole experience takes about three hours. Prices include all equipment, transportation, and the dive itself, which lasts about 40 minutes for both novices and experts (call a day or two in advance to reserve, tel. 081-877-1472, mobile 349-653-6323, www.futuromare.it, info@futuromare.it).

Boat Rental—You can rent motor boats big enough for four people (€150/day, plus gas—figure about €30 for a trip to Capri, more with a skipper; with your back to the ferry-ticket offices, it's to the left around the corner at Via Marina Piccola 43; tel. 081-807-2283, www.nauticasicsic.com).

Nightlife in Sorrento

English vacationers come here in droves (many have holidayed here annually for decades). The town is filled with pubs that try to help British guests feel right at home.

Pubs and Clubs

The English Inn offers both a streetside pub and a more refined-feeling garden out back—at least until the evening, when the stereo starts blaring. Order up baked beans on toast, fish-and-chips, or just a draft beer (daily, 8:30 until after midnight, Corso Italia 55, tel. 081-807-4357).

Photo offers a snapshot of contemporary Italy with a creative food and drink menu, DJ music, and people-watching among stylish Italians on vacation (described later, under "Eating in Sorrento").

The **Foreigners' Club** offers live Neapolitan songs, Sinatra-style classics, and jazzy elevator-type music nightly at 20:00 throughout the summer. It's just right for old-timers feeling frisky (in the center; described earlier under "Helpful Hints").

Theater Show

At **Teatro Tasso,** a hardworking troupe puts on *The Sorrento Musical,* a folk-music show that treats visitors to a schmaltzy dose of Neapolitan Tarantella music and dance—complete with "Funiculì Funiculà" and "Santa Loo-chee-yee-yah." The 75-minute Italian-language extravaganza features a cast of 14 playing guitar, violin, mandolin, and tambourines, and singing operatically from Neapolitan balconies...with Vesuvius erupting in the background. Your ticket includes a drink before and after the show. While tickets normally cost €25, Maurizio promises my readers tickets for €20 in 2013. He also offers readers a €40 dinner package (normally €50) that includes a four-course meal, drinks, and a seat at the show (discounts good only if you buy tickets directly from their box office and show this book, maximum 2 tickets or dinner packages per book; the earlier in the day you reserve, the better your seats; nightly April-Oct at 21:30, bar opens 45 minutes before show, dinner starts at 20:00 and must be reserved in advance—in person or by email, but not by phone, box office open virtually all day long, theater seats 350, facing Piazza Sant'Antonino in the old town, tel. 081-807-5525, info@teatro tasso.com).

Sleeping in Sorrento

Hotels here often charge the same for a room whether it has a view, balcony, or neither. At hotels that offer sea views, ask for a room *"con balcone, con vista sul mare"* (with a balcony, with a sea view). *"Tranquillo"* is taken as a request for a quieter room off the street. Hotels listed are either near the train station and city center or along the way to Punta del Capo, a 20-minute walk—or short bus ride—from the station (for locations, see the map on page 992). While many hotels close for the winter, you should have no trouble finding a room any time except in August, when the town is jammed and many hotel prices go way up. Most hotels have two rates: high season (April-Oct) and low. Outside of summer, prices can be soft—it doesn't hurt to ask for a discount (always show this book). Splurge for a hotel with air-conditioning if you wilt in the heat, but be aware that it often costs extra. Note: The spindly, more exotic, and more tranquil Amalfi Coast town of Positano (see next chapter) is also a good place to spend the night.

Sleep Code

(€1 = about $1.40, country code: 39)
S = Single, **D** = Double/Twin, **T** = Triple, **Q** = Quad, **b** = bathroom,
s = shower only. Unless otherwise noted, credit cards are accepted, English is spoken, and breakfast is included. A local tax of €1 per person, per night (more for fancier hotels) is not included in these rates.

To help you sort easily through these listings, I've divided the accommodations into three categories based on the price for a standard double room with bath:

$$$ Higher Priced—Most rooms €140 or more.
  $$ Moderately Priced—Most rooms between €80-140.
    $ Lower Priced—Most rooms €80 or less.

Prices can change without notice; verify the hotel's current rates online or by email.

In the Town Center

$$$ Hotel Antiche Mura, with 50 rooms and four stars, is sophisticated, elegant, and plush, offering all the amenities you could need. Surrounded by lemon trees, the pool and sundeck are an oasis. Just a block off the main square, it's cheaper than other hotels nearby, and also quieter because it's perched on the ledge of a dramatic ravine (small-windowed Db-€150, Db-€189, balcony Db-€250; Michele promises 15 percent off in 2013 if you reserve direct, mention this book, and pay cash; about a third cheaper Nov-March, includes impressive buffet breakfast, air-con, elevator, free Wi-Fi, parking-€10/day, a block inland from Piazza Tasso at Via Fuorimura 7, tel. 081-807-3523, fax 081-807-1323, www.hotel antichemura.com, info@hotelantichemura.com).

$$$ Plaza Sorrento is a new, contemporary-feeling, upscale refuge in the very center of town (next door to Antiche Mura). Its 65 well-soundproofed rooms, arranged on color-coded floors, are mod and minimalist, and the rooftop swimming pool is inviting. Their "comfort" and "superior" rooms offer views and balconies (for €20-40 more), but if you want views you'll find far better ones on Via Capo, described later (standard Db-€180, elevator, air-con, free Wi-Fi, Via Fuorimura 3, tel. 081-878-2831, www.plaza sorrento.com, info@plazasorrento.com).

$$ Casa Astarita B&B is a shining gem in the middle of town, with a crazy-quilt-tiled entryway. You'll find six bright, tranquil, air-conditioned rooms (three with little balconies) and a fully stocked communal fridge and sideboard for help-yourself breakfasts in the rustic-yet-elegant common room. Despite double-paned windows, pub noise can seep into the three front-facing, balcony rooms (Db-€115, Tb-€130, mention this book for these rates, free Internet access and Wi-Fi, 50 yards past the cathedral on Corso Italia at #67, tel. 081-877-4906, fax 081-877-0326, www.casastarita.com, info@casastarita.com, Annamaria and Alfonso). If there's no one at reception, ask at Hotel Mignon (described next)—the same family runs both hotels.

$$ Hotel Mignon rents 24 soothing blue rooms with pretty, tiled public spaces in a central location near the cathedral (Sb-€80, Db-€105, Tb-€130, these prices good with this book when you reserve direct, air-con, free Internet access and Wi-Fi, rooftop sundeck, some balconies but no views; from the cathedral, walk a block up Corso Italia to Via Sersale 9; tel. 081-807-3824, fax 081-877-4348, www.sorrentohotelmignon.com, info@sorrentohotelmignon.com, Paolo).

$$ Hotel del Corso is a funky Old World three-star hotel with 26 decent rooms. Family-run with few frills, it doesn't get any more central than this (Db-€120, Tb-€150, Qb-€170, email for specials, €10 off-season discount when you mention this book and pay cash, elevator, air-con, free Internet access, pay Wi-Fi in some rooms, rooftop sun terrace, self-service laundry, closed Dec-Feb, near Piazza Tasso at Corso Italia 134, tel. 081-807-1016, fax 081-807-3157, www.hoteldelcorso.com, info@hoteldelcorso.com, Luca and Imma).

$$ Il Palazzo Starace B&B, a lesser value than other hotels in this price range, offers seven tidy rooms in a little alley off Corso Italia (opposite Hotel del Corso, listed above), one block from Piazza Tasso (Db-€90, €10 extra for balcony, family room-€150, a bit higher in Aug, 10 percent off with cash and this book in 2013, includes small breakfast at a bar around the corner, air-con, no elevator but a luggage dumbwaiter; ring bell at Via Santa Maria della Pietà 9, then climb 3 floors; tel. 081-878-4031, mobile 338-276-1418, fax 081-532-9344, www.palazzostarace.com, info@palazzostarace.com, Giovanna).

$ Ulisse Deluxe Hostel is the best budget deal in town, with public areas that feel more like an elegant hotel than a hostel. The 56 marble-tiled rooms have big private bathrooms, so unless you choose to sleep in its dorm, the only thing hostel-like about this place is the price—it's an excellent value (Db-€70, Tb-€105, Qb-€140, €25/bunk in 2- to 8-bed single-sex dorm, these rates valid when you mention this book and reserve direct, breakfast-€7, air-con, elevator, free Wi-Fi, spa and pool use extra, Via del Mare 22, tel. 081-877-4753, fax 081-877-4093, www.ulissedeluxe.com, info@ulissedeluxe.com). The hostel is a 5-minute walk from the old-town action, hiding beneath the big parking lot—go downhill along the right side of the lot to find the entrance.

$ Hotel Nice rents 29 simple, cramped, cheap rooms with high ceilings 100 yards in front of the train station on the noisy main drag. This last resort is worth considering only for its very handy-to-the-train-station location. Alfonso promises that you can have a quiet room—which is critical given the thin windows and busy location—if you request it with your booking email (Db-€75, €85 in Aug; extra bed-€20; 10 percent discount when you book direct, mention this book, and pay cash; air-con, elevator, rooftop terrace, Wi-Fi, closed Nov-March, Corso Italia 257, tel. 081-878-1650, fax 081-878-3086, www.hotelnice.it, info@hotelnice.it).

$ Hostel Le Sirene, a tiny hostel four blocks from the train station, offers 50 of the cheapest beds in town (€18/bunk in 8- to 10-bed dorms with bath, Db-€65, includes tiny breakfast and linens, no curfew, open year-round, elevator, pay Internet access, free Wi-Fi, luggage storage, shared kitchen, Via degli Aranci 156, check in at bar next door, tel. 081-807-2925, fax 081-877-1371, www.hostellesirene.com, info@hostellesirene.com).

At the East End of Town

These hotels are only a few minutes' walk beyond the town center. To reach them, head a block in front of the train station, turn right onto Corso Italia, then left down Via Capasso (which eventually winds right and becomes Via Califano).

$$$ Grand Hotel Ambasciatori is a sumptuous four-star hotel with 100 rooms, a cliffside setting, a sprawling garden, and a pool. This is Humphrey Bogart land, with plush public spaces, a relaxing stay-a-while ambience, and a free elevator to its "private beach"—actually a sundeck built out over the water (prices vary wildly, but in high season generally: viewless Db-€200, sea-view Db-€350, 10 percent discount with this book if you book direct, also check website for specials, elevator, air-con in summer, balconies in most rooms, pay Internet access, free Wi-Fi, parking-€20/day, closed Nov-March, Via Califano 18, tel. 081-878-2025, fax 081-807-1021, www.ambasciatorisorrento.com, ambasciatori@man niellohotels.com).

$$$ Hotel La Meridiana Sorrento, an overpriced three-star option with everything but character, offers business-class public spaces and 45 soulless, dated rooms, including some with views (Db-€160, Tb-€190, Qb-€240, €10-20 extra for views and balconies, air-con, elevator, big rooftop terrace with grand views, next door to public Lemon Grove Garden at Via Rota 1, tel. 081-807-3535, fax 081-807-3484, www.lameridianasorrento.com, info@la meridianasorrento.com).

With a View on Via Capo

These hotels are outside of town, near the cape (straight out Corso Italia, which turns into Via Capo). Once you're set up, commuting into town by bus or on foot is easy. Hotel Minerva and Albergo Settimo Cielo are my favorite Sorrento splurges, while Hotel Désirée and Hotel Elios are better budget bets. If you're in Sorrento to stay put and luxuriate, these accommodations are perfect (although I'd rather luxuriate in Positano—see next chapter).

Getting to Via Capo: From the city center, it's a gradually uphill 15-minute walk (20 minutes from train station, last part is a bit steeper), a €20 taxi ride, or a cheap bus ride. An occasional Via Capo-bound bus leaves from the train station itself (about every 40 minutes, usually blue or green-and-white SITA buses, direction: Massa, don't take one heading for Positano/Amalfi). Many more buses leave from Piazza Tasso in the city center, a five-minute walk from the station (go down a block and turn left on Corso Italia; from far side of the piazza, look for red-and-white bus #A, about 3/hour). Tickets for either bus are sold at the station newsstand and tobacco shops (€2.40). Most Via Capo hotels are near the Hotel Belair bus stop. If you're headed to Via Capo after 19:30, when the center (and Piazza Tasso bus stop) is closed to traffic, catch the bus instead on Via degli Aranci (with your back to the station, wind left, up and around it; the bus stop is near Bar Paradise).

Getting from Via Capo into Town: Buses work great once you get the hang of them (and it's particularly gratifying to avoid the taxi racket). To reach downtown Sorrento from Via Capo, catch any bus heading downhill from Hotel Belair (3/hour, buses run all day and evening).

$$$ Hotel Minerva is like a sun-worshipper's temple. Catch the elevator at Via Capo 32. Getting off on the fifth floor, you'll step onto a spectacular terrace with outrageous Mediterranean views, a small cliff-hanging swimming pool, and a cold-water Jacuzzi—all complementing 60 large, tiled *limoncello* rooms with views (Db-€160, Tb-€200, €10 more for balcony, these discounted prices promised with this book through 2013 only if mentioned when you reserve, can be cheaper in shoulder season, air-con, free Internet access and Wi-Fi, parking-€15/day, closed Nov-March, Via Capo 30, tel. 081-878-1011, fax 081-878-1949, www.minerva sorrento.com, minerva@acampora.it).

$$$ Hotel La Tonnarella is an old-time Sorrentine villa with several terraces, stylish tiles, and indifferent service. Eighteen of its 24 rooms have views of the sea (non-view Db-€130, "superior" sea-view or balcony Db-€180, "deluxe" Db with view terrace-€200, exotic view suite with terrace-€310, email for best rates, €30/person half-pension available, air-con, Internet access and Wi-Fi, free parking, small beach with elevator access, closed Dec-Feb, Via

Capo 31, tel. 081-878-1153, fax 081-878-2169, www.latonnarella.it, info@latonnarella.it).

$$ Albergo Settimo Cielo ("Seventh Heaven") offers all the views and lazy resort trappings you could want, and is run by a family that really hustles to provide a fine value. At this old-fashioned cliff-hanger sitting 300 steps above Marina Grande, the reception is just off the waterfront side of the road, and the elevator passes down through four floors with 50 clean-and-comfortable rooms—all with grand views, and many with balconies. The rooms feel dated and spartan for the price, but you're paying for the views and warm welcome (Sb-€120, Db-€140, Tb-€180, Qb-€215, check website for specials or ask for 5 percent discount on these rates in 2013 when you mention this book when reserving, air-con in summer, free Internet access and Wi-Fi, free parking, inviting pool in the summer, sun terrace, Via Capo 27, tel. 081-878-1012, fax 081-807-3290, www.hotelsettimocielo.com, info@hotelsettimocielo .com, Giuseppe, sons Stefano and Massimo, and daughter Serena).

$$ Hotel Désirée is a modest affair, with reasonable rates, humbler vistas, and no traffic noise. The 22 basic rooms have high, ravine-facing or partial-sea views, and half come with balconies (all same price). Most rooms have fans, and there's a fine rooftop sunning terrace and lovable (if smellable) cats. Eco-friendly Corinna, daughter Cassandra, and receptionist Antonio are hugely helpful with tips on exploring the peninsula (Sb-€60, small Db-€75, Db-€85, Tb-€105, Qb-€115, lots of stairs with no elevator, free Internet access and Wi-Fi, laundry-€8, free parking, shares driveway and beach access with La Tonnarella, Via Capo 31, tel. & fax 081-878-1563, www.desireehotelsorrento.com, info@desireehotel sorrento.com).

$ Hotel Elios, warmly run by Gianna, is humble...much like a Sorrentine *nonna*'s house. It offers 14 simple but spacious rooms— 12 with balconies and views—a panoramic sun terrace, and a quiet atmosphere. She serves a small continental breakfast, and you're welcome to use the kitchen and dining room (Sb-€50, Db-€80, Tb-€100, extra bed-€20, family rooms, cash only, free Wi-Fi, free parking, closed Dec-March, Via Capo 33, tel. 081-878-1812, www .hotelelios.it, info@hotelelios.it).

Eating in Sorrento

Gourmet Splurges Downtown

In a town proud to have no McDonald's, consider eating well for a few extra bucks. Both of these places are worthwhile splurges run by a hands-on boss with a passion for good food and exacting service. Be prepared to relax and stay a while.

Ristorante il Buco, once the cellar of an old monastery, is now a small, dressy restaurant that serves delightfully presented, playful, and creative modern Mediterranean dishes under a grand, rustic arch. Peppe and his staff love to explain exactly what's on the plate. The dashing team of cooks builds sophisticated dishes with an emphasis on seafood in a state-of-the-art kitchen, while a plasma-screen TV out by the front door shows all the action. Peppe, who holds the only Michelin star in town, designs his menu around whatever's fresh, and travels in the winter to assemble a wine list sure to offer connoisseurs something new and memorable. Reservations are usually necessary to sit inside under their elegant vault (€16-20 pastas, €20-28 *secondi*, dinners run from about €50 plus wine, extravagant tasting *menu*s for €55-85, 10 percent discount when you show this book in 2013, always a good vegetarian selection, Thu-Tue 12:00-15:00 & 19:00-23:00, closed Wed and Jan; just off Piazza Sant'Antonino—facing the basilica, go under the grand arch on the left and immediately enter the restaurant at Il Rampa Marina Piccola 5; tel. 081-878-2354).

L'Antica Trattoria serves more traditional cuisine from an inviting but pricey menu in a *romantico* candlelit ambience. The atmosphere is sedate and a bit old-school pretentious, with formally attired waiters. Run by the same family since 1930, the restaurant has a trellised garden outside and intimate nooks inside (ideal for small groups). Walk around the labyrinthine interior before you select a place to sit. Aldo and sons will take care of you, while the Joe Cocker-esque resident mandolin player entertains. Their wine list features well-known wines from the region. They offer several fixed-price meals—including a €20 two-course lunch and a €39 four-course dinner—or you can order à la carte (€15-20 pastas, €26-29 *secondi*, 10 percent discount when you show this book in 2013, vegetarian options, daily 12:00-23:30, closed Mon Nov-Feb, air-con, reservations smart, Via Padre R. Giuliani 33, tel. 081-807-1082).

Eating Well and Cheaply Downtown

Inn Bufalito, which focuses on regional Campania specialties, backs up its motto: "Eating well is for everyone." Franco and his sharp staff serve up a changing menu of pizza, pasta, and all things buffalo, including a delicious selection of *mozzarella di bufala*. The smartly designed space has a modern, borderline-trendy, casual atmosphere and a fun indoor-outdoor vibe (€6-9 salads, €8-10 pastas, €9-14 *secondi*, no cover charge, daily 12:00-24:00, closed Tue off-season and closed entirely in Jan-Feb, Vico I Fuoro 21, tel. 081-365-6975).

Photo, a sleek and modern place, has a creative menu, secluded garden, and DJ music. Less traditional and more expensive, it's fun for a drink or a unique meal (May-Nov daily 18:00-late, Dec-April open Fri-Sat only, reservations smart, Via Correale 19, 4-minute walk from Piazza Tasso, tel. 081-877-3686).

Ristorante Pizzeria da Gigino, lively and congested, makes huge, tasty Neapolitan-style pizzas in their wood-burning oven (€6-10 pizzas and pastas, €8-12 *secondi*, daily 12:00-24:00, closed Jan-Feb; just off Piazza Sant'Antonino—take first road to the left of Sant'Antonino as you face him, pass under the archway, and take the first left to Via degli Archi 15; tel. 081-878-1927, Antonino).

Ristorante Pizzeria Lanterna Due offers an agreeable family-run atmosphere celebrating the "food, art, and music of Italian cooking," with a fun staff and decent food. Join the other tourists at the long line of tables along the alley, or in the air-conditioned interior (€8 pastas, €10 *secondi*, daily 12:00-15:30 & 18:00-23:00, Via Santa Maria delle Grazie 28, tel. 081-807-4521).

Meating, as its name implies, focuses on top-quality meats, from homemade sausages to giant steaks on a wood-fired grill. You'll find no seafood or pasta here, but there are a variety of vegetable dishes and delicious local cheeses, along with a reasonably priced selection of wine (€10-18 steaks, daily 11:30-15:00 & 18:30-24:00, closed Wed except in July-Sept, Via della Pietà 20, tel. 081-878-2891).

Pizzeria da Franco seems to be Sorrento's favorite place for basic, casual pizza in a fun, untouristy atmosphere. There's nothing fancy about this place—just locals on benches eating hot sandwiches and great pizzas served on waxed paper in a square tin. It's packed to the rafters with a youthful crowd that doesn't mind the plastic cups (€6-8 pizzas, €5 salads, daily 12:00-2:00 in the morning, just across from Lemon Grove Garden on busy Corso Italia at #265, tel. 081-877-2066).

Picnics: Markets and take-out pizzerias abound in the old town. If you fancy a picnic dinner on your balcony, on the hotel terrace, or in the Lemon Grove Garden, get a pizza to go at Pizzeria da Franco (listed above) or groceries at the **Decò supermarket** (Mon-Sat 8:30-20:30, Sun 9:30-13:30 & 17:00-20:30, Corso Italia 223).

Gelato: Near the train station, **Gelateria David** has many repeat customers (so many flavors, so little time). In 1957, Augusto Davide opened a *gelateria* in Sorrento, and his grandson, Mario, proudly carries on the tradition today (the gelato is still made on-site). Before choosing, sample *Profumi di Sorrento* (an explosive sorbet of mixed fruits), "Sorrento moon" (white almond with lemon zest), and lemon crème. They also serve simple meals at fair prices (daily 9:30-24:00, shorter hours in spring and fall, closed Nov-March, a block below the train station at Via Marziale 9, tel. 081-807-3649). Mario also offers gelato-making classes for a behind-the-scenes look at Italy's favorite dessert (€10/person, 4-person minimum, 1 hour, call or email ahead to reserve, gelateriadavid@yahoo.it).

Don't mistake this place for the similarly named Gelateria Davide, in the town center, owned by a distant relative, but not as good.

At **Gelateria Primavera,** another local favorite, Antonio and Alberta whip up 70 exotic flavors—and still have time to make pastries for the pope (and everybody else—check out the photos). Try the *noce* (pronounced NO-chay), made from local walnuts (€3 for up to three flavors, daily 9:00-2:00 in the morning, just west of Piazza Tasso at Corso Italia 142, tel. 081-807-3252).

Dinner with Sea Views

For a decent dinner *con vista,* head for a view terrace at one of these restaurants. To get to Marina Grande, where the first two are located, follow the directions from the cliffside square on the "Welcome to Sorrento" walk (described earlier). For a less scenic route, walk down Via del Mare, past the recommended Ulisse Deluxe Hostel, to the harbor. Either way, it's about a 15-minute stroll from downtown. You can also take bus #D from Piazza Tasso (€2.40).

Ristorante Delfino gets their seafood right off the fishermen's boats at Marina Grande, and serves it up in big portions to hungry locals in a quiet and bright pier restaurant. The cooking, service, and setting are all top-notch, and the prices are good. The restaurant is lovingly run by Luisa, her brothers Andrea and Roberto, and her husband Antonio. They take good care of their guests and give travelers who carry this book a little glass of *limoncello* to cap the experience. If you're here for lunch, take advantage of the wonderful sundeck—show this book to get an hour of relaxation and digestion on the lounge chairs (€11-16 pastas, €11-20 *secondi,* daily 11:30-15:30 & 18:30-23:00, closed Nov-March; at Marina Grande, facing the water, go all the way to the left and follow signs; tel. 081-878-2038).

Trattoria da Emilia, on the tranquil Marina Grande waterfront, is considerably more rustic, less expensive, and good for straightforward, typical Sorrentine home-cooking, including fresh fish, lots of fried seafood, and *gnocchi di mamma*—potato dumplings with meat sauce, basil, and mozzarella (€6-11 pastas, €7-12 *secondi,* daily 12:15-15:00 & 19:00-22:30, closed Tue Nov-Feb, no reservations taken, indoor and outdoor pier seating, cash only, tel. 081-807-2720).

The **Foreigners' Club Restaurant** has the best sea views in town (with a sprawling terrace under breezy palms), live music nightly at 20:00 (May-Oct), and passable meals. It's a good spot for dessert or an after-dinner *limoncello* (€7-8 pastas and pizzas, daily, bar opens at 9:30, meals served 11:00-23:00, Via Luigi de Maio 35, tel. 081-877-3263).

On Via Capo

Verde Mare is the locals' pick for a cheaper place (Thu-Tue 12:30-14:45 & 19:00-23:30, closed Wed, 300 yards uphill from La Tonnarella and other recommended hotels—see map on page 992, tel. 081-878-2589).

Sorrento Connections

It's impressively fast to zip by boat from Sorrento to most coastal towns and islands during the summer, when there are many more departures. In fact, it's quicker and easier for residents to get around by fast boat than by car or train (see "By Boat," later, and the map on page 989).

By Train and Bus

From Sorrento to Naples, Pompeii, and Herculaneum by Circumvesuviana Train: This commuter train runs twice hourly between Naples and Sorrento (www.vesuviana.it). From Sorrento, it's about 30 minutes to Pompeii, 50 minutes to Herculaneum (€2.10 one-way for either trip), and 70 minutes to Naples (€4 one-way). There's no round-trip discount, and the €12 all-day pass is generally not worthwhile (except on weekends, when it's called a "weekend pass" and is roughly half-price—€6.30). If there's a line at the train station, you can also buy tickets at the appropriately named Snack Bar (across from the main ticket office) or downstairs at the newsstand.

When returning to Naples' Centrale Station on the Circumvesuviana, get off at the next-to-the-last station, Garibaldi (Centrale station is just up the escalator). Bonus: When returning from Sorrento, your Circumvesuviana ticket includes travel on the Naples Metro or bus system within three hours of validation (no need to validate again). The trip is also covered by the Campania ArteCard—see page 934. The schedule is printed in the free *Surrentum* magazine (available at TI). For more information on the Circumvesuviana and theft precautions, see "Getting Around the Region" on page 966 of the Naples chapter. Note that the risk of theft is mostly limited to suburban Naples, but can be a problem anywhere. Going between Sorrento and Pompeii or Herculaneum is generally safer.

From Sorrento to Naples Airport: Six Curreri buses run daily to and from the airport; confirm the schedule at the TI (€10, pay driver, daily at 6:30, 8:30, 10:30, 12:00, 14:00, and 16:30, likely 2 additional departures May-Oct, 1.5 hours, departs from in front of train station, tel. 081-801-5420, www.curreriviaggi.it). Although it's possible to connect through Naples (either take a jet boat to Naples, then cross the street to catch the airport bus on Piazza

Municipio; or ride the Circumvesuviana to Naples' Centrale Station to catch the airport bus from Piazza Garibaldi), the direct bus is more convenient and reliable.

To the Amalfi Coast: See page 1023.

To Rome: Most people ride the Circumvesuviana 70 minutes to Naples, then catch the Frecciarossa express train to Rome. However, the direct Sorrento-Rome bus is cheaper, and can actually be more convenient. Marozzi buses leave Sorrento's train station daily for Rome's Tiburtina station (€17, Mon-Sat at 6:00 and 17:00, Sun at 17:00, off-season at 6:00 only, 4 hours; buy tickets by phone, at some travel agencies, or on board for a €3 surcharge; also stops at Pompei Scavi and Naples' Port Beverello, tel. 080-579-0111, www.marozzivt.it). A Curreri bus makes the trip as well, but only in the summer (€16, departs Mon-Sat at 6:30, 4 hours, tel. 081-801-5420, www.curreriviaggi.it).

By Boat

The number of boats that run per day varies according to the season. The frequency indicated here is for roughly mid-May through mid-October, with more boats per day in the peak of summer and fewer off-season. Check all schedules with the TI, your hotel, or online (visit the individual boat company websites—see below—or visit www.capritourism.com, select English, and click on "Shipping timetable"). The Caremar line, a subsidized state-run ferry company, takes cars, offers fewer departures, and is just a bit slower—but cheaper—than the other boat. All of the boats take several hundred people each—and frequently fill up.

From Sorrento to Capri: Boats run at least hourly. Your options include a fast **ferry** (*traghetto* or *nave veloce*, 4/day, 25 minutes, €13, run by Caremar, tel. 081-807-3077, www.caremar.it) or a slightly faster, pricier **jet boat** (*aliscafi*, 18/day, 20 minutes, €15, run by Gescab, tel. 081-807-1812, www.gescab.it). To minimize the crowds on Capri, it's best to buy your ticket at 8:00 and take the 8:25 jet boat (if you miss it, try to depart by 9:30 at the very latest). These early boats can be jammed, but it's worth it once you reach the island.

From Sorrento to Other Points: Naples (6/day, departs roughly every 2 hours, 35 minutes, €11; starting at 7:20), **Positano** (mid-April-mid-Oct only, 2-4/day, 35 minutes, €15), **Amalfi** (mid-April-mid-Oct only, 2-4/day, 1.25 hours, €15). For a slightly less touristy alternative to Capri, consider the nearby island of **Ischia** (1/day, Easter-Nov only, departure usually around 9:30, more frequent from Naples, 1 hour, €36 round-trip).

Getting to Sorrento's Port: To get from Sorrento's Piazza Tasso to Marina Piccola (the port), walk down the stairs near the statue's left side (about 10 minutes), or take the slightly longer road (with fewer stairs) that passes by the TI and Foreigners' Club. Or, from Piazza Sant'Antonino, catch a red-and-white bus #B or #C (3/hour, €1, buy ticket at tobacco shop and specify that you're going to the *porto*) or the little blue bus (4/hour, €1, buy ticket from driver). Boat tickets are sold only at the port.

Capri

Capri was made famous as the vacation hideaway of Roman emperors Augustus and Tiberius. In the 19th century, it was the haunt of

Romantic Age aristocrats on their Grand Tour of Europe. But these days, the island is a world-class tourist trap, packed with gawky nametag-wearing visitors searching for the rich and famous, and finding only their prices.

The "Island of Dreams" is a zoo in July and August—overrun with tacky, low-grade group tourism at its worst. Other times of year, while still crowded, it can provide a relaxing and scenic break from the cultural gauntlet of Italy.

Planning Your Time

This is the best see-everything-in-a-day plan from Sorrento: Take an early jet boat to Capri (buy ticket at 8:00, boat leaves at 8:25 and arrives at 8:45—smart). Go directly to the Blue Grotto, then catch a bus from the grotto to Anacapri and ride the chairlift to Monte Solaro. From the summit, return by chairlift (or hike down). Stroll out from the base of the chairlift to Villa San Michele for the view, then catch a bus to Capri town for the rest of your stay. At the end of the day, ride the funicular down to Marina Grande (kill time lazing on the free beach or wandering the yacht harbor) to catch the boat back to Sorrento.

Efficient travelers can make a quick trip here between destinations: Sail from Sorrento, check your bag at the harbor, see Capri, and boat directly from here to Naples.

If you buy a one-way ticket to Capri (there's no round-trip discount anyway), you'll have maximum schedule flexibility and can take either the ferry or the jet boat back. (Check times for the last return crossing upon arrival; on Capri, get a schedule from the TI or check at boat-ticket kiosk or automated boat-departure board.) During July and August, however, it's wise to get a round-trip boat

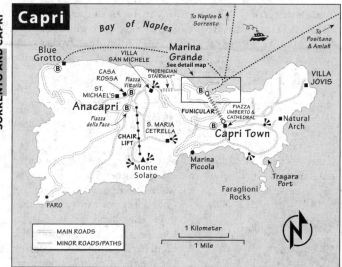

ticket with a late return (improving your odds of getting a spot on a boat when they're most crowded)—and you can use the ticket to return earlier if you like. Be 20 minutes early for the boat, or you can be bumped.

Day-trippers come down from Rome, creating a daily rush hour in each direction (arriving between 10:00-11:00, leaving around 17:00). The trip to the Blue Grotto is just a 20-minute boat ride from the arrival dock, but the commotion there can amount to a two-hour delay. If you're heading to Capri specifically to see the Blue Grotto, be sure to check that the tide isn't too high or the water too rough—ask the TI or your hotelier before heading over.

Orientation to Capri

First thing—pronounce it right: Italians say KAH-pree, not kah-PREE like the song or the pants. The island is small—just four miles by two miles—and is separated from the Sorrentine Peninsula by a narrow strait. Home to 13,000 people, there are only two towns to speak of: Capri and Anacapri. The island also has some scant Roman ruins and a few interesting churches and villas. But its chief attraction is its famous Blue Grotto, and its best activity is a chairlift up the island's Monte Solaro.

Arrival in Capri

For instructions on getting from Sorrento to Capri, see page 1010. Get oriented on the boat before you dock. As you near the harbor, Capri spreads out before you: The port is called **Marina Grande**

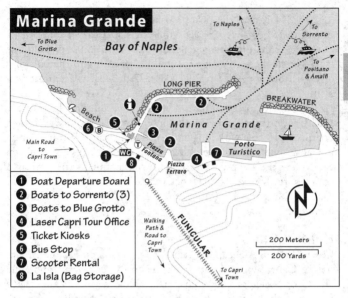

Marina Grande

To Naples

To Sorrento

To Blue Grotto

Bay of Naples

To Positano & Amalfi

LONG PIER

BREAKWATER

Beach

Marina Grande

Main Road to Capri Town

Porto Turistico

Piazza Fontana

WC

Piazza Ferraro

Walking Path & Road to Capri Town

FUNICULAR

To Capri Town

1 Boat Departure Board
2 Boats to Sorrento (3)
3 Boats to Blue Grotto
4 Laser Capri Tour Office
5 Ticket Kiosks
6 Bus Stop
7 Scooter Rental
8 La Isla (Bag Storage)

200 Meters
200 Yards

(TI, boats to Blue Grotto, buses to anywhere, funicular to the town of Capri). **Capri town** fills the ridge high above the harbor. The ruins of Emperor Tiberius' palace, **Villa Jovis,** cap the peak on the left. The dramatic *"Mamma mia!"* road arcs around the highest mountain on the island **(Monte Solaro)** on the right, leading up to **Anacapri** (the island's second town, just out of sight). Notice the old zigzag steps below that road. Until 1874, this was the only connection between Capri and Anacapri. (Though it's quite old, it's nowhere near as old as its nickname, "The Phoenician Stairway," implies.) The white house on the ridge above the zigzags is **Villa San Michele** (where you can go later for a grand view of boats like the one you're on now).

Upon arrival, get your bearings. Boats dock in two places: on the long pier and directly by the main street. If your boat arrives on the main street, take a right to get to the long pier. Stand with your back to the pier: The **funicular** is across the street. The fourth little shop to the right of the funicular (La Isla, sells clothes and souvenirs) provides **baggage storage** in the back of the store (€3/bag, daily 9:00-18:00, tel. 081-837-4575). If it's closed, try the upper funicular station in Capri town (bag storage near public WCs, €3/bag, daily 7:00-20:00; be aware that you may have to pay extra to take big bags up the funicular). The kiosk that sells **bus and funicular tickets** is to your right, in the cluster of buildings at the start of the pier. Behind that are kiosks that sell return **boat tickets** (for the two competing companies). Across the street and uphill from all this are the **public WCs.**

The **TI** is near the ticket kiosk, right by the stubby dock for Blue Grotto boats (April-Oct Mon-Sat 9:30-13:30 & 15:30-18:45, Sun 9:00-15:00, off-season generally daily 9:00-15:00; pick up free map—or the better €1 map if you'll be venturing to the outskirts of Capri town or Anacapri, tel. 081-837-0634, www.capritourism .com).

From the port, you have several transit options: boat to the Blue Grotto (best early—ideally upon arrival), bus to Capri town or Anacapri (often with long and frustrating lines), or funicular up to Capri town (4/hour, 5 minutes). If you have energy to burn, you can follow the steep paved footpath that connects the port area with Capri town. It starts a block inland from the ferry dock, near the Laser Capri office (follow the signs to *Capri centro*; allow 30 minutes).

Helpful Hints

Cheap Tricks: A cheap day trip to Capri is tough. From Sorrento to Capri by boat costs from €13 to €15 each way, and Blue Grotto tickets (plus transportation) come to €25.50—that's more than €50 per person. Taking the bus rather than the boat to the Blue Grotto saves about €9 per person (see "Blue Grotto," later). After the boats stop running, anyone willing to swim in can see the Blue Grotto for free (albeit technically illegally).

Best Real Hike: Serious hikers love the peaceful and scenic three-hour Fortress Hike, which takes you entirely away from the tourists. You'll walk under ruined forts along the rugged coast, from the Blue Grotto to the *faro* (lighthouse). From there, you can take a bus back to Anacapri (3/hour). The tourist office has a fine map/brochure.

Free Beach: Marina Grande has a free pebbly beach. You can get a shower at the bar for €1.

Local Guide: Giovanna Donadio is a good tour guide for Sorrento, Amalfi, and Capri (€100/half-day, €160/day, same price for any size group, mobile 338-466-0114, giovanna_dona @hotmail.com). Naples-based **Pina Esposito** also does tours of the entire region (see listing on page 938).

Boat Departure Schedule: A very handy electronic board lists all boats departing in the next hour or so from Capri. It's on the end of the building between the TI and boat-ticket kiosk (on the wall facing the mainland). This is the one way to know all the departure options coming up and to confirm your boat's departure time and dock number. The board includes a small chart that locates the many dock numbers in this confusing harbor.

Getting Around Capri

The buses and funicular are covered by the same ticket options: €1.80 per ride (two single tickets are the easiest option if going straight to Blue Grotto by public bus—one to get to Anacapri, then one to get to the Blue Grotto) or €8.60 for an all-day pass (includes deposit, turn it in at the end of the day to get €1 back). Single-ride tickets are often available at newsstands, tobacco shops, or from the driver. All-day passes and funicular tickets are usually sold only at official ticket offices. Consider an all-day pass if you plan to take more than five rides on the buses and funicular (possible if you go by bus to the Blue Grotto and spend some time in each town). Schedules are clearly posted at all bus stations. Taxis have steep and fixed rates (Marina Grande to Capri-€15; Marina Grande to Anacapri-€20). You can hire a taxi for about €70 per hour—negotiate.

Buses and Funicular from the Port at Marina Grande: Buses pick up just uphill from the ticket booth (you can also buy tickets from driver). Get in line under the appropriate sign: either under *San Costanzo* for going up to the town of **Capri** (at least 4/hour, 10 minutes), where you could then transfer to Anacapri (4/hour, 10 minutes, often a long queue for this Capri-Anacapri bus); or direct to **Anacapri** (sporadic schedule, but about every 40 minutes, 25 minutes). For most people, the best way from the port to Anacapri is to take the funicular to Capri (4/hour, on the quarter-hour, 5 minutes; if there's a long line, the bus might be quicker), and then bus from there to Anacapri.

Buses from Anacapri: To use the buses intelligently in Anacapri, you need to know that there are two stops: the town center (Piazza Vittoria) and the cemetery stop (Piazza della Pace—pronounced "PAH-chay"—just 200 yards farther down the main road; residents may refer to it by its former name, Piazza del Cimitero). Buses to **Capri town** (at least 4/hour) and the port, **Marina Grande** (less frequent), can be packed. Guarantee a place by catching the bus from the Piazza della Pace stop, one stop before most people get on (for either destination, catch the bus on the street corner across from the newsstand).

Getting to the Blue Grotto: You have two options—take the direct boat from Marina Grande or ride the bus from Anacapri (see "Blue Grotto," later).

Boat Trips Around the Island: Laser Capri runs quick trips around the island, passing stunning cliffs, caves, and views that most miss when they go only to the Blue Grotto. Their tiny ticket window faces dock #23 at Marina Grande, from where its boats offer three excursions: circle the island without grotto stop (1 hour, €16); circle the island with a grotto stop (2 hours, €16); and just to the grotto and back (about 1 hour, €13). The €12.50 grotto admission is always extra. If you have an hour to spare, the island circle is well worth the extra €3 (boats leave daily from 9:00 until 13:00 or possibly later—whenever Blue Grotto rowboats stop running, Via Don Giobbe Ruocco 45, tel. 081-837-5208, www.lasercapri .com). Another company, **Motoscafisti Capri,** offers the grotto trip for the same price (see listings under the "Blue Grotto," later).

Scooter Rental: If you like riding a scooter, this is the perfect way to have the run of the island—although the steep and narrow roads aren't ideal for novice riders. **Ciro** proudly rents 40 bright-yellow scooters with 50cc engines—strong enough to haul couples. Rental includes a map and instructions with parking tips and other helpful information (€15/hour, €55/day, €5 discount with this book for 2 hours or more in 2013; includes helmet, gas, and insurance; daily 9:30-19:00, look for the Ferrari sign at Via Don Giobbe Ruocco 55, Marina Grande, tel. 081-837-8018, mobile 338-360-6918, www.capriscooter.com).

Sights in Capri

Capri Town

This is a cute but extremely touristy shopping town. The *funiculare* drops you just around the corner from Piazza Umberto, the town's main square. The **TI** fills a closet under the bell tower on Piazza Umberto (less crowded than its sister on the port: Mon-Sat 8:30-20:30, Sun 9:00-15:00, shorter hours off-season, tel. 081-837-0686, WC and baggage storage downstairs behind TI). With your back to the funicular, the bus stop is 50 yards down Via Roma. The footpath to the port starts just behind the TI near the baggage storage (follow signs to *Il Porto*, 15-minute walk).

Capri's multi-domed Baroque **cathedral,** which faces the square, is worth a quick look. (Its multicolored marble floor at the altar was scavenged from the Emperor Tiberius's villa in the 19th century.)

To the left of City Hall (Municipio, lowest corner), a lane leads into the medieval part of town, which has plenty of eateries and is the starting point for the walk to Villa Jovis. The lane to the left of the cathedral (past Bar Tiberio, under the wide arch) has been dubbed "Rodeo Drive" by residents because it's the fashionable shopping strip. Walk a few minutes down Rodeo Drive (past Gelateria Buonocore at #35, with its tempting fresh waffle cones) to Quisisana Hotel, the island's top old-time hotel. From there, head left for fancy shops and villas, and right for gardens and views. Downhill and to the right, a five-minute walk leads to a lovely public garden, Giardini Augusto (free, daily 9:00-18:30).

Villa Jovis and the Emperor's Capri

Even before becoming emperor, Augustus loved Capri so much that he traded the family-owned Isle of Ischia to the (then-independent) Neapolitans in exchange for making Capri his personal property. Emperor Tiberius spent a decade here, 26-37 A.D. (Some figure he did so in order to escape being assassinated in Rome.)

Emperor Tiberius' ruined villa, Villa Jovis, is a scenic 45-minute hike from Capri town. You won't find any statues or mosaics here—just an evocative, ruined complex of terraces fitting a rocky perch over a sheer drop to the sea...and a lovely view. You can make out a large water reservoir for baths, the foundations of servants' quarters, and Tiberius' private apartments (fragments of marble flooring still survive). The ruined lighthouse dates from the Middle Ages.

Cost and Hours: €2, daily 9:00-16:00, possibly later in summer, closes earlier off-season, tel. 081-837-4549.

▲▲Blue Grotto

Three thousand tourists a day spend a couple of hours visiting Capri's Blue Grotto (Grotta Azzurra). I did—early (when the light

is best), without the frustration of crowds, and with choppy waves nearly making entrance impossible...and it was great.

The actual cave experience isn't much: a five-minute dinghy ride through a three-foot-high entry hole to reach a 60-yard-long cave, where the sun reflects brilliantly blue on its limestone bottom. But the experience—getting there, getting in, and getting back—is a scenic hoot. You get a fast ride on a 30-foot boat partway around the gorgeous island; along the way you see bird life and dramatic limestone cliffs with scant narration. You'll understand why Roman emperors appreciated the invulnerability of the island—it's surrounded by cliffs, with only one access point, and therefore easy to defend.

At the grotto's "distribution center," you pile into eight-foot dinghies with other tourists; from there, ruffian rowers elbow their way to the tiny hole, then pull fast and hard on the cable at the low point of the swells to squeeze you into the grotto. Then your man rows you around, spouting off a few descriptive lines and singing "O Sole Mio." Depending upon the strength of the sunshine that day, the blue light inside can be brilliant.

The grotto was actually an ancient Roman *nymphaeum*—a retreat for romantic hanky-panky. Many believe that, in its day, a tunnel led here directly from the palace, and that the grotto experience was enlivened by statues of Poseidon and company, placed half-underwater as if emerging from the sea. It was ancient Romans who smoothed out the entry hole that's still used to this day.

Typically, your boatman will extort an extra tip out of you before taking you back outside to your big boat (€1 is enough, but you don't need to pay a penny...you've already paid plenty).

Cost: Once you reach the grotto, you pay €8.50 for a rowboat to take you in for the five-minute row around the inside of the grotto (after your rower jockeys for position for at least 20 minutes), plus €4 to cover the admission to the grotto (€12.50 total for grotto visit, not counting €13 round-trip ride from port; again, tip entirely optional). While technically against the rules, some people dive in for free after the boats stop running—a magical experience and a favorite among locals.

Timing: When the waves or high tide make entering dangerous, the boats don't go in—the grotto can close without notice, sending tourists (flush with anticipation) home without a chance to squeeze through the little hole. (If this happens to you, consider the one-hour, €16 boat ride around the island—including a look at the Faraglioni Rocks—offered by both companies.)

If you're coming from Capri's port, allow 1-3 hours for the entire visit, depending on the chaos at the caves. Going with the first trip will get you there at the same time as the boatmen in their dinghies—who hitch a ride behind your boat—resulting in less chaos and a shorter wait at the entry point.

Getting There: You can either take the boat directly from Marina Grande, as most people do, or save money by taking the bus most of the way there.

By Boat from Marina Grande: Two companies make the boat trip from Marina Grande—Laser Capri and Motoscafisti Capri (€13 round-trip with either company, no discount for one-way; Motoscafista Capri—tel. 081-837-7714, www.motoscafisticapri.com; Laser Capri—tel. 081-837-5208, www.lasercapri.com). The first boats depart Marina Grande at 9:00, and they continue at least until 13:00—or often later, depending on when the rowboats stop running (likely 17:00 in summer, but earlier off-season). Boats don't run in stormy weather or during high tides—check weather and tide conditions *before* you purchase boat tickets.

By Bus via Anacapri: If you're on a budget, you can take the bus from Anacapri to the grotto (rather than a boat from Marina Grande). You'll save about €5 (assuming you're paying for round-trip bus fare from Marina Grande to Anacapri to Blue Grotto and back to the port), and see a beautiful, calmer side of the island. For info on getting to Anacapri, see "Getting Around Capri," earlier.

Anacapri-Blue Grotto buses depart only from the Piazza della Pace stop (not from the town center; the piazza is a 200-yard walk on the main road beyond the Piazza Vittoria bus stop in Anacapri). If you're coming from the town of Capri and want to transfer to the Blue Grotto buses, don't get off when the driver announces "Anacapri." Instead, ride one more stop to Piazza della Pace, then transfer to the Grotta Azzurra (Blue Grotto) bus (3/hour, 10 minutes). If in doubt, ask the driver or a local.

Getting Back to Marina Grande: You can take the boat back, or request to be dropped off on a small dock next to the grotto to return by bus to Anacapri (no discount for one-way boat ticket, stairs lead to bus stop with posted schedule, roughly 3/hour, 10 minutes, buy ticket from driver, €1.80).

Anacapri

Capri's second town has no sea views but some fun and interesting activities. From the busy Piazza Vittoria, where the bus drops you, head to the right of the statue of "Anacapri," and go 40 yards down the pedestrian street Via Orlandi to reach the tiny **TI** (Mon-Sat 9:00-15:00, closed Sun, often closed Nov-Easter, Via Orlandi 59, tel. 081-837-1524). Walk on this street for another 10 minutes or so, passing the Casa Rossa, St. Michael's Church, shops, and peaceful side streets. You'll also find a number of eateries, including a couple of good choices for quick, inexpensive pizza, panini, and other goodies: **Sciué Sciué** (informal seating or take-away, daily April-Nov, closed Dec-March, near the TI at #73, tel. 081-837-2068) and **Pizza e Pasta** (take-away only, daily March-Dec, closed Jan-Feb, just before the church at #157, tel. 328-623-8460).

For a sweeping island view just a few minutes away, go to the top of the stairs in Piazza Vittoria, and take the pedestrian path that heads left, past the deluxe Capri Palace Hotel (venture in if you can get past the treacherously eye-catching swimming pool windows), and below the Villa San Michele. (The view is even better from the villa—described next.)

Villa San Michele—The 19th-century mansion of Axel Munthe, Capri's grand personality, offers an insight into the scene here when this was the only comfortable refuge for Europe's artsy gay community. Oscar Wilde, D. H. Lawrence, and company hung out here back when being gay could land you in jail...or worse. Munthe, a Swedish doctor who lived here until 1949, left this impressive mansion littered with Roman statues, the Olivetum (museum of native birds and bugs), and a delightful garden. From the sphinx, you'll enjoy one of Capri's best views.

Cost and Hours: €6, May-Sept daily 9:00-18:00, closes earlier Oct-April, tel. 081-837-1401, www.villasanmichele.eu.

Casa Rossa (Red House)—This "Pompeiian-red," eccentric home is a hodgepodge of architectural styles, and the former residence of a Confederate colonel who moved to Capri after the American Civil War. Its small collection of 19th-century paintings of scenes from around the island recalls a time before mass tourism. Don't miss the top floor, with its three scarred ancient statues, which were recovered from the depths of the Blue Grotto in 1964.

Cost and Hours: €3; free with ticket stub from Blue Grotto, Villa San Michele, or Monte Solaro chairlift; June-Sept Tue-Sun 10:00-13:30 & 17:30-20:00, closed Mon; April-May Tue-Sun 10:00-17:00, closed Mon; Oct Tue-Sun 10:00-16:00, closed Mon; closed Nov-March, Via Orlandi 78, tel. 081-838-2193.

▲**St. Michael's Church**—This church has a remarkable majolica floor showing paradise on earth in a classic 18th-century Neapolitan style. The entire floor is ornately tiled, featuring an angel (with flaming sword) driving Adam and Eve from paradise. The devil is wrapped around the trunk of a beautiful tree. The animals—happily ignoring this momentous event—all have human expressions. For the best view, climb the spiral stairs from the postcard desk.

Cost and Hours: €2, daily 9:00-19:00, Nov-March until 14:00; in town center—after the TI, continue walking five minutes and look for the signs to *Chiesa Monumentale San Michele*; tel. 081-837-2396.

Faro—The lighthouse is a favorite place to enjoy the sunset, with a private beach, pool, small restaurants, and a few fishermen. Reach it by bus from Anacapri (3/hour, departs from Piazza della Pace stop).

▲▲**Chairlift up to Monte Solaro**—From Anacapri, ride the chairlift to the 1,900-foot summit of Monte Solaro for a commanding view of the Bay of Naples. Work on your tan as you float over hazelnut, walnut, chestnut, apricot, peach, kiwi, and fig trees, past a montage of tourists (mostly from cruise ships; when the grotto is closed—as it often is—they bring passengers here instead). As you ascend, consider how Capri's real estate has been priced out of the locals' reach. The ride takes 15 minutes each way, and you'll want at least 30 minutes on top.

Cost and Hours: €7.50 one-way, €10 round-trip, daily June-Oct 9:30-17:00, last run down at 17:30, closes earlier Nov-May, confirm schedule with TI, departs from top of the steps in Piazza Vittoria—the first Anacapri bus stop, tel. 081-837-1428.

At the Summit: You'll enjoy the best panorama possible: lush cliffs busy with seagulls enjoying the ideal nesting spot. The Faraglioni Rocks—with tour boats squeezing through every few minutes—are an icon of the island. The pink building nearest the rocks was an American R&R base during World War II. Eisenhower and Churchill met here. On the peak closest to Cape Sorrento, you can see the distant ruins of the Emperor Tiberius' palace, Villa Jovis. Pipes from the Sorrento Peninsula bring water to Capri (demand for fresh water here long ago exceeded the supply provided by the island's three natural springs). The Galli Islands mark the Amalfi Coast in the distance. Cross the bar terrace for views of Mount Vesuvius and Naples.

Hiking Down: A highlight for hardy walkers (provided you have strong knees and good shoes) is the 40-minute downhill hike from the top of Monte Solaro, through lush vegetation and ever-changing views, past the 14th-century Chapel of Santa Maria Cetrella (at the trail's only intersection, it's a 10-minute detour to the right), and back into Anacapri. The trail starts downstairs, past the WCs (last chance). Down two more flights of stairs, look for the sign to *Anacapri e Cetrella*—you're on your way. While the trail is well-established, you'll encounter plenty of uneven steps, loose rocks, and few signs.

Capri Connections

From Capri's Marina Grande by Boat to: Positano (mid-April-mid-Oct, 2-4/day, 35-50 minutes, €15.50-17; less off-season), **Amalfi** (mid-April-mid-Oct, 2-4/day, 50-75 minutes, €17-19), **Sorrento** (fast ferry: 4/day, 25 minutes, €13, jet boat: 18/day, 20 minutes, €15), **Naples** (roughly 2/hour, 45 minutes, €17), **Salerno** (mid-April-Sept, 2/day, 2 hours, €18.50). Confirm the schedule carefully—last boats usually leave between 18:00 and 20:10. All departing boats are listed at the port on a handy lighted schedule board, which notes exact dock locations for each departure (facing the taxis, the board is just around the corner from the TI).

AMALFI COAST and PAESTUM

With its stunning scenery, hill- and harbor-hugging towns, and historic ruins, Amalfi is Italy's coast with the most. The bus trip from Sorrento to Salerno along the breathtaking Amalfi Coast is one of the world's great bus rides. It will leave your mouth open and your camera's memory card full. You'll gain respect for the Italian engineers who built the roads in the 1800s—and even more respect for the bus drivers who drive it today. Cantilevered garages, hotels, and villas cling to the vertical terrain, and beautiful sandy coves tease from far below and out of reach. As you hyperventilate, notice how the Mediterranean, a sheer 500-foot drop below, really twinkles. All this beautiful scenery apparently inspires local Romeos and Juliets, with the evidence of late-night romantic encounters littering the roadside turnouts. Over the centuries, the spectacular scenery and climate have been a siren call for the rich and famous, luring Roman emperor Tiberius, Richard Wagner, Sophia Loren, Gore Vidal, and others to the Amalfi Coast's special brand of *la dolce vita*.

Planning Your Time

On a quick visit, use Sorrento (described in the previous chapter) as your home base and do the Amalfi Coast as a day trip. But for a small-town vacation from your vacation, spend a few more days on the coast, perhaps sleeping in Positano or Amalfi town.

Trying to decide between staying in Sorrento, Positano, or Amalfi? Sorrento is the largest of the three, with the best transportation connections. Positano is the most chic and picturesque, with a decent beach. The town of Amalfi has the most actual sights and the best hiking opportunities.

Getting Around the Amalfi Coast

10 Kilometers

10 Miles

To Rome

Naples

20·30-40m·€4.10
20·20m·€2.50
22·45m·€5

▲ Vesuvius

Ercolano
HERCU-LANEUM RUINS
20·20m·€2.10

Pompei Town

€6
POMPEII RUINS

Bay of Naples

To Palermo

Salerno

Sorrento
20·30m·€2.10

Ravello
20·25m·€2.40

€3.60

Positano
20·50m·€3.60

20·80m·€3.60

Amalfi
€7

To Paestum

20·50m·€3.60

4-6·30m·€7

6·35m·€17

20·45m·€11

22·20m·€14

4-6·35m·€7

Capri

2-4·35m·€15

2-4·35m·€17

Gulf of Salerno

AMALFI COAST

┼┼┼┼┼┼ Rail - Circumvesuviana	**Code:**
━ ━ ━ Main Rail Line	1st Number - Departures per day
━━━━ Bus	2nd Number - Length of trip in minutes
·········· Boats	3rd Number - Cost (one-way) in Euros
	Note: Slightly slower/cheaper boats exist on some routes.

Getting Around the Amalfi Coast

Amalfi Coast towns are pretty but are generally touristy, congested, overpriced, and a long hike above tiny, pebbly beaches. Most beaches are private, and access is expensive. Check and understand your bills in this greedy region. The real thrill here is the scenic Amalfi drive. This is treacherous stuff—even if you have a car, you may want to take the bus or hire a taxi. Brave souls

enjoy seeing the coast by scooter or motorbike (rent in Sorrento). The most logical springboard for this trip is Sorrento, but Positano and Amalfi work, too.

Many travelers do the Amalfi Coast as a round-trip by bus, but a good strategy is to go one way by bus and return by boat. For example, instead of busing from

Sorrento to Salerno (end of the line) and back, consider taking the bus to Salerno, then catching the ferry back to Amalfi or Positano, and then, from either town, hopping another ferry to Sorrento.

Perhaps the simplest option is to take the bus to Positano and boat from there back to Sorrento (or vice-versa). Note that ferry service for this trip decreases or may not exist at all off-season (mid-Oct–mid-April). Boats don't run in stormy weather.

Looking for exercise? Consider an Amalfi Coast hike (see "Hikes" on page 1044). Numerous trails connect the main towns along the coast with villages on the hills. Get a good map and/or book before you venture out.

By Bus

From Sorrento: SITA buses depart from Sorrento's train station nearly hourly (in peak season, 20/day, marked *Amalfi via Positano*) and stop at all Amalfi Coast towns (Positano in 50 minutes; Amalfi in another 50 minutes), ending up in Salerno, at the far end of the coast, in about three hours (easy transfer in Amalfi). Ticket prices vary with trip length (45-minute ride, good for trips within the city-€2.40; 1.5-hour ride, good to Positano-€3.60; 24-hour All Amalfi Coast ticket, good to Amalfi and beyond-€7.20; 3-day ticket-€18). For most trips, you'll want the 24-hour All Amalfi Coast ticket. In summer, buses start running as early as 6:30 and run as late as 22:00 (they stop running earlier off-season; check the schedule). Buy tickets at the tobacco shop nearest any bus stop before boarding.

An info booth is across from the bus stop (mid-April-Oct daily 8:30-13:30), but the tobacco shop/newsstand at street level inside the train station is more reliable (daily 7:00-13:30 & 14:30-20:00, also sells Circumvesuviana train tickets). If both are closed, try the appropriately named Snack Bar, upstairs in the station, or Bar Frisby, just down the hill.

Line up under the *Bus Stop SITA* sign (where a schedule is posted on the wall) across from the Sorrento train station (10 steps down). Carefully note the lettered codes that differentiate daily buses from weekend-only buses. *Giornaliero* means daily; *Feriale* notes Monday-Saturday departures; and *Festivo* is for Sundays and holidays. After 19:30 (and occasionally on Sundays—check the sign at the main bus stop), buses may leave from Via degli Aranci (with your back to the station, go left and wind around it; the bus stop is near Bar Paradise).

Leaving Sorrento, grab a seat on the right for the best views. If you return by bus, it's fun to sit directly behind the driver for a box seat with a view over the twisting hairpin action. Sitting toward the front will also help minimize carsickness.

Avoiding Crowds on the Bus: Buses are routinely unable

to handle the demand during summer months and holidays. Occasionally, an extra bus is added to handle the overflow. Generally, if you don't get on one bus, you're well-positioned to catch the next one (bring a book). Try to arrive early in the morning. Remember that buses start taking off as early as 6:30; beginning at 8:30, they leave about every 30 minutes. Departures between 9:00 and 11:00 are crowded and frustrating. Count the number of people in line: Buses pull into Sorrento empty and seat 48 (plus 25 standing).

Returning to Sorrento: The congestion can be so bad in the summer—particularly July and August—that return buses don't even stop in Positano (because they've been filled in Amalfi). Those trying to get back to Sorrento are stuck with taking an extortionist taxi or, if in Positano, hopping a boat...if one's running. If touring the coast by bus, do Positano first and come home from Amalfi to avoid the problem of full buses.

By Boat

Several companies compete for passengers, and usually claim to know nothing about their rivals' services. It's wise to check posted schedules, pick up ferry schedules from the TI, and confirm times to figure out the best plan. The boats servicing Sorrento, Positano, and Amalfi generally operate mid-April through mid-October (pick up schedule at TI, buy ticket on dock). Few boats run off-season.

From Salerno, ferries run from mid-April through September from Piazza Concordia to Amalfi (4-6/day, 35 minutes, €7), continuing to Positano (4-6/day, 70 minutes total, €11; tickets and info at TravelMar, Piazza Concordia, tel. 089-872-950, www.travelmar.it). Salerno's dock is conveniently located at the Amalfi Coast bus stop.

By Taxi

Given the hairy driving, impossible parking, congested buses, and potential fun, you might consider splurging to hire your own car and driver for the Amalfi day. (Don't bother for Pompeii, as the

Circumvesuviana train serves it conveniently and only licensed guides can take you into the site.)

The Monetti family—**Raffaele**, brother-in-law **Tony**, and cousin **Lorenzo**—have long taken excellent care of my readers' transportation needs from Sorrento. Sample trips and rates for their comfortable Mercedes

AMALFI COAST

Amalfi Coast & Paestum Area

500 Meters

500 Yards

S-31

VIA PIAVE

A-30

E-841

• Fisciano

Montecorvino
Rovella

Salerno

S-163 • Vietri

Cetara

S-18

A-3

S-164

S-18

S-175

WAR
CEMETERY

Battipaglia

La Picciola

S-18

of   Salerno

S-175A

S-30

N

Paestum

**PAESTUM
RUINS**

taxis: Amalfi Coast Day (Positano-Amalfi with time for lunch in Ravello), eight hours, €260; Amalfi Coast and Paestum, 10 hours, €360; transfer to Naples airport or train station, one hour, €110 (these prices are for up to three people, more for a larger van). If you're arriving by cruise ship, you can hire the Monettis for a custom excursion: From Sorrento, the prices are the same as the ones listed above, but they're a bit more from Naples (all-day loop from Naples port to Pompeii to the Amalfi Coast and back to Naples port: about 9 hours, €450/up to 3 people, €550/up to 8 people). To get these special prices (promised through 2013), mention this book. The Monettis also do other excursions and can take up to eight passengers—at a higher rate schedule—in their air-conditioned Mercedes van. Payment is by cash only. Their reservation system is simple and reliable (Raffaele's mobile 335-602-9158 or 338-946-2860, "office" run by Raffaele's English-speaking wife, Susanna, fax 081-807-4531, www.monettitaxi17.it, monettitaxi17 @libero.it).

Be careful: Many cabbies claim to be the Monettis. The real Monettis (Raffaele and Carmello are pictured on the previous page) drive Mercedes van-taxi #17, which is usually found at Sorrento's Piazza Tasso. Raffaele's dad, **Carmello** (a jolly, singing, in-love-with-life grandfatherly type who speaks only Italian) occasionally does trips; his specialty is helping Italian Americans find their families in southern Italy. Email him in advance if you want to find your long-lost relatives, and he can put together a meeting and transportation package. If you get in any kind of a jam, call Raffaele's mobile phone for information. **Umberto and Giovanni Benvenuto** offer transport, narrated tours, and shore excursions throughout the Amalfi Coast, as well as to Rome, Naples, Pompeii, and more. While as friendly as the Monettis, they're more upmarket and formal, with steeper rates explained on their website (tel. 081-007-2114 or 089-874-024, mobile 346-684-0226, US tel. 310-424-5640, www.benvenutolimos.com, info@benvenutolimos.com).

Sorrento Silver Star has professional drivers and several comfortable Mercedes cars and vans, and offers custom trips throughout the region at prices somewhere between the Monettis' and the Benvenutos' (tel. 081-877-1224, mobile 339-388-8143, www.sorrento silverstar.com, Luisa).

Anthony Buonocore is based in Amalfi but does excursions and transfers anywhere in the region in his eight-person Mercedes van (rates vary depending on trip, tel. 349-441-0336, www .amalfitransfer.com, buonocoreanthony@yahoo.it).

Rides Only: If you're hiring a cabbie off the street for a ride and not a tour, here are sample fares from Sorrento to Positano: up to four people one-way for about €80 in a car, or up to six people for €90 in a minibus. Figure on paying 50 percent more to Amalfi.

While taxis must use a meter within a city, a fixed rate is OK otherwise. Negotiate—ask about a round-trip.

Self-Guided Bus Tour

Hugging the Amalfi Coast

The trip from Sorrento to Salerno is one of the all-time great white-knuckle rides. Gasp from the right side of the bus as you

go out and from the left as you return to Sorrento. (Those on the wrong side really miss out.) Traffic is so heavy that private tour buses are only allowed to go in one direction (southbound from Sorrento)—summer traffic is infuriating. Fluorescent-vested policemen are posted at tough bends during peak hours to help fold in side-view mirrors and keep things moving.

Here's a loosely guided tour of what you're seeing, from west to east (note that many of these towns are described in greater detail later in this chapter):

Leaving Sorrento, the road winds up into the hills past lemon groves and hidden houses. Traveling the coast, you'll see several watchtowers placed within sight of each other, so that a relay of rooftop bonfires could spread word of a Saracen (Turkish pirate) attack. The gray-green trees are olives. Dark, green-leafed trees planted in dense groves are the source of the region's lemons—many destined to become *limoncello* liqueur. The black nets over the orange and lemon groves create a greenhouse effect, trapping warmth and humidity for maximum tastiness, while offering protection from hail and birds (preserving the peels used for *limoncello*).

Atop the ridge outside of Sorrento, look to your right: The two small islands after Sorrento are the **Galli Islands;** the bigger one, on the left, is Ulysses Island (see page 994 for the ancient connection). These islands, once owned by the famed ballet dancer Rudolf Nureyev, mark the boundary between the Bay of Naples and the Bay of Salerno. Technically, the Amalfi Coast drive begins here.

The limestone cliffs that plunge into the sea were traversed by an ancient trail that became a modern road in the mid-19th century. Fruit stands sell produce from farms and orchards just over the hill. Limestone absorbs the heat, making this south-facing coastline a suntrap, with temperatures as much as 10 degrees higher than in nearby Sorrento. Bougainvillea and geraniums grow like weeds here in the summer.

As you approach the exotic-looking town of **Positano,** you know you've reached the scenic heart of the Amalfi Coast. Views of Positano, the main stop along the coast, are dramatic on either side of town. Just south of Positano, **St. Peter's Hotel** (Il San Pietro di Positano, camouflaged below the tiny St. Peter's church) is just about the most posh stop on the coast. Notice the elevator to the beach and dock. Bring your credit card.

Praiano is notable for its cathedral, with the characteristic majolica-tiled roof and dome—a reminder of this region's respected ceramics industry. Just past the tunnel stands another Saracen watchtower.

Marina di Praiano is a tiny and unique fishing hamlet wedged into a tight ravine with a couple of good restaurants and some small hotels.

The next Saracen tower guarded the harbor of the Amalfi navy until the fleet was destroyed in 1343 by a tsunami caused by an earthquake.

The most striking stretch of coastline ends at **Amalfi** and **Atrani.** As you leave Amalfi, look up to the left. The white house that clings to a cliff (Villa Rondinaia) was home for many years to the writer Gore Vidal. Atop the cliff is the town of **Ravello.** From here, the western half of the Amalfi Coast is mostly wild and unpopulated until you hit **Salerno,** and, farther south, the striking Greek temples at **Paestum.**

Positano

According to legend, the Greek god Poseidon created Positano for Pasitea, a nymph he lusted after. History says the town was founded when ancient Greeks at Paestum decided to move out of the swamp (to escape the malaria carried by its mosquitoes). Specializing in scenery and sand, Positano hangs halfway between Sorrento and Amalfi town on the most spectacular stretch of the coast.

The village, a ▲▲▲ sight from a distance, is a pleasant gathering of cafés and expensive stores, with a good but pebbly beach. Positano is famous for its fashions—90 percent of its shops are women's clothing boutiques.

The "skyline" looks like it did a century ago. Notice the town's characteristic Saracen-inspired rooftop domes. Filled with sand, these provide low-tech insulation—to help buildings stay cool in summer and warm in winter. It's been practically impossible to get a building permit in Positano for 25 years now, and landowners who want to renovate can't make external changes. The steep stairs are a way of life for the 4,000 hardy locals. Only one street in Positano allows motorized traffic; the rest are steep pedestrian lanes. Because hotels don't take large groups (bus access is too difficult), this town—unlike Sorrento—has been spared the ravages of big-bus tourism.

AMALFI COAST

Consider seeing Positano as a day trip from Sorrento: Take the bus out and the afternoon ferry home, but be sure to check the boat schedules when you arrive—the last ferry often leaves before 18:00. Or spend the night to enjoy the magic of Positano. The town has a local flavor at night, when the grown-ups stroll and the kids play soccer on the church porch.

Orientation to Positano

Squished into a ravine, with narrow alleys that cascade down to the harbor, Positano requires you to stroll, whether you're going up or heading down. The center of town has no main square (unless you count the beach). There's little to do here but eat, window-shop, and enjoy the beach and views...hence the town's popularity.

Tourist Information

The TI is a half-block from the beach, in a small building at the bottom of the church steps (April-Sept Mon-Sat 9:00-17:00, Sun 9:00-14:00, shorter hours Oct-March, Via del Saracino 4, tel. 089-875-067, www.aziendaturismopositano.it).

Arrival in Positano

The main coast highway winds above the town. Regional SITA buses (blue or green-and-white) stop at two scheduled bus stops located at either end of town: Chiesa Nuova (at Bar Internazionale, near the Sorrento end of town; use this one only if you're staying at Brikette Hostel) and Sponda (nearer Amalfi town). Although both stops are near roads leading downhill through the town to the beach, Sponda is closer and less steep; from this stop, it's a 20-minute downhill stroll/shop/munch to the beach (and TI).

If you're catching the SITA bus back to Sorrento, be aware that it may leave from the Sponda stop up to five minutes before the printed departure. There's simply no room for the bus to wait,

AMALFI COAST

so in case the driver is early, you should be, too (€3.60, departures about hourly, daily 7:00-22:00, until 20:00 off-season). Buy tickets from the tobacco shop next to Bar Mulino Verde in the town center, or just below the bus stop at the Li Galli Bar or Total gas station (across from Hotel Marincanto).

If the walk up to the stop is too tough, take the dizzy little local red-and-white shuttle bus (marked *Interno Positano*), which constantly loops through Positano, connecting the lower town with the highway's two bus stops (2/hour, €1.20 at tobacco shop or €1.50 on board, catch it at convenient stop at the corner of Via Colombo and Via dei Mulini, heads up to Sponda). Bar Mulino Verde, located off Piazza dei Mulini (as close as cars, taxis, and the shuttle bus can get to the beach), is just across from the shuttle bus stop, with a fine, breezy terrace you can enjoy if you're waiting.

Drivers must go with the one-way flow, entering the town only at the Chiesa Nuova bus stop (closest to Sorrento) and exiting at Sponda. Driving is a headache here. Parking is worse.

Helpful Hints

Internet Access: Your best bet is at **La Brezza Internet,** on the west side of the beach (to the right as you face the water).

1. Hotel Marincanto
2. Hotel Savoia
3. Hotel Bougainville
4. Albergo California
5. Residence la Tavolozza
6. Brikette Hostel
7. Waterfront Eateries
8. Ristorante Bruno
9. To Ristorante Scirocco
10. Delicatessen
11. Vini e Panini
12. Music on the Rocks Club
13. La Zagara Café
14. Bar Mulino Verde & Bus Stop

AMALFI COAST

Local Guide: Christine Ornelas, an Australian lawyer who fell for a local and married into the Positano scene, has become the town historian. She weaves her interests into a fascinating three-hour walk through town. Christine's tour gives the town context and brings meaning to fun hidden history, while offering an overview of the local scene, tastings of local products, and tips on shopping, beaches, restaurants, and excursions (€25, 2 people-€45 with this book, April-Oct Mon-Sat at 10:30, email or call to confirm—she'll do the tour for even just a couple of people, mobile 334-232-2096, www.discover positano.it, christineornelas@gmail.com). Christine's walk starts at Piazza dei Mulini (outside the church, Chiesa del Rosario).

Self-Guided Walk

Welcome to Positano

While there's no real sightseeing in Positano, this short, guided stroll downhill will help you get your bearings from top to bottom.

• *Start at...*

Piazza dei Mulini: This is the upper town meeting point—as close to the beach as vehicles can get—and is also the lower stop for the little red-and-white shuttle bus (2/hour, departs on the hour and half-hour). Bar Mulino Verde is *the* local hangout—older people gather inside while the younger crowd congregates on the wisteria-draped terrace across the street. In this small town, gossiping is a big pastime.

Positano's ceramic and linen industries boomed when tourists discovered the place in the 1970s. The beach-inspired Moda Positano fashion label was first created as a break from the rigid dress code of the '50s. On this piazza, and throughout town, you'll find lots of ceramic and linen shops (and an abundance of ATMs), along with galleries featuring the work of local artists.

• *Wander downhill to the stepped fork in the road. You've reached...*

Midtown: At Enoteca Cuomo (#3), butcher Vincenzo stocks fine local red wines and is happy to explain their virtues. He also makes homemade sausages, salami, and *panini*—good for a quick lunch. The small set of stairs leads to the wonderful, recommended Delicatessen, where Emilia can fix you a good picnic. Their downstairs café (past the stairs, on the left at #13) sells an array of tempting edible souvenirs.

La Zagara (across the lane at #10) is a pastry shop by day and a piano bar by night. Tempting pastries such as the rum-drenched *babà* (a local favorite) fill the window display. After-hours, it's filled with traditional Neapolitan music and dancing. A bit farther downhill, Brunella (#24) is respected for traditional, quality, and locally made linens.

Across the street, Hotel Palazzo Murat fills what was a grand Benedictine monastery. Step into the plush courtyard to enjoy the scene. Continuing on, under a fragrant bougainvillea trellis, you'll come to "street merchants' gulch," where artisans display their goodies.

• *Continue to Piazza Flavio Gioia, with the big...*

Church of Santa Maria Assunta: This church originated as the abbey of Positano's 12th-century Benedictine monastery. Originally Romanesque, it was eventually abandoned (along with the entire lower town) out of fear of pirate attacks. When the coast was clear in the 18th century, the church was given an extreme Baroque makeover. Its dome is covered in colorful majolica tiles.

Inside (first chapel on left) is a fine manger scene *(presepe)*. Its original 18th-century figurines give you an idea of the folk costumes of the age. Above the main altar is the Black Madonna, an icon-like Byzantine painting, which was likely brought here in the 12th century by Benedictine monks. But locals prefer the romantic legend: Saracen pirates had it on their ship as plunder. A violent storm hit—sure to sink the evil ship. The painting of Mary spoke, saying, *"Posa, posa"* (lay me down), and the ship glided safely to this harbor. The pirates were so stricken they became Christians. Locals kept the painting, and the town became known as *Posatano* (recalling Mary's command). To the right of the altar, a small chapel holds a silver and copper bust of St. Vitus—the town patron who brought Christianity here in about A.D. 300 (this may be displayed nearby in a freestanding wooden altar). In the adjacent niche is a rare painting of Baby Jesus being circumcised (by Fabrizio Santafede, 1599), considered the finest historic painting in town.

Back outside, you'll see the bell tower, dating from 1707. Above the door, it sports a Romanesque relief scavenged from the original church. The scene—a wolf mermaid with seven little fish—was a reminder to worshippers of how integral the sea was to their livelihood.

• *Backtrack up the steps, circling the church around to the right.*

Around the Church: Around the side of the church, find the information board describing in English how this spot once held a Roman villa, buried when Mount Vesuvius erupted in A.D. 79. Only a few minor rooms have been excavated (a photograph shows one of the preserved frescoes). The rest await discovery—digging has ceased until there are enough funds to do it properly. The stairs (when open) lead down to a glass door that offers a peek into the church's crypt—originally the early church's altar. According to local legend, the Benedictines sat their dead brothers on the stone choir chairs here to decompose and remind all of their mortality.

• *Continue climbing down the steps arcing to the right. You'll eventually come to the little square facing the beach.*

Piazzetta: This is the local gathering point in the evening, as local boys hustle tourist girls into the nearby nightclub. Residents traded their historic baptistery font with Amalfi town for the two iron lions you see facing the beach. From here, you can look up and admire the colorful majolica tiles so typical of church domes in this region. Positano was once a notable naval power, with many shipyards along this beach. These eventually became fishermen's quarters and storehouses, and later, today's tourist restaurants. The Positano **beach,** called Spiaggia Grande, is half public (no shower) and half private.

• *On the far left side of the beach is...*

Music on the Rocks: This chic, recommended club is all that's left of the 1970s scene, when Positano really rocked. While it's dead until about 23:00, you're welcome to wander into the cool troglo-disco interior for a drink.

• *Wander across the beach. Beyond the kiosks that sell boat tickets, a path climbs up and over, past a 13th-century lookout fort from Saracen pirate days, to the next beach. It's a worthwhile little five-minute walk to...*

Fornillo Beach: This is where locals go for better swimming and to escape some of the tourist crowds.

• *Our walk is over. Time to relax.*

Sights in Positano

Beaches—Positano's pebbly and sandy primary beach, **Spiaggia Grande,** is colorful with umbrellas as it stretches wide around the cove. It's mostly private (€10-15/person, April-Oct, cost includes drink service and use of lounge chair and umbrella), with a free section near the middle, close to where the boats take off. The nearest WC is beneath the steps to the right (as you face the water).

Fornillo Beach, a less-crowded option just around the bend (to the west) of Spiaggia Grande, is favored by residents, with more affordable chair and umbrella rentals. This beach is lined by humble snack bars and lunch eateries.

Boat Trips—At the west end of Spiaggia Grande (to the right as you face the sea), booths sell at tickets to a number of destinations. Consider renting a rowboat or taking a boat tour to a nearby cave (La Grotta dello Smeraldo—Emerald Cave), fishing village (Nerano), or small islands.

Ferries run to Amalfi, Capri, and Sorrento; see "Positano Connections," page 1039.

Shopping—Locally produced linens and ceramics can be found at shops and galleries throughout town. **Ceramica Assunta,** one of the oldest ceramics stores in Positano, carries colorful Solimene dinnerware and more at two locations (Via Colombo 97 and Via Colombo 137, tel. 089-875-008). The young owner-artisan couple at **Sunflower Bottega d'Arte** make and paint their own ceramic designs. Two popular (and pricey) fashion boutiques are **Brunella** (Via Pasitea 72, tel. 089-875-228) and **Pepito's** (Via Pasitea 39, tel. 089-875-446).

Nightlife—The big-time action in the old town center is the impressive club **Music on the Rocks,** literally carved into the rocks on the beach (opens at 22:00 mid-April-Oct but party starts about 23:30, €10-20 cover charge includes a drink, go to dance or just check out the scene, Via Grotte Dell'Incanto 51, tel. 089-875-874, www.musicontherocks.it). For a more low-key atmosphere, café/pastry shop **La Zagara** hosts music nightly in summer (June-Sept, starts around 21:00, Via dei Mulini 10, tel. 089-875-964).

Sleeping in Positano

These hotels (but not the hostel) are all on or near Via Colombo, which leads from the SITA Sponda bus stop down into the village. Prices given are for the highest season (June-Sept)—at other

Sleep Code

(€1 = about $1.40, country code: 39)
S = Single, **D** = Double/Twin, **T** = Triple, **Q** = Quad, **b** = bathroom,
s = shower only. Unless otherwise noted, credit cards are
accepted, English is spoken, and breakfast is included.

To help you sort easily through these listings, I've divided
the accommodations into three categories based on the price
for a standard double room with bath:

$$$ Higher Priced—Most rooms €180 or more.
$$ Moderately Priced—Most rooms between €120-180.
$ Lower Priced—Most rooms €120 or less.

Prices can change without notice; verify the hotel's
current rates online or by email.

times, they become soft. Most places close in the winter (Dec-Feb
or longer). Expect to pay more than €20 a day to park.

$$$ Hotel Marincanto is a newly restored four-star hotel
with 32 rooms, impersonal service, and a bright breakfast ter-
race practically teetering on a cliff. Suites seem to be designed
for a *luna di miele*—honeymoon (Db-€220 mid-April–mid-Oct,
€170 off-season, more expensive superior rooms and suites, eleva-
tor, free Internet access and Wi-Fi, pool, private stairs to beach,
parking-€25/day, closed Nov-March, 50 yards below Sponda bus
stop at Via Colombo 50, tel. 089-875-130, fax 089-875-595, www
.marincanto.it, info@marincanto.it).

$$ Hotel Savoia is family-run, with 39 sizeable, breezy,
bright, simple rooms with tiles and older furnishings (viewless
Db-€120, view Db-€170, deluxe Db with balcony or terrace-€190,
at least €10/day less with this book in 2013, air-con, elevator, free
Wi-Fi, closed Nov-Feb, Via Colombo 73, tel. 089-875-003, fax
089-811-844, www.savoiapositano.it, info@savoiapositano.it,
Regina and daughters Mechy, Piera, and Cristina).

$$ Hotel Bougainville rents 16 comfortable rooms, half
with balconies. Everything's bright, modern, and tasteful (small-
windowed viewless Db-€119, regular viewless Db-€140, view
Db-€185, 5 percent off these rates if you book direct with this book
in 2013, check website for specials, air-con, pay Internet access
and Wi-Fi, closed Nov-March, Via Colombo 25, tel. 089-875-047,
www.bougainville.it, info@bougainville.it, friendly Marella).

$$ Albergo California has lofty views, 15 spacious rooms (all
with views), and a grand terrace draped with vines. The Cinque
family—Maria, John, and Antonio—will welcome you (view
Db-€160 June-Sept, €10 less April-May and Oct, prices promised

with this book through 2013, air-con, Wi-Fi, free parking, closed Nov-March, Via Colombo 141, tel. 089-875-382, fax 089-812-154, www.hotelcaliforniapositano.it, info@hotelcaliforniapositano.it).

$ Residence la Tavolozza is an attractive six-room hotel, warmly run by Celeste (cheh-LEHS-tay) and daughters Francesca (who speaks English) and Paola. Each cheerily tiled room comes with a view, a terrace, and silence. This is a good value (Db-€95-120 depending on size, these prices promised through 2013 with this book, families can ask for sprawling "Royal Apartment"—price varies depending on occupancy, cash only, call to confirm if arriving late, extra for lavish à la carte breakfast, air-con, closed Dec-Feb, Via Colombo 10, tel. & fax 089-875-040, www.la tavolozzapositano.it, celeste.dileva@tiscali.it).

$ Brikette Hostel offers your best cheap dorm-bed option in this otherwise ritzy town. Renting 35 beds and offering a great sun and breakfast terrace, it has a loose, youthful, rough-around-the-edges ambience (bunk in humble 10-bed dorm-€25, bunk in 8-bed dorm-€28, Db-€120, bigger family rooms, these prices with cash; hearty breakfast-€5, €5-7 dinners; free Wi-Fi, 11:00-14:30 lockout for cleaning, may be closed Dec-Feb, leave bus at Chiesa Nuova/Bar Internazionale stop and backtrack uphill 500 feet to Via G. Marconi 358, tel. & fax 089-875-857, www.brikette.com, info@brikette.com).

Eating in Positano

Positano is a very expensive place to dine. Little distinguishes the largely tourist-oriented options here, so take these recommendations with a grain of salt. You may do just as well looking for the view and menu that you like best. The options listed under "Picnics" are clearly the best values in town.

Waterfront Dining: The pizzerias and restaurants facing the beach, while overpriced, are pleasant and convenient. At the waterfront, several interchangeable restaurants with view terraces leave people fat and happy, albeit with lighter wallets (figure €15-20 pastas and *secondi*, plus pricey drinks and sides).

"Uptown": The unassuming, family-run **Ristorante Bruno** is handy if you don't want to hike down into the town center for dinner (€11-16 pastas, €16-20 *secondi*, daily 12:00-23:00, near the top of Via Colombo at #157, tel. 089-875-179).

"Way Uptown": **Ristorante Scirocco** is a worthy splurge, perched high above Positano with fantastic views and equally fine meals ranging from seafood to steak. Get there with enough daylight left to enjoy the scenery (€12 pastas, €18 *secondi*, €35 fixed-price meal, daily 12:00-15:00 & 19:00-24:00, closed Nov-Easter, call to arrange a free shuttle, Via Montepertuso 126, tel. 089-875-184).

Picnics: If a picnic dinner on your balcony or the beach sounds good, sunny Emilia at **Delicatessen** can supply the ingredients (*antipasto misto* to go at €1.40/100 grams, pasta for €1/100 grams, sandwiches made and sold by weight—about €3.50-5, she microwaves food and includes all the picnic ware, come early for best selection; daily March-Oct 7:00-22:00, Nov-Feb 8:00-20:00, just below car park at Via del Mulini 5, tel. 089-875-489). **Vini e Panini,** another small grocery, is a block from the beach a few steps above the TI. Daniela, the fifth-generation owner, speaks English and happily makes sandwiches to order. Choose from the "Caprese" (mozzarella and tomato), the "Positano" (mozzarella, tomato, and ham), or create your own (priced by weight, around €3.50 each). They also have a nice selection of well-priced regional wines (daily 8:00-20:00, until 22:00 in summer, closed mid-Nov-mid-March, just off church steps, tel. 089-875-175).

Positano Connections

Always check boat schedules, since the last boats often leave Positano before 18:00. The schedule varies drastically according to time of year; it's more reliable in summer than off-season, but be sure to check it with the TI. There's no real dock, so stormy weather can disrupt schedules. If you're thinking of taking a Capri trip from Positano, consider a boat that goes directly to the Blue Grotto (rather than dropping you in the port to catch another boat from there).

From Positano by Boat to: Amalfi (4-6/day, 30 minutes, €7, on TravelMar), **Capri** (mid-April-mid-Oct, 2-4/day, 35-50 minutes, €15.50-17, on Gescab; less off-season), **Sorrento** (mid-April-mid-Oct only, 2-4/day, 35 minutes, €15), **Salerno** (mid-April-Sept only, 4-6/day, 70 minutes, €11). Check schedules carefully as most boats run only mid-April to mid-October; few run off-season. Direct boats to **Naples** run several times a day in the summer (check with the TI); you can also change boats in Sorrento or Capri.

By Bus: See "Getting Around the Amalfi Coast—By Bus," on page 1024.

Near Positano: Marina di Praiano

Wedged into a tight ravine between Positano and Amalfi town, this tiny fishing hamlet has a pint-sized beach (half free, half pay), a couple of restaurants, and a few small hotels. All Sorrento-Positano buses stop at the top of the village. Parking is pricey (blue spots—€3/hour, pay and display). If you're staying here overnight, hotels can arrange a cheaper spot.

Sleeping in Marina di Praiano: Consider **$ La Conchiglia da Antonio,** a bar that rents 12 rooms across the ravine (Db-€60 in Oct-May, €90 in June-July, €110 in Aug, extra bed-€20, mention this book when reserving; includes small breakfast, air-con, parking-€10-20 depending on season, tel. 089-874-313, www.la conchigliapraiano.it, info@laconchigliapraiano.it). **$$ Hotel Alfonso a Mare** rents 15 rooms (Db-€130, €200 in Aug when it includes obligatory dinner, can be cheaper off-season, tel. 089-874-091, www.alfonsoamare.it, info@alfonsoamare.it).

Amalfi Town

The Amalfi Coast is named for this town. It was founded (according to legend) when the girlfriend of Hercules was buried here.

After Rome fell, Amalfi was one of the first cities to trade goods—coffee, carpets, and paper—between Europe and points east. Its heyday was the 10th and 11th centuries, when it was a powerful maritime republic—a trading power with a fleet that controlled this region and rivaled Genoa and Venice. The Republic of Amalfi founded a hospital in Jerusalem and claims to have founded the Knights of Malta order—even giving them the Amalfi cross, which became the famous Maltese cross. Amalfi minted its own coins and established "rules of the sea"—the basics of which survive today. Paper has been a vital industry here since the glory days in the Middle Ages. They'd pound rags into pulp in a big vat, pull it up using a screen, and air-dry it to create paper (the same technique used to make paper still sold in Amalfi shops). For a demonstration of this ancient technique, check out the Paper Museum (see "Sights in Amalfi Town," later).

In 1343, this little powerhouse was suddenly destroyed by a tsunami caused by an undersea earthquake. That disaster, com-

Flavio Gioia

You'll see a statue of Flavio Gioia towering above the chaos of cars and buses on the seaside piazza. Amalfi residents credit this hometown boy with the invention of the magnetic compass back in 1302, but historians can't verify that he actually existed. While an improvement to the compass did occur in Amalfi during that time period, Chinese and Arab navigators had been using rudimentary compasses for years. In Gioia's time, seamen placed a magnetized needle on the surface of a container of water as a kind of medieval GPS. If Gioia existed at all, he probably just figured out how to secure that needle inside a little box. Locals, however, have no doubt that Flavio Gioia was an inventor extraordinaire.

pounded by devastating plagues, left Amalfi a humble backwater. Today, its 7,000 residents live off tourism (and paper). Amalfi is not as picturesque as Positano or as well-connected as Sorrento, but take some time to explore the town. Amalfi's charms will reveal themselves, especially early and late in the day, when the tourist crowds dissipate.

Orientation to Amalfi Town

The waterfront of this town is dominated by a bus station, a parking lot, two gas stations, a statue of local boy Flavio Gioia—the purported inventor of the compass (see sidebar)—and a TI.

Amalfi, the most big-bus accessible of the towns along the coast, is a classic tourist trap. It's packed during the day with big-bus tours (whose drivers pay €50 an hour to park while their groups shop for *limoncello* and ceramics).

Before you enter the town, notice the colorful tile above the Porta della Marina gateway, showing off the domain of the maritime Republic of Amalfi. Just to the left, along the busy road, are a series of arches that indicate the long, narrow, vaulted halls of its arsenal—where ships were built in the 11th century.

Venture into the town, and you find its once rich and formidable medieval shell is filled with trendy shops, a main square sporting a springwater-spewing statue of St. Andrew, and a cathedral—the town's most important sight.

The farther you get away from the water, the more traditional Amalfi gets. The Paper Museum is a 10-minute walk up Via Lorenzo d'Amalfi, the main drag. From here, the road narrows and you can turn off onto a path leading to the shaded Valle dei Mulini; it's full of paper-mill ruins that recall this once proud and prosperous industry. The ruined castle clinging to the rocky ridge above Amalfi is Torre dello Ziro, a good lookout point for intrepid hikers (see "Hikes" on page 1044).

Tourist Information

The TI is about 100 yards south of the center, next to the post office; facing the sea, it's to the left (generally Mon-Fri 9:00-13:00 & 14:00-18:00, Sat 9:00-13:00, closed Sun, shorter hours off-season, Corso della Repubbliche Marinare 27, tel. 089-871-107, www .amalfitouristoffice.it).

Helpful Hints

Don't Get Stranded: Be warned—most of the year, the last bus back to Sorrento leaves at 20:00 (at 22:00 in June-July, at 23:00 in Aug, at 21:00 in Sept—but confirm times locally) and can be full. Without a public bus, your only option is a €100 taxi ride.

Internet Access: The travel agency **L'Altra Costiera,** on the main drag a block up from the church, has several terminals with Internet access (daily 9:00-21:00, Via Lorenzo d'Amalfi 34, tel. 089-873-6082).

Hiking Guidebook: The best book on hiking is *Sorrento Amalfi Capri Car Tours and Walks,* on sale at many local bookstores. It has useful color-coded maps and info on public transportation to the trailheads.

Baggage Storage: You can store your bag safely for €3 at the **Divina Costiera Travel Office** facing the waterfront square, across from the bus parking area (daily 8:00-13:00 & 14:00-19:30, tel. 089-872-467).

Laundry: The full-service **Lavalampo** offers same-day service (€5/kilo wash and dry, Mon-Sat 8:30-13:00 & 16:30-20:00, closed Thu afternoon and Sun; drop off before 9:30 and pick up same day). It's a four-minute walk up the main drag (#51) from the cathedral.

Speedboat Charters: To hire your own boat for a tour of the coastline from Amalfi (or to Capri), consider **Charter La Dolce Vita** (mobile 335-549-9365, www.amalficoastyacht.it).

Sights in Amalfi Town

Cathedral—This church is "Amalfi Romanesque" (a mix of Moorish and Byzantine flavors, built c. 1000-1300) with a fanciful Neo-Byzantine facade from the 19th century. Climb the imposing stairway—which functions as a handy outdoor theater for town events. The 1,000-year-old bronze door at the top was given to Amalfi by a wealthy local merchant who had it made in Constantinople.

Cost and Hours: €3, daily June-Sept 7:30-19:30, 9:00-18:00 in spring and fall, shorter hours off-season, closed Jan-Feb, from 10:00-17:00 access church through cloister, tel. 089-871-324. There's a fine, free WC at the top of the steps (through unmarked green door, just a few steps before ticket booth, ask for key at desk).

Visiting the Cathedral: Pick up the English flier as you enter. Visitors are directed on a one-way circuit through the cathedral complex with four stops.

This courtyard of 120 graceful columns—the **"Cloister of Paradise"**—was the cemetery for local nobles in the 13th century (note their stone sarcophagi). Don't miss the fine view of the bell tower and its majolica tiles.

The original ninth-century church, known as the **Basilica of the Crucifix,** is now a museum filled with the art treasures of the cathedral. The Angevin Mitre (Mitra Angioina), with a "pavement of tiny pearls" setting off its gold and gems, has been worn by bishops since the 14th century. On the far wall is a plank from a Saracen pirate ship that wrecked just outside of town in 1544 during a freak storm. Believers credit St. Andrew with causing the storm that saved the town from certain Turkish pillage and plunder.

Just as Venice needed Mark to get on the pilgrimage map, Amalfi needed St. Andrew—one of the apostles who, along with his brother (St. Peter), left their fishing nets to become the original "fishers of men." What are believed to be his remains (in the **Crypt of St. Andrew,** under the huge bronze statue) were brought here from Constantinople in 1206 during the Crusades—an indication of the wealth and importance of Amalfi back then.

The **cathedral** interior is notable for its fine 13th-century wooden crucifix. The painting behind it shows St. Andrew martyred on an X-shaped cross flanked by two Egyptian granite columns supporting a triumphal arch. Before leaving, check out the delicate mother-of-pearl crucifix (right of door in back).

▲**Paper Museum**—At this cavernous, cool 13th-century paper mill-turned-museum, a multilingual guide collects groups at the entrance (no particular times) for a 25-minute tour that recounts the history and process of papermaking, a long-time industry for the town of Amalfi.

Cost and Hours: €4, March-Oct daily 10:00-18:30, sporadic hours Nov-Feb; a 10-minute walk up the main street from the cathedral, look for signs to *Museo della Carta;* tel. 089-830-4561, www.museodellacarta.it.

Hikes

Amalfi is the starting point for several fine hikes (see "Hiking Guidebook," earlier). Here are two:

Hike #1—This loop trail leads up the valley past paper-mill ruins, ending in the tiny town of **Pontone;** you can get lunch there, and head back down to the town of Amalfi (allow 3 hours total). Bring a good map, since it's easy to veer off the main route. Start your hike by following the main road (Via Lorenzo d'Amalfi) away from the sea.

After the Paper Museum, jog right, then left to join the trail, which runs through the shaded woods along a babbling stream. Heed the signs that warn people to stay away from the ruins of paper mills (no matter how tempting), since many are ready to collapse on unwary hikers. Continue up to Pontone, where Trattoria l'Antico Borgo offers wonderful cuisine and a great view (Via Noce 4, tel. 089-871-469). After lunch, return to Amalfi via a steep stairway.

If you're feeling ambitious, before you head back to Amalfi, add a one-hour detour (30 minutes each way) to visit the ridge-hugging **Torre dello Ziro** (ask a local how to find the trail to this tower). You'll be rewarded with a spectacular view.

Hike #2—For an easier hike (more of a walk), head to the nearby town of **Atrani.** This village, just a 15-minute stroll beyond Amalfi town, is a world apart; its 1,500 residents consider themselves definitely *not* from Amalfi. Leave Amalfi via the main road, and stay on the water side until the sidewalk ends. Cross the street and head up the stairs; the paved route takes you over the hill, and drops you into Atrani in about 15 minutes. Piazza Umberto is the core of town, with cafés and a little grocery store that makes sandwiches. Amazingly, Atrani has none of the trendy resort feel of Amalfi, with relatively few tourists, a delightful town square, and a free, sandy beach (if you drive here, pay for parking at harbor). This town also has some recommended accommodations.

From Atrani, you can continue up to **Ravello** (see page 1046). But be warned: Unless you're part mountain goat, you'll probably prefer catching the bus to Ravello from Amalfi town instead.

Sleeping in Amalfi Town

(€1 = about $1.40, country code: 39)

Sleeps are better in Positano, but if you're marooned in Amalfi, here are some options. High season on the Amalfi Coast (especially July-Sept) demands the highest prices; prices listed here are peak-season rates (roughly April-Oct).

$$ Hotel La Bussola, a five-minute walk north along the harbor, rises above the ocean with 50 sunny rooms, most boasting terraces with a breezy sea view (Sb-€90, Db-€140, more in Aug-Sept, Signor Di Lieto offers a 10 percent Rick Steves discount in 2013 when you book direct, air-con, free Wi-Fi, parking-€15/day, Lungomare dei Cavalieri 16, tel. 089-871-533, www.labussolahotel .it, info@labussolahotel.it).

$ Hotel Amalfi, with 40 rooms and a garden, lacks warmth but is an acceptable choice (Db-€80-120, peaks at €160 Aug-Sept, €10 cash discount, air-con, Wi-Fi, roof-terrace breakfast, no sea views; 50 yards from cathedral—head up the pedestrian street and take staircase to the left before underpass, Via dei Pastai 3; tel. 089-872-440, fax 089-872-250, www.hamalfi.it, info@hamalfi.it).

$ Residenza del Duca is a fancy little seven-room boutique B&B taking advantage of its wonderful location in the heart of this touristy enclave (minuscule Sb-€60, Db-€90—or €130 in Aug-Sept, €10 discount with this book and cash, air-con, Wi-Fi, glimpses of ocean through the rooftops; 25 yards uphill from Piazza Duomo, take the first left, go up the stairs and follow the signs, then go up more stairs—over 70 total—to Via Mastalo II Duca 3; call for free luggage service—available April-Oct 8:00-20:00, tel. 089-873-6365, www.residencedelduca.it, info@residencedelduca .it, Andrea and Daniela).

Nearby in Atrani

Accommodation options are limited in Atrani, a small-town Amalfi hideaway without the glitz and hill-climbing of Positano (described under "Hike #2," earlier).

$ A'Scalinatella is a dingy, informal backpackers' hostel, with a honeycomb of cramped 3- to 10-bed dorms, way-over-priced private rooms, and a communal kitchen (dorm bed-€25, D-€60, Db-€90, prices very soft—ask for Rick Steves discount, cash only, 100 yards up from main square at #5 on Scalinatella Piazza Umberto I, tel. 089-871-492, www.hostelscalinatella.com, info@hostelscalinatella.com). It's run by English-speaking owners Filippo and Gabriele, who also rent rooms scattered all over town.

$ L'Argine Fiorito, which stands like a little castle overlooking a ravine at the top of town, rents five tidy and tiled rooms (Db-€100, extra bed-€35, tel. 089-873-6309, mobile 347-531-1158, www .larginefiorito.it, info@larginefiorito.it).

Ravello

Ravello sits atop a lofty perch 1,000 feet above the sea and offers an interesting church, two villas, and a chance to catch a glimpse of celebrities. American author Gore Vidal, who lived here for decades, is one of a sizable group of rich and famous artists—including Richard Wagner, D. H. Lawrence, Henry Wadsworth Longfellow, and Greta Garbo—who've succumbed to Ravello's charms.

To see the sights listed here, start at the bus stop and walk through the tunnel to the main square, where you'll find the church on the right, Villa Rufolo on the left, and the **TI** (daily May-Oct 10:00-18:00, shorter hours in winter, 100 yards from the square—follow signs to Via Roma 18, tel. 089-857-096, www.ravellotime.com). A 10-minute walk through the town (follow the signs) leads to Villa Cimbrone.

Sights in Ravello

Duomo—You can't miss Ravello's cathedral, located right on the main square. The main features of this church are the bronze doors, with 54 scenes of the life of Christ, the carved marble pulpit supported by six lions, and a chance to climb behind the altar for a close-up look at the relic of holy blood. The geometric designs show Arabic influence. The humble cathedral museum is two rooms of well-described carved marble that evoke the historical importance of the town.

Cost and Hours: Church—free, daily May-Oct 9:00-13:00 & 16:00-19:00, closes earlier off-season; museum—€3, daily 9:00-19:00, until 18:00 in winter; you can generally get into the church all day long via the museum, entrance on the right, tel. 089-858-311, www.chiesaravello.com.

Villa Rufolo—The villa, built in the 13th century, is only a barren ruin today. It has pleasant Arabic/Norman gardens, which provide a delightful frame for the commanding coastline view (you can enjoy the same view, without the entry fee, from the bus parking lot just below the villa). It's also one of the venues for Ravello's annual arts festival, which runs from July through September (www.ravellofestival.com). During the concert season (April-Oct), concertgoers perch on a bandstand on the edge of the cliff for a combination of wonderful music and dizzying views. Wagner visited here and was impressed enough to set the second act of his opera *Parsifal* in the villa's magical gardens. A concert on the cliff is a sublime experience.

Cost and Hours: Villa entry-€5, daily May-Sept 9:00-20:00, Oct-April 9:00 until sunset, may close earlier if hosting a concert, tel. 089-857-621, concert information tel. 089-858-149, www.ravello arts.org.

Villa Cimbrone—This villa, located at the other end of Ravello, was built in the 20th century by Englishman William Beckett. It offers extensive gardens and a killer view from the "Terrace of Infinity." Consider buying a picnic in town and discreetly munching it here, with magnificent Italian panoramas at your feet. A wander through the gardens will reveal reproductions of famous sculptures and lots of great views.

Cost and Hours: €6, daily 9:00-20:00, until 16:00 in winter, last entry 30 minutes before closing, tel. 089-858-072.

▲Hike to Amalfi Town from Villa Cimbrone—To walk downhill from Ravello's Villa Cimbrone to the town of Amalfi (a path for hardy hikers only—follow the TI's map), retrace your steps back toward town. Take the first left, which turns into a stepped path winding its way below the cliff. Pause here to look back up at the rock with a big white mansion—Villa La Rondinaia, where Gore Vidal lived for many years. Continue down the fairly steep path about 40 minutes to the town of Atrani, where several bars on the main square offer well-deserved refreshment. From here, it's about a 15-minute walk back to Amalfi (see "Hike #2" on page 1044).

Eating and Sleeping in Ravello

Ristorante Garden clings to the hillside and serves up unbeatable views of the coastline below—along with homemade pasta. Savor a relaxing lunch on their terrace. Make sure to save room for the local favorite, *delizia al limone*—calling it a "lemon cream puff" doesn't do it justice. If it's sold out, try another one of their tasty options (€13 pastas, €16 *secondi*, daily 12:00-15:00 & 19:30-22:00, closed Tue off-season and Jan, next to Villa Rufolo—facing the church walk to the right through the tunnel to Via Boccaccio 4, tel. 089-857-226). They also rent nine basic but comfortable rooms, all with balconies and the same sweeping views (Db-€120-140, air-con, Wi-Fi, www.gardenravello.com, info@gardenravello.com, Anna).

Ravello Connections

Ravello and the town of Amalfi are connected by a winding road and a bus. Coming from Amalfi town, buy your ticket at the bar on the waterfront, and ask where the bus stop is (buses usually stop to the left as you face the water, near the statue on the waterfront by Piazza Flavio Gioia). In Ravello, line up early, since the buses are often crowded (2/hour, 25 minutes, €2.40, buy ticket in tobacco shop; catch bus 100 yards off main square, just past tunnel).

Paestum

Paestum (PASTE-oom) has one of the best collections of Greek temples anywhere—and certainly the most accessible to Western Europe. Serenely situated, Paestum is surrounded by fields and wild-flowers, and has a sandy beach and only a modest commercial strip.

This town was founded as Poseidonia by Greeks in the sixth century B.C., and became a key stop on an important trade route. In the fifth century B.C., the Lucanians, a barbarous inland tribe, conquered Poseidonia, changed its name to Paistom, and tried to adopt the cultured ways of the Greeks. The Romans, who took over in the third century B.C., gave Paestum the name it bears today. The final conquerors of Paestum, malaria-carrying mosquitoes, kept the site wonderfully deserted for nearly a thousand years. Rediscovered in the 18th century, Paestum today offers the only well-preserved Greek ruins north of Sicily.

Planning Your Time
Allow two hours, including the museum. Depending on your interest and the heat, start with either the site or the museum. You'll enjoy the best light and smallest crowds late in the day.

Orientation to Paestum

Tourist Information: At the TI, next to the Paestum Archaeo-logical Museum, pick up a free info booklet of the site (TI open daily 9:00-16:00, tel. 0828-811-016, www.infopaestum.it).

Arrival at Paestum: Buses from Salerno (see "Paestum Connections," at the end of this chapter) stop near a corner of the ruins (at a little bar/café). Or, if you're arriving by train, exit the station and walk through the old city gate; the ruins are an eight-minute walk straight ahead.

Cost: €10, includes site and museum.

Hours: Both museum and site are open daily at 9:00 (except the first and third Mon of each month, when the museum is closed). Year-round, the museum closes at 19:30 (last ticket sold at 18:45). The site closes one hour before sunset (as late as 19:30 June-July, as early as 15:30 in Nov, last site ticket sold one hour before closing, tel. 0828-811-023).

Information: There's little English information at the site itself. Several mediocre guidebooks are offered at the museum's bookshop, including a €15 past-and-present guide. Dull €5 audio-guides are available to rent at the site entrance and cover both museum and site (ID required). Or you can follow my self-guided tours, below.

Local Guide: Silvia Braggio is a good guide who gives a fine two-hour walk of the site and museum (special rate with this book—€100, must arrange in advance, mobile 347-643-2307, www .silviaguide.it, silvia@silviaguide.it).

Eating: A couple of typical, touristy eateries flank the TI and site entrance. Your best lunch option is **Ristorante Nettuno** (quality food, reasonable prices, great setting, good temple views from tables, located at south entrance).

Entry: The site and museum have separate entrances. The museum, just outside the ruins, is in a cluster with the TI and a small paleo-Christian basilica. You can buy tickets either at the museum or at a less conveniently located ticket office near Ristorante Nettuno (at the south end of the site). On days when the museum is closed (first and third Monday of each month), you can buy tickets at the site entrances.

Self-Guided Tours

Paestum Archaeological Site

This tour begins at the Temple of Ceres, goes through the center of the Roman town past the Greek Memorial Tomb, circles around the other two Greek temples, then leaves the site to walk down the modern road to the Ekklesiasterion (which faces the museum). With this information, most visitors will not need to rent the audioguide or buy a book.

Background: While Paestum is famous for its marvelous Greek temples, much of what you see is Roman. Five elements of Greek Paestum survive: three misnamed temples, a memorial tomb, and a circular meeting place (or Ekklesiasterion). The rest, including the wall that defines the site, is Roman.

Paestum was once a seaport (the ocean is now about a mile away—the wall in the distance, which stretches about three miles, is about halfway to today's coastline). Only about a fifth of the site has been excavated. The Greek city, which archaeologists figure had a population of about 13,000, was first conquered by Lucanians (who were pretty crude and made almost no changes in

AMALFI COAST

the physical city), and then by the Romans (who completely made it over).

The remaining Greek structures survive because the Romans were superstitious—they respected sacred areas, and didn't mess with temples and tombs. While most old Christian churches are built upon Roman temples (it's just what people do when they conquer another culture), no Roman temple is built upon a Greek temple. Romans appreciated how religion could function as the opiate of the masses. As long as people paid their taxes and obeyed the emperor's dictates, the practical Romans had no problem with any religion. The three Greek temples that you'll see here today have stood for about 2,500 years.

• *Buy your ticket at the museum, then head to the right to find the site's north entrance. Once inside, stand in front of the...*

Temple of Ceres: All three Paestum temples have inaccurate names, coined by 19th-century archaeologists who based their

"discoveries" on wishful thinking. (While the Romans made things easy by leaving lots of inscriptions, the Greeks did not.) Those 1800s archaeologists wanted this temple to be devoted to Ceres, the goddess of agriculture. However, all the little votive statues found later, when modern archaeologists dug here, instead depicted a woman with a big helmet: Athena, goddess of wisdom and war. (The Greeks' female war goddess was also the goddess of wisdom—thinking...strategy...female. The Romans' masculine war god was Mars—just fighting.) Each temple is part of a sanctuary—an open, sacred space around the temple. Because regular people couldn't go into the temple, the altar logically stood outside.

The Temple of Ceres dates from 500 B.C. It's made of locally quarried limestone blocks. Good roads and shipping didn't come along until the Romans, so the Greeks' buildings were limited to local materials. The wooden roof is long gone. Like the other two temples, this one was once painted white, black, and red, and has an east-west orientation—facing the rising sun. This temple's *cella* (interior room) is gone, cleared out when it was used as a Christian church in the sixth century. In medieval times, Normans scavenged stones from here; chunks of these temples can be found in Amalfi's cathedral.

Walk around to the back side of the Temple of Ceres. The capitals broke in a modern earthquake, so a steel bar provides necessary support. Each of the Paestum temples is Doric style—with three stairs, columns without a base, and shafts that narrow at the top to a simple capital of a round then a square block. While there were no carved reliefs, colorful frescoes once decorated the pediments.

As you walk away, look back at the temple. Traditionally, Greeks would build a sanctuary of Athena on a city's highest spot (like the Parthenon in Athens, on the Acropolis). Paestum had no hill, so the Greeks created a mound. The hill was more impressive in its time because the Greek city level was substantially lower than the Roman pavement stones you'll walk on today.

• *From here, walk about 100 yards down Via Sacra toward the other Greek temples. To the left of the road, you'll see a little half-buried house with a tiled roof.*

Greek Memorial Tomb: This tomb (from 500 B.C.) survived because the Romans respected religious buildings. But the tomb was most inconveniently located, right in the middle of their growing city. So the practical Romans built a perimeter wall around it (visible today), added a fine tiled roof, and then buried the tomb.

There's a mystery here. Greeks generally buried their dead outside the city (as did Romans)—there are over a thousand ancient tombs outside Paestum's walls—yet this tomb was parked smack-dab in the center of town. When it was uncovered in 1952, no bodies were found inside. The tomb instead held nine perfectly preserved vases (now in the museum). Archaeologists aren't sure of the tomb's purpose. Perhaps it was a memorial dedicated to some great hero (like a city founder). Or perhaps it was a memorial to those lost when a neighboring community had to evacuate and settle as refugees here.

• *Continue walking down Via Sacra, the main drag of...*

Roman Paestum: Roman towns were garrison towns: rectangular with a grid street plan and two main streets cutting north-south and east-west, dividing the town into four equal sections. They were built by military engineers with a no-nonsense standard design. New excavations (on the left) have uncovered Roman-era lead piping. City administration buildings were on the left, and residential buildings were on the right.

Shortly after the road turns into a dirt path, you'll come to a big Roman pool that archaeologists believe was a sanctuary dedicated to Fortuna Virilis, goddess of luck and fertility. The strange stones likely supported a wooden platform for priests and statues of gods. Imagine young women walking down the ramp at the far end and through the pool, hoping to conceive a child.

The next big square is the Roman forum and ancient Paestum's main intersection. The road on the right led directly (and very practically) to the port. It made sense to have a direct connection to move freight between the sea and the center of town.

Until 2007, the vast field of ruins between the forum and the next temple (on the right) was covered in vegetation. It's recently been cleared, and cleaned of harmful lichen, which produce acids that dissolve limestone. Study the rocks: Yellow lichen is alive, black is dead. Even the great temples of Paestum were covered in this destructive lichen until 2000, when a two-year-long project cleaned them for the first time.

• *Ahead on the left are the so-called...*

Temples of Neptune and Hera: The **Temple of Neptune** dates from 450 B.C. and employs the Greek architectural trick

where the base line is curved up just a tad, to overcome the illusion of sagging caused by a straight base. The Athenians built their Parthenon (with a similar bowed-up base line) just 30 years after this. Many think this temple could have been their inspiration.

The adjacent **Temple of Hera,** dating from 550 B.C., is the oldest of Paestum's three temples and one of the oldest Greek temples still standing anywhere. Notice the change 100 years makes in the architectural styles: Archaic Doric in 550 B.C. versus Classic Doric in 450 B.C.

Archaeologists now believe the "Temple of Neptune" was actually devoted to a different god. Votive statues uncovered here suggest that Hera was the focus (perhaps this was a new and improved version of the adjacent, simpler, and older Temple of Hera). Or perhaps it was a temple to Zeus, Hera's husband, to honor the couple together.

Together, the two temples formed a single huge sanctuary with altars on the far (east) side. Walk around to the front. Notice how overbuilt the Temple of Hera appears. Its columns and capitals are closer together than necessary, as if the builders lacked confidence in their ability to span the distance between supports. Square pillars mark the corners of the *cella* inside. Temples with an odd number of columns (nine) had a single colonnade crossing in the center inside to support the wooden roof. More modern temples had six columns, with two colonnades passing through the *cella*. This left a line of vision open through the middle so that worshippers could see the big statue of the god.

By the way, in 1943, Allied paratroopers dropped in near here during the famous "Landing of Salerno." The Temple of Hera served as an Allied military tent hospital. From here the Allies pushed back the Nazis, marching to Naples, Cassino, and finally to Rome.

• *Leave the site and turn left on the modern road, Via Magna Grecia. The king of Naples built this Naples-to-Paestum road in 1829 to inspire his people with ancient temples. While he was modern in his appreciation of antiquity, his road project destroyed a swath of the ancient city. Just past the amphitheater, you'll find the...*

Ekklesiasterion: Immediately across the street from the museum is what looks like a sunken circular theater. This rare bit of ancient Greek ruins was the Ekklesiasterion, a meeting place where the Greeks would get together to discuss things and vote. Archaeologists believe that the agora (market) would also have been located here.

• *Across the street is the...*

Paestum Archaeological Museum

Paestum's museum offers the rare opportunity to see artifacts—dating from prehistoric to Greek to Roman times—at the site where they were discovered. These beautifully crafted works (with good English descriptions throughout) help bring Paestum to life.

Before stepping into the museum, notice the proud fascist architecture. While the building dates from 1954, the design is pre-WWII fascist. It seems to command that you *will* enjoy this history lesson.

The exhibit is on several levels. You'll find mostly Greek pieces on the ground floor (artifacts from the Temple of Hera in front, frescoes from tombs in the back), Paleolithic to Iron Age artifacts on the mezzanine level, and Roman art on the top floor (statues, busts, and inscriptions dating from the time of the Roman occupation). While Roman art is not unique to Paestum, the Greek collection is—so that's what you should focus on. Here are the highlights:

Temple Reliefs: Wrapping around the first room, the large carvings overhead once adorned a sanctuary of the goddess Hera (wife of Zeus) five miles outside the city. Some of the carvings show scenes from the life of Hercules.

• *In the back of this room are glass cases holding nine perfectly preserved...*

Vases: One ceramic and eight bronze, with artistic handles, these vases were found in Paestum's Greek Memorial Tomb (described earlier). Greek bronzes are rare because Romans often melted them down to make armor. These were discovered in 1952, filled with still-liquid honey and sealed with beeswax. The honey (as you can see in the display cases below) has since crystallized. Honey was a standard part of a funeral because, to ancient Greeks, honey symbolized immortality...it lasts forever.

• *The next room is filled with ancient Greek...*

Votive Offerings: These were dug up around the Temple of Hera. Such offerings are a huge help to modern archaeologists, since the figures worshippers brought to a temple are clues as to which god the temple honored. These votives depict a woman with a crown on a throne—clearly Hera. The clay votives were simple, affordable, and accessible to regular people.

• *The next room holds...*

Temple Ornaments: The temples were once adorned with decorations, such as these ornamental spouts that spurted rainwater out of lions' mouths. Notice the bits of the surviving black, red, and white paint, and the reconstructions showing archaeologists' best guesses as to how the original decorations might have looked.

• *In a glass case nearby, find the statue of...*

Zeus: This painted clay statue of Zeus dates from 520 B.C. The king of the gods was so lusty with his antics, he's still smirking.

• *Look out the museum's back window for a good...*

View of Ancient Paestum: The walls of ancient Paestum reach halfway to the mountain—a reminder that most of the site is still private property and yet to be excavated. The town up on the mountainside is Capaccio, established in the eighth century when inhabitants of the original city of Paestum were driven out by malaria and the city was abandoned.

• *Along the corridor are...*

Objects from Tombs: Over 1,000 tombs have been identified outside of the ancient city's wall. About 100 were found decorated with frescoes or containing objects such as these.

• *At the end of the corridor is...*

The Tomb of the Diver: This is the museum's treasure and the most precious Paestum find. Dating from 480 B.C., it's not only the

sole ancient Greek tomb fresco in the museum—it's the only one ever found in southern Italy. Discovered in 1968, it has five frescoed slabs (four sides and a lid; the bottom wasn't decorated). The Greeks saw death as a passage: diving from mortality into immortality...into an unknown world. Archaeologists believe that the pillars shown on the fresco represent the Pillars of Hercules at Gibraltar, which in ancient times defined the known world. The ocean beyond the Mediterranean was the great unknown...like the afterlife. The Greek banquet makes it clear that this was an aristocratic man.

• *After the Tomb of the Diver, a room displays...*

Lucanian Tomb Frescoes: The many other painted slabs in

the museum date from a later time, around 350 B.C., when Paestum fell under Lucanian rule. These frescoes are cruder than their earlier Greek counterpart. The people who conquered the Greeks tried to appropriate their art and style, but lacked the Greeks' distinctive light touch. Still, these offer fascinating glimpses into ancient life here at Paestum.

Sleeping in Paestum

(€1 = about $1.40, country code: 39)
Paestum at night, with views of the floodlit ruins, is magic.

$ Il Granaio dei Casabella, a converted old granary, is close to the action and reasonably priced. It has a beautiful garden, a nice restaurant, and views of one of the ancient temples from a corner of the property (Sb-€80, Db-€100, Tb-€125, Qb-€150, about €20 more per room mid-July-Aug, 10 percent discount for Rick Steves readers, free Wi-Fi, just west of the bus stop closest to Salerno at Via Tavernelle 84, tel. 0828-781-014, fax 0828-811-893, www.ilgranaiodeicasabella.com, info@ilgranaiodeicasabella.com, hospitable Celardo family).

$ Hotel Villa Rita is a tidy, quiet country hotel set on two acres within walking distance of the beach and the temples. It has 22 bright, modern, air-conditioned rooms; a kid-friendly swimming pool; and free parking (Sb-€70, Db-€90-100, €130 in Aug, third bed-€15, lunch or dinner-€16, Luigi promises a 10 percent discount with this book and cash in 2013, Wi-Fi, closed Nov-Feb, Via Nettuno 9, tel. 0828-811-081, fax 0828-722-555, www.hotel villarita.it, info@hotelvillarita.it). The hotel is a 10-minute walk west of the Hera entrance and public bus stop, and a 15-minute walk from the train station.

$ Hotel delle Rose, with 10 small, basic rooms with miniscule bathrooms, is near the Neptune entrance on the street bordering the ruins (Sb-€35, Db-€60, Luigi promises these prices in 2013 if you mention this book, Via Magna Grecia 193, tel. 0828-189-0778, www.hotelristorantedellerose.com, info@hotelristorantedellerose .com).

Nearby

$$ Agriturismo Seliano offers plush public spaces, a pool, and 14 spacious rooms on a peaceful, ramshackle, once-elegant farm estate that's been in the same family for 300 years (Db-€80-100, €120 in Aug, air-con, closed Nov-March; one mile north of ruins on main road—Via Magna Grecia—a small *Azienda Agrituristica Seliano* sign directs you down long dirt driveway, best for drivers; tel. 0828-723-634, www.agriturismoseliano.it, seliano@agriturismo seliano.it). They serve a fine lunch or dinner with produce fresh

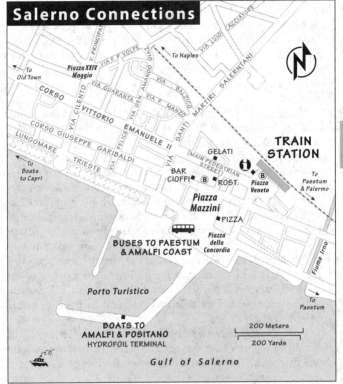

Salerno Connections

from the garden (€20 for guests or €25 for non-guests, price includes all your drinks). The place is run by Cecilia, an English-speaking baroness, and her family—including about a dozen dogs.

Paestum Connections

Salerno and Paestum

Salerno, the big city just north of Paestum, is the nearest transportation hub. From Naples or Sorrento, you'll change buses in Salerno to reach Paestum; from Naples or Pompeii, the train is easiest. Salerno's **TI** has bus, ferry, and train schedules (Mon-Sat 9:00-13:00 & 15:15-19:15, closed Sun, shorter hours off-season, on Piazza Veneto, just outside train station, tel. 089-231-432, toll-free 800-213-289, www.turismoinsalerno.it).

From Salerno to Paestum by Bus: Four companies (CSTP, SCAT, Giuliano, and Lettieri) offer a Salerno-Paestum bus service, all conveniently leaving from the same stop at Piazza della Concordia on the waterfront (2-3/hour, 50-70 minutes, schedules extremely sparse on Sun—better by train). Buy the €3 ticket on the bus, except for CSTP buses (buy these from the nearby tobacco shop). No clear schedule is posted at the Salerno stop. Simply ask a local or a bus representative at the stop for the next bus to Paestum; otherwise, get a schedule at the TI (more impartial, since they don't represent a particular company and their schedule shows all companies and times). Orange CSTP city buses use the same stop; ignore these.

When leaving Paestum, catch a northbound bus from either of the intersections that flank the ruins (see map on the previous page). Flag down any bus, ask "Salerno?" and buy the ticket on board (except for CSTP buses—buy ticket at bar closest to stop).

From Salerno to Paestum by Train: The train from Salerno to Paestum (nearly hourly, 35 minutes, direction: Paola or Sapri) runs less frequently than the buses, though it's a quicker ride because it's immune to traffic jams; check schedules at Salerno's TI or train station. Paestum's ruins are an eight-minute walk from the train station (from station, go through old city wall, ruins are straight ahead). If you plan to leave Paestum by train, buy your train ticket at the bar-café near the TI or various souvenir shops, because the station is not staffed (train schedules at TI). Leaving Paestum, trains bound for Salerno (direction: Battipaglia) usually continue to Naples.

From Naples to Salerno by Train: Trains run frequently (2/hour, 30-75 minutes), but don't board the extra-slow *diretto* train. Note that some trains stop at Pompeii, and some continue to Paestum—ideal if you want to avoid a transfer.

From Sorrento to Salerno by Bus: The scenic three-hour Amalfi Coast drive (blue or green-and-white SITA bus, in peak season 20/day, 3 hours, easy transfer in Amalfi) drops you at Piazza della Concordia (where you can catch a bus to Paestum—described earlier). The stop is a few blocks from the Salerno train station, where the TI is located.

Buses from Salerno to Amalfi (with an easy transfer to continue on to other Amalfi Coast stops and Sorrento) stop directly in front of Salerno's train station exit, on the median strip under the *Fermata SITA* sign. Buy your bus ticket at the newsstand inside the train station and tell the vendor your destination (prices vary). If it's closed, try the ticket windows in the train station or walk two blocks to Bar Cioffi (CHOH-fee), across the square from Piazza della Concordia (see map on previous page). Ticket vendors change periodically; if Bar Cioffi no longer sells tickets, ask anyone, such as a clerk at a tobacco shop or magazine shop, "Who sells bus tickets to _____?" by saying, *"Chi vende i biglietti dell'autobus per _____?"* (kee VEHN-dee ee beel-YET-tee del-OW-toh-boos pehr _____).

From Sorrento to Salerno by Train: Ride the Circumvesuviana to Naples' Centrale station (2/hour, 70 minutes) and catch the Salerno train (2/hour, 30-75 minutes).

From Salerno by Ferry to: Amalfi (4-6/day, 35 minutes, €7), **Positano** (4-6/day, 70 minutes, €11), **Capri** (2/day, 2 hours, €18.50). Boats run mid-April through September, with fewer boats off-season. Most ferries depart from Salerno's Piazza della Concordia, shown on the map on the previous page (Amalfi and Positano tickets and info at TravelMar, Piazza della Concordia, tel. 089-872-950, www.travelmar.it). Boats to Capri depart from the part of Salerno's port called Molo Manfredi, about a mile west of Piazza Concordia, and are operated by Gescab (www.gescab.it).

Drivers: While the Amalfi Coast is a thrill to drive off-season, summer traffic is miserable. From Sorrento, Paestum is 60 miles and three hours via the coast, but a much smoother two hours by autostrada. To reach Paestum from Sorrento via the autostrada, drive toward Naples, catch the autostrada (direction: Salerno), skirt Salerno (direction: Reggio), exit at Battipaglia, and drive straight through the roundabout. During your ride, you'll see many signs for *mozzarella di bufala*, cheese made from the milk of water buffalo. Try it here—it can't be any fresher.

ITALIAN HISTORY

Italy has a lot of history, so let's get started.

Origins of Rome (c. 753 B.C.-450 B.C.)

A she-wolf breastfed two human babies, Romulus and Remus, who grew to build the city of Rome in 753 B.C.—you buy that? Closer to fact, farmers and shepherds of the Latin tribe settled near the mouth of the Tiber River, a convenient trading location. The crude settlement was sandwiched between two sophisticated civilizations—Greek colonists to the south (Magna Grecia, or greater Greece), and the Etruscans of Tuscany, whose origins and language are largely still a mystery to historians (for more on the Etruscans, see page 650). Baby Rome was both dominated and nourished by these societies.

When an Etruscan king raped a Roman woman (509 B.C.), her husband led a revolt, driving out the Etruscan kings and replacing them with elected Roman senators and (eventually) a code of law ("Laws of the Twelve Tables," 450 B.C.). The Roman Republic was born.

The Roman Republic Expands
(c. 509 B.C.-A.D. 1)

Located in the center of the peninsula, Rome was perfectly situated for trading salt and wine. Roman businessmen, backed by a disciplined army, expanded through the Italian peninsula, establishing a Roman infrastructure as they went. Rome soon swallowed up its northern Etruscan neighbors, conquering them by force and absorbing their culture.

Next came Magna Grecia, with Rome's legions defeating the Greek general Pyrrhus after several costly "Pyrrhic" victories (c. 275 B.C.). Rome now ruled a united federation stretching from

Tuscany to the Italian peninsula, with a standard currency, a system of roads (including the Via Appia), and a standing army of a half-million soldiers ready for the next challenge: Carthage.

Carthage (modern-day Tunisia) and Rome fought the three bitter Punic Wars for control of the Mediterranean (264-201 B.C. and 146 B.C.). The balance of power hung precariously in the Second Punic War (218-201 B.C.), when Hannibal of Carthage crossed the sea to Spain with a huge army of men and elephants. He marched 1,200 miles overland, crossed the Alps, and forcefully penetrated Italy from the rear. Almost at the gates of the city of Rome, he was finally turned back. The Romans prevailed and, in the mismatched Third Punic War, they burned the city of Carthage to the ground (146 B.C.).

The well-tuned Roman legions easily subdued sophisticated Greece in three Macedonian Wars (215-146 B.C.). Though Rome conquered Greece, Greek culture dominated the Romans. From hairstyles to statues to temples to the evening's entertainment, Rome was forever "Hellenized," becoming the curators of Greek culture, passing it down to future generations.

By the first century B.C., Rome was master of the Mediterranean. Booty, cheap grain, and thousands of captured slaves poured in, transforming the economic model from small farmers to unemployed city dwellers living off tribute from conquered lands. The Republic had changed.

Civil Wars and the Transition to Empire (First Century B.C.)

With easy money streaming in and traditional roles obsolete, Romans bickered among themselves over their slice of the pie. Wealthy landowners (patricians, the ruling Senate) wrangled with the middle and working classes (plebeians) and with the growing population of slaves, who demanded greater say-so in government. In 73 B.C., Spartacus—a Greek-born soldier-turned-Roman slave who'd been forced to fight as a gladiator—escaped to the slopes of Mount Vesuvius, where he amassed an army of 70,000 angry slaves. After two years of fierce fighting across Italy, the Roman legions crushed the revolt and crucified 6,000 rebels along the Via Appia as a warning.

Amid the chaos of class war and civil war, charismatic generals who could provide wealth and security became dictators—men such as Sulla, Crassus, Pompey...and Caesar. Julius Caesar (100-44 B.C.) was a cunning politician, riveting speaker, conqueror of Gaul, author of *The Gallic Wars,* and lover of Cleopatra, Queen of Egypt. In his four-year reign, he reformed and centralized the government around himself. Disgruntled Republicans feared that he would make himself king. At his peak of power, they surrounded

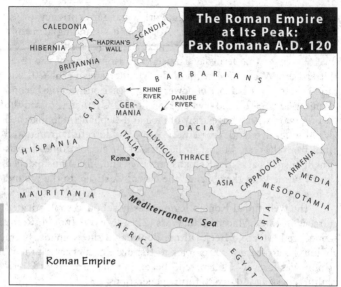

ITALIAN HISTORY

Caesar in the Senate on the "Ides of March" (March 15, 44 B.C.) and stabbed him to death.

Julius Caesar died, but the concept of one-man rule lived on in his adopted son. Named Octavian at birth, he defeated rival Mark Antony (another lover of Cleopatra, 31 B.C.) and was proclaimed Emperor Augustus (27 B.C.). Augustus outwardly followed the traditions of the Republic, while in practice he acted as a dictator with the backing of Rome's legions and the rubber-stamp approval of the Senate. He established his family to succeed him (making the family name "Caesar" a title), and set the pattern of rule by emperors for the next 500 years.

The Roman Empire (C. A.D. 1-500)

In his 40-year reign, Augustus ended Rome's civil wars and ushered in the Pax Romana: 200 years of prosperity and relative peace. Rome ruled an empire of 54 million people, stretching from Scotland to Africa, from Spain to the "Cradle of Civilization" (modern-day Iraq). Conquered peoples were welcomed into the fold of prosperity, linked by roads, common laws, common gods, education, and the Latin language. The city of Rome, with more than a million inhabitants, was decorated with Greek-style statues and monumental structures faced with marble. It was the marvel of the known world.

The empire prospered on a (false) economy of booty, slaves, and cheap imports. On the Italian peninsula, traditional small farms were swallowed up by large farming and herding estates.

In this "global economy," the Italian peninsula became just one province of many in a worldwide Latin-speaking empire, ruled by an emperor who was likely born elsewhere. The empire even survived the often turbulent and naughty behavior of emperors such as Caligula (r. 37-41) and Nero (r. 54-68).

Decline and Fall (A.D. 200-500)

Rome peaked in the second century A.D. under the capable emperors Trajan (r. 98-117), Hadrian (r. 117-138), and Marcus Aurelius (r. 161-180). For the next three centuries, the Roman Empire declined, shrinking in size and wealth, a victim of corruption, disease, an overextended army, a false economy, and the constant pressure of "barbarian" tribes pecking away at its borders. By the third century, the army had become the real power, handpicking figurehead emperors to do its bidding—in a 40-year span, 15 emperors were first saluted and then assassinated by fickle generals.

Trying to stall the disintegration, Emperor Diocletian (r. 284-305) split the empire into two administrative halves under two equal emperors. Constantine (r. 306-337) solidified the divide by moving the capital of the empire from decaying Rome to the new city of Constantinople (330, present-day Istanbul). Almost instantly, the once-great city of Rome became a minor player in imperial affairs. (The eastern "Byzantine" half of the empire would thrive and live on for another thousand years.) Constantine also legalized Christianity (313), and the once-persecuted cult soon became virtually the state religion, the backbone of Rome's fading hierarchy.

By 410, "Rome" had shrunk to just the city itself, surrounded by a protective wall. Barbarian tribes from the north and east poured in to loot and plunder. The city was sacked by Visigoths (410), vandalized by Vandals (455), and the pope had to plead with Attila the Hun for mercy (451). The peninsula's population fell to six million, trade and agriculture were disrupted, schools closed, and the infrastructure collapsed. Peasants huddled near powerful lords for protection from bandits, planting the seeds of medieval feudalism.

In 476, the last emperor sold his title for a comfy pension, and Rome fell like a huge column, kicking up dust that would plunge Europe into a thousand years of darkness. For the next 13 centuries, there would be no "Italy," just a patchwork of rural dukedoms and towns, victimized by foreign powers. Italy lay in shambles, helpless.

Invasions (A.D. 500-1000)

In 500 years, Italy suffered through a full paragraph of invasions: Lombards (568) and Byzantines (under Justinian, 536) occupied the north. In the south, Muslim Saracens (827) and Christian Normans (1061) established thriving kingdoms. Charlemagne, King of the Franks (a Germanic tribe), defeated the Lombards, and on Christmas Day A.D. 800, he knelt before the pope in St. Peter's in Rome to be crowned "Holy Roman Emperor." For the next thousand years, Italians would pledge nominal allegiance to weak, distant German kings as their "Holy Roman Emperor," an empty title meant to resurrect the glory of ancient Rome united with medieval Christianity.

Through all of the invasions and chaos, the glory of ancient Rome was preserved in the pomp, knowledge, hierarchy, and wealth of the Christian Church. Strong popes (Leo I, 440-461, and Gregory the Great, 590-604) ruled like small-time emperors, governing territories in central Italy called the Papal States.

Prosperity and Politics (A.D. 1000-1300)

Italy survived Y1K, and the economy picked up. Sea-trading cities like Venice, Genoa, Pisa, Naples, and Amalfi grew wealthy as middlemen between Europe and the Orient. During the Crusades (e.g., First Crusade 1097-1130), Italian ships ferried Europe's Christian soldiers eastward, then returned laden with spices and highly marked-up luxury goods from the Orient. Trade spawned banking, and Italians became capitalists, loaning money at interest to Europe's royalty. Italy pioneered a new phenomenon in Europe—cities *(comuni)* that were self-governing commercial centers. The medieval prosperity of the cities laid the foundation of the future Renaissance.

Politically, the Italian peninsula was dominated by two rulers—the pope in Rome and the German "Holy Roman Emperor" (with holdings in the north). It split Italy into two warring political parties: supporters of the popes (called Guelphs, centered in urban areas) and supporters of the emperors (Ghibellines, popular with the rural nobility).

The Unlucky 1300s

In 1309, the pope—enticed by Europe's fast-rising power, France—moved from Rome to Avignon, France. At one point, two rival popes reigned, one in Avignon and the other in Rome, and they excommunicated each other. The papacy eventually returned to Rome (1377), but the schism had created a breakdown in central authority that was exacerbated by an outbreak of bubonic plague (Black Death, 1347-1348), which killed a third of the Italian population.

In the power vacuum, new powers emerged in the independent cities. Venice, Florence, Milan, and Naples were under the protection and leadership of local noble families *(signoria)* such as the Medici in Florence. Florence thrived in the wool and dyeing

Church Architecture

History comes to life when you visit a centuries-old church. Even if you wouldn't know your apse from a hole in the ground, learning a few simple terms will enrich your experience. Note that not every church has every feature, and that a "cathedral" isn't a type of church architecture, but rather a designation for a church that's a governing center for a local bishop.

Aisles: The long, generally low-ceilinged arcades that flank the nave.

Altar: The raised area with a ceremonial table (often adorned with candles or a crucifix), where the priest prepares and serves the bread and wine for Communion.

Apse: The space beyond the altar, generally bordered with small chapels.

Barrel Vault: A continuous round-arched ceiling that resembles an extended upside-down U.

Choir: A cozy area, often screened off, located within the church nave and near the high altar, where services are sung in a more intimate setting.

Cloister: Covered hallways bordering a (usually square-shaped) open-air courtyard, traditionally where monks and nuns got fresh air.

Facade: The outer wall of the church's main (west) entrance, viewable from outside and generally highly decorated.

Groin Vault: An arched ceiling formed where two equal barrel vaults meet at right angles. Less common usage: term for a medieval jock strap.

Narthex: The area (portico or foyer) between the main entry and the nave.

Nave: The long, central section of the church (running west to east, from the entrance to the altar) where, in medieval times, the congregation stood through the service.

Transept: The north-south part of the church, which crosses (perpendicularly) the east-west nave. In a traditional Latin cross-shaped floor plan, the transept forms the "arms" of the cross.

West Portal: The main entry to the church (on the west end, opposite the main altar).

Top 10 Italians

Romulus: Breastfed on wolf milk, this legendary orphan grew to found the city of Rome (traditionally in 753 B.C.). Over the next seven centuries, his descendants dominated the Italian peninsula, ruling from Rome as a Republic.

Julius Caesar (100-44 B.C.): After conquering Gaul (France), subduing Egypt, and winning Cleopatra's heart, Caesar ruled Rome with king-like powers. In an attempt to preserve the Republic, senators stabbed him to death, but the concept of one-man rule lived on.

Augustus (born Octavian, 63 B.C.-A.D. 14): Julius's adopted son became the first of the Caesars that ruled Rome during its 500 years as a Europe-wide power. He set the tone for emperors both good (Trajan, Hadrian, Marcus Aurelius) and bad (Caligula, Nero, and dozens of others).

Constantine (c. 280-337 A.D.): Raised in a Christian home, this emperor legalized Christianity, almost instantly turning a persecuted sect into a Europe-wide religion. With the Fall of Rome, the Church was directed by strong popes and so guided Italians through the next thousand years of invasions, plagues, political decentralization, and darkness.

Lorenzo the Magnificent (1449-1492): Soldier, poet, lover, and ruler of Florence in the 1400s, this Renaissance Man embodied the "rebirth" of ancient enlightenment. Lorenzo's wealthy Medici family funded Florentine artists who pioneered a realistic 3-D style.

Michelangelo Buonarroti (1475-1564): His statue of David—slaying an ignorant brute—stands as a monumental symbol of Italian enlightenment. Along with fellow geniuses Leonardo da Vinci and Raphael, Michelangelo spread the Italian Renaissance (painting, sculpture, architecture, literature, and ideas) to a worldwide audience.

trade, which led to international banking, with branches in all of Europe's capitals. A positive side effect of the terrible Black Death was that the now-smaller population got a bigger share of the land, jobs, and infrastructure. By century's end, Italy was poised to enter its most glorious era since antiquity.

The Renaissance (1400s)

The Renaissance *(Rinascimento)*—the "rebirth" of ancient Greek and Roman art styles, knowledge, and humanism—began in Italy (c. 1400), and spread through Europe over the next two centuries. Many of Europe's most famous painters, sculptors, and thinkers—Michelangelo, Leonardo, Raphael, etc.—were Italian.

It was a cultural boom that changed people's thinking about

Giovanni Lorenzo Bernini (1598-1680): The "Michelangelo of Baroque" kept Italy a major exporter of sophisticated trends. Bernini's ornate statues and architecture decorated palaces of the rising power in France, even as Italy was reverting to an economically stagnant patchwork of foreign-ruled states.

Victor Emmanuel II (1820-1878): As the only Italian-born ruler on the peninsula, this King of Sardinia became the rallying point for Italian unification. Aided by the general Garibaldi, writer Mazzini, and politician Cavour (with a soundtrack by Verdi), he became the first ruler of a united, democratic Italy in September 1870. (The preceding proper nouns have since come to adorn streets and piazzas throughout Italy.)

Benito Mussolini (1883-1945): A kinder, gentler Hitler, he derailed Italy's fledgling democracy, becoming dictator of a fascist state, leading the country into defeat in World War II. No public places honor Mussolini, but many streets and piazzas throughout Italy bear the name of Giacomo Matteotti (1885-1924), a politician whose outspoken opposition to Mussolini got him killed by Fascists.

Federico Fellini (1920-1993): Fellini's films (*La Strada, La Dolce Vita, 8½*) chronicle Italy's postwar years in gritty black and white—the poverty, destruction, and disillusionment of the war followed by the optimism, decadence, and materialism of the economic boom. He captured the surreal chaos of Italy's abrupt social change from traditional Catholic to a secular, urban world presided over by Mafia bosses and weak government.

Top Italian Number 11 (?): Has Italy produced another recent citizen who's dominant enough to make his or her mark on the world? Could it be former Prime Minister Silvio Berlusconi, Italy's richest man? The late opera singer Luciano Pavarotti? Or big-pec'd model "Fabio" Lanzoni, named "Sexiest Man on Earth" by Cosmopolitan magazine? The world awaits.

every aspect of life. In politics, it meant democracy. In religion, it meant a move away from Church dominance and toward the assertion of man (humanism) and a more personal faith. Science and secular learning were revived after centuries of superstition and ignorance. In architecture, it was a return to the balanced columns and domes of Greece and Rome. In painting, the Renaissance meant 3-D realism.

Italians dotted their cities with publicly financed art—Greek gods, Roman-style domed buildings. They preached Greek-style democracy and explored the natural world. The cultural boom was financed by booming trade and lucrative banking. During the Renaissance, the peninsula once again became the trendsetting cultural center of Europe.

End of the Renaissance, France and Spain Invade (1500s)

In May 1498, Vasco da Gama of Portugal landed in India, having found a sea route around Africa. Italy's monopoly on trade with the East was broken. Portugal, France, Spain, England, and Holland—nation-states under strong central rule—began to overtake decentralized Italy. Italy's once-great maritime cities now traded in an economic backwater, just as Italy's bankers (such as the Medici in Florence) were going bankrupt. While the Italian Renaissance was all the rage throughout Europe, it declined in its birthplace. Italy—culturally sophisticated but weak and decentralized—was ripe for the picking by Europe's rising powers.

France and Spain invaded (1494 and 1495)—initially invited by Italian lords to attack their rivals—and began divvying up territory for their noble families. Italy also became a battleground in religious conflicts between Catholics and the new Protestant movement. In the chaos, the city of Rome was brutally sacked by foreign mercenary warriors (1527).

Foreign Rule (1600-1800)

For the next two centuries, most of Italy's states were ruled by foreign nobles, serving as prizes for the winners of Europe's dynastic wars. Italy ceased to be a major player in Europe, politically or economically. Italian intellectual life was often cropped short by a conservative Catholic Church trying to fight Protestantism. Galileo, for example, was forced by the Inquisition to renounce his belief that the earth orbited the sun (1633). But Italy did export Baroque art (Giovanni Lorenzo Bernini) and the budding new medium of opera.

The War of the Spanish Succession (1713)—a war in which Italy did not participate—gave much of northern Italy to Austria's ruling family, the Habsburgs (who now wore the crown of "Holy Roman Emperor"). In the south, Spain's Bourbon family ruled the Kingdom of Naples (known after 1816 as the Kingdom of the Two Sicilies), making it a culturally sophisticated but economically backward area, preserving a medieval, feudal caste system.

In 1720, a minor war (the War of Austrian Succession) created a new state at the foot of the Alps, called the Kingdom of Sardinia (a.k.a. the Kingdom of Piedmont, or Savoy). Ruled by the Savoy family, this was the only major state on the peninsula that was actually ruled by Italians. It proved to be a toehold to the future.

Italy Unites—The Risorgimento (1800s)

In 1796, Napoleon Bonaparte swept through Italy and changed everything. He ousted Austrian and Spanish dukes, confiscated Church lands, united scattered states, and crowned himself "King

Italian Unification

NOTE: Dates indicate the year of annexation to the Kingdom of Sardinia. After 1861, this became the Kingdom of Italy

SWITZERLAND

AUSTRIA

FRANCE

PIEDMONT

LOMBARDY (1859)

VENETIA (1866)

Venice

PARMA

MODENA

TUSCANY (1860)

Florence

STATES OF THE CHURCH (1870)

KINGDOM OF SARDINIA

Adriatic Sea

Rome

Naples

SARDINIA

KINGDOM OF THE TWO SICILIES (1860)

Mediterranean Sea

100 Kilometers
100 Miles

SICILY

ITALIAN HISTORY

of Italy" (1805). After his defeat (1815), Italy's old ruling order (namely, Austria and Spain) was restored. But Napoleon had planted a seed: What if Italians could unite and rule themselves like Europe's other modern nations?

For the next 50 years, a movement to unite Italy slowly grew. Called the Risorgimento—a word that means "rising again"—the movement promised a revival of Italy's glory. It started as a revolutionary, liberal movement—taking part in it was punishable by death. Members of a secret society called the Carbonari (led by a professional revolutionary named Giuseppe Mazzini) exchanged secret handshakes, printed fliers, planted bombs, and assassinated conservative rulers. Their small revolutions (1820-1821, 1831, 1848) were easily and brutally slapped down, but the cause wouldn't die.

Gradually, Italians of all stripes warmed to the idea of unification. Whether it was a united dictatorship, a united papal state, a united kingdom, or a united democracy, most Italians could agree that it was time for Spain, Austria, and France to leave.

The movement coalesced around the Italian-ruled Kingdom of Sardinia and its king, Victor Emmanuel II. In 1859, Sardinia's prime minister, Camillo Cavour, cleverly persuaded France to drive Austria out of northern Italy, leaving the region in Italian hands. A plebiscite (vote) was held, and several central Italian states (including some of the pope's) rejected their feudal lords and chose to join the growing Kingdom of Sardinia.

After victory in the north, Italy's most renowned Carbonari general, Giuseppe Garibaldi (1807-1882), steamed south with a thousand of his best soldiers (*I Mille*) and marched on the Spanish-ruled city of Naples (1860). The old order simply collapsed. In two short months, Garibaldi had achieved a seemingly impossible victory against a far superior army. Garibaldi sent a one-word telegram to the king of Sardinia: *"Obbedisco"* (I obey). The following year, an assembly of deputies from throughout Italy met in Turin and crowned Victor Emmanuel II "King of Italy." Only the pope in Rome held out, protected by French troops. When the city finally fell—easily—to the unification forces on September 20, 1870, the Risorgimento was complete. Italy went ape.

The Risorgimento was largely the work of four men: Garibaldi (the sword), Mazzini (the spark), Cavour (the diplomat), and Victor Emmanuel II (the rallying point). Today, street signs throughout Italy honor them and the dates of their great victories.

Mussolini and War (1900-1950)

Italy—now an actual nation-state, not just a linguistic region—entered the 20th century with a progressive government (a constitutional monarchy), a collection of colonies, and a flourishing northern half of the country. In the economically backward south (the Mezzogiorno), millions of poor peasants emigrated to the Americas. World War I (1915-1918) left 650,000 Italians dead, but being on the winning Allied side, survivors were granted possession of the alpine regions. In the postwar cynicism and anarchy, many radical political parties rose up—Communist, Socialist, Popular, and Fascist.

Benito Mussolini (1883-1945), a popular writer for socialist and labor-union newspapers, led the Fascists. ("Fascism" comes from Latin *fasci*, the bundles of rods that symbolized unity in ancient Rome.) Though only a minority (6 percent of the parliament in 1921), they intimidated the disorganized majority with organized violence by black-shirted Fascist gangs. In 1922, Mussolini seized the government (see "The March on Rome" sidebar) and began his rule as dictator for the next two decades.

Mussolini solidified his reign among Catholics by striking an agreement with the pope (Concordato, 1929), giving Vatican City

The March on Rome

In October 1922, Benito Mussolini, head of the newly formed Fascist Party, boldly proposed a coup d'état, saying: "Either the government will be given to us, or we will take it by marching on Rome." Throughout Italy, black-shirted Fascists occupied government buildings in their hometowns. Others grabbed guns, farming hoes, and kitchen knives and set off to converge on the outskirts of Rome. (Estimates of the size of the Fascist band range from 300 to the 300,000 of Fascist legend.) Mussolini sent the government an ultimatum to surrender. Though the Fascists were easily outmanned and outgunned by government forces, the show of force intimidated the king, Victor Emmanuel III, into avoiding a nasty confrontation. He invited Mussolini to Rome. Mussolini arrived the next day (by first-class train), was made prime minister, then marched his black-shirted troops triumphantly through the streets of Rome.

to the papacy, while Mussolini ruled Italy with the implied blessing of the Catholic Church. Italy responded to the great worldwide Depression (1930s) with big public works projects (including Rome's subway), government investment in industry, and an expanded army.

Mussolini allied his country with Hitler's Nazi regime, drawing an unprepared Italy into World War II (1940). Italy's lame army was never a factor in the war, and when Allied forces landed in Sicily (1943), Italians welcomed them as liberators. The Italians toppled Mussolini's government and surrendered to the Allies, but Nazi Germany sent troops to rescue Mussolini. The war raged on as Allied troops inched their way north against German resistance. Italians were reduced to dire poverty. In the last days of the war (April 1945), Mussolini was captured by the Italian resistance. They shot him and his girlfriend and hung their bodies upside down in a public square in Milan.

Postwar Italy

At war's end, Italy was physically ruined and extremely poor. The nation rebuilt in the 1950s and 1960s (the "economic miracle") with Marshall Plan aid from the United States. Many Italian men moved to northern Europe to find work; many others left farms and flocked to the cities. Italy regained its standing among nations, joining the United Nations, NATO, and what would become the European Union.

However, the government remained weak, changing on average once a year, shifting from right to left to centrist coalitions (it's had 62 governments since World War II). All Italians acknowledged that the real power lay in the hands of backroom politicians and organized crime—a phenomenon called *Tangentopoli*, or "Bribe City." The country remained strongly divided between the rich, industrial north and the poor, rural south.

Italian society changed greatly in the 1960s and 1970s, spurred by the liberal reforms of the Catholic Church at the Vatican II conference (1962-1965). The once-conservative Catholic country legalized divorce and contraception, and the birth rate plummeted. In the 1970s, the economy slowed thanks to inflation, strikes, and the worldwide energy crisis. Italy suffered a wave of violence from left- and right-wing domestic terrorists and organized crime, punctuated by the assassination of Prime Minister Aldo Moro (1978). A series of coalition governments in the 1980s brought some stability to the economy.

Italy Today

In the early 1990s, the judiciary launched a campaign to rid politics of corruption and Mafia ties. Though still ongoing, the investigation sent a message that Italy would no longer tolerate evils that were considered necessary just a generation earlier. As home to the Vatican, Italy keeps a close watch on the Catholic church's ongoing scandal of pedophile priests.

In 2001, controversial billionaire Silvio Berlusconi—the owner of many of Italy's media outlets and Italy's richest person—became prime minister, heading a center-right coalition. In 2003, he lost a close election, but in 2008, the 74-year-old Berlusconi was re-elected prime minister. Berlusconi's personal life made him a polarizing figure—he was accused of corruption and of consorting with women one-fourth his age—but his downfall came when Italy's economy started hitting the skids. By the end of 2011, Italy's debt load was the second worst in the euro zone, behind only Greece. To calm the markets, Berlusconi resigned. The government was taken over by former European Commissioner Mario Monti, who appointed a cabinet composed entirely of unelected professionals rather than politicians.

Like other European nations, Italy has run up big deficits by providing comfy social benefits without sufficient tax revenue, forcing the Italian government to tighten its belt. The Yale-trained Monti has his hands full enforcing austerity while trying to promote growth.

As you travel through Italy today, you'll encounter a fascinating country with a rich history and a per capita income that comes close to its neighbors to the north. Despite its ups and downs, Italy remains committed to Europe...yet it's as wonderfully Italian as ever.

APPENDIX

Contents

Tourist Information

The Italian national tourist offices in the US are a wealth of information. Before your trip, scan their website (www.italia.it) or contact the nearest branch to briefly describe your trip and request information. They'll mail you a general interest brochure and you can download many other brochures free of charge. If you have a specific problem, they're a good source of sympathy.

In New York: Tel. 212/245-5618, fax 212/586-9249, newyork @enit.it; 630 Fifth Ave. #1965, New York, NY 10111.

In Chicago: Tel. 312/644-0996, fax 312/644-3019, chicago @enit.it; 500 N. Michigan Ave. #506, Chicago, IL 60611.

In Los Angeles: Tel. 310/820-1898, fax 310/820-6357, los angeles@enit.it; 12400 Wilshire Blvd. #550, Los Angeles, CA 90025.

Worthwhile sites on Italy include the Italian Tourist Board site listed above, along with www.museionline.it (museums in Italy) and www.trenitalia.com (train info and schedules; also see "Trains—Schedules" on page 1086).

In **Italy,** your best first stop is generally the tourist information office (abbreviated **TI** in this book, and marked *i, turismo,* and *APT* in Italy). TIs are typically good places to get a city map, advice on public transit (including bus and train schedules), walking tours, special events, and nightlife. While Italian TIs are about half as helpful as those in other countries, their information is twice as important. Prepare a list of questions and a proposed plan to double-check. Many TIs have information on the entire country or at least the region, so try to pick up maps for destinations you'll be visiting later in your trip. If you're arriving in town after the TI closes, call ahead or pick up a map in a neighboring town. Since Italy is ever-changing, ask the local TI for a current list of the city's sights, hours, and prices.

Be wary of the travel agencies or special information services that masquerade as TIs but serve fancy hotels and tour companies. They're in the business of selling things you don't need.

While TIs are eager to book you a room, use their room-finding service only as a last resort. They are unable to give hard opinions on the relative value of one place over another. The accommodations stakes are too high to go potluck through the TI. Even if there's no "fee," you'll save yourself and your host money by going direct with the listings in this book.

Communicating

Hurdling the Language Barrier

Many Italians—especially those in the tourist trade and in big cities—speak some English. Still, you'll get more smiles and results by using at least a few Italian pleasantries. In smaller, non-touristy towns, Italian is the norm. Italians have an endearing habit of talking to you even if they know you don't speak their language—and yet, thanks to gestures and thoughtfully simplified words, it somehow works. Don't stop them to say you don't understand every word—just go along for the ride. For a list of survival phrases, see page 1115.

Note that Italian is pronounced much like English, with a few exceptions, such as: c followed by e or i is pronounced ch (to ask, *"Per centro?"*—To the center?—you say, pehr CHEHN-troh). In Italian, ch is pronounced like the hard c in Chianti (*chiesa*—church—is pronounced kee-AY-zah). Give it your best shot. Italians appreciate your efforts.

Telephones

Smart travelers use the telephone to reserve or reconfirm rooms, get tourist information, reserve restaurants, confirm tour times, or phone home. This section covers dialing instructions, phone cards,

APPENDIX

and types of phones (for more in-depth information, see www
.ricksteves.com/phoning).

How to Dial

Calling from the US to Italy, or vice versa, is simple—once you
break the code. The European calling chart later in this chapter
will walk you through it.

Dialing Domestically Within Italy

Italy has a direct-dial phone system (no area codes). To call anywhere within Italy, just dial the number. For example, the number
of one of my recommended Florence hotels is 055-289-592. That's
the number you dial whether you're calling it from Florence's train
station or from Rome.

If you're calling from a US mobile phone, try dialing the
number as if it's an international call—even if it isn't (see "Dialing
Internationally to or from Italy," next). If that doesn't work, try
dialing it as a domestic call.

Italy's landlines start with 0, and mobile lines start with 3.
The country's toll-free lines begin with 80. These 80 numbers—
called *freephone* or *numero verde* (green number)—can be dialed
free from any phone without using a phone card. Note that you
can't call Italy's toll-free numbers from the US, nor can you count
on reaching American toll-free numbers from Italy. Any Italian
phone number that starts with 8 but isn't followed by a 0 is a toll
call, generally costing €0.10-0.50 per minute.

Italian phone numbers vary in length; a hotel can have, say, an
eight-digit phone number and a nine-digit fax number.

Dialing Internationally to or from Italy

If you want to make an international call, follow these steps:

• Dial the international access code (00 if you're calling from
Europe, 011 from the US or Canada). If you're dialing from a
mobile phone, you can replace the international access code with
+, which works regardless of where you're calling from. (On many
mobile phones, you can insert a + by pressing and holding the 0
key.)

• Dial the country code of the country you're calling (39 for
Italy, or 1 for the US or Canada).

• Dial the local number. Note that in most European countries, you have to drop the zero at the beginning of the local
number—but in Italy, you dial it. (The European calling chart lists
specifics per country.)

Calling from the US to Italy: To call from the US to my recommended Florence hotel, dial 011 (the US international access
code), 39 (Italy's country code), then 055-289-592.

European Calling Chart

Just smile and dial, using this key:
AC = Area Code, LN = Local Number.

European Country	Calling long distance within ...	Calling from the US or Canada to ...	Calling from a European country to ...
Austria	AC + LN	011 + 43 + AC (without the initial zero) + LN	00 + 43 + AC (without the initial zero) + LN
Belgium	LN	011 + 32 + LN (without initial zero)	00 + 32 + LN (without initial zero)
Bosnia-Herzegovina	AC + LN	011 + 387 + AC (without initial zero) + LN	00 + 387 + AC (without initial zero) + LN
Britain	AC + LN	011 + 44 + AC (without initial zero) + LN	00 + 44 + AC (without initial zero) + LN
Croatia	AC + LN	011 + 385 + AC (without initial zero) + LN	00 + 385 + AC (without initial zero) + LN
Czech Republic	LN	011 + 420 + LN	00 + 420 + LN
Denmark	LN	011 + 45 + LN	00 + 45 + LN
Estonia	LN	011 + 372 + LN	00 + 372 + LN
Finland	AC + LN	011 + 358 + AC (without initial zero) + LN	999 (or other 900 number) + 358 + AC (without initial zero) + LN
France	LN	011 + 33 + LN (without initial zero)	00 + 33 + LN (without initial zero)
Germany	AC + LN	011 + 49 + AC (without initial zero) + LN	00 + 49 + AC (without initial zero) + LN
Gibraltar	LN	011 + 350 + LN	00 + 350 + LN
Greece	LN	011 + 30 + LN	00 + 30 + LN
Hungary	06 + AC + LN	011 + 36 + AC + LN	00 + 36 + AC + LN
Ireland	AC + LN	011 + 353 + AC (without initial zero) + LN	00 + 353 + AC (without initial zero) + LN

European Country	Calling long distance within ...	Calling from the US or Canada to ...	Calling from a European country to ...
Italy	LN	011 + 39 + LN	00 + 39 + LN
Montenegro	AC + LN	011 + 382 + AC (without initial zero) + LN	00 + 382 + AC (without initial zero) + LN
Morocco	LN	011 + 212 + LN (without initial zero)	00 + 212 + LN (without initial zero)
Netherlands	AC + LN	011 + 31 + AC (without initial zero) + LN	00 + 31 + AC (without initial zero) + LN
Norway	LN	011 + 47 + LN	00 + 47 + LN
Poland	LN	011 + 48 + LN	00 + 48 + LN
Portugal	LN	011 + 351 + LN	00 + 351 + LN
Slovakia	AC + LN	011 + 421 + AC (without initial zero) + LN	00 + 421 + AC (without initial zero) + LN
Slovenia	AC + LN	011 + 386 + AC (without initial zero) + LN	00 + 386 + AC (without initial zero) + LN
Spain	LN	011 + 34 + LN	00 + 34 + LN
Sweden	AC + LN	011 + 46 + AC (without initial zero) + LN	00 + 46 + AC (without initial zero) + LN
Switzerland	LN	011 + 41 + LN (without initial zero)	00 + 41 + LN (without initial zero)
Turkey	AC (if there's no initial zero, add one) + LN	011 + 90 + AC (without initial zero) + LN	00 + 90 + AC (without initial zero) + LN

APPENDIX

- The instructions above apply whether you're calling a land line or mobile phone.

- The international access code (the first numbers you dial when making an international call) is 011 if you're calling from the US or Canada. It's 00 if you're calling from virtually anywhere in Europe (except Finland, where it's 999 or another 900 number, depending on the phone service you're using).

- To call the US or Canada from Europe, dial 00, then 1 (the country code for the US and Canada), then the area code and number. In short, 00 + 1 + AC + LN = Hi, Mom!

Calling from any European country to the US: To call my office in Edmonds, Washington, from anywhere in Europe, I dial 00 (Europe's international access code), 1 (the US country code), 425 (Edmonds' area code), and 771-8303.

Mobile Phones

Traveling with a mobile phone is handy and practical. Whether you're using a smartphone or a conventional cell phone, the basics for how to make calls and send texts are the same. For specifics on using your smartphone to get online, see the sidebar.

Roaming with Your Mobile Phone: Your US mobile phone works in Europe if it's GSM-enabled, tri-band or quad-band, and on a calling plan that includes international calls. Phones from AT&T and T-Mobile, which use the same GSM technology that Europe does, are more likely to work overseas than Verizon or Sprint phones (if you're not sure, ask your service provider). Most US providers will charge you $1.29-1.99 per minute to make or receive calls while roaming internationally, and 20–50 cents to send or receive text messages. If you bother to sign up for an international calling plan with your provider, you'll save a few dimes per minute. Though pricey, roaming on your own phone is easy and can be a cost-effective way to keep in touch—especially on a short trip or if you won't be making many calls.

Buying and Using SIM Cards in Europe: You'll pay much cheaper rates if you put a European SIM card in your mobile phone; to do this, your phone must be electronically "unlocked" (ask your provider about this, buy an unlocked phone before you leave, or get one in Europe—see "Other Mobile-Phone Options," next). Then, in Europe, you can buy a fingernail-size **SIM card,** which gives you a European phone number. SIM cards are sold at mobile-phone stores and some newsstand kiosks for $5–10, and often include at least that much prepaid domestic calling time (making the card itself almost free). When you buy a SIM card in Italy, you'll need to show your passport.

Insert the SIM card in your phone (usually in a slot behind the battery or on the side) and it'll work like a European mobile phone. Before purchasing a SIM card, always ask about fees for domestic and international calls, roaming charges, and how to check your credit balance and buy more time. When you're in the SIM card's home country, domestic calls average 10-20 cents per minute, and incoming calls are free. Rates are higher if you're roaming in another country, and you may pay more to call a toll number than you would dialing from a fixed line.

Other Mobile-Phone Options: Many travelers like to carry two phones: both their own US mobile phone (allowing them to stay reachable on their own phone number) and a second, unlocked

Smartphones and Data Roaming

I take my smartphone to Europe, using it to make phone calls (sparingly) and send texts, but also to check email, listen to audiotours, and browse the Internet. If you're clever, you can do all this without incurring huge data-roaming fees. Here's how.

Many smartphones, such as the iPhone, Android, and BlackBerry, work in Europe (though some older Verizon iPhones don't). For voice calls and text messaging, smartphones work like any mobile phone (as described under "Roaming with Your Mobile Phone," opposite page)—unless you're connected to free Wi-Fi, in which case you can use Skype, Google Talk, or FaceTime to call for free (or at least very cheaply; see "Calling over the Internet," next page).

The (potentially) *really* expensive aspect of using smartphones in Europe is not voice calls or text messages, but sky-high rates for using data: checking email, browsing the Internet, streaming videos, using certain apps, and so on. If you don't proactively adjust your settings, these charges can mount up even if you're not actually using your phone—because the phone is constantly "roaming" to update your email and such. (One tip is to switch your email settings from "push" to "fetch," so you can choose when to download your emails rather than having them automatically "pushed" over the Internet to your device.)

The best solution: Disable data roaming entirely, and use your device to access the Internet only when you find free Wi-Fi (at your hotel, for example). Then you can surf the net to your heart's content, or make free (or extremely cheap) phone calls via Skype. You can manually turn off data roaming on your phone's menu (check under the "Network" settings). For added security, you can call and ask your service provider to temporarily suspend your data account entirely for the length of your trip.

Some travelers enjoy the flexibility of getting online even when they're not on free Wi-Fi. But be careful. If you simply switch on data roaming, you'll pay exorbitant rates of about $20 per megabyte (figure around 40 cents per email downloaded, or about $3 to view a typical web page)—much more expensive than it is back home. If you know you'll be doing some data roaming, it's far more affordable to sign up for a limited international data-roaming plan through your carrier (but be very clear on your megabyte limit to avoid inflated overage charges). In general, ask your provider in advance how to avoid unwittingly roaming your way to a huge bill.

European phone (which lets them do all their local calling at far cheaper rates). You could either bring two phones from home, or get one in Europe. If you have an old mobile phone sitting around, ask your provider for the "unlock code" so it can be used with European SIM cards. Or buy a cheap, basic phone before you go (search your favorite online shopping site for "unlocked quad-band GSM phone").

In Europe, basic phones are sold at hole-in-the-wall vendors at many airports and train stations, and at phone desks within larger department stores. Phones that are "locked" to work with a single provider start around $40; "unlocked" phones (which work with any SIM card) start around $60. Regardless of how you get your phone, remember that you'll need a SIM card to make it work.

Car-rental companies and mobile-phone companies offer the option to rent a mobile phone with a European number. While this seems convenient, hidden fees (such as high per-minute charges or expensive shipping costs) can really add up—which usually makes it a bad value. One exception is Verizon's Global Travel Program, available only to Verizon customers.

Calling over the Internet

Some things that seem too good to be true...actually are true. If you're traveling with a laptop, tablet, or smartphone, you can make free calls over the Internet to another wireless device, anywhere in the world, for free. (Or you can pay a few cents to call a telephone from your device). The major providers are Skype (www.skype .com, also available as a smartphone app), Google Talk (www .google.com/talk), and FaceTime (this app is preloaded on most Apple devices). You can get online at a Wi-Fi hotspot and use these apps to make calls without ringing up expensive roaming charges (though call quality can be spotty on slow connections). You can make Internet calls even if you're traveling without your own mobile device: Many European Internet cafés have Skype, as well as microphones and webcams, on their terminals—just log on and chat away.

Landline Telephones

As in the US, these days most Italians do the majority of their phoning on mobile phones. But you'll still encounter landlines in hotel rooms and at pay phones.

Hotel-Room Phones: Calling from your hotel room can be great for local calls and for international calls if you have an international phone card (described later). Otherwise, hotel-room phones can be an almost criminal rip-off for long-distance or international calls. Many hotels charge a fee for local and sometimes even "toll-free" numbers—always ask for the rates before you dial. Incoming calls are free, making this a cheap way for friends and family to stay in touch (provided they have a long-distance plan with good international rates—and a list of your hotels' phone numbers).

Public Pay Phones: Coin-op phones are virtually extinct. To make calls from public phones, you'll need a prepaid phone card, described below.

Metered Phones: In Italy, some call shops have phones with meters. You can talk all you want, then pay the bill when you leave—but be sure you know the rates before you have a lengthy conversation. Note that charges can be "per unit" rather than per minute; find out the length of a unit.

Types of Telephone Cards
There are two different kinds of phone cards: insertable and international. (Both types of phone cards work only in Italy. If you have a live card at the end of your trip, give it to another traveler to use up.)

Insertable Phone Cards: This type of card, usable only at pay phones, is sold by Italy's largest phone company, Telecom Italia. They give you the best deal for calls within Italy and are reasonable for international calls. You can buy Telecom cards (in denominations of €5 or €10) at tobacco shops, post offices, and machines near phone booths (many phone booths have signs indicating where the nearest phone-card sales outlet is located).

Rip off the perforated corner to "activate" the card, and then physically insert it into a slot in the pay phone. It displays how much money you have remaining on the card. Then just dial away. The price of the call is automatically deducted while you talk.

International Phone Cards: With these cards, phone calls from Italy to the US can cost less than a nickel a minute. The cards can also be used to make local calls, and work from any type of phone, including your hotel-room phone or a mobile phone with a European SIM card. To use the card, dial a toll-free access number, then enter your scratch-to-reveal PIN code. If you're calling from a hotel, be sure to dial the *freephone* number (starts with "80") provided on your card rather than the "local access" number (which will incur a charge; remember to ask your hotelier about rates before you call).

You can buy the cards at small newsstand kiosks, tobacco shops, Internet cafés, hostels, and hole-in-the-wall long-distance phone shops. Because there are so many brand names, simply ask for an international phone card (*carta telefonica prepagata internazionale,* KAR-tah teh-leh-FOHN-ee-kah pray-pah-GAH-tah inter-naht-zee-oh-NAH-lay). Tell the vendor where you'll be calling the most ("*per Stati Uniti*"—to America), and he'll select the brand with the best deal.

APPENDIX

Buy a lower denomination in case the card is a dud. I've had good luck with the Europa card, which offers up to 350 minutes from Italy to the US for €5. Some shops also sell cardless codes, printed right on the receipt.

Since you don't need the actual card or receipt to use the account, you can write down the access number and code and share it with friends.

US Calling Cards: These cards, such as the ones offered by AT&T, Verizon, or Sprint, are a rotten value and are being phased out. Try any of the options outlined earlier.

Useful Phone Numbers
Emergency Needs
English-Speaking Police Help: 113
Ambulance: 118
Road Service: 116

Embassies and Consulates
US Embassy in Rome: 24-hour emergency line—tel. 06-46741, non-emergency—tel. 06-4674-2420 answered Mon-Fri 15:00-17:00 (passport services Mon-Fri 8:30-12:00, Via Vittorio Veneto 121, www.usembassy.it)
US Consulates: Milan—tel. 02-290-351 (Via Principe Amedeo 2/10, http://milan.usconsulate.gov), **Florence**—tel. 055-266-951 (Lungarno Vespucci 38, http://florence.usconsulate.gov), **Naples**—tel. 081-583-8111 (Piazza della Repubblica, http://naples.usconsulate.gov)
Canadian Embassy in Rome: Tel. 06-854-441 (Mon-Fri 9:00-12:00, closed Sat-Sun, Via Zara 30, Rome, www.italy.gc.ca)
Canadian Consulates: Naples—tel. 081-401-338 (Via Carducci 29), **Padua**—tel. 049-876-4833 (Riviera Ruzzante 25). The website for all locations is www.italy.gc.ca.

Travel Advisories
US Department of State: Tel. 888-407-4747, from outside US tel. 1-202-501-4444, www.travel.state.gov
Canadian Department of Foreign Affairs: Canadian tel. 800-267-6788, from outside Canada tel. 1-613-996-8885, www.voyage.gc.ca
US Centers for Disease Control and Prevention: Tel. 800-CDC-INFO (800-232-4636), www.cdc.gov/travel

Directory Assistance
Telephone Help (in English; free directory assistance): 170
Directory Assistance (for €0.50, an Italian-speaking robot gives the number twice, very clearly): 12

Airports

Assisi: Perugia/San Egidio Airport (airport code: PEG)—tel. 075-592-141, www.airport.umbria.it

Florence: Amerigo Vespucci Airport (airport code: FLR)—tel. 055-306-1630 (for flight info, tel. 055-306-1700), www.aeroporto .firenze.it

Milan: Malpensa (airport code: MXP) and Linate (airport code: LIN) airports share the same phone number and website: tel. 02-74851, www.sea-aeroportimilano.it. Bergamo Airport (airport code: BGY)—tel. 035-326-323, www.sacbo.it

Naples: Naples International Airport (airport code: NAP)—tel. 081-789-6111, www.gesac.it

Pisa: Galileo Galilei Airport (airport code: PSA)—tel. 050-849-300, www.pisa-airport.com

Rome: Fiumicino Airport (airport code: FCO)—tel. 06-6595-3640; Ciampino Airport (airport code: CIA)—tel. 06-6595-9515. Both airports share the same website: www.adr.it

Venice: Marco Polo Airport (airport code: VCE)—tel. 041-260-9260, www.veniceairport.com; Treviso Airport (airport code: TSF)—tel. 042-231-5111, www.trevisoairport.it

Verona: Catullo Airport (also known as Verona-Villafranca, airport code: VRN)—tel. 045-809-5666, www.aeroportoverona.it

APPENDIX

Internet Access

It's useful to get online periodically as you travel—to confirm trip plans, check train or bus schedules, get weather forecasts, catch up on email, blog or post photos from your trip, or call folks back home (explained earlier, under "Calling over the Internet").

Your Mobile Device: The majority of accommodations in Italy offer Wi-Fi, as do many cafés, making it easy for you to get online with your laptop, tablet, or smartphone. Access is often free, but sometimes there's a fee.

Some hotel rooms and Internet cafés have high-speed Internet jacks that you can plug into with an Ethernet cable. A cellular modem—which lets your device access the Internet over a mobile network—provides more extensive coverage, but is much more expensive than Wi-Fi (in Italy, www.wind.it and www.tim.it offer pay-as-you-go mobile broadband).

Public Internet Terminals: Many accommodations offer a computer in the lobby with Internet access for guests. If you ask politely, smaller places may sometimes let you sit at their desk for a few minutes just to check your email. If your hotel doesn't have access, ask your hotelier to direct you to the nearest place to get online. Italian keyboards are a little different from ours; to type an @ symbol, press the "Alt Gr" key and the key that shows the @ symbol.

Security: Whether you're accessing the Internet with your own device or at a public terminal, using a shared network or computer comes with the potential for increased security risks. Be careful about storing personal information online, such as passport and credit-card numbers. If you're not convinced a connection is secure, avoid accessing any sites that could be vulnerable to fraud (e.g., online banking).

Mail

You can mail one package per day to yourself worth up to $200 duty-free from Europe to the US (mark it "personal purchases"). If you're sending a gift to someone, mark it "unsolicited gift." For details, visit www.cbp.gov and search for "Know Before You Go."

Mail service in Italy has improved over the last few years, but even so, mail nothing precious from an Italian post office. For quick transatlantic delivery in either direction, consider services such as DHL (www.dhl.com).

Transportation

By Car or Public Transportation?

Each has pros and cons. Public transportation is one of the few bargains in Italy. Cars are best for three or more traveling together (especially families with small kids), those packing heavy, and those scouring the countryside. Trains and buses are best for solo travelers, blitz tourists, city-to-city travelers, and those who don't want to drive in Europe. While a car gives you more freedom—enabling you to search for hotels more easily and carrying your bags for you—trains and buses zip you effortlessly and scenically from city to city, usually dropping you in the center, often near a TI.

Considering how handy and affordable Italy's trains and buses are (and that you're likely to go both broke and crazy driving in Italian cities), I'd do most of Italy by public transportation. If you want to drive, consider doing the big, intense stuff (Rome, Naples area, Milan, Florence, and Venice) by train or bus and renting a car for the hill towns of central Italy and for the Dolomites. A car is a worthless headache on the Riviera and in the Lake Como area.

In this section, I'll cover specifics on traveling by train, bus, and car in Italy.

Trains

To travel by train cheaply in Italy, you can simply buy tickets as you go. Ticket machines in stations work well and are easy to use (see "Buying Tickets," later), so you can usually avoid long lines at ticket windows. Pay all ticket costs in the station before you board or pay a penalty on the train.

Italy's Public Transportation

FRANCE

SWITZERLAND

GERMANY

To Paris
Chamonix
Luzern
Lugano
St. Moritz
Innsbruck
Salzburg
Mts.
La Palud
Domo-
dossola
Locarno
Brennero
San
Candido
AUSTRIA
Pre Saint
Didier
Aosta
Men.
Cortina
Villach
To Vienna
Modane
Stresa
Gallarate
Como
Varenna
Tirano
Bolzano
Cast.
Tarvisio
Jesenice
Torino
Milan
Bergamo
Riva
Trento
Conegliano
Udine
Bled
Desenzano
Verona
Vicenza
Gorizia
N.G. SLOVENIA
To
Nice
Santa
Margherita
Parma
Padua
Venice
Mon.
Trieste
Sez.
Ljubljana
Finale
Genoa
Vernazza
Modena
Ferrara
Ventimiglia
La Spezia
Bologna
CROATIA
CINQUE
TERRE
Pisa
Lucca
Ravenna
*Ligurian
Sea*
Livorno
Florence
Rimini
Pesaro
Empoli
Poggibonsi
Falconara
San Gimignano
Siena
Camucia
(Cortona)
Ancona
CORSICA
(FRANCE)
Piombino
Chiusi
Perugia
Assisi
*Adriatic
Sea*
Orvieto
Todi
Foligno
Split
Civita di Bag.
Spoleto
Orte
Porto
Torres
Civitavecchia
Pescara
Olbia
Rome
Chilivani
Anzio
Monte-
cassino
*Tyrrhenian
Sea*
To Dubrovnik,
Croatia
SARDINIA
Naples
Foggia
Capri
Pompeii
Bari
Cagliari
Sorrento
Salerno
Matera
Paestum
Potenza
Brindisi
Taranto
Metaponto
Lecce
Lamezia
Terme
To Corfu
& Patra,
Greece
Trapani
Palermo
Cefalù
Milazzo
Messina
Marsala
Crotone
Castelvetrano
Villa San Giovanni
Reggio Calabria
Tunis
TUNISIA
Agrigento
Caltanissetta
Taormina
Catania
SICILY
Siracusa
*Mediterranean
Sea*

	Rail
	Bus
	Boat
⊛	Airport (not all shown)

100 Kilometers

100 Miles

Train Costs in Italy

Map key: Approximate point-to-point one-way second-class rail fares in US dollars. First class costs 50 percent more.

Before deciding to get a railpass, add up the approximate ticket costs for your itinerary. If you'll be making short, inexpensive trips each day, you'll probably find it's cheaper to buy tickets as you go in Italy.

Types of Trains: Most trains in Italy are operated by the state-run Trenitalia company (a.k.a. Ferrovie dello Stato Italiane or FS). Since ticket prices depend on the speed of the train, it helps to know the different types of trains in Italy: pokey R *(regionali)*, medium-speed RV *(regionali espresso)*, and E *(espresso)*; fast IC (Intercity) and EC (Eurocity); and super-fast ES (Eurostar Italia, including Alta Velocità and Frecciarossa). If you're traveling with a railpass (covered later), note that reservations are optional for IC trains, but required for EC and international trains (€5) and ES trains (€10). You can't make reservations for regional trains.

Beginning in mid-2012, a brand-new, private train company called Italo began running fast trains on major routes in Italy, attempting to challenge Trenitalia's monopoly. Italo is focusing on the high-speed Venice-Milan-Bologna-Florence-Rome-Naples corridor, running trains at more or less the same speed as Trenitalia's high-speed trains, but often at lower fares. Italo does not currently accept railpasses. As this is a new venture, it's difficult to know how effective Italo will be—or if it'll even be around by the time you read this.

Schedules: At the train station, the easiest way to check schedules is at a handy automated ticket machine (described later, under "Buying Tickets"). Enter the desired date, time, and destination to see all of your options. Printed schedules are also posted at the station (departure posters are always yellow).

Newsstands sell up-to-date regional and all-Italy timetables

Deciphering Italian Train Schedules

At the station, look for the big yellow posters labeled *Partenze*—Departures. The white posters show arrivals.

Schedules are listed chronologically, hour by hour, showing the trains leaving the station throughout the day. Each schedule has columns:

- The first column *(Ora)* lists the time of departure.
- The next column *(Treno)* shows the type of train.
- The third column *(Classi Servizi)* lists the services available (first- and second-class cars, dining car, *cuccetta* berths, etc.) and, more important, whether you need reservations (usually denoted by an *R* in a box). Note that all Eurostar (ES) and Alta Velocita (AV) trains, many InterCity (IC) and EuroCity (EC) trains, and most international trains require reservations.
- The next column lists the destination of the train *(Principali Fermate Destinazioni),* often showing intermediate stops, followed by the final destination, with arrival times listed throughout in parentheses. Note that *your* final destination may be listed in fine print as an intermediate destination. For example, if you're going from Milan to Florence, scan the schedule and you'll notice that virtually all trains that terminate in Rome stop in Florence en route. Travelers who read the fine print end up with a far greater choice of trains.
- The next column *(Servizi Diretti e Annotazioni)* has pertinent notes about the train, such as "also stops in..." *(ferma anche a...),* "doesn't stop in..." *(non ferma a...),* "stops in every station" *(ferma in tutte le stazioni),* "delayed..." *(ritardo...),* and so on.
- The last column lists the track *(Binario)* the train departs from. Confirm the *binario* with an additional source: a ticket seller, the electronic board that lists immediate departures, TV monitors on the platform, or the railway officials who are usually standing by the train unless you really need them.

For any odd symbols on the poster, look at the key at the end. Some of the phrasing can be deciphered easily, such as *servizio periodico* (periodic service—doesn't always run). For the trickier ones, ask a local or railway official, try your *Rick Steves' Italian Phrase Book & Dictionary,* or simply take a different train.

You can also check schedules—for trains anywhere in Italy, not just from the station you're currently in—at the handy ticket machines. Enter the date and time of your departure (to or from any Italian station), and you can view all your options.

Open or Non-Reserved Ticket—Need to Validate

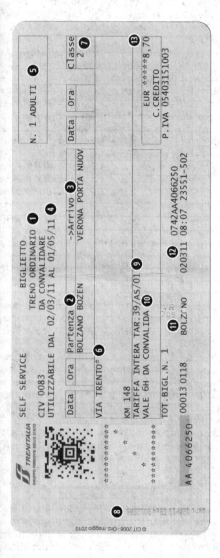

1 Open ticket for non-express trains, must be validated
2 Point of departure
3 Destination
4 Validity of ticket (use once within 2 months of purchase)
5 Number of passengers
6 Route
7 Class of travel (1 = 1ˢᵗ; 2 = 2ⁿᵈ)
8 Validation stamp
9 Full fare for non-express train
10 Once stamped, ticket is good for 1 trip within 6 hours
11 Location of ticket sale
12 Date ticket was purchased
13 Ticket cost

Reserved Ticket (Fast Train)—Need Not Validate

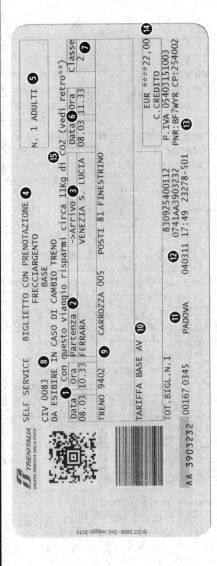

1. Departure date & time
2. Point of departure
3. Destination
4. "Ticket with reservation"
5. Number of passengers
6. Arrival date & time
7. Class of travel (1 = 1st; 2 = 2nd)
8. "Present to official if changing trains"
9. Train #, train car # & seat # (finestrino = window seat)
10. Fast-train fare (other types of trains can be cheaper and don't require reservations)
11. Location of ticket sale
12. Date ticket was purchased
13. Booking ID
14. Ticket cost
15. Amount of CO_2 usage reduced by this train trip

(€5, ask for the *orario ferroviaro*). On the Web, check www.tren italia.com and www.italotreno.it (domestic journeys only); for international trips, use www.bahn.com (Germany's excellent all-Europe website). Trenitalia offers a single all-Italy telephone number for train information (24 hours daily, toll tel. 892-021, in Italian only, consider having your hotelier call for you). For Italo trains, call 06-0708.

Point-to-Point Tickets

Train tickets are a good value in Italy. Sample fares are shown on page 1086, though fares can vary for the same journey, mainly depending on the time of day, the speed of the train, and more. **First-class** tickets cost 50 percent more than **second-class.** While second-class cars go as fast as their first-class neighbors, Italy is one country where I would consider the splurge of first class. The easiest way to "upgrade" a second-class ticket once on board a crowded train is to nurse a drink in the snack car.

Speed vs. Savings: For point-to-point tickets on major routes, fast trains save time, but charge a premium. For example, superfast Rome-Venice trains run hourly, cost €76 in second class, and make the trip in 3.75 hours, while less-frequent InterCity options cost €46 and take 6 hours. Speedy Rome-Florence trains take 1.5 hours and cost €45 in second class, compared to InterCity trains that take 3 hours and cost €30.

Discounts: Families with young children can get price breaks—kids ages 4 and under travel free; ages 4-11 at half-price. Ask for the "Offerta Familia" deal when buying tickets at a counter (or, at a ticket machine, choose "Yes" at the "Do you want ticket issue?" prompt, then choose "Familia"). With the discount, families of three to five people with at least one kid (age 12 or under) get 50 percent off the child fare, and 20 percent off the adult fare. The deal doesn't apply to all trains at all times, but it's worth checking out.

Discounts for youths and seniors require purchase of a separate card (Carta Verde for ages 12-26 costs €40; Carta Argento for ages 60 and over is €30), but the discount on tickets is so minor (10-15 percent respectively for domestic travel), it's not worth it for most.

Buying Tickets: Avoid train-station ticket lines whenever possible by using the automated ticket machines found in station halls. You'll be able to easily purchase tickets for travel within Italy (not international trains), make seat reservations, and even book a *cuccetta* (koo-CHEHT-tah; overnight berth).

Trenitalia's automated ticket machines (usually green-and-white, marked *Biglietto Veloce/Fast Ticket*) are user-friendly and found in all but the tiniest stations in Italy. You can pay by cash (they give change) or by debit or credit card (even for small amounts). Select English, then your destination. If you don't immediately see the city you're traveling to, keep keying in the spelling until it's listed. You can choose from first- and second-class seats, request tickets for more than one traveler, and (on the high-speed Eurostar trains) choose an aisle or window seat. If the machine prompts you—"Fidelity Card?"—choose no. Don't select a discount rate without being sure that you meet the criteria (for example, Americans are not eligible for any EU or resident discounts). If you need to validate your ticket, you can do it in the same machine if you're boarding your train right away.

For nearby destinations only, you can also buy tickets from the older, gray-and-blue machines marked *Rete regionale* (cash only, push button for English).

It's possible, but generally unnecessary, to buy Trenitalia tickets in advance online at www.trenitalia.com. Because most Italian trains run frequently and there's no deadline to buy tickets, you can keep your travel plans flexible by buying tickets as you go, or buy several tickets at one station when you are ready to reserve.

To buy tickets for high-speed **Italo** trains, look for a dedicated service counter (in most major rail stations), or a red automated ticket machine labeled *Italo*. You can also book Italo tickets by phone (tel. 06-0708) or online (www.italotreno.it).

If you buy a ticket for one train line, you must travel with only that company—your ticket is not valid on the competitor's train line. Survey your options carefully before you choose.

Note that you can't buy international tickets from machines; for this and anything else that requires a real person, try a local travel agency, a good alternative to station ticket windows plagued by long lines. Agencies also sell domestic tickets and make reservations. The cost is only a little more (they charge a small fee); it can be more convenient (if you find yourself near a travel agency while you're sightseeing); there are no crowds; and the language barrier can be smaller than at the station's ticket windows.

Validating Tickets: If your ticket includes a seat reservation on a specific train, you're all set and can just get on board. However, many tickets (especially for slower trains) are flexible—not tied to a particular train or specific reserved seat—and so must be validated before you board. You always need to validate the small, paper-slip tickets that you buy from newsstands or older ticket machines. Tickets from the newer machines must also be validated if they say *"Da convalidare"* near the top. To validate your ticket, stamp it in the yellow box near the platform. Once you validate a ticket, you must complete your trip within the timeframe shown on the ticket (within 6 hours for medium-distance trips; within 1.25 hours for short rides under 6 miles).If you forget to validate your ticket, go right away to the train conductor—before he comes to you—or you'll pay a fine. Note that you don't need to validate a railpass or e-ticket.

Railpasses

The **Italy Pass** for Italian State Railways may save you money if you're taking three long train rides or prefer first-class travel, but don't count on it for hop-on convenience on every train. Use the price map on page 1086 to add up your ticket costs (ticket prices on the map are for the fastest trains on a given route, many of which have reservation costs built in). Remember that railpasses are not valid on high-speed Italo trains.

Railpass travelers must make separate seat reservations for the fastest trains between major Italian cities (€10-15 each). Railpass travelers can just hop on InterCity trains (optional €5 reservation) and regional trains (no reservations possible). Making a reservation at a train station or travel agency is the same as the process to buy a ticket, so you may need to stand in line either way. Reservations for berths on overnight trains cost extra, aren't covered by railpasses, and aren't reflected on the ticket cost map.

A 23-country **Global Pass** can work well for an all-Europe trip, but is a bad value for travel exclusively in Italy. A cheaper version, the **Select Pass,** allows you to tailor a pass to your trip, provided you're traveling in three, four, or five adjacent countries directly connected by rail or ferry. For instance, with a three-country pass allowing 10 days of train travel within a two-month period ($730 for a single adult in 2012), you could choose France-Italy-Greece or Germany-Austria-Italy. A **France and Italy Pass** combines just those two countries. (If your route includes a connection in Switzerland, you'll pay extra—so the Select Pass is a better choice if you want to see the Alps). Note that none of these passes cover direct day or night trains between Italy and Paris, which require a separate ticket. Before you buy a Select Pass or France and Italy Pass, consider how many travel days you'll really need. Use the pass only for travel days that involve long hauls or several trips. Pay out of pocket for tickets on days you're taking only short, cheap rides.

For a summary of railpass deals and the latest prices, check my Guide to Eurail Passes at www.ricksteves.com/rail. If you decide to get a railpass, this guide will help you know you're getting the right one for your trip.

Train Tips

This section contains information on making seat reservations, storing baggage, avoiding theft, and dealing with strikes.

Seat Reservations: Trains can fill up, even in first class. If you're on a tight schedule, you'll want to reserve a few days ahead

Railpasses

Prices listed are for 2012 and are subject to change. For the latest prices, details, and train schedules (and easy online ordering), see my comprehensive *Guide to Eurail Passes* at www.ricksteves.com/rail.

"Saver" prices are per person for two or more people traveling together. "Youth" means under age 26. The fare for children 4–11 is half the adult individual fare or Saver fare. Kids under age 4 travel free.

ITALY PASS

	Individual 1st Class	Individual 2nd Class	Saver 1st Class	Saver 2nd Class	Youth 2nd Class
3 days in 2 months	$274	$223	$234	$192	$183
Extra rail days (max 7)	31-38	25-31	26-33	20-27	20-25

ITALY RAIL & DRIVE PASS

Any 3 rail days and 2 car days in 2 months.

Car Category	1st Class	2nd Class	Extra Car Day
Economy 2-Door	$384	$326	$69
Economy 4-Door	392	335	77
Compact	413	356	98
Intermediate	441	384	126
Economy Automatic	422	364	107
Premium	548	490	233
Extra rail days (max 3)	31	25	

Prices are per person, two traveling together. Solo travelers pay about 20 percent more. To order a Rail & Drive pass, call your travel agent or Rail Europe at 800-438-7245. *This pass is not sold by Europe Through the Back Door.*

FRANCE–ITALY PASS

	Individual 1st Class	Individual 2nd Class	Saver 1st Class	Saver 2nd Class	Youth 2nd Class
4 days in 2 months	$411	$353	$353	$300	$268
Extra rail days (max 6)	45-50	38-40	38-40	31-37	28-30

Be aware of your route. Direct Paris–Italy trains (day and overnight) and trains via Switzerland aren't covered by this pass.

GREECE–ITALY PASS

	Individual 1st Class	Individual 2nd Class	Saver 1st Class	Saver 2nd Class	Youth 2nd Class
4 days in 2 months	$384	$309	$327	$263	$252
Extra rail days (max 6)	38-40	30-32	32-34	25-27	25-27

Covers deck passage on overnight Superfast Ferries between Patras, Greece and Bari or Ancona, Italy (starts use of one travel day). Or 30-50% discount on Hellenic Mediterranean Line ferry with basic cabin Patras-Corfu-Brindisi (does not use a travel day). Does not cover travel to or on Greek islands, except a 30% discount on Blue Star Ferries. Very few trains run in Greece.

SELECTPASS

This pass covers travel in three adjacent countries. Please visit **www.ricksteves.com/rail** for four- and five-country options.

	Individual 1st Class	Saver 1st Class	Youth 2nd Class
5 days in 2 months	$486	$413	$317
6 days in 2 months	536	456	350
8 days in 2 months	633	539	413
10 days in 2 months	734	624	478

for fast trains (see "Types of Trains," earlier). Purchasing tickets or passholder reservations onboard a train comes with a nasty penalty. Buying them at the station can be a time-waster unless you use the automatic ticket machines.

If you don't need a reservation, and if your train originates at your departure point (e.g., you're catching the Milan-Venice train in Milan), arriving at least 15 minutes before the departure time will help you snare a seat.

Some major stations have train composition posters on the platforms showing where first- and second-class cars are located when the trains arrive (letters on the poster are supposed to correspond to letters posted over the platform—but they don't always). Since most trains now allow you to make reservations up to the time of departure, conductors no longer mark reserved seats with a card—instead, they simply post a list of the reservable and non-reservable seat rows (sometimes in English) in each train car's vestibule. This means that if you board a crowded train and get one of the last seats, you may be ousted when the reservation holder comes along.

Baggage Storage: Many stations have *deposito bagagli* where you can safely leave your bag for €8 per 12-hour period (payable when you pick up the bag, double-check closing hours). Due to security concerns, no Italian stations have lockers.

Theft Concerns: Italian trains are famous for their thieves. Never leave a bag unattended. Police do ride the trains, cutting down on theft. Still, for an overnight trip, I'd feel safe only in a *cuccetta* (a bunk in a special sleeping car with an attendant who keeps track of who comes and goes while you sleep—approximately €21 in a 6-bed compartment, €26 in a less-cramped four-bed compartment, €50 in a more private, double compartment).

Strikes: Strikes, which are common, generally last a day. Train employees will simply explain, *"Sciopero"* (strike). But in actuality, sporadic trains, following no particular schedule, lumber down the tracks during most strikes. When a strike is pending, travel agencies (and Web-savvy hoteliers) can check the Internet for you to see when the strike goes into effect and which trains will continue to run. Revised schedules may be posted in Italian at stations, and station personnel still working can often tell you what trains are expected to run. If I need to get somewhere and know a strike is imminent, I leave early (heading off the strike, which often begins at 9:00), or I just go to the station with extra patience in tow and hop on anything rolling in the direction I want to go.

Buses

You can usually get anywhere you want to in Italy by bus, as long as you're not in a hurry, and plan ahead using bus schedules (pick up at local TIs). For reaching small towns, buses are sometimes the only option if you don't have a car.

Buy bus tickets at newsstands or tobacco shops (with the big *T* signs). Confirm the departure point *("Dov'è la fermata?")*—some piazzas have more than one bus stop, so double-check that the posted schedule lists your destination and departure time. In general, orange buses are local city buses, and blue buses are for long distances.

Once the bus arrives, confirm the destination with the driver. You are expected to stow big backpacks underneath the bus (open the luggage compartment yourself if it's closed).

Sundays and holidays are problematic; even from large cities schedules are sparse, departing buses are jam-packed, and ticket offices are often closed. Plan ahead and buy your ticket in advance. Most travel agencies book bus (and train) tickets for just a small fee.

Renting a Car

If you're renting a car in Italy, bring your driver's license. You're also technically required to have an International Driving Permit—an official translation of your driver's license (sold at your local AAA office for $15 plus the cost of two passport-type photos; see www .aaa.com). While that's the letter of the law, I've often rented cars in Italy without having—or being asked to show—this permit.

Rental companies require you to be at least 21 years old and to have held your license for one year. Drivers under the age of 25 may incur a young-driver surcharge, and some rental companies do not rent to anyone 75 and over. If you're considered too young or old, look into leasing (described later), which has less-stringent age restrictions.

Research car rentals before you go. It's cheaper to arrange most car rentals from the US. Call several companies and look online to compare rates, or arrange a rental through your hometown travel agent.

Most of the major US rental agencies (including National, Avis, Budget, Hertz, and Thrifty) have offices in Italy. Also consider the two major Europe-based agencies, Europcar and Sixt. It can be cheaper to use a consolidator, such as Auto Europe (www .autoeurope.com) or Europe by Car (www.ebctravel.com), which compares rates at several companies to get you the best deal. However, my readers have reported problems with consolidators, ranging from misinformation to unexpected fees; because you're going through a middleman, it can be more challenging to resolve disputes that arise with the rental agency.

Regardless of the car-rental company you choose, always read the contract carefully. The fine print can conceal a host of common add-on charges—such as one-way drop-off fees, airport surcharges, or mandatory insurance policies—that aren't included in the "total price," but can be tacked on when you pick up your car. You may need to query rental agents pointedly to find out your actual cost.

For the best rental deal, rent by the week with unlimited mileage. To save money on fuel, ask for a diesel car. I normally rent the smallest, least-expensive model with a stick shift (cheaper than an automatic). An automatic transmission adds about 50 percent to the car-rental cost over a manual transmission. Almost all rentals are manual by default, so if you need an automatic, you must request one in advance; beware that these cars are usually larger models (not as maneuverable on narrow, winding roads). Roads and parking spaces are narrow in Italy, so you'll do yourself a favor by renting the smallest car that meets your needs.

For a three-week rental, allow $900 per person (based on two people sharing a car), including insurance, tolls, gas, and parking. For trips of this length, look into leasing (see page 1097); you'll save money on insurance and taxes.

You can sometimes get a GPS unit with your rental car or leased vehicle for an additional fee (around $15/day; be sure it's set to English and has all the maps you need before you drive off). Or, if you have a portable GPS device at home, consider taking it with you to Europe (buy and upload European maps before your trip). GPS apps are also available for smartphones, but downloading maps on one of these apps in Europe could lead to an exorbitant data-roaming bill (for more details, see the "Smartphones and Data Roaming" sidebar, earlier).

Big companies have offices in most cities; ask whether they can pick you up at your hotel. Small local rental companies can be cheaper but aren't as flexible. Compare pick-up costs (downtown can be cheaper than the airport) and explore drop-off options (south of Rome can be a problem). When selecting a location, don't trust the agency's description of "downtown" or "city center." In some cases, a "downtown" branch can be on the outskirts of the city—a long, costly taxi ride from the center. Before choosing, plug the addresses into a mapping website. You may find that the "train station" location is handier.

Returning a car at a big-city train station or downtown agency can be tricky; get precise details on the car drop-off location and hours. Note that rental offices usually close from midday Saturday until Monday.

When you pick up the rental car, check it thoroughly and

make sure any damage is noted on your rental agreement. Find out how your car's lights, turn signals, wipers, and fuel cap function, and know what kind of fuel the car takes. When you return the car, make sure the agent verifies its condition with you.

If you want a car for only a couple of days, a **rail-and-drive pass** (such as a EurailDrive, Select Pass Drive, or Italy Rail and Drive) can be put to thoughtful use. Certain areas are great by car, such as the Dolomites and the hill towns of Tuscany and Umbria, while most of Italy (including the Cinque Terre) is best by train. The basic Italy Rail and Drive Pass, which includes theft insurance and CDW (CDW described below), comes with two days of car rental and three days of rail in two months. While rail-and-drive passes are convenient, they're also pricey, particularly for solo travelers.

Car Insurance Options

When you rent a car, you're liable for a very high deductible, sometimes equal to the entire value of the car. Limit your financial risk in case of an accident by choosing one of these two options: Buy Collision Damage Waiver (CDW) coverage from the car-rental company (figure roughly 30 percent extra), or get coverage through your credit card (free, but more complicated).

In Italy, most car-rental companies' rates automatically include CDW coverage. Even if you try to decline CDW when you reserve your Italian car, you may find when you show up at the counter that you must buy it after all.

While each rental company has its own variation, basic CDW costs $15-35 a day and reduces your liability, but does not eliminate it. When you pick up the car, you'll be offered the chance to "buy down" the deductible to zero (for an additional $10-30/day; this is sometimes called "super CDW").

If you opt for credit-card coverage, there's a catch. You'll technically have to decline all coverage offered by the car-rental company, which means they can place a hold on your card for up to the full value of the car. In case of damage, it can be time-consuming to resolve the charges with your credit-card company. Before you decide on this option, quiz your credit-card company about how it works.

For more on car-rental insurance, see www.ricksteves.com/cdw.

Theft Insurance: Note that theft insurance (separate from CDW insurance) is mandatory in Italy. The insurance usually costs about $15-20 a day, payable when you pick up the car.

Leasing

For trips of three weeks or more, consider leasing (which automatically includes zero-deductible collision and theft insurance). By

APPENDIX

technically buying and then selling back the car, you save lots of money on tax and insurance. Leasing provides you a brand-new car with unlimited mileage and a 24-hour emergency assistance program. You can lease for as little as 21 days to as long as six months. Car leases must be arranged from the US. One of many companies offering affordable lease packages is Europe by Car (US tel. 800-223-1516, www.ebctravel.com).

Driving

Driving in Italy can be scary—a video game for keeps, and you only get one quarter. Italian drivers can be aggressive. They drive fast and tailgate as if it were required. They pass where Americans are taught not to—on blind corners and just before tunnels. Roads have narrow shoulders or none at all. Driving in the countryside is less stressful than driving through urban areas, but stay alert. On one-lane roads, larger vehicles have the right-of-way. If you're on a truckers' route, stifle your Good Samaritan impulse when you see provocatively dressed women standing by camper-vans at the side of the road; they're not having car trouble.

Road Rules: Stay out of restricted traffic zones or you'll risk huge fines. Car traffic is restricted in many city centers. Don't drive or park in any area that has a sign reading *Zona Traffico Limitato* (*ZTL*, often shown above a red circle, see image). If you do, your license plate can be photographed and a hefty (€100-plus) ticket mailed to your home without your ever having met a cop. Bumbling in and out of these zones can net you multiple fines. If your hotel is within a restricted area, it's best to ask your

hotelier to direct you to parking outside the zone. (Although your hotelier can register your car as an authorized vehicle permitted to enter the zone, this usually isn't worth the hassle).

As for other rules, seatbelts are mandatory, kids 12 and under need a child-safety or booster seat, and you should keep headlights on at all times outside of urban areas. It's illegal to drive while using your mobile phone without a hands-free headset. In Europe, you're not allowed to turn right on a red light, unless there is a sign or signal specifically authorizing it. Ask your car-rental company about these rules, or check the US State Department website (www.travel.state.gov, click on "International Travel," then specify "Italy" and click "Traffic Safety and Road Conditions").

Tolls: Italy's freeway system, the autostrada, is as good as our interstate system, but you'll pay about a dollar for every 10 minutes of use. (I paid €20 for the four-hour drive from Bolzano to Pisa.) While I favor the freeways because I feel they're safer, cheaper

Driving in Italy

AUSTRIA

SWITZERLAND

Brenner Pass

Villach

Mt. Blanc Tunnel

Lake Como (Varenna)

Dolomites (Bolzano)

SLOVENIA

70m·2h

260m·5h

110m·2.5h

160m·4.5h (via Cortina)

100m·1.5h

155m·2.5h

Trieste

95m·1.75h

145m·2.5h

30m·.75h

Verona

80m·1.5h

Venice

CROATIA

Milan

100m·1.75h

185m·3.25h

85m·2.5h

200m·4h

175m·2.75h

135m·2.5h

225m·4h

155m·3h

Ravenna

160m·2.75h

175m·.25h

115m·2h

Cinque Terre (La Spezia)

90m·1.75h

50m·1h

Florence

125m·2.25h

Ventimiglia

70m·1.5h

100m·2h

Pisa

45m·1h

80m·2h

Assisi

Siena

100m·1.75h

55m·1.5h

115m·2.25h

2.10m·4h

75m·1.5h

Orvieto

75m·1.5h

Note: Your times may vary based on traffic, construction and road conditions.

Rome

155m·2.5h

35m·1h

Naples

Salerno

30m·.75h

30m·1h

Sorrento

30m·1.5h

m = miles
h = hours

Paestum

APPENDIX

(saving time and gas), and less nerve-wracking than smaller roads, savvy local drivers know which toll-free *superstradas* are actually faster and more direct than the autostrada (e.g., Florence to Pisa). For more information, visit www.autostrade.it.

Fuel: Fuel is expensive—often about $8.50 per gallon. Diesel cars are more common in Europe than back home, so be sure you know what type of fuel your car takes before you fill up. Gas pumps are color-coded for unleaded *(senza piombo)* or diesel *(gasolio).* Autostrada rest stops are self-service stations open daily without a siesta break. Many 24-hour-a-day stations are entirely automated. Small-town stations are usually cheaper and offer full service but shorter hours.

Maps and Signage: A good map is essential. Learn the universal road signs (explained in charts in most road atlases and at service stations). Although roads are numbered on maps, actual road signs don't list route numbers. Instead, roads are indicated by blue signs with a city name on them (for example, if you want to take a road heading east out of Venice—marked route S-11 on your map—you'd follow signs to Padua, the next town along this road). The signs are inconsistent: They may direct you to the nearest big city or simply the next town along the route.

STOP AND LEARN THESE ROAD SIGNS

Speed Limit (km/hr) · Yield · No Passing · End of No Passing Zone

One Way · Intersection · Main Road · Freeway

Danger · No Entry · No Entry for Cars · All Vehicles Prohibited

Parking · No Parking · Customs · Peace

Theft: Cars are routinely vandalized and stolen. Thieves easily recognize rental cars and assume they are filled with a tourist's gear. Try to make your car look locally owned by hiding the "tourist-owned" rental-company decals and putting an Italian newspaper in your back window. Be sure all of your valuables are out of sight and locked in the trunk, or even better, with you or in your room.

Parking: White lines generally mean parking is free. Yellow lines mean that parking is reserved for residents only (who have permits). Blue lines mean you'll have to pay—usually €1.50 per hour (use machine, leave time-stamped receipt on dashboard). If there's no meter, there's probably a roving attendant who will take your money. Study the signs. Often the free zones have a 30- or 60-minute time limit. Signs showing a street cleaner and a day of the week indicate which day the street is cleaned; there's a €100 tow-fee incentive to learn the days of the week in Italian.

Zona disco has nothing to do with dancing. Italian cars come equipped with a time disk (a cardboard clock), which you set at your arrival time and lay on the dashboard so the attendant knows how long you've been parked. This is a fine system that all drivers should take advantage of. (If your rental car doesn't come with a *zona disco*, pick one up at a tobacco shop or just write your arrival time on a piece of paper and place it on the dashboard.)

Garages are safe, save time, and help you avoid the stress of parking tickets. Take the parking voucher with you to pay the cashier before you leave.

Cheap Flights

If you're visiting one or more cities on a longer European trip, or linking up far-flung Italian cities (such as Rome and Venice)

consider the affordable intra-European airlines. While trains are still the best way to connect places that are close together, a flight can save both time and money on long journeys. When comparing your options, factor in the time it takes to get to the airport and how early you'll need to arrive to check in before the flight. Most flights make sense only as an alternative to a train ride five or more hours in length.

The best comparison search engine for both international and intra-European flights is www.kayak.com. For inexpensive flights within Europe, try www.skyscanner.com or www.hipmunk.com. If you're not sure who flies to your destination, check its airport's website for a list of carriers.

Be aware of the potential drawbacks of flying on the cheap: nonrefundable and nonchangeable tickets, minimal or nonexistent customer service, treks to airports far outside town, and stingy baggage allowances with steep overage fees. If you're traveling with lots of luggage, a cheap flight can quickly become a bad deal. To avoid unpleasant surprises, read the small print before you book.

Resources

Resources from Rick Steves

Rick Steves' Italy 2013 is one of many books in my series on European travel, which includes country guidebooks, city guidebooks (Rome, Florence, Paris, London, etc.), Snapshot guides (excerpted chapters from my country guides), Pocket Guides (full-color little books on Rome and other big cities), and my budget-travel skills handbook, *Rick Steves' Europe Through the Back Door.* Most of my titles are available as ebooks. My phrase books—for Italian, French, German, Spanish, and Portuguese—are practical and budget-oriented. My other books include *Europe 101* (a crash course on art and history), *Mediterranean Cruise Ports* (how to make the most of your time in port), and *Travel as a Political Act* (a travelogue sprinkled with tips for bringing home a global perspective). A more complete list of my titles appears near the end of this book.

Video: My public television series, *Rick Steves' Europe,* covers European destinations in 100 shows, with 15 episodes on Italy. To watch episodes online, visit www.hulu.com/rick-steves-europe; for scripts and local airtimes, see www.ricksteves.com/tv.

Audio: My weekly public radio show, *Travel with Rick Steves,* features interviews with travel experts from around the world. I've

Begin Your Trip at www.ricksteves.com

At ricksteves.com, you'll discover a wealth of free information on European destinations, including fresh monthly news and helpful tips from thousands of fellow travelers. You'll find my latest guidebook updates (www.ricksteves.com/update), a monthly travel e-newsletter (easy and free to sign up), my personal travel blog, and my free Rick Steves Audio Europe smartphone app (if you don't have a smartphone, you can access the same content via podcasts). You can even follow me on Facebook and Twitter.

Our **online Travel Store** offers travel bags and accessories that I've designed specifically to help you travel smarter and lighter. These include my popular carry-on bags (roll-aboard and backpack versions), money belts, totes, toiletries kits, adapters, other accessories, and a wide selection of guidebooks, planning maps, and DVDs.

Choosing the right **railpass** for your trip—amid hundreds of options—can drive you nutty. We'll help you choose the best pass for your needs and ship it to you for free, plus give you a bunch of free extras.

Want to travel with greater efficiency and less stress? We organize **tours** with more than three dozen itineraries and more than 500 departures reaching the best destinations in this book...and beyond. Our Italy tours include "the best of" in 17 days, Village Italy in 14 days, South Italy in 13 days, Sicily in 10 days, Venice-Florence-Rome in 10 days, the Heart of Italy in nine days, My Way: Italy "unguided" tour in 13 days, and a week-long Rome tour. You'll enjoy great guides, a fun bunch of travel partners (with small groups of generally around 24-28), and plenty of room to spread out in a big, comfy bus. You'll find European adventures to fit every vacation length. For all the details, and to get our Tour Catalog and a free Rick Steves Tour Experience DVD (filmed on location during an actual tour), visit www.ricksteves.com or call us at 425/608-4217.

also produced free self-guided **audio tours** of the top sights and neighborhoods in Florence, Rome, Venice, and more. All of this audio content is available for free at Rick Steves Audio Europe, an extensive online library organized by destination. Choose whatever interests you, and download it for free via the Rick Steves Audio Europe

smartphone app, www.ricksteves.com/audioeurope, iTunes, or Google Play.

Maps

The black-and-white maps in this book are concise and simple, designed to help you locate recommended places and get to local TIs, where you can pick up more in-depth maps of cities and regions (usually free). Better maps are sold at newsstands and bookstores. Before you buy a map, look at it to be sure it has the level of detail you want. Drivers will want to pick up a good, detailed map in Europe (I'd recommend a 1:200,000- or 1:300,000-scale map).

Other Guidebooks

If you're like most travelers, this book is all you need. But if you're heading beyond my recommended destinations, $40 for extra maps and books can be money well-spent. If you'll be spending a lot of time in Italian cities, consider *Rick Steves' Florence & Tuscany, Rick Steves' Venice,* or *Rick Steves' Rome.*

The following books are worthwhile, though most are not updated annually; check the publication date before you buy. Lonely Planet's *Italy* is thorough, well-researched, and packed with travel information, maps, and hotel recommendations for various budgets. The similar *Rough Guide to Italy* is also good and more insightful, updated by British researchers. The highly opinionated *Let's Go: Italy,* researched by Harvard students, is great for students and vagabonds. If you're a low-budget train traveler interested in hosteling and the youth and nightlife scene (which I have largely ignored), get *Let's Go: Italy.* The Italy section in the bigger *Let's Go: Europe* is sparse.

Cultural and Sightseeing Guides: The colorful Eyewitness series, which focuses mainly on sights, has editions on Italy, its various regions, and the major cities. They're fun for their great graphics and photos, but they're relatively skimpy on content and weigh a ton. You can buy them in Italy (no more expensive than in the US) or simply borrow a book for a minute from other travelers at certain sights to make sure that you're aware of that place's highlights. The tall, green Michelin guides to Italy and Rome have minimal information on room and board, but include great maps for drivers and lots of solid, encyclopedic coverage of sights, customs, and culture (sold in English in Italy). The Cadogan guides to various parts of Italy offer a thoughtful look at the rich and confusing local culture, as does *Culture Shock: Italy*.

Recommended Books and Movies

To learn more about Italy past and present, check out a few of these books or films.

Nonfiction

For the classics of Italian history, look to Machiavelli's *The Prince* and *Florentine Histories*. Written in the 18th century, Edward Gibbon's *Decline and Fall of the Roman Empire* is the landmark history of ancient Rome.

Travelers' Tales Italy (Calcagno) is an excellent compilation of travel writing. Susan Cahill collected travelogues by female authors in *Desiring Italy*. In *Italian Days*, Barbara Grizzuti Harrison crafts travel essays on destinations ranging from Milan to Naples.

Italian Neighbors (Parks) describes life as an Englishman in a small Italian town, while *The Italians* (Barzini), written by an Italian, sheds light on the national character of this fascinating country.

Florence history buffs would enjoy reading the story of the Renaissance city's first family, *The House of Medici* (Hibbert). *Brunelleschi's Dome* (King) describes the trials involved with building Florence's magnificent Duomo. *Under the Tuscan Sun* was a bestseller for Frances Mayes (and is better than the movie of the same name).

Out of Paul Hofmann's multiple books about Italy, *The Seasons of Rome* is the favorite among readers. Elizabeth Gilbert's eloquent *Eat, Pray, Love* describes her time in Rome (in the "Eat" section). David Macaulay's illustrated books about the Eternal City—*Rome Antics* and *City: A Story of Roman Planning and Construction*—please both kids and adults.

For a solid overview of Venice, try *A History of Venice* (Norwich). Mary McCarthy's *Venice Observed* is a well-written memoir. In *The City of Falling Angels*, John Berendt tells the real-life mystery of the La Fenice Opera House fire.

For a true story about the Sicilian Mafia, consider *Excellent Cadavers* (Stille). *Midnight in Sicily* (Robb) offers a good general history of the Mob. In the memoir *Christ Stopped at Eboli: The Story of a Year*, Carlo Levi describes his banishment to southern Italy.

Pomp and Sustenance: Twenty-Five Centuries of Sicilian Food (Simeti) is both a cookbook and an historical overview. Gourmets also like *The Marling Menu-Master for Italy*.

Fiction

Fans of classical literature will want to read Dante's *Divine Comedy* and Boccaccio's *Decameron*. Among the Shakespeare plays set in Italy are *Romeo and Juliet* (Verona), *The Merchant of Venice*, *Much Ado About Nothing* (Sicily), *The Two Gentlemen of Verona*, and *The Taming of the Shrew* (Padua).

In his 18th-century collection of writings titled *Italian Journey*, Goethe describes his travels to Rome, Sicily, and Naples. Henry James often wrote stories with an Italian theme, and three recommended books—*The Wings of the Dove*, *Italian Hours*, and *The Aspern Papers and Other Stories*—use Venice as their backdrop. Another classic tale is Thomas Mann's *Death in Venice*.

For historical fiction that brings ancient Rome to life, try *The First Man in Rome* (McCullough) and *I, Claudius* (Graves). *Pompeii* (Harris), set in the ancient doomed city, tells of a young man's rescue attempt.

In the 19th and early 20th centuries, great European writers fell in love with Florence. Two great books from this time are George Eliot's *Romola* and E. M. Forster's *A Room with a View*. Modern novels with Florence as the setting include *The Passion of Artemisia* (Vreeland), *The Sixteen Pleasures* (Hellenga), *Birth of Venus* (Dunant), and *Galileo's Daughter* (Sobel).

If Venice is on your itinerary, consider reading *Invisible Cities* (Calvino), set in the city during Marco Polo's time; *The Passion* (Winterson), a complex tale of love; and *In the Company of the Courtesan* (Dunant), a chronicle of romantic intrigue in Renaissance Venice.

Regarded as one of the most important works of Italian literature, *The Leopard* (di Lampedusa) describes Sicilian life during the Risorgimento. *A Bell for Adano*, set in Sicily, won John Hersey the Pulitzer Prize in 1945. *A Soldier of the Great War* (Helprin)—which takes place partially in the Italian Alps and partially in Sicily—is a brutal tale set in World War I. *A Thread of Grace* (Russell) follows a group of Jews trying to find a safe haven in WWII Italy.

One of the best (and bestselling) murder mysteries is Umberto Eco's *The Name of the Rose*, set in a 14th-century Italian monastery. Mystery fans should also consider the books by Michael Dibdin, including *Ratking* (set in Umbria) and *Cabal* (Rome), *A Full Rich Death* (Florence), and *Dead Lagoon* (Venice). Dan Brown, the author of *The Da Vinci Code*, used Rome as the backdrop for his earlier murder mystery, *Angels and Demons*. Two Florentine-based mysteries are *The Dante Game* (Langton) and *Bella Donna* (Cherne). Donna Leon's detective stories often take place in Venice; *Death at La Fenice* is one of her most popular.

Films

Roberto Rossellini's *Open City* (1945) and Vittorio de Sica's *Bicycle Thieves* (1949), both classics of Italian Neorealism, continue to inspire audiences today.

In *Roman Holiday* (1953), Audrey Hepburn and Gregory Peck sightsee the city on his scooter. Two campy big-budget Hollywood flicks bring ancient Rome to life: *Ben-Hur* (1959) and *Spartacus* (1960). In *La Dolce Vita* (1961), Fellini captures the Roman character, while *Gladiator* (2000) was a crowd-pleaser and an Academy Award winner.

1900 (1977) is Bernardo Bertolucci's epic tale of life under fascism; it stars Robert De Niro and Gérard Depardieu.

A Room with a View (1986), a close adaptation of the classic novel, captures Florence's appeal to turn-of-the-century English travelers. Oscar-winning *Life Is Beautiful* (1997) has sections set in a Tuscan town.

Cinema Paradiso (1990), about a film projectionist and a little boy in post-WWII Sicily, won the Oscar for Best Foreign Picture. In *Enchanted April* (1991), filmed in Portofino, an all-star British cast fall in love, discuss relationships, eat well, and take naps in the sun. *Ciao, Professore!* (1994) shows the influence of a grade-school teacher in Southern Italy. In *Il Postino* (1995), poet Pablo Neruda befriends his Italian postman.

In *Bread and Tulips* (2000), a harassed Italian housewife discovers beauty, love, and her true self in Venice. For an adrenaline-laced chase scene through Venice's canals, see *The Italian Job* (2003).

The warm-hearted epic *Best of Youth* (2003), a story of two brothers, takes place in several Italian locations and gives you a good feel for the last several decades of Italian history. *Nuovomondo* (2006, also called *The Golden Door*) tells the story of Sicilian immigrants leaving home for Ellis Island.

Gorgeous Italian backdrops star in two 2010 movies: *Letters to Juliet*, shot in Verona and Siena, and the film adaptation of *Eat, Pray, Love*, with scenes in Naples and Rome.

Holidays and Festivals

In Italy, holidays seem to strike without warning. For instance, every town has a festival honoring its patron saint. The Vatican City in Rome closes for many lesser-known Catholic holidays—confirm their schedule at http://mv.vatican.va.

This list includes selected festivals in major cities in 2013, plus national holidays observed throughout Italy. Many sights and banks close down on national holidays—keep this in mind when planning your itinerary. Before planning a trip around a festival,

verify its dates by checking the festival's website or TI sites (www
.italia.it); www.whatsonwhen.com also lists many festival dates.

In Italy, hotels get booked up on Easter weekend (from Good
Friday through Easter Monday), April 25 (Liberation Day), May
1 (Labor Day), Ascension Day (May 9 in 2013), November 1 (All
Saint's Day), and on Fridays and Saturdays year-round. Some hotels
require you to book the full three-day weekend around a holiday.
For sports events, see www.sportsevents365.com for schedules and
ticket information.

Here are the major holidays in 2013:

Jan 1	New Year's Day
Jan 6	Epiphany
Jan	Fashion convention, Florence
Jan 26-Feb 12	Carnevale (Mardi Gras, www.carnevale .venezia.it), Venice
Early Feb	Carnevale Celebrations/Mardi Gras in Florence (costumed parades, street water fights, jousting competitions)
March 31	Easter Sunday (and Scoppio del Carro fireworks in Florence)
April 1	Easter Monday
Early April	Vinitaly (wine festival), Verona
April	Italy's Cultural Heritage Week (www .beniculturali.it)
April 21	City Birthday, Rome
April 25	Italian Liberation Day, St. Mark's Day, Venice
May 1	Labor Day
May 9	Feast of the Ascension Day
Mid-May	Cricket Festival, Florence (music, entertainment, food, crickets sold in cages)
Late May	Fashion convention, Florence
Late May-early June	Vogalonga Regatta, Venice
June 1-30	Annual Flower Display, Florence (carpet of flowers on the main square, Piazza della Signoria)
June 2	Anniversary of the Republic
June 16-17	Festival of St. Ranieri, Pisa
Mid-June-Aug	Verona Opera season
June 24	St. John the Baptist Day, Rome; Festival of St. John the Baptist, Florence (parades, dances, boat races); and Calcio Fiorentino (costumed soccer game on Florence's Piazza Santa Croce)
June 29	Sts. Peter and Paul's Day, most fervently celebrated in Rome

APPENDIX

2013

JANUARY
S	M	T	W	T	F	S
		1	2	3	4	5
6	7	8	9	10	11	12
13	14	15	16	17	18	19
20	21	22	23	24	25	26
27	28	29	30	31		

FEBRUARY
S	M	T	W	T	F	S
					1	2
3	4	5	6	7	8	9
10	11	12	13	14	15	16
17	18	19	20	21	22	23
24	25	26	27	28		

MARCH
S	M	T	W	T	F	S
					1	2
3	4	5	6	7	8	9
10	11	12	13	14	15	16
17	18	19	20	21	22	23
24/31	25	26	27	28	29	30

APRIL
S	M	T	W	T	F	S
	1	2	3	4	5	6
7	8	9	10	11	12	13
14	15	16	17	18	19	20
21	22	23	24	25	26	27
28	29	30				

MAY
S	M	T	W	T	F	S
			1	2	3	4
5	6	7	8	9	10	11
12	13	14	15	16	17	18
19	20	21	22	23	24	25
26	27	28	29	30	31	

JUNE
S	M	T	W	T	F	S
						1
2	3	4	5	6	7	8
9	10	11	12	13	14	15
16	17	18	19	20	21	22
23/30	24	25	26	27	28	29

JULY
S	M	T	W	T	F	S
	1	2	3	4	5	6
7	8	9	10	11	12	13
14	15	16	17	18	19	20
21	22	23	24	25	26	27
28	29	30	31			

AUGUST
S	M	T	W	T	F	S
				1	2	3
4	5	6	7	8	9	10
11	12	13	14	15	16	17
18	19	20	21	22	23	24
25	26	27	28	29	30	31

SEPTEMBER
S	M	T	W	T	F	S
1	2	3	4	5	6	7
8	9	10	11	12	13	14
15	16	17	18	19	20	21
22	23	24	25	26	27	28
29	30					

OCTOBER
S	M	T	W	T	F	S
		1	2	3	4	5
6	7	8	9	10	11	12
13	14	15	16	17	18	19
20	21	22	23	24	25	26
27	28	29	30	31		

NOVEMBER
S	M	T	W	T	F	S
					1	2
3	4	5	6	7	8	9
10	11	12	13	14	15	16
17	18	19	20	21	22	23
24	25	26	27	28	29	30

DECEMBER
S	M	T	W	T	F	S
1	2	3	4	5	6	7
8	9	10	11	12	13	14
15	16	17	18	19	20	21
22	23	24	25	26	27	28
29	30	31				

APPENDIX

Late June–early Sept	Florence's annual outdoor cinema season (contemporary films)
July 2	Palio horse race, Siena
Mid-July	Feast and Regatta of the Redeemer (held third weekend of month), Venice
Aug	Musical Weeks, Lake Maggiore
Aug 10	St. Lawrence Day, Rome
Aug 15	Assumption of Mary (Ferragosto)
Aug 16	Palio horse race, Siena
Sept	Chestnut Festivals (festivals, chestnut roasts), most towns, mainly north of Rome
Early Sept	Historical Regatta (held first weekend of month—Sept 7-8 in 2013), Venice; and Festa della Rificolona, Florence (children's procession with lanterns, street performances, parade)

Sept 13-14	Volto Santo (procession and fair), Lucca
Oct	Musica dei Popoli Festival, Florence (ethnic and folk music and dances)
Mid-Oct	Castelrotto Festival (held second week-end of month—Oct 12-13 in 2013), Dolomites
Nov 1	All Saints' Day
Nov 21	Feast of Our Lady of Good Health, Venice
Dec	Christmas Market, Rome, Piazza Navona; and crèches in churches throughout Italy
Dec 8	Feast of the Immaculate Conception
Dec 25	Christmas
Dec 26	St. Stephen's Day

Conversions and Climate

Numbers and Stumblers

- Europeans write a few of their numbers differently than we do. 1 = 1, 4 = 4, 7 = 7.
- In Europe, dates appear as day/month/year, so Christmas is 25/12/13.
- Commas are decimal points and decimals commas. A dollar and a half is 1,50, one thousand is 1.000, and there are 5.280 feet in a mile.
- When pointing, use your whole hand, palm down.
- When counting with fingers, start with your thumb. If you hold up your first finger to request one item, you'll probably get two.
- What Americans call the second floor of a building is the first floor in Europe.
- On escalators and moving sidewalks, Europeans keep the left "lane" open for passing. Keep to the right.

Roman Numerals

In the US, you'll see Roman numerals—which originated in ancient Rome—used for copyright dates, clocks, and the Super Bowl. In Italy, you're likely to observe these numbers chiseled on statues and buildings. If you want to do some numeric detective work, here's how: In Roman numerals, as in ours, the highest numbers (thousands, hundreds) come first, followed by smaller numbers. Many numbers are made by combining numerals into sets: V = 5, so VIII = 8 (5 plus 3). Roman numerals follow a subtraction principle for multiples of fours (4, 40, 400, etc.) and nines (9, 90, 900, etc.); the number four, for example, is written as IV

APPENDIX

(1 subtracted from 5), rather than IIII. The number nine is IX (1 subtracted from 10).

Rick Steves' Italy 2013—written in Italian with Roman numerals—would translate as *Rick Steves' Italia MMXIII*. Big numbers such as dates can look daunting at first. The easiest way to handle them is to read the numbers in discrete chunks. For example, Michelangelo was born in MCDLXXV. Break it down: M (1,000) + CD (100 subtracted from 500, or 400) + LXX (50 + 10 + 10, or 70) + V (5) = 1475. It was a very good year.

M = 1000	XL = 40
CM = 900	X = 10
D = 500	IX = 9
CD = 400	V = 5
C = 100	IV = 4
XC = 90	I = duh
L = 50	

Metric Conversions (approximate)

A kilogram is 2.2 pounds, and 1 liter is about a quart, or almost four to a gallon. A kilometer is six-tenths of a mile. I figure kilometers to miles by cutting them in half and adding back 10 percent of the original (120 km: 60 + 12 = 72 miles, 300 km: 150 + 30 = 180 miles).

1 foot = 0.3 meter	1 square yard = 0.8 square meter
1 yard = 0.9 meter	1 square mile = 2.6 square kilometers
1 mile = 1.6 kilometers	1 ounce = 28 grams
1 centimeter = 0.4 inch	1 quart = 0.95 liter
1 meter = 39.4 inches	1 kilogram = 2.2 pounds
1 kilometer = 0.62 mile	32°F = 0°C

Clothing Sizes

When shopping for clothing, use these US-to-European comparisons as general guidelines (but note that no conversion is perfect).

- Women's dresses and blouses: Add 30
  (US size 10 = European size 40)
- Men's suits and jackets: Add 10
  (US size 40 regular = European size 50)
- Men's shirts: Multiply by 2 and add about 8
  (US size 15 collar = European size 38)
- Women's shoes: Add about 30
  (US size 8 = European size 38-39)
- Men's shoes: Add 32-34
  (US size 9 = European size 41; US size 11 = European size 45)

APPENDIX

Italy's Climate

First line, average daily high; second line, average daily low; third line, average days without rain. For more detailed weather statistics for destinations in this book (as well as the rest of the world), check www.worldclimate.com.

	J	F	M	A	M	J	J	A	S	O	N	D
Rome												
	52°	55°	59°	66°	74°	82°	87°	86°	79°	71°	61°	55°
	40°	42°	45°	50°	56°	63°	67°	67°	62°	55°	49°	44°
	13	19	23	24	26	26	30	29	25	23	19	21
Milan and Florence												
	40°	46°	56°	65°	74°	80°	84°	82°	75°	63°	51°	43°
	32°	35°	43°	49°	57°	63°	67°	66°	61°	52°	43°	35°
	25	21	24	22	23	21	25	24	25	23	20	24
Venice												
	42°	46°	53°	62°	70°	76°	81°	80°	75°	65°	53°	46°
	33°	35°	41°	49°	56°	63°	66°	65°	61°	53°	44°	37°
	25	21	24	21	23	22	24	24	25	24	21	23

Temperature Conversion: Fahrenheit and Celsius

Europe takes its temperature using the Celsius scale, while we opt for Fahrenheit. For a rough conversion from Celsius to Fahrenheit, double the number and add 30. For weather, remember that 28°C is 82°F—perfect. For health, 37°C is just right.

Packing Checklist

Whether you're traveling for five days or five weeks, here's what you'll need to bring. Pack light to enjoy the sweet freedom of true mobility. Happy travels!

❑ 5 shirts: long- and short-sleeve
❑ 1 sweater or lightweight fleece
❑ 2 pairs pants
❑ 1 pair shorts
❑ 1 swimsuit
❑ 5 pairs underwear and socks
❑ 1 pair shoes
❑ 1 rainproof jacket with hood
❑ Tie or scarf
❑ Money belt
❑ Money—your mix of:
  ❑ Debit card (for ATM withdrawals)
  ❑ Credit card
  ❑ Hard cash (in easy-to-exchange $20 bills)
❑ Documents plus photocopies:
  ❑ Passport
  ❑ Printout of airline eticket
  ❑ Driver's license
  ❑ Student ID and hostel card
  ❑ Railpass/car rental voucher
  ❑ Insurance details
❑ Daypack
❑ Electronics—your choice of:
  ❑ Camera (and related gear)
  ❑ Computer/mobile devices (phone, MP3 player, ereader, etc.)
  ❑ Chargers for each of the above
  ❑ Plug adapter
❑ Empty water bottle

❑ Wristwatch and alarm clock
❑ Earplugs
❑ Toiletries kit
  ❑ Toiletries
  ❑ Medicines and vitamins
  ❑ First-aid kit
  ❑ Glasses/contacts/sunglasses (with prescriptions)
❑ Sealable plastic baggies
❑ Laundry soap
❑ Clothesline
❑ Small towel
❑ Sewing kit
❑ Travel information (guidebooks and maps)
❑ Address list (for sending postcards)
❑ Postcards and photos from home
❑ Notepad and pen
❑ Journal

If you plan to carry on your luggage, note that all liquids must be in 3.4-ounce or smaller containers and fit within a single quart-size sealable baggie. For details, see www.tsa.gov/travelers.

Hotel Reservation

To: _____   _____
              hotel   *email or fax*

From: _____   _____
              name   *email or fax*

Today's date: _____ / _____ / _____
                day   *month*   *year*

Dear Hotel _____ ,
Please make this reservation for me:

Name: _____

Total # of people: _____   # of rooms: _____   # of nights: _____

Arriving: _____ / _____ / _____   My time of arrival (24-hr clock): _____
             day *month* *year*   (I will telephone if I will be late)

Departing: _____ / _____ / _____
              day *month* *year*

Room(s): Single____   Double ____   Twin ____   Triple ____   Quad____

With: Toilet ____   Shower ____   Bath ____   Sink only ____

Special needs: View____   Quiet____   Cheapest ____   Ground Floor____

Please email or fax confirmation of my reservation, along with the type of
room reserved and the price. Please also inform me of your cancellation
policy. After I hear from you, I will quickly send my credit-card information
as a deposit to hold the room. Thank you.

_____
Name

_____
Address

_____
City   *State*   *Zip Code*   *Country*

Before hoteliers can make your reservation, they want to know the informa-
tion listed above. You can use this form as the basis for your email, or you can
photocopy this page, fill in the information, and send it as a fax (also available
online at www.ricksteves.com/reservation).

Italian Survival Phrases

Good day.	Buon giorno.	bwohn JOR-noh
Do you speak English?	Parla inglese?	PAR-lah een-GLAY-zay
Yes. / No.	Si. / No.	see / noh
I (don't) understand.	(Non) capisco.	(nohn) kah-PEES-koh
Please.	Per favore.	pehr fah-VOH-ray
Thank you.	Grazie.	GRAHT-seeay
You're welcome.	Prego.	PRAY-go
I'm sorry.	Mi dispiace.	mee dee-speeAH-chay
Excuse me.	Mi scusi.	mee SKOO-zee
(No) problem.	(Non) c'è un problema.	(nohn) cheh oon proh-BLAY-mah
Good.	Va bene.	vah BEHN-ay
Goodbye.	Arrivederci.	ah-ree-vay-DEHR-chee
one / two	uno / due	OO-noh / DOO-ay
three / four	tre / quattro	tray / KWAH-troh
five / six	cinque / sei	CHEENG-kway / SEHee
seven / eight	sette / otto	SEHT-tay / OT-toh
nine / ten	nove / dieci	NOV-ay / deeAY-chee
How much is it?	Quanto costa?	KWAHN-toh KOS-tah
Write it?	Me lo scrive?	may loh SKREE-vay
Is it free?	È gratis?	eh GRAH-tees
Is it included?	È incluso?	eh een-KLOO-zoh
Where can I buy / find...?	Dove posso comprare / trovare...?	DOH-vay POS-soh kohm-PRAH-ray / troh-VAH-ray
I'd like / We'd like...	Vorrei / Vorremmo...	vor-REHee / vor-RAY-moh
...a room.	...una camera.	OO-nah KAH-meh-rah
...a ticket to ____.	...un biglietto per ____.	oon beel-YEHT-toh pehr
Is it possible?	È possibile?	eh poh-SEE-bee-lay
Where is...?	Dov'è...?	DOH-veh
...the train station	...la stazione	lah staht-seeOH-nay
...the bus station	...la stazione degli autobus	lah staht-seeOH-nay DAYL-yee OW-toh-boos
...tourist information	...informazioni per turisti	een-for-maht-seeOH-nee pehr too-REE-stee
...the toilet	...la toilette	lah twah-LEHT-tay
men	uomini, signori	WOH-mee-nee, seen-YOH-ree
women	donne, signore	DON-nay, seen-YOH-ray
left / right	sinistra / destra	see-NEE-strah / DEHS-trah
straight	sempre diritto	SEHM-pray dee-REE-toh
When do you open / close?	A che ora aprite / chiudete?	ah kay OH-rah ah-PREE-tay / keeoo-DAY-tay
At what time?	A che ora?	ah kay OH-rah
Just a moment.	Un momento.	oon moh-MAYN-toh
now / soon / later	adesso / presto / tardi	ah-DEHS-soh / PREHS-toh / TAR-dee
today / tomorrow	oggi / domani	OH-jee / doh-MAH-nee

APPENDIX

In an Italian-speaking Restaurant

I'd like...	Vorrei...	vor-REHee
We'd like...	Vorremmo...	vor-RAY-moh
...to reserve...	...prenotare...	pray-noh-TAH-ray
...a table for one / two.	...un tavolo per uno / due.	oon TAH-voh-loh pehr OO-noh / DOO-ay
Non-smoking.	Non fumare.	nohn foo-MAH-ray
Is this seat free?	È libero questo posto?	eh LEE-bay-roh KWEHS-toh POH-stoh
The menu (in English), please.	Il menù (in inglese), per favore.	eel may-NOO (een een-GLAY-zay) pehr fah-VOH-ray
service (not) included	servizio (non) incluso	sehr-VEET-seeoh (nohn) een-KLOO-zoh
cover charge	pane e coperto	PAH-nay ay koh-PEHR-toh
to go	da portar via	dah POR-tar VEE-ah
with / without	con / senza	kohn / SEHN-sah
and / or	e / o	ay / oh
menu (of the day)	menù (del giorno)	may-NOO (dayl JOR-noh)
specialty of the house	specialità della casa	spay-chah-lee-TAH DEHL-lah KAH-zah
first course (pasta, soup)	primo piatto	PREE-moh peeAH-toh
main course (meat, fish)	secondo piatto	say-KOHN-doh peeAH-toh
side dishes	contorni	kohn-TOR-nee
bread	pane	PAH-nay
cheese	formaggio	for-MAH-joh
sandwich	panino	pah-NEE-noh
soup	minestra, zuppa	mee-NEHS-trah, TSOO-pah
salad	insalata	een-sah-LAH-tah
meat	carne	KAR-nay
chicken	pollo	POH-loh
fish	pesce	PEH-shay
seafood	frutti di mare	FROO-tee dee MAH-ray
fruit / vegetables	frutta / legumi	FROO-tah / lay-GOO-mee
dessert	dolci	DOHL-chee
tap water	acqua del rubinetto	AH-kwah dayl roo-bee-NAY-toh
mineral water	acqua minerale	AH-kwah mee-nay-RAH-lay
milk	latte	LAH-tay
(orange) juice	succo (d'arancia)	SOO-koh (dah-RAHN-chah)
coffee / tea	caffè / tè	kah-FEH / teh
wine	vino	VEE-noh
red / white	rosso / bianco	ROH-soh / beeAHN-koh
glass / bottle	bicchiere / bottiglia	bee-keeAY-ray / boh-TEEL-yah
beer	birra	BEE-rah
Cheers!	Cin cin!	cheen cheen
More. / Another.	Ancora un po.' / Un altro.	ahn-KOH-rah oon poh / oon AHL-troh
The same.	Lo stesso.	loh STEHS-soh
The bill, please.	Il conto, per favore.	eel KOHN-toh pehr fah-VOH-ray
tip	mancia	MAHN-chah
Delicious!	Delizioso!	day-leet-seeOH-zoh

For more user-friendly Italian phrases, check out *Rick Steves' Italian Phrase Book & Dictionary* or *Rick Steves' French, Italian, and German Phrase Book*.

APPENDIX

INDEX

INDEX

MAP INDEX

MAP INDEX

Audio Europe

RICK STEVES AUDIO EUROPE

Rick's Free Travel App

Get your FREE **Rick Steves Audio Europe**™ app to enjoy…

- Dozens of self-guided tours of Europe's top museums, sights and historic walks
- Hundreds of tracks filled with cultural insights and sightseeing tips from Rick's radio interviews
- All organized into handy geographic playlists
- For iPhone, iPad, iPod Touch, Android

With Rick whispering in your ear, Europe gets even better.

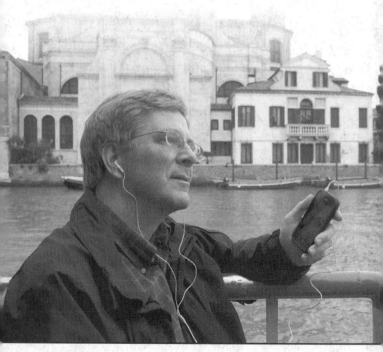

Find out more at ricksteves.com

Join a Rick Steves tour

Enjoy Europe's warmest welcome... with the flexibility and friendship of a small group getting to know Rick's favorite places and people. It all starts with our free tour catalog and DVD.

Great guides, small groups, no grumps.

Start your trip at

▸ Plan Your Trip

Browse thousands of articles and a wealth of money-saving tips for planning your dream trip. You'll find up-to-date information on Europe's best destinations, packing smart, getting around, finding rooms, staying healthy, avoiding scams and more.

▸ Eurail Passes

Find out, step-by-step, if a railpass makes sense for your trip—and how to avoid buying more than you need. Get free shipping on online orders

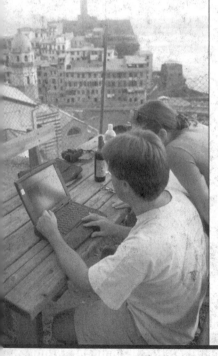

▸ Graffiti Wall & Travelers Helpline

Learn, ask, share—our online community of savvy travelers is a great resource for first-time travelers to Europe, as well as seasoned pros.

Rick Steves' Europe Through the Back Door, In

Rick Steves

www.ricksteves.com

Rick Steves guidebooks are published by Avalon Travel,
a member of the Perseus Books Group.

NOW AVAILABLE:
eBOOKS, DVD & BLU-RAY

eBOOKS

Nearly all Rick Steves guides are available as eBooks. Check with your favorite bookseller.

RICK STEVES' EUROPE DVDs

10 New Shows 2011–2012
Austria & the Alps
Eastern Europe
England & Wales
European Christmas
European Travel Skills & Specials
France
Germany, BeNeLux & More
Greece & Turkey
Iran
Ireland & Scotland
Italy's Cities
Italy's Countryside
Scandinavia
Spain
Travel Extras

BLU-RAY

Celtic Charms
Eastern Europe Favorites
European Christmas
Italy Through the Back Door
Mediterranean Mosaic
Surprising Cities of Europe

PHRASE BOOKS & DICTIONARIES

French
French, Italian & German
German
Italian
Portuguese
Spanish

JOURNALS

Rick Steves' Pocket Travel Journal
Rick Steves' Travel Journal

PLANNING MAPS

Britain, Ireland & London
Europe
France & Paris
Germany, Austria & Switzerland
Ireland
Italy
Spain & Portugal

Rick Steves books and DVDs are available at bookstores and through online booksellers.

Credits

Researchers

To update his four books on Italy, Rick relied on the help of...

Ben Cameron

Ben experienced his first taste of European travel when he was three, exploring medieval castles with his parents. Returning after graduation, he was hooked and has spent much of his time since exploring Europe independently and leading tours for Rick Steves. When not living out of his backpack, Ben splits his time between Rome and Seattle.

Cameron Hewitt

Cameron writes and edits guidebooks for Rick Steves, specializing in Eastern Europe. For this book, he swung through the urban jungle of Naples, beat the lines to climb the Campanile, plied the Tuscan countryside in search of *agriturismi,* and saw more frescoes than he could count. When he's not traveling, Cameron lives in Seattle with his wife Shawna.

Sarah Murdoch

Sarah has spent most of her adult life split between the US and Italy, ever since studying architecture in Rome during college. She is passionate about history, art, and pistachio gelato. When she isn't researching guidebooks or leading tours, she lives in Seattle with her patient husband Patrick and sons Lucca and Nicola.

Contributor
Gene Openshaw

Gene is the co-author of 10 Rick Steves' books. For this book, he wrote material on Italy's art, history, and contemporary culture. When not traveling, Gene enjoys composing music, recovering from his 1973 trip to Europe with Rick, and living everyday life with his daughter.

Images

Location	Photographer
Front color matter, title page: Varenna	David C. Hoerlein
Front color matter: Venice	Michael Potter
Front color matter: Venice	Laura VanDeventer
Venice: Church of San Giorgio Maggiore	David C. Hoerlein
Towns Near Venice: Verona's Roman Arena	David C. Hoerlein
The Dolomites: Alpe di Siusi	Julie Coen
The Lakes: Bellagio	Rick Steves
Milan: Cathedral (Duomo)	David C. Hoerlein
Cinque Terre: Corniglia	Rick Steves
Riviera Towns near the Cinque Terre: Portofino	David C. Hoerlein
Florence: View from Piazzale Michelangelo	Rick Steves
Pisa and Lucca: Pisa's Field of Miracles	Rick Steves
Siena: Il Campo	David C. Hoerlein
Hill Towns of Central Italy: San Gimignano	Rick Steves
Assisi: Basilica of St. Francis	Rick Steves
Orvieto & Civita: Civita di Bagnoregio	David C. Hoerlein
Rome: Piazza Navona	Rick Steves
Naples: Mt. Vesuvius	David C. Hoerlein
Sorrento and Capri: Capri	David C. Hoerlein
Amalfi Coast and Paestum: Positano	David C. Hoerlein

Rick Steves' Guidebook Series

City, Regional, and Country Guides

Rick Steves' Amsterdam, Bruges & Brussels
Rick Steves' Best of Europe
Rick Steves' Budapest
Rick Steves' Croatia & Slovenia
Rick Steves' Eastern Europe
Rick Steves' England
Rick Steves' Florence & Tuscany
Rick Steves' France
Rick Steves' Germany
Rick Steves' Great Britain
Rick Steves' Greece: Athens & the Peloponnese
Rick Steves' Ireland

Rick Steves' Istanbul
Rick Steves' Italy
Rick Steves' London
Rick Steves' Paris
Rick Steves' Portugal
Rick Steves' Prague & the Czech Republic
Rick Steves' Provence & the French Riviera
Rick Steves' Rome
Rick Steves' Scandinavia
Rick Steves' Spain
Rick Steves' Switzerland
Rick Steves' Venice
Rick Steves' Vienna, Salzburg & Tirol

Snapshot Guides

Excerpted from country guidebooks, the Snapshots Guides cover many of my favorite destinations, such as *Rick Steves' Snapshot Barcelona, Rick Steves' Snapshot Scotland,* and *Rick Steves' Snapshot Hill Towns of Central Italy.*

Pocket Guides

My new Pocket Guides are condensed, colorful guides to Europe's top cities, including Paris, London, Rome, and more. These combine the top self-guided walks and tours from my city guides with vibrant full-color photos, and are sized to slip easily into your pocket.

Rick Steves' Phrase Books

French
French/Italian/German
German
Italian
Portuguese
Spanish

More Books

Rick Steves' Europe 101: History and Art for the Traveler
Rick Steves' Europe Through the Back Door
Rick Steves' European Christmas
Rick Steves' Mediterranean Cruise Ports
Rick Steves' Postcards from Europe
Rick Steves' Travel as a Political Act

Avalon Travel
a member of the Perseus Books Group
1700 Fourth Street
Berkeley, CA 94710

Printed in Canada by Friesens. First printing October 2012.

ISBN 978-1-61238-379-8
ISSN 1084-4422

For the latest on Rick's lectures, guidebooks, tours, public radio show, and public television
series, contact Europe Through the Back Door, Box 2009, Edmonds, WA 98020, tel.
425/771-8303, fax 425/771-0833, www.ricksteves.com, rick@ricksteves.com.

Europe Through the Back Door
Managing Editor: Risa Laib
Editors: Jennifer Madison Davis, Glenn Eriksen, Tom Griffin, Cameron Hewitt, Suzanne
    Kotz, Cathy Lu, Gretchen Strauch
Editorial Interns: Emily Dugdale, Michael Maloy, Jessica Shaw
Researchers: Ben Cameron, Cameron Hewitt, Sarah Murdoch
Graphic Content Director: Laura VanDeventer
Maps & Graphics: David C. Hoerlein, Twozdai Hulse, Lauren Mills, Laura VanDeventer

Avalon Travel
Senior Editor and Series Manager: Madhu Prasher
Editor: Jamie Andrade
Assistant Editor: Nikki Ioakimedes
Copy Editor: Patrick Collins
Proofreader: Denise Silva
Indexer: Julie Kawabata
Production & Typesetting: McGuire Barber Design
Cover Design: Kimberly Glyder Design
Maps & Graphics: Kat Bennett, Mike Morgenfeld, Lohnes + Wright

Front Matter Color Photos: p. I Varenna © David C. Hoerlein; p. XIV, Venice © Michael
    Potter; p. XXIV, Venice © Laura VanDeventer
Front Cover Photo: Chianciano Terme, Tuscany © Dominic Bonuccelli
Additional Photography: Dominic Bonuccelli, Ben Cameron, Jennifer Hauseman,
    Cameron Hewitt, David C. Hoerlein, Anne Jenkins, Gene Openshaw, Michael Potter,
    Robyn Stencil, Rick Steves, Bruce VanDeventer, Laura VanDeventer, Les Wahlstrom
    (p.1023), Ian Watson, Tom Wallace (p.381), Wikimedia Commons, Deanna Woodruff

ABOUT THE AUTHOR

RICK STEVES

Since 1973, Rick Steves has spent 100 days every year exploring Europe. Along with writing and researching a bestselling series of guidebooks, Rick produces a public television series (Rick Steves' Europe), a public radio show (Travel with Rick Steves), and an app and podcast (Rick Steves Audio Europe); writes a nationally syndicated newspaper column; organizes guided tours that take over ten thousand travelers to Europe annually; and offers an information-packed website (www.ricksteves.com). With the help of his hardworking staff of 80 at Europe Through the Back Door—in Edmonds, Washington, just north of Seattle—Rick's mission is to make European travel fun, affordable, and culturally enlightening for Americans.

Connect with Rick:

facebook.com/RickSteves

twitter: @RickSteves

Foldout Color Map

The foldout map on the opposite page includes:
- A map of Italy on one side
- City maps, including Rome, Florence, Venice, and Siena on the other side